BaseBall america DIRECTORY 2004

Your Definitive Guide To The Game

Detailed Information On Baseball In All Leagues At All Levels!

Majors

Minors

Independent

International

College

Amateur

Published By Baseball America
Durham, North Carolina

Baseball america
DIRECTORY 2004

EDITOR
Allan Simpson
ASSOCIATE EDITOR
Chris Kline
ASSISTANT EDITORS
J.J. Cooper
Will Lingo
PRODUCTION DIRECTOR
Phillip Daquila
PRODUCTION ASSISTANTS
Matthew Eddy
Linwood Webb
ACCOUNT EXECUTIVE
Keith Dangel
SERVICE DIRECTORY MANAGER
Cliff Gardner
COVER DESIGN
Linwood Webb

Baseball America Inc.
PRESIDENT/CEO
Catherine Silver
VICE PRESIDENT/PUBLISHER
Lee Folger
EDITOR IN CHIEF
Allan Simpson
MANAGING EDITOR
Will Lingo
DESIGN & PRODUCTION DIRECTOR
Phillip Daquila

COVER PHOTOS
Tomas Perez and Luis Castillo by Morris Fostoff; Walt Jocketty by Larry Goren;
The Baseball Grounds of Jacksonville (Fla.) by Jay Metz

TABLE OF CONTENTS

MAJOR LEAGUES

Major League Baseball..33
American League 35
National League 35

Anaheim	36	Milwaukee	66
Arizona	38	Minnesota	68
Atlanta	40	Montreal	70
Baltimore	42	New York (NL)	72
Boston	44	New York (AL)	74
Chicago (NL)	46	Oakland	76
Chicago (AL)	48	Philadelphia	78
Cincinnati	50	Pittsburgh	80
Cleveland	52	St. Louis	82
Colorado	54	San Diego	84
Detroit	56	San Francisco	86
Florida	58	Seattle	88
Houston	60	Tampa Bay	90
Kansas City	62	Texas	92
Los Angeles	64	Toronto	94

Major League Standings and Schedules...97
Spring Training 109
Media...113

MINOR LEAGUES

Minor League Baseball 129

International	135	Midwest	187
Pacific Coast	143	South Atlantic	194
Eastern	152	New York-Penn	202
Southern	159	Northwest	209
Texas	165	Appalachian	214
California	170	Pioneer	219
Carolina	176	Arizona	224
Florida State	181	Gulf Coast	224

Minor League Schedules 225

INDEPENDENT LEAGUES

Atlantic	259	Northeast	270
Central	262	Northern	273
Frontier	265	Southwestern	277

Independent League Schedules 278

OTHER LEAGUES/ORGANIZATIONS

International Leagues 283
Winter Baseball...291
College Baseball..296
Amateur Baseball..343
High School Baseball..355
Youth Baseball...361

Agent Directory/Service Directory 368
Index With Phone/FAX Numbers 377

2004–2005
CALENDAR

2004

March

Sun	Mon	Tue	Wed	Thu	Fri	Sat
	1	2	3	4	5	6
7	8	9	10	11	12	13
14	15	16	17	18	19	20
21	22	23	24	25	26	27
28	29	30	31			

April

Sun	Mon	Tue	Wed	Thu	Fri	Sat
				1	2	3
4	5	6	7	8	9	10
11	12	13	14	15	16	17
18	19	20	21	22	23	24
25	26	27	28	29	30	

May

Sun	Mon	Tue	Wed	Thu	Fri	Sat
						1
2	3	4	5	6	7	8
9	10	11	12	13	14	15
16	17	18	19	20	21	22
23	24	25	26	27	28	29
30	31					

June

Sun	Mon	Tue	Wed	Thu	Fri	Sat
		1	2	3	4	5
6	7	8	9	10	11	12
13	14	15	16	17	18	19
20	21	22	23	24	25	26
27	28	29	30			

July

Sun	Mon	Tues	Wed	Thur	Fri	Sat
				1	2	3
4	5	6	7	8	9	10
11	12	13	14	15	16	17
18	19	20	21	22	23	24
25	26	27	28	29	30	31

August

Sun	Mon	Tue	Wed	Thu	Fri	Sat
1	2	3	4	5	6	7
8	9	10	11	12	13	14
15	16	17	18	19	20	21
22	23	24	25	26	27	28
29	30	31				

September

Sun	Mon	Tue	Wed	Thu	Fri	Sat
			1	2	3	4
5	6	7	8	9	10	11
12	13	14	15	16	17	18
19	20	21	22	23	24	25
26	27	28	29	30		

October

Sun	Mon	Tue	Wed	Thu	Fri	Sat
					1	2
3	4	5	6	7	8	9
10	11	12	13	14	15	16
17	18	19	20	21	22	23
24	25	26	27	28	29	30
31						

November

Sun	Mon	Tue	Wed	Thu	Fri	Sat
	1	2	3	4	5	6
7	8	9	10	11	12	13
14	15	16	17	18	19	20
21	22	23	24	25	26	27
28	29	30				

December

Sun	Mon	Tue	Wed	Thu	Fri	Sat
			1	2	3	4
5	6	7	8	9	10	11
12	13	14	15	16	17	18
19	20	21	22	23	24	25
26	27	28	29	30	31	

2005

January

Sun	Mon	Tue	Wed	Thu	Fri	Sat
						1
2	3	4	5	6	7	8
9	10	11	12	13	14	15
16	17	18	19	20	21	22
23	24	25	26	27	28	29
30	31					

February

Sun	Mon	Tue	Wed	Thu	Fri	Sat
		1	2	3	4	5
6	7	8	9	10	11	12
13	14	15	16	17	18	19
20	21	22	23	24	25	26
27	28					

March

Sun	Mon	Tue	Wed	Thu	Fri	Sat
		1	2	3	4	5
6	7	8	9	10	11	12
13	14	15	16	17	18	19
20	21	22	23	24	25	26
27	28	29	30	31		

April

Sun	Mon	Tue	Wed	Thu	Fri	Sat
					1	2
3	4	5	6	7	8	9
10	11	12	13	14	15	16
17	18	19	20	21	22	23
24	25	26	27	28	29	30

THE GAME'S GREATEST HITTERS

SILVER SLUGGER AWARD 2003

2003 SILVER SLUGGER TEAM

American League

1B	Carlos Delgado (3)	
2B	Bret Boone (2)	
3B	Bill Mueller	
SS	Alex Rodriguez (7)	
OF	Vernon Wells	
OF	Garret Anderson (2)	
OF	Manny Ramirez (6)	
C	Jorge Posada (4)	
DH	Edgar Martinez (5)	

National League

1B	Todd Helton (4)	
2B	Jose Vidro	
3B	Mike Lowell	
SS	Edgar Renteria (3)	
OF	Barry Bonds (11)	
OF	Albert Pujols (2)	
OF	Gary Sheffield (2)	
C	Javy Lopez	
P	Mike Hampton (5)	

Previous winners' total number of Silver Slugger Awards in parentheses.

HILLERICH & BRADSBY CO
SILVER SLUGGER AWARD
Louisville Slugger is proud to announce the 2003 Silver Slugger Team

Since 1884.

EVENTS CALENDAR

February 2004 – February 2005

FEBRUARY

28—Opening Day: Chinese Professional Baseball League.

MARCH

2—Major league teams may renew contracts of unsigned players (through March 11).
17—Opening Day: Mexican League.
27—Opening Day: Japan Pacific League.
30—Opening Series: Tampa Bay vs. New York in Tokyo, two-game series through March 31.

APRIL

2—Opening Day: China League.
2—Opening Day: Japan Central League.
4—Opening Day: American League (Boston at Baltimore).
5—Opening Day: American League (Chicago at Kansas City, Cleveland at Minnesota, Detroit at Toronto, Texas at Oakland).
5—Opening Day: National League (Milwaukee at St. Louis, Philadelphia at Pittsburgh, San Diego at Los Angeles, San Francisco at Houston).
5—Opening Day: Korean Baseball Organization.
6—Opening Day: American League (Anaheim at Seattle).
6—Opening Day: National League (Chicago at Cincinnati, Colorado at Arizona, Montreal at Florida, New York at Atlanta).
8—Opening Day: International League, Pacific Coast League, Eastern League, Southern League, Texas League, California League, Carolina League, Florida State League, Midwest League, South Atlantic League.
9—Montreal Expos vs. New York Mets in San Juan, P.R. (first of 22 Expos games in Puerto Rico)
12—National Classic High School Tournament at Fullerton, Calif. (through April 15).

MAY

1—Earliest date major league clubs may re-sign free agents who were not offered arbitration.
6—Opening Day: Atlantic League, Central League.
18—Perfect Game National Predraft Camp at Cedar Rapids, Iowa.
20—Opening Day: Northern League.
21—Opening Day: Frontier League.
22—NCAA Division II World Series at Montgomery, Ala. (through May 29).
22—Junior College Division III World Series at Batavia, N.Y. (through May 26).
26—Opening Day: Northeast League.
28—Opening Day: Southwestern League.
28—NCAA Division III World Series at Appleton, Wis. (through June 1).
28—NAIA World Series at Lewiston, Idaho (through June 4).
29—Junior College World Series at Grand Junction,

Minute Maid Park, site of the 2004 major league All-Star Game

Colo. (through June 4).
29—Junior College Division II World Series at Millington, Tenn. (through June 4).
31—Start of closed period for amateur draft.

JUNE

1—Opening Day: Atlantic Collegiate League, California Collegiate League, Southern Collegiate League.
2—Opening Day: Northwoods League.
3—Opening Day: Venezuelan Summer League.
3—Opening Day: Coastal Plain League, New York Collegiate League.
4—NCAA Division I Regionals at campus sites (through June 6).
4—Opening Day: Clark Griffith Collegiate League, Pacific International League, Valley League.
6—Opening Day: Dominican Summer League.
7—First interleague games (Cincinnati at Oakland, Houston at Seattle, Pittsburgh at Texas).
7—Amateur draft (through June 8).
8—Opening Day: Alaska League, Jayhawk League, Texas Collegiate League.
10—Opening Day: Central Illinois Collegiate League.
11—NCAA Division I Super Regionals at campus sites (through June 14).
11—Opening Day: New England Collegiate League.
12—Florida State League all-star game at Port St. Lucie, Fla.
12—Opening Day: Great Lakes League, Florida Collegiate Instructional League.
14—Hall of Fame Game at Cooperstown (Atlanta vs. Minnesota).
17—Opening Day: Cape Cod League.
18—58th College World Series at Omaha (through June 27/28).
18—Perfect Game National Showcase at St. Petersburg, Fla. (through June 20).
18—Opening Day: New York-Penn League, Northwest League, Pioneer League.

18—USA Baseball Junior Olympic Championships at Palm Beach County, Fla., and Peoria/Surprise, Ariz. (through June 26).

20—USA Baseball college team trials at Durham, N.C. (through June 22).

21—USA Baseball junior Tournament of Stars at Joplin, Mo. (through June 28).

21—Texas League all-star game at Midland, Texas.

21—Opening Day: Appalachian League, Gulf Coast League.

22—Midwest League all-star game at Cedar Rapids, Iowa.

22—Sunbelt Baseball Classic Series at Norman, Okla. (through June 26).

22—Opening Day: Arizona League.

29—California League/Carolina League all-star game at San Bernardino, Calif.; South Atlantic League all-star game at Charleston, S.C.

JULY

10—Japan All-Star Game I at Nagoya Dome.

11—6th All-Star Futures Game at Minute Maid Park, Houston.

11—Japan All-Star Game II at Nagano.

13—Southern League all-star game at Chattanooga, Tenn.

13—75th Major League All-Star Game at Minute Maid Park, Houston.

14—Atlantic League all-star game at Camden, N.J.; Frontier League all-star game at O'Fallon, Mo.

14—Triple-A all-star game at Pawtucket; Eastern League all-star game at Bowie, Md.

20—Central League/Northeast League all-star game at Fort Worth, Texas; Northern League all-star game at Joliet, Ill.

22—World University Championship at Tainan, Taiwan (through July 31).

25—Cape Cod League all-star game at Orleans, Mass.

25—Hall of Fame induction ceremonies, Cooperstown.

27—East Coast Professional Baseball Showcase at Wilmington, N.C. (through Aug. 1).

30—Women's World Cup at Edmonton, Alberta (through Aug. 8).

31—National Baseball Congress World Series at Wichita (through Aug. 14).

31—IBAF World Children's Baseball Fair at Hyogo Prefecture, Japan (through Aug. 5).

AUGUST

1—End of major league trading period without waivers.

4—Area Code Games at Long Beach (through Aug. 9).

6—Connie Mack World Series at Farmington, N.M. (through Aug. 12).

6—AFLAC High School Classic at Aberdeen, Md.

14—Babe Ruth 16-18 World Series at Newark, Ohio (through Aug. 21).

14—Pony League World Series at Washington, Pa.

(through Aug. 21).

15—Olympic Games baseball tournament at Athens, Greece (through Aug. 25).

20—Little League World Series at Williamsport, Pa. (through Aug. 29).

20—Babe Ruth 13-15 World Series at Longview, Wash. (through Aug. 28).

20—American Legion World Series at Corvallis, Oregon (through Aug. 24).

31—Postseason major league roster eligibility frozen.

SEPTEMBER

1—Major league roster limits expanded from 25 to 40.

3—World Junior Championship at Taipei, Taiwan (through Sept. 12).

OCTOBER

1—Baseball America/Perfect Game 16 and under Wood Bat Championship at Fort Myers, Fla. (through Oct. 4).

2—Opening Day: Arizona Fall League.

3—Major league season ends.

4—Beginning of major league trading period without waivers.

5—Major league Division Series begin.

12—League Championship Series begin.

16—Japan Series begins at home of Pacific League champion.

23—World Series begins.

24—Baseball America/Perfect Game World Wood Bat Championship (through Oct. 27).

NOVEMBER

19—Filing date, 40-man major league winter rosters.

DECEMBER

2—National High School Baseball Coaches Association convention at Grapevine, Texas. (through Dec. 5).

7—Deadline for major league clubs to offer eligible players salary arbitration.

10—102nd annual Winter Meetings at Anaheim (through Dec. 13).

13—Rule 5 major league/minor league drafts.

19—Deadline for players offered arbitration to accept.

20—Last date for major league clubs to tender contracts.

JANUARY 2005

6—American Baseball Coaches Association convention at Nashville (through Jan. 9).

7—NCAA National Convention at Dallas (through Jan. 11).

FEBRUARY

1—Caribbean Series at Mazatlan, Mexico (through Feb. 8).

RICE UNIVERSITY OWLS

TPX

2003 Wins: 58
First-Time National Champions
Bat Models: Louisville Slugger
TPX Response™ and
Louisville Slugger TPX Omaha®
2003 Numbers:
.313 Avg., 773 Hits, 51 HR, 449 RBI

The

Bats

Behind

The Stats.

ALEX RODRIGUEZ
TEXAS RANGERS

GENUINE C271
TEXAS RANGERS

Bat Model: Louisville Slugger
C271 Cupped
Finish: Black-Smith
Length: 34"
Weight: 31oz
Youngest player in Major League
history to reach 300 home runs.

BASEBALL AMERICA

ESTABLISHED 1981

PRESIDENT/CEO: Catherine Silver

VICE PRESIDENT/PUBLISHER: Lee Folger

EDITOR IN CHIEF: Allan Simpson

MANAGING EDITOR: Will Lingo
EXECUTIVE EDITOR: Jim Callis
SENIOR WRITER: Alan Schwarz
NATIONAL WRITER: John Manuel
NEWS EDITOR: J.J. Cooper
ASSOCIATE EDITOR: Will Kimmey
ASSISTANT EDITORS: Chris Kline, Alan Matthews
ADMINISTRATIVE ASSISTANT: Gary Martin

GENERAL MANAGER, BASEBALLAMERICA.COM: Kevin Goldstein

DESIGN AND PRODUCTION DIRECTOR: Phillip Daquila
PRODUCTION ASSISTANTS: Matthew Eddy, Linwood Webb

CUSTOMER SERVICE: Demetris Burns, Ronnie McCabe, Shirley McCabe, Jessica Ross
customerservice@baseballamerica.com

ADVERTISING SALES
ACCOUNT EXECUTIVE: Keith Dangel
MARKETPLACE MANAGER: Cliff Gardner
P.O. Box 2089, Durham, NC 27702
Telephone: (800) 845-2726; **FAX:** (919) 682-2880

BUSINESS STAFF
ECONOMIST: Bill Porter
MANAGER, FINANCE: Cara Callanan
FINANCIAL ADMINISTRATOR: Leon Lashway
LEGAL COUNSEL: Mike Ring

BASEBALL AMERICA INC.
Mailing Address: P.O. Box 2089, Durham, NC 27702
Street Address: 201 West Main Street, Suite 201, Durham, NC 27701
Telephone: (919) 682-9635 • **Toll-Free:** (800) 845-2726
FAX: (919) 682-2880
Website: BaseballAmerica.com

BASEBALL AMERICA, the nation's most complete all-baseball magazine, publishes 26 issues a year. Subscription rates are US $69.95 for one year, $104.90 for two years. Call or write for non-U.S. addresses.

BASEBALL AMERICA PUBLICATIONS

2004 Almanac: A comprehensive look at the 2003 season, featuring major and minor league statistics and commentary; 464 pages. **$16.95** ($19.95 spiral bound)

2004 Prospect Handbook: Detailed scouting reports and biographical sketches on 900 of the top prospects in the minor leagues; 512 pages. **$23.95**

2004 Super Register: A complete record, with biographical information, of every player who played professional baseball in 2003; 720 pages. **$64.95**

2004 Directory: Names, addresses, phone numbers, major and minor league schedules—vital to baseball insiders and fans; 384 pages. **$19.95** ($22.95 spiral bound)

2004 Great Parks: The Baseball America Calendar. **$13.95**

All prices in US funds. Add $8 for shipping and handling for first item and $2 for each additional item. Allow four weeks for delivery.

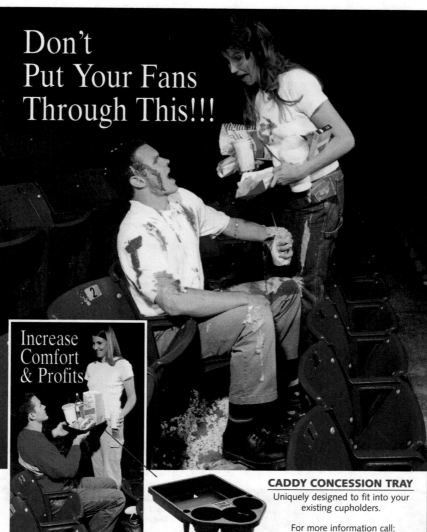

BASEBALL AMERICA
2003 AWARD WINNERS

MAJOR LEAGUES

Player of the Year
Barry Bonds, of, Giants
Executive of the Year
Brian Sabean, Giants
Rookie of the Year
Brandon Webb, rhp, Diamondbacks
Roland Hemond Award (Contributions to Scouting and Player Development)
George Kissell, Cardinals
Lifetime Achievement Award
300-game winners

MINOR LEAGUES

Organization of the Year
Florida Marlins
Player of the Year
Joe Mauer, c, Twins (Fort Myers/Florida State, New Britain/Eastern)
Manager of the Year
Dave Brundage, Mariners (San Antonio/Texas)
Executive of the Year
Chuck Domino, Reading Phillies (Eastern)
Team of the Year
Sacramento River Cats, Pacific Coast/Athletics
Bob Freitas Awards (Best Minor League Operations)
Triple-A: Pawtucket Red Sox (International)
Double-A: New Britain Rock Cats (Eastern)
Class A: Modesto A's (California)
Short-season: Spokane Indians (Northwest)
Classification Players of the Year
Triple-A: Bobby Crosby, ss, Athletics (Sacramento/Pacific Coast)
Double-A: Alexis Rios, of, Blue Jays (New Haven/Eastern)
High Class A: Josh Barfield, 2b, Padres (Lake Elsinore/California)

Baseball America's Major League Player of the Year
Giants left fielder Barry Bonds

Low Class A: Prince Fielder, 1b, Brewers (Beloit/Midwest)
Short-season: Vito Chiaravolloti, 1b, Blue Jays (Auburn/New York-Penn)
Rookie: Lou Palmisano, c, Brewers (Helena/Pioneer)

INDEPENDENT LEAGUES

Player of the Year
Jason Shelley, rhp, Rockford (Frontier)

WINTER LEAGUES

2003-2004 Player of the Year
Alexis Rios, of, Caguas (Puerto Rico/Blue Jays)

COLLEGES

Player of the Year
Rickie Weeks, 2b, Southern
Coach of the Year
George Horton, Cal State Fullerton
Freshman of the Year
Ryan Braun, ss, Miami

AMATEUR/YOUTH LEAGUES

Summer Player of the Year (College players)
Jered Weaver, rhp, Team USA
Youth Player of the Year (High school and younger)
Nick Adenhart, rhp, Williamsport, Md.
Ripken Baseball Youth Coach of the Year
Mary Sigler, Bolingbrook, Ill.

HIGH SCHOOLS

Player of the Year
Jeff Allison, rhp, Veterans Memorial HS, Peabody, Mass.
National Champion (Baseball America/National High School Baseball Coaches Association poll)
Chatsworth (Calif.) HS

Baseball America's Minor League Player of the Year
Twins catching prospect Joe Mauer

TRAVEL INFO
TOLL-FREE NUMBERS & WEBSITES

AIRLINES

Aeromexico	aeromexico.com	800-237-6639
Air Canada	aircanada.com	800-361-2159
Airtran Airways	airtran.com	800-247-8726
Alaska Airlines	alaskaair.com	800-426-0333
Aloha Airlines	alohaairlines.com	800-227-4900
America West	americawest.com	800-235-9292
American Airlines	aa.com	800-433-7300
Continental Airlines	continental.com	800-525-0280
Delta Air Lines	delta.com	800-221-1212
Japan Air Lines	jal.co.jp/en/	800-525-3663
Korean Air	koreanair.com	800-438-5000
Northwest Airlines	nwa.com	800-225-2525
Olympic Airways	olympic-airways.gr	800-223-1226
Qantas Airways	qantas.com	800-227-4500
Southwest Airlines	southwest.com	800-435-9792
United Airlines	ual.com	800-864-8331
U.S. Airways	usairways.com	800-428-4322

CAR RENTALS

Alamo	goalamo.com	800-732-3232
Avis	avis.com	800-331-1212
Budget	budget.com	800-527-0700
Dollar	dollar.com	800-800-4000
Enterprise	enterprise.com	800-325-8007
Hertz	hertz.com	800-654-3131
National	nationalcar.com	800-227-7368
Thrifty	thrifty.com	800-367-2277

HOTELS/MOTELS

Best Western	bestwestern.com	800-528-1234
Choice Hotels	choicehotels.com	800-424-6423
Clarion	choicehotels.com	800-221-2222
Comfort Inn	choicehotels.com	800-221-2222
Courtyard by Marriott	marriott.com	800-321-2211
Days Inn	daysinn.com	800-325-2525
Doubletree Hotels	doubletree.com	800-424-2900
Econo Lodge	choicehotels.com	800-424-4777
Embassy Suites	embassy-suites.com	800-362-2779
Fairfield (Marriott)	fairfieldinn.com	800-228-2800
Hampton Inn	hampton-inn.com	800-426-7866
Hilton Hotels	hilton.com	800-445-8667
Holiday Inn/ Holiday Inn Express	sixcontinentshotels.com	800-465-4329
Howard Johnson	hojo.com	800-654-2000
Hyatt Hotels	hyatt.com	800-228-9000
La Quinta	laquinta.com	800-531-5900
Marriott Hotels	marriott.com	800-228-9290
Omni Hotels	omnihotels.com	800-843-6664
Quality Inn	choicehotels.com	800-221-2222
Radisson Hotels	radisson.com	800-333-3333
Ramada Inns	ramada.com	800-228-2828
Red Lion	redlion.com	800-547-8010
Red Roof Inns	redroof.com	800-843-7663
Renaissance Hotels	renaissancehotels.com	800-468-3571
Residence Inn	marriott.com	800-331-3131
Rodeway Inn	choicehotels.com	800-228-2000
Sheraton Hotels	sheraton.com	800-325-3535
Sleep Inn	choicehotels.com	800-221-2222
Super 8 Motels	super8.com	800-800-8000
TravelLodge	travelodge.com	800-578-7878
Westin Hotels	starwood.com/westin	800-228-3000
Wyndham Hotels	wyndham.com	800-996-3426

RAIL

Amtrak	amtrak.com	800-872-7245

WHAT'S NEW
IN 2004

MAJOR LEAGUES

■ **BALLPARKS**
Philadelphia: Citizens Bank Park.
San Diego: Petco Park
■ **SPRING TRAINING**
Phillies move into new ballpark at Clearwater, Fla., complex: Bright House Networks Field.

MINOR LEAGUES

Triple-A
No significant changes.

Double-A
New Haven (Eastern) moves to Manchester, N.H. (New Hampshire Fisher Cats).
Orlando (Southern) moves to Montgomery, Ala. (Montgomery Biscuits).
■ **BALLPARKS**
Montgomery (Southern): Montgomery Riverwalk Stadium.

Class A
■ **NAME CHANGES**
Clearwater Phillies (Florida State) become Clearwater Threshers.
Quad City River Bandits (Midwest) become Swing of the Quad Cities.
South Georgia Waves (South Atlantic) become Columbus Catfish.
■ **BALLPARKS**
Clearwater Threshers (Florida State): Bright House Networks Field.

Short-Season
Martinsville (Appalachian) moves to Greeneville, Tenn. (Greeneville Astros).

Padres join Arizona League.
Orioles leave Gulf Coast League; Mets join Gulf Coast League.
■ **BALLPARK**
Greeneville (Appalachian): Pioneer Park.
■ **NICKNAME CHANGES**
Idaho Falls (Pioneer) from Padres to Chukars.
■ **AFFILIATION CHANGES**
Royals move second Arizona League affiliate to Idaho Falls (Pioneer).

INDEPENDENT LEAGUES

Arizona-Mexico League will not play in 2004.
Pensacola moves from Southeastern League to Central League.
Central League drops Springfield/Ozark and Rio Grande Valley, taking it from 10 teams to eight.
Cook County and Kenosha (Frontier) replaced by Springfield/Ozark and Windy City.
Berkshire (Northeast) replaced by New Haven County.
Southeastern League will not play in 2004.
Southwestern League will begin play in 2004.

FOREIGN/WINTER LEAGUES

Canadian League will not play in 2004.
Cordoba (Mexican) moves to Aguascaliente (Aguascaliente Rieleros).
Reynosa (Mexican) moves to San Luis (San Luis Tuneros).
Two Laredos (Mexican) moves to Tijuana (Tijuana Bulls).

COLLEGE

New summer college league, Texas Collegiate League, begins play at eight sites in Texas.

The Florida State League's latest diamond
Clearwater's Bright House Networks Field, home of the Threshers

2004 DRAFT ORDER

It's been 16 years since San Diego took righthander Andy Benes with the No. 1 overall pick in the 1988 draft. When they make the first pick again in June, the Padres will join the Mets by drafting No. 1 overall for the fifth time in the draft's 40-year history. This year's draft is scheduled for June 7–8. Teams draft in reverse order of their 2003 finish, with the National League up first. The Padres also drafted first in 1970, '72 and '74.

The order of selection in the second half of the first round (picks 16-30) has changed to reflect compensation for major league free agents who signed with new clubs during the offseason. The Twins will be the most active club, with five picks before the start of the second round. They receive two additional picks apiece for losing Eddie Guardado (Mariners) and LaTroy Hawkins (Twins).

Teams are awarded compensation in the form of draft picks based on the type of free agent involved. A team losing a Type A free agent gets the first-round pick of the team that signs the player, as well as a supplemental pick. A team losing a Type B free agent receives only the signing team's top pick. In both cases, a team selecting in the top half of the draft rotation cannot lose its first-round pick. The loss of a Type C free agent provides a team a pick between the second and third rounds.

Following is the order of selection for the first round and supplemental rounds, along with adjustments in the second and third rounds.

FIRST ROUND

Club	Pick From	For (Type)
1. Padres		
2. Tigers		
3. Mets		
4. Devil Rays		
5. Brewers		
6. Indians		
7. Reds		
8. Orioles		
9. Rockies		
10. Rangers		
11. Pirates		
12. Angels		
13. Expos		
14. Royals		
15. Diamondbacks		
16. Blue Jays		
17. Dodgers		
18. White Sox		
19. Cardinals		
20. Twins		
21. Phillies		
22. Twins	Mariners	Eddie Guardado (A)
23. Yankees	Astros	Andy Pettitte (A)
24. Athletics	Red Sox	Keith Foulke (A)
25. Twins	Cubs	LaTroy Hawkins (A)
26. Athletics		
27. Marlins		
28. Dodgers	Yankees	Paul Quantrill (A)
29. Royals	Giants	Michael Tucker (B)
30. Rangers	Braves	John Thomson (B)

SUPPLEMENTAL FIRST ROUND

31. Pirates		Matt Stairs (A)
32. Royals		Raul Ibanez (A)
33. Blue Jays		Kelvim Escobar (A)
34. Dodgers		Quantrill
35. White Sox		Bartolo Colon (A)
36. Twins		Guardado
37. Athletics		Foulke
38. Yankees		Pettitte
39. White Sox		Tom Gordon (A)

First overall pick in 2003 draft
Devil Rays outfielder Delmon Young

40. Twins		Hawkins
41. Athletics		Miguel Tejada (A)
42. Yankees		David Wells (A)

SECOND ROUND

43. Yankees	Padres	Wells
50. Athletics	Orioles	Tejada
54. White Sox	Angels	Colon
57. Pirates	Royals	Stairs
64. Royals	Mariners	Ibanez
70. White Sox	Yankees	Gordon

THIRD ROUND

84. Blue Jays	Angels	Escobar

BASEBALL
INFORMATION

BASEBALL TERMINOLOGY

■ Roster Limits
Major league rosters may include 40 players until Opening Day, when the number must be reduced to 25. The number returns to 40 on Sept. 1. The minimum number of active players maintained by each club throughout the season is 24.

■ Trading Regulations
The trading deadline is July 31. Trades may be made with any other major league club in the period from the end of the season through July 31 (midnight) without waivers.

■ Disabled Lists
There are two disabled lists, 15-day and 60-day. Players may be disabled retroactively, up to a maximum of 10 days, beginning with the day after the last day they played. A player on the 15-day DL may be shifted to the 60-day DL at any time. Players may be assigned to a minor league club for injury rehabilitation for a maximum of 20 days (30 days for pitchers).

15-day. There is no limit on the number of players per club.

60-day. There is no limit on the number of players per club, but it may be used only when a club is at the maximum of 40 players. Players carried on this list do not count against a club's control limit of 40 players. If a player is transferred to this list after Aug. 1, he must remain through the end of the season and postseason.

■ Options
When a player is on a major league club's 40-man roster and in the minor leagues, he is on "optional assignment." Players have three options and may be sent up and down as many times as the club chooses within those seasons but will only be charged with one option per season. When a player is "out of options," it means he's been on a 40-man roster during at least three different seasons and in his fourth pro season or later, he will have to clear irrevocable waivers in order to be sent down.

■ Waivers
If a player placed on major league waivers is not claimed by another team within two business days after waivers have been requested, then the player has "cleared waivers," and the team has secured waivers for the remainder of the waiver period. The team then can do one of two things:

1. Send him to the minors.
2. Trade him to another team, even if the trading deadline has passed, or do nothing at all.

Note: Any trades involving a 40-man roster player from July 31 to the end of the season may only involve players who have cleared major league waivers. If a player does not clear waivers—he is claimed by another team or teams—the club requesting waivers may withdraw the waiver request. If the club does not withdraw the waiver request, the player's contract is assigned as follows:

a. If only one claim is entered, the player's contract is assigned to the claiming club.

b. If more than one club in the same league makes claims, the club currently lower in the standings gets the player.

c. If clubs in both leagues claim the player, preference shall always go to the club in the same league as the club requesting waivers.

■ Designated for Assignment
This rule allows a club to open a roster spot for up to 10 days while waiting for a player to clear waivers.

Recalled vs. Contract Purchased

If a player is on the 40-man roster, he is "recalled." If not, then his contract is purchased from the minor league team. A player must be added to the 40-man roster when his contract is purchased.

■ Free agency
Six years of major league service are required to be eligible for free agency. A player has 15 days from the first day after the World Series to file for free agency.

By Dec. 7, a player's former club must offer to arbitrate or it becomes ineligible to sign the player. By Dec. 19, the player must accept the club's offer or on Jan. 9 the former club becomes ineligible to sign the player.

Six-year free agent (minor leagues). A player is eligible for free agency if he has played all or part of seven seasons in the major or minor leagues and is not placed on a major league team's 40-man roster as of Oct. 15.

■ Salary Arbitration
Three years of major league service are required for eligibility. A player with at least two years but less than three years of major league service will also be eligible if he ranks in the top 17 percent in total service in the class of players who have at least two but less than three years of major league service, however accumulated, but with at least 86 days of service accumulated during the immediately preceding season.

■ Rule 5 Draft
A player not on a major league 40-man roster as of Nov. 20 is eligible for the Rule 5 draft if:

1. The player was 18 or younger when he first signed a pro contract and this is the fourth Rule 5 draft since he signed.
2. The player was 19 or older when he first signed a pro contract and this is the third Rule 5 draft since he signed.

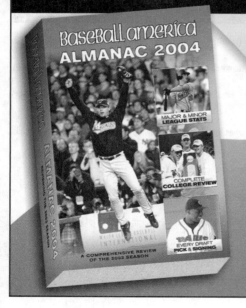

■ **Consecutive Game Hitting Streak**
    A consecutive game hitting streak shall not be terminated if all the player's plate appearances (one or more) result in a base on balls, hit-by-pitch, defensive interference or a sacrifice bunt. The streak shall terminate if the player has a sacrifice fly and no hit.

■ **Consecutive Games Played Streak**
    A consecutive games played streak shall be extended if the player plays one-half inning on defense, or if he completes a time at bat by reaching base or being put out.

■ **Major League Service**
    A full year of service in the major leagues constitutes 172 days.

■ **Rookie Qualifications**
    A player shall be considered a rookie if:
       1. He does not have more than 130 at-bats or 50 innings pitched in the major leagues during a previous season or seasons and,
       2. He has not accumulated more than 45 days on a major league roster during the 25-player limit, excluding time on the disabled list.

■ **Save Rule**
    A pitcher shall be credited with a save when he meets the following three conditions:
       1. He is the finishing pitcher in a game won by his club, and
       2. He is not the winning pitcher, and
       3. He qualifies under one of the following conditions:
          a. he enters the game with a lead of no more than three runs and pitches for at least one inning, or
          b. he enters the game with the potential tying run either on base, at bat or on deck, or
          c. he pitches effectively for at least three innings.
    Blown save. When a relief pitcher enters a game in a save situation and departs with the save situation no longer in effect because he has given up the lead, he is charged with a blown save.

■ **Qualifying Marks**
    Batting Championship. Major leagues—To qualify, a player must have a minimum of 502 plate appearances (3.1 plate appearances for each of the scheduled 162 games). Minor leagues—To qualify, a player must have accumulated 2.7 plate appearances for each scheduled game.
    Earned Run Average. Major leagues—To qualify, a pitcher must have at least 162 innings pitched and have the lowest ERA. Minor leagues—To qualify, a pitcher must have pitched a number of innings at least .8 times the number of scheduled games.
    Fielding Average. To qualify as a leader at the positions of first base, second base, third base, shortstop and outfield, a player must have appeared in a minimum of two-thirds of his team's games. For catcher, a player must have appeared in a minimum of one half of his team's games. For pitcher, the player with the highest average and the greatest number of total chances qualifies as the leader.

HOW TO FIGURE

■ **Batting Average**
    Divide the number of hits by the number of at-bats (H/AB).

■ **Earned Run Average**
    Multiply the number of earned runs by nine; take that number and divide it by the number of innings pitched (ER x 9/IP).

■ **Slugging Percentage**
    Divide the total bases of all safe hits by the total of times at bat. At-bats do not include walks, sacrifices, hit-by-pitches or times awarded first base because of interference or obstruction (TB/AB).

■ **On-Base Percentage**
    Add the total number of hits, walks and number of times hit by pitches and divide by the total of at-bats, walks, hit-by-pitches and sacrifice flies (H+BB+HBP/AB+BB+HBP+SF).

■ **Fielding Percentage**
    Divide the total number of putouts and assists by total chances—putouts, assists and errors (PO+A/PO+A+E).

■ **Winning Percentage**
    Divide the number of games won by the total games won and lost (W/W+L).

■ **Magic Number**
    Determine the number of games yet to be played, add one, and then subtract the number of games ahead in the loss column of the standings from the closest opponent.

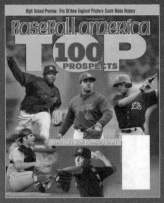

The Ultimate Reference Tool

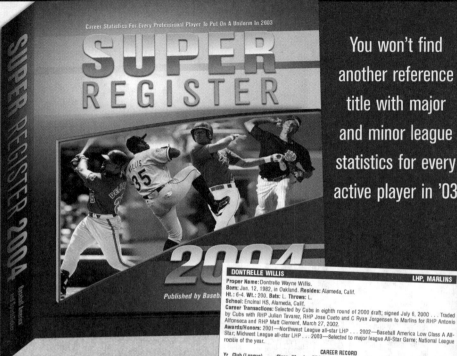

Career Statistics For Every Professional Player To Put On A Uniform In 2003

SUPER REGISTER

2004

Published by Baseb...

You won't find another reference title with major and minor league statistics for every active player in '03

DONTRELLE WILLIS   **LHP, MARLINS**

Proper Name: Dontrelle Wayne Willis.
Born: Jan. 12, 1982, in Oakland. **Resides:** Alameda, Calif.
Ht.: 6-4. **Wt.:** 200. **Bats:** L. **Throws:** L.
School: Encinal HS, Alameda, Calif.
Career Transactions: Selected by Cubs in eighth round of 2000 draft; signed July 6, 2000 . . . Traded by Cubs with RHP Julian Tavarez, RHP Jose Cueto and C Ryan Jorgensen to Marlins for RHP Antonio Alfonseca and RHP Matt Clement, March 27, 2002.
Awards/Honors: 2001—Northwest League all-star LHP . . . 2002—Baseball America Low Class A All-Star; Midwest League all-star LHP . . . 2003—Selected to major league All-Star Game; National League rookie of the year.

Yr	Club (League)	Class	W	L	ERA	G	GS	CG	SV	IP	H	R	ER	HR	BB	SO	AVG
00	Cubs (AZL)	R	3	1	3.86	9	1	0	0	28	26	15	12	0	8	22	.245
01	Boise (NWL)	A	8	2	2.98	15	15	0	0	94	76	36	31	1	19	77	.217
02	Kane County (Mid)	A	10	2	1.83	19	19	3	0	128	91	29	26	3	21	101	.200
	Jupiter (FSL)	A	2	0	1.80	5	5	0	0	30	24	7	6	2	3	27	.216
03	Carolina (SL)	AA	4	0	1.49	6	6	0	0	36	24	6	6	2	9	32	.194
	Florida (NL)	MAJ	14	6	3.30	27	27	2	0	161	148	61	59	13	58	142	.245
	MAJOR LEAGUE TOTALS		14	6	3.30	27	27	2	0	161	148	61	59	13	58	142	.245
	MINOR LEAGUE TOTALS		27	5	2.31	54	46	3	0	316	241	93	81	8	60	259	.210

T he 2004 Super Register features complete career statistics for every active player in Organized Baseball in 2003, from the youngest player in the Gulf Coast League to the oldest player in the major leagues.

Other books might list statistics for select minor leaguers, but you won't find another one that lists them all—more than 6,300 players, with transactions, awards and major and minor league totals. New categories in this edition: slugging and on-base percentages; home runs allowed and batting average against. Whether you get paid to follow players or just want to dominate your fantasy league, you'll want to have the 2004 Super Register on your bookshelf. Order now for $64.95 (plus shipping).

DRIVING DIRECTIONS

AMERICAN LEAGUE STADIUMS

ANGELS STADIUM, ANAHEIM
Highway 57 (Orange Freeway) to Orangewood exit, west on Orangewood, stadium on west side of Orange Freeway.

CAMDEN YARDS, BALTIMORE
From the north and east on I-95, take I-395 (exit 53), downtown to Russell Street; from the south or west on I-95, take exit 52 to Russell Street North.

FENWAY PARK, BOSTON
Massachusetts Turnpike (I-90) to Prudential exit (stay left), right at first set of lights, right on Dalton Street, left on Boylston Street, right on Ipswich Street.

U.S. CELLULAR FIELD, CHICAGO
Dan Ryan Expressway (I-90/94) to 35th Street exit.

JACOBS FIELD, CLEVELAND
From south, I-77 North to East Ninth Street exit, to Ontario Street; From east, I-90/Route 2 west to downtown, remain on Route 2 to East Ninth Street, left to stadium.

COMERICA PARK, DETROIT
I-75 to Grand River exit, follow service drive east to stadium, located off Woodward Avenue.

KAUFFMAN STADIUM, KANSAS CITY
From north or south, take I-435 to stadium exits. From east or west, take I-70 to stadium exits.

METRODOME, MINNESOTA
I-35W south to Washington Avenue exit or I-35W north to Third Street exit. I-94 East to I-35W north to Third Street exit or I-94 West to Fifth Street exit.

YANKEE STADIUM, NEW YORK
From I-95 North, George Washington Bridge to Cross Bronx Expressway to exit 1C; Major Deegan South (I-87) to exit G (161st Street); I-87 North to 149th or 155th Streets; I-87 South to 161st Street.

NETWORK ASSOCIATES COLISEUM, OAKLAND
From I-880, take either the 66th Avenue or Hegenberger Road exit.

SAFECO FIELD, SEATTLE
I-5 or I-90 to Fourth Avenue South exit.

TROPICANA FIELD, TAMPA BAY
I-275 South to St. Petersburg, exit 11, left onto Fifth Avenue, right onto 16th Street.

THE BALLPARK IN ARLINGTON, TEXAS
From I-30, take Ballpark Way exit, south on Ballpark Way; From Route 360, take Randol Mill exit, west on Randol Mill.

SKYDOME, TORONTO
From west, take QEW/Gardiner Expressway eastbound and exit at Spadina Avenue, north on Spadina one block, right on Bremner Boulevard. From east, take Gardiner Expressway westbound and exit at Spadina Avenue, north on Spadina one block, right on Bremner Boulevard.

NATIONAL LEAGUE STADIUMS

BANK ONE BALLPARK, ARIZONA
I-10 to Seventh Street exit, turn south; I-17 to Seventh Street, turn north.

TURNER FIELD, ATLANTA
I-75/85 northbound/southbound, take exit 246 (Fulton Street); I-20 westbound, take exit 58A (Capitol Avenue); I-20 eastbound, take exit 56B (Windsor Street), right on Windsor Street, left on Fulton Street.

WRIGLEY FIELD, CHICAGO
I-90/94 to Addison Street exit, follow Addison five miles to ballpark. One mile west of Lakeshore Drive, exit at Belmont going northbound, exit at Irving Park going southbound.

GREAT AMERICAN BALL PARK, CINCINNATI
I-75 southbound, take Second Street exit. Ballpark is located off Second Street at Main Street. I-71 southbound, take Third Street exit, right on Broadway. I-75/I-71 northbound, take Second Street exit—far right lane on Brent Spence Bridge. Ballpark is located off Second Street at Main Street.

COORS FIELD, COLORADO
I-70 to I-25 South to exit 213 (Park Avenue) or 212C (20th Street); I-25 to 20th Street, east to park.

PRO PLAYER STADIUM, FLORIDA
From south, Florida Turnpike extension to stadium exit; From north, I-95 to I-595 West to Florida Turnpike to stadium exit; From west, I-75 to I-595 to Florida Turnpike to stadium exit; From east, Highway 826 West to NW 27th Avenue, north to Dan Marino Blvd., right to stadium.

MINUTE MAID PARK, HOUSTON
From I-10 East, take Smith Street (exit 769A), left at Texas Ave., 0.6 miles to park at corner of Texas Ave. and Crawford St.; from I-10 West, take San Jacinto St. (exit 769B), right on Fannin St., left on Texas Ave., 0.3 miles to park; From Hwy. 59 North: take Gray Ave./Pierce Ave. exit, 0.3 miles on Gray St. to Crawford St., one mile to park.

DODGER STADIUM, LOS ANGELES
I-5 to Stadium Way exit, left on Stadium Way, right on Academy Road, left to Stadium Way to Elysian Park Avenue, left to stadium; I-110 to Dodger Stadium exit, left on Stadium Way, right on Elysian Park Avenue; US 101 to Alvarado exit, right on Sunset, left on Elysian Park Avenue.

MILLER PARK, MILWAUKEE
From airport/south, I-94 West to Madison exit, to stadium.

OLYMPIC STADIUM, MONTREAL
From New England, take I-87 North from Vermont to Quebec Highway 15 to the Jacques Cartier Bridge, exit left, right on Sherbrooke. From upstate New York, take I-81 North to Trans Canada Highway 401, east to Quebec Highway 20, north to Highway 40 to Boulevard Pie IX exit south to stadium. Access by subway from downtown Montreal to Pie IX Metro station.

SHEA STADIUM, NEW YORK
From Bronx and Westchester, take Cross Bronx Expressway to Bronx-Whitestone Bridge, then take bridge to Whitestone Expressway to Northern Boulevard/Shea Stadium exit. From Brooklyn, take Eastbound BQE to Eastbound Grand Central Parkway. From Long Island, take either Northern State Parkway or LIE to Westbound Grand Central Parkway. From northern New Jersey, take George Washington Bridge to Cross Bronx Expressway. From Southern New Jersey, take any of bridge crossings to Verazzano Bridge, and then take either Belt Parkway or BQE to Grand Central Parkway.

CITIZENS BANK PARK, PHILADELPHIA
From I-95 or I-76, take the Broad Street exit. The ballpark is on on the north side of Pattison Avenue, between 11th and Darien Streets.

PNC PARK, PITTSBURGH
From south, I-279 through Fort Pitt Tunnel, make left off bridge to Fort Duquesne Bridge, cross Fort Duquesne Bridge, follow signs to PNC Park. From north, I-279 to PNC Park (exit 12, left lane), follow directions to parking.

BUSCH STADIUM, ST. LOUIS
From Illinois, take I-55 South, I-64 West, I-70 West or US 40 West across the Mississippi River (Poplar Street Bridge) to Busch Stadium exit. In Missouri, take I-55 North, I-64 East, I-70 East, I-44 East or US 40 East to downtown St. Louis and Busch Stadium exit.

PETCO PARK, SAN DIEGO
Four major thoroughfares feed into and out of downtown in all directions: Pacific Highway, I-5, State Route 163 and State Route 94/Martin Luther King Freeway. In addition, eight freeway on- and off-ramps service the area immediately around the ballpark.

SBC PARK, SAN FRANCISCO
From Peninsula/South Bay, I-280 north (or U.S. 101 north to I-280 north) to Mariposa Street exit, right on Mariposa, left on Third Street. From East Bay (Bay Bridge), I-80/Bay Bridge to Fifth Street exit, right on Fifth Street, right on Folsom Street, right on Fourth Street, continue on Fourth Street to parking lots (across bridge). From North Bay (Golden Gate Bridge), U.S. 101 south/Golden Gate Bridge to Downtown/Lombard Street exit, right on Van Ness Ave., left on Golden Gate Ave., right on Hyde Street and across Market Street to Eighth Street, left on Bryant Street, right on Fourth Street.

MAJOR LEAGUE
BASEBALL

Mailing Address: 245 Park Ave., New York, NY 10167.
Telephone: (212) 931-7800. **Website:** www.mlb.com.
Commissioner: Allan H. "Bud" Selig.
Senior Executive Assistant to Commissioner: Kathy Dubinski. **Executive Protection Supervisor:** Earnell Lucas. **Administrative Assistant:** Sandy Ronback. **Office Assistant:** Lisa Steinman. **Supervisor, Security/Investigations:** Tom Christopher. **Assistant to the Commissioner:** Lori Keck.
President/Chief Operating Officer: Bob DuPuy.
Executive Vice President, Baseball Operations: Sandy Alderson. **Executive VP, Administration:** John McHale. **Executive VP, Labor Relations/Human Resources:** Robert Manfred. **Executive VP, Business:** Tim Brosnan. **Executive VP, Finance:** Jonathan Mariner.

Bud Selig

Baseball Operations
Senior Vice President, Baseball Operations: Jimmie Lee Solomon. **VP, Baseball Operations/Administration:** Ed Burns. **Senior Director, Major League Operations:** Roy Krasik. **Manager, Baseball Operations:** Jeff Pfeifer.
Manager, Waivers/Major League Records: Brian Small. **Senior Manager, Minor League Operations:** Sylvia Lind. **VP, International Baseball Operations:** Lou Melendez. **Manager, Dominican Operations:** Rafael Perez.
VP, On-Field Operations: Bob Watson.
Director, Umpire Administration: Tom Lepperd. **Director, Umpire Medical Services:** Mark Letendre. **Umpiring Supervisors:** Rich Garcia, Jim McKean, Steve Palermo, Frank Pulli, Rich Rieker, Marty Springstead.
Director, Arizona Fall League: Steve Cobb.
Director, Major League Scouting Bureau: Frank Marcos. **Assistant Director, Scouting Bureau:** Rick Oliver.

Security, Facilities
Senior Vice President, Security/Facilities: Kevin Hallinan. **Senior Director, Security Operations:** Dan Mullin. **Senior Manager, Facilities Operations:** Linda Pantell. **Manager, Security Operations:** Paul Padilla. **Manager, Investigations:** Leroy Hendricks.

Bob DuPuy

General Administration
Vice President, Accounting/Treasurer: Bob Clark. **VP, Finance:** Kathleen Torres. **Director, Risk Management/ Financial Reporting:** Anthony Avitable. **Manager, Payroll/Pension:** Rich Hunt.
Senior VP/General Counsel: Tom Ostertag. **Senior Manager, Records:** Mildred Delgado.
Senior VP/General Counsel: Ethan Orlinsky. **Deputy General Counsel:** Domna Candido, Jennifer Cohane. **Director, Quality Control:** Peggy O'Neill-Janosik.
VP, Information Technologies: Julio Carbonell. **Director, Operations/Technical Support:** Peter Surhoff. **Manager, Software Development:** John Moran. **Senior Manager, Enterprise Systems:** Mike Morris.
Senior Director, Baseball Assistance Team: Jim Martin.
Senior VP/General Counsel, Labor Relations: Frank Coonelly. **Deputy General Counsel, Labor:** Jennifer Gefsky. **Director, Salary/Contract Administration:** John Ricco.
VP, Strategic Planning for Recruitment/Diversity: Wendy Lewis. **Senior Manager, Diverse Business Partners:** Hanh Pham. **Director, Recruitment:** Denise Males. **Senior Director, Office Services:** Donna Hoder.
VP, Human Resources: Ray Scott. **Manager, Benefits/HRIS:** Diane Cuddy.

Sandy Alderson

Public Relations
Telephone: (212) 931-7878. **FAX:** (212) 949-5654.
Senior Vice President, Public Relations: Richard Levin. **Vice President, PR Operations:** Patrick Courtney. **Director, Marketing Communications:** Kathleen Fineout. **Senior Manager, Marketing Communications:** Carole Coleman. **Senior Manager, Baseball Information System:** Robert Doelger. **Manager, Media Relations:** Matthew Gould. **Manager, Marketing Communications:** Carmine Tiso. **Specialist, Baseball Information System:** John Blundell. **Specialist, Marketing Communications:** Matt Burton. **Senior Coordinator, Media Relations:** Dominick Balsamo. **Coordinator, Marketing Communications:** Paige Novack. **Senior Administrative Assistant:** Heather Flock. **Administrative Assistant:** Adriana Arcia. **Baseball Historian:** Jerome Holtzman.

Licensing
Senior Vice President, Licensing: Howard Smith.
VP, Adult Wearables/Authentics: Steve Armus. **VP, Collectibles/Cooperstown:** Colin Hagen. **Director, Licensing/Minor Leagues:** Eliot Runyon. **Senior Manager, Apparel Retail:** Adam Blinderman. **Director, Authentics:** Dennis Nolan. **Director, Novelties/Gifts:** Maureen Mason. **Director, New Technology/New Business:** Mike Napolitano. **Director, Business Affairs:** Geary Sellers. **Director, Non-Authentics:** Greg Sim. **Senior Manager, Presence Marketing:** Robin Jaffe.

Publishing and Photographs

Vice President, Publishing/Photographs: Don Hintze. **Editor, Publishing/Photographs:** Mike McCormick. **Art Director, Publications:** Faith Matorin. **Director, MLB Photographs:** Rich Pilling.

Special Events

Senior Vice President, Special Events: Marla Miller. **Directors, Special Events:** Morgan Littlefield, Brian O'Gara. **Managers, Special Events:** Eileen Buser, Christine Buckley, Joe Fitzgerald, Carolyn Taylor.

Broadcasting

Senior Vice President, Broadcasting: Chris Tully. **VP, Broadcast Administration/Operations:** Bernadette McDonald. **Director, Distribution Development:** Susanne Hilgefort. **Manager, Broadcast Administration/Operations:** Chuck Torres.

Community Affairs/Educational Programming

Vice President, Community Affairs/Educational Programming: Tom Brasuell. **Manager, Community Affairs/Educational Programming:** Jana Perry.

Advertising, Corporate Sales

Senior VP, Advertising/Marketing: Jacqueline Parkes. **Director, Marketing:** Mary Abrams. **Director, Research:** Dan Derian. **Senior Manager, Promotions:** Colleen LeMay. **Manager, Marketing:** Liana Bassin. **Vice President, Design Services:** Anne Occi.
Director, Local Sales: Joe Grippo.

Club Relations

Senior Vice President, Club Relations/Scheduling: Katy Feeney. **Coordinator, Club Relations/Scheduling:** Paul Kuo. **Senior Administrative Assistant, Club Relations/Scheduling:** Raxel Concepcion.
Senior VP, Club Relations: Phyllis Merhige. **Coordinator, Club Relations:** Michael Teevan.

Major League Baseball Productions

Office Address: 75 Ninth Ave., New York, NY 10011. **Telephone:** (212) 931-7777. **FAX:** (212) 931-7788.
Vice President/Executive Producer: Dave Gavant.
Senior Coordinating Producer: David Check. **Senior Manager Producer, Field Productions:** Steve Fortunato. **Managing Producer:** Adam Schlackman. **Senior Producer:** Jeff Spaulding. **Senior Writer:** Jeff Scott. **Director, Productions/Operations:** Shannon Valine. **Vice President, Productions Programming/Business Affairs:** Elizabeth Scott. **Manager, Videotape Library:** Frank Caputo.

International Business Operations

Mailing Address: 245 Park Ave., 34th Floor, New York, NY 10167. **Telephone:** (212) 931-7500. **FAX:** (212) 949-5795.
Senior Vice President, International Operations: Paul Archey. **VP, International Licensing/Sponsorship:** Shawn Lawson-Cummings. **Director, Broadcast Sales:** Italo Zanzi. **Managing Director, MLB Japan:** Jim Small. **Director, Australian Operations:** Thomas Nicholson. **Director, European Operations:** Clive Russell. **Director, Market Development/Events:** James Pearce. **Executive Producer, MLB International:** Russell Gabay.

MLB Advanced Media (MLB.com)

Office Address: 75 Ninth Ave., 5th Floor, New York, NY 10011. **Telephone:** (212) 485-3444. **FAX:** (212) 485-3456.
Chief Executive Officer: Bob Bowman.
Senior Vice President, Chief Marketing Officer: Holly Arnowitz, **Director, Ticketing:** Heather Benz. **VP, Multi-Media:** Jane Buford. **VP, Human Resources:** Leslie Knickerbocker. **Senior VP/Chief Technical Officer:** Joe Choti. **VP, Chief Financial Officer:** Jeff D'Onofrio. **Senior VP, Corporate Communications:** Jim Gallagher. **Senior VP, E-Commerce:** Noah Garden. **Senior VP/Editor-In-Chief, mlb.com:** Dinn Mann. **VP, Design:** Deck Rees. **Senior VP/General Counsel:** Michael Mellis, **Senior VP, Business Development:** George Kliavkoff. **VP, Sponsorship:** Mark Sage.

Umpires

Ted Barrett (Gilbert, AZ), Wally Bell (Boardman, OH), Joe Brinkman (Chiefland, FL), C.B. Bucknor (Brooklyn, NY), Mark Carlson (Channahon, IL), Gary Cederstrom (Minot, ND), Eric Cooper (Johnston, IA), Derryl Cousins (Hermosa Beach, CA), Terry Craft (Bradenton, FL), Jerry Crawford (Tiera Verde, FL), Fieldin Culbreth (Inman, SC), Phil Cuzzi (Nutley, NJ), Kerwin Danley (Los Angeles, CA), Gary Darling (Phoenix, AZ), Gerry Davis (Appleton, WI), Dana DeMuth (Gilbert, AZ), Laz Diaz (Orlando, FL), Mike DiMuro (Chandler, AZ), Bruce Dreckman (Marcus, IA), Doug Eddings (Las Cruces, NM), Paul Emmel (Bradenton, FL), Mike Everitt (Clive, IA), Andy Fletcher (Olive Branch, MS), Marty Foster (Beloit, WI), Bruce Froemming (Mequon, WI), Greg Gibson (Catlettsburg, KY), Brian Gorman (Camarillo, CA), Angel Hernandez (Loxahatchee, FL), John Hirschbeck (Youngstown, OH), Bill Hohn (Blue Bell, PA), Sam Holbrook (Lexington, KY), Marvin Hudson (Washington, GA), Dan Iassogna (Smyrna, GA), Jim Joyce (Beaverton, OR), Jeff Kellogg (Mattawan, MI), Ron Kulpa (Maryland Heights, MO), Jerry Layne (Winter Haven, FL), Alfonso Marquez (Gilbert, AZ), Randy Marsh (Edgewood, KY), Tim McClelland (West Des Moines, IA), Jerry Meals (Salem, OH), Chuck Meriwether (Nashville, TN), Bill Miller (San Clemente, CA), Ed Montague (San Mateo, CA), Paul Nauert (Lawrenceville, GA), Jeff Nelson (Windermere, FL), Brian O'Nora (Canfield, OH), Larry Poncino (Tucson, AZ), Tony Randazzo (Las Cruces, NM), Ed Rapuano (Boca Raton, FL), Rick Reed (Rochester Hills, MI), Mike Reilly (Battle Creek, MI), Charlie Reliford (Ashland, KY), Jim Reynolds (Osprey, FL), Brian Runge (Ramona, CA), Paul Schrieber (Scottsdale, AZ), Dale Scott (Portland, OR), Tim Timmons (New Albany, OH), Tim Tschida (Turtle Lake, WI), Larry Vanover (Owensboro, KY), Mark Wegner (Plant City, FL), Tim Welke (Kalamazoo, MI), Bill Welke (Marshall, MI), Hunter Wendelstedt (Daytona Beach, FL), Joe West (Ft. Lauderdale, FL), Mike Winters (Carlsbad, CA), Larry Young (Roscoe, IL).

EVENTS

2004 Major League All-Star Game: July 13 at Minute Maid Park, Houston.
2004 World Series: Begins Oct. 23 at winning league in All-Star Game.

AMERICAN LEAGUE

Years League Active: 1901-.
2004 Opening Date: March 30. **Closing Date:** Oct. 3.
Regular Season: 162 games.
Division Structure: East—Baltimore, Boston, New York, Tampa Bay, Toronto. **Central**—Chicago, Cleveland, Detroit, Kansas City, Minnesota. **West**—Anaheim, Oakland, Seattle, Texas.
Playoff Format: Three division champions and second-place team with best record meet in best-of-5 Division Series. Winners meet in best-of-7 League Championship Series.
All-Star Game: July 13, Minute Maid Park, Houston (American League vs. National League).
Roster Limit: 25, through Aug. 31 when rosters expand to 40.
Brand of Baseball: Rawlings.
Statistician: Elias Sports Bureau, 500 Fifth Ave., New York, NY 10110.

STADIUM INFORMATION

City	Stadium	LF	Dimensions CF	RF	Capacity	2003 Att.
Anaheim	Angel Stadium	365	406	365	45,050	3,061,093
Baltimore	Camden Yards	333	410	318	48,876	2,425,440
Boston	Fenway Park	310	390	302	33,871	2,724,165
Chicago	U.S. Cellular Field	300	400	335	44,321	1,939,594
Cleveland	Jacobs Field	325	405	325	43,863	1,729,911
Detroit	Comerica Park	346	422	330	40,000	1,368,245
Kansas City	Kauffman Stadium	330	400	330	40,529	1,753,211
Minnesota	Humphrey Metrodome	343	408	327	48,678	1,946,012
New York	Yankee Stadium	318	408	314	57,545	3,465,599
Oakland	Network Assoc. Coliseum	330	400	367	43,662	2,216,414
Seattle	Safeco Field	331	405	326	45,600	3,268,504
Tampa Bay	Tropicana Field	315	407	322	45,200	1,058,695
Texas	Ballpark in Arlington	334	400	325	49,166	2,094,394
Toronto	SkyDome	328	400	328	50,516	1,799,458

NATIONAL LEAGUE

Years League Active: 1876-.
2004 Opening Date: April 5. **Closing Date:** Oct. 3.
Regular Season: 162 games.
Division Structure: East—Atlanta, Florida, Montreal, New York, Philadelphia. **Central**—Chicago, Cincinnati, Houston, Milwaukee, Pittsburgh, St. Louis. **West**—Arizona, Colorado, Los Angeles, San Diego, San Francisco.
Playoff Format: Three division champions and second-place team with best record meet in best-of-5 Division Series. Winners meet in best-of-7 League Championship Series.
All-Star Game: July 13 at Minute Maid Park, Houston (National League vs. American League).
Roster Limit: 25, through Aug. 31 when rosters expand to 40.
Brand of Baseball: Rawlings.
Statistician: Elias Sports Bureau, 500 Fifth Ave., New York, NY 10110.

STADIUM INFORMATION

City	Stadium	LF	Dimensions CF	RF	Capacity	2003 Att.
Arizona	Bank One Ballpark	330	407	334	48,500	2,808,492
Atlanta	Turner Field	335	401	330	50,528	2,401,084
Chicago	Wrigley Field	355	400	353	38,884	2,952,620
Cincinnati	Great American Ball Park	328	404	325	42,263	2,355,266
Colorado	Coors Field	347	415	350	50,200	2,335,424
Florida	Pro Player Stadium	335	410	345	40,585	1,302,714
Houston	Minute Maid Park	315	435	326	42,000	2,455,239
Los Angeles	Dodger Stadium	330	395	330	56,000	3,138,626
Milwaukee	Miller Park	315	402	315	53,192	1,700,354
Montreal	Olympic Stadium	325	404	325	46,500	1,025,639
New York	Shea Stadium	338	410	338	55,777	2,172,771
Philadelphia	Citizens Bank Park	329	401	330	43,500	*2,259,943
Pittsburgh	PNC Park	335	400	335	48,044	1,636,752
St. Louis	Busch Stadium	330	402	330	49,676	2,910,386
San Diego	Petco Park	334	398	322	42,000	#2,030,083
San Francisco	SBC Park	335	404	307	40,800	3,264,888

*Attendance for Veterans Stadium in 2003
#Attendance for Qualcomm Stadium in 2003

ANAHEIM ANGELS

Office Address: Angel Stadium of Anaheim, 2000 Gene Autry Way, Anaheim, CA 92806.
Mailing Address: P.O. Box 2000, Anaheim, CA 92803.
Telephone: (714) 940-2000. FAX: (714) 940-2001.
Website: www.angelsbaseball.com.

Ownership

Operated by: Angels Baseball LP.
Chairman, Chief Executive Officer: Arturo Moreno.

Arte Moreno

BUSINESS OPERATIONS

President: Dennis Kuhl. Executive Administrative Assistant: Trish Pene.

Finance, Administration

Chief Financial Officer: Bill Beverage. Vice President, Finance/Administration: Molly Taylor. Senior Financial Analyst: Amy Langdale. Manager, Information Services: Al Castro. Senior Network Engineer: Neil Farris. Senior Customer Support Analyst: David Yun. Assistant Controller: Cris Fisher. Accountants: Lorelei Largey, Jean Ouyang. Assistant, Accounting: Linda Chubak.

Director, Human Resources: Jenny Price. Human Resources Coordinator: Cindy Williams. Assistant, Human Resources: Lidia Argomaniz.

Marketing, Corporate Sales

Senior Vice President, Sales/Marketing: John Carpino. Director, Corporate Sales: Richard McClemmy. Corporate Sales Managers: Paul LaFerla, Bill Pedigo, Sam Piccione, Sabrina Warner. Administrative Assistant: Maria Dinh.

Director, Marketing/Promotions: Robert Alvaradol. Director, Ticket/Suites Sales: Steve Shiffman. Manager, Suites/Guest Relations: Lynda Nelson. Senior Marketing Representative: Jennifer Randall. Marketing Representative: Joel Hobson. Marketing Coordinator/Designer: Nancy Herrera. Account Executives: Dan Carnahan, Lisa Gaspar, Mike Kirby, Damon Roschke, Keith Rowe. Group Sales Manager: Joe Furmanski. Group Sales Account Executives: Scott Booth, Ryan Redmond, Angel Rodriguez, Michael Sandoval, Carla Enriquez, Ernie Prukner. Telemarketing Supervisor: Tom DeTemple. Administrative Assistant, Marketing/Promotions: Monica Campanis. Administrative Assistants, Sales: Pat Lissy, Amy Fournier.

Manager, Entertainment: Peter Bull. Producer, Video/Scoreboard Operations: Robert Castillo. Associate Producer, Video/Scoreboard Operations: David Tsuruda.

Public Relations, Communications

Telephone: (714) 940-2014. FAX: (714) 940-2205.
Vice President, Communications: Tim Mead. Administrative Assistant: Unavailable.
Manager, Baseball Information: Larry Babcock. Manager, Media Services: Nancy Mazmanian. Manager, Community Development: Matt Bennett. Publicity/Broadcasting Manager: Aaron Tom. Publications Manager: Doug Ward. Media Relations Representatives: Eric Kay, Marty Sewell. Traveling Secretary/Media Representative: Tom Taylor. Speakers' Bureau: Bobby Grich, Clyde Wright. Club Photographers: Bob Binder, John Cordes, Debora Robinson.

Ballpark Operations

Director, Ballpark Operations: John Drum. Manager, Facility Services: Mike McKay. Assistant Operations Manager: Sam Maida.

Manager, Security: Keith Cleary. Manager, Field/Ground Maintenance: Barney Lopas. Purchasing Specialist: Ron Sparks. Office Specialist: Linda Fitzgerald. Purchasing Assistant: Suzanne Peters. Office Support Assistant: Calvin Ching. Receptionist: Jeannette Radillo.

PA Announcer: David Courtney. Organist: Peggy Duquesnel.

Ticketing

Manager, Ticket Operations: Sheila Brazelton. Assistant Ticket Manager: Susan Weiss. Supervisor, Ticketing: Eric Challman. Ticketing Representatives: Clancy Holligan, Kim Weaver.

Travel, Clubhouse

Clubhouse Manager: Ken Higdon. Assistant Clubhouse Manager: Keith Tarter. Visiting Clubhouse Manager: Brian Harkins.

Senior Video Coordinator: Diego Lopez. Video Coordinator: Ruben Montano.

GENERAL INFORMATION

Stadium (year opened): Angel Stadium of Anaheim (1998).
Home Dugout: Third Base. Playing Surface: Grass.
Team Colors: Red, dark red, blue and silver.
Player Representative: Jarrod Washburn.

Bill Stoneman

BASEBALL OPERATIONS

Vice President, General Manager: Bill Stoneman.
Assistant GM: Ken Forsch. **Special Assistants to GM:** Preston Gomez, Gary Sutherland. **Administrative Assistant, Scouting/ General Manager:** Laura Fazioli.

Major League Staff

Manager: Mike Scioscia.
Coaches: Bench—Joe Maddon; Pitching—Bud Black; Batting—Mickey Hatcher; First Base—Alfredo Griffin; Third Base—Ron Roenicke; Bullpen—Orlando Mercado; Bullpen Catcher—Steve Soliz.

Medical, Training

Medical Director: Dr. Lewis Yocum. **Team Physician:** Dr. Craig Milhouse.
Head Athletic Trainer: Ned Bergert. **Athletic Trainer:** Rick Smith.
Physical Therapist: Brian Scherr. **Strength/Conditioning Coach:** Brian Grapes. **Administrative Assistant:** Chris Titchenal.

Player Development

Telephone: (714) 940-2031. **FAX:** (714) 940-2203.
Director, Player Development: Tony Reagins. **Manager, Baseball Operations:** Abe Flores. **Mesa Operations:** Eric Blum. **Administrative Assistant, Player Development:** Juana Maria Arellano.
Field Coordinator: Bruce Hines. **Roving Instructors:** Mike Butcher (pitching), Trent Clark (strength/conditioning), Geoff Hostetter (training coordinator), Bill Lachemann (catching/special assignment), Bobby Mitchell (outfield/baserunning/bunting), Bobby Ramos (catching), Ty Van Burkleo (hitting).

Mike Scioscia

Farm System

Class	Farm Team	League	Manager	Coach	Pitching Coach
AAA	Salt Lake	Pacific Coast	Mike Brumley	Jim Eppard	Rich Bombard
AA	Arkansas	Texas	Tyrone Boykin	Todd Takayoshi	Kernan Ronan
High A	Rancho Cucamonga	California	Bobby Meacham	James Rowson	Keith Comstock
Low A	Cedar Rapids	Midwest	Bobby Magallanes	Justin Baughman	Erik Bennett
Rookie	Provo	Pioneer	Tom Kotchman	Kevin Ham	Zeke Zimmerman
Rookie	Mesa	Arizona	Brian Harper	Keith Johnson	Jack Uhey
Rookie	Angels	Dominican	Charlie Romero	Edgal Rodriguez	Santos Alcala

Scouting

Telephone: (714) 940-2038. **FAX:** (714) 940-2203.
Director, Amateur Scouting: Eddie Bane.
Director, Professional Scouting: Gary Sutherland.
Major League Scouts: Jay Hankins (Greenwood, MO), Rich Schlenker (Walnut Creek, CA), Brad Sloan (Brimfield, IL), Moose Stubing (Villa Park, CA), Dale Sutherland (La Crescenta, CA), John Van Ornum (Bass Lake, CA).
National Crosscheckers: Jeff Malinoff (Lopez, WA), Ric Wilson (Chandler, AZ). **Regional Supervisors:** West—William "Bo" Hughes (Sherman Oaks, CA). Midwest—Ron Marigny (Houston, TX). East—Marc Russo (Mooresville, NC).
Area Scouts: Arnold Braithwaite (Steger, IL), John Burden (Fairfield, OH), Karl Carswell (Kansas City, MO), Arnold Cochrane (Ponce, PR), Tim Corcoran (La Verne, CA), Jeff Crane (Tuscaloosa, AL), Bobby DeJardin (San Clemente, CA), Kevin Ham (El Paso, TX), Tom Kotchman (Seminole, FL), Dan Lynch (Marlboro, MA), Chris McAlphin (Huntersville, NC), Chad MacDonald (Arlington, TX), Dan Radcliffe (Green Belt, MD), Scott Richardson (Vacaville, CA), Jeff Scholzen (Hurricane, UT), Mike Silvestri (Davie, FL), Jack Uhey (Vancouver, WA).

Eddie Bane

International Supervisor: Clay Daniel (Jacksonville, FL).
International Scouts: Amador Arias (Venezuela), Luis Cuevas (Dominican Republic), Felipe Gutierrez (Mexico), Tak Kawamoto (Japan), Charlie Kim (Seoul, Korea), Alex Messier (Canada), Leo Perez (Dominican Republic), Carlos Porte (Venezuela), Dennys Suarez (Venezuela), Ramon Valenzuela (Dominican Republic), Grant Weir (Australia).

ARIZONA DIAMONDBACKS

Office Address: Bank One Ballpark, 401 E. Jefferson St., Phoenix, AZ 85004.
Mailing Address: P.O. Box 2095, Phoenix, AZ 85001.
Telephone: (602) 462-6500. **FAX:** (602) 462-6599.
Website: www.azdiamondbacks.com.

Ownership

Operated by: AZPB Limited Partnership.
Chairman of the Board: Jerry Colangelo.
Executive Committee: Bill Andrew, Bob Bohannon, Evy Chipman, Mike Chipman, George Getz, Jon Held, Dale Jensen, Ken Kendrick, Jeff Royer, Mel Shultz.

BUSINESS OPERATIONS

President: Richard Dozer. **Assistant to President:** Michelle Libonati.
General Counsel: Tom O'Malley.
Director, Human Resources: Peter Wong.

Jerry Colangelo

Finance

Senior Vice President, Finance: Tom Harris. **VP, Information Systems:** Bill Bolt.
Controller: Craig Bradley. **Assistant Controller:** Barbara Ragsdale. **Office Manager:** Pat Perez.

Marketing, Sales

Senior Vice President, Marketing/Sales: Scott Brubaker. **VP, Corporate Sales:** Mark Fernandez. **VP, Broadcasting:** Scott Geyer.
Director, Hispanic Marketing: Richard Saenz. **Tucson Operations Manager:** Jack Donovan. **Senior Director. Marketing:** Mike Malo. **Assistant, Marketing:** Maxine Royer.

Community Affairs

Director, Community Affairs: Karen Conway. **Senior Manager, Community Affairs:** Veronica Zapata Zendejas.

Public Relations, Communications

Telephone: (602) 462-6519. **FAX:** (602) 462-6527.
Director, Public Relations: Mike Swanson. **Manager, Publications:** Joel Horn. **Assistants to Director, Public Relations:** David Pape, Casey Wilcox. **Media Coordinator:** Susan Webner. **Staff Assistant:** Jeff Munn.

Stadium Operations

General Manager: Paige Peterson.
Vice President, Facilities Management: Alvan Adams. **VP, Event Services:** Russ Amaral. **VP, Security:** George Bevans. **Director, Suite Services:** Diney Mahoney. **Director, Ballpark Attractions:** Charlene Vazquez-Inzunza. **Assistant Managers, Guest Relations:** Summer Tennesen, Bryan White. **Director, Event Operations:** Jim Bochenek.
Head Groundskeeper: Grant Trenbeath.
PA Announcer: Jeff Munn. **Official Scorer:** Rodney Johnson.

Ticketing

Telephone: (602) 514-8400. **FAX:** (602) 462-4141.
Senior Vice President, Ticket Operations/Special Services: Dianne Aguilar.
VP, Sales/Group and Season Tickets: Rob Kiese. **Director, Ticket Operations:** Darrin Mitch.

Travel, Clubhouse

Director, Team Travel: Roger Riley. **Visitors Clubhouse:** Bob Doty.

GENERAL INFORMATION

Stadium (year opened): Bank One Ballpark (1998).
Home Dugout: Third Base. **Playing Surface:** Grass.
Team Colors: Purple, copper and turquoise.
Player Representative: Unavailable.

BASEBALL OPERATIONS

Telephone: (602) 462-6500. **FAX:** (602) 462-6599.
Senior Vice President, General Manager: Joe Garagiola Jr.
Vice President, Senior Assistant GM: Sandy Johnson. **Assistant GM:** Bob Miller.
Business Manager, Baseball Operations: Jeff Jacobs. **Assistant to GM:** Valerie Dietrich.

Major League Staff

Manager: Bob Brenly.
Coaches: Bench—Robin Yount; Pitching—Chuck Kniffin; Batting—Rick Schu; First Base—Glenn Sherlock; Third Base—Al Pedrique; Bullpen—Mark Davis.

Joe Garagiola Jr.

Medical, Training

Club Physicians: Dr. Michael Lee, Dr. Roger McCoy.
Head Trainer: Paul Lessard. **Assistant Trainer:** Dave Edwards. **Strength and Conditioning Coach:** David Page.

Minor Leagues

Telephone: (602) 462-4400. **FAX:** (602) 462-6421.
Director, Player Development: Tommy Jones. **Assistant Director, Player Development:** Fred Seymour. **Administrative Assistant, Player Development/Scouting:** Lisa Ventresca.
Coordinators: Dennis Lewallyn (pitching), Damon Berryhill (catching), Lee Tinsley (outfield), Jack Howell (hitting).
Head Trainer/Rehabilitation Coordinator: Greg Latta. **Tucson Complex Coordinator:** Bob Bensinger. **Rehabilitation Coach:** John Denny.

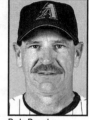

Bob Brenly

Farm System

Class	Farm Team	League	Manager	Coach	Pitching Coach
AAA	Tucson	Pacific Coast	Chip Hale	Lorenzo Bundy	Mike Parrott
AA	El Paso	Texas	Scott Coolbaugh	Damon Mashore	Mel Stottlemyre Jr.
High A	Lancaster	California	Wally Backman	Eric Fox	Dan Carlson
Low A	South Bend	Midwest	Tony Perezchica	Hector de la Cruz	Jeff Pico
Short season	Yakima	Northwest	Bill Plummer	Jay Gainer	Ed Vosberg
Rookie	Missoula	Pioneer	Jim Presley	Allen Campbell	Wellington Cepeda
Rookie	Diamondbacks	Dominican	Luis de los Santos	Juan Ballara	Jose Tapia

Scouting

Telephone: (602) 462-6518. **FAX:** (602) 462-6425.
Director, Scouting: Mike Rizzo. **Scouting Assistant:** Michele Copes.
Advance Scout: Mike Paul (Tucson, AZ).
Major League Scouts: Mack Babitt (Richmond, CA), Bryan Lambe (North Massapequa, NY), Jim Marshall (Paradise Valley, AZ).
Special Assignment Scout: Phil Rizzo (Rolling Meadows, IL).
Professional Scouts: Bill Earnhart (Point Clear, AL), Doug Gassaway (Blum, TX), Mike Piatnik (Winter Haven, FL), Mike Sgobba (Scottsdale, AZ).
National Supervisor: Kendall Carter (Scottsdale, AZ).
Regional Supervisors: East—Ed Durkin (Safety Harbor, FL); West—Kris Kline (Scottsdale, AZ).

Mike Rizzo

Scouts: Mark Baca (Temecula, CA), Ray Blanco (Miami, FL), Fred Costello (Livermore, CA), Trip Couch (Sugar Land, TX), Mike Daughtry (St. Charles, IL), Ed Gustafson (Spokane, WA), Scott Jaster (Midland, MI), Steve Kmetko (Phoenix, AZ), Hal Kurtzman (Van Nuys, CA), Greg Lonigro (Connellsville, PA), Steve McAllister (Chillicothe, IL), Howard McCullough (Greenville, NC), Matt Merullo (Madison, CT), Mike Valarezo (Cantonment, FL), Luke Wrenn (Lakeland, FL).
Director, Latin American Operations: Junior Noboa (Santo Domingo, DR). **Coordinator, Mexico:** Mike Sgobba (Scottsdale, AZ). **Venezuela Supervisor:** Miguel Nava (Tampa, FL).

ATLANTA BRAVES

Office Address: 755 Hank Aaron Dr., Atlanta, GA 30315.
Mailing Address: P.O. Box 4064, Atlanta, GA 30302.
Telephone: (404) 522-7630. **FAX:** (404) 614-1392.
Website: www.atlantabraves.com.

Ownership

Operated by: Atlanta National Baseball Club, Inc.
Owner: Time Warner.
Chairman Emeritus: Bill Bartholomay.
Chairman/President: Terry McGuirk. **Senior Vice President/Assistant to President:** Henry Aaron.

BUSINESS OPERATIONS

Executive Vice President, Business Operations: Mike Plant. **Senior VP, Sales/Marketing:** Derek Schiller. **VP/Team Counsel:** John Cooper.

Finance

Vice President, Controller: Chip Moore.

Marketing, Sales

Senior Director, Ticket Sales: Paul Adams. **Director, Corporate Sales:** Jim Allen.

Public Relations, Communications

Telephone: (404) 614-1556. **FAX:** (404) 614-1391.
Senior Vice President Public Relations/Communications: Greg Hughes. **Media Relations Manager:** Brad Hainje.
Administrative Assistant: Anne McAlister. **Assistants, Public Relations:** Adam Liberman, Meagan Swingle.

Stadium Operations

Director, Stadium Operations/Security: Larry Bowman. **Field Director:** Ed Mangan.
PA Announcer: Bill Bowers. **Official Scorers:** Mark Frederickson, Mike Stamus.
Director, Audio-Video Operations: Jennifer Berger.

Ticketing

Telephone: (800) 326-4000. **FAX:** (404) 614 -2480.
Director, Ticket Operations: Ed Newman.

Travel, Clubhouse

Director, Team Travel/Equipment Manager: Bill Acree. **Visiting Clubhouse Manager:** John Holland.

Terry McGuirk

GENERAL INFORMATION

Stadium (year opened): Turner Field (1997).
Home Dugout: First Base. **Playing Surface:** Grass.
Team Colors: Red, white and blue.
Player Representative: Unavailable.

BASEBALL OPERATIONS

Telephone: (404) 522-7630. **FAX:** (404) 614-3308.
Executive Vice President, General Manager: John Schuerholz.
VP/Assistant GM: Frank Wren. **Special Assistant to GM/Player Development:** Jose Martinez. **Executive Assistant:** Melissa Stone.

Major League Staff
Manager: Bobby Cox.
Coaches: Dugout—Pat Corrales; Pitching—Leo Mazzone; Batting—Terry Pendleton; First Base—Glenn Hubbard; Third Base—Fredi Gonzalez; Bullpen—Bobby Dews.

Medical, Training

John Schuerholz

Director, Medical Services: Dr. Joe Chandler.
Trainer: Jeff Porter. **Assistant Trainer:** Jim Lovell. **Strength/Conditioning Coach:** Frank Fultz.

Player Development
Telephone: (404) 522-7630. **FAX:** (404) 614-1350.
Director, Player Personnel: Dayton Moore. **Assistant, Player Personnel:** Tyrone Brooks. **Assistant Director, Player Development:** Marco Paddy. **Administrative Assistants:** Lena Burney, Chris Rice. **Baseball Operations Assistant:** Matt Price.
Field Coordinator, Instruction: Chino Cadahia. **Senior Pitching Supervisor:** Bill Fischer. **Supervisor, Field Operations:** Jim Beauchamp.
Roving Instructors: Mike Alvarez, (pitching), Rafael Belliard, (infield), Jeff Blauser (general), Franklin Stubbs, (hitting), Jack Voigt (baserunning/bunting), Phil Falco (strength/conditioning).

Bobby Cox

Farm System

Class	Farm Team	League	Manager	Coach	Pitching Coach
AAA	Richmond	International	Pat Kelly	Rick Albert	Guy Hansen
AA	Greenville	Southern	Brian Snitker	Mel Roberts	Dave Schuler
High A	Myrtle Beach	Carolina	Randy Ingle	Jack Maloof	Bruce Dal Canton
Low A	Rome	South Atlantic	Rocket Wheeler	Bobby Moore	Kent Willis
Rookie	Danville	Appalachian	Phillip Wellman	Luis Ortiz	Jim Czajkowski
Rookie	Kissimmee	Gulf Coast	Ralph Henriquez	S. Lezcano/J. Saul	D. Botelho/G. Luckert
Rookie	Braves I	Dominican	Jose Mota	Jose Vilar	Luis Alvarez
Rookie	Braves II	Dominican	Argenis Salazar	Tommy Herrera	Juan Rojas

Scouting
Telephone: (404) 614-1354. **FAX:** (404) 614-1350.
Director, Scouting: Roy Clark. **Administrative Assistant:** Dixie Keller.
Advance Scout: Bobby Wine (Norristown, PA).
Special Assignment Scouts: Dick Balderson (Englewood, CO), Jim Fregosi (Tarpon Springs, FL), Duane Larson (Knoxville, TN), Chuck McMichael (Grapevine, TX), Scott Nethery (Houston, TX), Paul Snyder (Murphy, NC), Jose Martinez (Miramar, FL). **Professional Scouts:** Rod Gilbreath (Lilburn, GA), Bob Wadsworth (Westminster, CA).
National Crosscheckers: John Flannery (Austin, TX), Tim Conroy (Monroeville, PA).
Regional Supervisors: Hep Cronin (Cincinnati, OH), Paul Faulk (Little River, SC), Kurt Kemp (Vancouver, WA).
Area Supervisors: Mike Baker (Santa Ana, CA), Daniel Bates (Phoenix, AZ), Billy Best

Dayton Moore

(Holly Springs, NC), Stu Cann (Bradley, IL), Sherard Clinkscales (Indianapolis, IN), Al Goetz (Duluth, GA), Ralph Garr (Missouri City, TX), J Harrison (Antelope, CA), Robert Lucas (Atlanta, GA), Darryl Monroe (Kansas City, MO), Alex Morales (Lake Worth, FL), J.J. Picollo (Mt. Laurel, NJ), John Ramey (Murrieta, CA), John Stewart (Granville, NY), Don Thomas (Baton Rouge, LA), Terry Tripp (Shawnee, OK).
International Supervisors: Phil Dale (Victoria, Australia), Julian Perez (Levittown, PR).
International Scouts: Roberto Aquino (Dominican Republic), Neil Burke (Australia), Richard Castro (Venezuela), Jeremy Chou (Taiwan), Jose Pedro Flores (Venezuela), Carlos Garcia (Colombia), Ruben Garcia (Venezuela), Lonnie Goldberg (Canada), Courtland Hall (Germany), David Latham (Japan), Jason Lee (Korea), Jose Leon (Venezuela), Luis Martinez (Venezuela), Luis Ortiz (Panama), Hiroyuki Oya (Japan), Rolando Petit (Venezuela), Elvis Pineda (Dominican Republic), Manuel Samaniego (Mexico), Miguel Teran (Colombia), Marvin Throneberry (Nicaragua), Carlos Torres (Venezuela).

BALTIMORE ORIOLES

Office Address: 333 W. Camden St., Baltimore, MD 21201.
Telephone: (410) 685-9800. **FAX**: (410) 547-6272.
E-Mail Address: fanservi@opacy.com.
Website: www.theorioles.com.

Ownership
Operated by: The Baltimore Orioles Limited Partnership, Inc.
Chairman/Chief Executive Officer: Peter G. Angelos.

BUSINESS OPERATIONS
Vice Chairman, Community Projects/Public Affairs: Thomas Clancy.
Vice Chairman, Chief Operating Officer: Joe Foss.
Executive Vice President: John Angelos.
VP/Special Liaison to Chairman: Lou Kousouris.
General Legal Counsel: Russell Smouse.
Director, Human Resources: Lisa Tolson. **Director, Information Systems:** James Kline.

Peter Angelos

Finance
Vice President, Chief Financial Officer: Robert Ames.
Controller: Edward Kabernagel.

Marketing, Sales
Vice President/Corporate Sales and Sponsorships: T.J. Brightman.

Public Relations, Communications
Telephone: (410) 547-6150. **FAX:** (410) 547-6272.
Executive Director, Communications: Spiro Alafassos.
Director, Public Relations: Bill Stetka. **Manager, Baseball Information**: Kevin Behan. **Manager, Communications**: Monica Pence.
Senior Director, Advertising/Promotions: Matthew Dryer. **Director, Events/Programs:** Kristen Schultz.
Director, Publishing/Creative Media: Jessica Fisher.

Ballpark Operations
Director, Ballpark Operations: Roger Hayden. **Manager, Event Operations**: Doug Rosenberger.
Director, Concession Operations: Robert Gallion.
Head Groundskeeper: Brian Kestranek.
PA Announcer: Dave McGowan. **Official Scorers**: Jim Henneman, Marc Jacobsen.

Fan, Ticket Services
Telephone: (410) 685-9800. **FAX:** (410) 547-6270.
Senior Director, Fan/Ticket Services: Don Grove. **Assistant Director, Sales:** Mark Hromalik.
Ticket Manager: Audrey Brown. **Systems Inventory Manager**: Steve Kowalski.

Travel, Clubhouse
Traveling Secretary: Phil Itzoe. **Equipment Manager (Home):** Jim Tyler. **Equipment Manager (Road):** Fred Tyler.
Umpires, Field Attendant: Ernie Tyler.

GENERAL INFORMATION
Stadium (year opened): Oriole Park at Camden Yards (1992).
Home Dugout: First Base. **Playing Surface**. Grass.
Team Colors: Orange, black and white.
Player Representative: Unavailable.

Jim Beattie

BASEBALL OPERATIONS

Telephone: (410) 547-6121. **FAX:** (410) 547-6271.
Executive Vice President, Baseball Operations: Jim Beattie. **VP, Baseball Operations:** Mike Flanagan.
Director, Baseball Administration: Ed Kenney Jr.
Executive Assistant to VP, Baseball Operations: Ann Lange.

Major League Staff

Manager: Lee Mazzilli.
Coaches: Bench—Sam Perlozzo; Pitching—Mark Wiley; Batting—Terry Crowley; First Base—Rick Dempsey; Third Base—Tom Trebelhorn; Bullpen—Elrod Hendricks.

Medical, Training

Club Physician: Dr. William Goldiner. **Club Physician, Orthopedics**: Dr. Charles Silberstein.
Head Athletic Trainer: Richie Bancells. **Assistant Athletic Trainer**: Brian Ebel.
Strength/Conditioning Coach: Tim Bishop.

Minor Leagues

Telephone: (410) 547-6120. **FAX:** (410) 547-6298.
Director, Minor League Operations: Doc Rodgers. **Assistant Director, Minor League Operations:** Tripp Norton. **Assistant, Minor League Operations:** Kevin Ibach.
Field/Hitting Coordinator: David Stockstill. **Medical Coordinator:** Dave Walker.
Strength/Conditioning Coach: Jay Shiner. **Facilities Coordinator:** Jaime Rodriguez. **Camp Coordinator:** Len Johnston. **Pitching Coordinator:** Dave Schmidt.
Roving Instructors: Jesus Alfaro (extended spring training manager), Moe Drabowsky (extended spring/rehab pitching), Andy Etchebarren (catching), Matt Martin (infield/baserunnng), Rosie Santizo (English and cultural literacy), Julio Vinas (hitting).

Lee Mazzilli

Farm System

Class	Farm Team	League	Manager	Coach	Pitching Coach
AAA	Ottawa	International	Tim Leiper	Dave Cash	Steve McCatty
AA	Bowie	Eastern	Dave Trembley	Butch Davis	Larry McCall
High A	Frederick	Carolina	Tom Lawless	Moe Hill	Scott McGregor
Low A	Delmarva	South Atlantic	Bien Figueroa	Don Werner	Doc Watson
Short season	Aberdeen	New York-Penn	Don Buford	Cedric Landrum/Jesus Alfaro	Andre Rabouin
Rookie	Bluefield	Appalachian	Gary Kendall	Len Johnston/Hensley Meulens	Larry Jaster
Rookie	Orioles	Dominican	Miguel Jabalera	Benny Adames	Robert Perez
Rookie	Orioles	Venezuela	Russell Vasquez	Luis Salazar	Carlos Leal

Scouting

Telephone: (410) 547-6187. **FAX:** (410) 547-6298.
Director, Scouting: Tony DeMacio.
Administrative Assistant: Marcy Zerhusen.
Advance Scout: Deacon Jones (Sugar Land, TX).
Professional Scouts: Todd Frohwirth (Waukesha, WI), Bruce Kison (Bradenton, FL), Gus Quattlebaum (Hermosa Beach, CA), Gary Roenicke (Nevada City, CA), Tim Thompson (Lewistown, PA), Fred Uhlman Sr. (Baltimore, MD).
National Crosschecker: Shawn Pender (Drexel Hill, PA).
Regional Crosscheckers: East—Jeff Taylor (Newark, DE), Central—Deron Rombach (Arlington, TX), West—Dave Blume (Elk Grove, CA).
Full-Time Scouts: Dean Albany (Baltimore, MD), Joe Almaraz (San Antonio, TX), Bill Bliss (Gilbert, AZ), Ty Brown (Ruther Glen, VA), Ralph Garr Jr. (Grand Prarie, TX), John Gillette (Kirkland, WA), Troy Hoerner (Gurnee, IL), Jim Howard (Clifton Park, NY), Dave Jennings (Daphne, AL), Ray Krawczyk (Corona, CA), Gil Kubski (Huntington Beach, CA), Lamar North (Rossville, GA), Nick Presto (West Palm Beach, FL), Harry Shelton (Ocoee, FL), Ed Sprague (Lodi, CA), Mike Tullier (River Ridge, LA), Dominic Viola (Cary, NC), Marc Ziegler (Columbus, OH).

Tony DeMacio

Director, Latin American Scouting: Carlos Bernhardt (San Pedro de Macoris, D.R.). **Supervisor, Central/South America, Lesser Antilles:** Jesus Halabi (Aruba).
International Scouts: Ubaldo Heredia (Venezuela), Salvador Ramirez (Dominican Republic), Arturo Sanchez (Venezuela), Mickey White (New Haven, CT).

BOSTON RED SOX

Office Address: Fenway Park, 4 Yawkey Way, Boston, MA 02215.
Telephone: (617) 267-9440. **FAX:** (617) 375-0944.
Website: www.redsox.com.

Ownership

Principal Owner: John Henry. **Chairman:** Tom Werner. **Vice Chairmen:** David Ginsberg, Les Otten.
President/Chief Executive Officer: Larry Lucchino.
Director: George Mitchell. **Chief Legal Officer, New England Sports Ventures:** Lucinda Treat.

BUSINESS OPERATIONS

Executive Vice President, Business Affairs: Mike Dee. **Executive VP, Public Affairs:** Dr. Charles Steinberg. **Senior VP, Fenway Affairs:** Larry Cancro. **Senior VP, Corporate Relations/Special Projects:** Meg Vaillancourt. **Special Assistant to Principal Owner:** Sylvia Moon.
Director, Human Resources/Office Administration: Michele Julian. **Administrative Assistants:** Adis Benitez, Christine Collins. **Receptionist:** Molly Walsh. **Mailroom Assistant:** Jared Pinkos.

Larry Lucchino

Finance, Legal

Vice President, Chief Financial Officer: Bob Furbush.
VP, Controller: Steve Fitch. **Administrator, Central Purchasing:** Eileen Murphy-Tagrin.
VP, Club Counsel: Elaine Steward. **Staff Counsel:** Jennifer Flynn. **Law Clerk:** Dina Conlin.

Sales, Marketing

Vice President, Sales/Corporate Partnerships: Sam Kennedy. **Director, Corporate Partnerships:** Joseph Januszewski. **Manager, Sponsor Services:** Troup Parkinson. **Coordinator, Sponsor Services:** Laura Reff. **Senior Manager, Season/Group Sales:** Corey Bowdre. **Senior Manager, Premium Sales:** Sean Curtin. **Premium Seating Sales Assistant:** Mark Rogoff. **Account Executives:** Kim Cameron, Tyler Fairchild, Jordan Kogler.
Director, Advertising/Television and Video Production: Tom Catlin. **Manager, Scoreboard/Video Production:** Danny Kischel. **Coordinator, Advertising:** Megan Kaiser. **Advertising/Production Assistants:** Jon Mancini, John Carter.
Director, Information Technology: Steve Conley. **Senior Systems Analyst:** Randy George.

Media, Community Relations

Director, Media Relations: Kevin Shea. **Director, Communications:** Glenn Geffner. **Coordinator, Media Relations:** Peter Chase. **Media Relations Assistant/Credentials:** Meghan McClure. **Media Relations Assistant:** Christopher Mearn.
Vice President, Publications/Archives: Dick Bresciani. **Executive Consultant, Public Affairs:** Lou Gorman. **Director, Publications:** Debbie Matson. **Manager, Publications/Archives:** Rod Oreste.
Manager, Community Relations: Vanessa Leyvas. **Director, Fan/Neighborhood Services:** Sarah McKenna. **Manager, Community Athletic Programs:** Ron Burton Jr. **Coordinator, Community Relations:** Sarah Stevenson. **Community Relations Assistant:** Colleen Reilly. **Red Sox Foundation Assistant:** Sheri Rosenberg.

Stadium Operations

Vice President, Stadium Operations: Joe McDermott.
VP, Planning/Development: Janet Marie Smith. **Coordinator, Planning/Development:** Paul Hanlon. **Director, Facilities Management:** Tom Queenan. **Facilities Maintenance:** Donnie Gardner, Glen McGlinchey, Ed Pistorino.
Director, Event Staff: Jeff Goldenberg. **Manager, Fenway Affairs:** Dan Lyons. **Superintendent, Park/Maintenance:** Joe Mooney. **Director, Grounds:** Dave Mellor. **Assistant Director, Grounds:** Charles Brunetti. **Stadium Operations:** Al Forester, Bob Levin.
PA Announcer: Ed Brickley. **Official Scorers:** Bruce Guindon, Dave O'Hara, Charles Scoggins.

Ticket Services, Operations

Telephone: (617) 267-1700, (617) 482-4769, (877) REDSOX-9. **FAX:** (617) 236-6640.
Senior Director, Business Services: Chuck Steedman. **Director, Ticket Services/Information:** Michael Schetzel. **Director, Ticket Operations:** Richie Beaton. **Manager, Season Ticket Services:** Joe Matthews. **Manager, Group/Premium Services:** Carole Alkins. **Manager, Fenway Tours/Events:** Marcita Thompson. **Manager, Ticket Services:** Marcell Saporita. **Manager, Ticket Accounting Administration:** Sean Carragher.

Travel, Clubhouse

Traveling Secretary: Jack McCormick. **Administrative Assistant:** Jean MacDougall. **Equipment Manager/Clubhouse Operations:** Joe Cochran. **Assistant Equipment Manager:** Edward Jackson. **Visiting Clubhouse Manager:** Tom McLaughlin. **Video/Advance Scouting Coordinator:** Billy Broadbent.

GENERAL INFORMATION

Stadium (first year): Fenway Park (1912).
Home Dugout: First Base. **Playing Surface:** Grass.
Team Colors: Navy blue, red and white.
Player Representative: Trot Nixon.

Theo Epstein

BASEBALL OPERATIONS

Telephone: (617) 267-9440. **FAX:** (617) 236-6649.
Senior Vice President, General Manager: Theo Epstein.
VP, Baseball Operations: Mike Port. **Assistant GM:** Josh Byrnes. **Special Assistant to GM/Scouting:** Bill Lajoie. **Special Assistant to GM/Player Development:** Craig Shipley. **Senior Baseball Operations Advisor:** Bill James. **Director, Baseball Operations/Assistant Director, Player Development:** Peter Woodfork. **Assistant, Baseball Operations:** Jed Hoyer.

Major League Staff

Manager: Terry Francona.
Coaches: Bench—Brad Mills; Pitching—Dave Wallace; Batting—Ron Jackson; First Base—Lynn Jones; Third Base—Dale Sveum; Bullpen—Euclides Rojas.

Medical, Training

Medical Director: Dr. William Morgan.
Head Trainer: Jim Rowe. **Assistant Trainer/Rehab Coordinator:** Chris Correnti. **Assistant Trainer:** Chang-Ho Lee.

Player Development

Telephone: (617) 267-9440. **FAX:** (617) 226-6695.
Director, Player Development: Ben Cherington. **Director, Minor League Administration:** Raquel Ferreira. **Administrative Assistant, Scouting/Player Development:** Victor Cruz. **Player Development Consultants:** Dick Berardino, Dwight Evans, Tommy Harper, Felix Maldonado, Frank Malzone, Bob Tewksbury, Charlie Wagner.
Coordinator, Florida Operations: Todd Stephenson. **Minor League Equipment Manager:** Mike Stelmach.
Roving Instructors/Coordinators: Orv Franchuk (hitting coordinator), Lou Frazier (outfield/baserunning), Glenn Gregson (pitching coordinator), Rob Leary (field), Johnny Pesky (special assignment), Jim Rice (instructor), Victor Rodriguez, John Sanders (catching), U.L. Washington (infield), Carl Yastrzemski (instructor), Dave Yeager (medical), Jim Young (medical). **Coordinator, Latin Field:** Victor Rodriguez.

Terry Francona

Farm System

Class	Farm Team	League	Manager	Coach	Pitching Coach
AAA	Pawtucket	International	Buddy Bailey	Mark Budaska	Mike Griffin
AA	Portland	Eastern	Ron Johnson	Russ Morman	Bob Kipper
High A	Sarasota	Florida State	Todd Claus	David Howard	Al Nipper
Low A	Augusta	South Atlantic	Chad Epperson	Cesar Hernandez	Ace Adams
Short season	Lowell	New York-Penn	Luis Alicea	Randy Phillips	Dave Tomlin
Rookie	Fort Myers	Gulf Coast	Ralph Treuel	Walter Miranda	Alan Mauthe
Rookie	Red Sox	Dominican	Nelson Paulino	Gilberto Reyes	J.Gonzalez/D. Reyes
Rookie	Red Sox	Venezuelan	Josman Robles	Unavailable	Carlos Perez

Scouting

Director, Amateur Scouting: David Chadd. **Assistant Director, Professional/International Scouting:** Tom Moore. **Director, Scouting Administration:** Jason McLeod. **Scouting Assistant:** Amiel Sawdaye.
Coordinator, Advance Scouting: Galen Carr. **Advance Scout:** Dave Jauss.
National Crosschecker: Ray Crone Jr. (Cedar Hill, TX). **Regional Crosscheckers:** Dave Finley (San Diego, CA), Mark Wasinger (El Paso, TX).
Pro Scouts: Murray Cook (Weston, FL), Jerry Dipoto (Overland Park, KS), Bill Latham (Trussville, AL), Joe McDonald (Lakeland, FL), Rene Mons (Manchester, NH), Gary Rajsich (Temecula, CA), Alan Regier (Gilbert, AZ), John Sanders (Woodstock, GA), Matt Sczesny (Deer Park, NY), Jerry Stephenson (Fullerton, CA).
Area Scouts: John Booher (Vancouver, WA), John DiPuglia (Lake Worth, FL), Rob English (Duluth, GA), Ray Fagnant (East Granby, CT), Danny Haas (Paducah, KY), Matt Haas (Cincinnati, OH), Nakia Hill (San Francisco, CA), Ernie Jacobs (Wichita, KS), Wally Komatsubara (Aiea, HI), Dan Madsen (Murrieta, CA), Joe Mason (Millbrook, AL), Darryl Milne (Denver, CO), James Orr (Orlando, FL), Jim Robinson (Arlington, TX), Jim Woodward (Claremont, CA), Jeff Zona (Mechanicsville, VA).

David Chadd

Consulting Scouts: Pat Anderson (Pine Bluff, AR), Ray Boone (Rancho Santa Fe, CA), Buzz Bowers (East Orleans, MA), Kelvin Bowles (Rocky Mount, VA), Cucho Rodriguez (San Juan, PR), Ed Roebuck (Lakewood, CA), Dick Sorkin (Potomac, MD), Terry Sullivan (La Grange, IL).
Coordinator, Latin American Scouting: Miguel Garcia. **Coordinator, Pacific Rim Scouting:** Jon Deeble. **Director, Dominican Operations:** Jesus Alou. **Director, Baseball Operations, Dominican Republic:** Elvio Jimenez.

CHICAGO CUBS

Office Address: Wrigley Field, 1060 W. Addison St., Chicago, IL 60613.
Telephone: (773) 404-2827. **FAX:** (773) 404-4129.
E-Mail Address: cubs@cubs.com.
Website: www.cubs.com.

Ownership

Operated by: Chicago National League Ball Club, Inc. **Owner:** Tribune Company.
Board of Directors: Dennis Fitzsimmons, Andy MacPhail.
President, Chief Executive Officer: Andy MacPhail.

BUSINESS OPERATIONS

Executive Vice President, Business Operations: Mark McGuire.
Director, Information Systems/Special Projects: Carl Rice. **PC Systems Analyst:** Sean True. **Senior Legal Counsel/Corporate Secretary:** Crane Kenney. **Executive Secretary, Business Operations:** Gayle Finney. **Director, Human Resources:** Jenifer Surma.

Andy MacPhail

Finance

Controller: Jodi Reischl. **Manager, Accounting:** Terri Lynn. **Payroll Administrator:** Mary Jane Iorio. **Senior Accountant:** Angela Boone.

Marketing, Broadcasting

Vice President, Marketing/Broadcasting: John McDonough.
Director, Promotions/Advertising: Jay Blunk. **Manager, Cubs Care/Community Relations:** Rebecca Polihronis. **Coordinator, Marketing/Community Affairs:** Mary Dosek. **Manager, Mezzanine Suites:** Louis Artiaga. **Manager, Special Events/Player Relations:** Joe Rios.

Media Relations, Publications

Telephone: (773) 404-4191. **FAX:** (773) 404-4129.
Director, Media Relations: Sharon Pannozzo. **Manager, Media Information:** Samantha Newby. **Assistant, Media Relations:** B.R. Koehnemann.
Director, Publications: Lena McDonagh. **Manager, Publications:** Jim McArdle. **Editorial Specialist, Publications:** Michael Huang. **Senior Graphic Designer:** Juan Alberto Castillo. **Graphic Design Specialist:** Joaquin Castillo. **Photographer:** Stephen Green.

Stadium Operations

Director, Stadium Operations: Paul Rathje.
Manager, Event Operations/Security: Mike Hill. **Coordinator, Event Operations/Security:** Julius Farrell. **Head Groundskeeper:** Roger Baird. **Facility Supervisor:** Bill Scott. **Coordinator, Office Services:** Randy Skocz. **Coordinator, Stadium Operations:** Danielle Alexa. **Switchboard Operator:** Brenda Morgan.
PA Announcer: Paul Friedman. **Official Scorers:** Bob Rosenberg, Don Friske.

Ticketing

Telephone: (773) 404-2827. **FAX:** (773) 404-4014.
Director, Ticket Operations: Frank Maloney. **Assistant Director, Ticket Sales:** Brian Garza. **Assistant Director, Ticket Services:** Joe Kirchen. **Vault Room Supervisor:** Cherie Blake.

Travel, Clubhouse

Traveling Secretary: Jimmy Bank.
Home Clubhouse Manager: Tom Hellmann. **Visiting Clubhouse Manager:** Michael Berkhart.

GENERAL INFORMATION

Stadium (year opened): Wrigley Field (1916).
Home Dugout: Third Base. **Playing Surface:** Grass.
Team Colors: Royal blue, red and white.
Player Representative: Mark Prior.

Jim Hendry

BASEBALL OPERATIONS

Telephone: (773) 404-2827. **FAX:** (773) 404-4111.
Vice President/General Manager: Jim Hendry.
Executive Assistant to President/GM: Arlene Gill.
Director, Baseball Operations: Scott Nelson. **Manager, Baseball Information:** Brian Williams.
Special Assistant to President: Billy Williams. **Special Assistants to GM:** Keith Champion (Ballwin, MO), Gary Hughes (Lantana, FL), Ken Kravec (Sarasota, FL), Ed Lynch (Scottsdale, AZ). **Scouting Consultant/Assistant to VP/GM:** Grady Little (Pinehurst, NC).

Major League Staff

Manager: Dusty Baker.
Coaches: Dugout—Dick Pole; Pitching—Larry Rothschild; Batting—Gary Matthews; First Base—Gene Clines; Third Base—Wendell Kim; Bullpen—Juan Lopez.

Medical, Training

Team Physicians: Dr. Stephen Adams, Dr. Michael Schafer.
Head Trainer: Dave Groeschner. **Assistant Trainer:** Sandy Krum. **Strength/Conditioning Coordinator:** Tim Buss.

Player Development

Telephone: (773) 404-4035. **FAX:** (773) 404-4147.
Director, Player Development/Latin American Operations: Oneri Fleita. **Coordinator, Minor League Operations:** Patti Kargakis.
Field Coordinator: Dave Bialas. **Pitching Coordinator:** Lester Strode.
Minor League Medical Coordinator: Greg Keuter.
Roving Instructors: Vince Coleman (outfield/baserunning), Jeff Huson (infield), Scott Servais (catching), Danny Stinnett (strength/conditioning), Dave Keller (hitting).

Dusty Baker

Farm System

Class	Farm Team	League	Manager	Coach	Pitching Coach
AAA	Iowa	Pacific Coast	Mike Quade	Pat Listach	Rick Kranitz
AA	West Tenn	Southern	Bobby Dickerson	Von Joshua	Alan Dunn
High A	Daytona	Florida State	Steve McFarland	Richie Zisk	Tom Pratt
Low A	Lansing	Midwest	Julio Garcia	Mike Micucci	Mike Anderson
Short season	Boise	Northwest	Tom Beyers	Ricardo Medina	David Haas
Rookie	Mesa	Arizona	Trey Forkerway	C. Martinez/F. Font	Rick Tronerud
Rookie	Cubs	Dominican	Ramon Caraballo	L. Vals/P. Cabrera	Leo Hernandez

Scouting

Telephone: (773) 404-2827. **FAX:** (773) 404-4147.
Director, Scouting: John Stockstill. **Administrative Assistant:** Patricia Honzik. **Assistant, Scouting:** Brian Williams.
Advance Scout: Bob Didier (Federal Way, WA). **Major League Scout:** Bill Harford (Chicago, IL). **Professional Scouts:** Tom Bourque (Cambridge, MA), Jim Crawford (Petal, MS), Demie Manieri (South Bend, IN), Joe Housey (Hollywood, FL), Mark Servais (LaCrosse, WI), Charlie Silvera (Millbrae, CA).
Special Assignment Scouts: Gene Handley (Huntington Beach, CA), Glen Van Proyen (Lisle, IL).
National Crosschecker: Brad Kelley (Glendale, AZ). **Crosscheckers:** Mark Adair (Florissant, MO), Mike Soper (Tampa, FL).
Full-Time Scouts: Billy Blitzer (Brooklyn, NY), Steve Fuller (Brea, CA), Al Geddes (Canby, OR), Steve Hinton (Mather, CA), Sam Hughes (Smyrna, GA), Brian Milner (Edgecliff Village, TX), Fred Petersen (Long Beach, CA), Rolando Pino (Pembroke Pines, FL), Pat Portugal (Tallahassee, FL), Steve Riha (Houston, TX), Tom Shafer (Overland Park, KS), Mitch Sokol (Phoenix, AZ), Keith Stohr (Orleans, MA), Billy Swoope (Norfolk, VA), Jose Trujillo (Puerto Rico), Stan Zielinski (Winfield, IL).
International Scouts: Hector Ortega (Venezuela), Jose Serra (Dominican Republic).

John Stockstill

CHICAGO WHITE SOX

Office Address: 333 W. 35th St., Chicago, IL 60616.
Telephone: (312) 674-1000. **FAX:** (312) 674-5116.
Website: www.whitesox.com.

Ownership
Operated by: Chicago White Sox, Ltd.
Chairman: Jerry Reinsdorf. **Vice Chairman:** Eddie Einhorn.
Board of Directors: Fred Brzozowski, Robert Judelson, Judd Malkin, Robert Mazer, Allan Muchin, Jay Pinsky, Larry Pogofsky, Lee Stern, Sanford Takiff, Burton Ury, Charles Walsh.
General Counsel: Allan Muchin.

Jerry Reinsdorf

BUSINESS OPERATIONS
Executive Vice President: Howard Pizer.
Special Assistant to Chairman: Dennis Gilbert. **Director, Information Services:** Don Brown.
Director, Human Resources: Moira Foy. **Assistant to Chairman:** Anita Fasano.
Administrator, Human Resources: Leslie Gaggiano.

Finance
Vice President, Administration/Finance: Tim Buzard. **Director, Finance:** Bill Waters. **Accounting Manager:** Chris Taylor.

Marketing, Sales
Senior Vice President, Marketing/Broadcasting: Rob Gallas. **Director, Marketing/Broadcasting:** Bob Grim. **Manager, Promotions/Marketing Services:** Sharon Sreniawski. **Manager, Scoreboard Operations/Production:** Jeff Szynal. **Manager, Broadcasting/Marketing Services:** Jo Simmons. **Manager, Sponsorship Sales:** Ryan Gribble. **Marketing Account Executives:** Dale Song, Gail Tucker. **Coordinator, Sponsorship Sales:** Stephanie Brewer. **Coordinator, Promotions/Marketing Services:** Amy Gullick. **Sponsorship Sales Administrator:** Jorie Sax.
Director, Ticket Sales: Jim Muno. **Manager, Ticket Sales:** Tom Sheridan. **Coordinator, Suite Sales:** Debbie Theobald. **Director, Advertising/Community Relations:** Christine O'Reilly. **Director, Marketing Communications:** Amy Kress. **Manager, Design Services:** Nicole Stack. **Manager, Community Relations:** Nicole Arceneaux. **Coordinator, Publications:** Kyle White. **Coordinator, Community Relations:** Danielle Disch. **Administrator, Community Relations:** Stephanie Carew.

Public Relations
Telephone: (312) 674-5300. **FAX:** (312) 674-5116.
Director, Public Relations: Scott Reifert. **Assistant Director, Media Relations:** Bob Beghtol. **Manager, Corporate Communications:** Katie Kirby. **Coordinator, Media Relations:** Unavailable. **Coordinator, Public Relations:** Vivian Stalling. **Coordinator, Publicity:** Ryan Barry.

Stadium Operations
Vice President, Stadium Operations: Terry Savarise. **Director, Park Operations:** David Schaffer. **Director, Guest Services/Diamond Suite Operations:** Julie Taylor.
Head Groundskeeper: Roger Bossard.
PA Announcer: Gene Honda. **Official Scorers:** Bob Rosenberg, Don Friske, Scott Reed.

Ticketing
Telephone: (312) 674-1000. **FAX:** (312) 674-5102.
Director, Ticket Operations: Bob Devoy. **Manager, Ticket Operations:** Mike Mazza. **Manager, Ticket Accounting Administration:** Ken Wisz.

Travel, Clubhouse
Manager, Team Travel: Ed Cassin. **Equipment Manager, Clubhouse Operations:** Vince Fresso. **Visiting Clubhouse:** Gabe Morell. **Umpires Clubhouse:** Joey McNamara.

GENERAL INFORMATION
Stadium (year opened): U.S. Cellular Field (1991).
Home Dugout: Third Base. **Playing Surface:** Grass.
Team Colors: Black, white and silver.
Player Representative: Unavailable.

Ken Williams

BASEBALL OPERATIONS

Senior Vice President/General Manager: Ken Williams.
Assistant GM: Rick Hahn. **Executive Advisor to GM:** Roland Hemond. **Special Assistant to GM:** Dave Yoakum. **Executive Assistant to GM:** Nancy Nesnidal.
Senior Director, Player Personnel: Duane Shaffer. **Director, Baseball Operations Systems:** Dan Fabian. **Assistant Director, Baseball Operations Systems:** Andrew Pinter. **Assistant, Baseball Operations:** J.J. Lally.

Major League Staff

Manager: Ozzie Guillen.
Coaches: Bench—Joe Nossek; Pitching—Don Cooper; Hitting—Greg Walker; First Base—Rafael Santana; Third Base—Joey Cora; Bullpen—Art Kusnyer.

Medical, Training

Senior Team Physician: Unavailable. **Head Trainer:** Herm Schneider. **Assistant Trainer:** Brian Ball. **Director, Conditioning:** Allen Thomas.

Player Development

Telephone: (312) 674-1000. **FAX:** (312) 674-5105.
Director, Player Development: David Wilder. **Assistant Director, Player Development:** Brian Porter.
Director, Minor League Administration: Grace Zwit. **Coordinator, Minor League Administration:** Kathy Potoski. **Manager, Clubhouse/Equipment:** Dan Flood.
Director, Instruction: Jim Snyder.
Roving Instructors/Coordinators: Kirk Champion (pitching), Mike Lum (hitting), Daryl Boston (outfield), Nick Leyva (infield), Tommy Thompson (catching), Chris Cron (bunting), Trung Cao (conditioning assistant). **Coordinator, Minor League Trainers/Rehabilitation:** Scott Takao.

Ozzie Guillen

Farm System

Class	Farm Team	League	Manager	Coach	Pitching Coach
AAA	Charlotte	International	Nick Capra	Gregg Ritchie	Curt Hasler
AA	Birmingham	Southern	Razor Shines	Manny Trillo	Juan Nieves
High A	Winston-Salem	Carolina	Ken Dominguez	Unavailable	J.R. Perdew
Low A	Kannapolis	South Atlantic	Chris Cron	Brandon Moore	Sean Snedeker
Rookie	Great Falls	Pioneer	John Orton	Mark Haley	Richard Dotson
Rookie	Bristol	Appalachian	Jerry Hairston	Ryan Long/C. DiMidio	Bill Kinneberg
Rookie	White Sox	Dominican	Denny Gonzalez	Unavailable	Unavailable

Scouting

Telephone: (312) 674-1000. **FAX:** (312) 451-5105.
Vice President, Free Agent/Major League Scouting: Larry Monroe.
Professional Scouts: Joe Butler (Temecula, CA), Dan Durst (Rockford, IL), Reggie Lewis (Elkton, MD), Larry Maxie (Upland, CA), Gary Pellant (Chandler, AZ), Billy Scherrer (Grand Island, NY), Daraka Shaheed (Vallejo, CA), Bill Young (Long Beach, CA).
National Crosschecker: Ed Pebley (Brigham City, UT). **Regional Supervisors:** East Coast—John Tumminia (Newburgh, NY), West Coast—Rick Ingalls (Long Beach, CA), Gulf Coast—Paul Provas (Arlington, TX), Midwest—Nathan Durst (Sycamore, IL).
Full-Time Area Scouts: Jayme Bane (Riverview, FL), Alex Cosmidis (Raleigh, NC), Curt Daniels (Vancouver, WA), Chuck Fox (Summit, NJ), Larry Grefer (Park Hills, KY), Matt Hattabaugh (Westminster, CA), Nick Hostetler (Atlanta, GA), Warren Hughes (Mobile, AL), George Kachigian (Coronado, CA), John Kazanas (Phoenix, AZ), Jose Ortega (Fort Lauderdale, FL), Mike Shirley (Anderson, IN) Alex Slattery (Maumelle, AR), Keith Staab (College Station, TX), Derek Valenzuela (Temecula, CA), Adam Virchis (Modesto, CA).
Part-Time Scouts: Tom Butler (East Rancho Dominguez, CA), Javier Centeno (Guaynabo, PR), E.J. Chavez (El Paso, TX), John Doldoorian (Whitinsville, MA), James Ellison (Georgetown, TX), Phil Gulley (Morehead, KY), Blair Henry (Roberts, WI), Jack Jolly (Murfreesboro, TN), Glen Murdock (Livonia, MI), Howard Nakagama (Salt Lake City, UT), Clay Overcash (Topeka KS), Al Otto (Schaumburg, IL), Mike Paris (Boone, IA), Ralph Reyes (Miami, FL), Rodney Walker (Linwood, WA).
Latin American Coordinator: Miguel Ibarra (Panama).
International Scouts: Roberto Espinoza (Venezuela), Denny Gonzalez (Dominican Republic).

Duane Shaffer

CINCINNATI REDS

Office Address: 100 Main St., Cincinnati, OH 45202.
Telephone: (513) 765-7000. **FAX:** (513) 765-7342.
Website: www.cincinnatireds.com.

Ownership

Operated by: The Cincinnati Reds, Inc.
Ownership Group: Gannett Co. Inc., Carl Lindner, Mrs. Louis Nippert, William Reik Jr., Marge Schott, George Strike.
Chief Executive Officer: Carl Lindner. **Chief Operating Officer:** John Allen. **Executive Assistant to Chief Operating Officer:** Joyce Pfarr.

John Allen

BUSINESS OPERATIONS

General Counsel: James Evans. **Secretary Counsel:** Karl Grafe.

Finance, Administration

Senior Director, Finance and Administration/Controller: Anthony Ward. **Accounting Manager:** Samantha Bailey. **Payroll Supervisor:** Brian Koniak. **Payroll Accountant:** Ayanna Goddard. **Staff Accountant:** Jason Randolph. **Accounts Payable:** Amanda Young. **Accounting Clerk:** Srey Pic.
Human Resources Manager: Stephanie Dicks. **Assistant, Human Resources:** Chaka Miller.
Administrator, Business/Broadcasting: Ginny Kamp.

Marketing, Sales

Director, Marketing: Cal Levy. **Director, Corporate Marketing:** Brad Blettner. **Manager, Scoreboard Operations:** Russ Jenisch. **Media Designer Scoreboard Operations:** David Storm. **Coordinator, Marketing Operations/Events:** Zach Bonkowski. **Manager, Promotions:** Lori Watt. **Marketing Assistant, Corporate Services:** Michelle Weisman.
Director, Season/Group Operations: Pat McCaffrey. **Director, Sales:** Jenny Gardner. **Manager, Group Tickets Operations:** Brad Callahan. **Manager, Season Tickets Operations:** Cyndi Strzynski. **Senior Account Executive:** Jodi Czanik. **Account Executives:** Chris Herrell, Patrick Korosec, Ryan Niemeyer, Ryan Rizzo. **Manager, Suite/Premium Service:** Unavailable. **Manager, Special Events:** Jennifer Green. **Coordinator, Consumer Sales:** Maya Wadleigh. **Coordinator, Riverfront Club/Sales:** Emily Price. **Coordinator, Season Operations:** Amanda Dollhausen. **Coordinator, Group Operations:** Eric Keller.
Manager, Merchandise: Amy Hafer. **Manager, Dugout Shop:** Dena Holland. **Manager, Game Day Retail:** Alicia King. **Assistant Manager, Dugout Shop:** Brian Stoehr. **Merchandise Inventory Control Clerk:** John Rieder. **Merchandise Accounting Assistant:** Shelley Haas. **Assistants, Merchandise:** Victoria Brink, Rhonda Hengehold.

Public Relations, Communications

Telephone: (513) 765-7800. **FAX:** (513) 765-7180.
Director, Media Relations: Rob Butcher. **Assistant Director, Media Relations:** Michael Vassallo. **Coordinator, Media Relations:** Larry Herms. **Assistant, Media Relations:** Jamie Ramsey.
Director, Creative Services: Ralph Mitchell. **Manager, Creative Services:** Dann Stupp. **Coordinator Production and Design:** Julie Hammel. **Manager, Community Relations:** Lorrie Platt.

Ballpark Operations

Senior Director, Ballpark Operations: Declan Mullin. **Assistant Director, Ballpark Operations:** Mike Maddox. **Chief Engineer:** Roger Smith. **Assistant to Chief Engineer:** Eric Dearing. **Superintendent, Ballpark Operations:** Bob Harrison.
Manager, Public Safety/Security: Kerry Rowland. **Security Personnel:** Dewitt Anderson, Tom Branigan, Tim Brown, Phillip Cook, Tom Cox, Debra Hall, Bill Summe. **Switchboard Manager:** Lauren Gaghan. **Switchboard Operator:** Jenny Niehaus.
Head Groundskeeper: Doug Gallant. **Assistant Groundskeeper:** Jon Phelps.

Ticketing

Telephone: (513) 765-7400. **FAX:** (513) 765-7119.
Director, Ticket Operations: John O'Brien. **Assistant Director, Ticket Operations:** Ken Ayer. **Ticket Operations Administration Manager:** Hallie Kinney. **Ticket Operations Accountant:** Jim Hall. **Ticket Operations Assistant:** Kevin Barnhill.

Travel, Clubhouse

Traveling Secretary: Gary Wahoff.
Senior Clubhouse/Equipment Manager: Bernie Stowe. **Reds Clubhouse/Equipment Manager:** Rick Stowe. **Visiting Clubhouse Manager:** Mark Stowe. **Reds Clubhouse Assistant:** Josh Stewart.

GENERAL INFORMATION

Stadium (year opened): The Great American Ballpark (2003).
Home Dugout: First Base. **Playing Surface:** Grass.
Team Colors: Red, white and black.
Player Representative: Unavailable.

Dan O'Brien

BASEBALL OPERATIONS

Telephone: (513) 765-7700. **FAX:** (513) 765-7799.
General Manager: Dan O'Brien.
Assistant GM: Dean Taylor. **Director, Baseball Operations:** Brad Kullman. **Senior Special Assistant to GM/Advance Scout:** Gene Bennett. **Special Assistants to GM:** Larry Barton Jr., Leland Maddox, Bill Wood. **Special Consultants to GM:** Johnny Bench, Ken Griffey Sr. **Executive Assistant to GM:** Debbie Bent. **Coordinator of Major League Scouting/Video Operations:** Nick Krall.

Major League Staff

Manager: Dave Miley.
Coaches: Bench—Jerry Narron; Pitching—Don Gullett; Hitting—Chris Chambliss; First Base—Randy Whisler; Third Base—Mark Berry; Bullpen—Tom Hume.

Medical, Training

Medical Director: Dr. Tim Kremchek.
Head Trainer: Mark Mann. **Assistant Trainer:** Tim Elser, Nick Kenney. **Strength/ Conditioning Coach:** Carlo Alvarez.

Player Development

Director, Player Development: Tim Naehring. **Assistant Director, Player Development:** Grant Griesser. **Senior Advisor:** Chief Bender. **Administrative Coordinator, Player Development:** Lois Hudson. **Manager, Florida Operations:** Jeff Maultsby. **Assistant Manager, Florida Operations:** Larry Mackin **Minor League Equipment Manager:** Tim Williamson.

Minor League Field Coordinator: Ron Oester. **Roving Coordinators:** Freddie Benavides (infield), Sammy Ellis (pitching), Rod McCray (outfield/baserunning), Leon Roberts (hitting). **Roving Hitting Instructors:** Jim Hickman. **Coordinator, Rehabilitation:** John Butler. **Coordinator, Medical:** Mark Farnsworth. **Coordinator, Strength/Conditioning:** Matt Krause.

Dave Miley

Farm System

Class	Farm Team	League	Manager	Coach(es)	Pitching Coach
AAA	Louisville	International	Rick Burleson	A.Garrett/J.Young	Mack Jenkins
AA	Chattanooga	Southern	Jayhawk Owens	Jamie Dismuke	Bill Moloney
High A	Potomac	Carolina	Edgar Caceres	Billy White	Ed Hodge
Low A	Dayton	Midwest	Alonzo Powell	Max Venable	Larry Pierson
Rookie	Billings	Pioneer	Donnie Scott	Chris Sabo	Vern Ruhle
Rookie	Sarasota	Gulf Coast	Luis Aguayo	Joe Ayrault/B.Williams	J.Garcia/B.Henry
Rookie	Reds	Dominican	Frank Laureano	Victor Franco	Manuel Solano
Rookie	Reds	Venezuela	Jose Villa	J.Torres/C. Barrios	Jose Villa

Scouting

Telephone: (513) 765-7700. **FAX:** (513) 765-7799.
Assistant GM, Professional Scouting: Dean Taylor. **Assistant, Professional Scouting:** Matt Arnold. **Professional Scouts:** Jason Angel, Leland Maddox, Greg McClain, Tom Mooney, Les Parker, Ross Sapp, Mike Williams.

Director, Amateur Scouting: Terry Reynolds. **Director, Scouting Administration:** Wilma Mann. **Administrative Assistant, Scouting:** Paul Pierson.

National Crosschecker: Butch Baccala (Weimar, CA). **Regional Crosscheckers:** East— Jim Thrift (Sarasota, FL); Midwest—Jim Gonzales (San Antonio, TX); West—Jeff Barton (Higley, AZ).

Scouting Supervisors: Jason Baker (Rome, N.Y.), Howard Bowens (Tacoma, WA), Jerry Flowers (Baton Rouge, LA), Mike Keenan (Chicago, IL), Craig Kornfeld (Rancho Santa Margarita, CA), Steve Kring (Charlotte, NC), Mike Misuraca (Sun City, CA), Steve Mondile (Wenonah, NJ), Jeff Morris (Tucson, AZ), Paul Pierson (Burlington, KY), Mike Powers (Sedona, AZ), Joe Siers (Wesley Chapel, FL), Reuben Smiley (Los Angeles, CA), Perry Smith (Charlotte, NC), Tom Wheeler (Martinez, CA), Brian Wilson (Albany, TX), Greg Zunino (Cape Coral, FL).

Terry Reynolds

Director, International Scouting: Johnny Almaraz. **International Scouts:** Oswaldo Alvarez (Mexico), Felix Delgado (Venezuela), Orlando Granda (Brazil), Victor Mateo (Dominican), Jorge Oquendo (Puerto Rico).

CLEVELAND INDIANS

Office Address: Jacobs Field, 2401 Ontario St., Cleveland, OH 44115.
Telephone: (216) 420-4200. **FAX:** (216) 420-4396.
Website: www.indians.com.

Ownership
Owner, Chief Executive Officer: Lawrence Dolan.
President: Paul Dolan.

BUSINESS OPERATIONS
Executive Vice President, Business: Dennis Lehman. **Senior Director, Human Resources/Customer Service:** Sara Lehrke.
Manager, Spring Training: Jerry Crabb.

Finance
Senior Vice President, Finance/Chief Financial Officer: Ken Stefanov.
Controller: Sarah Taylor. **Senior Director, Information Systems:** Dave Powell. **Director, Planning, Analysis/Reporting:** Rich Dorffer. **Manager, Accounting:** Karen Menzing.

Larry Dolan

Marketing, Merchandising
Vice President, Sales: Jon Starrett. **Director, Corporate Marketing:** Chris Previte. **Director, Marketing:** Sanaa Julien. **Manager, Publications/Graphic Design:** Bernadette Repko. **Manager, Brand Development/Special Events:** Dan Foust. **Manager, Scoreboard Operations:** Steve Warren. **Manager, Broadcasting:** Alex Slemc.
VP, Merchandising/Licensing: Jayne Churchmack. **Merchandise Manager:** Carol Schultz. **Buyers, Retail**: Iris Delgado, Karen Fox. **Retail Controller:** Marjorie Ruhl. **District Manager:** Joanne Kahr.

Public Relations, Communications
Telephone: (216) 420-4350. **FAX:** (216) 420-4396.
Vice President, Public Relations: Bob DiBiasio.
Director, Media Relations: Bart Swain. **Manager, Media Relations/Administration:** Susie Giuliano. **Manager, Media Relations:** Curtis Danburg. **Coordinator, Media Relations**: Jeff Sibel. **Press Box Supervisor:** John Krepop.
Coordinator, Public Relations: Angela Brdar.
Director, Community Relations: Latisha James. **Director, Charitable Programs**: Melissa Zapanta. **Coordinator, Public Relations:** Stephanie Hierro. **Manager, Community Relations:** John Carter.

Stadium Operations
Vice President, Ballpark Operations: Jim Folk. **Director, Ballpark Operations:** Jerry Crabb. **Manager, Facility Maintenance:** Chris Donahoe. **Head Groundskeeper:** Brandon Koehnke.
PA Announcers: Duane Robinson, Bob Tayak. **Official Scorers:** Hank Kozloski, Rick Rembielak, Chuck Murr, Chad Broski, Bob Price.

Ticketing
Telephone: (216) 420-4240, (216) 420-4487. **FAX:** (216) 420-4481.
Director, Ticket Services: Michael Thom. **Manager, Ticket System/Development:** Gail Liebenguth. **Manager, Public Sale:** Susan Leslie. **Coordinator, Vault/Processing:** Kelly Cruise. **Director, Ticket Sales:** Jim Willits. **Director, Luxury Seating:** Bill Lavelle. **Manager, Luxury Seating:** Larry Abel.

Travel, Clubhouse
Director, Team Travel: Mike Seghi.
Home Clubhouse/Equipment Manager: Tony Amato. **Assistant Home Clubhouse/Equipment Manager:** Tommy Foster. **Visiting Clubhouse Manager:** Cy Buynak. **Manager, Equipment Acquisition/Distribution:** Jeff Sipos.

GENERAL INFORMATION
Stadium (year opened): Jacobs Field (1994).
Home Dugout: Third Base. **Playing Surface:** Grass.
Team Colors: Navy blue, red and silver.
Player Representative: John McDonald.

Mark Shapiro

BASEBALL OPERATIONS

Telephone: (216) 420-4200. **FAX:** (216) 420-4321.
Executive Vice President, General Manager: Mark Shapiro.
Assistant GMs: Chris Antonetti, Neal Huntington. **Special Assistant to GM:** Charles Nagy.
Director, Player Personnel: Steve Lubratich. **Director, Professional Scouting:** DeJon Watson. **Senior Advisor, Baseball Operations:** Mike Hargrove. **Special Advisor, Baseball Operations:** Karl Kuehl. **Special Assistants, Baseball Operations:** Tim Belcher, Robby Thompson.
Director, Baseball Administration: Wendy Hoppel. **Executive Administrative Assistant, Baseball Operations:** Marlene Lehky. **Administrative Assistant, Baseball Operations:** Barbara Lessman. **Senior Coordinator, Baseball Systems:** Dan Mendlik. **Sport Psychologist/Director, Psychological Services:** Dr. Charles Maher.

Major League Staff

Manager: Eric Wedge.
Coaches: Bench—Buddy Bell; Pitching—Carl Willis; Batting—Eddie Murray; First Base—Jeff Datz; Third Base—Joel Skinner; Bullpen—Luis Isaac, Bullpen Catcher—Dan Williams, Baserunning/Outfield—Rick Manning.

Medical, Training

Director, Orthopaedic Services: Dr. Mark Schickendantz.
Head Trainer: Lonnie Soloff. **Assistant Trainer:** Rick Jameyson. **Senior Consultant, Athletic Training:** Paul Spicuzza. **Strength/Conditioning Coach:** Tim Maxey. **Director, Rehabilitation:** Jim Mehalik.

Player Development

Telephone: (216) 420-4308. **FAX:** (216) 420-4321.
Director, Player Development: John Farrell. **Director, Latin American Operations:** Ross Atkins. **Assistant Director, Player Development:** Mike Hazen. **Advisor, Player Development:** Johnny Goryl. **Assistant Director, Player Development/Latin American Operations:** Lino Diaz. **Mental Skills Coordinator:** John Couture. **Nutrition Consultant:** Jackie Berning.
Field Coordinator: Tim Tolman. **Coordinators:** Al Bumbry (outfield/baserunning), Ted Kubiak (defense), Jim Malone (strength/conditioning), Dave Miller (pitching), Derek Shelton (hitting).
Rehab/Medical Coordinator: Lee Kuntz.
Field Coordinator, Latin America: Minnie Mendoza.

Eric Wedge

Farm System

Class	Farm Team	League	Manager	Coach	Pitching Coach
AAA	Buffalo	International	Marty Brown	Carlos Garcia	Terry Clark
AA	Akron	Eastern	Brad Komminsk	Sean McNally	Steve Lyons
High A	Kinston	Carolina	Torey Lovullo	Wayne Kirby	Greg Hibbard
Low A	Lake County	South Atlantic	Luis Rivera	Jack Mull	Tony Arnold
Short-Season	Mahoning Valley	New York-Penn	Mike Sarbaugh	Chris Bando	Ken Rowe
Rookie	Burlington	Appalachian	Rouglas Odor	Unavailable	Ruben Niebla
Rookie	Indians	Dominican	Jose Stela	Jacobo Urena	Juan Jimenez
Rookie	Indians	Domincan	Junior Betances	Luis Chavez	Geovanny Veras

Scouting

Telephone: (216) 420-4309. **FAX:** (216) 420-4321.
Assistant GM, Scouting Operations: John Mirabelli.
Assistant Director, Scouting: Brad Grant.
Major League Scouts: Don Poplin (Norwood, NC), DeJon Watson (Phoenix, AZ).
Professional Scouts: Rodney Davis (Glendale, AZ), Robyn Lynch (Randolph, NJ), Dave Malpass (Huntington Beach, CA), Pat Murtaugh (Lafayette, IN), Jonathan Story (Melbourne, FL).
Special Assignment Scout: Chuck Tanner (New Castle, PA).
National Crosschecker: Jim Olander (Tucson, AZ).
Free-Agent Supervisors: Southeast—Jerry Jordan (Kingsport, TN), Northeast—Chuck Ricci (Myersville, MD), Midwest—Ken Stauffer (Katy, TX), West Coast—Paul Cogan (Rocklin, CA).
Full-Time Area Scouts: Scott Barnsby (Old Hickory, TN), Henry Cruz (Fajardo, PR), Mike Daly (Kansas City, MO), Joe Graham (Phoenix, AZ), Chris Jefts (Atlanta, GA), Don Lyle (Sacramento, CA), Bob Mayer (Somerset, PA), Scott Meaney (Humble, TX), Tim Moore (Greenville, NC), Les Pajari (Duluth, MN), Phil Rossi (Jessup, PA), Matt Ruebel (Oklahoma City, OK), Vince Sagisi (Encino, CA), Bill Schudlich (Dearborn, MI), Jason Smith (Long Beach, CA), Shawn Whalen (Vancouver, WA).
Director, Latin America Operations: Ross Atkins (Miami, FL).
Dominican Advisor: Winston Llenas (Dominican Republic). **Latin America Supervisors:** Henry Centeno (Venezuela), Felix Fermin (Dominican Republic), Johnny Martinez (Dominican Republic).

John Mirabelli

COLORADO ROCKIES

Office Address: 2001 Blake St., Denver, CO 80205.
Telephone: (303) 292-0200. **FAX:** (303) 312-2116.
Website: www.coloradorockies.com.

Ownership

Operated by: Colorado Rockies Baseball Club, Ltd.
Chairman: Jerry McMorris. **Vice Chairman, Chief Executive Officer:** Charles Monfort.
Vice Chairman: Richard Monfort. **Executive Assistant to Vice Chairmen:** Patricia Penfold.

BUSINESS OPERATIONS

President: Keli McGregor. **Executive Assistant to President:** Terry Douglass.
Senior Vice President, Business Operations: Greg Feasel. **Assistant to Senior VP:** Marcia McGovern. **Senior Director, Personnel/Administration:** Elizabeth Stecklein. **Director, Information Systems:** Bill Stephani.

Finance

Senior VP/Chief Financial Officer: Hal Roth. **Assistant to Senior VP/Chief Financial**
Officer: Tammy Vergara.

Charles Monfort

VP, Finance: Michael Kent. **Senior Director, Accounting:** Gary Lawrence. **Payroll Administrator:** Phil Emerson.
Accountant: Matt Vinnola. **Assistant, Finance Department:** Janet Glant.

Marketing, Sales

Senior Director, Corporate Sales: Marcy English Glasser. **Account Executives:** Kari Anderson, Shayne Cotner, Derrek Patrick, Paula Swanson-Dorr. **Coordinator, Corporate Sales:** Kathy Wilson.
Senior Director, Promotions/Broadcasting: Alan Bossart. **Assistant to Senior Director, Promotions/Broadcasting:** Elizabeth Coates.
Manager, Promotions: Jason Fleming. **Coordinator, Broadcasting/Video Services:** Brian Ives. **Assistant, Broadcasting/Video Services:** Dan Storey.
Senior Director, Community/Retail Operations: Jim Kellogg. **Assistant to Senior Director, Community/Retail Operations:** Kelly Hall. **Manager, Community Affairs:** Stacy Schafer. **Coordinator, Community Affairs:** Antigone Vigil.
Coordinator, Publications: Mike Kennedy. **Manager, Coors Field Receiving/Distribution Center:** Steve Tomlinson.

Public Relations, Communications

Telephone: (303) 312-2325. **FAX:** (303) 312-2319.
Senior Director, Communications/Public Relations: Jay Alves. **Assistant to Senior Director, Communications/Public Relations:** Irma Thumim. **Coordinators, Communications/Public Relations:** Billy Witter, Brendan McNicholas.

Stadium Operations

Vice President, Ballpark Operations: Kevin Kahn.
Director, Coors Field Administration/Development: Dave Moore. **Manager, Ballpark Services:** Mary Beth Benner.
Director, Guest Services: Steven Burke. **Scheduling/Payroll Assistant:** Beth Spiegel. **Supervisors, Guest Services:** Kathryn Coates, Brian Schneringer, Sandy Seta.
Director, Security: Don Lyon. **Senior Director, Engineering/Facilities:** James Wiener. **Assistant Director, Engineering:** Randy Carill. **Assistant Director, Facilities:** Dan Olsen.
Head Groundskeeper: Mark Razum. **Assistant Head Groundskeeper:** Jose Gonzalez. **Assistants, Groundskeeping:** Tim Holt, James Sowl.
PA Announcer: Kelly Burnham. **Official Scorers:** Dave Einspahr, Jack Rose.

Ticketing

Telephone: (303) 762-5437, (800) 388-7625. **FAX:** (303) 312-2115.
Vice President, Ticket Operations/Sales: Sue Ann McClaren. **Senior Director, Ticket Operations/Development:** Kevin Fenton. **Director, Ticket Operations/Finances:** Kent Hakes. **Assistant Director, Vault:** Scott Donaldson.
Senior Director, Ticket Sales/Advertising: Jill Roberts. **Coordinator, Advertising:** Angela Keenan. **Director, Ticket Services/Spring Training Business Operations:** Chuck Javernick. **Director, Group Sales:** Jeff Spector. **Director, Season Tickets:** Jeff Benner. **Supervisor, Ticket Services:** Michael Bishop. **Lead Representative:** Jake McKeown.

Travel, Clubhouse

Director, Major League Operations: Paul Egins.
Clubhouse/Equipment Manager: Dan McGinn. **Visiting Clubhouse Manager:** Keith Schulz. **Video Coordinator:** Mike Hamilton.

GENERAL INFORMATION

Stadium (year opened): Coors Field (1995).
Home Dugout: First Base. **Playing Surface:** Grass.
Team Colors: Purple, black and silver.
Player Representative: Unavailable.

Dan O'Dowd

BASEBALL OPERATIONS

Telephone: (303) 292-0200. **FAX:** (303) 312-2320.
Executive Vice President/General Manager: Dan O'Dowd. **Assistant to Executive VP/GM:** Adele Armagost. **Director, Baseball Administration:** Thad Levine.

Special Assistants to General Manager: Pat Daugherty (Aurora, CO), Marcel Lachemann (Penryn, CA), Kasey McKeon (Stoney Creek, NC).

Major League Staff

Manager: Clint Hurdle.

Coaches: Bench—Jamie Quirk; Pitching—Bob Apodaca; Hitting—Duane Espy; First Base—Dave Collins; Third Base—Sandy Alomar Sr.; Bullpen—Rick Mathews; Strength—Brad Andress; Video—Mike Hamilton; Bullpen Catcher: Mark Strittmatter.

Medical, Training

Medical Director: Dr. Richard Hawkins. **Club Physicians:** Dr. Tom Noonan, Dr. Allen Schreiber, Dr. Douglas Wyland. **Physical Therapist:** Mike Allen.

Head Trainer: Tom Probst. **Assistant Trainer:** Keith Dugger. **Rehabilitation Coordinator:** Scott Gehret.

Player Development

Telephone: (303) 292-0200. **FAX:** (303) 312-2320.
Senior Director, Player Personnel: Bill Geivett. **Assistant Director, Player Development:** Marc Gustafson. **Assistant Director, Player Development/Scouting:** Billy Eppler. **Assistant to Senior Director, Player Development:** Jody Ross.

Roving Instructors: Mike Gallego (infield), Jim Johnson (hitting), Brian Jordan (strength/conditioning), Fred Kendall (catching), Jim Wright (pitching).

Video Coordinator: Brian Jones. **Mental Skills Coach:** Ronn Svetich. **Coordinator, Cultural Development:** Lori Brown. **Equipment Manager:** Joe Tamowski.

Clint Hurdle

Farm System

Class	Farm Team	League	Manager	Coach	Pitching Coach
AAA	Colorado Springs	Pacific Coast	Marv Foley	Alan Cockrell	Bob McClure
AA	Tulsa	Texas	Tom Runnells	Darron Cox	Bo McLaughlin
HighA	Visalia	California	Stu Cole	Glenallen Hill	Jim Bennett
Low A	Asheville	South Atlantic	Joe Mikulik	Dave Hajek	Greg Booker
Short season	Tri-City	Northwest	Ron Gideon	Fred Ocasio	Butch Hughes
Rookie	Casper	Pioneer	P.J. Carey	Tony Diaz	Richard Palacios
Rookie	Rockies	Dominican	Mauricio Gonzalez	Edison Lora	Pablo Paredes
Rookie	Rockies	Venezuela	Maurio Mendez	Unavailable	Dilson Torres

Scouting

Telephone: (303) 292-0200. **FAX:** (303) 312-2320.
Senior Director, Scouting: Bill Schmidt. **Director, Professional Scouting:** Coley Brannon. **Assistant Director, Player Development/Scouting:** Billy Eppler. **Administrator, Scouting:** Zach Wilson.

Major League Scout: Will George (Woolwich Township, NJ). **Professional Scouts:** Mike Berger (Oakmont, PA), Jack Gillis (Sarasota, FL), Don Reynolds (Portland, OR), Art Pontarelli (Cranston, RI).

Special Assignment Scouts: Dave Holliday (Coalgate, OK), Terry Wetzel (Overland Park, KS). **National Crosscheckers:** Ty Coslow (Louisville, KY), Danny Montgomery (Charlotte, NC), **Scouting Advisor:** Dave Snow (Seal Beach, CA).

Full-Time Area Scouts: Todd Blyleven (Fountain Valley, CA), John Cedarburg (Fort Myers, FL), Scott Corman (Lexington, KY), Dar Cox (Frisco, TX), Jeff Edwards (Houston, TX), Mike Ericson (Glendale, AZ), Mike Garlatti (Edison, NJ), Mark Germann (Atkins, IA), Jeff Hipps (Long Beach, CA), Bert Holt (Visalia, CA), Damon Iannelli (Brandon, MS), Jay Matthews (Charlotte, NC), Jorge de Posada (Rio Piedras, PR), Ed Santa (Powell, OH), Gary Wilson (Sacramento, CA).

Bill Schmidt

Scouts: Steve Bernhardt (Perry Hall, MD), Norm DeBriyn (Fayetteville, AR), Casey Harvie (Lake Stevens, WA), Don Lindeberg (Anaheim, CA), Dave McQueen (Bossier City, LA).

Director, Latin America Operations: Rolando Fernandez. **Coordinator, Pacific Rim Scouting:** Kent Blasingame (Fountain Hills, AZ).

International Scouts: Phil Allen (Australia), Francisco Cartaya (Venezuela), Felix Feliz (Dominican Republic), Cristobal Giron (Panama), Carlos Gomez (Venezuela), Orlando Medina (Venezuela).

DETROIT TIGERS

Office Address: 2100 Woodward Ave., Detroit, MI, 48201.
Telephone: (313) 471-2000. **FAX:** (313) 471-2138.
Website: www.detroittigers.com.

Ownership

Operated by: Detroit Tigers, Inc.
Owner: Michael Ilitch.
President, Chief Executive Officer: Dave Dombrowski. **Special Assistants to President:** Al Kaline, Willie Horton. **Executive Assistant to President/CEO:** Patricia McConnell.
Senior Vice President: Jim Devellano.

BUSINESS OPERATIONS

Senior Vice President, Business Affairs: Jim Stapleton.
Senior Vice President, Sales: Duane McLean.
Executive Assistant to Senior VPs, Business Affairs/Sales: Tamara Mitin.

Mike Ilitch

Finance

Vice President, Chief Financial Officer: Steve Quinn. **Assistant to VP, Finance/CFO:** Peggy Bacarella.
Director, Finance: Kelli Kollman. **Manager, Accounting/Finance:** Karla Felton. **Accounts Payable Supervisor:** Sheila Wood. **Accounts Payable Coordinator:** Debbie Sword. **Purchasing Manager:** DeAndre Berry.
Senior Director, Information Technology: Cole Stewart.
Director, Human Resources: Lara Juras. **Director, Ballpark Operations:** Mike Churchill.
Senior Manager, Payroll Administration: Maureen Kraatz. **Payroll/Human Resources Coordinator:** Stephanie Duchane. **Mail Services:** Paul Kustra. **Switchboard Operator:** Janet Ware.

Marketing, Communications

Vice President, Public Affairs/Strategic Planning: Elaine Lewis. **Administrative Assistant, Public Affairs/Strategic Planning:** Tiffani Langford. **Director, Community Relations:** Celia Bobrowsky. **Coordinator, Community Relations:** Corey Bell.

Sales, Marketing

Manager, Corporate Sales: John Wolski. **Account Executive:** Jim Spadafore. **Corporate Sales Coordinator:** Jill Chamberlain.
Director, Marketing: Ellen Hill Zeringue. **Coordinator, Marketing:** Ed Sanchez.
Director, Promotions/In-Game Entertainment: Joel Scott. **Coordinator, Promotions/Special Events:** Eli Bayless.
Vice President, Corporate Suite Sales and Services/Hospitality: Charles Jones. **Manager, Suite Sales/Service:** Scot Pett. **Suite Services Coordinator:** Amy Howard.
Director, Fantasy Camps: Jerry Lewis.

Media Relations, Communications

Telephone: (313) 471-2114. **FAX:** (313) 471-2138.
Senior Director, Communications: Cliff Russell. **Coordinator, Media Relations:** Brian Britten. **Media Relations Assistant:** Rick Thompson. **Media Relations/Broadcast Manager:** Molly Light.

Park Operations

Vice President, Park Operations: Tim Padgett. **Director, Park Operations:** Mike Churchill.
Head Groundskeeper: Heather Nabozny. **Senior Manager, Park Operations:** Ed Goward. **Managers, Ballpark Services:** Allan Carrise, DuShawn Brandy. **Park Operations Coordinator:** Tessa Lawrence.
Scoreboard/Video Producer: Scott Fearncombe.

Ticketing

Telephone: (313) 471-2255.
Vice President, Ticket Sales/Service: Bob Raymond.
Manager, Ticket Sales: Steve Fox. **Manager, Group Sales:** Dwain Lewis.
Senior Director, Ticket Services: Ken Marchetti. **Administrator, Ticket Systems:** Sandra Sobotka.

Travel, Clubhouse

Traveling Secretary: Bill Brown
Manager, Home Clubhouse: Jim Schmakel. **Assistant Manager, Visiting Clubhouse:** John Nelson. **Clubhouse Assistant:** Tyson Steele.
Ballpark Video Operations: Jeremy Kelch.

GENERAL INFORMATION

Stadium (year opened): Comerica Park (2000).
Home Dugout: Third Base. **Playing Surface:** Grass.
Team Colors: Navy blue, orange and white.
Player Representative: Unavailable.

BASEBALL OPERATIONS

Telephone: (313) 471-2096. **FAX:** (313) 471-2099.
General Manager: Dave Dombrowski.
Vice President/Assistant GM: Al Avila. **Special Assistant to GM:** Steve Boros. **Administrative Assistant to VP/Assistant GM/Baseball Legal Counsel:** Eileen Surma.
VP, Player Personnel: Scott Reid.
Director, Baseball Administration: Dave Miller. **Assistant, Baseball Operations/Foreign Affairs:** Ramon Pena. **Assistant, Baseball Operations:** Mike Smith. **International Liaison:** Joe Alvarez.
VP/Baseball Legal Counsel: John Westhoff.

Dave Dombrowski

Major League Staff
Manager: Alan Trammell.
Coaches: Bench—Kirk Gibson; Pitching—Bob Cluck; Batting—Bruce Fields; First Base—Mick Kelleher; Third Base—Juan Samuel; Bullpen—Lance Parrish.

Medical, Training
Team Physicians: Dr. Kyle Anderson, Dr. David Collon, Dr. Michael Workings. **Director, Medical Services/Head Athletic Trainer:** Kevin Rand. **Assistant Athletic Trainer:** Steve Carter. **Administrative Assistant, Training/Conditioning:** Barbara McNulty. **Strength/Conditioning Coach:** Dennie Taft.

Player Development
Telephone, Detroit: (313) 471-2096. **FAX:** (313) 471-2099. **Telephone, Florida Operations:** (863) 686-8075. **FAX:** (863) 688-9589.
Director, Minor League Operations: Rick Bennett. **Senior Consultant, Minor League Operations:** Dave Miller. **Administrative Assistant, Minor Leagues:** Audrey Zielinski.
Field Coordinator: Glenn Ezell. **Roving Instructors:** Bill Freehan (catching), Javiar Gillett (strength/conditioning) Gene Roof (outfield/baserunning), Rafael Landestoy (infield), Jon Matlack (pitching), Brian Peterson (performance enhancement), Toby Harrah (hitting), Doug Teter (medical coordinator).

Alan Trammell

Farm System

Class	Farm Team	League	Manager	Coach	Pitching Coach
AAA	Toledo	International	Larry Parrish	Leon Durham	Jeff Jones
AA	Erie	Eastern	Rick Sweet	Pete Incaviglia	Mike Caldwell
High A	Lakeland	Florida State	Gary Green	Rich Morales	Britt Burns
Low A	West Michigan	Midwest	Matt Walbeck	Tony Jaramillo	A.J. Sager
Short season	Oneonta	New York-Penn	Mike Rojas	Basilio Cabrera	Bill Monbouquette
Rookie	Lakeland	Gulf Coast	Kevin Bradshaw	Scott Makarewicz	Greg Sabat
Rookie	Tigers	Dominican	Unavailable	Unavailable	Unavailable

Scouting
Telephone: (313) 471-2098. **FAX:** (313) 471-2099.
Director, Scouting: Greg Smith. **Administrative Assistant, Scouting:** Gwen Keating.
Major League Scouts: Scott Bream (Phoenix, AZ), Dick Egan (Phoenix, AZ), Rob Guzik (Latrobe, PA), Al Hargesheimer (Arlington Heights, IL), Mike Russell (Gulf Breeze, FL).
National Crosschecker: Curtis Dishman (Seabrook, TX). **Regional Supervisors:** Southeast—Steve Williams (Raleigh, NC), Northeast—Bob Cummings (Oak Lawn, IL), Midwest—Mike Hankins (Lee's Summit, MO), West—Joe Ferrone (Santa Clarita, CA).
Area Scouts: Bill Buck (Manassas, VA), Vaughn Calloway (Detroit, MI), Rolando Casanova (Miami, FL), Jerome Cochran (Slidell, LA), Tim Grieve (Katy, TX), Mike Herbert (Chicago, IL), Tom Hinkle (Atascadero, CA), Joe Hodges (Rockwood, TN), Lou Laslo (Maumee, OH), Marty Miller (Chicago, IL), Mark Monahan (Saline, MI), Steve Nichols (Mount Dora, FL), Brian Reid (Phoenix, AZ), Derrick Ross (Newington, CT), Dennis Sheehan (Glasco, NY), Steve Taylor (Shawnee, OK), Clyde Weir (Portland, MI), Rob Wilfong (San Dimas, CA), Harold Zonder (Louisville, KY).
Assistant, Baseball Operations/Foreign Affairs: Ramon Pena (Dominican Republic).

Greg Smith

FLORIDA MARLINS

Office Address: Pro Player Stadium, 2267 Dan Marino Blvd. Miami, FL 33056.
Telephone: (305) 626-7400. FAX: (305) 626-7428.
Website: www.floridamarlins.com.

Ownership

Chairman, Chief Executive Officer/Managing General Partner: Jeffrey Loria. Vice Chairman: Joel Mael.
President: David Samson. Executive Assistant to President: Beth McConville.
Special Assistants to President: Andre Dawson, Tony Perez.

BUSINESS OPERATIONS

Director, Human Resources: Ana Hernandez. Supervisor, Office Services: Karl Heard.
Senior Receptionist: Kathy Lanza. Receptionist: Christina Fredericks.

Finance

Senior Vice President, Chief Financial Officer: Michel Bussiere.
VP, Finance: Susan Jaison. Manager, Accounting: Barry LaChance. Manager, Business Information Systems: Ken Strand. Manager, Telecommunications: Sam Mora.

Jeffrey Loria

Marketing, Sales

Vice President, Marketing: Sean Flynn. Manager, Promotions: Matt Britten. Manager, Merchandise: Robyn Fogel.
VP, Sales: Dale Hendricks. Director, Corporate Sales: Brendan Cunningham. Director, Season/Group Sales: Pat McNamara. Manager, Season/Group Sales: Marty Mulford. Manager, Customer Service: Spencer Linden.
Manager, Executive Affairs: Michelle Azel.
Manager, Community Affairs: Angela Smith. Assistant, Player Relations: Manny Colon. Assistant, Community Affairs: Ron Sklar.
Executive Director, Florida Marlins Community Foundation: Nancy Olson. Assistant Director: Doug Harris.

Media Relations, Communications

Telephone: (305) 626-7429. FAX: (305) 626-7302.
Vice President, Communications/Broadcasting: P.J. Loyello.
Director, Media Relations: Steve Copses. Manager, Media Relations: Andrew Feirstein. Coordinator, Media Relations: Alex Horowitz. Assistant, Media Relations: Maria Armella.
Director, Broadcast Services: Suzanne Rayson.

Stadium Operations

Director, In-Game Entertainment: Gary Levy. Producer, Game Presentation: Matt Hagood. Associate Producer: Eric Ramirez. Coordinator, Creative Services: Robert Vigon. Video Archivist: Chris Myers. Organist: Lowery Ballew.
PA Announcer: Dick Sanford. Official Scorer: Ron Jernick.

Ticketing

Telephone: (305) 930-4487. FAX: (305) 626-7432.
Customer Service Manager: Spencer Linden. Customer Service Representative: David Argote.

Travel, Clubhouse

Director, Team Travel: Bill Beck.
Video Coordinator: Cullen McRae.
Equipment Manager: John Silverman. Assistant Equipment Manager: Mark Brown. Visiting Clubhouse Manager: Bryan Greenberg.

GENERAL INFORMATION

Stadium (year opened): Pro Player Park (1993).
Home Dugout: First Base. Playing Surface: Grass.
Team Colors: Teal, black and white.
Player Representative: Unavailable.

Larry Beinfest

BASEBALL OPERATIONS

Telephone: (305) 626-7400. **FAX:** (305) 626-7433.
Senior Vice President, General Manager: Larry Beinfest.
VP, Player Personnel: Dan Jennings. **Assistant GM:** Michael Hill. **Special Assistant to GM/Scouting Director:** Orrin Freeman. **Manager, Baseball Information Systems:** David Kuan. **Executive Assistant to GM:** Rita Filbert.
General Counsel: Derek Jackson.

Major League Staff

Manager: Jack McKeon.
Coaches: Dugout—Doug Davis; Pitching—Wayne Rosenthal; Batting—Bill Robinson; First Base—Perry Hill; Third Base—Jeff Cox; Bullpen—Tony Taylor; Bullpen Coordinator—Pierre Arsenault.

Medical, Training

Club Physician: Dr. Daniel Kanell. **Head Trainer:** Sean Cunningham. **Assistant Trainer:** Mike Kozak. **Director, Strength/Conditioning:** Paul Fournier.

Player Development

Senior Vice President/Director, International Operations: Fred Ferreria. **Assistant Director, International Operations:** Randy Kierce.
VP, Player Development and Scouting/Assistant General Manager: Jim Fleming. **Director, Player Development:** Marc DelPiano. **Assistant, Baseball Operations:** Brian Chattin. **Director, Minor League Operations:** Cheryl Evans.
Field Coordinator: John Pierson. **Coordinators:** Gene Bashem (strength/conditioning, rehabilitation), John Mallee (hitting), Dean Treanor (pitching), Bump Wills (infield).

Jack McKeon

Farm System

Class	Farm Team	League	Manager	Coach	Pitching Coach
AAA	Albuquerque	Pacific Coast	Tracy Woodson	Matt Stark	Jeff Schwarz
AA	Carolina	Southern	Ron Hassey	Edwin Rodriguez	Gil Lopez
High A	Jupiter	Florida State	Luis Dorante	Paul Sanagorski	Reid Cornelius
Low A	Greensboro	South Atlantic	Steve Phillips	Brandon Hyde	Scott Mitchell
Short season	Jamestown	New York-Penn	Benny Castillo	Matt Raleigh	Tom Signore
Rookie	Jupiter	Gulf Coast	Tim Cossins	Johnny Rodriguez	Gary Buckels

Scouting

Telephone: (305) 626-7400. **FAX:** (305) 626-7294.
Director, Scouting: Stan Meek (Norman, OK). **Assistant Director, Scouting:** Gregg Leonard.
Advance Scout: Joe Moeller (Manhattan Beach, CA).
Major League Scouts: Tommy Thompson (La Mesa, CA), Gene Watson.
National Crosschecker: Joe Jordan (Blanchard, OK). **Regional Supervisors:** East—Mike Cadahia (Miami Springs, FL), Central—David Crowson (College Station, TX), West—Scott Goldby (Yuba City, CA), Canada—Steve Payne (Barrington, RI).
Area Scouts: Alex Agostino (St. Bruno, Quebec), Matt Anderson (Williamsport, PA), Carlos Berroa (San Juan, PR), Brian Bridges (Atlanta, GA), Dennis Cardoza (Blanchard, OK), John Cole (Lake Forest, CA), Robby Corsaro (Adelanto, CA), Dave Dangler (Birmingham, AL), Kevin Delcovich (Edmond, OK), Scot Engler (Montgomery, IL), John Hughes (Walnut Creek, CA),

Stan Meek

John Martin (Tampa, FL), Joel Matthews (Concord, NC), Bob Oldis (Iowa City, IA), David Post (Hillsboro, OR), Scott Stanley (Phoenix, AZ).
International Supervisors: Carlos Acosta (Venezuela), Jesus Campos (Dominican Republic), A.B. Jesurun (Europe).
International Scouts: Wilmer Adrian (Venezuela), Evelio Areas (Nicaragua), Greg Burrows (Bahamas), Aristides Bustamonte (Panama/Costa Rica), Nelson Castro (Venezuela), Terry Chinnery (British West Indies), Enrique Constante (Dominican Republic), Nathan Davison (Australia), Scott Dawes, (Australia), Luis Fermin (Venezuela), Rene Garcia (Venezuela), Carlos Guzman (Guatemala), Jason Hewitt (Australia), Ton Hofstede (The Netherlands), Go Ikeda (Japan/Korea/Taiwan), Brian Lombard (South Africa), Roberto Marquez (Venezuela), Pedro Martinez (Venezuela), Willie Marrugo (Colombia), Ellerton Maynard (Virgin Islands), Spencer Mills (The Netherlands), Romulo Oliveros (Venezuela), Rene Picota (Panama), Carlos Rivero (Venezuela), Craig Stoves (Australia), Orlando Tejera (Venezuela), Francis Wanga (Bonaire).

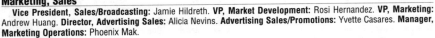

HOUSTON ASTROS

Office Address: Minute Maid Park, Union Station, 501 Crawford, Suite 400, Houston, TX 77002.
Mailing Address: P.O. Box 288, Houston, TX 77001.
Telephone: (713) 259-8000. **FAX:** (713) 259-8981.
E-Mail Address: fanfeedback@astros.mlb.com.
Website: www.astros.com.

Ownership
Operated by: McLane Group, LP.
Chairman, Chief Executive Officer: Drayton McLane.
Board of Directors: Drayton McLane, Bob McClaren, Sandy Sanford, Webb Stickney.

BUSINESS OPERATIONS
President, Business Operations: Pam Gardner. **Executive Assistants:** Eileen Colgin, Tracy Faucette.

Finance
Senior Vice President, Finance: Jackie Traywick.
Accounts Receivable: Mary Ann Bell. **Accounts Payable:** Irene Dumenil. **Manager, Payroll:** Ruth Kelly.

Drayton McLane

Marketing, Sales
Vice President, Sales/Broadcasting: Jamie Hildreth. **VP, Market Development:** Rosi Hernandez. **VP, Marketing:** Andrew Huang. **Director, Advertising Sales:** Alicia Nevins. **Advertising Sales/Promotions:** Yvette Casares. **Manager, Marketing Operations:** Phoenix Mak.

Public Relations, Communications
Telephone: (713) 259-8900. **FAX:** (713) 259-8981.
Senior Vice President, Communications: Jay Lucas.
Director, Media Relations: Jimmy Stanton. **Assistant Director, Media Relations:** Lisa Ramsperger.
VP, Community Development: Marian Harper. **Director, Business Communications:** Todd Fedewa. **Manager, Community Development:** Rita Suchma.
Director, Information Technology: Brad Bourland. **Network Administrator:** Rob Weaver.

Stadium Operations
Senior Vice President, Operations: Rob Matwick.
Vice President, Special Events: Kala Sorenson. **Senior Director, Engineering:** Bobby Forrest. **Director, Ballpark Entertainment:** Kirby Kander. **Assistant Director, Ballpark Entertainment:** Brock Jessel. **Director, Telecommunications/Broadcast Technology:** Mike Cannon. **Director, Customer Service:** Michael Kenny. **Conference Center/Special Events Sales:** Christine O'Beirne. **Manager, Minute Maid Park Tours:** Jennifer Ammel. **Manager, Safety/Security:** Kirk Benoit.
Director, Field Operations: Unavailable. **Assistant Groundskeeper:** Colin Castille.
PA Announcer: Bob Ford. **Official Scorers:** Rick Blount, Ivy McLemore, David Matheson, Trey Wilkinson.

Ticketing
Telephone: (713) 259-8500. **FAX:** (713) 259-8326.
Vice President, Ticket Services: John Sorrentino.
Director, Ticket Operations: Marcia Coronado. **Director, Box Office Operations:** Bill Cannon. **Manager, Sales Support:** Matt Rogers. **Manager, Premium Sales:** Andrea Levine-Spier.

Travel, Clubhouse
Director, Baseball Administration: Barry Waters. **Equipment Manager:** Dennis Liborio. **Assistant Equipment Managers:** Carl Schneider, Butch New. **Visiting Clubhouse Manager:** Steve Perry. **Umpires/Clubhouse Assistant:** Chuck New.

GENERAL INFORMATION
Stadium (year opened): Minute Maid Park (2000).
Home Dugout: First Base. **Playing Surface:** Grass.
Team Colors: Brick red, sand beige and black.
Player Representative: Morgan Ensberg.

Gerry Hunsicker

BASEBALL OPERATIONS
Telephone: (713) 259-8000. **FAX:** (713) 259-8600.
President, Baseball Operations: Tal Smith.
General Manager: Gerry Hunsicker. **Director, Baseball Administration:** Barry Waters. **Executive Assistant:** Traci Dearing.

Major League Staff
Manager: Jimy Williams.
Coaches: Bench—John Tamargo; Pitching—Burt Hooton; Batting—Harry Spilman; First Base—Jose Cruz Sr.; Third Base—Gene Lamont; Bullpen—Mark Bailey.

Medical, Training
Medical Director: Dr. David Lintner.
Head Trainer: Dave Labossiere. **Assistant Trainer:** Rex Jones. **Strength and Conditioning Coach:** Dr. Gene Coleman.

Player Development
Telephone: (713) 259-8922. **FAX:** (713) 259-8600.
Assistant General Manager/Director, Player Development: Tim Purpura.
Director, Minor League Administration: David Gottfried. **Minor League Administrator:** Jay Edmiston. **Administrative Assistant:** Monica Shak. **Assistant, Baseball Operations:** Carlos Perez.
Field Coordinator: Tom Wiedenbauer. **Minor League Coordinators:** Dewey Robinson (pitching), Jim Pankovits (defense), Pat Roessler (hitting).
Coordinator, Training/Conditioning: Pete Fagan. **Coordinator, Strength/Conditioning:** Nathan Lucero.

Jimy Williams

Farm System

Class	Farm Team	League	Manager	Coach	Pitching Coach
AAA	New Orleans	Pacific Coast	Chris Maloney	Gary Gaetti	Jim Hickey
AA	Round Rock	Texas	Jackie Moore	S. Berry/S. Owen	Joe Slusarski
High A	Salem	Carolina	Russ Nixon	Marc Ronan	Stan Boroski
Low A	Lexington	South Atlantic	Ivan DeJesus	Brian Dayett	Charley Taylor
Short season	Tri-City	New York-Penn	Gregg Langbehn	Jorge Orta	Bill Ballou
Rookie	Greeneville	Appalachian	Tim Bogar	Pete Rancont	Jack Billingham
Rookie	Astros	Dominican	Rafael Ramirez	Rodney Linares	Rick Aponte
Rookie	Astros	Venezuela	Mario Gonzalez	Omar Lopez	Oscar Padron

Scouting
Telephone: (713) 259-8921. **FAX:** (713) 259-8600.
Director, Scouting: David Lakey.
Assistant Director, Scouting: Pat Murphy. **Administrative Assistant, Scouting:** Charlie Norton.
Coordinator, Professional Scouting: Paul Ricciarini (Pittsfield, MA).
Advance Scout: Fred Nelson (Richmond, TX). **Special Assignment Scout:** Bob Skinner (San Diego, CA).
Major League Scouts: Stan Benjamin (Greenfield, MA), Gordy MacKenzie (Fruitland Park, FL), Walt Matthews (Texarkana, TX), Paul Weaver (Phoenix, AZ).
Professional Scouts: Ken Califano (Fredricksburg, VA), Brandy Davis (Newark, DE), Gene DeBoer (Brandon, WI), Joe Pittman (Columbus, GA), Tom Romenesko (Santee, CA), Scipio Spinks (Houston, TX).
National Supervisors: Kevin Burrell (Sharpsburg, GA), Tad Slowik (Arlington Heights, IL).
Regional Supervisors: East—Gerry Craft (St. Clairsville, OH), Central—Ralph Bratton (Dripping Springs, TX).
Area Scouts: Chuck Carlson (Orlando, FL), Larry D'Amato (Tualatin, OR) Tom DeLong (Ocala, FL), Doug Deutsch (Costa Mesa, CA), Ellis Dungan (Pensacola, FL), James Farrar (Shreveport, LA), David Henderson (Edmond, OK), Brian Keegan (Matthews, NC), Bob King (La Mesa, CA), Mike Maggart (Penn Yan, NY), Jerry Marik (Chicago, IL), Tom McCormack (University City, MO), Mel Nelson (Highland, CA), Rusty Pendergrass (Houston, TX), Bob Poole (Redwood City, CA), Mike Rosamond (Madison, MS), Mark Ross (Tucson, AZ), Joey Sola (Caguas, PR), Dennis Twombley (Redondo Beach, CA), Nick Venuto (Massillon, OH), Gene Wellman (Danville, CA).
Special Assistant to GM, International Scouting/Development: Andres Reiner. **Coordinator, Venezuela:** Pablo Torrealba. **Director, Dominican Operations:** Julio Linares.

David Lakey

KANSAS CITY ROYALS

Office Address: One Royal Way, Kansas City, MO 64129.
Mailing Address: P.O. Box 419969, Kansas City, MO 64141.
Telephone: (816) 921-8000. FAX: (816) 921-1366.
Website: www.kcroyals.com.

Ownership

Operated by: Kansas City Royals Baseball Club, Inc.
Chairman/Chief Executive Officer: David Glass. President: Dan Glass. Board of Directors: Ruth Glass, Don Glass, Dayna Martz, Julia Irene Kauffman, Herk Robinson.
Executive Vice President, Chief Operating Officer: Herk Robinson. Executive Administrative Assistant: Ginger Salem.
General Counsel: Dick Nixon.

BUSINESS OPERATIONS

Senior Vice President, Business Operations: Mark Gorris. Executive Administrative Assistant: Cindy Hamilton.

Finance

David Glass

Vice President, Finance/Administration: Dale Rohr. Senior Administrative Assistant: Janet Milone.
Senior Director/Controller: John Luther. Manager, Accounting: Sean Ritchie. Manager, Ticket Office/Concession Accounting: Lisa Kresha. Accounts Payable Coordinator: Sarah Kosfeld. Accounting Coordinator: Shelley Wilson.

Marketing, Community Relations

Vice President, Sales/Marketing: Charlie Seraphin. Senior Administrative Assistant: Emily Rand. Graphic Designer: Vic Royal.
Director, Community Relations: Shani Tate. Coordinator, Community Relations: Ben Aken.
Senior Director, Corporate Sales: Mike Phillips. Director, Corporate Sponsorships: Michele Kammerer. Senior Account Executive, Corporate Sales: Joy Gibson.
Director, Ticket Sales: Rick Amos. Manager, Lancer Program: Lyndy Elmore. Manager, Group Sales: Scott Wadsworth. Account Executives: Carl Keenan, Jeff Miller, Rachelle Smith.
Director, Advertising/Promotions: Kim Hillix. Manager, Advertising/Promotions: Curt Nelson.

Public Relations, Communications

Telephone: (816) 921-8000. FAX: (816) 921-5775.
Vice President, Broadcasting/Public Relations: David Witty. Director, Broadcast Services/Royals Alumni: Fred White. Director, Media Relations: Aaron Babcock. Manager, Broadcast/Media Services: Chris Stathos. Manager, Media Relations: Lora Grosshans.

Ballpark Operations

Vice President, Ballpark Operations/Development: Bob Rice. Director, Event Operations/Guest Relations: Chris Richardson. Administrative Assistant: Renee VanLaningham. Tour Coordinator: Morrie Carlson.
Director, Groundskeeping/Landscaping: Trevor Vance. Landscape Assistant: Anthony Bruce.
Director, Stadium Operations: Rodney Lewallen. Coordinator, Stadium Operations: Robin Taylor. Coordinator, Telephone Services: Kathy Butler. Coordinator, Mail Services: Larry Garrett. Manager, Stadium Services: Johnny Williams. Manager, Stadium Engineering: Chris Frank.
Director, Scoreboard Operations: David Szucs. Coordinator, Video Operations: Chris DeRuyscher.
PA Announcer: Mike McCartney. Official Scorers: Del Black, Alan Eskew.

Ticketing

Telephone: (816) 921-8000. FAX: (816) 504-4144.
Senior Director, Ticket Operations: Lance Buckley. Director, Ticket Services: Chris Darr. Director, Season Ticket Services: Joe Grigoli. Coordinator, Season Tickets: Mary Lee Martino. Manager, Call Center: John Fields. Coordinators, Ticket Office: Betty Bax, Jacque Tschirhart.
Cashier, Ticket Office: Andrew Coughlin.

Travel, Clubhouse

Director, Team Travel: Jeff Davenport.
Equipment Manager: Mike Burkhalter. Assistant Equipment Manager: Patrick Gorman. Visiting Clubhouse Manager: Chuck Hawke. Video Coordinator: Mark Topping.

GENERAL INFORMATION

Stadium (year opened): Ewing M. Kauffman Stadium (1973).
Home Dugout: First Base. Playing Surface: Grass.
Team Colors: Royal blue and white.
Player Representative: Unavailable.

Allard Baird

BASEBALL OPERATIONS
Telephone: (816) 921-8000. FAX: (816) 924-0347.
Senior Vice President/General Manager: Allard Baird. Vice President/Assistant GM: Muzzy Jackson. Senior Advisor to GM: Art Stewart. Assistant to GM: Brian Murphy. Special Assistants to GM: Pat Jones, Luis Medina. Manager, Major League Operations: Karol Kyte.
Vice President, Baseball Operations: George Brett. Director, Baseball Operations: Jin Wong.

Major League Staff
Manager: Tony Pena.
Coaches: Bench—Bob Schaefer; Pitching—John Cumberland; Batting—Jeff Pentland; First Base—Luis Silverio; Third Base—John Mizerock; Bullpen—Brian Poldberg.

Medical, Training
Team Physician: Dr. Steven Joyce. Associate Physicians: Dr. Tim Badwey, Dr. Mark Bernhardt, Dr. Dan Gurba, Dr. Thomas Phillips, Dr. Charles Rhoades.
Head Trainer: Nick Swartz. Assistant Trainer: Frank Kyte. Strength/Conditioning Coordinator: Chris Mihlfeld. Assistant Strength/Conditioning Coordinator: Jason Estep.

Minor Leagues
Telephone: (816) 921-8000. FAX: (816) 924-0347.
Director, Player Development: Shaun McGinn. Coordinator, Minor League Operations: Unavailable. Special Assistant, Baseball Operations: Joe Jones. Special Assignment, Player Development/Scouting: John Wathan.
Coordinator, Instruction: Jeff Garber. Roving Instructors: Keith Bodie (outfield/baserunning), Ron Clark (infield), Andre David (hitting), Jason Estep (strength/conditioning), Dale Gilbert (rehabilitation), Mike Mason (pitching), Joe Szekely (catching).
Latin American Strength/Conditioning Coordinator: Ryan Stoneberg. Minor League Equipment Coordinator: Johnny O'Donnell.

Tony Pena

Farm System

Class	Farm Team	League	Manager	Coach	Pitching Coach
AAA	Omaha	Pacific Coast	Mike Jirschele	Terry Bradshaw	Dave LaRoche
AA	Wichita	Texas	Frank White	Nelson Liriano	Larry Carter
High A	Wilmington	Carolina	Billy Gardner Jr.	Boots Day	Reggie Jackson
Low A	Burlington	Midwest	Jim Gabella	Patrick Anderson	Tom Burgmeier
Rookie	Idaho Falls	Pioneer	Brian Rupp	Pookie Wilson	Jose Bautista
Rookie	Surprise	Arizona	Lloyd Simmons	Tom Poquette	Royal Clayton
Rookie	Royals	Dominican	Julio Bruno	J. Tartabull/M. Garcia	Oscar Martinez/Carlos Martinez

Scouting
Telephone: (816) 921-8000. FAX: (816) 924-0347.
Senior Director, Scouting: Deric Ladnier. Manager, Scouting Operations: Linda Smith.
Professional Scouts: Brannon Bonifay (Stuart, FL), Orlando Estevez (Pembroke Pines, FL), Earl Winn (Bowling Green, KY).
Special Assignment Scout: Carlos Pascual (Miami, FL).
Regional Supervisors: Jeff McKay (Walterville, OR), Mike Paczik (Bethesda, MD), Junior Vizcaino (Wake Forest, NC), Dennis Woody (Danville, AR).
Area Supervisors: Bob Bishop (San Dimas, CA), Mike Brown (Chandler, AZ), Jason Bryans (Detroit, MI), Steve Connelly (Massapequa, NY), Albert Gonzalez (Coral Springs, FL), Spencer Graham (Raleigh, NC), Phil Huttmann (Kansas City, MO), Gary Johnson (Costa Mesa, CA), Cliff Pastornicky (Venice, FL), Johnny Ramos (Carolina, PR), Sean Rooney (Tinton Falls, NJ), Max Semler (Lake City, FL), Chet Sergo (Houston, TX), Greg Smith (Davenport, WA), Keith Snider (Stockton, CA), Gerald Turner (Euless, TX), Brad Vaughn (Griffithville, AR), Jon Weil (Atlanta, GA), Mark Willoughby (Hammond, LA).

Deric Ladnier

Coordinator, Latin America Operations: Albert Gonzalez (Coral Springs, FL). Dominican Republic Academy Administrator/Scouting: Pedro Silverio. Venezuelan Scouting Supervisor: Juan Carlos Indriago.
International Scouts: Wilmer Castillo (Venezuela), Luis Cordoba (Panama), Juan Lopez (Nicaragua), Ramon Martinez (Dominican Republic), Daurys Nin (Dominican Republic), Mike Randall (South Africa), Rafael Vasquez (Dominican Republic).

LOS ANGELES DODGERS

Office Address: 1000 Elysian Park Ave., Los Angeles, CA 90012.
Telephone: (323) 224-1500. **FAX:** (323) 224-1269.
Website: www.dodgers.com.

Ownership

Operated by: Los Angeles Dodgers, Inc.
Principal Owner/Chairman of the Board: Frank McCourt.
Vice Chairman: Jamie McCourt. **Senior Vice President:** Tommy Lasorda. **Senior VP, General Counsel:** Sam Fernandez. **Associate Counsel:** Christine Chrisman. **Secretary, Legal:** Irma Duenas.

BUSINESS OPERATIONS

Vice President, Human Resources/Administration: David Walkley.

Finance

Vice President, Chief Financial Officer: Cristine Hurley.
Director, Finance/Accounting: Amanda Shearer. **Manager, Payroll:** Rebecca Aguilar.
Chief Information Officer/Director, Management Information Systems: Mike Mularky.

Frank McCourt

Sales, Advertising, Client Services

Executive Vice President, Business Operations: Kris Rone. **Vice President, Sales:** Sergio del Prado. **Assistant Director, Group/Season Sales:** Lisa Johnson. **Director, Sponsorship Sales:** Jason Klein. **Director, Sponsorship Sales:** Karen Marumoto. **Manager, Advertising/Special Events:** Dan Brewster.

Public Relations, Communications

Senior Vice President, Communications: Derrick Hall. **VP, External Affairs:** Tommy Hawkins. **Director, Public Relations:** John Olguin. **Assistant Director, Public Relations:** Josh Rawitch. **Manager, Baseball Information:** Dave Tuttle. **Supervisor, Broadcast/Publications:** Paul Gomez. **Director, Community Affairs:** Erikk Aldridge. **Director, Community Relations:** Don Newcombe.

Stadium Operations

Vice President, Stadium Operations: Doug Duennes.
Director, Stadium Operations: Lon Rosenberg. **Assistant Director, Stadium Operations:** Charles Taylor. **Assistant Director, Stadium Operations/Turf and Grounds:** Eric Hansen.
PA Announcer: Eric Smith **Official Scorers:** Don Hartack, Gordie Verrell. **Organist:** Nancy Bea Hefley.

Ticketing

Telephone: (323) 224-1471. **FAX:** (323) 224-2609.
Director, Ticket Operations: Billy Hunter. **Director, Special Projects:** Debra Duncan.
Assistant Director, Ticket Operations: Chris Frumento.

Travel, Clubhouse

Director, Team Travel: Shaun Rachau. **Home Clubhouse Managers:** Dave Dickinson, Mitch Poole. **Visiting Clubhouse Manager:** Jerry Turner.

GENERAL INFORMATION

Stadium (year opened): Dodger Stadium (1962).
Home Dugout: Third Base. **Playing Surface:** Grass.
Team Colors: Dodger blue, red and white.
Player Representative: Paul LoDuca.

Paul DePodesta

BASEBALL OPERATIONS

Telephone: (323) 224-1500. **FAX:** (323) 224-1463.
Executive Vice President, General Manager: Paul DePodesta.
VP, Assistant GM: Kim Ng. **Special Assistant to GM:** Jeff Schugel.
Special Assistant to GM/Advance Scout: Mark Weidemaier (Tierre Verde, FL).
Senior Advisors, Baseball Operations: Joe Amalfitano, John Boles. **Assistant, Baseball Operations:** A.J. Preller. **Administrator, Baseball Operations:** Ellen Harrigan.
Vice President, Spring Training/Minor League Facilities: Craig Callan.
Director, Asian Operations: Acey Kohrogi. **Manager, Japanese Affairs:** Scott Akasaki. **Manager, Korean Affairs:** Curtis Jung. **Manager, Chinese/Taiwanese Affairs:** Vincent Liao.

Major League Staff

Manager: Jim Tracy.
Coaches: Bench—Jim Riggleman, Manny Mota; Pitching—Jim Colborn; Hitting—Tim Wallach; First Base—John Shelby; Third Base—Glenn Hoffman; Bullpen—Jim Lett.

Medical, Training

Team Physicians: Dr. Frank Jobe, Dr. Michael Mellman, Dr. Ralph Gambardella, Dr. Herndon Harding.
Head Trainer: Stan Johnston. **Assistant Trainer:** Matt Wilson. **Physical Therapist:** Pat Screnar. **Strength/Conditioning Coach:** Todd Clausen. **Muscle Therapist:** Bill Le Suer.

Player Development

Telephone: (323) 224-1431. **FAX:** (323) 224-1359.
Director, Player Development: Unavailable. **Assistant Director, Player Development:** Luchy Guerra. **Coordinator, Minor League Operations:** Chris Haydock.
Field Coordinator: Terry Collins.
Roving Coordinators: Mark Brewer (pitching), Del Crandall (advisor), Jon Debus (catching), Rick Honeycutt (pitching), Doug Jarrow (strength/conditioning), Bob Mariano (hitting), Kevin McNair (physical development), Gene Richards (outfield/baserunning), Jerry Royster (infield), John Shoemaker (roving instructor), Jason Steere (physical therapy).
Coordinators, Dominican Republic Operations: Victor Baez (field), Antonio Bautista (hitting), Martin Berroa (training), Luis Montalvo (infield). **Supervisor, Venezuelan Operations:** Camilo Pascual.

Jim Tracy

Farm System

Class	Farm Team	League	Manager	Coach	Pitching Coach
AAA	Las Vegas	Pacific Coast	Terry Kennedy	George Hendrick	Roger McDowell
AA	Jacksonville	Southern	Dino Ebel	Mariano Duncan	Marty Reed
High A	Vero Beach	Florida State	Scott Little	Juan Bustabad	Ken Howell
Low A	Columbus	South Atlantic	Dann Bilardello	Garey Ingram	Shawn Barton
Rookie	Ogden	Pioneer	Travis Barbary	Pat Harrison	Tim Kelly
Rookie	Vero Beach	Gulf Coast	Luis Salazar	Brian Traxler	George Culver
Rookie	Dodgers I	Dominican	Pedro Mega	Jose Mija	Hector Eduardo
Rookie	Dodgers II	Dominican	Juan Davalillo	Rafael Rijo	Carlos Gil

Scouting

Director, Amateur Scouting: Logan White. **Director, Professional Scouting:** Matt Slater.
Director, International Scouting: Rene Francisco. **Administrator, Scouting:** Jane Capobianco. **Coordinator, Scouting Operations:** Bill McLaughlin. **Senior Scouting Advisor:** Don Welke.
Major League Scout: Carl Loewenstine (Hamilton, OH).
Professional Scouts: Dan Freed (Lexington, IL), Vance Lovelace (Tampa, FL), Ron Rizzi (Joppa, MD).
Special Advisor to Amateur Scouting Director/National Crosschecker: Gib Bodet (San Clemente, CA). **National Crosschecker:** Tim Hallgren (Roanoke, TX).
Regional Supervisors: East—John Barr (Palm City, FL), Midwest—Gary Nickels (Naperville, IL), West Coast—Tom Thomas (Phoenix, AZ).
Special Assignment Scout: Tim Kelly (New Lenox, IL).
Area Scouts: Doug Carpenter (Jupiter, FL), Jim Chapman (Delta, B.C.), Bobby Darwin (Cerritos, CA), Scott Groot (Mission Viejo, CA), Clarence Johns (New Orleans, LA), Calvin Jones (Henderson, NV), Hank Jones (Vancouver, WA), Lon Joyce (Spartanburg, SC), John Kosciak (Milford, MA), Marty Lamb (Lexington, KY), Mike Leuzinger (Mansfield, TX), James Merriweather (Los Angeles, CA), Bill Pleis (Parrish, FL), Clair Rierson (Frederick, MD), Mark Sheehy (Sacramento, CA), Chris Smith (Montgomery, TX), Brian Stephenson (Phoenix, AZ), Mitch Webster (Great Bend, KS).
International Scouts: Mike Brito (Mexico), Tony Harris (Australia), Pat Kelly (Pacific Rim), Camilo Pascual (Venezuela).

Logan White

MILWAUKEE BREWERS

Office Address: Miller Park, One Brewers Way, Milwaukee, WI 53214.
Telephone: (414) 902-4400. **FAX:** (414) 902-4053.
Website: www.milwaukeebrewers.com.

Ownership
Operated by: Milwaukee Brewers Baseball Club.
Board of Directors: John Canning, Francis Croak, Mitchell Fromstein, Michael Grebe, Wendy Selig-Prieb, Richard Strup, Harris Turer. **Chairman:** Wendy Selig-Prieb.

BUSINESS OPERATIONS
Executive Vice President: Rick Schlesinger. **Assistant Vice President:** Geoff Campion.
Manager, Corporate Partner Services: Patty Harsch. **Manager, Human Resources:** Mariela Garcia-Danet. **Executive Assistant, Business Operations:** Adela Reeve. **Director, Entertainment:** Aleta Mercer.

Finance
Senior Vice President, Chief Financial Officer: Robert J. Quinn Jr. **Controller:** Joe Zidanic. **Director, Management Information Systems:** Dan Krautkramer. **Systems Administrator:** Tristan Benson.
Manager, Budget/Special Projects: Carol McInnes. **Payroll Coordinator/Accountant:** Brian Krueger. **Staff Accountants:** Wes Seidel, Vicki Wise. **Supervisor, Accounts Receivable/Payable:** Cathy Schwab.

Wendy Selig-Prieb

Corporate Affairs, Sales/Marketing
Vice President, Corporate Affairs: Laurel Prieb.
Directors, Corporate Sales: Tom Kozlowski, Amy Deering. **Manager, Corporate Sales/Promotions:** David Barnes. **Account Executive:** Jaclyn Habeck. **Administrative Assistant, Marketing:** Lisa Brzeski.

Public Relations, Communications
Telephone: (414) 902-4400. **FAX:** (414) 902-4053.
Director, Media Relations: Jon Greenberg. **Assistant Director, Media Relations:** Jason Parry. **Manager, Media Relations:** Nicole Saunches. **Publications Assistant:** Robbin Barnes.
Team Photographers: Scott Paulus, Jill Stolt. **Director, Broadcasting:** Tim Van Wagoner. **Manager, Audio/Video Productions:** Deron Anderson.
Director, Community Relations: Leonard Peace. **Coordinator, Community Relations:** Patricia Ramirez.

Stadium Operations
Vice President, Stadium Operations: Steve Ethier.
Director, Grounds: Gary Vanden Berg. **Manager, Grounds:** Raechal Volkening.
Coordinator, Guest Relations: Kristy Suworoff. **Coordinator, Telecommunications:** Tonya Powell. **Supervisor, Warehouse:** Patrick Rogo. **Supervisor, Maintenance:** James Broeker.
President, Brewers Charities: Lynn Sprangers.
PA Announcer: Robb Edwards. **Official Scorers:** Tim O'Driscoll, Wayne Franke.

Ticketing
Telephone: (414) 902-4000. **FAX:** (414) 902-4100.
Assistant Vice President, Ticket Sales: Jim Bathey, **Assistant Vice President, Ticket Services:** John Barnes. **Manager, Season Ticket/Group Sales:** Chris Barlow. **Administrative Assistant:** Irene Bolton. **Assistant Director, Ticket Services:** Nancy Jorgensen. **Manager, Ticket Services/Phone Center:** Glenn Kurylo. **Representative, Ticket Office Support Services:** Diane Schoenfeld. **Senior Account Executives:** Beau Bradle, Billy Friess, Bill Junker, Kara Kabitzke.

Travel, Clubhouse
Director, Team Travel: Dan Larrea.
Director, Clubhouse Operations/Equipment Manager: Tony Migliaccio. **Visiting Clubhouse Manager:** Phil Rozewicz. **Assistant, Home Clubhouse:** Mike Moulder. **Coordinator, Umpires Room:** Duane Lewis.

GENERAL INFORMATION

Stadium (year opened): Miller Park (2001).
Home Dugout: First Base. **Playing Surface:** Grass.
Team Colors: Navy blue, gold and white.
Player Representative: Wes Helms.

BASEBALL OPERATIONS
Executive Vice President, General Manager: Doug Melvin. **Assistant GM:** Gord Ash.
Senior Special Assistant to GM: Larry Haney (Barboursville, VA). **Special Assistant to GM/Scouting:** Dick Groch (Marysville, MI).
Senior Administrator, Baseball Operations: Barb Stark.

Major League Staff
Manager: Ned Yost.
Coaches: Bench—Rich Dauer. Pitching—Mike Maddux; Batting—Butch Wynegar; First Base—Dave Nelson; Third Base—Rich Donnelly; Bullpen—Bill Castro.

Medical, Training

Doug Melvin

Head Team Physician: Dr. William Raasch. **Head Athletic Trainer:** Roger Caplinger. **Assistant Athletic Trainer/Coordinator, Strength and Conditioning:** Dan Wright. **Assistant Athletic Trainer:** Paul Anderson.

Player Development
Telephone: (414) 902-4400. **FAX:** (414) 902-4059.
Special Assistant to GM/Player Development: Reid Nichols. **Assistant Director, Player Development:** Scott Martens. **Assistant to Player Development:** Mark Mueller.
Field Coordinator: Ed Sedar. **Coordinators:** Jim Rooney (pitching), Jim Skaalen (hitting), Frank Neville (trainers), Keith Wilson (strength/conditioning). **Roving Instructor:** Ed Romero (infield). **Equipment Manager:** J.R. Rinaldi. **Maryvale Clubhouse Manager:** Matt Bass. **Performance Enhancement Coordinator:** Dr. Jack Curtis.

Ned Yost

Farm System

Class	Farm Team	League	Manager	Coach	Pitching Coach
AAA	Indianapolis	International	Cecil Cooper	Bobby Randall	Stan Kyles
AA	Huntsville	Southern	Frank Kremblas	Sandy Guerrero	Fred Dabney
High A	High Desert	California	Mel Queen	Stanton Cameron	John Curtis
Low A	Beloit	Midwest	Don Money	Tony Diggs	Rich Sauveur
Rookie	Helena	Pioneer	Johnny Narron	Norberto Martin	Mark Littell
Rookie	Phoenix	Arizona	Mike Guerrero	Joel Youngblood	Steve Cline

Scouting
Telephone: (414) 902-4400. **FAX:** (414) 902-4059.
Director, Scouting: Jack Zduriencik. **Assistant Director, Scouting:** Tom Flanagan. **Administrative Assistant:** Amanda Klecker.
Special Assignment Scout: Lee Thomas (Chesterfield, MO).
Professional Scouts: Lary Aaron (Atlanta, GA), Hank Allen (Upper Marlboro, MD), Chris Bourjos (Scottsdale, AZ), Brad Delbarba (Fort Mitchell, KY), Larry Haney (Barboursville, VA), Toney Howell (Gurnee, IL), Rudy Terrasas (Santa Fe, TX), Leon Wurth (Nashville, TN).
National Crosscheckers: Larry Doughty (Leawood, KS), John Poloni (Tarpon Springs, FL).
Regional Supervisors: West Coast—Tom Allison (Austin, TX), Midwest—Jeff Cornell (Lee's Summit, MO), East Coast—Bobby Heck (Apopka, FL), Latin America—Fernando Arango (Dania, FL).

Jack Zduriencik

Area Supervisors: Charles Aliano (Land O' Lakes, FL), Tony Blengino (Magnolia, NJ), Grant Brittain (Hickory, NC), Jeff Brookens (Chambersburg, PA), Mike Farrell (Indianapolis, IN), Manolo Hernandez (Moca, PR), Brian Johnson (Avondale, AZ), Harvey Kuenn Jr. (New Berlin, WI), Justin McCray (Davis, CA), Ray Montgomery (Pearland, TX), Brandon Newell (Bellingham, WA), Larry Pardo (Miami, FL), Doug Reynolds (Tallahassee, FL), Corey Rodriguez (Hermosa Beach, CA), Bruce Seid (Aliso Viejo, CA), Jim Stevenson (Tulsa, OK).
Scouts: Edward Fastaia (Brooklyn, NY), Roger Janeaway (Englewood, OH), John Logan (Milwaukee, WI), Mike Rasdall (Colorado Springs, CO), Brad Stoll (Lawrence, KS).
International Scout: Richard Clemons (Canada).

MINNESOTA TWINS

Office Address: 34 Kirby Puckett Place, Minneapolis, MN 55415.
Telephone: (612) 375-1366. **FAX:** (612) 375-7480.
Website: www.twinsbaseball.com.

Ownership

Operated by: The Minnesota Twins.
Owner: Carl Pohlad. **Chairman, Executive Committee:** Howard Fox.
Executive Board: Jerry Bell, Kevin Cattoor, Carl Pohlad, James Pohlad, Robert Pohlad, William Pohlad, Dave St. Peter.
President, Minnesota Twins: Dave St Peter. **President, Twins Sports Inc:** Jerry Bell. **Executive Vice President, Twins Sports Inc.:** Kevin Cattoor. **Administrative Assistant to President/Office Manager:** Joan Boeser.

BUSINESS OPERATIONS

Human Resources

VP, Human Resources/Diversity: Raenell Dorn. **Payroll Manager:** Lori Beasley. **Human Resources Generalist:** Leticia Fuentes. **Cordinator, Workmans Compensation:** Tina Flowers.

Carl Pohlad

Finance

Chief Financial Officer: Kip Elliott. **Director, Financial Planning:** Andy Weinstein. **Director, Financial Reporting:** Michelle Stukel. **Accountant:** Jerry McLaughlin. **Accounts Payable:** Amy Fong. **Director, Information Systems:** Wade Navratil. **Director, Network/Baseball Information Systems:** John Avenson. **PC Support Specialist:** Erik Vermeulen. **Programmers/Analysts:** Tony Persio, Paul Samargia.

Marketing

Vice President, Marketing: Patrick Klinger. **Director, Advertising:** Nancy O'Brien. **Promotions Coordinator:** Chris Hodapp. **Director, Game Presentation:** Andy Price. **Director, Community Affairs:** Peter Martin. **Manager, Community Affairs:** Bryan Donaldson. **Coordinators, Community Affairs:** Gloria Westerdahl, Andrea Knutson.

Corporate Sales

Vice President, Corporate Partnerships: Eric Curry. **Managers, Corporate Sales:** Chad Jackson, Dick Schultz, Mark Zobel. **Account Executive:** Willie Wong. **Manager, Client Services:** Bodie Rykken. **Coordinators, Client Services:** Jordan Gross, Katie Hartman.

Ticket Sales

Director, Ticket Sales: Scott O'Connell. **Account Sales Executives:** Dan Craighead, Jeff Hibicke, Eric Hudson, Mike Leonard, Rob Malec, Chris Malek, Jason Stern. **Manager, Sales Administration:** Beth Vail.

Communications

Telephone: (612) 375-7471. **FAX:** (612) 375-7473.
Director, Communications: Brad Ruiter. **Manager, Media Relations:** Sean Harlin. **Assistant Manager, Media Relations:** Mike Herman. **Coordinator, Communications:** Molly Gallatin. **Official Scorer:** Tom Mee.

Stadium Operations

Vice President, Operations: Matt Hoy. **Director, Stadium Operations:** Dave Horsman. **Director, Special Events:** Heidi Sammon. **Manager, Stadium Operations:** Ric Johnson. **Manager, Security:** Dick Dugan. **Manager, Merchandise:** Matt Noll. **Manager, Roseville Pro Shop:** Joel Davis. **Manager, Minnetonka Pro Shop:** Courtney Pahlke. **Coordinator, Office Services:** John McEvoy. **Coordinator, Operations:** Jeff Flom. **Receptionist:** TaMica Tody. **PA Announcer:** Bob Casey.

Ticket Operations

Telephone: (612) 338-9467, (800) 338-9467. **FAX:** (612) 375-7464.
Director, Ticket Operations: Paul Froehle. **Manager, Box Office:** Mike Stiles. **Supervisor, Ticket Office:** Karl Dedenbach. **Coordinator, Ticket Office:** Mike Johnson. **Manager, Telemarketing:** Patrick Forsland.

Travel, Clubhouse

Traveling Secretary: Remzi Kiratli.
Equipment Manager: Jim Dunn. **Visitors Clubhouse:** Troy Matchan. **Internal Video Specialist:** Nyal Peterson.

GENERAL INFORMATION

Stadium (year opened): Hubert H. Humphrey Metrodome (1982).
Home Dugout: Third Base. **Playing Surface:** Artificial turf.
Team Colors: Burgundy, navy blue and white.
Player Representative: Unavailable.

Terry Ryan

BASEBALL OPERATIONS
Telephone: (612) 375-7484. **FAX:** (612) 375-7417.
Vice President, General Manager: Terry Ryan.
VP, Assistant GM: Bill Smith. **Assistant GM:** Wayne Krivsky. **Special Assistants to GM:** Larry Corrigan, Joe McIlvaine, Tom Kelly.
Director, Baseball Operations: Rob Antony. **Assistant Director, Baseball Operations:** Brad Steil. **Administrative Assistant, Major League Operations:** Juanita Lagos-Benson.

Major League Staff
Manager: Ron Gardenhire.
Coaches: Bench—Steve Liddle; Pitching—Rick Anderson; Batting—Scott Ullger; First Base—Jerry White; Third Base—Al Newman; Bullpen—Rick Stelmaszek.

Medical, Training
Club Physicians: Dr. Dan Buss, Dr. Vijay Eyunni, Dr. Tom Jetzer, Dr. John Steubs, Dr. Jon Hallberg.
Head Trainer: Jim Kahmann. **Assistant Trainer:** Rick McWane. **Strength and Conditioning Coach:** Randy Popple.

Player Development
Telephone: (612) 375-7488. **FAX:** (612) 375-7417.
Director, Minor Leagues: Jim Rantz. **Administrative Assistant, Minor Leagues:** Julie Rohloff.
Field Coordinator: Joe Vavra. **Roving Instructors:** Jim Dwyer (hitting), Rick Knapp (pitching).

Ron Gardenhire

Farm System

Class	Farm Team	League	Manager	Coach	Pitching Coach
AAA	Rochester	International	Phil Roof	Rick Miller	Bobby Cuellar
AA	New Britain	Eastern	Stan Cliburn	Jeff Carter	Stu Cliburn
High A	Fort Myers	Florida State	Jose Marzan	Floyd Rayford	Eric Rasmussen
Low A	Quad City	Midwest	Kevin Boles	Rudy Hernandez	Gary Lucas
Rookie	Elizabethton	Appalachian	Ray Smith	Jeff Reed	Jim Shellenback
Rookie	Fort Myers	Gulf Coast	Riccardo Ingram	Milt Cuyler	Steve Mintz
Rookie	Twins	Dominican	Nelson Norman	N. Prada/C. Almonic	Ivan Arteaga
Rookie	Twins	Venezuela	Asdrubal Estrada	Ramon Borrego	Pablo Torres

Scouting
Telephone: (612) 375-7525. **FAX:** (612) 375-7417.
Director, Scouting: Mike Radcliff (Overland Park, KS).
Administrative Assistant, Scouting: Jack Goin.
Special Assignment Scouts: Larry Corrigan (Fort Myers, FL), Cal Ermer (Chattanooga, TN).
Major League Scout: Bill Harford (Chicago, IL). **Coordinator, Professional Scouting:** Vern Followell (Buena Park, CA). **Advance Scout:** Bob Hegman (Lee's Summit, MO).
Scouting Supervisors: East—Earl Frishman (Tampa, FL), West—Deron Johnson (Sacramento, CA), Midwest—Joel Lepel (Plato, MN), Mike Ruth (Lee's Summit, MO).
Area Scouts: Kevin Bootay (Sacramento, CA), Marty Esposito (Robinson, TX), Sean Johnson (Chandler, AZ), John Leavitt (Garden Grove, CA), Bill Lohr (Centralia, WA), Bill Mele (El Segundo, CA), Gregg Miller (Chandler, OK), Billy Milos (Crown Point, IN), Tim O'Neil (Lexington, KY), Hector Otero (Trujillo Alto, PR), Mark Quimuyog (Lynn Haven, FL), Ricky Taylor (Hickory, NC), Brad Weitzel (Haines City, FL), Jay Weitzel (Salamanca, NY), John Wilson (Blairstown, NJ), Mark Wilson (Lindstrom, MN).
Director, International Scouting: Joe McIlvaine (Newtown Square, PA).
International Scouts: John Cortese (Italy), Gene Grimaldi (Europe), David Kim (South Korea), Jose Leon (Venezuela), Howard Norsetter (Australia, Europe), Yoshi Okamoto (Japan), Jim Ridley (Canada), Koji Takahashi (Japan).

Mike Radcliff

MONTREAL EXPOS

Office Address: Olympic Stadium, 4549 Pierre-de-Coubertin Ave., Montreal, Quebec H1V 3N7.
Mailing Address: P.O. Box 500, Station M, Montreal, Quebec H1V 3P2.
Telephone: (514) 253-3434. **FAX:** (514) 253-8282.
Website: www.montrealexpos.com.

Ownership
Operated by: Baseball Expos, LP.
President: Tony Tavares. **Executive Assistant:** Monique Chibok.

BUSINESS OPERATIONS
Executive Vice President, Business Affairs: Claude Delorme. **VP/General Manager, Space Coast Stadium:** Andy Dunn.

Sales, Marketing
Director, Ticket Sales: John DiTerlizzi. **Director, Administration/Sales and Marketing:** Chantal Dalpe. **Producer, Scoreboard Operations:** Chantal Burnett. **Coordinator, Special Events:** Martine Peters.

Tony Tavares

Media Relations, Communications
Director, Media Services: Monique Giroux. **Director, Baseball Information:** John Dever. **Coordinator, Media Relations:** Elias Makos. **Administrative Assistant:** Sina Gabrielli.

Stadium Operations
Director, Game Operations: Denis Pare. **Assistant Director, Game Operations:** Stephane Mercier. **Coordinator, Entertainment:** Jean-Simon Bibeau. **Director, Management Information System:** Yves Poulin. **Manager, Souvenirs:** Peggy O'Leary.
PA Announcer: Marc Leveille. **Official Scorers:** Serge Rivest, Michel Spinelli.

Ticketing
Director, Olympic Stadium Ticket Office: Frederique Brault. **Assistant Director, Ticket Office:** Steeve Michaud.

Travel, Clubhouse
Coordinator, Team Travel: Rob McDonald.
Equipment Manager: Mike Wallace. **Visiting Clubhouse:** Matt Rosenthal.

GENERAL INFORMATION
Stadium (year opened): Olympic Stadium (1977).
Home Dugout: First Base. **Playing Surface:** Artificial turf.
Team Colors: Blue, red and white.
Player Representative: Brian Schneider.

BASEBALL OPERATIONS

Vice President, General Manager: Omar Minaya.
Assistant GM/Director, Baseball Administration: Tony Siegle. **Administrative Assistant:** Marcia Schnaar.

Major League Staff

Manager: Frank Robinson.
Coaches: Dugout—Eddie Rodriguez; Pitching—Randy St. Claire; Batting—Tom McCraw; First Base/Outfield—Jerry Morales; Third Base/Infield—Manny Acta; Bullpen/Catchers—Bob Natal; Roving—Claude Raymond.

Medical, Training

Team Physician: Dr. Bruce Thomas.
Omar Minaya
Head Trainer: Ron McClain. **Assistant Trainer:** Tim Abraham.
Coordinator, Strength/Conditioning: Michael Arndt.

Player Development

Telephone: (514) 253-3434. **FAX:** (514) 253-8282.
Director, Player Development: Adam Wogan. **Coordinator, Minor League Administration:** Nick Manno.
Field Coordinator: Doug Sisson. **Roving Coordinators:** Frank Cacciatore (hitting), Jose Alguacil (infield), Brent Strom (pitching).
Manager, Florida Operations: Dan Wallin.

Frank Robinson

Farm System

Class	Farm Team	League	Manager	Coach	Pitching Coach
AAA	Edmonton	Pacific Coast	Dave Huppert	Mike Hart	Charlie Corbell
AA	Harrisburg	Eastern	Dave Machemer	Rob Ducey	Mark Grater
High A	Brevard County	Florida State	Tim Raines	Andy Skeels	Craig Bjornson
Low A	Savannah	South Atlantic	Bob Henley	Joel Chimelis	Ricky Bones
Short season	Vermont	New York-Penn	Unavailable	Joe Marchese	Franklin Bravo
Rookie	Melbourne	Gulf Coast	Aurturo DeFreites	Jose Alguacil	Tom Keating
Rookie	Expos	Dominican	Unavailable	Elvis Herrera	Manuel DeJesus

Scouting

Director, Amateur Scouting: Dana Brown. **Director, Pro Scouting:** Lee MacPhail IV.
Coordinator, Scouting: Brian Parker.
Advance Scout: Jerry Terrell (Blue Springs, MO). **Professional Scouts:** Jack Bloomfield (McAllen, TX), Manny Estrada (Brandon, FL), Carmen Fusco (Mechanicsburg, PA), Fred Mazuca (Tustin, CA), Mike Toomey (Gaithersburg, MD), Rick Williams (St. Petersburg, FL).
Regional Crosscheckers: East—Paul Tinnell (Cortez, FL), Midwest—Ray Jackson (Ocala, FL), West Coast—Charles Scott (Novato, CA).
Area Scouts: Anthony Arango (Los Angeles, CA), Russ Bove (Apopka, FL), Ray Corbett (College Station, TX), Zack Hoyrst (Lovejoy, GA), Larry Izzo (Deer Park, NY), Ben Jones (Fort Wayne, IN), Doug McMillan (Shingle Springs, CA), Lance Nichols (Dodge City, KS), Delvy Santiago (Vega Alta, PR), Alex Smith (Abingdon, MD), Fred Wright (Harrisburg, NC).

Dana Brown

Part-Time Scouts: Mike Alberts (Worcester, MA), Leslie Gonzalez (Arlington, TX), Wilmer Reid (Philadelphia, PA).
Director, Latin American Scouting/Development: Ismael Cruz. **Coordinator, Latin American Scouting/Development:** Pablo Cruz. **Coordinator, Dominican Republic:** Sandi Rosaro.

NEW YORK METS

Office Address: 123-01 Roosevelt Ave., Flushing, NY 11368.
Telephone: (718) 507-6387. FAX: (718) 507-6395.
Website: www.mets.com.

Ownership

Operated by: Sterling Mets, LP.
Board of Directors: Fred Wilpon, Saul Katz, Jeff Wilpon, Marvin Tepper, Arthur Friedman, Michael Katz, David Katz, Tom Osterman, Richard Wilpon, Stuart Sucherman, Steve Greenberg.
Chairman, Chief Executive Officer: Fred Wilpon. President: Saul Katz. Senior Executive Vice President, Chief Operating Officer: Jeff Wilpon.

BUSINESS OPERATIONS

Executive Vice President, Business Operations: David Howard. Senior Vice President, General Counsel: David Cohen.

Fred Wilpon

Finance

Chief Financial Officer: Mark Peskin. Vice President/Controller: Lenny Labita. Director, Information Systems: Dot Pope. Chief Accountant: Rebecca Mahadeva.

Marketing, Sales

Vice President, Corporate Sales/Services: Paul Danforth.
Director, Marketing: Tina Bucciarelli. Director, Marketing Productions: Tim Gunkel.
Director, Corporate Services: Jim Plummer. Manager, Marketing Communications: Jill Grabill. Director, Community Outreach: Jill Knee. Coordinator, Community Outreach: Chris Brown.

Media Relations

Telephone: (718) 565-4330. FAX: (718) 639-3619.
Vice President, Media Relations: Jay Horwitz. Manager, Media Relations: Shannon Dalton. Manager, Corporate/Media Services: Stella Fiore. Media Relations Specialists: Chris Tropeano, Ethan Wilson.

Stadium Operations

Vice President, Facilities: Karl Smolarz. Director, Stadium Operations: Kevin McCarthy. Manager, Stadium Operations: Sue Lucchi. Manager, Field Operations: Mike Williams.
PA Announcer: Roger Luce. Official Scorers: Joe Donnelly, Howie Karpin, Bill Shannon, Jordan Sprechman.

Ticketing

Telephone: (718) 507-8499. FAX: (718) 507-6396.
Vice President, Ticket Sales/Services: Bill Ianniciello.
Director, Ticket Operations: Dan DeMato. Assistant Director, Ticket Sales Development: Jamie Ozure. Manager, Corporate Ticket Sales: Marc Steir. Director, Group/Ticket Sales Services: Thomas Fersch. Manager, Group/Ticket Sales Services: Mark Phillips.

Travel, Clubhouse

Equipment Manager, Associate Travel Director: Charlie Samuels. Assistant Equipment Manager: Vinny Greco. Visiting Clubhouse Manager: Tony Carullo. Video Editor: Joe Scarola.

GENERAL INFORMATION

Stadium (year opened): Shea Stadium (1964).
Home Dugout: First Base. Playing Surface: Grass.
Team Colors: Blue and orange.
Player Representative: Vance Wilson.

Jim Duquette

BASEBALL OPERATIONS
Telephone: (718) 565-4315. **FAX:** (718) 507-6391.
Senior Vice President, General Manager: Jim Duquette.
Special Assistants to GM: Bruce Benedict, Al Goldis, Bill Livesey. **Executive Assistant to GM:** Denise Morris. **Baseball Operations Assistant:** Adam Fisher.

Major League Staff
Manager: Art Howe.
Coaches: Dugout—Don Baylor/Matt Galante; Pitching—Rick Peterson; Batting—Denny Walling; First Base/Outfield—Gary Pettis; Third Base/Infield—Bobby Floyd.

Medical, Training
Team Physician: Dr. Andrew Rokito. **Associate Team Physician:** Dr. Joe Bosco.
Head Trainer: Scott Lawrenson. **Assistant Trainer:** Mike Herbst. **Coordinator, Strength/Conditioning:** Rick Slate. **Assistant Coordinator, Fitness/Conditioning:** Jose Vazquez.

Player Development
Telephone: (718) 565-4302. **FAX:** (718) 205-7920.
Assistant General Manager/Director, Baseball and Scouting Operations: Gary LaRocque. **Director, Minor League Operations:** Kevin Morgan. **Assistant Director, Minor League Operations:** John Fantauzzi. **Assistant, Player Development:** Amy Neal.
Field Coordinator: Guy Conti. **Assistant Field Coordinator:** Tony Tijerina. **Infield Consultant:** Chico Fernandez. **Roving Instructors:** Mickey Brantley (hitting), Gary Carter (catching), Edgar Alfonzo (infield), Rick Paterson (outfield/baserunning), Rick Waits (pitching).
Advisor, Minor Leagues: Chuck Hiller. **Advisors, Baseball Operations:** Ray Rippelmeyer, Al Jackson. **Training Coordinator:** Bill Wagner. **Rehabilitation Coordinator:** Jason Wulf. **Coordinator, Strength/Conditioning:** Jason Craig. **Assistant Coordinator, Strength/Conditioning:** Ken Coward. **Equipment Manager:** Kevin Kierst. **Assistant Equipment Manager:** Jack Brenner.

Art Howe

Farm System
Class	Farm Team	League	Manager	Coach	Pitching Coach
AAA	Norfolk	International	John Stearns	Al LeBoeuf	Dan Warthen
AA	Binghamton	Eastern	Ken Oberkfell	Howard Johnson	Jerry Reuss
High A	St. Lucie	Florida State	Tim Teufel	Lamar Johnson	Rick Mahler
Low A	Capital City	South Atlantic	Jack Lind	Dave Hollins	Blaine Beatty
Short season	Brooklyn	New York-Penn	Leon Lee	Donovan Mitchell	Hector Berrios
Rookie	Kingsport	Appalachian	Mookie Wilson	Luis Natera	Unavailable
Rookie	Port St. Lucie	Gulf Coast	Brett Butler	Juan Lopez	Randy Niemann
Rookie	Mets	Dominican	Lillian Castro	M. Valdez/H. Sierra	Unavailable
Rookie	Mets	Venezuelan	Jesus Tiamo	Leo Hernandez	Jesus Hernaiz

Scouting
Telephone: Amateur—(718) 565-4311, Professional—(718) 803-4013. **FAX:** (718) 205-7920.
Director, Amateur Scouting: Jack Bowen. **Assistant, Amateur Scouting:** Elizabeth Gadsden. **Assistant, Professional/International Scouting:** Anne Fairbanks.
Professional Scouts: Duffy Dyer (Phoenix, AZ), Dave Engle (San Diego, CA), Howie Freiling (Apex, NC), Rod Fridley (Covington, VA), Roland Johnson (Newington, CT), Joe Nigro (Staten Island, NY).
National Crosscheckers: Paul Fryer (Calabasas, CA), Terry Tripp (Harrisburg, IL).
Regional Supervisors: West—Bob Minor (Garden Grove, CA), North—Gene Kerns (Hagerstown, MD), South—Joe DelliCarri (Longwood, FL).
Area Supervisors: Dave Birecki (Peoria, AZ), Quincy Boyd (Plainfield, IL), Erwin Bryant (Lexington, KY), Jon Bunnell (Tampa, FL), Larry Chase (Pearcy, AR), Rodney Henderson (Lexington, KY), Chuck Hensley Jr. (Sacramento, CA), Brian Hunter (Lake Elsinore, CA), Scott Hunter (Binghamton, NY), Steve Leavitt (Huntington Beach, CA), Dave Lottsfeldt (Richardson, TX), Marlin McPhail (Irmo, SC), Greg Morhardt (South Windsor, CT), Claude Pelletier (St. Lazare, Quebec), Jim Reeves (Camas, WA), Junior Roman (San Sebastian, PR), Bob Rossi (Baton Rouge, LA), Joe Salermo (Miami Beach, FL), Matt Wondolowski (Oakton, VA).
Director, International Scouting: Rafael Bournigal. **International Scouts:** Eddy Toledo (Dominican Republic), Gregorio Machado (Venezuela). **Director, Pacific Rim:** Isao O'Jimi (Japan).

Gary LaRocque

NEW YORK YANKEES

Office Address: Yankee Stadium, East 161st Street and River Avenue, Bronx, NY 10451.
Telephone: (718) 293-4300. **FAX:** (718) 293-8431.
Website: www.yankees.com.

Ownership
Principal Owner: George Steinbrenner. **General Partners:** Harold Steinbrenner, Henry Steinbrenner, Stephen Swindal.

BUSINESS OPERATIONS
President: Randy Levine.
Chief Operating Officer: Lonn Trost.
VP, Administration: Sonny Hight.

Finance
Vice President, Chief Financial Officer: Martin Greenspun. **Controller:** Robert Brown.

Marketing, Community Relations
Vice President, Marketing: Deborah Tymon.
VP, Corporate/Community Relations: Brian Smith.
Director, Sponsorship Sales/Services: Michael Tusiani.

George Steinbrenner

Media Relations, Publications
Telephone: (718) 579-4460. **FAX:** (718) 293-8414.
Senior Advisor: Arthur Richman. **Director, Media Relations/Publicity:** Rick Cerrone. **Assistant Director, Media Relations/Publicity:** Jason Zillo. **Coordinator, Media Relations:** Ben Tuliebitz. **Director, Publications/Multimedia:** Mark Mandrake.

Stadium Operations
Director, Stadium Operations: Kirk Randazzo. **Assistant Director, Stadium Operations:** Doug Behar. **Stadium Superintendent:** Pete Pullara.
Head Groundskeeper: Dan Cunningham. **Scoreboard/Broadcasting Manager:** Mike Bonner.
Director, Concessions/Hospitality: Joel White.
PA Announcer: Bob Sheppard. **Official Scorers:** Bill Shannon, Howie Karpin.

Ticketing
Telephone: (718) 293-6000. **FAX:** (718) 293-4841.
Vice President, Ticket Operations: Frank Swaine.
Senior Director, Ticket Operations: Irfan Kirimca.

Travel, Clubhouse
Traveling Secretary: David Szen.
Equipment Manager: Rob Cucuzza. **Visiting Clubhouse Manager:** Lou Cucuzza Jr.

GENERAL INFORMATION
Stadium (year opened): Yankee Stadium (1923).
Home Dugout: First Base. **Playing Surface:** Grass.
Team Colors: Navy blue and white.
Player Representative: Mike Mussina.

BASEBALL OPERATIONS

Telephone: (718) 293-4300. **FAX:** (718) 293-0015.
Senior Vice President/General Manager: Brian Cashman. **VP, Assistant GM:** Jean Afterman.
Senior VP, Baseball Operations: Mark Newman. **Senior VP/Player Personnel:** Gordon Blakeley. **Assistant Director, Baseball Operations:** Stephanie Carapazza.
VP/Senior Advisor: Gene Michael.
Special Assistant, Baseball Operations: Frank Howard, Jerry Krause.
Special Advisory Group: Yogi Berra, Reggie Jackson, Clyde King.

Major League Staff

Brian Cashman

Manager: Joe Torre.
Coaches: Dugout—Willie Randolph; Pitching—Mel Stottlemyre; Batting—Don Mattingly; First Base—Roy White; Third Base—Luis Sojo; Bullpen—Rich Monteleone; Catching—Gary Tuck.

Medical, Training

Team Physician, New York: Dr. Stuart Hershon. **Team Physician, Tampa:** Dr. Andrew Boyer.
Head Trainer: Gene Monahan. **Assistant Trainer:** Steve Donohue.
Strength and Conditioning Coach: Jeff Mangold.

Player Development

Florida Complex: 3102 N. Himes Ave., Tampa, FL. 33607. **Telephone:** (813) 875-7569. **FAX:** (813) 873-2302.
VP, Player Development/Scouting: Damon Oppenheimer.
VP, Player Personnel: Billy Connors. **Senior Administrator, Player Development:** Trevor Schaffer.
Head Trainer: Mark Littlefield. **Coordinator, Strength/Conditioning:** E.J. Amo. **Equipment Manager:** David Hays. **Clubhouse Manager:** Jack Terry.
Coordinator, Instruction: Rick Down. **Special Assignment Instructor:** Rob Thomson.

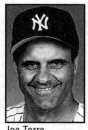

Joe Torre

Farm System

Class	Farm Club	League	Manager	Coach	Pitching Coach
AAA	Columbus	International	Bucky Dent	Kevin Long	Neil Allen
AA	Trenton	Eastern	Stump Merrill	Steve Braun	Gary Lavelle
High A	Tampa	Florida State	Bill Masse	Ty Hawkins	Greg Pavlick
Low A	Battle Creek	Midwest	Mitch Seoane	Bill Mosiello	Steve Renko
Short season	Staten Island	New York-Penn	Tommy John	Kevin Higgins	Dave Eiland
Rookie	Tampa	Gulf Coast	Oscar Acosta	Unavailable	Dwight Gooden
Rookie	Yankees	Dominican	Humberto Trejo	Freddie Tiburcio	Wilfredo Cordova
Rookie	Yankees	Dominican	Darwin Bracho	Carlos Mota	Jose Duran

Scouting

Telephone: (813) 875-7569. **FAX:** (813) 348-2302.
Vice President, Scouting: Lin Garrett.
Research Coordinator, Baseball Operations: John Coppolella.
Advance Scouts: Wade Taylor (Orlando, FL), Chuck Cottier (Tampa, FL).
Professional Scouts: Jim Benedict (Bradenton, FL), Ron Brand (Mesa, AZ), Joe Caro (Tampa, FL), Bill Emslie (Safety Harbor, FL), Tim McIntosh (Stockton, CA), Jeff Wetherby (Wesley Chapel, FL).
Regional Crosscheckers: East—Joe Arnold (Lakeland, FL), Midwest—Tim Kelly (New Lenox, IL), West—Greg Orr (Sacramento, CA).
Area Scouts: Mike Baker (Cave Creek, AZ), Brian Barber (Richmond, VA), Mark Batchko (Arlington, TX), Steve Boros (Kingwood, TX), John Cox (Redlands, CA), Mike Gibbons (Liberty Township, OH), Steve Lemke (Lincolnshire, IL), Jeff Patterson (Anaheim, CA), Cesar Presbott (Bronx, NY), Dan Radison (Deerfield Beach, FL), D.J. Svihlik (Birmingham, AL), Steve Swail (Charlotte, NC), Fay Thompson (Callejo, CA).

Lin Garrett

Coordinator, Latin American Scouting: Carlos Rios (Santo Domingo, DR). **Coordinator, Pacific Rim Scouting:** John Cox (Redlands, CA).
International Scouts: Ricardo Finol (Venezuela), Luis Gonzalez (Dominican Republic), Karl Heron (Panama), Ricardo Heron (Panama), Rudy Jabalera (Dominican Republic), Jose Luna (Dominican Republic), Victor Mata (Dominican Republic), Tito Quintero (Colombia), Dan Radison (Puerto Rico/Virgin Islands), Hector Rincones (Venezuela), Edgar Rodriguez (Nicaragua), Arquimedes Rojas (Venezuela), Cesar Suarez (Venezuela).

OAKLAND ATHLETICS

Office Address: 7000 Coliseum Way, Oakland, CA 94621.
Telephone: (510) 638-4900. **FAX:** (510) 562-1633.
Website: www.oaklandathletics.com.

Ownership

Operated by: Athletics Investment Group LLC (1996).
Co-Owner/Managing Partner: Steve Schott. **Owner/Partner:** Ken Hofmann.
President: Michael Crowley. **Executive Assistant to President:** Carolyn Jones.
General Counsel: Nick Rossi. **Assistant General Counsels:** Caleb Jay, Rob Schantz.

BUSINESS OPERATIONS

Steve Schott

Finance, Administration

Vice President, Finance: Paul Wong.
Director, Finance: Linda Rease. **Payroll Manager:** Kathy Leviege. **Senior Accountant:** Isabelle Mahaffey. **Staff Accountant:** Helga Mahlmann. **Ticket Accountant:** Chris James.
Director, Human Resources: Eleanor Yee. **Human Resources/Finance Coordinator:** Kim Chen.
Information Systems Manager: Debbie Dean. **Executive Office Receptionist:** Maggie Baptist.

Sales, Marketing

Vice President, Sales/Marketing: David Alioto.
Director, Corporate Sales: Franklin Lowe. **Corporate Account Managers:** Jill Golden, Kelle Venezia, Susan Weiglein. **Manager, Sales/Marketing:** Lisa Wood. **Manager, Interactive Marketing:** Cameron Stewart. **Coordinator, Sales/Marketing:** Lynne Tibbet. **Manager, Creative Services:** Mike Ono.
Director, Merchandising/Purchasing: Drew Bruno. **Manager, Merchandise Operations/Purchasing:** Colin Nicholas. **Manager, Merchandise Warehouse:** Doug Heater. **Manager, Merchandising:** Stephanie Moritz. **Coordinator, Merchandising:** Josh Vargo.

Public Relations, Communications

Telephone: (510) 563-2207. **FAX:** (510) 562-1633.
Vice President, Broadcasting/Communications: Ken Pries.
Director, Public Relations: Jim Young. **Manager, Media Relations:** Kristy Fick. **Manager, Baseball Information:** Mike Selleck. **Coordinator, Media Services:** Debbie Gallas. **Team Photographer:** Michael Zagaris. **Manager, Community Relations:** Detra Paige. **Coordinator, Community Relations/Broadcasting:** Warren Chu.

Stadium Operations

Vice President, Stadium Operations: David Rinetti.
Director, Stadium Operations: David Avila. **Manager, Stadium Operations:** Paul La Veau. **Manager, Stadium Operations Systems:** Eric Nelson. **Manager, Stadium Services:** Randy Duran. **Manager, Stadium Operations Events:** Kristy Ledbetter. **Coordinator, Stadium Services:** David Cochran. **Coordinator, Stadium Operations:** Shannon Bruener.
Director, In-Stadium Entertainment: Troy Smith. **Director, Multimedia Services:** David Don. **Coordinator, Multimedia Services:** Rick Ruvalcaba. **Coordinator, In-Stadium Entertainment:** Jeff Gass.
Head Groundskeeper: Clay Wood. **Arizona Groundskeeper:** Chad Huss.
PA Announcer: Roy Steele. **Official Scorers:** Chuck Dybdal, Art Santo Domingo.

Ticketing

Director, Ticket Operations: Steve Fanelli.
Senior Manager, Ticket Operations: Doug Vanderheyden. **Manager, Ticket Services:** Josh Ziegenbusch. **Manager, Box Office:** Anthony Silva. **Coordinator, Group Tickets:** David Adame. **Manager, Spring Training Marketing/Operations:** Mike Saverino. **Ticket Service Representatives:** Ryan Jones, Travis LoDolce, Molly Sklut, Matt Weiss.
Director, Premium Seating Services: Dayn Floyd. **Manager, Premium Seating Services:** Susie Campion.
Manager, Special Events: Adrienne Carew. **Assistant, Ticket Events:** Liam Miller. **Assistant, Corporate Events:** Jennifer Schultz.
Coordinator, Office Services: Julie Vasconcellos. **Assistant, Office Services:** Kathy French.
Senior Manager, Ticket Sales: Grant Christensen.

Travel, Clubhouse

Director, Team Travel: Mickey Morabito. **Travel Specialist:** Colleen Osterberg.
Equipment Manager: Steve Vucinich. **Visitors Clubhouse:** Mike Thalblum. **Assistant Equipment Manager:** Brian Davis. **Clubhouse Assistant:** William Angel. **Manager, Arizona Clubhouse:** Jesse Sotomayor.

GENERAL INFORMATION

Stadium (year opened): Network Associates Coliseum (1968).
Home Dugout: Third Base. **Playing Surface:** Grass.
Team Colors: Kelly green and gold.
Player Representative: Unavailable.

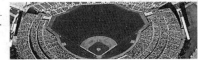

BASEBALL OPERATIONS
Vice President, General Manager: Billy Beane. **Assistant General Manager:** David Forst. **Special Assistants to GM:** Randy Johnson, Matt Keough. **Executive Assistant:** Betty Shinoda.
Director, Baseball Administration: Pamela Pitts. **Assistant, Baseball Operations:** Bryn Alderson.

Major League Staff
Manager: Ken Macha.
Coaches: Dugout—Chris Speier; Pitching—Curt Young; Batting—Dave Hudgens; First Base—Thad Bosley; Third Base—Ron Washington; Bullpen—Brad Fischer.

Billy Beane

Medical, Training
Team Physician: Dr. Allan Pont. **Team Orthopedist:** Dr. Jerrald Goldman. **Consulting Orthopedists:** Dr. John Frazier, Dr. Lewis Yocum. **Arizona Team Physician:** Dr. Fred Dicke.
Head Trainer: Larry Davis. **Assistant Trainer:** Steve Sayles. **Strength and Conditioning:** Clarence Cockrell.

Player Development
Telephone, Oakland: (510) 638-4900. **FAX:** (510) 563-2376.
Arizona Complex: Papago Park Baseball Complex, 1802 N. 64th St., Phoenix, AZ 85008. **Telephone:** (602) 949-5951. **FAX:** (602) 945-0557.
Director, Player Development: Keith Lieppman. **Director, Minor League Operations:** Ted Polakowski.
Director, Player Personnel: Billy Owens.
Roving Instructors: Juan Navarrete (infield), Ron Plaza, Ron Romanick (pitching), Greg Sparks (hitting).
Medical Coordinator: Jeff Collins. **Strength and Conditioning:** Chris Lantz.

Ken Macha

Farm System

Class	Farm Team	League	Manager	Coach	Pitching Coach
AAA	Sacramento	Pacific Coast	Tony DeFrancesco	Joe Sparks	Rick Rodriguez
AA	Midland	Texas	Webster Garrison	Brian McArn	Jim Coffman
High A	Modesto	California	Von Hayes	Eddie Williams	Scott Emerson
Low A	Kane County	Midwest	Dave Joppie	Aaron Nieckula	Fernando Arroyo
Short season	Vancouver	Northwest	Dennis Rogers	Todd Steverson	Craig Lefferts
Rookie	Phoenix	Arizona	Ruben Escalera	Juan Dilone	Mike Holmes
Rookie	Athletics I	Dominican	Unavailable	Unavailable	Unavailable
Rookie	Athletics II	Dominican	Unavailable	Unavailable	Unavailable

Scouting
Telephone: (510) 638-4900. **FAX:** (510) 563-2376.
Director, Scouting: Eric Kubota. **Assistant, Scouting:** Dan Feinstein.
Advance/Major League Scout: Bob Johnson (University Park, FL).
National Field Coordinator: Chris Pittaro (Robbinsville, NJ). **National Crosschecker:** Ron Vaughn (Corona, CA).
Scouting Supervisors: Midwest—Steve Bowden (Cypress, TX), West Coast—Will Schock (Oakland, CA).
Area Scouts: Steve Barningham (Dunedin, FL), Jeff Bittiger (Saylorsburg, NJ), Blake Davis (Dallas, TX), Ruben Escalera (San Juan, PR), Mike Holmes (Winston-Salem, NC), Scott Kidd (Rocklin, CA), Rick Magnante (Van Nuys, CA), Kelcey Mucker (Metairie, LA), Jim Pransky (Bettendorf, IA), Jeremy Schied (Phoenix, AZ), Rich Sparks (Sterling Heights, MI).
Coordinator, Dominican Republic: Raymond Abreu (Santo Domingo, DR).
International Scouts: Ruben Barradas (Venezuela), Juan Carlos De la Cruz (Dominican Republic), Angel Eusebio (Dominican Republic), Julio Franco (Venezuela), Juan Martinez (Dominican Republic), Fausto Pena (Dominican Republic), Bernardino Rosario (Dominican Republic), Oswaldo Troconis (Venezuela).

Eric Kubota

PHILADELPHIA PHILLIES

Office Address: Citizens Bank Park, One Citizens Bank Way, Philadelphia, PA 19148.
Telephone: (215) 463-6000. **FAX:** (215) 389-3050.
Website: www.phillies.com.

Ownership
Operated by: The Phillies.
President, Chief Executive Officer: David Montgomery. **Chairman:** Bill Giles.

BUSINESS OPERATIONS
Vice President, General Counsel: Bill Webb.
Director, Business Development: Joe Giles. **Director, Human Resources:** Terry DeRugeriis.

David Montgomery

Finance
Senior Vice President, Chief Financial Officer: Jerry Clothier.
Director, Finance/Accounting: John Nickolas. **Manager, Payroll Services:** Karen Wright.
Director, Information Systems: Brian Lamoreaux.

Marketing, Promotions
Vice President, Advertising Sales: David Buck.
Manager, Client Services/Alumni Relations: Debbie Nocito. **Manager, National Sales:** Rob MacPherson.
Manager, Advertising Sales: Scott Nickle. **Manager, Corporate Sales:** Brian Mahoney. **Director, Events:** Kurt Funk.
Director, Entertainment: Chris Long. **Director, Broadcasting/Video Services:** Rory McNeil. **Manager, Advertising/Internet Services:** Jo-Anne Levy-Lamoreaux.

Public Relations, Communications
Telephone: (215) 463-6000. **FAX:** (215) 389-3050.
Vice President, Public Relations: Larry Shenk.
Director, Media Relations: Leigh Tobin. **Director, Print/Creative Services:** Tina Urban. **Coordinator, Publications:** Christine Negley. **Media Relations Representative:** Greg Casterioto. **Media Relations Administrator:** Mary Ann Gettis. **Director, Community Relations:** Gene Dias. **Speakers' Bureau Representative:** Maje McDonnell. **Community/Fan Development Representative:** Dick Allen.

Stadium Operations
Vice President, Operations/Administration: Michael Stiles.
Director, Facility Management: Mike DiMuzio. **Director, Event Operations:** Eric Tobin. **Operations Assistant/Concessionaire Liaison:** Bruce Leith.
PA Announcer: Dan Baker. **Official Scorers:** Jay Dunn, Bob Kenney, John McAdams.

Ticketing
Telephone: (215) 463-1000. **FAX:** (215) 463-9878.
Vice President, Ticket Operations: Richard Deats.
Director, Ticket Department: Dan Goroff. **Director, Sales:** John Weber. **Director, Group Sales:** Kathy Killian.
Manager, Ticket Technology/Development: Chris Pohl. **Manager, Premium Seating:** Tom Mashek.
Manager, Phone Center: Phil Feather. **Manager, Citizens Bank Park Club Sales:** Derek Schuster. **Manager, Season Ticket Services:** Mike Holdren.

Travel, Clubhouse
Manager, Equipment/Team Travel: Frank Coppenbarger. **Assistant Equipment Manager:** Dan O'Rourke. **Manager, Visiting Clubhouse:** Kevin Steinhour. **Assistant, Home Clubhouse:** Phil Sheridan.

GENERAL INFORMATION
Stadium (year opened): Citizens Bank Park (2004).
Home Dugout: First Base. **Playing Surface:** Natural grass.
Team Colors: Red, blue and white.
Player Representative: Randy Wolf.

Ed Wade

BASEBALL OPERATIONS

Vice President, General Manager: Ed Wade.
Assistant GM: Ruben Amaro Jr. **Director, Baseball Administration:** Susan Ingersoll. **Computer Analysis:** Jay McLaughlin. **Senior Advisor to GM:** Dallas Green. **Special Assistant to GM:** Charlie Manuel.

Major League Staff

Manager: Larry Bowa.
Coaches: Dugout—Gary Varsho; Pitching—Joe Kerrigan; Batting—Greg Gross; First Base—Milt Thompson; Third Base—John Vukovich; Bullpen—Ramon Henderson; Catching Instructor—Mick Billmeyer.

Medical, Training

Director, Medical Services: Dr. Michael Ciccotti. **Assistant Director, Medical Services:** Dr. John McShane.
Head Trainer: Jeff Cooper. **Assistant Trainer:** Mark Andersen. **Conditioning Coordinator:** Scott Hoffman.

Player Development

Telephone: (215) 463-6000. **FAX:** (215) 755-9324.
Assistant GM, Scouting/Player Development: Mike Arbuckle.
Director, Minor League Operations: Steve Noworyta. **Assistant Director, Scouting:** Rob Holiday. **Administrative Assistant, Minor Leagues/Scouting:** Mike Ondo.
Director, Latin American Operations: Sal Artiaga. **Director, Florida Operations:** John Timberlake. **Assistant Director, Florida Operations:** Lee McDaniel.
Field Coordinator: Bill Dancy. **Coordinators:** Gorman Heimueller (pitching), Don Long (hitting), Dave Owen (infield), Jerry Martin (outfield/baserunning), Mike Compton (catching) Pat Sandora (conditioning), Scott Sheridan (trainers).

Larry Bowa

Farm System

Class	Farm Team	League	Manager	Coach	Pitching Coach
AAA	Scranton/W-B	International	Marc Bombard	Sal Rende	Rich Dubee
AA	Reading	Eastern	Greg Legg	John Morris	Rod Nichols
High A	Clearwater	Florida State	Mike Schmidt	Manny Amador	Steve Schrenk
Low A	Lakewood	South Atlantic	P.J. Forbes	Eric Richardson	Tom Filer
Short season	Batavia	New York-Penn	Luis Melendez	Jim Morrison	Warren Brusstar
Rookie	Clearwater	Gulf Coast	Roly deArmas	Tony Scott	Carlos Arroyo
Rookie	Phillies	Dominican	Sammy Mejia	Domingo Brito	Cesar Mejia
Rookie	Phillies	Venezuelan	Rafael DeLima	Silverio Navas	Lester Straker

Scouting

Telephone: (215) 218-5204. **FAX:** (215) 755-9324.
Director, Scouting: Marti Wolever (Papillion, NE).
Coordinators, Scouting: Jim Fregosi Jr. (Murrieta, CA), Mike Ledna (Arlington Heights, IL).
Director, Major League Scouts: Gordon Lakey (Barker, TX). **Major League Scout:** Jimmy Stewart (Odessa, FL). **Advance Scout:** Hank King (Limerick, PA). **Special Assignment Scout:** Bob Boone.
Professional Scouts: Sonny Bowers (Waco, TX), Ron Hansen (Baldwin, MD), Dean Jongewaard (Fountain Valley, CA), Dick Lawlor (Windsor, CT), Larry Rojas (Clearwater, FL), Del Unser (Dove Canyon, CA).
Scout/Instructor: Ruben Amaro Sr.
Regional Supervisors: East—Dean Decillis (Weston, FL), Central—Brian Kohlscheen (Norman, OK), West—Billy Moore (Alta Loma, CA).

Mike Arbuckle

Area Scouts: Sal Agostinelli (Kings Park, NY), Therron Brockish (Council Bluffs, IA), Darrell Conner (Riverside, CA), Joey Davis (Roseville, CA), Tim Kissner (Mountlake Terrace, WA), Jerry Lafferty (Kansas City, MO), Chip Lawrence (Somerfield, FL), Matt Lundin (Santa Ana, CA), Miguel Machado (Miami Lakes, FL), Paul Murphy (Wilmington, DE), Gene Schall (Harleysville, PA), Paul Scott (Frisco, TX), Mike Stauffer (Ridgeland, MS), Bob Szymkowski (Chicago, IL), Roy Tanner (Charleston, SC).
International Supervisor: Sal Agostinelli (Kings Park, NY).
International Scouts: Tomas Herrera (Mexico), Allan Lewis (Panama, Central America), Jesus Mendez (Venezuela), Wil Tejada (Dominican Republic).

PITTSBURGH PIRATES

Office Address: PNC Park at North Shore, 115 Federal St., Pittsburgh, PA 15212.
Mailing Address: P.O. Box 7000, Pittsburgh, PA 15212.
Telephone: (412) 323-5000. **FAX:** (412) 325-4412.
Website: www.pittsburghpirates.com.

Ownership
Operated by: Pittsburgh Pirates Acquisition, Inc.
Principal Owner: Kevin McClatchy.
Board of Directors: William Allen, Don Beaver, Frank Brenner, Chip Ganassi, Kevin McClatchy, Thomas Murphy Jr., Ogden Nutting.

BUSINESS OPERATIONS

Finance
Vice President, Finance: Jim Plake.
Controller: David Bowman. **Director, Office Services:** Patti Mistick. **Director, Information Technology:** Terry Zeigler.

Kevin McClatchy

Marketing, Sales
Vice President, Sales/Marketing: Mike Berry.
Director, Ticket Sales/Services: Jim Alexander. **Director, Merchandising:** Joe Billetdeaux. **Director, Promotions:** Rick Orienza. **Director, Corporate Sales:** Mike Egan. **Manager, Broadcasting:** Marc Garda.

Communications
Telephone: (412) 325-4976. **FAX:** (412) 325-4413.
Vice President, Communications: Patty Paytas. **VP, Corporate Projects:** Nelson Briles.
Director, Media Relations: Jim Trdinich. **Manager, Media Services:** Dan Hart. **Media Relations Assistant:** Patrick O'Connell.
Director, Community Development: Wende Torbert.
Alumni Liaison: Sally O'Leary. **In-Game Entertainment:** Eric Wolff, Alex Moser.

Stadium Operations
Vice President, PNC Park Operations/Facilities Management: Dennis DaPra.
Director, Operations: Chris Hunter. **Director, Security/Contract Services:** Jeff Podobnik. **Field Maintenance Manager:** Steve Peeler.
PA Announcer: Tim DeBacco. **Official Scorers:** Bob Hertzel, Evan Pattak, Bob Webb, Tony Krizmanich.

Ticketing
Telephone: (800) 289-2827. **FAX:** (412) 325-4404.
Manager, Ticket Services: Dave Wysocki.

Travel, Clubhouse
Traveling Secretary: Greg Johnson.
Equipment Manager/Home Clubhouse Operations: Roger Wilson. **Visitors Clubhouse Operations:** Kevin Conrad.

GENERAL INFORMATION
Stadium (year opened): PNC Park (2001).
Home Dugout: Third Base. **Playing Surface:** Grass.
Team Colors: Black, gold, red and white
Player Representative: Josh Fogg.

David Littlefield

BASEBALL OPERATIONS

Telephone: (412) 325-4743. **FAX:** (412) 325-4414.
Senior Vice President, General Manager: David Littlefield.
Assistant GM: Roy Smith. **Special Assistants to GM:** Louie Eljaua, Jesse Flores, Jax Robertson, Doug Strange, Pete Vuckovich.
Coordinator, Baseball Operations: Jon Mercurio. **Baseball Operations Assistant:** Bryan Minniti. **Administrative Assistant, Baseball Operations:** Jeannie Donatelli.

Major League Staff

Manager: Lloyd McClendon.
Coaches: Bench—Pete Mackanin; Pitching—Spin Williams; Batting—Gerald Perry; First Base—Rusty Kuntz; Third Base—John Russell; Bullpen—Bruce Tanner.

Medical, Training

Medical Director: Dr. Patrick DeMeo. **Team Physician:** Dr. Edward Snell.
Head Trainer: Brad Henderson. **Assistant Trainers:** Mark Rogow, Mike Sandoval. **Strength/Conditioning Coordinator:** Frank Velasquez.

Minor Leagues

Telephone: (412) 325-4737. **FAX:** (412) 325-4414.
Director, Player Development: Brian Graham. **Administrator, Minor Leagues:** Diane DePasquale.
Coordinator, Instruction: Jeff Banister. **Roving Instructors:** Doug Mansolino (infield), Jeff Manto (hitting), Gary Redus (outfield/baserunning), Gary Ruby (pitching), Ramon Sambo (Latin American field coordinator).
Director, Dominican Republic Academy: Esteban Beltre.

Lloyd McClendon

Farm System

Class	Farm Team	League	Manager	Coach	Pitching Coach
AAA	Nashville	Pacific Coast	Trent Jewett	Jeff Livesey	Darold Knowles
AA	Altoona	Eastern	Tony Beasley	John Wehner	Jeff Andrews
High A	Lynchburg	Carolina	Jay Loviglio	Greg Briley	Scott Lovekamp
Low A	Hickory	South Atlantic	Dave Clark	Matt Winters	Bob Milacki
Short-season	Williamsport	New York-Penn	Jeff Branson	Tom Prince	Ray Searage
Rookie	Bradenton	Gulf Coast	Woody Huyke	Ramon Sambo	Miguel Bonilla
Rookie	Pirates	Dominican	Ramon Zapata	Ceciliio Beltre	Leonardo Mejia
Rookie	Pirates	Venezuelan	Osmin Melendez	Unavailable	Unavailable

Scouting

Telephone: (412) 325-4738. **FAX:** (412) 325-4414.
Director, Scouting: Ed Creech.
Coordinator, Scouting Systems: Sandy Deutsch.
Advance Scout: Chris Lein (Boca Raton, FL).
National Supervisor: Jimmy Lester (Columbus, GA). **Regional Supervisors:** John Green (West Grove, PA), Scott Littlefield (Long Beach, CA), Mark McKnight (Acworth, GA).
Area Scouts: Tom Barnard (Houston, TX), Kevin Clouser (Seattle, WA), Steve Fleming (Louisa, VA), Duane Gustavson (Columbus, OH), Greg Hopkins (Beaverton, OR), Mike Kendall (Manhattan Beach, CA), Jaron Madison (Vallejo, CA), Jon Mecurio (Pittsburgh, PA), Jack Powell (Sweetwater, TN), Jim Rough (Wichita, KS), Everett Russell (Thibodaux, LA), Scott Sharp (Fort Lauderdale, FL), Rob Sidwell (Windermere, FL), Ted Williams (Glendale, AZ).
Part-Time Scouts: Elmer Gray (Pittsburgh, PA), Hank Krause (Akton, IA), Homer Newlin (Tallahassee, FL), William Price (Austin, TX), Tom Rogers (Clearwater, FL), Jose Rosario (Bayamon, PR), Jack Sharp (Dallas, TX).
Director, Latin American Scouting: Rene Gayo. **Supervisor, Dominican Republic:** Ramon Perez. **Supervisor, Venezuela:** Rodolfo Jose Petit.
Dominican Republic Scouts: Marciano Alvarez, Frank Tavares, Emmanuel Herrera.
International Scouts: Alex Zapata (Panama), Daniel Garcia (Colombia), Jose Pineda (Panama), Jesus Valdez (Mexico).

Ed Creech

ST. LOUIS CARDINALS

Office Address: 250 Stadium Plaza, St. Louis, MO 63102.
Telephone: (314) 421-3060. **FAX:** (314) 425-0640.
Website: www.stlcardinals.com.

Ownership
Operated by: St. Louis Cardinals, LLC.
General Partner: Bill DeWitt Jr. **Vice Chairman:** Fred Hanser. **Secretary/Treasurer:** Andrew Baur.
President: Mark Lamping.
Senior Administrative Assistant to Chairman: Grace Hale. **Senior Administrative Assistant to President:** Julie Laningham.

BUSINESS OPERATIONS
Vice President, Business Development: Bill DeWitt III.
VP, Public Affairs/Employee Relations: Marian Rhodes. **Manager, Office Administration/Human Resources Specialist:** Karen Brown.

Mark Lamping

Finance
Vice President, Controller: Brad Wood.
Director, Accounting: Deborah Pfaff. **Project/Payroll Manager:** Rex Carter. **Senior Accountant:** Michelle Flach.

Marketing, Sales
Senior Vice President, Sales/Marketing: Dan Farrell. **Administrative Assistant, Corporate Sales:** Gail Ruhling.
Senior Director, Corporate Sales: Thane van Breusegen. **Director, Target Marketing:** Ted Savage. **Corporate Sales Account Executives:** Matt Gifford, Valerie Kotys, Theron Morgan, Tony Simokaitis.

Public Relations, Community Relations
Telephone: (314) 421-3060. **FAX:** (314) 982-7399.
Director, Media Relations: Brian Bartow. **Assistant to Director, Media Relations:** Brad Hainje. **Coordinator, Media Services:** Melody Yount.
Director, Publications: Steve Zesch. **Publications Assistant:** Tom Raber.
VP, Community Relations: Marty Hendin. **Community Relations Representative:** Gabrielle Martin.
VP/Group Director, Community Outreach/Cardinals Care: Tim Hanser. **Coordinator, Cardinals Care:** Lucretia Payne. **Development Coordinator, Cardinals Care:** Anna Marie Wingron. **Youth Baseball Commissioner, Cardinals Care:** Keith Brooks.

Stadium Operations
Vice President, Stadium Operations: Joe Abernathy. **Administrative Assistant:** Nan Bommarito.
Director, Stadium Operations: Mike Bertani. **Director, Security/Special Services:** Joe Walsh. **Administrative Assistant, Security:** Hope Baker.
Director, Quality Assurance/Guest Services: Mike Ball. **Coordinator, Operations:** Cindy Richards.
Senior Director, Event Services: Vicki Bryant. **Administrative Assistant, Event Services:** Missy Tobey.
Head Groundskeeper: Bill Findley. **Assistant Head Groundskeeper:** Chad Casella.
PA Announcer: John Ulett. **Official Scorers:** Gary Mueller, Jeff Durbin, Mike Smith.

Ticketing
Telephone: (314) 421-2400. **FAX:** (314) 425-0649.
Vice President, Ticket Operations: Josie Arnold.
Senior Director, Ticket Sales: Joe Strohm.
Manager, Ticket Operations: Kim Kleeschulte. **Manager, Box Office:** Julie Baker. **Director, Season/Premium Ticket Sales:** Mark Murray. **Manager, Season Ticket Sales/Services:** Julia Kelley.
Director, Group Sales: Michael Hall. **Manager, Direct Ticket Sales:** Mary Clare Bena. **Supervisor, Customer Service:** Marilyn Mathews.

Travel, Clubhouse
Traveling Secretary: C.J. Cherre.
Equipment Manager: Rip Rowan. **Assistant Equipment Manager:** Buddy Bates. **Visiting Clubhouse Manager:** Jerry Risch. **Video Coordinator:** Chad Blair.

GENERAL INFORMATION
Stadium (year opened): Busch Stadium (1966).
Home Dugout: First Base. **Playing Surface:** Grass.
Team Colors: Red and white.
Player Representative: Steve Kline.

Walt Jocketty

BASEBALL OPERATIONS

Telephone: (314) 425-0687. **FAX:** (314) 425-0648.
Senior Vice President, General Manager: Walt Jocketty. **Assistant GM/Scouting Director:** John Mozeliak.
VP, Player Personnel: Jerry Walker. **VP/Special Assistant to GM:** Bob Gebhard. **VP, Baseball Development:** Jeff Luhnow. **Special Assistants to GM:** Red Schoendienst, Mike Jorgensen.
Senior Executive Assistant to GM: Judy Carpenter-Barada.

Major League Staff

Manager: Tony La Russa.
Coaches: Bench—Joe Pettini; Pitching—Dave Duncan; Batting—Mitchell Page; First Base—Dave McKay; Third Base—Jose Oquendo; Bullpen—Marty Mason.

Medical, Training

Senior Medical Advisor: Dr. Stan London. **Club Physician:** Dr. George Paletta.
Head Trainer: Barry Weinberg. **Assistant Trainer:** Mark O'Neal.

Player Development

Telephone: (314) 425-0628. **FAX:** (314) 425-0638.
Director, Player Development: Bruce Manno. **Director, Baseball Operations:** Scott Smulczenski. **Assistant Director, Player Development/Manager, Baseball Information:** John Vuch. **Administrative Assistant:** Judy Francis.
Player Development Advisor/Infield Instructor: George Kissell.
Field Coordinator: Bob Humphreys. **Coordinators:** Mark Riggins (pitching), Gene Tenace (hitting), Tom Spencer (baserunning/outfield).
Minor League Equipment Manager: Ernie Moore.

Tony La Russa

Farm System

Class	Farm Team	League	Manager	Coach	Pitching Coach
AAA	Memphis	Pacific Coast	Danny Sheaffer	Tommy Gregg	Dyar Miller
AA	Tennessee	Southern	Mark DeJohn	Steve Balboni	Blaise Ilsley
High A	Palm Beach	Florida State	Tom Nieto	Darrell Whitmore	Derek Lilliquist
Low A	Peoria	Midwest	Joe Cunningham	Ron Warner	Bryan Eversgerd
Short season	New Jersey	New York-Penn	Tommy Shields	Unavailable	Sid Monge
Rookie	Johnson City	Appalachian	Tom Kidwell	George Kissell	Al Holland

Scouting

Telephone: (314) 516-0152. **FAX:** (314) 425-0638.
Director, Professional Scouting: Marteese Robinson. **Administrative Assistant, Baseball Operations:** Linda Brauer.
Major League/Special Assignment Scouts: Bing Devine (St. Louis, MO), Mike Jorgensen (St. Louis, MO), Jim Leyland (Pittsburgh, PA), Marty Maier (St. Louis, MO).
Professional Scouts: Clark Crist (Tucson, AZ), Bill Harford (Chicago, IL), Chuck Fick (Newbury Park, CA), Marty Keough (Scottsdale, AZ), Mike Squires (Kalamazoo, MI).
National Crosscheckers: Fred McAlister (Katy, TX), Mike Roberts (Kansas City, MO).
Regional Crosscheckers: Jay North, (Vacaville, CA), Joe Rigoli (Parsippany, NJ), Roger Smith (Eastman, GA).
Area Supervisors: Clark Crist (Tucson, AZ), Steve Gossett (Broken Arrow, OK), Scott Melvin (Quincy, IL), Dan Ontiveros (Corona, CA), Tommy Shields (Lititz, PA), Mike Shildt (Charlotte, NC), Steve Turco (Largo, FL), Dane Walker (Canby, OR).
International Scouts: Enrique Brito (Venezuela), Roberto Diaz (Dominican Republic), Joel Randa (Puerto Rico).

John Mozeliak

SAN DIEGO PADRES

Office Address: PETCO Park, 100 Park Blvd., San Diego, CA 92101.
Mailing Address: P.O. Box 122000, San Diego, CA 92112.
Telephone: (619) 795-5000. FAX: (619) 795-5035
E-Mail Address: comments@padres.com.
Website: www.padres.com

Ownership
Operated by: Padres, LP.
Principal Owner, Chairman: John Moores. Co-Vice Chairman: Charlie Noell.
President/Chief Operating Officer: Dick Freeman

BUSINESS OPERATIONS
Executive Director, Human Resources/Administrative Services: Lucy Freeman.

Finance
Senior Vice President, Chief Financial Officer: Fred Gerson. VP, Controller: Dan Fumai.
Director, Information Systems: Joe Lewis.

Marketing, Sales
Executive Vice President, Business Operations: Steve Violetta.
Executive Director, Corporate Partnerships: Jim Ballweg. Assistant Director, Corporate
Sponsorships: Marty Gorsich.

John Moores

Public Relations, Community Relations
Telephone: (619) 795-5265. FAX: (619) 795-5266.
Executive Vice President, Communications: Jeff Overton.
Director, Media Relations: Luis Garcia. Assistant Director, Media Relations: Michael Uhlenkamp. Coordinator,
Publications: Steve Hoem. Coordinator, Media Relations: Dustin Morse.
Vice President, Community Relations: Michele Anderson.
Director, Padres Foundation: Sue Botos. Manager, Community Relations: Nhu Tran. Coordinator, Community
Relations: Sarah Rodriguez.

Stadium Operations
Executive Vice President/Managing Director, Ballpark Operations: Richard Andersen. VP, Ballpark Operations:
Mark Guglielmo.
Director, Security/Transportation: Ken Kawachi. Director, Landscape/Field Maintenance: Luke Yoder.
PA Announcer: Unavailable. Official Scorers: Dennis Smythe, Bill Zavestoski.

Ticketing
Telephone: (619) 795-8025. FAX: (619) 795-5034.
Executive Director, Ticket Sales: Mark Tilson.

Travel, Clubhouse
Director, Team Travel/Equipment Manager: Brian Prilaman. Home Clubhouse Operations: Tony Petricca. Visitors
Clubhouse Operations: David Bacharach.

GENERAL INFORMATION
Stadium (year opened): Petco Park (2004).
Home Dugout: First Base. Playing Surface: Grass.
Team Colors: Padres sand, navy blue, sky blue.
Player Representative: Unavailable.

BASEBALL OPERATIONS

Telephone: (619) 881-5076. **FAX:** (619) 795-5036.
Executive Vice President, General Manager: Kevin Towers.
Assistant GM: Fred Uhlman Jr. **Special Assistant to GM:** Ken Bracey.
Assistant, Major League Operations: Jeff Kingston. **Administrative Assistant:** Herta Bingham.

Major League Staff

Manager: Bruce Bochy.
Coaches: Bench—Tony Muser; Pitching—Darren Balsley; Batting—Dave Magadan; First Base—Davey Lopes; Third Base—Rob Picciolo; Bullpen—Darrel Akerfelds.

Kevin Towers

Medical, Training

Club Physician: Scripps Clinic medical staff.
Head Trainer: Todd Hutcheson. **Assistant Trainer:** Jim Daniel. **Strength/Conditioning Coach:** Joe Hughes.

Player Development

Telephone: (619) 795-5335. **FAX:** (619) 795-5036.
Director, Player Development: Tye Waller. **Director, Minor League Operations:** Priscilla Oppenheimer. **Assistant to Director, Player Development:** Juan Lara.
Special Assistant to GM/Field Coordinator: Bill Bryk.
Roving Instructors: Mike Couchee (pitching), Doug Dascenzo (outfield/baserunning), Tony Franklin (infield), Rob Deer (hitting). **Coordinator, Trainers:** Lance Cacanindin.

Bruce Bochy

Farm System

Class	Farm Team	League	Manager	Coach	Pitching Coach
AAA	Portland	Pacific Coast	Craig Colbert	Tommy Sandt	Tom Brown
AA	Mobile	Southern	Gary Jones	Jose Castro	Gary Lance
High A	Lake Elsinore	California	Rick Renteria	Mike Davis	Mike Harkey
Low A	Fort Wayne	Midwest	Randy Ready	Tom Tornincasa	Steve Webber
Short season	Eugene	Northwest	Roy Howell	Ben Oglivie	Dave Rajsich
Rookie	Peoria	Arizona	Carlos Lezcano	Luis Quinones	Wally Whitehurst
Rookie	Padres	Dominican	Pablo Martinez	Jose Mateo	Juan Melo

Scouting

Telephone: (619) 795-5243. **FAX:** (619) 795-5036.
Director, Scouting: Bill Gayton. **Assistant Director, Scouting:** Mike Wickham.
Major League Scouts: Ken Bracey (Morton, IL), Ray Crone (Waxahachie, TX), Moose Johnson (Arvada, CO), Ted Simmons (Wildwood, MO), Gene Thompson (Scottsdale, AZ).
Advance Scout: Jeff Gardner (Newport Beach, CA).
Professional Scouts: Steve Demeter (Parma, OH), Gail Henley (La Verne, CA), Ben McLure (Hummelstown, PA), Tom McNamara (Lakewood Ranch, FL), Van Smith (Belleville, IL), Elanis Westbrooks (Houston, TX).
National Crosschecker: Jay Darnell (Plano, TX). **Regional Crosscheckers:** West Coast—Chris Gwynn (Alta Loma, CA); East Coast—Scott Trcka (Hobart, IN); Midwest—Tim Holt (Allen, TX).
Scouting Supervisor, Independent Leagues: Mal Fichman.

Bill Gayton

Full-Time Scouts: Joe Bochy (Plant City, FL), Rich Bordi (Rohnert Park, CA), Josh Boyd (Richmond, VA), Jim Bretz (South Windsor, CT), Lane Decker (Piedmont, OK), Bob Filotei (Wilmer, AL), Dan Huston (Bellevue, WA), Bob Laurie (Plano, TX), Tim McWilliam (San Diego, CA), Billy Merkel (Columbia, TN), Mike Rikard (Durham, NC), Anup Sinha (Rancho Cucamonga, CA), Jeff Stewart (Normal, IL), Jake Wilson (Phoenix, AZ).
Part-Time Scouts: Robert Beattie (Sioux Falls, SD), Dan Bleiwas (Thornhill, Ontario), Leroy Dreyer (Brenham, TX), Robert Gutierrez (Carol City, FL), Don Hanson (Mandan, ND), William Killian (Stanwood, MA), Steve Oleschuck (Saint Laurent, Quebec), Chuck Pierce (Bakersfield, CA), Willie Ronda (Rio Piedras, PR), Cam Walker (Centerville, IA).
Director, Professional/International Scouting: Randy Smith (Scottsdale, AZ).
International Scouts: Ray Brown (Oceania/Pacific Islands), Jorge Carolus (Netherlands Antilles), Milton Croes (Caribbean), Marcial Del Valle (Colombia), Akira Ejiri (Japan), Felix Francisco (Dominican Republic), Elvin Jarquin (Nicaragua), Victor Magdaleno (Venezuela), Daniel Mavares (Colombia), Ricardo Montenegro (Panama), Francis Movica (Dominican Republic), Ricardo Petit (Venezuela), Ronald Petit (Venezuela), Robert Rowley (Panama), Jose Salado (Dominican Republic), Trevor Schumm (Australia), Basil Tarasko (Eastern Europe), Modesto Ulloa (Dominican Republic).

SAN FRANCISCO GIANTS

Office Address: SBC Park, 24 Willie Mays Plaza, San Francisco, CA 94107.
Telephone: (415) 972-2000. **FAX:** (415) 947-2800.
Website: sfgiants.com.

Ownership
Operated by: San Francisco Baseball Associates, LP.
President, Managing General Partner: Peter Magowan.
Senior General Partner: Harmon Burns. **General Partner:** William Neukom. **Special Assistant:** Willie Mays. **Senior Advisor:** Willie McCovey.

BUSINESS OPERATIONS
Executive Vice President, Chief Operating Officer: Larry Baer.
Senior VP, General Counsel: Jack Bair. **Vice President, Human Resources:** Joyce Thomas.

Peter Magowan

Finance
Senior Vice President, Chief Financial Officer: John Yee. **VP, Chief Information Officer:** Bill Schlough. **Director, Management Information Systems:** John Winborn.
VP, Finance: Lisa Pantages.

Marketing, Sales
Senior Vice President, Corporate Marketing: Mario Alioto. **VP, Corporate Sponsorship:** Jason Pearl. **Director, Special Events:** Valerie McGuire. **Manager, Promotions:** Alison Vidal. **Senior VP, Consumer Marketing:** Tom McDonald. **Director of Marketing/Entertainment:** Bryan Srabian. **Director, Client Relations:** Annemarie Hastings. **Director, Sales/Ticket Marketing:** Rob Sullivan. **Manager, Season Ticket Sales:** Craig Solomon. **VP and General Manager, Retail:** Connie Kullberg. **Director, Retail:** Derik Landry.

Media Relations, Community Relations
Telephone: (415) 972-2448. **FAX:** (415) 947-2800.
Manager, Media Relations: Jim Moorehead. **Director, Broadcasting/Media Services:** Maria Jacinto. **Director, Media Relations:** Blake Rhodes. **Coordinator, Media Relations:** Matt Hodson. **VP, Print Publications/Creative Services:** Nancy Donati. **VP, Communications:** Staci Slaughter. **Director, Public Affairs:** Shana Daum. **Manager, Photography/Archives:** Missy Mikulecky.

Ballpark Operations
Senior Vice President, Ballpark Operations: Jorge Costa. **VP, Guest Services:** Rick Mears. **Senior Director, Ballpark Operations:** Gene Telucci. **Manager, Maintenance:** Frank Peinado. **Security Manager:** Tinie Roberson. **Head Groundskeeper:** Scott MacVicar.
PA Announcer: Renel Brooks-Moon. **Official Scorers:** Chuck Dybdal, Art Santo Domingo, Al Talboy.

Ticketing
Telephone: (415) 972-2000. **FAX:** (415) 947-2500.
Vice President, Ticket Services/Client Relations: Russ Stanley. **Director, Ticket Services:** Devin Lutes. **Director, Luxury Suites:** Amy Quartaroli. **Manager, Ticket Services:** Bob Bisio. **Manager, Ticket Accounting:** Kem Easley. **Manager, Ticket Operations:** Anita Sprinkles. **Special Events Ticket Manager:** Todd Pierce.

Travel, Clubhouse
Director, Travel: Reggie Younger. **Assistant, Travel:** Mike Scardino. **Equipment Manager:** Miguel Murphy. **Visitors Clubhouse:** Harvey Hodgerney. Umpires Attendant: Richard Cacace.

GENERAL INFORMATION
Stadium (year opened): SBC Park (2000).
Home Dugout: Third Base. **Playing Surface:** Grass.
Team Colors: Black, orange and cream.
Player Representative: Chad Zerbe.

Brian Sabean

BASEBALL OPERATIONS

Telephone: (415) 972-1922. **FAX:** (415) 947-2737.
Senior Vice President, General Manager: Brian Sabean.
VP, Assistant GM: Ned Colletti. **Special Assistant to GM:** Ron Perranoski. **Executive Assistant, Baseball Operations:** Karen Sweeney. **Assistant, Baseball Operations:** Jeremy Shelley.

Major League Staff

Manager: Felipe Alou.
Coaches: Bench—Ron Wotus; Pitching—Dave Righetti; Batting—Joe Lefebvre; First Base—Luis Pujols; Third Base—Gene Glynn; Bullpen—Mark Gardner; Bullpen Catcher—Bill Hayes.

Medical, Training

Team Physicians: Dr. Robert Murray, Dr. Gary Fanton, Dr. Ken Akizuki.
Medical Director/Head Trainer: Stan Conte. **Assistant Trainers:** Mark Gruesbeck, Ben Potenziano.

Player Development

Telephone: (415) 972-1922. **FAX:** (415) 947-2929.
Vice President, Player Personnel: Dick Tidrow.
Director, Player Development: Jack Hiatt. **Director, Minor League Administration:** Bobby Evans. **Special Assistants, Player Personnel:** Jim Davenport, Ted Uhlaender.
Coordinator, Minor League Pitching: Bert Bradley. **Coordinator, Minor League Hitting:** Willie Upshaw.
Roving Instructors: Kirt Manwaring (catching), Darren Lewis (baserunning/outfield), Lee Smith (pitching).

Felipe Alou

Farm System

Class	Farm Team	League	Manager	Coach	Pitching Coach
AAA	Fresno	Pacific Coast	Fred Stanley	Steve Decker	Ross Grimsley
AA	Norwich	Eastern	Shane Turner	Roger La Francois	Bob Stanley
High A	San Jose	California	Lenn Sakata	F.P. Santangelo	Trevor Wilson
Low A	Hagerstown	South Atlantic	Mike Ramsey	Hector Torres	Maximino Leon
Short season	Salem-Keizer	Northwest	Joe Strain	Unavailable	Jerry Cram
Rookie	Scottsdale	Arizona	Bert Hunter	Leo Garcia	Will Malerich
Rookie	Giants	Dominican	Ramon Valdivia	Hector Ortiz	Yoryi Almengo

Scouting

Telephone: (415) 972-1922. **FAX:** (415) 947-2737.
Coordinator, Scouting: Matt Nerland.
Major League Scouts: Joe DiCarlo (Ringwood, NJ), Stan Saleski (Dayton, OH), Paul Turco Sr. (Sarasota, FL), Ted Uhlaender (Parshall, CO), Randy Waddill (Valrico, FL), Tom Zimmer (St. Petersburg, FL). **Advance Scout:** Pat Dobson (El Cajon, CA).
Special Assignment Scouts: Dick Cole (Costa Mesa, CA), Larry Osborne (Woodstock, GA).
National Crosschecker: Doug Mapson (Chandler, AZ). **Regional Crosscheckers:** Canada—Steve Arnieri (Barrington, IL), Southwest—Lee Carballo (Westchester, CA), East—Alan Marr (Sarasota, FL), East Coast—Bobby Myrick (Colonial Heights, VA), West Coast—Darren Wittcke (Gresham, OR).

Dick Tidrow

Area Scouts: Billy Castell (El Cerrito, CA); Rex Delanuez (Burbank, CA), John DiCarlo (Glenwood, NJ), Lee Elder (Martinez, GA), Charlie Gonzalez (Weston, FL), Tom Korenek (Houston, TX), Sean O'Connor (Natick, MA), John Shafer (Portland, OR), Joe Strain (Englewood, CO), Todd Thomas (Dallas, TX), Glenn Tufts (Bridgewater, MA), Paul Turco Jr. (Sarasota, FL), Harry Stavrenos (Soquel, CA), Matt Woodward (Seattle, WA).
Coordinator, International Operations: Rick Ragazzo (Leona Valley, CA).
Director, Dominican Republic Operations: Pablo Peguero (Santo Domingo, DR). **Special Assignment Scout:** Matty Alou (Santo Domingo, DR). **Venezuela Supervisor:** Ciro Villalobos (Zulia, VZ).
International Scouts: Marcos Briceno (Dominican Republic), Enrique Burgos (Panama), Jorge Diaz (Colombia), Philip Elhage (Curacao), Martin Hernandez (Venezuela), Juan Marquez (Venezuela), Luis Pena (Mexico), Jesus Stephens (Dominican Republic), Alex Torres (Nicaragua), Sebastian Urrieta (Venezuela).

SEATTLE MARINERS

Office Address: 1250 First Ave. S., Seattle, WA 98134.
Mailing Address: P.O. Box 4100, Seattle, WA 98194.
Telephone: (206) 346-4000. FAX: (206) 346-4400.
Website: www.seattlemariners.com.

Ownership
Operated by: Baseball Club of Seattle, LP.
Board of Directors: Minoru Arakawa, John Ellis, Chris Larson, Howard Lincoln, John McCaw, Frank Shrontz, Wayne Perry.
Chairman, Chief Executive Officer: Howard Lincoln. President, Chief Operating Officer: Chuck Armstrong.

Chuck Armstrong

BUSINESS OPERATIONS

Finance
Executive Vice President, Finance/Ballpark Operations: Kevin Mather.
Controller: Tim Kornegay. Assistant Controller: Greg Massey.
VP, Human Resources: Marianne Short. VP, Technology Servies: Larry Witherspoon.

Marketing, Sales
Executive Vice President, Business/Operations: Bob Aylward.
VP, Marketing: Kevin Martinez. Director, Marketing: Jon Schuller. Director, Promotions: Gregg Greene. Director, Retail Operations: Jim La Shell. Manager, Retail Operations: Jeff Ibach. Suite Sales: Moose Clausen.

Baseball Information, Communications
Telephone: (206) 346-4000. FAX: (206) 346-4400.
Vice President, Communications: Randy Adamack.
Director, Baseball Information: Tim Hevly. Administrative Assistant, Baseball Information: Kelly Munro.
Director, Public Information: Rebecca Hale. Assistant Director, Baseball Information: Matt Roebuck. Manager, Graphic Design: Carl Morton. Coordinator, International Media: Megan Barrett.
Manager, Community Relations: Gina Hasson. Manager, Community Programs: Sean Grindley.

Ticketing
Telephone: (206) 346-4001. FAX: (206) 346-4100.
Director, Ticket Services: Kristin Fortier. Manager, Ticket Operations: Connie McKay. Manager, Group/Suite Tickets Services: Steve Belling. Manager, Box Office: Malcolm Rogel. Director, Season Tickets/Group Sales: Bob Hellinger.

Stadium Operations
Vice President, Ballpark Operations: Neil Campbell. Director, Safeco Field Operations: Tony Pereira.
Head Groundskeeper: Bob Christopherson.
PA Announcer: Tom Hutyler. Official Scorer: Terry Mosher.

Travel, Clubhouse
Director, Team Travel: Ron Spellecy.
Clubhouse Manager: Ted Walsh. Visiting Clubhouse Manager: Henry Genzale.
Video Coordinator: Carl Hamilton.

GENERAL INFORMATION

Stadium (year opened): Safeco Field (1999).
Home Dugout: First Base. Playing Surface: Grass.
Team Colors: Northwest green, silver and navy blue.
Player Representative: Unavailable.

BASEBALL OPERATIONS

Executive Vice President, General Manager: Bill Bavasi.
VP, Baseball Administration: Lee Pelekoudas.
VP/Special Assistant to General Manager: Roger Jongewaard.
Special Consultant to Executive VP/GM: Pat Gillick.
Administrator, Baseball Operations: Debbie Larsen. **Baseball Operations Assistant/Systems Coordinator:** Jim Na.

Major League Staff

Manager: Bob Melvin.
Coaches: Dugout—Rene Lachemann; Pitching—Bryan Price; Batting—Paul Molitor; First Base—Mike Aldrete; Third Base—Dave Myers; Bullpen—Orlando Gomez.

Bill Bavasi

Medical, Training

Medical Director: Dr. Larry Pedegana. **Club Physician:** Dr. Mitchel Storey.
Head Trainer: Rick Griffin. **Assistant Trainer:** Tom Newberg. **Strength/Conditioning Coach:** Allen Wirtala.

Player Development

Telephone: (206) 346-4313. **FAX:** (206) 346-4300.
Vice President, Player Development/Scouting: Benny Looper.
Director, Minor League Operations: Greg Hunter. **Director, Player Development:** Frank Mattox. **Administrator, Player Development:** Jan Plein.
Coordinator, Minor League Instruction: Mike Goff. **Trainer Coordinator:** Mickey Clarizio.
Roving Instructors: Glenn Adams (hitting), James Clifford (strength/conditioning), Roger Hansen (catching), Buzzy Keller (special assignment), Cal McLish (special assignment), John Moses, Pat Rice (pitching), Jim Slaton (special assignment).

Bob Melvin

Farm System

Class	Farm Team	League	Manager	Coach	Pitching Coach
AAA	Tacoma	Pacific Coast	Dan Rohn	Terry Pollreisz	Rafael Chaves
AA	San Antonio	Texas	Dave Brundage	Gary Thurman	Scott Budner
High A	Inland Empire	California	Steve Roadcap	Henry Cotto	Dwight Bernard
Low A	Wisconsin	Midwest	Daren Brown	Dana Williams	Brad Holman
Short season	Everett	Northwest	Pedro Grifol	Darrin Gamer	Marcos Garcia
Rookie	Peoria	Arizona	Scott Steinmann	T. Cruz/A. Bottin	Gary Wheelock
Rookie	Mariners	Dominican	Bienvenido Liriano	Unavailable	Manuel Marrero
Rookie	Mariners	Venezuela	Jose Moreno		Luis Hernandez

Scouting

Telephone: (206) 346-4000. **FAX:** (206) 346-4300.
Vice President, Scouting: Bob Fontaine. **Administrator, Scouting:** Hallie Larson.
Special Assignments/Amateur Scouting: Tom Davis. **Scouting Assistant:** Jim Fitzgerald.
Advance Scout: Steve Peck (Scottsdale, AZ).
Director, Professional Scouting: Ken Compton (Cypress, CA).
Major League Scouts: David Garcia (El Cajon, CA), Bob Harrison (Long Beach, CA), Bill Kearns (Milton, MA), Charley Kerfeld (Chico, CA), Bob Miske (Amherst, NY), Chris Pelekoudas (Mesa, AZ), Steve Pope (Asheville, NC), Tim Schmidt (San Bernardino, CA).
National Crosschecker: Steve Jongewaard (Huntington Beach, CA).
Regional Supervisors: West—Ron Tostenson (El Dorado Hills, CA), East—John McMichen (Treasure Island, FL), Midwest—Carroll Sembera (Shiner, TX), Canada—Wayne Norton (Port Moody, B.C.).
Full-Time Scouts: Craig Bell (Asheboro, NC), Joe Bohringer (Ventura, CA), Phil Geisler (Bellevue, WA), Pedro Grifol (Miami, FL), Mark Leavitt (Maitland, FL), Mark Lummus (Cleburne, TX), Ken Madeja (Novi, MI), David May (Bear, DE), Rob Mummau (Winchester, VA), Stacey Pettis (Antioch, CA), Tim Reynolds (Irvine, CA), Alvin Rittman (Memphis, TN), Eric Robinson (Hiram, GA), Kyle Van Hook (Brenham, TX), Greg Whitworth (Phoenix, AZ).
Supervisor, Pacific Rim Operations: Ted Heid (Peoria, AZ). **Assistant Director, Pacific Rim Operations:** Hide Sueyoshi (Bellevue, WA).
Director, Latin America Scouting/Operations: Bob Engle (Tampa, FL). **Supervisors, Latin America Scouting:** Emilio Carrasquel (Venezuela), Patrick Guerrero (Dominican Republic).

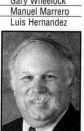

Bob Fontaine

Office Address: Tropicana Field, One Tropicana Dr., St. Petersburg, FL 33705.
Telephone: (727) 825-3137. **FAX:** (727)-825-3111.
Website: www.devilrays.com.

Ownership
Operated by: Tampa Bay Devil Rays, Ltd.
Managing General Partner, Chief Executive Officer: Vincent J. Naimoli. **Executive Assistant:** Diane Villanova.

BUSINESS OPERATIONS
Senior Vice President, Administration/General Counsel: John Higgins. **Senior VP, Business Operations:** David Auker. **Administrative Assistant:** Silvia Bynes. **VP, Employee/Guest Relations:** Jose Tavarez. **Benefits Coordinator:** Debra Perry.

Finance
Controller: Patrick Smith. **Supervisor, Accounting:** Sandra Faulkner. **Payroll Supervisor:** Jill Baetz. **Director, Business Administration:** Bill Wiener. **Coordinator, Purchasing:** Mike Yodis. **Accounts Payable Coordinator:** Sam Reams.

Vince Naimoli

Marketing, Sales
Vice President, Sales: Wayne Hodes. **Administrative Assistant:** Kristi Capone.
VP, Marketing: John Browne. **Senior Director, Corporate Sales/Broadcasting:** Larry McCabe. **Director, Corporate Sales:** Aaron Cohn. **Corporate Sales Account Representatives:** Danny Cooper, Wes Engram, Kraig Obarski, Brian Samillian. **Manager, Sponsorship Coordination:** Beth Bohnsack. **Director, Event Productions/Entertainment:** John Franzone. **Assistant Event Producer:** Stephanie Renica. **Matrix Producer:** Laura Cuozzo. **Video Producer:** Doug Elsberry. **Manager, Broadcast Operations:** Kevin Daigle. **Manager, Marketing/Advertising:** Brian Killingsworth. **Manager, Print/Graphic Production:** Charles Parker. **Graphic Designer/Photo Manager:** Erik Ruiz. **Manager, Video/Graphic Production:** Jason Rundle.

Public Relations
Telephone: (727) 825-3242. **FAX:** (727) 825-3111.
Vice President, Public Relations: Rick Vaughn. **Coordinator, Public Relations:** Carmen Molina. **Director, Media Relations:** Chris Costello. **Assistant, Media Relations:** Jason Latimer. **Director, Community Relations:** Liz-Beth Lauck. **Executive Director, Community Development:** Dick Crippen. **Website Manager:** Eric Helmer.

Stadium Operations
Vice President, Operations/Facilities: Rick Nafe. **Administrative Assistant:** Lorra Gillespie. **Building Superintendent:** Scott Kelyman. **Event Manager:** Tom Karac. **Event Coordinator:** Tom Buscemi. **Manager, Suites/Customer Liaison Services:** Cass Halpin. **Booking Coordinator:** Caren Gramley.
Head Groundskeeper: Dan Moeller. **Director, Audio/Visual Services:** Ron Golick.
PA Announcer: Bill Couch.

Ticketing
Director, Ticket Sales: Louis Ruvane. **Assistant Director, Ticket Sales:** David Gravenkemper. **Group Sales Account Executives:** Jake Dunlap, Lacy Keorner, Ben Krentzman, Dan Pasternak. **Account Executives, Ticket Sales:** Barry Jones, Kristin Aiello, Dean Huls, Laua Miller, Chris Montplaisir, Jerry Patterson, Bryan Ress, Jeremy White. **Power Hitter Program Coordinator:** John Heffernan. **Customer Service Coordinator:** Erin Buscemi. **Customer Service Representative:** Craig Champagne. **Director, Ticket Operations:** Robert Bennett. **Assistant Director, Ticket Operations:** Ken Mallory. **Ticket Operations:** Karen Smith. **Merchandise Manager:** Debbie Brooks.

Travel, Clubhouse
Director, Team Travel: Jeff Ziegler. **Equipment Manager, Home Clubhouse:** Chris Westmoreland. **Visitors Clubhouse:** Guy Gallagher.

GENERAL INFORMATION
Stadium (year opened): Tropicana Field (1998).
Home Dugout: First Base. **Playing Surface:** FieldTurf.
Team Colors: Black, blue and green.
Player Representative: Unavailable.

Chuck LaMar

BASEBALL OPERATIONS

Senior Vice President, Baseball Operations/ General Manager: Chuck LaMar.
Assistant GMs: Bart Braun, Scott Proefrock. **Director, Major League Administration:** Sandy Dengler. **Special Assistants to GM:** Hal McRae, Tim Wilken. **Senior Baseball Advisor:** Don Zimmer.
Video Coordinator: Chris Fernandez.

Major League Staff

Manager: Lou Piniella.
Coaches: Bench—John McLaren; Pitching—Chuck Hernandez; Batting—Lee Elia; First Base—Billy Hatcher; Third Base—Tom Foley; Bullpen—Matt Sinatro.

Medical, Training

Medical Director: Dr. James Andrews. **Medical Team Physician:** Dr. Michael Reilly. **Orthopedic Team Physician:** Dr. Koco Eaton.
Head Trainer: Ken Crenshaw. **Assistant Trainer:** Ron Porterfield. **Strength/Conditioning Coach:** Kevin Barr.

Minor Leagues

Telephone: (727) 825-3267. **FAX:** (727) 825-3493.
Director, Player Personnel/Scouting: Cam Bonifay. **Assistant, Player Development:** Mitch Lukevics. **Administrative Assistant, Player Development:** Denise Vega-Smith.
Field Coordinator: Jim Hoff. **Minor League Coordinators:** Paul Harker (medical/rehabilitation), Steve Henderson (hitting), Jerry Nyman (pitching). **Equipment Manager:** Tim McKechney.

Lou Piniella

Farm System

Class	Farm Team	League	Manager	Coach	Pitching Coach
AAA	Durham	International	Bill Evers	Richie Hebner	Joe Coleman
AA	Montgomery	Southern	Charlie Montoyo	Skeeter Barnes	Dick Bosman
High A	Bakersfield	California	Mako Oliveras	Ramon Ortiz	Xavier Hernandez
Low A	Charleston, SC	South Atlantic	Steve Livesey	Omer Munoz	Marty DeMerritt
Short season	Hudson Valley	New York-Penn	Dave Howard	Jorge Robles	Rafael Montalvo
Rookie	Princeton	Appalachian	Jamie Nelson	Manny Castillo	Nardi Contreras

Scouting

Telephone: (727) 825-3137. **FAX:** (727) 825-3300.
Assistant to Scouting Director: Nancy Berry.
Major League Scouts: Bart Johnson (Bridgeview, IL), Don Williams (Paragould, AR), Stan Williams (Lakewood, CA). **Major League Consultants:** Jerry Gardner (Los Alamitos, CA), Syd Thrift (Easton, MD), George Zuraw (Englewood, FL).
National Scouting Coordinator: R.J. Harrison (Phoenix, AZ).
Regional Scouting Coordinators: Dave Roberts (Portland, OR), Mac Siebert (Molino, FL). **Special Assignment Scout:** Benny Latino (Hammond, LA).
Scouting Supervisors: Rich Aude (Woodland Hills, CA), Jonathan Bonifay (Austin, TX), James Bonnici (Ortonville, MI), Skip Bundy (Birmingham, AL), Tom Couston (Chicago, IL), Rickey Drexler (Norman, OK), Kevin Elfering (Wesley Chapel, FL), Milt Hill (Cumming, GA), Hank King (Kinston, NC), Paul Kirsch (Sherwood, OR), Brad Matthews (Concord, NC), Fred Repke (Carson City, NV), Craig Weissmann (LaCosta, CA), Doug Witt (Glen Burnie, MD).
Area Scout: Joe Murphy (Rock Island, IL).
Director, International Scouting: Rudy Santin (Miami, FL). **International Scout:** Junior Ramirez (Dominican Republic).

Cam Bonifay

TEXAS RANGERS

Office Address: 1000 Ballpark Way, Arlington, TX 76011.
Mailing Address: P.O. Box 90111, Arlington, TX 76004.
Telephone: (817) 273-5222. **FAX:** (817) 273-5110.
Website: www.texasrangers.com.

Ownership
Owner: Southwest Sports Group, Inc.
Chairman, Chief Executive Officer: Tom Hicks.
President: Michael Cramer. **Executive Assistant:** Katy Terrill.
Executive Vice President/Chief Financial Officer: Joe Armes. **Executive Assistant:** Genee Darden.

Tom Hicks

BUSINESS OPERATIONS
Executive Vice President, Chief Operating Officer: Jeff Cogen. **Executive Assistant:** Amy Pettis.
Executive VP, Business Operations: Rick McLaughlin. **Executive Assistant:** Judy Southworth.
Senior VP, General Counsel: Casey Shilts. **Executive Assistant:** Amy Pettis.
Assistant VP, Human Resources: Terry Turner. **Manager, Staffing/Development:** Carla Clack. **Legal Assistant:** Brenda Conine Whittenberg.
Vice President, Information Technology: Steve McNeill. **Director, Application Systems:** Russell Smutzer.

Finance
Vice President, Finance: Kellie Fischer. **Executive Assistant, Finance:** Carolyn Corbett.
Assistant Controller: Starr Pritchard **Director, Treasury/Reporting:** Christie Steblein. **Manager, Payroll:** Donna Blaylock. **Manager, Purchasing:** Chelle Jezek. **Accounting Manager:** Donna Kee.

Marketing, Sales
Vice President, Sponsorship Sales: Brad Alberts. **Directors, Corporate Sales:** Jim Cochrane, Lillian Zars. **Director, Advertising Sales:** Grady Raskin. **Director, Broadcasting Sales Services:** Angie Swint. **Director, Corporate/Suite Sales:** Thomas Hicks Jr. **Manager, Corporate Sales Services:** Ginger Reed.
Executive VP, Marketing/Entertainment: Chuck Morgan. **Senior Director, Marketing:** Kelly Calvert. **Senior Director, Graphic Design:** Rainer Uhlir. **Director, Events:** Sherry Flow. **Director, Graphic Design:** Michelle Hays. **Director, Media:** Heidi Leonards. **Creative Director, Media:** Rush Olson. **Director, New Market Development:** Karin Synold.
Assistant Vice President, Merchandising: Todd Grizzle. **Director, Merchandising:** Diane Atkinson.

Public Relations, Communications
Telephone: (817) 273-5203. **FAX:** (817) 273-5110.
Senior Vice President, Communications: John Blake. **Senior Director, Baseball Media Relations:** Gregg Elkin. **Director, Publications:** Kurt Daniels. **Manager, Baseball Media Relations:** Rich Rice. **Assistant, Communications:** Jessica Beard.
VP, Community Development/Relations: Norm Lyons. **Director, Community Relations:** Taunee Paur Taylor. **Assistant Director, Community Relations:** Tyler Beckstrom.

Stadium Operations
Vice President, Event Operations/Security: John Hardin. **Senior Director, Customer Service:** Donnie Pordash. **Director, Baseball Programs/Youth Ballpark:** Breon Dennis. **Assistant Director, Security:** Mickey McGovern.
Assistant VP, Facilities Operations: Gib Searight. **Director, Grounds:** Tom Burns. **Director, Maintenance:** Mike Call. **Coordinator, Facility Services:** Duane Arber. **Coordinator, General Maintenance:** John Deardorff.
PA Announcer: Chuck Morgan. **Official Scorers:** John Mocek, Steve Weller.

Ticketing
Telephone: (817) 273-5100. **FAX:** (817) 273-5190.
Director, Ticket Services: Mike Lentz. **Manager, Ticket Operations:** David Larson. **Coordinator, Ticket Accounting Administration:** Ranae Lewis. **Coordinator, Season/Group Sales:** Jena Tunnell. **Coordinator, Box Office:** Ben Rogers.
Vice President, Ticket Sales: Andy Silverman. **Assistant VP, Luxury Suite Sales:** Paige Jackson.

Travel, Clubhouse
Director, Travel: Chris Lyngos.
Equipment/Home Clubhouse Manager: Zack Minasian. **Assistant Clubhouse Manager:** Dave Bales. **Visiting Clubhouse Manager:** Kelly Terrell. **Video Coordinator:** Josh Frasier.

GENERAL INFORMATION
Stadium (year opened): The Ballpark in Arlington (1994).
Home Dugout: First Base. **Playing Surface:** Grass.
Team Colors: Royal blue and red.
Player Representative: Jeff Zimmerman.

John Hart

BASEBALL OPERATIONS
Telephone: (817) 273-5222. **FAX:** (817) 273-5285.
Executive Vice President, General Manager: John Hart.
Special Assistants to GM: Dom Chiti, Jay Robertson.
Senior Advisor to GM: Tom Giordano.
Director, Major League Administration: Judy Johns.
Director, Baseball Operations: Jon Daniels. **Assistant, Baseball Operations:** Jake Krug.

Major League Staff
Manager: Buck Showalter.
Coaches: Dugout—Don Wakamatsu; Pitching—Orel Hershiser; Batting—Rudy Jaramillo; First Base—DeMarlo Hale; Third Base—Steve Smith; Bullpen—Mark Connor.

Medical, Training
Team Physician: Dr. Keith Meister. **Team Internist:** Dr. David Hunter.
Head Trainer/Medical Director: Jamie Reed. **Assistant Trainers:** Ray Ramirez. **Director, Strength/Conditioning:** Fernando Montes.

Player Development
Telephone: (817) 273-5224. **FAX:** (817) 273-5285.
Assistant General Manager, Player Development/Scouting: Grady Fuson.
Coordinator, Player Development: Bob Miscik. **Director, Minor League Operations:** John Lombardo. **Administrative Assistant, Player Development/Scouting:** Margaret Bales.
Roving Instructors: Ralph Dickinson (hitting), Kevin Harmon (medical/conditioning), Greg Riddoch (defense), Lee Tunnell (pitching), Jim Sundberg (catching).
Manager, Minor League Complex Operations: Chris Guth. **Assistant Equipment Manager:** Joe Catalano. **Administrative Assistant, Arizona Operations:** Marc Dallman.

Buck Showalter

Farm System

Class	Farm Team	League	Manager	Coach	Pitching Coach
AAA	Oklahoma	Pacific Coast	Bobby Jones	Bruce Crabbe	Glenn Abbott
AA	Frisco	Texas	Tim Ireland	Paul Carey	Steve Luebber
High A	Stockton	California	Arnie Beyeler	Todd Mensik	Andy Hawkins
Low A	Clinton	Midwest	Carlos Subero	Mike Boulanger	Stan Hilton
Short season	Spokane	Northwest	Darryl Kennedy	Derek Lee	David Chavarria
Rookie	Surprise	Arizona	Pedro Lopez	Brook Jacoby	Aris Tirado
Rookie	Rangers	Dominican	Guillermo Mercedes	Fermin Infante	Francisco Saneaux

Scouting
Telephone: (817) 273-5277. **FAX:** (817) 273-5243.
Coordinator, Scouting: Ron Hopkins (Seattle, WA). **Assistant, Scouting Operations:** Russ Ardolina.
Special Assignment Scout: Mel Didier (Phoenix, AZ). **Professional Scout:** Keith Boeck (Chandler, AZ)
Regional Crosscheckers: Kip Fagg (Gilbert, AZ), Dave Klipstein (Roanoke, TX), Doug Harris (Carlisle, PA).
Area Scouts: John Castleberry (High Point, NC), Guy DeMutis (Windermere, FL), Jay Eddings (Sperry, OK), Steve Flores (Temecula, CA), Tim Fortugno (Elk Grove, CA), Mark Giegler (Fenton, MI), Mike Grouse (Olathe, KS), Todd Guggiana (Long Beach, CA), Derek Lee (Homewood, IL), Gary McGraw (Gaston, OR), Rick Schroeder (Phoenix, AZ), Doug Simons (Decatur, AL), Randy Taylor (Katy, TX), Frankie Thon (Guaynabo, PR), Jeff Wood (New York, NY).
Part-time Scout: Ron Toenjes (Georgetown, TX).
Latin Coordinator: Manny Batista (Vega Alta, PR). **Dominican Program Coordinator:** Danilo Troncoso (La Romana, DR) **Dominican Program/English Instructor:** Dennys Sanchez. **Venezuela Scout Supervisor:** Marlon Nava (Zulia, VZ).
International Scouts: Andres Espinoso (Venezuela), Jesus Ovalle (Dominican Republic), Rodolfo Rosario (Dominican Republic), Edgar Suarez (Venezuela), Eduardo Thomas (Panama).

Grady Fuson

TORONTO BLUE JAYS

Office/Mailing Address: 1 Blue Jays Way, Suite 3200, Toronto, Ontario M5V 3M7.
Telephone: (416) 341-1000. **FAX:** (416) 341-1250.
E-Mail Address: bluejay@bluejays.ca.
Website: www.bluejays.com.

Ownership
Operated by: Toronto Blue Jays Baseball Club.
Principal Owner: Rogers Communications, Inc.
President, Chief Executive Officer: Paul Godfrey.

Paul Godfrey

BUSINESS OPERATIONS
Senior Vice President, Administration/Business Affairs: Lisa Novak. **Director, Business Affairs:** Matthew Shubar.

Finance
VP, Finance/Administration: Susan Brioux. **Controller:** Cathy McNamara-Mackay.
Director, Risk Management: Suzanne Joncas. **Manager, Payroll/Benefits:** Brenda Dimmer. **Manager, Budgeting/Forecasting:** Connie Ennis. **Accounting Analyst:** Shari Ralph. **Coordinator, Accounts Receivable:** Marion Sullivan. **Coordinator, Accounts Payable:** Andy Topolie. **Coordinator, Ticket Office Receivables:** Joseph Roach. **Coordinator, General Accounting:** Tony Phung. **Coordinator, Payroll/Benefits:** Lindsey Simonini.
Manager, Human Resources: Sarah Keenan.
Director, Information Technology: Jacques Farand. **Senior Systems Analyst:** Anthony Miranda. **Administrator, Network/Security:** Spencer Lui. **Information Systems Support:** Vidal Abad. **Ticket System Administrator:** Darlene Samakese.

Marketing, Sales
Director, Consumer Marketing: Jim Bloom. **Manager, Marketing Communications/Advertising:** Heidi Dunn. **Executive Producer, Game Entertainment:** Deb Belinsky. **Manager, Game Entertainment:** Tim Sullivan. **Manager, Promotions:** Brennan Anderson. **Coordinator, Promotions:** Greg Arbour.
Director, Stadium Merchandising: Michael Andrejek. **Manager, Purchasing/Mail Order Operations:** Helen Maunder. **Manager, Stadium Events:** Linda Mykytyshyn. **Manager, Bullpen Store:** Teresa Michalski.
Vice President, Corporate Partnerships/Business Development: Mark Lemmon. **Director, Corporate Sponsorships:** Robert Mackay. **Director, Corporate Marketing:** Wilna Behr. **Corporate Marketing Managers:** Susan Burrows, Honsing Leung, Bryan Reinblatt.

Media Relations, Communications
Telephone: (416) 341-1301/1303. **FAX:** (416) 341-1250.
Senior Vice President, Communications/External Relations: Rob Godfrey. **VP, Special Projects:** Howard Starkman.
Director, Communications: Jay Stenhouse. **Director, Public Relations:** Will Hill. **Manager, Baseball Information:** Michael Shaw. **Coordinator, Communications:** Sue Mallabon. **Communications Assistant:** Erik Grossman.

Stadium Operations
Director, Stadium Operations: Mario Coutinho. **Manager, Guest Relations:** Paul So. **Office Manager:** Anne Fulford.
Game Security Supervisor: John Booth. **Supervisor, Maintenance/Housekeeping Services:** Mick Bazinet.
PA Announcer: Murray Eldon. **Official Scorers:** Louis Cauz, Doug Hobbs, Neil MacCarl, Joe Sawchuk.

Ticketing
Telephone: (416) 341-1234. **FAX:** (416) 341-1177. .
Vice President, Ticket Sales/Service: Patrick Elster.
Senior Advisor/Director, Special Projects: Sheila Stella. **Director, Sales Strategy/Ticket Services:** Felix Paulick. **Director, Ticket Sales/Service:** Jason Diplock. **Manager, Ticket System/Box Office:** Doug Barr. **Manager, Database/System Administration:** Mark Nguyen. **Manager, Game Day Services:** John MacIntyre. **Manager, Group Development:** Shelby Nelson. **Manager, Consumer Sales:** Paul Fruitman. **Manager, Fan Loyalty:** Carrie Linton. **Manager, Premier Client Services:** Chris Gill.

Travel, Clubhouse
Manager, Team Travel: Bart Given.
Equipment Manager: Jeff Ross. **Clubhouse Manager:** Kevin Malloy. **Visiting Clubhouse Manager:** Len Frejlich. **Video Operations:** Robert Baumander.

GENERAL INFORMATION
Stadium (year opened): SkyDome (1989).
Home Dugout: Third Base. **Playing Surface:** Artificial turf.
Team Colors: Blue, metallic silver, metallic graphite, black and white.
Player Representative: Vernon Wells.

BASEBALL OPERATIONS

Senior Vice President, Baseball Operations/General Manager: J.P. Ricciardi. **VP, Baseball Operations/Assistant GM:** Tim McCleary. **Vice President:** Bobby Mattick. **Director, Player Personnel:** Tony Lacava. **Assistants to GM:** Keith Law, Chris Buckley.

Director, Florida Operations: Ken Carson. **Director, Team Safety:** Ron Sandelli. **Executive Assistant to GM:** Fran Brown. **Executive Assistant, Major League Operations:** Heather Connolly.

Major League Staff

Manager: Carlos Tosca.

Coaches: Bench—Joe Breeden; Pitching—Gil Patterson; Batting—Mike Barnett; First Base—John Gibbons; Third Base—Brian Butterfield; Bullpen—Bruce Walton. Bullpen Catcher—Alex Andreopoulos.

J.P. Ricciardi

Medical, Training

Head Trainer: George Poulis. **Assistant Trainer:** Dave Abraham. **Strength/Conditioning Coordinator:** Donovan Santas.

Player Development

Telephone: (727) 734-18007. **FAX:** (727) 734-8162.

Director, Player Development: Dick Scott.

Manager, Minor League Operations: Charlie Wilson.

Roving Instructors: Dane Johnson (pitching), Merv Rettenmund (hitting), Ernie Whitt.

Minor League Coordinators: Jay Inouye (training), Chris Joyner (strength/conditioning), Billy Wardlow (equipment).

Carlos Tosca

Farm System

Class	Farm Team	League	Manager	Coach	Pitching Coach
AAA	Syracuse	International	Marty Pevey	Ken Landreaux	Brad Arnsberg
AA	New Hampshire	Eastern	Mike Basso	Jim Bowie	Rick Adair
High A	Dunedin	Florida State	Omar Malave	Paul Elliott	Rick Langford
Low A	Charleston, WV	South Atlantic	Ken Joyce	Charles Poe	Tom Bradley
Short season	Auburn	New York-Penn	Dennis Holmberg	Dave Pano	James Keller
Rookie	Pulaski	Appalachian	Gary Cathcart	Justin Mashore	Unavailable
Rookie	Blue Jays	Dominican	Juan Bernhardt	Unavailable	Antonio Caceres
Rookie	Blue Jays	Venezuelan	Domingo Carrasquel	Hedbertt Hurtado	Oswald Peraza

Scouting

Telephone: (416) 341-1115. **FAX:** (416) 341-1245.

Director, Scouting: Jon Lalonde. **Director, Canadian Scouting/Amateur Baseball:** Kevin Briand. **Director, Latin America Operations:** Tony Arias (Miami, FL).

National Crosscheckers: Tom Clark (Shrewsbury, MA), Tim Huff (Cave Creek, AZ), Mike Mangan (Clermont, FL).

Professional Scouts: Sal Butera (Lake Mary, FL), Kimball Crossley (Providence, RI), Ted Lekas (Worcester, MA).

Scouting Coordinators: Andrew Tinnish (Tallahassee, FL), Alex Anthopoulos (Montreal, Quebec).

Area Scouts: Andy Beene (Center Point, TX), Matt Briggs (Ridgeland, MS), Tom Burns (Harrisburg, PA), Billy Gasparino (Los Angeles, CA), Joel Grampietro (Tampa, FL), Aaron Jersild (Chicago, IL), Alvin Morrow (Phoenix, AZ), Brandon Mozley (Sacramento, CA), Ty Nichols (Broken Arrow, OK), Demerius Pittman (Corona, CA), Jorge Rivera (Puerto Nevo, PR), Tom Tanous (Barrington, RI), Marc Tramuta (Charlotte, NC).

Jon Lalonde

International Scouts: Greg Brons (Saskatoon, Saskatchewan), Robinson Garces (Maracaibo, Venezuela), Jean Marc Mercier (Montreal, Quebec), Boris Miranda (Aquadulce, Panama), Rafael Moncada (Valencia, Venezuela), Juan Salavarria (Bolivar, Venezuela), Hilario Soriano (Santo Domingo, Dominican Republic), Greg Wade (Queensland, Australia).

MAJOR LEAGUE
SCHEDULES

2003 STANDINGS
SPRING TRAINING

AMERICAN LEAGUE

2003 STANDINGS

EAST	W	L	PCT	GB	Manager	General Manager
New York Yankees	101	61	.623	—	Joe Torre	Brian Cashman
*Boston Red Sox	95	67	.586	6	Grady Little	Theo Epstein
Toronto Blue Jays	86	76	.531	15	Carlos Tosca	J. P. Ricciardi
Baltimore Orioles	71	91	.438	30	Mike Hargrove	Jim Beattie/Mike Flanagan
Tampa Bay Devil Rays	63	99	.389	38	Lou Piniella	Chuck LaMar

CENTRAL	W	L	PCT	GB	Manager	General Manager
Minnesota Twins	90	72	.556	—	Ron Gardenhire	Terry Ryan
Chicago White Sox	86	76	.531	4	Jerry Manuel	Ken Williams
Kansas City Royals	83	79	.512	7	Tony Pena	Allard Baird
Cleveland Indians	68	94	.420	22	Eric Wedge	Mark Shapiro
Detroit Tigers	43	119	.265	47	Alan Trammell	Dave Dombrowski

WEST	W	L	PCT	GB	Manager	General Manager
Oakland Athletics	96	66	.593	—	Ken Macha	Billy Beane
Seattle Mariners	93	69	.574	3	Bob Melvin	Pat Gillick
Anaheim Angels	77	85	.475	19	Mike Scioscia	Bill Stoneman
Texas Rangers	71	91	.438	25	Buck Showalter	John Hart

*Won wild-card playoff berth

PLAYOFFS: Division Series (best-of-5)—New York defeated Minnesota 3-1; Boston defeated Oakland 3-2. **League Championship Series** (best-of-7)—New York defeated Boston 4-3.

NATIONAL LEAGUE

2003 STANDINGS

EAST	W	L	PCT	GB	Manager(s)	General Manager(s)
Atlanta Braves	101	61	.623	—	Bobby Cox	John Schuerholz
*Florida Marlins	91	71	.562	10	Jeff Torborg/Jack McKeon	Larry Beinfest
Philadelphia Phillies	86	76	.531	15	Larry Bowa	Ed Wade
Montreal Expos	83	79	.512	18	Frank Robinson	Omar Minaya
New York Mets	66	95	.410	34½	Art Howe	Steve Phillips/Jim Duquette

CENTRAL	W	L	PCT	GB	Manager(s)	General Manager
Chicago Cubs	88	74	.543	—	Dusty Baker	Jim Hendry
Houston Astros	87	75	.537	1	Jimy Williams	Gerry Hunsicker
St. Louis Cardinals	85	77	.525	3	Tony LaRussa	Walt Jocketty
Pittsburgh Pirates	75	87	.463	13	Lloyd McClendon	Dave Littlefield
Cincinnati Reds	69	93	.426	19	Bob Boone/Dave Miley	Jim Bowden
Milwaukee Brewers	68	94	.420	20	Ned Yost	Doug Melvin

WEST	W	L	PCT	GB	Manager	General Manager
San Francisco Giants	100	61	.621	—	Felipe Alou	Brian Sabean
Los Angeles Dodgers	85	77	.525	15½	Jim Tracy	Dan Evans
Arizona Diamondbacks	84	78	.519	16½	Bob Brenly	Joe Garagiola Jr.
Colorado Rockies	74	88	.457	26½	Clint Hurdle	Dan O'Dowd
San Diego Padres	64	98	.395	36½	Bruce Bochy	Kevin Towers

*Won wild-card playoff berth

PLAYOFFS: Division Series (best-of-5)—Chicago defeated Atlanta 3-2; Florida defeated San Francisco 3-1. **League Championship Series** (best-of-7)—Florida defeated Chicago 4-3.

WORLD SERIES
(Best-of-7)
Florida (National) defeated New York (American) 4-2.

AMERICAN LEAGUE

ANAHEIM ANGELS
Angel Stadium of Anaheim
■ **Standard Game Times:** 7:05 p.m.; Sun. 1:05.

APRIL	
6-**7-8**	at Seattle
9-10-**11**-12	at Texas
13-14-15	Seattle
16-17-**18**	Oakland
20-21-**22**	Texas
23-**24-25**	at Oakland
27-28-**29**	at Detroit
30	at Minnesota

MAY	
1-2	at Minnesota
3-4-5	Detroit
6-7-8-**9**	Tampa Bay
11-12-**13**	at Yankees
14-15-16	at Baltimore
18-19-20	Yankees
21-22-**23**	Baltimore
24	at Toronto
26-27	at Toronto
28-29-**30**	at White Sox

JUNE	
1-2	Boston
3-4-5-**6**	Cleveland
8-9-10	*Milwaukee
11-12-**13**	*Cubs
15-16-17	*at Pittsburgh
18-19-**20**	*at Houston
21-22-23-**24**	Oakland
25-**26-27**	*at Los Angeles
29-30	at Texas

JULY	
1	at Oakland

2-3-4	*Los Angeles
6-**7-8**	at White Sox
9-**10-11**	at Toronto
15-16-17-**18**	Boston
19-**20**	Cleveland
21-**22**	at Texas
23-**24-25**	at Seattle
26-27-28	Texas
29-30-31	Seattle

AUGUST	
1	Seattle
3-4-**5**	at Minnesota
6-7-8-9	at Kansas City
10-11-**12**	Baltimore
13-14-15	Detroit
17-18-**19**	at Tampa Bay
20-**21-22**	at Yankees
23-24-25	Kansas City
27-28-**29**	Minnesota
31	at Boston

SEPTEMBER	
1-2	at Boston
3-4-**5**	at Cleveland
7-8-9	Toronto
10-11-**12**	White Sox
13-14-15-16	at Seattle
17-**18-19**	Texas
20-21-22	Seattle
24-25-**26**	Oakland
27-28-29-**30**	at Texas

OCTOBER	
1-2-**3**	at Oakland

BALTIMORE ORIOLES
Oriole Park at Camden Yards
■ **Standard Game Times:** 7:05 p.m.; Sat. 4:35; Sun. 1:35.

APRIL	
4	Boston
6-**7-8**	Boston
9-10-**11**	at Tampa Bay
13-14-15	at Boston
16-**17-18**	at Toronto
20-21-22	Tampa Bay
23-**24-25**	Toronto
26-27-28-**29**	Seattle
30	at Cleveland

MAY	
1-2	at Cleveland
3-4-5	White Sox
7-**8-9**	Cleveland
11-12-**13**	at White Sox
14-15-16	Anaheim
18-19-20	at Seattle
21-22-23	at Anaheim
25-26-27	Yankees
28-29-**30**	at Detroit

JUNE	
1-2-**3**	at Yankees
4-**5-6**	Tampa Bay

8-9-10	*Arizona
11-**12-13**	*San Francisco
15-16-17	*at Los Angeles
18-19-**20**	*at Colorado
22-23-24	Yankees
25-**26-27**	*Atlanta
28-29-30	at Kansas City

JULY	
1	at Kansas City
2-3-4	*at Philadelphia
5-6-7	Tampa Bay
9-**10-11**	Kansas City
15-**16**-17-**18**	at Tampa Bay
19-**20**	at Kansas City
21-**22**	at Boston
23-24-**25**	Minnesota
26-27-28	Boston
29-30-**31**	at Yankees

AUGUST	
1	at Yankees
3-4	Seattle
6-**7-8-9**	Texas
10-11-**12**	at Anaheim

13-**14-15**	at Toronto
16-17-18	Oakland
20-**21-22**	Toronto
23-24-25-**26**	at Oakland
27-28-29	at Texas
31	at Tampa Bay

SEPTEMBER	
1-2	at Tampa Bay
3-4-5	at Yankees
6-7-8	Minnesota

BOSTON RED SOX
Fenway Park
■ **Standard Game Times:** 7:05 p.m.; Sat. 1:20, 7:05; Sun. 2:05.

APRIL	
4	at Baltimore
6-**7-8**	at Baltimore
9-10-11	Toronto
13-14-15	Baltimore
16-**17-18-19**	Yankees
20-21-22	at Toronto
23-**24-25**	at Yankees
27-28-29	Tampa Bay
30	at Texas

MAY	
1-2	at Texas
3-4-5-6	at Cleveland
7-**8-9**	Kansas City
10-11-12	Cleveland
13-14-**15-16**	at Toronto
18-19-20	at Tampa Bay
21-22-**23**	Toronto
25-26-27	Oakland
28-**29-30**	Seattle

JUNE	
1-2	at Anaheim
4-5-6	at Kansas City
8-9-10	*San Diego
11-**12-13**	*Los Angeles
15-16-**17**	*at Colorado
18-**19-20**	*at San Francisco
22-23-**24**	Minnesota
25-**26-27**	*Philadelphia
29-30	at Yankees

JULY	
1	at Yankees

2-3-4	*at Atlanta
6-**7-8**	Oakland
9-10-11	Texas
15-16-17-**18**	at Anaheim
19-20	at Seattle
21-**22**	Baltimore
23-**24-25**	Yankees
26-27-28	at Baltimore
30-31	at Minnesota

AUGUST	
1	at Minnesota
2-3-4	at Tampa Bay
6-**7-8**	at Detroit
9-10-11-**12**	Tampa Bay
13-14-**15**	White Sox
16-17-18	Toronto
20-**21-22**	at White Sox
23-24-25	at Toronto
26-27-28-**29**	Detroit
31	Anaheim

SEPTEMBER	
1-2	Anaheim
3-4-5	Texas
6-7-8	at Oakland
9-10-11-**12**	at Seattle
14-15-16	Tampa Bay
17-**18**-19	at Yankees
20-21-22-23	Baltimore
24-25-**26**	Yankees
27-28-29	at Tampa Bay

OCTOBER	
1-2-**3**	at Baltimore

CHICAGO WHITE SOX
U.S. Cellular Field
■ **Standard Game Times:** 7:05 p.m.; Sat. 6:05; Sun. 2:05.

APRIL	
5	at Kansas City
7	at Kansas City
8-9-10-11	at Seattle
13-14-15	Kansas City
16-17-**18**	at Tampa Bay
20-21-22	Yankees
23-**24-25**	Tampa Bay
27-28	Cleveland
29-30	Toronto

MAY	
1-2	Toronto
3-4-5	at Baltimore

7-**8-9**	at Toronto
11-12-**13**	Baltimore
14-15-**16**	Minnesota
17-18-19	at Cleveland
20-21-22-**23**	at Minnesota
25-26-27	Texas
28-29-**30**	Anaheim

JUNE	
1-2	at Oakland
4-**5-6**	at Seattle
8-9-10	*Philadelphia
11-12-**13**	*Atlanta
15-16-17	*at Florida

ANAHEIM ANGELS (continued)

13-**14-15**	at Toronto
16-17-18	Oakland
20-**21-22**	Toronto
23-24-25-**26**	at Oakland
27-28-29	at Tampa Bay
31	at Tampa Bay

SEPTEMBER	
1-2	at Tampa Bay
3-4-5	at Yankees
6-7-8	Minnesota

BALTIMORE ORIOLES (continued column)

10-11-**12**	Yankees
13	at Toronto
15-16	at Toronto
17-**18-19**	at Minnesota
20-21-22-23	at Boston
24-**25-26**	Detroit
27-28-29-30	Toronto

OCTOBER	
1-2-**3**	Boston

18-19-**20** ...... *at Montreal
21-22-23-**24** ...... Cleveland
25-26-27 .... *Cubs
29-30 .... at Minnesota

JULY
1 .... at Minnesota
2-3-4 .... *at Cubs
6-7-**8** .... Anaheim
9-10-**11** .... Seattle
15-16-**17-18** ..... at Oakland
19-20 .... at Texas
21-22 .... at Cleveland
23-**24-25** .... Detroit
26-27-**28** .... Minnesota
29-30-31 .... at Detroit

AUGUST
1 .... at Detroit
3-4-5 .... at Kansas City
6-7-**8-9** .... Cleveland
10-11-**12** .... Kansas City

CLEVELAND INDIANS
Jacobs Field
■ Standard Game Times: 7:05 p.m.; Sun. 1:05.

APRIL
5-6-7 .... at Minnesota
8-9-10-11 ..... at Kansas City
12 .... Minnesota
14-15 .... Minnesota
16-**17-18**-19 .... Detroit
20-21-22 .... Kansas City
23-**24-25** .... at Detroit
27-28 .... at White Sox
30 .... Baltimore

MAY
1-2 .... Baltimore
3-4-5-6 .... Boston
7-**8-9** .... at Baltimore
10-11-12 .... at Boston
14-**15-16** .... Tampa Bay
17-18-19 .... White Sox
21-22-**23** ...... at Tampa Bay
25-26-27 .... Seattle
28-29-**30** .... Oakland

JUNE
1-2 .... Texas
3-4-5-**6** .... at Anaheim
8-9-10 .... *Florida
11-12-**13** .... *Cincinnati
15-16-17 .... *at Mets
18-19-20 .... *at Atlanta
21-22-23-**24** .... at White Sox
25-26-27 .... *Colorado
29-30 .... at Detroit

JULY
1 .... at Detroit

DETROIT TIGERS
Comerica Park
■ Standard Game Times: 7:05 p.m.; Thur./Sat.–Sun. 1:05.

APRIL
5-6-7 .... at Toronto
8 .... Minnesota
10-11 .... Minnesota
13-14-**15** .... Toronto
16-**17-18**-19 ..... at Cleveland
20-21-**22** .... at Minnesota
23-**24-25** .... Cleveland
27-28-**29** .... Anaheim

13-14-**15** .... at Boston
17-18-19 .... Detroit
20-21-**22** .... Boston
23-24-25 .... at Detroit
26-27-28-**29** ...... at Cleveland
31 .... Oakland

SEPTEMBER
1-2 .... Oakland
3-4-**5** .... Seattle
6-7-8-9 .... at Texas
10-11-**12** .... at Anaheim
14-15-16 ...... at Minnesota
17-18-**19** .... Detroit
20-21-22 .... Minnesota
23-24-25-**26** ... Kansas City
27-28-29 .... at Detroit
30 .... at Kansas City

OCTOBER
1-2-**3** .... at Kansas City

2-3-**4** .... *at Cincinnati
5-6-**7-8** .... Texas
9-10-**11** .... Oakland
15-16-**17-18** .... at Seattle
19-**20** .... at Anaheim
21-22 .... White Sox
23-**24-25** .... Kansas City
26-27-28 .... Detroit
30-31 .... at Kansas City

AUGUST
1 .... at Kansas City
2-3-4-**5** .... at Toronto
6-**7-8-9** .... at White Sox
10-11-**12** .... Toronto
13-14-**15** .... Minnesota
16-17-18 .... at Texas
20-**21-22** .... at Minnesota
23-24-25 .... Yankees
26-27-28-**29** ..... White Sox
31 .... at Yankees

SEPTEMBER
1-2 .... at Yankees
3-4-**5** .... Anaheim
6 .... at Seattle
8 .... at Seattle
10-**11-12** .... at Oakland
14-15-16 .... Detroit
17-18-**19** .... Kansas City
20-21-22 .... at Detroit
23-24-25-**26** ..... Minnesota
27-28-29 ..... at Kansas City

OCTOBER
1-2-**3** .... at Minnesota

30 .... Seattle

MAY
1-2 .... Seattle
3-4-**5** .... at Anaheim
7-**8-9** .... at Texas
11-12-**13** .... Oakland
14-**15-16** .... Texas
18-19-**20** .... at Oakland
21-22-**23** .... at Seattle

25-26-**27** ..... at Kansas City
28-29-**30** .... Baltimore
31 .... Kansas City

JUNE
1-2-3 .... Kansas City
4-**5-6** .... at Minnesota
8-9-**10** .... *Atlanta
11-12-**13** .... *Florida
15-16-**17** ..... *at Philadelphia
18-19-**20** .... *at Mets
22-23-24 ..... at Kansas City
25-26-27 .... *Arizona
29-30 .... Cleveland

JULY
1 .... Cleveland
2-3-4 .... *at Colorado
5-6-7 .... at Yankees
8-9-**10-11** .... at Minnesota
15-16-**17-18** .... Yankees
19-20 ....Minnesota
21-**22** .... Kansas City
23-**24-25** .... at White Sox
26-27-28 .... at Cleveland
29-30-31 .... White Sox

KANSAS CITY ROYALS
Kauffman Stadium
■ Standard Game Times: 7:10 p.m.; Sat. 6:10; Sun. 2:10.

APRIL
5 .... White Sox
7 .... White Sox
8-9-10-11 .... Cleveland
13-14-15 ...... at White Sox
16-**17-18** .... at Minnesota
20-21-**22** .... at Cleveland
23-**24-25** .... Minnesota
27-28-**29** .... Texas
30 .... at Yankees

MAY
1-2 .... at Yankees
3-4-5 .... at Toronto
7-**8-9** .... at Boston
10-11-**12** .... Toronto
14-**15-16** .... Oakland
18-19-20 .... at Texas
21-**22-23** .... at Oakland
25-26-27 .... Detroit
28-**29-30** .... Minnesota
31 .... at Detroit

JUNE
1-2-3 .... at Detroit
4-**5-6** .... Boston
8-9-**10** .... *Montreal
11-**12-13** .... *Mets
15-16-**17** .... *at Atlanta
18-**19-20** ..... *at Philadelphia
22-23-**24** .... Detroit
25-26-**27** .... *St. Louis
28-29-30 .... Baltimore

JULY
1 .... Baltimore

AUGUST
1 .... White Sox
3-4-**5** .... Texas
6-7-**8** .... Boston
10-**11-12** .... at Oakland
13-14-**15** .... at Anaheim
17-18-19 ...... at White Sox
20-21-**22** .... Seattle
23-24-25 .... White Sox
26-27-**28-29** ...... at Boston
30-31 .... at Kansas City

SEPTEMBER
1 .... at Kansas City
3-4-**5** .... at Tampa Bay
6-7-8-9 .... Kansas City
10-11-**12**-13 ..... Minnesota
14-15-16 .... at Cleveland
17-**18-19** ...... at White Sox
20-21-22 .... Cleveland
24-**25-26** .... at Baltimore
27-28-29 .... White Sox

OCTOBER
1-2-**3** .... Tampa Bay

2-3-**4** .... *at San Diego
5-6-**7** .... at Minnesota
9-10-11 .... at Baltimore
15-16-**17-18** ..... Minnesota
19-**20** .... Baltimore
21-**22** .... at Detroit
23-24-**25** .... at Cleveland
27-28-29 ...... at Tampa Bay
30-31 .... Cleveland

AUGUST
1 .... Cleveland
3-4-5 .... White Sox
6-7-**8-9** .... Anaheim
10-**11-12** ...... at White Sox
13-**14-15** .... at Oakland
17-18-19 .... Seattle
20-21-**22** .... Texas
23-24-25 .... at Anaheim
26-27-**28-29** ...... at Seattle
30-31 .... Detroit

SEPTEMBER
1 .... Detroit
3-4-**5** .... at Minnesota
6-7-8-9 .... at Detroit
10-11-**12** .... Tampa Bay
13-14-**15** .... Yankees
17-**18-19** ...... at Cleveland
20-21-22 .... at Tampa Bay
23-24-25-**26** ...... at White Sox
27-28-29 .... Cleveland
30 .... White Sox

OCTOBER
1-2-**3** .... White Sox

MINNESOTA TWINS
Hubert H. Humphrey Metrodome
■ Standard Game Times: 7:10 p.m.; Sat 6:10, Sun. 1:10.

APRIL
5-6-7 .... Cleveland
8 .... at Detroit
10-11 .... at Detroit
12 .... at Cleveland

14-15 .... at Cleveland
16-17-**18** .... Kansas City
20-21-**22** .... Detroit
23-24-25 ..... at Kansas City
26-27-28 .... Toronto

30 .... Anaheim

MAY
1-2 .... Anaheim
4-5-6 .... at Seattle
7-8-9 .... at Oakland
11-12-13 .... Seattle
14-15-16 ...... at White Sox
17-18-19 ...... at Toronto
20-21-22-23 .... White Sox
25-26-27 ...... at Tampa Bay
28-29-30 ..... at Kansas City
31 .... Tampa Bay

JUNE
1-2-3 .... Tampa Bay
4-5-6 .... Detroit
8-9-10 .... *Mets
11-12-13 ...... *Philadelphia
15-16-17 ...... *at Milwaukee
18-19-20 .... *at Milwaukee
22-23-24 .... at Boston
25-26-27 .... *Milwaukee
29-30 .... White Sox

JULY
1 .... White Sox
2-3-4 .... *at Arizona
5-6-7 .... Kansas City
8-9-10-11 .... Detroit
15-16-17-18 .... at Kansas City

19-20 .... at Detroit
21-22 .... Tampa Bay
23-24-25 .... at Baltimore
26-27-28 ...... at White Sox
30-31 .... Boston

AUGUST
1 .... Boston
3-4-5 .... Anaheim
6-7-8-9 .... Oakland
10-11-12 .... at Seattle
13-14-15 .... at Cleveland
17-18-19 .... Yankees
20-21-22 .... Cleveland
23-24-25-26 .... at Texas
27-28-29 .... at Anaheim
31 .... Texas

SEPTEMBER
1-2 .... Texas
3-4-5 .... Kansas City
6-7-8 .... at Baltimore
10-11-12-13 ...... at Detroit
14-15-16 .... White Sox
17-18-19 .... Baltimore
20-21-22 ...... at White Sox
23-24-25-26 ..... at Cleveland
28-29-30 .... at Yankees

OCTOBER
1-2-3 .... Cleveland

NEW YORK YANKEES
Yankee Stadium

■ Standard Game Times: 7:05 p.m.; Sat.–Sun. 1:05.

MARCH
30-31 .... %Tampa Bay

APRIL
6-7 .... at Tampa Bay
8-9-10-11 .... White Sox
13-14 .... Tampa Bay
16-17-18-19 .... at Boston
20-21-22 ...... at White Sox
23-24-25 .... Boston
27-28-29 .... Oakland
30 .... Kansas City

MAY
1-2 .... Kansas City
4-5-6 .... at Seattle
7-8-9 .... at Seattle
11-12-13 .... Anaheim
14-15-16 .... Seattle
18-19-20 .... at Anaheim
21-22-23 .... at Texas
25-26-27 .... at Baltimore
28-29-30 .... at Tampa Bay

JUNE
1-2-3 .... Baltimore
4-5-6 .... Texas
8-9-10 .... *Colorado
11-12-13 .... *San Diego
15-16-17 .... *at Arizona
18-19-20 ..... *at Los Angeles
22-23-24 .... at Baltimore
25-26-27 .... *Mets
29-30 .... Boston

JULY
1 .... Boston

2-3-4 .... *at Mets
5-6-7 .... Detroit
8-9-10-11 .... Tampa Bay
15-16-17-18 ...... at Detroit
19-20 .... at Tampa Bay
21-22 .... Toronto
23-24-25 .... at Boston
26-27-28 .... at Toronto
29-30-31 .... Baltimore

AUGUST
1 .... Baltimore
3-4-5 .... Oakland
6-7-8-9 .... Toronto
10-11-12 .... at Texas
13-14-15 .... at Seattle
17-18-19 .... at Minnesota
20-21-22 .... Anaheim
23-24-25 .... at Cleveland
26-27-28-29 ..... at Toronto
31 .... Cleveland

SEPTEMBER
1-2 .... Cleveland
3-4-5 .... Baltimore
6-7-8-9 .... Tampa Bay
10-11-12 .... at Baltimore
13-14-15 ..... at Kansas City
17-18-19 .... Boston
21-22-23 .... Toronto
24-25-26 .... at Boston
28-29-30 .... Minnesota

OCTOBER
1-2-3 .... at Toronto

OAKLAND ATHLETICS
Network Associates Coliseum

■ Standard Game Times: 7:05 p.m.; Sat.–Sun. 1:05.

APRIL
5-6-7 .... Texas
9-10-11 .... Seattle
13-14-15 .... at Texas
16-17-18 .... at Anaheim
19-20-21-22 ...... at Seattle
23-24-25 .... Anaheim
27-28-29 .... at Yankees
30 .... at Tampa Bay

MAY
1-2 .... at Tampa Bay
4-5-6 .... Yankees
7-8-9 .... Minnesota
11-12-13 .... at Detroit
14-15-16 ......at Kansas City
18-19-20 .... Detroit
21-22-23 .... Kansas City
25-26-27 .... at Boston
28-29-30 .... at Cleveland

JUNE
1-2 .... White Sox
3-4-5-6 .... Toronto
7-8-9 .... *Cincinnati
11-12-13 .... *Pittsburgh
15-16-17 .... *at St. Louis
18-19-20 .... *at Cubs
21-22-23-24 .... at Anaheim
25-26-27 ... *San Francisco
29-30 .... Anaheim

JULY
1 .... Anaheim

2-3-4 ..... *at San Francisco
6-7-8 .... at Boston
9-10-11 .... at Cleveland
15-16-17-18 ..... White Sox
19-20 .... Toronto
21-22 .... at Seattle
23-24-25 .... Texas
26-27-28 .... Seattle
29-30-31 .... at Texas

AUGUST
1 .... at Texas
3-4-5 .... at Yankees
6-7-8-9 .... at Minnesota
10-11-12 .... Detroit
13-14-15 .... Kansas City
16-17-18 .... at Baltimore
20-21-22 ...... at Tampa Bay
23-24-25-26 ...... Baltimore
27-28-29 .... Tampa Bay
31 .... at White Sox

SEPTEMBER
1-2 .... at White Sox
3-4-5 .... at Yankees
6-7-8 .... Boston
10-11-12 .... Cleveland
13-14-15-16 .... Texas
17-18-19 .... at Seattle
21-22-23 .... at Texas
24-25-26 .... at Anaheim
27-28-29-30 .... Seattle

OCTOBER
1-2-3 .... Anaheim

SEATTLE MARINERS
Safeco Field

■ Standard Game Times: 7:05 p.m.; Sat. 1:05, 7:05; Sun. 1:05.

APRIL
6-7-8 .... Anaheim
9-10-11 .... at Oakland
13-14-15 .... at Anaheim
16-17-18 .... Texas
19-20-21-22 .... Oakland
23-24-25 .... at Texas
26-27-28-29 ..... at Baltimore
30 .... at Detroit

MAY
1-2 .... at Detroit
4-5-6 .... Minnesota
7-8-9 .... Yankees
11-12-13 ...... at Minnesota
14-15-16 .... at Yankees
18-19-20 .... Baltimore
21-22-23 .... Detroit
25-26-27 .... at Cleveland
28-29-30 .... at Boston
31 .... Toronto

JUNE
1-2 .... Toronto
4-5-6 .... White Sox
7-8-9 .... *Houston
11-12-13 .... *Montreal
15-16-17 .... *at Milwaukee
18-19-20 ..... *at Pittsburgh
22-23-24 .... at Texas
25-26-27 .... *San Diego
28-29-30 .... Texas

JULY
1 .... Texas
2-3-4 .... *at St. Louis
6-7-8 .... at Toronto
9-10-11 .... at White Sox
15-16-17-18 .... Cleveland
19-20 .... Boston
21-22 .... Oakland
23-24-25 .... Anaheim
26-27-28 .... at Oakland
29-30-31 .... at Anaheim

AUGUST
1 .... at Anaheim
3-4 .... at Minnesota
5-6-7-8 .... at Tampa Bay
10-11-12 .... Minnesota
13-14-15 .... Yankees
17-18-19 ...... at Kansas City
20-21-22 .... at Detroit
23-24-25 .... Tampa Bay
26-27-28-29 ..... Kansas City
31 .... at Toronto

SEPTEMBER
1-2 .... at Toronto
3-4-5 .... at White Sox
6 .... Cleveland
8 .... Cleveland
9-10-11-12 .... Boston
13-14-15-16 .... Anaheim
17-18-19 .... Oakland

20-21-22 .... at Anaheim
24-25-26 .... at Texas
27-28-29-**30** ..... at Oakland

TAMPA BAY DEVIL RAYS
Tropicana Field

■ Standard Game Times: 7:15 p.m.; Sat. 6:15; Sun. 1:15.

MARCH
30-31 .... %Yankees

APRIL
6-7 .... Yankees
9-10-11 .... Baltimore
13-14 .... at Yankees
16-17-**18** .... White Sox
20-21-22 .... at Baltimore
23-24-25 .... at White Sox
27-28-29 .... at Boston
30 .... Oakland

MAY
1-2 .... Oakland
3-4-5 .... at Texas
6-7-8-**9** .... at Anaheim
11-12-13 .... Texas
14-**15-16** .... at Cleveland
18-19-20 .... Boston
21-22-23 .... Cleveland
25-26-**27** .... Minnesota
28-29-**30** .... Yankees
31 .... at Minnesota

JUNE
1-2-3 .... at Minnesota
4-**5-6** .... at Baltimore
8-9-10 .... *San Francisco
11-12-**13** .... *Colorado
15-16-17 ..... *at San Diego
18-19-**20** .... *at Arizona
22-23-**24** .... at Toronto
25-26-**27** .... *Florida
28-29-30 .... Toronto

JULY
1 .... Toronto
2-3-**4** .... *at Florida
5-6-7 .... at Baltimore
8-9-**10-11** .... at Yankees
15-16-17-**18** ...... Baltimore
19-**20** .... Yankees
21-**22** .... at Minnesota
23-24-25 .... at Toronto
27-28-29 .... Kansas City
30-31 .... Toronto

AUGUST
1 .... Toronto
2-3-4 .... Boston
5-6-7-**8** .... Seattle
9-10-11-**12** .... at Boston
13-14-**15** .... at Texas
17-18-**19** .... Anaheim
20-21-**22** .... Oakland
23-24-25 .... at Seattle
27-28-**29** .... at Oakland
31 .... Baltimore

SEPTEMBER
1-2 ....Baltimore
3-4-**5** .... Detroit
6-7-8-**9** .... at Yankees
10-11-**12** ..... at Kansas City
14-15-16 .... at Boston
17-18-**19** .... at Toronto
20-21-**22** .... Kansas City
24-25-**26** .... Toronto
27-28-29 .... Boston

OCTOBER
1-2-**3** .... at Detroit

TEXAS RANGERS
The Ballpark in Arlington

■ Standard Game Times: 7:05 p.m.; Sun. 1:05.

APRIL
5-6-**7** .... at Oakland
9-10-11-12 ...... at Anaheim
13-14-**15** .... Oakland
16-17-**18** .... at Seattle
20-21-**22** .... at Anaheim
23-24-**25** .... Seattle
27-28-**29** ..... at Kansas City
30 .... Boston

MAY
1-2 .... Boston
3-4-5 .... Tampa Bay
7-8-**9** .... Detroit
11-12-**13** ...... at Tampa Bay
14-**15-16** .... at Detroit
18-19-20 .... Kansas City
21-22-**23** .... Yankees
25-26-**27** .... at White Sox
28-**29**-30 .... at Toronto
31 .... Boston

JUNE
1-2 .... at Cleveland
4-5-6 .... at Yankees
7-8-9 .... *Pittsburgh
11-12-**13** .... *St. Louis
15-16-17 ..... *at Cincinnati
18-19-**20** .... *at Florida
22-23-**24** .... Seattle
25-26-**27** .... *Houston
28-29-30 .... at Seattle

JULY
1 .... at Seattle
2-3-**4** .... *at Houston
5-6-7-**8** .... at Cleveland
9-10-**11** .... at Boston
16-17-18 .... Toronto
19-20 .... White Sox
21-**22** .... Anaheim
23-24-25 .... at Oakland
26-27-28 .... at Anaheim
29-30-31 .... Oakland

AUGUST
1 .... Oakland
3-4-**5** .... at Detroit
6-7-8-**9** .... at Baltimore
10-11-12 .... at Yankees
13-14-**15** .... Tampa Bay
16-17-18 .... Cleveland
20-21-**22** ..... at Kansas City
23-24-25-26 ..... Minnesota
27-28-29 .... Baltimore
31 .... at Minnesota

SEPTEMBER
1-2 .... at Minnesota
3-4-**5** .... at Boston
6-7-8-**9** .... White Sox
10-11-**12** .... Toronto
13-14-**15-16** ..... at Oakland
17-18-**19** .... at Anaheim
21-22-**23** .... Oakland
24-25-**26** .... Seattle
27-28-29-**30** .... Anaheim

OCTOBER
1-2-**3** .... at Seattle

TORONTO BLUE JAYS
SkyDome

■ Standard Game Times: 7:05 p.m.; Sat. (April-May) 1:05, (June-Oct.) 4:05; Sun. 1:05.

APRIL
5-6-7 .... Detroit
9-10-11 .... at Boston
13-14-**15** .... at Detroit
16-17-18 .... Baltimore
20-21-22 .... Boston
23-24-25 .... at Baltimore
26-27-28 ...... at Minnesota
29-30 .... at White Sox

MAY
1-2 .... at White Sox
3-4-5 .... Kansas City
7-**8-9** .... White Sox
10-11-12 ..... at Kansas City
13-14-**15-16** .... Boston
17-18-**19** .... Minnesota
21-22-23 .... at Boston
24 .... Anaheim
26-27 .... Anaheim
28-**29-30** .... Texas
31 .... at Seattle

JUNE
1-2 .... at Seattle
3-4-**5-6** .... at Oakland
8-9-10 .... *Los Angeles
11-12-**13** .... *Arizona
15-16-**17** ..... *at San Francisco
18-19-20 ..... *at San Diego
22-23-24 .... Tampa Bay
25-**26-27** .... *Montreal
28-29-30 ...... at Tampa Bay

JULY
1 .... at Tampa Bay
2-3-**4** .... *#at Montreal
6-7-8 .... Seattle
9-10-11 .... Anaheim
16-17-18 .... at Texas
19-**20** .... at Oakland
21-**22** .... at Yankees
23-24-25 .... Tampa Bay
26-27-28 .... Yankees
30-31 .... at Tampa Bay

AUGUST
1 .... at Tampa Bay
2-3-4-**5** .... Cleveland
6-7-8-**9** .... at Yankees
10-11-12 .... at Cleveland
13-**14-15** .... Baltimore
16-17-18 .... at Boston
20-**21-22** .... at Baltimore
23-24-25 .... Boston
26-27-**28-29** .... Yankees
31 .... Seattle

SEPTEMBER
1-2 .... Seattle
3-**4-5** .... Oakland
7-8-9 .... at Anaheim
10-11-**12** .... at Texas
13 .... Baltimore
15-16 .... Baltimore
17-**18-19** .... Tampa Bay
21-22-23 .... at Yankees
24-25-26 .... at Oakland
27-28-29-30 ..... at Baltimore

OCTOBER
1-2-**3** .... Yankees

NOTE: Dates in bold indicate afternoon games. All game times are subject to change. Gaps in dates indicate scheduled off-days but may be affected by rainouts.

* Interleague Series.
% at Tokyo, Japan.
# at San Juan, P.R.

NATIONAL LEAGUE

ARIZONA DIAMONDBACKS
Bank One Ballpark

■ **Standard Game Times:** 6:35 p.m.; 7:05; Sun. 1:35

APRIL	
6-7-8	Colorado
9-10-11	St. Louis
12	at Colorado
14-15	at Colorado
16-17-18	at San Diego
20-21-22	at Milwaukee
23-24-25	San Diego
26-27-28	Cubs
30	at Philadelphia

MAY	
1-2	at Philadelphia
4-5-6	at Cubs
7-8-9	Philadelphia
10-11-12-13	Mets
14-15-16	Montreal
18-19-20	at Atlanta
21-22-23-24	at Florida
25-26-27	at San Francisco
28-29-30	at Los Angeles
31	San Francisco

JUNE	
1-2-3	San Francisco
4-5-6	Los Angeles
8-9-10	*at Baltimore
11-12-13	*at Toronto
15-16-17	*Yankees
18-19-20	*Tampa Bay
21-22-23	at San Diego
25-26-27	*at Detroit
28-29-30	San Diego

JULY	
1	San Diego

2-3-4	*Minnesota
5-6-7	at Los Angeles
8-9-10-11	at San Francisco
15-16-17-18	Los Angeles
19-20	San Francisco
21-22	Houston
23-24-25	Colorado
26-27-28-29	at Houston
30-31	at Colorado

AUGUST	
1	at Colorado
3-4-5	Florida
6-7-8	Atlanta
10-11-12	at Montreal
13-14-15	at Mets
16-17-18	Pittsburgh
20-21-22	Cincinnati
23-24-25	at Pittsburgh
27-28-29	at Cincinnati
31	Los Angeles

SEPTEMBER	
1-2	Los Angeles
3-4-5	at San Francisco
7-8-9	at Los Angeles
10-11-12	San Francisco
13-14-15-16	Colorado
17-18-19	at St. Louis
21-22-23	at Colorado
24-25-26	at San Diego
27-28-29	Milwaukee

OCTOBER	
1-2-3	San Diego

ATLANTA BRAVES
Turner Field

■ **Standard Game Times:** 7:35 p.m.; Wed./Sat. 7:05; Sun. 1:05

APRIL	
6-7-8	Mets
9-10-11	Cubs
12	at Mets
14-15	at Mets
16-17-18	Florida
20-21-22	at Cincinnati
23-24-25	at Florida
26-27-28	at San Francisco
30	at Colorado

MAY	
1-2	at Colorado
4-5-6	San Diego
7-8-9	Houston
11-12-13	at St. Louis
14-15-16	at Milwaukee
18-19-20	Arizona
21-22-23	Los Angeles
24-25-26	at Montreal
27-28-29-30	at Philadelphia
31	Montreal

JUNE	
1-2	Montreal

3-4-5-6	Philadelphia
8-9-10	*at Detroit
11-12-13	*at White Sox
15-16-17	*Kansas City
18-19-20	*Cleveland
22-23-24	at Florida
25-26-27	*at Baltimore
28-29-30	Florida

JULY	
1	Florida
2-3-4	*Boston
5-6-7	#at Montreal
9-10-11	at Philadelphia
15-16-17-18	Montreal
19-20	Philadelphia
21-22	Pittsburgh
23-24-25	at Mets
26-27-28-29	at Pittsburgh
30-31	Mets

AUGUST	
1	Mets
3-4-5	at Houston
6-7-8	at Arizona

CINCINNATI REDS
Great American Ball Park

■ **Standard Game Times:** 7:10 p.m.; Sat. 7:10, 1:15; Sun. 1:15.

APRIL	
5	Cubs
7-8	Cubs
9-10-11	Pittsburgh
12	at Philadelphia
14-15	at Philadelphia
16-17-18-19	at Cubs
20-21-22	Atlanta
23-24-25-26	at Milwaukee
27-28	at Milwaukee
30	at Houston

MAY	
1-2-3	at Houston
4-5-6	Milwaukee
7-8-9	San Francisco
11-12-13	at San Diego
14-15-16	at Los Angeles
18-19-20	Colorado
21-22-23-24	Houston
25-26-27	Florida
28-29-30	at Montreal
31	at Florida

10-11-12	Milwaukee
13-14-15	St. Louis
16-17-18	at San Diego
19-20-21-22	at Los Angeles
24-25-26	Colorado
27-28-29-30	San Francisco
31	at Philadelphia

SEPTEMBER	
1	at Philadelphia
3-4-5	at Montreal

CHICAGO CUBS
Wrigley Field

■ **Standard Game Times:** 1:20 p.m., 7:05 p.m.; Fri. 2:20; Sat.–Sun. 1:20.

APRIL	
5	at Cincinnati
7-8	at Cincinnati
9-10-11	at Atlanta
12	Pittsburgh
14-15	Pittsburgh
16-17-18-19	Cincinnati
20-21-22	at Pittsburgh
23-24-25	Mets
26-27-28	at Arizona
30	at St. Louis

MAY	
1-2-3	at St. Louis
4-5-6	Arizona
7-8-9	Colorado
11-12-13	at Los Angeles
14-15-16	at San Diego
18-19-20	San Francisco
21-22-23	St. Louis
25-26	at Houston
28-29-30	at Pittsburgh
31	Houston

JUNE	
1-2	Houston
4-5-6	Pittsburgh
7-8-9-10	St. Louis
11-12-13	*at Anaheim
14-15-16-17	at Houston
18-19-20	*Oakland
22-23-24	at St. Louis
25-26-27	*at White Sox
29-30	Houston

JULY	
1	Houston

2-3-4	*White Sox
5-6-7	at Milwaukee
9-10-11	at St. Louis
15-16-17-18	Milwaukee
19-20	St. Louis
21-22	Cincinnati
23-24-25	at Philadelphia
26-27-28-29	at Milwaukee
30-31	Philadelphia

AUGUST	
1	Philadelphia
3-4-5	at Colorado
6-7-8	at San Francisco
10-11-12	San Diego
13-14-15	Los Angeles
17-18-19	at Milwaukee
20-21-22	at Houston
23-24-25	Milwaukee
26-27-28-29	Houston
30-31	at Montreal

SEPTEMBER	
1	at Montreal
3-4-5	at Florida
6-7-8	Montreal
10-11-12	Florida
13-14-15	Pittsburgh
16-17-18-19	at Cincinnati
21-22-23	at Pittsburgh
24-25-26	at Mets
27-28-29-30	Cincinnati

OCTOBER	
1-2-3	Atlanta

6-7-8-9	Philadelphia
10-11-12	Montreal
13-14-15-16	at Mets
17-18-19	at Florida
21-22-23	Cincinnati
24-25-26	Florida
27-28-29	Mets

OCTOBER	
1-2-3	at Cubs

JUNE	
1-2	at Florida
4-5-**6**	Montreal
7-8-9	*at Oakland
11-12-**13**	*at Cleveland
15-16-**17**	*Texas
18-19-**20**	at St. Louis
22-23-**24**	at Mets
25-26-**27**	Pittsburgh
29-30	Mets

JULY	
1	Mets
2-3-**4**	*Cleveland
5-6-7	at St. Louis
8-9-10-**11**	at Milwaukee
15-16-17-**18**	St. Louis
19-20	Milwaukee
21-22	at Cubs
23-24-**25**	at Pittsburgh
26-27-28	St. Louis
30-**31**	Houston

AUGUST	
1	Houston

COLORADO ROCKIES
Coors Field

■ **Standard Game Times:** 7:05 p.m.; Thurs. 1:05; Sat. (April-May, Sept.) 1:05, (June-Aug.) 6:05; Sun. 1:05.

APRIL	
6-7-8	at Arizona
9-10-**11**	at Los Angeles
12	Arizona
14-**15**	Arizona
16-**17**-**18**	at St. Louis
20-21-**22**	Los Angeles
23-**24**-**25**	Houston
26-27-**28**	Florida
30	Atlanta

MAY	
1-2	Atlanta
4-5-**6**	at Montreal
7-**8**-**9**	at Cubs
11-12-**13**	Pittsburgh
14-**15**-**16**-**17**	Philadelphia
18-19-20	at Cincinnati
21-22-**23**	at Mets
25-26-**27**	San Diego
28-29-**30**	at San Francisco
31	at San Diego

JUNE	
1-**2**	at San Diego
4-5-**6**-**7**	San Diego
8-9-**10**	*at Yankees
11-12-**13**	*at Tampa Bay
15-16-**17**	*Boston
18-19-**20**	*Baltimore
22-23-**24**	at Milwaukee
25-26-**27**	*at Cleveland
29-30	Milwaukee

JULY	
1	Milwaukee

FLORIDA MARLINS
Pro Player Stadium

■ **Standard Game Times:** 7:05 p.m.; Fri. 7:35; Sat. 6:05; Sun. 3:05.

APRIL	
6-7-8	Montreal
9-10-**11**	Philadelphia
13-14-15	#at Montreal

3-4-**5**	at San Francisco
6-7-**8**	at Colorado
10-11-**12**	Los Angeles
13-14-**15**	San Diego
16-17-18	at St. Louis
20-21-**22**	at Arizona
24-25-26	St. Louis
27-**28**-**29**	Arizona
30-31	Houston

SEPTEMBER	
1	Houston
3-4-**5**	at Milwaukee
6-7-8	at Houston
9-10-11-**12**	Milwaukee
13-14-**15**	Philadelphia
16-17-18-**19**	Cubs
21-22-23	at Atlanta
24-25-**26**	at Pittsburgh
27-**28**-**29**-**30**	at Cubs

OCTOBER	
1-**2**-3	Pittsburgh

2-3-**4**	*Detroit
5-6-7	at San Francisco
8-9-**10**-**11**	at San Diego
15-16-17-**18**	.. San Francisco
19-20	San Diego
21-**22**	at Los Angeles
23-24-**25**	at Arizona
26-27-28-**29**	.. Los Angeles
30-31	Arizona

AUGUST	
1	Arizona
3-4-**5**	Cubs
6-**7**-**8**	Cincinnati
9-10-11-12	.. at Philadelphia
13-14-**15**	at Pittsburgh
17-**18**-**19**	Mets
20-21-**22**	Montreal
24-25-26	at Atlanta
27-**28**-**29**	at Florida
31	at San Francisco

SEPTEMBER	
1-2	at San Francisco
3-4-**5**	at San Diego
7-8	San Francisco
9-10-**11**-**12**	San Diego
13-14-15-**16**	at Arizona
17-**18**-**19**	Los Angeles
21-22-**23**	Arizona
24-**25**-**26**	St. Louis
27-28-29-30	.. at Los Angeles

OCTOBER	
1-**2**-3	at Houston

16-17-**18**	at Atlanta
20-21-**22**	.... at Philadelphia
23-24-**25**	Atlanta
26-27-**28**	at Colorado

29-30	at San Francisco
MAY	
1-2	at San Francisco
4-5-6	Los Angeles
7-8-**9**	San Diego
11-12-13	at Houston
14-**15**-**16**	at St. Louis
18-19-20	Houston
21-**22**-**23**-24	Arizona
25-26-**27**	at Cincinnati
28-29-**30**	Mets
31	Cincinnati

JUNE	
1-2	Cincinnati
3-4-**5**-**6**	at Mets
8-9-10	*at Cleveland
11-12-**13**	*at Detroit
15-16-17	*White Sox
18-19-**20**	*Texas
22-23-24	Atlanta
25-26-**27**	*at Tampa Bay
28-29-30	at Atlanta

JULY	
1	at Atlanta
2-3-**4**	*Tampa Bay
5-6-7	Pittsburgh
9-10-**11**	Mets
16-17-**18**	at Pittsburgh
19-20	at Mets

HOUSTON ASTROS
Minute Maid Park

■ **Standard Game Times:** 7:05 p.m.; Sat. 6:05; Sun. 1:05.

APRIL	
5-6-7	San Francisco
9-**10**-**11**	at Milwaukee
12-13-**14**	at St. Louis
15-16-17-**18**	Milwaukee
20-21-22	St. Louis
23-**24**-**25**	at Colorado
27-**28**-**29**	at Pittsburgh
30	Cincinnati

MAY	
1-**2**-3	Cincinnati
4-5-**6**	Pittsburgh
7-8-**9**	at Atlanta
11-12-13	Florida
14-**15**-**16**	Mets
18-19-20	at Florida
21-22-**23**-24	.. at Cincinnati
25-26	Cubs
28-**29**-**30**	St. Louis
31	at Cubs

JUNE	
1-2	at Cubs
4-5-**6**	at St. Louis
7-8-9	*at Seattle
11-12-**13**	at Milwaukee
14-15-16-17	Cubs
18-19-**20**	*Anaheim
21-22-23-24	Pittsburgh
25-26-**27**	*at Texas
29-**30**	at Cubs

JULY	
1	at Cubs

21-**22**	at Philadelphia
23-24-**25**	at Montreal
26-27-28-**29**	... Philadelphia
30-31	Montreal

AUGUST	
1	Montreal
3-4-**5**	at Arizona
6-7-**8**	Milwaukee
10-11-12	St. Louis
13-14-**15**	at Milwaukee
16-17-18	at Los Angeles
20-21-**22**	at San Diego
24-25-26	San Francisco
27-28-**29**	Colorado
30-31	at Mets

SEPTEMBER	
1-2	at Mets
3-4-**5**	Cubs
7-8-**9**	Mets
10-**11**-**12**	at Cubs
13-14-15-16	Montreal
17-18-**19**	Atlanta
21-22-23	Philadelphia
24-25-**26**	at Atlanta
27-28-29	at Montreal
30	at Philadelphia

OCTOBER	
1-**2**-3	at Philadelphia

2-3-**4**	*Texas
5-6-7	at San Diego
8-9-10-**11**	.. at Los Angeles
16-17-**18**	San Diego
19-20	Los Angeles
21-**22**	at Arizona
23-24-**25**	Milwaukee
26-27-28-**29**	at Cincinnati
30-**31**	at Cincinnati

AUGUST	
1	at Cincinnati
3-4-5	Atlanta
6-7-**8**	Montreal
10-11-**12**	at Mets
13-14-**15**	at Montreal
17-18-**19**	at Philadelphia
20-21-**22**	Cubs
23-24-**25**	Philadelphia
26-27-28-**29**	at Cubs
30-31	at Cincinnati

SEPTEMBER	
1	at Cincinnati
3-4-**5**	Pittsburgh
6-7-8	Cincinnati
9-10-11-**12**	.. at Pittsburgh
14-15-16	at St. Louis
17-18-**19**	Milwaukee
21-22-23	.. at San Francisco
24-25-**26**	at Milwaukee
27-28-29	St. Louis

OCTOBER	
1-**2**-3	Colorado

LOS ANGELES DODGERS
Dodger Stadium

■ **Standard Game Times:** 7:10 p.m.; Sun. 1:10.

APRIL	
5-6-7	San Diego
9-10-**11**	Colorado
13-14-15	at San Diego
16-**17-18**	at San Francisco
20-21-**22**	at Colorado
23-24-**25**	San Francisco
27-28-29	Mets
30	Montreal

MAY	
1-**2**	Montreal
4-5-6	at Florida
7-8-9	at Pittsburgh
11-12-**13**	Cubs
14-15-**16**	Cincinnati
18-19-20	at Philadelphia
21-**22-23**	at Atlanta
25-26-**27**	at Milwaukee
28-29-30	Arizona
31	Milwaukee

JUNE	
1-2	Milwaukee
4-5-**6**	at Arizona
8-9-10	*at Toronto
11-**12-13**	*at Boston
15-16-17	*Baltimore
18-**19**-20	*Yankees
21-22-23-**24**	at San Francisco
25-**26-27**	*Anaheim
29-30	San Francisco

JULY	
1	San Francisco

2-3-4	*at Anaheim
5-6-7	Arizona
8-9-10-**11**	Houston
15-16-17-**18**	at Arizona
19-20	at Houston
21-**22**	Colorado
23-24-25	San Diego
26-27-28-**29**	at Colorado
30-31	at San Diego

AUGUST	
1	at San Diego
3-4-**5**	Pittsburgh
6-7-**8**	Philadelphia
10-11-**12**	at Cincinnati
13-14-15	at Cubs
16-17-18	Florida
19-20-**21-22**	Atlanta
23-24-25-26	at Montreal
27-**28-29**	at Mets
31	at Arizona

SEPTEMBER	
1-2	at Arizona
3-4-**5**	at St. Louis
7-8-9	Arizona
10-11-**12**	St. Louis
13-14-15-16	San Diego
17-**18-19**	at Colorado
21-22-23	at San Diego
24-25-**26**	at San Francisco
27-28-29-30	Colorado

OCTOBER	
1-2-**3**	San Francisco

MILWAUKEE BREWERS
Miller Park

■ **Standard Game Times:** 7:05 p.m.; Thur. (April-May) 12:05, (June-Sept.) 1:05; Sat. 1:05, 6:05; Sun. 1:05.

APRIL	
5-6-7-**8**	at St. Louis
9-10-11	Houston
12-13-**14**	at San Francisco
15-16-17-**18**	at Houston
20-21-**22**	Arizona
23-**24-25**	St. Louis
27-28	Cincinnati
30	Pittsburgh

MAY	
1-**2**	Pittsburgh
4-5-6	at Cincinnati
7-8-**9**	at Mets
11-12-**13**	Montreal
14-15-**16**	Atlanta
18-19-**20**	#at Montreal
21-22-23	at Pittsburgh
25-26-**27**	Los Angeles
28-29-**30**	San Diego
31	at Los Angeles

JUNE	
1-2	at Los Angeles
4-5-**6**	at San Diego
8-9-10	*at Anaheim
11-12-**13**	Houston
15-16-17	*Seattle
18-19-**20**	*Minnesota
22-23-24	Colorado
25-26-**27**	*at Minnesota

29-30	at Colorado

JULY	
1	at Colorado
2-3-4	at Pittsburgh
5-6-7	Cubs
8-9-10-**11**	Cincinnati
15-**16-17-18**	at Cubs
19-**20**	at Cincinnati
21-22	at St. Louis
23-24-**25**	at Houston
26-27-28-**29**	Cubs
30-31	Pittsburgh

AUGUST	
1	Pittsburgh
3-4-**5**	Mets
6-7-**8**	at Florida
10-11-12	at Atlanta
13-14-**15**	Florida
17-18-**19**	Cubs
20-21-**22**	Philadelphia
23-24-25	at Cubs
27-28-**29**	at Philadelphia
30-31	Pittsburgh

SEPTEMBER	
1-2	Pittsburgh
3-4-**5**	Cincinnati
6-7-**8**	at Pittsburgh
9-10-11-**12**	at Cincinnati
14-15-**16**	San Francisco

17-18-**19**	at Houston
20-21-22-**23**	St. Louis
24-25-**26**	Houston
27-28-**29**	at Arizona

OCTOBER	
1-2-**3**	at St. Louis

MONTREAL EXPOS
Olympic Stadium/Hiram Bithorn Stadium

■ **Standard Game Times:** Montreal—7:05 p.m.; Sun. 1:05. San Juan—7:05 p.m.; Sun. 1:35.

APRIL	
6-7-8	at Florida
9-10-**11**	#Mets
13-14-15	#Florida
16-**17-18**	at Philadelphia
19-20-21-**22**	at Mets
23-**24-25**	Philadelphia
26-27-28-29	at San Diego
30	at Los Angeles

MAY	
1-**2**	at Los Angeles
4-5-6	Colorado
7-8-**9**	St. Louis
11-12-**13**	at Milwaukee
14-15-**16**	at Arizona
18-19-**20**	#Milwaukee
21-**22-23**	#San Francisco
24-25-26	Atlanta
28-29-**30**	Cincinnati
31	at Atlanta

JUNE	
1-**2**	at Atlanta
4-5-**6**	at Cincinnati
8-9-**10**	*at Kansas City
11-12-**13**	*at Seattle
15-16-17	*Minnesota
18-19-**20**	*White Sox
22-23-24	Philadelphia
25-**26-27**	*at Toronto
28-29-30	at Philadelphia

JULY	
1	at Philadelphia

2-3-**4**	*#Toronto
5-6-7	#Atlanta
8-9-10-**11**	#Pittsburgh
15-16-17-**18**	at Atlanta
19-20	at Pittsburgh
21-**22**	at Mets
23-24-**25**	Florida
26-27-28-**29**	Mets
30-31	at Florida

AUGUST	
1	at Florida
3-4-5	at St. Louis
6-7-**8**	at Houston
10-11-12	Arizona
13-14-**15**	Houston
16-17-**18**	at San Francisco
20-21-**22**	at Colorado
23-24-25-26	Los Angeles
27-28-**29**	San Diego
30-31	Cubs

SEPTEMBER	
1	Cubs
3-4-**5**	Atlanta
6-7-**8**	at Cubs
10-11-**12**	at Atlanta
13-14-15-16	at Florida
17-18-**19**	at Philadelphia
21-22-23	Mets
24-25-**26**	Philadelphia
27-28-29	Florida

OCTOBER	
1-2-**3**	at Mets

NEW YORK METS
Shea Stadium

■ **Standard Game Times:** 7:10 p.m.; Sat. 1:10, 1:20, 7:10; Sun. 1:10.

APRIL	
6-7-8	at Atlanta
9-10-**11**	#at Montreal
12	at Atlanta
14-15	Atlanta
16-**17-18**	Pittsburgh
19-20-21-**22**	Montreal
23-24-**25**	at Cubs
27-28-29	at Los Angeles
30	at San Diego

MAY	
1-**2**	at San Diego
4-5-6	San Francisco
7-8-**9**	Milwaukee
10-11-12-13	at Arizona
14-15-**16**	at Houston
18-19-**20**	St. Louis
21-22-**23**	Colorado
25-26	Philadelphia
28-29-**30**	at Florida
31	at Philadelphia

JUNE	
1-2	at Philadelphia
3-4-**5-6**	Florida

8-9-10	*at Minnesota
11-**12-13**	*at Kansas City
15-16-17	*Cleveland
18-19-20	*Detroit
22-23-**24**	Cincinnati
25-**26-27**	*at Yankees
29-30	at Cincinnati

JULY	
1	at Cincinnati
2-3-**4**	*Yankees
5-6-7-**8**	at Philadelphia
9-10-**11**	at Florida
15-16-**17-18**	Philadelphia
19-20	Florida
21-**22**	Montreal
23-24-**25**	Atlanta
26-27-28-**29**	at Montreal
30-31	at Atlanta

AUGUST	
1	at Atlanta
3-4-**5**	at Milwaukee
6-7-**8**	at St. Louis
10-11-**12**	Houston
13-14-**15**	Arizona

17-18-**19** .... at Colorado
20-**21-22** .. at San Francisco
23-24-25-**26** .... San Diego
27-**28-29** ...... Los Angeles
30-31 .... Florida
SEPTEMBER
1-**2** .... Florida
3-4-**5** .... at Philadelphia
7-8-**9** .... at Florida

PHILADELPHIA PHILLIES
Citizens Bank Park

■ **Standard Game Times:** 1:05 p.m., 7:05; Sun. 1:35.

APRIL
5 .... at Pittsburgh
7-8 .... at Pittsburgh
9-10-**11** .... at Florida
12 .... Cincinnati
14-**15** .... Cincinnati
16-**17-18** .... Montreal
20-21-**22** .... Florida
23-**24-25** .... at Montreal
27-**28-29** .... at St. Louis
30 .... Arizona
MAY
1-2 .... Arizona
4-5-6 .... St. Louis
7-8-**9** .... at Arizona
11-12-**13** .. at San Francisco
14-**15-16-17** ... at Colorado
18-19-20 .... Los Angeles
21-22-**23** .... San Diego
25-26 .... at Mets
27-28-29-**30** .... Atlanta
31 .... Mets
JUNE
1-2 .... Mets
3-4-**5-6** .... at Atlanta
8-9-10 .... *at White Sox
11-12-13 ..... *at Minnesota
15-16-**17** .... *Detroit
18-19-**20** ...... *Kansas City
22-23-**24** .... at Montreal
25-**26-27** .... *at Boston
28-29-30 .... Montreal
JULY
1 .... Montreal

PITTSBURGH PIRATES
PNC Park

■ **Standard Game Times:** 7:05 p.m.; Sun. 1:35.

APRIL
5 .... Philadelphia
7-8 .... Philadelphia
9-**10-11** .... at Cincinnati
12 .... at Cubs
14-**15** .... at Cubs
16-**17-18** .... at Mets
20-21-22 .... Cubs
23-24-**25-26** ...... Cincinnati
27-**28-29** .... Houston
30 .... at Milwaukee
MAY
1-**2** .... at Milwaukee
4-5-**6** .... at Houston
7-8-**9** .... Los Angeles
11-12-**13** .... at Colorado
14-**15-16** . at San Francisco
18-19-20 .... San Diego
21-22-**23** .... Milwaukee

10-**11-12** .... Philadelphia
13-14-15-16 .... Atlanta
17-18-**19** ...... at Pittsburgh
21-22-23 .... at Montreal
24-25-**26** .... Cubs
27-28-**29** .... at Atlanta
OCTOBER
1-2-**3** .... Montreal

2-3-4 .... *Baltimore
5-6-7-8 .... Mets
9-**10-11** .... Atlanta
15-16-**17-18** .... at Mets
19-20 .... at Atlanta
21-**22** .... Florida
23-**24-25** .... Cubs
26-27-28-**29** ...... at Florida
30-31 .... at Cubs
AUGUST
1 .... at Cubs
3-4-5 .... at San Diego
6-**7-8** .... at Los Angeles
9-10-11-12 .... Colorado
13-**14-15** ..... San Francisco
17-18-**19** .... Houston
20-21-**22** ...... at Milwaukee
23-24-**25** .... at Houston
27-28-29 .... Milwaukee
31 .... Atlanta
SEPTEMBER
1 .... Atlanta
3-4-**5** .... Mets
6-7-8-9 .... at Atlanta
10-**11-12** .... at Mets
13-14-15 .... at Cincinnati
17-18-**19** .... Montreal
21-22-23 .... at Florida
24-25-**26** .... at Montreal
27-28-29 .... Pittsburgh
30 .... Florida
OCTOBER
1-2-**3** .... Florida

25-26-**27** .... at St. Louis
28-29-**30** .... Cubs
31 .... St. Louis
JUNE
1-2-**3** .... St. Louis
4-5-6 .... at Cubs
7-8-9 .... *at Texas
11-**12-13** .... *at Oakland
15-16-17 .... *Anaheim
18-19-**20** .... *Seattle
21-22-23-24 .... at Houston
25-26-27 .... at Cincinnati
28-29-**30** .... St. Louis
JULY
2-3-**4** .... Milwaukee
5-6-7 .... at Florida
8-9-10-**11** .... at Montreal
16-**17-18** .... Florida
19-20 .... Montreal

21-**22** .... at Atlanta
23-24-**25** .... Cincinnati
26-27-28-**29** .... Atlanta
30-31 .... at Milwaukee
AUGUST
1 .... at Milwaukee
3-4-**5** .... at Los Angeles
6-**7-8** .... at San Diego
10-11-12 ..... San Francisco
13-14-**15** .... Colorado
16-17-18 .... at Arizona
19-20-21-**22** .... at St. Louis
23-24-25 .... Arizona
27-28-**29** .... St. Louis

30-31 .... at Milwaukee
SEPTEMBER
1-**2** .... at Milwaukee
3-4-**5** .... at Houston
6-7-8 .... Milwaukee
9-10-11-**12** .... Houston
13-14-**15** .... at Cubs
17-18-**19** .... Mets
21-22-**23** .... Cubs
24-25-26 .... Cincinnati
27-28-29 .... at Philadelphia
OCTOBER
1-2-**3** .... at Cincinnati

ST. LOUIS CARDINALS
Busch Stadium

■ **Standard Game Times:** 7:10 p.m.; Thurs. (April-May) 12:10; Sat. 1:15, 6:15; Sun. 1:15.

APRIL
5-6-**7-8** .... Milwaukee
9-10-**11** .... at Arizona
12-13-**14** .... Houston
16-**17-18** .... Colorado
20-21-22 .... at Houston
23-**24-25** ...... at Milwaukee
27-28-29 .... Philadelphia
30 .... Cubs
MAY
1-2-**3** .... Cubs
4-5-6 .... at Philadelphia
7-8-**9** .... at Montreal
11-12-**13** .... Atlanta
14-**15-16** .... Florida
18-19-**20** .... at Mets
21-22-23 .... at Cubs
25-26-27 .... Pittsburgh
28-29-**30** .... at Houston
31 .... at Pittsburgh
JUNE
1-2-**3** .... at Pittsburgh
4-5-6 .... Houston
7-**8-9-10** .... at Cubs
11-12-**13** .... *at Texas
15-16-17 .... *Oakland
18-19-**20** .... Cincinnati
22-23-24 .... Cubs
25-26-**27** ... *at Kansas City
28-29-**30** ...... at Pittsburgh
JULY
2-3-**4** .... *Seattle

5-6-7 .... Cincinnati
9-**10-11** .... Cubs
15-16-**17-18** .. at Cincinnati
19-**20** .... at Cubs
21-22 .... Milwaukee
23-**24-25** ..... San Francisco
26-27-28 .... Cincinnati
30-31 ...... at San Francisco
AUGUST
1 .... at San Francisco
3-4-5 .... Montreal
6-**7-8** .... Mets
10-11-12 .... at Florida
13-**14-15** .... at Atlanta
16-17-18 .... Cincinnati
19-20-21-**22** ..... Pittsburgh
24-25-26 .... Cincinnati
27-**28-29** .... at Pittsburgh
31 .... San Diego
SEPTEMBER
1-2 .... San Diego
3-4-**5** .... Los Angeles
6-**7-8** .... at San Diego
10-11-**12** ... at Los Angeles
14-15-16 .... Houston
17-**18-19** .... Arizona
20-21-22-**23** . at Milwaukee
24-**25-26** .... at Colorado
27-28-29 .... at Houston
30 .... Milwaukee
OCTOBER
1-2-**3** .... Milwaukee

SAN DIEGO PADRES
PETCO Park

■ **Standard Game Times:** 7:05 p.m.; Sun. 1:05.

APRIL
5-6-**7** .... at Los Angeles
8 .... San Francisco
10-11 .... San Francisco
13-14-15 .... Los Angeles
16-17-18 .... Arizona
19-20-21-**22** .. at San Francisco
23-**24-25** .... at Arizona
26-27-28-29 .... Montreal
30 .... Mets
MAY
1-**2** .... Mets
4-5-**6** .... at Atlanta
7-8-**9** .... at Florida
11-12-13 .... Cincinnati

14-15-**16** .... Cubs
18-19-20 .... at Pittsburgh
21-22-**23** ...... at Philadelphia
25-26-**27** .... at Colorado
28-29-**30** ...... at Milwaukee
31 .... Colorado
JUNE
1-2 .... Colorado
4-5-6 .... Milwaukee
8-9-10 .... *at Boston
11-**12-13** .... *at Yankees
15-16-17 ..... *Tampa Bay
18-19-**20** .... *Toronto
21-22-**23** .... Arizona
25-26-**27** .... *at Seattle

28-29-30 .... at Arizona

JULY
1 .... at Arizona
2-3-**4** .... *Kansas City
5-6-7 .... Houston
8-9-**10-11** .... Colorado
16-17-**18** .... at Houston
19-20 .... at Colorado
21-**22** ...... at San Francisco
23-24-25 .... at Los Angeles
26-27-28-29 . San Francisco
30-31 .... Los Angeles

AUGUST
1 .... Los Angeles
3-4-5 .... Philadelphia
6-7-**8** .... Pittsburgh
10-**11-12** .... at Cubs
13-14-**15** .... at Cincinnati

SAN FRANCISCO GIANTS
SBC Park

■ **Standard Game Times:** 7:15 p.m.; Thurs. 12:35, 7:15; Sat. 1:05, 7:15; Sun. 1:05.

APRIL
5-6-7 .... at Houston
8 .... at San Diego
10-11 .... at San Diego
12-13-**14** .... Milwaukee

16-**17-18** .... Los Angeles
19-20-21-**22** ..... San Diego
23-24-**25** .... at Los Angeles
26-27-28 .... Atlanta
29-30 .... Florida

16-17-18 .... Atlanta
20-21-**22** .... Florida
23-24-25-**26** .... at Mets
27-28-**29** .... at Montreal
31 .... at St. Louis

SEPTEMBER
1-2 .... at St. Louis
3-4-**5** .... Colorado
6-7-**8** .... St. Louis
9-10-**11-12** ..... at Colorado
13-14-15-16 .. at Los Angeles
17-**18-19** .. at San Francisco
21-22-23 .... Los Angeles
24-25-**26** .... Arizona
28-29-30 ..... San Francisco

OCTOBER
1-2-**3** .... at Arizona

MAY
1-**2** .... Florida
4-5-6 .... at Mets
7-**8-9** .... at Cincinnati
11-12-**13** .... Philadelphia
14-**15-16** .... Pittsburgh
18-19-**20** .... at Cubs
21-22-**23** ...... #at Montreal
25-26-27 .... Arizona
28-29-**30** .... Colorado
31 .... at Arizona

JUNE
1-2-3 .... at Arizona
4-5-**6-7** .... at Colorado
8-9-10 .... *at Tampa Bay
11-**12-13** ...... *at Baltimore
15-16-17 .... *Toronto
18-**19-20** .... *Boston
21-22-23-**24** .. Los Angeles
25-26-**27** .... *at Oakland
29-30 .... at Los Angeles

JULY
1 .... at Los Angeles
2-**3-4** .... *Oakland
5-6-7 .... Colorado
8-9-10-**11** .... Arizona
15-16-17-**18** ... at Colorado

19-20 .... at Arizona
21-**22** .... San Diego
23-**24-25** .... at St. Louis
26-27-28-29 . at San Diego
30-31 .... St. Louis

AUGUST
1 .... St. Louis
3-4-**5** .... Cincinnati
6-7-**8** .... Cubs
10-11-12 ...... at Pittsburgh
13-**14-15** .... at Philadelphia
16-17-**18** .... Montreal
20-**21-22** .... Mets
24-25-26 .... at Florida
27-**28-29-30** .... at Atlanta
31 .... Colorado

SEPTEMBER
1-2 .... Colorado
3-4-**5** .... Arizona
7-8 .... at Colorado
10-11-**12** .... at Arizona
14-15-**16** ...... at Milwaukee
17-**18-19** .... San Diego
21-22-23 .... Houston
24-**25-26** .... Los Angeles
28-29-30 .... at San Diego

OCTOBER
1-2-**3** .... at Los Angeles

NOTE: Dates in **bold** indicate afternoon games. All game times are subject to change. Gaps in dates indicate scheduled off-days but may be affected by rainouts.

* Interleague Series
# at San Juan, P.R.

INTERLEAGUE
SCHEDULE

June 7
Cincinnati at Oakland
Houston at Seattle
Pittsburgh at Texas

June 8
Arizona at Baltimore
Atlanta at Detroit
Cincinnati at Oakland
Colorado at New York Yankees
Florida at Cleveland
Houston at Seattle
Los Angeles at Toronto
Milwaukee at Anaheim
Montreal at Kansas City
New York Mets at Minnesota
Philadelphia at Chicago White Sox
Pittsburgh at Texas
San Diego at Boston
San Francisco at Tampa Bay

June 9
Arizona at Baltimore
Atlanta at Detroit
Cincinnati at Oakland
Colorado at New York Yankees
Florida at Cleveland
Houston at Seattle
Los Angeles at Toronto
Milwaukee at Anaheim
Montreal at Kansas City
New York Mets at Minnesota
Philadelphia at Chicago White Sox
Pittsburgh at Texas
San Diego at Boston
San Francisco at Tampa Bay

June 10
Arizona at Baltimore
Atlanta at Detroit
Colorado at New York Yankees
Florida at Cleveland
Los Angeles at Toronto
Milwaukee at Anaheim
Montreal at Kansas City
New York Mets at Minnesota
Philadelphia at Chicago White Sox
San Diego at Boston
San Francisco at Tampa Bay

June 11
Arizona at Toronto
Atlanta at Chicago White Sox
Chicago Cubs at Anaheim
Cincinnati at Cleveland
Colorado at Tampa Bay
Florida at Detroit
Los Angeles at Toronto
Montreal at Seattle
New York Mets at Kansas City
Philadelphia at Minnesota
Pittsburgh at Oakland
St. Louis at Texas

San Diego at New York Yankees
San Francisco at Baltimore

June 12
Arizona at Toronto
Atlanta at Chicago White Sox
Chicago Cubs at Anaheim
Cincinnati at Cleveland
Colorado at Tampa Bay
Florida at Detroit
Los Angeles at Toronto
Montreal at Seattle
New York Mets at Kansas City
Philadelphia at Minnesota
Pittsburgh at Oakland
St. Louis at Texas
San Diego at New York Yankees
San Francisco at Baltimore

June 13
Arizona at Toronto
Atlanta at Chicago White Sox
Chicago Cubs at Anaheim
Cincinnati at Cleveland
Colorado at Tampa Bay
Florida at Detroit
Los Angeles at Toronto
Montreal at Seattle
New York Mets at Kansas City
Philadelphia at Minnesota
Pittsburgh at Oakland
St. Louis at Texas
San Diego at New York Yankees
San Francisco at Baltimore

June 15
Anaheim at Pittsburgh
Baltimore at Los Angeles
Boston at Colorado
Chicago White Sox at Florida
Cleveland at New York Mets
Detroit at Philadelphia
Kansas City at Atlanta
Minnesota at Montreal
New York Yankees at Arizona
Oakland at St. Louis
Seattle at Milwaukee
Tampa Bay at San Diego
Texas at Cincinnati
Toronto at San Francisco

June 16
Anaheim at Pittsburgh
Baltimore at Los Angeles
Boston at Colorado
Chicago White Sox at Florida
Cleveland at New York Mets
Detroit at Philadelphia
Kansas City at Atlanta
Minnesota at Montreal
New York Yankees at Arizona
Oakland at St. Louis
Seattle at Milwaukee

Tampa Bay at San Diego
Texas at Cincinnati
Toronto at San Francisco

June 17
Anaheim at Pittsburgh
Baltimore at Los Angeles
Boston at Colorado
Chicago White Sox at Florida
Cleveland at New York Mets
Detroit at Philadelphia
Kansas City at Atlanta
Minnesota at Montreal
New York Yankees at Arizona
Oakland at St. Louis
Seattle at Milwaukee
Tampa Bay at San Diego
Texas at Cincinnati
Toronto at San Francisco

June 18
Anaheim at Houston
Baltimore at Colorado
Boston at San Francisco
Chicago White Sox at Montreal
Cleveland at Atlanta
Detroit at New York Mets
Kansas City at Philadelphia
Minnesota at Milwaukee
New York Yankees at Los Angeles
Oakland at Chicago Cubs
Seattle at Pittsburgh
Tampa Bay at Arizona
Texas at Florida
Toronto at San Diego

June 19
Anaheim at Houston
Baltimore at Colorado
Boston at San Francisco
Chicago White Sox at Montreal
Cleveland at Atlanta
Detroit at New York Mets
Kansas City at Philadelphia
Minnesota at Milwaukee
New York Yankees at Los Angeles
Oakland at Chicago Cubs
Seattle at Pittsburgh
Tampa Bay at Arizona
Texas at Florida
Toronto at San Diego

June 20
Anaheim at Houston
Baltimore at Colorado
Boston at San Francisco
Chicago White Sox at Montreal
Cleveland at Atlanta
Detroit at New York Mets
Kansas City at Philadelphia
Minnesota at Milwaukee
New York Yankees at Los Angeles
Oakland at Chicago Cubs

Seattle at Pittsburgh
Tampa Bay at Arizona
Texas at Florida
Toronto at San Diego

June 25
Anaheim at Los Angeles
Arizona at Detroit
Atlanta at Baltimore
Chicago Cubs at Chicago White Sox
Colorado at Cleveland
Florida at Tampa Bay
Houston at Texas
Milwaukee at Minnesota
Montreal at Toronto
New York Mets at New York Yankees
Philadelphia at Boston
St. Louis at Kansas City
San Diego at Seattle
San Francisco at Oakland

June 26
Anaheim at Los Angeles
Arizona at Detroit
Atlanta at Baltimore
Chicago Cubs at Chicago White Sox
Colorado at Cleveland
Florida at Tampa Bay
Houston at Texas
Milwaukee at Minnesota
Montreal at Toronto
New York Mets at New York Yankees
Philadelphia at Boston
St. Louis at Kansas City

San Diego at Seattle
San Francisco at Oakland

June 27
Anaheim at Los Angeles
Arizona at Detroit
Atlanta at Baltimore
Chicago Cubs at Chicago White Sox
Colorado at Cleveland
Florida at Tampa Bay
Houston at Texas
Milwaukee at Minnesota
Montreal at Toronto
New York Mets at New York Yankees
Philadelphia at Boston
St. Louis at Kansas City
San Diego at Seattle
San Francisco at Oakland

July 2
Baltimore at Philadelphia
Boston at Atlanta
Chicago White Sox at Chicago Cubs
Cleveland at Cincinnati
Detroit at Colorado
Kansas City at San Diego
Los Angeles at Anaheim
Minnesota at Arizona
New York Yankees at New York Mets
Oakland at San Francisco
Seattle at St. Louis
Tampa Bay at Florida
Texas at Houston
#Toronto at Montreal

July 3
Baltimore at Philadelphia
Boston at Atlanta
Chicago White Sox at Chicago Cubs
Cleveland at Cincinnati
Detroit at Colorado
Kansas City at San Diego
Los Angeles at Anaheim
Minnesota at Arizona
New York Yankees at New York Mets
Oakland at San Francisco
Seattle at St. Louis
Tampa Bay at Florida
Texas at Houston
#Toronto at Montreal

July 4
Baltimore at Philadelphia
Boston at Atlanta
Chicago White Sox at Chicago Cubs
Cleveland at Cincinnati
Detroit at Colorado
Kansas City at San Diego
Los Angeles at Anaheim
Minnesota at Arizona
New York Yankees at New York Mets
Oakland at San Francisco
Seattle at St. Louis
Tampa Bay at Florida
Texas at Houston
#Toronto at Montreal

At San Juan, P.R.

SPRING TRAINING
ARIZONA CACTUS LEAGUE

ANAHEIM ANGELS
Major League Club
Complex Address (first year): Diablo Stadium (1993), 2200 W. Alameda, Tempe, AZ 85282. Telephone: (602) 438-4300. FAX: (602) 438-7950. **Seating Capacity:** 9,785. **Location:** I-10 to exit 153B (48th Street), south one mile on 48th Street to Alameda Drive, left on Alameda.

Minor League Clubs
Complex Address: Gene Autry Park, 4125 E. McKellips, Mesa, AZ 85205. Telephone: (480) 830-4137. FAX: (480) 438-7950. **Hotel Address:** Lake View Apartments, 1849 S. Power Rd., Mesa, AZ 85206.

ARIZONA DIAMONDBACKS
Major League Club
Complex Address (first year): Tucson Electric Park (1998), 2500 Ajo Way, Tucson, AZ 85713. Telephone: (520) 434-1400. FAX: (520) 434-1443. **Seating Capacity:** 11,000. **Location:** I-10 to exit 262 (Park Street) or 263 (Kino Street), south to Ajo Way, left (east) on Ajo Way to park.
Hotel Address: Radisson Suites, 6555 E. Speedway, Tucson, AZ 85710. Telephone: (520) 721-7100.

Minor League Clubs
Complex Address: Kino Veterans Memorial Sportspark, 3600 S. Country Club, Tucson, AZ 85713. Telephone: (520) 434-1400. FAX: (520) 434-1443. **Hotel Address:** Holiday Inn, 181 W. Broadway, Tucson, AZ 85701. Telephone: (520) 624-8711.

CHICAGO CUBS
Major League Club
Complex Address (first year): HoHoKam Park (1979), 1235 N. Center St., Mesa, AZ 85201. Telephone: (480) 668-0500. FAX: (480) 668-4541. **Seating Capacity:** 8,963. **Location:** Main Street (U.S. Highway 60) to Center Street, north 1½ miles on Center Street.
Hotel Address: Best Western Dobson Ranch Inn, 1666 S. Dobson Rd., Mesa, AZ 85202. Telephone: (480) 831-7000.

Minor League Clubs
Complex Address: Fitch Park, 160 E. Sixth Place, Mesa, AZ 85201. Telephone: (480) 668-0500. FAX: (480) 668-4501. **Hotel Address:** Best Western Mezona, 250 W. Main St., Mesa, AZ 85201. Telephone: (480) 834-9233.

CHICAGO WHITE SOX
Major League Club
Complex Address (first year): Tucson Electric Park (1998), 2500 E. Ajo Way, Tucson, AZ 85713. Telephone: (520) 434-1300. FAX: (520) 434-1151. **Seating Capacity:** 11,000. **Location:** I-10 to exit 262 (Park Street) or 263 (Kino Street), south to Ajo Way, left (east) on Ajo Way to park.
Hotel Address: Doubletree Guest Suites, 6555 E. Speedway Blvd., Tucson, AZ 85710. Telephone: (520) 721-7100.

Minor League Clubs
Complex Address: Same as major league club. **Hotel Address:** Ramada Palo Verde, 5251 S. Julian Dr., Tucson, AZ 85706. Telephone: (520) 294-5250.

COLORADO ROCKIES
Major League Club
Complex Address (first year): Hi Corbett Field (1993), 3400 E. Camino Campestre, Tucson, AZ 85716. Telephone: (520) 322-4500. **Seating Capacity:** 9,500. **Location:** I-10 to Broadway exit, east on Broadway to Randolph Park.
Hotel Address: Hilton Tucson East, 7600 Broadway, Tucson, AZ 85710.

Minor League Clubs
Complex Address: Same as major league club. **Hotel Address:** Clarion Hotel, 102 N. Alvernon, Tucson, AZ 85711. Telephone: (520) 795-0330.

KANSAS CITY ROYALS
Major League Club
Complex Address (first year): Surprise Stadium (2003), 15946 N. Bullard Ave., Surprise, AZ 85374. **Telephone:** (623) 266-8000. **FAX:** (623) 266-8012. **Seating Capacity:** 10,700. **Location:** I-10 West to Route 101 North, 101 North to Bell Road, left on Bell for five miles, stadium on left.
Hotel Address: Wingate Inn & Suites, 1188 N. Dysart Rd., Avondale, AZ 85323. Telephone: (623) 547-1313.

Minor League Clubs
Complex/Hotel Address: Same as major league club.

MILWAUKEE BREWERS
Major League Club
Complex Address (first year): Maryvale Baseball Park (1998), 3600 N. 51st Ave., Phoenix, AZ 85031. Telephone: (623) 245-5555. FAX: (623) 247-7404. **Seating Capacity:** 9,000. **Location:** I-10 to exit 139 (51st Ave.), north on 51st Ave.; I-17 to exit 202 (Indian School Road), west on Indian School Road.
Hotel Address: Sheraton Four Points, 10220 N. Metro Parkway East, Phoenix, AZ 85051. Telephone: (623) 997-5900.

Minor League Clubs
Complex Address: Maryvale Baseball Complex, 3805 N. 53rd Ave., Phoenix, AZ 85031. Telephone: (623) 245-5600. FAX: (623) 849-8941. **Hotel Address:** Town Place Suites, 5223 S. Priest Dr., Tempe, AZ 85283. Telephone: (480) 345-7889.

OAKLAND ATHLETICS
Major League Club
Complex Address (first year): Phoenix Municipal Stadium (1982), 5999 E. Van Buren, Phoenix, AZ 85008. Telephone: (602) 225-9400. FAX: (602) 225-9473. **Seating Capacity:** 8,500. **Location:** I-10 to exit 153 (48th Street), HoHoKam Expressway to Van Buren Street (U.S. Highway 60), right on Van Buren; park two miles on right.
Hotel Address: Doubletree Suites Hotel, 320 N. 44th St., Phoenix, AZ 85008. Telephone: (602) 225-0500.
Minor League Clubs
Complex Address: Papago Park Baseball Complex, 1802 N. 64th St., Phoenix, AZ 85008. Telephone: (480) 949-5951. FAX: (480) 945-0557. **Hotel Address:** Fairfield Inn, 5101 N. Scottsdale Rd., Scottsdale, AZ 85251. Telephone: (480) 945-4392.

SAN DIEGO PADRES
Major League Club
Complex Address (first year): Peoria Sports Complex (1994), 8131 W. Paradise Lane, Peoria, AZ 85382. Telephone: (623) 486-7000. FAX: (623) 412-9382. **Seating Capacity:** 10,000. **Location:** I-17 to Bell Road exit, west on Bell to 83rd Ave.
Hotel Address: Comfort Suites, 8473 W. Paradise Lane, Peoria, AZ 85382. Telephone: (623) 334-3993.
Minor League Clubs
Complex Address: Same as major league club.
Hotel Address: Sheraton Crescent, 2620 W. Dunlap Ave., Phoenix, AZ 85021. Telephone: (623) 943-8200.

SAN FRANCISCO GIANTS
Major League Club
Complex Address (first year): Scottsdale Stadium (1981), 7408 E. Osborn Rd., Scottsdale, AZ 85251. Telephone: (480) 990-7972. FAX: (480) 990-2643. **Seating Capacity:** 10,500. **Location:** Scottsdale Road to Osborne Road, east on Osborne ½ mile.
Hotel Address: Courtyard Marriott, 3311 N. Scottsdale Rd., Scottsdale, AZ 85251. Telephone: (480) 429-7785.
Minor League Clubs
Complex Address: Indian School Park, 4415 N. Hayden Road at Camelback Road, Scottsdale, AZ 85251. Telephone: (480) 990-0052. FAX: (480) 990-2349.
Hotel Address: Days Inn, 4710 N. Scottsdale Rd., Scottsdale, AZ 85351. Telephone: (480) 947-5411.

SEATTLE MARINERS
Major League Club
Complex Address (first year): Peoria Sports Complex (1993), 15707 N. 83rd Ave., Peoria, AZ 85382. Telephone: (623)776-4800. FAX: (623) 776-4829. **Seating Capacity:** 10,000. **Location:** I-17 to Bell Road exit, west on Bell to 83rd Ave.
Hotel Address: LaQuinta Inn & Suites, 16321 N. 83rd Ave., Peoria, AZ 85382 **Telephone:** (623) 487-1900.
Minor League Clubs
Complex Address: Peoria Sports Complex (1993), 15707 N. 83rd Ave., Peoria, AZ 85382. **Telephone:** (602) 412-9000. **FAX:** (602) 412-9382.
Hotel Address: Hampton Inn, 8408 W. Paradise Lane, Peoria, AZ 85382. Telephone: (623) 486-9918.

TEXAS RANGERS
Major League Club
Complex Address (first year): Surprise Stadium (2003), 15754 N. Bullard Ave., Surprise, AZ 85374. **Telephone:** (623) 266-9600. **FAX:** (623) 266-8120. **Seating Capacity:** 10,714. **Location:** I-10 West to Route 101 North, 101 North to Bell Road, left at Bell for five miles, stadium on left.
Hotel Address: Windmill Suites at Sun City West, 12545 W. Bell Rd., Surprise, AZ 85374. Telephone: (623) 583-0133.
Minor League Clubs
Complex Address: Same as major league club.
Hotel Address: Hampton Inn, 2000 N. Litchfield Rd., Goodyear, AZ 85338. Telephone: (623) 536-1313.

FLORIDA GRAPEFRUIT LEAGUE

ATLANTA BRAVES
Major League Club
Stadium Address (first year): Disney's Wide World of Sports Complex (1998), Cracker Jack Stadium, 700 S. Victory Way, Kissimmee, FL 34747. Telephone: (407) 939-2200. **Seating Capacity:** 9,500. **Location:** I-4 to exit 25B (Highway 192 West), follow signs to Magic Kingdom/Wide World of Sports Complex, right on Victory Way.
Hotel Address: World Center Marriott, World Center Drive, Orlando, FL 32821. Telephone: (407) 239-4200.
Minor League Clubs
Complex Address: Same as major league club. Telephone: (407) 939-2232. FAX: (407) 939-2225. **Hotel Address:** Days Suites, 5820 W. Hwy. 92, Kissimmee, FL 34746. Telephone: (407) 396-7900.

BALTIMORE ORIOLES
Major League Club
Complex Address (first year): Fort Lauderdale Stadium (1996), 1301 NW 55th St., Fort Lauderdale, FL 33309. Telephone: (954) 776-1921. FAX: (954) 776-9116. **Seating Capacity:** 8,340. **Location:** I-95 to exit 32 (Commercial Blvd.), West on Commercial, right on Orioles Blvd. (NW 55th Street), stadium on left.

Hotel Address: Sheraton Suites, 555 NW 62nd St., Fort Lauderdale, FL 33309. Telephone: (954) 772-5400.
Minor League Clubs
Complex Address: Twin Lakes Park, 6700 Clark Rd., Sarasota, FL 34241. Telephone: (941) 923-1996. FAX: (941) 922-3751. **Hotel Address:** Ramada Inn Osprey, 1660 S. Tamiami Trail, Sarasota, FL 34229. Telephone: (941) 966-2121.

BOSTON RED SOX
Major League Club
Complex Address (first year): City of Palms Park (1993), 2201 Edison Ave., Fort Myers, FL 33901. Telephone: (239) 334-4799. FAX: (239) 334-6060. **Seating Capacity:** 6,990. **Location:** I-75 to exit 39, three miles west to Tuttle Ave., right on Tuttle to 12th Street, stadium on left.
Hotel Address: Homewood Suites Hotel, 5255 Big Pine Way, Fort Myers, FL 33907. Telephone: (239) 275-6000.
Minor League Clubs
Complex Address: Red Sox Minor League Complex, 4301 Edison Ave., Fort Myers, FL 33916. Telephone: (239) 461-4500. FAX: (239) 332-8107. **Hotel Address:** Ramada Inn, 2500 Edwards Dr., Fort Myers, FL 33901. Telephone: (239) 337-0300.

CINCINNATI REDS
Major League Club
Complex Address (first year): Ed Smith Stadium (1998), 12th Street and Tuttle Avenue, Sarasota, FL 34237. Telephone: (941) 955-6501. FAX: (941) 955-6365. **Seating Capacity:** 7,500. **Location:** I-75 to exit 39, west on Fruitville Road (Route 780) for four miles, right on Tuttle.
Hotel Address: Marriott Residence Inn, 1040 University Pkwy., Sarasota, FL 34234. Telephone: (941) 358-1468. FAX: (941) 358-0850.
Minor League Clubs
Complex Address: Same as major league club. **Hotel Address:** Wellesley Inn, 1803 N. Tamiami Trail, Sarasota, FL 34234. Telephone: (941) 366-5128.

CLEVELAND INDIANS
Major League Club
Complex Address: Chain O' Lakes Park (1993), Cypress Gardens Blvd. at U.S. 17, Winter Haven, FL 33880. Telephone: (863) 293-5405. FAX: (863) 291-5772. **Seating Capacity:** 7,000. **Location:** U.S. 17 (3rd Street) south through Winter Haven to Cypress Gardens Blvd.
Hotel Address: Holiday Inn, 1150 Third St. SW, Winter Haven, FL 33880. Telephone: (863) 294-4451.
Minor League Clubs
Complex Address/Hotel: Same as major league club.

DETROIT TIGERS
Major League Club
Complex Address (first year): Joker Marchant Stadium (1946), 2301 Lakeland Hills Blvd., Lakeland, FL 33805. Telephone: (863) 686-8075. FAX: (863) 688-9589. **Seating Capacity:** 9,000. **Location:** I-4 to exit 19 (Lakeland Hills Blvd.), left 1½ miles.
Hotel Address: Wellesley Inn, 3520 Hwy. 98 N., Lakeland, FL 33805. Telephone: (863) 859-3399.
Minor League Clubs
Complex/Hotel Address: Tigertown, 2125 N. Lake Ave., Lakeland, FL 33805. Telephone: (863) 686-8075. FAX: (863) 688-9589.

FLORIDA MARLINS
Major League Club
Complex Address (first year): Roger Dean Stadium (1998), 4751 Main St., Jupiter, FL 33458. Telephone: (561) 775-1818. **Seating Capacity:** 7,000. **Location:** I-95 to exit 58, east on Donald Ross Road for ¼ mile.

Hotel Address: Hampton Inn, 401 RCA Blvd., Palm Beach Gardens, FL 33410. Telephone: 561-625-8880. FAX: (561) 625-6766.
Minor League Clubs
Complex Address: Same as major league club.
Hotel Address: Fairfield Inn, 6748 W. Indiantown Road, Jupiter, FL 33458. Telephone: (561) 748-5252.

HOUSTON ASTROS
Major League Club
Complex Address (first year): Osceola County Stadium (1985), 631 Heritage Park Way, Kissimmee, FL 34744. Telephone: (321) 697-3150. FAX: (321) 697-3199. **Seating Capacity:** 5,300. **Location:** From Florida Turnpike South, take exit 244, west on U.S. 192, right on Bill Beck Boulevard; From Florida Turnpike North, take exit 242, west on U.S. 192, right on Bill Beck Blvd.; From I-4, take exit onto 192 East for 12 miles, stadium on left; From 17-92 South, take U.S. 192, left for three miles.
Minor League Clubs
Complex Address: 1000 Bill Beck Blvd., Kissimmee, FL 34744. Telephone: (321) 697-3100. FAX: (321) 697-3195. **Hotel Address:** Four Points Sheraton, 4018 West Vine St. (U.S. 192), Kissimmee, FL 34741. Telephone: (321) 870-2000.

LOS ANGELES DODGERS
Major League Club
Complex Address (first year): Holman Stadium (1948). **Seating Capacity:** 6,500. **Location:** Exit I-95 to Route 60 East, left on 43rd Avenue, right on 26th Street.
Hotel Address: Dodgertown, 4001 26th St., Vero Beach, FL 32960. Telephone: (772) 569-4900. FAX: (772) 567-0819.
Minor League Clubs
Complex/Hotel Address: Same as major league club.

MINNESOTA TWINS
Major League Club
Complex Address (first year): Lee County Sports Complex/Hammond Stadium (1991), 14100 Six Mile Cypress Pkwy., Fort Myers, FL 33912. Telephone: (239) 768-4282. FAX: (239) 768-4211. **Seating Capacity:** 7,500. **Location:** Exit 21 off I-75, west on Daniels Parkway, left on Six Mile Cypress Parkway.
Hotel Address: Radisson Inn, 12635 Cleveland Ave., Fort Myers, FL 33907. Telephone: (239) 936-4300.
Minor League Clubs
Complex Address/Hotel: Same as major league club.

MONTREAL EXPOS
Major League Club
Complex Address (first year): Space Coast Stadium (2003), 5800 Stadium Pkwy., Viera, FL 32940. Telephone: (321) 633-9200. **Seating Capacity:** 7,200. **Location:** I-95 southbound to Fiske Blvd. (exit 74), south on Fiske/Stadium Parkway to stadium; I-95 northbound to State Road #509/Wickham Road (exit 73), left off exit, right on Lake Andrew Drive and follow to complex.
Hotel Address: Melbourne Airport Hilton, 200 Rialto Place, Melbourne, FL 32901. Telephone: (321) 768-0200
Minor League Clubs
Complex Address: Carl Berger Complex, 5600 Stadium Pkwy., Viera, FL 32940. **Telephone:** (321) 633-8119. **Hotel Address:** Imperial Hotel & Conference Center, 8298 N. Wickman Rd., Viera, FL 32940. Telephone: (321) 255-0077.

NEW YORK METS
Major League Club
Complex Address (first year): Tradition Field (1987), 525 NW Peacock Blvd., Port St. Lucie, FL 34986. Telephone: (772) 871-2100. FAX: (772) 878-9802. **Seating Capacity:** 7,347. **Location:** Exit 121 (St. Lucie West Boulevard) off I-95, east ½ mile, left on NW Peacock Boulevard.
Hotel Address: Holiday Inn, 10120 South Federal Hwy., Port St. Lucie, FL 34952. Telephone: (772) 337-2200.
Minor League Clubs
Complex/Hotel Address: Same as major league club. Telephone: (772) 871-2152.

NEW YORK YANKEES
Major League Club
Complex Address (first year): Legends Field (1996), One Steinbrenner Dr., Tampa, FL 33614. Telephone: (813) 875-7753. FAX: (813) 673-3199. **Seating Capacity:** 10,000. **Location:** I-275 to Martin Luther King, west on Martin Luther King to Dale Mabry.
Hotel Address: Radisson Bay Harbor Inn, 770 Courtney Campbell Causeway, Tampa, FL 33607. Telephone: (813) 281-8900.
Minor League Clubs
Complex Address: Yankees Player Development/Scouting Complex, 3102 N. Himes Ave., Tampa, FL 33607. Telephone: (813) 875-7569. FAX: (813) 873-2302. **Hotel Address:** Holiday Inn Express, 4732 N. Dale Mabry, Tampa, FL 33614.

PHILADELPHIA PHILLIES
Major League Club
Complex Address (first year): Bright House Networks Field (2004), 601 N. Old Coachman Rd., Clearwater, FL 33765. Telephone: (727) 467-4457. **FAX:** (727) 712-4498. **Seating Capacity:** 8,500. **Location:** U.S. Highway 19 North, left on Drew Street, right on Old Coachman Road, ballpark on right.
Hotel: None.
Minor League Clubs
Complex Address: Carpenter Complex, 651 N. Old Coachman Rd., Clearwater, FL 33765. Telephone: (727) 799-0503. FAX: (727) 726-1793. **Hotel Addresses:** Hampton Inn, 21030 U.S. Highway 19 North, Clearwater, FL 34625. Telephone: (727) 797-8173; Econolodge, 21252 U.S. Highway 19, Clearwater, FL 34625. Telephone: (727) 799-1569.

PITTSBURGH PIRATES
Major League Club
Stadium Address (first year): McKechnie Field

(1969), 17th Ave. West and Ninth Street West, Bradenton, FL 34205. **Seating Capacity:** 6,562. **Location:** U.S. 41 to 17th Ave, west to 9th Street.
Complex/Hotel Address: Pirate City, 1701 27th St. E., Bradenton, FL 34208. Telephone: (941) 747-3031. FAX: (941) 747-9549.
Minor League Clubs
Complex/Hotel Address: Same as major league club.

ST. LOUIS CARDINALS
Major League Club
Complex Address (first year): Roger Dean Stadium (1998), 4795 University Dr., Jupiter, FL 33458. Telephone: (561) 775-1818. FAX: (561) 799-1380. **Seating Capacity:** 6,871. **Location:** I-95 to exit 58, east on Donald Ross Road for ¼ mile.
Hotel Address: Palm Beach Gardens Marriott, 4000 RCA Blvd., Palm Beach Gardens, FL 33410. Telephone: (561) 622-8888.
Minor League Clubs
Complex: Same as major league club. **Hotel:** Doubletree Hotel, 4431 PGA Blvd., Palm Beach Gardens, FL 33410. Telephone: (561) 622-2260.

TAMPA BAY DEVIL RAYS
Major League Club
Stadium Address (first year): Progress Energy Park/Home of Al Lang Field (1998), 180 Second Ave. SE, St. Petersburg, FL 33701. Telephone: (727) 825-3137. FAX: (727) 825-3167. **Seating Capacity:** 6,438. **Location:** I-275 to exit 23C, left on First Street South to Second Avenue South, stadium on right.
Complex/Hotel Address: Raymond A. Naimoli Complex, 7901 30th Ave. N., St. Petersburg, FL 33710. Telephone: (727) 384-5517.
Minor League Clubs
Complex/Hotel Address: Same as major league club.

TORONTO BLUE JAYS
Major League Club
Stadium Address (first year): Knology Park (1977), 373 Douglas Ave. #A, Dunedin, FL 34698. Telephone: (727) 733-9302. **Seating Capacity:** 5,509. **Location:** From I-275, north on Highway 19, left on Sunset Point Road for 4 miles, right on Douglas Avenue, stadium one mile on right.
Minor League Clubs
Complex Address: Bobby Mattick Training Facility at Englebert Complex, 1700 Solon Ave., Dunedin, FL 34698. Telephone: (727) 743-8007. **Hotel Address:** Red Roof Inn, 3200 U.S. 19 N., Clearwater, FL 34684. Telephone: (727) 786-2529.

MEDIA
INFO

MEDIA INFORMATION

ANAHEIM ANGELS
Radio Announcers: English—Rory Markas, Terry Smith. Spanish—Ivan Lara, Jose Mota. **Flagship Station:** KSPN 710-AM, KTWQ 1090-AM (Spanish).
TV Announcers: Rex Hudler, Steve Physioc. **Flagship Stations:** KCAL Channel 9, Fox Sports Net (regional cable).
NEWSPAPERS, Daily Coverage (beat writers): Long Beach Press-Telegram, Los Angeles Times (Ross Newhan, Mike DiGiovanna), Orange County Register (Mark Saxon), Riverside Press-Enterprise (Matt Tresaugue), San Gabriel Valley Tribune (Joe Haakenson), Inland Valley Daily Bulletin.

BALTIMORE ORIOLES
Radio Announcers: Jim Hunter, Fred Manfra, Chuck Thompson. **Flagship Station:** WBAL 1090-AM.
TV Announcers: Jim Palmer, Michael Reghi. **Flagship Stations:** WJZ-TV, WNUV-TV, Comcast SportsNet.
NEWSPAPERS, Daily Coverage (beat writers): Baltimore Sun (Joe Christensen, Roch Kubatko), Washington Post (Dave Sheinin), Washington Times (Duff Durkin), York, Pa., Daily Record (Dan Connolly).

BOSTON RED SOX
Radio Announcers: Joe Castiglione, Jerry Trupiano. **Flagship Station:** WEEI 850-AM.
TV Announcers: WSBK 38—Sean McDonough, Jerry Remy; NESN—Don Orsillo, Jerry Remy. **Flagship Stations:** WSBK 38, New England Sports Network (regional cable).
NEWSPAPERS, Daily Coverage (beat writers): Boston Globe (Bob Hohler, Gordon Edes), Boston Herald (Howard Bryant, Jeff Horrigan, Tony Massarotti, Mike Silverman), Providence Journal (Steve Krasner, Sean McAdam), Worcester Telegram (Bill Ballou, Phil O'Neill), Hartford Courant (Paul Doyle, Dave Heuschkel).

CHICAGO WHITE SOX
Radio Announcers: John Rooney, Ed Farmer. **Flagship Station:** WMVP/ESPN Radio 1000-AM.
TV Announcers: Ken Harrelson, Darrin Jackson. **Flagship Stations:** WGN TV-9, WCIU-TV, FOX Sports Net Chicago (regional cable).
NEWSPAPERS, Daily Coverage (beat writers): Chicago Sun-Times (Doug Padilla), Chicago Tribune, Arlington Heights Daily Herald (Scot Gregor), Daily Southtown (Joe Cowley).

CLEVELAND INDIANS
Radio Announcers: Tom Hamilton, Mike Hegan, Matt Underwood. **Flagship Station:** WTAM 1100-AM.
TV Announcers: Rick Manning, John Sanders, Mike Hegan. **Flagship Station:** Fox Sports Net.
NEWSPAPERS, Daily Coverage (beat writers): Cleveland Plain Dealer (Paul Hoynes), Lake County News-Herald (Jim Ingraham), Akron Beacon-Journal (Sheldon Ocker), Canton Repository (Andy Call).

DETROIT TIGERS
Radio Announcers: Dan Dickerson, Jim Price. **Flagship Station:** WXYT 1270-AM.
TV Announcers: Rod Allen, Mario Impemba. **Flagship Station:** Fox Sports Net Detroit (regional cable).
NEWSPAPERS, Daily Coverage (beat writers): Detroit Free Press (John Lowe, Gene Guidi), Detroit News (Tom Gage), Oakland Press (Crystal Evola, Pat Caputo), Booth Newspapers (Danny Knobler), Windsor Star (Jim Parker).

KANSAS CITY ROYALS
Radio Announcers: Ryan Lefebvre, Denny Matthews. **Flagship Station:** WHB 810-AM.
TV Announcers: Bob Davis, Paul Splittorff. **Flagship Stations:** Royals Television Network.
NEWSPAPERS, Daily Coverage (beat writers): Kansas City Star (Dick Kaegel, Bob Dutton), MLB.com (Chris Shaeffer, Robert Falkoff).

MINNESOTA TWINS
Radio Announcers: Herb Carneal, John Gordon, Dan Gladden. **Flagship Station:** WCCO 830-AM.
TV Announcers: Bert Blyleven, Dick Bremer. **Flagship Station:** Victory Sports.
NEWSPAPERS, Daily Coverage (beat writers): St. Paul Pioneer Press (Gordon Wittenmyer), Minneapolis Star Tribune (LaVelle Neal).

NEW YORK YANKEES
Radio Announcers: John Sterling, Charley Steiner. **Flagship Station:** WCBS 880-AM.
TV Announcers: Michael Kay, Jim Kaat, Ken Singleton, Paul O'Neill, Fred Hickman, Suzyn Waldman. **Flagship Stations:** YES! Network (Yankees Entertainment & Sports), WCBS-TV, Ch. 2.
NEWSPAPERS, Daily Coverage (beat writers): New York Daily News (Anthony McCarron), New York Post (George King), New York Times (Tyler Kepner), Newark Star-Ledger (Dan Graziano), The Bergen Record, Newsday (Pete Caldera, Ken Davidoff), Hartford Courant (Dom Amore), The Journal News (John Delcos).

OAKLAND ATHLETICS
Radio Announcers: Bill King, Ray Fosse, Ken Korach. **Flagship Station:** KFRC 610-AM.
TV Announcers: Ray Fosse, Hank Greenwald, Tim Roye, Glen Kuiper. **Flagship Stations:** KICU, FOX Sports Net (regional cable).
NEWSPAPERS, Daily Coverage (beat writers): San Francisco Chronicle (Susan Slusser), Oakland Tribune (Josh Suchon), Contra Costa Times (Rick Hurd), Sacramento Bee (Kevin Yamamura), San Jose Mercury-News (Chris Haft),

Santa Rosa Press Democrat (Jeff Fletcher).

SEATTLE MARINERS

TV/Radio Announcers: Ron Fairly, Dave Henderson, Dave Niehaus, Rick Rizzs, Dave Valle.
Flagship Stations: KOMO 1000-AM (radio), FOX Sports Net Northwest (TV).
NEWSPAPERS, Daily Coverage (beat writers): Seattle Times (Bob Finnigan, Larry Stone), Seattle Post-Intelligencer (John Hickey), Tacoma News Tribune (Larry LaRue), The Everett Herald (Kirby Arnold), Kyodo News (Keizo Konishi), Nikkan Sports (Mamoru Shikama), MLB.com (Jim Street).

TAMPA BAY DEVIL RAYS

Radio Announcers: Paul Olden, Charlie Slowes. **Flagship Station:** WFLA 970-AM.
TV Announcers: DeWayne Staats, Joe Magrane. **Flagship Stations:** PAX-TV Fox SportsNet (regional cable).
NEWSPAPERS, Daily Coverage (beat writers): St. Petersburg Times (Marc Topkin), Tampa Tribune (Carter Gaddis), Bradenton Herald (Roger Mooney), Port Charlotte Sun-Herald (John Fineran), Lakeland Ledger (Dick Scanlan), Sarasota Herald-Tribune (Dennis Maffazoli).

TEXAS RANGERS

Radio Announcers: English—Eric Nadel, Victor Rojas; Spanish—Eleno Ornelas, Jose Guzman. **Flagship Station:** KRLD 1080-AM (English), KESS 1270-AM (Spanish).
TV Announcers: Josh Lewin, Tom Grieve. **Flagship Stations:** KDFI, KDFW, Fox Sports Southwest (regional cable).
NEWSPAPERS, Daily Coverage (beat writers): Dallas Morning News (Evan Grant, Ken Daley), Fort Worth Star-Telegram (T.R. Sullivan, Kathleen O'Brien), MLB.com (Jesse Sanchez).

TORONTO BLUE JAYS

Radio Announcers: Tom Cheek, Jerry Howarth. **Flagship Station:** The Fan 590-AM.
TV Announcers: Sportsnet—Rob Faulds, John Cerutti, Tom Candiotti. TSN—Rod Black, Pat Tabler. **Flagship Stations:** Rogers SportsNet (cable), The Sports Network.
NEWSPAPERS, Daily Coverage (beat writers): Toronto Sun (Mike Rutsey, Bob Elliott, Mike Ganter), Toronto Star (Geoff Baker, Richard Griffin, Alan Ryan, Mark Zwolinski), Globe and Mail (Larry Millson, Jeff Blair).

NATIONAL LEAGUE

ARIZONA DIAMONDBACKS

Radio Announcers: English—Thom Brennaman, Jeff Munn, Ken Phelps, Greg Schulte; Spanish—Miguel Quintana, Oscar Soria, Richard Saenz. **Flagship Stations:** KTAR 620-AM (English), KSUN 1400-AM (Spanish).
TV Announcers: Thom Brennaman, Mark Grace, Joe Garagiola, Greg Schulte. **Flagship Stations:** KTVK-TV 3, FOX Sports Net Arizona (regional cable).
Newspapers, Daily Coverage (beat writers): Arizona Republic (Bob McManaman), East Valley Tribune (Ed Price), Arizona Daily Star (Jack Magruder), Tucson Citizen (Ken Brazzle).

ATLANTA BRAVES

Radio Announcers: Skip Caray, Don Sutton, Joe Simpson, Pete Van Wieren. **Flagship Station:** WSB 750-AM.
TV Announcers: TBS—Skip Caray, Pete Van Wieren, Don Sutton, Joe Simpson; Fox Sports Net—Bob Rathbun, Tom Paciorek. **Flagship Stations:** TBS (national cable); Fox Sports Net South, Turner South (regional cable).
NEWSPAPERS, Daily Coverage (beat writers): Atlanta Journal-Constitution (Guy Cartwright, Dave O'Brien), Morris News (Bill Zack).

CHICAGO CUBS

Radio Announcers: Pat Hughes, Ron Santo. **Flagship Station:** WGN 720-AM.
TV Announcers: Chip Caray, Steve Stone. **Flagship Stations:** WGN Channel 9 (national cable), Fox Sports Net Chicago (regional cable), WCIU-TV Channel 26 (local).
NEWSPAPERS, Daily Coverage (beat writers): Chicago Tribune (Paul Sullivan, Phil Rogers), Chicago Sun-Times (Mike Kiley), Arlington Daily Herald (Bruce Miles), Daily Southtown (Jeff Vorva).

CINCINNATI REDS

Radio Announcers: Mary Brennaman, Joe Nuxhall. **Flagship Station:** WLW 700-AM.
TV Announcers: George Grande, Chris Welsh. **Flagship Station:** Fox Sports Net (regional cable).
NEWSPAPERS, Daily Coverage (beat writers): Cincinnati Enquirer (John Fay), Cincinnati Post (Tony Jackson), Dayton Daily News (Hal McCoy), Columbus Dispatch (Jim Massie).

COLORADO ROCKIES

Radio Announcers: Jack Corrigan, Jeff Kingery. **Flagship Station:** KOA 850-AM.
TV Announcers: Drew Goodman, George Frazier. **Flagship Station:** KTVD Channel 20 (UPN), Fox Sports Net (regional cable).
NEWSPAPERS, Daily Coverage (beat writers): Rocky Mountain News (Tracy Ringolsby, Jack Etkin), Denver Post (Troy Renck, Mike Klis), Boulder Daily Camera (Barney Hutchinson).

FLORIDA MARLINS

Radio Announcers: English—Jon Sciambi, Dave Van Horne. Spanish—Felo Ramirez, Yiky Quintana. **Flagship Stations:** WQAM 560-AM, WQBA 1140-AM (Spanish).
TV Announcers: Len Kasper, Tommy Hutton. **Flagship Stations:** PAX TV, Fox Sports Net (regional cable).
NEWSPAPERS, Daily Coverage (beat writers): Miami Herald (Kevin Baxter, Clark Spencer), Fort Lauderdale Sun-Sentinel (Mike Berardino, Juan Rodriguez), Palm Beach Post (Joe Capozzi). Spanish—El Nuevo Herald (Jorge Ebro).

HOUSTON ASTROS

Radio Announcers: English—Alan Ashby, Milo Hamilton; Spanish—Francisco Ernesto Ruiz, Alex Trevino. **Flagship Station:** KTRH 740-AM (English).

TV Announcers: Bill Brown, Jim Deshaies, Bill Worrell. **Flagship Station:** Fox Sports Net (regional cable).

NEWSPAPERS, Daily Coverage (beat writers): Houston Chronicle (Jesus Ortiz, Richard Justice), Beaumont Enterprise (Paula Hunt), Port Arthur News (Tom Halliburton), The Herald Coaster (Bill Hartman), MLB.com (Alyson Footer, Jim Molony).

LOS ANGELES DODGERS

Radio Announcers: English—Vin Scully, Rick Monday, Ross Porter; Spanish—Jaime Jarrin, Fernando Valenzuela, Pepe Yniguez. **Flagship Stations:** KFWB 980-AM, KWKW 1330-AM (Spanish).

TV Announcers: Vin Scully, Rick Monday, Ross Porter. **Flagship Station:** KCOP Channel 13, Fox Sports Net 2 (regional cable).

NEWSPAPERS, Daily Coverage (beat writers): Los Angeles Times (Ross Newhan, Jason Reid), South Bay Daily Breeze (Bill Cizek), Los Angeles Daily News (Tony Jackson), Orange County Register (Bill Plunkett), Riverside Press-Enterprise, La Opinion (Carlos Alvarado).

MILWAUKEE BREWERS

Radio Announcers: Bob Uecker, Jim Powell. **Flagship Station:** WTMJ 620-AM.

TV Announcers: Bill Schroeder, Daron Sutton. **Flagship Station:** Fox Sports Net.

NEWSPAPERS, Daily Coverage (beat writers): Milwaukee Journal Sentinel (Tom Haudricourt, Drew Olson).

MONTREAL EXPOS

Radio Announcers: English—Elliott Price, Mitch Melnick. French—Jacques Doucet, Marc Griffin. **Flagship Stations:** TEAM 990-AM (English), COOL 98.5-FM (French).

TV Announcers: French—Denis Casavant, Roger Brulotte. **Flagship Station:** Reseau des sports (RDS).

NEWSPAPERS, Daily Coverage (beat writers): English—Montreal Gazette (Stephanie Myles, Jack Todd, Pat Hickey). French—Canadian Press (Michel Lajeunesse, Richard Milo), La Presse (Marc-Antoine Godin, Pierre Ladouceur, Jean-Francois Begin), Le Journal de Montreal (Serge Touchette, Daniel Cloutier).

NEW YORK METS

Radio Announcers: Gary Cohen, Ed Coleman, Howie Rose. **Flagship Station:** WFAN 660-AM.

TV Announcers: Fran Healy, Keith Hernandez, Ralph Kiner, Matt Loughlin, Dave O'Brien, Ted Robinson, Tom Seaver. **Flagship Stations:** WPIX-TV, Fox Sports New York (regional cable), Madison Square Garden (regional cable).

NEWSPAPERS, Daily Coverage (beat writers): New York Times (Lee Jenkins), New York Daily News, New York Post (Mark Hale), Newsday (Dave Lennon), Newark Star-Ledger (Dave Waldstein), The Bergen Record (Jorge Arangue Jr.), The News Journal (Pete Abraham).

PHILADELPHIA PHILLIES

Radio Announcers: Larry Andersen, Scott Graham, Harry Kalas, Tom McCarthy, Chris Wheeler. **Flagship Station:** WPEN 950-AM.

TV Announcers: Larry Andersen, Harry Kalas, Chris Wheeler. **Flagship Stations:** WPSG UPN-57, Comcast SportsNet (regional cable).

NEWSPAPERS, Daily Coverage (beat writers): Philadelphia Inquirer (Todd Zolecki, Jim Salisbury), Philadelphia Daily News (Paul Hagen, Marcus Hayes), Bucks County Courier Times (Randy Miller), Camden Courier-Post (Kevin Roberts), Delaware County Times (Dennis Deitch), Wilmington News-Journal (Edward de la Fuente), Trenton Times (Chris Edwards).

PITTSBURGH PIRATES

Radio Announcers: Steve Blass, Greg Brown, Lanny Frattare, Bob Walk. **Flagship Station:** KDKA 1020-AM.

TV Announcers: Steve Blass, Greg Brown, Lanny Frattare, Bob Walk. **Flagship Station:** Fox Sports Net Pittsburgh (regional cable).

NEWSPAPERS, Daily Coverage (beat writers): Pittsburgh Post-Gazette (Bob Dvorchak), Pittsburgh Tribune-Review (Joe Rutter), Beaver County Times (John Perrotto).

ST. LOUIS CARDINALS

Radio Announcers: Mike Shannon, Wayne Hagin. **Flagship Station:** KMOX 1120-AM.

TV Announcers: Joe Buck , Al Hrabosky, Dan McLaughlin, Rick Horton, Bob Carpenter. **Flagship Stations:** KPLR Channel 11, Fox Sports Midwest (regional cable).

NEWSPAPER, Daily Coverage (beat writers): St. Louis Post-Dispatch (Joe Strauss, Rick Hummel), Belleville, Ill., News-Democrat (Joe Ostermeier, David Wilhelm).

SAN DIEGO PADRES

Radio Announcers: Jerry Coleman, Ted Leitner. **Flagship Station:** The Mighty 1090-AM.

TV Announcers: Matt Vasgersian, Mark Grant, Rick Sutcliffe. **Flagship Stations:** Channel 4 Padres (cable), KUSI TV-9/51.

NEWSPAPERS, Daily Coverage (beat writers): San Diego Union-Tribune (Tom Krasovic, Bill Center), North County Times (Brian Hiro, John Maffei), Associated Press (Bernie Wilson), MLB.com (Mike Scarr).

SAN FRANCISCO GIANTS

Radio Announcers: Mike Krukow, Duane Kuiper, Jon Miller, Greg Papa, Dave Flemming. **Flagship Station:** KNBR 680-AM.

TV Announcers: FOX—Mike Krukow, Duane Kuiper; KTVU—Jon Miller, Duane Kuiper, Mike Krukow, Greg Papa. **Flagship Stations:** KTVU-TV 2, FOX Sports Net (regional cable).

NEWSPAPERS, Daily Coverage (beat writers): San Francisco Chronicle (Henry Schulman), San Jose Mercury News (David Kiefer), Contra Costa Times (Joe Roderick), Sacramento Bee (Nick Peters), Oakland Tribune (Andrew Baggarly), Santa Rosa Press Democrat (Jeff Fletcher).

NATIONAL MEDIA
INFORMATION

BASEBALL STATISTICS

ELIAS SPORTS BUREAU INC.
Official Major League Statistician

Mailing Address: 500 Fifth Ave., Suite 2140, New York, NY 10110. **Telephone:** (212) 869-1530. **FAX:** (212) 354-0980. **Website:** www.esb.com.
President: Seymour Siwoff.
Executive Vice President: Steve Hirdt. **Vice President:** Peter Hirdt. **Data Processing Manager:** Chris Thorn.

THE SPORTS NETWORK
Official Minor League Statistician

Mailing Address: 2200 Byberry Rd., Suite 200, Hatboro, PA 19040. **Telephone:** (215) 441-8444. **FAX:** (215) 441-5767. **Website:** www.sportsnetwork.com.
President, Chief Executive Officer: Mickey Charles.
Managing Director, Operations: Phil Sokol. **Director, Technology:** Bruce Michaels. **Director, Sales:** Ken Zajac.

SPORTSTICKER-BOSTON
Mailing Address: Boston Fish Pier, West Bldg. #1, Suite 302, Boston, MA 02210. **Telephone:** (617) 951-0070. **FAX:** (617) 737-9960.
Director, Minor League Operations: Jim Keller. **Assistant Director, Minor League Operations:** Michael Walczak. **Programmer Analysts:** John Foley, Walter Kent. **Senior Bureau Manager:** Don Goss. **Bureau Managers:** Bryan Evans, Will Morin, Brian Rabuffetti, Marshall Wright. **Associate Bureau Manager:** Mark Padden. **Associate Bureau Editor:** Jon Mailloux. **Senior Editor:** Joe Barbieri. **Editor:** Matt Santillo.
Historical Consultant: Bill Weiss.

STATS, Inc.
Mailing Address: 8130 Lehigh Ave., Morton Grove, IL 60053. **Telephone:** (847) 583-2100. **FAX:** (847) 470-9140. **Website:** biz.stats.com.
Chief Executive Officer: Gary Walrath. **Senior Vice Presidents:** Steve Byrd, Robert Schur. **Sales:** Jim Capuano, Greg Kirkorsky. **Director, Marketing:** Walter Lis. **Director, Sports Operations:** Allan Spear. **Manager, Baseball Operations:** Jeff Chernow.

TELEVISION NETWORKS

ESPN/ESPN2

- Baseball Tonight
- Sunday Night Baseball
- Monday Night Baseball
- Wednesday Night Doubleheaders
- Wednesday Afternoon Baseball
- Opening Day, Holidays
- Home Run Derby, All-Star Game programming
- Spring Training Games

Mailing Address, ESPN Connecticut: ESPN Plaza, 935 Middle St., Bristol, CT 06010. **Telephone:** (860) 766-2000. **FAX:** (860) 766-2213.
Mailing Address, ESPN New York Executive Offices: 77 W. 66th St., New York, NY, 10023. **Telephone:** (212) 456-7777. **FAX:** (212) 456-2930.
President: George Bodenheimer.
Executive Vice President, Administration: Ed Durso. **Executive VP, Production/Technical Operations:** Steve Anderson. **Executive VP, Programming/Production:** Mark Shapiro.
Senior Vice President/Executive Editor: John Walsh. **Senior VP, Programming:** Len Deluca. **Director, Programming:** Mike Ryan. **Senior VP, Remote Production:** Jed Drake. **Senior Coordinating Producer, Remote Production:** Tim Scanlan. **Coordinating Producer, Remote Production:** Pat Cavanagh. **Senior VPs/Co-Managing Editors, Studio Production:** Bob Eaton, Norby Williamson. **Senior Coordinating Producer, Baseball Tonight:** Jay Levy.

ESPN.com
Vice President, Executive Editor: John Marvel.

ESPN Classic
Executive Producer: Jim Cohen.

ESPN International, ESPN Deportes
Senior Vice President/Managing Director, ESPN International: Russell Wolf. **VP, Operations/International Production:** Jodi Markley.

Communications

Senior Vice Presidents: Rosa Gatti, Chris Laplaca. **Director:** Diane Lamb. **Publicist:** Nate Smeltz.
Commentators, Sunday Night Baseball: Play-by-play—Jon Miller. Analyst—Joe Morgan.
Commentators, ESPN Deportes: Play-by-play—Ernesto Jerez. Analysts— Candy Maldanado Jr., Roberto Clemente Jr.

Other Commentators: Dave Barnett, Chris Berman, Jeff Brantley, Tom Candiotti, Bob Carpenter, Rob Dibble, Peter Gammons, Tony Gwynn, David Justice, Tim Kurkjian, Buck Martinez, Gary Miller, Dave O'Brien, Karl Ravech, Harold Reynolds, Dan Shulman, Jayson Stark, Rick Sutcliffe.

FOX SPORTS

- Saturday Game of the Week
- All-Star Game, 2004-2006
- Division Series, 2004-2006
- American League Championship Series, 2004-2006
- National League Championship Series, 2004-2006
- World Series, 2004-2006

Mailing Address, Los Angeles: Fox Network Center, Building 101, Fifth floor, 10201 West Pico Blvd., Los Angeles, CA 90035. **Telephone:** (310) 369-6000. **FAX:** (310) 969-9467.
Mailing Address, New York: 1211 Avenue of the Americas, 28th Floor, New York, NY 10036. **Telephone:** (212) 556-2500. **FAX:** (212) 354-6902. **Website:** www.foxsports.com.
Chairman/Chief Executive Officer, Fox Sports Television Group: David Hill. **President, Executive Producer:** Ed Goren. **Chief Operating Officer:** Larry Jones. **Executive Vice President, Production/Coordinating Studio Producer:** Scott Ackerson. **Executive VP, Marketing:** Neal Tiles. **Senior VP, Production/Senior Producer:** Bill Brown. **VP, Production:** Jack Simmons. **VP, Operations/MLB on Fox:** Jerry Steinberg. **Director, Production Services/MLB on FOX:** Lynn King. **Studio Producer, MLB on Fox:** Gary Lang. **Studio Director, MLB on Fox:** Bob Levy.
Senior VP, Communcations: Lou D'Ermilio. **Director, Communications:** Dan Bell. **Manager, Communications:** Tim Buckman. **Publicist:** Ileana Pena.
Broadcasters: Thom Brennaman, Joe Buck, Josh Lewin, Kevin Kennedy, Steve Lyons, Tim McCarver, Jeanne Zelasko.

FOX SPORTS NET

- Regional Coverage

Mailing Address: 10201 W. Pico Blvd., Building 101, Los Angeles, CA 90035. **Telephone:** (310) 369-1000. **FAX:** (310) 969-6049.
President, Chief Executive Officer/Fox Sports Television Group: David Hill. **President, Fox Sports Net/Fox Sports Cable Networks:** Bob Thompson. **Chief Operating Officer, Fox Sports Net:** Randy Freer. **President, Advertising Sales, Fox Cable Networks:** Lou LaTorre. **Executive VP, Programming/Production:** George Greenberg. **Manager, Communications:** Justin Simon. **Publicist:** Emily Corliss.

Other Television Networks

ABC SPORTS

Mailing Address: 47 West 66th St., New York, NY 10023. **Telephone:** (212) 456-4878. **FAX:** (212) 456-2877. **Website:** www.abcsports.com.
President, ABC Sports: Howard Katz. **Senior Vice President, Programming:** Loren Matthews. **VP, Media Relations:** Mark Mandel. **Publicist, Media Relations:** Adam Freifeld.

CBS SPORTS

Mailing Address: 51 W. 52nd St., New York, NY 10019. **Telephone:** (212) 975-5230. **FAX:** (212) 975-4063.
President, CBS Sports: Sean McManus. **Executive Producer:** Tony Petitti. **Senior Vice Presidents, Programming:** Mike Aresco, Rob Correa. **Vice President, Communications:** Leslie Anne Wade.

NBC SPORTS

Mailing Address: 30 Rockefeller Plaza, Suite 1558, New York, NY 10112. **Telephone:** (212) 664-2014. **FAX:** (212) 664-6365.
Chairman, NBC Sports: Dick Ebersol. **President, NBC Sports:** Ken Schanzer.
Vice President, Sports Communications: Kevin Sullivan.

Superstations

ROGERS SPORTSNET (Canada)

Mailing Address: 333 Bloor St. East, Toronto, Ontario M4W 1G9. **Telephone:** (416) 332-5600. **FAX:** (416) 332-5767. **Website:** www.sportsnet.ca.
President, Rogers Media: Tony Viner. **President, Rogers Sportsnet:** Doug Beeforth. **Vice President, Communications:** Jan Innes. **Director, Communications/Promotions:** Dave Rashford.

THE SPORTS NETWORK (Canada)

Mailing Address: Bell Globemedia Inc., 9 Channel Nine Court, Scarborough, Ontario M1S 4B5. **Telephone:** (416) 332-5000. **FAX:** (416) 332-4337. **Website:** www.tsn.ca
Executive Producer, News: Marc Milliere. **Senior Vice President, Programming:** Phil King. **Executive Producer:** Paul McLean. **VP, Production:** Rick Chisholm. **Communications Manager:** Andrea Goldstein. **Executive Producer, tsn.ca:** Mike Day.

TBS
(Atlanta Braves)

Mailing Address: One CNN Center, P.O. Box 105366, Atlanta, GA 30348. **Telephone:** (404) 827-1700. **FAX:** (404) 827-1593. **Website:** www.superstation.com.
Executive Producer: Glenn Diamond.

WGN
(Chicago Cubs, Chicago White Sox)

Mailing Address: 2501 W Bradley Pl., Chicago, IL 60618. **Telephone:** (773) 528-2311. **FAX:** (773) 528-6050. **Website:** www.wgntv.com.
Director, Programming: Bob Vorwald.

RADIO NETWORKS

ESPN RADIO

- Game of the Week
- Sunday Night Baseball
- All-Star Game
- Division Series
- League Championship Series
- World Series

Mailing Address: ESPN Plaza, 935 Middle St., Bristol, CT 06010. **Telephone:** (860) 766-2000. **FAX:** (860) 589-5523.
General Manager: Bruce Gilbert. **Executive Producer, Remote Broadcasts:** John Martin. **Chief Engineer:** Tom Evans. **Director, Operations:** Keith Goralski. **Program Director:** Pete Gianesini. **Marketing/Promotions Coordinator:** Janet Alden. **Vice President, Sports/ABC Radio Network:** T. J. Lambert.
Commentators: Joe D'Ambrosio, Dave Barnett, Dave Campbell, Rob Dibble, Jim Durham, Jon Miller, Chris Moore, Joe Morgan, Harold Reynolds, Dan Shulman.

ABC SPORTS RADIO

Mailing Address: 125 West End Ave., Sixth Floor, New York, NY 10023. **Telephone:** (212) 456-5185. **Studio:** (800) 221-4559. **E-Mail Address:** abcsportsradio@abc.com.
Vice President, Radio: Steve Jones. **General Manager, News/Sports:** Michael Rizzo. **Operations Manager:** Cliff Bond. **Producers:** Andrew Bogusch, Eric Duetsch, Howie Karpin, Mike Kirk, Tim McDermott, Yvette Michael, Tushar Saxena. Steve White. **Anchors:** Todd Ant, John Cloghessy, Johnny Holliday.

SPORTING NEWS RADIO NETWORK

Mailing Address: P.O. Box 509, Techny, IL 60082. **Telephone:** (847) 509-1661. **Producers Line:** (800) 224-2004. **FAX:** (847) 509-1677. **Website:** www.sportingnewsradio.com.
President: Chris Brennan. **Executive Vice President, Affiliate Relations:** Chuck Duncan. **Executive VP, Sales:** Bill Peterson. **Sports Directors:** Matt Nahigian, Ryan Williams. **Executive Producers:** Randy Merkin, Jen Williams.

SPORTS BYLINE USA

Mailing Address: 300 Broadway, Suite 8, San Francisco, CA 94133. **Telephone:** (415) 434-8300. **Guest Line:** (800) 358-4457. **Studio Line:** (800) 878-7529. **FAX:** (415) 391-2569. **E-Mail Address:** byline@pacbell.net. **Website:** www.sportsbyline.com.
President: Darren Peck. **Executive Producer:** Alex Murillo.

NEWS ORGANIZATIONS

ASSOCIATED PRESS

Mailing Address: 50 Rockefeller Plaza, New York, NY 10020. **Telephone:** (212) 621-1630. **FAX:** (212) 621-1639. **Website:** www.ap.org.
Sports Editor: Terry Taylor. **Deputy Sports Editor:** Aaron Watson. **Sports Photo Editor:** Mike Feldman. **Baseball Writers:** Ron Blum, Josh Dubow, Ben Walker.

BLOOMBERG SPORTS NEWS

Address: 400 College Road East, P.O. Box 888, Princeton, NJ 08540. **Telephone:** (609) 750-4691. **FAX:** (609) 897-8397.
Sports Editor: Jay Beberman. **Deputy Sports Editor:** Mike Sillup.

CANADIAN PRESS

Mailing Address, Toronto: 36 King St. East, Toronto, Ontario M5C 2L9. **Mailing Address, Montreal:** 215 Saint-Jacques St., Suite 100, Montreal, Quebec H2Y 1M6. **Telephone:** (416) 364-0321 (Toronto), (514) 849-3212 (Montreal). **FAX:** (416) 364-0207 (Toronto), (514) 849-7693 (Montreal). **E-Mail Address:** sports@cp.org.
Sports Editor: Neil Davidson. **Baseball Writer:** Pierre Lebrun. **Sports Writer, Montreal:** Bill Beacon.

SPORTSTICKER

Mailing Address: Harborside Financial Center, 800 Plaza Two, Jersey City, NJ 07311. **Telephone:** (201) 309-1200. **FAX:** (201) 860-9742. **E-Mail Address:** newsroom@sportsticker.com.
News Director: Chris Bernucca. **Assistant News Director:** Daren Smith. **Baseball Editor:** Anthony Mormile. **Director, Customer Marketing/Communications:** Lou Monaco.

PRESS ASSOCIATIONS

BASEBALL WRITERS ASSOCIATION OF AMERICA
Mailing Address: 78 Olive St., Lake Grove, NY 11755. **Telephone:** (631) 981-7938. **FAX:** (631) 585-4669. **E-Mail Address:** bbwaa@aol.com.
President: Drew Olson (Milwaukee Journal-Sentinel). **Vice President:** Ken Daley (Dallas Morning News). **Secretary-Treasurer:** Jack O'Connell (Hartford Courant).
Board of Directors: Mark Gonzalez (Arizona Republic), Paul Hagen (Philadelphia Daily News), Rick Hummel (St. Louis Post-Dispatch), Dave Sheinen (Washington Post).

NATIONAL COLLEGIATE BASEBALL WRITERS ASSOCIATION
Mailing Address: 2201 Stemmons Fwy., 28th Floor, Dallas, TX 75207. **Telephone:** (214) 753-0102. **FAX:** (214) 753-0145. **E-Mail Address:** bo@big12sports.com.
Executive Director, Newsletter Editor: Bo Carter (Big 12 Conference).
President: Jeff Hurd (Western Athletic Conference). **First Vice President:** Mike Montore (Southern Mississippi). **Second VP:** Todd Lamb (Ohio State). **Third VP:** Dave Fanucchi (USA Baseball). **Secretary/Treasurer:** Russ Anderson (Conference USA).

NEWSPAPERS/PERIODICALS

USA TODAY
Mailing Address: 7950 Jones Branch Dr., McLean, VA 22108. **Telephone/Baseball Desk:** (703) 854-5286, 854-5954, 854-3706, 854-3744, 854-3746. **FAX:** (703) 854-2072. **Website:** www.usatoday.com.
Publishing Frequency: Daily (Monday-Friday).
Baseball Editors: Cesar Brioso, Peter Barzilai, Matt Cimento, John Tkach. **Baseball Columnist:** Hal Bodley. **Baseball Writers:** Mel Antonen, Rod Beaton, Mike Dodd, Gary Graves, Chuck Johnson.

THE SPORTING NEWS
Mailing Address: 10176 Corporate Square Dr., Suite 200, St. Louis, MO 63132. **Telephone:** (314) 997-7111. **FAX:** (314) 997-0765. **Website:** www.sportingnews.com.
Publishing Frequency: Weekly.
Senior Vice President/Editorial Director: John Rawlings. **Executive Editor:** Bob Hille. **Managing Editor:** Stan McNeal. **Senior Writer:** Ken Rosenthal. **Senior Editor:** Tom Gatto. **Senior Photo Editor:** Paul Nisely.

SPORTS ILLUSTRATED
Mailing Address: 135 W. 50th St., New York, NY 10020. **Telephone:** (212) 522-1212. **FAX, Editorial:** (212) 522-4543. **FAX, Public Relations:** (212) 522-4832. **Website:** www.si.com.
Publishing Frequency: Weekly.
Managing Editor: Terry McDonnell. **Senior Editor:** Larry Burke. **Associate Editor:** B.J. Schecter. **Senior Writers:** Jeff Pearlman, Tom Verducci. **Staff Writer:** Danny Habib. **Writers/Reporters:** Albert Chen, Gene Menez.
Vice President, Communications: Art Berke.

USA TODAY SPORTS WEEKLY
Mailing Address: 7950 Jones Branch Dr., McLean, VA 22108. **Telephone:** (800) 872-1415, (703) 854-6319. **FAX:** (703) 854-2034. **Website:** www.usatoday.com.
Publishing Frequency: Weekly.
Publisher/Executive Editor: Lee Ivory. **Managing Editor:** Tim McQuay. **Deputy Managing Editor:** Scott Zucker. **Senior Editor:** Frank Cooney. **Operations Editor:** Amanda Tinkham Boltax. **Senior Writers:** Bob Nightengale, Paul White, Lisa Winston. **Writers:** Chris Colston, Steve DiMeglio, Seth Livingstone.

STREET AND SMITH'S SPORTS BUSINESS JOURNAL
Mailing Address: 120 W. Morehead St., Suite 310, Charlotte, NC 28202. **Telephone:** (704) 973-1400. **FAX:** (704) 973-1401. **Website:** www.sportsbusinessjournal.com.
Publishing Frequency: Weekly.
Publisher: Richard Weiss. **Editor-in-Chief:** Abraham Madkour. **Managing Editor:** Ross Nethery.

ESPN THE MAGAZINE
Mailing Address: 19 E. 34th St., Seventh Floor, New York, NY 10016. **Telephone:** (212) 515-1000. **FAX:** (212) 515-1290. **Website:** www.espn.com.
Publishing Frequency: Bi-weekly.
Executive Editor: Steve Wulf. **Senior Editor:** Jon Scher. **General Editor:** Ed McGregor. **Senior Writers:** Jeff Bradley, Peter Gammons, Tim Keown, Tim Kurkjian, Buster Olney. **Photo Editor:** Nik Kleinberg. **Deputy Photo Editor:** John Toolan. **Manager, Communications:** Ashley Swadel.

BASEBALL AMERICA
Address: 201 West Main St., Suite 201, Durham, NC 27702. **Mailing Address:** P.O. Box 2089, Durham, NC 27702. **Telephone:** (919) 682-9635. **FAX:** (919) 682-2880.
Publishing Frequency: Bi-weekly.
President: Catherine Silver. **Publisher:** Lee Folger. **Editor in Chief:** Allan Simpson. **Managing Editor:** Will Lingo. **Executive Editor:** Jim Callis. **Senior Writer:** Alan Schwarz.

BASEBALL DIGEST
Mailing Address: 990 Grove St., Evanston, IL 60201. **Telephone:** (847) 491-6440. **FAX:** (847) 491-6203. **E-Mail Address:** bkuenster@centurysports.net. **Website:** www.centurysports.net/baseball.

Publishing Frequency: Monthly, April through January.
Publisher: Norman Jacobs. **Editor:** John Kuenster. **Managing Editor:** Bob Kuenster.

COLLEGIATE BASEBALL

Mailing Address: P.O. Box 50566, Tucson, AZ 85703. **Telephone:** (520) 623-4530. **FAX:** (520) 624-5501. **E-Mail Address:** editor@baseballnews.com. **Website:** www.baseballnews.com.
Publishing Frequency: Bi-weekly, January-June; September, October.
Publisher: Lou Pavlovich. **Editor:** Lou Pavlovich Jr.

JUNIOR BASEBALL MAGAZINE

Mailing Address: P.O. Box 9099, Canoga Park, CA 91309. **Telephone:** (818) 710-1234. **Customer Service:** (888) 487-2448. **FAX:** (818) 710-1877. **E-Mail Address:** editor@juniorbaseball.com. **Website:** www.juniorbaseball.com.
Publishing Frequency: Bi-monthly.
Publisher/Editor: Dave Destler. **Publishing Director:** Dayna Destler.

SPORTS ILLUSTRATED FOR KIDS

Mailing Address: 135 W. 50th St., Fourth Floor, New York, NY 10020. **Telephone:** (212) 522-1212. **FAX:** (212) 522-0120. **Website:** www.sikids.com.
Publishing Frequency: Monthly.
Publisher: Peter Krieger. **Managing Editor:** Neil Cohen. **Assistant Managing Editor:** Peter Kay. **Senior Editor:** John Rolfe.

BASEBALL PARENT

Mailing Address: 4437 Kingston Pike, Suite 2204, Knoxville, TN 37919. **Telephone:** (865) 523-1274. **FAX:** (865) 673-8926. **E-Mail Address:** baseparent@aol.com. **Website:** www.baseball-parent.com.
Publishing Frequency: January, March, April, May, June, July.
Publisher/Editor: Wayne Christensen.

BASEBALL ANNUALS

ATHLON SPORTS BASEBALL

Mailing Address: 220 25th Ave. N., Suite 200, Nashville, TN 37203. **Telephone:** (615) 327-0747. **FAX:** (615) 327-1149. **E-Mail Address:** info@athlonsports.com. **Website:** www.athlonsports.com.
Chief Executive Officer: Roger Di Silvestro. **President:** Charles Allen. **Managing Editor:** Charlie Miller. **Senior Editor:** Rob Doster. **Editor:** Mitch Light.

STREET AND SMITH'S BASEBALL YEARBOOK

Mailing Address: 120 West Morehead St., Suite 230, Charlotte, NC 28202. **Telephone:** (704) 973-1575. **FAX:** (704) 973-1576. **E-Mail Address:** annuals@streetandsmiths.com. **Website:** www.streetandsmiths.com.
Publisher: Mike Kallay. **Managing Editor:** Scott Smith.

SPORTING NEWS BASEBALL YEARBOOK

Mailing Address: 10176 Corporate Square Dr., Suite 200, St. Louis, MO 63132. **Telephone:** (314) 997-7111. **FAX:** (314) 997-0765.
Editor: John Rawlings. **Executive Editor:** Bob Hille. **Managing Editor:** Stan McNeal. **Senior Editor:** Don Armstrong. **Senior Writers:** Ken Rosenthal, Michael Knisley. **Photo Editor:** Paul Nisely.

SPRING TRAINING BASEBALL YEARBOOK

Mailing Address: Vanguard Publications, P.O. Box 667, Chapel Hill, NC 27514. **Telephone:** (919) 967-2420. **FAX:** (919) 967-6294. **E-Mail Address:** vanguard3@mindspring.com. **Website:** www.springtrainingmagazine.com.
Publisher: Merle Thorpe. **Editor:** Myles Friedman.

Baseball Encyclopedias

THE BASEBALL ENCYCLOPEDIA

Mailing Address: Barnes & Noble Publishing Inc., 122 Fifth Ave., 5th Floor, New York, NY 10011. **Telephone:** (212) 633-3516. **FAX:** (212) 633-3327. **E-Mail Address:** jboudinot@bn.com. **Website:** www.247baseball.com.
Editors: Pete Palmer, Gary Gillette.

THE SPORTS ENCYCLOPEDIA: BASEBALL

Mailing Address: St. Martin's Press, 175 Fifth Ave., New York, NY 10010. **Telephone:** (212) 764-5151. **E-Mail Address:** joseph.rinaldi@stmartins.com. **Website:** www.stmartins.com.
Authors: David Neft, Richard Cohen, Michael Neft. **Editor:** Marc Resnick.

TOTAL BASEBALL

Mailing Address: SportClassic Books, Sport Media Publishing, 21 Carlaw Ave., Toronto, ON M4M 2R6. **Telephone:** (416) 466-0418. **FAX:** (416) 466-9530. **E-Mail Address:** info@sportclassicbooks.com. **Website:** www.sportclassic-books.com.
Editors: John Thorn, Phil Birnbaum, Bill Deane.

HOBBY PUBLICATIONS

BECKETT INC.
Beckett Baseball Collector

Mailing Address: 15850 Dallas Pkwy., Dallas, TX 75248. **Telephone:** (972) 991-6657, (800) 840-3137. **FAX:** (972)

991-8930. **Website:** www.beckett.com.

Chief Executive Officer, Publisher: James Beckett. **President, Beckett.com:** Mark Harwell. **Editor:** Mike Payne.

KRAUSE PUBLICATIONS

Mailing Address: 700 E. State St., Iola, WI 54990. **Telephone:** (715) 445-4612. **FAX:** (715) 445-4087. **Website:** www.krause.com, www.collect.com, www.fantasysportsmag.com.

Publisher: Dean Listle.

Editor, Fantasy Sports: Greg Ambrosius. **Editor, Sports Collectors Digest:** T.S. O'Connell. **Editor, Tuff Stuff:** Rocky Landsverk.

TEAM PUBLICATIONS

COMAN PUBLISHING
Diehard (Boston Red Sox), Mets Inside Pitch (New York Mets)

Mailing Address: P.O. Box 2331, Durham, NC 27702. **Telephone:** (919) 688-0218. **FAX:** (919) 682-1532.

Publisher: Stuart Coman. **Managing Editor:** Steve Downey.

VINE LINE
(Chicago Cubs)

Mailing Address: Chicago Cubs Publications, 1060 W. Addison St., Chicago, IL 60613. **Telephone:** (773) 404-2827. **FAX:** (773) 404-4129. **E-Mail Address:** jmcardle@cubs.com.

Managing Editor: Lena McDonagh. **Editor:** Jim McArdle.

YANKEES MAGAZINE
(New York Yankees)

Mailing Address: Yankee Stadium, Bronx, NY 10451. **Telephone:** (800) 469-2657.

Publisher/Director, Publications and Media: Mark Mandrake. **Managing Editor:** Glenn Slavin.

INDIANS INK
(Cleveland Indians)

Mailing Address: P.O. Box 539, Mentor, OH 44061. **Telephone:** (440) 953-2200. **FAX:** (440) 953-2202.

Editor: Frank Derry.

OUTSIDE PITCH
(Baltimore Orioles)

Mailing Address: P.O. Box 27143, Baltimore, MD 21230. **Telephone:** (410) 234-8888, (800) 342-4737. **FAX:** (410) 234-1029. **Website:** www.outsidepitch.com.

Publisher: David Simone. **Editor:** David Hill.

REDS REPORT
(Cincinnati Reds)

Mailing Address: Columbus Sports Publications, P.O. Box 12453, Columbus, OH 43212. **Telephone:** (614) 486-2202. **FAX:** (614) 486-3650.

Publisher: Frank Moskowitz. **Editor:** Mark Rae.

OTHER
INFO

GENERAL
INFORMATION

MAJOR LEAGUE BASEBALL PLAYERS ASSOCIATION

Mailing Address: 12 E. 49th St., 24th Floor, New York, NY 10017. **Telephone:** (212) 826-0808. **FAX:** (212) 752-4378. **Website:** www.bigleaguers.com.
Year Founded: 1966.
Executive Director: Donald Fehr.
Chief Operating Officer: Gene Orza. **General Counsel:** Mike Weiner. **Assistant General Counsel:** Jeff Fannell, Doyle Pryor, Robert Lenaghan. **Assistant General Counsel, Licensing:** Evie Goldstein.
Special Assistants: Tony Bernazard, Bobby Bonilla, Phil Bradley, Steve Rogers, Allyne Price.
Director, Business Affairs/Licensing: Judy Heeter. **General Manager, Licensing:** Richard White. **Director, Communications:** Greg Bouris. **Manager, Marketing Services:** Melissa Persaud. **Category Manager, Trading Cards/Collectibles:** Evan Kaplan. **Category Manager, Apparel/Novelties:** Nancy Willis. **Category Director, Interactive Games:** John Olshan. **Communications Coordinator:** Chris Dahl. **Contract Administrator:** Cindy Abercrombie. **Managing Officer:** Martha Child.
Executive Board: Player representatives of the 30 major league clubs.
Association Representatives: Tony Clark, Mark Loretta.

SCOUTING

MAJOR LEAGUE SCOUTING BUREAU

Mailing Address: 3500 Porsche Way, Suite 100, Ontario, CA 91764. **Telephone:** (909) 980-1881. **FAX:** (909) 980-7794.
Year Founded: 1974.
Director: Frank Marcos. **Assistant Director:** Rick Oliver. **Office Coordinator:** Joanne Costanzo. **Administrative Assistant:** Debbie Keedy.
Board of Directors: Sandy Alderson (Major League Baseball), Dave Dombrowski (Tigers), Bob Gebhard (Cardinals), Roland Hemond (White Sox), Frank Marcos, Omar Minaya (Expos), Randy Smith (Padres), Jimmie Lee Solomon (Major League Baseball), Art Stewart (Royals), Kevin Towers (Padres).
Scouts: Rick Arnold (Centre Hall, PA), Andy Campbell (Chandler, AZ), Mike Childers (Lexington, KY), Dick Colpaert (Utica, MI), Craig Conklin (Cayucos, CA), Dan Cox (Santa Ana, CA), Dan Dixon (Temecula, CA), J.D. Elliby (Glen Allen, VA), Jim Elliott (Winston-Salem, NC), Art Gardner (Walnut Grove, MS), Rusty Gerhardt (New London, TX), Dennis Haren (San Diego, CA), Doug Horning (Schererville, IN), Don Jacoby (Winter Haven, FL), Brad Kohler (Bethlehem, PA), Don Kohler (Asbury, NJ), Mike Larson (Waseca, MN), Wayne Mathis (Kansas City, MO), Jethro McIntyre (Pittsburg, CA), Paul Mirocke (Wesley Chapel, FL), Carl Moesche (Gresham, OR), Tim Osborne (Woodstock, GA), Gary Randall (Rock Hill, SC), Willie Romay (Miami Springs, FL), Kevin Saucier (Pensacola, FL), Pat Shortt (South Hempstead, NY), Craig Smajstrla (Pearland, TX), Christie Stancil (Raleigh, NC), Ed Sukla (Irvine, CA), Marv Thompson (Corona, CA), Jim Walton (Shattuck, OK).
Supervisor, Canada: Walt Burrows (Brentwood Bay, BC). **Canadian Scouts:** Curtis Bailey (Red Deer, AB), Jason Chee-Aloy (Toronto, ON), Gerry Falk (Carman, MB), Bill Green (Vancouver, BC), Sean Gulliver (St. John's, NF), Ian Jordan (Kirkland, QC), Ken Lenihan (Bedford, NS), Dave McConnell (Kelowna, BC), Dan Mendham (Dorchester, ON), Todd Plaxton (Saskatoon, SK), Jasmin Roy (Longueuil, QC), Tony Wylie (Anchorage, AK).
Supervisor, Puerto Rico: Pepito Centeno (Bayamon, PR).

PROFESSIONAL BASEBALL SCOUTS FOUNDATION

Mailing Address: 9665 Wilshire Blvd., Suite 801, Beverly Hills, CA 90212. **Telephone:** (310) 858-1935, (310) 271-2617. **E-Mail Addresses:** dennis@pbsfonline.com, lisa@pbsfonline.com. **Website:** www.professionalbaseball scoutsfoundation.com
Chairman: Dennis Gilbert. **Chief Financial Officer:** Joey Behrstock.
Directors: Roland Hemond, Dave Yoakum, Tracy Ringolsby, Harry Minor, Roberta Mazur, Tommy Lasorda, Lisa Jackson, Gary Hughes, Dan Evans, Dale Sutherland, Ray Poitevint, John Young, Bill Gayton, Derek Hall.

SCOUT OF THE YEAR FOUNDATION

Mailing Address: P.O. Box 211585, West Palm Beach, FL 33421. **Telephone:** (561) 798-5897. **FAX:** (561) 798-4644. **E-Mail Address:** bertmazur@aol.com.
President: Roberta Mazur. **Vice President:** Tracy Ringolsby. **Treasurer:** Ron Mazur II.
Board of Advisers: Joe L. Brown, Bob Fontaine, Pat Gillick, Roland Hemond, Gary Hughes, Tommy Lasorda, Allan Simpson, Ron Shapiro, Ted Spencer, Bob Watson.

SCOUTING SERVICES

INSIDE EDGE, INC.

Mailing Address: 5049 Emerson Ave. S., Minneapolis, MN 55419. **Telephone:** (800) 858-3343. **FAX:** (508) 526-6145. **E-Mail Address:** insideedge@aol.com. **Website:** inside-edge.com.
Partners: Jay Donchetz, Randy Istre.

PROSPECTS PLUS/THE SCOUTING REPORT

(A Joint Venture of Baseball America and Perfect Game USA)

Mailing Address: Baseball America, P.O. Box 2089, Durham, NC 27702. **Telephone:** (800) 845-2726. **FAX:** (919) 682-2880. **E-Mail Addresses:** allansimpson@baseballamerica.com; pgjerry@qwest.net. **Website:** www.baseballamerica.com; www.perfectgame.org

Editor, Baseball America: Allan Simpson. **Director, Perfect Game USA:** Jerry Ford.

SKILLSHOW, INC.

Mailing Address: 290 King of Prussia Rd., Suite 102, Radnor, PA 19087. **Telephone:** (610) 687-9072. **FAX:** (610) 687-9629. **E-Mail Address:** info@skillshow.com. **Website:** www.skillshow.com.

Chief Executive Officer: Tom Koerick Jr. **President/Director, Sales:** Tom Koerick Sr. **Vice President, Marketing:** Louis Manon.

UMPIRES

WORLD UMPIRES ASSOCIATION

Mailing Address: P.O. Box 760, Cocoa, FL 32923. **Telephone:** (920) 969-1580. **FAX:** (321) 633-7018. **E-Mail Address:** questions@worldumpires.com.

Year Founded: 2000.

President: John Hirschbeck. **Vice President:** Joe Brinkman. **Secretary/Treasurer:** Jeff Nelson. **Labor Counsel:** Joel Smith. **Administrator:** Phil Janssen.

Board of Directors: Randy Marsh, Tim McClelland, Bill Welke, Dale Scott, Mark Hirschbeck, Mike Winters.

PROFESSIONAL BASEBALL UMPIRE CORPORATION

Office Address: 201 Bayshore Dr. SE, St. Petersburg, FL 33701. **Mailing Address:** P.O. Box A, St. Petersburg, FL 33731. **Telephone:** (727) 822-6937. **FAX:** (727) 821-5819.

President: Mike Moore. **Treasurer/Vice President, Administration:** Pat O'Conner. **Secretary/General Counsel:** Scott Poley. **Administrator:** Eric Krupa. **Assistant to Administrator:** Lillian Dixon.

Executive Director, PBUC: Mike Fitzpatrick (Kalamazoo, MI).

Field Evaluators/Instructors: Dennis Cregg (Webster, MA), Mike Felt (Lansing, MI), Cris Jones (Wheat Ridge, CO), Jorge Bauza, (San Juan, PR), Larry Reveal (Chesapeake, VA).

UMPIRE DEVELOPMENT SCHOOLS
Harry Wendelstedt Umpire School

Mailing Address: 88 S. St. Andrews Dr., Ormond Beach, FL 32174. **Telephone:** (386) 672-4879. **FAX:** (386) 672-3212. **E-Mail Address:** admin@umpireschool.com. **Website:** www.umpireschool.com.

Operators: Harry Wendelstedt, Hunter Wendelstedt.

Jim Evans Academy of Professional Umpiring

Mailing Address: 12741 Research Blvd., Suite 401, Austin, TX 78759. **Telephone:** (512) 335-5959. **FAX:** (512) 335-5411. **E-Mail Address:** jimsacademy@earthlink.net. **Website:** www.umpireacademy.com.

Operator: Jim Evans.

TRAINERS

PROFESSIONAL BASEBALL ATHLETIC TRAINERS SOCIETY

Mailing Address: 400 Colony Square, Suite 1750, 1201 Peachtree St., Atlanta, GA 30361. **Telephone:** (404) 875-4000. **FAX:** (404) 892-8560. **E-Mail Address:** rmallernee@mallernee-branch.com. **Website:** www.pbats.org.

Year Founded: 1983.

President: Jamie Reed (Texas Rangers). **Secretary:** Jim Rowe (Boston Red Sox). **Treasurer:** Tom Probst (Colorado Rockies). **American League Representative:** Kevin Rand (Detroit Tigers). **American League Assistant Trainer Representative:** Brian Ebel (Baltimore Orioles). **National League Representative:** Jeff Porter (Atlanta Braves). **National League Assistant Trainer Representative:** Rex Jones (Houston Astros).

General Counsel: Rollin Mallernee.

EQUIPMENT

LENA BLACKBURN RUBBING MUD
(Official rubbing mud of Major League Baseball)

Mailing Address: 186 Forge Rd., Delran, NJ 08075. **Telephone:** (856) 764-7501. **FAX:** (856) 461-4089. **E-Mail Address:** lbrubmud@aol.com.

President: James Bintliff.

MUSEUMS

BABE RUTH BIRTHPLACE and OFFICIAL ORIOLES MUSEUM

Office Address: 216 Emory St., Baltimore, MD 21230. **Telephone:** (410) 727-1539. **FAX:** (410) 727-1652. **E-Mail Address:** info@baberuthmuseum.com. **Website:** www.baberuthmuseum.com.

Year Founded: 1973.

Executive Director: Mike Gibbons. **Curator:** Greg Schwalenberg.

Museum Hours: April-October, 10 a.m.-5 p.m. (10 a.m.-7 p.m. for Baltimore Orioles home games); November-March, 10 a.m.-4 p.m.

CANADIAN BASEBALL HALL OF FAME and MUSEUM

Museum Address: 386 Church St., St. Marys, Ontario N4X 1C2. **Mailing Address:** P.O. Box 1838, St. Marys, Ontario N4X 1C2. **Telephone:** (519) 284-1838. **FAX:** (519) 284-1234. **E-Mail Address:** baseball@baseballhalloffame.ca.

Website: www.baseballhalloffame.ca.
Year Founded: 1983.
President/Chief Executive Officer: Tom Valcke. **Director, Operations:** Scott Crawford. **Curator:** Carl McCoomb.
Museum Hours: May—Sat. 10:30 a.m.-4:30 p.m.; Sun. noon-4 p.m.; June 1-Oct. 9—Mon.-Sat. 10:30 a.m.-4:30 p.m.; Sun. noon-4 p.m.
2004 Induction Ceremonies: June 26.
Boys/Girls Weeklong Camps: July.

FIELD OF DREAMS MOVIE SITE

Address: 28963 Lansing Rd., Dyersville, IA 52040. **Telephone:** (888) 875-8404. **FAX:** (319) 875-7253. **E-Mail Address:** shoelessjoe@fieldofdreamsmoviesite.com. **Website:** www.fieldofdreamsmoviesite.com.
Year Founded: 1989.
Manager, Business/Marketing: Betty Boeckenstedt.
Hours: April-November, 9 a.m.-6 p.m.

PETER McGOVERN LITTLE LEAGUE MUSEUM

Office Address: Route 15 S., Williamsport, PA 17701. **Mailing Address:** P.O. Box 3485, Williamsport, PA 17701. **Telephone:** (570) 326-3607. **FAX:** (570) 326-2267. **E-Mail Address:** museum@littleleague.org. **Website:** www.little-league.org/museum.
Year Founded: 1982.
Director/Curator: Mike Miller. **Business/Office Manager:** Tracey Yeagle.
Museum Hours: Memorial Day-Sept. 30, 10 a.m.-7 p.m. (Sun. noon-7 p.m.); October-May, Mon., Thurs. and Fri. 10 a.m.-5 p.m.; Sat. noon-5 p.m.; Sun. noon-4 p.m.

LOUISVILLE SLUGGER MUSEUM

Office Address: 800 W. Main St., Louisville, KY 40202. **Telephone:** (502) 588-7228. **FAX:** (502) 585-1179. **Website:** www.sluggermuseum.org.
Year Founded: 1996.
Executive Director: Anne Jewell.
Museum Hours: Mon.-Sat., 9 a.m.-5 p.m.; Sunday (April-Nov.), noon-5 p.m.; closed Christmas Eve through New Year's Day.

THE NATIONAL PASTIME: MUSEUM OF MINOR LEAGUE BASEBALL

(Under Development)
Museum Address: 175 Toyota Plaza, Suite 300, Memphis, TN 38103. **Telephone:** (901) 722-0207. **FAX:** (901) 527-1642. **E-Mail Address:** dchase@memphisredbirds.com. **Website:** www.memphisredbirds.com/autozone_park/museum.html.
Founders: Dean Jernigan, Kristi Jernigan.
Executive Director: Dave Chase.

NATIONAL BASEBALL HALL OF FAME AND MUSEUM

Office Address: 25 Main St., Cooperstown, NY 13326. **Mailing Address:** P.O. Box 590, Cooperstown, NY 13326. **Telephone:** (888) 425-5633, (607) 547-7200. **FAX:** (607) 547-2044. **E-Mail Address:** info@baseballhalloffame.org. **Website:** www.baseballhalloffame.org.
Year Founded: 1939.
Chairman: Jane Forbes Clark. **Vice Chairman:** Joe Morgan. **President:** Dale Petroskey. **Senior Vice President:** Bill Haase. **VP, Communications/Education:** Jeff Idelson. **VP/Chief Curator:** Ted Spencer. **Executive Director, Retail Marketing:** Barbara Shinn. **Curator, Collections:** Peter Clark. **Librarian:** Jim Gates. **Controller:** Fran Althiser. **Director, Public Relations:** Brad Horn.
Museum Hours: Memorial Day Weekend-Labor Day—9 a.m.-9 p.m.; remainder of year—9 a.m.-5 p.m. Open daily except Thanksgiving, Christmas, New Year's Day.
2004 Hall of Fame Induction Ceremonies: July 25, 1:30 p.m. **Hall of Fame Game:** June 14, 2 p.m., Atlanta Braves vs. Minnesota Twins.

NEGRO LEAGUES BASEBALL MUSEUM

Mailing Address: 1616 E. 18th St., Kansas City, MO 64108. **Telephone:** (816) 221-1920. **FAX:** (816) 221-8424. **E-Mail Address:** bsamuels@nlbm.com. **Website:** www.nlbm.com.
Year Founded: 1990.
Chairman: Buck O'Neil. **President:** Mark Bryant. **Vice President:** Bruce Boeger. **Secretary:** Mamie Hughes. **Treasurer:** Dewy Alexander.
Executive Director: Don Motley. **Marketing Director/Assistant to the Executive Director:** Bob Kendrick. **Curator/Education Director:** Raymond Doswell. **Office Manager:** Barbara Samuels.
Museum Hours: Tues.-Sat. 9 a.m.-6 p.m.; Sun. noon-6 p.m. Closed Monday.

TED WILLIAMS MUSEUM and HITTERS HALL OF FAME

Mailing Address: 2455 N. Citrus Hills Blvd., Hernando, FL 34442. **Telephone:** (352) 527-6566. **FAX:** (352) 527-4163. **Website:** twmuseum.com.
Executive Director: Dave McCarthy. **Museum Director:** Mike Colabelli.
Museum Hours: Tues.-Sun., 10 a.m.-4 p.m.

RESEARCH

SOCIETY FOR AMERICAN BASEBALL RESEARCH

Mailing Address: 812 Huron Rd., Suite 719, Cleveland, OH 44115. **Telephone:** (216) 575-0500. **FAX:** (216) 575-0502. **E-Mail Address:** info@sabr.org. **Website:** www.sabr.org.
Year Founded: 1971.
President: Dick Beverage. **Vice President:** Stew Thornley. **Treasurer:** F.X. Flinn. **Secretary:** Neil Traven. **Directors:** Daniel Ginsburg, Rodney Johnson, Norman Macht, Andy McCue.
Executive Director: John Zajc. **Membership Services:** Ryan Chamberlain. **Publications Director:** Jim Charlton. **Administrative Assistant/Lending Library:** Eileen Canepari.

ALUMNI ASSOCIATIONS

MAJOR LEAGUE BASEBALL PLAYERS ALUMNI ASSOCIATION

Mailing Address: 1631 Mesa Ave., Suite B, Colorado Springs, CO 80906. **Telephone:** (719) 477-1870. **FAX:** (719) 477-1875. **E-Mail Address:** postoffice@mlbpaa.com. **Website:** www.baseball-legends.com.
President: Brooks Robinson. **Chief Executive Officer:** Dan Foster.
Board of Directors: Sandy Alderson, Nellie Briles, Jerry Dipoto, Denny Doyle, Don Fehr, Greg Gagne, Jim "Mudcat" Grant, Rich Hand, Jim Hannan (chairman), Ken Sanders, Bob Tewksbury, Jose Valdivielso, Fred Valentine (vice chairman).
Legal Counsel: Sam Moore. **Vice President, Player Appearances:** Chris Torgusen. **VP, Special Events:** Geoffrey Hixson. **VP, Special Events—Youth Programming:** Lance James. **Director, Administration:** Chandra Tracy.

MINOR LEAGUE BASEBALL ALUMNI ASSOCIATION

Mailing Address: P.O. Box A, St. Petersburg, FL 33731. **Telephone:** (727) 822-6937. **FAX:** (727) 825-3785. **E-Mail Address:** alumni@minorleaguebaseball.com. **Website:** www.minorleaguebaseball.com. **President:** Mike Moore.

ASSOCIATION OF PROFESSIONAL BALL PLAYERS OF AMERICA

Mailing Address: 1820 W. Orangewood Ave., Suite 206, Orange, CA 92868. **Telephone:** (714) 935-9993. **FAX:** (714) 935-0431. **E-Mail Address:** ballplayersassn@aol.com. **Website:** www.apbpa.org.
Year Founded: 1924.
President: Roland Hemond. **First Vice President:** Tal Smith. **Second VP:** Dick Wagner. **Third VP:** Bob Kennedy. **Secretary/Treasurer:** Dick Beverage. **Administrative Assistant:** Patty Helmsworth.
Directors: Sparky Anderson, Mark Grace, Tony Gwynn, Orel Hershiser, Whitey Herzog, Tony La Russa, Tom Lasorda, Brooks Robinson, Nolan Ryan, Tom Seaver.

BASEBALL ASSISTANCE TEAM (BAT)

Mailing Address: 245 Park Ave., 34th Floor, New York, NY 10167. **Telephone:** (212) 931-7823, (866) 605-4594. **FAX:** (212) 949-5691.
Year Founded: 1986.
President, Chief Executive Officer: Earl Wilson. **Vice Presidents:** Steve Garvey, Bob Gibson, Larry Gorman, Ed Stack. **Chairman:** Bobby Murcer.
Executive Director: James Martin. **Secretary:** Thomas Ostertag. **Treasurer:** Jonathan Mariner. **Consultant:** Sam McDowell.

MINISTRY

BASEBALL CHAPEL

Mailing Address: P.O. Box 302, Springfield, PA 19064.**Telephone:** (610) 690-2474. **E-Mail Address:** office@baseballchapel.org. **Website:** www.baseballchapel.org.
Year Founded: 1973.
President: Vince Nauss.
Director, Latin America: Rich Sparling. **Assistant Director:** Kyle Abbott. **Coordinator, Baseball Family:** Colleen Endres.
Board of Directors: Don Christenson, Greg Groh, Dave Howard, Jim Lane, Mike Matheny, Chuck Murphy, Vince Nauss, Bill Sampen, Tye Waller, Walt Wiley (chairman).

TRADE, EMPLOYMENT

THE BASEBALL TRADE SHOW

Mailing Address: P.O. Box A, St. Petersburg, FL 33731. **Telephone:** (727) 822-6937, (727) 456-1718. **FAX:** (727) 825-3785.
Manager, Exhibition Services/Alumni Association: Noreen Brantner.
2004 Convention: Dec. 10-12 at Anaheim.

PROFESSIONAL BASEBALL EMPLOYMENT OPPORTUNITIES

Mailing Address: P.O. Box A, St. Petersburg, FL 33731. **Telephone:** (866) 397-7236. **FAX:** (727) 821-5819. **E-Mail:** info@pbeo.com. **Website:** www.pbeo.com.
Contact: Scott Kravchuk.

MEN'S SENIOR BASEBALL LEAGUE/MEN'S ADULT BASEBALL LEAGUE

Mailing Address: One Huntington Quadrangle, Suite 3N07, Mellville, NY 11747. **Telephone:** (631) 753-6725. **FAX:** (631) 753-4031. **E-Mail Address:** info@msblnational.com. **Website:** www.msblnational.com.

President: Steve Sigler. **Vice President:** Gary D'Ambrisi.

Las Vegas Open: 18 and over, 28 and over, 38 and over, 48 and over, 58 and over, May 29-31, Las Vegas. **2004 World Series:** 18 and over, 28 and over, 38 and over, 48 and over, 58 and over, 65 and over, father/son, Oct. 17-Nov. 6, Phoenix. **Fall Classic:** 18 and over, 28 and over, 38 and over, 48 and over, Nov. 5-13, St. Petersburg, FL.

NATIONAL ADULT BASEBALL ASSOCIATION

Mailing Address: 3609 S. Wadsworth Blvd., Suite 135, Lakewood, CO 80235. **Telephone:** (800) 621-6479. **FAX:** (303) 639-6605. **E-Mail:** nabanational@aol.com. **Website:** www.dugout.org.

President: Shane Fugita.

Memorial Day Tournament: 18 and over, 30 and over, 40 and over, 50 and over, May 29-31, Las Vegas. **Atlantic City Tournament:** 18 and over, 28 and over, 38 and over, May 29-31, Atlantic City, NJ. **Hall of Fame Tournament (Wood Bat):** 18 and over, 28 and over, July 3-6, Cooperstown, NY. **Mile High Classic (Wood Bat):** 18 and over, 28 and over, 38 and over, July 3-5, Denver. **Gold Rush Tournament:** 18 and over, 28 and over, 38 and over, 48 and over, Sept. 4-6, Sacramento, CA. **NABA World Championship Series:** 18 and over, 28 and over, 38 and over, 48 and over, Oct. 5-16, Phoenix. **NABA Over 50 Baseball National Fun Tournament:** 48 and over, 58 and over, Nov. 1-6, Las Vegas.

ROY HOBBS BASEBALL

Mailing Address: 2048 Akron Peninsula Rd., Akron, OH 44313. **Telephone:** (330) 923-3400. **FAX:** (330) 923-1967. **E-Mail Address:** royhobbs@royhobbs.com. **Website:** www.royhobbs.com.

President: Tom Giffen. **Vice President:** Ellen Giffen.

2004 World Series (all in Fort Myers, FL): 28 and over, Oct. 30-Nov. 6; 38 and over, Nov. 6-13; 48 and over, Nov. 13-20; 55 and over, Oct. 30-Nov. 6; 60 and over, Nov. 13-20.

AMATEUR ATHLETIC UNION WOMEN'S BASEBALL

Mailing Address: 2048 Akron Peninsula Rd., Akron, OH 44313. **Telephone:** (330) 923-3400. **FAX:** (330) 923-1967. **Website:** www.uswb.org.

National Women's Baseball Chair: Tom Giffen. **Committee Members:** Adriane Adler, Tina Beining, Christi Hill, John Kovach, Cherie Leatherwood, Robin Wallace.

2004 National Championship: Nov. 3-7 at Fort Myers, FL.

LOS ANGELES DODGERS ADULT BASEBALL CAMP

Mailing Address: Dodgertown, P.O. Box 2887, Vero Beach, FL 32961. **Telephone:** (772) 569-4900, (800) 334-7529. **FAX:** (772) 229-6708. **E-Mail Address:** nancyg@ladodgers.com. **Website:** www.ladabc.com.

Camp Administrator: Nancy Gollnick.

RANDY HUNDLEY'S FANTASY BASEBALL CAMPS

Mailing Address: 128 S Northwest Hwy., Palatine, IL 60067. **Telephone/FAX:** (847) 991-9595. **E-Mail Address:** rhundley@home.com. **Website:** www.cubsfantasycamps.com.

Camp Coordinator: Barb Kozuh.

PHILLIES ADULT PHANTASY BASEBALL CAMP

Mailing Address: P.O. Box 505, Haverford, PA 19041. **Telephone:** (610) 520-3400. **E-Mail Address:** clandosky@esfcamps.com **Website:** www.philliesacademy.com.

Camp Coordinator: Kurt Funk.

DONRUSS CO.
Donruss, Leaf, Playoff

Mailing Address: 2300 E. Randoll Mill, Arlington, TX 76011. **Telephone:** (817) 983-0300. **FAX:** (817) 983-0400. **E-Mail Address:** info@donruss.com. **Website:** www.donruss.com.

FLEER/SKYBOX INTERNATIONAL

Mailing Address: 1120 Route 73 S., Suite 300, Mount Laurel, NJ 08054. **Telephone:** (800) 343-6816 . **FAX:** (856) 231-0383. **E-Mail Address:** info@fleer.com. **Website:** www.fleer.com.

GRANDSTAND CARDS

Mailing Address: 22647 Ventura Blvd., #192, Woodland Hills, CA 91364. **Telephone:** (818) 992-5642. **FAX:** (818) 348-9122. **E-Mail Address:** gscards1@pacbell.net. **Website:** www.grandstandcards.com.

THE TOPPS CO.
Bowman, Topps

Mailing Address: One Whitehall St., New York, NY 10004. **Telephone:** (212) 376-0300. **FAX:** (212) 376-0623. **Website:** www.topps.com.

UPPER DECK

Mailing Address: 5909 Sea Otter Place, Carlsbad, CA 92008. **Telephone:** (800) 873-7332. **FAX:** (760) 929-6548. **E-Mail Address:** customer_service@upperdeck.com. **Website:** www.upperdeck.com.

MINOR LEAGUE
BASEBALL

NATIONAL ASSOCIATION
OF PROFESSIONAL BASEBALL LEAGUES

Office Address: 201 Bayshore Dr. SE, St. Petersburg, FL 33701. **Mailing Address:** P.O. Box A, St. Petersburg, FL 33731. **Telephone:** (727) 822-6937. **FAX:** (727) 821-5819. **Website:** www.milb.com.

Year Founded: 1901.
President, Chief Executive Officer: Mike Moore.
Vice President: Stan Brand (Washington, D.C.).
Treasurer, Chief Operating Officer/VP, Administration: Pat O'Conner. **Assistant to VP, Administration:** Mary Wooters.
Secretary/General Counsel: Scott Poley. **Administrator, Legal Affairs:** Sandie Olmsted.
Special Counsel: George Yund (Cincinnati, OH).

Mike Moore

Executive Director, Business Operations: Misann Ellmaker.
Director, Baseball Operations: Tim Brunswick.
Director, Media Relations: Jim Ferguson. **Assistant Director, Media Relations:** Steve Densa.
Director, Business/Finance: Eric Krupa. **Assistant to Director, Business/Finance:** Lillian Patterson. **Manager, Accounting:** Jeff Carrier.
Director, Information Technology: Rob Colamarino.
Official Statistician: The Sports Network, 2200 Byberry Rd., Suite 200, Hatboro, PA 19040. Telephone: (215) 441-8444.
2004 Winter Meetings: Dec. 10-13 at Anaheim, CA.

Affiliated Members/Council of League Presidents

Class AAA

League	President	Telephone	FAX Number
International	Randy Mobley	(614) 791-9300	(614) 791-9009
Mexican	Raul Gonzalez	(011-52) 555-1007	(011-52) 555-1007
Pacific Coast	Branch Rickey	(719) 636-3399	(719) 636-1199

Class AA

League	President	Telephone	FAX Number
Eastern	Joe McEacharn	(207) 761-2700	(207) 761-7064
Southern	Don Mincher	(770) 321-0400	(770) 321-0037
Texas	Tom Kayser	(210) 545-5297	(210) 545-5298

High Class A

League	President	Telephone	FAX Number
California	Joe Gagliardi	(408) 369-8038	(408) 369-1409
Carolina	John Hopkins	(336) 691-9030	(336) 691-9070
Florida State	Chuck Murphy	(386) 252-7479	(386) 252-7495

Low Class A

League	President	Telephone	FAX Number
Midwest	George Spelius	(608) 364-1188	(608) 364-1913
South Atlantic	John Moss	(704) 739-3466	(704) 739-1974

Short-Season Class A

League	President	Telephone	FAX Number
New York-Penn	Ben Hayes	(727) 576-6300	(727) 576-6307
Northwest	Bob Richmond	(208) 429-1511	(208) 429-1525

Rookie Advanced

League	President	Telephone	FAX Number
Appalachian	Lee Landers	(704) 873-5300	(704) 873-4333
Pioneer	Jim McCurdy	(509) 456-7615	(509) 456-0136

Rookie

League	President	Telephone	FAX Number
Arizona	Bob Richmond	(208) 429-1511	(208) 429-1525
Dominican Summer	Freddy Jana	(011-809) 563-3233	(011-809) 563-3233
Gulf Coast	Tom Saffell	(941) 966-6407	(941) 966-6872
Venezuela Summer	Saul Gonzalez	(011-58) 41-24-0321	(011-58) 41-24-0705

PROFESSIONAL BASEBALL
PROMOTION CORPORATION

Office Address: 201 Bayshore Dr. SE, St. Petersburg, FL 33701. **Mailing Address:** P.O. Box A, St. Petersburg, FL 33731. **Telephone:** (727) 822-6937. **FAX/Marketing:** (727) 894-4227. **FAX/Licensing:** (727) 825-3785.

President, Chief Executive Officer: Mike Moore.

Treasurer, Chief Operating Officer/VP, Administration: Pat O'Conner.

Executive Director, Business Operations: Misann Ellmaker. **Senior Assistant Director, Special Operations:** Kelly Ryan. **Assistant Director, Special Operations:** Scott Kravchuk.

Director, Licensing: Brian Earle. **Assistant Director, Licensing:** Tina Gust.

Director, Marketing: Rod Meadows. **Senior Manager, Marketing Administration:** Derek Johnson. **Account Manager, Marketing:** Jen Morris. **Club Coordinator, Marketing:** Melissa Keilen.

Professional Baseball Employment Opportunities Contact: Scott Kravchuk. **Manager, Exhibition Services/Alumni Association:** Noreen Brantner. **Manager, Trademarks/Contracts:** Susan Pinckney. **Assistant, Special Operations:** Jill Rusinko. **Administrative Assistant, Special Operations:** Jeannette Machicote.

PROFESSIONAL BASEBALL
UMPIRE CORPORATION

Office Address: 201 Bayshore Dr. SE, St. Petersburg, FL 33701. **Mailing Address:** P.O. Box A, St. Petersburg, FL 33731. **Telephone:** (727) 822-6937. **FAX:** (727) 821-5819.

President: Mike Moore.

Treasurer/Vice President, Administration: Pat O'Conner. **Secretary/General Counsel:** Scott Poley.

Administrator: Eric Krupa. **Assistant to Administrator:** Lillian Patterson.

Executive Director, PBUC: Mike Fitzpatrick (Kalamazoo, MI).

Field Evaluators/Instructors: Dennis Cregg (Webster, MA), Mike Felt (Lansing, MI), Cris Jones (Wheat Ridge, CO), Jorge Bauza (San Juan, PR), Larry Reveal (Chesapeake, VA).

GENERAL
INFORMATION

	Teams	Regular Season Games	Open. Day	Clos. Day	All-Star Games Date	Site
International	14	144	April 8	Sept. 6	*July 14	Pawtucket
Pacific Coast	16	144	April 8	Sept. 6	*July 14	Pawtucket
Eastern	12	142	April 8	Sept. 6	July 14	Bowie
Southern	10	140	April 8	Sept. 6	July 13	Chattanooga
Texas	8	140	April 8	Sept. 5	June 21	Midland
California	10	140	April 8	Sept. 5	#June 29	Inland Empire
Carolina	8	140	April 8	Sept. 5	#June 29	Inland Empire
Florida State	12	140	April 8	Sept. 5	June 12	St. Lucie
Midwest	14	140	April 8	Sept. 6	June 22	Cedar Rapids
South Atlantic	16	140	April 8	Sept. 6	June 29	Charleston, S.C.
New York-Penn	14	76	June 18	Sept. 4	None	
Northwest	8	76	June 18	Sept. 5	Aug. 3	Spokane
Appalachian	10	68	June 21	Aug. 30	None	
Pioneer	8	76	June 18	Sept. 6	None	
Arizona	9	56	June 22	Aug. 30	None	
Gulf Coast	12	60	June 21	Aug. 28	None	

*Triple-A All-Star Game
#California League vs. Carolina League

MINOR LEAGUES

2003 STANDINGS *Split-season champion. #Wild card.

INTERNATIONAL LEAGUE — AAA

EAST	W	L	PCT	GB	Manager
Pawtucket (Red Sox)	83	61	.576	—	Buddy Bailey
#Ottawa (Orioles)	79	65	.549	4	Gary Allenson
Scranton/Wilkes Barre (Phillies)	73	70	.510	9½	Marc Bombard
Buffalo (Indians)	73	70	.510	9½	Marty Brown
Rochester (Twins)	68	75	.476	14½	Phil Roof
Syracuse (Blue Jays)	62	79	.440	19½	Omar Malave
WEST	**W**	**L**	**PCT**	**GB**	**Manager(s)**
Louisville (Reds)	79	64	.552	—	Dave Miley/Rick Burleson
Columbus (Yankees)	76	68	.528	3½	Bucky Dent
Toledo (Tigers)	65	78	.455	14	Larry Parrish
Indianapolis (Brewers)	64	78	.451	14½	Cecil Cooper
SOUTH	**W**	**L**	**PCT**	**GB**	**Manager**
Durham (Devil Rays)	73	67	.521	—	Bill Evers
Charlotte (White Sox)	74	70	.514	1	Nick Capra
Norfolk (Mets)	67	76	.469	7½	Bobby Floyd
Richmond (Braves)	64	79	.448	10½	Pat Kelly

GOVERNORS' CUP PLAYOFFS—Semifinals: Durham defeated Louisville 3-1 and Pawtucket defeated Ottawa 3-2 in best-of-5 series. **Final:** Durham defeated Pawtucket 3-0 in best-of-5 series.

PACIFIC COAST LEAGUE — AAA

AMERICAN CONFERENCE

EAST	W	L	PCT	GB	Manager(s)
Nashville (Pirates)	81	62	.566	—	Trent Jewett
New Orleans (Astros)	71	73	.493	10½	Chris Maloney
Oklahoma (Rangers)	70	72	.493	10½	Bobby Jones
Memphis (Cardinals)	64	79	.448	17	Tom Spencer/Danny Sheaffer
NORTH	**W**	**L**	**PCT**	**GB**	**Manager**
Edmonton (Expos)	73	69	.514	—	Dave Huppert
Portland (Padres)	69	75	.479	5	Rick Sweet
Salt Lake (Angels)	68	75	.479	5½	Mike Brumley
Tacoma (Mariners)	66	78	.458	8	Dan Rohn

PACIFIC CONFERENCE

CENTRAL	W	L	PCT	GB	Manager
Albuquerque (Marlins)	74	70	.514	—	Dean Treanor
Colorado Springs (Rockies)	73	70	.510	½	Rick Sofield
Iowa (Cubs)	70	72	.493	3	Mike Quade
Omaha (Royals)	70	73	.490	3½	Mike Jirschele
SOUTH	**W**	**L**	**PCT**	**GB**	**Manager**
Sacramento (Athletics)	92	52	.639	—	Tony DeFrancesco
Las Vegas (Dodgers)	76	66	.535	15	John Shoemaker
Tucson (Diamondbacks)	73	71	.507	19	Al Pedrique
Fresno (Giants)	55	88	.385	36½	Fred Stanley

PLAYOFFS—Semifinals: Sacramento defeated Edmonton 3-0 and Nashville defeated Albuquerque 3-1 in best-of -5 series. **Final:** Sacramento defeated Nashville 3-0 in best-of-5 series.

EASTERN LEAGUE — AA

NORTH	W	L	PCT	GB	Manager
New Haven Ravens (Blue Jays)	79	63	.556	—	Marty Pevey
#New Britain Rock Cats (Twins)	73	68	.518	5½	Stan Cliburn
Portland Seadogs (Red Sox)	72	70	.507	7	Ron Johnson
Trenton Thunder (Yankees)	70	71	.496	8½	Stump Merrill
Binghamton Mets (Mets)	63	78	.447	15½	John Stearns
Norwich Navigators (Giants)	62	79	.440	16½	Shane Turner
SOUTH	**W**	**L**	**PCT**	**GB**	**Manager**
Akron Aeros (Indians)	88	53	.624	—	Brad Komminsk
#Altoona Curve (Pirates)	78	63	.553	10	Dale Sveum
Erie Seawolves (Tigers)	72	70	.507	16½	Kevin Bradshaw
Bowie Baysox (Orioles)	69	72	.489	19	Dave Trembley
Reading Phillies (Phillies)	62	79	.440	26	Gregg Legg
Harrisburg Senators (Expos)	60	82	.423	28½	Dave Machemer

PLAYOFFS—Semifinals: Akron defeated Altoona 3-1 and New Haven defeated New Britain 3-2 in best-of-5 series. **Final:** Akron defeated New Haven 3-0 in best-of-5 series.

SOUTHERN LEAGUE　　　　AA

EAST	W	L	PCT	GB	Manager
*Carolina (Marlins)	80	58	.580	—	Tracy Woodson
#Tennessee (Cardinals)	72	67	.518	8½	Marc DeJohn
Greenville (Braves)	68	70	.493	12	Brian Snitker
Jacksonville (Dodgers)	66	73	.475	14½	Dino Ebel
Orlando (Devil Rays)	65	72	.474	14½	Charlie Montoyo
WEST	**W**	**L**	**PCT**	**GB**	**Manager**
*Huntsville (Brewers)	75	63	.543	—	Frank Kremblas
*Birmingham (White Sox)	73	64	.533	1½	Wally Backman
Chattanooga (Reds)	66	74	.471	10½	Phillip Wellman
West Tenn (Cubs)	65	73	.471	10½	Bobby Dickerson
Mobile (Padres)	61	77	.442	14	Craig Colbert

PLAYOFFS—Semifinals: Carolina defeated Tennessee 3-1 and Huntsville defeated Birmingham 3-2 in best-of-5 series. **Final:** Carolina defeated Huntsville 3-2 in best-of-5 series.

TEXAS LEAGUE　　　　AA

EAST	W	L	PCT	GB	Manager
Tulsa (Rockies)	74	64	.536	—	Marv Foley
*Frisco (Rangers)	73	67	.521	2	Tim Ireland
*Wichita (Royals)	71	69	.507	4	Keith Bodie
Arkansas (Angels)	70	70	.500	5	Tyrone Boykin
WEST	**W**	**L**	**PCT**	**GB**	**Manager**
**San Antonio (Mariners)	88	51	.633	—	Dave Brundage
Midland (Athletics)	69	70	.496	19	Greg Sparks
El Paso (Diamondbacks)	67	73	.479	21½	Scott Coolbaugh
Round Rock (Astros)	46	94	.329	42½	Jackie Moore

PLAYOFFS—Semifinals: Frisco defeated Wichita 3-0 in best-of-5 series; San Antonio received a first-round bye. **Finals:** San Antonio defeated Frisco 4-1 in best-of-7 series.

CALIFORNIA LEAGUE　　　　HIGH A

NORTH	W	L	PCT	GB	Manager
*Visalia (Rockies)	79	61	.564	—	Stu Cole
*Stockton (Rangers)	77	63	.550	2	Arnie Beyeler
#Modesto (Athletics)	74	66	.529	5	Rick Rodriguez
Bakersfield (Devil Rays)	70	70	.500	9	Omer Munoz
San Jose (Giants)	58	82	.414	21	Jack Lind
SOUTH	**W**	**L**	**PCT**	**GB**	**Manager**
*Inland Empire (Mariners)	78	62	.557	—	Steve Roadcap
#Lake Elsinore (Padres)	75	65	.536	3	Jeff Gardner
*Rancho Cucamonga (Angels)	74	66	.529	4	Bobby Meacham
Lancaster (Diamondbacks)	73	67	.521	5	Mike Aldrete
High Desert (Brewers)	42	98	.300	36	Tim Blackwell

PLAYOFFS—Quarterfinals: Inland Empire defeated Lake Elsinore 2-0 and Visalia defeated Modesto 2-0 in best-of-3 series. **Semifinals:** Inland Empire defeated Rancho Cucamonga 3-1 and Stockton defeated Visalia 3-2 in best-of-5 series. **Final:** Inland Empire defeated Stockton 3-0 in best-of-five series.

CAROLINA LEAGUE　　　　HIGH A

NORTH	W	L	PCT	GB	Manager
*Wilmington (Royals)	80	60	.571	—	Billy Gardner
*Lynchburg (Pirates)	76	59	.563	1½	Dave Clark
Potomac (Reds)	62	77	.446	17½	Jayhawk Owens
Frederick (Orioles)	60	75	.444	17½	Tom Lawless
SOUTH	**W**	**L**	**PCT**	**GB**	**Manager**
Salem (Astros)	73	65	.529	—	John Massarelli
*Kinston (Indians)	73	66	.532	½	Torey Lovullo
*Winston-Salem (White Sox)	71	67	.514	2	Razor Shines
Myrtle Beach (Braves)	56	82	.406	17	Randy Ingle

PLAYOFFS—Semifinals: Winston-Salem defeated Kinston 2-0 and Lynchburg defeated Wilmington 2-0 in best-of-3 series. **Final:** Winston-Salem defeated Lynchburg 3-0 in best-of-5 series.

FLORIDA STATE LEAGUE　　　　HIGH A

EAST	W	L	PCT	GB	Manager
*St. Lucie (Mets)	77	62	.554	—	Ken Oberkfell
*Jupiter (Marlins)	76	62	.551	½	Luis Dorante
Brevard County (Expos)	65	66	.496	8	Doug Sisson
Daytona Cubs (Cubs)	66	71	.482	10	Rick Kranitz
Vero Beach (Dodgers)	62	69	.473	11	Scott Little
Palm Beach (Cardinals)	54	84	.391	22½	Tom Nieto
WEST	**W**	**L**	**PCT**	**GB**	**Manager**
*Dunedin Blue Jays (Blue Jays)	78	62	.557	—	Mike Basso

	W	L	PCT	GB	
Clearwater Phillies (Phillies)	72	61	.541	2½	Roly deArmas
*Fort Myers Miracle (Twins)	73	63	.537	3	Jose Marzan
Tampa Yankees (Yankees)	68	64	.515	6	Bill Masse
Sarasota Red Sox (Red Sox)	63	67	.485	10	Tim Leiper
Lakeland Tigers (Tigers)	55	78	.414	19½	Gary Green

PLAYOFFS—Semifinals: St. Lucie defeated Jupiter 2-0 and Dunedin defeated Fort Myers 2-1 in best-of-3 series. **Final:** St. Lucie defeated Dunedin 3-1 in best-of-5 series.

MIDWEST LEAGUE — LOW A

EAST	W	L	PCT	GB	Manager
#Battle Creek (Yankees)	73	64	.533	—	Mitch Seoane
*South Bend (Diamondbacks)	72	64	.529	½	Von Hayes
*Fort Wayne (Padres)	71	66	.518	2	Gary Jones
#Lansing (Cubs)	69	66	.511	3	Julio Garcia
West Michigan (Tigers)	67	73	.479	7½	Phil Regan
Dayton (Reds)	61	78	.439	13	Donnie Scott

WEST	W	L	PCT	GB	Manager
*Kane County (Athletics)	80	59	.576	—	Webster Garrison
*Beloit (Brewers)	75	61	.551	3½	Don Money
#Wisconsin (Mariners)	69	66	.511	9	Daren Brown
#Clinton (Rangers)	69	66	.511	9	Carlos Subero
Cedar Rapids (Angels)	66	72	.478	13½	Todd Claus
Peoria (Cardinals)	65	73	.471	14½	Joe Cunningham
Burlington (Royals)	64	74	.464	15½	Joe Szekley
Quad City (Twins)	59	78	.431	20	Jeff Carter

PLAYOFFS—Quarterfinals: Lansing defeated South Bend 2-0, Battle Creek defeated Fort Wayne 2-0, Beloit defeated Wisconsin 2-0 and Clinton defeated Kane County 2-1 in best-of-3 series. **Semifinals:** Lansing defeated Battle Creek 2-0 and Beloit defeated Clinton 2-1 in best-of-3 series. **Final:** Lansing defeated Beloit 3-0 in best-of-5 series.

SOUTH ATLANTIC LEAGUE — LOW A

NORTH	W	L	PCT	GB	Manager
**Lake County (Indians)	97	43	.693	—	Luis Rivera
#Lexington (Astros)	75	63	.543	21	Russ Nixon
Hagerstown (Giants)	68	67	.504	26½	Mike Ramsey
Greensboro (Marlins)	67	69	.493	28	Steve Phillips
Delmarva (Orioles)	67	71	.486	29	Stan Hough
Charleston, W.Va. (Blue Jays)	57	76	.429	36½	Mark Meleski
Lakewood (Phillies)	57	81	.413	39	Buddy Biancalana
Kannapolis (White Sox)	55	82	.401	40½	John Orton

SOUTH	W	L	PCT	GB	Manager
*Hickory (Pirates)	82	54	.603	—	Tony Beasley
*Rome (Braves)	78	61	.561	5½	Rocket Wheeler
Charleston, S.C. (Devil Rays)	77	62	.554	6½	Mako Oliveras
Asheville (Rockies)	74	65	.532	9½	Joe Mikulik
Capital City (Mets)	73	65	.529	10	Tony Tijerina
South Georgia (Dodgers)	64	72	.471	18	Dann Bilardello
Savannah (Expos)	58	80	.420	25	Joey Cora
Augusta (Red Sox)	49	87	.360	33	Russ Morman

PLAYOFFS—Semifinals: Lake County defeated Lexington 2-0 and Rome defeated Hickory 2-1 in best-of-3 series. **Finals:** Rome defeated Lake County 3-1 in best-of-5 series.

NEW YORK-PENN LEAGUE — SHORT-SEASON A

McNAMARA	W	L	PCT	GB	Manager
Brooklyn (Mets)	47	28	.627	—	Tim Teufel
#Williamsport (Pirates)	46	30	.605	1½	Andy Stewart
Aberdeen (Orioles)	38	38	.500	9½	Joe Almaraz
Hudson Valley (Devil Rays)	37	37	.500	9½	Dave Howard
New Jersey (Cardinals)	31	42	.425	15	Tommy Shields
Staten Island (Yankees)	29	43	.403	16½	Andy Stankiewicz

STEDLER	W	L	PCT	GB	Manager(s)
Oneonta (Tigers)	45	30	.600	—	Randy Ready
Tri-City (Astros)	44	32	.579	1½	Ivan DeJesus
Lowell (Red Sox)	39	35	.527	5½	Jon Deeble/Lynn Jones
Vermont (Expos)	19	56	.253	26	Dave Barnett

PINCKNEY	W	L	PCT	GB	Manager
Auburn (Blue Jays)	56	18	.757	—	Dennis Holmberg
Mahoning Valley (Indians)	38	36	.514	18	Ted Kubiak
Batavia (Phillies)	30	45	.400	26½	Luis Melendez
Jamestown (Marlins)	22	51	.301	33½	Benny Castillo

PLAYOFFS—Semifinals: Williamsport defeated Auburn 2-0 and Brooklyn defeated Oneonta 2-1 in best-of-3 series. **Final:** Williamsport defeated Brooklyn 2-0 in best-of-3 series.

NORTHWEST LEAGUE
SHORT-SEASON A

NORTH	W	L	PCT	GB	Manager
Spokane (Rangers)	50	26	.658	—	Darryl Kennedy
Yakima (Diamondbacks)	45	31	.592	5	Bill Plummer
Tri-City (Rockies)	33	43	.434	17	Ron Gideon
Boise (Cubs)	27	49	.355	23	Steve McFarland
SOUTH	**W**	**L**	**PCT**	**GB**	**Manager**
Salem-Keizer (Giants)	43	33	.566	—	Joe Strain
Eugene (Padres)	39	37	.513	4	Roy Howell
Vancouver (Athletics)	35	41	.461	8	Dennis Rogers
Everett (Mariners)	32	44	.421	11	Pedro Grifol

PLAYOFF: Spokane defeated Salem-Keizer 3-0 in best-of-5 final for league championship.

APPALACHIAN LEAGUE
ROOKIE ADVANCED

EAST	W	L	PCT	GB	Manager
Martinsville (Astros)	42	23	.646	—	Jorge Orta
Danville (Braves)	36	30	.545	6½	Kevin McMullan
Burlington (Indians)	37	31	.544	6½	Rouglas Odor
Bluefield (Orioles)	23	40	.365	18	Don Buford
Princeton (Devil Rays)	23	41	.359	18½	Jamie Nelson
WEST	**W**	**L**	**PCT**	**GB**	**Manager**
Elizabethton (Twins)	42	24	.636	—	Ray Smith
Pulaski (Blue Jays)	38	29	.567	4½	Paul Elliot
Bristol (White Sox)	33	33	.500	9	Jerry Hairston
Johnson City (Cardinals)	27	36	.429	13½	Ron Warner
Kingsport (Mets)	25	39	.391	16	Mookie Wilson

PLAYOFF: Elizabethton defeated Martinsville 2-1 in best-of-3 series for league championship.

PIONEER LEAGUE
ROOKIE ADVANCED

NORTH	W	L	PCT	GB	Manager(s)
**Helena (Brewers)	48	28	.632	—	Ed Sedar
#Billings (Reds)	41	35	.539	7	Rick Burleson/Jay Sorg
Great Falls (White Sox)	38	38	.500	10	Chris Cron
Missoula (Diamondbacks)	36	40	.474	12	Tony Perezchica
SOUTH	**W**	**L**	**PCT**	**GB**	**Manager**
**Provo (Angels)	54	22	.710	—	Tom Kotchman
#Ogden (Dodgers)	35	41	.461	19	Travis Barbary
Casper (Rockies)	28	48	.368	26	P.J. Carey
Idaho Falls (Padres)	24	52	.316	30	Carlos Lezcano

PLAYOFFS—Semifinals: Billings def. Helena 2-1; Provo def. Ogden 2-1 in best-of-3 series. **Final:** Billings def. Provo 2-0 in best-of-3.

ARIZONA LEAGUE
ROOKIE

	W	L	PCT	GB	Manager
*Rangers	35	14	.714	—	Pedro Lopez
*Royals-1	31	18	.633	4	Kevin Boles
Mariners	29	19	.604	5½	Scott Steinmann
Royals-2	32	22	.593	5½	Lloyd Simmons
Giants	25	24	.510	10	Bert Hunter
Cubs	25	24	.510	10	Carmelo Martinez
Angels	20	29	.408	15	Brian Harper
Athletics	15	33	.313	19½	Ruben Escalera
Brewers	15	34	.306	20	Hector Torres

PLAYOFF: Royals-1 defeated Rangers in one-game playoff.

GULF COAST LEAGUE
ROOKIE

EAST	W	L	PCT	GB	Manager
Braves	38	22	.633	—	Ralph Henriquez
Dodgers	29	31	.483	9	Luis Salazar
Marlins	26	32	.448	11	Tim Cossins
Expos	25	33	.431	12	Bobby Henley
NORTH	**W**	**L**	**PCT**	**GB**	**Manager**
Pirates	36	20	.643	—	Woody Huyke
Tigers	28	29	.491	8½	Howard Bushong
Yankees	26	31	.456	10½	Dan Radison
Phillies	23	33	.411	13	Ruben Amaro
SOUTH	**W**	**L**	**PCT**	**GB**	**Manager**
Red Sox	33	26	.559	—	Ralph Treuel
Orioles	32	28	.553	1½	Jesus Alfaro
Twins	28	31	.475	5	Rudy Hernandez
Reds	26	34	.433	7½	Edgar Caceres

PLAYOFFS—Semifinal: Braves defeated Red Sox in one-game playoff. **Final:** Braves defeated Pirates 2-0 in best-of-3 series.

INTERNATIONAL
LEAGUE

Office Address: 55 S. High St., Suite 202, Dublin, OH 43017.
Telephone: (614) 791-9300. **FAX:** (614) 791-9009.
E-Mail Address: office@ilbaseball.com. **Website:** www.ilbaseball.com.
Years League Active: 1884-.

President/Treasurer: Randy Mobley.
Vice Presidents: Harold Cooper, Dave Rosenfield (Norfolk),
Tex Simone (Syracuse), George Sisler Jr. **Corporate Secretary:**
Max Schumacher (Indianapolis).

Directors: Bruce Baldwin (Richmond), Don Beaver (Charlotte), George Habel (Durham), Joe Napoli (Toledo), Ray Pecor Jr. (Ottawa), Bob Rich Jr. (Buffalo), Dave Rosenfield (Norfolk), Ken Schnacke (Columbus), Max Schumacher (Indianapolis), Naomi Silver (Rochester), John Simone (Syracuse), Mike Tamburro (Pawtucket), Gary Ulmer (Louisville), Tom Van Schaack (Scranton/Wilkes-Barre).

Assistant to President: Nathan Blackmon. **Office Manager:** Loretta Holland.
2004 Opening Date: April 8. **Closing Date:** Sept. 6.
Regular Season: 144 games.

Division Structure: North—Buffalo, Ottawa, Pawtucket, Rochester, Scranton/Wilkes-Barre, Syracuse. **West**—Columbus, Indianapolis, Louisville, Toledo. **South**—Charlotte, Durham, Norfolk, Richmond.

Randy Mobley

Playoff Format: West champion plays South champion in best-of-5 series; wild-card club (non-division winner with best record) plays North champion in best-of-5 series. Winners meet in best-of-5 series for Governors' Cup championship.

All-Star Game: July 14 at Pawtucket (IL vs. Pacific Coast League).
Roster Limit: 23; 24 for first 30 days of season and after Aug. 9. **Player Eligibility Rule:** No restrictions.
Brand of Baseball: Rawlings ROM-INT.
Statistician: The Sports Network, 2200 Byberry Rd., Suite 200, Hatboro, PA 19040.
Umpires: Bob Bainter (Taylorville, IL), Damien Beal (Gainesville, FL), Michael Belin (Tampa, FL), Tyler Bolick (Woodstock, GA), Kevin Causey (Riverview, FL), Ben Clanton (Nesbit, MS), Brad Cole (Jacksonville, FL), Dan Cricks (Palm Bay, FL), Dusty Dellinger (Landis, NC), Peter Durfee (Tucson, AZ), Chad Fairchild (Sarasota, FL), Mike Fichter (Munster, IN), Troy Fullwood (Hampton, VA), Ray Gregson (Jefferson, LA), Brian Hale (Trussville, AL), Matt Hollowell (Jupiter, FL), James Hoye (Brookpark, OH), Chris Hubler (Durant, IA), Darren Hyman (Moline, IL), Adrian Johnson (Trinity, FL), Trey Nelson (Lincoln, NE), David Riley (Neenah, WI), Darren Spagnardi (Lexington, NC), Neil Taylor (Dunedin, FL), Darin Williams (Beebe, AR).

STADIUM INFORMATION

Club	Stadium	Dimensions			Capacity	2003 Att.
		LF	CF	RF		
Buffalo	Dunn Tire Park	325	404	325	21,050	551,916
Charlotte	Knights	325	400	325	10,000	268,374
Columbus	Cooper	355	400	330	15,000	480,445
Durham	Durham Bulls Athletic	305	400	327	10,000	501,855
Indianapolis	Victory Field	320	402	320	15,500	550,319
Louisville	Louisville Slugger Field	325	400	340	13,200	661,986
Norfolk	Harbor Park	333	410	338	12,067	480,963
Ottawa	Lynx	325	404	325	10,332	182,852
Pawtucket	McCoy	325	400	325	10,031	569,106
Richmond	The Diamond	330	402	330	12,134	446,882
Rochester	Frontier Field	335	402	325	10,868	418,014
Scranton/WB	Lackawanna County	330	408	330	10,982	427,445
Syracuse	P&C	330	400	330	11,604	356,303
Toledo	Fifth Third Field	320	412	326	8,943	517,331

BUFFALO BISONS

Office Address: 275 Washington St., Buffalo, NY 14203.
Telephone: (716) 846-2000. **FAX:** (716) 852-6530.
E-Mail Address: info@bisons.com. **Website:** www.bisons.com.
Affiliation (first year): Cleveland Indians (1995). **Years in League:** 1886-90, 1912-70, 1998-.

OWNERSHIP, MANAGEMENT

Operated by: Rich Products Corp.
Chairman: Robert Rich Sr. **Principal Owner, President:** Robert Rich Jr.
President, Rich Entertainment Group: Melinda Rich. **President, Rich Baseball Operations:** Jon Dandes. **Vice President/Treasurer:** David Rich. **VP/Secretary:** William Gisel.
VP/General Manager: Mike Buczkowski. **VP, Finance:** Joseph Segarra. **Corporate Counsel:** Jill Bond, William Grieshober. **Director, Public Relations/Marketing:** Tom Burns. **Director, Sales:** Christopher Hill. **Director, Stadium Operations:** Tom Sciarrino. **Controller:** John Rupp. **Manager, Ticket Office/Accounting:** Rita Clark. **Accounting Assistant:** Amy Delaney. **Accountants:** Kevin Parkinson, Erin Turkasz, Nicole Winiarski. **Manager, Ticket Operations:** Mike Poreda. **Marketing/Game Day Assistant:** Mike Sciortino. **Ticketing Account Executives:** Kristen Burwell, Mark Gordon, Burt Mirti, Frank Mooney, Anthony Sprague. **Account Executives:** Kathleen Delisanti, Jim Harrington, Brendan Kelly. **Coordinator, Sales:** Susan Kirk. **Manager, Merchandise:** Kathleen Wind. **Manager, Office Services:** Margaret Russo. **Executive Assistant:** Tina Sarcinelli. **Director, Food/Beverages:** John Corey. **Assistant Concessions Manager:** Roger Buczek. **Assistant Manager, Pettibones Grill:** Mary Jo Crowe. **Head Groundskeeper:** Kari Briggs. **Chief Engineer:** Pat Chella. **Home Clubhouse/Equipment Manager:** Scott Lesher. **Visiting Clubhouse Manager:** Mike Crouse.

FIELD STAFF

Manager: Marty Brown. **Coach:** Carlos Garcia. **Pitching Coach:** Terry Clark. **Trainer:** Nick Paparesta.

GAME INFORMATION

Radio Announcers: Jim Rosenhaus, Duke McGuire. **No. of Games Broadcast:** Home-72, Away-72. **Flagship Station:** WWKB 1520-AM.
PA Announcer: John Summers. **Official Scorers:** Mike Kelly, Kevin Lester.
Stadium Name (year opened): Dunn Tire Park (1988). **Location:** From north, take I-190 to Elm Street exit, left onto Swan Street. From east, take I-90 West to exit 51 (Route 33) to end, exit at Oak Street, right onto Swan Street. From west, take I-90 East, exit 53 to I-190 North, exit at Elm Street, left onto Swan Street. **Standard Game Times:** 7:05 p.m.; Thur. 1:05; Sat. 2:05, 7:05; Sun 2:05.
Visiting Club Hotel: Downtown Holiday Inn, 620 Delaware Ave., Buffalo, NY 14202. Telephone: (716) 886-2121.

CHARLOTTE KNIGHTS

Office Address: 2280 Deerfield Dr., Fort Mill, SC 29715.
Telephone: (704) 357-8071. **FAX:** (704) 329-2155.
E-Mail Address: knights@charlotteknights.com. **Website:** www.charlotteknights.com.
Affiliation (first year): Chicago White Sox (1999). **Years in League:** 1993-.

OWNERSHIP, MANAGEMENT

Operated by: Knights Baseball, LLC.
Principal Owners: Bill Allen, Don Beaver, Derick Close.
President: Don Beaver.
Vice President/General Manager: Bill Blackwell. **Assistant GM:** Jon Percival. **Director, Group Sales/Ticket Operations:** Sean Owens. **Director, Media/Community Relations:** Ryan Gerds. **Director, Creative Services:** Mike Riviello. **Director, Broadcasting/Team Travel:** Matt Swierad. **Director, Corporate Accounts:** Dick Fox. **Business Manager:** Katie Smith. **Corporate Account Managers:** John Watkins, Brooke Varner. **Group Event Coordinators:** Bryan Stefani, Jon Davis, Sean O'Connor, Natalie Pope. **Box Office Coordinator:** Kelly Crawford. **Operations Manager:** Tom Humrickhouse. **Office Manager:** Stephanie ReVille. **Merchandise Manager:** Jennifer Lude. **Mascot Coordinator:** Billy Yandle. **Head Groundskeeper:** Eddie Busque. **Assistant Groundskeeper:** Brandon Landreth. **Facility Maintenance Manager:** Joe Sistare. **Clubhouse Manager:** John Bare.

FIELD STAFF

Manager: Nick Capra. **Coach:** Gregg Ritchie. **Pitching Coach:** Curt Hasler. **Trainer:** Scott Johnson.

GAME INFORMATION

Radio Announcer: Matt Swierad. **No. of Games Broadcast:** Home-72, Away-72. **Flagship Station:** WFNZ 610-AM.
PA Announcer: Unavailable. **Official Scorers:** Brent Stastny, Ed Walton, Sam Copeland.
Stadium Name (year opened): Knights Stadium (1990). **Location:** Exit 88 off I-77, east on Gold Hill Road. **Standard**

Game Times: 7:15 p.m.; Sun. 2:15.
 Visiting Club Hotel: Hilton Garden Inn, 425 Town Center Blvd., Pineville NC 28134. Telephone: (704) 889-3279.

COLUMBUS CLIPPERS

Office Address: 1155 W. Mound St., Columbus, OH 43223.
Telephone: (614) 462-5250. **FAX:** (614) 462-3271.
E-Mail Address: info@clippersbaseball.com. **Website:** www.clippersbaseball.com.
Affiliation (first year): New York Yankees (1979). **Years in League:** 1955-70, 1977-.

OWNERSHIP, MANAGEMENT

Operated by: Columbus Baseball Team, Inc.
Principal Owner: Franklin County, Ohio.
Board of Directors: Ralph Anderson, Donald Borror, Stephen Cheek, Wayne Harer, Richard Smith, Cathy Lyttle, John Wolfe.
President, General Manager: Ken Schnacke. **Assistant GM:** Mark Warren. **Director, Stadium Operations:** Steve Dalin. **Director, Ticket Operations:** Scott Ziegler. **Director, Group Sales:** Ty Debevoise. **Director, Marketing:** Mark Galuska. **Director, Promotions:** Jason Kidik. **Director, Broadcasting:** Todd Bell. **Director, Advertising:** Keif Fetch. **Director, Communications:** Joe Santry. **Director, Community/Media Relations:** Unavailable. **Director, Merchandising:** Krista Oberlander. **Director, Finance:** Bonnie Badgley. **Assistant Director, Group Sales:** Tom Hampton. **Assistant Director, Promotions:** Dan Scali. **Assistant to GM:** Judi Timmons. **Administrative Assistants:** Kelly Ryther, Brittney Heimann.

FIELD STAFF

Manager: Bucky Dent. **Coaches:** Jack Hubbard, Kevin Long. **Pitching Coach:** Neil Allen. **Trainer:** Darren London.

GAME INFORMATION

Radio Announcers: Todd Bell, Gary Richards. **No. of Games Broadcast:** Home-72, Away-72. **Flagship Station:** WSMZ 103.1-FM.
PA Announcer: Rich Hanchette. **Official Scorers:** Unavailable.
Stadium Name (year opened): Cooper Stadium (1977). **Location:** From north/south, I-71 to I-70 West, exit at Mound Street. From west, I-70 East, exit at Broad Street, east to Glenwood, south to Mound Street. From east, I-70 West, exit at Mound Street. **Standard Game Times:** 7:05 p.m.; Fri. 7:05/7:25; Sat. 6:05/7:05; Sun. 1:05.
Visiting Club Hotels: Radisson Hotel, 7007 N. High St., Columbus, OH 43085. Telephone: (614) 436-0700. Sheraton Suites-Columbus, 201 Hutchinson Ave., Columbus, OH 43235. Telephone: (614) 781-7316. Holiday Inn, 175 Hutchinson Ave., Columbus, OH 43235. Telephone: (614) 431-4457.

DURHAM BULLS

Office Address: 409 Blackwell St., Durham, NC 27701.
Mailing Address: P.O. Box 507, Durham, NC 27702.
Telephone: (919) 687-6500. **FAX:** (919) 687-6560.
Website: www.durhambulls.com.
Affiliation (first year): Tampa Bay Devil Rays (1998). **Years in League:** 1998-.

OWNERSHIP, MANAGEMENT

Operated by: Capitol Broadcasting Co., Inc.
President, Chief Executive Officer: Jim Goodmon.
Vice President: George Habel. **VP, Legal Counsel:** Mike Hill.
General Manager: Mike Birling. **Assistant General Manager:** Jon Bishop. **Manager, Sales:** Chip Hutchinson.
Account Executives, Sponsorship: Brian French, Shannon Haire, Sandy Speagle.
Coordinator, Sponsorship Services: Nicola Mattis. **Director, Media Relations/Promotions:** Matt DeMargel. **Director, Multimedia Operations:** Aaron Bare. **Assistant, Media Relations:** Dan Carr. **Assistant, Community Relations/Promotions:** Christy Holleman. **Director, Ticket Services:** Brad Lanphear. **Business Development Coordinators:** Tadd Hall, Sheldon Leonard, Tim Seaton. **Group Sales Assistants:** Kevin Crittendon, Dustin Hickman, Brooke Robinson, Mary Beth Warfford. **Director, Stadium Operations:** Mike Tilly. **Supervisor, Operations:** Derek Walsh. **Manager, Merchandise:** Allan Long. **General Manager, Concessions:** Jamie Jenkins. **Assistant GM, Concessions:** Tammy Scott. **Head Groundskeeper:** Jimmy Simpson. **Manager, Business:** Rhonda Carlisle. **Accountants:** Theresa Stocking, Delesia Rogers. **Director, Security:** Ed Sarvis. **Administrative Assistant:** Libby Hamilton. **Receptionist/Secretary:** Barbara Goss. **Box Office Sales:** Jerry Mach.

FIELD STAFF

Manager: Bill Evers. **Coach:** Richie Hebner. **Pitching Coach:** Joe Coleman. **Trainer:** Tom Tisdale.

GAME INFORMATION

Radio Announcers: Steve Barnes, Neil Solondz. **No. of Games Broadcast:** Home-72, Away-72. **Flagship Station:** WDNC 620-AM.

PA Announcer: Bill Law. **Official Scorer:** Brent Belvin.

Stadium Name (year opened): Durham Bulls Athletic Park (1995). **Location:** From Raleigh, I-40 West to Highway 147 North, exit 12B to Willard, two blocks on Willard to stadium. From I-85, Gregson Street exit to downtown, left on Chapel Hill Street, right on Mangum Street. **Standard Game Times:** 7 p.m.; Sun. 5.

Visiting Club Hotel: Durham Marriott at the Civic Center, 201 Foster St., Durham, NC 27701. Telephone: (919) 768-6000.

INDIANAPOLIS
INDIANS

Office Address: 501 W. Maryland St., Indianapolis, IN 46225.
Telephone: (317) 269-3542. **FAX:** (317) 269-3541.
E-Mail Address: indians@indyindians.com **Website:** www.indyindians.com.
Affiliation (first year): Milwaukee Brewers (2000). **Years in League:** 1963, 1998-.

OWNERSHIP, MANAGEMENT

Operated by: Indians, Inc.
Chairman, President: Max Schumacher.
General Manager: Cal Burleson. **Assistant GM, Operations:** Randy Lewandowski. **Director, Corporate Development:** Bruce Schumacher. **Director, Marketing:** Chris Herndon. **Director, Ticket Operations:** Mike Schneider. **Director, Ticket Sales:** Matt Guay. **Manager, Box Office:** Kerry Vick. **Director, Public Relations/Account Executive:** Mike Wolinsky. **Director, Community Relations:** Traci Vernon. **Director, Merchandising:** Mark Schumacher. **Marketing Coordinator:** Nicole Stevens. **Group Sales Executives:** Michael Blackert, Samantha Coghill. **Director, Broadcasting:** Howard Kellman. **Director, Business Operations:** Brad Morris. **Director, Stadium/Baseball Operations:** Scott Rubin. **Director, Suiteholder Services:** Dave McGhee. **Control Room Coordinator:** Adam Lane. **Facility Director:** Bill Sampson. **Director, Stadium Maintenance:** Tim Hughes. **Maintenance Assistant:** Allan Danehy. **Head Groundskeeper:** Jamie Mehringer. **Administrative Assistant:** Stu Tobias. **Equipment/Clubhouse Manager:** J.R. Rinaldi. **Director, Food Services:** Carey Landis.

FIELD STAFF

Manager: Cecil Cooper. **Coach:** Bobby Randall. **Pitching Coach:** Stan Kyles. **Trainer:** Jeff Paxson.

GAME INFORMATION

Radio Announcers: Howard Kellman, Brian Giffin. **No. of Games Broadcast:** Home-72, Away-72. **Flagship Station:** WXNT 1430-AM.

PA Announcer: Bruce Schumacher. **Official Scorers:** Kim Rogers, Tom Akins, Mark Walpole.

Stadium Name (year opened): Victory Field (1996). **Location:** I-70 to West Street exit, north on West Street to ballpark; I-65 to Martin Luther King and West Street exit, south on West Street to ballpark. **Standard Game Times:** 7 p.m.; Sun. 2/6.

Visiting Club Hotel: The Comfort Inn, 530 S. Capitol, Indianapolis, IN 46225. Telephone: (317) 631-9000.

LOUISVILLE
BATS

Office Address: 401 E. Main St., Louisville, KY 40202.
Telephone: (502) 212-2287. **FAX:** (502) 515-2255.
E-Mail Address: info@batsbaseball.com. **Website:** www.batsbaseball.com.
Affiliation (first year): Cincinnati Reds (2000). **Years in League:** 1998-.

OWNERSHIP, MANAGEMENT

Operated by: Louisville Baseball Club, Inc.
Board of Directors: Ed Glasscock, Jack Hillerich, Kenny Huber, Jim Morrissey, Tom Musselman, Dale Owens, Bob Stallings, Dan Ulmer, Gary Ulmer.
Chairman: Dan Ulmer. **President:** Gary Ulmer.
Vice President/General Manager: Dale Owens. **Assistant GM/Director, Marketing:** Greg Galiette. **Director, Baseball Operations:** Mary Barney. **Director, Stadium Operations:** Scott Shoemaker. **Director, Ticket Sales:** James Breeding. **Director, Broadcasting:** Jim Kelch. **Controller:** Michele Anderson. **Manager, Tickets:** George Veith. **Director, Public/Media Relations:** Svend Jansen. **Director, Suite Level Services:** Graham Honaker. **Manager, Ticket Accounting:** Earl Stubblefield. **Coordinator, Group Sales:** Bryan McBride. **Senior Account Executives:** Jason Abraham, Courtney Myers, Russell Pol, Jason Hartings, Hal Norwood. **Assistant Director, Public/Media Relations:** Megan Dimond. **Manager, Community Relations:** Karrie Harper. **Assistant Manager, Tickets:** Kyle Reh. **Operations Assistant:** Doug Randol. **Account Executive:** Matt Andrews. **Sales Representatives:** A.T. Simmons, Matt Wilmes.

Administrative Assistant: Jodi Tischendorf. **Head Groundskeeper:** Tom Nielsen. **Assistant Groundskeeper:** Brad Smith.

FIELD STAFF
Manager: Rick Burleson. **Coaches:** Adrian Garrett, Jeff Young. **Pitching Coach:** Mack Jenkins. **Trainer:** Steve Baumann.

GAME INFORMATION
Radio Announcers: Jim Kelch, Matt Andrews. **No. of Games Broadcast:** Home-72, Away-72. **Flagship Station:** WGTK 970-AM.
PA Announcer: Charles Gazaway. **Official Scorer:** Ken Horn.
Stadium Name (year opened): Louisville Slugger Field (2000). **Location:** I-64 and I-71 to I-65 South/North to Brook Street exit, right on Market Street, left on Jackson Street, stadium on Main Street between Jackson and Preston. **Standard Game Times:** 7:15 p.m.; Sat: 6:15; Sun: 1:15/6:15.
Visiting Club Hotel: Ramada Inn Riverside, 700 W Riverside Dr., Jeffersonville, IN 47130. Telephone: (812) 284-6711.

NORFOLK
TIDES

Office Address: 150 Park Ave., Norfolk, VA 23510.
Telephone: (757) 622-2222. **FAX:** (757) 624-9090.
Website: www.norfolktides.com.
Affiliation (first year): New York Mets (1969). **Years in League:** 1969-.

OWNERSHIP, MANAGEMENT
Operated by: Tides Baseball Club, LP.
President: Ken Young.
General Manager: Dave Rosenfield. **Director, Media Relations:** Robin Wentz. **Director, Community Relations:** Heather Harkins. **Manager, Merchandising:** Mark Kaczorowski. **Coordinator, Sales/Promotions:** Ben Giancola. **Director, Ticket Operations:** Glenn Riggs. **Director, Video Operations:** Jody Cox. **Director, Group Sales:** Dave Harrah. **Coordinator, Group Sales:** Stephanie Brammer. **Business Manager:** Mike Giedlin. **Director, Stadium Operations:** John Slagle. **Assistant, Stadium Operations:** Matt Newbold. **Ticket Manager:** Linda Waisanen. **Administrative Assistant:** Jenn Moore. **Equipment/Clubhouse Manager:** Stan Hunter. **Head Groundskeeper:** Ken Magner. **Assistant Groundskeeper:** Keith Collins.

FIELD STAFF
Manager: John Stearns. **Coach:** Al LeBoeuf. **Pitching Coach:** Dan Warthen. **Trainer:** Brian Chicklo.

GAME INFORMATION
Radio Announcers: Jeff McCarragher, John Castleberry. **No. of Games Broadcast:** Home-72, Away-72. **Flagship Station:** ESPN 1310-AM, WFOG 1050-AM.
PA Announcer: Don Bolger. **Official Scorer:** Unavailable.
Stadium Name (year opened): Harbor Park (1993). **Location:** Exit 9, 11A or 11B off I-264, adjacent to the Elizabeth River in downtown Norfolk. **Standard Game Times:** 7:15 p.m.; Sun. (April-June) 1:15, (July-Sept.) 6:15.
Visiting Club Hotels: Sheraton Waterside, 777 Waterside Dr., Norfolk, VA 23510. Telephone: (757) 622-6664. Doubletree Club Hotel, 880 N. Military Hwy., Norfolk, VA 23502. Telephone: (757) 461-9192.

OTTAWA
LYNX

Office Address: Lynx Stadium, 300 Coventry Rd., Ottawa, Ontario K1K 4P5.
Telephone: (613) 747-5969. **FAX:** (613) 747-0003.
E-Mail Address: lynx@ottawalynx.com. **Website:** www.ottawalynx.com.
Affiliation (first year): Baltimore Orioles (2003). **Years in League:** 1951-54, 1993-.

OWNERSHIP, MANAGEMENT
Operated By: Ottawa Lynx Company.
Principal Owner: Ray Pecor.
General Manager: Kyle Bostwick. **Assistant GM:** Mark Sluban. **Office Administrator:** Lorraine Charrette. **Director, Media/Public Relations:** Brian Morris. **Director, Ticket Operations:** Melissa Rumble. **Sales Account Executive:** Don Charrette. **Group Sales Coordinators:** Dominic Chagnon, Sarah Dokken. **Equipment Manager:** John Bryk. **Visiting Clubhouse Manager:** Jason Ross. **Head Groundskeepers:** Matt Horan, Steve Bennett.

FIELD STAFF
Manager: Tim Leiper. **Coach:** Dave Cash. **Pitching Coach:** Steve McCatty. **Trainer:** P.J. Mainville.

GAME INFORMATION

Radio: Unavailable.

PA Announcer: Jeff Lefebvre. **Official Scorer:** Frank Calamatas.

Stadium Name (year opened): Lynx Stadium (1993). **Location:** Highway 417 to Vanier Parkway exit, Vanier Parkway north to Coventry Road to stadium. **Standard Game Times:** 7:05 p.m.; Sat. 6:05; Sun./holidays 1:05.

Visiting Club Hotel: Chimo Hotel, 1199 Joseph Cyr Rd., Ottawa, Ontario K1K 3P5. Telephone: (613) 744-1060.

PAWTUCKET
RED SOX

Office Address: One Ben Mondor Way, Pawtucket, RI 02860.

Mailing Address: P.O. Box 2365, Pawtucket, RI 02861.

Telephone: (401) 724-7300. **FAX:** (401) 724-2140.

E-Mail Address: info@pawsox.com. **Website:** www.pawsox.com.

Affiliation (first year): Boston Red Sox (1973). **Years in League:** 1973-.

OWNERSHIP, MANAGEMENT

Operated by: Pawtucket Red Sox Baseball Club, Inc.

Chairman: Ben Mondor. **President:** Mike Tamburro.

Vice President/General Manager: Lou Schwechheimer. **VP, Chief Financial Officer:** Matt White. **VP, Sales/Marketing:** Michael Gwynn. **VP, Stadium Operations:** Mick Tedesco. **VP, Public Relations:** Bill Wanless. **Assistant to GM:** Daryl Jasper. **Director, Ticket Operations:** Mike McAtee. **Manager, Finance:** Kristy Batchelder. **Director, Community Relations:** Jeff Bradley. **Director, Merchandising:** Eric Petterson. **Director, Media Services:** Jeff Quimette. **Director, Warehouse Operations:** Dave Johnson. **Director, Concession Services:** Jim Hogan. **Administrative Assistant:** Patricia Lapinski. **Account Executive:** John Garcia. **Secretary:** Jackie Dryer. **Clubhouse Manager:** Chris Parent. **Head Groundskeeper:** Casey Erven. **Assistant Groundskeeper:** Matt McKinnon. **Facility Operations:** Kevin Galligan. **Executive Chef:** Dom Rendine.

FIELD STAFF

Manager: Buddy Bailey. **Coach:** Mark Budaska. **Pitching Coach:** Mike Griffin. **Trainer:** Bill Coffey.

GAME INFORMATION

Radio Announcer: Andy Freed. **No. of Games Broadcast:** Home-72, Away-72. **Flagship Station:** WSKO 790-AM.

PA Announcer: Jim Martin. **Official Scorer:** Bruce Guindon.

Stadium Name (year opened): McCoy Stadium (1946). **Location:** From north, Route 95 South to exit 2A in Massachusetts (Newport Ave./Pawtucket), follow Newport Ave. for 2 miles, right on Columbus Ave., follow Columbus Ave. for one mile, stadium on right. From south, Route 95 North to exit 28 (School Street), right at bottom of exit ramp, through two sets of lights, left onto Pond Street, right on Columbus Ave., stadium entrance on left. From west, (Worcester), Route 146 South to Route 295 North to Route 95 South and follow directions from north. From east (Fall River), Route 195 West to Route 95 North and follow directions from south. **Standard Game Times:** 7 p.m.; Sat. 6, Sun. 1.

Visiting Club Hotel: Comfort Inn, 2 George St., Pawtucket, RI 02860. Telephone: (401) 723-6700.

RICHMOND
BRAVES

Office Address: 3001 North Blvd., Richmond, VA 23230.

Mailing Address: P.O. Box 6667, Richmond, VA 23230.

Telephone: (804) 359-4444. **FAX:** (804) 359-0731.

E-Mail Address: info@rbraves.com. **Website:** www.rbraves.com.

Affiliation (first year): Atlanta Braves (1966). **Years in League:** 1884, 1915-17, 1954-64, 1966-.

OWNERSHIP, MANAGEMENT

Operated by: Atlanta National League Baseball, Inc.

General Manager: Bruce Baldwin. **Assistant GM:** Toby Wyman. **Office Manager:** Joanne Curnutt. **Receptionist:** Janet Zimmerman. **Manager, Stadium Operations:** Rob Bordner. **Manager, Field Maintenance:** Chad Mulholland. **Manager, Public Relations:** Todd Feagans. **Assistant Manager, Community Relations:** Elizabeth Snavely. **Assistant Manager, Promotions and Entertainment:** Noir Fowler. **Manager, Corporate Sales:** Bobby Holland. **Manager, Ticket Sales:** Ben Terry. **Assistant Manager, Ticket Sales:** Bryan Jones. **Assistant Manager, Group Sales:** Meghan Lynch. **Clubhouse Manager:** Nicholas Leto.

FIELD STAFF

Manager: Pat Kelly. **Coach:** Rick Albert. **Pitching Coach:** Guy Hansen. **Trainer:** Jay Williams.

GAME INFORMATION

Radio Announcers: Robert Fish. **No. of Games Broadcast:** Home-72, Away-72. **Flagship Station:** WXGI 950-AM.

PA Announcer: Mike Blacker. **Official Scorers:** Leonard Alley, Roscoe Puckett.

Stadium Name (year opened): The Diamond (1985). **Location**: Exit 78 (Boulevard) at junction of I-64 and I-95, follow signs to park. **Standard Game Times:** 7 p.m.; Sat. 4; Sun. 2.
Visiting Club Hotel: Quality Inn, 8008 W. Broad St., Richmond, VA 23230. Telephone: (804) 346-0000.

ROCHESTER
RED WINGS

Office Address: One Morrie Silver Way, Rochester, NY 14608.
Telephone: (585) 454-1001. **FAX:** (585) 454-1056, (585) 454-1057.
E-Mail Address: info@redwingsbaseball.com **Website**: www.redwingsbaseball.com.
Affiliation (first year): Minnesota Twins (2003). **Years in League:** 1885-89, 1891-92, 1895-.

OWNERSHIP, MANAGEMENT

Operated by: Rochester Community Baseball.
Chairman, Chief Operating Officer: Naomi Silver. **President, Chief Executive Officer**: Gary Larder.
General Manager: Dan Mason. **Assistant GM**: Will Rumbold. **Controller**: Darlene Giardina. **Operations Coordinator**: Mary Goldman. **Head Groundskeeper**: Gene Buonomo. **Director, Media/Public Relations**: Chuck Hinkel. **Director, Marketing**: Nick Sciarratta. **Group/Picnic Director**: Parker Allen. **Director, Promotions**: Matt Cipro. **Director, Game Day Production**: Brian Golding. **Director, Ticket Sales**: Joe Ferrigno. **Director, Merchandising**: Lisa Cardilli. **Director, Human Resources**: Paula LoVerde. **Account Executive**: Rose Marie Bianco **APAR Manager**: Liz Ammons. **Executive Secretary**: Ginny Colbert. **Director, Food Services**: Jeff Dodge. **Manager, Suites/Catering**: Jennifer Pierce. **Catering Sales Manager**: Sarah Bradley. **Manager, Concessions**: Jeff DeSantis. **Business Manager, Concessions**: Dave Bills. **Clubhouse Operations**: Terry Costello. **Account Representative**: Zach Holmes. **Night Secretary**: Cathie Costello.

FIELD STAFF

Manager: Phil Roof. **Coach**: Rich Miller. **Pitching Coach:** Bobby Cuellar. **Trainer:** Dave Pruemer.

GAME INFORMATION

Radio Announcers: Josh Whetzel, Joe Altobelli. **No. of Games Broadcast**: Home-72, Away-72. **Flagship Stations**: WHTK 1280-AM, WHAM 1180-AM.
PA Announcer: Pete McKenzie. **Official Scorer**: Lary Bump.
Stadium Name: Frontier Field (1997). **Location**: I-490 East to exit 12 (Brown/Broad Street) and follow signs. I-490 West to exit 14 (Plymouth Ave.) and follow signs. **Standard Game Times**: 7:05 p.m.; Sun 1:35.
Visiting Club Hotel: Crown Plaza, 70 State St., Rochester, NY 14608. Telephone: (585) 546-3450.

SCRANTON/WILKES-BARRE
RED BARONS

Office Address: 235 Montage Mountain Rd., Moosic, PA 18507.
Mailing Address: P.O. Box 3449, Scranton, PA 18505.
Telephone: (570) 969-2255. **FAX:** (570) 963-6564.
E-Mail Address: barons@epix.net. **Website:** www.redbarons.com.
Affiliation (first year): Philadelphia Phillies (1989). **Years in League:** 1989-.

OWNERSHIP, MANAGEMENT

Operated by: Lackawanna County Stadium Authority.
Chairman: Bill Jenkins.
General Manager: Tom Van Schaack. **Director, Media/Public Relations:** Mike Cummings. **Director, Promotions:** Unavailable. **Executive Assistant:** Kelly Byron. **Director, Stadium Operations:** Jeremy Ruby. **Director, Sales/Marketing:** Ron Prislupski. **Senior Account Representatives:** Ned Gavlick, Jack Gowron, Joe Shaughnessy, Travis Spencer, Jennette LePori. **Director, Ticket Sales:** Ann Marie Nocera. **Director, Merchandising:** Ray Midura. **Director, Food Services:** Rich Sweeney. **Clubhouse Operations:** Red Brower, Rich Revta. **Director, Special Projects:** Karen Healey. **Office Manager:** Donna Kunda. **Controller:** Vicki Lamberton. **Head Groundskeeper:** Bill Casterline.

FIELD STAFF

Manager: Marc Bombard. **Coach:** Sal Rende **Pitching Coach:** Rich Dubee. **Trainer:** Brian Cammarota.

GAME INFORMATION

Radio Announcer: Kent Westling. **No. of Games Broadcast:** Home-72, Away-72. **Flagship Station:** WWDL 104.9-FM.
PA Announcer: Johnny Davies. **Official Scorers:** Bob McGoff, Jeep Fanucci.
Stadium Name (Year Opened): Lackawanna County Stadium (1989). **Location:** I-81 to exit 182 (Davis Street/Montage Mountain Road), take Montage Mountain Road one mile to stadium. **Standard Game Times:** 7 p.m.; Sun. 2/6.
Visiting Club Hotel: Radisson at Lackawanna Station, 700 Lackawanna Ave., Scranton, PA 18503. Telephone: (570) 342-8300.

SYRACUSE
SKYCHIEFS

Office Address: P&C Stadium, One Tex Simone Dr., Syracuse, NY 13208.
Telephone: (315) 474-7833. **FAX:** (315) 474-2658.
E-Mail Address: baseball@skychiefs.com. **Website:** www.skychiefs.com.
Affiliation (first year): Toronto Blue Jays (1978). **Years in League:** 1885-89, 1891-92, 1894-1901, 1918, 1920-27, 1934-55, 1961-.

OWNERSHIP, MANAGEMENT

Operated by: Community Owned Baseball Club of Central New York, Inc.
Chairman: Richard Ryan. **President:** Donald Waful. **Vice President/Treasurer:** Anton Kreuzer. **Vice President/Chief Operating Officer:** Anthony "Tex" Simone.
General Manager: John Simone. **Assistant GM, Sales:** Unavailable. **Assistant GM, Business:** Don Lehtonen. **Director, Group Sales:** Victor Gallucci. **Director, Operations:** H.J. Refici. **Director, Corporate Sales/Community Relations:** Andy Gee. **Associate Director, Group/Corporate Sales:** Mike Voutsinas. **Director, Merchandising:** Wendy Shoen. **Director, Ticket Office:** Jon Blumanthal. **Team Historian:** Ron Gersbacher. **Receptionist:** Priscilla Venditti. **Field Maintenance:** Jim Jacobson.

FIELD STAFF

Manager: Marty Pevey. **Coach:** Ken Landreaux. **Pitching Coach:** Brad Arnsberg. **Trainer:** Jon Woodworth.

GAME INFORMATION

Radio Announcer: Bob McElligott. **No. of Games Broadcast:** Home-72, Away-72. **Flagship Station:** WFBL 1390-AM.
PA Announcer: Jim Donovan. **Official Scorer:** Unavailable.
Stadium Name (year opened): P&C Stadium (1997). **Location:** New York State Thruway to exit 36 (I-81 South), to 7th North Street exit, left on 7th North, right on Hiawatha Boulevard. **Standard Game Times:** 7 p.m.; Sun. 6.
Visiting Club Hotel: Ramada Inn, 1305 Buckley Rd., Syracuse, NY 13212. Telephone: (315) 457-8670.

TOLEDO
MUD HENS

Office Address: 406 Washington St., Toledo, OH 43604.
Telephone: (419) 725-4367. **FAX:** (419) 725-4368.
E-Mail Address: mudhens@mudhens.com. **Website:** www.mudhens.com.
Affiliation (first year): Detroit Tigers (1987). **Years in League:** 1889, 1965-.

OWNERSHIP, MANAGEMENT

Operated by: Toledo Mud Hens Baseball Club, Inc.
Chairman, President: Michael Miller. **Vice President:** David Huey. **Secretary/Treasurer:** Charles Bracken.
General Manager: Joseph Napoli. **Assistant GM/Director, Corporate Sales:** Scott Jeffer. **Assistant GM/Director, Marketing and Advertising:** Neil Neukam. **Assistant GM, Ticket Sales/Operations:** Erik Ibsen. **Chief Financial Officer:** Bob Eldridge. **Director, Promotions:** Kerri White. **Director, Public/Media Relations:** Jason Griffin. **Manager, Season Ticket Sales/Services:** Thom Townley. **Manager, Community Relations:** Cheri Bohnsack. **Corporate Sales Associate:** Neil Stein. **Season Ticket/Group Sales Associates:** Steve Dolinar, Chris Hole, John Mulka, Brian Perkins, Greg Setola, Nathan Steinmetz. **Manager, Video Board Operations:** Mike Ramirez. **Manager, Merchandising:** Dan Berns. **Assistant Manager, Merchandising:** Craig Katz. **Manager, Stadium Operations:** Kirk Sausser. **Assistant Manager, Operations:** Melissa Ball. **Business Manager:** Dorothy Welniak. **Office Manager:** Carol Hamilton. **Maintenance Supervisor:** L.C. Bates. **Maintenance Assistant:** Erick Coleman. **Head Groundskeeper:** Jeff Limburg. **Assistant Groundskeeper:** Kris Fawcett. **Clubhouse Manager:** Joe Sarkisian. **Team Historian:** John Husman.

FIELD STAFF

Manager: Larry Parrish. **Coach:** Leon Durham. **Pitching Coach:** Jeff Jones. **Trainer:** Matt Rankin.

GAME INFORMATION

Radio Announcers: Jim Weber, Frank Gilhooley. **No. of Games Broadcast:** Home-72, Away-72. **Flagship Station:** WLQR 1470-AM.
PA Announcer: Bobb Vergeils. **Official Scorers:** Jeff Businger, Ron Kleinfelter, Guy Lammers.
Stadium Name (year opened): Fifth Third Field (2002). **Location:** From Ohio Turnpike 80/90, exit 54 (4A) to I-75 North, follow I-75 North to exit 201-B, left onto Erie Street, right onto Washington Street. From Detroit, I-75 South to exit 202-A, right onto Washington Street. From Dayton, I-75 North to exit 201-B, left onto Erie Street, right onto Washington Street. From Ann Arbor, Route 23 South to I-475 East, I-475 East to I-75 South, I-75 South to exit 202-A, right onto Washington Street. **Standard Game Times:** 7 p.m.; Sun. 2.
Visiting Club Hotel: Radisson, 101 North Summit, Toledo, OH 43604. Telephone: (419) 241-3000.

PACIFIC COAST
LEAGUE

CLASS AAA

Mailing Address: 1631 Mesa Ave., Suite A, Colorado Springs, CO 80906.
Telephone: (719) 636-3399. **FAX:** (719) 636-1199.
E-Mail Address: office@pclbaseball.com. **Website:** www.pclbaseball.com.

President: Branch B. Rickey.
Vice President: Don Logan (Las Vegas).
Directors: Don Beaver (New Orleans), Sam Bernabe (Iowa), Hilary Buzas-Drammis (Salt Lake), Hugh Campbell (Edmonton), John Carbray (Fresno), George Foster (Tacoma), Al Gordon (Nashville), Bob Goughan (Colorado Springs), Dean Jernigan (Memphis), Tom Lasley (Portland), Don Logan (Las Vegas), Matt Minker (Omaha), Tim O'Toole (Oklahoma), Art Savage (Sacramento), Ken Young (Albuquerque), Jay Zucker (Tucson).
Director, Operations: George King. **Office Manager:** Melanie Fiore. **Operations Assistant:** Steve Hurlbert.
2004 Opening Date: April 8. **Closing Date:** Sept. 6.
Regular Season: 144 games.
Division Structure. American Conference—Central: Albuquerque, Colorado Springs, Iowa, Omaha. **Eastern:** Memphis, Nashville, New Orleans, Oklahoma. **Pacific Conference—Southern:** Fresno, Las Vegas, Sacramento, Tucson. **Northern:** Edmonton, Portland, Salt Lake, Tacoma.

Branch Rickey

PACIFIC COAST LEAGUE

Playoff Format: Northern champion plays Southern champion, and Central champion plays Eastern champion in best-of-5 semifinal series. Winners meet in best-of-5 series for league championship.
All-Star Game: July 14 at Pawtucket, RI (PCL vs. International League).
Roster Limit: 23; 24 for first 30 days of season and after Aug. 9. **Player Eligibility Rule:** No restrictions.
Brand of Baseball: Rawlings ROM.
Statistician: The Sports Network, 2200 Byberry Rd., Suite 200, Hatboro, PA 19040.
Umpires: Ramon Armendariz (Vista, CA), David Aschwege (Lincoln, NE), Lance Barksdale (Jackson, MS), Angel Campos (Ontario, CA), Greg Chittenden (Springfield, MO), Frank Coffland (San Antonio, TX), Steve Cox (Tulsa, OK), Adam Dowdy (Pontiac, IL), Robert Drake (Mesa, AZ), Chris Guccione (Brighton, CO), Andy Hergesheimer (Columbia Falls, MT), Mike Jost (Tucson, AZ), Cameron Keller (Westminster, CO), Kevin Kelley (St. Louis, MO), Brian Knight (Helena, MT), Scott Letendre (Shasta, CA), Mark Mauro (San Mateo, CA), John McMasters (Tacoma, WA), Casey Moser (Iowa Park, TX), Michael Muchlinski (Ephrata, WA), Shawn Rakos (Pacific, WA), Travis Reininger (Brighton, CO), Jack Samuels (Orange, CA), Kevin Sweeney (Rio Rancho, NM), Todd Tichenor (Holcomb, KS), Ryan West (Littleton, CO), Mark Winters (Springfield, IL), Jim Wolf (West Hills, CA).

STADIUM INFORMATION

Club	Stadium	Dimensions LF	CF	RF	Capacity	2003 Att.
Albuquerque	Albuquerque Sports	360	410	340	10,510	576,867
Colorado Springs	Sky Sox	350	400	350	9,000	253,548
Edmonton	TELUS Field	340	420	320	9,200	333,792
Fresno	Grizzly Stadium	324	402	335	12,500	522,174
Iowa	Sec Taylor	335	400	335	10,800	490,150
Las Vegas	Cashman Field	328	433	323	9,334	326,243
Memphis	AutoZone Park	319	400	322	14,200	749,446
Nashville	Herschel Greer	327	400	327	10,700	387,345
New Orleans	Zephyr Field	333	405	332	11,000	379,819
Oklahoma	Southwestern Bell	325	400	325	13,066	380,051
Omaha	Rosenblatt	332	408	332	24,000	304,421
Portland	PGE Park	319	405	321	19,810	438,931
Sacramento	Raley Field	330	405	325	14,111	766,326
Salt Lake	Franklin Covey	345	420	315	15,500	474,647
Tacoma	Cheney	325	425	325	9,600	327,927
Tucson	Tucson Electric	340	405	340	11,000	286,657

ALBUQUERQUE
ISOTOPES

Office Address: 1601 Avenida Cesar Chavez SE, Albuquerque, NM 87106.
Telephone: (505) 924-2255. **FAX:** (505) 242-8899.
E-Mail Address: info@albuquerquebaseball.com. **Website:** www.albuquerque-baseball.com.
Affiliation (first year): Florida Marlins (2003). **Years in League:** 1972-2000, 2003-.

OWNERSHIP, MANAGEMENT

Operated by: Albuquerque Baseball Club, LLC.
President: Ken Young. **Secretary/Treasurer:** Emmett Hammond.
General Manager: John Traub. **Director, Sales/Marketing:** Nick LoBue. **Director, Accounting:** Barbara Campbell. **Director, Stadium Operations:** Drew Stuart. **Director, Group Sales/Season Tickets:** Jennifer Steger. **Manager, Merchandise:** Chrissy Baines. **Assistant Manager, Merchandise:** Darrell McKay. **Box Office Manager:** Daniel Luna. **Coordinator, Media Relations:** David Bearman. **Coordinator, Community Relations:** Melissa Gomez. **Corporate Sales/Marketing:** Chris Holland, Cheryl Hull. **Coordinator, Special Projects:** Paul Hartenberger. **Ticket Sales:** Adam Beggs, Amy Borkstrom. **Office Manager:** Kristien Camp. **General Manager, Ovations Food Services:** Jay Satenspiel. **Head Groundskeeper:** Jarad Alley. **Home Clubhouse Operations:** Gerald Bass. **Visiting Clubhouse Operations:** Rick Pollack. **Stadium Operations Intern:** Eddie Enriquez.

FIELD STAFF

Manager: Tracy Woodson. **Coach:** Matt Stark. **Pitching Coach:** Jeff Schwarz. **Trainer:** Greg Harrel.

GAME INFORMATION

Radio Announcer: Bob Socci. **No. of Games Broadcast:** Home-72, Away-72. **Flagship Station:** KNML 610-AM.
PA Announcer: Unavailable. **Official Scorers:** Gary Herron, John Miller.
Stadium Name (year opened): Isotopes Park (2003). **Location:** From 1-25, exit east on Avenida Cesar Chavez SE to University Boulevard; from I-40, exit south on University Boulevard SE to Avenida Cesar Chavez. **Standard Game Times:** 7:11 p.m.; Sun. (April-May) 1:35, (June-Sept.) 6:05.
Visiting Club Hotel: Holiday Inn Mountain View, 2020 Menaul NE, Albuquerque, NM 87107. Telephone: (505) 884-2511.

COLORADO SPRINGS
SKY SOX

Office Address: 4385 Tutt Blvd., Colorado Springs, CO 80922.
Telephone: (719) 597-1449. **FAX:** (719) 597-2491.
E-Mail Address: info@skysox.com. **Website:** www.skysox.com.
Affiliation (first year): Colorado Rockies (1993). **Years in League:** 1988-.

OWNERSHIP, MANAGEMENT

Operated by: Colorado Springs Sky Sox, Inc.
Principal Owner: David Elmore.
President/General Manager: Bob Goughan. **Senior Vice President, Administration:** Sam Polizzi. **Senior VP, Operations:** Dwight Hall. **Senior VP, Marketing:** Rai Henniger. **Senior VP, Stadium Operations:** Mark Leasure. **Coordinator, Special Events:** Brien Smith. **Assistant GM, Public Relations:** Gabe Ross. **Director, Finance:** Karen Jewell. **Director, Broadcast Operations:** Dan Karcher. **Assistant GM, Community Relations:** Corey Wynn. **Assistant GM, Merchandise/Account Manager:** Murlin Whitten. **Group Sales Director:** Dan Schaefer. **Group Sales/Ticket Operations:** Chip Dreamer. **Promotions/Public Relations Coordinator:** Kazuhito Oki. **Home Clubhouse Manager:** Ricky Grima. **Visiting Clubhouse Manager:** Greg Grimaldo. **Marketing Representatives:** Gina D'Ambrosio, Yu Matsumoto, George Shellem, Wade Shuman, Eric Speicher, Joe-Michael Wright.

FIELD STAFF

Manager: Marv Foley. **Coach:** Alan Cockrell. **Pitching Coach:** Bob McClure. **Trainer:** Jeremy Moeller.

GAME INFORMATION

Radio Announcers: Dan Karcher, Dick Chase. **No. of Games Broadcast:** Home-72, Away-72. **Flagship Station:** KRDO 1240-AM.
PA Announcer: Chip Dreamer. **Official Scorer:** Marty Grantz.
Stadium Name (year opened): Sky Sox Stadium (1988). **Location:** I-25 South to Woodmen Road exit, east on Woodmen to Powers Boulevard, right on Powers to Barnes Road. **Standard Game Times:** 7:05 p.m.; Sun. 1:35.
Visiting Club Hotel: LeBaron Hotel Downtown Colorado Springs, 314 W. Bijou St., Colorado Springs, CO 80905. Telephone: (800) 477-8610.

EDMONTON TRAPPERS

Office Address: 10233 96th Ave., Edmonton, Alberta T5K 0A5.
Telephone: (780) 414-4450. **FAX:** (780) 414-4475.
E-Mail Address: trappers@trappersbaseball.com. **Website:** www.trappersbaseball.com.
Affiliation (first year): Montreal Expos (2003). **Years in League:** 1981-.

OWNERSHIP, MANAGEMENT

Operated by: Edmonton Trapper Baseball Club.
Owner: Edmonton Eskimo Football Club. **President/Chief Executive Officer:** Hugh Campbell.
Chief Operating Officer: Rick LeLacheur **Assistant General Manager:** Dennis Henke. **Office Manager:** Nancy Yeo. **Executive Assistant to COO:** Cathy Fiss. **Account Executives:** Ken Charuk, Del Schjefte. **Manager, Baseball Information:** Gary Tater. **Baseball Operations Assistant:** Fraser Murray. **Manager, Tickets:** Unavailable. **Manager, Merchandise:** Darin Kowalchuk. **Manager, Marketing/Community Relations:** Karen Gurba. **Manager, Ticket Operations:** Kendra Morten. **Stadium Manager:** Don Benson. **Head Groundskeeper:** Tom Archibald. **Home Clubhouse Manager:** Dan Rosnau. **Visiting Clubhouse Manager:** Ian Rose.

FIELD STAFF

Manager: Dave Huppert. **Coach:** Mike Hart. **Pitching Coach:** Charlie Corbell. **Trainer:** Mike Quinn.

GAME INFORMATION

Radio Announcer: Al Coates. **No. of Games Broadcast:** Unavailable. **Flagship Station:** CHQT 880-AM.
PA Announcers: Ron Rimer, Bill Cowen. **Official Scorers:** Al Coates, Gary Tater.
Stadium Name (year opened): TELUS Field (1995). **Location:** From north, 101st Street to 96th Avenue, left on 96th, one block east; From south, Calgary Trail North to Queen Elizabeth Hill, right across Walterdale Bridge, right on 96th Avenue. **Standard Game Times:** 7:05 p.m.; Sun. 1:35.
Visiting Club Hotel: Sutton Place, 10235 101st St., Edmonton, Alberta T5J 3E9. Telephone: (780) 428-7111.

FRESNO GRIZZLIES

Office Address: 1800 Tulare St., Fresno, CA 93721.
Telephone: (559) 442-1994. **FAX:** (559) 264-0795.
E-Mail Address: info@fresnogrizzlies.com. **Website:** www.fresnogrizzlies.com.
Affiliation (first year): San Francisco Giants (1998). **Years in League:** 1998-.

OWNERSHIP, MANAGEMENT

Operated by: Fresno Diamond Group, LLC.
President: Pat Filipone. **Vice President:** Gerry McKearney.
General Manager: Bill Gorman. **VP, Tickets:** Andrew Stuebner. **Director, Community Relations:** Heather Raburn. **Director, Marketing:** Erin Deis. **Assistant, Promotions/Community Relations:** Erin Moroney. **Director, Ticketing:** Victor Felan. **Director, Business Development:** Stacie Johnson. **Director, Group Sales:** Brian Merrell. **Account Executive:** Shane Scott. **Account Executive/Merchandise Manager:** Brian Sheets. **Ticket Office Assistant:** Karen Thomas. **Director, Sales:** Patrick Cassidy. **Director, Corporate Sales:** Mike Maiorana. **Corporate Account Assistant:** Michelle Sanchez. **Employee Service/Events Manager:** Gayle Prezioso. **Manager, Operations:** Chris Althoff. **Chief Building Engineer:** Steve Hummer. **Head Groundskeeper:** Jim Silva. **Manager, Housekeeping:** Jerry Benebides. **Assistant Operations Manager:** Harvey Kawasaki. **Director, Human Resources:** Theresa Graham. **Booking Manager:** Misty Piell. **Financial Assistant:** Bret Harrison. **Office Manager/Receptionist:** Janet Anderson. **GM, Food Services:** Michael Doocey. **Assistant GM, Food Services:** Kevin Watson. **Executive Chef:** Steve Kretz. **Warehouse Manager:** Henry Lockwood.

FIELD STAFF

Manager: Fred Stanley. **Coach:** Steve Decker. **Pitching Coach:** Ross Grimsley. **Trainer:** Richard Stark.

GAME INFORMATION

Radio Announcers: Doug Greenwald (English), Jess Gonzalez (Spanish). **No. of Games Broadcast:** Home-72, Away-72. **Flagship Stations:** KAAT 103.1-FM (English), KGST 1600-AM (Spanish).
PA Announcer: Brian Anthony. **Official Scorer:** Unavailable.
Stadium Name (year opened): Grizzlies Stadium (2002). **Location:** From 99 North, take Fresno Street exit, left on Fresno Street, left on Inyo or Tulare to stadium; from 99 South, take Fresno Street exit, left on Fresno Street, right on Broadway to H Street; from 41 North, take Van Ness exit towards downtown Fresno, left on Van Ness, left on Inyo or Tulare, stadium is straight ahead; from 41 South, take Tulare exit, stadium is located at Tulare and H Streets, or take Van Ness exit, right on Van Ness, left on Inyo or Tulare, stadium is straight ahead. **Standard Game Times:** 7:05 p.m.; Sun. (April-June 15) 2:05.
Visiting Club Hotel: Unavailable.

IOWA
CUBS

Office Address: 1 Line Drive, Des Moines, IA 50309.
Telephone: (515) 243-6111. **FAX:** (515) 243-5152.
E-Mail Address: info@iowacubs.com. **Website:** www.iowacubs.com.
Affiliation (first year): Chicago Cubs (1981). **Years in League:** 1969-.

OWNERSHIP, MANAGEMENT

Operated by: Raccoon Baseball Inc.
Chairman, Principal Owner: Michael Gartner. **Executive Vice President:** Michael Giudicessi.
President, General Manager: Sam Bernabe. **VP, Assistant GM:** Jim Nahas. **VP, Chief Financial Officer:** Sue Tollefson. **VP/Director, Stadium Operations:** Tom Greene. **VP/Director, Broadcast Operations:** Deene Ehlis. **Director, Media Relations:** Jeff Lantz. **Coordinator, Public Relations:** Matt Nordby. **Director, Community Relations:** Matt Johnson. **Coordinators, Group Sales:** Katie Egli, Ryan Ulrich. **Director, Sales:** Rich Gilman. **Director, Luxury Suites:** Brent Conkel. **Manager, Stadium Operations:** Jeff Tilley. **Corporate Sales Executives:** Greg Ellis, Julie Lofdahl. **Corporate Relations:** Red Hollis. **Manager, Broadcast Operations:** David Raymond. **Head Groundskeeper:** Chris Schlosser. **Director, Merchandise:** Chad Mescher. **Coordinator, Merchandise:** Rick Giudicessi. **Accountant:** Lori Auten. **Manager, Cub Club:** Rick Cooper. **Office Manager**: Jenn Hoffman.

FIELD STAFF

Manager: Mike Quade. **Coach:** Pat Listach. **Pitching Coach:** Rick Kranitz. **Trainer:** Ed Halbur.

GAME INFORMATION

Radio Announcers: Deene Ehlis, David Raymond. **No. of Games Broadcast:** Home-72, Away-72. **Flagship Station:** KXNO 1460-AM.
PA Announcers: Corey Coon, Mark Pierce, Geoff Conn. **Official Scorers:** Dirk Brinkmeyer, Brian Gibson, Mike Mahon.
Stadium Name (year opened): Sec Taylor Stadium (1992). **Location:** I-80 or I-35 to I-235, to Third Street exit, south on Third Street, left on Tuttle Street. **Standard Game Times:** 7:05 p.m.; Sun. 1:05.
Visiting Club Hotel: Valley West Inn, 3535 Westown Pkwy., West Des Moines, IA 50266. Telephone: (515) 225-2524.

LAS VEGAS
51s

Office Address: 850 Las Vegas Blvd. N., Las Vegas, NV 89101.
Telephone: (702) 386-7200. **FAX:** (702) 386-7214.
E-Mail Address: info@lv51.com. **Website:** www.lv51.com.
Affiliation (first year): Los Angeles Dodgers (2001). **Years in League:** 1983-.

OWNERSHIP, MANAGEMENT

Operated by: Mandalay Baseball Properties.
Chief Executive Officer: Hank Stickney.
Managing Director: Ken Stickney. **Chairman:** Peter Guber. **Vice Chairman:** Paul Schaeffer. **President, MBP Teams Division:** Jon Spoelstra.
President, General Manager: Don Logan. **Vice President, Finance/Controller:** Allen Taylor. **VP, Operations/Security:** Nick Fitzenreider. **Director, Ticket Sales:** Tom D'Abruzzo. **Director, Business Development:** Derek Eige. **Director, Ticket Operations:** Mike Rodriguez. **Director, Corporate Sponsorships:** Mike Hollister. **Director, Merchandise:** Laurie Wanser. **Director, Broadcasting:** Russ Langer. **Manager, Corporate Marketing Sales:** Brandon Raphael. **Managers, Corporate Marketing:** Scott Christiansen, Matt Amoia, Jeff Lukich. **Manager, Group Accounts:** Manny Gomez. **Manager, Community Relations:** Larry Brown. **Manager, Baseball Administration:** Denise Korach. **Media Relations Director:** Jim Gemma. **Special Assistant to GM:** Bob Blum. **Administrative Assistant:** Michelle Taggart.

FIELD STAFF

Manager: Terry Kennedy. **Coach:** George Hendrick. **Pitching Coach:** Roger McDowell. **Trainer:** Jason Mahnke.

GAME INFORMATION

Radio Announcer: Russ Langer. **No. of Games Broadcast:** Home-72, Away-72. **Flagship Station:** KENO 1460-AM.
PA Announcer: Dan Bickmore. **Official Scorer:** Kevin Force.
Stadium Name (year opened): Cashman Field (1983). **Location:** I-15 to US 95 exit (Downtown), east to Las Vegas Boulevard North exit, One-half mile north to Cashman Field. **Standard Game Times:** 7:10 p.m.; Sun. 12:05 p.m..
Visiting Club Hotel: Golden Nugget Hotel & Casino, 129 Fremont St., Las Vegas, NV 89101. Telephone: (702) 385-7111.

MEMPHIS REDBIRDS

Office Address: 175 Toyota Plaza, Suite 300, Memphis, TN 38103.
Telephone: (901) 721-6000. **FAX:** 901-892-1222.
Website: www.memphisredbirds.com.
Affiliation (first year): St. Louis Cardinals (1998). **Years in League:** 1998-.

OWNERSHIP, MANAGEMENT

Operated by: Memphis Redbirds Baseball Foundation, Inc. **Founders:** Dean Jernigan, Kristi Jernigan. **President/General Manager:** Dave Chase. **Assistant GM:** Steele Ford. **Controller:** Garry Condrey. **Accounting Specialist:** Deborah Boyle. **Human Resources Specialist:** Pam Abney. **Manager, Information Technology:** P.J. McGhee. **VP, Marketing:** Kerry Sewell. **Director, Game Entertainment:** Kim Jackson. **Director, Communications:** John Lambert. **Coordinator, Communications:** Nick Benyo. **Coordinator, Media Relations:** Molly Darnofall. **Graphic Designer:** Iris Horne. **Mascot Coordinator:** Chris Pegg. **Director, Broadcasting:** Tom Stocker. **Senior VP, Sales:** Pete Rizzo. **Executive Assistant:** Rhonda Anderson. **Director, Retail Operations:** Dana Loughridge. **Retail Assistant:** Starr Taiani. **Sales Executive:** Rob Edgerton. **Sales Coordinator:** Zhanelle Whitley. **Sales Representative:** Lisa Shurden. **VP, Community Relations:** Reggie Williams. **Coordinator, Community Relations:** Emma Glover. **Programs Coordinator, Community Relations:** Andres Diaz. **Director, Field Operations:** Steve Horne. **Groundskeepers:** Ed Collins, Jeff Vincent. **Director, Ticket Sales:** Don Rovak. **Ticket Manager:** Brady Bruhn. **Manager, Season Tickets:** Cathy Allen. **Coordinator, Group Sales:** Justin Marek. **Chief Engineer:** Danny Abbott. **Manager, Stadium Operations:** Asim Thomas. **Coordinator, Operations:** Tony Martin. **Office Coordinator:** Trina Ross.

FIELD STAFF

Manager: Danny Sheaffer. **Coach:** Tommy Gregg. **Pitching Coach:** Dyar Miller. **Trainer:** Aaron Bruns.

GAME INFORMATION

Radio Announcers: Tom Stocker, Steve Selby. **No. of Games Broadcast:** Home-72, Away-72. **Flagship Station:** WHBQ 560-AM.
PA Announcer: Tim Van Horn. **Official Scorer:** J.J. Guinozzo.
Stadium Name (year opened): AutoZone Park (2000). **Location:** North on I-240, exit at Union Avenue West, approx. 1½ miles to park. **Standard Game Times:** 7:05 p.m.; Sat. 6:05; Sun. 2:05.
Visiting Club Hotel: Sleep Inn at Court Square, 40 N. Front, Memphis, TN 38103. Telephone: (901) 522-9700.

NASHVILLE SOUNDS

Office Address: 534 Chestnut St., Nashville, TN 37203.
Telephone: (615) 242-4371. **FAX:** (615) 256-5684.
E-Mail Address: info@nashvillesounds.com. **Website:** www.nashvillesounds.com.
Affiliation (first year): Pittsburgh Pirates (1998). **Years in League:** 1998-.

OWNERSHIP, MANAGEMENT

Operated by: AmeriSports.
President/Owner: Al Gordon.
General Manager: Glenn Yaeger. **Assistant GM, Operations:** Jason Hise. **Assistant GM, Sales:** Chris Snyder. **Director, Accounting:** Barb Walker. **Director, Sales:** Joe Hart. **Director, Ticketing:** Ricki Schlabach. **Director, Media Relations:** Doug Scopel. **Director, Marketing/Promotions:** Brandon Vonderharr. **Director, Stadium Operations:** Ken Thomas. **Director, Food/Beverage:** Mark Lawrence. **Director, Corporate Sales:** Jason Bennett. **Manager, Church/Youth Programs:** Brent High. **Assistant Manager, Church/Youth Programs:** Rob DeLucas. **Manager, Community Relations:** Sarah Barthol. **Manager, Sponsorships/Marketing:** Julie Hager. **Manager, Customer Service:** Claudia Weber. **Manager, Mascot/Entertainment:** Buddy Yelton. **Manager, Ticket Sales:** Patrick Ventura. **Assistant Manager, Food/Beverage:** Scott Chapman. **Office Manager:** Sharon Ridley. **Broadcaster:** Chuck Valenches. **Home Clubhouse Manager:** Steve Humphrey. **Visitors Clubhouse Manager:** Cory Sifford. **Head Groundskeeper:** Chris Pearl.

FIELD STAFF

Manager: Trent Jewett. **Coach:** Jeff Livesey. **Pitching Coach:** Darold Knowles. **Trainer:** Jose Ministral.

GAME INFORMATION

Radio Announcer: Chuck Valenches. **No. of Games Broadcast:** Home-72, Away-72. **Flagship Station:** WANT 98.9-FM.
PA Announcer: Unavailable. **Official Scorers:** Eric Jones, Matt Wilson.
Stadium Name (year opened): Herschel Greer Stadium (1978). **Location:** I-65 to Wedgewood exit, west to Eighth Avenue, right on Eighth to Chestnut Street, right on Chestnut. **Standard Game Times:** 7 p.m.; Wed. 12; Sat. 6; Sun. (April-May) 2, (June-Aug.) 6.
Visiting Club Hotel: Holiday Inn Select, 2613 West End Ave., Nashville, TN 37203. Telephone: (615) 327-4707.

NEW ORLEANS
ZEPHYRS

Office Address: 6000 Airline Dr., Metairie, LA 70003.
Telephone: (504) 734-5155. **FAX:** (504) 734-5118.
E-Mail Address: zephyrs@zephyrsbaseball.com. **Website:** www.zephyrsbaseball.com.
Affiliation (first year): Houston Astros (1997). **Years in League:** 1998-.

OWNERSHIP, MANAGEMENT

Operated by: New Orleans Zephyrs Baseball Club, LLC.
Managing Partner/President: Don Beaver.
Vice President/General Manager: Dan Rajkowski. **Assistant GM:** Mike Schline. **Director, Community Relations:** Marc Allen. **Director, Broadcasting:** Tim Grubbs. **Director, Operations:** Jon Peterson. **Director, Corporate Sales:** Alex Sheffield. **Director, Marketing:** Ian Dallimore. **Director, Corporate Events/Merchandising:** Pattie Feder. **Director, Special Events:** Todd Covino. **Director, Ticket Operations:** Preston Gautrau. **Director, Finance:** Kim Topp. **Personal Assistant to VP/GM:** Jessica DeOro. **Assistant Director, Marketing:** Jamie Burchfield. **Sales Executive:** David Cole. **Group Sales Representatives:** Jason Adzigian, Jody van de Sande, Ray Cotrufo, Adam Wasch. **Media Relations:** Kevin Maney. **Media Manager:** Ron Swoboda. **Head Groundskeeper:** Thomas Marks. **Assistant Groundskeeper:** Craig Shaffer. **Maintenance Coordinator:** Bill Rowell. **Assistant Director, Operations:** Todd Wilson. **GM, Food Services:** George Messina. **Assistant GM, Food Services:** Kristy Palermo. **Administrative Assistant, Food Services:** Priscilla Arbello.

FIELD STAFF

Manager: Chris Maloney. **Coach:** Gary Gaetti. **Pitching Coach:** Jim Hickey. **Trainer:** Mike Freer.

GAME INFORMATION

Radio Announcers: Tim Grubbs, Ron Swoboda, Herman Rodriguez (Spanish). **No. of Games Broadcast:** Home-72, Away-72; Spanish: Home-38. **Flagship Station:** WTIX 690-AM, WSLA 1560-AM, WFNO 830-AM (Spanish).
PA Announcer: Doug Moreau. **Official Scorer:** J.L. Vangilder.
Stadium Name (year opened): Zephyr Field (1997). **Location:** I-10 West toward Baton Rouge, exit at Clearview Parkway (exit 226) and continue south, right on Airline Drive (U.S. 61 North) for 1 mile, stadium on left; From airport, take Arline Drive (U.S. 61) east for 4 miles, stadim on right. **Standard Game Times:** 7:05 p.m.; Sat. 6:05, Sun. (April-May) 2:05, (June-Sept.) 5:05.
Visiting Club Hotel: Best Western Landmark, 2601 Severn Ave., Metairie, LA 70002. Telephone: (504) 888-9500.

OKLAHOMA
REDHAWKS

Mailing Address: SBC Bricktown Ballpark, 2 S. Mickey Mantle Dr., Oklahoma City, OK 73104.
Telephone: (405) 218-1000. **FAX:** (405) 218-1001.
E-Mail Address: info@oklahomaredhawks.com. **Website:** www.oklahomaredhawks.com.
Affiliation (first year): Texas Rangers (1983). **Years in League:** 1963-1968, 1998-.

OWNERSHIP, MANAGEMENT

Operated by: Oklahoma Baseball Club, LLC
Principal Owner: Robert Funk.
Managing General Partner: Scott Pruitt. **Assistant General Manager, Chief Financial Officer:** Steve McEwen. **Assistant GM, Operations:** Mike Prange. **Assistant GM, Sales and Marketing:** John Allgood. **Assistant GM, Guest Services/Event Management:** Nancy Simmons. **Director, Communications:** Justin Tinder **Director, Facility Operations:** Harlan Budde. **Director, Food/Beverage:** Samuel Brooks. **Senior Accountant:** Nicole Lamb. **Group Sales Manager:** Kristin Packnett. **Baseball Operations:** Mike Pomeroy. **Senior Account Executive:** Brandon Baker. **Account Executive:** Cheynne Deupree. **Head Groundskeeper:** Monte McCoy.

FIELD STAFF

Manager: Bobby Jones. **Coach:** Bruce Crabbe. **Pitching Coach:** Glenn Abbott. **Trainer:** Chris DeLucia

GAME INFORMATION

Radio Announcer: David Garrett. **No. of Games Broadcast:** Home-72, Away-72. **Flagship Station:** KEBC 1340-AM
PA Announcer: Randy Kemp. **Official Scorers:** Bob Colon, Mike Treps.
Stadium Name (year opened): SBC Bricktown Ballpark (1998). **Location:** At interchange of I-235 and I-40, take Reno exit, east on Reno. **Standard Game Times:** 7:05 p.m.; Sun. 2:05.
Visiting Club Hotel: Westin Hotel, One N. Broadway, Oklahoma City, OK 73102. Telephone: (405) 235-2780.

OMAHA
ROYALS

Office Address: Rosenblatt Stadium, 1202 Bert Murphy Ave., Omaha, NE 68107.
Telephone: (402) 734-2550. **FAX:** (402) 734-7166.
E-Mail Address: info@oroyals.com. **Website:** www.oroyals.com.
Affiliation (first year): Kansas City Royals (1969). **Years in League:** 1998-.

OWNERSHIP, MANAGEMENT
Operated by: Omaha Royals Limited Partnership.
Principal Owners: Matt Minker, Warren Buffett, Walter Scott. **Managing General Partner, President:** Matt Minker.
Senior Vice President, General Manager: Doug Stewart. **VP, Sales/Assistant GM:** Matt Brown. **Vice President, Business/Baseball Operations:** Kyle Fisher. **Director, Broadcasting:** Mark Nasser. **Director, Media Relations:** Kevin McNabb. **Director, Ticket Operations/Group Sales:** Don Wilson. **Director, Merchandise/Promotions:** Cassie Duncan. **Assistant Director, Marketing:** Rose Swenson. **Sponsorship Sales Representatives:** Angela Bonella, Jim Hochstrasser. **Manager, Community Relations:** Chad Tettenborn. **Assistant Director, Ticket Operations:** Jeff Gogerty. **Ticket Sales Representative:** Brock Shaw. **Assistant, Ticket Operations:** Bob Brown. **Administrative Assistants:** Kay Besta, Lois Biggs. **Head Groundskeeper:** Jesse Cuevas. **General Manager, Concessions:** Ryan Slane.

FIELD STAFF
Manager: Mike Jirschele. **Coach:** Terry Bradshaw. **Pitching Coach:** Dave LaRoche. **Trainer:** Jeff Stevenson.

GAME INFORMATION
Radio Announcers: Mark Nasser, Kevin McNabb. **No. of Games Broadcast:** Home-72, Away-72. **Flagship Station:** KOSR 1490-AM.
PA Announcer: Bill Jensen. **Official Scorer:** Rob White.
Stadium Name (year opened): Rosenblatt Stadium (1948). **Location:** I-80 to 13th Street exit, one block south. **Standard Game Times:** 7:05 p.m.; Sat. 6:05; Sun. 1:35.
Visiting Club Hotel: Hilton Omaha, 1001 Cass St., Omaha, NE 68102. Telephone: (402) 342-4313.

PORTLAND
BEAVERS

Office Address: 1844 SW Morrison, Portland, OR 97205.
Telephone: (503) 553-5400. **FAX:** (503) 553-5405.
E-Mail Address: info@pdxpfe.com. **Website:** www.portlandbeavers.com.
Affiliation (first year): San Diego Padres (2001). **Years in League:** 1903-1917, 1919-1972, 1978-1993, 2001-.

OWNERSHIP, MANAGEMENT
Operated by: Unavailable.
General Manager: Jack Cain. **Director, Communications:** Chris Metz. **Director, Sales:** Ripper Hatch. **Director, Operations:** Ken Puckett. **Director, Promotions/Travel:** Jennifer Gartz. **Director, Finance:** Kim Veys. **Manager, Corporate Marketing:** Todd McKee. **Manager, Community Outreach/Client Services:** Keri Stoller. **Manager, Group Sales:** Ben Hoel. **Manager, Accounting:** Diane Rogers. **Manager, Facility Maintenance:** Dave Tankersley. **Coordinator, Client Services/Sponsorship:** Jaimee Bremner. **Coordinator, Ticket Sales:** Katrina Marshall. **Coordinator, Media Relations:** Collin Romer. **Coordinator, Ticket Renewals:** Dan Zusman. **Account Executive, Group Sales:** Kim Berger. **Accounts Receivable/Payroll Administrator:** Amy Camp. **Accounts Payable Administrator:** Laura Close. **Receptionist:** Nika Altotsky. **Head Groundskeeper:** Jessie Smith.

FIELD STAFF
Manager: Craig Colbert. **Coach:** Tommy Sandt. **Pitching Coach:** Tom Brown. **Trainer:** John Maxwell.

GAME INFORMATION
Radio Announcers: Bill Schonely, Rich Burk. **No. of Games Broadcast:** Home-72, Away-72. **Flagship Station:** Unavailable.
PA Announcer: Mike Stone. **Official Scorer:** Blair Cash.
Stadium Name: PGE Park (1926). **Location:** I-405 to West Burnside exit, SW 20th Street to park. **Standard Game Times:** 7:05 p.m.; Sun. 2:05.
Visiting Club Hotel: Portland Marriott-Downtown, 1401 SW Naito Pkwy., Portland, OR 97201. Telephone: (503) 226-7600.

SACRAMENTO
RIVER CATS

Office Address: 400 Ballpark Dr., West Sacramento, CA 95691.
Telephone: (916) 376-4700. **FAX:** (916) 376-4710.
E-Mail Address: info@rivercats.com. **Website:** www.rivercats.com
Affiliation (first year): Oakland Athletics (2000). **Years in League:** 1903, 1909-11, 1918-60, 1974-76, 2000-.

OWNERSHIP, MANAGEMENT

Owned by: Sacramento River Cats Baseball Club, LLC.
Principal Owner, Chief Executive Officer: Art Savage.
President, Chief Operating Officer: Alan Ledford. **Executive Vice Presidents:** Bob Hemond, Warren Smith. **Senior VP, General Manager:** Gary Arthur. **Senior VP, Sales/Marketing:** Tom Glick. **Senior VP, Chief Financial Officer:** Dan Vistica. **General Counsel:** Matt Re. **VP, Corporate Partnerships:** Darrin Gross. **Assistant GM:** Mike Gazda. **Director, Stadium/Grounds:** Matt LaRose. **Director, Ticket Operations:** Scott Gephart. **Director, Community Relations:** Tony Asaro. **Director, Finance/Accounting:** Rita Ward. **Director, Guest Services/Employee Relations:** Kristi Goldby. **Director, Marketing:** Bret Smith. **Director, Ticket Sales:** Andy Fiske. **Manager, Merchandise:** Trish Dolan. **Manager, Game Entertainment:** Paul Flanigan. **Manager, Promotions:** Jamie Von Sossen. **Manager, Grounds:** Roy Hayes. **Manager, Baseball/Stadium Operations:** Matt Thomas. **Manager, Special Events:** Karolen LaRose. **Manager, Guest Services:** Larisa Collins. **Manager, Luxury Suites/Service:** Josh Morin. **Manager, Season Tickets:** Bob Dunham. **Manager, Business Development:** Cory Dolich. **Manager, Group Sales:** Justin Piper. **Manager, Inside Sales:** Scott Prebola. **Manager, Ticket Operations:** Larry Martinez. **Manager, Corporate Services:** Scott Druskin. **Executive Assistant/Team Travel:** Pat Berger.

FIELD STAFF

Manager: Tony DeFrancesco. **Coach:** Joe Sparks. **Pitching Coach:** Rick Rodriguez. **Trainer:** Walt Horn.

GAME INFORMATION

Radio Announcers: Johnny Doskow (English), Jose Reynoso (Spanish). **No. of Games Broadcast:** Home-72, Away-72 (English); Home-72, Away-28 (Spanish). **Flagship Stations:** KSTE 650-AM (English), KSQR 1240-AM (Spanish).
PA Announcer: Greg Lawson. **Official Scorers:** Mark Honbo, Brian Berger.
Stadium Name (year opened): Raley Field (2000). **Location:** I-5 to Business-80 West, exit at Jefferson Boulevard. **Standard Game Times:** 7:05 p.m.
Visiting Club Hotel: Holiday Inn, Capital Plaza, 300 J St., Sacramento, CA 95814. **Telephone:** (916) 446-0100.

SALT LAKE
STINGERS

Office Address: 77 W. 1300 South, Salt Lake City, UT 84115.
Mailing Address: P.O. Box 4108, Salt Lake City, UT 84110.
Telephone: (801) 485-3800. **FAX:** (801) 485-6818.
E-Mail Address: info@stingersbaseball.com. **Website:** www.stingersbaseball.com.
Affiliation (first year): Anaheim Angels (2001). **Years in League:** 1915-25, 1958-65, 1970-84, 1994-.

OWNERSHIP, MANAGEMENT

Owned by: Buzas Baseball Inc.
Principal Owners: Helen Buzas, Hilary Buzas-Drammis, Jason Buzas.
President: Hilary Buzas-Drammis.
Vice President, General Manager: Dorsena Picknell. **VP/Assistant General Manager:** Brad Tammen. **Director, Media/Public Relations:** Gary Tomlinson. **Director, Ticket Operations:** Richard Lahr. **Director, Corporate/Group Sales:** Mike Daniels. **Account Executives:** David Elkin, Will Erickson, Darren Feller, Steven Joseph Kun, Blake Paranial. **Manager, Concessions:** Jeff Koller. **Concessions Office Manager:** Melinda Gregory. **Office Manager:** Julie Empey.

FIELD STAFF

Manager: Mike Brumley. **Coach:** Jim Eppard. **Pitching Coach:** Rich Bombard. **Trainer:** Adam Nevala.

GAME INFORMATION

Radio Announcer: Steve Klauke. **No. of Games Broadcast:** Home-72, Away-72. **Flagship Station:** KWUN 1230-AM.
PA Announcer: Jeff Reeves. **Official Scorers:** Bruce Hilton, Howard Nakagama.
Stadium Name (year opened): Franklin Covey Field (1994). **Location:** I-15 to 1300 South exit, east to West Temple; exit TRAX at "Ball Park" station, one block east. **Standard Game Times:** 6:30 p.m. (April-May); 7 (June-Aug.); Sun. 2.
Visiting Club Hotel: Sheraton City Centre, 150 W. 500 South, Salt Lake City, UT 84101. **Telephone:** (801) 401-2000.

TACOMA RAINIERS

Office Address: 2502 S. Tyler St., Tacoma, WA 98405.
Telephone: (253) 752-7707. **FAX:** (253) 752-7135.
Website: www.tacomarainiers.com.
Affiliation: Seattle Mariners (1995). **Years in League:** 1904-1905, 1960-.

OWNERSHIP, MANAGEMENT

Operated by: George's Pastime, Inc.
President: George Foster.
Board of Directors: George Foster, Jeff Foster, Jonathan Foster, Sue Foster, Mark Kanai, Jack Pless.
Community Fund President: Margaret McCormick.
General Manager: Dave Lewis. **Chief Financial Officer:** Laurie Yarbrough. **Assistant GM, Baseball Operations:** Kevin Kalal. **Assistant GM, Stadium Operations:** Philip Cowan. **Director, Marketing:** Rachel Marecle. **Director, Sales:** Tim Sexton. **Director, Promotions:** Nate Kelley. **Group Sales Coordinator:** Cory Carbary. **Account Executive:** Shane Santman. **Director, Food/Beverage:** Corey Brandt. **Director, Merchandise:** Kathy Baxter. **Manager, Tickets:** Darrin Miller. **Staff Accountant:** Jacquie Sonnenfeld. **Office Manager:** Patti Stacy. **Head Groundskeeper:** Ryan Schutt. **Maintenance Supervisor:** Jim Smith. **Clubhouse Manager:** Jeff Bopp. **Assistant Clubhouse Manager:** Jake Parker.

FIELD STAFF

Manager: Dan Rohn. **Coach:** Terry Pollreisz. **Pitching Coach:** Rafael Chaves. **Trainer:** Rob Nodine.

GAME INFORMATION

Radio Broadcaster: Mike Curto. **No. of Games Broadcast:** Home-72, Away-72. **Flagship Station:** KHHO 850-AM.
PA Announcer: Jeff Randall. **Official Scorekeeper:** Darin Padur.
Stadium name (year opened): Cheney Stadium (1960). **Location:** From I-5, take exit 132 (Highway 16 West) for 1.2 miles to 19th Street East exit, right on Tyler Street for ½ mile. **Standard Game Times:** 7:05 p.m.; (April-May) 6:05; Sun., holidays 1:35.
Visiting Club Hotel: La Quinta Inn, 1425 E. 27th St., Tacoma, WA 98421. Telephone (253) 383-0146.

TUCSON SIDEWINDERS

Office Address: 2500 E. Ajo Way, Tucson, AZ 85713.
Mailing Address: P.O. Box 27045, Tucson, AZ 85726.
Telephone: (520) 434-1021. **FAX:** (520) 889-9477.
E-Mail Address: mail@tucsonsidewinders.com. **Website:** www.tucsonsidewinders.com.
Affiliation (first year): Arizona Diamondbacks (1998). **Years in League:** 1969-.

OWNERSHIP, MANAGEMENT

Operated by: Tucson Baseball LLC.
Principal Owner/Chief Executive Officer: Jay Zucker.
General Manager: Rick Parr. **Executive Assistant:** Deanna Ruiz. **Director, Stadium Operations:** Matthew Burke. **Director, Broadcasting:** Brett Dolan. **Director, Group Sales:** Brian Moss. **Group Sales Representatives:** Kimberly Levin, Andrew Kirk. **Director, Community Relations:** Sergio Pedroza. **Director, Media Relations:** Landon Vincent. **Director, Inside Sales:** Sandy Davis. **Director, Sales/Marketing:** Sean Smock. **Account Executives, Sales/Marketing:** Nick Wesoky, Jessica Withers. **Administrative Assistant:** Stacy Griffitts.

FIELD STAFF

Manager: Chip Hale. **Coach:** Lorenzo Bundy. **Pitching Coach:** Mike Parrott. **Trainer:** Greg Barber.

GAME INFORMATION

Radio Announcer: Brett Dolan. **No. of Games Broadcast:** Home-72, Away-72. **Flagship Station:** KTZR 1450-AM.
PA Announcer: Dale Lopez. **Official Scorer:** Unavailable.
Stadium Name (year opened): Tucson Electric Park (1998). **Location:** From northwest, I-10 to Ajo exit, east on Ajo to stadium; from southeast, I-10 to Palo Verde exit, north to Ajo, west to stadium. **Standard Game Times:** 7 p.m.; (April-May) 6:30; Sun. 6:30.
Visiting Club Hotel: Viscount Suite Hotel, 4855 E. Broadway, Tucson, AZ 85711. Telephone: (520) 745-6500.

EASTERN LEAGUE

CLASS AA

Office Address: 511 Congress St., 7th Floor, Portland, ME 04101.
Mailing Address: P.O. Box 9711, Portland, ME 04104.
Telephone: (207) 761-2700. **FAX:** (207) 761-7064.
E-Mail Address: elpb@easternleague.com. **Website:** www.easternleague.com.
Years League Active: 1923-.

President, Treasurer: Joe McEacharn.
Vice President, Secretary: Rick Brenner
Assistant to President: Bill Rosario.
Directors: Greg Agganis (Akron), Bill Dowling (New Britain), Charles Eshbach (Portland), Joe Finley (Trenton), Barry Gordon (Norwich), Chuck Greenberg (Altoona), Greg Martini (Harrisburg), Frank Miceli (Bowie), Shawn Smith (New Hampshire), Craig Stein (Reading), Hank Stickney (Erie), Mike Urda (Binghamton).
2004 Opening Date: April 8. **Closing Date:** Sept. 6.
Regular Season: 142 games.
Division Structure: North—Binghamton, New Britain, New Hampshire, Norwich, Portland, Trenton. **South**—Akron, Altoona, Bowie, Erie, Harrisburg, Reading.
Playoff Format: Top two teams in each division meet in best-of-5 series. Winners meet in best-of-5 series for league championship.

Joe McEacharn

All-Star Game: July 14 at Bowie.
Roster Limit: 23; 24 until 30th day of season and after Aug. 9. **Player Eligibility Rule:** No restrictions.
Brand of Baseball: Rawlings ROM-EL.
Statistician: The Sports Network, 2200 Byberry Rd., Suite 200, Hatboro, PA 19040.
Umpires: Scott Barry (Quincy, MI), Chris Conroy (Williamstown, MA), John Coons (Streator, IL), Brandon Cooper (Louisville, KY), Rob Healey (Cranston, RI), Joe Judkowitz (Coral Springs, FL), Jason Klein (Orange, CT), Ben Lindquist (Jamestown, NY), Keith McConkey (Thorold, Ontario), Josh Miller (Coral Springs, FL), Brent Persinger (Lexington, KY), Daniel Reyburn (DeWitt, MI), Brent Rice (Jackson, MI), Jeff Spisak (Portage, MI), Art Stewart (Frankport, IL), David Uyl (Caledonia, IL), Andrew Vincent (Simsbury, CT).

STADIUM INFORMATION

| Club | Stadium | Dimensions | | | Capacity | 2003 Att. |
		LF	CF	RF		
Akron	Canal Park	331	400	337	9,297	445,603
Altoona	Blair County Ballpark	315	400	325	7,200	365,376
Binghamton	NYSEG	330	400	330	6,012	211,533
Bowie	Prince George's	309	405	309	10,000	324,913
Erie	Jerry Uht Park	312	400	328	6,000	197,656
Harrisburg	RiverSide	335	400	335	6,300	257,898
New Britain	New Britain	330	400	330	6,146	268,532
*New Hampshire	Gill	312	400	312	4,000	140,922
Norwich	Thomas J. Dodd	309	401	309	6,275	158,622
Portland	Hadlock Field	315	400	330	6,975	405,021
Reading	First Energy	330	400	330	9,000	465,717
Trenton	Waterfront Park	330	407	330	6,341	427,567

* Played 2003 season in New Haven, Conn.

AKRON
AEROS

Office Address: 300 S. Main St., Akron, OH 44308.
Telephone: (330) 253-5151. **FAX:** (330) 253-3300.
E-Mail Adress: info@akronaeros.com. **Website:** www.akronaeros.com.
Affiliation (first year): Cleveland Indians (1989). **Years in League:** 1989-.

OWNERSHIP, MANAGEMENT

Operated by: Akron Professional Baseball, Inc.
Principal Owners: Mike Agganis, Greg Agganis.
Chief Executive Officer: Greg Agganis. **Executive Vice President/General Manager:** Jeff Auman. **Vice President:** Drew Cooke. **Chief Financial Officer:** Bob Larkins. **Director, Public Relations:** James Carpenter. **Director, Corporate Sales:** Dan Burr. **Director, Ticket Sales:** Kim Usselman-Fogel. **Manager, Package Sales:** Kevin Snyder. **Senior Account Representative, Group Sales:** Thomas Craven. **Account Representatives, Group Sales:** Keith Solar, Matt Kurilec. **Director, Merchandising:** Kris Roukey. **Director, Field/Stadium Maintenance:** Matt Duncan. **Director, Player Facilities:** Fletcher Wilkes. **Office Manager:** Arlene Vidumanksy.

FIELD STAFF

Manager: Brad Komminsk. **Coach:** Sean McNally. **Pitching Coach:** Steve Lyons. **Trainer:** Todd Tomczyk.

GAME INFORMATION

Radio Announcer: Jim Clark. **No. of Games Broadcast:** Home-71, Away-71. **Flagship Station:** FOX Sports 1350-AM.
PA Announcer: Joe Jastrzemski. **Official Scorer:** Tom Liggett.
Stadium Name (year opened): Canal Park (1997). **Location:** From I-76 East or I-77 South, exit onto Route 59 East, exit at Exchange/Cedar, right onto Cedar, left at Main Street. From I-76 West or I-77 North, exit at Main Street/Downtown, follow exit onto Broadway Street, left onto Exchange Street, right at Main Street. **Standard Game Times:** 7:05 p.m.; Sat. (April) 2:05; Sun. 2:05.
Visiting Club Hotel: Radisson Hotel Akron City Centre, 20 W. Mill St., Akron, OH 44308. Telephone: (330) 384-1500.

ALTOONA
CURVE

Office Address: 1000 Park Ave., Altoona, PA 16602.
Mailing Address: P.O. Box 1029, Altoona, PA 16603.
Telephone: (877) 99-CURVE, (814) 943-5400. **FAX:** (814) 942-9132, (814) 943-9050.
E-Mail Address: frontoffice@altoonacurve.com. **Website:** www.altoonacurve.com.
Affiliation (first year): Pittsburgh Pirates (1999). **Years in League:** 1999-.

OWNERSHIP, MANAGEMENT

Operated by: Curve Baseball, LP.
President, Managing Partner: Chuck Greenberg. **General Manager:** Todd Parnell. **Assistant GM:** Rick Janac. **Senior Director, Ticketing/New Business Development:** Brent Boznanski. **Director, Broadcasting:** Rob Egan. **Director, Media Relations:** Jason Dambach. **Director, Community Relations:** Elsie Zengel. **Director, Merchandising:** Larry Grimaldi. **Director, Ballpark Operations:** Kirk Stiffler. **Director, Finance:** Machelle Noel. **Director, Entertainment:** Bob Masewicz. **Director, Group Sales:** Jeff Garner. **Ticketing Associates:** Jeff Adams, Corey Homan, Derek Martin, Doug Nelson, Chris Phillips. **Information Services Specialist/Graphic Designer:** Bill Edevane. **Assistant Director, Ballpark Operations/Merchandising:** Ben Rothrock. **Head Groundskeeper:** Patrick Coakley. **Assistant Groundskeeper:** Matt Neri. **Director, Food Services:** Eric Shoup. **Assistant Manager, Concessions:** Yvonne Hunter. **Clubhouse Operations:** Jake Hundt (home), Ken Thomas (visitors).

FIELD STAFF

Manager: Tony Beasley. **Coach:** John Wehner. **Pitching Coach:** Jeff Andrews. **Trainer:** Jason Palmer.

GAME INFORMATION

Radio Announcers: Rob Egan, Jason Dambach. **No. of Games Broadcast:** Home-71, Away-71. **Flagship Station:** WFBG 1290-AM.
PA Announcer: Rich DeLeo. **Official Scorer:** Ted Beam.
Stadium Name (year opened): Blair County Ballpark (1999). **Location:** I-99 to Frankstown Road exit. **Standard Game Times:** 7:05 p.m., (April-May) 6:35; Sun. 6:05, (April-May) 3:05.
Visiting Club Hotel: Ramada Inn of Altoona, Route 220 and Plank Road, Altoona, PA 16602. Telephone: (814) 946-1631.

BINGHAMTON
METS

Office Address: 211 Henry St., Binghamton, NY 13901.
Mailing Address: P.O. Box 598, Binghamton, NY 13902.
Telephone: (607) 723-6387. **FAX:** (607) 723-7779.
E-Mail Address: bmets@bmets.com. **Website:** www.bmets.com.
Affiliation (first year): New York Mets (1992). **Years in League:** 1923-37, 1940-63, 1966-68, 1992-.

OWNERSHIP, MANAGEMENT
Operated by: Binghamton Mets Baseball Club, Inc.
Principal Owners: Bill Maines, David Maines, George Scherer, Michael Urda.
President: Michael Urda.
General Manager: Bill Terlecky. **Assistant GM:** Scott Brown. **Director, Business Operations:** Jim Weed. **Director, Stadium Operations:** Richard Tylicki. **Manager, Stadium Operations:** Scott Gruver. **Director, Sales/Community Relations:** Robert O'Brien. **Group Sales:** Mike Catalano, Erin Rurey. **Coordinator, Special Events:** Dan Abashian. **Merchandising Manager:** Lisa Shattuck. **Director, Broadcasting:** Matt Park. **Office Manager:** Rebecca Brown. **Administrative Assistant:** Nancy Wiseman.

FIELD STAFF
Manager: Ken Oberkfell. **Coach:** Howard Johnson. **Pitching Coach:** Jerry Reuss. **Trainer:** Unavailable.

GAME INFORMATION
Radio Announcer: Matt Park. **No. of Games Broadcast:** Home-71, Away-71. **Flagship Station:** WNBF 1290-AM.
PA Announcer: Roger Neel. **Official Scorer:** Steve Kraly.
Stadium Name (year opened): NYSEG Stadium (1992). **Location:** I-81 to exit 4S (Binghamton), Route 11 exit to Henry Street. **Standard Game Times:** 7 p.m.; (April-May) 6; Sat. 6; Sun. 1:30.
Visiting Club Hotel: Holiday Inn Arena, 8 Hawley St., Binghamton, NY 13901. Telephone: (607) 722-1212.

BOWIE
BAYSOX

Office Address: 4101 NE Crain Hwy., Bowie, MD 20716.
Telephone: (301) 805-6000. **FAX:** (301) 464-4911.
E-Mail Address: info@baysox.com. **Website:** www.baysox.com.
Affiliation (first year): Baltimore Orioles (1993). **Years In League:** 1993-.

OWNERSHIP, MANAGEMENT
Operated by: Comcast-Spectacor.
Directors: Peter Luukko, Frank Miceli.
General Manager: Mike Munter. **Director, Ticket Operations/Group Events:** Brian Shallcross. **Director, Marketing:** Phil Wrye. **Director, Communications:** Andy Frankel. **Assistant Director, Marketing:** Kristen Daffin. **Assistant Director, Ticket Operations/Group Events:** Addie Staebler. **Manager, Ticket Office:** Charlene Fewer. **Director, Stadium Operations:** Phil Laws. **Head Groundskeeper:** Matt Parrott. **Account Managers, Group Events:** Clark Baker, Pete Sekulow, Matt Murphy, Mike Zatchey, Lauran Dathe. **Corporate Partnerships:** Bill Snitcher. **Bookkeeper:** Carol Terwillger. **Assistant, Ticket Operations:** Sandra Kemmel. **Assistant, Box Office:** Marsha Darbouze. **Assistant, Communications:** Ryan Sakamoto. **Assistant, Marketing:** Heather Fales.

FIELD STAFF
Manager: Dave Trembley. **Coach:** Butch Davis. **Pitching Coach:** Larry McCall. **Trainer:** Mark Shires.

GAME INFORMATION
Radio Announcer: Dave Collins. **No. of Games Broadcast:** Unavailable. **Flagship Station:** Unavailable.
PA Announcers: Thom Jones, Byron Hudtloff. **Official Scorer:** Jeff Hertz.
Stadium Name (year opened): Prince George's Stadium (1994). **Location:** ¼ mile south of U.S. 50-U.S. 301 interchange at Bowie. **Standard Game Times:** 7:05 p.m.; Sun. (April-June) 1:05, (July-Aug.) 6:05.
Visiting Club Hotel: Best Western-Annapolis, 2520 Riva Rd., Annapolis, MD 21401. Telephone: (410) 224-2800.

ERIE
SEAWOLVES

Office Address: 110 E. 10th St., Erie, PA 16501.
Mailing Address: P.O. Box 1776, Erie, PA 16507.
Telephone: (814) 456-1300. **FAX:** (814) 456-7520.

EASTERN LEAGUE

E-Mail Address: rmagee@seawolves.com. **Website:** www.seawolves.com.
Affiliation (first year): Detroit Tigers (2001). **Years in League:** 1999-.

OWNERSHIP, MANAGEMENT

Operated by: Mandalay Baseball Properties.
General Manager: John Frey. **Head Groundskeeper:** Brandon Schanz. **Assistant GM/Business Development:** Matt Bresee. **Director, Marketing/Promotions:** Rob Magee. **Director, Ticket Operations:** Mark Pirrello. **Director, Group Sales:** Joe Etling. **Director, Concessions/Stadium Operations:** Ragen Walker. **Ticket Sales Representatives:** Becky Obradovic, Ross Swaldo. **Accountant:** Shannon Sterling. **Administrative Assistant:** Christine Brown.

FIELD STAFF

Manager: Rick Sweet. **Coach:** Pete Incaviglia. **Pitching Coach:** Mike Caldwell. **Trainer:** Rob Sonnenberg.

GAME INFORMATION

Radio Announcer: Mike Antonellis. **No. of Games Broadcast:** Home-71, Away-71. **Flagship Station:** WFNN 1330-AM.
PA Announcer: Dean Pepicello. **Official Scorer:** Les Caldwell.
Stadium Name (year opened): Jerry Uht Park (1995). **Location:** U.S. 79 North to East 12th Street exit, left on State Street, right on 10th Street. **Standard Game Times:** 7:05 p.m.; (April-May) 6:35; Sun. 1:05.
Visiting Club Hotel: Avalon Hotel, 16 W. 10th St., Erie, PA 16501. Telephone: (814) 459-2220.

HARRISBURG
SENATORS

Office Address: Commerce Bank Park, City Island, Harrisburg, PA 17101.
Mailing Address: P.O. Box 15757, Harrisburg, PA 17105.
Telephone: (717) 231-4444. **FAX:** (717) 231-4445.
E-Mail Address: hbgsenator@aol.com. **Website:** www.senatorsbaseball.com.
Affiliation (first year): Montreal Expos (1991). **Years in League:** 1924-35, 1987-.

OWNERSHIP, MANAGEMENT

Operated by: Harrisburg Civic Baseball Club, Inc.
Chairman: Greg Martini.
General Manager: Todd Vander Woude. **Assistant GM, Baseball Operations:** Mark Mattern. **Assistant GM, Business Operations:** Mark Clarke. **Director, Facilities Operations:** Tim Foreman. **Director, Concessions Operations:** Steve Leininger. **Manager, Concessions:** Traci Kirkhoff. **Director, Ticket Sales:** Tom Wess. **Director, Group Sales:** Brian Egli. **Associate, Group Sales:** Craig Hazelwood. **Director, Picnic Operations:** Carol Baker. **Associate, Ticket Sales:** Mark Brindle. **Turf Manager:** Ryan Schmidt.

FIELD STAFF

Manager: Dave Machemer. **Coach:** Rob Ducey. **Pitching Coach:** Mark Grater. **Trainer:** Rich Ramirez.

GAME INFORMATION

Radio Announcer: Unavailable. **No. of Games Broadcast:** Home-71, Away-71. **Flagship Station:** WKBO 1230-AM.
PA Announcer: Chris Andree. **Official Scorer:** Dave Wright.
Stadium Name (year opened): Commerce Bank Park (1987). **Location:** I-83, exit 23 (Second Street) to Market Street, bridge to City Island. **Standard Game Times:** 6:35 p.m.; Sat. 6:05; Sun. 1:05.
Visiting Club Hotel: Hilton Hotel, One N. Second St., Harrisburg, PA 17101. Telephone: (717) 233-6000.

NEW BRITAIN
ROCK CATS

Office Address: 230 John Karbonic Way, New Britain, CT 06051.
Mailing Address: P.O. Box 1718, New Britain, CT 06050.
Telephone: (860) 224-8383. **FAX:** (860) 225-6267.
E-Mail Address: rockcats@rockcats.com. **Website:** www.rockcats.com.
Affiliation (first year): Minnesota Twins (1995). **Years in League:** 1983-.

OWNERSHIP, MANAGEMENT

Operated by: New Britain Baseball Club, Inc.
Principal Owners: Bill Dowling, Coleman Levy.
Chairman of The Board: Coleman Levy.
President, General Manager: Bill Dowling. **Assistant GMs:** Evan Levy, John Willi. **Controller:** Paula Perdelwitz. **Director, Broadcasting:** Jeff Dooley. **Director, Ticket Operations:** Peter Colon. **Account Executives:** Matt Person, Elizabeth Saye, Dennis Meehan, Nicole Palmieri. **Coordinator, Stadium Operations/Home Clubhouse Manager:** Rich Grajewski. **Assistant Manager, Operations:** Brian Gannon. **Administrative Assistant:** Luke Pawlak. **Visiting Clubhouse Manager:** Tyler Greco.

FIELD STAFF

Manager: Stan Cliburn. **Coach:** Jeff Carter. **Pitching Coach:** Stu Cliburn. **Trainer:** Tony Leo.

GAME INFORMATION

Radio Announcers: Jeff Dooley, Dan Lovallo. **No. of Games Broadcast:** Home-71, Away-71. **Flagship Station:** WDRC 1360-AM.

PA Announcer: Don Shamber. **Official Scorer:** Unavailable.

Stadium Name (year opened): New Britain Stadium (1996). **Location:** From I-84, take Route 72 East (exit 35) or Route 9 South (exit 39A), left at Ellis Street (exit 25), left at South Main Street, stadium one mile on right. From Route 91 or Route 5, take Route 9 North to Route 71 (exit 24), first exit.

Standard Game Times: 7:05 p.m.; (April-June) 6:35; Sun. 1:35.

Visiting Club Hotel: Super 8, 1 Industrial Park Rd., Cromwell, CT 06416. Telephone: (860) 632-8888.

NEW HAMPSHIRE
FISHER CATS

Office Address: 1000 Elm St., Manchester, NH 03101.
Mailing Address: P.O. Box 120, Manchester, NH 03101.
Telephone: (603) 641-2005. **FAX:** (603) 641-2055.
E-Mail Address: baseballinfo@nhfishercats.com. **Website:** www.nhfishercats.com.
Affiliation (first year): Toronto Blue Jays (2004). **Years in League:** 2004-

OWNERSHIP, MANAGEMENT

Operated By: 6 to 4 to 3, LLC.
Principal Owner: Drew Weber.
President, General Manager: Shawn Smith. **Controller:** Patricia Owens. **Assistant GM:** Jeff Tagliaferro. **Director, Corporate Events:** John Egan. **Director, Baseball/Event Operations:** Mike Biagini. **Director, Media Relations:** Tim Wood. **Director, Marketing/Entertainment:** Kirsten Larsen. **Director, Food/Beverage:** Tim Restall. **Director, Group Sales:** Erik Lesniak. **Community Relations/Group Sales Specialist:** Kendra Krauss. **Ticket Assistants:** Eric Johnson, Brent Weigler, Christi McCusker, Pat Martin.

FIELD STAFF

Manager: Mike Basso. **Coach:** Jim Bowie. **Pitching Coach:** Rick Adair. **Trainer:** Jeff Stay.

GAME INFORMATION

Radio Announcer: Mike Murphy. **No. of Games Broadcast:** Home-71, Away-71. **Flagship Station:** WKXL 1450-AM.
PA Announcer: Unavailable. **Official Scorer:** Unavailable.
Stadium Name (year opened): Gill Stadium (1913). **Location:** From I-93, take exit 8 (Bridge Street). Stay on Bridge Street for 1 mile, then left on Beech Street past JFK Ice Arena, Gill Stadium on left. **Standard Game Times:** 7:05 p.m.; (April-May) 6:05; Sat. 5:05; (April-May) 1:05; Sun. 1:05.
Visiting Club Hotel: Comfort Inn, 298 Queen City Ave., Manchester, NH 03102. Telephone: (603) 668-2600.

NORWICH
NAVIGATORS

Office Address: 14 Stott Ave., Norwich, CT 06360.
Mailing Address: P.O. Box 6003, Yantic, CT 06389.
Telephone: (860) 887-7962. **FAX:** (860) 886-5996.
E-Mail Address: tater@gators.com. **Website:** www.gators.com.
Affiliation (first year): San Francisco Giants (2003). **Years in League:** 1995-.

OWNERSHIP, MANAGEMENT

Operated by: Minor League Sports Enterprises, LP.
Chairman: Barry Gordon. **President:** Hank Smith.
General Manager: Keith Hallal. **Assistant GM/Director, Marketing:** Tom Hinsch. **Director, Finance:** Richard Darling. **Senior Director, Stadium Operations:** John Gilbert. **Director, Group Sales:** Brad Favreau. **Group Sales Manager:** Mike Uden. **Director, Merchandise/Internet:** John Fleming. **Ticket Manager:** Neil Frisch. **Director, Media/Broadcasting:** Shawn Holliday. **Business Development:** Bob Garguilo. **Marketing/Media Relations Assistant:** Alyssa Gerlando. **Office Manager:** Michelle Sadowski. **Stadium Superintendent:** Chris Berube. **Head Groundskeeper:** Kyle Lewis.

FIELD STAFF

Manager: Shane Turner. **Coach:** Roger La Francois. **Pitching Coach:** Bob Stanley. **Trainer:** Patrick Serbus.

GAME INFORMATION

Radio Announcer: Shawn Holliday. **No. of Games Broadcast:** Home-71, Away-71. **Flagship Station:** Unavailable.
PA Announcer: Ed Weyant. **Official Scorer:** Gene Gumbs.

Stadium Name (year opened): Sen. Thomas J. Dodd Memorial Stadium (1995). Location: I-395 to exit 82, follow signs to Norwich Industrial Park, stadium is in back of industrial park. Standard Game Times: 7:05 p.m.; Mon., Tue., Thur. (April-May) 6:35; Wed. (April-May) 12:35; Sat. (April-May) 1:05; Sun. 1:05.
Visiting Club Hotel: Days Inn-Niantic, 265 Flanders Rd., Niantic, CT 06357. Telephone: (860) 739-6921.

PORTLAND
SEA DOGS

Office Address: 271 Park Ave., Portland, ME 04102.
Mailing Address: P.O. Box 636, Portland, ME 04104.
Telephone: (207) 874-9300. FAX: (207) 780-0317.
E-Mail Address: seadogs@portlandseadogs.com. Website: www.seadogs.com.
Affiliation (first year): Boston Red Sox (2003). Years in League: 1994-.

OWNERSHIP, MANAGEMENT
Operated By: Portland, Maine Baseball, Inc.
Principal Owner, Chairman: Daniel Burke.
President, General Manager: Charles Eshbach. Vice President/Assistant GM: John Kameisha. Assistant GM, Business Operations: Jim Heffley. Assistant GM, Sales/Marketing: Jim Beaudoin. Director, Public Relations: Chris Cameron. Director, Business Development/Promotions Coordinator: Geoff Iacuessa. Director, Group Sales: Greg Hughes. Director, Ticketing: Dave Strong. Manager, Box Office: Jason Lemont. Director, Broadcasting: Todd Jamison. Director, Food Services: Mike Scorza. Director, Video Operations: Unavailable. Special Events Coordinator: Kelli Heffley. Special Projects: Peter Drivas. Office Manager: Judy Bray. Administrative Assistants: Greg Cross, Kate Farren, Chris Hakala, Jaime Keiller, Kate Lawrence, Mike Roy, John Youngblood. Clubhouse Managers: Craig Candage Jr., Craig Candage Sr., Rick Goslin. Head Groundskeeper: Rick Anderson.

FIELD STAFF
Manager: Ron Johnson. Coach: Russ Morman. Pitching Coach: Bob Kipper. Trainer: Unavailable.

GAME INFORMATION
Radio Announcers: Todd Jamison, Steve Pratt. No. of Games Broadcast: Home-71, Away-71. Flagship Station: WMTW 870-AM.
PA Announcer: Dean Rogers. Official Scorer: Mike Beveridge.
Stadium Name (year opened): Hadlock Field (1994). Location: From South, I-295 to exit 5, merge onto Congress Street, left at St. John Street, merge right onto Park Ave.; From North, I-295 to exit 6A, right onto Park Ave. Standard Game Times: 7 p.m.; (April-May) 6; Sat. 6; (April-May) 1; Sun. 1.
Visiting Club Hotel: DoubleTree Hotel, 1230 Congress St., Portland, ME 04102. Telephone: (207) 774-5611.

READING
PHILLIES

Office Address: Route 61 South/1900 Centre Ave., Reading, PA 19601.
Mailing Address: P.O. Box 15050, Reading, PA 19612.
Telephone: (610) 375-8469. FAX: (610) 373-5868.
E-Mail Address: info@readingphillies.com. Website: www.readingphillies.com.
Affiliation (first year): Philadelphia Phillies (1967). Years in League: 1933-35, 1952-61, 1963-65, 1967-.

OWNERSHIP, MANAGEMENT
Operated By: E&J Baseball Club, Inc.
Principal Owner, President: Craig Stein.
General Manager: Chuck Domino. Assistant GM: Scott Hunsicker. Director, Stadium Operations/Concessions: Andy Bortz. Director, Maintenance/Game Staff Operations: Troy Potthoff. Director, Stadium Grounds: Dan Douglas. Office Manager: Deneen Giesen. Controller: Kristyne Haver. Director, Ticket Operations: Joe Pew. Director, Merchandise: Kevin Sklenarik. Director, Box Office Operations: Mike Becker. Manager, Group Sales: Ryan Bardi. Group Sales Specialists: Christie Chrisanthon, Mike Robinson. Director, Group Sales/Fan Development: Ashley Forlini. Director, Communications: Rob Hackash. Communications Assistant: Andy Kauffman. Director, New Business Development: Joe Bialek. Sales/Client Services: Matt Jackson. Sales/Special Events: Ben Rupp.

FIELD STAFF
Manager: Greg Legg. Coach: John Morris. Pitching Coach: Rod Nichols. Trainer: Joel Kennedy.

GAME INFORMATION
Radio Announcer: Steve Degler. No. of Games Broadcast: Home-71, Away-71. Flagship Station: WIOV 1240-AM.
PA Announcer: Dave Bauman. Official Scorer: John Lemcke.
Stadium Name (year opened): FirstEnergy Stadium (1950). Location: From east, take Pennsylvania Turnpike West to Morgantown exit, to 176 North, to 422 West, to Route 12 East, to Route 61 South exit. From west, take 422 East to Route 12 East, to Route 61 South exit. From north, take 222 South to Route 12 exit, to Route 61 South exit. From

south, take 222 North to 422 West, to Route 12 East exit at Route 61 South. **Standard Game Times:** 7:05 p.m.; Mon.-Thurs. (April-May) 6:35; Sun. 1:05.
Visiting Club Hotel: Wellesley Inn, 910 Woodland Ave., Wyomissing, PA 19610. Telephone: (610) 374-1500.

TRENTON
THUNDER

Office Address: One Thunder Rd., Trenton, NJ 08611.
Telephone: (609) 394-3300. **FAX:** (609) 394-9666.
E-Mail Address: office@trentonthunder.com. **Website:** www.trentonthunder.com.
Affiliation (second year): New York Yankees (2003). **Years in League:** 1994-.

OWNERSHIP, MANAGEMENT
Operated by: Garden State Baseball, LLP.
General Manager/Chief Operating Officer: Rick Brenner. **Assistant GM:** Brad Taylor. **Executive Director, Marketing:** Eric Lipsman. **Chief Financial Officer:** Steve Ripa. **Director, Stadium Operations:** Josh Watson. **Director, Merchandising:** Joe Pappalardo. **Director, Media Relations/Broadcasting:** Dan Loney. **Director, Ticket Operations:** Matt Pentima. **Director, Group Sales:** Brian Cassidy. **Director, Public Relations:** Bill Cook. **Office Manager:** Ed Zacharewicz. **Manager, Ticket Operations:** Brian Sloan. **Production Manager:** Aaron Wygonik. **Assistant Controller:** Mike Langer. **Managers, Group Sales:** Brian Fox, Nancy Kraus, Jason Schubert. **Conference Center Specialist/Group Sales Manager:** Vicky Rhinesmith. **Assistant, Ticket Office:** Kathy Gallagher. **Assistant, Media Relations:** Ellen Donahue. **Assistant, Merchandise:** Shannon Noonan. **Assistant, Stadium Operations:** Howard Wilensky. **Interns:** Ivan Alber, Adam Alterman, Gary Canuso, Robert Dellasala, John Dooley, Mark Evans, Lorna Gifis, Christopher Jones, Blake Kanickij, Howard Kline, Jaclyn Levi, Brian Mintzer, Andrew Moses, Rob Ortega, Ed Pettola, Jamie Pilka, Ana Maria Raducan, Ross Rodriguez, Matthew Schwartz, Jeremy Seglem, Jocelyn Tutrani, Andrew Wilson. **Head Groundskeeper:** Unavailable. **Clubhouse Manager:** Chris Root.

FIELD STAFF
Manager: Stump Merrill. **Coach:** Steve Braun. **Pitching Coach:** Gary Lavelle. **Trainer:** Greg Spratt.

GAME INFORMATION
Radio Announcers: Dan Loney, Steve Rudenstein. **Flagship Station:** WBUD 1260-AM. **No. of Games Broadcast:** Home-71, Away-71.
PA Announcer: Bill Bromberg. **Official Scorers:** Jay Dunn, Mike Maconi.
Stadium Name (year opened): Samuel J. Plumeri Sr. Field at Mercer County Waterfront Park (1994). **Location:** From 1-95, take Route 1 North to Route 29 South, stadium entrance just before tunnel. **Standard Game Times:** 7:05 p.m.; Sun. 1:35.
Visiting Club Hotel: McIntosh Hotel, 3270 Brunswick Pike, Lawrenceville, NJ 08648. Telephone: (609) 896-3700.

SOUTHERN
LEAGUE

CLASS AA

Mailing Address: 2551 Roswell Rd., Suite 330, Marietta, GA 30062.
Telephone: (770) 321-0400. **FAX:** (770) 321-0037.
E-Mail Address: soleague@earthlink.net. **Website:** www.southernleague.com.
Years League Active: 1964-.

President: Don Mincher.
Vice President: Steve DeSalvo. **Secretary-Treasurer:** Lori Webb.

Directors: Peter Bragan Jr. (Jacksonville), Steve Bryant (Carolina), Frank Burke (Chattanooga), Steve DeSalvo (Greenville), Tom Dickson (Montgomery), Tony Ensor (Birmingham), Doug Kirchhofer (Tennessee), Robert Lozinak (West Tenn), Miles Prentice (Huntsville), Bill Shanahan (Mobile).

Vice President, Operations: Lori Webb. **Coordinator, Media Relations:** Joey Elger.
2004 Opening Date: April 8. **Closing Date:** Sept. 6.
Regular Season: 140 games.
Division Structure: East—Carolina, Chattanooga, Greenville, Jacksonville, Tennessee.
West—Birmingham, Huntsville, Mobile, Montgomery, West Tenn.

Playoff Format: First-half division champions play second-half division champions in best-of-5 series. Winners meet in best-of-5 series for league championship.
All-Star Game: July 13 at Chattanooga.

Don Mincher

Roster Limit: 23; 24 until 30th day of season and after Aug. 9. **Player Eligibility Rule:** No restrictions.
Brand of Baseball: Rawlings.
Statistician: The Sports Network, 2200 Byberry Rd., Suite 200, Hatboro, PA 19040.
Umpires: Brandon Bushee (Tocsin, IL), Scott Chamberlain (Strawberry Plains, TN), Michael Estabrook (Tampa, FL), Rusty Griffin (Gillsville, GA), Robert Hansen (Aberdeen, SD), Brian Kennedy (Greenville, NC), Scott Kennedy (Louisville, KY), Brian Martin (Mooresville, NC), Maria Pagageorgiou (Rock Island, IL), Pete Pedersen, Andrew Roberts (Birmingham, AL), Jamie Roebuck (Connelly Springs, NC), R.J. Thompson (Ooltewah, TN), Garrett Watson (Reno, NV), John Woods (Orlando, FL).

STADIUM INFORMATION

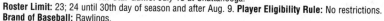

Club	Stadium	LF	CF	RF	Capacity	2003 Att.
Birmingham	Hoover Metropolitan	340	405	340	10,800	276,717
Carolina	Five County	330	400	330	6,500	204,867
Chattanooga	BellSouth Park	325	400	330	6,160	237,235
Greenville	Greenville Municipal	335	400	335	7,027	183,564
Huntsville	Davis Municipal	345	405	330	10,200	198,416
Jacksonville	Baseball Grounds	321	420	317	11,000	359,979
Mobile	Hank Aaron	325	400	310	6,000	219,007
*Montgomery	Riverwalk Stadium	314	401	332	6,000	150,051
Tennessee	Smokies Park	330	400	330	6,000	268,033
West Tenn	Pringles Park	310	395	320	6,000	224,698

* Played 2003 season in Orlando, Fla.

BIRMINGHAM
BARONS

BIRMINGHAM

Barons

BASEBALL

Office Address: 100 Ben Chapman Dr., Hoover, AL 35244.
Mailing Address: P.O. Box 360007, Birmingham, AL 35236.
Telephone: (205) 988-3200. **FAX:** (205) 988-9698.
E-Mail Address: barons@barons.com. **Website:** www.barons.com.
Affiliation (first year): Chicago White Sox (1986). **Years in League:** 1964-65, 1967-75, 1981-.

OWNERSHIP, MANAGEMENT
Operated by: Elmore Sports Group, Ltd.
Principal Owner: Dave Elmore.
President, General Manager: Tony Ensor. **Assistant GM:** Jonathan Nelson. **Director, Operations:** Chris Jenkins.
Head Groundskeeper: Luke Davis. **Director, Broadcasting:** Curt Bloom. **Director, Media Relations:** Mike Hobson.
Director, Sales: Martie Cordaro. **Director, Season Tickets:** Jim Stennett. **Director, Group Sales:** Dave Endress.
Director, Food Services: Eric Crook. **Corporate Events Planners:** Michael Peppers, James Young. **Office Manager:** Kecia Arnold.

FIELD STAFF
Manager: Razor Shines. **Coach:** Manny Trillo. **Pitching Coach:** Juan Nieves. **Trainer:** Joe Geck.

GAME INFORMATION
Radio Announcer: Curt Bloom. **No. of Games Broadcast:** Home-70, Away-70. **Flagship Station:** WYDE 101.1-FM.
PA Announcer: Chris Champion. **Official Scorer:** Unavailable.
Stadium Name (year opened): Hoover Metropolitan Stadium (1988). **Location:** I-459 to Highway 150 (exit 10) in Hoover. **Standard Game Times:** 7 p.m.; Wed (April-June) 11 a.m.; Sun. (April-June) 2; (July-Aug.) 6.
Visiting Club Hotel: Riverchase Inn, 1800 Riverchase Dr., Birmingham, AL 35244. Telephone: (205) 985-7500.

CAROLINA
MUDCATS

Office Address: 1501 N.C. Hwy. 39, Zebulon, NC 27597.
Mailing Address: P.O. Drawer 1218, Zebulon, NC 27597.
Telephone: (919) 269-2287. **FAX:** (919) 269-4910.
E-Mail Address: muddy@gomudcats.com. **Website:** www.gomudcats.com.
Affiliation (first year): Florida Marlins (2003). **Years in League:** 1991-.

OWNERSHIP, MANAGEMENT
Operated by: Carolina Mudcats Professional Baseball Club, Inc.
Principal Owner: Steve Bryant.
General Manager: Joe Kremer. **Assistant GM:** Eric Gardner. **Director, Broadcasting:** Patrick Kinas. **Director, Stadium Operations:** Ben Layton. **Director, Sales:** Will Barfield. **Director, Group Sales:** Elizabeth Henderson. **Director, Tickets:** Erin Wallace. **Director, Special Events:** Nathan Priddy. **Head Groundskeeper:** John Packer. **Office Manager:** Jackie DiPrimo. **Community Relations/Marketing:** Brian DeWine. **Director, Food/Beverage:** David Turska. **Group Sales Associates:** Kelly Korte, Hampton Terry, Chris MacLean. **Coordinator, Video Production:** Scott Timmreck.

FIELD STAFF
Manager: Ron Hassey. **Coach:** Edwin Rodriguez. **Pitching Coach:** Gil Lopez. **Trainer:** Steve Miller.

GAME INFORMATION
Radio Announcer: Patrick Kinas. **No. of Games Broadcast:** Home-70, Away-70. **Flagship Station:** Unavailable.
PA Announcer: Duke Sanders. **Official Scorer:** John Hobgood.
Stadium Name (year opened): Five County Stadium (1991). **Location:** From Raleigh, U.S. 64 East to 264 East, exit at Highway 39 in Zebulon. **Standard Game Times:** 7:15 p.m.; Sun. 4; (April, May, Sept) 2.
Visiting Club Hotel: Country Inn and Suites, 2715 Capital Blvd., Raleigh, NC 27604. Telephone: (919) 872-5000.

CHATTANOOGA
LOOKOUTS

Office Address: 201 Power Alley, Chattanooga, TN 37402.
Mailing Address: P.O. Box 11002, Chattanooga, TN 37401.
Telephone: (423) 267-2208. **FAX:** (423) 267-4258.
E-Mail Address: lookouts@lookouts.com. **Website:** www.lookouts.com.

Affiliation (first year): Cincinnati Reds (1988). **Years in League:** 1964-65, 1976-.

OWNERSHIP, MANAGEMENT

Operated by: Scenic City Baseball, LLC.
Principal Owners: Daniel Burke, Frank Burke, Charles Eshbach.
President/General Manager: Frank Burke. **Assistant GM:** Brad Smith. **Director, Business Administration:** Jack Mitchell. **Director, Group Sales:** Bill Wheeler. **Director, Merchandising:** Sally Violin. **Director, Sales/Media Relations:** John Maedel. **Director, Ticketing Operations:** Ben Slater. **Director, Concessions:** Debbie Triplett. **Director, Stadium Operations:** Allen Key. **Head Groundskeeper:** Bo Henley. **Broadcasting Assistant:** Claude Dicks.

FIELD STAFF

Manager: Jayhawk Owens. **Coach:** Jamie Dismuke. **Pitching Coach:** Bill Moloney. **Trainer:** Steve Bauman

GAME INFORMATION

Radio Announcer: Larry Ward. **No. of Games Broadcast:** Home-70, Away-70. **Flagship Station:** WDOD 1310-AM. **PA Announcer:** John Maedel. **Official Scorers:** Wirt Gammon, Andy Paul
Stadium Name (year opened): BellSouth Park (2000). **Location:** From I-24, take U.S. 27 North to exit 1C (4th Street), first left onto Chestnut Street, left onto Third Street. **Standard Game Times:** 7:15 p.m.; Wed. 12:15; Sun. 2:15. **Visiting Club Hotel:** Holiday Inn, 2345 Shallowford Rd., Chattanooga, TN 37412. Telephone: (423) 855-2898.

GREENVILLE
BRAVES

Office Address: One Braves Ave., Greenville, SC 29607.
Mailing Address: P.O. Box 16683, Greenville, SC 29606.
Telephone: (864) 299-3456. **FAX:** (864) 277-7369.
Website: www.gbraves.com.
Affiliation (first year): Atlanta Braves (1984). **Years in League:** 1984-.

OWNERSHIP, MANAGEMENT

Operated by: Atlanta National League Baseball Club, Inc. **Principal Owner:** Time Warner.
General Manager: Steve DeSalvo. **Assistant GM:** Jim Bishop. **Director, Media/Public Relations:** Mark Hauser. **Head Groundskeeper:** Matt Taylor. **Director, Community Relations:** Brenda Yoder. **Director, Food Services:** Brian Prochilo. **Office Manager:** Patti Rice.

FIELD STAFF

Manager: Brian Snitker. **Coach:** Mel Roberts. **Pitching Coach:** Dave Schuler. **Trainer:** Mike Graus.

GAME INFORMATION

Radio Announcer: Mark Hauser. **No. of Games Broadcast:** Home-70, Away-70. **Flagship Station:** WCCP 104.9-FM. **PA Announcer:** Chris Lee. **Official Scorer:** John Burton.
Stadium Name (year opened): Greenville Municipal Stadium (1984). **Location:** I-85 to exit 46 (Mauldin Road), east two miles. **Standard Game Times:** Unavailable.
Visiting Club Hotel: Quality Inn, 50 Orchard Park Dr., Greenville, SC 29615. Telephone: (864) 297-9000.

HUNTSVILLE
STARS

Office Address: 3125 Leeman Ferry Rd., Huntsville, AL 35801.
Mailing Address: P.O. Box 2769, Huntsville, AL 35804.
Telephone: (256) 882-2562. **FAX:** (256) 880-0801.
E-Mail Address: info@huntsvillestars.com. **Website:** www.huntsvillestars.com.
Affiliation (first year): Milwaukee Brewers (1999). **Years In League:** 1985-.

OWNERSHIP, MANAGEMENT

Operated by: Huntsville Stars, LLC.
President: Miles Prentice.
General Manager: Bryan Dingo. **Assistant GM:** Robin Bellizzi. **Director, Broadcasting/Sales:** Robert Portnoy. **Director, Marketing/Community Relations:** Wes Robertson. **Director, Ticketing:** Rob Norton. **Director, Field Maintenance:** Darren Seebold. **Director, Stadium Operations:** Unavailable. **Group Sales Executives:** Jennifer Betsayad, Daniel Petre, Gary Ward. **Office Manager/Assistant, Community Relations:** Earl Grilliot.

FIELD STAFF

Manager: Frank Kremblas. **Coach:** Sandy Guerrero. **Pitching Coach:** Fred Dabney. **Trainer:** Greg Barajas.

GAME INFORMATION

Radio Announcer: Robert Portnoy. **No. of Games Broadcast:** Home-70, Away-70. **Flagship Station:** WTKI 1450-AM.

PA Announcer: Todd Blass. **Official Scorer:** Don Rizzardi.
Stadium Name (year opened): Joe W. Davis Municipal Stadium (1985). **Location:** I-65 to I-565 East, south on Memorial Parkway to Drake Avenue exit, right on Don Mincher Drive. **Standard Game Times:** 7:05 p.m.; Tues.-Wed. (April-June 20) 12:05; Sun. (April-June 20) 2:05; (June 22-Sept.) 6:05.
Visiting Club Hotel: La Quinta Inn, 3141 University Dr., Huntsville, AL 35805. Telephone: (256) 533-0756.

JACKSONVILLE
SUNS

Office Address: 301 A. Philip Randolph Blvd, Jacksonville, FL 32202.
Mailing Address: P.O. Box 4756, Jacksonville, FL 32201.
Telephone: (904) 358-2846. **FAX:** (904) 358-2845.
E-Mail Address: jaxsuns@bellsouth.net. **Website:** www.jaxsuns.com.
Affiliation (second year): Los Angeles Dodgers (2001). **Years In League:** 1970-.

OWNERSHIP, MANAGEMENT
Operated by: Baseball Jax, Inc.
Principal Owner, President: Peter Bragan Sr. **President:** Mary Frances Bragan.
VP/General Manager: Peter Bragan Jr. **Assistant GM:** Kirk Goodman. **Director, Ticket Operations:** Karlie Evatt. **Director, Broadcasting:** Joe Block. **Director, Community Relations:** Tana Stavinoha. **Director, Group Sales:** Justin Rossi. **Director, Food Services:** David Leathers. **Executive Assistant:** Suzanne Roper. **Director, Stadium Operations:** Shannon Leach. **Director, Merchandise:** Traci Barbour. **Manager, Box Office:** Lana Lundell. **Manager, Sales:** Bill Schumpp. **Office Manager:** Barbara O'Berry. **Business Manager:** Craig Barnett. **Manager, Merchandise:** Brady Ballard. **Administrative Assistants:** Kate Mata, Jennifer Pedersen.

FIELD STAFF
Manager: Dino Ebel. **Coach:** Mariano Duncan. **Pitching Coach:** Marty Reed. **Trainer:** Tony Cordova. **Strength/Conditioning:** Ron Quintana

GAME INFORMATION
Radio Announcer: Joe Block. **No. of Games Broadcast:** Home-70, Away-70. **Flagship Station:** AM 930 The Fox.
PA Announcer: John Leard. **Official Scorer:** Jason Eliopulos.
Stadium Name (year opened): The Baseball Grounds of Jacksonville (2003). **Location:** I-95 South to Martin Luther King Parkway exit, follow Gator Bowl Blvd. around Alltel Stadium; I-95 North to Exit 347 (Emerson Street), go right to Hart Bridge Expressway, take Sports Complex exit, left at light to stop sign, take left and follow around Alltel Stadium; From Mathews Bridge, take A. Philip Randolph exit, right on A. Philip Randolph, straight to stadium. **Standard Game Times:** 7:05 p.m; Wed. 1:05; Fri. 7:35; Sun. 3:05, 5:05.
Visiting Club Hotel: Adam's Mark Jacksonville, 225 Coastline Dr., Jacksonville, FL 32202. Telephone: (904) 633-9095.

MOBILE
BAYBEARS

Office Address: Hank Aaron Stadium, 755 Bolling Bros. Blvd., Mobile, AL 36606.
Telephone: (251) 479-2327. **FAX:** (251) 476-1147.
E-Mail Address: baybears@mobilebaybears.com. **Website:** www.mobile baybears.com.
Affiliation (first year): San Diego Padres (1997). **Years in League:** 1966, 1970, 1997-.

OWNERSHIP, MANAGEMENT
Operated by: HWS Group.
Principal Owner: Mike Savit.
President/General Manager: Bill Shanhan. **Vice President/General Sales Manager:** Travis Toth. **Assistant GM, Finance:** Betty Adams. **Assistant GM Ticket Operations:** Doug Stephens. **Assistant GM, Facility Operations/Head Groundskeeper:** Pat White. **Media Relations:** Tom Nichols. **Director, Group Sales:** Jeff Long. **Director, Marketing:** Kirstin Rayborn. **Director, Merchandising:** Mandy Schmitz. **Director, Stadium Operations:** Grant Barnett. **Director, Corporate Development:** Karen Blackwell. **Director, Baseball Operations:** Jason Kirksey. **Director, Banquet Facilities:** Mike Callahan. **Sales Representative/Customer Service:** LaLoni Taylor. **Charities Coordinator/Graphic Designer:** Jennifer Wirtz. **Assistant Groundskeeper:** Nick Krause. **Stadium Operations Assistant:** Wade Vadakin. **Internet Liaison/Team Chaplain:** Lorin Barr. **Sales Representative:** Ira Yates. **Interns:** Mike Meier, Jason Ward. **Clubhouse Manager:** A.J. Niland.

FIELD STAFF
Manager: Gary Jones. **Coach:** Jose Castro. **Pitching Coach:** Gary Lance. **Trainer:** Will Sinon.

GAME INFORMATION

Radio Announcer: Tom Nichols. **No. of Games Broadcast:** Home-70, Away-70. **Flagship Station:** WABB 1480-AM. **PA Announcers:** Jay Hasting, Matt McCoy. **Official Scorer:** Unavailable.

Stadium Name (year opened): Hank Aaron Stadium (1997). **Location:** I-65 to exit 1A (Government Street East), right at Satchel Paige Drive, right at Bolling Bros. Boulevard. **Standard Game Times:** 7:05 p.m.; Sun. (April-May) 2:05; (June-Aug.) 6:05.

Visiting Club Hotel: Adam's Mark Mobile, 64 S. Water St., Mobile, AL 36602. Telephone: (251) 438-4000.

MONTGOMERY
BISCUITS

Office Address: 200 Coosa St., Montgomery, AL 36104.
Telephone: (334) 323-2255. **FAX:** (334) 323-2225.
E-Mail Address: info@biscuitsbaseball.com. **Website:** www.biscuitsbaseball.com.
Affiliation (first year): Tampa Bay Devil Rays (2004). **Years in League:** 1965-1980, 2004-.

OWNERSHIP, MANAGEMENT

Operated by: Montgomery Professional Baseball, LLC.
Principal Owners: Tom Dickson, Sherrie Myers.
General Manager, Operations: Greg Rauch. **GM, Sales/Marketing:** Megan Frazer. **Director, Sales:** Patrick Day. **Marketing Assistants:** Jim Tocco, Elizabeth Booksh. **Sales Service Managers:** Gretchen Pickle, Marla Terranova. **Corporate Account Executives:** Travis Burkett, Kerry Cranford. **Box Office Manager:** Scott Howland. **Director, Food Service:** Nick Kavalauskas. **Season Ticket Coordinator/Head Concierge:** Kent Rose. **Business Manager:** Becky Haynes. **Retail Manager:** Monte Meyers. **Head Groundskeeper:** Rob McKay. **Director, Operations:** Steve Blackwell. **Group Sales Representatives:** Cody Berry, Casey Huddleston, Eric Clements. **Marketing/Operations Coordinator:** Hope Fussell. **Sales/Marketing Intern:** DeAndrae Watson.

FIELD STAFF

Manager: Charlie Montoyo. **Coach:** Skeeter Barnes. **Pitching Coach:** Dick Bosman. **Trainer:** Matt Lucero.

GAME INFORMATION

Radio Announcer: Jim Tocco. **No. of Games Broadcast:** Home-70, Away-70. **Flagship Station:** WLWI 1440-AM. **PA Announcer:** Unavailable. **Official Scorer:** Travis Jarome.

Stadium Name (year opened): Montgomery Riverwalk Stadium (2004). **Location:** I-65 to exit 172, east on Herron Street, left on Coosa Street. **Standard Game Times:** 7:05 p.m.; Sun. (April-June) 2:05; (July-Sept.) 6:05.

Visiting Club Hotel: Unavailable.

TENNESSEE
SMOKIES

Office Address: 3540 Line Dr., Kodak, TN 37764.
Telephone: (865) 286-2300. **FAX:** (865) 523-9913.
E-Mail Address: info@smokiesbaseball.com. **Website:** www.smokiesbaseball.com.
Affiliation (first year): St. Louis Cardinals (2003). **Years in League:** 1964-67, 1972-.

OWNERSHIP, MANAGEMENT

Operated by: SPBC, LLC.
President: Doug Kirchhofer.
General Manager: Brian Cox. **Assistant GM:** Mark Seaman. **Director, Communications/Marketing:** Jeff Shoaf. **Director, Broadcasting/Media Relations:** Tom Hart. **Director, Sales:** Jon Zeitz. **Corporate Sales Executive:** Kevin Hill. **Director, Stadium Operations:** Brian Webster. **Director, Ticket Operations:** Misty Yoder. **Director, Community Relations:** Lauren Chesney. **Director, Field Operations:** Ross D'Lugos. **Assistance Director, Field Operations:** Bob Shoemaker. **Director, Group Sales:** Jon Kuka. **Group Sales Representatives:** Gabe Bowman, Tom Luebbe, Keli Mayes. **Business Manager:** Suzanne French. **Merchandise Assistant:** Latosha Pryor **Operations Assistants:** Steve Stone, Jason Testa, Brian LeHeup, Ryan Herrig. **Administrative Assistants:** Kay Campbell, Tolena Trout.

FIELD STAFF

Manager: Mark DeJohn. **Coach:** Steve Balboni. **Pitching Coach:** Blaise Ilsley. **Trainer:** Christophe Conroy.

GAME INFORMATION

Radio Announcer: Tom Hart. **No. of Games Broadcast:** Home-70, Away-70. **Flagship Stations:** WNOX 99.1-FM, WSEV 105.5-FM.

PA Announcer: George Yardley. **Official Scorers:** Paul Barger, Randy Corrado.

Stadium Name (year opened): Smokies Park (2000). **Location:** I-40 to exit 407, Highway 66 North. **Standard Game Times:** 7:15 p.m.; Sun. 5.

Visiting Club Hotel: Days Inn-Exit 407, 3402 Winfield Dunn Pkwy., Kodak TN 37764. Telephone: (865) 933-4500.

WEST TENN
DIAMOND JAXX

Office Address: 4 Fun Place, Jackson, TN 38305.
Telephone: (731) 988-5299. **FAX:** (731) 988-5246.
E-Mail Address: fun@diamondjaxx.com. **Website:** www.diamondjaxx.com.
Affiliation (first year): Chicago Cubs (1998). **Years in League:** 1998-.

OWNERSHIP, MANAGEMENT

Operated by: Lozinak Baseball Properties, LLC.
General Manager: Jeff Parker. **Director, Operations:** Robert Jones. **Director, Broadcasting/Media Relations:** Ron Potesta. **Director, Advertising/Ticket Sales:** Dave Jojola. **Manager, Ticketing/Merchandise:** Jason Compton. **Manager, Community Affairs/Group Sales:** Abigail Gerhard. **Manager, Advertising Sales/Promotions:** Kevin Huffine. **Group Sales Associates:** Stephanie Pierce, John-Michael Tolar. **Advertising/Marketing Sales Associate:** Todd Roll. **Administrative Assistant:** Jackie Nelson. **Head Groundskeeper:** Justin Spillman. **Assistant, Groundscrew:** Steve Hamilton. **Concessions Manager:** Barbara Kaylor. **Clubhouse Manager:** Unavailable.

FIELD STAFF

Manager: Bobby Dickerson. **Coach:** Von Joshua. **Pitching Coach:** Alan Dunn. **Trainer:** Justin Sharpe.

GAME INFORMATION

Radio Announcer: Ron Potesta. **No. of Games Broadcast:** Home-70, Away-70. **Flagship Station:** WTNE 97.7-FM. **PA Announcer:** John Schofield. **Official Scorer:** Tracy Brewer.
Stadium Name (year opened): Pringles Park (1998). **Location:** From I-40, take exit 85 South to F.E. Wright Drive, left onto Ridgecrest Extended. **Standard Game Times:** 7:05 p.m.; 6:35 (April-May); Sun. 1:05, (April) 2:05, (August) 6:05.
Visiting Club Hotel: Doubletree Hotel, 1770 Hwy. 45 Bypass, Jackson, TN 38305. Telephone: (731) 664-6900.

TEXAS LEAGUE

CLASS AA

Mailing Address: 2442 Facet Oak, San Antonio, TX 78232.
Telephone: (210) 545-5297. **FAX:** (210) 545-5298.
E-Mail Address: texasleague@sbcglobal.net. **Website:** www.texas-league.com.
Years League Active: 1888-1890, 1892, 1895-1899, 1902-1942, 1946-.

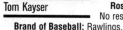

President, Treasurer: Tom Kayser.
Vice President: Monty Hoppel. **Corporate Secretary:** Mike McCall. **Administrative Assistant:** Gary Livingston.
Directors: Bobby Brett (El Paso), Jon Dandes (Wichita), Chuck Lamson (Tulsa), Jay Miller (Round Rock), Miles Prentice (Midland), Hank Stickney (Frisco), Bill Valentine (Arkansas), Burl Yarbrough (San Antonio).
2004 Opening Date: April 8. **Closing Date:** Sept. 5.
Regular Season: 140 games (split-schedule).
Division Structure: East—Arkansas, Frisco, Tulsa, Wichita. **West**—El Paso, Midland, Round Rock.
Playoff Format: First-half division champions play second-half division champions in best-of-5 series. Winners meet in best-of-7 series for league championship.
All-Star Game: June 21 at Midland.

Tom Kayser

Roster Limit: 23; 24 for first 30 days of season and after Aug. 9. **Player Eligibility Rule:** No restrictions.
Brand of Baseball: Rawlings.
Statistician: The Sports Network, 2200 Byberry Rd., Suite 200, Hatboro, PA 19040.
Umpires: Paul Chandler (Silverdale, WA), Delfin Colon (Houston, TX), Rodney Galloway (Houston, TX), Chris Griffith (Keller, TX), Jonathan Kaylor (Grain Valley, MO), Jason Kiser (Columbia, MO), Joe Stegner (Boise, ID), Jason Stein (Forth Worth, TX), Chris Tiller (Tyler, TX), Hitoshi Uchikawa (Osaka, Japan), Anthony Waters (Coppell, TX), A.J. Wendel (Arlington, TX).

STADIUM INFORMATION

Club	Stadium	Dimensions			Capacity	2003 Att.
		LF	CF	RF		
Arkansas	Ray Winder Field	330	390	345	6,083	187,401
El Paso	Cohen	340	410	340	9,725	224,821
Frisco	Dr. Pepper/Seven-Up Ballpark	330	410	322	10,000	666,977
Midland	First America Bank Ballpark	330	410	322	6,669	270,627
Round Rock	The Dell Diamond	330	400	325	10,000	685,973
San Antonio	Nelson Wolff Municipal	310	402	340	6,200	305,235
Tulsa	Drillers	335	390	340	11,003	273,155
Wichita	Lawrence-Dumont	344	401	312	6,055	153,665

ARKANSAS TRAVELERS

Office Address: Ray Winder Field at War Memorial Park, Little Rock, AR 72205.
Mailing Address: P.O. Box 55066, Little Rock, AR 72215.
Telephone: (501) 664-1555. FAX: (501) 664-1834.
E-Mail Address: travs@travs.com. Website: www.travs.com.
Affiliation (first year): Anaheim Angels (2001). Years In League: 1966-.

OWNERSHIP, MANAGEMENT

Operated by: Arkansas Travelers Baseball Club, Inc.
President: Bert Parke.
Executive Vice President, General Manager: Bill Valentine. Assistant GM: Pete Laven. Director, Concessions: Troy Russell. Director, Stadium Operations: George Reynolds. Director, Media Relations/Broadcasting: Phil Elson. Office Manager: John Paige. Park Superintendent: Greg Johnston. Assistant Park Superintendent: Reggie Temple. Bookkeeper: Nena Valentine.

FIELD STAFF

Manager: Tyrone Boykin. Coach: Todd Takayoshi. Pitching Coach: Kernan Ronan. Trainer: Jamie Welch.

GAME INFORMATION

Radio Announcer: Phil Elson. No. of Games Broadcast: Home-70, Away-70. Flagship Station: KDXE 1380-AM.
PA Announcer: Kevin Cruise. Official Scorers: Tim Cooper, Dan Floyd.
Stadium Name (year opened): Ray Winder Field (1932). Location: I-630 to Fair Park Boulevard exit, north off exit, right after zoo. Standard Game Times: 7:10 p.m., DH 6:30; Sun. 2.
Visiting Club Hotel: La Quinta Inn, 4100 East McCain Blvd., North Little Rock, AR 72117. Telephone: (501) 945-0808.

EL PASO DIABLOS

Office Address: 9700 Gateway North Blvd., El Paso, TX 79924.
Telephone: (915) 755-2000. FAX: (915) 757-0671.
E-Mail Address: awheeler@diablos.com. Website: www.diablos.com.
Affiliation (first year): Arizona Diamondbacks (1999). Years in League: 1962-70, 1972-.

OWNERSHIP, MANAGEMENT

Operated by: Brett Sports.
Principal Owners: Bobby Brett, Peter Gray, Bill Pereira.
Vice President, General Manager: Andrew Wheeler. VP, Sales/Marketing: Kevin Farlow. VP, Tickets: Brent Miles. Director, Season Tickets: Derrel Ebert. Director, Group Sales: Manuel Gomez. Manager, Box Office: Tina Arrambide. Director, Broadcasting: Matt Hicks. Director, Business Operations: Melissa Wheeler. Head Groundskeeper: Tony Lee. Director, Stadium Operations: Jimmy Hicks. Director, Spanish Broadcasting: Miguel Flores. Account Executive: Brett Pollock. Coordinator, Promotions/Public Relations: Kathy Sarver. Account Representatives: Miguel Flores, Matt Hicks, Bernie Ricono, Monica Ortega.

FIELD STAFF

Manager: Scott Coolbaugh. Coach: Damon Mashore. Pitching Coach: Mel Stottlemyre Jr. Trainer: Rodger Fleming.

GAME INFORMATION

Radio Announcers: Matt Hicks, Brett Pollock (English); Miguel Flores (Spanish). No. of Games Broadcast: Home-70, Away-70. Flagship Station: KHEY 1380-AM.
PA Announcer: Paul Torres. Official Scorer: Bernie Olivas.
Stadium Name (year opened): Cohen Stadium (1990). Location: I-10 to U.S. 54 (Patriot Freeway), east to Diana exit to Gateway North Boulevard. Standard Game Time: 6:30 p.m.
Visiting Club Hotel: Best Western Airport Inn, 7144 Gateway Blvd. E., El Paso, TX 79915. Telephone: (915) 779-7700.

FRISCO ROUGHRIDERS

Office Address: 7300 RoughRiders Trail, Frisco, TX 75034.
Telephone: (972) 731-9200. FAX: (972) 731-7455.

E-Mail Address: info@ridersbaseball.com. **Website:** www.ridersbaseball.com. **Affiliation (first year):** Texas Rangers (2003). **Years in League:** 2003-.

OWNERSHIP, MANAGEMENT

Operated by: Mandalay Sports Entertainment.
Principal Owners: Mandalay Sports Entertainment, Southwest Sports Group.
President, General Manager: Mike McCall. **Senior VP, Sponsorships:** Scott Sanju. **VP, Marketing/Ticket Sales:** Lynn Wittenburg. **VP, Communications:** Shellie Johnson. **VP, Stadium Operations:** Mike deMaine. **Director, Group Sales:** Marcia Steinberg. **Director, Finance:** Sally Morris. **Director, Ticket Sales:** Brent Stehlik. **Director, Quality Control:** Dick Harmon. **Director, Sponsor Services:** Rebecca King. **Sponsor Promotions:** Todd McVeigh. **Suite Services Coordinator:** Kristin Yanowski. **Corporate Marketing Managers:** Michael Byrnes, Michael Drake, Brandon Raphael, Chuck Flannagan, Matt Goodman, Jason Cohen. **Customer Account Managers:** Jennifer Jimenez, Danielle Rush, Will Rhodes. **Group Sales Managers:** Carrie Caldwell, Kai Murray, Michael Davidow. **Communications Coordinator:** Blake Reedy. **Head Groundskeeper:** Blake Shinn. **Box Office Manager:** John Krivacic. **Director, Stadium Operations:** Mike Bonasia. **Director of Game Entertainment:** Tony Canepa. **Creative Director:** Aaron Artman. **Executive Assistant, President:** Jennifer Knaup **Receptionist:** Collette Robbins.

FIELD STAFF

Manager: Tim Ireland. **Coach:** Paul Carey. **Pitching Coach:** Steve Luebber. **Trainer:** Unavailable.

GAME INFORMATION

Radio Announcer: Scott Garner **No. of Games Broadcast:** Home-70, Away-70. **Radio Station:** KBTK 1700-AM.
PA Announcer: Ken Buckner. **Official Scorer:** Unavailable.
Stadium Name (year opened): Dr Pepper/Seven Up Ballpark (2003). **Location:** Dallas North Tollway to State Highway 121. **Standard Game Times:** 7 p.m.; Fri.-Sat. 7:30; Sun. (April-May) 2, (June-Aug.) 6.
Visiting Club Hotel: Hampton Inn & Suites, 3199 Parkwood Blvd., Frisco, TX 75034. Telephone: (972) 712-8400.

MIDLAND
ROCKHOUNDS

Office Address: 5514 Champions Dr., Midland, TX 79706.
Mailing Address: 5514 Champions Dr., Midland, TX 79706.
Telephone: (432) 520-2255. **FAX:** (432) 520-8326.
Website: www.midlandrockhounds.org.
Affiliation (first year): Oakland Athletics (1999). **Years in League:** 1972-.

OWNERSHIP, MANAGEMENT

Operated By: Midland Sports, Inc.
Principal Owners: Miles Prentice, Bob Richmond.
President: Miles Prentice. **Executive Vice President:** Bob Richmond.
General Manager: Monty Hoppel. **Assistant GM:** Jeff VonHolle. **Assistant GM, Marketing/Tickets:** Jamie Richardson. **Assistant GM, Corporate Sales:** Harold Fuller. **Director, Broadcasting/Publications:** Bob Hards. **Director, Advertising:** Erick Chapman. **Executive Director, Midland Concessions:** Dave Baur. **Concessions Assistant:** Edwin White. **Director, Merchandising/Manager, Stadium Facilities:** Ray Fieldhouse. **Director, Business Operations:** Eloisa Galvan. **Manager, Season Ticket Sales:** Kevin Smith. **Director, Group Sales:** Bob Flannery. **Box Office Ticket Manager:** Stacy Fielding. **Director, Team Operations:** Joe Harrell. **Head Groundskeeper:** Monty Sowell. **Assistant Groundskeeper:** Erick Ferland. **Director, Community Relations:** Brittney Holum.

FIELD STAFF

Manager: Webster Garrison. **Coach:** Brian McArn. **Pitching Coach:** Jim Coffman. **Trainer:** Brian Thorson.

GAME INFORMATION

Radio Announcer: Bob Hards. **No. of Games Broadcast:** Home-70, Away-70. **Flagship Station:** KCRS 550-AM.
PA Announcer: Ace O'Connel. **Official Scorer:** Bobby Dunn.
Stadium Name (year opened): First American Bank Ballpark (2002). **Location:** From I-20, exit Loop 250 North to Highway 191 intersection. **Standard Game Times:** 7 p.m.; Sunday (April-May) 2, (June-Aug.) 6.
Visiting Club Hotel: Holiday Inn Hotel and Suites, 4300 W. Hwy. 80, Midland, TX 79703. Telephone: (432) 697-3181.

ROUND ROCK
EXPRESS

Office Address: 3400 Palm Valley Blvd., Round Rock, TX 78664.
Mailing Address: P.O. Box 5309, Round Rock, TX 78683.
Telephone: (512) 255-2255. **FAX:** (512) 255-1558.
E-Mail Address: info@rrexpress.com. **Website:** www.roundrockexpress.com.

Affiliation (first year): Houston Astros (2000). **Years in League:** 2000-.

OWNERSHIP, MANAGEMENT
Operated by: Round Rock Baseball, Inc.
Principal Owners: Eddie Maloney, J. Con Maloney, Nolan Ryan, Reid Ryan, Don Sanders.
Chairman, President: Reid Ryan.
Vice President, General Manager: Jay Miller. **Chief Financial Officer:** Reese Ryan. **Assistant GM, Sales/Marketing:** Dave Fendrick. **Controller:** Debbie Coughlin. **Assistant GM, Promotions/Stadium Entertainment:** Derrick Grubbs. **Director, Media/Public Relations:** Kirk Dressendorfer. **Media Relations Coordinator:** Mark Swanson. **Director, Merchandising:** Sue Denny. **Director, Ticket Operations:** Ross Scott. **Director, United Heritage Center:** Scott Allen. **Assistant Director, United Heritage Center:** Laura Whatley. **Director, Group Sales:** Henry Green. **Director, Sales:** Gary Franke. **Director, Customer Relations:** George Smith. **Account Executives:** Clint Bell, LaBaron Graham. **Receptionist:** Wendy Gordon. **Head Groundskeeper:** Dennis Klein. **Director, Broadcasting:** Mike Capps. **Clubhouse Manager:** Unavailable.

FIELD STAFF
Manager: Jackie Moore. **Coaches:** Spike Owen, Sean Berry. **Pitching Coach:** Joe Slusarski. **Trainer:** Jamey Snodgrass.

GAME INFORMATION
Radio Announcer: Mike Capps. **No. of Games Broadcast:** Home-70, Away-70. **Flagship Station:** KWNX 1260-AM.
PA Announcer: Derrick Grubbs. **Official Scorer:** Jim Van Geffen.
Stadium Name (year opened): The Dell Diamond (2000). **Location:** I-35 North to exit 253 (Highway 79 East/Taylor), stadium on left approximately 3½ miles. **Standard Game Times:** 7:05 p.m.; Sun. (April-May) 2:05, (June-Sept.) 6:05.
Visiting Club Hotel: Hilton Garden Inn, 2310 N. IH-35, Round Rock, TX 78681. Telephone: (512) 341-8200.

SAN ANTONIO
MISSIONS

Office Address: 5757 Hwy. 90 W., San Antonio, TX 78227.
Telephone: (210) 675-7275. **FAX:** (210) 670-0001.
E-Mail Address: sainfo@samissions.com. **Website:** www.samissions.com.
Affiliation (third year): Seattle Mariners (2001). **Years In League:** 1888, 1892, 1895-99, 1907-42, 1946-64, 1968-.

OWNERSHIP, MANAGEMENT
Operated by: Elmore Sports Group.
Principal Owner: Dave Elmore.
President: Burl Yarbrough. **General Manager:** David Gasaway. **Assistant GMs:** Jeff Long, Jeff Windle, Doug Campbell. **Controller:** Marc Frey. **Stadium Manager:** Tom McAfee. **Director, Media Relations:** Mickey Holt. **Community Relations:** Wesley Ratliff. **Manager, Group Sales:** Bill Gerlt. **Coordinator, Group Sales:** Leif Peterson. **Director, Box Office:** Tiffany Johnson. **Director, Broadcasting:** Roy Acuff. **Account Executives:** Jose Melendez, Andy Peal, Stu Paul, Emmy Roberts. **Office Manager:** Delia Rodriguez. **Merchandising:** Karen Sada. **Clubhouse Operations:** Matt Martinez (home), Jim Vasaldua (visitors).

FIELD STAFF
Manager: Dave Brundage. **Coach:** Gary Thurman. **Pitching Coach:** Scott Budner. **Trainer:** Chris Gorosics.

GAME INFORMATION
Radio Announcers: Roy Acuff, Stu Paul. **No. of Games Broadcast:** Home-70, Away-70. **Flagship Station:** KKYX 680-AM.
PA Announcer: Stan Kelly. **Official Scorer:** David Humphrey.
Stadium Name (year opened): Nelson W. Wolff Municipal Stadium (1994). **Location:** From I-10, I-35 or I-37, take U.S. 90 West to Callaghan Road exit, stadium on right. **Standard Game Times:** 7:05 p.m.; Sun. 6:05.
Visiting Club Hotel: Red Roof Inn, 1011 E. Houston St., San Antonio, TX 78205. Telephone: (210) 229-9973.

TULSA
DRILLERS

Office Address: 4802 E. 15th St., Tulsa, OK 74112.
Telephone: (918) 744-5998. **FAX:** (918) 747-3267.
E-Mail Address: mail@tulsadrillers.com. **Website:** www.tulsadrillers.com.
Affiliation (first year): Colorado Rockies (2003). **Years in League:** 1933-42, 1946-65, 1977-.

OWNERSHIP, MANAGEMENT
Operated by: Tulsa Baseball, Inc.
Principal Owner, President: Went Hubbard.

Executive Vice President, General Manager: Chuck Lamson. **Assistant GM:** Mike Melega. **Bookkeeper:** Cheryll Couey. **Office Manager:** D.D. Bristol. **Director, Promotions/Merchandise:** Jason George. **Manager, Ticket Sales:** Jeremy Lawson. **Director, Public/Media Relations:** Brian Carroll. **Director, Stadium Operations/Group Sales:** Mark Hilliard. **Operations Manager:** Cary Stidham. **Head Groundskeeper:** Gary Shepherd. **Assistant Group Ticket Sales:** Leslie Ahrberg. **Ticket Sales Assistant:** Kristine Garner. **Public Relations/Operations Assistant:** Ben Slavens. **Promotions/Merchandise Assistant:** Jackie Marshall.

FIELD STAFF
Manager: Tom Runnells. **Coach:** Darron Cox. **Pitching Coach:** Bo McLaughlin. **Trainer:** Beau Clay.

GAME INFORMATION
Radio Announcer: Mark Neely. **No. of Games Broadcast:** Home-70, Away-70. **Flagship Station:** KAKC 1300-AM. **PA Announcer:** Kirk McAnany. **Official Scorers:** Bruce Howard, Larry Lewis.
Stadium Name (year opened): Drillers Stadium (1981). **Location:** Three miles north of I-44 and 1½ miles south of I-244 at 15th Street and Yale Avenue. **Standard Game Times:** 7:05 p.m.; Sun. (April-June) 2:05, (July-Aug.) 6:05.
Visiting Club Hotel: Hampton Inn, 3209 S. 79th E. Ave., Tulsa, OK 74145. Telephone: (918) 663-1000.

WICHITA
WRANGLERS

Office Address: 300 S. Sycamore, Wichita, KS 67213.
Mailing Address: P.O. Box 1420, Wichita, KS 67201.
Telephone: (316)-267-3372. **FAX:** (316)-267-3382.
E-Mail Address: wranglers@wichitawranglers.com. **Website:** www.wichitawranglers.com.
Affiliation (first year): Kansas City Royals (1995). **Years in League:** 1987-.

OWNERSHIP, MANAGEMENT:
Operated By: Wichita Baseball, Inc.
Principal Owner: Rich Products Corp.
Chairman: Robert Rich Sr. **President:** Robert Rich Jr. **Executive Vice President:** Melinda Rich.
General Manager: Eric Edelstein. **Assistant GM, Director of Stadium/Baseball Operations:** Josh Robertson. **Assistant GM, Director of Sales/Marketing:** Kyle Ebers. **Director, Business Operations:** Sindy Dick. **Manager, Marketing/Media Relations:** Matt Rogers. **Assistant, Marketing/Media Relations:** Staci Flinchbaugh. **Assistant, Stadium/Baseball Operations:** Mike Quick. **Senior Account Executive:** Robert Slaughter. **Account Executive:** Justin Cole. **Ticket Manager:** Stephanie White. **Game Day/Merchandise Manager:** Ryanne Rogers.

FIELD STAFF
Manager: Frank White. **Coach:** Nelson Liriano. **Pitching Coach:** Larry Carter. **Trainer:** Charles Leddon.

GAME INFORMATION
Radio Announcers: Rick Page, Brian Goldberg. **No. of Games Broadcast:** Home-70, Away-70. **Flagship Station:** WKME 93.5-FM.
PA Announcer: Unavailable. **Official Scorer:** Ted Woodward.
Stadium Name (year opened): Lawrence-Dumont Stadium (1934). **Location:** I-35 to Kellogg Avenue West, North on Broadway, West on Lewis. **Standard Game Times:** 7 p.m.; Sun. 6, (April-May) 2.
Visiting Club Hotel: La Quinta-Towne East, 7700 E. Kellogg, Wichita, KS 67207. Telephone: (316)-681-2881.

CALIFORNIA
LEAGUE

CLASS A ADVANCED

Office Address: 2380 S. Bascom Ave., Suite 200, Campbell, CA 95008.
Telephone: (408) 369-8038. **FAX:** (408) 369-1409.
E-Mail Address: cabaseball@aol.com. **Website:** www.californialeague.com.
Years League Active: 1941-1942, 1946-.

President/Treasurer: Joe Gagliardi.
Vice President: Mike Ellis (Lancaster). **Corporate Secretary:** John Oldham.
Directors: Bobby Brett (High Desert), Chris Chen (Modesto), Mike Ellis (Lancaster), Gary Jacobs (Lake Elsinore), Jack Patton (Bakersfield), Tom Seidler (Visalia), Chris Lampe (San Jose), Dave Oldham (Inland Empire), Hank Stickney (Rancho Cucamonga), Tom Volpe (Stockton).
Director, Marketing: Pete Thureson. **League Administrator:** Kathleen Kelly. **Director, Umpire Development:** John Oldham.
2004 Opening Date: April 8. **Closing Date:** Sept. 6.
Regular Season: 140 games (split-schedule).
Division Structure: North—Bakersfield, Modesto, San Jose, Stockton, Visalia. **South**—High Desert, Inland Empire, Lake Elsinore, Lancaster, Rancho Cucamonga.

Joe Gagliardi

Playoff Format: Six teams. First-half champions in each division earn first-round bye; second-half champions meet wild card with next best overall record in best-of-3 quarterfinals. Winners meet first-half champions in best-of-5 semifinals. Winners meet in best-of-5 series for league championship.
All-Star Game: June 29 at Inland Empire (California League vs. Carolina League).
Roster Limit: 25 active. **Player Eligibility Rule:** No more than two players and one player-coach on active list may have more than six years experience.
Brand of Baseball: Rawlings.
Statistician: The Sports Network, 2200 Byberry Rd., Suite 200, Hatboro, PA 19040. Telephone: (214) 441-8444.
Umpires: Aaron Banks, Brandon Coony (Andrews, TX), Stephen Fritz (Montclair, CA), Jeffrey Latter (Lincoln, NE), Brandon Leopoldus (Colorado Springs, CO), Jeffrey Macias, Robert Morris (Red Water, TX), David Rackley, David Sparling, Jacob Uhlenhopp (Nevada, IA).

STADIUM INFORMATION

		Dimensions				
Club	Stadium	LF	CF	RF	Capacity	2003 Att.
Bakersfield	Sam Lynn Ballpark	328	354	328	4,200	90,099
High Desert	Mavericks	340	401	340	3,808	126,705
Inland Empire	Arrowhead Credit Union	330	410	330	5,000	217,866
Lake Elsinore	The Diamond	330	400	310	7,866	240,166
Lancaster	Lancaster Municipal	350	410	350	4,500	151,616
Modesto	Thurman Field	312	400	319	4,000	148,195
R. Cucamonga	Epicenter	335	400	335	6,615	296,118
San Jose	Municipal	340	390	340	4,000	154,927
Stockton	Billy Hebert Field	325	392	335	3,500	75,609
Visalia	Recreation Park	320	405	320	1,647	62,898

BAKERSFIELD
BLAZE

Office Address: 4009 Chester Ave., Bakersfield, CA 93301.
Mailing Address: P.O. Box 10031, Bakersfield, CA 93389.
Telephone: (661) 322-1363. **FAX:** (661) 322-6199.
E-Mail Address: blaze1@bakersfieldblaze.com. **Website:** www.bakersfieldblaze.com.
Affiliation: Tampa Bay Devil Rays (2001). **Years In League:** 1941-42, 1946-75, 1978-79, 1982-.

OWNERSHIP, MANAGEMENT
Principal Owner/President: Pat Patton.
Vice President, General Manager: Jack Patton. **Assistant GMs:** Brian Thomas, Susan Wells. **Director, Baseball Operations:** Joe Foye. **Head Groundskeeper:** Leon Williams. **Director, Community Relations:** Paul Sheldon. **Director, Special Projects:** Cricket Whitaker. **Office Manager:** Seve Niron. **Director, Radio Broadcasting:** Mark Roberts.

FIELD STAFF
Manager: Mako Oliveras. **Coach:** Ramon Ortiz. **Pitching Coach:** Xavier Hernandez. **Trainer:** Chris Tomashoff.

GAME INFORMATION
Radio Announcers: Mark Roberts, Brian Thomas. **No. of Games Broadcast:** Home-70, Away-70. **Flagship Station:** KGEO 1230-AM.
PA Announcer: John Bryan. **Official Scorer:** Tim Wheeler.
Stadium Name (year opened): Sam Lynn Ballpark (1941). **Location:** Highway 99 to California Avenue, east three miles to Chester Avenue, north two miles to stadium. **Standard Game Time:** 7:15 p.m.
Visiting Club Hotel: Holiday Inn Select, 801 Truxtun Ave., Bakersfield, CA 93301. Telephone: (661) 323-1900.

HIGH DESERT
MAVERICKS

Office Address: 12000 Stadium Way, Adelanto, CA 92301.
Telephone: (760) 246-6287. **FAX:** (760) 246-3197.
E-Mail Address: mavsinfo@hdmavs.com. **Website:** www.hdmavs.com.
Affiliation (first year): Milwaukee Brewers (2001). **Years in League:** 1991-.

OWNERSHIP, MANAGEMENT
Operated by: High Desert Mavericks, Inc.
Principal Owner: Bobby Brett. **President:** Andy Billig.
General Manager: Bruce Mann. **Director, Season Tickets:** Annie Montgomery. **Group Sales Coordinator:** Alex Ackles. **Account Executive:** Nate Liberman. **Marketing Account Executive:** Stacy Burns. **Director, Broadcasting:** Mike Lindskog. **Office Manager:** Robin Buckles. **Head Groundskeeper:** Tino Gonzales. **Clubhouse Manager:** Unavailable.

FIELD STAFF
Manager: Mel Queen. **Coach:** Stanton Cameron. **Pitching Coach:** John Curtis. **Trainer:** Matt Toth.

GAME INFORMATION
Radio Announcer: Mike Lindskog. **No. of Games Broadcast:** Home-70, Away-70. **Flagship Station:** KRAK 910-AM.
PA Announcer: Kevin Piscotti. **Official Scorer:** Jack Tucker.
Stadium Name (year opened): Mavericks Stadium (1991). **Location:** I-15 North to Highway 395 to Adelanto Road. **Standard Game Times:** 7:05 p.m.; Sun. (April-May) 3:05, (June-Aug.) 5:05.
Visiting Club Hotel: Ramada Inn, I-15 and Palmdale Road, Victorville, CA 92392. Telephone: (760) 245-6565.

INLAND EMPIRE
66ERS

Office Address: 280 South E St., San Bernardino, CA 92401.
Telephone: (909) 888-9922. **FAX:** (909) 888-5251.
Website: www.ie66ers.
Affiliation (first year): Seattle Mariners (2001). **Years in League:** 1941, 1987-.

OWNERSHIP, MANAGEMENT
Operated by: Inland Empire 66ers Baseball Club of San Bernardino.
Principal Owners: David Elmore, Donna Tuttle.
President/General Manager: Dave Oldham. **Vice President/Assistant GM:** Paul Stiritz. **Vice President:** John Stein. **Chief Financial Officer:** Brett Tyndale. **Director, Broadcasting:** Mike Saeger. **Assistant Director, Broadcasting:** Mike

Wagenheim. **Director, Food and Beverage/Stadium Manager**: Joe Henderson. **Assistant Food/Beverage Director:** Joe Hudson. **Assistant Stadium Manager**: Ryan English. **Director, Tickets:** Seneca Manzo. **Manager, Ticket Operations:** Steve James. **Director, Corporate Communications:** Laura Tolbirt. **Director, Community Relations:** Jill Sheehan. **Group Party Coordinators:** Melanie Barkley, Adam Corley, Scott Deeds, Travis Fech. **Head Groundskeeper:** Jessie Sandoval.

FIELD STAFF

Manager: Steve Roadcap. **Coach:** Henry Cotto. **Pitching Coach:** Dwight Bernard. **Trainer:** Andrew Nelson.

GAME INFORMATION

Radio Announcer: Mike Saeger. **No. of Games Broadcast:** Mon.-Sat. games only. **Flagship Station:** KVCR 91.9-FM. **PA Announcer:** J.J. Gould. **Official Scorer:** Unavailable.
Stadium Name (year opened): Arrowhead Credit Union Park (1996). **Location:** From south, I-215 to 2nd Street exit, east on 2nd, right on G Street. From north, I-215 to 3rd Street exit, left on Rialto, right on G Street. **Standard Game Times:** 7:05 p.m.; Sun. (April-May) 2:05, (June-Aug.) 6:05.
Visiting Club Hotel: Radisson Hotel, 295 North E St., San Bernardino, CA 92401. Telephone: (909) 381-6181.

LAKE ELSINORE
STORM

Office Address: 500 Diamond Dr., Lake Elsinore, CA 92530.
Mailing Address: P.O. Box 535, Lake Elsinore, CA 92531.
Telephone: (909) 245-4487. **FAX:** (909) 245-0305.
E-Mail Address: info@stormbaseball.com. **Website:** www.stormbaseball.com.
Affiliation (first year): San Diego Padres (2001). **Years in League:** 1994-.

OWNERSHIP, MANAGEMENT

Operated by: Storm, LLC.
Principal Owner: Gary Jacobs.
President/General Manager: Dave Oster. **Assistant GM/Vice President, Marketing:** Chris Jones. **Special Assistant to President:** Kathy Mair. **Assistant GM, Stadium Operations:** Bruce Kessman. **Assistant GM, Community Development:** Tracy Beskid. **Director, Corporate Sales:** Paul Engl. **Director, Broadcasting:** Sean McCall. **Director, Media/Public Relations:** Jon Fusco. **Director, Graphic Communications:** Mark Beskid. **Director, Merchandising:** Donna Grunow. **Director, Food/Beverage:** Steven Wassman. **Assistant Director, Food/Beverage:** Frank White. **Director, Group Sales:** Robyn Wassman. **Director, Ticket Operations:** Corrine Roberge. **Assistant Director, Stadium Operations:** Ben Schwartzhoff. **Assistant Director, Sales:** Eric Roth. **Director, Business Administration:** Yvonne Hunneman. **Office Manager:** Jo Equila. **Director, Field Maintenance:** Francisco Castaneda. **Clubhouse Manager:** Kyle Ross.

FIELD STAFF

Manager: Rick Renteria. **Coach:** Mike Davis. **Pitching Coach:** Mike Harkey. **Trainer:** Jason Haeussinger.

GAME INFORMATION

Radio Announcer: Sean McCall. **No. of Games Broadcast:** Home-70, Away-70. **Flagship Station:** Unavailable. **PA Announcer:** Unavailable. **Official Scorer:** Dennis Bricker.
Stadium Name (year opened): The Diamond (1994). **Location:** From I-15, exit at Diamond Drive, west one mile to stadium. **Standard Game Times:** 7:05 p.m.; Wed. 6:05; Sun. (first half) 2:05, (second half) 6:05.
Visiting Club Hotel: Lake Elsinore Hotel and Casino, 20930 Malaga St., Lake Elsinore, CA 92530. Telephone: (909) 674-3101.

LANCASTER
JETHAWKS

Office Address: 45116 Valley Central Way, Lancaster, CA 93536.
Telephone: (661) 726-5400. **FAX:** (661) 726-5406.
E-Mail Address: info@jethawks.com. **Website:** www.jethawks.com.
Affiliation (first year): Arizona Diamondbacks (2001). **Years in League:** 1996-.

OWNERSHIP, MANAGEMENT

Operated By: Clutch Play Baseball, LLC.
Chairman: Horn Chen. **President:** Mike Ellis.
General Manager: Brad Seymour. **Director, Sales/Marketing**: Matt Allen. **Communications Manager:** Dan Hubbard. **Office Administrator:** Bonnie Ward. **Stadium Operations Manager:** John Laferney. **Director, Ticketing:** Joe Reinsch. **Promotions Manager:** Michelle Pouzol. **Account Executive:** Craig Czubik. **Merchandising Manager**: Anita Kaye. **Head Groundskeeper:** Dave Phatenhaur.

FIELD STAFF

Manager: Wally Backman. **Coach:** Eric Fox. **Pitching Coach:** Dan Carlson. **Trainer:** Adam Weyer.

GAME INFORMATION

Radio Announcer: Dan Hubbard. **No. of Games Broadcast:** Home-70, Away-70. **Flagship Station:** KTPI 1340-AM. **PA Announcers:** Mitchell Chase, Dave Kelli. **Official Scorer:** David Guenther.

Stadium Name (year opened): Lancaster Municipal Stadium (1996). **Location:** Highway 14 in Lancaster to Avenue I exit, west one block to stadium. **Standard Game Times:** 7:15 p.m., (April-May) 6:30; Sun (April–May) 2, (June–Sept) 6.

Visiting Club Hotel: Best Western Antelope Valley Inn, 44055 North Sierra Hwy., Lancaster, CA 93534 . Telephone: (661) 948-4651.

MODESTO
A's

Office Address: 601 Neece Dr., Modesto, CA 95351.
Mailing Address: P.O. Box 883, Modesto, CA 95353.
Telephone: (209) 572-4487. **FAX:** (209) 572-4490.
E-Mail Address: fun@modestoathletics.com. **Website:** www.modestoathletics.com.
Affiliation (first year): Oakland Athletics (1975). **Years in League:** 1946-64, 1966-.

OWNERSHIP, MANAGEMENT

Operated by: Modesto A's Baseball Club, Inc.
Principal Owner, President: Chris Chen.
Vice President, Business Development: Tim Marting. **VP, Administration**: Greg Coleman.
General Manager: Michael Gorrasi. **Assistant GM, Sales/Marketing:** Mike Malinas. **Director, Group Sales:** Daniel Plantier. **Director, Broadcasting:** Paul Chiofar. **Director, Tickets**: Bob Angus. **Office/Accounting Manager:** Debra Baucom. **Director, Operations:** Alex Schwerin.

FIELD STAFF

Manager: Von Hayes. **Coach:** Eddie Williams. **Pitching Coach:** Scott Emerson. **Trainer:** Javier Alvidrez.

GAME INFORMATION

Radio Announcer: Paul Chiofar. **No. of Games Broadcast:** Home-50, Away-50. **Flagship Station:** KESP 970-AM. **PA Announcer:** Unavailable. **Official Scorer:** Unavailable.

Stadium Name (year opened): John Thurman Field (1952). **Location:** Highway 99 in southwest Modesto to Tuolomne Boulevard exit, west on Tuolomne for one block to Neece Drive, left for ¼ mile to stadium. **Standard Game Times:** 7:05 p.m.; Sun. (April-June) 1:05, (July-Aug.) 5:05.

Visiting Club Hotel: Ramada Inn, 2001 W. Orangeburg Ave., Modesto, CA 95350. Telephone: (209) 521-9000.

RANCHO CUCAMONGA
QUAKES

RANCHO CUCAMONGA

Quakes

PROFESSIONAL BASEBALL CLUB

Office Address: 8408 Rochester Ave., Rancho Cucamonga, CA 91730.
Mailing Address: P.O. Box 4139, Rancho Cucamonga, CA 91729.
Telephone: (909) 481-5000. **FAX:** (909) 481-5005.
E-Mail Address: rcquakes@aol.com. **Website:** www.rcquakes.com.
Affiliation (first year): Anaheim Angels (2001). **Years in League:** 1993-.

OWNERSHIP, MANAGEMENT

Operated by: Valley Baseball Inc.
Principal Owners: Jack Cooley, Mark Harmon, Hank Stickney.
Chairman: Hank Stickney.
General Manager: North Johnson. **Assistant GM/Director, Ticket Sales:** Chris Bitters. **Assistant GM/Director, Concessions:** Tom Backemeyer. **Director, Finance:** Jessica Thompson. **Head Groundskeeper:** Rex Whitney. **Director, Broadcasting/Media Relations:** Jason Anaforian. **Director, Community Relations:** Moriah Vierkant. **Director, Group Sales:** Scott Carter. **Director, Entertainment/Publications:** Kristin Beernink. **Director, Guest Relations:** Linda Rathfon. **Manager, Stadium Operations:** Ryan Ross. **Manager, Sponsorship Services:** Brandon Tanner. **Manager, Group Sales:** Dan Wesolowski. **Manager, Corporate Sales:** Tim Renyo. **Manager, Ticket Office:** Heather Lint. **Ticket Sales Representative:** Jan Selasky. **Administrative Assistant:** Stacie Lord.

FIELD STAFF

Manager: Bobby Meacham. **Coach:** James Rowson. **Pitching Coach:** Keith Comstock. **Trainer:** Armando Rivas.

GAME INFORMATION

Radio Announcer: Jason Anaforian. **No. of Games Broadcast:** Home-70, Away-70. **Flagship Station:** KWRM 1370-AM.

PA Announcer: David Jeremiah. **Official Scorer:** Larry Kavanaugh.
   Stadium Name (year opened): The Epicenter (1993). **Location:** I-10 to I-15 North, exit at Foothill Boulevard, left on Foothill, left on Rochester to stadium. **Standard Game Times:** 7:15 p.m.; Sun. (first half) 2:15, (second half) 5:15.
   Visiting Club Hotel: Best Western Heritage Inn, 8179 Spruce Ave., Rancho Cucamonga, CA 91730. Telephone: (909) 466-1111.

SAN JOSE
GIANTS

   Office Address: 588 E. Alma Ave., San Jose, CA 95112.
   Mailing Address: P.O. Box 21727, San Jose, CA 95151.
   Telephone: (408) 297-1435. **FAX:** (408) 297-1453.
   E-Mail Address: sanjosegiants@sjgiants.com **Website:** www.sjgiants.com.
   Affiliation (first year): San Francisco Giants (1988). **Years in League:** 1942, 1947-58, 1962-76, 1979-.

OWNERSHIP, MANAGEMENT
   Operated by: Progress Sports Management.
   Principal Owners: Heidi Cox, Richard Beahrs. **Chief Operating Officer:** Chris Lampe
   General Manager: Mark Wilson. **Assistant GM:** Dave Moudry. **Director, Marketing/Promotions:** Mike McCarroll. **Director, Public Relations:** Erik Holland. **Director, Sales:** Linda Pereira. **Director, Guest Services:** Zach Walter. **Ticket Director/Group Sales:** Chris DiGiorgio. **Director, Game Day Operations:** Jeremy Schwimmer. **Manager, Stadium Operations:** Leyton Lampe.

FIELD STAFF
   Manager: Lenn Sakata. **Coach:** F.P. Santangelo. **Pitching Coach:** Trevor Wilson. **Trainer:** Brett Allen.

GAME INFORMATION
   Radio Announcer: Rocky Koplik. **No. of Games Broadcast:** Saturdays and Sundays. **Flagship Station:** KSFB 1220-AM.
   PA Announcer: Brian Burkett. **Official Scorer:** John Pletsch.
   Stadium Name (year opened): Municipal Stadium (1942). **Location:** From I-280, 10th Street exit to Alma, left on Alma, stadium on right. From U.S. 101, Tully Road exit to Senter, right on Senter, left on Alma, stadium on left. **Standard Game Times:** 7 p.m.; Sat. 5; Sun. 1.
   Visiting Club Hotel: Pruneyard Inn, 1995 S. Bascom Ave., Campbell, CA 95008. Telephone: (408) 559-4300.

STOCKTON
PORTS

   Office Address: Billy Hebert Field at Oak Park, Alpine and Sutter Streets, Stockton, CA 95204.
   Mailing Address: P.O. Box 8365, Stockton, CA 95208.
   Telephone: (209) 644-1900. **FAX:** (209) 644-1931.
   E-Mail Address: info@stocktonports.com. **Website:** www.stocktonports.com.
   Affiliation (first year): Texas Rangers (2003). **Years in League:** 1941, 1946-72, 1978-.

OWNERSHIP, MANAGEMENT
   Operated by: 7th Inning Stretch, LLC.
   Chairman, Chief Executive Officer: Tom Volpe.
   Vice President, General Manager: John Katz. **Assistant GM:** Trevor Fawcett. **Director, Sales/Marketing:** Jamie Brown. **Director, Promotions:** Brandon Winslow. **Clubhouse Manager:** Victor Zapien.

FIELD STAFF
   Manager: Arnie Beyeler. **Coach:** Todd Mensik. **Pitching Coach:** Andy Hawkins. **Trainer:** Brian Bobier.

GAME INFORMATION
   Radio Announcer: Unavailable. **No. of Games Broadcast:** Away-70. **Flagship Station:** Unavailable.
   PA Announcer: Unavailable. **Official Scorer:** Unavailable.
   Stadium Name (year opened): Billy Hebert Field (1927). **Location:** From I-5/99, take Crosstown Freeway (Highway 4) to El Dorado Street, north on El Dorado to Alpine, right on Alpine Street, left on Alvarado into Oak Park, first left to stadium. **Standard Game Times:** 7:05 p.m.; Sun. (first half) 1:05, (second half) 5:05.
   Visiting Club Hotel: Best Western Stockton Inn, 4219 Waterloo Rd., Stockton, CA 95215. Telephone: (209) 931-3131.

VISALIA
OAKS

Office Address: 440 N. Giddings St., Visalia, CA 93291.
Telephone: (559) 625-0480. **FAX:** (559) 739-7732.
E-Mail Address: oaksbaseball@hotmail.com. **Website:** www.oaksbaseball.com.
Affiliation (first year): Colorado Rockies (2003). **Years in League:** 1946-62, 1968-75, 1977-.

OWNERSHIP, MANAGEMENT
Operated by: Top of the Third, Inc.
Principal Owners: Tom Seidler, Kevin O'Malley.
General Manager: Jennifer Whiteley. **Director, Broadcasting/Media Relations:** David Skoczen. **Group Sales Executive:** John Drigotas. **Director, Concessions:** Don Cary. **Head Groundskeeper:** Ken Peterson.

FIELD STAFF
Manager: Stu Cole. **Coach:** Glenallen Hill. **Pitching Coach:** Jim Bennett. **Trainer:** Heath Townsend.

GAME INFORMATION
Radio Announcer: David Skoczen. **No. of Games Broadcast:** Home-70, Away-70. **Flagship Station:** KJUG 1270-AM.
PA Announcer: Matt White. **Official Scorer:** Harry Kargenian.
Stadium Name (year opened): Recreation Park (1946). **Location:** From Highway 99, take 198 East to Mooney Boulevard exit, left on Giddings Avenue. **Standard Game Times:** 6:35 p.m.; Fri.-Sat. 7:05; Sun. 1:35.
Visiting Club Hotel: Radisson Hotel, 300 S. Court St. Visalia, CA 93291. Telephone: (559) 636-1111.

CAROLINA LEAGUE

CLASS A ADVANCED

Office Address: 1806 Pembroke Rd., Greensboro, NC 27408.
Mailing Address: P.O. Box 9503, Greensboro, NC 27429.
Telephone: (336) 691-9030. **FAX:** (336) 691-9070.
E-Mail Address: office@carolinaleague.com. **Website:** www.carolinaleague.com.
Years League Active: 1945-.

President/Treasurer: John Hopkins.
Vice Presidents: Kelvin Bowles (Salem), Calvin Falwell (Lynchburg). **Corporate Secretary:** Matt Minker (Wilmington).
Directors: Kelvin Bowles (Salem), Calvin Falwell (Lynchburg), George Habel (Myrtle Beach), Peter Luukko (Frederick), Cam McRae (Kinston), Matt Minker (Wilmington), Billy Prim (Winston-Salem), Art Silber (Potomac).
Administrative Assistants: Michael Albrecht, Marnee Larkins.
2004 Opening Date: April 8. **Closing Date:** Sept. 6.
Regular Season: 140 games (split-schedule).
Division Structure: North—Frederick, Lynchburg, Potomac, Wilmington. **South—**Kinston, Myrtle Beach, Salem, Winston-Salem.
Playoff Format: First-half division champions play second-half division champions in best-of-3 series (team that wins both halves plays wild-card). Division champions meet in best-of-5 series for Mills Cup.

John Hopkins

All-Star Game: June 29 at San Bernardino, CA (Carolina League vs. California League).

Roster Limit: 25 active. **Player Eligibility Rule:** No age limit. No more than two players and one player-coach on active list may have six or more years of prior minor league service.
Brand of Baseball: Rawlings.
Statistician: The Sports Network; 2200 Byberry Rd., Suite 200, Hatboro, PA 19040.
Umpires: John Blackburn (Brick, NJ), John Brammer (State College, PA), Steve Bretz (Lansing, MI), Fran Burke (Apex, NC), Charles Carillo (Staten Island, NY), Jason Day (Carlyle, IL), Stephen McMullen (Hainesport, NJ), Karreem Mebane (Hamden, CT).

STADIUM INFORMATION

Club	Stadium	Dimensions			Capacity	2003 Att.
		LF	CF	RF		
Frederick	Harry Grove	325	400	325	5,400	285,048
Kinston	Grainger	335	390	335	4,100	103,433
Lynchburg	City	325	390	325	4,000	91,935
Myrtle Beach	Coastal Federal	325	405	328	4,324	203,443
Potomac	Pfitzner	315	400	315	6,000	160,238
Salem	Salem Memorial	325	401	325	6,300	175,155
Wilmington	Frawley	325	400	325	6,532	315,134
Winston-Salem	Ernie Shore	325	400	325	6,000	124,454

FREDERICK
KEYS

Office Address: 21 Stadium Dr., Frederick, MD 21703.
Mailing Address: P.O. Box 3169, Frederick, MD 21705.
Telephone: (301) 662-0013. **FAX:** (301) 662-0018.
E-Mail Address: info@frederickkeys.com **Website:** www.frederickkeys.com.
Affiliation (first year): Baltimore Orioles (1989). **Years in League:** 1989-.

OWNERSHIP, MANAGEMENT
Operated by: Comcast-Spectacor.
Directors: Peter Luukko, Frank Miceli.
General Manager: Joe Pinto. **Assistant GM:** Gina Stepoulos. **Director, Marketing:** Mark Fine. **Assistant Director, Marketing:** Keri Scrivani. **Manager, Communications:** Chris McMurry. **Communications Assistant:** Nick Carita. **Director, Stadium Operations:** Dave Wisner. **Senior Account Manager:** Mark Zeigler. **Account Managers:** Shaun O'Neal, Ernie Stepoulos. **Ticket Operations:** Ed Maurer. **Box Office Manager:** Joan Dubord. **Box Office Assistant:** Jennifer Smoral. **Events Coordinators:** Kelly Crum, Kevin DeLauter, Deanna Davis. **Administrative Assistant:** Barb Freund. **Bookkeeper:** Tami Hetrick. **Clubhouse Manager:** George Bell. **GM, Food Services:** Chris Inouye. **Assistant GM, Food Services:** Shannon Tauzier. **Head Groundskeeper:** Tommy Long.

FIELD STAFF
Manager: Tom Lawless. **Coach:** Moe Hill. **Pitching Coach:** Scott McGregor. **Trainer:** Trek Schuler.

GAME INFORMATION
Radio: None.
PA Announcer: Unavailable. **Official Scorer:** George Richardson.
Stadium Name (year opened): Harry Grove Stadium (1990). **Location:** From I-70, take exit 54 (Market Street), left at light. From I-270, take exit 32 (I-70 Baltimore/Hagerstown) towards Baltimore (I-70 East), to exit 54, left at Market Street. **Standard Game Times:** 7:05 p.m.; Sun. 2:05.
Visiting Club Hotel: Comfort Inn, 420 Prospect Blvd., Frederick, MD 21701. Telephone: (301) 695-6200.

KINSTON
INDIANS

Office Address: 400 E. Grainger Ave., Kinston, NC 28501.
Mailing Address: P.O. Box 3542, Kinston, NC 28502.
Telephone: (252) 527-9111. **FAX:** (252) 527-0498.
E-Mail Address: info@kinstonindians.com. **Website:** www.kinstonindians.com.
Affiliation (first year): Cleveland Indians (1987). **Years in League:** 1956-57, 1962-74, 1978-.

OWNERSHIP, MANAGEMENT
Operated by: Slugger Partners, LP.
Principal Owners: Cam McRae, North Johnson.
Chairman: Cam McRae. **President:** North Johnson
General Manager: Clay Battin. **Assistant GM:** Shari Massengill. **Director, Sales:** Kamryn Hollar. **Director, Food/Beverage:** Sarah Frazier. **Head Groundskeeper:** Tommy Walston. **Clubhouse Operations:** Robert Smeraldo. **Team Photographer:** Carl Kline.

FIELD STAFF
Manager: Torey Lovullo. **Coach:** Wayne Kirby. **Pitching Coach:** Greg Hibbard. **Trainer:** Jeff Desjardins.

GAME INFORMATION
Radio Announcer: Rob Sinclair **No. of Games Broadcast:** Home-70, Away-70. **Flagship Station:** WRNS 960-AM.
PA Announcer: Jeff Diamond. **Official Scorer:** Unavailable.
Stadium Name (year opened): Grainger Stadium (1949). **Location:** From west, take U.S. 70 Business (Vernon Avenue), left on East Street; from east, take U.S. 70 West, right on Highway 58, right on Vernon Avenue, right on East Street. **Standard Game Times:** 7 p.m.; Sun. (April-June) 2, (July-Aug.) 5.
Visiting Club Hotel: Hampton Inn, Highway 70 Bypass, Kinston NC 28504. Telephone: (252) 523-1400.

LYNCHBURG
HILLCATS

Office Address: Lynchburg City Stadium, 3180 Fort Ave., Lynchburg, VA 24501.
Mailing Address: P.O. Box 10213, Lynchburg, VA 24506.

Telephone: (434) 528-1144. **FAX:** (434) 846-0768.
E-Mail Address: hillcats@lynchburg-hillcats.com. **Website:** www.lynchburg-hillcats.com.
Affiliation (first year): Pittsburgh Pirates (1995). **Years in League:** 1966-.

OWNERSHIP, MANAGEMENT

Operated by: Lynchburg Baseball Corp.
President: Calvin Falwell.
General Manager: Paul Sunwall. **Assistant GM:** Ronnie Roberts. **Director, Group Sales/Promotions:** Kevin Donahue. **Head Groundskeeper/Sales:** Darren Johnson. **Director, Broadcasting/Publications:** Matt Provence. **Assistant Director, Broadcasting:** Jon Schaeffer. **Stadium Operations/Concessions Director:** Chris Johnson. **Ticket Manager:** Todd Sauer. **Group Sales Assistant:** Robert Finley. **Assistant Groundskeeper:** Ray Lewis. **Office Manager:** Diane Tucker.

FIELD STAFF

Manager: Jay Loviglio. **Coach:** Greg Briley. **Pitching Coach:** Scott Lovekamp. **Trainer:** Dave Powell.

GAME INFORMATION

Radio Announcers: Matt Provence, Jon Schaeffer. **No. of Games Broadcast:** Home-70, Away-70. **Flagship Station:** WKDE 105.5-FM.
PA Announcer: Chuck Young. **Official Scorers:** Malcolm Haley, Chuck Young.
Stadium Name (year opened): Lynchburg City Stadium (1940). **Location:** U.S. 29 South to The Merritt Hutchinson Stadium (exit 6); U.S. 29 North to The Merritt Hutchinson Stadium (exit 4). **Standard Game Times:** 7:05 p.m.; Sun. (first half) 2:05, (second half) 6:05.
Visiting Club Hotel: Best Western, 2815 Candlers Mountain Rd., Lynchburg, VA 24502. Telephone: (434) 237-2986.

MYRTLE BEACH
PELICANS

Office Address: 1251 21st Ave. N., Myrtle Beach, SC 29577.
Telephone: (843) 918-6002. **FAX:** (843) 918-6001.
E-Mail Address: info@myrtlebeachpelicans.com. **Website:** www.myrtlebeachpelicans.com.
Affiliation (first year): Atlanta Braves (1999). **Years in League:** 1999-.

OWNERSHIP, MANAGEMENT

Operated by: Capitol Broadcasting Company.
Principal Owner: Jim Goodmon. **Vice President:** George Habel.
Vice President, General Manager: Matt O'Brien. **Senior Director, Sales:** Tony Zefiretto. **Senior Director, Operations:** David Frost. **Director, Corporate Sales:** Neil Fortier. **Community Relations:** Angela Barwick. **Coordinator, Group Sales:** Ody Perez. **Director, Broadcasting:** Garry Griffith. **Accounting Manager:** Anne Frishmuth. **Director, Ticket Operations:** Richard Graves. **Manager, Group Sales:** Glenn Fallon. **Ticket Sales Representative:** Randy Menken. **Retail Manager:** Richard Graves. **Director, Facility Operations:** Chris Ball. **Administrative Assistant, Media:** Angela Barwick. **Assistant Groundskeeper:** Tracy Schneweis. **Clubhouse Manager:** Mark Conrad.

FIELD STAFF

Manager: Randy Ingle. **Coach:** Jack Maloof. **Pitching Coach:** Bruce Dal Canton. **Trainer:** Mike Dart.

GAME INFORMATION

Radio Announcers: Garry Griffith, Ryan Ibbotson. **No. of Games Broadcast:** Home-70, Away-70. **Flagship Station:** The TEAM 93.9-FM, 93.7-FM, 1050-AM.
PA Announcer: Unavailable. **Official Scorer:** Bill Walsh.
Stadium Name (year opened): Coastal Federal Field (1999). **Location:** U.S. Highway 17 Bypass to 21st Avenue North, ½ mile to stadium. **Standard Game Time:** 7:05 p.m.
Visiting Club Hotel: Holiday Inn Express-Broadway at the Beach, U.S. Highway 17 Bypass & 29th Avenue North; Myrtle Beach, SC 29578. Telephone: (843) 916-4993.

POTOMAC
CANNONS

Office Address: 7 County Complex Ct., Woodbridge, VA 22192.
Mailing Address: P.O. Box 2148, Woodbridge, VA 22195.
Telephone: (703) 590-2311. **FAX:** (703) 590-5716.
E-Mail Address: cannonswin@aol.com. **Website:** www.potomaccannons.com.
Affiliation (first year): Cincinnati Reds (2003). **Years in League:** 1978-.

OWNERSHIP, MANAGEMENT

Operated by: Prince William Professional Baseball Club, Inc.

Principal Owner: Art Silber. **President:** Lani Silber Weiss.
General Manager: Jay Richardson. **Director, Operations:** Eric Enders. **Director, Marketing:** Eric Fiscus. **Director, Ticket Operations:** Brian Keller. **Director, Community Relations:** Liz Braswell. **Director, Group Sales:** Garrett Fahrmann. **Sales/Promotions Coordinator:** Kim LaFollette. **Director, Food Services:** Kristian Hawkins. **Director, Broadcasting:** Dan Laing. **Outside Sales Representative:** Don Wallace. **Head Groundskeeper:** Mike Lundy.

FIELD STAFF
Manager: Edgar Caceres. **Coach:** Billy White. **Pitching Coach:** Ed Hodge. **Trainer:** Ryusi Araki.

GAME INFORMATION
Radio: None.
PA Announcer: Dave Sher. **Official Scorer:** Dave Vincent.
Stadium Name (year opened): G. Richard Pfitzner Stadium (1984). **Location:** From I-95, take exit 158B and continue on Prince William Parkway for 5 miles, right into County Complex Court. **Standard Game Times:** 7:05 p.m.; Sun. 1:35.
Visiting Club Hotel: Best Western Potomac Mills, 14619 Potomac Mills Rd., Woodbridge, VA 22192. Telephone: (703) 494-4433.

SALEM
AVALANCHE

Office Address: 1004 Texas St., Salem, VA 24153.
Mailing Address: P.O. Box 842, Salem, VA 24153.
Telephone: (540) 389-3333. **FAX:** (540) 389-9710.
E-Mail Address: info@salemavalanche.com. **Website:** www.salemavalanche.com.
Affiliation (first year): Houston Astros (2003). **Years in League:** 1968-.

OWNERSHIP, MANAGEMENT
Operated by: Salem Professional Baseball Club, Inc.
Principal Owner/President: Kelvin Bowles.
General Manager: Jamie Toole. **Assistant GMs:** Chris Allen, Todd Lange. **Director, Finance:** Brian Bowles. **Director, Group Sales:** Tim Schuster. **Director, Stadium Operations:** Chris Deines. **Director, Tickets:** Rashad West. **Director, Merchandising:** Tim Burnham. **Director, Food Service:** Allen Lawrence. **Director, Media/Public Relations:** Mick Gillispie. **Head Groundskeeper:** Unavailable. **Sales Associates:** Nick Basso, Brad Cassady, Kyle Droppers, Matt Krantz.

FIELD STAFF
Manager: Russ Nixon. **Coach:** Marc Ronan. **Pitching Coach:** Stan Boroski. **Trainer:** Mike Smith.

GAME INFORMATION
Radio Announcer: Mick Gillispie. **No. of Games Broadcast:** Home-69, Away-71. **Flagship Stations:** WGMN 1240-AM, WVGM 1320-AM.
PA Announcer: Adam Ranzer. **Official Scorer:** Bob Teitlebaum.
Stadium Name (year opened): Salem Memorial Baseball Stadium (1995). **Location:** I-81 to exit 141 (Route 419), follow signs to Salem Civic Center Complex. **Standard Game Times:** 7:05 p.m.; Sun. (April-June) 2:05, (July-Aug) 6:05.
Visiting Club Hotel: Comfort Inn Airport, 5070 Valley View Blvd., Roanoke VA 24012. Telephone: (540) 527-2020.

WILMINGTON
BLUE ROCKS

Office Address: 801 S. Madison St., Wilmington, DE 19801.
Telephone: (302) 888-2015. **FAX:** (302) 888-2032.
E-Mail Address: info@bluerocks.com. **Website:** www.bluerocks.com.
Affiliation (first year): Kansas City Royals (1993). **Years in League:** 1993-.

OWNERSHIP, MANAGEMENT
Operated by: Wilmington Blue Rocks, LP.
President: Matt Minker.
General Manager: Chris Kemple. **Assistant GM:** Andrew Layman. **Director, Sales/Marketing:** Chris Parise. **Assistant, Marketing:** Matt Genna. **Director, Merchandise:** Jim Beck. **Assistant, Merchandise:** Lauren Kendall. **Director, Broadcasting/Media Relations:** Steve Lenox. **Assistant, Media Relations:** John Sadak. **Director, Publications/Promotions:** Tripp Baum. **Director, Community Relations:** Dave Brown. **Assistant, Community Relations:** Steve Datz. **Director, Group Sales:** Jen Francis. **Assistant Director, Group Sales:** Melissa Golden. **Executive, Sales/Group Sales:** Kevin Linton. **Director, Ticket Sales:** Jared Forma. **Ticket Office Assistants:** Kevin Geist, Tom Ellis. **Director, Field Operations:** Steve Gold. **Assistant Groundskeeper:** Brad DiMascio. **Office Manager:** Terra Crump. **Centerplate General Manager:** Bobby Dichiaro. **Centerplate Office Manager:** Nicole Houtman.

FIELD STAFF

Manager: Billy Gardner Jr. **Coach:** Boots Day. **Pitching Coach:** Reggie Jackson. **Trainer:** Steve Guadalupe.

GAME INFORMATION

Radio Announcers: Steve Lenox, John Sadak. **No. of Games Broadcast:** Home-70, Away-70. **Flagship Station:** WWTX 1290-AM.

PA Announcer: John McAdams. **Official Scorers:** E.J. Casey, Jay Dunn, Dick Shute.

Stadium Name (year opened): Judy Johnson Field at Daniel S. Frawley Stadium (1993). **Location:** I-95 North to Maryland Ave. (exit 6), right onto Maryland Ave., right on Read Street, right on South Madison Street to ballpark; I-95 South to Maryland Ave. (exit 6), left at Martin Luther King Blvd., right on South Madison Street. **Standard Game Times:** 7:05 p.m.; Sun. 1:35.

Visiting Club Hotel: Quality Inn-Skyways, 147 N. DuPont Hwy., New Castle, DE 19720. Telephone: (302) 328-6666.

WINSTON-SALEM
WARTHOGS

Office Address: 401 Deacon Blvd., Winston-Salem, NC 27105.
Mailing Address: P.O. Box 4488, Winston-Salem, NC 27115.
Telephone: (336) 759-2233. **FAX:** (336) 759-2042.
E-Mail Address: warthogs@warthogs.com. **Website:** www.warthogs.com.
Affiliation (first year): Chicago White Sox (1997). **Years in League:** 1945-.

OWNERSHIP, MANAGEMENT

Operated by: Sports Menagerie, Corp.
Co-Owners: Billy Prim, Andrew Filipowski.
President: Guy Schuman. **General Manager, Baseball Operations:** Ryan Manuel. **Special Assistant to GM:** David Beal. **Chief Financial Operator:** Kurt Gehsmann. **Office Manager:** Amanda Elbert. **Director, Broadcasting/Media Relations:** Alan York. **Director, Community Relations:** Wil Loftis. **Director, Merchandise/Tickets:** Amanda Williams. **Account Executives:** Shaun McElhinny, Sarcanda Bellissimo, Vinny Pannutti. **Interns:** Mike Moore, Cory Harpin, Katie Kurts, George Brown, Nicole Miller, Cass Ferguson, Keith Gavin.

FIELD STAFF

Manager: Ken Dominguez. **Coach:** Unavailable. **Pitching Coach:** J.R Perdew. **Trainer:** Josh Fallin.

GAME INFORMATION

Radio Announcers: Alan York, Mike Moore. **No. of Games Broadcast:** Home-70, Away-70. **Flagship Station:** WSJS 600—AM.

PA Announcer: Unavailable. **Official Scorer:** Unavailable.

Stadium Name (year opened): Ernie Shore Field (1956). **Location:** I-40 Business to Cherry Street exit, north through downtown, right on Deacon Boulevard, park on left. **Standard Game Times:** 7 p.m.; Wed. 12; Sun. 2.

Visiting Club Hotel: Ramada Plaza, 3050 University Pkwy., Winston-Salem, NC 27106. Telephone: (336) 723-2911.

FLORIDA STATE
LEAGUE

CLASS A ADVANCED

Street Address: 103 E. Orange Ave., Daytona Beach, FL 32114.
Mailing Address: P.O. Box 349, Daytona Beach, FL 32115.
Telephone: (386) 252-7479. **FAX:** (386) 252-7495.
E-Mail Address: fslbaseball@cfl.rr.com. **Website:** www.floridastateleague.com.
Years League Active: 1919-1927, 1936-1941, 1946-.

President, Treasurer: Chuck Murphy.
Vice Presidents: Ken Carson (Dunedin), Rob Rabenecker (Jupiter).
Corporate Secretary: David Hood.
Directors: Sammy Arena (Tampa), Brian Barnes (Jupiter), Ken Carson (Dunedin), Ben Cherington (Sarasota), Andy Dunn (Brevard County), Chris Easom (Palm Beach), Marvin Goldklang (Fort Myers), Trevor Gooby (Vero Beach), Ron Myers (Lakeland), Andrew Rayburn (Daytona), Paul Taglieri (St. Lucie), John Timberlake (Clearwater).
Office Secretary: Peggy Catigano.
2004 Opening Date: April 8. **Closing Date:** Sept. 5.
Regular Season: 140 games (split-schedule).
Division Structure: East—Brevard County, Daytona, Jupiter, Palm Beach, St. Lucie, Vero Beach. **West**—Clearwater, Dunedin, Fort Myers, Lakeland, Sarasota, Tampa.
Playoff Format: First-half division champions play second-half champions in best-of-3 series. Winners meet in best-of-5 series for league championship.

Chuck Murphy

All-Star Game: June 12 at St. Lucie.
Roster Limit: 25. **Player Eligibility Rule:** No age limit. No more than two players and one player-coach on active list may have six or more years of prior minor league service.
Brand of Baseball: Rawlings.
Statistician: The Sports Network, 2200 Byberry Rd., Suite 200, Hatboro, PA 19040.
Umpires: Joshua Carlisle (New Philadelphia, OH), Scott Childers (Augusta, GA), Steven Cummings (Satsuma, FL), Jason Dunn (Caruthersville, MO), Eric Eckert (Ballwin, MO), Mike Edwards III (Chesapeake, VA), Edwin Hickox (Daytona Beach, FL), Joseph Maiden (West Hills, CA), Jonathan Merry (Gainesville, GA), Todd Paskiet (DeLand, FL), Brian Reilly (Lansing, MI), J.D. Robertson (Hampton, CA), Chris Thomas (Versailles, KY).

STADIUM INFORMATION

| Club | Stadium | Dimensions | | | Capacity | 2003 Att. |
		LF	CF	RF		
Brevard County	Space Coast	340	404	340	7,500	83,314
Clearwater	Bright House Networks	330	400	330	8,500	63,655
Daytona	Jackie Robinson Ballpark	317	400	325	4,000	97,362
Dunedin	Dunedin	335	400	315	6,106	42,752
Fort Myers	Hammond	330	405	330	7,500	110,356
Jupiter	Roger Dean	330	400	325	6,871	90,080
Lakeland	Joker Marchant	340	420	340	7,100	30,832
Palm Beach	Roger Dean	330	400	325	6,871	68,210
St. Lucie	Thomas J. White	338	410	338	7,500	81,154
Sarasota	Ed Smith	340	400	340	7,500	49,684
Tampa	Legends Field	318	408	314	10,386	67,565
Vero Beach	Holman	340	400	340	6,500	57,339

BREVARD COUNTY
MANATEES

Office Address: 5800 Stadium Pkwy., Melbourne, FL 32940.
Telephone: (321) 633-9200. **FAX:** (321) 633-9210.
E-Mail Address: info@spacecoaststadium.com. **Website:** www.manatees
baseball.com.
Affiliation (first year): Montreal Expos (2002). **Years in League:** 1994-.

OWNERSHIP, MANAGEMENT
Operated by: Montreal Expos.
Vice President, Brevard Operations: Andy Dunn. **Assistant General Manager:** Trey Fraser. **Director, Sales, Marketing/Promotions:** Buck Rogers. **Director, Ticket Operations/Public Relations:** Jeff Weinhold. **Manager, Sales/Promotions/Internships:** Calvin Funkhouser. **Manager, Groups/Special Events:** Babs Rogers. **Manager, Sales/Marketing:** Mark Hughes. **Account Executives:** Brett Handelman, Tyler Hubbard, Joe McGrail, Ross Mehalko, Amanda Turner, John Van Vleet. **Office Manager:** Lilya McAtee. **Head Groundskeeper:** Doug Lopas. **Assistant Groundskeeper:** Roger Manuel. **Facilities Engineer:** Charles Bunch. **Director, Chocolate Moose:** Roy Lake. **Office Manager, Concessions:** Siv Donovan.

FIELD STAFF
Manager: Tim Raines. **Coach:** Andy Skeels. **Pitching Coach:** Craig Bjornson. **Trainer:** Steve Gober.

GAME INFORMATION
Radio: None.
PA Announcer: Pat Hernan. **Official Scorer:** Ron Jernick.
Stadium Name (year opened): Space Coast Stadium (1994). **Location:** I-95 North to Wickham Road (exit 191), left on Wickham, right on Lake Andrew Drive, left onto Judge Fran Jameson Way, right on Stadium Parkway; I-95 South to Fiske Boulevard (exit 195), left on Fiske, follow Fiske/Stadium Parkway to ballpark. **Standard Game Times:** 7:05 p.m.; Sun. 1:35.
Visiting Club Hotel: Baymont Inn & Suites, 7200 George T. Edwards Dr., Melbourne, FL 32940. Telephone: (321) 242-9400.

CLEARWATER
THRESHERS

Office Address: 601 N. Old Coachman Rd, Clearwater, FL 33765.
Mailing Address: 601 N. Old Coachman Rd, Clearwater, FL 33765.
Telephone: (727) 467-4457. **FAX:** (727) 712-4498. **Website:** www.threshers
baseball.com.
Affiliation (first year): Philadelphia Phillies (1985). **Years in League:** 1985-.

OWNERSHIP, MANAGEMENT
Operated by: The Philadelphia Phillies.
Chairman: Bill Giles. **President:** David Montgomery.
Director, Florida Operations: John Timberlake. **Assistant Director, Florida Operations:** Lee McDaniel. **Business Manager:** Dianne Gonzalez. **General Manager:** John Cook. **Director, Sales:** Dan McDonough. **Coordinator, Ticketing/Media:** Jason Adams. **Coordinator, Merchandising/Special Events:** Carrie Jenkins. **Manager, Food/Beverage:** Dan Madden. **Group Sales:** Jennifer Mastry. **Stadium Operations:** Jay Warren. **Ticket Manager:** Kevin Brahm. **Office Manager:** De De Angelillis. **Head Groundskeeper:** Opie Cheek. **Clubhouse Operations:** Cliff Armbruster.

FIELD STAFF
Manager: Mike Schmidt. **Coaches:** Manny Amador, Dan Roberts. **Pitching Coach:** Steve Schrenk. **Trainer:** Sean Fcasni.

GAME INFORMATION
Radio: None.
PA Announcer: Don Guckian. **Official Scorer:** Larry Wiederecht.
Stadium Name (year opened): Bright House Networks Field (2004). **Location:** U.S. 19 North and Drew Street in Clearwater. **Standard Game Times:** 7:05 p.m.; Sun. 2:05.
Visiting Club Hotel: Econo Lodge, 21252 U.S. 19 N., Clearwater, FL 33765. Telephone: (727) 796-3165.

DAYTONA
CUBS

Office Address: 105 East Orange Ave., Daytona Beach, FL 32114.
Telephone: (386) 257-3172. **FAX:** (386) 257-3382.

E-Mail Address: info@daytonacubs.com. **Website:** www.daytonacubs.com.
Affiliation (first year): Chicago Cubs (1993). **Years in league:** 1920-24, 1928, 1936-41, 1946-73, 1977-87, 1993-.

OWNERSHIP/MANAGEMENT

Operated by: Big Game Florida, LLC.
Principal Owner/President: Andrew Rayburn.
General Manager: Michael Swope. **Assistant GM:** Bill Papierniak. **Director, Media:** Kyle Bushn. **Director, Stadium Operations:** Erik Malvik.

FIELD STAFF

Manager: Steve McFarland. **Coach:** Richie Zisk. **Pitching Coach:** Tom Pratt. **Trainer:** Steve Melendez

GAME INFORMATION

Radio Announcers: Bo Fulginiti, Kyle Bushn. **No. of Games Broadcast:** Home-70, Away-70. **Flagship Station:** WELE 1380-AM.
PA Announcer: Tim Lecras. **Official Scorer:** Lyle Fox.
Stadium Name (year opened): Jackie Robinson Ballpark (1930). **Location:** I-95 to International Speedway Blvd. exit (Route 92), east to Beach Street, south to Orange Ave., east to ballpark; A1A North/South to Orange Ave., west to ballpark. **Standard Game Times:** 7 p.m.; Sun. 1.
Visiting Club Hotel: Treasure Island Resort, 2025 S. Atlantic Ave., Daytona Beach Shores, FL 32118. Telephone: (386) 255-8371.

DUNEDIN
BLUE JAYS

Office Address: 373-A Douglas Ave., Dunedin, FL 34698.
Telephone: (727) 733-9302. **FAX:** (727) 734-7661.
E-Mail Address: feedback@dunedinbluejays.com. **Website:** www.dunedin bluejays.com.
Affiliation (first year): Toronto Blue Jays (1987). **Years in League:** 1978-79, 1987-.

OWNERSHIP, MANAGEMENT

Operated by: Toronto Blue Jays.
Director, Florida Operations/General Manager: Ken Carson. **Assistant GM:** Carrie Johnson. **Manager, Ticket Sales:** Russ Williams. **Manager, Group Sales:** Jay Eylward. **Office Manager:** Pat Smith. **Sales Representatives:** Lizz Curll, James O'Brien. **Head Groundskeeper:** Steve Perry. **Clubhouse Operations:** Mickey McGee.

FIELD STAFF

Manager: Omar Malave. **Coach:** Paul Elliott. **Pitching Coach:** Rick Langford. **Trainer:** Mike Frostad.

GAME INFORMATION

Radio: None.
PA Announcers: Ed Groth, Dave Bell. **Official Scorer:** Bobby Porter.
Stadium Name (year opened): Dunedin Stadium (1977). **Location:** From I-275, north on Highway 19, left on Sunset Point Road for 4½ miles, right on Douglas Avenue, stadium is ½ mile on right. **Standard Game Times:** 7 p.m.; Sun. 2.
Visiting Club Hotel: Econo Lodge, 21252 US 19 N, Clearwater, FL 34625. Telephone: (727) 799-1569.

FORT MYERS
MIRACLE

Office Address: 14400 Six Mile Cypress Pkwy., Fort Myers, FL 33912.
Telephone: (239) 768-4210. **FAX:** (239) 768-4211.
E-Mail Address: miracle@miraclebaseball.com. **Website:** www.miraclebaseball.com.
Affiliation: Minnesota Twins (1993). **Years in League:** 1926, 1978-87, 1991-.

OWNERSHIP, MANAGEMENT

Operated by: Greater Miami Baseball Club, LP.
Principal Owner/Chairman: Marvin Goldklang. **Chief Executive Officer:** Mike Veeck. **President:** Linda McNabb.
General Manager: Steve Gliner. **Assistant GM:** Andrew Seymour. **Director, Business Operations:** Suzanne Reaves. **Manager, Sales/Marketing:** Terry Simon. **Head Groundskeeper:** Keith Blasingim. **Manager, Media Relations/Broadcasting:** Sean Aronson. **Sales Representative:** Stephen Kaufman. **Manager, Food/Beverage:** John Acquavella. **Assistant Manager, Food/Beverage:** Chris Milewski.

FIELD STAFF

Manager: Jose Marzan. **Coach:** Floyd Rayford. **Pitching Coach:** Eric Rasmussen. **Trainer:** Larry Bennese.

GAME INFORMATION

Radio Announcer: Sean Aronson. **No of Games Broadcast:** Home-70, Away-70. **Flagship Station:** ESPN 770-AM. **PA Announcer:** Sean Fox. **Official Scorer:** Benn Norton.

Stadium Name (year opened): William H. Hammond (1991). **Location:** Exit 131 off I-75, west on Daniels Parkway, left on Six Mile Cypress Parkway. **Standard Game Times:** 7:05 p.m.; Sun. 1:05.

Visiting Club Hotel: Wellesley Inn and Suites, 4400 Ford St. Extension, Fort Myers, FL 33909. Telephone: (239) 278-3949.

JUPITER
HAMMERHEADS

Office Address: 4751 Main St., Jupiter, FL 33458.
Telephone: (561) 775-1818. **FAX:** (561) 691-6886.
E-Mail Address: info@rogerdeanstadium.com. **Website:** www.jupiterhammer
heads.com.
Affiliation (first year): Florida Marlins (2002). **Years in League:** 1998-.

OWNERSHIP, MANAGEMENT

Owned by: Florida Marlins.
Operated by: Jupiter Stadium, LTD.
General Manager, JSL: Rob Rabenecker. **Executive Assistant to GM, JSL:** Carol McAteer.
GM, Jupiter Hammerheads: Brian Barnes. **Associate GM:** Chris Easom. **Director, Sales/Marketing:** Jennifer Brown. **Manager, Merchandising:** Jordan Sproat. **Manager, Stadium Building:** Jorge Toro. **Manager, Facility Operations:** Marshall Jennings. **Assistant Manager, Facility Operations:** Johnny Simmons. **Office Manager:** Louise Helkowski. **Manager, Tickets:** Tim Stoyle. **Manager, Marketing:** Matt McKenna. **Marketing Sales Executive:** Sandi O'Malley. **Sales Representatives:** Brentley Childs, Ivar Isacsson, Amanda Sinclair. **Press Box Coordinator:** Chris Tunno. **Stadium Operations Assistant:** Bryan Knapp. **Interns:** Danielle Antoszeski, Caitlin Bakum, Blake Englert, Scott Hodge, Katie Hyslop, Chris LaRoy, Matthew Monstrola, Lainey Ruskay, Ben Rustine, Amanda Welcomer.

FIELD STAFF

Manager: Luis Dorante. **Coach:** Paul Sanagorski. **Pitching Coach:** Reid Cornelius. **Trainer:** Brad LaRosa.

GAME INFORMATION

Radio: None.
PA Announcers: John Frost, Dick Sanford. **Official Scorer:** Blake Englert.
Stadium Name (year opened): Roger Dean Stadium (1998). **Location:** I-95 to exit 83, east on Donald Ross Road for ¼ mile.
Standard Game Times: 7:05 p.m.; Sun. 4:05, (April–May) 1:05.
Visiting Club Hotel: Waterford Hotel & Conference Center, 11360 U.S. Hwy. 1, North Palm Beach, FL 33408. Telephone: (561) 624-7186.

LAKELAND
TIGERS

Office Address: 2125 N. Lake Ave., Lakeland, FL 33805.
Mailing Address: P.O. Box 90187, Lakeland, FL 33804.
Telephone: (863) 686-8075. **FAX:** (863) 688-9589.
E-Mail Address: info@lakelandtigers.net.
Affiliation (first year): Detroit Tigers (1967). **Years in League:** 1919-26, 1953-55, 1960, 1962-64, 1967-.

OWNERSHIP, MANAGEMENT

Operated by: Detroit Tigers.
Principal Owner: Mike Ilitch. **President:** Dave Dombrowski. **Director, Florida Operations:** Ron Myers.
General Manager: Todd Pund. **Assistant GM:** Shannon Follett. **Ticket Operations:** Unavailable. **Director, Merchandising/Concessions:** Kay LaLonde. **Director, Tiger Town Cafeteria:** Agnes Proctor. **Clubhouse Operations:** Dan Price. **Head Groundskeeper:** Bryan French.

FIELD STAFF

Manager: Gary Green. **Coach:** Rich Morales. **Pitching Coach:** Britt Burns. **Trainer:** Chris McDonald.

GAME INFORMATION

Radio: None.
PA Announcer: Shari Szabo. **Official Scorer:** Sandy Shaw.
Stadium Name (year opened): Joker Marchant Stadium (1966). **Location:** I-4 to Exit 33, left 1½ miles. **Standard Game Times:** 7 p.m.; Sun. 1.
Visiting Club Hotel: Baymont Inns and Suites, 4315 Lakeland Park Dr., Lakeland, FL 33809. Telephone: (863) 815-0606.

PALM BEACH
CARDINALS

Office Address: 4751 Main St., Jupiter, FL 33458.
Telephone: (561) 775-1818. **FAX:** (561) 691-6886.
E-Mail Address: info@rogerdeanstadium.com. **Website:** www.palmbeach cardinals.com.
Affiliation (first year): St. Louis Cardinals (2003). **Years in League:** 2003-.

OWNERSHIP, MANAGEMENT

Owned by: St. Louis Cardinals.
Operated by: Jupiter Stadium, LTD.
General Manager, JSL: Rob Rabenecker. **Executive Assistant to GM, JSL:** Carol McAteer.
GM, Palm Beach Cardinals: Chris Easom. **Associate GM:** Brian Barnes. **Director, Sales/Marketing:** Jennifer Brown. **Manager, Merchandising:** Jordan Sproat. **Manager, Stadium Building:** Jorge Toro. **Manager, Facility Operations:** Marshall Jennings. **Assistant Manager, Facility Operations:** Johnny Simmons. **Office Manager:** Louise Helkowski. **Manager, Tickets:** Tim Stoyle. **Manager, Marketing:** Matt McKenna. **Marketing Sales Executive:** Sandi O'Malley. **Sales Representatives:** Brentley Childs, Ivar Isacsson, Amanda Sinclair. **Press Box Coordinator:** Chris Tunno. **Stadium Operations Assistant:** Bryan Knapp. **Interns:** Danielle Antoszeski, Caitlin Bakum, Blake Englert, Scott Hodge, Katie Hyslop, Chris LaRoy, Matthew Monstrola, Lainey Ruskay, Ben Rustine, Amanda Welcomer.

FIELD STAFF

Manager: Tom Nieto. **Coach:** Darrell Whitmore. **Pitching Coach:** Derek Lilliquist. **Trainer:** Kevin Crawmer.

GAME INFORMATION

Radio: None.
PA Announcers: John Frost, Dick Sanford. **Official Scorer:** Chris Tunno.
Stadium Name (year opened): Roger Dean Stadium (1998). **Location:** I-95 to exit 83, east on Donald Ross Road for ¼ mile.
Standard Game Times: 7:05 p.m.; Sun. 4:05, (April–May) 1:05.
Visiting Club Hotel: Waterford Hotel & Conference Center, 11360 U.S. Hwy. 1, North Palm Beach, FL 33408. Telephone: (561) 624-7186.

ST. LUCIE
METS

Office Address: 525 NW Peacock Blvd., Port St. Lucie, FL 34986.
Telephone: (772) 871-2100. **FAX:** (772) 878-9802.
Website: www.stluciemets.com.
Affiliation (first year): New York Mets (1988). **Years in League:** 1988-.

OWNERSHIP, MANAGEMENT

Operated by: Sterling Mets, LP.
Chairman: Fred Wilpon. **President:** Saul Katz. **Executive Vice President/Chief Operating Officer:** Jeff Wilpon.
Director, Florida Operations/General Manager: Paul Taglieri. **Assistant GM, Stadium Operations:** Traer Van Allen. **Assistant GM, Marketing/Public Relations:** Ari Skalet. **Director, Food Services:** Chip Wheeler. **Office Assistant:** Cynthia Malaspino. **Account Executive:** Brian Paupeck. **Administrative Assistant:** Paula Sloan. **Head Groundskeeper:** Tommy Bowes. **Clubhouse Manager:** Jack Brenner.

FIELD STAFF

Manager: Tim Teufel. **Coach:** Lamar Johnson. **Pitching Coach:** Rick Mahler. **Trainer:** Mike Lopriore.

GAME INFORMATION

Radio: None.
PA Announcer: Kevin Driscoll. **Official Scorer:** Bob Adams.
Stadium Name (year opened): Tradition Field (1988). **Location:** Exit 121 (St. Lucie West Blvd.) off I-95, east ½ mile, left on NW Peacock Blvd. **Standard Game Times:** 7 p.m.; Sun 1.
Visiting Club Hotel: Holiday Inn, 10120 S. Federal Hwy., Port St. Lucie, FL 34952. Telephone: (772) 337-2200.

SARASOTA
RED SOX

Office Address: 2700 12th St., Sarasota, FL 34237.
Mailing Address: P.O. Box 2816, Sarasota, FL 34230.

Telephone: (941) 365-4460. **FAX:** (941) 365-4217.
Affiliation (first year): Boston Red Sox (1994). **Years in League:** 1927, 1961-65, 1989-.

OWNERSHIP, MANAGEMENT

Operated by: Red Sox of Florida, Inc. **Principal Owner:** Boston Red Sox.
General Manager: Todd Stephenson. **Assistant GM:** Dana Forsberg. **Director, Operations/Marketing:** Bryan Oberle. **Manager, Ticketing:** Mike Chasanoff. **Clubhouse Manager:** Richard Bryce.

FIELD STAFF

Manager: Todd Claus. **Coach:** David Howard. **Pitching Coach:** Al Nipper. **Trainer:** Unavailable.

GAME INFORMATION

Radio: None.
PA Announcers: Alex Topp, Joe Mercurio. **Official Scorer:** Howard Spungen.
Stadium Name (year opened): Ed Smith Stadium (1989). **Location:** I-75 to exit 210, three miles west to Tuttle Avenue, right on Tuttle ½ mile to 12th Street, stadium on left. **Standard Game Times:** 7:05 p.m.; Sun. 1.
Visiting Club Hotel: AmericInn and Suites, 5931 Fruitville Rd., Sarasota, FL 34232. Telephone: (941) 342-8778.

TAMPA
YANKEES

Office Address: One Steinbrenner Dr., Tampa, FL 33614.
Telephone: (813) 875-7753. **FAX:** (813) 673-3174.
E-Mail Address: sarena@yankees.com.
Affiliation (first year): New York Yankees (1994). **Years in League:** 1919-27, 1957-1988, 1994-.

OWNERSHIP, MANAGEMENT

Operated by: New York Yankees, LP.
Principal Owner: George Steinbrenner.
General Manager: Sammy Arena. **Assistant GM:** Julie Kremer. **Director, Stadium Operations:** Dean Holbert. **Director, Sales/Marketing:** Howard Grosswirth. **Account Representative:** Heath Hardin. **Director, Ticket Sales:** Vance Smith. **Head Groundskeeper:** Ritchie Anderson.

FIELD STAFF

Manager: Billy Masse. **Coach:** Ty Hawkins. **Pitching Coach:** Greg Pavlick. **Trainer:** Mike Wickland.

GAME INFORMATION

Radio: None.
PA Announcer: Steve Hague. **Official Scorer:** Unavailable.
Stadium Name (year opened): Legends Field (1996). **Location:** I-275 to Martin Luther King, west on Martin Luther King to Dale Mabry. **Standard Game Times:** 7 p.m.; Sun. 1.
Visiting Club Hotel: Holiday Inn Express, 4732 N. Dale Mabry Hwy., Tampa, FL 33614. Telephone: (813) 877-6061.

VERO BEACH
DODGERS

Office Address: 4101 26th St., Vero Beach, FL 32960.
Mailing Address: P.O. Box 2887, Vero Beach, FL 32961.
Telephone: (772) 569-4900. **FAX:** (772) 567-0819.
E-Mail Address: info@vbdodgers.com. **Website:** www.vbdodgers.com.
Affiliation (first year): Los Angeles Dodgers (1980). **Years in League:** 1980-.

OWNERSHIP, MANAGEMENT

Operated by: Los Angeles Dodgers.
President: Bob Daly.
General Manager: Trevor Gooby. **Assistant GM:** Jeff Singer. **Head Groundskeeper:** Steve Carlsward. **Director, Ticket Sales:** Louise Boissy. **Manager, Concessions/Souvenirs:** Kathy Bond. **Secretary:** Carmen Thompson. **Advertising Secretary:** Betty Rollins. **Administrative Assistants:** Emily Christy, Ryan Dobson, Adrienne Midgely, Tim Patykula.

FIELD STAFF

Manager: Scott Little. **Coach:** Juan Bustabad. **Pitching Coach:** Ken Howell. **Trainer:** Chris Hiatt.

GAME INFORMATION

Radio Announcer: Greg Detter. **No. of Games Broadcast:** Home-70, Away-70. **Flagship Station:** WTTB 1490-AM.
PA Announcers: Joe Sanchez, Steve Stone. **Official Scorer:** Randy Phillips.
Stadium Name (year opened): Holman Stadium (1953). **Location:** I-95 to Route 60 East, left on 43rd Avenue, right on Aviation Boulevard. **Standard Game Times:** 7 p.m.; Sun. (April-June) 1.
Visiting Club Hotel: Key West Inn, 1580 U.S. 1, Sebastian, FL 32958. Telephone: (772) 388-8588.

MIDWEST LEAGUE

Office Address: 1118 Cranston Rd., Beloit, WI 53511.
Mailing Address: P.O. Box 936, Beloit, WI 53512.
Telephone: (608) 364-1188. **FAX:** (608) 364-1913.
E-Mail Address: mwl@midwestleague.com. **Website:** www.midwestleague.com.
Years League Active: 1947-.

President, Treasurer: George Spelius.
Vice President: Ed Larson. **Legal Counsel/Secretary:** Richard Nussbaum.
Directors: Andrew Appleby (Fort Wayne), Sam Bernabe (Battle Creek), Lew Chamberlin (West Michigan), Dennis Conerton (Beloit), Tom Dickson (Lansing), Kevin Krause (Quad City), Alan Levin (South Bend), Robert Murphy (Dayton), Doug Smith (Clinton), Rocky Vonachen (Peoria), Dave Walker (Burlington), Mike Woleben (Kane County), Rob Zerjav (Wisconsin), Unavailable (Cedar Rapids).
League Administrator: Holly Voss.
2004 Opening Date: April 8. **Closing Date:** Sept. 6.
Regular Season: 140 games (split-schedule).
Division Structure: East—Battle Creek, Dayton, Fort Wayne, Lansing, South Bend, West Michigan. **West**—Beloit, Burlington, Cedar Rapids, Clinton, Kane County, Peoria, Quad City, Wisconsin.

George Spelius

Playoff Format: Eight teams qualify. First-half and second-half division champions and wild-card teams meet in best-of-3 quarterfinal series. Winners meet in best-of-3 series for division championship. Division champions meet in best-of-5 final for league championship.
All-Star Game: June 22 at Cedar Rapids.
Roster Limit: 25 active. **Player Eligibility Rule:** No age limit. No more than two players and one player-coach on active list may have more than five years experience.
Brand of Baseball: Rawlings ROM-MID.
Statistician: The Sports Network; 2200 Byberry Rd., Suite 200, Hatboro, PA 19040.
Umpires: Chris Bakke, Jeremy Barbe (Wichita, KS), Cory Blaser, Darren Budahn, Robert Davidson, Brian Frisch, Scott Jarrad, Barry Larson (Lewiston, ID), Eric Loveless, Nicholas Monaco, Jason Nakaishi, Robert Price, Mark Ripperger, Will Robinson (Jonesboro, AR).

STADIUM INFORMATION

Club	Stadium	Dimensions			Capacity	2003 Att.
		LF	CF	RF		
Battle Creek	C.O. Brown	322	402	333	6,000	93,314
Beloit	Pohlman Field	325	380	325	3,500	96,431
Burlington	Community Field	338	403	318	3,500	59,427
Cedar Rapids	New Veterans Memorial	315	400	325	6,000	174,451
Clinton	Alliant Energy Field	335	390	325	2,500	81,535
Dayton	Fifth Third Field	338	402	338	7,230	590,382
Fort Wayne	Memorial	330	400	330	6,516	257,013
Kane County	Philip B. Elfstrom	335	400	335	7,400	516,133
Lansing	Oldsmobile Park	305	412	305	11,000	364,623
Peoria	O'Brien Field	310	400	310	7,500	246,370
Quad City	John O'Donnell	340	390	340	5,200	132,983
South Bend	Coveleski Regional	336	405	336	5,000	203,690
West Michigan	Fifth Third Ballpark	327	402	327	10,900	361,545
Wisconsin	Fox Cities	325	405	325	5,500	198,001

BATTLE CREEK
YANKEES

Office Address: 1392 Capital Ave. NE, Battle Creek MI 49017.
Telephone: (269) 660-2287. **FAX:** (269) 660-2288.
E-Mail Address: info@battlecreekyankees.com. **Website:** www.battlecreek
yankees.com
Affiliation (first year): New York Yankees (2003). **Years in League:** 1995-.

OWNERSHIP, MANAGEMENT
Operated by: Riverside Baseball, LLC.
Executive Director: Sam Bernabe.
Assistant General Manager: David Darkey. **Director, Stadium Operations:** Luke Kuboushek. **Director, Media Relations:** Scott Sailor. **Director, Corporate Sales:** Tim Wilson. **Director, Baseball Operations:** Jacob Bolton. **Director, Technology:** Michael Gartner. **Sports Turf Manager:** Len Matthews.

FIELD STAFF
Manager: Mitch Seoane. **Coach:** Bill Mosiello. **Pitching Coach:** Steve Renko. **Trainer:** Unavailable.

GAME INFORMATION
Radio: www.battlecreekyankees.com
PA Announcer: Roy LaFountain. **Official Scorer:** Geoff Henson.
Stadium Name (year opened): C.O. Brown Stadium (1990). **Location:** I-94 to exit 98B (downtown), to Capital Avenue and continue five miles to stadium. **Standard Game Times:** 7 p.m., (April-May) 6; Sun. 2.
Visiting Club Hotel: Comfort Inn, 2590 Capital Ave. SW, Battle Creek MI 49017. Telephone: (269) 965-3201.

BELOIT
SNAPPERS

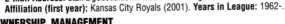

Office Address: 2301 Skyline Dr., Beloit, WI 53511.
Mailing Address: P.O. Box 855, Beloit, WI 53512.
Telephone: (608) 362-2272. **FAX:** (608) 362-0418.
E-Mail Address: snappy@snappersbaseball.com. **Website:** www.snappersbaseball.com.
Affiliation (first year): Milwaukee Brewers (1982). **Years in League:** 1982-.

OWNERSHIP, MANAGEMENT
Operated by: Beloit Professional Baseball Association, Inc.
Chairman: Dennis Conerton. **President:** Marcy Olsen.
General Manager: Brian Barkowski. **Assistant GM/Promotions:** Dave Costello. **Assistant GM/Gameday Operations:** Jeff Vohs. **Director, Group Sales:** Scott Koontz **Director, Community/Media Relations:** Jeremy Neuman

FIELD STAFF
Manager: Don Money. **Coach:** Tony Diggs. **Pitching Coach:** Rich Sauveur. **Trainer:** Alan Diamond.

GAME INFORMATION
Radio Announcer: Unavailable. **No. of Games Broadcast:** Unavailable. **Flagship Station:** WTJK 1380-AM.
PA Announcer: Dave Costello. **Official Scorer:** Unavailable.
Stadium Name (year opened): Pohlman Field (1982). **Location:** I-90 to exit 185-A, right at Cranston Road for 1½ miles; I-43 to Wisconsin 81 to Cranston Road, right at Cranston for 1½ miles. **Standard Game Times:** 7 p.m., (April-May) 6:30; Sun. 2.
Visiting Club Hotel: Econo Lodge, 2956 Milwaukee Rd., Beloit, WI 53511. Telephone: (608) 364-4000.

BURLINGTON
BEES

Office Address: 2712 Mt. Pleasant St., Burlington, IA 52601.
Mailing Address: P.O. Box 824, Burlington, IA 52601.
Telephone: (319) 754-5705. **FAX:** (319) 754-5882.
E-Mail Address: staff@gobees.com. **Website:** www.gobees.com.
Affiliation (first year): Kansas City Royals (2001). **Years in League:** 1962-.

OWNERSHIP, MANAGEMENT
Operated by: Burlington Baseball Association, Inc.
President: Dave Walker.

General Manager: Chuck Brockett. **Assistant GM, Baseball Operations:** Randy Wehofer. **Assistant GM, Sales/Marketing:** Adam Small. **Director, Group Outings:** Trish Renken. **Head Groundskeeper:** Dave Vander Heyden.

FIELD STAFF
Manager: Jim Gabella. **Coach:** Patrick Anderson. **Pitching Coach:** Tom Burgmeier. **Trainer:** Mark Stubblefield.

GAME INFORMATION
Radio Announcer: Randy Wehofer. **No. of Games Broadcast:** Home-70, Away-70. **Flagship Stations:** KBUR 1490-AM, KBKB 1360-AM.
PA Announcer: Bob Engberg. **Official Scorer:** Scott Logas.
Stadium Name (year opened): Community Field (1947). **Location:** From U.S. 34, take U.S. 61 North to Mt. Pleasant Street, east ⅛ mile. **Standard Game Times:** 7 p.m.; Sat. (April-May) 6; Sun. 2.
Visiting Club Hotel: Pzazz Best Western, 3001 Winegard Dr., Burlington, IA 52601. Telephone: (319) 753-2223.

CEDAR RAPIDS
KERNELS

Office Address: 950 Rockford Rd. SW, Cedar Rapids, IA 52404.
Mailing Address: P.O. Box 2001, Cedar Rapids, IA 52406.
Telephone: (319) 363-3887. **FAX:** (319) 363-5631.
E-Mail Address: kernels@kernels.com. **Website:** www.kernels.com.
Affiliation (first year): Anaheim Angels (1993). **Years in League:** 1962-.

OWNERSHIP, MANAGEMENT
Operated by: Cedar Rapids Baseball Club, Inc.
President: Unavailable.
General Manager: Jack Roeder. **Chief Operating Officer:** Doug Nelson. **Director, Merchandising:** Nancy Cram. **Head Groundskeeper:** Jesse Roeder. **Director, Ticket/Group Sales:** Andrea Murphy. **Director, Marketing/Public Relations:** Mike Koolbeck. **Director, Broadcasting:** John Rodgers. **Director, Finance/Human Resources:** Charlie Patrick. **Director, Graphics/Technology:** Andrew Pantini. **Sales Account Executives:** Jessica Fergesen, Zach Melton, Loni Thorsten. **Concessions Manager:** Dave Soper. **Clubhouse Operations:** Ron Plein.

FIELD STAFF
Manager: Bobby Magallanes. **Coach:** Justin Baughman. **Pitching Coach:** Erik Bennett. **Trainer:** Brian Reinker.

GAME INFORMATION
Radio Announcer: John Rodgers. **No. of Games Broadcast:** Home-70, Away-70. **Flagship Station:** KCRG 1600-AM.
PA Announcer: Dale Brodt. **Official Scorer:** Al Gruwell.
Stadium Name (year opened): Veterans Memorial Stadium (2002). **Location:** I-380 to Wilson Ave. exit, west to Rockford Road, right one mile to corner of 8th Ave. and 15th Street SW. **Standard Game Times:** 7 p.m., (April-May, Sept.) 6:30 p.m.; Sat. (April-May) 5, (June-Aug.) 7; Sun. 2.
Visiting Club Hotel: Best Western Village Inn, 100 F Ave. NW, Cedar Rapids, IA 52405. Telephone: (319) 366-5323.

CLINTON
LUMBERKINGS

Office Address: Alliant Energy Field, Sixth Avenue and First Street, Clinton, IA 52732.
Mailing Address: P.O. Box 1295, Clinton, IA 52733.
Telephone: (563) 242-0727. **FAX:** (563) 242-1433.
E-Mail Address: lumberkings@lumberkings.com. **Website:** www.lumberkings.com.
Affiliation (first year): Texas Rangers (2003). **Years in League:** 1956-.

OWNERSHIP, MANAGEMENT
Operated by: Clinton Baseball Club, Inc.
Chairman: Don Roode. **President:** Doug Smith.
General Manager: Ted Tornow. **Director, Sales/Promotions:** Troy Russell. **Groundskeeper:** Unavailable.

FIELD STAFF
Manager: Carlos Subero. **Coach:** Mike Boulanger. **Pitching Coach:** Stan Hilton. **Trainer:** Mark Ryan.

GAME INFORMATION
Radio Announcer: Chris Lake. **No. of Games Broadcast:** Home-70, Away-70. **Flagship Station:** KCLN 1390-AM.
PA Announcer: Morty Kriner. **Official Scorer:** Spike Tuss.
Stadium Name (year opened): Alliant Energy Field (1937). **Location:** Highway 30 East to Sixth Avenue North, right on Sixth, cross railroad tracks, stadium on right. **Standard Game Times:** 7 p.m.; Sat. (April-May) 2; Sun. 2.
Visiting Club Hotel: Super 8 Motel, 1711 Lincoln Way, Clinton, IA 52732. Telephone: (563) 242-8870.

DAYTON
DRAGONS

Office Address: Fifth Third Field, 220 N. Patterson Blvd., Dayton, OH 45402.
Telephone: (937) 228-2287. FAX: (937) 228-2284.
E-Mail Address: dragons@daytondragons.com. Website: www.daytondragons.com.
Affiliate (first year): Cincinnati Reds (2000). Years in League: 2000-present.

OWNERSHIP, MANAGEMENT
Operated by: Dayton Professional Baseball, LLC.
Owners: Hank Stickney, Ken Stickney, Peter Guber, Paul Schaeffer, Earvin "Magic" Johnson, Archie Griffin.
President: Robert Murphy. Executive Vice President: Eric Deutsch.
VP, Baseball/Stadium Operations: Gary Mayse. VP, Sponsorships: Mark Clayton. Director, Ticket Sales: John Davis. Director, Team Accounting: Jim Goodrich. Staff Accountant: Dorothy Day. Director, Entertainment: Shari Sharkins. Director, Marketing: Jim Francis. Director, Media Relations/Broadcasting: Mike Vander Wood. Corporate Marketing Managers: Michael Blanton, Jermaine Gage, Laura Rose, Mark Wilhelm. Marketing Managers: Brad Eaton, Shannon Johnson, Jeff Thompson, Emily Tincher. Manager, Box Office: Sally Ledford. Operations Manager: Joe Eaglowski. Facilities Manager: Joe Elking. Head Groundskeeper: Ryan Kaspitzke.

FIELD STAFF
Manager: Alonzo Powell. Coach:. Max Venable. Pitching Coach: Larry Pierson. Trainer: Randy Brackney.

GAME INFORMATION
Radio Announcer: Mike Vander Wood. No. of Games Broadcast: Home-70, Away-70. Flagship Station: WING 1410-AM.
PA Announcer: Unavailable. Official Scorers: Matt Lindsay, Jim Scott.
Stadium Name (year opened): Fifth Third Field (2000). Location: I-75 South to downtown Dayton, left at First Street; I-75 North, right at First Street exit. Standard Game Times: 7 p.m.; Sun. 2.
Visiting Club Hotel: Unavailable.

FORT WAYNE
WIZARDS

Office Address: 1616 E. Coliseum Blvd., Fort Wayne, IN 46805.
Telephone: (260) 482-6400. FAX: (260) 471-4678.
E-Mail: wizards@fortwaynewizards.com. Website: www.fortwaynewizards.com
Affiliation (first year): San Diego Padres (1999). Years in League: 1993-.

OWNERSHIP, MANAGEMENT
Operated by: General Sports and Entertainment, LLC.
Owner: Andrew Appleby.
General Manager: Mike Nutter. Assistant GM, Business Operations: Brian Schackow. Senior Assistant GM: David Lorenz. Director, Marketing/Graphic Design: Michael Limmer. Director, Community/Media Relations: Jared Parcell. Director, Ticket Operations: Michael Moody. Director, Broadcasting: Terry Byrom. Group Sales Representatives: Kevin Duplaga, Brad Shank, Mike Williams, Jeff Wing. Corporate Sales Representatives: Jared Parcell, David Lorenz, Terry Byrom, Brian Schackow, Mike Nutter. Group Sales Representative: Jeff Bierly. Office Manager: Cathy Tinney.

FIELD STAFF
Manager: Randy Ready. Coach: Tom Tornincasa. Pitching Coach: Steve Webber. Trainer: Paul Navarro.

GAME INFORMATION
Radio Announcers: Terry Byrom, Kent Hormann. No. of Games Broadcast: Home-70, Away-70. Flagship Station: WKJG 1380-AM.
PA Announcer: Jared Parcell. Official Scorers: Mike Maahs; Mike Jewell.
Stadium Name (year opened): Memorial Stadium (1993). Location: Exit 112A (Coldwater Road South) off I-69 to Coliseum Blvd., left to stadium. Standard Game Times: 6 p.m., (June-July) 7; Wed. 11, (June-July) 12; Sat. 4, (June-July) 6; Sun. 2.
Visiting Club Hotel: Best Western Luxbury, 5501 Coventry Lane, Fort Wayne, IN 46804. Telephone: (260) 436-0242.

KANE COUNTY
COUGARS

Office Address: 34W002 Cherry Lane, Geneva, IL 60134.
Telephone: (630) 232-8811. FAX: (630) 232-8815.
E-Mail Address: info@kccougars.com. Website: www.kccougars.com.

Affiliation (first year): Oakland Athletics (2003). **Years in League:** 1991-.

OWNERSHIP, MANAGEMENT

Operated by: Cougars Baseball Partnership/American Sports Enterprises, Inc.
President: Mike Woleben. **Vice President:** Mike Murtaugh.
VP/General Manager: Jeff Sedivy. **Assistant GMs:** Curtis Haug, Jeff Ney. **Business Manager:** Mary Almlie. **Comptroller:** Doug Czurylo. **Concessions Accountant:** Chris McGorry. **Director, Ticket Operations:** Amy Mason. **Assistant Director, Ticket Operations:** Mike Gilreath. **Season Ticket Coordinator:** Lindsey Bast. **Ticket Operations:** Steve McNelley. **Director, Ticket Sales:** Michael Patterson. **Account Executives:** David Edison, Kurt Hasenbalg, Marty Henry, Greg Hofer, Patti Savage. **Director, Food/Beverage:** Rich Essegian. **Director, Catering:** Mike Klafehn. **Concessions Supervisor:** Tim Howe. **Director, Public Relations:** Kari Kuefler. **Design, Graphics:** Emmet Broderick, Todd Koenitz. **Manager, Advertising:** Bill Baker. **Manager, Merchandise:** Leif Anderson. **Head Groundskeeper:** Ryan Nieuwsma. **Assistant Groundskeeper:** Brad Anderson. **Office Manager:** Carol Huppert. **Facilities Management:** Jeff Snyder. **Head of Security:** Dan Klinkhammer. **Clubhouse Manager:** Unavailable.

FIELD STAFF

Manager: Dave Joppie. **Coach:** Aaron Nieckula. **Pitching Coach:** Fernando Arroyo. **Trainer:** Justin Whitehouse.

GAME INFORMATION

Radio Announcer: Unavailable. **No. of Games Broadcast:** Home-70, Away-70. **Flagship Station:** WBIG 1280-AM. **PA Announcer:** Kevin Sullivan. **Official Scorer:** Bill Baker.
Stadium Name (year opened): Philip B. Elfstrom Stadium (1991). **Location:** From east or west, I-88 (East-West Tollway) to Farnsworth Road North exit, north five miles to Cherry Lane, left into stadium complex; from north, Route 59 south to Route 64 (North Ave.), west to Kirk Road, south past Route 38 to Cherry Lane, right into stadium complex; from northwest, I-90 to Randall Road South exit, south to Fabyan Parkway, east to Kirk Road, north to Cherry Lane, left into stadium complex. **Standard Game Times:** 7 p.m., (April-May 13) 6; Sat. (April-May 13) 4, (May 14-Sept.) 6; Sun. 2.
Visiting Club Hotel: Unavailable.

LANSING
LUGNUTS

Office Address: 505 E. Michigan Ave., Lansing, MI 48912.
Telephone: (517) 485-4500. **Fax:** (517) 485-4518.
E-Mail Address: info@lansinglugnuts.com. **Website:** www.lansinglugnuts.com.
Affiliation (first year): Chicago Cubs (1999). **Years In League:** 1996-.

OWNERSHIP, MANAGEMENT

Operated by: Take Me Out to the Ballgame, LLC.
Principal Owners: Tom Dickson, Sherrie Myers.
General Manager: Jeff Calhoun. **Director, Marketing:** Darla Bowen. **Director, Food Service:** Dave Parker. **Manager, Tickets:** Chris Troub. **Director, Retail:** Cherie Hargitt. **Director, Sales:** Nick Grueser. **Broadcaster/Marketing Assistant:** Seth VanHoven. **Marketing Assistant:** Ben Broder. **Head Groundskeeper:** Nate Lyster.. **Group Sales Representatives:** Mike MacKenzie, Nick Brzenzinski. **Corporate Account Executives:** Jim LaPorte, Nathan Greene. **Sponsorship Service Representative:** Valerie Claus. **Business Manager:** Suzanne Green. **Front Desk Administrator:** Sharon Jackson. **Sales Intern:** Bianca Richards.

FIELD STAFF

Manager: Julio Garcia. **Coach:** Mike Micucci. **Pitching Coach:** Mike Anderson. **Trainer:** Chuck Baughman.

GAME INFORMATION

Radio Announcer: Seth VanHoven. **No. of Games Broadcast:** Home-65, Away-65 (no weekday day games). **Flagship Station:** The Ticket 92.7-FM.
PA Announcer: J.J. Wright. **Official Scorer:** Mike Clark.
Stadium Name (year opened): Oldsmobile Park (1996). **Location:** I-96 East/West to U.S. 496, exit at Larch Street. **Standard Game Times:** 7:05 p.m., (April-May) 6:05; Sun. 2:05.
Visiting Club Hotel: Unavailable.

PEORIA
CHIEFS

Office Address: 730 SW Jefferson, Peoria, IL 61602.
Telephone: (309) 680-4000. **FAX:** (309) 680-4080.
Website: www.peoriachiefs.com.
Affiliation (first year): St. Louis Cardinals (1995). **Years in League:** 1983-.

OWNERSHIP/MANAGEMENT

Operated by: Peoria Chiefs Community Baseball Club, LLC.
President, General Manager: Rocky Vonachen. **Vice President:** Mark Moehlenkamp. **Director, Guest**

Services/Account Executive: Howard Yates. **Manager, Box Office:** Ryan Sivori. **Manager, Entertainment/Events:** Autum Vorhees. **Manager, Broadcast/Media:** Nathan Baliva. **Account Executives:** George Moore, Jeremy Wieburg.

FIELD STAFF
Manager: Joe Cunningham. **Coach:** Ron Warner. **Pitching Coach:** Bryan Eversgerd. **Trainer:** James Spinale.

GAME INFORMATION
Radio Announcer: Nathan Baliva. **No. of Games Broadcast:** Home-70, Away-70. **Flagship Station:** WOAM 1350-AM. **PA Announcer:** Unavailable. **Official Scorers:** Unavailable.
Stadium Name (year opened): O'Brien Field (2002). **Location:** From South/East, I-74 to exit 93 (Jefferson Street), west one mile, stadium is one block west of Kumpf Boulevard on left. From North/West, I-74 to exit 91 (Glendale Avenue), straight through stoplight and follow Kumpf Boulevard left for five blocks, right on Jefferson Street, stadium on left. **Standard Game Times:** 6:30 p.m.; (April-May 22, Aug. 23-Sept. 2) 6; Fri.-Sat. 7; Sun. 2.
Visiting Club Hotel: Holiday Inn City Centre, 500 Hamilton Blvd., Peoria, IL 61602. Telephone: (309) 674-2500.

SWING OF THE QUAD CITIES

Office Address: 209 S. Gaines St., Davenport, IA 52802.
Mailing Address: P.O. Box 3496, Davenport, IA 52808.
Telephone: (563) 324-3000. **FAX:** (563) 324-3109.
E-Mail Address: jazzed@swingbaseball.com. **Website:** www.swingbaseball.com.
Affiliation (first year): Minnesota Twins (1999). **Years in League:** 1960-.

OWNERSHIP, MANAGEMENT
Operated by: Seventh Inning Stretch, LLC.
Principal Owner, President: Kevin Krause.
Vice President/General Manager: Dave Ziedelis. **Director, Baseball Operations:** Andy Duyvejonck. **Director, Stadium Operations:** Keith Vaske. **Director, Promotions:** Josh Eagan. **Director, Sales:** Michael Corrigan. **Ticket Manager:** Eileen Connors. **Director, Food/Beverage:** James Johnson. **Manager, Merchandise:** Betsy Gladish. **Director, Broadcasting/Media Relations:** Andrew Rudnik. **Account Executives:** Geoff Brigham, Chris Nietupski. **Office Manager:** Carrie Brus. **Head Groundskeeper:** Andy Duyvejonck.

FIELD STAFF
Manager: Kevin Boles. **Coach:** Rudy Hernandez. **Pitching Coach:** Gary Lucas. **Trainer:** Chad Jackson.

GAME INFORMATION
Radio Announcer: Andrew Rudnik. **No. of Games Broadcast:** Home-70, Away-70. **Flagship Station:** Unavailable. **PA Announcer:** Unavailable. **Official Scorer:** Unavailable.
Stadium Name (year opened): John O'Donnell Stadium (1931). **Location:** From I-74, take State Street exit, west onto River Drive, south on Gaines Street. From I-80, take Brady/Harrison Street exit south, west onto River Drive, south on Gaines Street. **Standard Game Times:** 7 p.m.; Sun. 2.
Visiting Club Hotel: Unavailable.

SOUTH BEND
SILVER HAWKS

Office Address: 501 W. South St., South Bend, IN 46601.
Mailing Address: P.O. Box 4218, South Bend, IN 46634.
Telephone: (574) 235-9988. **FAX:** (574) 235-9950.
E-Mail Address: hawks@silverhawks.com. **Website:** www.silverhawks.com.
Affiliation (first year): Arizona Diamondbacks (1997). **Years in League:** 1988-.

OWNERSHIP, MANAGEMENT
Operated by: Palisades Baseball, Ltd.
Principal Owner: Alan Levin. **Executive Vice President:** Erik Haag. **Chief Financial Officer:** Mick Rauch. **Director, Finance:** Cheryl Case.
General Manager: Christian Carlson. **Assistant GM/Operations:** Tim Arseneau. **Director, Sales:** Tony Wittrock. **Manager, Box Office:** Stephen Hinkel. **Director, Operations:** Mike Cook. **Assistant Director, Operations:** Ben Beaver. **Director, Marketing:** Greg Boyd. **Account Executives:** Billy Richards, Ian Zelenski. **Office Manager:** Brandy Beehler. **Director, Media Relations:** Mike Lockert. **Head Groundskeeper:** Joel Reinebold.

FIELD STAFF
Manager: Tony Perezchica. **Coach:** Hector de la Cruz. **Pitching Coach:** Jeff Pico. **Trainer:** Scott Jones.

GAME INFORMATION
Radio Announcer: Mike Lockert. **No. of Games Broadcast:** Unavailable. **Flagship Station:** Unavailable. **PA Announcer:** Unavailable. **Official Scorer:** Unavailable.

Stadium Name (year opened): Stanley Coveleski Regional Stadium (1988). **Location:** I-80/90 toll road to exit 77, take US 31/33 south to South Bend, to downtown (Main Street), to Western Avenue, right on Western, left on Taylor. **Standard Game Times:** 7 p.m., (April-May) 6:30; Sun. 1:30.

Visiting Club Hotel: Holiday Inn-University Area, 515 Dixie Way North, South Bend, IN 46637. Telephone: (574) 272-6600.

WEST MICHIGAN
WHITECAPS

Office Address: 4500 W. River Dr., Comstock Park, MI 49321.
Mailing Address: P.O. Box 428, Comstock Park, MI 49321.
Telephone: (616) 784-4131. **FAX:** (616) 784-4911.
E-Mail Address: playball@whitecaps-baseball.com. **Website:** www.whitecaps-baseball.com.
Affiliation (first year): Detroit Tigers (1997). **Years in League:** 1994-.

OWNERSHIP, MANAGEMENT

Operated by: Whitecaps Professional Baseball Corp.
Principal Owners: Denny Baxter, Lew Chamberlin.
Chief Executive Officer, Managing Partner: Lew Chamberlin. **Chief Financial Officer:** Denny Baxter. **President:** Scott Lane.

Vice President, Operations: Jim Jarecki. **VP, Sales/Marketing:** John Guthrie. **Director, Ticket Sales:** Steve McCarthy. **Manager, Operations:** Matt Costello. **Managers, Human Resources:** Ellen Chamberlin, Tina Porcelli. **Manager, Food/Beverage:** Matt Timon. **Manager, Sales:** Dan McCrath. **Manager, Promotions:** Mickey Graham. **Manager, Group Sales Operations:** Kerri Troyer. **Manager, Website/Merchandise:** Lori Ashcroft. **Manager, Public Relations:** Jamie Farber. **Manager, Ticket Operations:** Steve Klein. **Head Groundskeeper:** Ryan Baumbach. **Manager, Facility Maintenance:** Dutch VanSingel. **Coordinator, Media Relations:** Dewayne Hankins. **Coordinator, Special Events:** Jason Lewandowski. **Corporate Sales:** Rick Berkey, Trevor Tkach. **Ticket Sales Consultants:** Alanna Kuhn, Candace Lutz, Scott Lutz, Chad Sayen. **Assistant, Accounts Receivable:** Barb Renteria. **Assistant, Food/Beverage:** Bill Moore. **Receptionists:** Kim Castle, Susie Former. **Ticket Sales Interns:** Ashley Chalk, Craig Yust. **Ticket Sales/Reading Club Intern:** Jocelynn Clemings,

FIELD STAFF

Manager: Matt Walbeck. **Coach:** Tony Jaramillo. **Pitching Coach:** A.J. Sager. **Trainer:** Chris Vernon.

GAME INFORMATION

Radio Announcer: Rick Berkey. **No. of Games Broadcast:** Home-70, Away-70. **Flagship Station:** WBBL 1340-AM
PA Announcers: Bob Wells, Mike Newell. **Official Scorers:** Mike Dean, Don Thomas.
Stadium Name (year opened): Fifth Third Ballpark (1994). **Location:** U.S. 131 North from Grand Rapids to exit 91 (West River Drive). **Standard Game Times:** 7 p.m., (April-May) 6:35; Sat. (April-May) 2; Sun. 2.
Visiting Club Hotel: Days Inn-Downtown, 310 Pearl St. NW, Grand Rapids, MI 49504. Telephone: (616) 235-7611.

WISCONSIN
TIMBER RATTLERS

TIMBER **Rattlers** ™

Office Address: 2400 N. Casaloma Dr., Appleton, WI 54913.
Mailing Address: P.O. Box 7464, Appleton, WI 54912.
Telephone: (920) 733-4152. **FAX:** (920) 733-8032.
E-Mail Address: info@timberrattlers.com. **Website:** www.timberrattlers.com.
Affiliation (first year): Seattle Mariners (1993). **Years in League:** 1962-.

OWNERSHIP, MANAGEMENT

Operated by: Appleton Baseball Club, Inc.
Chairman: Dave Anderson.
President, General Manager: Rob Zerjav. **Director, Operations:** Tom Kulczewski. **Controller:** Cathy Spanbauer. **Director, Community/Media Relations:** Nikki Becker. **Director, Promotions/Graphic Design:** Angie Ceranski. **Manager, Merchandise/Internet Specialist:** Logan Waetje. **Director, Ticket Sales:** Andrew Podlasik. **Managers, Group Sales:** Darren Feller, Peter Schueppert, Lisa Nortman. **Director, Sales:** Laurie Schill. **Managers, Corporate Sales:** Nicole DeBoth, Chris Mehring. **Office Manager:** Mary Robinson. **Head Groundskeeper:** Jesse Mallmann.

FIELD STAFF

Manager: Daren Brown. **Coach:** Dana Williams. **Pitching Coach:** Brad Holman. **Trainer:** Jeremy Clipperton.

GAME INFORMATION

Radio Announcer: Chris Mehring. **No. of Games Broadcast:** Home-70, Away-70. **Flagship Station:** WJMQ 92.3-FM.
PA Announcer: Matt Wittlin. **Official Scorer:** Jay Grusznski.
Stadium Name (year opened): Fox Cities Stadium (1995). **Location:** Highway 41 to Highway 15 (OO) exit, west to Casaloma Drive, left to stadium. **Standard Game Times:** 7:05 p.m., (April-May) 6:35; Sun. 1:05.
Visiting Club Hotel: Microtel Inn & Suites, 321 Metro Dr., Appleton, WI 54913. Telephone: (920) 997-3121.

SOUTH ATLANTIC
LEAGUE

CLASS A

Office Address: 504 Crescent Hill, Kings Mountain, NC 28086.
Mailing Address: P.O. Box 38, Kings Mountain, NC 28086.
Telephone: (704) 739-3466. **FAX:** (704) 739-1974.
E-Mail Address: saleague@bellsouth.net. **Website:** www.southatlanticleague.com.
Years League Active: 1904-1964, 1979 -.

President/Secretary-Treasurer: John Moss.
Vice President: Ron McKee (Asheville).
Directors: Don Beaver (Hickory), Cooper Brantley (Greensboro), Rita Carfagna (Lake County), Tom Dickson (Charleston, WV), Joseph Finley (Lakewood), Marv Goldklang (Charleston, SC), Larry Hedrick (Kannapolis), David Heller (Columbus), Frank Miceli (Delmarva), Ron McKee (Asheville), Chip Moore (Rome), Rich Mozingo (Capital City), Rich Neumann (Hagerstown), Michael Savit (Augusta), Ken Silver (Savannah), Alan Stein (Lexington).
Director, Administration: Elaine Moss. **Administrative Assistant:** Patrick Heavner.
2004 Opening Date: April 8. **Closing Date:** Sept. 6.
Regular Season: 140 games (split-schedule).
Division Structure: North—Charleston WV, Delmarva, Hagerstown, Hickory, Kannapolis, Lake County, Lakewood, Lexington. **South**—Asheville, Augusta, Capital City, Charleston SC, Columbus, Greensboro, Rome, Savannah.

John Moss

Playoff Format: First-half and second-half division champions meet in best-of-3 semifinal series. Winners advance to best-of-5 series for league championship.
All-Star Game: June 29 at Charleston, SC.
Roster Limit: 25 active. **Player Eligibility Rule:** No age limit. No more than two players and one player-coach on active list may have more than five years of experience.
Brand of Baseball: Rawlings.
Statistician: The Sports Network, 2200 Byberry Rd., Suite 200, Hatboro, PA 19040.
Umpires: Frederick Alexander, Lance Barrett, Russell Barrett, John Bennett (Sarasota, FL), Jason Bradley (Blackshear, GA), William Coble (Graham, NC), James Collins, Tim Donald, Trevor Grieve (Toronto, Ontario), Thomas Hallion , Nathan Huber (Louisville, KY), Richard Laird, Mark Lollo, Billy Parker, James Pearson (Mansfield, LA), Justin Vogel (Jacksonville, FL).

STADIUM INFORMATION

Club	Stadium	Dimensions LF	CF	RF	Capacity	2003 Att.
Asheville	McCormick Field	328	402	300	4,000	143,596
Augusta	Lake Olmstead	330	400	330	4,322	131,650
Capital City	Capital City	330	395	320	6,000	102,149
Charleston, SC	Riley Ballpark	306	386	336	5,800	259,007
Charleston, WV	Watt Powell Park	340	406	330	4,500	95,590
Columbus	Golden Park	330	415	330	5,000	30,565
Delmarva	Perdue	309	402	309	5,200	228,344
Greensboro	War Memorial	327	401	327	7,500	164,589
Hagerstown	Municipal	335	400	330	4,600	100,865
Hickory	L.P. Frans	330	401	330	5,062	176,366
Kannapolis	Fieldcrest Cannon	330	400	310	4,700	92,321
Lake County	Eastlake Ballpark	320	400	320	7,273	437,515
Lakewood	FirstEnergy Park	325	400	325	6,588	445,838
Lexington	Applebee's Park	320	401	318	6,033	370,656
Rome	State Mutual Stadium	335	400	330	5,100	246,718
Savannah	Grayson	290	410	310	8,000	103,443

ASHEVILLE
TOURISTS

Office Address: McCormick Field, 30 Buchanan Pl., Asheville, NC 28801.
Mailing Address: P.O. Box 1556, Asheville, NC 28802.
Telephone: (828) 258-0428. **FAX:** (828) 258-0320.
E-Mail Address: touristsbb@mindspring.com. **Website:** www.theashevilletourists.com.
Affiliation (first year): Colorado Rockies (1994). **Years in League:** 1976-.

OWNERSHIP, MANAGEMENT
Operated by: Asheville Tourists Baseball, Inc.
Principal Owners: Peter Kern, Ron McKee.
President: Peter Kern.
General Manager: Ron McKee. **Assistant GMs:** Chris Smith, Larry Hawkins. **Director, Business Operations:** Carolyn McKee. **Director, Media Relations:** Bill Ballew. **Director, Tickets/Merchandising:** Margarita Turner. **Concessions Manager:** Ben Ashby. **Head Groundskeeper:** Patrick Schrimplin.

FIELD STAFF
Manager: Joe Mikulik. **Coach:** Dave Hajek. **Pitching Coach:** Greg Booker. **Trainer:** Heath Townsend.

GAME INFORMATION
Radio: None.
PA Announcer: Rick Diggler. **Official Scorers:** Wilt Browning, Mike Gore.
Stadium Name (year opened): McCormick Field (1992). **Location:** I-240 to Charlotte Street South exit, south one mile on Charlotte, left on McCormick Place. **Standard Game Times:** 7 p.m.; Sun. 2.
Visiting Club Hotel: Holiday Inn East, 1450 Tunnel Rd., Asheville, NC 28805. Telephone: (828) 298-5611.

AUGUSTA
GREENJACKETS

Office Address: 78 Milledge Rd., Augusta, GA 30904.
Mailing Address: P.O. Box 3746, Augusta, GA 30904.
Telephone: (706) 736-7889. **FAX:** (706) 736-1122.
E-Mail Address: grnsox@aol.com. **Website:** www.greenjackets.net.
Affiliation (first year): Boston Red Sox (1999). **Years in League:** 1988-.

OWNERSHIP, MANAGEMENT
Operated by: H.W.S. Baseball, LLC.
Chief Executive Officer: Michael Savit. **Chief Operating Officer:** Jeffrey Savit. **Executive Vice President:** Chris Scheuer.
General Manager: Nick Brown. **Director, Stadium Operations:** David Ryther Jr. **Director, Marketing:** Andrew Harrell. **Director, Media Relations:** John Butts. **Director, Ticket Sales:** Frank Coppola. **Groundskeeper:** Unavailable.

FIELD STAFF
Manager: Chad Epperson. **Coach:** Cesar Hernandez. **Pitching Coach:** Ace Adams. **Trainer:** Jim Jochim.

GAME INFORMATION
Radio: None.
PA Announcer: Scott Skadan. **Official Scorer:** Steve Cain.
Stadium Name (year opened): Lake Olmstead Stadium (1995). **Location:** I-20 to exit 199 (Washington Road), east to Broad Street, left onto Milledge Road, stadium on right. **Standard Game Times:** 7:15 p.m.; Sun. 2:15.
Visiting Club Hotel: Holiday Inn-West, 1075 Stevens Creek Rd., Augusta, GA 30907. Telephone: (706) 738-8811.

CAPITAL CITY
BOMBERS

CAPITAL CITY
BOMBERS

Office Address: 301 S. Assembly St., Columbia, SC 29201.
Mailing Address: P.O. Box 7845, Columbia, SC 29202.
Telephone: (803) 256-4110. **FAX:** (803) 256-4338.
E-Mail Address: info@bomberball.com. **Website:** www.bomberball.com.
Affiliation (first year): New York Mets (1983). **Years in League:** 1960-61, 1983-.

OWNERSHIP, MANAGEMENT
Operated by: RB3, LLC.
President: Rich Mozingo.

General Manager: Tim Swain. **Assistant GM/Director, Media:** Mark Bryant. **Assistant GM, Ticket Operations:** Brian Kenna. **Director, Stadium Operations/Head Groundskeeper:** Bob Hook. **Director, Corporate Ticket Sales:** Henry Chastain. **Director, Group Sales:** Pete Ehmke.

FIELD STAFF

Manager: Jack Lind. **Coach:** Dave Hollins. **Pitching Coach:** Blaine Beatty. **Trainer:** Unavailable.

GAME INFORMATION

Radio: None.
PA Announcer: Unavailable. **Official Scorer:** Julian Gibbons.
Stadium Name (year opened): Capital City Stadium (1991). **Location:** I-26 East to Columbia, Elmwood Avenue to Assembly Street, right on Assembly for four miles; I-77 South to Columbia, exit at State Road 277 (Bull Street), right on Elmwood, left on Assembly. **Standard Game Times:** 7:05 p.m.; Sun., 2:05.
Visiting Club Hotel: Travelodge, 2210 Bush River Rd., Columbia, SC 29210. Telephone: (803) 798-9665.

CHARLESTON, S.C.
RIVERDOGS

RIVERDOGS

Office Address: 360 Fishburne St., Charleston, SC 29403.
Mailing Address: P.O. Box 20849, Charleston, SC 29413.
Telephone: (843) 723-7241. **FAX:** (843) 723-2641.
E-Mail Address: dogsrus@riverdogs.com. **Website:** www.riverdogs.com.
Affiliation (first year): Tampa Bay Devil Rays (1997). **Years in League:** 1973-78, 1980-.

OWNERSHIP, MANAGEMENT

Operated by: The Goldklang Group/South Carolina Baseball Club, LP.
Principal Owners: Marv Goldklang, Mike Veeck, Bill Murray.
General Manager: Derek Sharrer. **Assistant GM:** Andy Lange. **Director, Stadium Operations:** Ben Danosky. **Director, Promotions:** Stacy Wagner. **Coordinator, Media Relations:** Dan Lehv. **Business Manager:** Aubra Carlton. **Director, Special Events:** Dale Stickney. **Director, Food/Beverage:** Jason Kerton. **Director, Technology Services:** Chris Ginnett. **Office Manager:** Kristal Lessington. **Director, Community Relations:** Danielle Swigart. **Coordinator, Sales:** Harold Craw. **Director, Merchandise:** Kristi Tolley. **Manager, Food/Beverage:** Amy Ferris. **Manager, Ticket:** Trevor Wood. **Manager, Sales:** Rob McAdams. **Head Groundskeeper:** Melissa Slingerland. **Intern, Broadcast/Media:** Keith Yimoyines.

FIELD STAFF

Manager: Steve Livesey. **Coach:** Omer Muñoz. **Pitching Coach:** Marty DeMerritt. **Trainer:** Unavailable.

GAME INFORMATION

Radio Announcer: Dan Lehv. **No. of Games Broadcast:** Home-70, Away-70. **Flagship Station:** WQSC 1340-AM.
PA Announcer: Ken Carrington. **Official Scorer:** Chuck Manka.
Stadium Name (year opened): Joseph P. Riley Jr. Ballpark (1997). **Location:** From U.S. 17, take Lockwood Drive North, right on Fishburne Street. **Standard Game Times:** 7:05 p.m.; Sun. 2:05.
Visiting Club Hotel: Howard Johnson Riverfront, 250 Spring St., Charleston, SC 29403. Telephone: (843) 722-4000.

CHARLESTON, W. VA.
ALLEY CATS

Office Address: 3403 MacCorkle Ave. SE, Charleston, WV 25304.
Telephone: (304) 344-2287. **FAX:** (304) 344-0083.
E-Mail Address: team@charlestonalleycats.com. **Website:** www.charleston alleycats.com.
Affiliation (first year): Toronto Blue Jays (2001). **Years in League:** 1987-.

OWNERSHIP, MANAGEMENT

Operated by: Charleston Professional Baseball Club, LLC.
Principal Owners: Tom Dickson, Sherrie Myers.
General Manager: Andy Milovich. **Assistant GM:** Christopher Hahn. **Business Manager:** Erica Alvarado. **Director, Food Operations:** Justin Meadows. **Director, Ticketing/Operations:** Chad Hodson. **Sales Intern:** Brian Harrigan. **Sponsorship Sales Intern:** William Haynes.

FIELD STAFF

Manager: Ken Joyce. **Coach:** Charles Poe. **Pitching Coach:** Tom Bradley. **Trainer:** Voon Chong.

GAME INFORMATION

Radio: None.
PA Announcer: Donald Cook. **Official Scorer:** Eric Bailey.
Stadium Name (year opened): Watt Powell Park (1949). **Location:** From north/west, I-64/77 to exit 98 (35th Street

Bridge), cross bridge, ballpark is at MacCorkle Avenue; From south/east, I-64/77 to exit 95 (MacCorkle Avenue), take MacCorkle Avenue West ramp (Route 61 North), stadium is 21⁄2 miles on left. **Standard Game Times:** 6:05 p.m., 7:05; Sun. 2:05.

Visiting Club Hotel: Ramada Plaza Hotel, 2nd Avenue and B Street, South Charleston, WV 25303. Telephone: (304) 744-4641.

COLUMBUS
CATFISH

Office Address: Golden Park, 100 Fourth St., Columbus, GA 31901.
Telephone: (706) 571-8866. **FAX:** (706) 571-9984.
E-Mail Address: info@columbuscatfish.com. **Website:** www.columbuscatfish.com.
Affiliation (third year): Los Angeles Dodgers (2002). **Years in League:** 1991-.

OWNERSHIP, MANAGEMENT
Operated by: Main Street Baseball, LLC.
Owner: David Heller.
General Manager: Chris Gallas. **Director, Ticket Operations:** Nick Papas. **Director, Media/Community Relations:** Megan Thomas. **Director, Stadium Operations:** John Evans. **Director, Broadcasting:** Nathan Raynor.

FIELD STAFF
Manager: Dann Bilardello. **Coach:** Garey Ingram. **Pitching Coach:** Shawn Barton. **Trainer:** Carlos Olivas.

GAME INFORMATION
Radio Announcer: Nathan Raynor. **No. of Games Broadcast:** Home-70, Away-70. **Flagship Station:** WDAK 540- AM.
Stadium Name (year opened): Golden Park. **Location:** I-85 South to exit 1 (Victory Drive), west to Fourth Street, in South Commons complex on left. **Standard Game Times:** 7 p.m.; Sun. (April-May) 2, (June-Aug.) 6.
Visiting Club Hotel: Holiday Inn North, 2800 Manchester Expwy., Columbus, GA 31904. Telephone: (706) 324-0231.

DELMARVA
SHOREBIRDS

Office Address: 6400 Hobbs Rd., Salisbury, MD 21804.
Mailing Address: P.O. Box 1557, Salisbury, MD 21802.
Telephone: (410) 219-3112. **FAX:** (410) 219-9164.
E-Mail Address: information@theshorebirds.com. **Website:** www.theshorebirds.com.
Affiliation (first year): Baltimore Orioles (1997). **Years in League:** 1996-.

OWNERSHIP, MANAGEMENT
Operated by: Comcast-Spectacor.
Directors: Peter Luukko, Frank Miceli.
General Manager: Steve Yaros. **Assistant GM:** Unavailable. **Director, Stadium Operations:** Deandre Ewell. **Head Groundskeeper:** Unavailable. **Director, Media/Public Relations:** Chris Schenk. **Director, Broadcasting:** Ryan Sachs. **Director, Marketing:** Sharine Iacono. **Corporate Account Representatives:** Ryan Sachs, Megan Kirchhoff. **Manager, Accounting:** Gail Potts. **Ticket Manager:** Randy Brown. **Director, Ticket Operations:** Randy Brown. **Ticket Sales Representatives:** Kris Rutledge, Erin Dunn, Tom Denlinger. **Office Manager:** Dana Holyfield. **Community Relations Manager/Customer Service:** Norb Sadilek. **Senior Group Events Manager:** Jason Hall. **Corporate Sales Manager:** Jimmy Sweet.

FIELD STAFF
Manager: Bien Figueroa. **Coach:** Don Werner. **Pitching Coach:** Steve "Doc" Watson. **Trainer:** Joe Benge.

GAME INFORMATION
Radio Announcer: Ryan Sachs. **No. of Games Broadcast:** Home-70, Away-70. **Flagship Station:** WTDK 107.1-FM.
PA Announcer: Jim Whittemore. **Official Scorer:** Unavailable.
Stadium Name (year opened): Arthur W. Perdue Stadium (1996). **Location:** From U.S. 50 East, right on Hobbs Road; From U.S. 50 West, left on Hobbs Road. **Standard Game Times:** 6:35 p.m.; Sun. 1:05.
Visiting Club Hotel: Best Value Inn 2625 N. Salisbury Blvd., Salisbury, MD 21801. Telephone: (410) 742-7194.

GREENSBORO
BATS

Office Address: 510 Yanceyville St., Greensboro, NC 27405.
Telephone: (336) 333-2287. **FAX:** (336) 273-7350.

E-Mail Address: bats@greensborobats.com. **Website:** www.greensborobats.com.
Affiliation (first year): Florida Marlins (2003). **Years in League:** 1979-.

OWNERSHIP, MANAGEMENT
Operated by: Greensboro Baseball, LLC.
Principal Owners: Cooper Brantley, Bill Lee, Pat Pittard, Len White.
President, General Manager: Donald Moore **Assistant GM:** Tom Howe. **Director, Stadium Operations/Head Groundskeeper:** Jake Holloway. **Director, Media Relations:** Josh Flickinger. **Director, Finance:** Carolyn Powell. **Office Manager/Director, Merchandise:** Sue DeRocco. **Executive Assistant to GM:** Rosalee Brewer. **Director, Group Sales:** Kim Benningfield

FIELD STAFF
Manager: Steve Phillips. **Coach:** Brandon Hyde. **Pitching Coach:** Scott Mitchell. **Trainer:** Steve Miller.

GAME INFORMATION
Radio Announcer: Andy Durham. **No. of Games Broadcast:** Home-70. **Flagship Station:** WPET 950-AM.
PA Announcer: Jim Scott. **Official Scorer:** Paul Wirth.
Stadium Name (year opened): War Memorial Stadium (1926). **Location:** I-40/I-85 to Highway 29, north to Lee Street, west to Bennett Avenue, right on Bennett. **Standard Game Times:** 7 p.m.; Sun. 5.
Visiting Club Hotel: Howard Johnson Hotel, 3030 High Point Rd., Greensboro, NC 27403. Telephone: (336) 294-4920.

HAGERSTOWN
SUNS

**HAGERSTOWN
SUNS**

Office Address: 274 E. Memorial Blvd., Hagerstown, MD 21740.
Telephone: (301) 791-6266. **FAX:** (301) 791-6066.
E-Mail Address: info@hagerstownsuns.com. **Website:** www.hagerstownsuns.com.
Affiliation (first year): San Francisco Giants (2001). **Years in League:** 1993-.

OWNERSHIP, MANAGEMENT
Operated by: Mandalay Sports Entertainment.
Principal Owners: Hank Stickney, Ken Stickney, Peter Guber, Paul Schaeffer.
General Manager: Kurt Landes. **Assistant GM:** Will Smith. **Director, Business Operations:** Carol Gehr. **Director, Stadium Operations:** Mike Showe. **Director, Food/Beverage:** Chris Matthias. **Director, Marketing:** C.J. Johnson. **Director, Group Sales:** Mike Tarleton. **Manager, Media Relations:** Jason Gordon. **Assistant Manager, Media Relations:** Jay Burnham. **Interns:** Yoshiaki Itoi, Michele Wagner. **Clubhouse Manager:** Unavailable.

FIELD STAFF
Manager: Mike Ramsey. **Coach:** Hector Torres. **Pitching Coach:** Maximino Leon. **Trainer:** Jeffrey Shanley.

GAME INFORMATION
Radio Announcers: Jason Gordon, Jay Burnham. **No. of Games Broadcast:** Home-70, Away-70. **Flagship Station:** WHAG 1410-AM.
PA Announcer: Rick Reeder. **Official Scorer:** Chris Spaid.
Stadium Name (year opened): Municipal Stadium (1931). **Location:** Exit 32B (U.S. 40 West) on I-70 West, left at Eastern Boulevard; Exit 6A (U.S. 40 East) on I-81 South, right at Cleveland Ave. **Standard Game Times:** 7:05 p.m., (April-May) 6:35; Sun. 1:35.
Visiting Club Hotel: Clarion Hotel, 901 Dual Hwy., Hagerstown, MD 21740. Telephone: (301) 733-5100.

HICKORY
CRAWDADS

**HICKORY
CRAWDADS**

Office Address: 2500 Clement Blvd. NW, Hickory, NC 28601.
Mailing Address: P.O. Box 1268, Hickory, NC 28603.
Telephone: (828) 322-3000. **FAX:** (828) 322-6137.
E-Mail Address: crawdad@hickorycrawdads.com. **Website:** www.hickorycrawdads.com.
Affiliation (first year): Pittsburgh Pirates (1999). **Years in League:** 1952, 1960, 1993-.

OWNERSHIP, MANAGEMENT
Operated by: Hickory Baseball, Inc.
Principal Owners: Don Beaver, Luther Beaver, Charles Young.
President: Don Beaver.
General Manager: David Haas. **Assistant GM:** Jeremy Neisser. **Ticket Manager:** Brad Dail. **Director, Operations:** Harry Schroeder. **Director, Merchandise:** Barbara Beatty. **Office Manager/Special Events:** Jeanna Homesley. **Director, Broadcasting/Media Relations:** Dave Friedman. **Director, Public Relations:** Amanda Starnes. **Account Executives:** Patrick Bell, Reid Twine, Ezera Lenk, Dan Brokos, Alex Dalmas, Matt Lewis.

FIELD STAFF

Manager: Dave Clark. **Coach:** Matt Winters. **Pitching Coach:** Bob Milacki. **Trainer:** Bryan Housand.

GAME INFORMATION

Radio Announcer: David Friedman. **No. of Games Broadcast:** Home-70, Away-70. **Flagship Station:** WMNC 92.1-FM. **PA Announcers:** JuJu Phillips, Steve Fisher. **Official Scorer:** Gary Olinger.
Stadium Name (year opened): L.P. Frans Stadium (1993). **Location:** I-40 to exit 123 (Lenoir North), 321 North to Clement Blvd., left for ½ mile. **Standard Game Times:** 7 p.m., 6:30 (school nights); Sun. (April-May) 2, (June-Aug.) 6.
Visiting Club Hotel: Red Roof Inn, 1184 Lenoir Rhyne Blvd., Hickory, NC 28602. Telephone: (828) 323-1500.

KANNAPOLIS
INTIMIDATORS

Office Address: 2888 Moose Rd., Kannapolis, NC 28083.
Mailing Address: P.O. Box 64, Kannapolis, NC 28082.
Telephone: (704) 932-3267. **FAX:** (704) 938-7040.
E-Mail Address: info@intimidatorsbaseball.com. **Website:** www.intimidatorsbaseball.com.
Affiliation (first year): Chicago White Sox (2001). **Years in League:** 1995-.

OWNERSHIP, MANAGEMENT

Operated by: Carolina Baseball, Inc.
Principal Owners: Larry Hedrick, Bruton Smith, estate of Dale Earnhardt. **President:** Billy Raines. **Vice President:** Craig Detwiler.
General Manager: Tim Mueller. **Associate GM:** Randy Long. **Assistant GM, Stadium Operations:** Jaime Pruitt. **Director, Media Relations/Broadcasting:** Michael Pacheco. **Director, Tickets/Group Sales/Community Relations:** Tracy Snelbaker. **Director, Merchandise:** Sean Feeney.

FIELD STAFF

Manager: Chris Cron. **Coach:** Brandon Moore. **Pitching Coach:** Sean Snedeker. **Trainer:** Tomas Vera.

GAME INFORMATION

Radio Announcer: Mike Pacheco. **No. of Games Broadcast:** Home-70, Away-70. **Flagship Station:** WRKB 1460-AM. **PA Announcer:** John Homa. **Official Scorer:** Tom Reilly.
Stadium Name (year opened): Fieldcrest Cannon Stadium (1995). **Location:** Exit 63 on I-85, west on Lane Street to Stadium Drive. **Standard Game Times:** 7:05 p.m.; Sun. 5:05.
Visiting Club Hotel: Hampton Inn, 612 Dickens Place NE, Concord, NC 28025. Telephone: (704) 793-9700.

LAKE COUNTY
CAPTAINS

Office Address: 35300 Vine St., Eastlake, OH 44095.
Mailing Address: P.O. Box 7129, Eastlake, OH 44095.
Telephone: (440) 975-8085. **FAX:** (440) 975-8958.
E-Mail Address: info@captainsbaseball.com. **Website:** www.captainsbaseball.com.
Affiliation (first year): Cleveland Indians (2003). **Years in League:** 2003-.

OWNERSHIP, MANAGEMENT

Operated by: Cascia, LLC.
Principal Owner, President: Rita Murphy Carfagna. **Vice President:** Ray Murphy. **Secretary/Treasurer:** Peter Carfagna.
Vice President, Baseball Operations/General Manager: Casey Stump. **Assistant GM, Sales/Marketing:** Gary Thomas. **Assistant GM, Operations:** Paul Siegwarth. **Assistant GM, Public Relations:** Katie Dannemiller. **Director, Merchandise:** Scott Beaman. **Director, Ticket Sales:** Kevin Brodzinski. **Sports Turf Manager:** Greg Elliott. **Director, Community Relations:** Kate Furman. **Controller:** Ken Fogel. **Business Manager:** Priscilla Hyclak. **Assistant Sports Turf Manager:** Josh Klute. **Director, Promotions:** Joel Koch. **Ticket Account Manager:** Julia LaManna. **Director, Special Projects:** Bill Levy. **Director, Stadium Operations:** Rob LoPresti. **Senior Corporate Account Manager:** Steven Minner. **Director, Client Services:** Josh Myers. **Corporate Account Manager:** Becki Rath. **Assistant Box Office Manager:** Morris Seiden. **Manager, Food Service:** Linda Stringham. **Concession Manager:** Ashley Teichart. **Director, Broadcasting/Media Relations:** Dave Wilson. **Account Executives:** Beth West, Jeff Hull, Matt Phillips. **Interns:** Josh Bailey, Ken Brown, Brock Richards, Courtney Strah, Charles White.

FIELD STAFF

Manager: Luis Rivera. **Coach:** Jack Mull. **Pitching Coach:** Tony Arnold. **Trainer:** Michael Salazar.

GAME INFORMATION

Radio Announcers: Dave Wilson, Craig Deas. **No. of Games Broadcast:** Home-70, Away-70. **Flagship Station:** WELW 1330-AM.

PA Announcer: Ray Milavec. **Official Scorer:** Fred Heyer.
Stadium Name (year opened): Eastlake Ballpark (2003). **Location:** From Route 2 East, exit at Ohio 91, stadium is ½ mile north. **Standard Game Times:** 7:05 p.m.; Sat. (April-May) 2:05; Sun. 2:05.
Visiting Club Hotel: Hampton Inn-Wickliffe, 28611 Euclid Ave., Wickliffe, OH 44092. Telephone: (440) 944-4030.

LAKEWOOD
BLUECLAWS

Office Address: 2 Stadium Way, Lakewood, NJ 08701.
Telephone: (732) 901-7000. **FAX:** (732) 901-3967.
E-Mail Address: info@lakewoodblueclaws.com. **Website:** www.lakewood blueclaws.com.
Affiliation: Philadelphia Phillies (2001). **Years In League:** 2001-.

OWNERSHIP, MANAGMENT
Operated by: American Baseball Company, LLC.
President: Joseph Finley. **Partners:** Joseph Caruso, Joseph Plumeri, Craig Stein.
General Manager: Geoff Brown. **Assistant GM:** John Clark. **Director, Marketing:** Mike Ryan. **Executive Director, Marketing:** Eric Lipsman. **Director, Production:** Clint Wulfekotte. **Director, Media/Public Relations:** Unavailable. **Director, Ticket Sales:** Jeremy Fishman. **Director, Operations:** Brandon Marano. **Manager, Community Relations:** Jim DeAngelis. **Ticket Manager:** Hal Hansen. **Operations Manager:** Joe Scalise. **Director, Group Sales:** Keri Conway. **Group Sales Managers:** Annette Ballina, Zak Boenig, Michelle Casserly, Nelson Constantino. **Director, Merchandising:** Brian Reider. **Chief Financial Officer:** Steve Ripa. **Assistant Controller:** Denise Casazza. **Head Groundskeeper:** Bill Butler. **Assistant Groundskeeper:** Ryan Radcliffe. **Office Manager:** Robin Hill. **Assistants:** Westley Bailey, Dan DeYoung, Michael Goddard, Mike Hyland, Jim McNamara, Elizabeth Metcalf, Alicia Pishnick, Ben Wagner.

FIELD STAFF
Manager: P.J. Forbes. **Coach:** Eric Richardson. **Pitching Coach:** Tom Filer. **Trainer:** Unavailable.

GAME INFORMATION
Radio Announcer: Ben Wagner. **No. of Games Broadcast:** Home-70, Away-70. **Flagship Station:** WOBM 1160-AM. **PA Announcer:** Kevin Clark. **Official Scorer:** Lisa Clark.
Stadium Name (year opened): FirstEnergy Park (2001). **Location:** Route 70 to New Hampshire Ave., north on New Hampshire for 2½ miles to ballpark. **Standard Game Times:** 7:05 p.m., Mon.-Thur. (April-May) 6:35; Sat. (April) 1:05; Sun 1:05, (July-Aug.) 5:05.
Visiting Team Hotel: Super 8, 2016 Hwy. 37 W., Manchester Township, NJ. Telephone: (732) 657-7100.

LEXINGTON
LEGENDS

Office Address: 207 Legends Lane, Lexington, KY 40505.
Mailing Address: P.O. Box 11458, Lexington, KY 40575.
Telephone: (859) 252-4487. **FAX:** (859) 252-0747.
E-Mail Address: webmaster@lexingtonlegends.com. **Website:** www.lexingtonlegends.com.
Affiliation (first year): Houston Astros (2001). **Years in League:** 2001-.

OWNERSHIP, MANAGEMENT
Operated by: Lexington Professional Baseball Company.
Principal Owner: Brad Redmon. **President, Chief Executive Officer:** Alan Stein. **Chief Financial Officer:** Stacy Martin. **General Manager:** Gary Durbin. **Director, Stadium Operations/Human Resources:** Shannon Kidd. **Director, Marketing/Media Relations:** Christi Clay. **Director, Special Events:** Rick Bryant. **Director, Field Maintenance:** Steve Kundick. **Box Office Manager:** Missy Carl. **Director, Group Sales:** Beth Goldenberg. **Comptroller:** Jeff Black. **Senior Sales Executive:** Kevin Kulp. **Advertising Sales Executives:** Tyler Oliver, Mike Martin. **Director, Ticket Operations:** Kevin Shelton.

FIELD STAFF
Manager: Ivan DeJesus. **Coach:** Bryan Dayett. **Pitching Coach:** Charley Taylor. **Trainer:** Eric Montague.

GAME INFORMATION
Radio Announcer: Larry Glover. **No. of Games Broadcast:** Home-70, Away-70. **Flagship Station:** WLXG 1300-AM. **PA Announcer:** Unavailable. **Official Scorer:** Kenny Bourne.
Stadium Name (year opened): Applebee's Park (2001). **Location:** From I-64/75, take exit 113, right onto North Broadway toward downtown Lexington for 1.2 miles, past New Circle Road (Highway 4), right into stadium, located adjacent to Northland Shopping Center. **Standard Game Times:** 7:05 p.m.; Mon.-Thur. (April-May) 6:35; Sun. (April-May) 2:05, (June-Aug.) 6:05.
Visiting Club Hotel: Ramada Inn and Conference Center, 2143 N. Broadway, Lexington, KY 40505. Telephone: (859) 299-1261.

ROME BRAVES

Office Address: State Mutual Stadium, 755 Braves Blvd, Rome, GA 30161.
Mailing Address: P.O. Box 5515, Rome, GA 30162.
Telephone: (706) 368-9388. **FAX:** (706) 368-6525.
E-Mail Address: rome.braves@turner.com. **Website:** www.romebraves.com.
Affiliation (first year): Atlanta Braves (2003). **Years in League:** 2003-.

OWNERSHIP, MANAGEMENT

Operated by: Atlanta National League Baseball Club, Inc.
Principal Owner: Time Warner. **President:** Terry McGuirk.
General Manager: Michael Dunn. **Assistant GM:** Jim Jones. **Stadium Operations Manager:** Eric Allman. **Director, Ticket Sales:** Terry Morgan. **Director, Food/Beverage:** Dave Atwood. **Manager, Community Relations:** Erin White. **Administrative Manager:** Kristie Hancock. **Account Representatives:** Dave Butler, Jennifer Collins. **Head Groundskeeper:** Andrew Wright. **Executive Chef:** Curtis Morris. **Receptionist:** Starla Roden. **Retail Manager:** Unavailable.

FIELD STAFF

Manager: Rocket Wheeler. **Coach:** Bobby Moore. **Pitching Coach:** Kent Willis. **Trainer:** Drew Van Dam.

GAME INFORMATION

Radio Announcer: Bryan Evans. **No. of Games Broadcast:** Home-70, Away-70. **Flagship Stations:** WLAQ 1410-AM, WATG 95.7-FM.
PA Announcer: Eddie Brock. **Official Scorer:** Ron Taylor.
Stadium Name (year opened): State Mutual Stadium (2003). **Location:** I-75 North to exit 290 (Rome/Canton), left off exit and follow Highway 411/Highway 20 to Rome, right at intersection of Highway 411 and Highway 1 (Veterans Memorial Highway), stadium is at intersection of Veterans Memorial Highway and Riverside Parkway.
Standard Game Times: 7 p.m.; Sun. 2.
Visiting Club Hotel: Days Inn, 840 Turner McCall Blvd., Rome, GA 30161. Telephone: (706) 295-0400.

SAVANNAH SAND GNATS

Office Address: 1401 E. Victory Dr., Savannah, GA 31404.
Mailing Address: P.O. Box 3783, Savannah, GA 31414.
Telephone: (912) 351-9150. **Fax:** (912) 352-9722.
E-Mail Address: shep21@aol.com. **Website:** www.sandgnats.com.
Affiliation (first year): Montreal Expos (2003). **Years in League:** 1962, 1984-.

OWNERSHIP, MANAGEMENT

Operated by: Savannah Big Time Baseball, LLC.
President: Kenneth Silver.
Chief Operating Officer, General Manager: Ken Shepard. **Assistant GM, Sales/Marketing:** Marty Wheeler. **Director, Merchandising:** Unavailable. **Director, Public Relations:** Frank Novak. **Director, Special Events/Promotions:** Paul Lucas. **Assistant Director, Promotions/Public Relations:** Jennifer Mixon. **Assistant, Promotions/Public Relations:** Brian Sheaffer. **Director, Ticket Operations:** Ryan Eason. **Ticket Manager:** Kyle Davis. **Director, Field Operations/Groundskeeper:** Bryan Glover. **Director, Finance:** Clarissa Tillman. **Clubhouse Manager:** John White. **Operations Manager:** Matt Barry. **Assistant, Operations:** Damian Burgess

FIELD STAFF

Manager: Bob Henley. **Coach:** Joel Chimelis. **Pitching Coach:** Ricky Bones. **Trainer:** Beth Jarrett.

GAME INFORMATION

Radio: None.
PA Announcer: Unavailable. **Official Scorer:** Marcus Holland.
Stadium Name (year opened): Grayson Stadium (1941). **Location:** I-16 to 37th Street exit, left on 37th, right on Abercorn Street, left on Victory Drive; From I-95 to exit 16 (Savannah/Pembroke), east on 204, right on Victory Drive, stadium is on right in Daffin Park. **Standard Game Times:** 7 p.m.; Mon.-Thurs. (April-May) 6:35; Sun. (April-May) 2, (June-Sept.) 5.
Visiting Club Hotel: Days Inn–Oglethorpe Mall, 114 Mall Blvd., Savannah, GA 31406. Telephone: (912) 352-4455.

NEW YORK-PENN LEAGUE

SHORT-SEASON CLASS A

Mailing Address: 9410 International Court N., St. Petersburg, FL 33716
Telephone: (727) 576-6300 **FAX:** (727) 576-6307
E-Mail Address: nypenn@attglobal.net **Website:** www.nypennleague.com
Years League Active: 1939-.

Ben Hayes

President: Ben Hayes

Vice President: Sam Nader (Oneonta). **Treasurer:** Bill Gladstone (Tri-City). **Corporate Secretary:** Tony Torre (New Jersey).

Directors: Tim Bawmann (Lowell), David Burke (Hudson Valley), Steve Cohen (Brooklyn), Eric Edelstein (Jamestown), Jeff Eiseman (Aberdeen), Joshua Getzler (Staten Island), Bill Gladstone (Tri-City), Barry Gordon (New Jersey), Alan Levin (Mahoning Valley), Paul Marriott (Batavia), Sam Nader (Oneonta), Ray Pecor (Vermont), Leo Pinckney (Auburn), Paul Velte (Williamsport).

League Administrator: Debbie Carlisle. **League Historian:** Charles Wride.

2004 Opening Date: June 18. **Closing Date:** Sept. 4.

Regular Season: 76 games.

Division Structure: McNamara—Aberdeen, Brooklyn, Hudson Valley, New Jersey, Staten Island, Williamsport. **Pinckney—**Auburn, Batavia, Jamestown, Mahoning Valley. **Stedler—**Lowell, Oneonta, Tri-City, Vermont.

Playoff Format: Division champions and wild card team meet in best-of-3 semifinals. Winners meet in best-of-3 series for league championship.

All-Star Game: None. **Hall of Fame Game:** July 24 at Cooperstown, NY (Tri-City vs. Oneonta).

Roster Limit: 30 active, but only 25 may be in uniform and eligible to play in any given game.

Player Eligibility Rule: No more than four players who are 23 or older; no more than three players on active list may have four or more years of prior service.

Brand of Baseball: Rawlings.

Statistician: The Sports Network, 2200 Byberry Rd., Suite 200, Hatboro, PA 19040.

Umpires: Unavailable.

STADIUM INFORMATION

		Dimensions				
Club	**Stadium**	**LF**	**CF**	**RF**	**Capacity**	**2003 Att.**
Aberdeen	Ripken	310	400	310	6,000	234,143
Auburn	Falcon Park	330	400	330	2,800	65,047
Batavia	Dwyer	325	400	325	2,600	42,801
Brooklyn	KeySpan Park	315	412	325	7,500	307,383
Hudson Valley	Dutchess	325	400	325	4,494	146,613
Jamestown	Diethrick Park	335	410	353	3,324	53,469
Lowell	LeLacheur Park	337	400	302	5,000	175,000
Mahoning Valley	Cafaro Field	335	405	335	6,000	141,889
New Jersey	Skylands Park	330	392	330	4,356	117,220
Oneonta	Damaschke Field	350	406	350	4,200	48,905
Staten Island	Richmond County Bank	325	400	325	6,500	163,432
Tri-City	Joseph L. Bruno	325	400	325	5,000	103,984
Vermont	Centennial Field	330	405	323	4,400	101,431
Williamsport	Bowman Field	345	405	350	4,200	83,346

ABERDEEN
IRONBIRDS

Office Address: 873 Long Drive, Aberdeen, MD 21001.
Telephone: (410) 297-9292. **FAX:** (410) 297-6653.
E-Mail Address: info@ironbirdsbaseball.com. **Website:** www.ironbirdsbaseball.com.
Affiliation (first year): Baltimore Orioles (2002). **Years in League:** 2002-.

OWNERSHIP, MANAGEMENT
Operated by: Ripken Professional Baseball, LLC.
Principal Owner: Cal Ripken.
General Manager: Jeff Eiseman. **Assistant GM:** Aaron Moszer. **Director, Sales:** Amy Venuto. **Manager, Public Relations/Broadcasting:** Steve Spadafino.

FIELD STAFF
Manager: Don Buford. **Coaches:** Cedric Landrum, Jesus Alfaro. **Pitching Coach:** Andre Rabouin. **Trainer:** Spencer Elliot.

GAME INFORMATION
Radio Announcer: Steve Spadafino. **No. of Games Broadcast:** Home-38, Away-30. **Flagship Station:** WAMD 970-AM.
PA Announcer: Andrew Holly. **Official Scorers:** Doug Young, Joe Stetka.
Stadium Name (year opened): Ripken Stadium (2002). **Location:** I-95 to exit 85 (Route 22), left on Route 22, first right on Gilbert Road, stadium ¼ mile on right. **Standard Game Times:** 7:05 p.m.; Sun. 1:05.
Visiting Club Hotel: Wingate Inn, Riverside Parkway, Aberdeen, MD 21001. Telephone: (410) 272-2929.

AUBURN
DOUBLEDAYS

Office Address: 130 N. Division St., Auburn, NY 13021.
Telephone: (315) 255-2489. **FAX:** (315) 255-2675.
E-Mail Address: ddays@auburndoubledays.com. **Website:** www.auburndouble days.com.
Affiliation (first year): Toronto Blue Jays (2001). **Years in League:** 1958-80, 1982-.

OWNERSHIP, MANAGEMENT
Operated by: Auburn Community Non-Profit Baseball Association, Inc.
Chairman: Tom Ganey. **President:** Leo Pinckney.
General Manager: Jason Smorol. **Assistant GM:** Carl Gutelius. **Head Groundskeeper:** Rich Wild. **Director, Media/Public Relations:** Unavailable.

FIELD STAFF
Manager: Dennis Holmberg. **Coach:** Dave Pano. **Pitching Coach:** James Keller. **Trainer:** Tommy Craig.

GAME INFORMATION
Radio Announcer: Unavailable. **No of Games Broadcast:** Away-38. **Flagship Station:** WDWN 89.1-FM
PA Announcer: Unavailable. **Official Scorer:** Unavailable.
Stadium Name (year opened): Falcon Park (1995). **Location:** I-90 to exit 40, right on Route 34 for 8 miles to York Street, right on York, left on North Division Street. **Standard Game Times:** 7 p.m.; Sun. 6.
Visiting Club Hotel: Microtel, 12 Seminary Ave., Auburn, NY 13021. Telephone: (315) 253-5000.

BATAVIA
MUCKDOGS

Office Address: Dwyer Stadium, 299 Bank St., Batavia, NY 14020.
Telephone: (585) 343-5454. **FAX:** (585) 343-5620.
E-Mail Address: info@muckdogs.com. **Website:** www.muckdogs.com.
Affiliation (first year): Philadelphia Phillies (1988). **Years in League:** 1939-53, 1957-59, 1961-.

OWNERSHIP, MANAGEMENT
Operated by: Genesee County Baseball Club.
President: Dennis Dwyer.
General Manager: Paul Marriott. **Assistant GM:** Unavailable. **Director, Media/Public Relations:** Chuck Wade. **Director, Community Relations:** Linda Crook. **Clubhouse Operations:** Tony Pecora.

FIELD STAFF
Manager: Luis Melendez. **Coach:** Jim Morrison. **Pitching Coach:** Warren Brusstar. **Trainer:** Unavailable.

GAME INFORMATION
Radio Announcer: Chuck Wade. **No. of Games Broadcast:** Away-38. **Flagship Station:** WBSU 89.1-FM
PA Announcer/Official Scorer: Wayne Fuller.
Stadium Name (year opened): Dwyer Stadium (1996). **Location:** I-90 to exit 48, left on Route 98 South, left on Richmond Avenue, left on Bank Street. **Standard Game Times:** 7:05 p.m.
Visiting Club Hotel: Days Inn of Batavia, 200 Oak St., Batavia, NY 14020. Telephone: (585) 343-1440.

BROOKLYN
CYCLONES

Office/Mailing Address: 1904 Surf Ave., Brooklyn, NY 11224.
Telephone: (718) 449-8497. **FAX:** (718) 449-6368.
E-Mail Address: info@brooklyncyclones.com. **Website:** www.brooklyncyclones.com.
Affiliation (first year): New York Mets (2001). **Years in League:** 2001-.

OWNERSHIP, MANAGEMENT
Operated by: Brooklyn Baseball Co., LLC.
Managing Member: Fred Wilpon. **Senior Executive Vice President/Chief Operating Officer:** Jeff Wilpon.
General Manager: Steve Cohen. **Assistant GM:** Kevin Mahoney. **Director, Sales:** Gary Perone. **Manager, Media Relations:** Dave Campanaro. **Producer, Video Entertainment/Account Executive:** Vic Christopher. **Account Executive/Group Sales, Community Relations:** Robert Field. **Account Executive:** Marty Haber. **Manager, Brooklyn Baseball Gallery/Community Relations:** Anna Isaacson. **Manager, Merchandise:** Kevin Jimenez. **Bookkeeper:** Tatiana Kanevsky. **Manager, Operations:** Vladimir Lipsman. **Receptionist/Community Relations:** Sharon Lundy-Ross. **Manager, Tickets:** Chris Parsons. **Head Groundskeeper:** Kevin Ponte. **Maintenance/Grounds Crew:** George Reeder. **Administrative Assistant:** Barbara Spina. **Manager, Promotions/Entertainment:** Howie Wolpoff.

FIELD STAFF
Manager: Leon Lee. **Coach:** Donovan Mitchell. **Pitching Coach:** Hector Berrios. **Trainer:** Unavailable.

GAME INFORMATION
Radio Announcer: Warner Fusselle. **No. of Games Broadcast:** Home-38, Away-38. **Flagship Station:** Unavailable.
PA Announcer: Dominick Alagia. **Official Scorer:** David Freeman.
Stadium Name (year opened): KeySpan Park (2001). **Location:** Belt Parkway to Cropsey Avenue South, continue on Cropsey until it becomes West 17th Street, continue to Surf Avenue, stadium on south side of Surf Avenue. By subway, west to Stillwell Avenue/Coney Island Station. **Standard Game Times:** 7 p.m., Sat. 6, Sun. 5.
Visiting Club Hotel: Comfort Inn, 8315 Fourth Ave., Brooklyn, NY 11209. Telephone: (718) 238-3737.

HUDSON VALLEY
RENEGADES

Office Address: Dutchess Stadium, Route 9D, Wappingers Falls, NY 12590.
Mailing Address: P.O. Box 661, Fishkill, NY 12524.
Telephone: (845) 838-0094. **FAX:** (845) 838-0014.
E-Mail Address: info@hvrenegades.com. **Website:** www.hvrenegades.com.
Affiliation (first year): Tampa Bay Devil Rays (1996). **Years in League:** 1994-.

OWNERSHIP, MANAGEMENT
Operated by: Keystone Professional Baseball Club, Inc.
Principal Owner: Marv Goldklang.
President: Mike Veeck. **General Manager:** David Burke. **Vice President/Assistant GM:** Kathy Butsko. **Assistant GM:** Derek Sharp. **Director, Ticket Operations:** Bonnie Johnson. **Director, Food Services:** Joe Ausanio. **Director, Business Operations:** Jennifer Vitale. **Director, Entertainment:** Stephen Colvin. **Director, Special Events/Renegades Charitable Foundation:** Rick Zolzer. **Head Groundskeeper/Director, Stadium Maintenance:** Tom Hubmaster. **Director, Client Services/Media Relations:** Thomas Butkier. **Director, Community Relations:** Danielle Wachter. **Director, Ticket Sales:** Corey Whitted. **Administrative Assistant, Tickets:** Jermaine Stevens. **Sales Associate:** Tyler Tumminia. **Assistant Director, Food Services:** Unavailable. **Client Services, Renegades Charitable Foundation:** Rich McClane. **Assistant Groundskeeper:** Jay Martin. **Clubhouse Manager:** James Brignall.

FIELD STAFF
Manager: Dave Howard. **Coach:** Jorge Robles. **Pitching Coach:** Rafael Montalvo. **Trainer:** Unavailable.

GAME INFORMATION
Radio Announcer: Sean Ford. **No. of Games Broadcast:** Home-38, Away-38. **Flagship Stations:** WBNR 1260-AM, WLNA 1420-AM.

PA Announcer: Rick Zolzer. **Official Scorer:** James Bouffard.
Stadium Name (year opened): Dutchess Stadium (1994). **Location:** I-84 to exit 11 (Route 9D North), north one mile to stadium. **Standard Game Times:** 7:11 p.m.; Sun. 5:11.
Visiting Club Hotel: The Wellesley Inn, Route 9, Fishkill, NY 12524. Telephone (845) 896-4995.

JAMESTOWN
JAMMERS

Office Address: 485 Falconer St., Jamestown, NY 14701.
Mailing Address: P.O. Box 638, Jamestown, NY 14702.
Telephone: (716) 664-0915. **FAX:** (716) 664-4175.
E-Mail Address: email@jamestownjammers.com. **Website:** www.jamestownjammers.com.
Affiliation (first year): Florida Marlins (2002). **Years in League:** 1939-57, 1961-73, 1977-.

OWNERSHIP, MANAGEMENT
Operated by: Rich Baseball Operations.
Principal Owner, President: Robert Rich Jr. **Chairman:** Robert Rich Sr. **President, Rich Baseball Operations:** Jonathon Dandes.
General Manager: Matthew Drayer. **Director, Sales/Marketing:** George Sisson. **Director, Baseball Operations:** Benjamin Burnett. **Head Groundskeeper:** Jamie Bloomquist. **Director, Food Services:** Rich Ruggerio.

FIELD STAFF
Manager: Benny Castillo. **Coach:** Matt Raleigh. **Pitching Coach:** Tom Signore. **Trainer:** Frank Briceland

GAME INFORMATION
Radio Announcer: Unavailable. **No. of Games Broadcast:** Away-38. **Flagship Station:** Unavailable.
PA Announcer: Unavailable. **Official Scorer:** Jim Riggs.
Stadium Name (year opened): Russell E. Diethrick Jr. Park (1941). **Location:** From I-90, south on Route 60, left on Buffalo Street, left on Falconer Street. **Standard Game Times:** 7:05 p.m.; Sun. 4:05.
Visiting Club Hotel: Red Roof Inn, 1980 E. Main St., Falconer, NY 14733. Telephone: (716) 665-3670.

LOWELL
SPINNERS

Office Address: 450 Aiken St., Lowell, MA 01854.
Telephone: (978) 459-2255. **FAX:** (978) 459-1674.
E-Mail Address: generalinfo@lowellspinners.com. **Website:** www.lowellspinners.com.
Affiliation (first year): Boston Red Sox (1996). **Years in League:** 1996-.

OWNERSHIP, MANAGEMENT
Operated by: Diamond Action, Inc.
Chief Executive Officer: Drew Weber.
President: Shawn Smith.
General Manager: Tim Bawmann. **Vice President Business Operations:** Brian Lindsay. **Controller:** Priscilla Harbour. **Director, Stadium Operations:** Dan Beaulieu. **Assistant Director, Stadium Operations:** Gareth Markey. **Director, Corporate Communications:** Jon Goode. **Director, Merchandising:** Joann Weber. **Merchandising Manager:** Justin Panarese. **Director, Ticket Sales:** Shannon Feehan. **Director, Ticket Group Sales:** Jon Healy. **Head Groundskeeper:** Rick Walker. **Clubhouse Manager:** Del Christman.

FIELD STAFF
Manager: Luis Alicea. **Coach:** Randy Phillips. **Pitching Coach:** Dave Tomlin. **Trainer:** David Yeager.

GAME INFORMATION
Radio: Unavailable.
PA Announcer: Matt Steinberg. **Official Scorers:** Dave Rourke, Rusty Eggen, Bob Ellis.
Stadium Name (year opened): Edward LeLacheur Park (1998). **Location:** From Routes 495 and 3, take exit 35C (Lowell Connector), follow connector to exit 5B (Thorndike Street) onto Dutton Street, past city hall, left onto Father Morrissette Boulevard, right on Aiken Street. **Standard Game Times:** 7:05 p.m.; Sat.-Sun. 5:05.
Visiting Club Hotel: Doubletree Inn, 50 Warren St., Lowell, MA 01852. Telephone: (978) 452-1200.

MAHONING VALLEY
SCRAPPERS

Office Address: 111 Eastwood Mall Blvd., Niles, OH 44446.
Mailing Address: P.O. Box 1357, Niles, OH 44446.
Telephone: (330) 505-0000. **FAX:** (330) 505-9696.
E-Mail Address: mvscrappers@onecom.com. **Website:** www.mvscrappers.com.
Affiliation (first year): Cleveland Indians (1999). **Years in League:** 1999-.

OWNERSHIP, MANAGEMENT
Operated by: Palisades Baseball, Ltd.
Managing General Partner: Alan Levin. **Executive Vice President:** Erik Haag. **Chief Financial Officer:** Mick Rauch.
General Manager: Dave Smith. **Director, Business Development:** Joe Gregory. **Director, Stadium Operations:** Chris Walsh. **Director, Ticket Operations:** Jordan Taylor. **Manager, Box Office:** Heather Safarek. **Accountant:** Debbie Primmer. **Director, Promotions/Marketing:** Jim Riley. **Ticket Sales Representatives:** John Muszkewycz, Scott MacDonald. **Director, Concessions:** Jeff Meehan. **Director, Client Services:** Mike Brent.

FIELD STAFF
Manager: Mike Sarbaugh. **Coach:** Chris Bando. **Pitching Coach:** Ken Rowe. **Trainer:** Chad Wolfe.

GAME INFORMATION
Radio Announcer: Greg Gania. **No. of Games Broadcasts:** Home-38, Away-38. **Flagship Station:** WNIO 1390-AM.
PA Announcer: Ryan Pritt. **Official Scorer:** Al Thorne.
Stadium Name (year opened): Cafaro Field (1999). **Location:** I-80 to 11 North to 82 West to 46 South, stadium located behind Eastwood Mall. **Standard Game Times:** 7 p.m.; Sun. 2.
Visiting Club Hotel: Unavailable.

NEW JERSEY
CARDINALS

Office Address: 94 Championship Place, Suite 2, Augusta, NJ 07822.
Telephone: (973) 579-7500. **FAX:** (973) 579-7502.
E-Mail Address: office@njcards.com. **Website:** www.njcards.com.
Affiliation (first year): St. Louis Cardinals (1994). **Years in League:** 1994-.

OWNERSHIP, MANAGEMENT
Operated by: Minor League Heroes, LP.
Chairman: Barry Gordon. **President:** Marc Klee.
Vice President, General Manager: Tony Torre. **Assistant GM:** Herm Sorcher. **Head Groundskeeper:** Ralph Naife.
Director, Marketing/Merchandising: Bob Commentucci. **Director, Ticket Operations:** Bob Mischler. **Director, Group Sales:** Matt Millet. **Director, Sponsorships/Group Sales:** Gregg Kubala. **Director, Community Relations/Group Sales:** Lisa Howell. **Director, Finance:** Tullia Mowery.

FIELD STAFF
Manager: Tom Shields. **Coach:** Unavailable. **Pitching Coach:** Sid Monge. **Trainer:** Unavailable.

GAME INFORMATION
Radio Announcers: Phil Pepe, Joel Konya. **No. of Games Broadcast:** Unavailable. **Flagship Station:** Unavailable.
PA Announcer: Mike Griffone. **Official Scorer:** Ken Hand.
Stadium Name (year opened): Skylands Park (1994). **Location:** In New Jersey, I-80 to exit 34B (Route 15 North) to Route 565 East; From Pennsylvania, I-84 to Route 6 (Matamoras) to Route 206 North to Route 565 East. **Standard Game Times:** 7:15 p.m.; Sat.-Sun. 5.
Visiting Club Hotel: Wellesley Inn, 1255 Route 10, Whippany, NJ 07981. Telephone: (973) 539-8350.

ONEONTA
TIGERS

Office Address: 95 River St., Oneonta, NY 13820.
Telephone: (607) 432-6326. **FAX:** (607) 432-1965.
E-Mail Address: naderas@telenet.net. **Website:** www.oneontatigers.com.
Affiliation (first year): Detroit Tigers (1999). **Years in League:** 1966-.

OWNERSHIP, MANAGEMENT
Operated by: Oneonta Athletic Corp., Inc.

President, General Manager: Sam Nader. Director, Business/Stadium Operations: John Nader. Controller: Sidney Levine. Head Groundskeepers: Dan Obergufell, Mike Dunn. Director, Media/Public Relations: Alice O'Conner. Director, Marketing/Merchandising: Suzanne Longo. Director, Special Projects: Mark Nader. Director, Operations/Ticket Sales: Bob Zeh. Director, Food Services: Brad Zeh.

FIELD STAFF
Manager: Mike Rojas. Coach: Basilio Cabrera. Pitching Coach: Bill Monbouquette. Trainer: Dustin Campbell.

GAME INFORMATION
Radio: None.
PA Announcer: John Horne. Official Scorer: Tom Heitz.
Stadium Name (year opened): Damaschke Field (1906). Location: Exit 15 off I-88. Standard Game Times: 7 p.m.; Sun. 6.
Visiting Club Hotel: Oasis Motor Inn, 366 Chestnut St., Oneonta, NY 13820. Telephone: (607) 432-6041.

STATEN ISLAND
YANKEES

Stadium Address: 75 Richmond Terrace, Staten Island, NY 10301.
Telephone: (718) 720-9265. FAX: (718) 273-5763.
E-Mail Address: siyanks@siyanks.com. Website: www.siyanks.com.
Affiliation: New York Yankees (1999). Years in League: 1999-.

OWNERSHIP, MANAGEMENT
Operated by: Staten Island Minor League Holdings, LLC.
Principal Owners: Josh Getzler, Phyllis Getzler, Stan Getzler.
Chairman: Stan Getzler. President: Henry Steinbrenner. Chief Operating Officer: Josh Getzler.
General Manager: Jeff Dumas. Assistant GM: Jane Rogers. Director, Media Relations: Jim Mauceri. Bookkeeper: Ruth Rizzo. Director, Tickets: Dominic Costantino. Technical Director: John Davison. Director, Group Sales: Dan Yaeger. Director, Stadium Operations: Dave McCausland. Director, Concerts/Stadium Events: Joe Ricciutti. Head Groundskeeper: Unavailable. Director, Community Relations: Jessica Rohde.

FIELD STAFF
Manager: Tommy John. Coach: Kevin Higgins. Pitching Coach: Dave Eiland. Trainer: Unavailable.

GAME INFORMATION
Radio Announcer: Unavailable. No. of Games Broadcast: Home-38, Away-38. Flagship Station: Unavailable.
PA Announcer: Unavailable. Official Scorer: Richard Senzel.
Stadium Name (year opened): Richmond County Bank Ballpark at St. George (2001). Location: St. George located in Staten Island, next to Staten Island Ferry Terminal. Standard Game Times: 7:05 p.m.; Sun 5:05.
Visiting Club Hotel: The Navy Lodge, 408 North Path Rd., Staten Island, NY 10305. Telephone: (718) 442-0413.

TRI-CITY
VALLEYCATS

Stadium Address: 80 Vandenburgh Ave., Troy, NY 12180.
Mailing Address: P.O. Box 694, Troy, NY 12181.
Telephone: (518) 629-2287. FAX: (518) 629-2299.
E-Mail Address: info@tcvalleycats.com. Website: www.tcvalleycats.com.
Affiliation: Houston Astros (2001). Years in League: 2002-.

OWNERSHIP, MANAGEMENT
Operated by: National Pastime Corporation.
Principal Owners: Martin Barr, John Burton, William Gladstone, Richard Murphy, Alfred Roberts, Stephen Siegel.
President: William Gladstone.
General Manager: Richard Murphy. Director, Sales/Marketing: Peter Rosenberg Account Executives: Brett Gilmore, Aaron Donahue, Stacey Elsasser Director, Corporate Communications: Eileen McCarthy.

FIELD STAFF
Manager: Gregg Langbehn. Coach: Jorge Orta. Pitching Coach: Bill Ballou. Trainer: Adam Thomas.

GAME INFORMATION
Radio Announcer: Unavailable. No. of Games Broadcast: Home-38, Away-38. Flagship Station: Unavailable.
PA Announcer: Unavailable. Official Scorer: Unavailable.
Stadium Name (year opened): Hudson Valley Community College (2002). Location: From north, I-87 to exit 7 (Route 7), go east approximately 1½ miles to I-787 South, to Route 378 East, go over bridge to Route 4, right to Route 4 south, one mile to Hudson Valley Community College campus on left. From south, I-87 to exit 23 (I-787), I-787 north six miles to exit for Route 378 east, Route 378 over bridge to Route 4, go right to Route 4 South, one mile to Hudson

Valley Community College campus on left. From east, Massachusetts Turnpike to exit B-1 (I-90), go nine miles to Exit 8 (Defreestville), left off ramp to Route 4 North, Route 4 North for five miles, Hudson Valley Community College on right. From West, I-90 to exit 24 (I-90 East), I-90 east for six miles to I-787 North (Troy), take I-787 North for 2.2 miles to exit for Route 378 East, take Route 378 over bridge to Route 4,, right to Route 4 south for one mile to Hudson Valley Community College campus on left. **Standard Game Times:** 7 p.m.; Sun. 6.

Visiting Club Hotel: Unavailable.

VERMONT
EXPOS

Office Address: 1 Main St., Suite 4, Winooski, VT 05404.
Telephone: (802) 655-4200. **FAX:** (802) 655-5660.
E-Mail Address: mail@vermontexpos.com. **Website:** www.vermontexpos.com.
Affiliation (first year): Montreal Expos (1994). **Years in League:** 1994-.

OWNERSHIP, MANAGEMENT

Operated by: Vermont Expos, Inc.
Principal Owner, President: Ray Pecor. **Vice President:** Kyle Bostwick.
General Manager: C.J. Knudsen. **Director, Stadium Operations:** Jim O'Brien. **Head Groundskeeper:** Chris Baker. **Director, Public Relations/Promotions:** Adrienne Wilson. **Director, Media Relations:** Paul Stanfield. **Director, Sales:** Shawn Quinn. **Director, Ticket Operations/Design:** Nate Cloutier. **Director, Food Services:** Steve Bernard. **Director, Special Projects:** Onnie Matthews. **Clubhouse Operations:** Phil Schelzo.

FIELD STAFF

Manager: Unavailable. **Coach:** Joe Marchese. **Pitching Coach:** Franklin Bravo. **Trainer:** Unavailable.

GAME INFORMATION

Radio Announcer: George Commo. **No. of Games Broadcast:** Home-25, Away-25. **Flagship Station:** WVAA 1390-AM.
PA Announcer: Rich Haskell. **Official Scorer:** Ev Smith.
Stadium Name (year opened): Centennial Field (1922). **Location:** I-89 to exit 14W, right on East Avenue for one mile, right at Colchester Avenue. **Standard Game Times:** 7:05 p.m.; Sun. 5:05.
Visiting Club Hotel: University Inn & Suites, 5 Dorset St., South Burlington, VT 05403. Telephone: (802) 863-5541.

WILLIAMSPORT
CROSSCUTTERS

Office Address: Bowman Field, 1700 W. Fourth St., Williamsport, PA 17701.
Mailing Address: P.O. Box 3173, Williamsport, PA 17701.
Telephone: (570) 326-3389. **FAX:** (570) 326-3494.
E-Mail Address: mail@crosscutters.com. **Website:** www.crosscutters.com.
Affiliation (first year): Pittsburgh Pirates (1999). **Years in League:** 1968-72, 1994-.

OWNERSHIP, MANAGEMENT

Operated by: Geneva Cubs Baseball, Inc.
Principal Owners: Paul Velte, John Schreyer. **President:** Paul Velte. **Vice President:** John Schreyer.
General Manager: Doug Estes. **Director, Marketing/Public Relations:** Gabe Sinicropi. **Director, Food/Beverage:** Bill Gehron. **Director, Ticket Operations/Community Relations:** Kelle Renninger. **Assistant, Ticket Operations:** Kathryn Hettler **Assistant, Public Relations:** Charlie Hepp **Assistant, Stadium Operations:** Unavailable. **Head Groundskeeper:** Unavailable. **Clubhouse Manager:** Unavailable.

FIELD STAFF

Manager: Jeff Branson. **Coach:** Tom Prince. **Pitching Coach:** Ray Searage. **Trainer:** Bob Westwood.

GAME INFORMATION

Radio Announcer: Unavailable. **No. of Games Broadcast:** Unavailable. **Flagship Station:** WRLC 91.7-FM.
PA Announcer: Rob Thomas. **Official Scorer:** John Green
Stadium Name (year opened): Bowman Field (1923). **Location:** From south, Route 15 to Maynard Street, right on Maynard, left on Fourth Street for one mile; From north, Route 15 to Fourth Street, left on Fourth. **Standard Game Time:** 7:05 p.m.
Visiting Club Hotel: Holiday Inn, 1840 E. Third St., Williamsport, PA 17701. Telephone: (570) 326-1981.

NORTHWEST
LEAGUE

SHORT-SEASON CLASS A

Office Address: 910 Main St., Suite 351, Boise, ID 83702.
Mailing Address: P.O. Box 1645, Boise, ID 83701.
Telephone: (208) 429-1511. **FAX:** (208) 429-1525.
E-Mail Address: bobrichmond@worldnet.att.net.
Years League Active: 1954-.

President, Treasurer: Bob Richmond.
Vice President: Fred Herrmann (Vancouver). **Corporate Secretary:** Jerry Walker (Salem-Keizer).
Directors: Bob Beban (Eugene), Bobby Brett (Spokane), Fred Herrmann (Vancouver), Mike McMurray (Yakima), Mark Schuster (Tri-City), Mark Sperandio (Everett), Dan Walker (Boise), Jerry Walker (Salem-Keizer).
Administrative Assistant: Rob Richmond.
2004 Opening Date: June 17. **Closing Date:** Sept. 4.
Regular Season: 76 games.
Division Structure: East—Boise, Spokane, Tri-City, Yakima. **West**—Eugene, Everett, Salem-Keizer, Vancouver.
Playoff Format: Division winners meet in best-of-5 series for league championship.
All-Star Game: None.

Bob Richmond

Roster Limit: 30 active, 35 under control. **Player Eligibility Rule:** No more than four players 23 or older. No more than three players on active list may have four or more years of prior service.
Brand of Baseball: Rawlings.
Statistician: The Sports Network, 2200 Byberry Rd., Suite 200, Hatboro, PA 19040.
Umpires: Unavailable.

STADIUM INFORMATION

Club	Stadium	Dimensions			Capacity	2003 Att.
		LF	CF	RF		
Boise	Memorial	335	405	335	4,500	104,156
Eugene	Civic	335	400	328	6,800	130,657
Everett	Everett Memorial	330	395	330	3,682	110,043
Salem-Keizer	Volcanoes	325	400	325	4,100	119,556
Spokane	Seafirst	335	398	335	7,162	170,640
Tri-City	Pasco	335	400	335	3,730	58,976
Vancouver	Nat Bailey	335	395	335	6,500	137,026
Yakima	Yakima County	295	406	295	3,000	60,037

BOISE HAWKS

Office Address: 5600 Glenwood St., Boise, ID 83714.
Telephone: (208) 322-5000. **FAX:** (208) 322-6846.
Website: www.boisehawks.com.
Affiliation (first year): Chicago Cubs (2001). **Years in League:** 1975-76, 1978, 1987-.

OWNERSHIP, MANAGEMENT

Operated by: Boise Hawks Baseball Club LCC.
President/General Manager: Dan Walker.
Vice President, Sales/Marketing: Todd Rahr. **Controller:** Lee Ryan. **Stadium Operations/Head Groundskeeper:** Boyd Mauer. **Director, Customer Service/Administrative Assistant:** Dina Duncan. **Director, Media Relations:** Dan Walker. **Ticketing Account Executive:** Dorothy Gutierrez.

FIELD STAFF

Manager: Tom Beyers. **Coach:** Ricardo Medina. **Pitching Coach:** David Haas. **Trainer:** David Grines.

GAME INFORMATION

Radio Announcer: Mike Safford. **No. of Games Broadcast:** Home-38, Away-38. **Flagship Station:** KTIK 1350-AM.
PA Announcer: Dave Hahn. **Official Scorer:** Liza Safford.
Stadium Name (year opened): Memorial Stadium (1989). **Location:** I-84 to Cole Road, north to Western Idaho Fairgrounds at 5600 North Glenwood St. **Standard Game Times:** 7:05 p.m.; Sun. 6:05.
Visiting Club Hotel: Holiday Inn, 3300 Vista Ave., Boise, ID 83705. **Telephone:** (208) 344-8365.

EUGENE EMERALDS

Office Address: 2077 Willamette St., Eugene, OR 97405.
Mailing Address: P.O. Box 5566, Eugene, OR 97405.
Telephone: (541) 342-5367. **FAX:** (541) 342-6089.
E-Mail Address: ems@go-ems.com. **Website:** www.go-ems.com.
Affiliation (first year): San Diego Padres (2001). **Years in League:** 1955-68, 1974-.

OWNERSHIP, MANAGEMENT

Operated by: Elmore Sports Group, Ltd.
Principal Owner: David Elmore.
President, General Manager: Bob Beban. **Assistant General Managers:** Sergio Apodaca, Bryan Beban. **Director, Business Operations:** Eileen Beban. **Director, Food Services:** Jeph Mitchell. **Director, Tickets/Special Events:** Brandy Evenson. **Director, Stadium Operations:** David Puente. **Grounds Superintendent:** Peter Lockwood.

FIELD STAFF

Manager: Roy Howell. **Coach:** Ben Oglivie. **Pitching Coach:** Dave Rajsich. **Trainer:** Jo Jo Tarantino.

GAME INFORMATION

Radio Announcer: Dennis Higgins. **No. of Games Broadcast:** Home-38, Away-38. **Flagship Station:** KPNW 1120-AM.
PA Announcer: Unavailable. **Official Scorer:** Unavailable.
Stadium Name (year opened): Civic Stadium (1938). **Location:** From I-5, take I-105 to Exit 2, stay left and follow to downtown, cross over Ferry Street Bridge to Eighth Avenue, left on Pearl Street, south to 20th Avenue. **Standard Game Times:** 7:05 p.m.; Sun. 5:05.
Visiting Club Hotel: Unavailable.

EVERETT AQUASOX

Mailing Address: 3802 Broadway, Everett, WA 98201.
Telephone: (425) 258-3673. **FAX:** (425) 258-3675.
E-Mail Address: aquasox@aquasox.com. **Website:** www.aquasox.com.
Affiliation (first year): Seattle Mariners (1995). **Years in League:** 1984-.

OWNERSHIP, MANAGEMENT

Operated by: Farm Club Sports, Inc.
President: Mark Sperandio. **Vice President:** Joan Sperandio.

Director, Operations: Dan Lewis. **Director, Corporate Sales:** Brian Sloan. **Director, Broadcasting/Advertising Sales Associate:** Pat Dillon. **Director, Ballpark Operations:** Jason Jarett. **Director, Ticket Services:** Dave Roberts. **Director, Information Systems/Group Sales Associate:** Matt Nystrom. **Director, Food/Beverage:** Cathy Bierman. **Group Sales Associates:** Victoria Dearborn, Todd Holterhoff. **Director, Media Relations:** Amy Randall.

FIELD STAFF
Manager: Pedro Grifol. **Coach:** Darrin Garner. **Pitching Coach:** Marcos Garcia. **Trainer:** Spyder Webb.

GAME INFORMATION
Radio Announcer: Pat Dillon. **No. of Games Broadcast:** Home-38, Away-38. **Flagship Station:** KSER 90.7-FM. **PA Announcer:** Tom Lafferty. **Official Scorer:** Pat Castro.
Stadium Name (year opened): Everett Memorial Stadium (1984). **Location:** I-5, exit 192. **Standard Game Times:** 7:05 p.m.; Sun 4:05.
Visiting Club Hotel: Best Western Cascadia Inn, 2800 Pacific Ave., Everett, WA 98201. Telephone: (425) 258-4141.

SALEM-KEIZER
VOLCANOES

Street Address: 6700 Field of Dreams Way NE, Keizer, OR 97307.
Mailing Address: P.O. Box 20936, Keizer, OR 97307.
Telephone: (503) 390-2225. **FAX:** (503) 390-2227.
E-Mail Address: probasebal@aol.com. **Website:** www.volcanoesbaseball.com.
Affiliation (first year): San Francisco Giants (1997). **Years in League:** 1997-.

OWNERSHIP, MANAGEMENT
Operated By: Sports Enterprises, Inc.
Principal Owners: Jerry Walker, Bill Tucker.
President, General Manager: Jerry Walker. **Vice President, Operations:** Rick Nelson. **Manager, Corporate Sales/Director, Promotions:** Lisa Walker. **Corporate Sponsorships:** Steve Wertz, Amanda Hauge. **Director, Sales/Media Relations:** Pat Lafferty. **Director, Community Relations:** Unavailable. **Director, Ticket/Group Sales:** Greg Herbst. **Manager, Corporate Sales:** Robert Boyd. **Director, Merchandising/Ticket Office Operations:** Brienne Meaghers.

FIELD STAFF
Manager: Joe Strain. **Coach:** None. **Pitching Coach:** Jerry Cram. **Trainer:** Larry Duensing.

GAME INFORMATION
Radio Announcer: Pat Lafferty. **No. of Games Broadcast:** Home-38, Away-38. **Flagship Station:** KYKN 1430-AM. **PA Announcer:** Dave Jarvis. **Official Scorer:** Dawn Hills.
Stadium Name (year opened): Volcanoes Stadium (1997). **Location:** I-5 at exit 260 (Chemawa Road), west one block to Radiant Drive, north six blocks to stadium. **Standard Game Times:** 6:35 p.m.; Fri-Sat. 7:05; Sun. 5:05.
Visiting Club Hotel: Comfort Suites, 630 Hawthorne Ave. SE, Salem, OR 97301. Telephone: (503) 585-9705.

SPOKANE
INDIANS

Office Address: 602 N. Havana, Spokane, WA 99202.
Mailing Address: P.O. Box 4758, Spokane, WA 99220.
Telephone: (509) 535-2922. **FAX:** (509) 534-5368.
E-Mail Address: mail@spokaneindiansbaseball.com. **Website:** www.spokaneindiansbaseball.com.
Affiliation (first year): Texas Rangers (2003). **Years in League:** 1972, 1983-.

OWNERSHIP, MANAGEMENT
Operated by: Longball, Inc.
Principal Owners: Bobby Brett, George Brett, J.B. Brett.
President: Andrew Billig.
Vice President, General Manager: Paul Barbeau. **VP, Sponsorships:** Otto Klein. **Assistant GM, Ticket Sales:** Paul Zilm. **Assistant GM, Operations:** Chris Duff. **Assistant GM, Concessions:** Lesley DeHart. **Director, Group Sales:** Brian Burton. **Director, Season Ticket Sales:** Scott Litle. **Director, Promotions:** Jared Rose. **Director, Accounting:** Greg Sloan. **Account Executives:** Josh Roys, Jake Shapansky. **Coordinator, Group Sales:** Sara Matuska. **Coordinator, Promotions:** Brad Poe. **Head Groundskeeper:** Bret Whiteman. **Assistant Director, Stadium Operations:** Larry Blumer.

FIELD STAFF
Manager: Darryl Kennedy. **Coach:** Derek Lee. **Pitching Coach:** David Chavarria. **Trainer:** Cesar Roman.

GAME INFORMATION
Radio Announcer: Bob Robertson. **No. of Games Broadcast:** Home-38, Away-38. **Flagship Station:** KFAN 790-AM. **PA Announcer:** Unavailable. **Official Scorer:** Unavailable.

Stadium Name (year opened): Avista Stadium at Spokane County Fair and Expo Center (1958). **Location:** From west, I-90 to exit 283B (Thor/Freya), east on 3rd Avenue, left onto Havana; from east, I-90 to Broadway exit, right onto Broadway, left onto Havana. **Standard Game Time:** 6:30 p.m.

Visiting Club Hotel: West Coast Ridpath Hotel, 515 W. Sprague, Spokane, WA 99201. Telephone: (509) 838-2711.

TRI-CITY
DUST DEVILS

Office Address: 6200 Burden Rd., Pasco, WA 99301.
Telephone: (509) 544-8789. **FAX:** (509) 547-9570.
E-Mail Address: info@dustdevilsbaseball.com. **Website:** www.dustdevilsbase-ball.com.
Affiliation (first year): Colorado Rockies (2001). **Years in League:** 1955-1974, 1983-1986, 2001-.

OWNERSHIP, MANAGEMENT
Operated by: Portland Family Entertainment.
Vice President, General Manager: Brian Rogers. **Assistant GM:** Jody Sellers. **Director, Ticket Sales:** Matt Nash. **Director, Group Sales/Community Relations:** Nikki Pruett. **Office Manager:** Teri Miller.

FIELD STAFF
Manager: Ron Gideon. **Coach:** Freddie Ocasio. **Pitching Coach:** Butch Hughes. **Trainer:** Scott Murayama.

GAME INFORMATION
Radio Announcer: Tom Barket. **No. of Games Broadcast:** Home-38, Away-38. **Flagship Station:** KJOX 970-AM. **PA Announcer:** Shane Edinger. **Official Scorer:** Tony Wise.
Stadium Name (year opened): Dust Devils Stadium (1995). **Location:** I-182 to exit 9 (Road 68), north to Burden Rd., right to stadium. **Standard Game Times:** 7:05 p.m.; 6:05 Sun.
Visiting Club Hotel: Red Lion Hotel-Columbia Center, 1101 N. Columbia Center Blvd., Kennewick, WA 99336. Telephone: (509) 783-0611.

VANCOUVER
CANADIANS

Office Address: 4601 Ontario St., Vancouver, British Columbia V5V 3H4.
Telephone: (604) 872-5232. **FAX:** (604) 872-1714.
E-Mail Address: staff@canadiansbaseball.com. **Website:** www.canadiansbaseball.com.
Affiliation (first year): Oakland Athletics (2000). **Years in League:** 2000-.

OWNERSHIP, MANAGEMENT
Operated by: National Sports Organization, Inc.
Principal Owners: Dwain Cross, Fred Herrmann, Bud Kaufman.
President/General Manager: Dan Kilgras. **Director, Ticket Operations/Account Executive:** Delany Dunn. **Manager, Corporate Sales/Group Events:** Ben Ekren. **Director, Stadium Operations:** Bill Posthumus. **Ticket Manager:** Anne Slusser. **Account Executive:** Jeff Dye. **Clubhouse Manager:** Trevor Reid. **Director, Finance:** Carol Miner.

FIELD STAFF
Manager: Dennis Rogers. **Coach:** Todd Steverson. **Pitching Coach:** Craig Lefferts. **Trainer:** Jeff Collins.

GAME INFORMATION
Radio: The Team 1040-AM.
PA Announcer: Delany Dunn. **Official Scorer:** Pat Karl.
Stadium Name (year opened): Nat Bailey Stadium (1951). **Location:** From downtown, take Cambie Street Bridge, left on East 29th Avenue, left on Clancy Loringer Way, right to stadium; from south, take Highway 99 to Oak Street, right on 41st Avenue, left on Ontario to 30th Avenue. **Standard Game Times:** 7:05 p.m.; 1:05 Sun.
Visiting Club Hotel: Rosedale on Robson Suite Hotel, 838 Hamilton St., Vancouver, B.C. V6B 6A2. Telephone: (800) 661-8870, (604) 689-8033.

YAKIMA
BEARS

Office Address: 8 N. 2nd St., Yakima, WA 98901.
Mailing Address: P.O. Box 483, Yakima, WA 98907.
Telephone: (509) 457-5151. **FAX:** (509) 457-9909.
E-Mail Address: info@yakimabears.com. **Website:** www.yakimabears.com.

Affiliation (first year): Arizona Diamondbacks (2001). **Years in League:** 1955-66, 1990-.

OWNERSHIP, MANAGEMENT

Operated by: Short Season, LLC.
President: Mike McMurray.
Managing Partners: Mike McMurray, Mike Ellis, Josh Weinman, Myron Levin, Jim McCurdy.
General Manager: Bob Romero. **Assistant GM:** K.L. Wombacher. **Ticket/Group Sales:** Teddi Fowler. **Director, Stadium Operations:** Casey Steiner.
Head Groundskeeper: Bob Garretson. **Clubhouse Operations:** Aaron Arndt. **Administrative Assistants:** Joe Stapleton, Todd Sund, Lydia Turner.

FIELD STAFF

Manager: Bill Plummer. **Coach:** Jay Gainer. **Pitching Coach:** Ed Vosberg. **Trainer:** Unavailable.

GAME INFORMATION

Radio Announcer: Chad Goldberg. **No. of Games Broadcast:** Home-38, Away-38. **Flagship Station:** KUTI 1460-AM.
PA Announcer: Todd Lyons. **Official Scorer:** Mike McMurray.
Stadium Name (year opened): Yakima County Stadium (1993). **Location:** I-82 to exit 34 (Nob Hill Boulevard), west to Fair Avenue, right on Fair, right on Pacific Avenue. **Standard Game Times:** 7:05 p.m.; Sun. 6:05.
Visiting Club Hotel: Best Western Ahtanum Inn, 2408 Rudkin Rd., Union Gap, WA 98903. Telephone: (509) 248-9700.

APPALACHIAN
LEAGUE

APPALACHIAN LEAGUE
of professional baseball clubs

Mailing Address: 283 Deerchase Circle, Statesville, NC 28625.
Telephone: (704) 873-5300. **FAX:** (704) 873-4333.
E-Mail Address: appylg@direcway.com.
Years League Active: 1921-25, 1937-55, 1957-.

President, Treasurer: Lee Landers. **Corporate Secretary:** Jim Holland (Princeton).
Directors: Cam Bonifay (Princeton), John Farrell (Burlington), Dave Wilder (Bristol), Len Johnston (Bluefield), Bruce Manno (Johnson City), Dayton Moore (Danville), Kevin Morgan (Kingsport), Tim Purpura (Greeneville), Jim Rantz (Elizabethton), Dick Scott (Pulaski).
League Administrator: Bobbi Landers.
2004 Opening Date: June 21. **Closing Date:** Aug. 30.
Regular Season: 68 games.
Division Structure: East—Bluefield, Burlington, Danville, Princeton, Pulaski. **West**—Bristol, Elizabethton, Greeneville, Johnson City, Kingsport.
Playoff Format: Division winners meet in best-of-3 series for league championship.
All-Star Game: None.
Roster Limit: 35 active. **Player Eligibility Rule:** No more than two years of prior minor league service. No more than 15 players 21 years of age or older, provided no more than two of the 15 are 23 years of age or older. No more than 12 of the 21-year-olds may be listed on lineup card for any game.

Lee Landers

Brand of Baseball: Rawlings.
Statistician: The Sports Network, 2200 Byberry Rd., Suite 200, Hatboro, PA 19040.
Umpires: Unavailable.

Club	Stadium	Dimensions			Capacity	2003 Att.
		LF	CF	RF		
Bluefield	Bowen Field	335	365	335	2,250	22,853
Bristol	DeVault Memorial	325	400	310	2,000	19,770
Burlington	Burlington Athletic	335	410	335	3,000	37,380
Danville	Dan Daniel Memorial	330	400	330	2,588	35,621
Elizabethton	Joe O'Brien Field	335	414	326	1,500	24,004
*Greeneville	Pioneer Park	331	400	331	2,400	27,821
Johnson City	Howard Johnson	320	410	320	2,500	31,261
Kingsport	Hunter Wright	330	410	330	2,500	19,108
Princeton	Hunnicutt Field	330	396	330	1,950	26,339
Pulaski	Calfee Park	335	405	310	2,500	21,828

*Club operated in Martinsville, Va., in 2003

BLUEFIELD
ORIOLES

Office Address: 2003 Stadium Dr., Bluefield, WV 24701.
Mailing Address: P.O. Box 356, Bluefield, WV 24701.
Telephone: (276) 326-1326. **FAX:** (276) 326-1318.
Affiliation (first year): Baltimore Orioles (1958). **Years in League:** 1946-55, 1957-

OWNERSHIP, MANAGEMENT
Operated by: Bluefield Baseball Club, Inc.
Director: Len Johnston (Baltimore Orioles).
Vice President: Cecil Smith. **Secretary:** M.K. Burton. **Counsel:** David Kersey.
President, General Manager: George McGonagle. **Controller:** Charles Peters. **Director, Special Projects:** Tuillio Ramella.

FIELD STAFF
Manager: Gary Kendall. **Coaches:** Len Johnston, Hensley Muelens. **Pitching Coach:** Larry Jaster. **Trainer:** Patrick Wesley.

GAME INFORMATION
Radio Announcer: Buford Early. **No. of Games Broadcast:** Away-34. **Flagship Station:** WHIS 1440-AM.
PA Announcer: Dave Crosier. **Official Scorer:** Will Prewitt.
Stadium Name (year opened): Bowen Field (1939). **Location:** I-77 to Bluefield exit, Route 290 to Route 460 West, right onto Leatherwood Lane, left at first light, past Chevron station and turn right, stadium ¼ mile on left. **Standard Game Times:** 7 p.m., DH 6; Sun. 6, DH 5.
Visiting Club Hotel: East River Mountain Inn, 3175 E. Cumberland Rd., Bluefield, WV 24701. Telephone: (276) 325-5421

BRISTOL
WHITE SOX

Office Address: 1501 Euclid Ave., Bristol, VA 24201.
Mailing Address: P.O. Box 1434, Bristol, VA 24203.
Telephone: (540) 645-7275. **FAX:** (540) 669-7686.
E-Mail Address: bwsox@3wave.com. **Website:** www.bristolsox.com.
Affiliation (first year): Chicago White Sox (1995). **Years in League:** 1921-25, 1940-55, 1969-.

OWNERSHIP, MANAGEMENT
Operated by: Chicago White Sox.
Director: Dave Wilder (Chicago White Sox).
President: Boyce Cox. **General Manager:** Robert Childress.

FIELD STAFF
Manager: Jerry Hairston. **Coaches:** Chet DeMidio, Ryan Long. **Pitching Coach:** Bill Kinneberg. **Trainer:** Darren Wheeler.

GAME INFORMATION
Radio: None.
PA Announcer: Boyce Cox. **Official Scorer:** Allen Shepherd.
Stadium Name (year opened): DeVault Memorial Stadium (1969). **Location:** I-81 to exit 3 onto Commonwealth Ave., right on Euclid Ave. for ½ mile. **Standard Game Time:** 7 p.m.
Visiting Club Hotel: Ramada Inn, 2122 Euclid Ave., Bristol, VA 24201. Telephone: (540) 669-7171.

BURLINGTON
INDIANS

Office Address: 1450 Graham St., Burlington, NC 27217.
Mailing Address: P.O. Box 1143, Burlington, NC 27217.
Telephone: (336) 222-0223. **FAX:** (336) 226-2498.
E-Mail Address: info@btribebaseball.com. **Website:** www.btribebaseball.com.
Affiliation (first year): Cleveland Indians (1986). **Years in League:** 1986-.

OWNERSHIP, MANAGEMENT
Operated by: Burlington Baseball Club, Inc.

Director: John Farrell (Cleveland Indians).
President: Miles Wolff. **Vice President:** Dan Moushon.
General Manager: Mark Cryan. **Assistant GM:** Jeremy Auker. **Director, Media Relations:** Gene Brtalik.

FIELD STAFF

Manager: Rouglas Odor. **Coach:** Unavailable. **Pitching Coach:** Ruben Niebla. **Trainer:** Teddy Blackwell.

GAME INFORMATION

Radio Announcer: Unavailable. **No. of Games Broadcast:** Home-34, Away-34. **Flagship Station:** WBAG 1150-AM.
PA Announcer: Byron Tucker. **Official Scorer:** David Williams.
Stadium Name (year opened): Burlington Athletic Stadium (1960). **Location:** I-40/85 to exit 145, north on Route 100 (Maple Avenue) for 1½ miles, right on Mebane Street for 1 1/2 miles, right on Beaumont, left on Graham. **Standard Game Time:** 7 p.m.
Visiting Club Hotel: Holiday Inn-Outlet Center, 2444 Maple Ave., Burlington, NC 27215. Telephone: (336) 229-5203.

DANVILLE
BRAVES

Office Address: Dan Daniel Memorial Park, 302 River Park Dr., Danville, VA 24540.
Mailing Address: P.O. Box 378, Danville, VA 24543.
Telephone: (434) 797-3792. **FAX:** (434) 797-3799.
E-Mail Address: info@dbraves.com. **Website:** www.dbraves.com.
Affiliation (first year): Atlanta Braves (1993). **Years in League:** 1993-.

OWNERSHIP, MANAGEMENT

Operated by: Atlanta National League Baseball Club, Inc.
Director: Dayton Moore (Atlanta Braves).
General Manager: David Cross. **Assistant GM:** Bob Kitzmiller. **Office Manager:** Shelby Tate. **Head Groundskeeper:** Richard Gieselman.

FIELD STAFF

Manager: Phillip Wellman. **Coach:** Luis Ortiz. **Pitching Coach:** Jim Czajkowski. **Trainer:** Tyson Burton.

GAME INFORMATION

Radio: None.
PA Announcer: Unavailable. **Official Scorer:** Sam Ferguson.
Stadium Name (first year): American Legion Field Post 325 Field at Dan Daniel Memorial Park (1993). **Location:** U.S. 58 to U.S. 29 S. Bypass, follow signs to park; U.S. 29 bypass to Dan Daniel Park exit (River Park Drive), follow signs to park. **Standard Game Times:** 7 p.m.; Sun. 4.
Visiting Club Hotel: Innkeeper-West, 3020 Riverside Dr., Danville, VA 24541. Telephone: (434) 799-1202.

ELIZABETHTON
TWINS

Office Address: 208 N. Holly Lane, Elizabethton, TN 37643.
Mailing Address: 136 S. Sycamore St., Elizabethton, TN 37643.
Telephone: (423) 547-6441. **FAX:** (423) 547-6442.
E-Mail Address: etwins@preferred.com. **Website:** www.elizabethtontwins.com.
Affiliation (first year): Minnesota Twins (1974). **Years in League:** 1937-42, 1945-51, 1974-.

OWNERSHIP, MANAGEMENT

Operated by: City of Elizabethton.
Director: Jim Rantz (Minnesota Twins).
President: Harold Mains.
General Manager: Mike Mains. **Clubhouse Operations:** David McQueen. **Head Groundskeeper:** David Nanney.
Director, Ticket Sales: Sherri Campbell. **Director, Group Sales:** J Harold Ray. **Director, Merchandising:** Linda Church.
Director, Food Services: Cindy Walker.

FIELD STAFF

Manager: Ray Smith. **Coach:** Jeff Reed. **Pitching Coach:** Jim Shellenback. **Trainer:** Unavailable.

GAME INFORMATION

Radio Announcer: Frank Santore. **No. of Games Broadcast:** Home-34, Away-6. **Flagship Station:** WBEJ 1240-AM.
PA Announcer: Tom Banks. **Official Scorer:** Bill Crow.
Stadium Name (year opened): Joe O'Brien Field (1974). **Location:** I-81 to I-181, exit at Highway 321/67, left at Holly Lane. **Standard Game Times:** 7 p.m., DH 6.
Visiting Club Hotel: Days Inn, 505 W. Elk Ave., Elizabethton, TN 37643. Telephone: (423) 543-3344.

GREENEVILLE
ASTROS

Office Address: 135 Shiloh Rd., Greeneville, TN 37743.
Mailing Address: P.O. Box 5192, Greeneville, TN 37743.
Telephone: (423) 638-0411. **FAX:** (423) 638-9450.
E-Mail Address: info@greenevilleastros.com. **Website:** www.greenevilleastros.com.
Affiliation (first year): Houston Astros (2004). **Years in League:** 2004-.

OWNERSHIP, MANAGEMENT
Operated by: Houston Astros Baseball Club.
Director: Tim Purpura (Houston Astros).
General Manager: Lynsi House. **Assistant GM:** Omar Roque. **Account Executive:** John Doyle. **Head Groundskeeper:** Unavailable. **Clubhouse Operations:** Unavailable.

FIELD STAFF
Manager: Tim Bogar. **Coach:** Pete Rancont. **Pitching Coach:** Jack Billingham. **Trainer:** John Patton.

GAME INFORMATION
Radio Announcer: Unavailable. **No. of Games Broadcast:** Home-34. **Flagship Station:** Unavailable.
PA Announcer: Unavailable. **Official Scorer:** Unavailable.
Stadium Name (year opened): Pioneer Park (2004). **Location:** On campus of Tusculum College. **Standard Game Times:** 7 p.m; Sun. 6.
Visiting Club Hotel: Unavailable.

JOHNSON CITY
CARDINALS

Office Address: 111 Legion St., Johnson City, TN 37601.
Mailing Address: P.O. Box 179, Johnson City, TN 37605.
Telephone: (423) 461-4866. **FAX:** (423) 461-4864.
E-Mail Address: jccardinalsbb@aol.com. **Website:** www.jccardinals.com.
Affiliation (first year): St. Louis Cardinals (1975). **Years in League:** 1911-13, 1921-24, 1937-55, 1957-61, 1964-.

OWNERSHIP, MANAGEMENT
Operated by: Johnson City Sports Foundation, Inc.
President: Dr. Jeff Banyas.
Director: Bruce Manno (St. Louis Cardinals).
General Manager: Brandon Cross. **Clubhouse Operations:** Pat Kramer. **Groundskeeper:** Mike Whitson.

FIELD STAFF
Manager: Tommy Kidwell. **Coach:** George Kissell. **Pitching Coach:** Al Holland. **Trainer:** Allen Thompson.

GAME INFORMATION
Radio: Unavailable. **No. of Games Broadcast:** Home-34. **Flagship Station:** WKPT 1590-AM.
PA Announcer: Unavailable. **Official Scorer:** Unavailable.
Stadium Name (year opened): Howard Johnson Field (1956). **Location:** I-181 to exit 32, left on East Main, through light onto Legion Street. **Standard Game Times:** 7 p.m.
Visiting Club Hotel: Holiday Inn, 101 W. Springbrook Dr., Johnson City, TN 37601. Telephone: (423) 282-4611.

KINGSPORT
METS

Office Address: 433 E. Center St., Kingsport, TN 37664.
Mailing Address: P.O. Box 1128, Kingsport, TN 37662.
Telephone: (423) 378-3744. **FAX:** (423) 392-8538.
E-Mail Address: info@kmets.com. **Website:** www.kmets.com.
Affiliation (first year): New York Mets (1980). **Years in League:** 1921-25, 1938-52, 1957, 1960-63, 1969-82, 1984-.

OWNERSHIP, MANAGEMENT
Operated by: S&H Baseball, LLC.
Director: Kevin Morgan (New York Mets).
President: Rick Spivey. **Vice President:** Steve Harville.
General Manager: Roman Stout. **Director, Housing:** Peggy Lozier.

FIELD STAFF

Manager: Mookie Wilson. **Coach:** Luis Natera. **Pitching Coach:** Unavailable. **Trainer:** Michael Suski.

GAME INFORMATION

Radio: None.
PA Announcer: Don Spivey. **Official Scorer:** Eddie Durham.
Stadium Name (year opened): Hunter Wright Stadium (1995). **Location:** I-81 to I-181 North, exit 11E (Stone Drive), left on West Stone Drive (U.S. 11W), right on Granby Road. **Standard Game Times:** 7 p.m., DH 6.
Visiting Club Hotel: Ramada Inn, 2005 Lamasa Dr., Kingsport, TN 37660. Telephone: (423) 245-0271.

PRINCETON
DEVIL RAYS

Office Address: Hunnicutt Field, Old Bluefield Road, Princeton, WV 24740.
Mailing Address: P.O. Box 5646, Princeton, WV 24740.
Telephone: (304) 487-2000. **FAX:** (304) 487-8762.
E-Mail Address: raysball@sunlitsurf.com. **Website:** www.princetondevilrays.com.
Affiliation (first year): Tampa Bay Devil Rays (1997). **Years in League:** 1988-.

OWNERSHIP, MANAGEMENT

Operated by: Princeton Baseball Association, Inc.
Director: Cam Bonifay (Tampa Bay Devil Rays).
President: Dewey Russell.
General Manager: Jim Holland. **Director, Stadium Operations:** Mick Bayle. **Head Groundskeeper:** Frankie Bailey.
Account Representative: Paul Lambert. **Clubhouse Manager:** Matt Gallant.

FIELD STAFF

Manager: Jamie Nelson. **Coach:** Manny Castillo. **Pitching Coach:** Nardi Contreras. **Trainer:** Unavailable.

GAME INFORMATION

Radio Announcer: Uavailable. **No. of Games Broadcast:** Away-34. **Flagship Station:** WAEY 1490-AM.
PA Announcer: Dave Ebert. **Official Scorer:** Dick Daisey.
Stadium Name (year opened): Hunnicutt Field (1988). **Location:** Exit 9 off I-77, U.S. 460 West to downtown exit, left on Stafford Drive, stadium located behind Mercer County Technical Education Center. **Standard Game Times:** 7 p.m., DH 5:30; Sun. 4.
Visiting Club Hotel: Days Inn, I-77 and Ambrose Lane, Princeton, WV 24740. Telephone: (304) 425-8100.

PULASKI
BLUE JAYS

Mailing Address: P.O. Box 676, Pulaski, VA 24301.
Telephone: (540) 980-1070. **FAX:** (540) 980-1850.
E-Mail Address: mail@pulaskibluejays.com. **Website:** www.pulaskibluejays.com.
Affiliation (first year): Toronto Blue Jays (2003). **Years in League:** 1946-50, 1952-55, 1957-58, 1969-77, 1982-92, 1997-.

OWNERSHIP, MANAGEMENT

Operated by: Pulaski Baseball, Inc.
General Manager: Tom Compton. **Assistant GM:** Shawn Hite.

FIELD STAFF

Manager: Gary Cathcart. **Coach:** Justin Mashore. **Pitching Coach:** Antonio Caceres. **Trainer:** Andrew Muccino.

GAME INFORMATION

Radio: None.
PA Announcer: Andy French. **Official Scorer:** Edgar Williams.
Stadium Name (year opened): Calfee Park (1935). **Location:** I-81 to exit 89B (Route 11), north to Pulaski, right on Pierce Avenue. **Standard Game Time:** 7 p.m.
Visiting Club Hotel: Comfort Inn, 4424 Cleburne Blvd., Dublin, VA 24084. Telephone: (540) 674-1100.

PIONEER
LEAGUE

Office Address: 157 S. Lincoln Ave., Spokane, WA 99201.
Mailing Address: P.O. Box 2564, Spokane, WA 99220.
Telephone: (509) 456-7615. **FAX:** (509) 456-0136.
E-Mail Address: fanmail@pioneerleague.com. **Website:** www.pioneerleague.com.
Years League Active: 1939-42, 1946-.

President/Secretary-Treasurer: Jim McCurdy.
Vice President: Mike Ellis (Missoula).
Directors: Dave Baggott (Ogden), Mike Ellis (Missoula), D.G. Elmore (Helena), Larry Geske (Great Falls), Kevin Greene (Idaho Falls), Kevin Haughian (Casper), Rob Owens (Provo), Bob Wilson (Billings).
Administrative Assistant: Teryl MacDonald.
2004 Opening Date: June 18. **Closing Date:** Sept. 6.
Regular Season: 76 games (split-schedule).
Division Structure: North—Billings, Great Falls, Helena, Missoula. **South**—Casper, Idaho Falls, Ogden, Provo.
Playoff Format: First-half division winners play second-half division winners in best-of-3 series. Winners meet in best-of-3 series for league championship.
All-Star Game: None.

Jim McCurdy

Roster Limit: 35 active, 30 dressed for each game. **Player Eligibility Rule:** No more than 17 players 21 and older, provided that no more than two are 23 or older. No player on active list may have three or more years of prior minor league service.
Brand of Baseball: Rawlings.
Statistician: The Sports Network, 2200 Byberry Rd., Suite 200, Hatboro, PA 19040.
Umpires: Unavailable.

STADIUM INFORMATION

Club	Stadium	Dimensions			Capacity	2003 Att.
		LF	CF	RF		
Billings	Cobb Field	335	405	325	4,200	122,090
Casper	Mike Lansing Field	355	400	345	2,500	51,427
Great Falls	Legion Park	335	414	335	3,800	114,603
Helena	Kendrick Legion Field	335	400	325	1,700	47,493
Idaho Falls	McDermott Field	340	400	350	2,928	57,854
Missoula	Lindborg-Cregg	320	400	320	2,200	51,236
Ogden	Lindquist Field	335	396	334	5,000	126,706
Provo	Larry H. Miller Field	345	400	345	2,000	56,856

BILLINGS
MUSTANGS

Office Address: Cobb Field, 901 N. 27th St., Billings, MT 59101.
Mailing Address: P.O. Box 1553, Billings, MT 59103.
Telephone: (406) 252-1241. **FAX:** (406) 252-2968.
E-Mail Address: mustangs@billingsmustangs.com. **Website:** www.billingsmustangs.com.
Affiliation (first year): Cincinnati Reds (1974). **Years in League:** 1948-63, 1969-.

OWNERSHIP, MANAGEMENT
Operated by: Billings Pioneer Baseball Club, Inc.
Chairman: Ron May.
President, General Manager: Bob Wilson. **Assistant GM:** Gary Roller. **Head Groundskeeper:** Dave Graves. **Director, Sales:** Allen Reynolds. **Director, Broadcasting:** Chris Rushin. **Director, Clubhouse Operations:** George Kimmet.

FIELD STAFF
Manager: Donnie Scott. **Coach:** Chris Sabo. **Pitching Coach:** Vern Ruhle. **Trainer:** Unavailable.

GAME INFORMATION
Radio Announcer: Chris Rushin. **No. of Games Broadcast:** Home-38, Away-38. **Flagship Station:** KBUL 970-AM.
PA Announcer: Adam Bryant. **Official Scorer:** Matt Bender.
Stadium Name (year opened): Cobb Field (1948). **Location:** I-90 to 27th Street North exit, north to Ninth Avenue North. **Standard Game Times:** 7 p.m.; Sun. 4.
Visiting Club Hotel: Rimrock Inn, 1203 N. 27th St., Billings, MT 59101. Telephone: (406) 252-7107.

CASPER
ROCKIES

Office Address: 330 Kati Lane, Casper, WY 82602.
Mailing Address: P.O. Box 1293, Casper, WY 82602.
Telephone: (307) 232-1111. **FAX:** (307) 265-7867.
E-Mail Address: baseball@casperrockies.com. **Website:** www.casperrockies.com.
Affiliation (first year): Colorado Rockies (2001). **Years in League:** 2001-.

OWNERSHIP, MANAGEMENT
Operated by: Casper Professional Baseball Club, LLC.
Principal Owner, Chief Executive Officer: Kevin Haughian.
President, General Manager: Mary Schmidt. **Assistant GM/Director, Operations:** Todd Titus. **Assistant GM/Manager, Corporate Sales:** Danny Tetzlaff.

FIELD STAFF
Manager: P.J. Carey. **Coach:** Tony Diaz. **Pitching Coach:** Richard Palacios. **Trainer:** Unavailable.

GAME INFORMATION
Radio: KWYY 95.5-FM.
PA Announcer: Unavailable. **Official Scorer:** Unavailable.
Stadium Name (year opened): Mike Lansing Field (2002). **Location:** I-25 to Poplar Street exit, north on Poplar Street, right into Crossroads Park. **Standard Game Times:** 7:05 p.m.; Sun. 5:05.
Visiting Club Hotel: Parkway Plaza, 123 W. "E" St., Casper, WY 82601. Telephone (307) 235-1777.

GREAT FALLS
WHITE SOX

Office/Stadium Address: 1015 25th St. N., Great Falls, MT 59401.
Mailing Address: P.O. Box 1621, Great Falls, MT 59403.
Telephone: (406) 452-5311. **FAX:** (406) 454-0811.
E-Mail Address: whitesox@greatfallswhitesox.com. **Website:** www.greatfallswhitesox.com.
Affiliation (first year): Chicago White Sox (2003). **Years in League:** 1948-1963, 1969-.

OWNERSHIP/MANAGEMENT
Operated by: Great Falls Baseball Club, Inc.
President: Larry Geske.
General Manager: Jim Keough. **Assistant GM:** Ginger Burcham. **Head Groundskeeper:** Carl Christofferson.

FIELD STAFF
Manager: John Orton. **Coach:** Mark Haley. **Pitching Coach:** Richard Dotson. **Trainer:** Kevin Pillifant.

GAME INFORMATION
Radio Announcer: Michael Purpura. **No. of Games Broadcast:** Home-38, Away-38. **Flagship Station:** KMON 560-AM.

PA Announcer: Tim Paul. **Official Scorer:** Mike Lewis.

Stadium Name (Year Opened): Legion Park (1956). **Location:** From I-15, take 10th Ave. South (exit 281) for four miles to 26th Street, left to 8th Ave. North, left to 25th Street North, right to ballpark. **Standard Game Times:** 7 p.m.; Sun. 4.

Visiting Club Hotel: Midtown Hotel, 526 Second Ave. N., Great Falls, MT 59401. Telephone: (406) 453-2411.

HELENA BREWERS

Office Address: 1300 N. Ewing, Helena, MT 59601.
Mailing Address: P.O. Box 6756, Helena, MT 59604.
Telephone: (406) 495-0500. **FAX:** (406) 495-0900.
E-Mail Address: info@helenabrewers.net. **Website:** www.helenabrewers.net.
Affiliation (first year): Milwaukee Brewers (2003). **Years in League:** 1978-2000, 2003-.

OWNERSHIP, MANAGEMENT
Operated by: Helena Baseball Club LLC.
Principal Owner: D.G. Elmore.
General Manager: Paul Fetz. **Assistant GM:** Travis Brower. **Director, Broadcasting/Media Relations:** Unavailable.

FIELD STAFF
Manager: Johnny Narron. **Coach:** Norberto Martin. **Pitching Coach:** Mark Littell. **Trainer:** Masa Koyanagi.

GAME INFORMATION
Radio Announcer: Unavailable. **No. of Games Broadcast:** Home-38, Away-38. **Flagship Station:** KCAP 1340-AM.
PA Announcer: Unavailable. **Official Scorer:** Unavailable.
Stadium Name (year opened): Kindrick Field (1939). **Location:** Cedar Street exit off I-15, west to Main Street, left at Memorial Park. **Standard Game Time:** 7:05 p.m.
Visiting Club Hotel: Red Lion Colonial Hotel, 2301 Colonial Drive, Helena, MT 59601. Telephone: (406) 443-2100.

IDAHO FALLS CHUKARS

Office Address: 568 W. Elva, Idaho Falls, ID 83402.
Mailing Address: P.O. Box 2183, Idaho Falls, ID 83403.
Telephone: (208) 522-8363. **FAX:** (208) 522-9858.
E-Mail Address: chukars@ifchukars.com. **Website:** www.ifchukars.com.
Affiliation (first year): Kansas City Royals (2004). **Years in League:** 1940-42, 1946-.

OWNERSHIP, MANAGEMENT
Operated by: The Elmore Group.
Principal Owner: David Elmore.
President, General Manager: Kevin Greene. **Assistant GM, Merchandise:** Marcus Loyola. **Director, Public Relations/Concessions:** Nathaniel Peck. **Director, Corporate Sales:** Andrea Villalpando. **Head Groundskeeper:** Christopher Michaels.

FIELD STAFF
Manager: Brian Rupp. **Coach:** Pookie Wilson. **Pitching Coach:** Jose Bautista. **Trainer:** Unavailable.

GAME INFORMATION
Radio Announcers: John Balginy, Jim Garshow. **No. of Games Broadcast:** Home-38, Away-38. **Flagship Station:** KUPI 980-AM.
PA Announcer: Tim Hagerty. **Official Scorer:** John Balginy.
Stadium Name (year opened): McDermott Field (1976). **Location:** I-15 to West Broadway exit, left onto Memorial Drive, right on Mound Avenue, ¼ mile to stadium. **Standard Game Times:** 7:15 p.m.; Sun. 5.
Visiting Club Hotel: Unavailable.

MISSOULA
OSPREY

Office Address: 700 Cregg Lane, Missoula, MT 59801.
Telephone: (406) 543-3300. FAX: (406) 543-9463.
E-Mail Address: generalmgr@missoulaosprey.com. Website: www.missoula
osprey.com.
Affiliation (first year): Arizona Diamondbacks (1999). Years in League: 1956-60, 1999-.

OWNERSHIP, MANAGEMENT

Operated by: Mountain Baseball, LLC.
President: Mike Ellis. Executive Vice President: Judy Ellis.
VP/General Manager: Matt Ellis. Assistant GMs: Chris Hale, Jared Amoss. Director, Finance/Human Resources: Shelly Ellis. Manager, Group Sales: Thom Carter. Director, Merchandise: Lori Hale. Office Administrator: Stephanie Johnston. Clubhouse Manager: Unavailable.

FIELD STAFF

Manager: Jim Presley. Coach: Allen Campbell. Pitching Coach: Wellington Cepeda. Trainer: Dave Philbreck.

GAME INFORMATION

Radio Announcer: Tim Boulware. No. of Games Broadcast: Home-38, Away-38. Flagship Station: 1340-AM.
PA Announcer: Patrick Nikolay. Official Scorer: Unavailable.
Stadium Name (year opened): Missoula Civic Stadium (2004). Location: Orange Street to Cregg Lane, west on Cregg Lane, stadium west of McCormick Park. Standard Game Times: 7:05 p.m.; Sun. 5:05.
Visiting Club Hotel: Campus Inn, 744 E. Broadway, Missoula, MT 59802. Telephone: (406) 549-5134.

OGDEN
RAPTORS

Office Address: 2330 Lincoln Ave., Ogden, UT 84401.
Telephone: (801) 393-2400. FAX: (801) 393-2473.
E-Mail Address: homerun@ogden-raptors.com. Website: www.ogden-raptors.com.
Affiliation (first year): Los Angeles Dodgers (2003). Years in League: 1939-42, 1946-55, 1966-74, 1994-.

OWNERSHIP, MANAGEMENT

Operated by: Ogden Professional Baseball, Inc.
Principal Owners: Dave Baggott, John Lindquist.
Chairman, President: Dave Baggott. General Manager: Joe Stein. Controller: Carol Spickler. Head Groundskeeper: Ken Kopinski. Director, Merchandising: Geri Kopinski.

FIELD STAFF

Manager: Travis Barbary. Coach: Pat Harrison. Pitching Coach: Tim Kelly. Trainer: Robert Picard.

GAME INFORMATION

Radio Announcer: Brian Petrotta. No. of Games Broadcast: Home-38, Away-38. Flagship Station: KXOL 1660-AM.
PA Announcer: Pete Diamond. Official Scorer: Dennis Kunimura.
Stadium Name (year opened): Lindquist Field (1997). Location: I-15 North to 21st Street exit, east to Lincoln Avenue, south three blocks to park. Standard Game Times: 7 p.m.; Sun. 1.
Visiting Club Hotel: Marriott, 247 24th St., Odgen, UT 84401. Telephone: (801) 627-1190.

PROVO
ANGELS

Office Address: 1516 N. Technology Way, Building D, 2nd Floor, Orem, UT 84097.
Telephone: (801) 377-2255. FAX: (801) 377-2345.
E-Mail Address: fan@provoangels.com. Website: www.provoangels.com.
Affiliation: Anaheim Angels (2001). Years in League: 2001-.

OWNERSHIP/MANAGEMENT

Operated by: Never Say Never, Inc.
Principal Owners: Rob Owens, Linda Gach Ray.
Chairman: Linda Gach Ray. President: Rob Owens.
General Manager: Dave Jacobsen. Assistant General Manager: Ryan Pace.

FIELD STAFF

Manager: Tom Kotchman. **Coach:** Kevin Ham. **Pitching Coach:** Zeke Zimmerman. **Trainer:** Aaron Wells.

GAME INFORMATION

Radio Announcer: Unavailable. **No. of Games Broadcast:** Home-38, Away-38. **Flagship Station:** Unavailable. **PA Announcers:** Tyler Maesom, Jeff Hanson. **Official Scorer:** Sara Harris.

Stadium Name (year opened): Larry H. Miller Field at Miller Park (2001). **Location:** Exit 272 (University Parkway) off 1-15, east four miles to Brigham Young University campus, stadium on right. **Standard Game Times:** 7:05 p.m.; DH 6:05; Mon. 5:05.

Visiting Club Hotel: Provo Days Inn, 1675 N. 200 West, Provo, UT 84604. Telephone: (801) 375-8600.

ARIZONA LEAGUE

Office Address: 910 Main St., Suite 351, Boise, ID 83702.
Mailing Address: P.O. Box 1645, Boise, ID 83701.
Telephone: (208) 429-1511. **FAX:** (208) 429-1525. **E-Mail Address:** bobrichmond@worldnet.att.net.
Years League Active: 1988-.
President/Treasurer: Bob Richmond.
Vice President: Bobby Evans (Giants). **Corporate Secretary:** Ted Polakowski (Athletics).
Administrative Assistant: Rob Richmond.
2004 Opening Date: June 22. **Closing Date:** Aug. 30. **Standard Game Times:** 10:30 a.m.; (Night Games)—7 p.m.
Division Structure: None.
Regular Season: 56 games (split-schedule).
Playoff Format: First-half winner meets second-half winner in one-game championship.
All-Star Game: None.
Roster Limit: 35 active. **Player Eligibility Rule:** No more than 12 players 20 or older, no more than eight players 21 or older, and no more than four players of any age not selected in 2004 first-year draft. No more than two years of prior service if a player is under the age of 20; unless a player is switching from a position player to a pitcher.
Brand of Baseball: Rawlings.
Statistician: The Sports Network, 2200 Byberry Rd., Suite 200, Hatboro, PA 19040.

Clubs	Playing Site	Manager	Coach	Pitching Coach
Angels	Gene Autry Park, Mesa	Brian Harper	Keith Johnson	Jack Uhey
Athletics	Papago Park Sports Complex, Phoenix	Ruben Escalera	Juan Dilone	Mike Holmes
Brewers	Maryvale Baseball Complex, Phoenix	Mike Guerrero	Joel Youngblood	Steve Cline
Cubs	Fitch Park, Mesa	Trey Forkerway	C.Martinez/F. Font	Rick Tronerud
Giants	Scottsdale Stadium, Scottsdale	Bert Hunter	Leo Garcia	Will Malerich
Mariners	Peoria Sports Complex, Peoria	Scott Steinmann	T. Cruz/A. Bottin	Gary Wheelock
Padres	Peoria Sports Complex, Peoria	Carlos Lezcano	Luis Quinones	Wally Whitehurst
Rangers	Surprise Recreation Campus	Pedro Lopez	Brook Jacoby	Aris Tirado
Royals	Surprise Recreation Campus	Lloyd Simmons	Tom Poquette	Royal Clayton

GULF COAST LEAGUE

Office Address: 1503 Clower Creek Dr., Suite H-262, Sarasota, FL 34231.
Telephone: (941) 966-6407. **FAX:** (941) 966-6872.
Years League Active: 1964-.
President/Secretary-Treasurer: Tom Saffell.
First Vice President: Steve Noworyta (Phillies). **Second Vice President:** Jim Rantz (Twins).
Administrative Assistant: Bill Ventolo.
2004 Opening Date: June 19. **Closing Date:** Aug. 28.
Regular Season: 60 games.
Division Structure: East—Dodgers, Expos, Marlins, Mets. **North**—Braves, Phillies, Tigers, Yankees. **South**—Pirates, Reds, Red Sox, Twins.
Playoff Format: Division winner with best regular season record plays winner of one-game playoff between other two division winners in best-of-3 series for championship.
Roster Limit: 35 active, but only 30 eligible for each game. **Player Eligibility Rule:** No more than eight players 20 or older, no more than two players 21 or older, and no more than four players of any age who were eligible but passed over in the 2004 draft. No more than two years of prior service, excluding Rookie leagues outside the United States and Canada; a third year is allowed for players under 20.
Brand of Baseball: Rawlings.
Statistician: The Sports Network, 2200 Byberry Rd., Suite 200, Hatboro, PA 19040.

Clubs	Playing Site	Manager	Coach(es)	Pitching Coach
Braves	Disney's Wide World of Sports, Orlando	Ralph Henriquez	S. Lezcano/J. Saul	D. Botelho/G. Luckett
Dodgers	Dodgertown, Vero Beach	Luis Salazar	Brian Traxler	George Culver
Expos	Carl Barger Baseball Complex, Melbourne	Arturo DeFreites	Jose Alguacil	Tom Keating
Marlins	Roger Dean Stadium, Jupiter	Tim Cossins	Johnny Rodriguez	Gary Buckels
Mets	St. Lucie Sports Complex, St. Lucie	Brett Butler	Juan Lopez	Randy Niemann
Phillies	Carpenter Complex, Clearwater	Roly DeArmas	Tony Scott	Carlos Arroyo
Pirates	Pirate City Complex, Bradenton	Woody Huyke	Ramon Sambo	Miguel Bonilla
Reds	Ed Smith Stadium, Sarasota	Luis Aguayo	J. Ayrault/B. Williams	J. Garcia/B. Henry
Red Sox	City of Palms Park, Fort Myers	Ralph Treuel	Walter Miranda	Alan Mauthe
Tigers	Tigertown, Lakeland	Kevin Bradshaw	Scott Makarewicz	Greg Sabat
Twins	Lee County Stadium, Fort Myers	Riccardo Ingram	Milt Cuyler	Steve Mintz
Yankees	Yankee Complex, Tampa	Oscar Acosta	Unavailable	Dwight Gooden

CLASS AAA
INTERNATIONAL LEAGUE

BUFFALO

APRIL
8-9-10-10 .. at Pawtucket
12-13-14 ...... at Scranton
16-17-18 .... Ottawa
19-20-21-22 .... Scranton
23-24-25 .... at Ottawa
26-27-28-29 .. at Rochester
30 .... Pawtucket

MAY
1-2-3 .... Pawtucket
4-5-6-7 .... Rochester
8-9-10-11 .... at Columbus
13-14-15-16 .. at Columbus
17-18-19-20 .... Louisville
21-22-23-24 ...... Norfolk
25-26-27-28 .. at Richmond
29-30-31 .... at Norfolk

JUNE
1 ...... at Norfolk
3-4-5-6 .... Columbus
7-8-9-10 .... Charlotte
11-12 .... Rochester
13-14 .... at Ottawa
15-16-17-18 .. at Louisville
19-20-21-22 .. Indianapolis
24-25-26-27 ...... Durham
28-29-30 .. at Indianapolis

JULY
1 .... at Indianapolis
2-3 .... Syracuse
4 .... at Syracuse
5-6-7-8 .... at Charlotte
9-10-10-11 .... at Durham
15-16-17-18 ...... Scranton
19-20-21-22 .. Richmond
23-24-25 .... at Syracuse
27-28-29-30 .... Toledo
31 .... Ottawa

AUGUST
1 .... Ottawa
3-3-4 .... Syracuse
5-6 .... at Scranton
7-8 .... at Syracuse
9-10 .... at Rochester
11-12 .... Pawtucket
13-14-15 .... Ottawa
16-17-18-19 .. at Pawtucket
20-21-22 ...... at Scranton
23-24 .... Pawtucket
25-26 .... Rochester
27-28 .... at Syracuse
29-30-31 .... Syracuse

SEPTEMBER
2-3-4 .... at Ottawa
5-6 .... at Rochester

CHARLOTTE

APRIL
8-9 .... at Columbus
10-11-12-13 .. at Toledo
14-15 .... Columbus

16-17-18-19 .... Toledo
21-22-23 .... at Richmond
24-25 .... at Norfolk
26-27 .... Norfolk
28-29 .... Richmond
30 .... Louisville

MAY
1-2-3 .... Louisville
4-5-6-7 .. at Indianapolis
8-9-10-11 .... at Louisville
13-14-15-16 .. Pawtucket
17-18-19-20 .. at Scranton
21-22-23-24 .. at Pawtucket
25-26-27-28 .... Syracuse
29 ....Richmond
31 .... Richmond

JUNE
1-2 .... Richmond
3-4-5-6 .... at Syracuse
7-8-9-10 .... at Buffalo
11-12-13-14 .. Indianapolis
15-16-17-18 .... Ottawa
19-20-21-22 .. at Rochester
24-25-26-27 .. at Ottawa
28-29-30 .... Scranton

JULY
1 .... Scranton
2-3 .... at Durham
4 .... Durham
5-6-7-8 .... Buffalo
9-10-11-11 ...... Rochester
15-16-17-18 .. at Columbus
19-20 .... Indianapolis
21-22-23-24 .. at Norfolk
25-26 .... at Durham
27-28-29-30 .. Columbus
31 .... Durham

AUGUST
1 .... Durham
3-4 .... at Louisville
5-6 .... at Toledo
7-8 .... at Indianapolis
9-10 .... Louisville
11-12 .... Toledo
13-14 .... Durham
15-16 .... at Durham
17-18 .... at Norfolk
19-20 .... at Richmond
21-22-23-24 ...... Norfolk
26-27 .... at Durham
28-29 .... Richmond
30-31 .... Norfolk

SEPTEMBER
1-2-3 .... at Richmond
4-5-6 .... Durham

COLUMBUS

APRIL
8-9 .... Charlotte
10-10 .... Durham
12-13 .... Durham
14-15 .... at Charlotte
16-17-18-19 .. at Durham

21-22-23 .... Louisville
24-25 .... Indianapolis
26-27 .... Toledo
28-29 ....at Toledo
30 .... at Norfolk

MAY
1-2-3 .... at Norfolk
4-5-6-7 ..... at Richmond
8-9-10-11 .... Norfolk
13-14-15-16 ..... Buffalo
17-18-19-20 .... at Indy
21-22-23-24 ...... Ottawa
25-26-27-28 .... Scranton
29-30-31 .... at Ottawa

JUNE
1 .... at Ottawa
3-4-5-6 ...... at Buffalo
7-8-9-10 .... Rochester
11-12-13-14 .. at Richmond
15-16-17-18 .. at Rochester
19-20-21-22 .. at Syracuse
24-25 .... Toledo
26-27 .... at Toledo
28-29-30 .... Syracuse

JULY
1 .... Syracuse
2-2 .... Toledo
3 .... at Toledo
4-5-6-7 .... at Scranton
8-9-10-11 .... at Louisville
15-16-17-18 .... Charlotte
19-20-21-22 .. Pawtucket
23-24 .... at Durham
25-26 .... at Richmond
27-28-29-30 .. at Charlotte
31 .... at Pawtucket

AUGUST
1-2-3 .... at Pawtucket
5-6 .... Indianapolis
7-8 .... Durham
9-10 .... at Indianapolis
11-12 .... Indianapolis
13-14 .... Norfolk
15-16 .... Richmond
17-18 .... at Louisville
19-20 .... at Norfolk
21-22 .... Indianapolis
23-24-25 .... Louisville
26-27 ...... at Indianapolis
28-29 .... at Louisville
30-31 .... Louisville

SEPTEMBER
2-3 .... Toledo
4-5-6 .... at Toledo

DURHAM

APRIL
8-9 .... at Toledo
10-10 .... at Columbus
12-13 .... at Columbus
14-15 .... Toledo
16-17-18-19 .. Columbus
21-22-23 .... at Norfolk

24-25-26-27 .. at Richmond
28-29 .... Norfolk
30 .... Richmond

MAY
1-2-3 .... Richmond
4-5-6-7 .... Louisville
8-9-10-11 .. at Rochester
13-14-15-16 .. at Scranton
17-18-19-20 .. Pawtucket
21-22-23-24 .... at Indy
25-26-27-28 .. at Louisville
29-30-31 .... Syracuse

JUNE
1 .... Syracuse
3-4-5-6 .... Norfolk
7-8-9-10 .. at Syracuse
11-12-13-14 .. at Pawtucket
15-16-17-18 .. Indianapolis
19-20-21-22 .... Ottawa
24-25-26-27 .. at Buffalo
28-29-30 .... at Ottawa

JULY
1 .... at Ottawa
2-3 .... Charlotte
4 .... at Charlotte
5-6-7-8 .... Rochester
9-10-10-11 .... Buffalo
15-16-17-18 .... at Toledo
19-20 .... at Norfolk
21-22 .... Indianapolis
23-24 .... Columbus
25-26 .... Charlotte
27-28-29-30 .... Scranton
31 .... at Charlotte

AUGUST
1 .... at Charlotte
3-4 .... at Indianapolis
5-6 .... at Louisville
7-8 .... at Columbus
9-10 .... Richmond
11-12 .... Louisville
13-14 .... at Charlotte
15-16 .... Charlotte
17-18-19-20 .... Toledo
21-22-23-24 .. at Richmond
26-27 .... Charlotte
28-29 .... Norfolk
30-31 .... Richmond

SEPTEMBER
1-2-3 .... at Norfolk
4-5-6 .... at Charlotte

INDIANAPOLIS

APRIL
8-9 .... at Norfolk
10-11-12-13 .. at Richmond
15 .... Norfolk
16-17-18-19 .. Richmond
21-22-23 .... at Toledo
24-25 .... at Columbus
26-27 .... at Louisville
28-29 .... Louisville
30 .... Toledo

MAY
1-2-3 .... Toledo
4-5-6-7 .... Charlotte
8-9-10-11 .... at Ottawa
13-14-15-16 .. at Rochester
17-18-19-20 .. Columbus
21-22-23-24 ...... Durham
25-26-27-28 .. at Pawtucket
29-30-31 ...... at Scranton

JUNE
1 .... at Scranton
3-4-5-6 .... Rochester
7-8-9-10 .... Scranton
11-12-13-14 .. at Charlotte
15-16-17-18 .. at Durham
19-20-21-22 .. at Buffalo
24-25-26-27 ... Syracuse
28-29-30 .... Buffalo

JULY
1 .... Buffalo
2 .... at Louisville
3-4 .... Louisville
5-6-6-7 .... at Syracuse
8-9-10-11 .... Ottawa
15-16-17-18 .. Pawtucket
19-20 .... at Charlotte
21-22 .... at Durham
23-24 .... at Richmond
25-26-27-28 .. at Norfolk
29-29-30 .... Norfolk
31 .... at Toledo

AUGUST
1 .... at Toledo
3-4 .... Durham
5-6 .... at Columbus
7-8 .... Charlotte
9-10 .... Columbus
11-12 .... at Columbus
13-14 .... at Louisville
15-16 .... Norfolk
17-18 .... Richmond
19-20 .... Louisville
21-22 .... at Columbus
23-24-25 .... at Toledo
26-27 .... Columbus
28-29-30-31 ...... Toledo

SEPTEMBER
2 .... at Louisville
3-4 .... Louisville
5-6 .... at Louisville

LOUISVILLE
APRIL
8-9 .... at Richmond
10-11-12-13 .. at Norfolk
14-15 .... Richmond
16-17-18-19 ...... Norfolk
21-22-23 .... at Columbus
24-25 .... Toledo
26-27 .... Indianapolis
28-29 ...... at Indianapolis
30 .... at Charlotte

MAY
1-2-3 .... at Charlotte
4-5-6-7 .... at Durham
8-9-10-11 .... Charlotte
13-14-15-16 .... Toledo
17-18-19-20 .. at Buffalo

21-22-23-24 .. at Syracuse
25-26-27-28 ...... Durham
29-30-31 .... Pawtucket

JUNE
1 .... Pawtucket
3-4-5-6 .... at Scranton
7-8-9-10 .... at Pawtucket
11-12-13-14 ...... Buffalo
15-16-17-18 ...... Buffalo
19-20-21-22 .... at Toledo
24-25-26-27 .. Rochester
28-29-30 ..... at Richmond

JULY
1 .... at Richmond
2 .... Indianapolis
3-4 .... at Indianapolis
5-6-6-7 .... Ottawa
8-9-10-11 .... Columbus
15-16-17-18 .... Syracuse
19-20-21-22 ... at Toledo
23-24-25-26 .. at Rochester
27-28-29-30 .. Richmond
31 .... Norfolk

AUGUST
1 .... Norfolk
3-4 .... Charlotte
5-6 .... Durham
7-8 .... at Norfolk
9-10 .... at Charlotte
11-12 .... at Durham
13-14 .... Indianapolis
15-16 .... at Toledo
17-18 .... Columbus
19-20 ...... at Indianapolis
21-22 .... at Toledo
23-24-25 .... at Columbus
26-27 .... Toledo
28-29 .... Columbus
30-31 .... at Columbus

SEPTEMBER
2 .... Indianapolis
3-4 .... Indianapolis
5-6 .... Indianapolis

NORFOLK
APRIL
8-9 .... Indianapolis
10-11-12-13 .... Louisville
15 .... at Indianapolis
16-17-18-19 .. at Louisville
21-22-23 .... Durham
24-25 .... Charlotte
26-27 .... at Charlotte
28-29 .... at Durham
30 .... Columbus

MAY
1-2-3 .... Columbus
4-5-6-7 .... at Toledo
8-9-10-11 .. at Columbus
13-14-15-16 .... Syracuse
17-18-19-20 .. Rochester
21-22-23-24 .. at Buffalo
25-26-27-28 .. at Rochester
29-30-31 .... Buffalo

JUNE
1 .... Buffalo
3-4-5-6 .... at Durham
7-8-9-10 .... Ottawa

11-12-13-14 .... Toledo
15-16-17-18 .. at Syracuse
19-20-21-22 .. at Pawtucket
24-25-26-27 .... Scranton
28-29-30 .... Pawtucket

JULY
1 .... Pawtucket
2 .... Richmond
3-4-5 .... at Richmond
6-7 .... Richmond
8-9-10-11 .... at Scranton
15-16-17-18 .... at Ottawa
19-20 .... Durham
21-22-23-24 .... Charlotte
25-26-27-28 .. Indianapolis
29-29-30 .. at Indianapolis
31 .... at Louisville

AUGUST
1 .... at Louisville
2-3 .... at Toledo
4 .... Richmond
5 .... at Richmond
6 .... Richmond
7-8 .... Louisville
9-10 .... Toledo
11 .... at Richmond
13-14 .... at Columbus
15-16 ...... at Indianapolis
17-18 .... Charlotte
19-20 .... Columbus
21-22-23-24 .. at Charlotte
25-26 .... Richmond
27 .... Richmond
28-29 .... at Durham
30-31 .... at Charlotte

SEPTEMBER
1-2-3 .... Durham
4-5 .... Richmond
6 .... at Richmond

OTTAWA
APRIL
8-9-10-11 .... Scranton
12-13-14 .... Syracuse
16-17-18 .... at Buffalo
19-20-21-22 .. at Syracuse
23-24-25 .... Buffalo
26-27-28-29 .. Pawtucket
30 .... at Scranton

MAY
1-2-3 .... at Scranton
4-5-6-7 ...... at Pawtucket
8-9-10-11 .... Indianapolis
13-14-15-16 .... Richmond
17-18-19-20 ... at Toledo
21-22-23-24 .. at Columbus
25-26-27-28 .... Toledo
29-30-31 .... Columbus

JUNE
1 .... Columbus
3-4-5-6 ...... at Richmond
7-8-9-10 .... at Norfolk
11-12 .... Syracuse
13-14 .... Buffalo
15-16-17-18 .. at Charlotte
19-20-21-22 .. at Durham
24-25-26-27 .. Charlotte
28-29-30 .... Durham

JULY
1 .... Durham
2-3-4 .... at Rochester
5-6-6-7 .... at Louisville
8-9-10-11 .. at Indianapolis
15-16-17-18 ...... Norfolk
19-20-21-22 ... Louisville
23-24-25-26 .. at Pawtucket
28-29-30 .... Rochester
31 .... at Buffalo

AUGUST
1 .... at Buffalo
2-3-4 .... at Rochester
5-6 .... at Syracuse
7-8-9-10 .... Pawtucket
11-12 .... at Rochester
13-14-15 ...... at Buffalo
17-17 .... Rochester
18-19 .... Scranton
20-21-22 .... Syracuse
23-24-25-26 .. at Scranton
27-28-29 .... Rochester
31 .... Scranton

SEPTEMBER
1 .... Scranton
2-3-4 .... Buffalo
5-6 .... at Syracuse

PAWTUCKET
APRIL
8-9-10-10 .... Buffalo
12-13-14 .... at Rochester
15-16-17-18 .. at Syracuse
19-20-21 .... Rochester
23-24-25 .... Syracuse
26-27-28-29 .. at Ottawa
30 .... at Buffalo

MAY
1-2-3 .... at Buffalo
4-5-6-7 .... Ottawa
8-9-10-11 .... Scranton
13-14-15-16 .. at Charlotte
17-18-19-20 .. at Durham
21-22-23-24 .... Charlotte
25-26-27-28 .. Indianapolis
29-30-31 .... at Louisville

JUNE
1 .... at Louisville
3-4-5-6 .... at Toledo
7-8-9-10 .... Louisville
11-12-13-14 ...... Durham
15-16-17-17-18 .. at Scran.
19-20-21-22 ...... Norfolk
24-25-26-27 .. Richmond
28-29-30 .... at Norfolk

JULY
1 .... at Norfolk
2-3 .... Scranton
4-5-6-7 .... Toledo
8-9-10-11 .. at Richmond
15-16-17-18 .... at Indy
19-20-21-22 .. at Columbus
23-24-25-26 .... Ottawa
27-28-29-30 .. at Syracuse
31 .... Columbus

AUGUST
1-2-3 .... Columbus
5-6 .... Rochester

7-8-9-10 .... at Ottawa
11-12 .... at Buffalo
13-14-15 .... Syracuse
16-17-18-19 ...... Buffalo
20-21-22 .... at Rochester
23-24 .... at Buffalo
25-26 .... Syracuse
27-28-29 .... at Scranton
30-31 .... at Rochester

SEPTEMBER
2-3-4 .... Rochester
5-6 .... Scranton

RICHMOND
APRIL
8-9 .... Louisville
10-11-12-13 .. Indianapolis
14-15 .... at Louisville
16-17-18-19 .... at Indy
21-22-23 .... Charlotte
24-25-26-27 ...... Durham
28-29 .... at Charlotte
30 .... at Durham

MAY
1-2-3 .... at Durham
4-5-6-7 .... Columbus
8-9-10-11 .... Syracuse
13-14-15-16 ..... at Ottawa
17-18-19-20 .. at Syracuse
21-22-23-24 .. Rochester
25-26-27-28 ...... Buffalo
29 .... at Charlotte
31 .... at Charlotte

JUNE
1-2 .... at Charlotte
3-4-5-6 .... Ottawa
7-8-9-10 ...... at Toledo
11-12-13-14 .. at Columbus
15-16-17-18 .... Toledo
19-20-21-22 .. at Scranton
24-25-26-27 .. at Pawtucket
28-29-30 ...... Louisville

JULY
1 .... Louisville
2 .... at Norfolk
3-4-5 .... Norfolk
6-7 .... at Norfolk
8-9-10-11 ..... Pawtucket
15-16-17-18 .. at Rochester
19-20-21-22 .. at Buffalo
23-24 .... Indianapolis
25-26 .... Columbus
27-28-29-30 .. at Louisville
31 .... Scranton

AUGUST
1-2-3 .... Scranton
4 .... at Norfolk
5 .... Norfolk
6 .... at Norfolk
7-8 .... Toledo
9-10 .... at Durham
11 .... Norfolk
13-14 .... at Toledo
15-16 .... at Columbus
17-18 ...... at Indianapolis
19-20 .... Charlotte
21-22-23-24 ...... Durham
25-26 .... Norfolk

27 .... at Norfolk
28-29 .... at Charlotte
30-31 .... at Durham

SEPTEMBER
1-2-3 .... Charlotte
4-5 .... at Norfolk
6 .... Norfolk

ROCHESTER
APRIL
8-9 .... at Syracuse
10-11 .... Syracuse
12-13-14 ...... Pawtucket
15-16-17-18 .. at Scranton
19-20-21 .... at Pawtucket
23-24-25 .... Scranton
26-27-28-29 ...... Buffalo
30 .... at Syracuse

MAY
1-2-3 .... at Syracuse
4-5-6-7 .... at Buffalo
8-9-10-11 .... Durham
13-14-15-16 .. Indianapolis
17-18-19-20 .. at Norfolk
21-22-23-24 .. at Richmond
25-26-27-28 ...... Norfolk
29-30-31 .... Toledo

JUNE
1 .... Toledo
3-4-5-6 .. at Indianapolis
7-8-9-10 .... at Columbus
11-12 .... at Buffalo
13-14 .... Syracuse
15-16-17-18 .. Columbus
19-20-21-22 .... Charlotte
24-25-26-27 .. at Louisville
28-29-30 .... at Toledo

JULY
1 .... at Toledo
2-3-4 .... Ottawa
5-6-7-8 .... at Durham
9-10-11-11 .. at Charlotte
15-16-17-18 .. Richmond
19-20 .... Scranton
21-22 .... at Scranton
23-24-25-26 .. Louisville
28-29-30 .... at Ottawa
31 .... Syracuse

AUGUST
1 .... Syracuse
2-3-4 .... Ottawa
5-6 .... at Pawtucket
7-8 .... at Scranton
9-10 .... Buffalo
11-12 .... Ottawa
13-14-15 .... Scranton
17-17 .... at Ottawa
18-19 .... Syracuse
20-21-22 .... Pawtucket
23-24 .... at Syracuse
25-26 .... at Buffalo
27-28-29 .... Ottawa
30-31 .... Pawtucket

SEPTEMBER
2-3-4 .... at Pawtucket
5-6 .... Buffalo

SCRANTON/W-B
APRIL
8-9-10-11 .... at Ottawa
12-13-14 .... Buffalo
15-16-17-18 .. Rochester
19-20-21-22 .. at Buffalo
23-24-25 .... at Rochester
26-27-28-29 .... Syracuse
30 .... Ottawa

MAY
1-2-3 .... Ottawa
5-6-7 .... at Syracuse
8-9-10-11 .. at Pawtucket
13-14-15-16 .... Durham
17-18-19-20 ... Charlotte
21-22-22-23 .... at Toledo
25-26-27-28 .. at Columbus
29-30-31 .... Indianapolis

JUNE
1 .... Indianapolis
3-4-5-6 .... Louisville
7-8-9-10 .. at Indianapolis
11-12-13-14 .. at Louisville
15-16-17-17-18 ...... Paw.
19-20-21-22 .. Richmond
24-25-26-27 .. at Norfolk
28-29-30 ...... at Charlotte

JULY
1 .... at Charlotte
2-3 .... at Pawtucket
4-5-6-7 .... Columbus
8-9-10-11 ...... Norfolk
15-16-17-18 .. at Buffalo
19-20 .... at Rochester
21-22 .... Rochester
23-24-25-26 .. Toledo
27-28-29-30 .. at Durham
31 .... at Richmond

AUGUST
1-2-3 .... at Richmond
5-6 .... Buffalo
7-8 .... Rochester
9-10-11-12 ...... Syracuse
13-14-15 .... at Rochester
16-17 .... at Syracuse
18-19 .... at Ottawa
20-21-22 .... Buffalo
23-24-25-26 .. Ottawa
27-28-29 ...... Pawtucket
31 .... at Ottawa

SEPTEMBER
1 .... at Ottawa
2-3-4 .... at Syracuse
5-6 .... at Pawtucket

SYRACUSE
APRIL
8-9 .... Rochester
10-11 .... at Rochester
12-13-14 .... at Ottawa
15-16-17-18 .. Pawtucket
19-20-21-22 .... Ottawa
23-24-25 .... at Pawtucket
26-27-28-29 .. at Scranton
30 .... Rochester

MAY
1-2-3 .... Rochester

5-6-7 .... Scranton
8-9-10-11 .. at Richmond
13-14-15-16 .. at Norfolk
17-18-19-20 .. Richmond
21-22-23-24 .... Louisville
25-26-27-28 .. at Charlotte
29-30-31 ...... at Durham

JUNE
1 .... at Durham
3-4-5-6 .... Charlotte
7-8-9-10 .... Durham
11-12 .... at Rochester
13-14 .... at Rochester
15-16-17-18 ...... Norfolk
19-20-21-22 .. Columbus
24-25-26-27 ... at Indy
28-29-30 ..... at Columbus

JULY
1 .... at Columbus
2-3 .... at Buffalo
4 .... Buffalo
5-6-6-7 ...... Indianapolis
8-9-10-11 .... Toledo
15-16-17-18 .. at Louisville
19-20-21-22 .. at Toledo
23-24-25 .... Buffalo
27-28-29-30 .. Pawtucket
31 .... at Rochester

AUGUST
1 .... at Rochester
3-3-4 .... at Buffalo
5-6 .... Ottawa
7-8 .... Buffalo
9-10-11-12 .. at Scranton
13-14-15 .... at Pawtucket
16-17 .... Scranton
18-19 .... at Rochester
20-21-22 ..... at Ottawa
23-24 .... Rochester
25-26 ...... at Pawtucket
27-28 .... Buffalo
29-30-31 .... at Buffalo

SEPTEMBER
2-3-4 .... Scranton
5-6 .... Ottawa

TOLEDO
APRIL
8-9 .... Durham
10-11-12-13 .... Charlotte
14-15 .... at Durham
16-17-18-19 .. at Charlotte
21-22-23 .... Indianapolis
24-25 .... at Louisville
26-27 .... at Columbus
28-29 .... Columbus
30 .... at Indianapolis

MAY
1-2-3 .... at Indianapolis
4-5-6-7 .... Norfolk
8-9-10-11 .... Buffalo
13-14-15-16 .. at Louisville
17-18-19-20 .... Ottawa
21-22-22-23 .. at Scranton
25-26-27-28 .... at Ottawa
29-30-31 .... at Rochester

JUNE
1 .... at Rochester

3-4-5-6 .... Pawtucket	**JULY**	31 .... Indianapolis	15-16 .... Louisville

3-4-5-6 .... Pawtucket
7-8-9-10 .... Richmond
11-12-13-14 .. at Norfolk
15-16-17-18 .. at Richmond
19-20-21-22 .... Louisville
24-25 .... at Columbus
26-27 .... Columbus
28-29-30 .... Rochester

JULY
1 .... Rochester
2-2 .... at Columbus
3 .... Columbus
4-5-6-7 ...... at Pawtucket
8-9-10-11 .... at Syracuse
15-16-17-18 ...... Durham
19-20-21-22 .... Syracuse
23-24-25-26 .. at Scranton
27-28-29-30 .. at Buffalo

31 .... Indianapolis
AUGUST
1 .... Indianapolis
2-3 .... Norfolk
5-6 .... Charlotte
7-8 .... at Richmond
9-10 .... at Norfolk
11-12 .... at Charlotte
13-14 .... Richmond

15-16 .... Louisville
17-18-19-20 .. at Durham
21-22 .... Louisville
23-24-25 .... Indianapolis
26-27 .... at Louisville
28-29-30-31 .... at Indy
SEPTEMBER
2-3 .... at Columbus
4-5-6 .... Columbus

PACIFIC COAST LEAGUE

ALBUQUERQUE
APRIL
8-9-10-11 .... at Memphis
12-13-14-15 .... Nashville
16-17-18-19 .... Memphis
20-21-22-23 .. at Nashville
24-25-26-27 .. at Omaha
29-30 .... Iowa
MAY
1-2 .... Iowa
3-4-5-6 ... at Col. Springs
7-8-9-10 .... Omaha
11-12-13-14 .. at Salt Lake
15-16-17-18 ..at Edmonton
20-21-22-23 .. Las Vegas
24-25-26-27 ...... Tucson
28-29-30-31 .. at Memphis
JUNE
1-2-3-4 ...... New Orleans
5-6-7-8 ...... at Oklahoma
10-11-12-13 .... Nashville
14-15-16-17 ...... Iowa
18-19-20-21 .. at Nashville
22-23-24-25 .. Oklahoma
26-27-28-29 .. at New Orl.
JULY
1-2-3 .... Col. Springs
4-5-6-7 .... at Iowa
8-9-10-11 .... Memphis
15-16-17-18 .. at Oklahoma
19-20-21-22 .. New Orleans
23-24-25-26 ...... Omaha
27-28-29-30 .. at Portland
31 .... at Tacoma
AUGUST
1-2-3 .... at Tacoma
5-6-7-8 .... Sacramento
9-10-10-11 .... Fresno
13-14-15-16 ...... at Iowa
17-18-19-20 .. at Omaha
21-22-23-24 .. at Col. Spr.
25-26-27-28-29 .. Col. Spr.
30-31 .... at New Orleans
SEPTEMBER
1-2 .... at New Orleans
3-4-5-6 .... Oklahoma

COL. SPRINGS
APRIL
8-9-10-11 .... at Nashville
12-13-14-15 .. at Memphis
16-17-18-19 .... Nashville
20-21-22-23 .... Memphis
24-25-26-27 ...... at Iowa

29-30 .... at Omaha
MAY
1-2 .... at Omaha
3-4-5-6 ...... Albuquerque
7-8-9-10 .... Iowa
11-12-13-14 .. at Edmonton
15-16-17-18 .. at Salt Lake
20-21-22-23 ...... Tucson
24-25-26-27 .. Las Vegas
28-29-30-31 .. at Nashville
JUNE
1-2-3-4 .... at Memphis
5-6-7-8 .... Omaha
10-11-12-13 .. at New Orl.
14-15-16-17 .. Oklahoma
18-19-20-21 ...... at Iowa
22-23-24-25 .. Memphis
26-27-28-29 .... Nashville
JULY
1-2-3 ...... at Albuquerque
4-5-6-7 .... Omaha
8-9-10-11 ...... Oklahoma
15-16-17-18 .. at New Orl.
19-20-21-22 .. at Oklahoma
23-24-25-26 .... Iowa
27-28-29-30 .. at Tacoma
31 .... at Portland
AUGUST
1-2-3 .... at Portland
5-6-7-8 .... Fresno
9-10-10-11 .. Sacramento
13-14-15-16 .. at Omaha
17-18-19-20 .. New Orleans
21-22-23-24 .... Alb.
25-26-27-28-29 .. at Alb.
30-31 .... at Oklahoma
SEPTEMBER
1-2 .... at Oklahoma
3-4-5-6 ...... New Orleans

EDMONTON
APRIL
8-9-10-11 .... Sacramento
12-13-14-15 .... Fresno
16-17-18-19 .... at Sacra.
20-21-22-23 .... at Fresno
24-25-26-27 ...... Tacoma
29-30 .... Portland
MAY
1-2 .... Portland
3-4-5-6 .... at Tacoma
7-8-9-10 ...... at Portland
11-12-13-14 .. Col. Spr.
15-16-17-18 .. Albuquerque

20-21-22-23 .. at New Orl.
24-25-26-27 .. at Oklahoma
28-29-30-31 .. Sacramento
JUNE
1-2-3-4 ...... at Las Vegas
5-6-7-8 .... at Sacramento
10-11-12-13 .. Las Vegas
14-15-16-17 ...... Tucson
18-19-20-21 .. at Las Vegas
22-23-24-25 .. at Tucson
26-27-28-29 ...... Portland
30 .... Salt Lake
JULY
1-2 .... Salt Lake
4-5-6-7 .... at Portland
8-9-10-11 .... Tucson
15-16-17-18 .. at Salt Lake
19-20-21-22 .... Fresno
23-24-25-26 ...... Tacoma
27-28-29-30 .. at Nashville
31 .... at Nashville
AUGUST
1-2-3 .... at Nashville
5-6-7-8 .... at Iowa
9-10-10-11 .... Omaha
13-14-15-16 .. at Tacoma
17-18-19-20 .. at Salt Lake
21-22-23-24 .... at Tucson
25-26-27-28-29 .. Salt Lake
30-31 .... Las Vegas
SEPTEMBER
1-2 .... Las Vegas
3-4-5-6 .... at Fresno

FRESNO
APRIL
8-9-10-11 .... at Salt Lake
12-13-14-15 .. at Edmonton
16-17-18-19 .... Salt Lake
20-21-22-23 .. Edmonton
24-25-26-27 .. at Tucson
29-30 .... Las Vegas
MAY
1-2 .... Las Vegas
3-4-5-6 .... at Sacramento
7-8-9-10 .... Tucson
11-12-13-14 ...... at Iowa
15-16-17-18 .. at Omaha
20-21-22-23 .... Memphis
24-25-26-27 ...... Nashville
28-29-30-31 .. at Salt Lake
JUNE
1-2-3-4 .... at Portland
5-6-7-8 .... Salt Lake

10-11-12-13 .... Portland
14-15-16-17 ... at Sacra.
18-19-20-21 .. at Portland
22-23-24-25 ...... Tacoma
26-27-28-29 .. Las Vegas
JULY
1-2-3 .... at Las Vegas
4-5-6-7 .... Sacramento
8-9-10-11 ...... at Tacoma
15-16-17-18 ...... Tacoma
19-20-21-22 .. at Edmonton
23-24-25-26 .. at Tucson
27-28-29-30 .. Oklahoma
31 .... New Orleans
AUGUST
1-2-3 .... New Orleans
5-6-7-8 .... at Col. Springs
9-10-10-11 .... at Alb.
13-14-15-16 ...... Tucson
17-18-19-20 .. at Tacoma
21-22-23-24 .. Sacramento
25-26-27-28-29 ... at L.V.
30-31 .... Portland
SEPTEMBER
1-2 .... Portland
3-4-5-6 .... Edmonton

IOWA
APRIL
8-9-10-11 .. New Orleans
12-13-14-15 .. Oklahoma
16-17-18-19 .. at New Orl.
20-21-22-23 .. at Oklahoma
24-25-26-27 .. Col. Spr.
29-30 .... at Albuquerque
MAY
1-2 .... at Albuquerque
3-4-5-6 .... Omaha
7-8-9-10 .. at Col. Springs
11-12-13-14 .... Fresno
15-16-17-18 .. Sacramento
20-21-22-23 .. at Portland
24-25-26-27 .. at Tacoma
28-29-30-31 .. Oklahoma
JUNE
1-2-3-4 .... at Nashville
5-6-7-8 .... Memphis
10-11-12-13 .. at Oklahoma
14-15-16-17 .... at Alb.
18-19-20-21 .... Col. Spr.
22-23-24-25 .... Nashville
26-27-28-29 .. at Memphis
JULY
1-2-3 .... at Omaha

4-5-6-7 ...... Albuquerque
8-9-10-11 .. New Orleans
15-16-17-18 .. at Memphis
19-20-21-22 .. at Nashville
23-24-25-26 .. at Col. Spr.
27-28-29-30 ...... Tucson
31 .... Las Vegas

AUGUST
1-2-3 .... Las Vegas
5-6-7-8 .... Edmonton
9-10-10-11 .. at Salt Lake
13-14-15-16 .... Alb.
17-18-19-20 .. Nashville
21-22-23-24 .. at New Orl.
25-26-27-28-29 .. at Memphis
30-31 .... Memphis

SEPTEMBER
1-2 .... Memphis
3-4-5-6 .... Omaha

LAS VEGAS
APRIL
8-9-10-11 .... Portland
12-13-14-15 ...... Tacoma
16-17-18-19 .. at Portland
20-21-22-23 .. at Tacoma
24-25-26-27 .. Sacramento
29-30 .... at Fresno

MAY
1-2 .... at Fresno
3-4-5-6 .... Tucson
7-8-9-10 .. at Sacramento
11-12-13-14 .. New Orleans
15-16-17-18 .. Oklahoma
20-21-22-23 .... at Alb.
24-25-26-27 .. at Col. Spr.
28-29-30-31 ...... Tacoma

JUNE
1-2-3-4 .... Edmonton
5-6-7-8 .... at Tacoma
10-11-12-13 .. at Edmonton
14-15-16-17 .... Portland
18-19-20-21 .. Edmonton
22-23-24-25 .. at Salt Lake
26-27-28-29 .... at Fresno

JULY
1-2-3 .... Fresno
4-5-6-7 .... at Tucson
8-9-10-11 .... Salt Lake
15-16-17-18 .. at Portland
19-20-21-22 ...... Tucson
23-24-25-26 .. Sacramento
27-28-29-30 .. at Omaha
31 .... at Iowa

AUGUST
1-2-3 .... at Iowa
5-6-7-8 .... Memphis
9-10-10-11 ...... Nashville
13-14-15-16 .. at Sacra.
17-18-19-20 .. at Tucson
21-22-23-24 .. at Salt Lake
25-26-27-28-29 .. Fresno
30-31 .... at Edmonton

SEPTEMBER
1-2 .... at Edmonton
3-4-5-6 .... Salt Lake

MEMPHIS
APRIL
8-9-10-11 .. Albuquerque
12-13-14-15 .... Col. Spr.
16-17-18-19 .... at Alb.
20-21-22-23 .... at Col. Spr.
24-25-26-27 .. New Orleans
29-30 .... Oklahoma

MAY
1-2 .... Oklahoma
3-4-5-6 .... at Nashville
7-8-9-10 .. at New Orleans
11-12-13-14 .... Portland
15-16-17-18 ...... Tacoma
20-21-22-23 ..... at Fresno
24-25-26-27 .... at Sacra.
28-29-30-31 .... Alb.

JUNE
1-2-3-4 ...... Col. Springs
5-6-7-8 .... at Iowa
10-11-12-13 .. at Omaha
14-15-16-17 .. New Orleans
18-19-20-21 ...... Omaha
22-23-24-25 ... at Col. Spr.
26-27-28-29 .... Iowa

JULY
1-2-3 .... at Oklahoma
4-5-6-7 .... Nashville
8-9-10-11 .... at Alb.
15-16-17-18 .... Iowa
19-20-21-22 .. at Omaha
23-24-25-26 .. at New Orl.
27-28-29-30 .. Edmonton
31 .... Salt Lake

AUGUST
1-2-3 .... Salt Lake
5-6-7-8 ...... at Las Vegas
9-10-10-11 .... at Tucson
13-14-15-16 .. at Nashville
17-18-19-20 .. Oklahoma
21-22-23-24 ...... Omaha
25-26-27-28-29 .. at Okla.
30-31 .... at Iowa

SEPTEMBER
1-2 .... at Iowa
3-4-5-6 .... Nashville

NASHVILLE
APRIL
8-9-10-11 .. Col. Springs
12-13-14-15 .... at Alb.
16-17-18-19 .. at Col. Spr.
20-21-22-23 .... Alb.
24-25-26-27 .. Oklahoma
29-30 .... at New Orleans

MAY
1-2 ...... at New Orleans
3-4-5-6 .... Memphis
7-8-9-10 .... at Oklahoma
11-12-13-14 ...... Tacoma
15-16-17-18 .... Portland
20-21-22-23 .... at Sacra.
24-25-26-27 .... at Fresno
28-29-30-31 .... Col. Spr.

JUNE
1-2-3-4 .... Iowa
5-6-7-8 .. at New Orleans
10-11-12-13 .... at Alb.
14-15-16-17 ...... Omaha
18-19-20-21 .... at Alb.
22-23-24-25 ...... at Iowa
26-27-28-29 .. at Col. Spr.

JULY
1-2-3 .... New Orleans
4-5-6-7 ...... at Memphis
8-9-10-11 ...... Omaha
15-16-17-18 .. at Omaha
19-20-21-22 .... Iowa
23-24-25-26 .. at Oklahoma
27-28-29-30 .. Salt Lake
31 .... Edmonton

AUGUST
1-2-3 .... Edmonton
5-6-7-8 ...... at Tucson
9-10-10-11 .. at Las Vegas
13-14-15-16 .... Memphis
17-18-19-20 ...... at Iowa
21-22-23-24 ... Oklahoma
25-26-27-28-29 .. New Orl.
30-31 .... at Omaha

SEPTEMBER
1-2 .... at Omaha
3-4-5-6 .... at Memphis

NEW ORLEANS
APRIL
8-9-10-11 .... at Iowa
12-13-14-15 .. at Omaha
16-17-18-19 .... Iowa
20-21-22-23 ...... Omaha
24-25-26-27 .. at Memphis
29-30 .... Nashville

MAY
1-2 .... Nashville
3-4-5-6 ...... at Oklahoma
7-8-9-10 .... Memphis
11-12-13-14 .. at Las Vegas
15-16-17-18 .. at Tucson
20-21-22-23 .. Edmonton
24-25-26-27 .. Salt Lake
29-29-30-31 .. at Omaha

JUNE
1-2-3-4 .. at Albuquerque
5-6-7-8 .... Nashville
10-11-12-13 .. Col. Spr.
14-15-16-17 .. at Memphis
18-19-20-21 .. at Oklahoma
22-23-24-25 ...... Omaha
26-27-28-29 .... Alb.

JULY
1-2-3 .... at Nashville
4-5-6-7 .... Oklahoma
8-9-10-11 ...... at Iowa
15-16-17-18 .... Col. Spr.
19-20-21-22 .... at Alb.
23-24-25-26 .... Memphis
27-28-29-30 .. at Sacra.
31 .... at Fresno

AUGUST
1-2-3 .... Fresno
5-6-7-8 .... Portland
9-10-10-11 .... Tacoma
13-14-15-16 .. Oklahoma
17-18-19-20 .. at Col. Spr.

21-22-23-24 .... Iowa
25-26-27-28-29 .. at Nash.
30-31 .... Albuquerque

SEPTEMBER
1-2 .... Albuquerque
3-4-5-6 .... at Col. Springs

OKLAHOMA
APRIL
8-9-10-10 ...... at Omaha
12-13-14-15 ...... at Iowa
16-17-18-19 ...... Omaha
20-21-22-23 .... Iowa
24-25-26-27 .. at Nashville
29-30 .... at Memphis

MAY
1-2 .... at Memphis
3-4-5-6 ...... New Orleans
7-8-9-10 .... Nashville
11-12-13-14 .. at Las Vegas
15-16-17-18 .. at Tucson
20-21-22-23 .... Salt Lake
24-25-26-27 .. Edmonton
28-29-30-31 ...... at Iowa

JUNE
1-2-3-4 .... at Omaha
5-6-7-8 ...... Albuquerque
10-11-12-13 .... Iowa
14-15-16-17 .. at Col. Spr.
18-19-20-21 .. New Orleans
22-23-24-25 .... at Alb.
26-27-28-29 ...... Omaha

JULY
1-2-3 .... Memphis
4-5-6-7 .. at New Orleans
8-9-10-11 .... at Col. Spr.
15-16-17-18 .... Alb.
19-20-21-22 .... Col. Spr.
23-24-25-26 .. Nashville
27-28-29-30 .... at Fresno
31 .... at Sacramento

AUGUST
1-2-3 .... at Sacramento
5-6-7-8 .... Tacoma
9-10-10-11 ...... Portland
13-14-15-16 .. at New Orl.
17-18-19-20 .. at Memphis
21-22-23-24 .. at Nashville
25-26-27-28-29 .. Memphis
30-31 .... Col. Springs

SEPTEMBER
1-2 .... Col. Springs
3-4-5-6 .. at Albuquerque

OMAHA
APRIL
8-9-10-10 ...... Oklahoma
12-13-14-15 .. New Orleans
16-17-18-19 .. at New Orl.
20-21-22-23 .. at New Orl.
24-25-26-27 .... Alb.
29-30 .... Col. Springs

MAY
1-2 .... Col. Springs
3-4-5-6 .... at Iowa
7-8-9-10 .. at Albuquerque
11-12-13-14 .. Sacramento

15-16-17-18 .... Fresno
20-21-22-23 .. at Tacoma
24-25-26-27 .. at Portland
28-29-30-31 .. New Orleans

JUNE
1-2-3-4 .... Oklahoma
5-6-7-8 .. at Col. Springs
10-11-12-13 .... Memphis
14-15-16-17 .. at Nashville
18-19-20-21 .. at Memphis
22-23-24-25 .. at New Orl.
26-27-28-29 .. at Oklahoma

JULY
1-2-3 .... Iowa
4-5-6-7 .... at Col. Springs
8-9-10-11 .... at Nashville
15-16-17-18 .... Nashville
19-20-21-22 .... Memphis
23-24-25-26 .... at Alb.
27-28-29-30 .. Las Vegas
31 .... Tucson

AUGUST
1-2-3 .... Tucson
5-6-7-8 .... at Salt Lake
9-10-10-11 .. at Edmonton
13-14-15-16 .... Col. Spr.
17-18-19-20 .... Alb.
21-22-23-24 .. at Memphis
25-26-27-28-29 ...... Iowa
30-31 .... Nashville

SEPTEMBER
1-2 .... Nashville
3-4-5-6 .... at Iowa

PORTLAND
APRIL
8-9-10-11 .. at Las Vegas
12-13-14-15 .. at Tucson
16-17-18-19 .. Las Vegas
20-21-22-23 ...... Tucson
24-25-26-27 at Salt Lake
29-30 .... at Edmonton

MAY
1-2 .... at Edmonton
3-4-5-6 .... Salt Lake
7-8-9-10 .... Edmonton
11-12-13-14 .. at Memphis
15-16-17-18 .. at Nashville
19-20-21-22 .... Iowa
24-25-26-27 ...... Omaha
28-29-30-31 .. at Tucson

JUNE
1-2-3-4 .... Fresno
5-6-7-8 .... Tucson
10-11-12-13 .... at Fresno
14-15-16-17 .. at Las Vegas
18-19-20-21 .... Fresno
22-23-24-25 .. Sacramento
26-27-28-29 .. at Edmonton

JULY
1-2-3 .... at Tacoma
4-5-6-7 .... Edmonton
8-9-10-11 .. at Sacramento
15-16-17-18 .. Las Vegas
19-20-21-22 ...... Tacoma
23-24-25-26 .. at Salt Lake
27-28-29-30 .... Alb.

31 .... Col. Springs
AUGUST
1-2-3 .... Col. Springs
5-6-7-8 .. at New Orleans
9-10-10-11 .. at Oklahoma
13-14-15-16 .... Salt Lake
17-18-19-20 .... at Sacra.
21-22-23-24 ...... Tacoma
25-26-27-28-29 .. at Tac.
30-31 .... at Fresno

SEPTEMBER
1-2 .... at Fresno
3-4-5-6 .... Sacramento

SACRAMENTO
APRIL
8-9-10-11 .. at Edmonton
12-13-14-15 .. at Salt Lake
16-17-18-19 .. Edmonton
20-21-22-23 .... Salt Lake
24-25-26-27 .. at Las Vegas
29-30 .... at Tucson

MAY
1-2 .... at Tucson
3-4-5-6 .... Fresno
7-8-9-10 .... Las Vegas
11-12-13-14 .. at Omaha
15-16-17-18 ...... at Iowa
20-21-22-23 .... Nashville
24-25-26-27 .... Memphis
28-29-30-31 .. at Edmonton

JUNE
1-2-3-4 .... at Tacoma
5-6-7-8 .... Edmonton
10-11-12-13 .. at Salt Lake
14-15-16-17 .... Fresno
18-19-20-21 ...... Tacoma
22-23-24-25 .. at Portland
26-27-28-29 ...... Tacoma

JULY
1-2-3 .... Tucson
4-5-6-7 .... at Fresno
8-9-10-11 .... Portland
15-16-17-18 .. at Tucson
19-20-21-22 .... Salt Lake
23-24-25-26 .. at Las Vegas
27-28-29-30 .. New Orleans
31 .... Oklahoma

AUGUST
1-2-3 .... Oklahoma
5-6-7-8 .. at Albuquerque
9-10-10-11 .. at Col. Spr.
13-14-15-16 .. Las Vegas
17-18-19-20 .... Portland
21-22-23-24 .. at Tucson
25-26-27-28-29 .. Tucson
30-31 .... at Tacoma

SEPTEMBER
1-2 .... at Tacoma
3-4-5-6 .... at Portland

SALT LAKE
APRIL
8-9-10-11 .... Fresno
12-13-14-15 .. Sacramento
16-17-18-19 .... at Fresno
20-21-22-23 .... at Sacra.

24-25-26-27 .... Portland
29-30 .... Tacoma

MAY
1-2 .... Tacoma
3-4-5-6 .... at Portland
7-8-9-10 .... at Tacoma
11-12-13-14 .... Alb.
15-16-17-18 .... Col. Spr.
20-21-22-23 .. at Oklahoma
24-25-26-27 .. at New Orl.
28-29-30-31 .... Fresno

JUNE
1-2-3-4 .... at Tucson
5-6-7-8 .... at Fresno
10-11-12-13 .. Sacramento
14-15-16-17 .. at Tacoma
18-19-20-21 ...... Tucson
22-23-24-25 .. Las Vegas
26-27-28-29 .. at Tucson
30 .... at Edmonton

JULY
1-2 .... at Edmonton
4-5-6-7 .... Tacoma
8-9-10-11 .. at Las Vegas
15-16-17-18 .. Edmonton
19-20-21-22 .... at Sacra.
23-24-25-26 .... Portland
27-28-29-30 at Nashville
31 .... at Memphis

AUGUST
1-2-3 .... at Memphis
5-6-7-8 .... Omaha
9-10-10-11 .... Iowa
13-14-15-16 .. at Portland
17-18-19-20 .. Edmonton
21-22-23-24 .. Las Vegas
25-26-27-28-29 .. at Edmon.
30-31 .... Tucson

SEPTEMBER
1-2 .... Tucson
3-4-5-6 ...... at Las Vegas

TACOMA
APRIL
8-9-10-11 ...... at Tucson
12-13-14-15 .. at Las Vegas
16-17-18-19 ...... Tucson
20-21-22-23 .. Las Vegas
24-25-26-27 .. at Edmonton
29-30 .... at Salt Lake

MAY
1-2 .... at Salt Lake
3-4-5-6 .... Edmonton
7-8-9-10 .... Salt Lake
11-12-13-14 .. at Nashville
15-16-17-18 .. at Memphis
20-21-22-23 ...... Omaha
24-25-26-27 .... Iowa
28-29-30-31 .. at Las Vegas

JUNE
1-2-3-4 .... Sacramento
5-6-7-8 .... Las Vegas
10-11-12-13 .. at Tucson
14-15-16-17 .... Salt Lake
18-19-20-21 .... at Sacra.
22-23-24-25 .... at Fresno
26-27-28-29 .... at Sacra.

JULY
1-2-3 .... Portland
4-5-6-7 .... at Salt Lake
8-9-10-11 .... Fresno
15-16-17-18 .... at Fresno
19-20-21-22 .. at Portland
23-24-25-26 .. at Edmonton
27-28-29-30 .... Col. Spr.
31 .... Albuquerque

AUGUST
1-2-3 .... Albuquerque
5-6-7-8 .... at Oklahoma
9-10-10-11 .. at New Orl.
13-14-15-16 .. Edmonton
17-18-19-20 .... Fresno
21-22-23-24 .. Portland
25-26-27-28-29 .. Portland
30-31 .... Sacramento

SEPTEMBER
1-2 .... Sacramento
3-4-5-6 .... Tucson

TUCSON
APRIL
8-9-10-11 .... Tacoma
12-13-14-15 .... Portland
16-17-18-19 .. at Tacoma
20-21-22-23 .. at Portland
24-25-26-27 ...... Fresno
29-30 .... Sacramento

MAY
1-2 .... Sacramento
3-4-5-6 ...... at Las Vegas
7-8-9-10 .... at Fresno
11-12-13-14 .. Oklahoma
15-16-17-18 .. New Orleans
20-21-22-23 .. at Col. Spr.
24-25-26-27 ...... at Alb.
28-29-30-31 .... Portland

JUNE
1-2-3-4 .... Salt Lake
5-6-7-8 .... at Portland
10-11-12-13 .... Tacoma
14-15-16-17 .. at Edmonton
18-19-20-21 .. at Salt Lake
22-23-24-25 .. Edmonton
26-27-28-29 .. Salt Lake

JULY
1-2-3 ...... at Sacramento
4-5-6-7 .... Las Vegas
8-9-10-11 .. at Edmonton
15-16-17-18 .. Sacramento
19-20-21-22 .. at Las Vegas
23-24-25-26 .... Fresno
27-28-29-30 ...... at Iowa
31 .... at Omaha

AUGUST
1-2-3 .... at Omaha
5-6-7-8 .... Nashville
9-10-10-11 ...... Memphis
13-14-15-16 .... at Fresno
17-18-19-20 .. Las Vegas
21-22-23-24 .. Edmonton
25-26-27-28-29 .. at Sacra.
30-31 .... at Salt Lake

SEPTEMBER
1-2 .... at Salt Lake
3-4-5-6 .... at Tacoma

CLASS AA
EASTERN LEAGUE

AKRON

APRIL
8-9-10-11 .... Reading
12-13-14 ...... Harrisburg
15-16-17-18 .. at Reading
19-20-21 .. at Harrisburg
23-24-25 ...... New Britain
26-27-28 .... New Hamp.
29-30 .... at Trenton

MAY
1-2 .... at Trenton
3-4-5 ...... at New Hamp.
6-7-8-9 .... Portland
11-12-13 .... Bowie
14-15-16 .... at Altoona
17-18-19-20 .... at Bowie
21-22-23 .... Altoona
25-26-27 .... at Erie
28-29-30-31 .. at Harrisburg

JUNE
1-2-3 .... Erie
4-5-6 .... Altoona
7-8-9 .... at Reading
10-11-12-13 .. at Norwich
15-16-17 .... Binghamton
18-19-20 ...... Harrisburg
21-22-23-24 .. at Altoona
25-26-27 .... Bowie
28-29-30 .. at Binghamton

JULY
1-2-3-4 .... at Portland
6-7-8 .... Reading
9-10-11-12 .... at Erie
15-16-17-18 .... Erie
19-20-21-22 ...... Trenton
23-24-25 ...... at Reading
27-28-29 .... at Altoona
30-31 .... Reading

AUGUST
1 .... Reading
2-3-4-5 .... Altoona
6-7-8 .... at Bowie
9-10-11 .... at New Britain
13-14-15 .... at Erie
16-17-18 .... Erie
19-20-21-22 .... Norwich
24-25-26 .... at Bowie
27-28-29 .. at Harrisburg
30-31 .... Bowie

SEPTEMBER
1-2 .... Bowie
3-4-5-6 .... Harrisburg

ALTOONA

APRIL
8-9-10-11 .... Portland
12-13-14 .... Norwich
15-16-17-18 .... at H'burg
19-20-21 .... Bowie
23-24-25 .. at Binghamton

26-27-28 ...... at Norwich
29-30 .... Erie

MAY
1-2 .... Erie
3-4-5 .... Binghamton
6-7-8-9 .... at Bowie
10-11-12 .... at Erie
14-15-16 .... Akron
17-18-19-20 .. at Trenton
21-22-23 .... at Akron
25-26-27 .... Reading
28-29-30-31 .. New Britain

JUNE
1-2-3 .... at Bowie
4-5-6 .... at Akron
7-8-9 .... Harrisburg
10-11-12-13 .. at Reading
15-16-17 .. at Harrisburg
18-19-20 .... Erie
21-22-23-24 .... Akron
25-26-27 .... at Erie
28-29-30 ...... at Reading

JULY
1-2-3-4 .... Harrisburg
6-7-8 .... New Hampshire
9-10-11-12 .. at Portland
15-16-17-18 ...... Reading
19-20-21 .... Erie
23-24-25 .... at Bowie
27-28-29 .... Akron
30-31 .... Bowie

AUGUST
1 .... Bowie
2-3-4-5 .... at Akron
6-7-8 .... Harrisburg
10-11-12 at New Hamp.
13-14-15 ...... at Reading
16-17-18 .. at Harrisburg
19-20-21-22 .... Bowie
23-24-25-26 .... at Erie
27-28-29 .... Reading
30-31 .... Trenton

SEPTEMBER
1-2 .... Trenton
3-4-5-6 .... at New Britain

BINGHAMTON

APRIL
8-9-10-11 .... Norwich
12-13-14 .... Erie
15-16-17-18 .. at Portland
19-20-21 .. at New Britain
23-24-25 .... Altoona
26-27-28 .... Trenton
29-30 ...... at New Hamp.

MAY
1-2 .... at New Hampshire
3-4-5 .... at Altoona
6-7-8-9 .... New Britain
11-12-13 .... Norwich
14-15-16 .. at New Hamp.

17-18-19-20 .... at H'burg
21-22-23 .... New Hamp.
24-25-26 ...... at Portland
28-29-30-31 ...... Trenton

JUNE
1-2-3 .... Portland
4-5-6 .... at New Britain
7-8-9 .... Norwich
10-11-12-13 .... at Bowie
15-16-17 .... at Akron
18-19-20 .... Portland
21-22-23-24 .. at Norwich
25-26-27 .... at Trenton
28-29-30 .... Akron

JULY
1-2-3-4 .... at Reading
5-6-7 .... at Erie
9-10-11-12 .... Bowie
15-16-17-18 .. at New Brit.
19-20-21-22 .. New Hamp.
23-24-25 ...... New Britain
27-28-29 ...... at Portland
30-31 .... New Britain

AUGUST
1 .... New Britain
2-3-4-5 .... at Trenton
6-7-8 .... Trenton
9-10-11 ...... at Norwich
13-14-15 .. at New Hamp.
16-17-18 .... New Hamp.
19-20-21-22 .. Harrisburg
24-25-26 ...... at Norwich
27-28-29 .... at Trenton
30-31 .... Portland

SEPTEMBER
1-2 .... Portland
3-4-5-6 .... Reading

BOWIE

APRIL
8-9-10-11 ..... Harrisburg
12-13-14 .... Reading
15-16-17-18 .... at Erie
19-20-21 .... at Altoona
23-24-25 .... Portland
26-27-28 .... Harrisburg
29-30 .... at Harrisburg

MAY
1-2 .... at Harrisburg
3-4-5 .... Erie
6-7-8-9 .... Reading
11-12-13 .... at Akron
14-15-16 ...... at Trenton
17-18-19-20 .... Akron
21-22-23 .... Erie
25-26-27 .. at New Britain
28-29-30-31 .. at Reading

JUNE
1-2-3 .... Altoona
4-5-6 .... Reading
7-8-9 .... at Erie

17-18-19-20 .... at H'burg
21-22-23 .... New Hamp.
24-25-26 ...... at Portland
28-29-30-31 ...... Trenton

JUNE
1-2-3 .... Portland
4-5-6 .... at New Britain
7-8-9 .... Norwich
10-11-12-13 .... at Bowie
15-16-17 .... at Akron
18-19-20 .... Portland
21-22-23-24 .. at Norwich
25-26-27 .... at Trenton
28-29-30 .... Akron

JULY
1-2-3-4 .... at Reading
5-6-7 .... at Erie
9-10-11-12 .... Bowie
15-16-17-18 .. at New Brit.
19-20-21-22 .. New Hamp.
23-24-25 ...... New Britain
27-28-29 ...... at Portland
30-31 .... New Britain

AUGUST
1 .... New Britain
2-3-4-5 .... at Trenton
6-7-8 .... Trenton
9-10-11 ...... at Norwich
13-14-15 .. at New Hamp.
16-17-18 .... New Hamp.
19-20-21-22 .. Harrisburg
24-25-26 ...... at Norwich
27-28-29 .... at Trenton
30-31 .... Portland

SEPTEMBER
1-2 .... Portland
3-4-5-6 .... Reading

10-11-12-13 .. Binghamton
15-16-17 ...... at Portland
18-19-20 ...... at Reading
21-22-23-24 .. New Hamp.
25-26-27 .... at Akron
28-29-30 .... Trenton

JULY
1-2-3-4 .... Erie
6-7-8 .... at Harrisburg
9-10-11-12 .... at Bing.
15-16-17-18 .. at Norwich
19-20-21-22 ...... Reading
23-24-25 .... Altoona
27-28-29 .... at Erie
30-31 .... at Altoona

AUGUST
1 .... at Altoona
2-3-4-5 .... at New Hamp.
6-7-8 .... Akron
9-10-11 .... Harrisburg
13-14-15 .. at Harrisburg
16-17-18 ...... at Reading
19-20-21-22 .. at Altoona
24-25-26 .... Akron
27-28-29 ...... New Britain
30-31 .... at Akron

SEPTEMBER
1-2 .... at Akron
3-4-5-6 .... Norwich

ERIE

APRIL
8-9-10-11 ...... at Trenton
12-13-14 .. at Binghamton
15-16-17-18 .... Bowie
20-21 .... at Reading
23-24-25 .... New Hamp.
26-27-28 .... New Britain
29-30 .... at Altoona

MAY
1-2 .... at Altoona
3-4-5 .... at Bowie
6-7-8-9 .... Harrisburg
10-11-12 .... Altoona
14-15-16 .. at New Britain
17-18-19-20 .. at Norwich
21-22-23 .... at Bowie
25-26-27 .... Akron
28-29-30-31 .... Norwich

JUNE
1-2-3 .... at Akron
4-5-6 .... Harrisburg
7-8-9 .... Bowie
10-11-12-13 .... at H'burg
15-16-17 .... at Altoona
18-19-20 .... at Altoona
21-22-23-24 .... Portland
25-26-27 .... Altoona
28-29-30 .. at Harrisburg

JULY
1-2-3-4 .... at Bowie

5-6-7 .... Binghamton
9-10-11-12 .... Akron
15-16-17-18 .... at Akron
19-20-21 .... at Altoona
23-24-25 ...... Harrisburg
27-28-29 .... Bowie
30-31 .... at Harrisburg

AUGUST
1 .... at Harrisburg
2-3-4-5 .... at Portland
6-7-7-8 ...... at Reading
9-10-11 .... Reading
13-14-15 .... Akron
16-17-18 .... at Akron
19-20-21-22 ...... Reading
23-24-25-26 ...... Altoona
27-28-29 .. at New Hamp.
30-31 .... at Reading

SEPTEMBER
1-2 .... at Reading
3-4-5-6 .... Trenton

HARRISBURG

APRIL
8-9-10-11 .... at Bowie
12-13-14 .... at Akron
15-16-17-18 ...... Altoona
19-20-21 .... Akron
23-24-25 ..... at Norwich
26-27-28 .... at Bowie
29-30 .... Bowie

MAY
1-2 .... Bowie
3-4-5 .... Portland
6-7-8-9 .... at Erie
11-12-13 ...... at Reading
14-15-16 .... Norwich
17-18-19-20 .. Binghamton
21-22-23 ...... at Portland
25-26-27 .... at Trenton
28-29-30-31 .... Akron

JUNE
1-2-3 .... Trenton
4-5-6 .... at Erie
7-8-9 .... at Altoona
10-11-12-13 .... Erie
15-16-17 .... Altoona
18-19-20 .... at Akron
21-22-23-24 .. at Reading
25-26-27 .... Reading
28-29-30 .... Erie

JULY
1-2-3-4 .... at Altoona
6-7-8 .... Bowie
9-10-11-12 .. at New Hamp.
15-16-17-18 .. New Hamp.
19-20-21-22 .. at New Brit.
23-24-25 .... at Erie
27-28-29 .... Reading
30-31 .... Erie

AUGUST
1 .... Erie
2-3-4-5 .... Reading
6-7-8 .... at Altoona
9-10-11 .... at Bowie
13-14-15 .... Bowie

16-17-18 .... Altoona
19-20-21-22 ...... at Bing.
24-25-26 ...... at Reading
27-28-29 .... Akron
30-31 .... New Britain

SEPTEMBER
1-2 .... New Britain
3-4-5-6 .... at Akron

NEW BRITAIN

APRIL
8-9-10-11 .... New Hamp.
12-13-14 .... Portland
15-16-17-18 .. at Norwich
19-20-21 .... Binghamton
23-24-25 ...... at Akron
26-27-28 .... at Erie
29-30 .... Reading

MAY
1-2 .... Reading
3-4-5 .... Trenton
6-7-8-9 .. at Binghamton
11-12-13 ...... at Portland
14-15-16 .... Erie
17-18-19-20 .... Portland
21-22-23 ...... at Norwich
25-26-27 .... Bowie
28-29-30-31 .. at Altoona

JUNE
1-2-3 ...... at New Hamp.
4-5-6 .... Binghamton
7-8-9 ...... at New Hamp.
10-11-12-13 .. at Portland
15-16-17 .... Trenton
18-19-20 .... Norwich
21-22-23-24 .. at Trenton
25-26-27 .... Norwich
28-29-30 .. at New Hamp.

JULY
1 ...... at New Hampshire
2-3-4-5 .... Trenton
6-7-8 .... at Norwich
9-10-11-12 ... at Reading
15-16-17-18 .. Binghamton
19-20-21-22 .. Harrisburg
23-24-25 .. at Binghamton
27-28-29 ...... New Hamp.
30-31 .... at Binghamton

AUGUST
1 .... at Binghamton
2-3-4-5 .... Norwich
6-7-8 .... Portland
9-10-11 .... Akron
12-13-14 .... at Trenton
16-17-18 ...... at Portland
20-21-22 ...... New Hamp.
24-25-26 .... at Trenton
27-28-29 .... at Bowie
30-31 .... at Harrisburg

SEPTEMBER
1-2 .... at Harrisburg
3-4-5-6 .... Altoona

NEW HAMPSHIRE

APRIL
8-9-10-11 .. at New Britain

12-13-14 .... at Trenton
15-16-17-18 ..... Trenton
19-20-21 .... Norwich
23-24-25 .... at Erie
26-27-28 .... at Akron
29-30 .... Binghamton

MAY
1-2 .... Binghamton
3-4-5 .... Akron
6-7-8-9 .... at Reading
11-12-13 .... at Trenton
14-15-16 .... Binghamton
17-18-19-20 ...... Reading
21-22-23 .. at Binghamton
24-25-26 .... Norwich
28-29-30-31 .... Portland

JUNE
1-2-3 .... New Britain
4-5-6 .... at Portland
7-8-9 .... New Britain
10-11-12-13 .. at Trenton
15-16-17 ...... at Norwich
18-19-20 .... Trenton
21-22-23-24 ... at Bowie
25-26-27 .... Portland
28-29-30 ...... New Britain

JULY
1 .... New Britain
2-3-4-5 .... at Norwich
6-7-8 .... at Altoona
9-10-11-12 .... Harrisburg
15-16-17-18 .... at H'burg
19-20-21-22 ... at Bing.
23-24-25 .... Trenton
27-28-29 .. at New Britain
30-31 .... Portland

AUGUST
1 .... Portland
2-3-4-5 .... Bowie
6-7-8 .... at Norwich
10-11-12 .... Altoona
13-14-15 .... Binghamton
16-17-18 .. at Binghamton
20-21-22 .. at New Britain
24-25-26 ...... at Portland
27-28-29 .... Erie
30-31 .... Norwich

SEPTEMBER
1-2 .... Norwich
3-4-5-6 .... at Portland

NORWICH

APRIL
8-9-10-11 .. at Binghamton
12-13-14 .... at Altoona
15-16-17-18 .. New Britain
19-20-21 at New Hamp.
23-24-25 ...... Harrisburg
26-27-28 .... Altoona
29-30 .... at Portland

MAY
1-2 .... at Portland
3-4-5 .... Reading
6-7-8-9 .... Trenton
11-12-13 .. at Binghamton
14-15-16 .. at Harrisburg

17-18-19-20 .... Erie
21-22-23 ...... New Britain
24-25-26 .. at New Hamp.
28-29-30-31 .... at Erie

JUNE
1-2-3 .... at Reading
4-5-6 .... Trenton
7-8-9 ...... at Binghamton
10-11-12-13 .... Akron
15-16-17 ...... New Britain
18-19-20 .. at New Britain
21-22-23-24 .. Binghamton
25-26-27 .. at New Britain
28-29-30 ...... at Portland

JULY
1 .... New Britain
2-3-4-5 .... at Norwich
6-7-8 .... Altoona
9-10-11-12 .... Harrisburg
15-16-17-18 .... at H'burg
19-20-21-22 ... at Bing.
23-24-25 .... Trenton
27-28-29 .. at New Britain
30-31 .... at Trenton

AUGUST
1 .... at Trenton
2-3-4-5 .. at New Britain
6-7-8 .... New Hamp.
9-10-11 .... Binghamton
13-14-15 .... Portland
16-17-18 .... at Akron
19-20-21-22 .... at Akron
24-25-26 .... Binghamton
27-28-29 .... Portland
30-31 ...... at New Hamp.

SEPTEMBER
1-2 .... at New Hampshire
3-4-5-6 .... at Bowie

PORTLAND

APRIL
8-9-10-11 ...... at Altoona
12-13-14 .. at New Britain
15-16-17-18 .. Binghamton
19-20-21 .... Trenton
23-24-25 .... at Bowie
26-27-28 ...... at Reading
29-30 .... Norwich

MAY
1-2 .... Norwich
3-4-5 .... at Harrisburg
6-7-8-9 .... at Akron
11-12-13 ..... New Britain
14-15-16 .... Reading
17-18-19-20 .. at New Brit.
21-22-23 ..... Harrisburg
24-25-26 ...... Binghamton
28-29-30-31 ...... at N.H.

JUNE
1-2-3 ...... at Binghamton
4-5-6 .... New Hamp.
7-8-9 .... at New Britain
10-11-12-13 .. New Britain
15-16-17 .... Bowie
18-19-20 .. at Binghamton
21-22-23-24 .... at Erie
25-26-27 .. at New Hamp.

JULY
1-2-3-4 .... Akron
6-7-8 .... at Trenton
9-10-11-12 .... Altoona
15-16-17-18 .. at Trenton
19-20-21-22 .. at Norwich
23-24-25 .... Norwich
27-28-29 ...... Binghamton
30-31 .. at New Hampshire

AUGUST
1 ...... at New Hampshire
2-3-4-5 .... Erie
6-7-8 ..... at New Britain
9-10-11 .... Trenton
13-14-15 ...... at Norwich
16-17-18 ...... New Britain
19-20-21-22 ...... Trenton
24-25-26 .... New Hamp.
27-28-29 ...... at Norwich
30-31 ...... at Binghamton

SEPTEMBER
1-2 ...... at Binghamton
3-4-5-6 .... New Hamp.

READING
APRIL
8-9-10-11 .... at Akron
12-13-14 .... at Bowie
15-16-17-18 .... Akron
20-21 .... Erie
23-24-25 ...... at Trenton
26-27-28 .... Portland

29-30 ...... at New Britain

MAY
1-2 .... at New Britain
3-4-5 .... at Norwich
6-7-8-9 .... New Hamp.
11-12-13 ...... Harrisburg
14-15-16 ...... at Portland
17-18-19-20 .... at N.H.
21-22-23 .... Trenton
25-26-27 .... at Altoona
28-29-30-31 .... Bowie

JUNE
1-2-3 .... Norwich
4-5-6 .... at Bowie
7-8-9 .... Akron
10-11-12-13 ...... Altoona
15-16-17 .... at Erie
18-19-20 .... Bowie
21-22-23-24 .. Harrisburg
25-26-27 .. at Harrisburg
28-29-30 .... Altoona

JULY
1-2-3-4 ...... Binghamton
6-7-8 .... at Akron
9-10-11-12 .. New Britain
15-16-17-18 .. at Altoona
19-20-21-22 .... at Bowie
23-24-25 .... Akron
27-28-29 .. at Harrisburg
30-31 .... at Akron

AUGUST
1 .... at Akron

2-3-4-5 ...... at Harrisburg
6-7-7-8 .... Erie
9-10-11 .... at Erie
13-14-15 .... Altoona
16-17-18 .... Bowie
19-20-21-22 .... at Erie
24-25-26 .... Harrisburg
27-28-29 ...... at Altoona
30-31 .... Erie

SEPTEMBER
1-2 .... Erie
3-4-5-6 .. at Binghamton

TRENTON
APRIL
8-9-10-11 .... Erie
12-13-14 .... New Hamp.
15-16-17-18 ...... at N.H.
19-20-21 ...... at Portland
23-24-25 .... Reading
26-27-28 .. at Binghamton
29-30 .... Akron

MAY
1-2 .... Akron
3-4-5 .... at New Britain
6-7-8-9 .... at Norwich
11-12-13 .... New Hamp.
14-15-16 .... Bowie
17-18-19-20 ...... Altoona
21-22-23 ...... at Reading
25-26-27 ...... Harrisburg
28-29-30-31 ...... Bing.

JUNE
1-2-3 .... at Harrisburg
4-5-6 .... at Norwich
7-8-9 .... Portland
10-11-12-13 .. New Hamp.
15-16-17 .. at New Britain
18-19-20 .. at New Hamp.
21-22-23-24 .. Binghamton
25-26-27 .... Binghamton
28-29-30 .... at Bowie

JULY
2-3-4-5 .... at New Britain
6-7-8 .... Portland
9-10-11-12 ...... Norwich
15-16-17-18 .... Portland
19-20-21-22 .... at Akron
23-24-25 .. at New Hamp.
27-28-29 ...... New Britain
30-31 .... Norwich

AUGUST
1 .... Norwich
2-3-4-5 ...... Binghamton
6-7-8 ...... at Binghamton
9-10-11 ...... at Portland
12-13-14 ...... New Britain
16-17-18 ...... Portland
19-20-21-22 .. at Portland
24-25-26 .... New Britain
27-28-29 .... Binghamton
30-31 .... at Altoona

SEPTEMBER
1-2 .... at Altoona
3-4-5-6 .... at Erie

SOUTHERN LEAGUE

BIRMINGHAM
APRIL
8-9-10-11 ...... West Tenn
12-13-14 .. Montgomery
16-17-18 ...... at Carolina
19-20-21-22 ...... at Tenn.
23-24-25-26 .. Greenville
27-28-29-30 .. at W. Tenn

MAY
1-2-3-4 ...... Chattanooga
6-7-8-9 .... at Mobile
10-11-12-13 .... at Mont.
14-15-16-17 ...... Mobile
18-19-20-21 .. Huntsville
22-23-24-25 .. at Greenville
27-28-29-30 .... at J'ville

JUNE
1-1-2-3 .... West Tenn
4-5-6-7 ...... Montgomery
8-9-10-11 .. at Huntsville
12-13-14 .... at West Tenn
17-18-19-20 .. Huntsville
23-24-25 .. at Jacksonville
26-27-28 .. Montgomery
30 .... Tennessee

JULY
1-2-3 .... Tennessee
4-5-6-7 .... at Mobile
8-9-10-11 .. at Chattanooga

15-16-17-18 .. Jacksonville
19-20-21-22 .. at W. Tenn
23-24-25-26 .. Huntsville
27-28-29-30 .. Montgomery
31 .... at Huntsville

AUGUST
1-2-3 .... at Huntsville
5-6-7-8 .... West Tenn
9-10-11-12 .... Mobile
13-14-15-16 .... at Mont.
17-18-19-20 .... Carolina
21-22-23-24 .. at Huntsville
26-27-28-29 .... at Mobile
30-31 .... Chattanooga

SEPTEMBER
1-2 .... Chattanooga
3-4-5-6 .. at Montgomery

CAROLINA
APRIL
8-9-10-10 .... at Mobile
12-13-14 .... at Huntsville
16-17-18 .... Birmingham
19-20-21-22 .. Chattanooga
23-24-25-26 ...... at J'ville
27-28-29-30 .. at Greenville

MAY
1-2-3-4 .... Mobile
6-7-8-9 .... Greenville

10-11-12-13 .... at Chatt.
14-15-16-17 ...... at Tenn.
18-19-20-21 .. Chattanooga
22-23-24-25 .. Tennessee
27-28-29-30 .. at W. Tenn
31 .... at Tennessee

JUNE
1-2-3 .... at Tennessee
4-5-6-7 ...... Jacksonville
8-9-10-11 ...... Tennessee
12-13-14-15 ...... at J'ville
17-18-19-20 .. West Tenn
23-24-25 .. at Chattanooga
26-27-28-29 .... at J'ville
30 .... Chattanooga

JULY
1-2-3 .... Chattanooga
4-5-6 .... Jacksonville
8-9-10-11 .. at Montgomery
15-16-17-18 .. Tennessee
19-20-21-22 .. Greenville
23-24-25-26 .... at Chatt.
27-28-29-30 .. at Greenville
31 .... Montgomery

AUGUST
1-2-3 .... Montgomery
5-6-7-8 .... Huntsville
9-10-11-12 .. at W. Tenn
13-14-15-16 .. at W. Tenn
17-18-19-20 ...... at Birm.

21-22-23-24 .. Chattanooga
26-27-28-29 .. at Greenville
30-31 .... Tennessee

SEPTEMBER
1-2 .... Tennessee
3-4-5-6 ...... Jacksonville

CHATTANOOGA
APRIL
8-9-10-11 ...... Greenville
12-13-14 ...... Tennessee
16-17-18 .... at Greenville
19-20-21-22 .. at Carolina
23-24-25-26 .. West Tenn
27-28-29-30 .. Huntsville

MAY
1-2-3-4 .. at Birmingham
6-7-8-9 ...... at Tennessee
10-11-12-13 .... Carolina
14-15-16-17 ...... at J'ville
18-19-20-21 .. at Carolina
22-23-24-25 .. Montgomery
27-28-29-30 .. Tennessee
31 .... Mobile

JUNE
1-2-3 .... Mobile
4-5-6-7 ...... at Huntsville
8-9-10-11 .. Jacksonville
12-13-14-15 ... at Mobile

17-18-19-20 .. at Greenville
23-24-25 .... Carolina
26-27-28 .. at Tennessee
30 .... at Carolina

JULY
1-2-3 .... at Carolina
4-5-6-7 .... Greenville
8-9-10-11 .. Birmingham
15-16-17-18 .. at Greenville
19-20-21-22 ...... at J'ville
23-24-25-26 .... Greenville
27-28-29-30 .... Jacksonville
31 .... at Tennessee

AUGUST
1-2-3 .... at Tennessee
5-6-7-8 .. at Montgomery
9-10-11-12 .. at West Tenn
13-14-15-16 .. Greenville
17-18-19-20 .. Jacksonville
21-22-23-24 .. at Carolina
26-27-28-29 .. Tennessee
30-31 ..... at Birmingham

SEPTEMBER
1-2 .... at Birmingham
3-4-5-6 .... Huntsville

GREENVILLE

APRIL
8-9-10-11 .. at Chattanooga
12-13-14 .. at Jacksonville
16-17-18 .... Chattanooga
19-20-21-22 .. Jacksonville
23-24-25-26 ...... at Birm.
27-28-29-30 .... Carolina

MAY
1-2-3-4 .... Tennessee
6-7-8-9 .... at Carolina
10-11-12-13 .. Jacksonville
14-15-16-17 .. at Huntsville
18-19-20-21 .. Montgomery
22-23-24-25 .. Birmingham
27-28-29-30 .... at Mont.
31 .... at Jacksonville

JUNE
1-2-3 .. at Jacksonville
4-5-6-7 ...... at Tennessee
8-9-10-11 .... Mobile
12-13-14-15 .... at Mont.
17-18-19-20 .. Chattanooga
23-24-25 .. at West Tenn
26-27-28 .... Huntsville
30 .... Jacksonville

JULY
1-2-3 .... Jacksonville
4-5-6-7 .. at Chattanooga
8-9-10-11 .. at Tennessee
15-16-17-18 .. Chattanooga
19-20-21-22 .. at Carolina
23-24-24-26 .. Tennessee
27-28-29-30 ...... Carolina
31 .... at Jacksonville

AUGUST
1-2-3 .... at Jacksonville
5-6-7-8 .... at Mobile
9-10-11-12 .. Jacksonville
13-14-15-16 .... at Chatt.
17-18-19-20 .. Tennessee
21-22-23-24 ...... at Tenn.
26-27-28-29 ...... Carolina
30-31 ...... at Jacksonville

SEPTEMBER
1-2 .... at Jacksonville
3-4-5-6 .... West Tenn

HUNTSVILLE

APRIL
8-9-10-11 .. Montgomery
12-13-14 .... Carolina
16-17-18 .. at Montgomery
19-20-21-22 .. at W. Tenn
23-24-25-25 .. Tennessee
27-28-29-30 .... at Chatt.

MAY
1-2-3-4 .... West Tenn
6-7-8-9 .. at Jacksonville
10-11-12-13 .. at Mobile
14-15-16-17 .. Greenville
18-19-20-21 ...... at Birm.
22-23-24-25 .. Jacksonville
27-28-29-30 ...... Mobile
31 .... at Montgomery

JUNE
1-2-3 ...... at Montgomery
4-5-6-7 ...... Chattanooga
8-9-10-11 .. Birmingham
12-13-14-15 ...... at Tenn.
17-18-19-20 ...... at Birm.
23-24-25 .... Tennessee
26-27-28 .... at Greenville
30 .... Mobile

JULY
1-2-3 .... Mobile
4-5-6-7 .. at Montgomery
8-9-10-11 .... Mobile
15-16-17-18 .. Montgomery
19-20-21-22 .... at Mobile
23-24-25-26 ...... at Birm.
27-28-29-30 .. at W. Tenn
31 .... Birmingham

AUGUST
1-2-3 .... Birmingham
5-6-7-8 ...... at Carolina
9-10-11-12 .. Montgomery
13-14-15-16 .. at Mobile
17-18-19-20 .. West Tenn
21-22-23-24 .. Birmingham
26-27-28-29 .. Montgomery
30-31 .... Greenville

SEPTEMBER
1-2 .... Greenville
3-4-5-6 .... at Carolina

MOBILE

APRIL
8-9-10-10 .... Carolina
12-13-14 ...... West Tenn
16-17-18 .. at Tennessee
19-20-21-22 .... at Mont.
23-24-25-26 .. Montgomery
27-28-29-30 .... at J'ville

MAY
1-2-3-4 .... at Carolina
6-7-8-9 ...... Birmingham
10-11-12-13 .. Huntsville
14-15-16-17 .... at Birm.
18-19-20-21 .. Jacksonville
22-23-24-25 .. at W. Tenn
27-28-29-30 .. at Huntsville
31 .... at Chattanooga

JUNE
1-2-3 ...... at Chattanooga
4-5-6-7 .... West Tenn
8-9-10-11 .. at Greenville
12-13-14-15 .. Chattanooga
17-18-19-20 .. Montgomery
23-24-25 .. at Montgomery
26-27-28 ...... West Tenn

30 .... at Huntsville

JULY
1-2-3 .... at Huntsville
4-5-6-7 ...... Birmingham
8-9-10-11 .. at Huntsville
15-16-17-17 .. at W. Tenn
19-20-21-22 .. Huntsville
23-24-25-26 .. Jacksonville
27-28-29-30 .. Tennessee
31 .... at West Tenn

AUGUST
1-2-3 .... at West Tenn
5-6-7-8 .... Greenville
9-10-11-12 .... at Birm.
13-14-15-16 .. Greenville
17-18-19-20 .. Montgomery
21-22-23-24 ...... at J'ville
26-27-28-29 .. Birmingham
30-31 .... at Montgomery

SEPTEMBER
1-2 .... at Montgomery
3-4-5-6 ...... at Tennessee

MONTGOMERY

APRIL
8-9-10-11 .. at Huntsville
12-13-14 .. at Birmingham
16-17-18 .... Huntsville
19-20-21-22 .... at Mobile
23-24-25-26 .... at Mobile
27-28-29-30 .. Tennessee

MAY
1-2-3-4 ...... Jacksonville
6-7-8-9 ...... at West Tenn
10-11-12-13 .. Birmingham
14-15-16-17 .. West Tenn
18-19-20-21 .. at Greenville
22-23-24-25 .... at Chatt.
27-28-29-30 .. Greenville
31 .... Huntsville

JUNE
1-2-3 .... Huntsville
4-5-6-7 .. at Birmingham
8-9-10-11 .. at Huntsville
12-13-14-15 .. Greenville
17-18-19-20 .... at Mobile
23-24-25 .... Mobile
26-27-28 .. at Birmingham
30 .... at West Tenn

JULY
1-2-3 .... at West Tenn
4-5-6-7 .... Huntsville
8-9-10-11 .... Carolina
15-16-17-18 .. at Huntsville
19-20-21-22 ...... at Tenn.
23-24-25-26 .. West Tenn
27-28-29-30 ...... at Birm.
31 .... at Carolina

AUGUST
1-2-3 .... at Carolina
5-6-7-8 ...... Chattanooga
9-10-11-12 .. at Huntsville
13-14-15-16 .. Birmingham
17-18-19-20 .... at Mobile
21-22-23-24 .. West Tenn

JACKSONVILLE

APRIL
8-9-10-11 ...... Tennessee
12-13-14 .... Greenville
16-17-18 .. at West Tenn
19-20-21-22 .. at Greenville
23-24-25-26 ...... Carolina
27-28-29-30 .... Mobile

MAY
1-2-3-4 .. at Montgomery
6-7-8-9 .... Huntsville
10-11-12-13 .. at Greenville
14-15-16-17 .. Chattanooga
18-19-20-21 .... at Mobile
22-23-24-25 .. at Huntsville
27-28-29-30 .. Birmingham
31 .... Greenville

JUNE
1-2-3 .... Greenville
4-5-6-7 .... at Carolina
8-9-10-11 .. at Chattanooga
12-13-14-15 ...... Carolina
17-18-19-20 ...... at Tenn.
23-24-25 ...... Birmingham
26-27-28-29 ...... Carolina
30 .... at Greenville

JULY
1-2-3 .... at Carolina
4-5-6 .... at Carolina
8-9-10-11 ...... West Tenn
15-16-17-18 ...... at Birm.
19-20-21-22 .. Chattanooga
23-24-25-26 .. at Mobile
27-28-29-30 .... at Chatt.
31 .... Greenville

AUGUST
1-2-3 .... Greenville
5-6-7-8 .... Tennessee
9-10-11-12 .. at Greenville
13-14-15-16 ...... at Tenn.
17-18-19-20 ...... at Chatt.
21-22-23-24 .... Mobile
26-27-28-29 .. Montgomery
30-31 .... Greenville

SEPTEMBER
1-2 .... Greenville
3-4-5-6 .... at Carolina

TENNESSEE (continued)

26-27-28-29 ...... at J'ville
30-31 .... Mobile

SEPTEMBER
1-2 .... Mobile
3-4-5-6 ...... Birmingham

TENNESSEE

APRIL
8-9-10-11 .. at Jacksonville
12-13-14 .. at Chattanooga
16-17-18 .... Mobile
19-20-21-22 .. Birmingham
23-24-25-25 .. at Huntsville
27-28-29-30 .... at Mont.

MAY
1-2-3-4 .... at Carolina
6-7-8-9 ...... Chattanooga
10-11-12-13 .. at W. Tenn
14-15-16-17 ..... Carolina
18-19-20-21 .. West Tenn
22-23-24-25 .. at Carolina
27-28-29-30 .... at Chatt.
31 .... Carolina

JUNE
1-2-3 .... Carolina

4-5-6-7 .... Greenville
8-9-10-11 .... at Carolina
12-13-14-15 .. Huntsville
17-18-19-20 .. Jacksonville
23-24-25 .... at Huntsville
26-27-28 .... Chattanooga
30 .... at Birmingham

JULY
1-2-3 ...... at Birmingham
4-5-6-7 .... West Tenn
8-9-10-11 ..... Greenville
15-16-17-18 .. at Carolina
19-20-21-22 .. Montgomery
23-24-24-26 .. at Greenville
27-28-29-30 .... at Mobile
31 .... Chattanooga

AUGUST
1-2-3 .... Chattanooga
5-6-7-8 .. at Jacksonville
9-10-11-12 .... Carolina
13-14-15-16 .. Jacksonville
17-18-19-20 .. at Greenville
21-22-23-24 .. Greenville
26-27-28-29 .... at Chatt.
30-31 .... at Carolina

SEPTEMBER
1-2 .... at Carolina
3-4-5-6 .... Mobile

WEST TENN

APRIL
8-9-10-11 .. at Birmingham
12-13-14 ..... at Mobile
16-17-18 .... Jacksonville
19-20-21-22 .. Huntsville
23-24-25-26 .... at Chatt.
27-28-29-30 .. Birmingham

MAY
1-2-3-4 ...... at Huntsville
6-7-8-8 ...... Montgomery
10-11-12-13 .. Tennessee
14-15-16-17 .... at Mont.
18-19-20-21 .... at Tenn.
22-23-24-25 .... Mobile
27-28-29-30 ..... Carolina

JUNE
1-1-2-3 .. at Birmingham
4-5-6-7 .... at Mobile
8-9-10-11 .. Montgomery
12-13-14 .... Birmingham

17-18-19-20 .. at Carolina
23-24-25 .... Greenville
26-27-28 ..... at Mobile
30 .... Montgomery

JULY
1-2-3 .... Montgomery
4-5-6-7 ...... at Tennessee
8-9-10-11 .. at Jacksonville
15-16-17-17 .... Mobile
19-20-21-22 .. Birmingham
23-24-25-26 .... at Mont.
27-28-29-30 .. Huntsville
31 .... Mobile

AUGUST
1-2-3 .... Mobile
5-6-7-8 .. at Birmingham
9-10-11-12 .. Chattanooga
13-14-15-16 ...... Carolina
17-18-19-20 .. at Huntsville
21-22-23-24 .... at Mont.
26-27-28-29 .. Huntsville
30-31 .... at Huntsville

SEPTEMBER
1-2 .... at Huntsville
3-4-5-6 ...... at Greenville

TEXAS LEAGUE

ARKANSAS

APRIL
8-9-10-11-12-13 .. at Wich.
14-15-16-17 ...... at Tulsa
18-19-20-21 ...... Wichita
22-23-24-25 .... Tulsa
27-28-29-30 .. at Midland

MAY
1-2-3-4 .... at El Paso
6-7-8-9 .... Midland
10-11-12-13 ...... El Paso
14-15-16-17 ...... at Tulsa
18-19-20-21 .... Frisco
22-23-24-25 ...... Wichita
26-27-28-29 .... at Frisco
30-31 .... at Wichita

JUNE
1-2 .... at Wichita
4-5-6-7 ...... Round Rock
8-9-10-11 .. San Antonio
12-13-14-15 .. at R. Rock
16-17-18-19 .. at San Ant.
23-24-25-26 .. at Wichita
28-29-30 .... Round Rock

JULY
1 .... Round Rock
2-3-4-5 .. at San Antonio
6-7-8-9 .... at Tulsa
10-10-12-13 ...... Wichita
14-15-16-17 .... Frisco
18-19-20-21 .. at R. Rock
22-23-24-24 .. San Antonio
27-28-29-30 .... Frisco
31-31 .... Tulsa

AUGUST
2-3 .... Tulsa

5-6-7-8 .... at Frisco
9-10-11-12-13-14 .. Tulsa
16-17-18-19 .. at El Paso
20-21-22-23 .. at Midland
25-26-27-28 ...... El Paso
29-30-31 .... Midland

SEPTEMBER
1 .... Midland
2-3-4-5 .... at Frisco

EL PASO

APRIL
8-9-10-11-12-13 .. R. Rock
14-15-16-17 .. San Antonio
18-19-20-21 .. at R. Rock
22-23-24-25 .. at San Ant.
27-28-29-30 .... Frisco

MAY
1-2-3-4 .... Arkansas
6-7-8-9 .... at Frisco
10-11-12-13 .. at Arkansas
14-15-16-17 .. San Antonio
18-19-20-21 ...... Midland
22-23-24-25 .. at R. Rock
26-27-28-29 .. at Midland
30-31 .... Round Rock

JUNE
1-2 .... Round Rock
4-5-6-7 .... Tulsa
8-9-10-11 .... Wichita
12-13-14-15 ...... at Tulsa
16-17-18-19 .. at Wichita
23-24-25-26 .. at San Ant.
27-28-29-30 .... Tulsa

JULY
2-3-4-5 .... Wichita
6-7-8-9 .. at San Antonio

10-11-12-13 .. Round Rock
14-15-16-17 ...... Midland
18-19-20-21 ...... at Tulsa
22-23-24-25 .. at Wichita
27-28-29-30 .. at Midland
31 .... San Antonio

AUGUST
1-2-3 .... San Antonio
5-6-7-8 .... at Midland
9-10-11-12-13-14 .. at R. R.
16-17-18-19 .... Arkansas
20-21-22-23 .... Frisco
25-26-27-28 .. at Arkansas
29-30-31 .... at Frisco

SEPTEMBER
1 .... at Frisco
2-3-4-5 .... Midland

FRISCO

APRIL
8-9-10-11-12-13 .. at Tulsa
14-15-16-17 .. at Wichita
18-19-20-21 .... Tulsa
22-23-24-25 ...... Wichita
27-28-29-30 .. at El Paso

MAY
1-2-3-4 .... at Midland
6-7-8-9 .... El Paso
10-11-12-13 ...... Midland
14-15-16-17 .. at Wichita
18-19-20-21 .. at Arkansas
22-23-24-25 .... Tulsa
26-27-28-29 ...... Arkansas
31 .... at Tulsa

JUNE
1-2-3 .... at Tulsa
4-5-6-7 ...... San Antonio

8-9-10-11 .. Round Rock
12-13-14-15 .. at San Ant.
16-17-18-19 .. at R. Rock
23-24-25-26 ...... at Tulsa
28-29-30 .. San Antonio

JULY
1 .... San Antonio
2-3-4-5 ...... Round Rock
6-7-8-9 .... at Wichita
10-11-12-13 .... Tulsa
14-15-16-17 .. at Arkansas
18-19-20-21 .. at San Ant.
22-23-24-25 .. at R. Rock
27-28-29-30 .. at Arkansas
31 .... Wichita

AUGUST
1-2-3 .... Wichita
5-6-7-8 .... Arkansas
9-10-11-12-13-14 .. Wichita
16-17-18-19 .. at Midland
20-21-22-23 .. at El Paso
25-26-27-28 ...... Midland
29-30-31 .... El Paso

SEPTEMBER
1 .... El Paso
2-3-4-5 .... Arkansas

MIDLAND

APRIL
8-9-10-11-12-13 .. San Ant.
14-15-16-17 .. Round Rock
18-19-20-21 .. at San Ant.
22-23-24-25 .. at R. Rock
27-28-29-30 .... Arkansas

MAY
1-2-3-4 .... Frisco
6-7-8-9 .... at Arkansas

10-11-12-13 .... at Frisco
14-15-16-17 .. Round Rock
18-19-20-21 .. at El Paso
22-23-24-25 .. San Antonio
26-27-28-29 ...... El Paso
31 .... at San Antonio

JUNE
1-2-3 ..... at San Antonio
4-5-6-7 .... Wichita
8-9-10-11 .... Tulsa
12-13-14-15 .. at Wichita
16-17-18-19 ...... at Tulsa
23-24-25-26 .. at R. Rock
28-29-30 .... Wichita

JULY
1 .... Wichita
2-3-4-5 .... Tulsa
6-7-8-9 .. at Round Rock
10-11-12-13 .. San Antonio
14-15-16-17 .. at El Paso
18-19-20-21 .. at Wichita
22-23-24-25 ...... at Tulsa
27-28-29-30 ...... El Paso
31 .... Round Rock

AUGUST
1-2-3 .... Round Rock
5-6-7-8 .... El Paso
9-10-11-12-13-14 .. at S.A.
16-17-18-19 .... Frisco
20-21-22-23 .... Arkansas
25-26-27-28 .... at Frisco
29-30-31 .... at Arkansas

SEPTEMBER
1 .... at Arkansas
2-3-4-5 .... at El Paso

ROUND ROCK
APRIL
8-9-10-11-12-13 .. at E. P.
14-15-16-17 .. at Midland
18-19-20-21 ...... El Paso
22-23-24-25 ...... Midland
27-28-28 .... at Tulsa
30 .... at Tulsa

MAY
1-2-3-4 .... at Wichita
6-7-8-9 .... Tulsa
10-11-12-13 ...... Wichita
14-15-16-17 .. at Midland
18-19-20-21 .. at San Ant.
22-23-24-25 ...... El Paso
26-27-28-29 .. San Antonio
30-31 .... at El Paso

JUNE
1-2 .... at El Paso

4-5-6-7 .... at Arkansas
8-9-10-11 .... at Frisco
12-13-14-15 .... Arkansas
16-17-18-19 .... Frisco
23-24-25-26 ...... Midland
28-29-30 .... at Arkansas

JULY
1 .... at Arkansas
2-3-4-5 .... at Frisco
6-7-8-9 .... Midland
10-11-12-13 .. at El Paso
14-15-16-17 .. at San Ant.
18-19-20-21 .... Arkansas
22-23-24-25 .... Frisco
27-28-29-30 .. San Antonio
31 .... at Midland

AUGUST
1-2-3 .... at Midland
5-6-7-8 ...... San Antonio
9-10-11-12-13-14 .. El Paso
16-17-18-19 ...... at Tulsa
20-21-22-23 .. at Wichita
25-26-27-28 .... Tulsa
29-30-31 .... Wichita

SEPTEMBER
1 .... Wichita
2-3-4-5 .. at San Antonio

SAN ANTONIO
APRIL
8-9-10-11-12-13 .. at Mid.
14-15-16-17 .. at El Paso
18-19-20-21 ...... Midland
22-23-24-25 ...... El Paso
27-28-29-30 .. at Wichita

MAY
1-2-3-4 .... at Tulsa
6-7-8-9 .... Wichita
10-11-12-13 .... Tulsa
14-15-16-17 .. at El Paso
18-19-20-21 .. Round Rock
22-23-24-25 .. at Midland
26-27-28-29 .. at R. Rock
31 .... Midland

JUNE
1-2-3 .... Midland
4-5-6-7 .... at Frisco
8-9-10-11 .... at Arkansas
12-13-14-15 .... Frisco
16-17-18-19 .. Arkansas
23-24-25-26 ...... El Paso
28-29-30 .... at Frisco

JULY
1 .... at Frisco
2-3-4-5 .... Arkansas

6-7-8-9 .... El Paso
10-11-12-13 .. at Midland
14-15-16-17 .. Round Rock
18-19-20-21 .... Frisco
22-23-24-24 .. at Arkansas
27-28-29-30 .. at R. Rock
31 .... at El Paso

AUGUST
1-2-3 .... at El Paso
5-6-7-8 .. at Round Rock
9-10-11-12-13-14 .. Mid.
16-17-18-19 .. at Wichita
20-21-22-23 ...... at Tulsa
25-26-27-28 ...... Wichita
29-30-31 .... Tulsa

SEPTEMBER
1 .... Tulsa
2-3-4-5 ...... Round Rock

TULSA
APRIL
8-9-10-11-12-13 .. Frisco
14-15-16-17 .... Arkansas
18-19-20-21 .... at Frisco
22-23-24-25 .. at Arkansas
27-28-28-30 .. Round Rock

MAY
1-2-3-4 ...... San Antonio
6-7-8-9 .. at Round Rock
10-11-12-13 .. at San Ant.
14-15-16-17 .... Arkansas
18-19-20-21 ...... Wichita
22-23-24-25 .... at Frisco
26-27-28-29 .. at Wichita
31 .... Frisco

JUNE
1-2-3 .... Frisco
4-5-6-7 .... at El Paso
8-9-10-11 ...... at Midland
12-13-14-15 ...... El Paso
16-17-18-19 ...... Midland
23-24-25-26 .... Frisco
28-29-30 .... at El Paso

JULY
2-3-4-5 .... at Midland
6-7-8-9 .... Arkansas
10-11-12-13 .... at Frisco
14-15-16-17 ...... Wichita
18-19-20-21 ...... El Paso
22-23-24-25 ...... Midland
27-28-29-30 .. at Wichita
31-31 .... at Arkansas

AUGUST
2-3 .... at Arkansas
5-6-7-8 .... Wichita

9-10-11-12-13-14 .. at Ark.
16-17-18-19 .. Round Rock
20-21-22-23 .. San Antonio
25-26-27-28 .. at R. Rock
29-30-31 .. at San Antonio

SEPTEMBER
1 .... at San Antonio
2-3-4-5 .... at Wichita

WICHITA
APRIL
8-9-10-11-12-13 .. Arkan.
14-15-16-17 .... Frisco
18-19-20-21 .. at Arkansas
22-23-24-25 .... at Frisco
27-28-29-30 .. San Antonio

MAY
1-2-3-4 ...... Round Rock
6-7-8-9 .. at San Antonio
10-11-12-13 .. at R. Rock
14-15-16-17 .... Frisco
18-19-20-21 ...... at Tulsa
22-23-24-25 .. at Arkansas
26-27-28-29 .... Tulsa
30-31 .... Arkansas

JUNE
1-2 .... Arkansas
4-5-6-7 .... at Midland
8-9-10-11 ...... at El Paso
12-13-14-15 ...... Midland
16-17-18-19 ...... El Paso
23-24-25-26 .... Arkansas
28-29-30 ...... at Midland

JULY
1 .... at Midland
2-3-4-5 .... at El Paso
6-7-8-9 .... Frisco
10-10-12-13 .. at Arkansas
14-15-16-17 ...... at Tulsa
18-19-20-21 ...... Midland
22-23-24-25 ...... El Paso
27-28-29-30 .... Tulsa
31 .... at Frisco

AUGUST
1-2-3 .... at Frisco
5-6-7-8 .... at Tulsa
9-10-11-12-13-14 .. at Fris.
16-17-18-19 .. San Antonio
20-21-22-23 .. Round Rock
25-26-27-28 .. at San Ant.
29-30-31 .. at Round Rock

SEPTEMBER
1 .... at Round Rock
2-3-4-5 .... Tulsa

CLASS A
CALIFORNIA LEAGUE

BAKERSFIELD
APRIL
9-10-11 .... Rancho Cuca.
13-14-15 .... at I.E.
16-17-18 .. at High Desert
19-20-21-22 .... Stockton
23-24-25 .. Lake Elsinore
27-28-29 ...... at Stockton
30 .... Modesto
MAY
1-2 .... Modesto
3-4-5-6 .... at San Jose
7-8-9-10 .... at Visalia
11-12-13 .... Stockton
14-15-16-17 .... Modesto
18-19-20 .... at San Jose
21-22-23-24 .. at Modesto
25-26-27 .... San Jose
28-29-30 .... at Visalia
31 .... Visalia
JUNE
1-2-3 .... Visalia
4-5-6 .... at Modesto
8-9-10 .... San Jose
11-12-13 .... Visalia
14-15-16-17 .. at Stockton
18-19-20 .... Lancaster
21-22-23 .... Modesto
24-25-26-26 .. at Stockton
JULY
1-2-3 .... Stockton
4 .... at Lancaster
6-7 .... at Lancaster
8-9-10-11 .... San Jose
13-14-15 .... High Desert
16-17-18 ...... at Modesto
19-20-21 .... San Jose
22-23-24-25 .. at Modesto
26-27-28-29 .. at San Jose
30-31 .... Modesto
AUGUST
1-2 .... Modesto
3-4-5 .... at Lake Elsinore
6-7-8 .... at Rancho Cuca.
10-11-12 .... at San Jose
13-14-15 .... at Visalia
17-18-19 .. Inland Empire
20-21-22-23 .... Stockton
24-25-26 .... Visalia
27-28-29 .... at Visalia
31 .... at Stockton
SEPTEMBER
1-2 .... at Stockton
3-4-5-6 .... Visalia

HIGH DESERT
APRIL
8-9-10-11 .. at Lancaster
12-13-14-15 .... R.C.
16-17-18 ...... Bakersfield
19-20-21-22 .... at R.C.
23-24-25 .. Rancho Cuca.
27-28-29 .... at L.E.

30 .... Lancaster
MAY
1-2 .... Lancaster
3-4-5-6 .... Lake Elsinore
7-8-9 .... at Lancaster
10-11-12-13 .... at I.E.
14-15-16 .. Lake Elsinore
18-19-20 .. Inland Empire
21-22-23-24 .... at L.E.
25-26-27 .... Stockton
28-29-30 .... at I.E.
JUNE
1-2-3 .... at Modesto
4-5-6 .... at Visalia
7-8-9-10 .... Lancaster
11-12-13 .... at I.E.
15-16-17 .. at Rancho Cuca.
18-19-20 .... San Jose
21-22-23 .... at R.C.
24-25-26 .. Inland Empire
JULY
1-2-3 .... at San Jose
4 .... Rancho Cucamonga
5-6-7-8 .. at Rancho Cuca.
9-10-11 .. Lake Elsinore
13-14-15 ... at Bakersfield
16-17-18 ...... at Stockton
19-20-21-22 .. Lancaster
23-24-25 .. Inland Empire
26-27-28-29 .... at I.E.
30-31 ..... Rancho Cuca.
AUGUST
1 .... Rancho Cucamonga
3-4-5 .... Visalia
6-7-8 .... at Lancaster
10-11-12 .... Modesto
13-14-15-16 .... I.E.
17-18-19 .... at L.E.
20-21-22 .... Lancaster
23-24-25-26 .. Lake Elsi.
27-28-29 .... at L.E.
31 .. Rancho Cucamonga
SEPTEMBER
1-2 .. Rancho Cucamonga
3-4-5-6 ...... at Lancaster

INLAND EMPIRE
APRIL
8 .... Lake Elsinore
9-10-11 .. at Lake Elsinore
13-14-15 ...... Bakersfield
16-17-18 .. Lake Elsinore
19-20-21-22 .. at Lancaster
23-24-25-26 .. Lancaster
27-28-29 .... at Visalia
30 .. at Rancho Cucamonga
MAY
1-2-3 .... at Rancho Cuca.
4-5-6 .... at Stockton
7-8-9 .... at San Jose
10-11-12-13 .. High Desert
14-15-16 .... at R.C.
18-19-20 .. at High Desert

21-22-23 .... Lancaster
25-26-27 .... at L.E.
28-29-30 .... High Desert
31 .. Rancho Cucamonga
JUNE
1-2-3 .... Rancho Cuca.
4-5-6 .... at Lancaster
8-9-10 .... Modesto
11-12-13 .... High Desert
14-15-16 .. Lake Elsinore
17 .... at Lake Elsinore
18-19-20 .. Rancho Cuca.
21-22-23 .... at L.E.
24-25-26 .. at High Desert
JULY
1-2-3 .... at Rancho Cuca.
4-5-6-7 .... Lake Elsinore
8-9-10-11 ...... Lancaster
12-13-14-15 .... at L.E.
16-17-18 .... at Lancaster
20-21-22 .. Lake Elsinore
23-24-25 .. at High Desert
26-27-28-29 .. High Desert
30-31 .... Stockton
AUGUST
1 .... Stockton
2-3-4-5 .. at Rancho Cuca.
6-7-8 .... Visalia
10-11-12 .... Lancaster
13-14-15-16 .... at H.D.
17-18-19 .. at Bakersfield
20-21-22 ...... at Modesto
24-25 ...... Rancho Cuca.
27-28-29 .... San Jose
30-31 .... at Lancaster
SEPTEMBER
1-2 .... at Lancaster
3-4-5-6 .... Rancho Cuca.

LAKE ELSINORE
APRIL
8 .... at Inland Empire
9-10-11 .... Inland Empire
12-13-14-15 .. at Lancaster
16-17-18 .... at I.E.
20-21-22 .... at Visalia
23-24-25 .. at Bakersfield
27-28-29 .... High Desert
30 .... San Jose
MAY
1-2 .... San Jose
3-4-5-6 .... at High Desert
7-8-9 .... Rancho Cuca.
11-12-13 .... Lancaster
14-15-16 .. at High Desert
18-19-20 .... at I.E.
21-22-23-24 .. High Desert
25-26-27 .. Inland Empire
28-29-30 .... at R.C.
31 .... Lancaster
JUNE
1-2-3 .... Lancaster
4-5-6 .... at Rancho Cuca.

21-22-23 .... Lancaster
25-26-27 .... at L.E.
28-29-30 .... High Desert
31 .. Rancho Cucamonga
JUNE
1-2-3 .... Rancho Cuca.
4-5-6 .... at Lancaster
8-9-10 .... Modesto
11-12-13 .... High Desert
14-15-16 .. Lake Elsinore
17 .... at Lake Elsinore
18-19-20 .. Rancho Cuca.
21-22-23 .... at L.E.
24-25-26 .. at High Desert
JULY
1-2-3 .... at Rancho Cuca.
4-5-6-7 .... Lake Elsinore
8-9-10-11 ...... Lancaster
12-13-14-15 .... at L.E.
16-17-18 .... at Lancaster
20-21-22 .. Lake Elsinore
23-24-25 .. at High Desert
26-27-28-29 .. High Desert
30-31 .... Stockton
AUGUST
1 .... Stockton
2-3-4-5 .. at Rancho Cuca.
6-7-8 .... Visalia
10-11-12 .... Lancaster
13-14-15-16 .... at H.D.
17-18-19 .. at Bakersfield
20-21-22 ...... at Modesto
24-25 ...... Rancho Cuca.
27-28-29 .... San Jose
30-31 .... at Lancaster
SEPTEMBER
1-2 .... at Lancaster
3-4-5-6 .... Rancho Cuca.

7-8-9-10 .. Rancho Cuca.
11-12-13 ...... at Modesto
14-15-16 .... at I.E.
17 .... Inland Empire
18-19-20 .... Stockton
21-22-23 .. Inland Empire
24-25-26 .... at Lancaster
JULY
1-2-3 .... Lancaster
4-5-6-7 .. at Inland Empire
9-10-11 .. at High Desert
12-13-14-15 .... I.E.
16-17-18 .... at R.C.
20-21-22 .... at I.E.
23-24-25 .... Visalia
27-28-29 .... at Lancaster
30-31 .... Lancaster
AUGUST
1-2 .... Lancaster
3-4-5 .... Bakersfield
6-7-8 .... Modesto
10-11-12 .. Rancho Cuca.
13-14-15-16 .... at R.C.
17-18-19 .... High Desert
20-21-21-22 .... R.C.
23-24-25-26 .. at High Des.
27-28-29 .... High Desert
31 .... at San Jose
SEPTEMBER
1-2 .... at San Jose
3-4-5-6 .... at Stockton

LANCASTER
APRIL
8-9-10-11 .... High Desert
12-13-14-15 .. Lake Elsi.
16-17-18 .... at R.C.
19-20-21-22 .... I.E.
23-24-25-26 .... at I.E.
27-28-29 ...... at Modesto
30 .... at High Desert
MAY
4-5-6 .... Rancho Cuca.
7-8-9 .... High Desert
11-12-13 .. at Lake Elsi.
14-15-16 .... Visalia
18-19-20 .. Lake Elsinore
21-22-23 .... at I.E.
24-25-26-27 .... R.C.
28-29-30 .... Stockton
31 .... at Lake Elsinore
JUNE
1-2-3 ...... at Lake Elsinore
4-5-6 .... Inland Empire
7-8-9-10 .. at High Desert
11-12-13 .... at R.C.
15-16-17 .... at San Jose
18-19-20 .. at Bakersfield
21-22-23 .... at Visalia
24-25-26 .. Lake Elsinore
JULY
1-2-3 ...... at Lake Elsinore
4 .... Bakersfield

BASEBALL AMERICA 2004 DIRECTORY • 237

6-7 .... Bakersfield
8-9-10-11 .... at I.E.
13-14-15 .. Rancho Cuca.
16-17-18 .. Inland Empire
19-20-21-22 .... at H.D.
23-24-25-26 .... R.C.
27-28-29 .. Lake Elsinore
30-31 .... at Lake Elsinore

AUGUST
1-2 .... at Lake Elsinore
3-4-5 .... at Stockton
6-7-8 .... High Desert
10-11-12 .... at I.E.
13-14-15 .... Modesto
17-18-19 .... at R.C.
20-21-22 .. at High Desert
23-24-25 .... San Jose
26-27-28-29 .... at R.C.
30-31 ...... Inland Empire

SEPTEMBER
1-2 .... Inland Empire
3-4-5-6 .... High Desert

MODESTO
APRIL
9-10-11 .... at Stockton
12-13-14-15 .... San Jose
16-17-18 .... Stockton
19-20-21-22 .. at San Jose
23-24-25-26 .... Stockton
27-28-29 .... Lancaster
30 .... at Bakersfield

MAY
1-2 .... at Bakersfield
4-5-6 .... Visalia
7-8-8-9 .... at Stockton
11 .... San Jose
12 .... at San Jose
13 .... San Jose
14-15-16-17 .... at B'field
18-19-20 .. Rancho Cuca.
21-22-23-24 .. Bakersfield
25-26-27 .... at Visalia
28 .... at San Jose
29 .... San Jose
30 .... at San Jose

JUNE
1-2-3 .... High Desert
4-5-6 .... Bakersfield
8-9-10 .. at Inland Empire
11-12-13 .. Lake Elsinore
14-15-16-17 .... at Visalia
18-19-20 .... Visalia
21-22-23 .. at Bakersfield
24-25-26 .... Visalia

JULY
1-2-3 .... at Visalia
4-5-6-7 .... San Jose
9-10-11 .... at Stockton
12 .... at San Jose
14-15 .... at San Jose
16-17-18 ...... Bakersfield
19-20-21 .... at R.C.
22-23-24-25 .. Bakersfield
26-27-28-29 .. at Visalia
30-31 .... at Bakersfield

AUGUST
1-2 .... at Bakersfield
3-4-5 .... San Jose

6-7-8 .... at Lake Elsinore
10-11-12 .. at High Desert
13-14-15 .... at Lancaster
17-18-19-19 .... Stockton
20-21-22 .. Inland Empire
24-25-26 ...... at Stockton
27-28-29 .... Stockton
30-31 .... Visalia

SEPTEMBER
1-2 .... Visalia
3-4-5-6 ...... at San Jose

RANCHO CUCAMONGA
APRIL
9-10-11 .... at Bakersfield
12-13-14-15 .... at H.D.
16-17-18 .... Lancaster
19-20-21-22 .. High Desert
23-24-25 .. at High Desert
26-27-28-29 .... San Jose
30 .... Inland Empire

MAY
1-2-3 .... Inland Empire
4-5-6 .... at Lancaster
7-8-9 .... at Lake Elsinore
11-12-13 .... Visalia
14-15-16 .. Inland Empire
18-19-20 ...... at Modesto
21-22-23 ...... at Stockton
24-25-26-27 .. at Lancaster
28-29-30 .. Lake Elsinore
31 .... at Inland Empire

JUNE
1-2-3 ... at Inland Empire
4-5-6 .... Lake Elsinore
7-8-9-10 .. at Lake Elsinore
11-12-13 .... Lancaster
15-16-17 .... High Desert
18-19-20 .. at Inland Emp.
21-22-23 .... High Desert
25-26-27 .... at San Jose

JULY
1-2-3 .... Inland Empire
4 .... at High Desert
5-6-7-8 .... High Desert
9-10-11 .... at Visalia
13-14-15 ..... at Lancaster
16-17-18 .. Lake Elsinore
19-20-21 .... Modesto
23-24-25-26 .. at Lancaster
27-28-29 .... Stockton
30-31 ...... at High Desert

AUGUST
1 .... at High Desert
2-3-4-5 .... Inland Empire
6-7-8 .... Bakersfield
10-11-12 ... at Lake Elsi.
13-14-15-16 .. Lake Elsi.
17-18-19 .... Lancaster
20-21-22 ...... Lake Elsi.
24-25 .. at Inland Empire
26-27-28-29 .. Lancaster
31 .... at High Desert

SEPTEMBER
1-2 .... at High Desert
3-4-5-6 .. at Inland Empire

SAN JOSE
APRIL
8-9-10-11 .... at Visalia
12-13-14-15 .. at Modesto
16-17-18 .... Visalia
19-20-21-22 .... Modesto
23-24-25 .... at Visalia
26-27-28-29 .... at R.C.
30 .... at Lake Elsinore

MAY
1-2 .... at Lake Elsinore
3-4-5-6 .... Bakersfield
7-8-9 .... Inland Empire
11 .... at Modesto
12 .... Modesto
13 .... at Modesto
14-15-16 .... at Stockton
18-19-20 ...... Bakersfield
21-22-23-24 .... Visalia
25-26-27 .. at Bakersfield
28 .... Modesto
29 .... at Modesto
30 .... Modesto
31 .... Stockton

JUNE
1-2 .... Stockton
3-4-5-6 .... at Stockton
8-9-10 ...... at Bakersfield
11-12-13 .... Stockton
15-16-17 .... Lancaster
18-19-20 .. at High Desert
21-22-23 .... Stockton
25-26-27 .. Rancho Cuca.

JULY
1-2-3 .... High Desert
4-5-6-7 ...... at Modesto
8-9-10-11 .. at Bakersfield
12, 14-15 .... Modesto
16-17-18 .... Visalia
19-20-21 .. at Bakersfield
23-24-25 ...... at Visalia
26-27-28-29 .. Bakersfield
30-31 .... at Visalia

AUGUST
1-2 .... at Visalia
3-4-5 .... at Modesto
6-7-8-9 .... Stockton
10-11-12 ...... Bakersfield
13-14-15 ...... at Stockton
16-17-18 ...... at Modesto
19-20-21-22 .... Visalia
23-24-25 .... at Lancaster
27-28-29 .. at Inland Emp.
31 .... Lake Elsinore

SEPTEMBER
1-2 .... Lake Elsinore
3-4-5-6 .... Modesto

STOCKTON
APRIL
9-10-11 .... Modesto
12-13-14-15 ..... San Jose
16-17-18 ...... at Modesto
19-20-21-22 .... at B'field
23-24-25-26 .. at Modesto
27-28-29 ...... Bakersfield
30 .... at Visalia

MAY
1-1-2 .... at Visalia
4-5-6 .... Inland Empire
7-8-8-9 .... Modesto
11-12-13 .. at Bakersfield
14-15-16 .... San Jose
18-19-20 .... at Visalia
21-22-23 .. Rancho Cuca.
25-26-27 .. at High Desert
28-29-30 .... at Lancaster
31 .... at San Jose

JUNE
1-2 .... at San Jose
3-4-5-6 .... San Jose
8-9-10 .... Visalia
11-12-13 .... at San Jose
14-15-16-17 .. Bakersfield
18-19-20 .... at Lake Elsi.
21-22-23 .... at Visalia
24-25-26-26 .. Bakersfield

JULY
1-2-3 .... at Bakersfield
4-5-6-7 .... Visalia
9-10-11 .... Modesto
12-13-14-15 .. at Visalia
16-17-18 .... High Desert
20-21-22 .... at Visalia
23-24-25 .... San Jose
27-28-29 .... at R.C.
30-31 .. at Inland Empire

AUGUST
1 .... Inland Empire
3-4-5 .... Lancaster
6-7-8-9 .... at San Jose
10-11-12 .... Visalia
13-14-15 .... San Jose
17-18-19-19 .. at Modesto
20-21-22-23 ... at B'field
24-25-26 .... Modesto
27-28-29 ...... at Modesto
31 .... Bakersfield

SEPTEMBER
1-2 .... Bakersfield
3-4-5-6 .... Lake Elsinore

VISALIA
APRIL
8-9-10-11 .... San Jose
12-13-14-15 .. at Stockton
16-17-18 .... at San Jose
20-21-22 .. Lake Elsinore
23-24-25 .... San Jose
27-28-29 .. Inland Empire
30 .... Stockton

MAY
1-1-2 .... Stockton
4-5-6 .... at Modesto
7-8-9-10 ...... Bakersfield
11-12-13 .... at R.C.
14-15-16 ..... at Lancaster
17-18-19-20 ...... Stockton
21-22-23-24 .. at San Jose
25-26-27 .... Modesto
28-29-30 ...... Bakersfield
31 .... at Bakersfield

JUNE
1-2-3 .... at Bakersfield
4-5-6 .... High Desert
8-9-10 .... at Stockton

11-12-13 .. at Bakersfield
14-15-16-17 .... Modesto
18-19-20 ..... at Modesto
21-22-23 ...... Lancaster
24-25-26 ..... at Modesto

JULY
1-2-3 .... Modesto

4-5-6-7 .... at Stockton
9-10-11 .... Rancho Cuca.
12-13-14-15 .... Stockton
16-17-18 .... at San Jose
20-21-22 .... Stockton
23-24-25 .... at Lake Elsi.
26-27-28-29 .... Modesto
30-31 .... San Jose

AUGUST
1-2 .... San Jose
3-4-5 ...... at High Desert
6-7-8 .... at Inland Empire
10-11-12 ..... at Stockton
13-14-15 ...... Bakersfield
16-17-18 .... San Jose

19-20-21-22 .. at San Jose
24-25-26 .. at Bakersfield
27-28-29 ..... Bakersfield
30-31 .... at Modesto

SEPTEMBER
1-2 .... at Modesto
3-4-5-6 .... at Bakersfield

CAROLINA LEAGUE

FREDERICK
APRIL
9-10-11 .... at Lynchburg
12-13-14-15 .... Salem
16-17-18 .... Kinston
19-20-21 .... at Salem
23-24-25 ...... Wilmington
26-27-28-29 .... at W-S
30 .... at Potomac
MAY
1-2 .... at Potomac
3-4-5-6 .. Winston-Salem
7-8-9 .... Potomac
10-11-12-13 ...... at M.B.
14-15-16 ...... at Kinston
17-18-19 .. Myrtle Beach
21-22-23 ...... Lynchburg
24-25-26 .. at Wilmington
27-28-29-30 .... at Lynch.
31 .... Salem
JUNE
1-2 .... Salem
3-4-5-6 .... Kinston
7-8-9 .... at Salem
10-11-12-13 .. Wilmington
15-16-17 .. at Win.-Salem
18-19-20 ...... at Potomac
21-22-23 ...... Win.-Salem
25-26-27 .... Potomac
JULY
1-2-3 .... at Myrtle Beach
4-5-6 ...... at Lynchburg
7-8-9 .... Myrtle Beach
10-11-12 ...... Lynchburg
14-15-16-17 .... at Wilm.
19-20-21-22 .. at Kinston
23-24-25 .... Salem
26-27-28 .... Kinston
29-30-31 ...... at Potomac
AUGUST
1 .... at Potomac
2-3-4 .... Wilmington
5-6-7 .. at Winston-Salem
8-9-10-11 .... at Salem
13-14-15 .... Win.-Salem
16-17-18-19 .... Wilmington
20-21-22 .. at Myrtle Beach
24-25-26 .... at Kinston
27-28-29-30 .... M.B.
31 .... Lynchburg
SEPTEMBER
1-2-3 .... Lynchburg
4-5-6 .... at Wilmington

KINSTON
APRIL
9-10-11 .. Winston-Salem

12-13-14-15 .... Potomac
16-17-18 .... at Frederick
19-20-21 .. at Wilmington
23-24-25 .. Myrtle Beach
26-27-28-29 .. Lynchburg
30 .... at Salem
MAY
1-2 .... at Salem
3-4-5-6 ...... at Lynchburg
7-8-9 .... Salem
10-11-12-13 .. at Potomac
14-15-16 .... Frederick
17-18-19 ...... Wilmington
21-22-23 .. at Win.-Salem
24-25-26 .... Salem
27-28-29-30 .. Win.-Salem
31 .... Potomac
JUNE
1-2 .... Potomac
3-4-5-6 .... at Frederick
7-8-9 .... at Wilmington
10-11-12-13 .. Myrtle Bch.
15-16-17 ...... Lynchburg
18-19-20 .... at M.B.
22-23-24 .. at Lynchburg
25-26-27 .... at Salem
JULY
1-2-3 .... at Wilmington
4-5-6 .. at Winston-Salem
7-8-9 .... Wilmington
10-11-12 .. Winston-Salem
14-15-16-17 .... at Frederick
19-20-21-22 .... Potomac
23-24-25 .... Potomac
26-27-28 .... at Frederick
29-30-31 .. at Wilmington
AUGUST
1 .... at Wilmington
2-3-4 .... Myrtle Beach
5-6-7 .... Lynchburg
9-10-11-12 .... at M.B.
13-14-15 .. at Lynchburg
16-17-18-19 .... Salem
20-21-22 ...... at Potomac
24-25-26 .... Frederick
27-28-29-30 .. Wilmington
31 ...... at Winston-Salem
SEPTEMBER
1-2-3 .. at Winston-Salem
4-5-6 .... at Myrtle Beach

LYNCHBURG
APRIL
9-10-11 .... Frederick
12-13-14-15 .. Wilmington
16-17-18 .. at Win.-Salem
19-20-21 ...... at Potomac
23-24-25 .... Kinston

26-27-28-29 .. at Kinston
30 .... at Myrtle Beach
MAY
1-2 .... at Myrtle Beach
3-4-5-6 .... Kinston
7-8-9 ...... Myrtle Beach
10-11-12-13 .... at Wilm.
14-15-16 .. Winston-Salem
17-18-19 .... Potomac
21-22-23 .... at Frederick
24-25-26 .... at M.B.
27-28-29-30 .... Frederick
31 .... Wilmington
JUNE
1-2 .... Wilmington
3-4-5-6 .. at Winston-Salem
7-8-9 .... at Potomac
10-11-12-13 .... Salem
15-16-17 .... at Kinston
18-19-20 .... at Salem
22-23-24 .... Kinston
25-26-27 .. Myrtle Beach
JULY
1-2-3 .... at Wilmington
4-5-6 .... Frederick
7-8-9 .... Salem
10-11-12 .... at Frederick
14-15-16-17 ...... at M.B.
19-20-21-22 .. Win.-Salem
23-24-25 ...... Wilmington
26-27-28 .. at Win.-Salem
29-30-31 .... at Salem
AUGUST
1 .... at Salem
2-3-4 .... Potomac
5-6-7 .... at Kinston
8-9-10-11 .... at Potomac
13-14-15 .... Kinston
16-17-18-19 .... M.B.
20-21-22 .. at Wilmington
24-25-26 ...... Win.-Salem
27-28-29-30 .. Potomac
31 .... at Frederick
SEPTEMBER
1-2-3 .... at Frederick
4-5-6 .... at Salem

MYRTLE BEACH
APRIL
8-9-10-11 .... Wilmington
12-13-14-15 .... at W-S
16-17-18 .... Potomac
19-20-21 .. Winston-Salem
23-24-25 .... at Kinston
26-27-28-29 .... Salem
30 .... Lynchburg

MAY
1-2 .... Lynchburg
3-4-5-6 .... at Salem
7-8-9 .... at Lynchburg
10-11-12-13 .... Frederick
14-15-16 .... at Potomac
17-18-19 .... at Frederick
20-21-22 .. at Wilmington
24-25-26 ...... Lynchburg
28-29-30 ...... Wilmington
31 ...... at Winston-Salem
JUNE
1-2 .... at Winston-Salem
3-4-5-6 ...... at Potomac
7-8-9 ...... Winston-Salem
10-11-12-13 .. at Kinston
15-16-17 .... at Salem
18-19-20 .... Kinston
22-23-24 .... Salem
25-26-27 .. at Lynchburg
JULY
1-2-3 .... Frederick
4-5-6 .... at Potomac
7-8-9 .... at Frederick
10-11-12 .... Wilmington
14-15-16-17 .. Lynchburg
19-20-21-22 .... at Wilm.
23-24-25 .. at Win.-Salem
26-27-28 .... Potomac
29-30-31 .. Win.-Salem
AUGUST
1 .... Winston-Salem
2-3-4 .... at Kinston
5-6-7 .... Salem
9-10-11-12 .... Kinston
13-14-15 .... at Salem
16-17-18-19 .... at Lynch.
20-21-22 .... Frederick
24-25-26 .. at Wilmington
27-28-29-30 at Frederick
31 .... Potomac
SEPTEMBER
1-2-3 .... Potomac
4-5-6 .... Kinston

POTOMAC
APRIL
9-10-11 .... at Salem
12-13-14-15 .. at Kinston
16-17-18 .. at Myrtle Beach
19-20-21 ...... Lynchburg
23-24-25 .. at Win.-Salem
26-27-28-29 .. Wilmington
30 .... Frederick

MAY
1-2 .... Frederick
3-4-5-6 .... at Wilmington

7-8-9 .... at Frederick
10-11-12-13 ..... Kinston
14-15-16 .. Myrtle Beach
17-18-19 .. at Lynchburg
21-22-23 .... at Salem
24-25-26 .... Win.-Salem
27-28-29-30 .... Salem
31 .... at Kinston

JUNE
1-2 .... at Kinston
3-4-5-6 ...... Myrtle Beach
7-8-9 .... Lynchburg
10-11-12-13 .... at W-S
14-15-16 ..... Wilmington
18-19-20 ...... Frederick
22-23-24 .. at Wilmington
25-26-27 .... at Frederick

JULY
1-2-3 .... Kinston
4-5-6 ...... Myrtle Beach
7-8-9 .. at Winston-Salem
10-11-12 .... at Salem
15-16-17-18 .. Win.-Salem
19-20-21-22 .... Salem
23-24-25 .... at Kinston
26-27-28 .... at M.B.
29-30-31 .... Frederick

AUGUST
1 .... Frederick
2-3-4 .... at Lynchburg
5-6-7 .... Wilmington
8-9-10-11 ...... Lynchburg
13-14-15 .. at Wilmington
16-17-18-19 ..... at Fred.
20-21-22 .... Kinston
24-25-26 .... Salem
27-28-29-30 .... at Lynch.
31 .... at Myrtle Beach

SEPTEMBER
1-2-3 ... at Myrtle Beach
4-5-6 ..... Winston-Salem

SALEM
APRIL
9-10-11 .... Potomac
12-13-14-15 .. at Frederick
16-17-18 .. at Wilmington
19-20-21 .... Frederick
23-24-25 .. at Lynchburg
26-27-28-29 ...... at M.B.
30 .... Kinston

MAY
1-2 .... Kinston
3-4-5-6 ..... Myrtle Beach
7-8-9 .... at Kinston
11-12-13 .. at Win.-Salem
14-15-16 ..... Wilmington
17-18-19-20 .. Win.-Salem
21-22-23 .... Potomac
24-25-26 .... at Kinston
27-28-29-30 .. at Potomac
31 .... at Frederick

JUNE
1-2 .... at Frederick
3-4-5-6 .... at Wilmington
7-8-9 .... Frederick
10-11-12-13 ... at Lynch.
15-16-17 .. Myrtle Beach
18-19-20 ...... Lynchburg
22-23-24 .... at M.B.
25-26-27 .... Kinston

JULY
1-2-3 ..... Winston-Salem
4-5-6 .... at Wilmington
7-8-9 .... at Lynchburg
10-11-12 .... Potomac
14-15-16-17 ...... Kinston
19-20-21-22 .. at Potomac
23-24-25 .... at Frederick
26-27-28 ..... Wilmington
29-30-31 ...... Lynchburg

AUGUST
1 .... Lynchburg
2-3-4 .. at Winston-Salem
5-6-7 .... at Myrtle Beach
8-9-10-11 .... Frederick
13-14-15 .. Myrtle Beach
16-17-18-19 .. at Kinston
20-21-22 .... Win.-Salem
24-25-26 ...... at Potomac
27-28-29-30 .... at W-S
31 .... Wilmington

SEPTEMBER
1-2-3 .... Wilmington
4-5-6 .... Lynchburg

WILMINGTON
APRIL
8-9-10-11 .... at M.B.
12-13-14-15 ... at Lynch.
16-17-18 .... Salem
19-20-21 .... Kinston

23-24-25 .... at Frederick
26-27-28-29 .. at Potomac
30 .... Winston-Salem

MAY
1-2 .... Winston-Salem
3-4-5-6 .... Potomac
7-8-9 .. at Winston-Salem
10-11-12-13 .. Lynchburg
14-15-16 .... at Salem
17-18-19 .... at Kinston
20-21-22 .. Myrtle Beach
24-25-26 .... Frederick
28-29-30 .. at Myrtle Beach
31 .... at Lynchburg

JUNE
1-2 .... at Lynchburg
3-4-5-6 .... Salem
7-8-9 .... Kinston
10-11-12-13 .. at Frederick
14-15-16 ..... Win.-Salem
18-19-20 .. at Wilmington
21-22-23 .... at Frederick
25-26-27 ...... Wilmington

JULY
1-2-3 .... at Salem
4-5-6 .... Kinston
7-8-9 .... Potomac
10-11-12 .... at Kinston
15-16-17-18 .. at Potomac
19-20-21-22 ... at Lynch.
23-24-25 .. Myrtle Beach
26-27-28 ...... Lynchburg
29-30-31 .... at M.B.

AUGUST
1 .... at Myrtle Beach
2-3-4 .... Salem
5-6-7 .... Frederick
9-10-11-12 .. at Wilmington
13-14-15 .... at Frederick
16-17-18-19 .. Wilmington
20-21-22 .... at Salem
24-25-26 .. at Lynchburg
27-28-29-30 .... Salem
31 .... Kinston

SEPTEMBER
1-2-3 .... Kinston
4-5-6 .... at Potomac

WINSTON-SALEM
APRIL
9-10-11 .... at Kinston

12-13-14-15 .... M.B.
16-17-18 ...... Lynchburg
19-20-21 .. at Myrtle Beach
23-24-25 .... Potomac
26-27-28-29 .... Frederick
30 .... at Wilmington

MAY
1-2 .... at Wilmington
3-4-5-6 .... Potomac
7-8-9 .. at Winston-Salem
10-11-12-13 .. Lynchburg
14-15-16 .. at Frederick
17-18-19 .... at Kinston
20-21-22 .. Myrtle Beach
24-25-26 ...... at Salem
28-29-30 .. at Myrtle Beach
31 .... at Lynchburg

JUNE
1-2 .... Myrtle Beach
3-4-5-6 .... Lynchburg
7-8-9 .. at Myrtle Beach
10-11-12-13 .... Potomac
15-16-17 .... Frederick
18-19-20 .. at Wilmington
21-22-23 .... at Frederick
25-26-27 ...... Wilmington

JULY
1-2-3 .... at Salem
4-5-6 .... Kinston
7-8-9 .... Potomac
10-11-12 .... at Kinston
15-16-17-18 .. at Potomac
19-20-21-22 ... at Lynch.
23-24-25 .. Myrtle Beach
26-27-28 ...... Lynchburg
29-30-31 .... at M.B.

AUGUST
1 .... at Myrtle Beach
2-3-4 .... Salem
5-6-7 .... Frederick
9-10-11-12 .. at Wilmington
13-14-15 .... at Frederick
16-17-18-19 .. Wilmington
20-21-22 .... at Salem
24-25-26 .. at Lynchburg
27-28-29-30 .... Salem
31 .... Kinston

SEPTEMBER
1-2-3 .... Kinston
4-5-6 .... at Potomac

FLORIDA STATE LEAGUE

BREVARD COUNTY
APRIL
8-9 .... at Daytona
10-11 .... Daytona
12-13 .... St. Lucie
14-15 ...... at Palm Beach
16-17 .... Jupiter
18-19-20-21 .. at Daytona
22-23 .... Vero Beach
24-25 .... St. Lucie
26-27-28-29 .. at Ft. Myers
30 .... Tampa

MAY
1-2-3 .... Tampa
4-5 .... Vero Beach
6-7 .... at Vero Beach
8-9-10-11 .... Daytona
12-13-14-15 .. at Lakeland
17-17 .... Palm Beach
18-19 .... at Jupiter
20-21 .... at St. Lucie
22-23 .... Jupiter
24-25-26-27 .... Dunedin
28-29 .... at St. Lucie
30 .... at Jupiter
31 .... at Palm Beach

JUNE
1 .... at Palm Beach
2-3-4-5 .... at Sarasota
7-8-9-10 .... Clearwater
14-15-16 .. at Vero Beach
17 .... Vero Beach
18-19 .... Palm Beach
20 .... at Jupiter
22-23-24-25 .... at Tampa
26-27-28-29 .... Jupiter
30 .... Daytona

JULY
1-2 .... Vero Beach
3 .... Daytona

4 .... at Daytona
5-6-7-8 .... at Dunedin
9-10 .... at Daytona
12-13-14-15 .... Sarasota
16-17-18-19 .. Fort Myers
20-21-22-23 .. at C'water
24 .... at Daytona
26-27-28-29 .. at Palm Bch.
30-31 .... Lakeland

AUGUST
1-2 .... Lakeland
3 .... Palm Beach
4 .... at St. Lucie
5-6 .... at Jupiter

[continued column 1]

7 .... at Daytona
9-10 .... St. Lucie
11-12 .... at St. Lucie
13-14 .... St. Lucie
16 .... at St. Lucie
17 .... at Vero Beach
18-19 .... Palm Beach
20-21 ...... at Vero Beach
23 .... Daytona
24-25 ...... at Vero Beach
26-27-28 .... Daytona
30 .... at Daytona
31 .... at Jupiter

SEPTEMBER
1 .... at Jupiter
2-3-4 .... Vero Beach
5 .... Palm Beach

CLEARWATER
APRIL
8 .... Dunedin
9 .... at Dunedin
10-11 .... Dunedin
12-13-14-15 .. Fort Myers
16-17 .... at Dunedin
18-19 .... at Fort Myers
20-21 .... at Sarasota
22-23 .... Dunedin
24-25 .... Sarasota
26-27-28-29 .... at Tampa
30 .... Palm Beach

MAY
1-2-3 .... Palm Beach
4-5-6-7 .... Jupiter
8-9 .... at Lakeland
10-11 .... Lakeland
12 .... Dunedin
13 .... at Dunedin
14-15 ...... at Fort Myers
17-17-18-19 .. at Daytona
20-21-22-23 .. at Vero Bch.
24-25-26-27 .... St. Lucie
28-29 .... Sarasota
30 .... at Sarasota
31 .... at Dunedin

JUNE
1 .... at Dunedin
2-3 .... Lakeland
4-5 .... at Lakeland
7-8-9-10 .. at Brev. County
14 .... Tampa
15 .... at Tampa
16-17-18-19 .... Tampa
20 .... at Tampa
22-23-24-25 .. at St. Lucie
26-27-28-29 .. at Palm Bch.
30 .... Tampa

JULY
1 .... Tampa
2 .... at Dunedin
3 .... Dunedin
4 .... at Dunedin
5-6-7-8 .... Daytona
9-10 .... Lakeland
12-13-14-15 .... at Jupiter
16-17-18-19   Vero Beach
20-21-22-23 .. Brev. County
24 .... Dunedin
26-27 .... at Fort Myers

[continued column 2]

28-29 .... Fort Myers
30 .... at Dunedin
31 .... at Tampa

AUGUST
1 .... at Tampa
2 .... Dunedin
3-4 .... at Dunedin
5-6 .... at Fort Myers
7 .... Sarasota
9-10 .... Fort Myers
11 .... at Tampa
12-13 .... at Sarasota
14 .... Tampa
16 .... at Sarasota
17-18 .... Tampa
19-20 .... at Lakeland
21 .... at Dunedin
23 .... Dunedin
24 .... at Sarasota
25-26 .... Dunedin
27-28 .... Lakeland
30-31 .... Sarasota

SEPTEMBER
1 .... Sarasota
2-3 .... at Lakeland
4-5 .... at Tampa

DAYTONA
APRIL
8-9 .... Brevard County
10-11   at Brevard County
12-13 .... at Jupiter
14-15 .... at St. Lucie
16-17 .... St. Lucie
18-19-20-21 .. Brev. County
22-23-24-25 .. at Palm Bch.
26-27-28-29 .. at Sarasota
30 .... at Lakeland

MAY
1-2-3 .... at Lakeland
4-5-6-7 .... Dunedin
8-9-10-11 .. at Brev. County
12-13 .... St. Lucie
14-15 .... at St. Lucie
17-17-18-19 .. Clearwater
20-21-22-23 .... Tampa
24-25-26-27 .. at Ft. Myers
28-29 .... Jupiter
30-31 ...... at Vero Beach

JUNE
1 .... at Vero Beach
2-3 .... Jupiter
4-5 .... at Jupiter
7-8-9-10 ...... Vero Beach
14-15-16-17 .. Palm Beach
18 .... Vero Beach
19-20 ...... at Vero Beach
22-23-24-25 .... Sarasota
26-27-28-29 .. Fort Myers
30 ...... at Brevard County

JULY
1-2 .... at Jupiter
3 .... at Brevard County
4 .... Brevard County
5-6-7-8 ...... at Clearwater
9-10 ...... Brevard County
12 .... Vero Beach
13-14-15 .. at Vero Beach
16-17-18-19 .. at Dunedin

[continued column 3]

20-21-22-23 .... Lakeland
24 .... Brevard County
26-27-28-29 .... at Tampa
30-31 ...... at Vero Beach

AUGUST
1-2 .... Vero Beach
3-4 .... Daytona
5-6 .... St. Lucie
7 .... Brevard County
9-10-11-12 .. at Palm Beach
13-14 .... Jupiter
16-17 .... Jupiter
18-19 .... Vero Beach
20-21 .... at St. Lucie
23 ...... at Brevard County
24-25 .... at St. Lucie
26-27-28 at Brev. County
30 .... Brevard County
31 .... Palm Beach

SEPTEMBER
1-2-3 .... Palm Beach
4-5 .... St. Lucie

DUNEDIN
APRIL
8 .... at Clearwater
9 .... Clearwater
10-11 ...... at Clearwater
12-13 .... Sarasota
14 .... at Tampa
15 .... at Lakeland
16-17 .... Clearwater
18 .... Lakeland
19 .... Tampa
20-21 .... Lakeland
22-23 .... at Clearwater
24-25 .... at Lakeland
26-27-28-29 .... Jupiter
30 .... St. Lucie

MAY
1-2-3 .... St. Lucie
4-5-6-7 .... at Daytona
8-9-10-11 .. at Vero Beach
12 .... at Clearwater
13 .... Clearwater
14-15 .... at Tampa
17-17 .... Fort Myers
18-19 .... at Sarasota
20-21 ...... at Fort Myers
22-23 .... Fort Myers
24-25-26-27 .... at B.C.
28 .... Lakeland
29 .... at Lakeland
30 .... Tampa
31 .... Clearwater

JUNE
1 .... Clearwater
2-3 .... at Tampa
4-5 .... at Tampa
7-8-9-10 ...... Palm Beach
14 .... at Sarasota
15 .... Tampa
16-17 .... Sarasota
18-19 ...... at Fort Myers
20 .... at Sarasota
22-23-24-25 .. at Palm Bch.
26-27-28-29 .. at St. Lucie
30 .... at Sarasota

[continued column 4]

JULY
1 .... Lakeland
2 .... Clearwater
3 .... at Clearwater
4 .... Clearwater
5-6-7-8 .. Brevard County
9-10 .... at Tampa
12-13 .... Fort Myers
14-15 .... at Fort Myers
16-17-18-19 ...... Daytona
20-21-22-23 .. at Jupiter
24 .... at Clearwater
26-27-28-29 Vero Beach
30 .... Clearwater
31 .... Sarasota

AUGUST
1 .... Sarasota
2 .... at Clearwater
3-4 .... Clearwater
5 .... Tampa
6-7 .... Lakeland
9-10 .... at Sarasota
11-12-13-14 .. at Lakeland
16 .... Tampa
17-18 .... Sarasota
19-20 .... Tampa
21 .... Clearwater
23 .... at Clearwater
24 .... Tampa
25-26 ...... at Clearwater
27-28 .... at Fort Myers
30-31 .... at Tampa

SEPTEMBER
1 .... at Tampa
2-3 .... Fort Myers
4-5 .... at Sarasota

FORT MYERS
APRIL
8-9 .... Sarasota
10-11 .... at Sarasota
12-13-14-15 .. at C'water
16-17 .... at Lakeland
18-19 .... Clearwater
20-21 .... Tampa
22-23 .... at Lakeland
24-25 .... at Sarasota
26-27-28-29 .. Brev. County
30 .... at Sarasota

MAY
1 .... at Sarasota
3 .... Sarasota
4-5-6-7 .... at St. Lucie
8-9-10-11 .. at Palm Beach
12-13 .... at Tampa
14-15 .... Clearwater
17-17 .... at Dunedin
18-19 .... Lakeland
20-21 .... at Dunedin
22-23 .... at Dunedin
24-25-26-27 ...... Daytona
28-29 .... Tampa
30-31 .... Lakeland

JUNE
1 .... at Lakeland
2-3-4-5 .... Vero Beach
6-7-8 .... Jupiter
9-10 .... at Sarasota
14-15-16-17 .... at Jupiter

18-19 .... Dunedin
20 .... Lakeland
22-23-24-25 .. at Vero Bch.
26-27-28-29 .. at Daytona
30 .... at Sarasota

JULY
1 .... at Sarasota
2-3 .... Sarasota
4 .... at Sarasota
5-6-7-8 .... Palm Beach
9-10 .... Sarasota
12-13 .... at Dunedin
14-15 .... Dunedin
16-17-18-19 ...... at B.C.
20-21-22-23 .... St. Lucie
24 .... Sarasota
26-27 .... Clearwater
28-29 .... at Clearwater
30-31 .... Jupiter

AUGUST
1-2 .... Jupiter
3-4 .... Tampa
5-6 .... Clearwater
7 .... at Tampa
9-10 .... at Clearwater
11 .... at Sarasota
12-13 .... Tampa
14 .... Sarasota
16-17-18 ...... at Lakeland
19-20 .... at Sarasota
21 .... at Tampa
23-24 .... at Lakeland
25-26 .... at Tampa
27-28 .... Dunedin
30-31 .... Lakeland

SEPTEMBER
1 .... Lakeland
2-3 .... at Dunedin
4-5 .... Lakeland

JUPITER

APRIL
8 .... at Palm Beach
9-10-11 ...... Palm Beach
12-13 .... Daytona
14-15 ...... at Vero Beach
16-17 .. at Brevard County
19-20 .... St. Lucie
21-22-23 ..... at St. Lucie
24-25 ...... at Vero Beach
26-27-28-29 .. at Dunedin
30 .... Vero Beach

MAY
1-2-3 .... Vero Beach
4-5-6-7 ...... at Clearwater
8-9-10-11 .... at Tampa
12-13 ...... at Palm Beach
14-15 .... Palm Beach
17-17 .... St. Lucie
18-19 .... Brevard County
20-21 ...... at Palm Beach
22-23 .. at Brevard County
24-25-26-27 .... Sarasota
28-29 .... at Daytona
30 .... Brevard County
31 .... at St. Lucie

JUNE
1 .... at St. Lucie
2-3 .... at Daytona

4-5 .... Daytona
6 .... at St. Lucie
7-8-9-10 .... Lakeland
14-15-16-17 .. Fort Myers
18-19 .... St. Lucie
20 .... Brevard County
22-23-24-25 .. at Lakeland
26-27-28-29 .... at B.C.
30 .... Palm Beach

JULY
1-2 .... Daytona
3 .... at Palm Beach
4 .... Palm Beach
5-6-7-8 .... Tampa
9-10 .... at St. Lucie
12-13-14-15 .. Clearwater
16-17-18-19 .. at St. Lucie
20-21-22-23 ... Dunedin
24 .... St. Lucie
26-27-28-29 .. at Sarasota
30-31 .... at Fort Myers

AUGUST
1-2 .... at Fort Myers
3-4 .... Daytona
5-6 .... Brevard County
7 .... St. Lucie
9-10-11-12 .. at Vero Beach
13-14 .... at Daytona
16-17 .... at Daytona
18-19 .... St. Lucie
20-21 .... Palm Beach
23-24-25 .. at Palm Beach
26-27-28-29 .. Vero Beach
30 .... at Palm Beach
31 .... Brevard County

SEPTEMBER
1 .... Brevard County
2-3 .... St. Lucie
4 .... Palm Beach

LAKELAND

APRIL
8 .... Tampa
9 .... at Tampa
10 .... Tampa
11-12 .... at Tampa
13 .... Tampa
14 .... at Sarasota
15 .... Dunedin
16-17 .... Fort Myers
18 .... at Dunedin
19 .... Sarasota
20-21 .... at Dunedin
22-23 .... Fort Myers
24-25 .... Dunedin
26-27-28-29 .. at Palm Bch.
30 .... Daytona

MAY
1-2-3 .... Daytona
4-5 .... Tampa
6-7 .... at Tampa
8-9 .... Clearwater
10-11 .... at Clearwater
12-13-14-15 .. Brev. County
17-17 .... Sarasota
18-19 .... at Fort Myers
20-21 .... Sarasota
22-23 .... at Sarasota
24-25-26-27 .. Vero Beach

28 .... at Dunedin
29 .... Dunedin
30-31 .... at Fort Myers

JUNE
1 .... Fort Myers
2-3 .... at Clearwater
4-5 .... Clearwater
7-8-9-10 .... at Jupiter
14-15-16-17 .. at St. Lucie
18-19 .... at Sarasota
20 .... at Fort Myers
22-23-24-25 .... Jupiter
26-27-28-29 .... Tampa
30 .... at Dunedin

JULY
1 .... at Dunedin
2 .... at Tampa
3 .... Tampa
4 .... at Tampa
5-6-7-8 .... at Vero Beach
9-10 .... at Clearwater
12-13-14-15 .. Palm Beach
16-17-18-19 .. at Sarasota
20-21-22-23 .. at Daytona
24 .... at Tampa
26-27-28-29 .... St. Lucie
30-31 .. at Brevard County

AUGUST
1-2 .... at Brevard County
3-4-5 .... Sarasota
6-7 .... at Dunedin
9-10 .... at Tampa
11-12-13-14 .... Dunedin
16-17-18 ...... Fort Myers
19-20 .... Clearwater
21 .... at Sarasota
23-24 .... Fort Myers
25-26 .... Sarasota
27-28 ...... at Clearwater
30-31 .... at Fort Myers

SEPTEMBER
1 .... at Fort Myers
2-3 .... Clearwater
4-5 .... at Fort Myers

PALM BEACH

APRIL
8 .... Jupiter
9-10-11 .... at Jupiter
12-13 .... at Vero Beach
14-15 .... Brevard County
16-17 .... Vero Beach
18-19-20 .. at Vero Beach
21 .... at Vero Beach
22-23-24-25 ...... Daytona
26-27-28-29 .... Lakeland
30 .... at Clearwater

MAY
1-2-3 ...... at Clearwater
4-5-6-7 .... Sarasota
8-9-10-11 .... Fort Myers
12-13 .... Jupiter
14-15 .... at Jupiter
16 .... St. Lucie
17-17 .. at Brevard County
19 .... at St. Lucie
20-21 .... Jupiter
22-23 .... St. Lucie
#24-25-26-27 .. at Tampa

28-29 .... Vero Beach
30 .... at St. Lucie
31 .... Brevard County

JUNE
1 .... Brevard County
2-3 .... St. Lucie
4-5 .... at St. Lucie
7-8-9-10 ...... at Dunedin
14-15-16-17 .. at Daytona
18-19 .. at Brevard County
20 .... at St. Lucie
22-23-24-25 .... Dunedin
26-27-28-29 .. Clearwater
30 .... at Jupiter

JULY
1-2 .... at St. Lucie
3 .... Jupiter
4 .... at Jupiter
5-6-7-8 .... at Fort Myers
9-10 .... Vero Beach
12-13-14-15 .. at Lakeland
16-17-18-19 .... Tampa
20-21-22-23 .. at Sarasota
24 .... at Vero Beach
26-27-28-29 .. Brev. County
30-31 .... St. Lucie

AUGUST
1-2 .... St. Lucie
3 .... at Brevard County
4-5-6-7 .... at Vero Beach
9-10-11-12 .... Daytona
13-14 .... Vero Beach
16 .... Vero Beach
17 .... St. Lucie
18-19 .. at Brevard County
20-21 .... at Jupiter
23-24-25 .... Jupiter
26-27-28 ..... at St. Lucie
30 .... Jupiter
31 .... at Daytona

SEPTEMBER
1-2-3 .... at Daytona
4 .... at Jupiter
5 .... at Brevard County

ST. LUCIE

APRIL
8 .... Vero Beach
9 .... at Vero Beach
10 .... Vero Beach
11 .... at Vero Beach
12-13 .. at Brevard County
14-15 .... Daytona
16-17 .... at Daytona
19-20 .... at Jupiter
21-22-23 .... Jupiter
24-25 .. at Brevard County
26 .... at Vero Beach
27 .... Vero Beach
28 .... at Vero Beach
29 .... Vero Beach
30 .... at Dunedin

MAY
1-2-3 .... at Dunedin
4-5-6-7 .... Fort Myers
8-9-10-11 .... Sarasota
12-13 .... Daytona
14-15 .... Daytona
17-17 .... at Jupiter

19 .... Palm Beach
20-21 .... Brevard County
22-23 ...... at Palm Beach
24-25-26-27 .. at C'water
28-29 ...... Brevard County
30 .... Palm Beach
31 .... Jupiter

JUNE
1 .... Jupiter
2-3 .... at Palm Beach
4-5 .... Palm Beach
6 .... Jupiter
7-8-9-10 .... at Tampa
14-15-16-17 .... Lakeland
18-19 .... at Jupiter
20 .... Palm Beach
22-23-24-25 .. Clearwater
26-27-28-29 .. Dunedin
30 .... at Vero Beach

JULY
1-2 .... Palm Beach
3 .... at Vero Beach
4 .... Vero Beach
5-6-7-8 .... at Sarasota
9-10 .... Jupiter
12-13-14-15 ...... Tampa
16-17-18-19 ...... Jupiter
20-21-22-23 .. at Ft. Myers
24 .... at Jupiter
26-27-28-29 .. at Lakeland
30-31 .... at Palm Beach

AUGUST
1-2 .... at Palm Beach
3 .... Vero Beach
4 .... Brevard County
5-6 .... at Daytona
7 .... at Jupiter
9-10 .. at Brevard County
11-12 .. at Brevard County
13-14 .. at Brevard County
16 .... Brevard County
17 .... at Palm Beach
18-19 .... at Jupiter
20-21 .... Daytona
23 .... Vero Beach
24-25 .... Daytona
26-27-28 .... Palm Beach
30 .... Vero Beach
31 .... at Vero Beach

SEPTEMBER
1 .... at Vero Beach
2-3 .... at Jupiter
4-5 .... at Daytona

SARASOTA
APRIL
8-9 .... at Fort Myers
10-11 .... Fort Myers
12-13 .... at Dunedin
14 .... Lakeland
15-16 .... Tampa
17-18 .... at Tampa
19 .... at Lakeland
20-21 .... Clearwater
22-23 .... at Tampa
24-25 ...... at Clearwater
26-27-28-29 ..... Daytona
30 .... Fort Myers

MAY
1 .... Fort Myers
3 .... at Fort Myers
4-5-6-7 .... at Palm Beach
8-9-10-11 .... at St. Lucie
12-13-14-15 .. Vero Beach
17-17 .... at Lakeland
18-19 .... Dunedin
20-21 .... at Lakeland
22-23 .... Lakeland
24-25-26-27 ... at Jupiter
28-29 .... at Clearwater
30 .... Clearwater
31 .... Tampa

JUNE
1 .... Tampa
2-3-4-5 .. Brevard County
6-7-8 .... at Fort Myers
9-10 .... Fort Myers
14 .... Dunedin
15 .... Clearwater
16-17 .... at Dunedin
18-19 .... Lakeland
20 .... Dunedin
22-23-24-25 .. at Daytona
26-27-28-29 .. at Vero Bch.
30 .... Fort Myers

JULY
1 .... Fort Myers
2-3 .... at Fort Myers
4 .... Fort Myers
5-6-7-8 .... St. Lucie
9-10 .... at Fort Myers
12-13-14-15 .... at B.C.
16-17-18-19 .... Lakeland
20-21-22-23 .. Palm Beach
24 .... at Fort Myers
26-27-28-29 .... Jupiter
30 .... Tampa
31 .... at Dunedin

AUGUST
1 .... at Dunedin
2 .... at Tampa
3-4-5 .... at Lakeland
6 .... at Tampa
7 .... at Clearwater
9-10 .... Dunedin
11 .... Fort Myers
12-13 .... Clearwater
14 .... at Fort Myers
16 .... Clearwater
17-18 .... at Dunedin
19-20 .... Fort Myers
21 .... Lakeland
23 .... Tampa
24 .... Clearwater
25-26 .... at Lakeland
27-28 .... Tampa
30-31 .... at Clearwater

SEPTEMBER
1 .... at Clearwater
2-3 .... at Tampa
4-5 .... Dunedin

TAMPA
APRIL
8 .... at Lakeland
9 .... Lakeland
10 .... at Lakeland

11-12 .... Lakeland
13 .... at Lakeland
14 .... Tampa
15-16 .... at Sarasota
17-18 .... Sarasota
19 .... at Dunedin
20-21 .... at Fort Myers
22-23 .... Sarasota
24-25 .... Fort Myers
26-27-28-29 .. Clearwater
30 .... at Brevard County

MAY
1-2-3 .. at Brevard County
4-5 .... at Lakeland
6-7 .... Lakeland
8-9-10-11 .... Jupiter
12-13 .... Fort Myers
14-15 .... Dunedin
17-18-19 .. at Vero Bch.
20-21-22-23 .. at Daytona
#24-25-26-27 .. Palm Beach
28-29 .... at Fort Myers
30 .... at Dunedin
31 .... at Sarasota

JUNE
1 .... at Sarasota
2-3 .... Dunedin
4-5 .... at Dunedin
7-8-9-10 .... St. Lucie
14 .... at Clearwater
15 .... at Dunedin
16-17-18-19 .. at C'water
20 .... Clearwater
22-23-24-25 .. Brev. County
26-27-28-29 .. at Lakeland
30 .... at Clearwater

JULY
1 .... at Clearwater
2 .... Lakeland
3 .... at Lakeland
4 .... Lakeland
5-6-7-8 .... at Jupiter
9-10 .... Dunedin
12-13-14-15 .. at St. Lucie
16-17-18-19 .. at Palm Bch.
20-21-22-23 .. Vero Beach
24 .... Lakeland
26-27-28-29 ..... Daytona
30 .... at Sarasota
31 .... Clearwater

AUGUST
1 .... Clearwater
2 .... Sarasota
3-4 .... at Fort Myers
5 .... at Dunedin
6 .... Sarasota
7 .... Fort Myers
9-10 .... Lakeland
11 .... Clearwater
12-13 .... at Fort Myers
14 .... at Clearwater
16 .... at Dunedin
17-18 .... at Dunedin
19-20 .... at Dunedin
21 .... Fort Myers
23 .... at Sarasota
24 .... at Dunedin
25-26 .... Fort Myers
27-28 .... at Sarasota

30-31 .... Dunedin
SEPTEMBER
1 .... Dunedin
2-3 .... Sarasota
4-5 .... Clearwater

VERO BEACH
APRIL
8 .... at St. Lucie
9 .... St. Lucie
10 .... at St. Lucie
11 .... St. Lucie
12-13 .... Palm Beach
14-15 .... Jupiter
16-17 .... at Palm Beach
18-19-20 .. Palm Beach
21 .... at Palm Beach
22-23 .. at Brevard County
24-25 .... Jupiter
26 .... St. Lucie
27 .... at St. Lucie
28 .... St. Lucie
29 .... at St. Lucie
30 .... at Jupiter

MAY
1-2-3 .... at Jupiter
4-5 .... at Brevard County
6-7 ...... Brevard County
8-9-10-11 .... Dunedin
12-13-14-15 .. at Sarasota
17-17-18-19 ...... Tampa
20-21-22-23 .. Clearwater
24-25-26-27 .. at Lakeland
28-29 ..... at Palm Beach
30-31 .... Daytona

JUNE
1 .... Daytona
2-3-4-5 .... at Fort Myers
7-8-9-10 .... at Daytona
14-15-16 .. Brevard County
17 ...... at Brevard County
18 .... at Daytona
19-20 .... Daytona
22-23-24-25 .. Fort Myers
26-27-28-29 .... Sarasota
30 .... St. Lucie

JULY
1-2 .... at Brevard County
3 .... St. Lucie
4 .... at St. Lucie
5-6-7-8 .... Lakeland
9-10 .... at Palm Beach
12 .... at Daytona
13-14-15 .... Daytona
16-17-18-19 .. at C'water
20-21-22-23 .. at Tampa
24 .... Palm Beach
26-27-28-29 .. at Dunedin
30-31 .... Daytona

AUGUST
1-2 .... at Daytona
3 .... at St. Lucie
4-5-6-7 ...... Palm Beach
9-10-11-12 .... Jupiter
13-14 ...... at Palm Beach
16 .... at Palm Beach
17 .... Brevard County
18-19 .... at Daytona
20-21 .... Brevard County

23 .... at St. Lucie	30 .... at St. Lucie	**SEPTEMBER**	2-3-4 .. at Brevard County
24-25 .... Brevard County	31 .... St. Lucie	1 .... St. Lucie	
26-27-28-29 .... at Jupiter		# Games to be played at Dunedin	

MIDWEST LEAGUE

BATTLE CREEK

APRIL
8-9-10 .... Lansing
12-13-14-15 .. Fort Wayne
16-17-18-19 .. at W. Mich.
20-21-22-23 .. at Ft. Wayne
24-25-26-27 .... W. Mich.
29-30 .... at Kane County

MAY
1-2 .... at Kane County
3-4-5-6 .... Clinton
7-8-9-10 .... at Wisconsin
11-12-13-14 .. Quad City
15-16-17-18 ..... S. Bend
20-21-22-23 ...... at Beloit
24-25-26-27 .. at S. Bend
28-29-30-31 .. Burlington

JUNE
1-2-3-4 .... at Dayton
5-6-7-8 .... at Peoria
10-11-12-13 .... Peoria
14-15-16-17 .. Cedar Rap.
18-19-20 ...... at Lansing
24-25-26-27 .. at Fort Wayne
28-29-30 .. at Fort Wayne

JULY
1 .... at Fort Wayne
2-3 ...... at West Michigan
4-5-6-7 .... Peoria
8-9-10-11 .... Beloit
14-15 .. at West Michigan
16-17-18-19 .. at Quad City
20-21-22-23 .... W. Mich.
24-25-26-27 .. at Clinton
29-30-31 ...... Wisconsin

AUGUST
1 .... Wisconsin
2-3-4 .... Lansing
5-6-7-8 .. at Cedar Rapids
9-10-11-12 .. at South Bend
13-14-15 ...... at Lansing
17-18-19-20 .. Kane County
21-22-23-24 ...... at Burl.
26-27-28-29 .. South Bend
30-31 .... at Dayton

SEPTEMBER
1-2 .... at Dayton
3-4-5-6 .... Dayton

BELOIT

APRIL
8-9-10 .... Quad City
12-13-14-15 ...... Peoria
16-17-18-19 .. at Ft. Wayne
20-21-22-23 .. at Lansing
24-25-26-27 .. Wisconsin
29-30 .... at Clinton

MAY
1-2 .... at Clinton
3-4-5-6 ...... at Wisconsin
7-8-9-10 .... Kane County
11-12-13-14 Cedar Rap.

15-16-17-18 ...... at Burl.
20-21-22-23 .. Battle Creek
24-25-26-27 .. at Kane Co.
28-29-30-31 .... W. Mich.

JUNE
1-2-3-4 .... South Bend
5-6-7-8 .... at Dayton
10-11-12-13 .. at Ced. Rap.
14-15-16-17 ...... Clinton
18-19-20 ...... at Quad City
24-25-26-27 .. Kane County
28-29-30 .. at Burlington

JULY
1 .... at Burlington
2-3 ...... Fort Wayne
4-5-6-7 .. at South Bend
8-9-10-11 .. at Battle Creek
14-15 .... Fort Wayne
16-17-18-19 ..... Lansing
20-21-22-23 .. at Cedar Rap.
24-25-26-27 .. at Wisconsin
29-30-31 .... Clinton

AUGUST
1 .... Clinton
2-3-4 .... at Quad City
5-6-7-8 .... Dayton
9-10-11-12 .... Wisconsin
13-14-15 ...... Quad City
17-18-19-20 .. at W. Mich.
21-22-23-24 .... at Peoria
26-27-28-29 .. at Kane Co.
30-31 .... Burlington

SEPTEMBER
1-2 .... Burlington
3-4-5-6 .... Peoria

BURLINGTON

APRIL
8-9-10 ...... Kane County
12-13-14-15 .. Wisconsin
16-17-18-19 .. Quad City
20-21-22-23 .. at Wisconsin
24-25-26-27 .... Clinton
29-30 .... at Quad City

MAY
1-2 .... at Quad City
3-4-5-6 .... at South Bend
7-8-9-10 .. at Cedar Rapids
11-12-13-14 ...... Lansing
15-16-17-18 .... Beloit
20-21-22-23 .... Dayton
24-25-26-27 .... at Peoria
28-29-30-31 .. at Battle Cr.

JUNE
1-2-3-4 .... Cedar Rapids
5-6-7-8 .... at Clinton
10-11-12-13 .. Fort Wayne
14-15-16-17 .. at W. Mich.
18-19-20 .. at Kane County
24-25-26-27 .... W. Mich.
28-29-30 .... Beloit

JULY
1 .... Beloit
2-3 .... Clinton
4-5-6-7 .... at Fort Wayne
8-9-10-11 ...... at Lansing
14-15 .... Clinton
16-17 .... Cedar Rapids
18 .... Cedar Rapids
19 .... Cedar Rapids
20-21-22-23 .. at Wisconsin
24-25 .... at Cedar Rapids
26 .... Cedar Rapids
27 .... at Cedar Rapids
29-30-31 .... Quad City

AUGUST
1 .... Quad City
2-3-4 .... Kane County
5-6-7-8 .... at Peoria
9-10-11-12 ...... Peoria
13-14-15 .. at Kane County
17-18-19-20 .. at Clinton
21-22-23-24 .. Battle Creek
26-27-28-29 .. at Dayton
30-31 .... at Beloit

SEPTEMBER
1-2 .... at Beloit
3-4-5-6 .... South Bend

CEDAR RAPIDS

APRIL
8-9-10 .... Peoria
12-13-14-15 ...... Clinton
16-17-18-19 .. at Kane Co.
20-21-22-23 .. at Clinton
24-25 .... Kane County
26-27 .... Quad City
29-30 .. at West Michigan

MAY
1-2 ...... at West Michigan
3-4-5-6 .... Fort Wayne
7-8-9-10 .... Burlington
11-12-13-14 ..... at Beloit
15-16-17-18 .. at Wisconsin
20-21 .... Quad City
22-23 .... Kane County
24-25-26-27 ...... Dayton
28-29-30-31 ...... Lansing

JUNE
1-2-3-4 ..... at Burlington
5-6-7-8 .... at South Bend
10-11-12-13 ..... at Peoria
14-15-16-17 .. at Battle Cr.
18-19-20 .... at Peoria
24-25-26-27 .. Quad City
28-29-30 .... at Quad City

JULY
1 .... at Quad City
2-3 .... at Wisconsin
4-5-6-7 .... Clinton
8-9-10-11 .... Wisconsin
14-15 .... at Burlington
16-17 .... at Burlington

18 .... Burlington
19 .... at Burlington
20-21-22-23 .... Beloit
24-25 .... Burlington
26 .... at Burlington
27 .... at Burlington
29-30-31 .. at Kane County

AUGUST
1 .... at Kane County
2-3-4 .... at Peoria
5-6-7-8 .... Battle Creek
9-10-11-12 .. at Dayton
13-14-15 .... Peoria
17-18-19-20 .. South Bend
21-22-23-24 .. at Lansing
26-27-28-29 .. at Clinton
30-31 ...... at Fort Wayne

SEPTEMBER
1-2 .... at Fort Wayne
3-4-5-6 .. West Michigan

CLINTON

APRIL
8-9-10 ...... at Wisconsin
12-13-14-15 .. at Cedar Rap.
16-17-18-19 .... Dayton
20-21-22-23 .. Cedar Rap.
24-25-26-27 ...... at Burl.
29-30 .... Beloit

MAY
1-2 .... Beloit
3-4-5-6 .... at Battle Creek
7-8-9-10 .... at W. Mich.
11-12-13-14 .... Peoria
15-16-17-18 ...... Lansing
20-21-22-23 .. at S. Bend
24-25-26-27 .. Fort Wayne
28-29-30-31 .. at Quad City

JUNE
1-2-3-4 ...... Kane County
5-6-7-8 .... Burlington
10-11-12-13 .... at Peoria
14-15-16-17 ...... at Beloit
18-19-20 ...... Wisconsin
24-25-26-27 .. South Bend
28-29-30 ...... at Lansing

JULY
1 .... at Lansing
2-3 .... at Burlington
4-5-6-7 .. at Cedar Rapids
8-9-10-11 .... Peoria
14-15 .... at Burlington
16-17-18-19 .. at Dayton
20-21-22-23 .. Kane County
24-25-26-27 .. Battle Creek
29-30-31 .... at Beloit

AUGUST
1 .... at Beloit
2-3-4 .... at Wisconsin
5-6-7-8 .. West Michigan
9-10-11-12 ... at Kane Co.
13-14-15 ...... at Wisconsin

17-18-19-20 .. Burlington
21-22-23-24 .. at Ft. Wayne
26-27-28-29 Cedar Rap.
30-31 .... Quad City

SEPTEMBER
1-2 .... Quad City
3-4-5-6 ...... at Quad City

DAYTON
APRIL
8-9-10 .... West Michigan
12-13-14-15 ...... Lansing
16-17-18-19 .. at Clinton
20-21-22-23 .. Quad City
24-25-26-27 Fort Wayne
29-30 .... at Lansing
MAY
1-2 .... at Lansing
3-4-5-6 ...... Kane County
7-8-9-10 .. at South Bend
11-12-13-14 .. South Bend
15-16-17-18 .... Peoria
20-21-22-23 ...... at Burl.
24-25-26-27 .. at Ced. Rap.
28-29-30-31 .. at Ft. Wayne
JUNE
1-2-3-4 .... Battle Creek
5-6-7-8 .... Beloit
10-11-12-13 .. at Battle Cr.
14-15-16-17 .. Wisconsin
18-19-20 ...... at W. Mich.
24-25-26-27 ...... Lansing
28-29-30 .. at Wisconsin
JULY
1 .... at Wisconsin
2-3 .... at South Bend
4-5-6-7 .... Quad City
8-9-10-11 .... South Bend
14-15 ...... at South Bend
16-17-18-19 ...... Clinton
20-21 ...... at Fort Wayne
22-23 .... Fort Wayne
24-25-26-27 .. at Lansing
29-30 ...... Fort Wayne
31 .... at Fort Wayne
AUGUST
1 .... at Fort Wayne
2-3-4 .. at West Michigan
5-6-7-8 .... at Beloit
9-10-11-12 .. Cedar Rapids
13-14-15 .. West Michigan
17-18-19-20 .. at Clinton
21-22-23-24 .. at Kane Co.
26-27-28-29 .. Burlington
30-31 .... Battle Creek
SEPTEMBER
1-2 .... Battle Creek
3-4-5-6 .... at Battle Creek

FORT WAYNE
APRIL
8-9-10 .... at South Bend
12-13-14-15 .. at Battle Cr.
16-17-18-19 ...... Beloit
20-21-22-23 .. Battle Creek
24-25-26-27 .. at Dayton
29-30 .... Wisconsin
MAY
1-2 .... Wisconsin

3-4-5-6 .. at Cedar Rapids
7-8-9-10 .... at Quad City
11-12-13-14 .... W. Mich.
15-16-17-18 .. Kane County
20-21-22-23 .. at Lansing
24-25-26-27 .. at Clinton
28-29-30-31 ...... Dayton
JUNE
1-2-3-4 .. at West Michigan
5-6-7-8 .... Lansing
10-11-12-13 ...... at Burl.
14-15-16-17 .... Peoria
18-19-20 .... South Bend
24-25-26-27 .. at Battle Cr.
28-29-30 .... Battle Creek
JULY
1 .... Battle Creek
2-3 .... at Beloit
4-5-6-7 .... Burlington
8-9-10-11 .. West Michigan
14-15 .... at Beloit
16-17-18-19 .... at Peoria
20-21 .... Dayton
22-23 .... at Dayton
24-25-26-27 .. at Kane Co.
29-30 .... at Dayton
31 .... Dayton
AUGUST
1 .... Dayton
2-3-4 .... South Bend
5-6 .... at Lansing
7-8 .... Lansing
9-10-11-12 .. at W. Mich.
13-14-15 .. at South Bend
17-18-19-20 .. Quad City
21-22-23-24 ...... Clinton
26-27 .... at Lansing
28-29 .... Lansing
30-31 ...... Cedar Rapids
SEPTEMBER
1-2 .... Cedar Rapids
3-4-5-6 ...... at Wisconsin

KANE COUNTY
APRIL
8-9-10 ...... at Burlington
12-13-14-15 .. Quad City
16-17-18-19 .. Cedar Rap.
20-21-22-23 .... at Peoria
24-25 .... at Cedar Rapids
26-27 .... Peoria
29-30 .... Battle Creek
MAY
1-2 .... Battle Creek
3-4-5-6 .... at Dayton
7-8-9-10 .... at Beloit
11-12-13-14 .. Wisconsin
15-16-17-18 .. at Ft. Wayne
20-21 .... Peoria
22-23 .... at Cedar Rapids
24-25-26-27 .... Beloit
28-29-30-31 .. South Bend
JUNE
1-2-3-4 .... at Clinton
5-6-7-8 .. West Michigan
10-11-12-13 .. at Quad City
14-15-16-17 .. at Lansing
18-19-20 ...... Burlington
24-25-26-27 ...... at Beloit

28-29-30 .... at Peoria
JULY
1 .... at Peoria
2-3 .... at Quad City
4-5-6-7 .... Wisconsin
8-9-10-11 ...... Quad City
14-15 .... Quad City
16-17-18-19 .. at W. Mich.
20-21-22-23 .. at Clinton
24-25-26-27 .. Fort Wayne
29-30-31 .. Cedar Rapids
AUGUST
1 .... Cedar Rapids
2-3-4 .... at Burlington
5-6-7-8 ...... at Wisconsin
9-10-11-12 .... Clinton
13-14-15 ...... Burlington
17-18-19-20 .. at Battle Cr.
21-22-23-24 ...... Dayton
26-27-28-29 .. Beloit
30-31 .... at South Bend
SEPTEMBER
1-2 .... at South Bend
3-4-5-6 .... Lansing

LANSING
APRIL
8-9-10 .... at Battle Creek
12-13-14-15 .. at Dayton
16-17-18-19 .. South Bend
20-21-22-23 .... at S. Bend
24-25-26-27 .. at S. Bend
29-30 .... Dayton
MAY
1-2 .... Dayton
3-4-5-6 ...... at Quad City
7-8-9-10 .... Peoria
11-12-13-14 ...... at Burl.
15-16-17-18 .. at Dayton
20-21-22-23 .. Fort Wayne
24-25-26-27 .... W. Mich.
28-29-30-31 .. at Ced. Rap.
JUNE
1-2-3-4 .... Wisconsin
5-6-7-8 .. at Fort Wayne
10-11-12-13 .. at W. Mich.
14-15-16-17 .. Kane County
18-19-20 .... Battle Creek
24-25-26-27 .. at Dayton
28-29-30 .... Clinton
JULY
1 .... Clinton
2-3 .... at Peoria
4-5-6-7 .. West Michigan
8-9-10-11 ...... Burlington
14-15 .... at Peoria
16-17-18-19 ...... at Beloit
20-21-22-23 .. South Bend
24-25-26-27 ...... Dayton
29-30-31 .. at South Bend
AUGUST
1 .... at South Bend
2-3-4 ...... at Battle Creek
5-6 .... Fort Wayne
7-8 .... at Fort Wayne
9-10-11-12 .... Quad City
13-14-15 .... Battle Creek
17-18-19-20 .. at Wisconsin

21-22-23-24 .. Cedar Rap.
26-27 .... Fort Wayne
28-29 ...... at Fort Wayne
30-31 .. at West Michigan
SEPTEMBER
1-2 ...... at West Michigan
3-4-5-6 .. at Kane County

PEORIA
APRIL
8-9-10 .. at Cedar Rapids
12-13-14-15 ...... at Beloit
16-17-18-19 .. at Wisconsin
20-21-22-23 .. Kane County
24-25 .... Quad City
26-27 .... at Kane County
29-30 .... South Bend
MAY
1-2 .... South Bend
3-4-5-6 .. West Michigan
7-8-9-10 .... at Lansing
11-12-13-14 .. at Clinton
15-16-17-18 .. at Dayton
20-21 .... at Kane County
22-23 .... Quad City
24-25-26-27 .. Burlington
28-29-30-31 .. Wisconsin
JUNE
2-3-4 ...... at Quad City
5-6-7-8 .... Battle Creek
9 .... at Quad City
10-11-12-13 ...... Clinton
14-15-16-17 .. at Ft. Wayne
18-19-20 .. Cedar Rapids
24-25-26-27 .. at Wisconsin
28-29-30 .. Kane County
JULY
1 .... Kane County
2-3 .... Lansing
4-5-6-7 .. at Battle Creek
8-9-10-11 .. at Clinton
14-15 .... Lansing
16-17-18-19 .. Fort Wayne
20-21-22-23 .. Quad City
24-25-26-27 .. at S. Bend
29-30-31 ...... at W. Mich.
AUGUST
1 .... at West Michigan
2-3-4 .... Cedar Rapids
5-6-7-8 .... Burlington
9-10-11-12 .. at Burlington
13-14-15 .. at Cedar Rapids
17-18-19-20 ...... Dayton
21-22-23-24 .... Beloit
26-27-28-29 .. at Quad City
30-31 .... Wisconsin
SEPTEMBER
1-2 .... Wisconsin
3-4-5-6 .... at Beloit

QUAD CITY
APRIL
8-9-10 .... at Beloit
12-13-14-15 .. at Kane Co.
16-17-18-19 ...... at Burl.
20-21-22-23 .. at Dayton
24-25 .... at Peoria
26-27 .... at Cedar Rapids
29-30 .... Burlington

MAY

1-2	Burlington
3-4-5-6	Lansing
7-8-9-10	Fort Wayne
11-12-13-14	at Battle Cr.
15-16-17-18	at W. Mich.
20-21	at Cedar Rapids
22-23	at Peoria
24-25-26-27	Wisconsin
28-29-30-31	Clinton

JUNE

2-3-4	Peoria
5-6-7-8	at Wisconsin
10-11-12-13	Kane County
14-15-16-17	at S. Bend
18-19-20	Beloit
24-25-26-27	at Ced. Rap.
28-29-30	Cedar Rapids

JULY

1	Cedar Rapids
2-3	Kane County
4-5-6-7	at Dayton
8-9-10-11	at Kane County
14-15	Kane County
16-17-18-19	Battle Creek
20-21-22-23	at Peoria
24-25-26-27	W. Mich.
29-30-31	at Burlington

AUGUST

1	at Burlington
2-3-4	Beloit
5-6-7-8	South Bend
9-10-11-12	at Lansing
13-14-15	at Beloit
17-18-19-20	at Ft. Wayne
21-22-23-24	Wisconsin
26-27-28-29	Peoria
30-31	at Clinton

SEPTEMBER

1-2	at Clinton
3-4-5-6	Clinton

SOUTH BEND

APRIL

8-9-10	Fort Wayne
12-13-14-15	W. Mich.
16-17-18-19	at Lansing
20-21-22-23	at W. Mich.
24-25-26-27	Lansing
29-30	at Peoria

MAY

1-2	at Peoria
3-4-5-6	Burlington
7-8-9-10	Dayton
11-12-13-14	at Dayton
15-16-17-18	at Battle Cr.
20-21-22-23	Clinton
24-25-26-27	Battle Creek
28-29-30-31	at Kane Co.

JUNE

1-2-3-4	at Beloit
5-6-7-8	Cedar Rapids
10-11-12-12	at Wisconsin
14-15-16-17	at Fort Wayne
18-19-20	at Fort Wayne
24-25-26-27	at Clinton
28-29	West Michigan
30	at West Michigan

JULY

1	at West Michigan
2-3	Dayton
4-5-6-7	Beloit
8-9-10-11	at Dayton
14-15	Dayton
16-17-18-19	Wisconsin
20-21-22-23	at Lansing
24-25-26-27	Peoria
29-30-31	Lansing

AUGUST

1	Lansing
2-3-4	at Fort Wayne
5-6-7-8	at Quad City
9-10-11-12	Battle Creek
13-14-15	Fort Wayne
17-18-19-20	at Ced. Rap.
21-22	at West Michigan
23-24	West Michigan
26-27-28-29	at Battle Cr.
30-31	Kane County

SEPTEMBER

1-2	Kane County
3-4-5-6	at Burlington

WEST MICHIGAN

APRIL

8-9-10	at Dayton
12-13-14-15	at S. Bend
16-17-18-19	Battle Creek
20-21-22-23	South Bend
24-25-26-27	at Battle Cr.
29-30	Cedar Rapids

MAY

1-2	Cedar Rapids
3-4-5-6	at Peoria
7-8-9-10	Clinton
11-12-13-14	at Ft. Wayne
15-16-17-18	Quad City
20-21-22-23	at Wisconsin
24-25-26-27	at Lansing
28-29-30-31	at Beloit

JUNE

1-2-3-4	Fort Wayne
5-6-7-8	at Kane County
10-11-12-13	Lansing
14-15-16-17	Burlington
18-19-20	Dayton
24-25-26-27	at Burl.
28-29	at South Bend
30	South Bend

JULY

1	South Bend
2-3	Battle Creek
4-5-6-7	at Lansing
8-9-10-11	at Fort Wayne
14-15	Battle Creek
16-17-18-19	Kane County
20-21-22-23	at Battle Cr.
24-25-26-27	at Quad City
29-30-31	Peoria

AUGUST

1	Peoria
2-3-4	Dayton
5-6-7-8	at Clinton
9-10-11-12	Fort Wayne
13-14-15	at South Bend
17-18-19-20	Beloit
21-22	South Bend
23-24	at South Bend
26-27-28-29	Wisconsin
30-31	Lansing

SEPTEMBER

1-2	Lansing
3-4-5-6	at Cedar Rapids

WISCONSIN

APRIL

8-9-10	Clinton
12-13-14-15	at Burl.
16-17-18-19	Peoria
20-21-22-23	Burlington
24-25-26-27	at Beloit
29-30	at Fort Wayne

MAY

1-2	at Fort Wayne
3-4-5-6	Beloit
7-8-9-10	Battle Creek
11-12-13-14	at Ft. Wayne
15-16-17-18	Cedar Rap.
20-21-22-23	W. Mich.
24-25-26-27	at Quad City
28-29-30-31	at Beloit

JUNE

1-2-3-4	Fort Wayne
5-6-7-8	at Kane County
10-11-12-13	Lansing
14-15-16-17	Burlington
18-19-20	Dayton
24-25-26-27	at Burl.
28-29	at South Bend
30	South Bend

JULY

1	South Bend
2-3	Battle Creek
4-5-6-7	at Lansing
8-9-10-11	at Fort Wayne
14-15	Battle Creek
16-17-18-19	Kane County
20-21-22-23	at Battle Cr.
24-25-26-27	at Quad City
29-30-31	Peoria

AUGUST

1	Peoria
2-3-4	Dayton
5-6-7-8	at Clinton
9-10-11-12	Fort Wayne
13-14-15	at South Bend
17-18-19-20	Beloit
21-22	South Bend
23-24	at South Bend
26-27-28-29	Wisconsin
30-31	Lansing

SEPTEMBER

1-2	Lansing
3-4-5-6	at Cedar Rapids

SOUTH ATLANTIC LEAGUE

ASHEVILLE

APRIL

8-9-10-11	at Savannah
12-13-14	at Augusta
15-16-17-18	Char., SC
20-21-22-23	at Lexington
24-25-26-27	at Char., WV
28-29-30	Columbus

MAY

1-2-3-4	Rome
5-6-7-8	at Charleston, SC
10-11-12-13	Hickory
14-15-16-17	Kannapolis
19-20-21	at Rome
22-23-24-25	at Columbus
26-27-28-29	Savannah
30-31	at Greensboro

JUNE

1	at Greensboro
2-3-4	Capital City
5-6-7	Greensboro
9-10-11	at Capital City
12-13-14	Greensboro
15-16-17	Augusta
18-19-20	at Greensboro
22-23-24	at Capital City
25-26-27	at Savannah

JULY

1-2-3-4	Columbus
5-6-7-8	Capital City
9-10-11-12	at Augusta
14-15-16	Capital City
17-18-19	Augusta
20-21-22	at Greensboro
23-24-25	at Augusta
26-27-28	Greensboro
29-30-31	Rome

AUGUST

2-3-4-5	at Lake County
6-7-8-9	at Hagerstown
11-12-13-14	Delmarva
15-16-17-18	Lakewood
19-20-21-22	at Char., SC
23-24-25	Savannah
26-27-28-29	Char., SC
31	at Rome

SEPTEMBER

1-2	at Rome
3-4-5-6	at Columbus

AUGUSTA

APRIL

8-9-10-11	at Rome
12-13-14	Asheville
15-16-17-18	Columbus
20-21-22-23	at Hickory
24-25-26-27	at Kann.
28-29-30	Charleston, SC

MAY

1-2-3-4	Savannah
5-6-7-8	at Columbus
10-11-12-13	Char., WV
14-15-16-17	Lexington
19-20-21	at Char., SC
22-23	Savannah

24-25 .... at Savannah
26-27-28-29 .... Rome
30-31 ...... at Capital City
JUNE
1 .... at Capital City
2-3-4 .... Greensboro
5-6-7 .... Capital City
9-10-11 .. at Greensboro
12-13-14 ...... Capital City
15-16-17 ...... at Asheville
18-19-20 .. at Capital City
22-23-24 .... Greensboro
25-26-27 .... at Columbus
JULY
1-2 .... Capital City
3-4 .... at Capital City
5-6-7-8 .... at Greensboro
9-10-11-12 ...... Asheville
14-15-16 .. at Greensboro
17-18-19 ...... at Asheville
20-21-22 ...... Capital City
23-24-25 .... Asheville
26-27-28 .. at Capital City
29-30-31 .. Charleston, SC
AUGUST
2-3-4-5 ...... at Lakewood
6-7-8-9 .... at Delmarva
11-12-13-14 .. Hagerstown
15-16-17-18 .. Lake County
19-20-21-22 .... at Rome
23-24-25 .... Columbus
26-27-28-29 .... Rome
31 ...... at Charleston, SC
SEPTEMBER
1-2 ..... at Charleston, SC
3-4-5-6 ...... at Savannah

CAPITAL CITY
APRIL
8-9-10-11 .. at Columbus
12-13-14 .... Greensboro
15-16-17-18 .... Rome
20-21-22-23 .... at Kann.
24-25-26-27 .. at Hickory
28-29-30 .... Savannah
MAY
1-2 .... Charleston, SC
3-4 ...... at Charleston, SC
5-6-7-8 .... at Rome
10-11-12-13 .. Lexington
14-15-16-17 .. Char., WV
19-20-21 .. at Savannah
22-23 .. at Charleston, SC
24-25 ...... Charleston, SC
26-27-28-29 .. Columbus
30-31 .... Augusta
JUNE
1 .... Augusta
2-3-4 .... at Asheville
5-6-7 .... at Augusta
9-10-11 .... Asheville
12-13-14 ...... at Augusta
15-16-17 .. at Greensboro
18-19-20 .... Augusta
22-23-24 .... Asheville
25-26-27 .... at Rome
JULY
1-2 .... at Augusta

3-4 .... Augusta
5-6-7-8 .... at Asheville
9-10-11-12 .. Greensboro
14-15-16 ...... at Asheville
17-18-19 .... Greensboro
20-21-22 ...... at Augusta
23-24-25 .. at Greensboro
26-27-28 .... Augusta
29-30-31 .... Savannah
AUGUST
2-3-4-5 .... at Delmarva
6-7-8-9 ...... at Lakewood
11-12-13-14 .. Lake County
15-16-17-18 .. Hagerstown
19-20-21-22 .. at Columbus
23-24-25 .... Rome
26-27-28-29 .. Columbus
31 .... at Savannah
SEPTEMBER
1-2 .... at Savannah
3-4 ...... at Charleston, SC
5-6 .... Charleston, SC

CHARLESTON, SC
APRIL
8-9-10-11 .... Greensboro
12-13-14 .... at Savannah
15-16-17-18 .. at Asheville
20-21-22-23 .. Hagerstown
24-25-26-27 .. Lake County
28-29-30 .... at Augusta
MAY
1-2 .... at Capital City
3-4 .... Capital City
5-6-7-8 .... Asheville
10-11-12-13 .. at Delmarva
14-15-16-17 .. at Lakewood
19-20-21 .... Augusta
22-23 .... Capital City
24-25 ...... at Capital City
26-27-28-29 .... at G'boro
31 .... at Columbus
JUNE
1-2 .... at Columbus
3-4-5 .... Rome
6-7-8 .... Columbus
9-10-11 ...... at Savannah
12-13-14 ...... Columbus
15-16-17 .... Savannah
18-19-20 .... at Rome
22-23-24 .... at Columbus
25-26-27 .... Greensboro
JULY
1 .... at Savannah
2 .... Savannah
3 .... Savannah
4 .... Savannah
5-6-7-8 .... Columbus
9-10-11-12 .. at Savannah
14-15-16 .... Rome
17-18-19 .... at Savannah
20-21-22 .... Rome
23-24-25 .... Savannah
26-27-28 .... at Rome
29-30-31 ...... at Augusta
AUGUST
2-3-4-5 .. Charleston, WV
6-7-8-9 .... Lexington
11-12-13-14 .. at Hickory

15-16-17-18 .... at Kann.
19-20-21-22 .... Asheville
23-24-25 .. at Greensboro
26-27-28-29 .. at Asheville
31 .... Augusta
SEPTEMBER
1-2 .... Augusta
3-4 .... Capital City
5-6 .... at Capital City

CHARLESTON, WV
APRIL
8-9-10-11 .... Delmarva
12-13-14 .... at Lakewood
15-16-17-18 .. at H'town
20-21-22-23 .. Greensboro
24-25-26-27 .... Asheville
29-30 .... at Delmarva
MAY
1-2 .... at Delmarva
3-4 .... Lakewood
5-6-7 .... Hagerstown
8-9 .... Lakewood
10-11-12-13 .. at Augusta
14-15-16-17 .. at Cap. City
19-20-21 .... Lake County
22-23 .... at Lexington
24-25-26 ...... Kannapolis
27-28 .... Lexington
29-30-31 .. at Lake County
JUNE
2-3-4 .... at Hickory
5-6 .... at Kannapolis
7-8-9 .... Hickory
10-11 .... Kannapolis
12-13-14 .... at Lexington
15-16-17 .. at Kannapolis
18-19-20 .... Lexington
22-23-24 .... at Hickory
25-26-27 .... Lexington
JULY
1-2-3-4 .... at Delmarva
5-6 .... at Lakewood
7-8 .... Lakewood
9-10-11-12 ...... Delmarva
14-15-16 .. at Lake County
17-18-19-20-21 .. Hickory
22-23 .... at Lexington
24-25-26 .... at Hickory
27-28 .... Lakewood
29-30-31 .... Hagerstown
AUGUST
2-3-4-5 .. at Charleston, SC
6-7-8-9 ...... at Savannah
11-12-13-14 .. Columbus
15-16-17-18 .... Rome
20-21-22 .. at Hagerstown
23-24 .... at Lakewood
25-26-27 ...... Kannapolis
28-29 .... at Lexington
30-31 .... Lexington
SEPTEMBER
1-2-3 .... at Kannapolis
4-5-6 .... Lake County

COLUMBUS
APRIL
8-9-10-11 .... Capital City
12-13-14 .... Rome

15-16-17-18 .. at Augusta
20-21-22-23 .... Delmarva
24-25-26-27 .. Lakewood
28-29-30 .... at Asheville
MAY
1-2-3-4 .... at Greensboro
5-6-7-8 .... Augusta
10-11-12-13 ..... at L. C.
14-15-16-17 .. at H'town
19-20-21 .... Greensboro
22-23-24-25 .... Asheville
26-27-28-29 .. at Cap. City
31 .... Charleston, SC
JUNE
1-2 .... Charleston, SC
3-4-5 .... at Savannah
6-7-8 .. at Charleston, SC
9-10-11 .... Rome
12-13-14 .... at Char., SC
15-16-17 .... at Rome
18-19-20 .... Savannah
22-23-24 .. Charleston, SC
25-26-27 .... Augusta
JULY
1-2-3-4 .... at Asheville
5-6-7-8 .. at Charleston, SC
9-10-11-12 .... Rome
14-15-16 .... Savannah
17-18-19 .... at Rome
20-21-22 .... Savannah
23-24-25 .... at Rome
26-27-28 .... at Savannah
29-30-31 .. at Greensboro
AUGUST
2-3-4-5 .... Hickory
6-7-8-9 ...... Kannapolis
11-12-13-14 .. at Char., WV
15-16-17-18 .. at Lexington
19-20-21-22 .. Capital City
23-24-25 ...... at Augusta
26-27-28-29 .. at Cap. City
31 .... Greensboro
SEPTEMBER
1-2 .... Greensboro
3-4-5-6 .... Asheville

DELMARVA
APRIL
8-9-10-11 .. at Char., WV
12-13-14 ...... Kannapolis
15-16-17-18 .. Lexington
20-21-22-23 .. at Columbus
24-25-26-27 .... at Rome
29-30 .... Charleston, WV
MAY
1-2 .... Charleston, WV
3-4 .... at Kannapolis
5-6-7 .... at Lexington
8-9 .... at Lexington
10-11-12-13 .... Char., SC
14-15-16-17 .. Savannah
19-20-21 .... at Hickory
22-23 .... Lake County
24-25-26 .... at Hagerstown
27-28 ...... at Lake County
29-30-31 .... Hickory
JUNE
2-3-4 ...... at Hagerstown

5-6 .... Lake County
7-8-9 .... Hagerstown
10-11 .... at Lake County
12-13-14 .... at Lakewood
15-16-17 .... Hagerstown
18-19-20 .... Lakewood
22-23-24 .... Lake County
25-26-27 .... Lakewood

JULY
1-2-3-4 .. Charleston, WV
5-6 .... Hickory
7-8 .... at Hickory
9-10-11-12 .. at Char., WV
14-15-16 ...... Kannapolis
17-18 ..... at Lake County
19-20 .... Hagerstown
21-22-23 .... Lake County
24-25-26 .. at Hagerstown
27-28 .... at Hickory
29-30-31 ..... at Lexington

AUGUST
2-3-4-5 .... Capital City
6-7-8-9 .... Augusta
11-12-13-14 at Asheville
15-16-17-18 ... at G'boro
20-21-22 .... Lexington
23-24 .... Hickory
25-26-27 .... Lakewood
28-29-30 .. at Lake County
31 .... at Lakewood

SEPTEMBER
1 .... at Lakewood
2-3 .... Lakewood
4-5-6 .... at Kannapolis

GREENSBORO
APRIL
8-9-10-11 .... at Char., SC
12-13-14 .. at Capital City
15-16-17-18 .. Savannah
20-21-22-23 .. at Char., WV
24-25-26-27 at Lexington
28-29-30 .... Rome

MAY
1-2-3-4 .... Columbus
5-6-7-8 ...... at Savannah
10-11-12-13 .. Kannapolis
14-15-16-17 ...... Hickory
19-20-21 .. at Columbus
22-23-24-25 .... at Rome
26-27-28-29 .... Char., SC
30-31 .... Asheville

JUNE
1 .... Asheville
2-3-4 .... at Augusta
5-6-7 .... at Asheville
9-10-11 .... Augusta
12-13-14 ..... at Asheville
15-16-17 ...... Capital City
18-19-20 .... Asheville
22-23-24 ...... at Augusta
25-26-27 .... at Char., SC

JULY
1-2-3-4 .... Rome
5-6-7-8 .... Augusta
9-10-11-12 at Capital City
14-15-16 .... Augusta
17-18-19 .. at Capital City
20-21-22 .... Asheville

23-24-25 ..... Capital City
26-27-28 ...... at Asheville
29-30-31 .... Columbus

AUGUST
2-3-4-5 .... at Hagerstown
6-7-8-9 .. at Lake County
11-12-13-14 .. Lakewood
15-16-17-18 .... Delmarva
19-20-21-22 .. at Savannah
23-24-25 .. Charleston, SC
26-27-28-29 .. Savannah
31 .... at Columbus

SEPTEMBER
1-2 .... at Columbus
3-4-5-6 .... at Rome

HAGERSTOWN
APRIL
8-9-10-11 ... at Lexington
12-13-14 .... Delmarva
15-16-17-18 .. Char., WV
20-21-22-23 .. at Char., SC
24-25-26-27 .. at Savannah
29-30 .... Lexington

MAY
1-2 .... Lexington
3-4 .... at Hickory
5-6-7 .. at Charleston, WV
8-9 .... at Hickory
10-11-12-13 .... Rome
14-15-16-17 .. Columbus
19-20-21 .. at Kannapolis
22-23 .... Lakewood
24-25-26 .... Delmarva
27-28 .... at Lakewood
29-30-31 ...... Kannapolis

JUNE
2-3-4 .... Delmarva
5-6 .... at Lakewood
7-8-9 .... at Delmarva
10-11 .... Lakewood
12-13-14 .... Lake County
15-16-17 .... at Delmarva
18-19-20 .. at Lake County
22-24 .... Lakewood
25-26-27 .. at Lake County

JULY
1-2-3-4 .... Hickory
5-6 .... Kannapolis
7-8 .... at Kannapolis
9-10-11-12 .... at Hickory
14-15-16 .... Lexington
17-18 .... Lakewood
19-20 .... at Delmarva
21-22-23 .... at Lakewood
24-25-26 .... Lakewood
27-28 .... at Kannapolis
29-30-31 .... at Char., WV

AUGUST
2-3-4-5 .... Greensboro
6-7-8-9 .... Asheville
11-12-13-14 .. at Augusta
15-16-17-18 .. at Cap. City
20-21-22 .. Charleston, WV
23-24 .... Kannapolis
25-26-27 .... Lake County
28-29-30 .... at Lakewood
31 .... at Lake County

SEPTEMBER
1 .... at Lake County
2-3 .... Lake County
4-5-6 .... at Lexington

HICKORY
APRIL
8-9-10-11 ... Lake County
12-13-14 .. at Hagerstown
15-16-17-18 .. at Lakewood
20-21-22-23 ...... Augusta
24-25-26-27 .. Capital City
29-30 ...... at Lake County

MAY
1-2 .... at Lake County
3-4 .... Hagerstown
5-6-7 .... Lakewood
8-9 .... Hagerstown
10-11-12-13 .. at Asheville
14-15-16-17 .... at G'boro
19-20-21 .... Delmarva
22-23 .... Kannapolis
24-25-26 .... at Lexington
27-28 .... at Kannapolis
29-30-31 .... at Delmarva

JUNE
2-3-4 .... Charleston, WV
5-6 .... Lexington
7-8-9 .. at Charleston, WV
10-11 .... at Lexington
12-13-14 ...... Kannapolis
15-16-17 .... Lexington
18-19-20 .. at Kannapolis
22-23-24 .. Charleston, WV
25-26-27 .. at Kannapolis

JULY
1-2-3-4 .... at Hagerstown
5-6 .... at Delmarva
7-8 .... Delmarva
9-10-11-12 .. Hagerstown
14-15-16 .... at Lakewood
17-18-19-20-21 .. at Char., WV
22-23 .... Kannapolis
24-25-26 .. Charleston, WV
27-28 .... Hagerstown
29-30-31 .... Lake County

AUGUST
2-3-4-5 ...... at Columbus
6-7-8-9 .... at Rome
11-12-13-14 .... Char., SC
15-16-17-18 .. Savannah
20-21-22 .. at Lake County
23-24 .... at Delmarva
25-26-27 .... Lexington
28-29 .... at Kannapolis
30-31 .... at Hickory

SEPTEMBER
1-2-3 .... at Lexington
4-5-6 .... Lakewood

KANNAPOLIS
APRIL
8-9-10-11 ...... Lakewood
12-13-14 .... at Delmarva
15-16-17-18 ...... at L. C.
20-21-22-23 .. Capital City
24-25-26-27 ...... Augusta
29-30 .... at Lakewood

MAY
1-2 .... at Lakewood
3-4 .... Delmarva
5-6-7 .... Lake County
8-9 .... Delmarva
10-11-12-13 .... at G'boro
14-15-16-17 .. at Asheville
19-20-21 .... Hagerstown
22-23 .... at Hickory
24-25-26 .... at Char., WV
27-28 .... Hickory
29-30-31 .. at Hagerstown

JUNE
2-3-4 .... at Lexington
5-6 .... Charleston, WV
7-8-9 .... Lexington
10-11 .. at Charleston, WV
12-13-14 .... at Hickory
15-16-17 .. Charleston, WV
18-19-20 .... Hickory
22-23-24 .... at Lexington
25-26-27 .... Hickory

JULY
1-2-3-4 .. at Lake County
5-6 .... at Hagerstown
7-8 .... Hagerstown
9-10-11-12 .. Lake County
14-15-16 .... at Delmarva
17-18-19-20-21 ...... Lex.
22-23 .... at Hickory
24-25-26 .... at Lexington
27-28 .... Hagerstown
29-30-31 .... Lakewood

AUGUST
2-3-4-5 .... at Rome
6-7-8-9 ...... at Columbus
11-12-13-14 .... Savannah
15-16-17-18 .... Char., SC
23-24 ...... at Hagerstown
25-26-27 .... at Char., WV
28-29 .... Hickory
30-31 .... at Hickory

SEPTEMBER
1-2-3 .... Charleston, WV
4-5-6 .... Delmarva

LAKE COUNTY
APRIL
8-9-10-11 ...... at Hickory
12-13-14 .... Lexington
15-16-17-18 .. at Savannah
20-21-22-23 .. at Savannah
24-25-26-27 .. at Char., SC
29-30 .... Hickory

MAY
1-2 .... Hickory
3-4 .... at Lexington
5-6-7 .... at Kannapolis
8-9 .... at Lexington
10-11-12-13 .. Columbus
14-15-16-17 .... Rome
19-20-21 .... at Char., WV
22-23 .... at Lexington
24-25-26 .... Lakewood
27-28 .... Delmarva
29-30-31 .. Charleston, WV

JUNE
2-3-4 .... at Lakewood
5-6 .... at Delmarva
7-8-9 .... Lakewood
10-11 .... Delmarva
12-13-14 .. at Hagerstown
15-16-17 .... at Lakewood
18-19-20 .... Hagerstown
22-23-24 .... at Delmarva
25-26-27 .... Hagerstown

JULY
1-2-3-4 .... Kannapolis
5-6 .... Lexington
7-8 .... at Lexington
9-10-11-12 .. at Kannapolis
14-15-16 .. Charleston, WV
17-18 .... Delmarva
19-20 .... at Lakewood
21-22-23 .... at Delmarva
24-25-26 .... Lakewood
27-28 .... at Lexington
29-30-31 .... at Hickory

AUGUST
2-3-4-5 .... Asheville
6-7-8-9 .... Greensboro
11-12-13-14 .. at Cap. City
15-16-17-18 .. at Augusta
20-21-22 .... Hickory
23-24 .... Lexington
25-26-27 .. at Hagerstown
28-29-30 .... Delmarva
31 .... Hagerstown

SEPTEMBER
1 .... Hagerstown
2-3 .... at Hagerstown
4-5-6 .. at Charleston, WV

LAKEWOOD

APRIL
8-9-10-11 .. at Kannapolis
12-13-14 .. Charleston, WV
15-16-17-18 ...... Hickory
20-21-22-23 .... at Rome
24-25-26-27 .. at Columbus
29-30 .... Kannapolis

MAY
1-2 .... Kannapolis
3-4 .... at Charleston, WV
5-6-7 .... at Hickory
8-9 .... at Charleston, WV
10-11-12-13 .. Savannah
14-15-16-17 .... Char., SC
19-20-21 .... at Lexington
22-23 ...... at Hagerstown
24-25-26 .. at Lake County
27-28 .... Hagerstown
29-30-31 .... Lexington

JUNE
2-3-4 .... Lake County
5-6 .... Hagerstown
7-8-9 ...... at Lake County
10-11 ...... at Hagerstown
12-13-14 .... Delmarva
15-16-17 .... Lake County
18-19-20 .... at Delmarva
22-23-24 .. at Hagerstown
25-26-27 .... Delmarva

JULY
1-2-3-4 .... Lexington
5-6 .... Charleston, WV
7-8 .... at Charleston, WV
9-10-11-12 .. at Lexington
14-15-16 .... Hickory
17-18 ...... at Hagerstown
19-20 .... Lake County
21-22-23 .... Hagerstown
24-25-26 .. at Lake County
27-28 .. at Charleston, WV
29-30-31 .. at Kannapolis

AUGUST
2-3-4-5 .... Augusta
6-7-8-9 .... Capital City
11-12-13-14 .... at G'boro
15-16-17-18 .. at Asheville
20-21-22 ...... Kannapolis
23-24 .... Charleston, WV
25-26-27 .... at Delmarva
28-29-30 .... Hagerstown
31 .... Delmarva

SEPTEMBER
1 .... Delmarva
2-3 .... at Delmarva
4-5-6 .... at Hickory

LEXINGTON

APRIL
8-9-10-11 .... Hagerstown
12-13-14 .. at Lake County
15-16-17-18 .. at Delmarva
20-21-22-23 .... Asheville
24-25-26-27 .. Greensboro
29-30 ...... at Hagerstown

MAY
1-2 .... at Hagerstown
3-4 .... Lake County
5-6-7 .... Delmarva
8-9 .... Lake County
10-11-12-13 .. at Cap. City
14-15-16-17 .. at Augusta
19-20-21 .... Lakewood
22-23 .... Charleston, WV
24-25-26 .... Hickory
27-28 .. at Charleston, WV
29-30-31 .... at Lakewood

JUNE
2-3-4 .... Kannapolis
5-6 .... at Hickory
7-8-9 .... at Kannapolis
10-11 .... Hickory
12-13-14 .. Charleston, WV
15-16-17 .... at Hickory
18-19-20 .... at Char., WV
22-23-24 ...... Kannapolis
25-26-27 .... at Char., WV

JULY
1-2-3-4 ...... at Lakewood
5-6 .... at Lake County
7-8 .... Lake County
9-10-11-12 .... Lakewood
14-15-16 .. at Hagerstown
17-18-19-20-21 .. at Kann.
22-23 .... Charleston, WV
24-25-26 ...... Kannapolis
27-28 .... Lake County
29-30-31 .... Delmarva

AUGUST
2-3-4-5 ...... at Savannah
6-7-8-9 .. at Charleston, SC
11-12-13-14 .... Rome
15-16-17-18 .. Columbus
20-21-22 .... at Delmarva
23-24 ...... at Lake County
25-26-27 .... at Hickory
28-29 .... Charleston, WV
30-31 at Charleston, WV

SEPTEMBER
1-2-3 .... Hickory
4-5-6 .... Hagerstown

ROME

APRIL
8-9-10-11 .... Augusta
12-13-14 .... at Columbus
15-16-17-18 .. at Cap. City
20-21-22-23 .. Lakewood
24-25-26-27 .... Delmarva
28-29-30 .. at Greensboro

MAY
1-2-3-4 .... at Asheville
5-6-7-8 .... Capital City
10-11-12-13 .. at H'town
14-15-16-17 ...... at L. C.
19-20-21 .... Asheville
22-23-24-25 .. Greensboro
26-27-28-29 .. at Augusta
31 .... Savannah

JUNE
1-2 .... Savannah
3-4-5 .. at Charleston, SC
6-7-8 .... at Savannah
9-10-11 ...... at Columbus
12-13-14 .... Savannah
15-16-17 .... Columbus
18-19-20 .. Charleston, SC
22-23-24 .... at Savannah
25-26-27 ...... Capital City

JULY
1-2-3-4 .... at Greensboro
5-6-7-8 .... Savannah
9-10-11-12 .. at Columbus
14-15-16 .... at Char., SC
17-18-19 .... Columbus
20-21-22 .... at Char., SC
23-24-25 .... Columbus
26-27-28 .. Charleston, SC
29-30-31 ...... at Asheville

AUGUST
2-3-4-5 .... Kannapolis
6-7-8-9 .... Hickory
11-12-13-14 .. at Lexington
15-16-17-18 .. at Char., WV
19-20-21-22 ...... Augusta
23-24-25 .. at Capital City
26-27-28-29 .. at Augusta
31 .... Asheville

SEPTEMBER
1-2 .... Asheville
3-4-5-6 .... Greensboro

SAVANNAH

APRIL
8-9-10-11 .... Asheville
12-13-14 .. Charleston, SC
15-16-17-18 .... at G'boro
20-21-22-23 .. Lake County
24-25-26-27 .. Hagerstown
28-29-30 .. at Capital City

MAY
1-2-3-4 .... at Augusta
5-6-7-8 .... Greensboro
10-11-12-13 .. at Lakewood
14-15-16-17 .. at Delmarva
19-20-21 ...... Capital City
22-23 .... at Augusta
24-25 .... Augusta
26-27-28-29 .. at Asheville
31 .... at Rome

JUNE
1-2 .... at Rome
3-4-5 .... Columbus
6-7-8 .... Rome
9-10-11 .. Charleston, SC
12-13-14 .... at Rome
15-16-17 .... at Char., SC
18-19-20 .... at Columbus
22-23-24 .... Rome
25-26-27 .... Asheville

JULY
1 .... Charleston, SC
2 .... at Charleston, SC
3 .... Charleston, SC
4 .... at Charleston, SC
5-6-7-8 .... at Rome
9-10-11-12 ...... Char., SC
14-15-16 .... at Columbus
17-18-19 .. Charleston, SC
20-21-22 .... at Columbus
23-24-25 .... at Char., SC
26-27-28 .... Columbus
29-30-31 .. at Capital City

AUGUST
2-3-4-5 .... Lexington
6-7-8-9 .. Charleston, WV
11-12-13-14 .... at Kann.
15-16-17-18 .. at Hickory
19-20-21-22 .. Greensboro
23-24-25 ...... at Asheville
26-27-28-29 .... at G'boro
31 .... Capital City

SEPTEMBER
1-2 .... Capital City
3-4-5-6 .... Augusta

SHORT-SEASON CLASS A
NEW YORK-PENN LEAGUE

ABERDEEN

JUNE
18-19-20	.. Staten Island
21-22	...... at New Jersey
23-24-25	...... Jamestown
26-27-28	.... at Lowell
29-30	.... Staten Island

JULY
1-2	.... Hudson Valley
3-4	.... New Jersey
5-6-7	.... at Oneonta
9-10-11	.. at Williamsport
12-13-14	.. Hudson Valley
15-16	.. at Hudson Valley
17-18-19	...... New Jersey
20-21-22	.... Williamsport
23-24-25	.... at Brooklyn
26-27	.... Brooklyn
29-30-31	.... Auburn

AUGUST
1-2-3	.... Brooklyn
4-5-6	.... at Batavia
7-8-9	.... Vermont
10-11-12	.. at Williamsport
13-14	.... at Staten Island
15-16	.... at Brooklyn
18-19-20	.. at Hudson Val.
21-22-23	.. at Staten Island
24-25-26	.. at Mahon. Val.
27-28-29	...... Williamsport
30-31	.... Tri-City

SEPTEMBER
1	.... Tri-City
2-3-4	.... at New Jersey

AUBURN

JUNE
18-19-20	.. at Mahon. Val.
21-22	.. Mahoning Valley
23-24-25	...... Williamsport
26-27-28	.. at New Jersey
29-30	...... at Mahon. Val.

JULY
1-2	.. at Mahoning Valley
3	.... Batavia
4	.... at Batavia
5-6-7	.... Brooklyn
9-10-11	.... at Jamestown
12	.... at Batavia
13	.... Batavia
14	.... at Batavia
15	.... Batavia
16	.... at Batavia
17-18-19	.... Tri-City
20-21-22	.... Lowell
23-24-25	.. at Jamestown
26-27	.... Jamestown
29-30-31	.... at Aberdeen

AUGUST
1-2-3	.... Mahoning Valley

BATAVIA

JUNE
18	.... at Jamestown
19	.... at Jamestown
20	.... at Jamestown
21	.... Jamestown
22	.... at Jamestown
23-24-25	...... New Jersey
26-27-28	.... at Tri-City
29	.... at Jamestown
30	.... Jamestown

JULY
1	.... at Jamestown
2	.... Jamestown
3	.... at Auburn
4	.... Auburn
5-6-7	...... at Williamsport
9-10-11	.. at Mahon. Val.
12	.... Auburn
13	.... at Auburn
14	.... Auburn
15	.... at Auburn
16	.... Auburn
17-18-19	...... at Vermont
20-21-22	.... Oneonta
23-24-25	.. at Mahon. Val.
26-27	.. Mahoning Valley
29-30-31	.. at Staten Island

AUGUST
1	.... Jamestown
2	.... at Jamestown
3	.... Jamestown
4-5-6	.... Aberdeen
7-8-9	.... Lowell
10	.... at Auburn
11	.... Auburn
12	.... at Auburn
13-14	.. Mahoning Valley
15-16	...... at Mahon. Val.
18	.... Jamestown
19	.... at Jamestown
20	.... Jamestown
21	.... Auburn
22	.... at Auburn
23	.... Auburn
24-25-26	.. Hudson Valley
27	.... at Auburn
28	.... Auburn
29	.... Auburn
30-31	.... at Oneonta

SEPTEMBER
1	.... at Oneonta
2-3-4	.... Jamestown

BROOKLYN

JUNE
18-19-20	.. at Williamsport
21	.... at Hudson Valley
22	.... Hudson Valley
23-24-25	.... at Tri-City
26-27-28	...... Mahon. Val.
29	.... at Hudson Valley
30	.... at Hudson Valley

JULY
1	.... New Jersey
2	.... at New Jersey
3-4	.... Williamsport
5-6-7	.... at Auburn
9	.... Staten Island
10	.... at Staten Island
11	.... Staten Island
12-13-14	.... Williamsport
15-16	.... at Williamsport
17	.... Hudson Valley
18	.... at Hudson Valley
19	.... Hudson Valley
20-21-22	...... at Vermont
23-24-25	.... Aberdeen
26-27	.... at Aberdeen
29-30-31	.... Lowell

AUGUST
1-2-3	.... at Aberdeen
4-5-6	.... at Jamestown
7	.... New Jersey
8	.... at New Jersey
9	.... New Jersey
10	.... Staten Island
11	.... at Staten Island
12	.... Staten Island
13	.... New Jersey
14	.... at New Jersey
15-16	.... Aberdeen
18	.... at Staten Island
19	.... Staten Island
20	.... at Staten Island
21	.... at New Jersey
22	.... New Jersey
23	.... at New Jersey
24-25-26	.... Oneonta
27	.... Staten Island
28-29	.... at Staten Island
30-31	.... Batavia

AUBURN (continued)

JUNE
21	.... Auburn
22	.... at Auburn
23	.... Auburn
24-25-26	.. Hudson Valley
27	.... at Auburn
28	.... Auburn
29	.... at Auburn
30-31	.... at Brooklyn

SEPTEMBER
1	.... at Brooklyn
2-3-4	.... Mahoning Valley

HUDSON VALLEY

JUNE
18	.... at New Jersey
19	.... New Jersey
20	.... at New Jersey
21	.... Brooklyn
22	.... at Brooklyn
23-24-25	.... Vermont
26-27-28	...... Jamestown
29	.... Brooklyn
30	.... Brooklyn

JULY
1-2	.... at Aberdeen
3	.... at Staten Island
4-5	.... at Staten Island
6	.... at Staten Island
7	.... Staten Island
9	.... New Jersey
10	.... at New Jersey
11	.... New Jersey
12-13-14	.... at Aberdeen
15-16	.... Aberdeen
17	.... at Brooklyn
18	.... Brooklyn
19	.... at Brooklyn
20-21-22	.. at Mahon. Val.
23	.... at Staten Island
24	.... Staten Island
25	.... at Staten Island
26	.... Staten Island
27	.... at Staten Island
29-30-31	...... at Oneonta

AUGUST
1-2-3	...... at Williamsport
4-5-6	.... Auburn
7-8-9	.... Tri-City
10	.... at New Jersey
11	.... New Jersey
12	.... at New Jersey
13-14	.... Williamsport
15-16	.... at Williamsport
18-19-20	.... Aberdeen
21-22-23	...... Williamsport
24-25-26	.... at Batavia
27	.... New Jersey
28	.... at New Jersey
29	.... New Jersey
30-31	.... at Lowell

SEPTEMBER
1	.... at Lowell
2	.... Brooklyn
3	.... at Brooklyn
4	.... Brooklyn

JAMESTOWN

JUNE
18 .... Batavia
19 .... at Batavia
20 .... Batavia
21 .... at Batavia
22 .... Batavia
23-24-25 .... at Aberdeen
26-27-28 .. at Hudson Val.
29 .... Batavia
30 .... at Batavia

JULY
1 .... Batavia
2 .... at Batavia
3-4 ...... Mahoning Valley
5-6-7 .... at Lowell
9-10-11 .... Auburn
12-13-14 .... Mahon. Val.
15-16 ...... at Mahon. Val.
17-18-19 .... Oneonta
20-21-22 .. at New Jersey
23-24-25 .... Auburn
26-27 .... at Auburn
29-30-31 .... Vermont

AUGUST
1 .... at Batavia
2 .... Batavia
3 .... at Batavia
4-5-6 .... Brooklyn
7-8-9 .... Williamsport
10-11-12 .. at Mahon. Val.
13-14 .... at Auburn
15-16 .... Auburn
18 .... at Batavia
19 .... Batavia
20 .... at Batavia
21-22-23 .. at Mahon. Val.
24-25-26 ...... at Tri-City
27-28-29 .... Mahon. Val.
30-31 .... Staten Island

SEPTEMBER
1 .... Staten Island
2-3-4 .... at Auburn

LOWELL

JUNE
18-19-20 .... Tri-City
21-22 .... at Vermont
23-24-25 .... Mahon. Val.
26-27-28 .... Aberdeen
29-30 .... at Oneonta

JULY
1-2 .... Oneonta
3-4 .... at Tri-City
5-6-7 .... Jamestown
9-10-11 .... at Tri-City
12-13-14-15-16 .. Vermont
17-18-19 .. at Williamsport
20-21-22 .... at Auburn
23-24-25 .... Vermont
26-27 .... Tri-City
29-30-31 ...... at Brooklyn

AUGUST
1-2-3 .... Oneonta
4-5-6 .... at Staten Island
7-8-9 .... at Batavia

10-11-12 ...... at Vermont
13-14 .... Tri-City
15-16 .... at Oneonta
18-19-20 .... Oneonta
21-22-23 .... at Tri-City
24-25-26 ...... New Jersey
27-28-29 ...... at Oneonta
30-31 .... Hudson Valley

SEPTEMBER
1 .... Hudson Valley
2-3-4 .... at Vermont

MAHONING VALLEY

JUNE
18-19-20 .... Auburn
21-22 .... at Auburn
23-24-25 .... at Lowell
26-27-28 ...... at Brooklyn
29-30 .... Auburn

JULY
1-2 .... Auburn
3-4 .... at Jamestown
5-6-7 .... Vermont
9-10-11 .... Batavia
12-13-14 .. at Jamestown
15-16 .... Jamestown
17-18-19 .. at Staten Island
20-21-22 .. Hudson Valley
23-24-25 .... Batavia
26-27 .... at Batavia
29-30-31 ...... New Jersey

AUGUST
1-2-3 .... at Auburn
4-5-6 .... Tri-City
7-8-9 .... at Oneonta
10-11-12 .... Jamestown
13-14 .... at Batavia
15-16 .... Batavia
18-19-20 .... at Auburn
21-22-23 .... Jamestown
24-25-26 .... Aberdeen
27-28-29 .. at Jamestown
30-31 .... at Williamsport

SEPTEMBER
1 .... at Williamsport
2-3-4 .... at Batavia

NEW JERSEY

JUNE
18 .... Hudson Valley
19 .... at Hudson Valley
20 .... Hudson Valley
21-22 .... Aberdeen
23-24-25 .... at Batavia
26-27-28 .... Auburn
29-30 ..... at Williamsport

JULY
1 .... at Brooklyn
2 .... Brooklyn
3-4 .... at Aberdeen
5-6-7 .... Tri-City
9 .... at Hudson Valley
10 .... at Hudson Valley
11 .... at Hudson Valley
12 .... at Staten Island
13 .... Staten Island

14 .... at Staten Island
15 .... Staten Island
16 .... at Staten Island
17-18-19 ..... at Aberdeen
20-21-22 ...... Jamestown
23-24 .... Williamsport
25-26-27 .. at Williamsport
29-30-31 .. at Mahon. Val.

AUGUST
1 .... Staten Island
2 .... at Staten Island
3 .... Staten Island
4-5-6 .... at Oneonta
7 .... at Brooklyn
8 .... Brooklyn
9 .... at Brooklyn
10 .... Hudson Valley
11 .... at Hudson Valley
12 .... Hudson Valley
13 .... at Brooklyn
14 .... Brooklyn
15 .... at Staten Island
16 .... Staten Island
18-19-20 .... Williamsport
21 .... Brooklyn
22 .... at Brooklyn
23 .... Brooklyn
24-25-26 .... at Lowell
27 .... at Hudson Valley
28 .... Hudson Valley
29 .... at Hudson Valley
30-31 .... Vermont

SEPTEMBER
1 .... Vermont
2-3-4 .... Aberdeen

ONEONTA

JUNE
18-19-20 .... Vermont
21-22 .... Tri-City
23-24-25 .. at Staten Island
26-27-28 .. at Williamsport
29-30 .... Lowell

JULY
1-2 .... at Lowell
3-4 .... Vermont
5-6-7 .... Aberdeen
9-10-11 .... at Vermont
12-13-14 .... Tri-City
15-16 .... at Tri-City
17-18-19 .. at Jamestown
20-21-22 .... at Batavia
23-24-25 .... Tri-City
26-27 .... at Vermont
29-30-31 .. Hudson Valley

AUGUST
1-2-3 .... at Lowell
4-5-6 .... New Jersey
7-8-9 ... Mahoning Valley
10-11-12 .... at Tri-City
13-14 .... at Vermont
15-16 .... Lowell
18-19-20 .... at Lowell
21-22-23 .... Vermont
24-25-26 ..... at Brooklyn
27-28-29 .... Lowell
30-31 .... Auburn

SEPTEMBER
1 .... Auburn
2-3-4 .... at Tri-City

STATEN ISLAND

JUNE
18-19-20 .... at Aberdeen
21-22 .... Williamsport
23-24-25 .... Oneonta
26-27-28 ...... at Vermont
29-30 .... at Aberdeen

JULY
1-2 .... at Williamsport
3 .... Hudson Valley
4-5 ...... at Hudson Valley
6 .... Hudson Valley
7 .... at Hudson Valley
9 .... at Brooklyn
10 .... Brooklyn
11 .... at Brooklyn
12 .... New Jersey
13 .... at New Jersey
14 .... New Jersey
15 .... at New Jersey
16 .... New Jersey
17-18-19 ..... Mahon. Val.
20-21-22 .... at Tri-City
23 .... Hudson Valley
24 .... at Hudson Valley
25 .... Hudson Valley
26 .... at Hudson Valley
27 .... Hudson Valley
29-30-31 .... Batavia

AUGUST
1 .... at New Jersey
2 .... New Jersey
3 .... at New Jersey
4-5-6 .... Lowell
7-8-9 .... at Auburn
10 .... at Brooklyn
11 .... Brooklyn
12 .... at Brooklyn
13-14 .... Aberdeen
15 .... New Jersey
16 .... at New Jersey
18 .... Brooklyn
19 .... at Brooklyn
20 .... Brooklyn
21-22-23 .... Aberdeen
24-25-26 .... Williamsport
27 .... at Brooklyn
28-29 .... Brooklyn
30-31 ...... at Jamestown

SEPTEMBER
1 .... at Jamestown
2-3-4 ...... at Williamsport

TRI-CITY

JUNE
18-19-20 .... at Lowell
21-22 .... at Oneonta
23-24-25 .... Brooklyn
26-27-28 .... Batavia
29-30 .... at Vermont

JULY
1-2 .... Vermont

3-4	.... Lowell
5-6-7	.... at New Jersey
9-10-11	.... Lowell
12-13-14	...... at Oneonta
15-16	.... at Lowell
17-18-19	.... at Auburn
20-21-22	.. Staten Island
23-24-25	...... at Oneonta
26-27	.... at Lowell
29-30-31	.... Williamsport

AUGUST

1-2-3	.... Vermont
4-5-6	.. at Mahoning Valley
7-8-9	.. at Hudson Valley
10-11-12	.... Oneonta
13-14	.... at Lowell
15-16	.... Vermont
18-19-20	...... at Vermont
21-22-23	.... Lowell
24-25-26	...... Jamestown
27-28-29	...... at Vermont
30-31	.... at Aberdeen

SEPTEMBER

| 1 | .... at Aberdeen |

| 2-3-4 | .... Oneonta |

VERMONT

JUNE

18-19-20	...... at Oneonta
21-22	.... Lowell
23-24-25	.. at Hudson Val.
26-27-28	.. Staten Island
29-30	.... Tri-City

JULY

1-2	.... at Tri-City
3-4	.... at Oneonta
5-6-7	.. at Mahoning Valley
9-10-11	.... Oneonta
12-13-14-15-16	.. at Lowell
17-18-19	.... Batavia
20-21-22	.... Brooklyn
23-24-25	.... at Lowell
26-27	.... Oneonta
29-30-31	.. at Jamestown

AUGUST

| 1-2-3 | .... at Tri-City |
| 4-5-6 | .... Williamsport |

7-8-9	.... at Aberdeen
10-11-12	.... Lowell
13-14	.... Oneonta
15-16	.... at Tri-City
18-19-20	.... Tri-City
21-22-23	...... at Oneonta
24-25-26	.... Auburn
27-28-29	.... Tri-City
30-31	...... at New Jersey

SEPTEMBER

| 1 | .... at New Jersey |
| 2-3-4 | .... Lowell |

WILLIAMSPORT

JUNE

18-19-20	.... Brooklyn
21-22	.... at Staten Island
23-24-25	.... at Auburn
26-27-28	.... Oneonta
29-30	.... New Jersey

JULY

| 1-2 | .... Staten Island |
| 3-4 | .... at Brooklyn |

5-6-7	.... Batavia
9-10-11	.... Aberdeen
12-13-14	...... at Brooklyn
15-16	.... Brooklyn
17-18-19	.... Lowell
20-21-22	.... at Aberdeen
23-24	...... at New Jersey
25-26-27	...... New Jersey
29-30-31	...... at Tri-City

AUGUST

1-2-3	...... Hudson Valley
4-5-6	.... at Vermont
7-8-9	.... at Jamestown
10-11-12	.... Aberdeen
13-14	.. at Hudson Valley
15-16	...... Hudson Valley
18-19-20	.. at New Jersey
21-22-23	.. at Hudson Val.
24-25-26	.. at Staten Island
27-28-29	.... at Aberdeen
30-31	.. Mahoning Valley

SEPTEMBER

| 1 | .... Mahoning Valley |
| 2-3-4 | .... Staten Island |

NORTHWEST LEAGUE

BOISE

JUNE

18-19-20	.... Spokane
21-22-23-24-25	.. at Van.
26-27-28-29-30	...... Eugene

JULY

1-2-3	.... at Spokane
4-5-6	.... Tri-City
7-8-9-10-11	.... at Eugene
13-14-15-16-17	.. Van.
18-19-20	.... at Yakima
21-22-23	.... Spokane
24-25-26-27-28	.. at Salem
29-30-31	.... Everett

AUGUST

1-2	.... Everett
5-6-7	.... at Yakima
8-9-10	.... at Tri-City
11-12-13-14-15	.. Salem
16-17-18	.... Yakima
20-21-22	...... at Spokane
23-24-25-26-27	.. at Everett
28-29-30	.... at Tri-City
31	.... Tri-City

SEPTEMBER

| 1-2 | .... Tri-City |
| 3-4-5 | .... Yakima |

EUGENE

JUNE

18-19-20	.. at Salem-Keizer
21-22-23-24-25	.. Tri-City
26-27-28-29-30	.. at Boise

JULY

1-2-3	.... Salem-Keizer
4-5-6	.... at Salem-Keizer
7-8-9-10-11	.... Boise
13-14-15-16-17	.. at Spok.

18-19-20-21-22-23	.. Everett
24-25-26-27-28	.. at Yakima
29-30-31	.... Spokane

AUGUST

1-2	.... Spokane
5-6-7	.... at Everett
8-9-10-11-12	...... Yakima
13-14-15	.... at Everett
16-17-18	.. at Vancouver
20-21-22	...... Vancouver
23-24-25-26-27	.. at Tri-City
28-29-30	.. Salem-Keizer
31	.... at Vancouver

SEPTEMBER

| 1-2 | .... at Vancouver |
| 3-4-5 | .... Vancouver |

EVERETT

JUNE

18-19-20	.... Vancouver
21-22-23-24-25	.. at Yakima
26-27-28-29-30	.. Spokane

JULY

1-2-3	.... at Vancouver
4-5-6	.... Vancouver
7-8-9-10-11	.. at Tri-City
13-14-15-16-17	.. Yakima
18-19-20-21-22-23	.. at Eug.
24-25-26-27-28	.. Tri-City
29-30-31	.... at Boise

AUGUST

1-2	.... at Boise
5-6-7	.... Eugene
8-9-10-11-12	.. at Spokane
13-14-15	.... Eugene
16-17-18	.. at Salem-Keizer
20-21-22	.. Salem-Keizer
23-24-25-26-27	.... Boise
28-29-30	.. at Vancouver

| 31 | .... Salem-Keizer |

SEPTEMBER

| 1-2 | .... at Everett |
| 3-4-5 | .... Everett |

SPOKANE

JUNE

18-19-20	.... at Boise
21-22-23-24-25	...... Salem
26-27-28-29-30	.. at Everett

JULY

| 1-2-3 | .... Boise |

4-5-6	.... Yakima
7-8-9-10-11	.. at Vancouver
13-14-15-16-17	.. Eugene
18-19-20	.... at Tri-City
21-22-23	.... at Boise
24-25-26-27-28	...... Van.
29-30-31	.... at Eugene

AUGUST

1-2	.... at Eugene
5-6-7	.... Tri-City
8-9-10-11-12	...... Everett
13-14-15	.... at Yakima
16-17-18	.... at Tri-City
20-21-22	.... Boise
23-24-25-26-27	.. at S-K
28-29-30	.... Yakima
31	.... at Yakima

SEPTEMBER

| 1-2 | .... at Yakima |
| 3-4-5 | .... Tri-City |

TRI-CITY

JUNE

18-19-20	.... Yakima
21-22-23-24-25	.. at Eugene
26-27-28-29-30	...... Van.

JULY

1-2	.... at Yakima
3	.... Yakima
4-5-6	.... at Boise
7-8-9-10-11	.... Everett
13-14-15-16-17	.. at S-K
18-19-20	.... Spokane
21	.... at Yakima
22-23	.... Yakima
24-25-26-27-28	.. at Everett
29-30-31	.. Salem-Keizer

AUGUST

| 1-2 | .... Salem-Keizer |

5-6-7 .... at Spokane
8-9-10 .... Boise
11-12-13-14-15 .. at Van.
16-17-18 .... Spokane
20-21-22 .... at Yakima
23-24-25-26-27 .. Eugene
28-29-30 .... Boise
31 .... at Boise

SEPTEMBER
1-2 .... at Boise
3-4-5 .... at Spokane

VANCOUVER

JUNE
18-19-20 .... at Everett
21-22-23-24-25 .... Boise
26-27-28-29-30 .. at Tri-City

JULY
1-2-3 .... Everett
4-5-6 .... at Everett
7-8-9-10-11 ...... Spokane
13-14-15-16-17 .. at Boise
18-19-20-21-22-23 .. S-K
24-25-26-27-28 .. at Spokane
29-30-31 .... Yakima

AUGUST
1-2 .... Yakima
5-6-7-8-9-10 .... at Salem
11-12-13-14-15 .. Tri-City
16-17-18 .... Eugene
20-21-22 .... at Eugene
23-24-25-26-27 .. at Yakima
28-29-30 .... Everett
31 .... Eugene

SEPTEMBER
1-2 .... Eugene
3-4-5 .... at Eugene

YAKIMA

JUNE
18-19-20 .... at Tri-City
21-22-23-24-25 .. Everett
26-27-28-29-30 .. at S-K

JULY
1-2 .... Tri-City
3 .... at Tri-City
4-5-6 .... at Spokane
7-8-9-10-11 .. Salem-Keizer
13-14-15-16-17 .. at Everett
18-19-20 .... Boise
21 .... Tri-City

22-23 .... at Tri-City
24-25-26-27-28 .. Eugene
29-30-31 .. at Vancouver

AUGUST
1-2 .... at Vancouver
5-6-7 .... Boise
8-9-10-11-12 .. at Eugene
13-14-15 .... Spokane
16-17-18 .... at Boise
20-21-22 .... Tri-City
23-24-25-26-27 ...... Van.
28-29-30 ...... at Spokane
31 .... Spokane

SEPTEMBER
1-2 .... Spokane
3-4-5 .... at Boise

ROOKIE LEAGUES
APPALACHIAN LEAGUE

BLUEFIELD

JUNE
21	Princeton
22-23-24	at Danville
25-26-27	at Kingsport
28-29-30	Danville

JULY
1-2-3	at Princeton
4-5-6	at Greeneville
7-8-9	Pulaski
10-11-12	at Burlington
14-15-16	Elizabethton
17-18-19	Johnson City
20-21-22	at Burlington
23-24-25	Danville
26-27-28	Pulaski
29-30-31	at Princeton

AUGUST
1	Princeton
3-4-5	at Pulaski
6-7-8	at Elizabethton
9-10-11	Burlington
12-13	Princeton
14	at Princeton
15-16-17	at Bristol
19-20-21	Bristol
22-23-24	at Johnson City
25-26-27	Greeneville
28-29-30	Kingsport

BRISTOL

JUNE
21	at Pulaski
22-23-24	Elizabethton
25-26-27	Burlington
28	at Elizabethton
29-30	Elizabethton

JULY
1-2	at Greeneville
3	Greeneville
4-5	at Kingsport
6	Kingsport
7	at Johnson City
8-9	Johnson City
10-11-12	Danville
14-15-16	at Princeton
17-18-19	at Pulaski
20-21-22	Greeneville
23-24-25	at Elizabethton
26-27-28	Kingsport
29-30-31	Johnson City

AUGUST
1	Pulaski
3-4-5	at Kingsport
6-7-8	Princeton
9-10-11	at Greeneville
12-13-14	at Johnson City
15-16-17	Bluefield
19-20-21	at Bluefield
22-23-24	Pulaski
25-26-27	at Danville

BURLINGTON

JUNE
21	at Danville
22-23-24	Greeneville
25-26-27	at Bristol
28-29-30	at Pulaski

JULY
1	Danville
2-3	at Danville
4-5-6	Princeton
7-8-9	at Kingsport
10-11-12	Bluefield
14-15-16	at Danville
17-18-19	Princeton
20-21-22	Bluefield
23-24-25	at Greeneville
26-27-28	at Johnson City
29-30-31	Elizabethton

AUGUST
1	at Danville
3-4-5	Johnson City
6-7-8	Danville
9-10-11	at Bluefield
12-13-14	at Elizabethton
15-16-17	Pulaski
19-20-21	at Pulaski
22-23-24	at Princeton
25-26-27	Kingsport
28-29-30	Bristol

DANVILLE

JUNE
21	Burlington
22-23-24	Bluefield
25-26-27	at Johnson City
28-29-30	at Bluefield

JULY
1	at Burlington
2-3	Burlington
4	at Pulaski
5-6	Pulaski
7-8-9	at Princeton
10-11-12	at Bristol
14-15-16	Burlington
17-18-19	Kingsport
20	Pulaski
21-22	at Pulaski
23-24-25	at Bluefield
26-27-28	Elizabethton
29-30-31	Greeneville

AUGUST
1	Burlington
3-4-5	at Elizabethton
6-7-8	at Burlington
9-10-11	Pulaski
12-13-14	at Greeneville
15-16-17	at Princeton
19-20-21	Princeton
22-23-24	at Kingsport

ELIZABETHTON

JUNE
21	Greeneville
22-23-24	at Bristol
25-26-27	Princeton
28	Bristol
29-30	at Bristol

JULY
1-2-3	Pulaski
4	Johnson City
5-6	at Johnson City
7	at Greeneville
8-9	Greeneville
10-11	Kingsport
12	at Kingsport
14-15-16	at Bluefield
17-18-19	at Greeneville
20-21-22	Johnson City
23-24-25	Bristol
26-27-28	at Danville
29-30-31	at Burlington

AUGUST
1	at Greeneville
3-4-5	Danville
6-7-8	Bluefield
9-10-11	at Johnson City
12-13-14	Burlington
15-16-17	at Kingsport
19-20-21	Kingsport
22-23-24	Greeneville
25-26-27	at Pulaski
28-29-30	at Princeton

GREENEVILLE

JUNE
21	at Elizabethton
22-23-24	at Burlington
25-26-27	Pulaski
28	Kingsport
29-30	at Kingsport

JULY
1-2	Bristol
3	at Bristol
4-5-6	Bluefield
7	Elizabethton
8-9	at Elizabethton
10-11	Johnson City
12	at Johnson City
14-15-16	Kingsport
17-18-19	Elizabethton
20-21-22	at Bristol
23-24-25	Burlington
26-27-28	at Princeton
29-30-31	at Danville

AUGUST
1	Elizabethton
3-4-5	Princeton
6-7-8	at Kingsport

JOHNSON CITY

JUNE
21	Kingsport
22-23-24	at Kingsport
25-26-27	Danville
28-29-30	Princeton

JULY
1	at Kingsport
2-3	Kingsport
4	at Elizabethton
5-6	Elizabethton
7	Bristol
8-9	at Bristol
10-11	at Greeneville
12	Greeneville
14-15-16	Pulaski
17-18-19	at Bluefield
20-21-22	at Elizabethton
23-24	Kingsport
25	at Kingsport
26-27-28	Burlington
29-30-31	at Bristol

AUGUST
1	Kingsport
3-4-5	at Burlington
6-7-8	at Pulaski
9-10-11	Elizabethton
12-13-14	Bristol
15-16-17	at Greeneville
19-20-21	Greeneville
22-23-24	Bluefield
25-26-27	at Princeton
28-29-30	at Danville

KINGSPORT

JUNE
21	at Johnson City
22-23-24	Johnson City
25-26-27	Bluefield
28	at Greeneville
29-30	Greeneville

JULY
1	Johnson City
2-3	at Johnson City
4-5	Bristol
6	at Bristol
7-8-9	Burlington
10-11	at Elizabethton
12	Elizabethton
14-15-16	at Greeneville
17-18-19	at Danville
20-21-22	Princeton
23-24	at Johnson City

BLUEFIELD (cont.)

28-29-30	at Burlington

BRISTOL (cont.)

25-26-27	Bristol
28-29-30	Johnson City

ELIZABETHTON (cont.)

9-10-11	Bristol
12-13-14	Danville
15-16-17	Johnson City
19-20-21	at Johnson City
22-23-24	at Elizabethton
25-26-27	at Bluefield
28-29-30	at Pulaski

25 .... Johnson City
26-27-28 .... at Bristol
29-30-31 .... Pulaski

AUGUST
1 .... at Johnson City
3-4-5 .... Bristol
6-7-8 .... Greeneville
9-10-11 .... Princeton
12-13-14 .... at Pulaski
15-16-17 .... Elizabethton
19-20-21 .. at Elizabethton
22-23-24 .... Danville
25-26-27 .. at Burlington
28-29-30 ..... at Bluefield

PRINCETON
JUNE
21 .... at Bluefield
22-23-24 .... Pulaski

25-26-27 .. at Elizabethton
28-29-30 .. at Johnson City

JULY
1-2-3 .... Bluefield
4-5-6 .... at Burlington
7-8-9 .... Danville
10-11-12 .... at Pulaski
14-15-16 .... Bristol
17-18-19 .. at Burlington
20-21-22 .... at Kingsport
23-24-25 .... at Pulaski
26-27-28 .... Greeneville
29-30-31 .... Bluefield

AUGUST
1 .... at Bluefield
3-4-5 .... at Greeneville
6-7-8 .... at Bristol
9-10-11 .... Kingsport

12-13 .... at Bluefield
14 .... Bluefield
15-16-17 .... Danville
19-20-21 ..... at Danville
22-23-24 ..... Burlington
25-26-27 .. Johnson City
28-29-30 .... Elizabethton

PULASKI
JUNE
21 .... Bristol
22-23-24 .... at Princeton
25-26-27 .. at Greeneville
28-29-30 .... Burlington

JULY
1-2-3 .... at Elizabethton
4 .... Danville
5-6 .... at Danville
7-8-9 .... at Bluefield

10-11-12 .... Princeton
14-15-16 .. at Johnson City
17-18-19 .... Bristol
20 .... at Danville
21-22 .... Danville
23-24-25 .... Princeton
26-27-28 ...... at Bluefield
29-30-31 .... at Kingsport

AUGUST
1 .... at Bristol
3-4-5 .... Bluefield
6-7-8 .... Johnson City
9-10-11 .... at Danville
12-13-14 .... Kingsport
15-16-17 .. at Burlington
19-20-21 ..... Burlington
22-23-24 ...... at Bristol
25-26-27 .... Elizabethton
28-29-30 ..... Greeneville

PIONEER LEAGUE

BILLINGS
JUNE
18-19-20 .... Helena
21-22 .... Great Falls
23-24-25-26 .... at G. F.
28-29 .... at Missoula
30 .... Great Falls

JULY
1 .... Great Falls
2-3-4 .... Missoula
5-6 .... Helena
7-8-9 .... at Missoula
10-11-12 .... at Helena
14-15-16 ...... Idaho Falls
17-18-19-20 .... Casper
21-22-23-24 .... at I. F.
25-26-27 .... at Casper
28-29-30 .... Helena
31 .... Great Falls

AUGUST
1-2-3 .... Great Falls
5-6 .... at Helena
7-8-9-10 .... at Great Falls
11-12 .... Missoula
13-14-15 .... at Missoula
16-17-18-19 .... Ogden
20-21-22 .... Provo
24-25-26 .... at Ogden
27-28-29 .... at Provo
30 .... at Provo

SEPTEMBER
1-2-3 .... Missoula
4-5-6 .... at Helena

CASPER
JUNE
18-19-20-21-22 .... Provo
23-24-25-26 .... at Ogden
28-29-30 ...... Idaho Falls

JULY
1-2 .... Ogden
3-4-5-6-7 .. at Idaho Falls
8-9-10 .... at Provo

12-13 .... at Ogden
14-15-16 .. at Great Falls
17-18-19-20 .. at Billings
21-22-23-24 .. Great Falls
25-26-27 .... Billings
28-29-30-31 .... at Ogden

AUGUST
2-3-4 .... Idaho Falls
5-6-7-8 .... Ogden
9-10-11 ... at Idaho Falls
12-13-14 .... at Provo
16-17-18-19 .... Helena
20-21-22 .... Missoula
24-25-26-27 at Missoula
28-29-30 .... at Helena
31 .... at Provo

SEPTEMBER
1 .... at Provo
2-3-4 .... Provo
5-6 .... Idaho Falls

GREAT FALLS
JUNE
18-19-20 .... Missoula
21-22 .... at Billings
23-24-25-26 ..... Billings
28-29 .... at Helena
30 .... at Billings

JULY
1 .... at Billings
2-3-4 .... Helena
5-6 .... Missoula
7-8-9 .... at Helena
10-11-12 ...... at Missoula
14-15-16 .... Casper
17-18-19-20 .. Idaho Falls
21-22-23-24 .. at Casper
25-26-27 .. at Idaho Falls
28-29-30 .... Missoula
31 .... at Billings

AUGUST
1-2-3 .... at Billings
5-6 .... at Missoula
7-8-9-10 .... Billings

11-12 .... Helena
13-14-15 .... at Helena
16-17-18-19 .... Provo
20-21-22 .... Ogden
24-25-26 .... at Provo
27-28-29-30 .... at Ogden

SEPTEMBER
1-2-3 .... Helena
4-5-6 .... at Missoula

HELENA
JUNE
18-19-20 .... at Billings
21-22-23-24 .... Missoula
25-26 .... at Missoula
28-29 .... Great Falls
30 .... at Missoula

JULY
1 .... at Missoula
2-3-4 .... at Great Falls
5-6 .... at Billings
7-8-9 .... Great Falls
10-11-12 .... Billings
14-15-16 .... at Ogden
17, 19-20 .... at Provo
21-22-23-24 .... Ogden
25-26-27 .... Provo
28-29-30 ..... at Billings
31 .... at Missoula

AUGUST
1-2-3 .... at Missoula
5-6 .... Billings
7-8-9-10 .... Missoula
11-12 .... at Great Falls
13-14-15 ...... Great Falls
16-17-18-19 .. at Casper
20-21-22 .. at Idaho Falls
24-25-26-27 .. Idaho Falls
28-29-30 .... Casper

SEPTEMBER
1-2-3 .... at Great Falls
4-5-6 .... Billings

IDAHO FALLS
JUNE
18-19-20 .... Ogden
21-22 .... at Ogden
23-24-25-26 .... at Provo
28-29-30 .... at Casper

JULY
1-2 .... Provo
3-4-5-6-7 .... Casper
8-9-10 .... at Ogden
12-13 .... Provo
14-15-16 ...... at Billings
17-18-19-20 .... at G. F.
21-22-23-24 ...... Billings
25-26-27 ...... Great Falls
28-29-30-31 .... at Provo

AUGUST
2-3-4 .... at Casper
5-6-7-8 .... Provo
9-10-11 .... Casper
12-13-14 .... at Ogden
16-17-18-19 .... Missoula
20-21-22 .... Helena
24-25-26-27 .. at Helena
28-29-30 ...... at Missoula
31 .... Ogden

SEPTEMBER
1-2-3-4 .... Ogden
5-6 .... at Casper

MISSOULA
JUNE
18-19-20 .. at Great Falls
21-22-23-24 ... at Helena
25-26 .... Helena
28-29 .... Billings
30 .... Helena

JULY
1 .... Helena
2-3-4 .... at Billings
5-6 .... at Great Falls
7-8-9 .... Billings
10-11-12 ...... Great Falls

14-15-16 .... at Provo
17-18-19-20 .... at Ogden
21-22-23-24 .... Provo
25-26-27 .... Ogden
28-29-30 .. at Great Falls
31 .... Helena

AUGUST
1-2-3 .... Helena
5-6 .... Great Falls
7-8-9-10 .... at Helena
11-12 .... at Billings
13-14-15 .... Billings
16-17-18-19 .... at I. F.
20-21-22 .... at Casper
24-25-26-27 .... Casper
28-29-30 ...... Idaho Falls

SEPTEMBER
1-2-3 .... at Billings
4-5-6 .... Great Falls

OGDEN
JUNE
18-19-20 .. at Idaho Falls
21-22 .... Idaho Falls
23-24-25-26 .... Casper
28-29-30 .... at Provo

JULY
1-2 .... at Casper
3-4-5 .... Provo
6-7 .... at Provo
8-9-10 .... Idaho Falls
12-13 .... at Casper
14-15-16 .... Helena
17-18-19-20 .... Missoula
21-22-23-24 .... at Helena
25-26-27 ...... at Missoula
28-29-30-31 .... Casper

AUGUST
2-3-4 .... at Provo
5-6-7-8 .... at Casper
9-10-11 .... Provo

12-13-14 ...... Idaho Falls
16-17-18-19 .. at Billings
20-21-22 .. at Great Falls
24-25-26 .... Billings
27-28-29-30 .. Great Falls
31 .... at Idaho Falls

SEPTEMBER
1-2-3-4 .... at Idaho Falls
5-6 .... Provo

PROVO
JUNE
18-19-20-21-22 .. at Casper
23-24-25-26 .. Idaho Falls
28-29-30 .... Ogden

JULY
1-2 .... at Idaho Falls
3-4-5 .... at Ogden
6-7 .... Ogden
8-9-10 .... Casper
12-13 .... at Casper

14-15-16 .... Missoula
17 .... Helena
19-19-20 .... Helena
21-22-23-24 .. at Missoula
25-26-27 .... at Helena
28-29-30-31 .. Idaho Falls

AUGUST
2-3-4 .... Ogden
5-6-7-8 .... at Idaho Falls
9-10-11 .... at Ogden
12-13-14 .... Casper
16-17-18-19 .. at Great Falls
20-21-22 .... at Billings
24-25-26 ..... Great Falls
27-28-28 .... Billings
30 .... Billings
31 .... Casper

SEPTEMBER
1 .... Casper
2-3-4 .... at Casper
5-6 .... at Ogden

INDEPENDENT
LEAGUES

INDEPENDENT
LEAGUES

2003 STANDINGS #Wild-card

ATLANTIC LEAGUE

NORTH	W	L	PCT	GB
*Bridgeport	73	53	.579	—
*Nashua	71	55	.563	2
Long Island	67	59	.532	6
Pennsylvania	30	95	.240	42½

SOUTH	W	L	PCT	GB
*Camden	78	48	.619	—
*Somerset	67	59	.532	11
Atlantic City	63	63	.500	15
Newark	54	71	.432	23½

PLAYOFFS—Semifinals: Somerset defeated Camden 2-0 and Nashua defeated Bridgeport 2-1 in best-of-3 series. **Final:** Somerset defeated Nashua 3-2 in best-of-5 series.

CENTRAL LEAGUE

EAST	W	L	PCT	GB
*Jackson	59	37	.615	—
*Fort Worth	51	43	.543	7
Shreveport	51	44	.537	7½
Springfield/Ozark	40	56	.417	19
Alexandria	40	56	.417	19

WEST	W	L	PCT	GB
*Edinburg	58	38	.563	—
#Amarillo	48	46	.511	9
San Angelo	47	48	.495	10½
Coastal Bend	46	50	.479	12
Rio Grande Valley	37	59	.385	21

PLAYOFFS—Semifinals: Amarillo defeated Edinburg 3-2 and Jackson defeated Fort Worth 3-2 in best-of-5 series. **Final:** Jackson defeated Amarillo 3-0 in best-of-5 series.

FRONTIER LEAGUE

EAST	W	L	PCT	GB
Chillicothe	54	31	.635	—
#Washington	54	34	.614	1½
#Evansville	51	37	.580	4½
Richmond	50	39	.562	6
Kalamazoo	33	56	.371	23
Florence	27	61	.307	28½

WEST	W	L	PCT	GB
Gateway	50	38	.568	—
Rockford	48	42	.533	3
Kenosha	47	42	.528	3½
River City	43	47	.478	9
Cook County	42	48	.467	9
Mid-Missouri	33	57	.367	18

PLAYOFFS—Semifinals: Gateway defeated Washington 2-0 and Evansville defeated Chillicothe 2-1 in best-of-3 series. **Final:** Gateway defeated Evansville 3-0 in best-of-5 series.

NORTHERN LEAGUE

EAST	W	L	PCT	GB
*Winnipeg	55	34	.618	—
*St. Paul	52	38	.578	3½
#Schaumburg	47	41	.534	7½
Joliet	40	48	.455	14½
Gary Southshore	36	54	.400	20½

WEST	W	L	PCT	GB
**Fargo-Moorhead	62	28	.689	—
Kansas City	43	46	.483	18½
Lincoln	41	49	.456	21
Sioux Falls	37	51	.420	24
Sioux City	33	57	.367	29

PLAYOFFS—Semifinals: Winnipeg defeated St. Paul 3-2 and Fargo defeated Schaumburg 3-2 in best-of-5 series. **Final:** Fargo defeated Winnipeg 3-1 in best-of-5 series.

NORTHEAST LEAGUE

NORTH	W	L	PCT	GB
*North Shore	51	39	.567	—
#Brockton	50	39	.562	½
*Quebec	49	40	.517	1½
Bangor	42	49	.462	9½

SOUTH	W	L	PCT	GB
**New Jersey	52	37	.584	—
Elmira	42	46	.477	9½
Berkshire	41	51	.446	12½
Allentown	32	58	.356	20½

PLAYOFFS: Semifinals—North Shore defeated Quebec 3-0 and Brockton defeated New Jersey 3-1 in best-of-5 series. **Finals—**Brockton defeated North Shore 3-0 in best-of-5 series.

SOUTHEASTERN LEAGUE

	W	L	PCT	GB
Pensacola	42	23	.646	—
Baton Rouge	38	31	.551	6
Montgomery	35	32	.522	8
Macon	33	35	.485	11½
Houma	28	34	.452	12½
Selma	23	44	.343	21

PLAYOFFS: Semifinals—Pensacola defeated Macon 2-0 and Baton Rouge defeated Montgomery 2-1 in best-of-3 series. **Final—**Baton Rouge defeated Pensacola 3-1 in best-of-5 series.

ATLANTIC
LEAGUE

Mailing Address: 401 N. Delaware Ave., Camden, NJ 08102.
Telephone: (856) 541-9400. **FAX:** (856) 541-9410.
E-Mail Address: atllge@aol.com. **Website:** www.atlanticleague.com.
Year Founded: 1998.

Chief Executive Officer: Frank Boulton.
Executive Director: Joe Klein.
Vice President: Mickey Herbert (Bridgeport).
Directors: Mark Berson (Newark), Frank Boulton (Long Island), Chris English (Nashua), Mickey Herbert (Bridgeport), Steve Kalafer (Somerset), Peter Kirk (Keystone Baseball/Pennsylvania), Tony Rosenthal (Atlantic City), Steve Shilling (Camden).
2004 Opening Date: May 6. **Closing Date:** Sept. 19
Regular Season: 126 games (split-schedule).
Division Structure: North—Bridgeport, Long Island, Nashua, Pennsylvania. **South**—Atlantic City, Camden, Newark, Somerset.
Playoff Format: First-half division winners meet second-half winners in best-of-3 series. Winners meet in best-of-5 final for league championship.
All-Star Game: July 14 at Camden.
Roster Limit: 25. **Eligibility Rule:** No restrictions.
Brand of Baseball: Rawlings.
Statistician: SportsTicker-Boston, Boston Fish Pier, West Bldg. #1, Suite 302, Boston, MA 02210.

ATLANTIC CITY
SURF

Office Address: 545 N. Albany Ave., Atlantic City, NJ 08401.
Telephone: (609) 344-8873. **FAX:** (609) 344-7010.
E-Mail Address: surf@acsurf.com. **Website:** www.acsurf.com.

Operated by: Jersey Shore Professional Baseball, Inc.
General Manager: Mario Perrucci. **Assistant GM/Director, Group Sales:** John Kiphorn. **Assistant Director, Group Sales:** Frank Dougherty. **Director, Media Relations/Marketing:** Chuck Betson. **Assistant Director, Media Relations:** Amy Dalrymple. **Director, Ticket Sales:** Kevin Skelly. **Director, Merchandising/Stadium Operations:** Danny Petrazzolo. **Director, Promotions/Community Relations:** Carl Grider. **Director, Finance:** Tom Clark. **Director, Baseball Operations:** Jeff Ball. **Clubhouse Operations:** Bob Schaffer.
Manager: Mitch Williams. **Coaches:** Tim Lindecamp, Greg Luzinski.

GAME INFORMATION

Radio Announcer: Jacob Issac. **No. of Games Broadcast:** Home-72, Away-54. **Flagship Station:** WUSS 1490-AM.
PA Announcer: Greg Maiuro. **Official Scorer:** Brian McCormick.
Stadium Name (year opened): The Sandcastle (1998). **Location:** Atlantic City Expressway to exit 2, east on Routes 40/322. **Standard Game Times:** 6:35 p.m.; Sun. 1:35, (May-June, Sept.) 5:05.
Visiting Club Hotel: Fairfield Inn, 405 White Horse Pike, Absecon, NJ. Telephone: (609) 646-5000.

BRIDGEPORT
BLUEFISH

Office Address: 500 Main St., Bridgeport, CT 06604.
Telephone: (203) 345-4800. **FAX:** (203) 345-4830.
E-Mail Address: rdelvecchio@bridgeportbluefish.com. **Website:** www.bridgeport bluefish.com.

Operated by: Bridgeport Bluefish Professional Baseball Club, LLC.
Owners: Charlie Dowd, Mickey Herbert, Ken Paul.
President, Chief Executive Officer: Mickey Herbert. **Senior Vice President:** Ken Paul.
General Manager: Charlie Dowd. **Assistant GM:** Rick DelVecchio. **Senior Account Executive:** John Harris. **Manager, Ticketing:** Joe Skarupa. **Assistant Manager, Ticketing:** Rebecca Ramos. **Ticketing Assistants:** Kim Pizighelli, Megan Watson, John Williams. **Controller:** Tammy Nolin. **Director, Operations:** John Cunningham. **Coordinator, Accounting:** Alison Mester. **Manager, Camps/Special Events:** Jen Davis. **Head Groundskeeper:** Craig Veeder.
Manager: Jose Lind. **Coaches:** Unavailable. **Trainer:** Pat LeGault.

GAME INFORMATION

Radio Announcer: Jeff Holtz. **No. of Games Broadcast:** Unavailable. **Flagship Station:** WVOF 88.5-FM.
PA Announcer: Bill Jensen. **Official Scorer:** Al Carbone.
Stadium Name (year opened): The Ballpark at Harbor Yard (1998). **Location:** I-95 to exit 27, Route 8/25 to exit 1.
Standard Game Times: 6:35 p.m., Sun. 1:35.
Visiting Club Hotel: Holiday Inn Bridgeport, 1070 Main St., Bridgeport, CT 06604. **Telephone:** (203) 334-1234.

CAMDEN
RIVERSHARKS

Office Address: 401 N. Delaware Ave., Camden, NJ 08102.
Telephone: (856) 963-2600. **FAX:** (856) 963-8534.
E-Mail Address: riversharks@riversharks.com. **Website:** www.riversharks.com.

Operated by: Camden Baseball, LLC.
Principal Owner: Steve Shilling.
General Manager: John Brandt. **Assistant GM, Operations:** Matt Kastel. **Assistant GM, Marketing:** David Brady.
Controller: Mary Anne McStravick. **Community Relations:** Amy Whilldin. **Office Manager:** Patty MacLuckie.
Accounting: Shannon Sloan. **Receptionist:** Dolores Rozier. **Ticket Operations:** Randy Newsome. **Director, Community Partnerships:** Sean Baedke. **Director, Corporate Partnerships:** Adam Lorber. **Senior Account Executives:** Al Barbieri, Brad Strauss. **Director, Ticket Sales:** Randy Mintz. **Group Sales:** Robert Nehring, Danielle Martinez. **Merchandise Manager:** Ryan Arnold. **Manager, Media Relations:** Don Delaney. **Head Groundskeeper:** Chris Walsh.
Manager: Wayne Krenchicki. **Coach:** Victor Torres. **Pitching Coach:** Steve Foucault. **Trainer:** Unavailable.

GAME INFORMATION

Radio: Unavailable.
PA Announcer: Kevin Casey. **Official Scorer:** Dick Shute.
Stadium Name (year opened): Campbell's Field (2001). **Location:** From Philadelphia, go right on 6th Street, right after Ben Franklin Bridge toll booth, right on Cooper Street until it ends at Delaware Ave. From Camden, I-676 to exit 5B, follow signs to field. **Standard Game Times:** 6:35 p.m., Sun. 1:35.
Visiting Club Hotel: Holiday Inn, Route 70 and Sayer Avenue, Cherry Hill, NJ 08002. Telephone: (856) 663-5300.

LONG ISLAND
DUCKS

Mailing Address: 3 Court House Dr., Central Islip, NY 11722.
Telephone: (631) 940-3825. **FAX:** (631) 940-3800.
E-Mail Address: info@liducks.com. **Website:** www.liducks.com.

Operated by: Long Island Ducks Professional Baseball, LLC.
Principal Owner, Chief Executive Officer: Frank Boulton. **Owner/Senior Vice President, Baseball Operations:** Bud Harrelson.
General Manager: Michael Hirsch. **Assistant GM:** Doug Cohen. **Controller:** Alex Scannella. **Manager, Media Relations:** Michael Pfaff. **Manager, Group Sales:** Mike Pacella. **Manager, Promotions:** Arlow Moreland. **Manager, Ticket Sales:** Ben Harper. **Manager, Community Relations:** Jaslyn Alicea. **Manager, Operations:** Andrew Washington. **Business Manager:** Gerry Anderson. **Manager, Clubhouse Operations:** Jimmy Russell. **Assistant Manager, Tickets:** Mike Fucci. **Coordinator, Administration:** Michele Connizzo. **Facilities:** Jon Archer.
Field Manager: Don McCormack. **Coach:** Bud Harrelson. **Pitching Coach:** Dave LaPoint. **Trainers:** Tony Amin, Adam Lewis.

GAME INFORMATION

Radio Announcers: Chris King, David Weiss. **No. of Games Broadcast:** 60. **Flagship Station:** WLIE 540-AM.
PA Announcers: Pitt Schultz, Bob Ottone. **Official Scorers:** Joe Donnelly, Red Foley.
Stadium Name (year opened): Citibank Park (2000). **Location:** Southern State Parkway east to Carleton Avenue North (exit 43 A), right onto Courthouse Drive, stadium behind Federal Courthouse Complex. **Standard Game Times:** 7:05 p.m.; Sun. 1:35.
Visiting Club Hotel: Huntington Hilton, 598 Broad Hollow Rd., Melville, NY 11747. Telephone: (631) 845-1000.

NASHUA
PRIDE

Office Address: 67 Amherst St., Nashua, NH 03064.
Telephone: (603) 883-2255. **FAX:** (603) 883-0880.

E-Mail Address: info@nashuapride.com. **Website:** www.nashuapride.com

Operated by: Nashua Pride Professional Baseball, LLC.
Principal Owner, President: Chris English.
General Manager: Todd Marlin. **Director, Promotions/Community Relations:** Eric Slack. **Director, Operations:** Joe Izzo. **Ticket Manager:** Jeff Farrar. **Coordinator, Community Partnership:** Greg Nota. **Manager, Media Relations:** Brian Moynahan. **Office Manager:** Bev Taylor. **Merchandise/Operations Intern:** Tony Rodriguez.
Manager: Butch Hobson. **Pitching Coach:** Rick Wise.

GAME INFORMATION

Radio Announcer: Unavailable. **No. of Games Broadcast:** Unavailable. **Flagship Station:** WSNH 900-AM.
PA Announcer: Ken Cail. **Official Scorer:** Roger Pepin.
Stadium Name (year opened): Historic Holman Stadium (1937). **Location:** Route 3 to exit 7E (Amherst Street), one mile on left. **Standard Game Time:** 6:35 p.m.
Visiting Club Hotel: Unavailable.

NEWARK
BEARS

Office Address: 450 Broad St., Newark, NJ 07102.
Telephone: (973) 848-1000. **FAX:** (973) 621-0095.
Website: www.newarkbears.com.

Operated by: Newark Bears Professional Baseball Club, Inc.
Owners: Steven Kalafer, Marc Berson.
General Manager: Dean Rivera. **Assistant GM:** Melissa Manfre. **Director, Player Personnel:** Pete Filson. **Director, Public Relations:** Kevin McKearney. **Corporate Sales Manager:** Julio Arriaga. **Controller:** Matthew DeMelia. **Manager, Stadium Operations:** Eddie Enderle. **Manager, Ticket Operations:** Keith Butler. **Manager, Group Sales:** Brian Schimpf. **Manager, Community Relations:** Mark Gallego. **Head Groundskeeper:** Unavailable.
Manager: Bill Madlock. **Pitching Coach:** Pete Filson.

GAME INFORMATION

Radio Announcer: Jim Cerny. **No. of Games Broadcast:** Unavailable. **Flagship Station:** Unavailable.
PA Announcer: Steve Boland. **Official Scorer:** Unavailable.
Stadium Name (year opened): Bears & Eagles Riverfront Stadium (1999). **Location:** New Jersey Parkway North/South to exit 145 (280 East), to exit 15; New Jersey Turnpike North/South to 280 West, to exit 15A. **Standard Game Times:** 7:05 p.m., Sat. 6:05, Sun. 1:35.
Visiting Club Hotel: Wellesley Inn & Suites, 265 Route 3 East, Clifton, NJ 07014. Telephone: (973) 778-6500.

PENNSYLVANIA
ROAD WARRIORS

The franchise will be operated by the Atlantic League as a road team during the 2004 season.
Manager: Bert Pena. **Coaches:** Unavailable.

SOMERSET
PATRIOTS

Office Address: One Patriots Park, Bridgewater, NJ 08807.
Telephone: (908) 252-0700. **FAX:** (908) 252-0776.
Website: www.somersetpatriots.com.

Operated by: Somerset Patriots Baseball Club, LLC.
Principal Owners: Steven Kalafer, Jack Cust, Byron Brisby, Don Miller.
Chairman: Steven Kalafer.
President, General Manager: Patrick McVerry. **Vice President, Ticketing:** Brendan Fairfield. **VP, Marketing:** Dave Marek. **VP, New Business Development:** Chris Bryan. **Controller:** Wayne Seguin. **Head Groundskeeper:** Ray Cipperly. **Director, Public Relations:** Marc Russinoff. **Director, Operations:** Rob Lukachyk. **Account Representatives:** Kenny Blattenbauer, John Gibson, Dan Neville. **Director, Community Relations:** Rich Reitman. **Director, Ticket Sales:** Bryan Iwicki. **Group Sales:** Chris Grundman, Matthew Kopas, Victoria Siesta. **Manager, Ticket Sales:** Chris Aubertin. **Executive Assistant to GM:** Michele DaCosta. **Manager, Operations:** Mike Kinahan. **Accountants:** Stephanie Diez, Wendi Miervaldis. **Receptionist:** Lorraine Ott.

Director, Player Procurement: Adam Gladstone. **Manager:** Sparky Lyle. **Pitching Coach:** John Montefusco. **Trainer:** Mike Curran.

GAME INFORMATION
Radio Announcer: Lou Brogno. **No. of Games Broadcast:** Home-72, Away-54. **Flagship Station:** WCTC 1450-AM. **PA Announcers:** Paul Spychala. **Official Scorers:** Dave Dedrick, John Nolan.
Stadium Name (year opened): Commerce Bank Ballpark (1999). **Location:** Route 287 North to exit 13B/Route 287 South to exit 13 (Somerville Route 28 West); follow signs to ballpark. **Standard Game Times:** 7:05 p.m., Sun. 1:35.
Visiting Club Hotel: Somerset Ramada, 60 Cottontail Lane, Somerset, NJ 08873. Telephone: (732) 560-9880.

CENTRAL
LEAGUE

Mailing Address/Baseball Operations: 1415 Hwy. 54 West, Suite 210, Durham, NC 27707.
Telephone: (919) 401-8150. **FAX:** (919) 401-8152.
Mailing Address/Business Operations: P.O. Box 2712, Colorado Springs, CO 87901.
Telephone: (719) 520-0060. **FAX:** (719) 520-0221.
E-Mail Address: info@centralleaguebaseball.com. **Website:** www.centralleaguebaseball.com.
Year Founded: 1994.

Commissioner: Miles Wolff. **Vice President, Baseball Operations:** Dan Moushon. **Director, Media Relations:** Gene Brtalik. **Supervisor, Umpires:** Kevin Winn.
2004 Opening Date: May 6. **Closing Date:** Aug. 21.
Regular Season: 96 games (split schedule).
Division Structure: East—Fort Worth, Jackson, Pensacola, Shreveport. **West**—Amarillo, Coastal Bend, Edinburg, San Angelo.
Playoff Format: First-half division winners meet second-half division winners in best-of-5 series. Winners meet in best-of-5 series for league championship.
All-Star Game: July 20 at Fort Worth (Central League vs. Northeast League).
Roster Limit: 22. **Player Eligibility Rule:** Minimum of five first-year players; maximum of four veterans with at least four years of professional experience.
Brand of Baseball: Rawlings.
Statistician: SportsTicker-Boston, Boston Fish Pier, West Bldg. #1, Suite 302, Boston, MA 02210.

AMARILLO
DILLAS

Mailing Address: P.O. Box 31241, Amarillo, TX 79120.
Telephone: (806) 342-3455. **FAX:** (806) 467-9894.
Website: www.dillas.com.

Vice President, General Manager: Ric Sisler. **Director, Sales/Marketing:** Mark Lee. **Director, Business Operations/Sales:** Nick Barkley. **Director, Ticket Sales:** Nick Barkley. **Office/Ticket Manager:** Beverly Sanders. **Manager, Grounds/Operations:** Jeff Schenck.
Manager: Unavailable. **Coaches:** Unavailable.

GAME INFORMATION
Radio Announcer: Unavailable. **No. of Games Broadcast:** Home-48, Away-48. **Flagship Station:** KPUR 1440-AM. **PA Announcer:** Joe Frank Wheeler. **Official Scorer:** Jeff Schenck.
Stadium Name: Amarillo National Dilla Villa. **Location:** I-40 to Grand Ave. North exit, left at 3rd Ave. **Standard Game Times:** 7:05 p.m., Sun. 5:05.
Visiting Club Hotel: Ramada Limited, 1620 I-40 East, Amarillo, TX 79103. Telephone: 806-374-2020.

COASTAL BEND
AVIATORS

Mailing Address: 1151 E. Main Ave., Robstown, TX 78380.
Telephone: (361) 387-8585. **FAX:** (361) 387-3535.
Website: www.aviatorsbaseball.com.

General Manager: George Stavrenos. **Assistant GM:** Shane Tritz. **Director, Stadium Operations:** Leroy Gonzalez. **Director, Media Relations:** Rory Miller. **Office Manager:** Brandi Ramone. **Director, Sales/Marketing:** Ray Hunt. **Sales**

Executives: Javier Limon.
Manager: Unavailable. **Coach:** Unavailable.

GAME INFORMATION
Radio Announcer: Rory Miller. **No. of Games Broadcast:** Home-48, Away-48. **Flagship Stations:** KSIX 1230-AM, KPUS 104.5-FM.
PA Announcer: Unavailable. **Official Scorer:** Unavailable.
Stadium Name (year opened): Aviators Stadium (2003). **Location:** 12 miles west of downtown Corpus Christi at junction of Highway 77 and Highway 44. **Standard Game Times:** 7:05 p.m., Sun. 6:05.
Visiting Club Hotel: Unavailable.

EDINBURGH
ROADRUNNERS

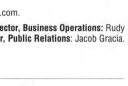

Office Address: 920 N. Sugar Rd., Edinburg, TX 78539.
Mailing Address: P.O. Box 4119, Edinburg, TX 78540.
Telephone: (956) 289-8800. **FAX:** (956) 289-8833.
E-Mail Address: winstonayala@yahoo.com. **Website:** www.roadrunnersbaseball.com.

General Manager: Winston Ayala. **Director, Sales/Marketing:** Bob Flanagan. **Director, Business Operations:** Rudy Rodriguez. **Manager, Sales:** Mike Patrick. **Sales Executive:** Jeremy Martin. **Director, Public Relations**: Jacob Gracia. **Office Manager:** Imelda Palacios.
Manager: Chad Tredaway. **Assistant Coaches:** Reggie Tredaway, John Harris.

GAME INFORMATION
Radio: Unavailable.
PA Announcer: Tony Forina. **Official Scorer:** Unavailable.
Stadium Name (year opened): Edinburg Stadium (2001). **Location:** Highway 281, left at Schuinor Street to Sugar Road, stadium on right. **Standard Game Time:** 7:05 p.m.
Visiting Club Hotel: Unavailable.

FORT WORTH
CATS

Mailing Address: P.O Box 4411, Fort Worth, TX 76106.
Telephone: (817) 226-2287. **FAX:** (817) 534-4620.
E-Mail Address: info@fwcats.com. **Website:** www.fwcats.com.

Operated By: Texas Independent Baseball.
Principal Owner: Carl Bell.
President, Chief Operating Officer: Marty Scott. **Vice President, General Manager:** Monty Clegg. **VP/Director, Sales and Marketing:** John Dittrich. **VP, Special Projects:** Maury Wills. **Assistant GM:** Kevin Forrester. **Director, Media Relations:** David Hatchett. **Operations Manager:** John Bilbow. **Manager, Group Sales:** Dana St. Germain. **Office Manager:** Stacy Navarro. **Manager, Community Relations:** Candiss Caudle. **Ticket Manager:** Sunni Watson. **Account Executive:** Shayne Forsyth. **Stadium Manager:** Gary Grimsley.
Director, Player Development: Barry Moss.
Manager: Wayne Terwilliger. **Coach:** Unavailable. **Pitching Coach:** Dan Smith. **Trainer:** Danny Wheat.

GAME INFORMATION
Radio Announcers: John Nelson, David Hatchett, Emil Moffatt. **No. of Games Broadcast:** Home-48, Away-48. **Flagship Station:** KTFW 1460-AM
PA Announcer: Frankie Gasca. **Official Scorer:** Bruce Unrue.
Stadium Name (year opened): LaGrave Field (2002). **Location:** From 1-30, take 1-35 North to North Side Drive exit, left (west) off exit to Main Street, left (south) on Main, left (east) onto NE Sixth Street. **Standard Game Times:** 7:05 p.m.; Sun. 2:05.
Visiting Club Hotel: Clarion Hotel, 600 Commerce St., Fort Worth, TX 76102. Telephone: (871) 332-6900.

JACKSON
SENATORS

Office Address: 1200 Lakeland Dr., Jackson, MS 39216.
Mailing Address: P.O. Box 4934, Jackson, MS 39296.
Telephone: (601) 362-2294. **FAX:** (601) 362-9577.

E-Mail Address: info@jacksonsenators.com. **Website:** www.jacksonsenators.com.

Operated By: Texas Independent Baseball.
Principal Owner: Carl Bell. **President, Chief Operating Officer:** Marty Scott.
   Vice President, General Manager: Craig Brasfield. **Assistant GM/Director, Sales and Marketing:** Chet Carey. **Assistant GM/Director, Stadium Operations:** Andrew Aguilar. **Controller/Director, Merchandising:** Carrie Brasfield. **Director, Group Sales/Ticket Operations:** Amanda Stringer. **Director, Media Relations/Broadcasting:** Ben Ingram. **Director, Food/Beverage:** Gary Starkey. **Head Groundskeeper:** Ken Estes. **Administrative Assistant:** Lane Smith.
   Manager: Dan Shwam. **Coaches:** James Frisbee, Tim Dowdy. **Trainer:** John Dussouy.

GAME INFORMATION
   Radio Announcer: Ben Ingram. **No. of Games Broadcast:** Home-48, Away-48. **Flagship Station:** ESPN 1240-AM.
   PA Announcer: Glen Waddle. **Official Scorer:** Denny Hales.
   Stadium Name (year opened): Smith-Wills Stadium (1975). **Location:** I-55 to Lakeland Drive, left at Cool Papa Bell Drive. **Standard Game Times:** 7:05 p.m.; Sun. 2:05, 6:05.
   Visiting Club Hotel: Unavailable.

PENSACOLA
PELICANS

Mailing Address: 913 Gulf Breeze Parkway, Suite 36, Gulf Breeze, FL 32561.
Telephone: (850) 934-8444. **FAX:** (850) 934-8744.
E-Mail Address: tony@pensacolapelicans.com. **Website:** www.pensacola pelicans.com.

Owner: Quint Studer. **President:** Rishy Studer.
General Manager: Tony Atchley. **Director, Corporate Sales:** Talmadge Nunnari. **Administrative Assistant:** Annee Imle. **Assistant Manager:** Lorie Pratt. **Director, Group Sales:** Jason Liebert.
Manager: Bernie Carbo. **Coach:** Unavailable. **Trainer:** Unavailable.

GAME INFORMATION
   Radio Announcer: Unavailable. **No. of Games Broadcast:** Home-48, Away-48. **Flagship Station:** Unavailable.
   PA Announcer: Unavailable. **Official Scorer:** Unavailable.
   Stadium Name: Pelican Park. **Location:** Highway 65 to CC&J exit, right on 17th Street, follow signs to stadium. **Standard Game Time:** 7:05 p.m.
   Visiting Club Hotel: Unavailable.

SAN ANGELO
COLTS

Office Address: 1600 University Ave., San Angelo, TX 76904.
Telephone: (325) 942-6587. **FAX:** (325) 947-9480.
E-Mail Address: colts@zipnet.us. **Website:** www.sanangelocolts.com.

Operated by: San Angelo Colts Baseball Club, LLC.
President, Executive General Manager: Harlan Bruha.
   General Manager: Paula Dowler. **Ticket/Merchandise Manager:** Paige Jackson. **Account Representative:** Kari Rumfield. **Assistant GM, Sales/Marketing Manager:** Susan Page. **Stadium Superintendent:** Joe Stapp.
   Manager: Toby Rumfield. **Coach:** Unavailable. **Trainer:** Jeff Mann.

GAME INFORMATION
   Radio Announcer: Mark Moesner. **No. of Games Broadcast:** Home-48, Away-48. **Flagship Station:** KKSA 1260-AM.
   PA Announcer: Unavailable. **Official Scorer:** Unavailable.
   Stadium Name (year opened): Colts Stadium (2000). **Location:** From north/south, take U.S. 87 to Knickerbocker Road, west to stadium; From east/west, take U.S. 67 to U.S. 87 South, to Knickerbocker Road, west to stadium. **Standard Game Time:** 7:05 p.m.
   Visiting Club Hotel: Howard Johnson, 415 W. Beauregard Blvd., San Angelo, TX 76903. Telephone: (915) 653-2995.

SHREVEPORT
SPORTS

Mailing Address: 2901 Pershing Blvd, Shreveport, LA 71109.
Telephone: (318) 636-5555. **FAX:** (318) 636-5670.
Website: www.shreveportsports.com.

Owners: Gary Elliston, Carl Bell.
General Manager: Brian Viselli. **Assistant GM:** Jeff Stewart. **Account Executives:** Dan Kelleher, Zach Viselli.
Director, Media Relations: Dave Nitz. **Corporate Sales:** Jeff Stewart. **Public Relations/Merchandise:** Laurie Oliphint.
Manager: Terry Bevington. **Coach:** John Barlow.

GAME INFORMATION

Radio Announcer: Dave Nitz. **No. of Games Broadcast:** Home-48, Away-48. **Flagship Station:** Unavailable.
PA Announcer: Unavailable. **Official Scorer:** Unavailable.
Stadium Name (year opened): Fair Grounds Field (1986). **Location:** Hearne Ave. (U.S. 171) exit off I-20 at Louisiana State Fairgrounds. **Standard Game Times:** 7:05 p.m., Sun. 2:05.
Visiting Club Hotel: Unavailable.

FRONTIER LEAGUE

Office Address: 408 W. U.S. Hwy 40, Suite 100, Troy, IL 62294.
Mailing Address: P.O. Box 62, Troy, IL 62294.
Telephone: (618) 667-8000. **FAX:** (618) 667-8524.
E-Mail Address: office@frontierleague.com. **Website:** www.frontierleague.com.
Year Founded: 1993.

Commissioner: Bill Lee.
Chairman of the Board: Chris Hanners (Chillicothe).
President: Rich Sauget (Gateway). **Vice Presidents:** John Swiatek (Washington), Duke Ward (Richmond).
Corporate Secretary/Treasurer: Bob Wolfe. **Legal Counsel/Deputy Commissioner:** Kevin Rouch.
Director of Development: Leo Trich.
Directors: Bill Bussing (Evansville), Dave Ciarrachi (Rockford), Tim Clegg (Springfield/Ozark), Chris Hanners (Chillicothe), Chuck Hildebrant (Florence), Kevin Rhomberg (Windy City), Rich Sauget (Gateway), John Swiatek (Washington), Duke Ward (Richmond), Gary Wendt (Mid-Missouri), Ken Wilson (River City), Bill Wright (Kalamazoo).
2004 Opening Date: May 21. **Closing Date:** Aug. 30.
Regular Season: 96 games.
Division Structure: East—Chillicothe, Evansville, Florence, Kalamazoo, Richmond, Washington. **West**—Gateway, Mid-Missouri, River City, Rockford, Springfield/Ozark, Windy City.
Playoff Format: Top two teams in each division meet in best-of-5 semifinal series. Winners meet in best-of-5 series for league championship.
All-Star Game: July 14 at River City.
Roster Limit: 24. **Eligibility Rule:** Minimum of 10 first-year players; maximum of seven players with one year professional experience; maximum of two players with two years of experience and maximum of three players with three or more years of experience. No player may be 27 prior to May 30.
Brand of Baseball: Wilson.
Statistician: SportsTicker-Boston, Boston Fish Pier, West Bldg. #1, Suite 302, Boston, MA 02210.

CHILLICOTHE PAINTS

Office Address: 59 N. Paint St., Chillicothe, OH 45601.
Telephone: (740) 773-8326. **FAX:** (740) 773-8338.
E-Mail Address: paints@bright.net. **Website:** www.chillicothepaints.com.

Operated by: Chillicothe Paints Professional Baseball Association, Inc.
Principal Owner: Chris Hanners. **President:** Shirley Bandy.
Vice President, General Manager: Bryan Wickline. **Stadium Superintendent:** Jim Miner. **Director, Finance:** Maleine Davis. **Director, Sales/Marketing:** John Wend. **Director of Game Day Operations/Group Sales:** Morgan West.
Director, Merchandise: Logan Hanners. **Director, Concessions:** Jody Clary. **Head Groundskeeper:** Jim Miner.
Field Manager: Jamie Keefe. **Coach:** Marty Dunn. **Trainer:** Aaron Schreiner.

GAME INFORMATION

Radio Announcer: Ryan Mitchell. **No. of Games Broadcast:** Home-48, Away-48. **Flagship Station:** WXIZ 100.9-FM.
PA Announcer: John Wend. **Official Scorer:** Aaron Lemaster.
Stadium Name (year opened): V.A. Memorial Stadium (1993). **Location:** Route 23 to Bridge Street, west on Route 35, north on Route 104. **Standard Game Times:** 7:05 p.m., Sun. 6:05.
Visiting Club Hotel: Days Inn of Chillicothe, 1250 N. Bridge St., Chillicothe, OH 45601. Telephone: (740) 775-7000.

EVANSVILLE
OTTERS

Office Address: 1701 N. Main St., Evansville, IN 47711.
Mailing Address: P.O. Box 3565, Evansville, IN 47734.
Telephone: (812) 435-8686. **FAX:** (812) 435-8688.
E-Mail Address: ottersbb@evansville.net. **Website:** www.evansvilleotters.com.

Operated by: Evansville Baseball, LLC.
President: Bill Bussing. **Senior Vice President:** Pat Rayburn.
Vice President, General Manager: Steve Tahsler. **VP/Director, Baseball Operations:** Gary Jones. **Director, Ticketing:** Andrew Aldenderfer. **Facilities Manager:** Mike Duckworth. **Account Executives:** Joel Padfield, Chad Cooper. **Promotions Director:** Eric Egan. **Assistant, Operations:** Tammy Berg. **Head Groundskeeper:** Joe Parker.
Manager: Greg Jelks. **Pitching Coach:** Jeff Pohl. **Trainer:** Jed Arsensau.

GAME INFORMATION
Radio Announcer: Chad Cooper. **No. of Games Broadcast:** Home-48, Away-48. **Flagship Station:** WUEV 91.5-FM.
PA Announcer: Eric Stone. **Official Scorer:** Steve Rhoads.
Stadium Name (year opened): Bosse Field (1915). **Location:** U.S. 41 to Diamond Ave. West, left at Heidelbach Ave.
Standard Game Times: 7:05 p.m., Sun. 6:05.
Visiting Club Hotel: Unavailable.

FLORENCE
FREEDOM

Office Address: 7950 Freedom Way, Florence, KY 41042.
Telephone: (859) 594-4487. **FAX:** (859) 647-4639.
Website: florencefreedom.com.

Operated by: Northern Kentucky Professional Baseball.
President, Managing Partner: Chuck Hildebrandt. **General Manager:** Connie Hildebrandt. **Director, Marketing:** Erin England.
Manager: Tom Browning. **Coach:** Mike Easler. **Pitching Coach:** Chris Hook. **Trainer:** Bill Tweehaus.

GAME INFORMATION
Radio: Unavailable.
PA Announcer: Unavailable. **Official Scorer:** Unavailable.
Stadium (year opened): Florence Freedom Field (2004). **Location:** I-71/75 South to exit 180, left onto U.S. 42, right on Freedom Way; I-71/75 North to exit 180. **Standard Game Time:** 7:05 p.m.
Visiting Club Hotel: Microtel Inns and Suites, 7490 Woodspoint Dr., Florence, KY 41042. Telephone: (859) 746-8100.

GATEWAY
GRIZZLIES

Mailing Address: 2301 Grizzlie Bear Blvd., Sauget, IL 62206.
Telephone: (618) 337-3000. **FAX:** (618) 332-3625.
E-Mail Address: grizzlies@accessus.net. **Website:** www.gatewaygrizzlies.com.

Operated by: Gateway Baseball, LLC.
Managing Officer: Richard Sauget.
General Manager: Tony Funderburg. **Assistant GM:** Steven Gomric. **Director, Ticket Operations:** Eric Wittenauer **Office Operations:** Brent Pownall. **Corporate Sales Associate:** Joe Pott. **Director, Media/Community Relations:** Patti LaBrott. **Assistant, Media Relations/Coordinator, Advertising:** Marlena Huenefeld. **Director, Promotions:** Jackie Marko. **Director, Stadium Operations/Corporate Sales Associate:** C.J. Hendrickson. **Assistant Director, Stadium Operations/Corporate Sales Associate:** Andrew Collmeyer **Director, Merchandise/Ticket Sales Associate:** Kelly Kicielinski. **Head Groundskeeper/Corporate Sales Associate:** Craig Kuhl. **Communities Relations Associate/Clubhouse Manager:** John Aebischer. **Interns:** Yumi Blackburn, Ian Calhoun, Wade DeVries, Nicole Drury, Ben Galvin, Mike Kennedy, Todd Peden, Katie Rule
Manager: Danny Cox. **Coaches:** Tim Mueth, Neil Fiala. **Trainer:** Geof Manzo.

GAME INFORMATION
Radio Announcer: Joe Pott. **No of Games Broadcast:** Home-48, Away-48. **Flagship Station:** WSMI 106.1-FM.
PA Announcer: Tom Calhoun. **Official Scorer:** Amanda Haas.
Stadium Name (year opened): GMC Stadium (2002). **Location:** I-255 at exit 15 (Mousette Lane). **Standard Game**

Times: 7:05 p.m., Sun. 6:05.
Visiting Club Hotel: The Casino Queen Hotel and Casino, 200 Front St., East St. Louis, IL 62201. Telephone: (618) 874-5000.

KALAMAZOO
KINGS

Mailing Address: 251 Mills St., Kalamazoo, MI 49001.
Telephone: (269) 388-8326. **FAX:** (269) 388-8333.
E-Mail Address: kalamazookings@kalamazookings.com. **Website:** www.kalamazoo kings.com.

Operated by: Team Kalamazoo, LLC.
Owners: Bill Wright, Mike Seelye, Pat Seelye, Joe Rosenhagen, Ed Bernard, Scott Hocevar.
General Manager/Managing Partner: Joe Rosenhagen. **Fundraising Coordinator/Community Relations:** Chris Peake. **Sales Manager:** Becky Smith. **Administrative Assistant:** Lucille Comartin.
Director, Baseball Operations/Field Manager: Fran Riordan. **Pitching Coach:** Unavailable.

GAME INFORMATION
Radio Announcers: Robert Ford, Ryan Maguire. **No. of Games Broadcast:** Home-48, Away-48. **Flagship Station:** WQSN 1660-AM.
PA Announcers: Jim Lefler, Tom Dukesherer. **Official Scorer:** Jason Zerban.
Stadium Name (year opened): Homer Stryker Field (1995). **Location:** I-94 to Sprinkle Road (exit 80), north on Sprinkle Road, left on Business Loop 94, left on Kings Highway, right on Mills Street, park on right. **Standard Game Times:** 6:35 p.m., Sun. 5:35.
Visiting Club Hotel: Days Inn Airport Hotel, 3522 Sprinkle Rd., Kalamazoo, MI 49002. Telephone: (269) 381-7070.

MID-MISSOURI
MAVERICKS

Mailing Address: 810 E. Walnut, Columbia, MO 65201.
Telephone: (573) 256-4004. **FAX:** (573) 256-4003.
E-Mail Address: homerun@socket.net. **Website:** Unavailable.

Operated by: Columbia Professional Baseball LLC.
President: Gary Wendt.
Director, Community Relations: Ann Wilhelm. **Director, Office/Ticket Operations:** Christine Heath. **Director, Media Relations:** Jeff Johnson.
Manager: Jack Clark. **Coach:** Unavailable. **Trainer:** James Oyler.

GAME INFORMATION
Radio Announcer: Jeff Johnson. **No. of Games Broadcast:** Home-48, Away-48. **Flagship Station:** KTGR 1580-AM.
PA Announcer: Unavailable. **Official Scorer:** Unavailable.
Stadium Name (year opened): Taylor Stadium (2000). **Location:** I-70 to Providence Road exit, south to Research Park Drive, right to stadium. **Standard Game Times:** 7:05 p.m., Sun. 6:05.
Visiting Club Hotel: Regency Downtown Hotel, 1111 E. Broadway, Columbia, MO 65201.

RICHMOND
ROOSTERS

Mailing Address: 201 NW 13th St., Richmond, IN 47374.
Telephone: (765) 935-7529. **FAX:** (765) 962-7047.
E-Mail Address: staff@richmondroosters.com. **Website:** www.richmond roosters.com.

Operated by: Richmond Roosters Baseball, LLC.
Owner/President: Allen Brady.
Vice President/General Manager: Deanna Beaman. **Assistant GM:** Todd Garrison. **Director, Baseball Operations:** John Cate. **Director, Ticket Sales:** Andrew Dickerson. **Director, Groups:** Tom Linehan. **Head Groundskeeper:** Cindy Cate. **Clubhouse Operations:** Unavailable. **Office Manager:** LaDonna White.
Manager: Chris Mongiardo. **Coach:** Unavailable. **Trainer:** Unavailable.

GAME INFORMATION
Radio Announcer: Unavailable. **No. of Games Broadcast:** Home-48, Away-48. **Flagship Stations:** WKBV 1490-AM,

WCNB 1580-AM, Star 98.3-FM.
PA Announcer: Scott Beaman. **Official Scorer:** Unavailable.
Stadium Name (year opened): McBride Stadium (1936). **Location:** I-70 to exit 149A (Williamsburg Pike), right on West Main Street, right on NW 13th Street. **Standard Game Times:** 6:35 p.m.; Sun. 4:35.
Visiting Club Hotel: Unavailable.

RIVER CITY
RASCALS

Office Address: 900 Ozzie Smith Dr., O'Fallon, MO 63366.
Mailing Address: P.O. Box 662, O'Fallon, MO 63366.
Telephone: (636) 240-2287. **FAX:** (636) 240-7313.
E-Mail Address: info@rivercityrascals.com. **Website:** www.rivercityrascals.com.

Operated by: Missouri River Baseball, LLC.
Managing Partner: Ken Wilson.
General Manager: Matt Jones. **Assistant GM:** Steve Chanez. **Director, Corporate Sales:** Allen Gossett. **Director, Merchandising:** Bobby Rhoden. **Director, Ticket Sales/Operations:** Bryan Goodall. **Director, Community/Media Relations:** Wendy Rackovan. **Director, Group Sales:** Alan Jackson. **Group Sales Associates:** Grant Wilson, Travis Young. **Head Groundskeeper:** Chris Young.
Manager: Randy Martz. **Coaches:** Brian Lewis, Mike Barger. **Trainer:** Unavailable.

GAME INFORMATION
Radio Announcer: Phil Giubileo. **No. of Games Broadcast:** Home-48, Away-48. **Flagship Station:** KSLQ 104.5-FM.
PA Announcer: Joe Sutton. **Official Scorer:** Keith Deshurley.
Stadium Name (year opened): T.R. Hughes Ballpark (1999). **Location:** I-70 to exit 219, north on T.R. Hughes Road and follow signs to ballpark. **Standard Game Times:** 7:05 p.m., Sun. 6:05.
Visiting Club Hotel: Hilton Garden Inn, 2310 Technology Dr., O'Fallon, MO 63366. Telephone: (636) 625-2700.

ROCKFORD
RIVERHAWKS

Office Address: 101 15th Ave., Rockford, IL 61104.
Telephone: (815) 964-2255. **FAX:** (815) 964-2462.
E-Mail Address: playball@rockfordriverhawks.com. **Website:** www.rockford riverhawks.com.

Operated by: Rockford Baseball, LLC.
Managing Partner: Dave Ciarrachi.
Vice President: John Dittrich **General Manager:** Mike Babcock. **Assistant GM:** Todd Fulk.
Director, Broadcasting: Bill Czaja. **Director, Sales/Scouting:** Cory Dirksen. **Head Groundskeeper:** Unavailable.
Manager: Bob Koopmann. **Coaches:** J.D. Arndt, Sam Knaack. **Trainer:** Unavailable.

GAME INFORMATION
Radio Announcer: Bill Czaja. **No. of Games Broadcast:** Home-48, Away-48. **Flagship Station:** WRHL 102.3-FM.
PA Announcer: Scott Bentley. **Official Scorer:** Aaron Nester.
Stadium Name: Marinelli Field (1988). **Location:** From north, I-90 South to I-39 South (U.S. 51 South exit), continue on U.S. 20 West for six miles to Illinois Highway 2 (North Main), north on North Main for two miles, right on 15th Ave. From east, I-90 North to U.S. 20 West to Illinois Highway 2 (North Main), north on North Main for two miles, right on 15th Ave. **Standard Game Times:** 7:05 p.m., Sun 3:05.
Visiting Club Hotel: Sweden House Lodge, 4605 E. State St., Rockford, IL 61107. Telephone: (815) 398-4130.

SPRINGFIELD-OZARK
DUCKS

Office Address: 4400 N. 17th St., Ozark, MO 65721.
Mailing Address: P.O. Box 1472, Ozark, MO 65721.
Telephone: (417) 581-2868. **FAX:** (417) 581-8342.
Website: www.ducksprobaseball.com.

Owned by: American Sports Entertainment.
General Manager: Tim Clegg. **Manager, Corporate Sales:** Eric Day. **Director, Stadium Operations:** Daniel Ochsner. **Director, Group Sales:** Shirley Jaeger. **Director, Ticket Sales:** Woody Schuler.

Manager: Greg Tagert. **Coach:** Unavailable. **Trainer:** Gary Turbak.

GAME INFORMATION
Radio Announcer: Dave Klopfer. **No. of Games Broadcast:** Home-48, Away-48. **Flagship Station:** Unavailable.
PA Announcer: Matt Puccio. **Official Scorer:** Unavailable.
Stadium Name (year opened): Price Cutter Park (1999). **Location:** Highway 65 to CC&J exit, right on 17th Street, follow signs to stadium. **Standard Game Times:** 7:15 p.m., Sun. 4:15.
Visiting Club Hotel: Clarion Hotel, 3333 S. Glenstone Ave., Springfield, MO 65804. Telephone: (417) 883-6550.

WASHINGTON
WILD THINGS

Office Address: Falconi Field, One Washington Federal Way, Washington, PA 15301.
Telephone: (724) 250-9555. **FAX:** (724) 250-2333.
E-Mail Address: info@washingtonwildthings.com. **Website:** www.washington wildthings.com.

Owned by: Sports Facilites, LLC. **Managing Partner:** Stu Williams.
Operated by: Washington Frontier League Baseball, LLC. **Managing Partners:** Jeff Coury, John Swiatek. **President/Chief Executive Officer:** John Swiatek.
General Manager: Ross Vecchio. **Director, Marketing:** Christine Blaine. **Director, Merchandise:** Scott Eafrati.
Director, Sales/Service: Jeff Ptak. **Director, Stadium Operations:** Steve Zavacky. **Account Representative:** Ricci Rich.
Manager: John Massarelli. **Coach:** Ryan Ellis. **Pitching Coach:** Mark Mason. **Trainer:** Craig Castor.

GAME INFORMATION
Radio Announcers: Bob Gregg, Ned Bowdern. **No. of Games Broadcast:** Home-48, Away-48. **Flagship Station:** WJPA 95.3-FM.
PA Announcer: Bill DiFabio. **Official Scorer:** Skip Hood.
Stadium Name (year opened): Falconi Field (2002). **Location:** I-70 to exit 15 (Chesnut Street), right on Chesnut Street to Washington Crown Center Mall, right at mall entrance, right on to Mall Drive to stadium. **Standard Game Times:** 7:05 p.m., Sun. 6:05.
Visiting Club Hotel: Holiday Inn Meadow Lands, 340 Racetrack Rd., Washington, PA 15301. Telephone: (724) 222-6200.

WINDY CITY
THUNDERBOLTS

Office Address: 14011 South Kenton Ave., Crestwood, IL 60445.
Telephone: (708) 489-2255. **FAX:** (708) 489-2999.
E-Mail Address: info@thunderbolts.com. **Website:** www.wcthunderbolts.com.

Owned by: Crestwood Professional Baseball, LLC.
President: Kevin Rhomberg.
General Manager: Unavailable. **Assistant GM:** Matt Wilson. **Director, Administration:** Georgia Klioris. **Director, Ticket Sales:** Unavailable. **Account Executive/Promotions and Media Relations:** Mike Lucas. **Account Executive/Stadium Operations:** Brian Hooper. **Account Executive/Community Relations:** Shauna Fiegel.
Manager: Steve Maddock. **Coaches:** Joe Charboneau, Greg Beck, Jason Klinger. **Trainer:** Unavailable.

GAME INFORMATION
Radio: Unavailable.
PA Announcer: Unavailable. **Official Scorer:** Unavailable.
Stadium Name (year opened): Hawkinson Ford Field (1999) **Location:** I-294 to Cicero Ave. exit (Route 50), south for 1½ miles, left at Midlothian Turnpike, right on Kenton Ave. **Standard Game Times:** 7 p.m., Sun. 6.
Visiting Club Hotel: Georgio's Comfort Inn, 8800 W. 159th St., Orland Park, IL 60462. **Telephone:** (708) 403-1100.

NORTHEAST
LEAGUE

Office Address: 1415 Hwy. 54 West, Suite 210, Durham, NC 27707.
Telephone: (919) 401-8150. **FAX:** (919) 401-8152.
E-Mail Address: info@northeastleague.com. **Website:** www.northeastleague.com.
Year Founded: 1995.

Commissioner: Miles Wolff. **President:** Dan Moushon. **Director, Media Relations:** Gene Brtalik.
Supervisor, Umpires: Tony Carilli.
2004 Opening Date: May 26. **Closing Date:** Sept. 6.
Regular Season: 92 games (split-schedule).
Division Structure: North—Bangor, Brockton, North Shore, Québec. **South**—Allentown, Elmira, New Haven, New Jersey.
Playoff Format: First-half division winners meet second-half division winners in best-of-5 series. Winners meet in best-of-5 series for league championship.
All-Star Game: July 20 at Fort Worth, Texas (Northeast League vs. Central League).
Roster Limit: 22. **Eligibility Rule:** Minimum of five first-year players; maximum of four veterans with at least four years of professional experience.
Brand of Baseball: Rawlings.
Statistician: SportsTicker-Boston, Boston Fish Pier, West Bldg. #1, Suite 302, Boston, MA 02210.

ALLENTOWN
AMBASSADORS

Office Address: 1511-1525 Hamilton St., Allentown, PA 18102.
Telephone: (610) 437-6800. **FAX:** (610) 437-6804.
E-Mail Address: info@ambassadorbaseball.com. **Website:** www.ambassador baseball.com.

Operated by: Allentown Ambassadors Professional Baseball, Inc.
Principal Owners: Peter Karoly, Lauren Angstadt.
President/General Manager: Clyde Smoll. **Vice President, Sales/Marketing:** Michael Jermain. **Director, Ticket Operations:** Charlene Small. **Director, Media Relations:** Jim Brinckman. **Director, Player Personnel:** Vic Davilla.
Manager: Ed Ott. **Coaches:** Tim Nieman, Ryan Bordenick. **Pitching Coach:** Steve Shirley.

GAME INFORMATION

Radio Announcer: Unavailable. **No. of Games Broadcast:** Home-46, Road-46. **Flagship Station:** WXLV 90.3-FM.
PA Announcer: Adam Helman. **Official Scorer:** Cara Singley.
Stadium Name (year opened): Bicentennial Park (1930). **Location:** I-78 to Lehigh Street, north on Lehigh for two miles toward downtown. **Standard Game Times:** 7:05 p.m., Sun. 5:05.
Visiting Club Hotel: Days Inn & Conference Center, 1151 Bulldog Dr., Allentown, PA 18104. Telephone: (610) 395-3731.

BANGOR
LUMBERJACKS

Office Address: 663 Stillwater Ave., Bangor, ME 04401.
Telephone: (207) 947-1900. **FAX:** (207) 947-9900.
E-Mail Address: info@bangorlumberjacks.com. **Website:** www.bangorlumber jacks.com.

Operated by: Lumberjack Baseball, LLC.
Principal Owner: Chip Hutchins.
General Manager: Curt Jacey. **Director, Operations:** Doug Collyer. **Sales:** Ryan Conley, Lesile Trott. **Office Assistant:** Kendra Peterson.
Director, Player Procurement: Nick Belmonte.
Manager: Kash Beauchamp. **Coach:** Kevin Pincavitch.

GAME INFORMATION

Radio: None.
PA Announcer: Unavailable. **Official Scorer:** Unavailable.
Stadium Name (year opened): John Winkin Baseball Complex (2003) **Location:** I-95 to exit 48, right on Broadway, left on Husson Avenue to entrance to Husson College, straight ahead 1 mile. **Standard Game Times:** 6:30 p.m., Sun. 2.
Visiting Club Hotel: Best Inn, 570 Main St., Bangor, ME 04401. Telephone: (207) 942-1234.

BROCKTON ROX

Office Address: 1 Lexington Ave, Brockton, MA 02301.
Mailing Address: P.O. Box 7547, Brockton, MA 02303.
Telephone: (508) 559-7000. **FAX:** (508) 587-2802.
Website: www.brocktonrox.com.

Principal Owner: Van Schley. **President:** Jim Lucas.
General Manager: Dave Echols. **Assistant GM:** David Sacchetti. **Director, Corporate Sales:** Gary MacKinnon.
Manager, Box Office: Drew Cunningham. **Ticket Sales Representatives:** Andy Crossley, Brian Voelkel. **Bookkeeper:** Mary Scarlett. **Director, Food/Beverages:** Unavailable. **Director, Promotions/Merchandise:** Jim Pfander. **Director, Media Relations:** Ryan Smith. **Groundskeeper:** Tom Hassett. **Receptionist:** Dawn Brunetti. **Director, Community Relations:** Andrea Thrubis. **Director, Special Events:** Danni Barrall.
Manager: Ed Nottle. **Coach:** Unavailable. **Trainer:** Ralph Evans.

GAME INFORMATION
Radio Announcer: Larry Blucher. **No. of Games Broadcast:** Home-46, Away-46. **Flagship Station:** WBET 1460-AM.
PA Announcer: John Dolan. **Official Scorer:** Jim Seavey.
Stadium name (year opened): Campanelli Stadium (2002). **Directions:** Route 24 North/South to Route 123 East, stadium 2 miles on right. **Standard Game Times:** 7:11 p.m.; Sun. (May-June) 2:05, (July-Sept.) 5:05.
Visiting Club Hotel: Residence Inn, 124 Liberty St., Brockton, MA 02301. Telephone: (508) 583-3600.

ELMIRA PIONEERS

Office Address: 546 Luce St., Elmira, NY 14904.
Telephone: (607) 734-1270. **FAX:** (607) 734-0891.
E-Mail Address: pioneers@elmirapioneers.com. **Website:** www.elmirapioneers.com.

Operated by: Elmira Baseball, LLC.
President: Phil Kramer.
General Manager: Tom Sullivan. **Sales/Marketing:** Unavailable. **Head Groundskeeper:** Dale Storch. **Director, Operations:** Ferrell Butler.
Manager: Unavailable. **Coach:** Unavailable.

GAME INFORMATION
Radio: Unavailable.
PA Announcer: Unavailable. **Official Scorer:** Unavailable.
Stadium Name (year opened): Dunn Field (1939). **Location:** I-86 (Route 17) to exit 56 (Church Street), left on Madison Ave., left on Maple Ave., left on Luce Street. **Standard Game Times:** 7:05 p.m.; Sun. 1:05.
Visiting Club Hotel: Holiday Inn Elmira-Riverview, 760 E. Water, Elmira, NY 14901. Telephone: (607) 734-4211.

NEW HAVEN COUNTY CUTTERS

Office Address: 252 Derby Ave., West Haven, CT 06516.
Telephone: (203) 777-5636. **FAX:** (203) 777-4369.

Operated by: Flying Bats and Balls, LLC.
Principal Owner: Jonathan Fleisig.
President: Rick Handelman.
General Manager: Tim Kelly. **Assistant GM:** Marie Heikkinen Webb.
Manager: Jarvis Brown. **Coach:** Unavailable. **Trainer:** Unavailable.

GAME INFORMATION
Radio: Unavailable.
PA Announcer: Unavailable. **Official Scorer:** Unavailable.
Stadium Name (year opened): Yale Field (1927). **Directions:** From I-95, take eastbound exit 44 or westbound exit 45 to Route 10 and follow the Yale Bowl signs. From Merritt Parkway, take exit 57, follow to 34 East. **Standard Game Times:** 7:05 p.m., Sun. 2:05.
Visiting Club Hotel: Unavailable.

NEW JERSEY
JACKALS

Office Address: One Hall Dr., Little Falls, NJ 07424.
Telephone: (973) 746-7434. **FAX:** (973) 655-8021.
E-Mail Address: info@jackals.com. **Website:** www.jackals.com.

Operated by: Floyd Hall Enterprises, LLC.
Principal Owner, Chairman: Floyd Hall. **President:** Greg Lockard.
General Manager: Larry Hall. **Director, Business Operations:** Jennifer Fertig. **Director, Media/Public Relations:** Unavailable. **Head Groundskeeper:** Aldo Licitra. **Director, Sales/Marketing:** Kenneth Yudman. **Director, Ticket Sales:** Keri Mackie. **Sales Representative:** Matt Abel. **Clubhouse Operations:** Wally Brackett.
Manager: Joe Calfapietra. **Coach:** Unavailable. **Pitching Coach:** Brian Drahman. **Trainer:** Unavailable.

GAME INFORMATION

Radio Announcer: Unavailable. **No. of Games Broadcast:** Home-46, Away-46. **Flagship Station:** WPSC 88.7-FM.
PA Announcer: Unavailable. **Official Scorer:** Kim DeRitter.
Stadium Name (year opened): Yogi Berra Stadium (1998). **Location:** Route 80 or Garden State Parkway to Route 46, take Valley Road exit to Montclair State University. **Standard Game Times:** 7:05 p.m.; Sun. (May-June) 2:05, (July-Sept.) 5:05.
Visiting Club Hotel: Wellesley Inn, 265 Route 3 East, Clifton, NJ 07014. Telephone: (973) 778-6500.

NORTH SHORE
SPIRIT

Office Address: 365 Western Ave, Lynn, MA 01904.
Mailing Address: P.O. Box 8120, Lynn, MA 01904.
Telephone: (781) 592-0007. **FAX:** (781) 592-0004.
E-Mail Address: info@northshorespirit.com. **Website:** www.northshorespirit.com.

Operated by: Spirit of New England Baseball Club, LLC.
Principal Owner: Nicholas Lopardo.
General Manager: Ben Wittkowski. **Assistant GM/Director, Sales and Marketing:** Brent Connolly. **Operations Director/Ticket Sales:** Andy Seguin. **Director, Entertainment:** Chris Ames. **Senior Account Executive:** Kevin Kelly. **Account Executive:** Bryce Scottron. **Media Relations:** Nicki Reilly. **Group Sales:** Luis Breazeale. **Director, Baseball Administration:** Heather Pellegrini. **Administrative/Advertising Assistant:** Courtney Desrosiers. **Operations Assistant:** Tim Seguin.
Manager: John Kennedy. **Coaches:** Rich Gedman, Frank Carey, Jim Tgettis. **Pitching Coach:** Dick Radatz. **Strength/Conditioning Coach:** Paul Melanson.

GAME INFORMATION

Radio Announcer: Don Boyle. **No. of Games Broadcast:** Home-46, Away-46. **Flagship Station:** WESX 1230-AM.
PA Announcer: Unavailable. **Official Scorer:** Unavailable.
Stadium Name (year opened): Fraser Field (1940). **Location:** Route 129 (Lynn exit) into Lynn on Lynnfield Street, left at Chestnut Street; right at Western Ave. (Route 107), stadium on right. **Standard Game Times:** 7:05 p.m., Sun. 2:05.
Visiting Club Hotel: Sheraton Ferncroft, 50 Ferncroft Rd., Danvers, MA 01923. Telephone: (978) 777-2500.

QUEBEC
LES CAPITALES

Office Address: 100 Rue du Cardinal Maurice-Roy, Quebec City, Quebec G1K 8Z1.
Telephone: (418) 521-2255. **FAX:** (418) 521-2266.
E-Mail Address: baseball@capitalesdequebec.com. **Website:** www.capitales dequebec.com.

President: Miles Wolff.
General Manager: Nicolas Labbé. **Director, Business Operations:** Rémi Bolduc. **Director, Media/Public Relations:** Alexandre Harvey. **Sales/Marketing:** Ed Sweeney. **Director, Ticket Sales:** Nathalie Gauthier.
Manager: Daren Bush. **Coaches:** Stéphan Bédard, Joey Rhodes.

GAME INFORMATION

Radio: Unavailable.
PA Announcer: Damien Miville-Deschênes. **Official Scorer:** Stéphan Lévesque.
Stadium Name (year opened): Stade Municipal de Québec (1938). **Location:** Highway 40 to Highway 173 (Centre-Ville) exit 2 to Parc Victoria. **Standard Game Times:** 7:05 p.m., Sun. 1:05.

Visiting Club Hotel: Hotel du Nord, 640 St. Vallier W., Quebec City, Quebec G1N 1C5. Telephone: (418) 522-1554.

NORTHERN
LEAGUE

Office Address: 306 West Seventh St., Suite 400, Fort Worth, TX 76107.
Telephone: (817) 378-9898. **FAX:** (817) 378-9805.
E-Mail Address: info@northernleague.com. **Website:** www.northernleague.com.

Commissioner: Mike Stone. **Director, Baseball Operations:** Mike Marshall.
Directors: Jim Abel (Lincoln), John Ehlert (Kansas City), Rich Ehrenreich (Schaumburg), Marv Goldklang (St. Paul), Michael Hansen (Joliet), Sam Katz (Winnipeg), John Roost (Sioux City), Mike Tatoian (Gary), Bruce Thom (Fargo-Moorhead), Ben Zurawl (Sioux Falls).
Supervisor, Umpires: Butch Fisher.
2004 Opening Date: May 20. **Closing Date:** Sept. 5.
Regular Season: 96 games (split-schedule).
Division Structure: North—Fargo-Moorhead, St. Paul, Sioux City, Sioux Falls, Winnipeg. **South**—Gary, Joliet, Kansas City, Lincoln, Schaumburg.
Playoff Format: First-half division winners play second-half division winners in best-of-5 series. Winners meet in best-of-5 series for league championship.
All-Star Game: July 20 at Joliet.
Roster Limit: 22. **Eligibility Rule:** Minimum of five first-year players; maximum of four veterans with at least four years of professional experience.
Brand of Baseball: Rawlings.
Statistician: Sports Ticker-Boston, Boston Fish Pier, West Bldg. #1, Suite 302, Boston, MA 02210.

FARGO-MOORHEAD
REDHAWKS

Office Address: 1515 15th Ave. N., Fargo, ND 58102.
Telephone: (701) 235-6161. **FAX:** (701) 297-9247.
E-Mail Address: redhawks@fmredhawks.com. **Website:** www.fmredhawks.com.

Operated by: Fargo Baseball, LLC.
Ownership: Otter Tail Corporation.
President: Bruce Thom.
Vice President/General Manager: Lee Schwartz. **Vice President/Director, Sales:** Brad Thom. **Director, Baseball Operations:** Josh Buchholz. **Senior Accountant:** Sue Wild. **Accounting Assistant:** Tina Lesmeister. **Stadium Superintendent/Head Groundskeeper:** Blair Tweet. **Director, Promotions:** Kristie Schwan. **Director, Merchandise/Special Events, Advertising:** Sara Garaas. **Office Manager:** Jenny Vangerud. **Director, Ticket Sales:** Nicole Ellis. **Assistant, Media Relations:** Mitch Hoff. **Clubhouse Operations:** Brent Tehven.
Manager/Director, Player Procurement: Doug Simunic. **Assistant Director, Player Procurement/Consultant:** Jeff Bittiger. **Pitching Coach:** Steve Montgomery. **Coach:** Bucky Burgau. **Trainer:** Don Bruenjes.

GAME INFORMATION

Radio Announcer: Jack Michaels. **No. of Games Broadcast:** Home-48, Away-48. **Flagship Station:** WDAY 970-AM.
PA Announcer: Merrill Piepkorn. **Official Scorer:** Rob Olson.
Stadium Name (year opened): Newman Outdoor Field (1996). **Location:** I-29 North to exit 67, right on 19th Ave. North, right on Albrecht Blvd. **Standard Game Times:** 7:05 p.m., Sun. 2:05.
Visiting Club Hotel: Comfort Inn West, 3825 9th Ave. SW, Fargo, ND 58103. Telephone: (701) 282-9596.

GARY SOUTHSHORE
RAILCATS

Office Address: One Stadium Plaza, Gary, IN 46402.
Telephone: (219) 882-2255. **FAX:** (219) 882-2259.
E-Mail Address: info@railcatsbaseball.com Website: www.railcatsbaseball.com.

Operated by: SouthShore Baseball, LLC. **Principal Owners:** Victory Sports Group, LLC.
Chairman: George Huber. **President, Chief Executive Officer:** Mike Tatoian.
Vice President, General Manager: Roger Wexelberg. **Assistant GM:** Kevin Spudic. **Director, Community/Special Sales Program:** Aukesha Henry. **Director, Marketing/ Promotions:** Jim Smith. **Director, Media/Broadcasting:** Alan

Garrett. **Director, Facilities:** Mike Figg **Director, Ticket Operations/Sales:** Sierra Foster. **Corporate Sales Manager:** Milton Thaxton. **Manager, Group Sales:** Mike Smith, **Manager, Merchandise:** Janine Kurpiel. **Groundskeeper:** Mike Faust. **Executive Assistant:** Tomika Hicks

Manager: Garry Templeton. **Coaches:** Brent Bowers, Joe Gates **Pitching Coach:** Wally Widelski.

GAME INFORMATION

Radio Announcer: Alan Garrett. **No. of Games Broadcast:** Home-48, Away-48. **Flagship Station:** WEFM 95.5-FM.

Stadium Name (year opened): U.S. Steel Yard (2003). **Location:** I-65 to I-90 West (toll), one mile to Broadway South, left on Fifth Street. **Standard Game Times:** 7 p.m., Sat. 6, Sun. 1.

Visiting Club Hotel: Trump Hotel, 21 Buffington Harbor Dr., Gary, IN 46406. **Telephone:** (219) 977-9999

JOLIET
JACKHAMMERS

Office Address: 1 Mayor Art Schultz Dr., Joliet, IL 60432.
Telephone: (815) 726-2255. **FAX:** (815) 726-9223.
E-Mail Address: info@jackhammerbaseball.com. **Website:** www.jackhammer baseball.com.

Operated by: Joliet Professional Baseball Club, LLC.

Chairman: Peter Ferro. **Vice Chairman:** Charles Hammersmith. **Chief Executive Officer/General Counsel:** Michael Hansen. **Chief Financial Officer/President:** John Costello.

Executive Vice President/General Manager: Steve Malliet. **VP, Sales:** Bob Lapinski. **Assistant GM:** Kelly Sufka. **Ticket Sales Manager:** Rich Kuchar. **Ticket Operations Manager:** Chad Therrien. **Ticket Sales Executive:** Kyle Kreger. **Director, Broadcasting/Media Relations:** Bryan Dolgin. **Director, Community Relations/Promotions:** Sarah Heth. **Corporate Sales Manager:** Karen Crichton. **Director, Field/Stadium Operations:** Jeff Eckert. **Director, Accounting/Human Resources:** Penny Roach. **Administrative Assistant:** Teresa Dyer.

Manager: Jeff Isom. **Coach/Player Development Coordinator:** Mike Pinto. **Pitching Coach:** Rich Hyde. **Trainer:** Scott Wilson.

GAME INFORMATION

Radio Announcers: Bryan Dolgin, Mark Vasko. **No. of Games Broadcast:** Home-48, Away-48. **Flagship Stations:** WJOL 1340-AM.

PA Announcer: Jake Blues. **Official Scorer:** Dave Laketa.

Stadium Name (year opened): Silver Cross Field (2002). **Location:** I-80 to Chicago Street/Route 53 North exit, go ½ mile on Chicago Street until it dead ends into Washington Street, right on Washington to Jefferson Street/U.S. 52, right on Jefferson, ballpark on left. **Standard Game Times:** 7:05 p.m., Sun. 2:05.

Visiting Club Hotel: Hampton Inn, 3555 Mall Loop Dr., Joliet, IL 60431. Telephone: (815) 439-9500.

KANSAS CITY
T-BONES

Office Address: 1800 Village West Pkwy., Kansas City, KS 66111.
Telephone: (913) 328-2255. **FAX:** (913) 328-5652.
E-Mail Address: batterup@tbonesbaseball.com. **Website:** www.tbonesbaseball.com.

Operated By: T-Bones Baseball Club, LLC.

Owner, President: John Ehlert. **Vice President:** Adam Ehlert.

General Manager: Rick Muntean. **VP, Marketing/Corporate Partnerships:** Kevin Battle. **Director, Stadium Operations:** Chris Browne. **Assistant, Stadium Operations:** Matt Pellant. **Director, Merchandising:** Tracy Lewis. **Director, Media Relations:** Loren Foxx. **Director, Promotions:** Justin Stancil. **Director, Group Sales:** Brandon Smith. **Head Groundskeeper:** Matt Mattes. **Manager, Sales:** Mike Meyer. **Marketing, Sponsorship Support:** Darci Vonfeldt. **Bookkeeper:** Vicki Vickers. **Executive Assistant:** Valerie Stuckey.

Manager: Al Gallagher. **Coaches:** Darryl Motley, Ray Brown, Eddie Pearson. **Pitching Coach:** Danny Jackson. **Trainer:** Unavailable.

GAME INFORMATION

Radio Announcer: Unavailable. **No. of Games Broadcast:** Home-48, Away-48. **Flagship Station:** Unavailable.

PA Announcer: Unavailable. **Official Scorer:** Unavailable.

Stadium Name (year opened): Community America Ballpark (2003). **Location:** State Avenue West off I-435, corner of 110th and State Avenue. **Standard Game Times:** 7:05 p.m., Sun. 5:05.

Visiting Club Hotel: Holiday Inn Express, 12601 West 95th St., Lenexa, KS 66215. Telephone: (913) 888-6670.

LINCOLN
SALTDOGS

Office Address: 403 Line Dr., Suite A, Lincoln, NE 68508.
Telephone: (402) 474-2255. **FAX:** (402) 474-2254.
E-Mail Address: info@saltdogs.com. **Website:** www.saltdogs.com.

Owner: Jim Abel. **President:** Charlie Meyer.
Vice President, General Manager: Tim Utrup. **Assistant GM/Director, Marketing:** Bret Beer. **Director, Media Relations:** Jason Wostrel. **Director, Marketing:** Jamie Von Sossan. **Director, Merchandising:** Anne Kurtzer. **Director, Ticketing:** Tim Petersen. **Assistant Directors, Sales:** Stephanie Erwin, Kendall Christensen. **Director, Stadium Operations:** Ryan Lockhart. **Athletic Turf Management:** Dan Bergstom. **Office Manager:** Jeanette Eagleton.
Manager: Tim Johnson. **Coaches:** Mike Busch, Mike Workman. **Trainer:** Unavailable.

GAME INFORMATION
Radio Announcers: Bill Doleman, John Baylor. **No. of Games Broadcast:** Home-48, Away-48. **Flagship Station:** KFOR 1240-AM.
PA Announcer: Unavailable. **Official Scorer:** Unavailable.
Stadium Name (year opened): Haymarket Park (2001). **Location:** I-80 to Cornhusker Highway West, left on First Street, right on Sun Valley Blvd., left on Line Drive. **Standard Game Times:** 7:05 p.m., Sun. 6:05.
Visiting Club Hotel: Embassy Suites, 1040 P St., Lincoln, NE 68508. Telephone: (402) 474-1111.

ST. PAUL
SAINTS

Office Address: 1771 Energy Park Dr., St. Paul, MN 55108.
Telephone: (651) 644-3517. **FAX:** (651) 644-1627.
E-Mail Address: funsgood@saintsbaseball.com. **Website:** www.saintsbaseball.com.

Operated By: St. Paul Saints Baseball Club, Inc.
Principal Owners: Marv Goldklang, Mike Veeck, Bill Murray.
Chairman: Marv Goldklang. **President:** Mike Veeck.
Vice President, General Manager: Bill Fanning. **VP, Business Development:** Tom Whaley. **Assistant GM, Operations:** Bill Fisher. **Director, Group Sales:** Eben Yager. **Coordinator, Group Sales:** Matt Bomberg. **Director, Corporate Sales/New Business Development:** John Kuhn. **Director, Media Relations/Internet:** Dave Wright. **Director, Community Relations:** Paul Tarnowski. **Ticket Manager:** Ryan Wiese. **Manager, Corporate Sales:** Matt Hansen. **Coordinator, Promotions:** Stephanie Harris. **Director, Food Services:** Tom Farrell. **Controller:** Wayne Engel. **Office Manager:** Jennifer Jansen. **Accountant:** Leesa Anderson. **Director, Stadium Operations:** Bob Klepperich. **Head Groundskeeper:** Connie Rudolph.
Manager: George Tsamis. **Coaches:** Ben Fleetham, Jackie Hernandez, Lamarr Rogers, T.J. Wiesner. **Trainer:** Chris Strickland.

GAME INFORMATION
Radio Announcer: Kris Atteberry. **No. of Games Broadcast:** Home-48, Away-48. **Flagship Station:** KSNB 950-AM.
PA Announcer: Unavailable. **Official Scorer:** Brock Kline.
Stadium Name (year opened): Midway Stadium (1982). **Location:** From I-94, take Snelling Avenue exit, north on Snelling, west onto Energy Park Drive. **Standard Game Times:** 7:05 p.m., Sun. 1:05.
Visiting Club Hotel: Holiday Inn North, 1201 West County Rd. E., St. Paul, MN 55112. Telephone: (651) 636-4123.

SCHAUMBURG
FLYERS

Office Address: 1999 S. Springinsguth Rd., Schaumburg, IL 60193.
Telephone: (847) 891-2255. **FAX:** (847) 891-6441.
E-Mail Address: info@flyersbaseball.com. **Website:** www.flyersbaseball.com.

Principal Owners: Richard Ehrenreich, John Hughes, Gregory Smith. **Managing Partner/President:** Richard Ehrenreich.
General Manager: Rick Rungaitis. **Assistant GM, Sales/Marketing:** Tom O'Reilly. **Director, Media Relations:** Matt McLaughlin. **Manager, Group Sales:** Robin Lemke. **Ticket Manager:** Scott Boor. **Director, Operations:** Eric Tholen. **Director, Graphics/Publications:** Shannan Kelly. **Director, Community Relations/Promotions:** Kristy Paukner. **Director, Merchandising/Schaumburg Club:** Angela Burg. **Director, Stadium Operations/Head Groundskeeper:** Eric Fasbender. **Director, Accounting/Human Resources:** Ben Burke. **Clubhouse Manager:** Greg Garofalo.
Manager: Andy McCauley. **Coach:** Gregg Neuman. **Pitching Coach:** Jim Boynewicz. **Trainer:** Mike Hickey.

GAME INFORMATION

Radio Announcer: Matt McLaughlin. **No. of Games Broadcast:** Home-48, Away-48. **Flagship Station:** WONC 89.1-FM. **PA Announcer:** Steve Brandy. **Official Scorers:** Tim Calderwood, Greg Swiderski.

Stadium Name (year opened): Alexian Field (1999). **Location:** From north, I-290 to Elgin-O'Hare Expressway (Thorndale), west on expressway to Irving Park Road exit, left on Springinsguth under expressway, stadium on left; From south, U.S. 20 West (Lake Street) to Elgin-O'Hare Expressway (Thorndale), east on expressway, right on Springinsguth Road. **Standard Game Times:** 7:05 p.m.; Sat. 6:20; Sun. 1:20.

Visiting Club Hotel: Radisson Hotel-Arlington Heights. 75 W. Algonquin Rd., Arlington Heights, IL 60005. Telephone: (847) 364-7600.

SIOUX CITY
EXPLORERS

Office Address: 3400 Line Dr., Sioux City, IA 51106.
Telephone: (712) 277-9467. **FAX:** (712) 277-9406.
E-Mail Address: siouxcityxs@yahoo.com. **Website:** www.xsbaseball.com.

Operated by: Sioux City Explorers Baseball Club, LLC.
General Manager: Chuck Robbins. **Office Manager:** Stephanie Sexton. **Assistant GM:** Luke Nielsen. **Director, Stadium Operations:** Jesse Underwood. **Director, Broadcasting:** Paul Guggenheimer. **Director, Ticketing/Merchandise:** Mike Gorsett.
Manager: Jay Kirkpatrick. **Pitching Coach:** Joe Georger. **Trainer:** Brandon Marreel.

GAME INFORMATION

Radio Announcer: Paul Guggenheimer. **No. of Games Broadcast:** Home-48, Away-48. **Flagship Station:** KSCJ 1360-AM.

PA Announcer: Lew Roberts. **Official Scorer:** Brent Frady.

Stadium Name (year opened): Lewis and Clark Park (1993). **Location:** I-29 to Singing Hills North, right on Line Drive. **Standard Game Times:** 7:05 p.m., Sun. 5:05.

Visiting Club Hotel: Best Western, 130 Nebraska St., Sioux City, IA 51101. Telephone: (712) 277-1550.

SIOUX FALLS
CANARIES

Office Address: 1001 N. West Ave., Sioux Falls, SD 57104.
Telephone: (605) 333-0179. **FAX:** (605) 333-0139.
E-Mail Address: canaries@canariesbaseball.com. **Website:** www.canaries baseball.com.

Operated by: Sioux Falls Canaries Professional Baseball Club, LLC.
Principal Owner, Chairman: Ben Zuraw. **President:** Jeff Loebl.
General Manager: John Hindle. **Assistant GM:** Larry McKenney. **Manager, Communications:** Unavailable. **Manager, Marketing/Promotions:** Unavailable. **Manager, Sales:** Barb Brown. **Manager, Food/Beverage:** Julie Malmberg. **Office/Ticket Manager:** Rachel Wiersma. **Clubhouse Manager:** Unavailable.
Manager/Director, Player Personnel: Doc Edwards. **Coaches:** Jeff Ware, Billy Williams. **Trainer:** Brian Pickering.

GAME INFORMATION

Radio Announcer: Unavailable. **No. of Games Broadcast:** Home-48, Away-48. **Flagship Station:** KWSN 1230-AM. **PA Announcer:** Dan Christopherson. **Official Scorer:** Unavailable.

Stadium Name (year opened): Sioux Falls Stadium (1964). **Location:** I-29 to Russell Street, south one mile, right on West Avenue. **Standard Game Times:** 7:04 p.m., Sun. 5:04.

Visiting Club Hotel: Baymont Inn, 3200 Meadow Ave., Sioux Falls, SD 57106. Telephone: (605) 362-0835.

WINNIPEG
GOLDEYES

Office Address: One Portage Ave. E., Winnipeg, Manitoba R3B 3N3.
Telephone: (204) 982-2273. **FAX:** (204) 982-2274.
E-Mail Address: goldeyes@goldeyes.com. **Website:** www.goldeyes.com.

Operated by: Winnipeg Goldeyes Baseball Club, Inc.
Principal Owner, President: Sam Katz.
General Manager: Andrew Collier. **Director, Marketing:** Dan Chase. **Director, Communications:** Jonathan Green.

Director, Promotions: Barb McTavish. **Director, Sales:** Lorraine Maciboric. **Director, Group Sales:** Tracy Smith. **Account Representatives:** Paul Edmonds, Regan Katz, Dave Loat, Darren McCabe, Dennis McLean. **Director, Merchandising:** Carol Orchard. **Comptroller:** Judy Jones. **Facility Manager:** Scott Horn. **Administrative Assistants:** Heather Mann-O'Hara, Angela Sanche. **Head Groundskeeper:** Don Ferguson.

Manager/Director, Player Procurement: Hal Lanier. **Coach:** Tom Vaeth. **Pitching Coach:** Rick Forney. **Trainer:** Dong Lien.

Game Information

Radio Announcer: Paul Edmonds. **No. of Games Broadcast:** Home-33, Road-33. **Flagship Station:** CJOB 680-AM. **PA Announcer:** Ron Arnst. **Official Scorer:** Steve Eitzen.

Stadium Name (year opened): CanWest Global Park (1999). **Location:** Pembina Highway (Route 75), east on River Ave., north on Main Street, east on Water Ave. **Standard Game Times:** 7:05 p.m., Sun. 1:35.

Visiting Club Hotel: Ramada Marlborough, 331 Smith St., Winnipeg, Manitoba R3B 2G9 Telephone: (204) 942-6411.

SOUTHWESTERN
LEAGUE

Office Address: 525 E. Madrid, Suite 9, Las Cruces, NM 88001. **Telephone:** (505) 523-4165. **FAX:** (501) 634-6181. **E-Mail Address:** leagueoffice@swlbaseball.com. **Website:** swlbaseball.com. **Year Founded:** 2004.

President: Bob Lipp. **Vice-President:** T.K. Karabatsos.
Regular Season: 54 games.
Member Clubs: Unavailable.
2004 Opening Date: May 28. **Closing Date:** July 28.
Playoff Format: Top two teams meet in best-of-5 series for league championship.
All-Star Game: None.
Roster Limit: 22. **Player Eligibility Rule:** No restrictions.
Brand of Baseball: Unavailable.
Official Statistician: SportsTicker-Boston, Boston Fish Pier, West Bldg. #1, Suite 302, Boston, MA 02210.

INDEPENDENT SCHEDULES

HOME GAMES ONLY

ATLANTIC LEAGUE

ATLANTIC CITY
MAY
7-8-9 .... Nashua
11-12-13 .. Pennsylvania
14-15-16 .... Bridgeport
18-19-20 .. Pennsylvania
25-26-27 .... Somerset
JUNE
3-4-5 .... Newark
6-7-8 .... Long Island
18-19-20 .... Newark
22-23-24 .. Nashua
25-26-27 .. Pennsylvania
JULY
1-2-3 .... Pennsylvania
4-4-6 .... Camden
16-17-18 .... Somerset
19-20-21 .... Newark
22-23-24 .... Long Island
31 .... Nashua
AUGUST
1-2 .... Nashua
10-11-12 .. Pennsylvania
13-14-15 .. Bridgeport
17-18-19 .. Pennsylvania
23-24-25 .... Somerset
26-27-28 .... Camden
SEPTEMBER
4-5-5 .... Long Island
14-15-16 ...... Bridgeport
17-18-19 .... Camden

BRIDGEPORT
MAY
18-19-20 .... Newark
21-22-23 .. Pennsylvania
25-26-27 .... Nashua
28-29-30 .... Long Island
JUNE
6-7-8 .... Camden
9-10-11 ...... Atlantic City
15-16-17 .... Somerset
18-19-20 .. Pennsylvania
28-29-30 .... Atlantic City
JULY
1-2-3 .... Newark
4-5-6 .... Pennsylvania
7-8-9 .... Nashua
10-11-12 .... Long Island
22-23-24 .... Camden
25-26-27 ... Atlantic City
28-29-30 .. Pennsylvania
AUGUST
3-4-5 .... Pennsylvania
6-7-8 .... Somerset
17-18-19 .... Long Island
23-24-25 .... Nashua
26-27-28 .... Newark
SEPTEMBER
4-5-6 .... Camden
7-8-9 .... Somerset
17-18-19 .. Pennsylvania

CAMDEN
MAY
6-7-8-9 ..... Pennsylvania
11-12-13 ..... Bridgeport
21-22-23 .... Atlantic City
25-26-27 .... Newark
28-29-30 .... Somerset
JUNE
3-4-5 .... Somerset
9-10-11 ...... Long Island
12-13-14 .... Nashua
15-16-17 .. Pennsylvania
23-24 .... Pennsylvania
25-26-27 ...... Bridgeport
JULY
7-8-9 .... Newark
10-11-12 .. Atlantic City
25-26-27 .... Nashua
28-29-30 .... Nashua
31 .... Pennsylvania
AUGUST
1-2 .... Pennsylvania
6-7-8 .... Long Island
10-11-12 ...... Bridgeport
20-21-22 .... Atlantic City
23-24-25 .... Newark
SEPTEMBER
1-2-3 .... Somerset
7-8-9 .... Long Island
10-11-12 .... Nashua
14-15-16 .. Pennsylvania

LONG ISLAND
MAY
11-12-13 .... Somerset
14-15-16 .... Camden
21-22-23 .... Nashua
25-26-27 .. Pennsylvania
31 .... Pennsylvania
JUNE
1-2 .... Pennsylvania
3-4-5 .... Bridgeport
12-13-14 .... Atlantic City
15-16-17 .... Newark
25-26-27 .... Somerset
28-29-30 .... Camden
JULY
4-5-6 .... Nashua
7-8-9 .... Pennsylvania
16-17-18 .. Pennsylvania
19-20-21 ...... Bridgeport
28-29-30 .... Atlantic City
31 .... Newark
AUGUST
1-2 .... Newark
10-11-12 .... Somerset
13-14-15 .... Camden
20-21-22 .... Nashua
23-24-25 .. Pennsylvania
29-30-31 .. Pennsylvania
SEPTEMBER
1-2-3 .... Bridgeport
10-11-12 .... Atlantic City
14-15-16 .... Newark

NASHUA
MAY
14-15-16 .... Somerset
18-19-20 .... Camden
28-29-30 .. Pennsylvania
31 .... Bridgeport
JUNE
1-2 .... Bridgeport
3-4-5 .... Pennsylvania
6-7-8 .... Newark
15-16-17 .... Atlantic City
18-19-20 .... Long Island
28-29-30 .... Somerset
JULY
1-2-3 .... Camden
10-11-12 .. Pennsylvania
16-17-18 ...... Bridgeport
19-20-21 .. Pennsylvania
22-23-24 .... Newark
25-26-27 .... Somerset
AUGUST
3-4-5 .... Long Island
6-7-8 .... Atlantic City
17-18-19 .... Camden
26-27-28 .. Pennsylvania
29-30-31 ...... Bridgeport
SEPTEMBER
1-2-3 .... Pennsylvania
4-5-6 .... Newark
7-8-9 .... Atlantic City
17-18-19 .... Long Island

NEWARK
MAY
6-7-8-9 .... Long Island
11-12-13 .... Nashua
14-15-16 .. Pennsylvania
28-29-30 .... Atlantic City
31 .... Camden
JUNE
1-2 .... Camden
9-10-11 .... Pennsylvania
12-13-14 ...... Bridgeport
23-24 .... Long Island
25-26-27 .... Nashua
28-29-30 .. Pennsylvania
JULY
4-5-6 .... Somerset
10-11-12 .... Somerset
16-17-18 .... Camden
25-26-27 .... Long Island
28-29-30 .... Somerset
AUGUST
3-4-5 .... Atlantic City
6-7-8 .... Pennsylvania
10-11-12 .... Nashua
13-14-15 .. Pennsylvania
20-21-22 ...... Bridgeport
29-30-31 .... Camden
SEPTEMBER
1-2-3 .... Atlantic City
7-8-9 .... Pennsylvania
10-11-12 ...... Bridgeport

PENNSYLVANIA
No home dates

SOMERSET
MAY
6-7-8 .... Bridgeport
18-19-20 .... Long Island
21-22-23 .... Newark
31 .... Atlantic City
JUNE
1-2 .... Atlantic City
6-7-8 .... Pennsylvania
9-10-11 .... Nashua
12-13-14 .. Pennsylvania
18-19-20 .... Camden
22-23-24 ...... Bridgeport
JULY
1-2-3 .... Long Island
7-8-9 .... Atlantic City
19-20-21 .... Camden
22-23-24 .. Pennsylvania
31 .... Bridgeport
AUGUST
1-2 .... Bridgeport
3-4-5 .... Camden
13-14-15 .... Nashua
17-18-19 .... Newark
20-21-22 .. Pennsylvania
26-27-28 .... Long Island
29-30-31 .... Atlantic City
SEPTEMBER
4-5-6 .... Pennsylvania
10-11-12 .. Pennsylvania
14-15-16 .... Nashua
17-18-19 .... Newark

CENTRAL LEAGUE

AMARILLO

MAY
6-7-8-9 .... Fort Worth
10-11-12 ...... Shreveport
21-22-23 .... Jackson
24-25-26-27 .. Coastal Bend

JUNE
4-4-5-6 .... Pensacola
15-16-17 .... Edinburg
18-19-20-21 .. San Angelo
27-28-29-30 .. Fort Worth

JULY
2-3-4-4 .... Shreveport
12-13-14 .... Jackson
16-17-18 .. Coastal Bend
30-31 .... Pensacola

AUGUST
1 .... Pensacola
10-11-12-13 .... Edinburg
15-16-17 ...... San Angelo

COASTAL BEND

MAY
6-7-8 .... Jackson
15-16 .... Fort Worth
17-18-19-20 .. Pensacola
31 .... Edinburg

JUNE
1-2 .... Edinburg
11-12-13-14 .. Shreveport
15-16-17 ...... San Angelo
23-24-25-26 .. Amarillo
27-28-29-30 ...... Jackson

JULY
9-10-11 .... Pensacola
12-13-14 ...... Fort Worth
28-29 .... Edinburg

AUGUST
6-7-8-9 .... Shreveport
11-12-13-14 .. San Angelo
16 .... Edinburg
18-19-20-21 .... Amarillo

EDINBURG

MAY
14-15-16 .... Pensacola
17-18-19-20 .. Fort Worth
28-29-30 .... Amarillo

JUNE
3-4-5-6 .... San Angelo
8-9-10 .... Shreveport
18-19-20-21 .. Coastal Bend
23-24-25-26 ...... Jackson

JULY
6-7-8 .... Pensacola
9-10-11 .... Fort Worth
22-23-24-25 .... Amarillo
26-27 .... Coastal Bend
30-31 .... San Angelo

AUGUST
1 .... San Angelo
3-4-5 .... Shreveport
15 .... Coastal Bend
18-19-20-21 ...... Jackson

FORT WORTH

MAY
10-11-12 .... Edinburg
13-14 .... Coastal Bend
21-22 .... Coastal Bend
24-25-26 ...... San Angelo
28-29-30 .... Pensacola

JUNE
3-4-5-6 .... Jackson
8-9-10 .... Amarillo
18-19-20-21-22 .. Shreveport

JULY
2-3-4-5 .... Edinburg
6-7-8 .... Coastal Bend
16-17-18 ...... San Angelo
22-23-24-25 .. Pensacola
30-31 .... Jackson

AUGUST
1 .... Jackson
3-4-5 .... Amarillo

JACKSON

MAY
10-11-12 ...... San Angelo
14-15-16 .... Amarillo
24-25-26-27 .... Edinburg
28-29-30 ...... Shreveport

JUNE
7-8-9-10 .... Coastal Bend
11-12-13-14 .. Fort Worth
18-19-20-21 .. Pensacola

JULY
2-3-4-5 .... San Angelo
6-7-8 .... Amarillo
16-17-18 .... Edinburg
22-23-24-25 .. Shreveport

AUGUST
2-3-4 .... Coastal Bend
6-7-8-9 .... Fort Worth
15-16-17 ...... Pensacola

PENSACOLA

MAY
6-7-8-9 .... Edinburg
10-11-12 .. Coastal Bend
22-22-23 ...... San Angelo
25-26-27 ...... Shreveport
31 .... Jackson

JUNE
1-2 .... Jackson
11-12-12-13 .... Amarillo
15-16-17 ...... Fort Worth
28-29-30 ...... Edinburg

JULY
1 .... Edinburg
2-2-3-4 ...... Coastal Bend
13-14-15 ...... San Angelo
16-17-18 ...... Shreveport
26-27-28 .... Jackson

AUGUST
6-6-7-8 .... Amarillo
11-12-13-14 .. Fort Worth

SAN ANGELO

MAY
13-14-15 ...... Shreveport
17-18-19-20 ...... Jackson
28-29 .... Coastal Bend
31 .... Amarillo

JUNE
1-2 .... Amarillo
7-8-9 .... Pensacola
11-12-13-14 .... Edinburg
23-24-25-26 .. Fort Worth

JULY
6-7-8 .... Shreveport
9-10-11 .... Jackson
22-23-24-25 .. Coastal Bend
26-27-28 .... Amarillo

AUGUST
2-3-4 .... Pensacola
6-7-8-9 .... Edinburg
18-19-20-21 .. Fort Worth

SHREVEPORT

MAY
6-7-8-9 .... San Angelo
17-18-19-20 .... Amarillo
21-22-23 .... Edinburg

JUNE
1-2 .... Fort Worth
3-4-5-6 .. Coastal Bend
15-16-17 .... Jackson
23-24-25-26 .. Pensacola
28-29-30 ...... San Angelo

JULY
1 .... San Angelo
9-10-11 .... Amarillo
13-14-15 .... Edinburg
27-28-29 ...... Fort Worth
30-31 .... Coastal Bend

AUGUST
1 .... Coastal Bend
11-12-13-14 ...... Jackson
18-19-20-21 .. Pensacola

15-16-17 ...... Shreveport

FRONTIER LEAGUE

CHILLICOTHE

MAY
28-29-30 .... Washington
31 .... Florence

JUNE
1-2 .... Florence
9-10-11 .... Kalamazoo
12-13-14 .... Florence
18-19-20 .... Evansville
22-23-24 .... Gateway
28-29-30 .... Washington

JULY
1-2-3 .... Kalamazoo
7-8-9 .... Richmond
16-17-18 ...... Kalamazoo

EVANSVILLE

MAY
21-22-23 .... Florence
25-26-27 ...... Chillicothe
29-29-30 ...... Kalamazoo

JUNE
6-7-8 .... Washington
9-10-11 .... Florence
15-16-17 ...... Kalamazoo
25-26-27 ...... Chillicothe

JULY
1-2-3 .... Richmond
10-11-12 ...... Chillicothe
22-23-24 .... Washington
28-29-30 .... Florence

AUGUST
4-5-6 ...... Mid-Missouri
10-11-12 .... Washington
13-14-15 .... Richmond
22-23-24 ...... Kalamazoo
25-26-27 .... Richmond

22-23-24 .... Richmond
25-26-27 .... Washington
31 .... Evansville

AUGUST
1-2 .... Evansville
10-11-12 .... Florence
16-17-18 .... Evansville
22-23-24 .... Richmond

FLORENCE

JUNE
18-19-20 .... Washington
22-23-24 .... River City
28-29-30 .... Evansville

JULY
4-5-6 .... Chillicothe
7-8-9 .... Kalamazoo
10-11-12 .... Washington
16-17-18 .... Evansville
19-20-21 ...... Chillicothe
25-26-27 .... Richmond
31 .... Kalamazoo

AUGUST
1-2 .... Kalamazoo

7-8-9 .... Richmond
13-14-15 ..... Washington
16-17-18 ...... Kalamazoo
19-20-21 .... Richmond
25-26-27 ...... Chillicothe
28-29-30 .... Evansville

GATEWAY
MAY
28-29-30 .... Rockford
JUNE
3-4-5 .... Windy City
9-10-11 .... Mid-Missouri
15-16-17 ...... S'field/Ozark
18-19-20 .... Rockford
25-26-27 ...... Windy City
JULY
1-2-3 .. Springfield/Ozark
4-5-6 .... River City
10-11-12 .... S'field/Ozark
19-20-21 .. Mid-Missouri
25-26-27 ...... Windy City
31 .... River City
AUGUST
1-2 .... River City
4-5-6 .... Chillicothe
10-11-12 .... Rockford
19-20-21 .... River City
22-23-24 .. Mid-Missouri

KALAMAZOO
MAY
25-26-27 .... Florence
31 .... Richmond
JUNE
1-2 .... Richmond
3-4-5 .... Chillicothe
6-7-8 .... Florence
12-13-14 .... Washington
18-19-20 .... Richmond
25-26-27 ...... Washington
JULY
4-5-6 .... Evansville
10-11-12 .... Richmond
22-23-24 .... Florence
25-26-27 .... Evansville
AUGUST
4-5-6 .. Springfield/Ozark
7-8-9 .... Evansville
13-14-15 ...... Chillicothe
19-20-21 ...... Chillicothe
25-26-27 .... Washington

MID-MISSOURI
MAY
25-26-27 .... Gateway
28-29-30 .... River City
JUNE
6-7-8 .. Springfield/Ozark
15-16-17 ...... Windy City
22-23-24 .... Evansville
25-26-27 .... Rockford
JULY
1-2-3 .... Windy City
7-8-9 .... Gateway
16-17-18 ..... S'field/Ozark
22-23-24 .... River City
25-26-27 .... Rockford
AUGUST
7-8-9 .... Gateway
13-14-15 ...... Windy City
19-20-21 ..... S'field/Ozark
25-26-27 .... River City
28-29-30 .... Rockford

RICHMOND
MAY
21-22-23 ...... Chillicothe
28-29-30 .... Florence
JUNE
3-4-5 .... Evansville
6-7-8 .... Chillicothe
12-13-14 .... Evansville
15-16-17 .... Florence
25-26-27 .... Florence
28-29-30 ...... Kalamazoo
JULY
4-5-6 .... Washington
16-17-18 .... Washington
19-20-21 ...... Evansville
28-29-30 ...... Chillicothe
AUGUST
4-5-6 .... Rockford
10-11-12 ..... Kalamazoo
16-17-18 ..... Washington
28-29-30 ...... Kalamazoo

RIVER CITY
MAY
21-22-23 .... Gateway
25-26-27 ...... Windy City
31 .... Rockford
JUNE
1-2 .... Rockford
6-7-8 .... Gateway
12-13-14 .... S'field/Ozark

18-19-20 .. Mid-Missouri
28-29-30 .. Mid-Missouri
JULY
7-8-9 .... Windy City
16-17-18 .... Gateway
25-26-27 .... S'field/Ozark
28-29-30 .... Rockford
AUGUST
4-5-6 .... Florence
10-11-12 .. Mid-Missouri
13-14-15 .... Rockford
22-23-24 ...... Windy City
28-29-30 .... S'field/Ozark

ROCKFORD
MAY
25-26-27 .... S'field/Ozark
JUNE
3-4-5 .... Mid-Missouri
6-7-8 .... Windy City
12-13-14 .. Mid-Missouri
15-16-17 .... River City
22-23-24 .... Richmond
28-29-30 .... Gateway
JULY
1-2-3 .... River City
7-8-9 .. Springfield/Ozark
10-11-12 .... River City
16-17-18 ...... Windy City
22-23-24 .... Gateway
31 .... Windy City
AUGUST
1-2 .... Windy City
7-8-9 .. Springfield/Ozark
16-17-18 .. Mid-Missouri
25-26-27 .... Gateway

SPRINGFIELD/OZARK
MAY
21-22-23 .. Mid-Missouri
31 .... Gateway
JUNE
3-4-5 .... River City
9-10-11 .... Rockford
22-23-24 ...... Kalamazoo
25-26-27 .... River City
JULY
4-5-6 .... Mid-Missouri
19-20-21 .... Rockford
22-23-24 ...... Windy City
28-29-30 .... Gateway
31 .... Mid-Missouri

AUGUST
1-2 .... Mid-Missouri
10-11-12 ...... Windy City
13-14-15 .... Gateway
16-17-18 .... River City
22-23-24 .... Rockford
25-26-27 ...... Windy City

WASHINGTON
MAY
21-22-23 ...... Kalamazoo
25-26-27 .... Richmond
31 .... Evansville
JUNE
1-2 .... Evansville
3-4-5 .... Florence
9-10-11 .... Richmond
15-16-17 ...... Chillicothe
22-23-24 ...... Windy City
JULY
1-2-3 .... Florence
7-8-9 .... Evansville
19-20-21 .... Kalamazoo
28-29-30 ...... Kalamazoo
31 .... Richmond
AUGUST
1-2 .... Richmond
7-8-9 .... Chillicothe
19-20-21 .... Evansville
22-23-24 .... Florence
28-29-30 ...... Chillicothe

WINDY CITY
MAY
21-22-23 .... Rockford
28-29-30 .... S'field/Ozark
31 .... Mid-Missouri
JUNE
1-2 .... Mid-Missouri
9-10-11 .... River City
12-13-14 .... Gateway
18-19-20 .... S'field/Ozark
28-29-30 .... S'field/Ozark
JULY
4-5-6 .... Rockford
10-11-12 .. Mid-Missouri
19-20-21 .... River City
28-29-30 .. Mid-Missouri
AUGUST
4-5-6 .... Washington
7-8-9 .... River City
16-17-18 .... Gateway
19-20-21 .... Rockford
28-29-30 .... Gateway

NORTHEAST LEAGUE

ALLENTOWN
JUNE
3-4-5-6 ...... North Shore
8-9-10 .... Quebec
18-19-20 .... Brockton
28-29-30 .... Bangor
JULY
1-2-3-4 .... Elmira
8-9-10-11 .... New Jersey
12-13-14 ...... New Haven
26-27-28 .... North Shore
29-30-31 .... Brockton
AUGUST
1 .... Brockton

9-10-11 .... Quebec
20-21-22 .... Bangor
23-24-25 .... Elmira
SEPTEMBER
1-2-3 .... New Haven
4-5-6 .... New Jersey

BANGOR
JUNE
3-4-5-6 .... New Jersey
7-8-9 .... Elmira
18-19-20 ...... New Haven
22-23-24 .... Allentown

JULY
2-3-4 .... Quebec
8-9-10-11 .. North Shore
12-13-14 .... Brockton
26-27-28 ...... New Haven
29-30-31 .... Elmira

AUGUST
1 .... Elmira
9-10-11 .... New Jersey
12-13-14-15 .. Allentown
24-25-26 .... Quebec

SEPTEMBER
1-2-3 .... North Shore
4-5-6 .... Brockton

BROCKTON
MAY
27-28-29-30 ...... Quebec
31 .... Bangor

JUNE
1-2 .... Bangor
11-12-13 ...... New Haven
14-15-16-17 .. North Shore
25-26-27 ...... New Jersey
28-29-30 .... Elmira

JULY
5-6-7 .... Allentown
16-17-18 ...... New Jersey
22-23-24-25 ...... Bangor

AUGUST
2-3-4 .... Quebec
5-6-7 .... North Shore
16-17-18 ...... New Haven
20-21-22 .... Elmira
27-28-29-30 .. Allentown

ELMIRA
MAY
27-28-29-30 .. New Haven
31 .... North Shore

JUNE
1-2 .... North Shore
11-12-13 .... Quebec
15-16-17 .... Allentown
21-22-23 .... Brockton
25-26-27 .... Bangor

JULY
5-6-7 .... New Jersey
16-17-18 .... Quebec
22-23-24-25 .. North Shore

AUGUST
2-3-4 .... New Jersey
5-6-7 .... Allentown
12-13-14-15 .... Brockton
17-18-19 .... Bangor
27-28-29-30 .. New Haven

NEW HAVEN
MAY
31 .... Allentown

JUNE
1-2 .... Allentown
3-4-5-6 .... Brockton
14-15-16-17 .. New Jersey
21-22-23 .... Quebec
25-26-27 .... North Shore

JULY
5-6-7 .... Bangor
8-9-10-11 .... Elmira
16-17-18 .... Bangor
29-30-31 .... Quebec

AUGUST
1 .... Quebec
2-3-4 .... Allentown
9-10-11 .... Brockton
20-21-22 .... North Shore
23-24-25 ...... New Jersey

SEPTEMBER
4-5-6 .... Elmira

NEW JERSEY
MAY
27-28-29-30 ...... Bangor

JUNE
7-8-9 .... Brockton
11-12-13 .... Allentown
18-19-20 .... Quebec
28-29-30 .... North Shore

JULY
2-3-4 .... New Haven
12-13-14 .... Elmira
22-23-24-25 .. Allentown
26-27-28 .... Brockton

AUGUST
5-6-7 .... New Haven
12-13-14-15 ...... Quebec
17-18-19 .... North Shore
27-28-29-30 ...... Bangor

SEPTEMBER
1-2-3 .... Elmira

NORTH SHORE
MAY
26-27-28-29 .. Allentown

JUNE
8-9-10 .... New Haven
11-12-13 .... Bangor

(next column)
18-19-20 .... Elmira
22-23-24 ...... New Jersey

JULY
2-3-4 .... Brockton
5-6-7 .... Quebec
16-17-18 .... Allentown
29-30-31 ...... New Jersey

AUGUST
1 .... New Jersey
2-3-4 .... Bangor
9-10-11 .... Elmira
12-13-14-15 .. New Haven
24-25-26 .... Brockton
27-28-29-30 ...... Quebec

QUEBEC
MAY
31 .... New Jersey

JUNE
1-2 .... New Jersey
3-4-5-6 .... Elmira
14-15-16-17 ...... Bangor
25-26-27 .... Allentown
28-29-30 ...... New Haven

JULY
8-9-10-11 .... Brockton
12-13-14 .... North Shore
22-23-24-25 .. New Haven
26-27-28 .... Elmira

AUGUST
5-6-7 .... Bangor
16-17-18 .... Allentown
20-21-22 ...... New Jersey

SEPTEMBER
1-2-3 .... Brockton
4-5-6 .... North Shore

NORTHERN LEAGUE

FARGO-MOORHEAD
JUNE
2-3-4-5 .... Gary
6-7-8-9 .... Sioux Falls
14-15-16 .... St. Paul
28-29-30 .... Sioux City

JULY
1-2-3-4 .... Winnipeg
8-9-10-11 .... Kansas City
13-14-15 .... Winnipeg
16-17-18 ...... Sioux Falls
26-27-28-29 ...... Lincoln
30-31 .... Schaumburg

AUGUST
1-2 .... Schaumburg
8-9-10-11 ...... Sioux City
12-13-14-15 ...... St. Paul
25-26-27-28 .... Joliet

GARY
MAY
24-25-26-27 ...... Lincoln
28-29-30-31 .... Joliet

JUNE
10-11-12-13 .. Kansas City
14-15 .... Schaumburg
18-19-20-21 .. Sioux Falls
23-24 .... Schaumburg

JULY
9-10-11 .... Sioux City
22-23-24-25 ...... St. Paul
26-27-28-29 .... Joliet

AUGUST
4-5-6-7 .. Fargo-Moorhead
13-14-15 .... Lincoln
17-18-19 .... Winnipeg
20-21-22-23 .. Schaumburg

SEPTEMBER
3-4-5 .... Kansas City

JOLIET
MAY
20-21-22-23 .... Gary
24-25-26 .. Fargo-Moorhead

JUNE
2-3-4-5 ...... Schaumburg
6-7-8-9 .... Kansas City
18-19-20-21 ...... St. Paul

JULY
5-6-7-8 .... Sioux City
9-10-11 .... Lincoln
16-17-18 .... Lincoln
22-23-24-25 .. Kansas City

AUGUST
8-9-10-11 .... Gary
16-17-18-19 .. Sioux Falls
20-21-22-23 .. Winnipeg

SEPTEMBER
3-4-5 .... Schaumburg

KANSAS CITY
MAY
20-21-22-23 ...... Lincoln
24-25-26-27 .. Schaumburg

JUNE
2-3-4-5 .... St. Paul
15-16-17 .... Winnipeg
23-24-25-26 .. Sioux Falls
28-29-30 .... Joliet

JULY
5-6-7 .... Gary
15-16-17-18 .. Schaumburg
30-31 .... Gary

(next column)
AUGUST
1-2 .... Gary
4-5-6-7 .... Joliet
17-18-19 .... F-M
25-26-27-28 .. Sioux City
29-30-31 .... Lincoln

SEPTEMBER
1 .... Lincoln

LINCOLN
MAY
28-29-30-31 .. Kansas City

JUNE
7-8-9 .... Schaumburg
14-15-16-17 .... Joliet
18-19-20-21 .... Winnipeg
23-24-25-26 .... F-M

JULY
2-3-4 .... Gary
12-13-14-15 .... Gary
30-31 .... Joliet

AUGUST
1-2 .... Joliet
9-10-11-12 .. Schaumburg
16-17-18-19 .. Sioux City

20-21-22 .... Kansas City
25-26-27-28 ...... St. Paul

SEPTEMBER
3-4-5 .... Sioux Falls

ST. PAUL

MAY
24-25-26-27 .... Winnipeg
28-29-30-31 .... F-M

JUNE
11-12-13 .... Lincoln
23-24-25-26 .. Sioux City
27-28-29-30 .... Gary

JULY
1-2-3-4 .... Sioux Falls
9-10-11 ...... Schaumburg
16-17-18 .... Winnipeg
26-27-28-29 .. Sioux Falls
30-31 .... Sioux City

AUGUST
1-2 .... Sioux City
8-9-10-11 .... Kansas City
20-21-22 .... F-M
29-30-31 .... Joliet

SEPTEMBER
1 .... Joliet

SCHAUMBURG

MAY
20-21-22-23 .... F-M

JUNE
10-11-12-13 .. Sioux City
16-17 .... Gary
18-19-20-21 .. Kansas City
25-26 .... Gary

JULY
2-3-4 .... Joliet
5-6-7-8 .... Lincoln
12-13-14 .... Joliet
22-23-24-25 ...... Lincoln
26-27-28-29 .. Kansas City

AUGUST
13-14-15 ...... Sioux Falls
16-17-18 .... St. Paul
25-26-27-28 .... Winnipeg
29-30-31 .... Gary

SEPTEMBER
1 .... Gary

SIOUX CITY

MAY
20-21-22-23 .... Winnipeg
24-25-26-27 .. Sioux Falls

JUNE
2-3-4-5 .... Lincoln

6-7-8-9 .... St. Paul
18-19-20-21 .... F-M

JULY
2-3-4 .... Kansas City
13-14-15 .... St. Paul
16-17-18 .... Gary
26-27-28-29 .... Winnipeg

AUGUST
4-5-6-7 ...... Schaumburg
13-14-15 .... Joliet
20-21-22-23 .. Sioux Falls

SEPTEMBER
2-3-4-5 .. Fargo-Moorhead

SIOUX FALLS

MAY
20-21-22 .... St. Paul
28-29-30-31 .. Schaumburg

JUNE
2-3-4-5 .... Winnipeg
10-11-12-13 .... Joliet
14-15-16 ...... Sioux City
27-28-29-30 ...... Lincoln

JULY
5-6-7 .... Fargo-Moorhead
12-13-14 .... Kansas City
22-23-24-25.... Sioux City
30-31 .... Winnipeg

AUGUST
1-2 .... Winnipeg
4-5-6-7 .... St. Paul
25-26-27-28 .... Gary
29-30-31 .... F-M

SEPTEMBER
1 .... Fargo-Moorhead

WINNIPEG

MAY
28-29-30-31 .. Sioux City

JUNE
6-7-8 .... Gary
10-11-12-13 .... F-M
23-24-25-26 .... Joliet
28-29-30 .... Schaumburg

JULY
5-6-7-8 .... St. Paul
9-10-11 .... Sioux Falls
22-23-24-25 .... F-M

AUGUST
4-5-6-7 .... Lincoln
8-9-10-11 .... Sioux Falls
12-13-14-15   Kansas City
30-31 .... Sioux City

SEPTEMBER
1 .... Sioux City
2-3-4-5 .... St. Paul

INTERNATIONAL
LEAGUES

FOREIGN LEAGUES

2003 STANDINGS

AMERICAS

MEXICAN LEAGUE
TRIPLE-A CLASSIFICATION

EAST	W	L	PCT	GB
*Mexico City Red Devils	68	40	.630	—
Monterrey Sultans	66	43	.606	2½
+Saltillo Sarape Makers	62	45	.579	5½
Puebla Parrots	62	48	.564	7
Two Laredos Owls	53	56	.486	15½
Monclova Steelers	49	59	.454	19
Reynosa Broncos	43	63	.406	24
Laguna Cowboys	39	71	.355	30

WEST	W	L	PCT	GB
*+Angelopolis Tigers	72	35	.673	—
Yucatan Lions	61	45	.575	10½
Oaxaca Warriors	57	52	.523	16
Campeche Pirates	55	51	.519	16½
Veracruz Reds	50	54	.481	20½
Tabasco Cattlemen	49	59	.454	23½
Cancun Lobstermen	44	63	.415	28
Cordoba Coffee Growers	29	75	.265	41½

*First-half champion +Second-half champion

PLAYOFFS—Quarterfinals (best-of-7): Oaxaca defeated Yucatan 4-0; Mexico City Red Devils defeated Puebla 4-3; Tigers defeated Campeche 4-2; and Monterrey defeated Saltillo 4-3. **Semifinals** (best-of-7): Mexico City Red Devils defeated Monterrey 4-2 and Tigers defeated Oaxaca 4-2. **Final** (best-of-7): Mexico City Red Devils defeated Tigers 4-1.

DOMINICAN SUMMER LEAGUE
ROOKIE CLASSIFICATION

SANTO DOMINGO EAST	W	L	PCT	GB
Diamondbacks	46	19	.708	—
Cardinals	38	27	.585	8
Rockies	38	28	.576	8½
Dodgers I	33	31	.516	12½
Giants	34	34	.500	13½
Tigers	29	39	.426	18½
Red Sox I	28	38	.424	18½
Diamondbacks/Expos	17	47	.266	28½

SANTO DOMINGO NORTH	W	L	PCT	GB
Athletics II	43	25	.632	—
Dodgers II	38	28	.576	4
Phillies	37	32	.536	6½
Brewers	34	32	.515	8
Athletics I	26	40	.394	16
Red Sox II	23	44	.343	19½

SANTO DOMINGO WEST	W	L	PCT	GB
Yankees I	48	18	.727	—
Padres	35	31	.530	13
Twins	33	35	.485	16
Yankees II	29	36	.446	18½
Reds	27	37	.422	20
Mets	26	41	.388	22½

SAN PEDRO de MACORIS	W	L	PCT	GB
Pirates	39	25	.609	—
Blue Jays	39	27	.591	1

	W	L	PCT	GB
Angels	34	30	.531	5
Astros	33	33	.500	7
Cubs	31	34	.477	8½
Orioles	28	37	.431	11½
Rangers	24	42	.364	16

CIBAO	W	L	PCT	GB
Indians II	41	24	.631	—
White Sox	41	26	.612	1
Braves II	39	27	.591	2½
Indians I	39	29	.574	3½
Braves I	36	28	.563	4½
Mariners	28	36	.438	12½
Royals	20	44	.313	20½
Marlins	18	48	.273	23½

PLAYOFFS—Quarterfinal (sudden death): Yankees I defeated Athletics II 1-0. **Semifinals** (best-of-3): Pirates defeated Yankees I 2-1 and Diamondbacks defeated Indians II 2-0. **Final** (best-of-5): Pirates defeated Diamondbacks 3-1.

VENEZUELAN SUMMER LEAGUE
ROOKIE CLASSIFICATION

BARQUISIMETO	W	L	PCT	GB
San Felipe (Indians)	45	15	.750	—
Yaritagua (Orioles)	32	28	.575	13
Chivacoa (Pirates)	23	36	.392	21½
Cocorote (Blue Jays/Marlins)	19	40	.325	25½

VALENCIA	W	L	PCT	GB
Aguirre (Mariners)	40	17	.695	—
Mariara (Phillies)	34	25	.575	7
Tronconero 2 (Mets)	33	26	.558	8
Venoco (Astros)	31	25	.551	8½
Tronconero 1 (Padres/Twins)	24	35	.408	17
Cagua (Brewers/Reds)	13	47	.217	28½

PLAYOFF (best-of-3)—San Felipe defeated Aguirre 2-1.

CANADA

EAST	W	L	PCT	GB
London (Ont.) Monarchs	20	13	.606	—
Niagara (Ont.) Stars	15	15	.500	3½
Trois-Rivieres (Quebec) Saints	14	17	.452	5
Montreal Royales	10	22	.313	9½

WEST	W	L	PCT	GB
Calgary (Alta.) Outlaws	24	13	.649	—
Saskatoon (Sask.) Legends	22	15	.595	2
Kelowna (B.C.) Heat	18	19	.486	6
Victoria (B.C.) Capitals	13	22	.371	10

NOTE: League suspended operations July 20; Calgary crowned champion.

CUBA

Group A	W	L	PCT	GB
Pinar del Rio	56	34	.622	—
Isla de la Juventud	41	48	.461	14½
Matanzas	41	49	.456	15
Metropolitans	41	49	.456	15

Group B	W	L	PCT	GB
Industriales	66	23	.742	—
Cienfuegos	52	38	.578	14½

Havana	51	39	.567	15½
Sancti Spiritus	49	41	.544	17½

Group C	W	L	PCT	GB
Villa Clara	56	34	.622	—
Camaguey	44	46	.489	12
Ciego de Avila	37	53	.411	19
Las Tunas	25	65	.278	31

Group D	W	L	PCT	GB
Granma	45	45	.500	—
Santiago de Cuba	44	46	.489	1
Holguin	43	47	.478	2
Guantanamo	28	62	.311	17

PLAYOFFS—Quarterfinals (best-of-5): Villa Clara defeated Santiago 3-2; Granma defeated Camaguey 3-1; Industriales defeated Havana 3-1 and Pinar del Rio defeated Cienfuegos 3-2. **Semifinals** (best-of-7): Villa Clara defeated Granma 4-2; Industriales defeated Pinar del Rio 4-1. **Final** (best-of-7): Industriales defeated Villa Clara 4-0.

ASIA

JAPANESE LEAGUES

CENTRAL	W	L	T	PCT	GB
Hanshin	87	51	2	.630	—
Chunichi	73	66	1	.525	14½
Yomiuri	71	66	3	.518	15½
Yakult	71	66	3	.518	15½
Hiroshima	67	71	2	.486	20
Yokohama	45	94	1	.324	42½

PACIFIC	W	L	T	PCT	GB
Fukuoka Daiei	82	55	3	.599	—
Seibu	77	61	2	.558	5½
Osaka Kintetsu	74	64	2	.536	8½
Chiba Lotte	68	69	3	.496	14
Nippon Ham	62	74	4	.456	19½
Orix	48	88	4	.353	33½

PLAYOFF (best-of-7)—Fukuoka Daiei defeated Hanshin 4-3.

KOREA BASEBALL ORGANIZATION

	W	L	T	PCT	GB
Hyundai	80	51	2	.611	—
Kia	78	50	5	.609	2
Samsung	76	53	4	.589	4
SK	66	64	3	.508	14
Hanwha	63	65	5	.492	17
LG	60	71	2	.458	20
Doosan	57	74	2	.435	23

Lotte		39	91	3	.300	41

PLAYOFFS—Quarterfinal (best-of-3): SK defeated Samsung 2-0. **Semifinal** (best-of-5): SK defeated Kia 3-0. **Final** (best-of-7): Hyundai defeated SK 4-3.

TAIWAN LEAGUES

	W	L	T	PCT	GB
#Brother	63	31	6	.670	—
+Sinon	62	32	6	.660	1
Uni-President	54	39	7	.581	8½
China	51	43	6	.543	12
Macoto	30	64	6	.319	33
First Financial	20	71	9	.220	41½

+ First-half champion #Second-half champion

PLAYOFF (best-of-7)—Brother defeated Sinon 4-2.

EUROPE

ITALY

	W	L	PCT	GB
Bologna	42	12	.778	—
Rimini	36	18	.667	6
Modena	36	18	.667	6
Grosseto	35	19	.648	7
Nettuno	31	23	.574	11
Parma	23	31	.426	19
San Marino	23	31	.426	19
Anzio	21	33	.389	21
Reggiana	15	39	.278	27
Firenze	8	46	.148	34

PLAYOFF (best-of-7)—Modena defeated Rimini 4-3.

NETHERLANDS

PLAYOFF POOL	W	L	T	PCT	GB
Neptunus	33	7	2	.810	—
Hoofddorp Pioniers	31	10	1	.750	2½
HCAW	29	13	0	.690	5
Hague Tornado's	22	19	1	.536	11½
Kinheim	16	24	2	.405	17
Amsterdam Pirates	14	28	0	.333	20

RELEGATION POOL	W	L	T	PCT	GB
PSV Eindhoven	18	1	1	.925	—
Almere	12	7	1	.625	6
Oosterhout Twins	10	10	0	.500	8½
Sparta/Feyenoord	8	11	1	.425	10
Quick	6	13	1	.325	12
RCH	4	16	0	.200	14½

PLAYOFF (best-of-5)—Neptunus defeated Hague 3-2.

AMERICAS

MEXICO

MEXICAN LEAGUE

Member, National Association

Class AAA

NOTE: *The Mexican League is a member of the National Association of Professional Baseball Leagues and has a Triple-A classification. However, its member clubs operate largely independent of the 30 major league teams, and for that reason the league is listed in the international section.*

Mailing Address: Angel Pola No. 16, Col. Periodista, CP 11220, Mexico, D.F. **Telephone:** (011-52) 555-557-1007. **FAX:** (011-52) 555-395-2454. **E-Mail Address:** mbl@prodigy.net.mx. **Website:** www.lmb.com.mx.

Years League Active: 1955-.

President: Raúl González Rodríguez. **Operations Manager:** Nestor Alba Brito.

2004 Opening Date: March 17. **Closing Date:** June 23.

Regular Season: 100 games (split-schedule).

Division Structure: North—Laguna, Mexico City, Monclova, Monterrey, Puebla, San Luis, Saltillo, Tijuana. **South**—Aguascalientes, Angelopolis, Campeche, Cancún, Oaxaca, Tabasco, Veracruz, Yucatan.

Playoff Format: Top six teams in each division qualify, with top two teams in each division receiving byes to the second round. First, second and semifinal rounds are best-of-7 series. Division finalists meet in best-of-7 series for league championship.

All-Star Game: May 6 at Torreon, Coahuila (Laguna).

Roster Limit: 28. **Roster Limit, Imports:** 5.

Statistician: The Sports Network, 2200 Byberry Rd., Suite 200, Hatboro, PA 19040.

AGUASCALIENTES RAILROADMEN

Office Address: Calle Manuel Madrigal y Juan de la Barrera, Colonia Heroes, Aguascalientes, Aguascalientes CP 20250. **Telephone:** (011-52) 449-918-6694. **E-Mail Address:** rieleros@lmb.com.mx. **Website:** www.rieleros-deaguascalientes.com

President: Jean Paul Mansur. **Chief Executive Officer:** Jaime Blacnarte. **General Manager:** Antelmo Hernandez.

Manager: Juan Jose Pacho.

ANGELOPOLIS TIGERS

Office Address: Blvd. Díaz Ordaz, #811 Mezzanine A Plaza Dorada, Col. Anzures, CP 72530, Puebla, Puebla. **Telephone:** (011-52) 222-237-1670. **FAX:** (011-52) 222-237-0148. **E-Mail Address:** tigres@tigrescapitalinos.com.mx. **Website:** www.tigrescapitalinos.com.mx.

President: Cuauhtémoc Rodriguez. **General Manager:** Iram Campos Lara.

Manager: Mario Mendoza.

CAMPECHE PIRATES

Office Address: Unidad Deportiva 20 de Noviembre, Local 4, CP 24000, Campeche, Campeche. **Telephone:** (011-52) 981-816-6071. **FAX:** (011-52) 981-816-3807. **E-Mail Address:** piratasc@prodigy.net.mx.

President: Gabriel Escalante Castillo. **General Manager:** Maria del Socorro Morales.

Manager: Francisco Estrada.

CANCUN LOBSTERMEN

Office Address: Av. De la Costa #40 S.M. L27, Mza. 11, CP 77500, Cancún, Quintana Roo. **Telephone:** (011-52) 998-884-9069. **FAX:** (011-52) 998-884-9069. **E-Mail Address:** cancunbeisbol@yahoo.com. **Website:** www.cancunbeisbol.com.

President: Chara Mansur Beltran. **Chief Executive Officer:** Angel Del Campo. **General Manager:** Ruben de la Cruz Herrera.

Manager: Alex Taveras.

LAGUNA COWBOYS

Office Address: Juan Gutenberg s/n, Col. Centro, CP 27000, Torreon, Coahuila. **Telephone:** (011-52) 871-718-5515. **FAX:** (011-52) 871-717-4335. **E-Mail Address:** unionlag@prodigy.net.mx. **Website:** www.vaqueroslaguna.com.

President: Jose Antonio Mansur Beltran. **General Manager:** Carlos Gomez del Campo.

Manager: Unavailable.

MEXICO CITY RED DEVILS

Office Address: Av. Cuauhtemoc # 451-101, Col. Narvarte, CP 03020, Mexico DF **Telephone:** (011-52) 555-639-8722. **FAX:** (011-52) 555-639-9722. **E-Mail Address:** diablos@diablos-rojos.com.mx. **Website:** www.diablos.com.mx.

President: Roberto Mansur Galán. **General Manager:** Eduardo de la Cerda.

Manager: Bernie Tatis.

MONCLOVA STEELERS

Office Address: Cuauhtemoc #299, Col. Ciudad Deportiva, CP 25750, Monclova, Coahuila. **Telephone:** (011-52) 866-636-2334. **FAX:** (011-52) 866-636-2688. **E-Mail Address:** acererosdelnorte@prodigy.net.mx. **Website:** www.acereros.com.mx.

President: José Maiz Garcia. **General Manager:** Roberto Madgaleno Ramîrez.

Manager: Fernando Elizondo.

MONTERREY SULTANS

Office Address: Av. Manuel Barragan s/n, Estadio Monterrey, CP 66460, Monterrey, Nuevo Leon. **Telephone:** (011-52) 818-351-8022, (011-52) 818-351-9467. **FAX:** (818) 351-9186. **E-Mail Address:** sultanes@sultanes.com.mx.

President: José Maiz García. **General Manager:** Roberto Magdaleno Ramírez.

Manager: Dan Firova.

OAXACA WARRIORS

Office Address: Privada del Chopo #105, Fraccionamiento El Chopo, CP 68050, Oaxaca, Oaxaca. **Telephone:** (011-52) 951-515-5522. **FAX:** (011-52) 951-515-4966. **E-Mail Address:** guerreros@guerrerosdeoaxaca.com. **Website:** www.guerrerosdeoaxaca.com.

President: Vicente Pérez Avellá Villa. **General Manager:** Guillermo Rodriguez Velazquez.

Manager: Houston Jimenez.

PUEBLA PARROTS

Office Address: Parque Hermanos Serdan, Unidad Deportiva 5 de Mayo s/n, Col. Maravillas, CP 72220, Puebla, Puebla. **Telephone:** (011-52) 222-222-2116. **FAX:** (011-52) 222-222-2117. **E-Mail Address:** oficina@pericosdepuebla.com.mx. **Website:** www.pericos

depuebla.com.mx.
President: Ricardo Henaine Mezher. **President:** Samuel Lozano Molina. **General Manager:** Francisco Minjarez.
Manager: Enrique Reyes.

SALTILLO SARAPE MAKERS
Office Address: Blvd. Nazario Ortiz Garza Esquina con Blvd. Jesus Sanchez, Col. Ciudad Deportiva, CP 25280, Saltillo, Coahuila. **Telephone:** (011-52) 844-416-9455. **FAX:** (011-52) 844-439-0550. **E-Mail Address:** sley@grupoley.com. **Website:** www.saraperos.com.mx.
President: Juan Manuel Ley. **General Manager:** Carlos de la Garza.
Manager: Raul Cano.

SAN LUIS TUNEROS
Office Address: Av. Himno Nacional #400, Col. Himno Nacional, San Luis Potosi, CP 78280. **Telephone:** (011-52) 444-812-4940. **FAX:** (011-52) 444-812-4939. **E-Mail Address:** Unavailable. **Website:** Unavailable.
President: Marcello De Los Santos. **General Manager:** Leo Clayton.
Manager: Chico Rodriguez.

TABASCO CATTLEMEN
Office Address: Explanada de la Ciudad Deportiva, Parque de Beisbol Centenario del 27 de Febrero, Col. Atasta de Serra, CP 86100, Villahermosa, Tabasco. **Telephone:** (011-52) 993-352-2787. **FAX:** (011-52) 993-352-2788. **E-Mail Address:** olmecastab@prodigy.net.mx.
President: Maximo Evia Ramirez. **General Manager:** Juan Antonio Balmaceda.
Manager: Juan Navarrete.

TIJUANA BULLS
Office Address: Paseo Centenario #10310, Int. 302 Zona Rio, Tijuana, Baja California. **Telephone:** (011-52) 664-682-3256. **FAX:** (011-52) 664-682-3255. **E-Mail Address:** Unavailable. **Website:** www.torostijuana.com.
President: Martín Reyes Madrigal. **General Manager:** Francisco Reyes Madrigal.
Manager: Carlos Hernandez.

VERACRUZ REDS
Office Address: Av. Jacarandas s/n, Esquina España, Fraccionamiento Virginia, CP 94294, Boca del Rio, Veracruz. **Telephone:** (011-52) 229-935-5004. **FAX:** (011-52) 229-935-5008. **E-Mail Address:** rojosdelaguila@terra.com.mx. **Website:** www.rojosdelaguila.com.mx.
President: Gustavo Sousa Escamilla. **General Manager:** Carlos Nahun Hernández.
Manager: Rolando Camarero.

YUCATAN LIONS
Office Address: Calle 50 #406-B, Entre 35 y 37, Col. Jesus Carranza, CP 97109, Merida, Yucatán. **Telephone:** (999) 926-3022. **FAX:** (999) 926-3631. **E-Mail Addresses:** leonesy@sureste.com, leonesy@cablered.net.mx. **Website:** www.leones.yucatan.com.mx.
President: Gustavo Ricalde Durán. **General Manager:** Jose Rivero Ancona.
Manager: Eddie Diaz.

DOMINICAN REPUBLIC
DOMINICAN SUMMER LEAGUE
Member, National Association
Rookie Classification
Mailing Address: Calle Segunda No. 64, Reparto Antilla, Santo Domingo, Dominican Republic. **Telephone/FAX:** (809) 532-3619.
Years League Active: 1985-.
President: Freddy Jana. **Administrative Assistant:** Orlando Diaz.
2004 Member Clubs: Angels, Diamondbacks, Braves I, Braves II, Orioles, Red Sox, Cubs, White Sox, Reds, Indians, Rockies, Tigers, Marlins, Astros, Royals, Dodgers I, Dodgers II, Brewers, Twins, Expos, Mets, Yankees I, Yankees II, Athletics I, Athletics II, Phillies, Pirates, Cardinals, Padres, Giants, Mariners, Rangers, Blue Jays.
2004 Opening Date: June 6. **Closing Date:** Aug. 31.
Regular Season: 70-72 games, depending on divisions.
Playoff Format: Four division winners meet in best-of-3 series; winners meet in best-of-5 series for league championship.
Roster Limit: 30 active. **Player Eligibility Rule:** No more than eight players 20 or older and no more than two players 21 or older. At least 10 players must be pitchers. No more than four years of prior service, excluding Rookie leagues outside the U.S. and Canada.

VENEZUELA
VENEZUELAN SUMMER LEAGUE
Member, National Association
Rookie Classification
Mailing Address: C.C. Caribbean Plaza Modulo 8, P.A. Local 173-174, Valencia, Carabobo, Venezuela. **Telephone:** (011-58) 241-824-0321, (011) 58-241-824-0980. **FAX:** (011-58) 241-824-0705. **Website:** www.venezuelansummerleague.com.
Years League Active: 1997-.
Administrator: Saul Gonzalez Acevedo. **Coordinator, Valencia Division:** Ramon Fereira. **Coordinator, Barquisimeto Division:** Jose Rafael Ramos. **Statistics, Barquisimeto:** Diego Matheus, Luis Matheus, Jose Suarez. **Statistics, Valencia:** Franklin Moreno Celis.
2004 Member Clubs, Division Structure: **Barquisimeto**—Chivacoa, Cocorote, San Felipe, Yaritagua. **Valencia**—Aguirre, Cagua, Mariana, Venoco, Troconero 1, Tronconero 2.
2004 Opening Date: June 3. **Closing Date:** Aug. 26.
Regular Season: 60 games.
Playoffs: Best-of-3 series between division champions for league championship.
Roster Limit: 30 active. **Player Eligibility Rule:** No player on active list may have more than three years of minor league service. Open to players from all Latin American Spanish-speaking countries except Mexico, the Dominican Republic and Puerto Rico.

ASIA

CHINA

CHINA BASEBALL LEAGUE

Mailing Address: 5, Tiyuguan Road, Beijing 100763, Peoples Republic of China. **Telephone:** (011-86) 10-85826002. **FAX:** (011-86) 10-85825994. **E-Mail Address:** Cga_cra@263.net.

Years League Active: 2002-.

Commissioner/Executive Director: Yang Jie. **Secretary General, CBL/China Baseball Association:** Shen Wei. **Vice Chairman:** Tom McCarthy.

Member Clubs: Beijing Tigers, Shanghai Golden Eagles, Tianjin Lions, Guangdong Leopards.

Regular Season: 24 games.

2004 Opening Date: April 2. **Closing Date:** June 27 (playoffs through July 11).

Import Rule: Only three import players may be active at any time.

JAPAN

Mailing Address: Imperial Tower, 14F, 1-1-1 Uchisaiwai-cho, Chiyoda-ku, Tokyo 100-0011. **Telephone:** 03-3502-0022. **FAX:** 03-3502-0140.

Commissioner: Yasuchika Negoro.

Executive Secretary: Kazuo Hasegawa. **Executive Director, Public Relations:** Kunio Shimoda. **Executive Director, Baseball Operations:** Masaru Madate. **Assistant Directors, International Affairs:** Nobby Ito, Tack Nakajima.

Japan Series: Best-of-7 series between Central and Pacific League champions, begins Oct. 16 at home of Pacific League club.

All-Star Series: July 10 at Nagoya Dome; July 11 at Nagano.

Roster Limit: 70 per organization (one major league club, one minor league club). Major league club is permitted to register 28 players at a time, though just 25 may be available for each game.

Roster Limit, Imports: 4 (2 position players and 2 pitchers; 3 position players and 1 pitcher or 3 pitchers and 1 position player) in majors; unlimited in minors.

CENTRAL LEAGUE

Mailing Address: Asahi Bldg. 3F, 6-6-7 Ginza, Chuo-ku, Tokyo 104-0061. **Telephone:** 03-3572-1673. **FAX:** 03-3571-4545.

President: Hajime Toyokura.

Secretary General: Hideo Okoshi. **Planning Department:** Masaaki Nagino. **Public Relations:** Kazu Ogaki.

2004 Opening Date: April 2. **Closing Date:** Sept. 30.

Regular Season: 140 games.

Playoff Format: None.

CHUNICHI DRAGONS

Mailing Address: Chunichi Bldg. 6F, 4-1-1 Sakae, Naka-ku, Nagoya 460-0008. **Telephone:** 052-252-5226. **FAX:** 052-263-7696.

Chairman: Bungo Shirai. **President:** Junnosuke Nishikawa. **General Manager:** Kazumasa Ito. **Field Manager:** Hiromitsu Ochiai.

2004 Foreign Players: Domingo Guzman, Omar Linares (Cuba), Alex Ochoa, Marc Valdes, Martin Vargas.

HANSHIN TIGERS

Mailing Address: 1-47 Koshien-cho, Nishinomiya-shi, Hyogo-ken 663-8152. **Telephone:** 0798-46-1515. **FAX:** 0798-40-0934.

Chairman: Shunjiro Kuma. **President/General Manager:** Katsuyoshi Nozaki. **Field Manager:** Akinobu Okada.

2004 Foreign Players: George Arias, Mike Kinkade, Ramon Morel, Jerrod Riggan, Jeff Williams.

HIROSHIMA TOYO CARP

Mailing Address: 5-25 Motomachi, Naka-ku, Hiroshima 730-8508. **Telephone:** 082-221-2040. **FAX:** 082-228-5013.

President: Hajime Matsuda. **General Manager:** Junro Anan. **Field Manager:** Koji Yamamoto.

2004 Foreign Players: John Bale, Chris Brock, Tom Davey, Greg LaRocca, Andy Sheets.

YAKULT SWALLOWS

Mailing Address: Shimbashi MCV Bldg. 5F, 5-13-5 Shimbashi, Minato-ku, Tokyo 105-0004. **Telephone:** 03-5470-8915. **FAX:** 03-5470-8916.

Chairman: Sumiya Hori. **President:** Yoshikazu Tagiku. **General Manager:** Kesatoku Kurashima. **Field Manager:** Tsutomu Wakamatsu.

2004 Foreign Players: Jason Beverlin, Billy Martin, Daniel Matsumoto (Brazil), Tony Mounce, Alex Ramirez.

YOKOHAMA BAYSTARS

Mailing Address: Kannai Arai Bldg, 7F, 1-8 Onoe-cho, Naka-ku, Yokohama 231-0015. **Telephone:** 045-681-0811. **FAX:** 045-661-2500.

Chairman: Yukio Sunahara. **President:** Takashi Ohori. **General Manager:** Yoshio Noguchi. **Field Manager:** Daisuke Yamashita.

2004 Foreign Players: Eddie Gaillard, Scott Mullen, Tyrone Woods. **Coach:** John Turney.

YOMIURI GIANTS

Mailing Address: Takebashi 3-3 Bldg., 3-3 Kanda Nishiki-cho, Chiyoda-ku, Tokyo 101-8462. **Telephone:** 03-3295-7711. **FAX:** 03-3295-7708.

Chairman: Tsuneo Watanabe. **President:** Hideaki Miyama. **General Manager:** Makoto Doi. **Field Manager:** Tsuneo Horiuchi.

2004 Foreign Players: Chris Latham, Roberto Petagine, Matt Randel, Tuffy Rhodes, Julio Santana, Brian Sikorski.

PACIFIC LEAGUE

Mailing Address: Asahi Bldg. 9F, 6-6-7 Ginza, Chuo-ku, Tokyo 104-0061. **Telephone:** 03-3573-1551. **FAX:** 03-3572-5843.

President: Tadao Koike. **Secretary General:** Shigeru Murata. **Administration Department:** Katsuhisa Matsuzaki.

2004 Opening Date: March 27. **Closing Date:** Sept. 22.

Regular Season: 135 games.

Playoff Format—Stage 1: 2nd-place team meets 3rd-place team in best-of-3 series. Stage 2: Winner meets 1st-place team in best-of-5 series for league championship.

CHIBA LOTTE MARINES

Mailing Address: WBG Marive West 26F, 2-6 Nakase, Mihama-ku, Chiba-shi, Chiba-ken 261-8587. **Telephone:**

043-297-2101. **FAX:** 043-297-2181.

Chairman: Takeo Shigemitsu. **General Manager:** Tomoichi Kawakita. **Field Manager:** Bobby Valentine.

2004 Foreign Players: Benny Agbayani, Matt Franco, Nathan Minchey, Dan Serafini, Lee Seung Yeop (Korea). **Coaches:** Frank Ramppen, Tom Robson.

FUKUOKA DAIEI HAWKS

Mailing Address: Fukuoka Dome, Hawks Town, Fukuoka 810-0065. **Telephone:** 092-844-1189. **FAX:** 092-844-4600.

Chairman: Tadashi Nakauchi. **President:** Takeshi Kotsuka. **General Manager:** Ryuzo Setoyama. **Field Manager:** Sadaharu Oh.

2004 Foreign Players: Anderson Gomes, Lindsay Gulin, Brandon Knight, Hector Mercado, Pedro Valdes, Julio Zuleta.

NIPPON HAM FIGHTERS

Mailing Address: 1 Hitsujigaoka, Toyohira-ku, Sapporo 062-0045. **Telephone:** 011-857-3939. **FAX:** 011-857-3900.

President: Junji Iwamura. **General Manager:** Takeshi Kojima. **Field Manager:** Trey Hillman.

2004 Foreign Players: Angel Echevarria, Carlos Mirabal, Ryan Rupe. **Coaches:** Mike Brown, Gary Denbo.

ORIX BLUEWAVE

Mailing Address: Yahoo! BB, Midoridai, Suma-ku, Kobe 654-0163. **Telephone:** 078-795-1203. FAX: 078-795-1505.

Chairman: Yoshihiko Miyauchi. **President:** Yutaka Okazoe. **General Manager:** Katsuhiro Nakamura. **Field Manager:** Haruki Ihara.

2004 Foreign Players: Roosevelt Brown, Trey Moore, Jose Ortiz, Jason Phillips, KooDae-Sung (Korea).

OSAKA KINTETSU BUFFALOES

Mailing Address: Midosuji Grand Bldg., 2-2-3 Namba, Chuo-ku, Osaka 542-0076. **Telephone:** 06-6212-9744. **FAX:** 06-6212-6834.

Chairman: Wa Tashiro. **President:** Mitsuru Nagai. **General Manager:** Tetsuya Kobayashi. **Field Manager:** Masataka Nashida.

2004 Foreign Players: Larry Barnes, Kevin Beirne, Jeremy Powell.

SEIBU LIONS

Mailing Address: 2135 Kami-Yamaguchi, Tokorozawa-shi, Saitama-ken 359-1189. **Telephone:** 04-2924-1155. **FAX:** 04-2928-1919.

Chairman: Yoshiaki Tsutsumi. **General Manager:** Yoshio Hoshino. **Field Manager:** Tsutomu Ito.

2004 Foreign Players: Alex Cabrera, Chang Chi-Chie (Taiwan), Jose Fernandez, Hsu Ming-chieh (Taiwan).

KOREA

KOREA BASEBALL ORGANIZATION

Mailing Address: 946-16 Dokokdong, Kangnam-gu, Seoul, Korea. **Telephone:** (02) 3460-4643. **FAX:** (02) 3460-4649.

Years League Active: 1982-.

Commissioner: Park Yong-oh. **Secretary General:** Choi Young-eun.

Assistant Manager: Park Chan-keun.

2004 Opening Date: April 5. **Closing Date:** Unavailable.

Regular Season: 132 games.

Division Structure: None.

Korean Series: Regular-season champion automatically qualifies for Korean Series. Fourth- and third-place teams meet in best-of-3 series with winner advancing to meet second-place team in best-of-5 series, with winner meeting first-place team in best-of-7 championship.

Roster Limit: 27 active through Sept. 1, when rosters expand to 32. **Imports:** 2 active.

DOOSAN BEARS

Mailing Address: Chamsil Baseball Stadium, 10 Chamsil-1 dong, Songpa-ku, Seoul, Korea 138-221. **Telephone:** (02) 2240-1777. **FAX:** (02) 2240-1788.

General Manager: Kun Koo Kang.

KIA TIGERS

Mailing Address: Kwangju Shi, Seo-gu, Daebang-dong 266, 2nd floor, Zip 502-807.**Telephone:** (062) 370-1878. **FAX:** (062) 525-5350.

General Manager: Jeong Jae-kong.

HANHWA EAGLES

Mailing Address: 22-1 Youngjeon-dong, Dong-ku, Taejeon, Korea 300-200. **Telephone:** (042) 637-6001. **FAX:** (042) 632-2929.

General Manager: Kyung Yon Hwang.

HYUNDAI UNICORNS

Mailing Address: Hyundai Haesang Bldg., 9th Floor, 1014 Kwonseon-dong, Kwonseon-ku, Suwon, Kyung Ki, Korea 441-390. **Telephone:** (032) 433-7979. **FAX:** (032) 435-3108.

General Manager: Jeong Jae-ho.

LG TWINS

Mailing Address: Chamsil Baseball Stadium, 10 Chamsil-1 dong, Songpa-ku, Seoul, Korea 138-221. **Telephone:** (02) 2005-5760, (02) 2005-5801.

General Manager: You Song-min.

LOTTE GIANTS

Mailing Address: 930 Sajik-Dong Dongrae-Ku, Pusan, Korea. **Telephone:** 51-505-7422-3. **FAX:** 51-506-0090.

General Manager: Chul Hwa Lee.

SAMSUNG LIONS

Mailing Address: 184-3, Sunhwari, Jinryangyup, Kyungsan, Kyung Buk, Korea 712-830. **Telephone:** (053) 859-3114. **FAX:** (053) 859-3117.

General Manager: Jong Man Kim.

SK WYVERNS

Mailing Address: 1456-1 Kuwol-dong, Namdong-ku, Inchon, Korea 405-220. **Telephone:** (032) 422-7949. **FAX:** (032) 429-4565.

General Manager: Myung Yung-chul.

TAIWAN

CHINESE PROFESSIONAL BASEBALL LEAGUE

Mailing Address: 2F, No. 32, Pateh Road, Sec. 3, Taipei, Taiwan. **Telephone:** 886-2-2577-6992. **FAX:** 886-2-2577-2606. **Website:** www.cpbl.com.tw.

Years League Active: 1990-.

Commissioner: Harvey Chen. **Secretary General:** Wayne Lee.

Member Clubs: Brother Elephants (Taipei), China Trust Whales (Chiayi City), President Lions (Tainan), Sinon Bulls (Taichung), La New Bears (Kaohsiung), Makoto Cobras (Taipei).

Regular Season: 100 games (split-schedule).

2004 Opening Date: Feb. 28. **Closing Date:** Oct. 31.

Championship Series: Top two teams meet in best-of-7 series, Nov. 6-14.

Import Rule: Only three import players may be active, and only two may be on the field at the same time.

EUROPE

ITALY

ITALTIAN SERIE A/1

Mailing Address: Federazione Italiana Baseball/Softball, Viale Tiziano 70, 00196 Roma, Italy. **Telephone:** 39-06-36858376. **FAX:** 39-06-36858201. **Website:** www.baseball-softball.it.
President: Riccardo Fraccari. **General Secretary:** Marcello Standoli.

ANZIO

Mailing Address: Via delle Felci 4, 00040 Lavinio (Roma). **Telephone:** 39-06-981-9087. **Website:** www.anziobc.it
President: Roberto Monaco. **Manager:** Carlo Morville.

BOLOGNA

Mailing Address: Piazzale Atleti Azzurri d'Italia, 40122 Bologna. **Telephone:** 39-051-479618. **FAX:** 39-051-554000. **E-Mail Address:** fortitudobaseball@tin.it. **Website:** www.fortitudobaseball.com.
President: Stefano Michelini. **Manager:** Mauro Mazzotti.

FIRENZE

Mailing Address: Via le M. Fanti 18, 50137 Firenze. **Telephone:** 39-055-422-0872. **E-Mail Address:** info@fiorentinabaseball.it **Website:** www.fiorentinabaseball.it
President: Pier Paulo Vita. **Manager:** Alberto Martinez.

GROSSETO

Mailing Address: Via della Repubblica 2, 58100 Grosseto. **Telephone:** 39-0564-494149. **FAX:** 39-0564-476750 **Website:** www.bbcgrosseto.it
President: Claudio Banchi. **Manager:** Pedro Medina.

MODENA

Mailing Address: Casella Postale 69, 41010 Saliceto Panaro, Modena. **Telephone:** 39-059-371655. **FAX:** 39-059-365300. **E-Mail Address:** modenabc@tin.it **Website:** www.modenabaseball.com
President: Giovanni Tinti. **Manager:** Mauro Paglioli.

NETTUNO

Mailing Address: Stadio Steno Borghese, Via Scipione Borghese, 00048 Nettuno (Roma). **Telephone/FAX:** 39-06-9854966. **E-Mail Address:** info@nettunobaseball.net **Website:** www.nettunobaseball.net
President: Cesare Augusto Spigoni. **Manager:** Ruggero Bagialemani.

PARMA

Mailing Address: Via Donatore 4, Collecchio, 43044 Parma. **Telephone:** 39-335-604-8969. **FAX:** 39-0521-802601. **E-Mail Address:** baseballcity@hotmail.com. **Website:** www.eteamz.com/cusparma.
President: Rossano Rinaldi. **Manager:** Chris Catanoso.

REGGIO EMILIA

Mailing Address: Via Petit Bon 1, 42100 Reggio Emilia. **Telephone/FAX:** 39-0522 558156. **E-Mail Address:** info@reggiobaseball.it **Website:** www.reggiobaseball.it
President: Graziella Casali. **Manager:** Gilberto Gerali.

RIMINI

Mailing Address: Via Monaco 2, 47900 Rimini. **Telephone/FAX:** 39-0541-741761. **E-Mail Address:** info@baseballrimini.com. **Website:** www.baseballrimini.com.
President: Cesare Zangheri. **Manager:** Michele Romano.

SAN MARINO

Mailing Address: Via Piana 37, 47031 Republic of San Marino **Telephone:** 39-0549-991170. **FAX:** 39-0549-991247.
President: Giorgio Pancotti. **Manager:** Doriano Bindi

NETHERLANDS

DUTCH MAJOR LEAGUE

Mailing Address: Koninklijke Nederlandse Baseball en Softball Bond (Royal Dutch Baseball and Softball Association), "Twinstate II", Perkinsbaan 15, 3439 ND Nieuwegein, Holland. **Telephone:** 31-(0) 30- 607-6070. **FAX:** 31-30- 294-3043. **Website:** www.knbsb.nl
President: Hans Meijer.

ALMERE '90

Mailing Address: B.S.C. Almere '90, Estafettelaan 2, 1318 EG Almere. **Telephone:** +31 (0) 36-549 95 40. **Website:** www.almere90.nl

AMSTERDAM PIRATES

Mailing Address: Sportpark Ookmeer, Herman Bonpad 5, 1067 SN Amsterdam. **Telephone:** +31 (0) 20-616 21 51. **Website:** www.amsterdam-pirates.nl.

DEN HAAG TORNADOS

Mailing Address: Steenwijklaan 500, 2541 RL Den Haag. **Telephone:** +31 (0) 70-366 97 22. **Website:** www.svado.nl

HCAW

Mailing Address: Mr. Cocker HCAW, Postbus 1321, 1400 BH Bussum. **Telephone:** +31 (0) 35-693- 14 30. **Website:** www.hcaw.nl.

HOOFDDORP PIONIERS

Mailing Address: Postbus 475, 2130 AL Hoofddorp. **Telephone:** +31 (0) 23-561 35 57. **Website:** www.hoofddorp-pioniers.nl

KINHEIM

Mailing Address: Gemeentelijk Sportpark, Badmintonpad, 2023 BT Haarlem. **Telephone:** +31 (0) 23-526 00 21. **Website:** www.kinheim.net

NEPTUNUS

Mailing Address: Sportclub Neptunus, Postbus 35064, 3005 DB Rotterdam. **Telephone:** +31 (0) 10-437 53 69. **Website:** www.neptunussport.com.

SPARTA/FEYENOORD

Mailing Address: Postbus 9211, 3007 AE Rotterdam. **Telephone:** +31 (0) 10-479-04 83. **Website:** www.spartafeyenoord.com

TWINS

Mailing Address: Postbus 4085, 4900 CB Oosterhout. **Telephone:** +31 (0) 162-433760. **Website:** www.twins-sc.com

WINTER
LEAGUES

2003-2004
STANDINGS

CARIBBEAN SERIES

	W	L	Pct.	GB
Dominican Republic	5	1	.857	—
Mexico	4	2	.666	1
Venezuela	3	3	.500	2
Puerto Rico	0	6	.000	5

DOMINICAN LEAGUE

REGULAR SEASON	W	L	PCT	GB
Licey	30	20	.600	—
Aguilas	28	22	.560	2
Gigantes	26	24	.520	4
Azucareros	26	24	.520	4
Estrellas	25	25	.500	5
Escogido	15	35	.300	15
ROUND-ROBIN	W	L	PCT	GB
Licey	11	4	.733	—
Gigantes	9	6	.600	2
Aguilas	9	6	.600	2
Azucareros	1	14	.083	10

CHAMPIONSHIP SERIES (best-of-5): Licey defeated Gigantes 3-1.

MEXICAN PACIFIC LEAGUE

	W	L	PCT	GB
*Mazatlan	40	28	.588	—
Obregon	39	29	.574	1
Culiacan	38	30	.559	2
*Hermosillo	36	30	.545	3
Guasave	33	33	.500	6
Navojoa	32	36	.471	8
Mochis	27	41	.397	13
Mexicali	25	43	.368	15

  * Split season champion

PLAYOFFS—Quarterfinals (best-of-7): Obregon defeated Navojoa 4-1; Culiacan defeated Guasave 4-2 and Hermosillo defeated Mazatlan 4-3. **Semifinals** (best-of-7): Culiacan defeated Hermosillo 4-2 and Obregon defeated Mazatlan 4-2. **Final** (best-of-7): Culiacan defeated Obregon 4-1.

PUERTO RICAN LEAGUE

	W	L	PCT	GB
Caguas	28	20	.583	—
Ponce	28	21	.571	½

Santure	27	23	.540	2
San Juan	27	23	.540	2
Carolina	24	25	.490	4 ½
Mayaguez	14	36	.280	15
Round-Robin	W	L	PCT	GB
Caguas	9	3	.750	—
Ponce	8	4	.667	1
Santure	6	6	.500	3
San Juan	1	11	.083	8

CHAMPIONSHIP SERIES (best-of-9): Ponce defeated Caguas 5-2.

VENEZUELAN LEAGUE

WEST	W	L	PCT	GB
Occidente	35	27	.565	—
Aragua	34	28	.548	1
Lara	30	32	.484	5
Zulia	22	40	.355	13
EAST	W	L	PCT	GB
La Guaira	33	28	.541	—
Caracas	33	29	.532	½
Oriente	32	29	.525	1
Magallanes	28	34	.452	5 ½
ROUND-ROBIN	W	L	PCT	GB
Oriente	9	5	.643	—
Aragua	9	5	.643	—
La Guaira	7	6	.538	1 ½
Caracas	5	8	.385	3 ½
Occidente	4	10	.286	5

CHAMPIONSHIP SERIES (best-of-7): Aragua defeated Oriente 4-2.

ARIZONA FALL LEAGUE

AMERICAN	W	L	PCT	GB
Mesa Solar Sox	20	13	.606	—
Peoria Saguaros	18	16	.529	2 ½
Scottsdale Scorpions	16	15	.516	3
NATIONAL	W	L	PCT	GB
Mesa Desert Dogs	18	13	.581	—
Grand Canyon Rafters	13	19	.406	5 ½
Peoria Javelinas	9	24	.273	10
*Team USA	9	3	.750	

  *Ineligible for league championship

PLAYOFF (sudden death): Mesa Solar Sox defeated Mesa Desert Dogs 1-0.

WINTER BASEBALL

CARIBBEAN BASEBALL CONFEDERATION

(Confederacion de Beisbol Profesional del Caribe)

Mailing Address: Frank Feliz Miranda No. 1 Naco, Santo Domingo, Dominican Republic. **Telephone:** (809) 562-4737, 562-4715. **FAX:** (809) 565-4654.
Commissioner: Juan Fco. Puello Herrera. **Secretary:** Benny Agosto.
Member Countries: Dominican Republic, Mexico, Puerto Rico, Venezuela.
2005 Caribbean Series: Feb. 1-8 at Mazatlan, Mexico.

DOMINICAN LEAGUE

Office Address: Estadio Quisqueya, 2da. Planta, Ens. La Fe, Santo Domingo, D.N., Dominican Republic. **Mailing Address:** Apartado Postal 1246, Santo Domingo, D.N., Dominican Republic. **Telephone:** (809) 567-6371, (809) 563-5085. **FAX:** (809) 567-5720. **E-Mail Address:** info@beisboldominicano.com. **Website:** www.beisboldominicano.com.
Years League Active: 1951-.
President: Dr. Leonardo Matos Berrido. **Administrator:** Marcos Rodriguez. **Public Relations Director:** Jorge Torres.
2004 Opening Date: Oct. 19. **Closing Date:** Dec 27.
Regular Season: 50 games.
Playoff Format: Top four teams meet in 18-game round-robin. Top two teams advance to best-of-7 series for league championship. Winner advances to Caribbean Series.
Roster Limit: 30. **Roster Limit, Imports:** 7.

AGUILAS CIBAENAS

Office Address: Estadio Cibao, Aveniba Imbert, Santiago, Dom. Rep. **Mailing Address:** EPS B-225, P.O. Box 02-5360, Miami, FL 33102. **Telephone:** (809) 575-4310, (809) 575-1810. **FAX:** (809) 575-8250. **E-Mail Address:** a.cibaenas@codetel.net.do. **Website:** www.lasaguilas.com.
President: Winston Llenas. **General Manager:** Reynaldo Bisono.
2003-2004 Manager: Felix Fermin.

AZUCAREROS DEL ESTE

Mailing Address: Estadio Francisco Micheli, La Romana, Dom. Rep. **Telephone:** (809) 556-6188. **FAX:** (809) 550-1550. **E-Mail Address:** arturo.miguel@codetel.net.do. **Website:** www.azucarerosdeleste.com
President: Arturo Gil. **General Manager:** Carlos Bernhardt.
2003-2004 Manager: Luis Silverio.

LEONES DEL ESCOGIDO

Office Address: Estadio Quisqueya, Ens. la Fe, Santo Domingo, Dom. Rep. **Mailing Address:** P.O. Box 1287, Santo Domingo, Dom. Rep. **Telephone:** (809) 565-1910. **FAX:** (809) 567-7643. **E-Mail Address:** info@escogido.com. **Website:** www.escogido.com.do.
President: Daniel Aquino Mendez. **General Manager:** Ramon Pena.
2003-2004 Manager: Nick Leyva.

ESTRELLAS ORIENTALES

Office Address: Av. Lope de Vega No. 45, Ens. Piantini, Santo Domingo, Dom. Rep. **Telephone:** (809) 246-4077. **FAX:** (809) 529-7752. **E-Mail Address:** estrellasdeoriente@hotmail.com. **Website:** www.estrellasdeoriente.com
President: Carlos Juan Musa-Hazim. **General**

Manager: Pablo Peguero.
2003-2004 Manager: Dino Ebel.

TIGRES DE LICEY

Office Address: Estadio Quisqueya, Santo Domingo, Dom. Rep. **Mailing Address:** P.O. Box 1321, Santo Domingo, Dom. Rep. **Telephone:** (809) 567-3090. **FAX:** (809) 542-7714. **E-Mail Address:** oficina@licey.com. **Website:** www.licey.com.
President: Emigolo Garrido. **General Manager:** Fernando Ravelo Jana.
2003-2004 Manager: Manny Acta.

GIGANTES DEL CIBAO

Office Address: Estadio Julian Javier, San Francisco de Macoris, Dom. Rep. **Mailing Address:** Ave. Luperon No. 25, Zona Industrial de Herrera, Santo Domingo, Dom. Rep. **U.S. Mailing Address:** EPS No. F-1447, P.O. Box 02-5301, Miami, FL 33102. **Telephone:** (809) 588-8882. **FAX:** (809) 588-8733. **Website:** www.gigantesdelcibao.com.
President: Stan Javier. **General Manager:** Junior Noboa.
2003-2004 Manager: Miguel Dilone.

MEXICAN PACIFIC LEAGUE

Mailing Address: Av. Insurgentes No. 847 Sur, Interior 402, Edificio San Carlos, Col. Centro, CP 80120, Culiacan, Sinaloa. **Telephone/FAX:** (011-52) 667-761-25-70, (011-52) 667-761-25-71. **E-Mail Address:** ligadelpacifico@imparcial.com.mx. **Website:** www.ligadelpacifico.com.mx.
Years League Active: 1958-.
President: Renato Vega Alvarado. **General Manager:** Oviel Dennis Gonzalez.
2003-2004 Opening Date: Oct. 12. **Closing Date:** Dec. 30.
Regular Season: 68 games.
Playoff Format: Six teams advance to best-of-7 quarterfinals. Three winners and losing team with best record advance to best-of-7 semifinals. Winners meet in best-of-7 series for league championship. Winner advances to Caribbean World Series.
Roster Limit: 30. **Roster Limit, Imports:** 5.

TOMATEROS DE CULIACAN

Street Address: Av. Alvaro Obregon 348 Sur, CP 8000, Culiacan, Sinaloa, Mexico. **Telephone/FAX:** (011-52) 667-712-2446, (011-52) 667-715-6828. **E-Mail Address:** tomateros@infosel.com.mx.
President: Juan Manuel Ley Lopez. **General Managers:** Luis Carlos Joffroy.
2003-2004 Manager: Francisco Estrada.

ALGODONEROS DE GUSAVE

Mailing Address: Obregon No. 43, CP 81000, Guasave, Sinaloa, Mexico. **Telephone:** (011-52) 687-

872-29-98. **FAX:** (011-52) 687-872-14-31. **E-Mail Address:** algodon@debate.com.mx.
President: Carlos Chavez. **General Manager:** Joaquin Valenzuela.
2003-2004 Manager: Raul Cano.

NARANJEROS DE HERMOSILLO
Mailing Address: Blvd. Solidaridad s/n, Estadio Hector Espino, E/Jose S. Healey Y Blvd., Luis Encinas, CP 83188, Hermosillo, Sonora, Mexico. **Telephone:** (011-52) 662-260-69-32, (011-52) 662-260-69-33. **FAX:** (011-52) 662-260-69-31. **E-Mail Address:** cquintero@mazon.mazon.com.mx.
President: Enrique Mazon Rubio. **General Manager:** Marco Antonio Manzo.
2003-2004 Manager: Lee Sigman.

CANEROS DE LOS MOCHIS
Mailing Address: Francisco I. Madero No. 116 Oriente, CP 81200, Los Mochis, Sinaloa, Mexico. **Telephone:** (011-52) 668-812-86-02. **FAX:** (011-52) 668-812-67-40. **E-Mail Address:** verdes@infosel.net.mx.
President: Mario Lopez Valdez. **General Manager:** Antonio Castro Chavez.
2003-2004 Manager: Juan Francisco Rodriguez.

VENADOS DE MAZATLAN
Mailing Address: Gutierrez Najera No. 821, CP 82000, Mazatlan, Sinaloa, Mexico. **Telephone:** (011-52) 669-981-17-10. **FAX:** (011-52) 669-981-17-11. **E-Mail Address:** club@venados.com.mx.
President: Jesus Ismael Barros Cebreros. **General Manager:** Alejandro Lizarraga Osuna.
2003-2004 Manager: Dan Fivora.

AGUILAS DE MEXICALI
Mailing Address: Estadio De Beisbol De La Cd. Deportiva, Calz. Cuautemoc s/n, Las Fuentes Mexicali, Baja, CA, Mexico. **Telephone:** (011-52) 686-567-0040. **FAX:** (011-52) 686-567-5129. **E-Mail Address:** aguilas2@telnor.net
President: Dio Alberto Murrillo. **General Manager:** Jesus Sommers.
2003-2004 Manager: Lorenzo Bundy.

MAYOS DE NAVOJOA
Mailing Address: Rosales No. 102, E/Pesqueira Y no Reeleccion, CP 85830, Navojoa, Sonora, Mexico. **Telephone:** (011-52) 642-422-14-33. **FAX:** (011-52) 642-422-89-97. **E-Mail Address:** clubmayos@hotmail.com.
President: Victor Cuevas Garibay. **General Manager:** Lauro Villalobos.
2003-2004 Manager: Bernie Tatis.

YAQUIS DE OBREGON
Mailing Address: Calle Guerrero y Michoacan, Estadio de Beisbol Tomas Oroz Gaytan, CP 85130, Ciudad Obregon, Sonora, Mexico. **Telephone:** (011-52) 644-413-77-66. **FAX:** (011-52) 644-414-11-56. **E-Mail Address:** clubyaquisdeobregon@yahoo.com.mx.
President: Luis Alfonso Lugo Platt. **General Manager:** Roberto Diaz Gonzalez.
2003-2004 Manager: Tim Johnson.

PUERTO RICAN LEAGUE
Office Address: Avenida Munoz Rivera 1056, Edificio First Federal, Suite 501, Rio Piedras, PR 00925. **Mailing Address:** P.O. Box 191852, San Juan, PR 00019. **Telephone:** (787) 765-6285, 765-7285. **FAX:** (787) 767-3028.
Years League Active: 1938-.
President: Joaquin Monserrate Matienzo. **Executive Director:** Benny Agosto.
2003-2004 Opening Date: Oct. 30. **Closing Date:** Jan. 8.
Regular Season: 54 games.
Playoff Format: Top four teams meet in best-of-7 semifinal series. Winners meet in best-of-9 series for league championship. Winner advances to Caribbean World Series.
Roster Limit: 28. **Roster Limit, Imports:** 9.

CRIOLLOS DE CAGUAS
Mailing Address: P.O. Box 1415, Caguas, PR 00726. **Telephone:** (787) 258-2222. **FAX:** (787) 743-0545.
President, General Manager: Enrique Hernandez. **Vice President:** Jenaro Marchand.
2003-2004 Manager: Mako Oliveras.

CAROLINA GIANTS
Mailing Address: Roberto Clemente Stadium, P.O. Box 366246, San Juan, PR 00936. **Telephone:** (787) 643-4351, 643-2511. **FAX:** (787) 731-7051.
President: Benjamin Rivera. **General Manager:** Johnny Ramos.
2003-2004 Managers: Steve Liddle.

MAYAGUEZ INDIANS
Mailing Address: 3089 Marina Station, Mayaguez, PR 00681. **Telephone:** (787) 834-6111, 834-5211. **FAX:** (787) 834-7480.
President, General Manager: Daniel Aquino.
2003-2004 Manager: Edgardo Romero.

LEONES DE PONCE
Mailing Address: P.O. Box 363148, San Juan, PR 00936. **Telephone:** (787) 848-8884. **FAX:** (787) 848-0050.
President: Antonio Munoz Jr.
2003-2004 Manager: Jose Cruz Sr.

SAN JUAN SENATORS
Mailing Address: Unavailable. **Telephone:** (787) 773-0759, (787) 773-0758. **FAX:** (787) 703-0756.
President: Carlos Baerga.
2003-2004 Manager: Unavailable.

CANGREJEROS DE SANTURCE
Mailing Address: P.O. Box 1077, Hato Rey, PR 00919. **Telephone:** (787) 772-9573. **FAX:** (787) 772-9574.
President: Joaqin Monserrate Matienzo.
2003-2004 Manager: Wally Backman.

VENEZUELAN LEAGUE
Mailing Address: Avenida Casanova, Centro Comercial "El Recreo," Torre Sur, Piso 3, Oficinas 6 y 7, Sabana Grande, Caracas, Venezuela. **Telephone:** (011-58) 212-761-4932. **FAX:** (011-58) 212-761-7661. **Website:** www.lvbp.com.
Years League Active: 1946-.
President: Ramon Guillermo Aveledo. **General Manager:** Jose Domingo Alvarez.
Division Structure: East—Caracas, La Guaira, Magallanes, Oriente. **West**—Aragua, Lara, Pastora, Zulia.
2003-2004 Opening Date: Oct. 16. **Closing Date:** Dec. 30.
Regular Season: 62 games.
Playoff Format: Top two teams in each division, plus a wild-card team, meet in 16-game round-robin series. Top two finishers meet in best-of-7 series for league

championship. Winner advances to Caribbean Series.
Roster Limit: 26. **Roster Limit, Imports:** 7.

ARAGUA TIGERS

Mailing Address: Estadio Jose Perez Colmenares, Calle Campo Elias, Barrio Democratico, Maracay, Aragua, Venezuela. **Telephone:** (011-58) 243-554-4134. **FAX:** (011-58) 243-553-8655. **E-Mail Address:** tigres@telcel.net.ve. **Website:** www.tigresdearagua.com.ve.
President, General Manager: Rafael Rodriguez.
2003-2004 Manager: Buddy Bailey.

CARACAS LIONS

Mailing Address: Av. Francisco de Miranda, Centro Seguros la Paz, Piso 4, ofc. 42-C, La California Norte. **Telephone:** (011-58) 212-238-7733. **FAX:** (011-58) 212-238-0691. **E-Mail Address:** contacto@leones.com. **Website:** www.leones.com.
President: Ariel Prat. **General Manager:** Oscar Prieto.
2003-2004 Manager: Omar Malave.

LA GUAIRA SHARKS

Mailing Address: Primera Transversal, Urbanizacion Miramar Pariata, Maiquetia, Vargas, Venezuela. **Telephone:** (011-58) 212-332-5579. **FAX:** (011-58) 212-332-3116. **E-Mail Address:** tiburones@cantv.net. **Website:** www.tiburones.com.
President: Percy Chacin Armando Arratia. **General Manager:** Carlos Moreno.
2003-2004 Manager: Luis Salazar.

LARA CARDINALS

Mailing Address: Av. Rotaria, Estadio Antonio Herrera Gutiérrez, Barquisimeto, Lara, Venezuela. **Telephone:** (011-58) 251-442-4543. **FAX:** (011-58) 251-442-1921. **E-Mail Address:** contacto@cardenalesdelara.com. **Website:** www.cardenalesdelara.com.
President, General Manager: Humberto Oropeza.
2003-2004 Manager: Dan Rohn.

MAGALLANES NAVIGATORS

Mailing Address: Centro Comercial Caribbean Plaza, Modulo 8, Local 173, Valencia, Carabobo, Venezuela. **Telephone:** (011-58) 241-824-0980. **FAX:** (011-58) 241-824-0705. **E-Mail address:** Magallanes@telcel.net.ve. **Website:** www.magallanes.com
President: Dr. Jorge Latoche. **General Manager:** Roberto Ferrari.
2003-2004 Manager: Phil Regan.

ORIENTE CARIBBEANS

Mailing Address: Avenida Estadio Alfonso Carrasquel, Oficina Caribes de Oriente, Centro Comercial Novocentro, Piso 2, Local 2-4, Puerto la Cruz, Anzoategui, Venezuela. **Telephone:** (011-58) 281-266-2536. **FAX:** (011-58) 281-266-7054. **Website:** caribesb-bc.com
President: Aurelio Fernandez-Concheso. **Vice President:** Pablo Ruggeri.
2003-2004 Manager: Dave Machemer.

PASTORA DE LOS LLANOS

Mailing Address: Estadio Bachiller Julio Hernandez Molina, Avenida Romulo Gallegos, Aruare, Portuguesa, Venezuela. **Telephone:** (011-58) 255-622-2945. **Fax:** (011-58) 255-621-8595.
President, General Manager: Enrique Finol.
2003-2004 Manager: Luis Dorante.

ZULIA EAGLES

Mailing Address: Avenida 8 con Calle 81, Urb. Santa Rita, Edificio Las Carolinas, Mezzanine Local M-3, Maracaibo, Zulia, Venezuela. **Telephone:** (011-58) 261-797-9834, (011-58) 261-798-0541. **FAX:** (011-58) 261-798-0579. **Website:** www.aguilas.com.
President: Lucas Rincon Colmenares. **General Manager:** Luis Rodolfo Machado Silva.
2003-2004 Manager: Pete Mackanin.

OTHER WINTER LEAGUES

ARIZONA FALL LEAGUE

Mailing Address: 10201 S. 51st St., Suite 230, Phoenix, AZ 85044. **Telephone:** (480) 496-6700. **FAX:** (480) 496-6384. **E-Mail Address:** afl@mlb.com **Website:** www.mlb.com.
Years League Active: 1992-.
Operated by: Major League Baseball.
Executive Vice President: Steve Cobb. **Executive Assistant:** Joan McGrath.
Division Structure: East—Mesa, Phoenix, Scottsdale; **West**—Grand Canyon, Maryvale, Peoria.
2004 Opening Date: Oct. 2. **Closing Date:** Nov. 15.
Regular Season: 52 games.
Playoff Format: Division champions meet in one-game championship.
Roster Limit: 30. Players with less than one year of major league service are eligible.

GRAND CANYON RAFTERS

Mailing Address: See league address.
Working Agreements: Detroit Tigers, Minnesota Twins, New York Yannkees, St. Louis Cardinals, San Francisco Giants.
2003 Manager: Andy Stankiewicz (Yankees).

MESA DESERT DOGS

Mailing Address: See league address.
Working Agreements: Boston Red Sox, Cleveland Indians, Oakland Athletics, Philadelphia Phillies,

Pittsburgh Pirates.
2003 Manager: Tony Beasley (Pirates).

MESA SOLAR SOX

Mailing Address: See league address.
Working Agreements: Atlanta Braves, Baltimore Orioles, Chicago Cubs, Colorado Rockies, Tampa Bay Devil Rays.
2003 Manager: Pat Kelly (Braves).

PEORIA JAVELINAS

Mailing Address: See league address.
Working Agreements: Chicago White Sox, Kansas City Royals, Montreal Expos, Seattle Mariners, Toronto Blue Jays.
2003 Manager: Frank White (Royals).

PEORIA SAGUAROS

Mailing Address: See league address.
Working Agreements: Milwaukee Brewers, Florida Marlins, New York Mets, San Diego Padres, Texas Rangers.
2003 Manager: Frank Kremblas (Brewers).

SCOTTSDALE SCORPIONS

Mailing Address: See league address.
Working Agreements: Anaheim Angels, Arizona Diamondbacks, Cincinnati Reds, Houston Astros, Los Angeles Dodgers.
2003 Manager: Rick Burleson (Reds).

COLLEGES

COLLEGE BASEBALL

NATIONAL COLLEGIATE ATHLETIC ASSOCIATION

Mailing Address: P.O. Box 6222, Indianapolis, IN 46206. **Telephone:** (317) 917-6222. **FAX:** (317) 917-6826, 917-6857. **E-Mail Addresses:** dpoppe@ncaa.org (Dennis Poppe), rbuhr@ncaa.org (Randy Buhr), dworlock@ncaa.org (David Worlock), jhamilton@ncaa.org (J.D. Hamilton), Sean Straziscar (sstraziscar@ncaa.org). **Websites:** www.ncaa.org, www.ncaasports.com.

President: Myles Brand. **Managing Director, Baseball:** Dennis Poppe. **Assistant Director, Championships:** Randy Buhr. **Media Contact, College World Series:** David Worlock. **Contact, Statistics:** Sean Straziscar.

Chairman, Division I Baseball Committee: Charlie Carr (senior associate athletic director, Florida State). **Division I Baseball Committee:** Skip Bertman (athletic director, Louisiana State), Rudy Davalos (AD, New Mexico), Mike Gaski (baseball coach, UNC Greensboro), Robert Staub (senior associate AD, Alabama-Birmingham), Robert Steitz (senior associate AD, Villanova), Brian Colleary (AD, Duquesne), Chris Monasch (commissioner, America East Conference), Bill Rowe (AD, Southwest Missouri State), Bob Todd (baseball coach, Ohio State).

Chairman, Division II Baseball Committee: Skip Fite (baseball coach, Augusta State). **Chairman, Division III Baseball Committee:** Eric Etchison (baseball coach, Maryville, Tenn.).

2005 National Convention: Jan. 7-11 at Dallas

2004 Championship Tournaments
NCAA Division I

58th College World Series	Omaha, NE, June 18-27/28
Super Regionals (8)	June 11-14
Regionals (16)	June 4-6

NCAA Division II

37th World Series	Montgomery, AL, May 22-29
Regionals (8)	Campus sites, May 13-15

NCAA Division III

29th World Series	Appleton, WI, May 28-June 1
Regionals (8)	Campus sites, May 20-23

NATIONAL ASSOCIATION OF INTERCOLLEGIATE ATHLETICS

Mailing Address: 23500 W. 105th St., P.O. Box 1325, Olathe, KS 66051. **Telephone:** (913) 791-0044. **FAX:** (913) 791-9555. **Website:** www.naia.org.

Chief Executive Officer: Steve Baker. **Director, Championship Events:** Natalie Cronkhite. **Publicity Director:** Mark Chiarucci.

2004 Championship Tournament

NAIA World Series	Lewiston, ID, May 28-June 4

NATIONAL JUNIOR COLLEGE ATHLETIC ASSOCIATION

Mailing Address: P.O. Box 7305, Colorado Springs, CO 80933. **Telephone:** (719) 590-9788. **FAX:** (719) 590-7324. **Website:** www.njcaa.org.

Executive Director: George Killian. **Director, Division I Baseball Tournament:** Jamie Hamilton. **Director, Division II Tournament:** John Daigle. **Director, Division III Tournament:** Barry Bower.

2004 Championship Tournaments
Division I

World Series	Grand Junction, CO, May 29-June 4

Division II

World Series	Millington, TN, May 29-June 4

Division III

World Series	Batavia, NY, May 22-26

CALIFORNIA COMMUNITY COLLEGE COMMISSION ON ATHLETICS

Mailing Address: 2017 O St., Sacramento, CA 95814. **Telephone:** (916) 444-1600. **FAX:** (916) 444-2616. **E-Mail Address:** info@coasports.org. **Website:** www.coasports.org.

Commissioner of Athletics: Joanne Fortunato. **Associate Commissioner, Athletics:** Stuart Van Horn. **Director, Sports Information:** David Eadie.

2004 Championship Tournament

State Championship	Fresno City College, May 29-31.

AMERICAN BASEBALL COACHES ASSOCIATION

Office Address: 108 S. University Ave., Suite 3, Mount Pleasant, MI 48858. **Telephone:** (989) 775-3300. **FAX:** (989) 775-3600. **E-Mail Address:** abca@abca.org. **Website:** www.abca.org.

Executive Director: Dave Keilitz. **Assistant to Executive Director:** Betty Rulong. **Membership/Convention Coordinator:** Nick Phillips. **Assistant Coordinator:** Juahn Clark.

Chairman: Glen Tuckett (Brigham Young University). **President:** Danny Hall (Georgia Tech).

2005 National Convention: Jan. 6-9 at Nashville, TN (Opryland Hotel).

AMERICA EAST CONFERENCE

Mailing Address: 10 High St., Suite 860, Boston, MA 02110. **Telephone:** (617) 695-6369. **FAX:** (617) 695-6385. **E-Mail Address:** bourque@americaeast.com. **Website:** www.americaeast.com.

Baseball Members (First Year): Albany (2002), Binghamton (2002), Hartford (1990), Maine (1990), Maryland-Baltimore County (2004), Northeastern (1990), Stony Brook (2002), Vermont (1990).

Assistant Commissioner/Communications: Matt Bourque.

2004 Tournament: Four teams, double-elimination. May 27-29 at Orono, ME (University of Maine).

ATLANTIC COAST CONFERENCE

Office Address: 4512 Weybridge Lane, Greensboro, NC 27407. **Mailing Address:** P.O. Drawer ACC, Greensboro, NC 27417. **Telephone:** (336) 851-6062. **FAX:** (336)854-8797. **E-Mail Address:** ayakola@theacc.org. **Website:** www.theacc.com.

Baseball Members (First Year): Clemson (1953), Duke (1953), Florida State (1992), Georgia Tech (1980), Maryland (1953), North Carolina (1953), North Carolina State (1953), Virginia (1953), Wake Forest (1953).

Director of Public Relations: Amy Yakola.

2004 Tournament: Nine teams, double-elimination. May 25-30 at Salem, VA (Salem Memorial Stadium).

ATLANTIC SUN CONFERENCE

Mailing Address: 3370 Vineville Ave., Suite 108-B, Macon, GA 31204. **Telephone:** (478) 474-3394. **FAX:** (478) 474-4272. **E-Mail Address:** dpierce@atlanticsun.org. **Website:** www.atlanticsun.org.

Baseball Members (First Year): Belmont (2002), Campbell (1994), UCF (1992), Florida Atlantic (1993), Gardner-Webb (2003), Georgia State (1983), Jacksonville (1999), Lipscomb (1994), Mercer (1978), Stetson (1985), Troy State (1998).

Assistant Commissioner, Media/Championships: Devlin Pierce. **Assistant Director, Communications:** Mike Holmes.

2004 Tournament: Six teams, double-elimination. May 26-29 at DeLand, FL (Stetson University).

ATLANTIC 10 CONFERENCE

Mailing Address: 230 S. Broad St., Suite 1700, Philadelphia, PA 19102. **Telephone:** (215) 545-6678. **FAX:** (215) 545-3342. **E-Mail Address:** shaug@atlantic10.org. **Website:** www.atlantic10.org.

Baseball Members (First Year): Dayton (1996), Duquesne (1977), Fordham (1996), George Washington (1977), LaSalle (1996), Massachusetts (1977), Rhode Island (1981), Richmond (2002), St. Bonaventure (1980), Saint Joseph's (1983), Temple (1983), Xavier (1996).

Director, Baseball Communications: Stephen Haug.

2004 Tournament: Six teams, double-elimination. May 26-29 at Norwich, CT (Thomas J. Dodd Memorial Stadium).

BIG EAST CONFERENCE

Mailing Address: 222 Richmond St., Suite 110, Providence, RI 02903. **Telephone:** (401) 272-9108. **FAX:** (401) 751-8540. **E-Mail Address:** rcarolla@bigeast.org. **Website:** www.bigeast.org.

Baseball Members (First Year): Boston College (1985), Connecticut (1985), Georgetown (1985), Notre Dame (1996), Pittsburgh (1985), Rutgers (1996), St. John's (1985), Seton Hall (1985), Villanova (1985), Virginia Tech (2001), West Virginia (1996).

Director, Communications: Rob Carolla.

2004 Championship: Four teams, double-elimination. May 27-29 at Bridgewater, NJ (Commerce Bank Ballpark).

BIG SOUTH CONFERENCE

Mailing Address: 6428 Bannington Dr., Suite A, Charlotte, NC 28226. **Telephone:** (704) 341-7990. **FAX:** (704) 341-7991. **E-Mail Address:** jasonc@bigsouth.org. **Website:** www.bigsouthsports.com.

Baseball Members (First Year): Birmingham-Southern (2002), Charleston Southern (1983), Coastal Carolina (1983), High Point (1999), Liberty (1991), UNC Asheville (1985), Radford (1983), Virginia Military Institute (2004), Winthrop (1983),

Director, Public Relations: Jason Corriher.

2004 Tournament: Six teams, double-elimination. May 25-29 at Rock Hill, SC (Winthrop University).

BIG TEN CONFERENCE

Mailing Address: 1500 W. Higgins Rd., Park Ridge, IL 60068. **Telephone:** (847) 696-1010. **FAX:** (847) 696-1110. **E-Mail Address:** schipman@bigten.org. **Website:** www.bigten.org.

Baseball Members (First Year): Illinois (1896), Indiana (1906), Iowa (1906), Michigan (1896), Michigan State (1950), Minnesota (1906), Northwestern (1898), Ohio State (1913), Penn State (1992), Purdue (1906).

Associate Director, Communications: Scott Chipman.

2004 Tournament: Six teams, double-elimination. May 26-29 at regular-season champion.

BIG 12 CONFERENCE

Mailing Address: 2201 Stemmons Freeway, 28th Floor, Dallas, TX 75207. **Telephone:** (214) 753-0102. **FAX:** (214) 753-0145. **E-Mail Address:** bo@big12sports.com. **Website:** www.big12sports.com.

Baseball Members (First Year): Baylor (1997), Kansas (1997), Kansas State (1997), Missouri (1997), Nebraska (1997), Oklahoma (1997), Oklahoma State (1997), Texas (1997), Texas A&M (1997), Texas Tech (1997).

Assistant Commissioner, Media Relations: Bo Carter.

2004 Tournament: Eight teams, double-elimination. May 26-30 at Arlington, TX (The Ballpark at Arlington).

BIG WEST CONFERENCE

Mailing Address: 2 Corporate Park, Suite 206, Irvine, CA 92606. **Telephone:** (949) 261-2525. **FAX:** (949) 261-2528. **E-Mail Address:** cramos@bigwest.org. **Website:** www.bigwest.org.

Baseball Members (First Year): Cal Poly (1997), UC Irvine (2002), UC Riverside (2002), UC Santa Barbara (1970), Cal State Fullerton (1975), Cal State Northridge (2001), Long Beach State (1970), Pacific (1972).

Assistant Director, Information: Chris Ramos.

2004 Tournament: None.

COLONIAL ATHLETIC ASSOCIATION

Mailing Address: 8625 Patterson Ave., Richmond, VA 23229. **Telephone:** (804) 754-1616. **FAX:** (804) 754-1830. **E-Mail Address:** rwashburn@caasports.com. **Website:** www.caasports.com.

Baseball Members (First Year): Delaware (2002), George Mason (1986), Hofstra (2002), James Madison (1986), UNC Wilmington (1986), Old Dominion (1992), Towson (2002), Virginia Commonwealth (1996), William & Mary (1986).

Sports Information Director: Rob Washburn.

2004 Tournament: Six teams, double-elimination. May 26-29 at Wilmington, NC (Brooks Field).

CONFERENCE USA

Mailing Address: 35 E. Wacker Dr., Suite 650, Chicago, IL 60601. **Telephone:** (312) 553-0483. **FAX:** (312) 553-0495. **E-Mail Address:** rdanderson@c-usa.org. **Website:** www.c-usasports.com.

Baseball Members (First Year): Alabama-Birmingham (1996), Charlotte (1996), Cincinnati (1996), East Carolina (2002), Houston (1997), Louisville (1996), Memphis (1996), Saint Louis (1996), South Florida (1996), Southern Mississippi (1996), Texas Christian (2002), Tulane (1996).

Assistant Commisioner, Media Relations: Russell Anderson.

2004 Tournament: Eight teams, double-elimination. May 26-30 at Houston (University of Houston).

HORIZON LEAGUE

Mailing Address: 201 S. Capitol Ave., Suite 500, Indianapolis, IN 46225.

Telephone: (317) 237-5622. **FAX:** (317) 237-5620. **E-Mail Address:** tstarowitz@horizonleague.org. **Website:** www.horizonleague.org.

Baseball Members (First Year): Butler (1979), Cleveland State (1994), Detroit (1980), Illinois-Chicago (1994), Wisconsin-Milwaukee (1994), Wright State (1994), Youngstown State (2002).

Director, Communications: Todd Starowitz.

2004 Tournament: Seven teams, double-elimination. May 25-29 at Youngstown, OH (Youngstown State University).

IVY LEAGUE

Mailing Address: 228 Alexander Rd., Second Floor, Princeton, NJ 08544.

Telephone: (609) 258-6426. **FAX:** (609) 258-1690. **E-Mail Address:**info@ivyleaguesports.com. **Website:** www.ivyleaguesports.com.

Baseball Members (First Year): Rolfe—Brown (1948), Dartmouth (1930), Harvard (1948), Yale (1930). **Gehrig**—Columbia (1930), Cornell (1930), Pennsylvania (1930), Princeton (1930).

Assistants, Public Information: Eddy Lentz, LaKesha Whitaker.

2004 Tournament: Best-of-3 series between division champions. May 8-9 at team with best overall record.

METRO ATLANTIC ATHLETIC CONFERENCE

Mailing Address: 712 Amboy Ave., Edison, NJ 08837. **Telephone:** (732) 738-5455. **FAX:** (732) 738-8366. **E-Mail Address:** jill.skotarczak@maac.org. **Website:** www.maacsports.com.

Baseball Members (First Year): Canisius (1990), Fairfield (1982), Iona (1982), LeMoyne (1990), Manhattan (1982), Marist (1998), Niagara (1990), Rider (1998), St. Peter's (1982), Siena (1990).

Director, Media Relations: Jill Skotarczak

2004 Tournament: Four teams, double-elimination. May 27-29 at Fishkill, NY (Dutchess Stadium).

MID-AMERICAN CONFERENCE

Mailing Address: 24 Public Square, 15th Floor, Cleveland, OH 44113. **Telephone:** (216) 566-4622. **FAX:** (216) 858-9622. **E-Mail Address:** bmcgowan@mac-sports.com. **Website:** www.mac-sports.com.

Baseball Members (First Year): Akron (1992), Ball State (1973), Bowling Green State (1952), Buffalo (2001), Central Michigan (1971), Eastern Michigan (1971), Kent State (1951), Marshall (1997), Miami

(1947), Northern Illinois (1997), Ohio (1946). Toledo (1950), Western Michigan (1947).

Associate Director, Media Relations: Bryan McGowan.

2004 Tournament: Six teams (top two in each division, two wild-card teams with next best conference winning percentage), double-elimination. May 26-29 at team with best conference winning percentage.

MID-CONTINENT CONFERENCE

Mailing Address: 340 W. Butterfield Rd., Suite 3-D, Elmhurst, IL 60126. **Telephone:** (630) 516-0661. **FAX:** (630) 516-0673. **E-Mail Address:** hamilton@mid-con.com. **Website:** www.mid-con.com.

Baseball Members (First Year): Centenary (2004), Chicago State (1994), Oakland (2000), Oral Roberts (1998), Southern Utah (2000), Valparaiso (1984), Western Illinois (1984).

Director, Media Relations: Tony Hamilton.

2004 Tournament: Four teams, double-elimination. May 27-29 at Shreveport, LA (Centenary College).

MID-EASTERN ATHLETIC CONFERENCE

Mailing Address: 102 N. Elm St., Suite 401, P.O. Box 21205, Greensboro, NC 27420. **Telephone:** (336) 275-9961. **FAX:** (336) 275-9964. **E-Mail Address:** conawayl@themeac.com. **Website:** www.meacsports.com.

Baseball Members (First Year): North—Coppin State (1985), Delaware State (1970), Maryland-Eastern Shore (1970). **South**—Bethune-Cookman (1979), Florida A&M (1979), Norfolk State (1998), North Carolina A&T (1970).

Director, Media Relations: LeCounte Conaway.

2004 Tournament: Seven teams, double-elimination. April 29-May 1 at Orlando, FL (Disney Wide World of Sports Complex).

MISSOURI VALLEY CONFERENCE

Mailing Address: 1818 Chouteau Ave., St. Louis, MO 63103. **Telephone:** (314) 421-0339. **FAX:** (314) 421-3505. **E-Mail Address:** fricke@mvc.org. **Website:** www.mvc.org.

Baseball Members (First Year): Bradley (1955), Creighton (1976), Evansville (1994), Illinois State (1980), Indiana State (1976), Northern Iowa (1991), Southern Illinois (1974), Southwest Missouri State (1990), Wichita State (1945).

Assistant Director, Communications: Erica Fricke.

2004 Tournament: Six teams, double-elimination. May 26-29 at Springfield, MO (Southwest Missouri State).

MOUNTAIN WEST CONFERENCE

Mailing Address: 15455 Gleneagle Dr., Suite 200B, Colorado Springs, CO 80921. **Telephone:** (719) 488-4040. **FAX:** (719) 487-7241. **E-Mail Address:** rchristian@themwc.com. **Website:** www.themwc.com.

Baseball Members (First Year): Air Force (2000), Brigham Young (2000), Nevada-Las Vegas (2000), New Mexico (2000), San Diego State (2000), Utah (2000).

Assistant Director, Communications: Ron Christian.

2004 Tournament: Six teams, double-elimination. May 26-29 at Las Vegas, NV (Earl E. Wilson Stadium).

NORTHEAST CONFERENCE

Mailing Address: 200 Cottontail Lane, Vantage Court North, Somerset, NJ 08873. **Telephone:** (732) 469-0440. **FAX:** (732) 469-0744. **E-Mail Address:** rratner@northeastconference.org. **Website:** www.northeastconference.org.

Baseball Members (First Year): Central Connecticut State (1999), Fairleigh Dickinson (1981), Long Island (1981), Monmouth (1985), Mount St. Mary's (1989), Quinnipiac (1999), Sacred Heart (2000), St. Francis, N.Y.

(1981), Wagner (1981).
Associate Commissioner: Ron Ratner.
2004 Tournament: Four teams, double-elimination. May 21-23 at Lakewood, NJ (First Energy Park).

OHIO VALLEY CONFERENCE

Mailing Address: 278 Franklin Rd., Suite 103, Brentwood, TN 37027. **Telephone:** (615) 371-1698. **FAX:** (615) 371-1788. **E-Mail Address:** kmelcher@ovc.org. **Website:** www.ovcsports.com.

Baseball Members (First Year): Austin Peay State (1962), Eastern Illinois (1996), Eastern Kentucky (1948), Jacksonville State (2003), Morehead State (1948), Murray State (1948), Samford (2003), Southeast Missouri State (1991), Tennessee-Martin (1992), Tennessee Tech (1949).

Assistant Commissioner: Kim Melcher.
2004 Tournament: Six teams, double-elimination. May 26-29 at Paducah, KY (Brooks Stadium).

PACIFIC-10 CONFERENCE

Mailing Address: 800 S. Broadway, Suite 400, Walnut Creek, CA 94596. **Telephone:** (925) 932-4411. **FAX:** (925) 932-4601. **E-Mail Address:** shitchcock@pac-10.org. **Website:** www.pac-10.org.

Baseball Members (First Year): Arizona (1979), Arizona State (1979), California (1916), UCLA (1928), Oregon State (1916), Southern California (1922), Stanford (1917), Washington (1916), Washington State (1917).

Public Relations Intern: Steve Hitchcock.
2004 Tournament: None.

PATRIOT LEAGUE

Mailing Address: 3773 Corporate Pkwy., Suite 190, Center Valley, PA 18034. **Telephone:** (610) 289-1950. **FAX:** (610) 289-1952. **E-Mail Address:** kpetersen@patriotleague.com. **Website:** www.patriotleague.com.

Baseball Members (First Year): Army (1993), Bucknell (1991), Holy Cross (1991), Lafayette (1991), Lehigh (1991), Navy (1993).

Assistant Director, Media Relations: Kristina Petersen.
2004 Tournament: Top three teams; No. 2 plays No. 3 in one-game playoff. Winner faces No. 1 team in best-of-3 series at No. 1 seed, May 8-9.

SOUTHEASTERN CONFERENCE

Mailing Address: 2201 Richard Arrington Blvd. N., Birmingham, AL 35203. **Telephone:** (205) 458-3000. **FAX:** (205) 458-3030. **E-Mail Address:** cdunlap@sec.org. **Website:** www.secsports.com.

Baseball Members (First Year): East—Florida (1933), Georgia (1933), Kentucky (1933), South Carolina (1992), Tennessee (1933), Vanderbilt (1933). **West**—Alabama (1933), Arkansas (1992), Auburn (1933), Louisiana State (1933), Mississippi (1933), Mississippi State (1933).

Assistant Director, Media Relations: Chuck Dunlap.
2004 Tournament: Eight teams, modified double-elimination. May 26-30 at Birmingham, AL (Hoover Metropolitan Stadium).

SOUTHERN CONFERENCE

Mailing Address: 905 E. Main Street, Suite 6, Spartanburg, SC 29302. **Telephone:** (864) 591-5100. **FAX:** (864) 591-3448. **E-Mail Address:** sshutt@socon.org. **Website:** www.soconsports.com.

Baseball Members (First Year): Appalachian State (1971), Charleston (1998), The Citadel (1936), Davidson (1991), East Tennessee State (1978), Elon (2004), Furman (1936), Georgia Southern (1991), UNC Greensboro (1997), Western Carolina (1976), Wofford (1997).

Associate Commissioner, Public Affairs: Steve Shutt.

2004 Tournament: Eight teams, double-elimination. May 26-29 at Charleston, SC (The Citadel).

SOUTHLAND CONFERENCE

Mailing Address: 1700 Alma Dr., Suite 550, Plano, TX 75075. **Telephone:** (972) 422-9500. **FAX:** (972) 422-9225. **E-Mail Address:** bludlow@southland.org. **Website:** www.southland.org.

Baseball Members (First Year): Lamar (1999), Louisiana-Monroe (1983), McNeese State (1973), Nicholls State (1992), Northwestern State (1988), Sam Houston State (1988), Southeastern Louisiana (1998), Texas State (1988), Texas-Arlington (1964), Texas-San Antonio (1992).

Baseball Contact/Assistant Commissioner: Bruce Ludlow.
2004 Tournament: Six teams, double-elimination. May 26-29 at Hammond, LA (Southeastern Louisiana University).

SOUTHWESTERN ATHLETIC CONFERENCE

Mailing Address: A.G. Gaston Building, 1527 Fifth Ave. N., Birmingham, AL 35203. **Telephone:** (205) 252-7573, ext. 111. **FAX:** (205) 252-9997. **E-Mail Address:** wdooley@swac.org. **Website:** www.swac.org.

Baseball Members (First Year): East—Alabama A&M (2000), Alabama State (1982), Alcorn State (1962), Jackson State (1958), Mississippi Valley State (1968). **West**—Arkansas-Pine Bluff (1999), Grambling State (1958), Prairie View A&M (1920), Southern (1934), Texas Southern (1954).

Assistant Commissioner, Media Relations: Wallace Dooley.
2004 Tournament: Six teams, double-elimination. May 6-9 at Houston, TX (Baseball USA—The Yard).

SUN BELT CONFERENCE

Mailing Address: 601 Poydras St., Suite 2355, New Orleans, LA 70130.
Telephone: (504) 299-9066. **FAX:** (504) 299-9068. **E-Mail Address:** willson@sunbeltsports.org. **Website:** www.sunbeltsports.org.

Baseball Members (First Year): Arkansas-Little Rock (1991), Arkansas State (1991), Florida International (1999), Louisiana-Lafayette (1991), Middle Tennessee (2001), New Mexico State (2001), New Orleans (1976, 1991), South Alabama (1976), Western Kentucky (1982).

Director, Service Bureau: Judy Willson.
2004 Tournament: Eight teams, double-elimination. May 26-29 at Mobile, Ala. (University of South Alabama).

WEST COAST CONFERENCE

Mailing Address: 1200 Bayhill Dr., Suite 302, San Bruno, CA 94066. **Telephone:** (650) 873-8622. **FAX:** (650) 873-7846. **E-Mail Addresses:** bwalker@westcoast.org. **Website:** www.wccsports.com.

Baseball Members (First Year): Gonzaga (1996), Loyola Marymount (1968), Pepperdine (1968), Portland (1996), Saint Mary's (1968), San Diego (1979), San Francisco (1968), Santa Clara (1968).

Assistant Commissioner: Brad Walker.
2004 Tournament: Division champions meet in best-of-3 series, May 28-30.

WESTERN ATHLETIC CONFERENCE

Mailing Address: 9250 East Costilla Ave., Suite 300, Englewood, CO 80112. **Telephone:** (303) 799-9221. **FAX:** (303) 799-3888. **E-Mail Address:** wac@wac.org. **Website:** www.wacsports.com.

Baseball Members (First Year): Fresno State (1993), Hawaii (1980), Louisiana Tech (2002), Nevada (2001),

Rice (1997), San Jose State (1997). **Commissioner:** Karl Benson. **Senior Associate Commissioner:** Jeff Hurd. **Director, Sports Information:**

Dave Chaffin.
2004 Tournament: None.

NCAA DIVISION II CONFERENCES

CALIFORNIA COLLEGIATE ATHLETIC ASSOCIATION

Mailing Address: 800 S. Broadway, Suite 309, Walnut Creek, CA 94596. **Telephone:** (925) 472-8299. **FAX:** (925) 472-8887. **Website:** www.goccaa.org.

Baseball Members: UC Davis, UC San Diego, Cal State Dominguez Hills, Cal State Los Angeles, Cal Poly Pomona, Cal State San Bernardino, Cal State Stanislaus, Chico State, Grand Canyon, San Francisco State, Sonoma State.

CAROLINAS-VIRGINIA ATHLETIC CONFERENCE

Mailing Address: 26 Cub Dr., Thomasville, NC 27360. **Telephone:** (336) 884-0482. **FAX:** (336) 884-0315. **E-Mail Address:** CVAC@triad.rr.com. **Website:** www.cvac.net.

Baseball Members: Anderson, Barton, Belmont Abbey, Coker, Erskine, Limestone, Mount Olive, Pfeiffer, St. Andrews Presbyterian.

CENTRAL ATLANTIC COLLEGIATE CONFERENCE

Mailing Address: NJIT Sports Information, University Heights, Newark, NJ 07102. **Telephone:** (973) 596-8324. **FAX:** (973) 596-8440. **E-Mail Address:** mentone@adm.njit.edu. **Website:** www.caccathletics. org.

Baseball Members: Bloomfield, Caldwell, Dominican (N.Y.), Felician, New Jersey Institute of Technology, Nyack, University of the Sciences in Philadelphia, Teikyo-Post, Wilmington (Del.).

CENTRAL INTERCOLLEGIATE ATHLETIC ASSOCIATION

Mailing Address: 303 Butler Farm Rd., Suite 102, Hampton, VA 23666. **Telephone:** (757) 865-0071. **FAX:** (757) 865-8436. **E-Mail Address:** TheCiaa@aol.com. **Website:** www.theciaa.com.

Baseball Members: Elizabeth City State, Saint Augustine's, Saint Paul's, Shaw, Virginia State.

GREAT LAKES INTERCOLLEGIATE ATHLETIC CONFERENCE

Mailing Address: 1110 Washington Ave., Bay City, MI 48708. **Telephone:** (989) 894-2529. **FAX:** (989) 894-2825. **E-Mail Address:** tomjb@gliac.org. **Website:** www.gliac.org.

Baseball Members: Ashland, Findlay, Gannon, Grand Valley State, Hillsdale, Mercyhurst, Northwood, Saginaw Valley State, Wayne State (Mich.).

GREAT LAKES VALLEY CONFERENCE

Mailing Address: Pan Am Plaza, Suite 560, 201 S. Capitol Ave., Indianapolis, IN 46225. **Telephone:** (317) 237-5636. **FAX:** (317) 237-5632. **E-Mail Address:** jnglvc@aol.com. **Website:** www.glvcsports.com.

Baseball Members: Bellarmine, Indianapolis, Kentucky Wesleyan, Lewis, Missouri-Saint Louis, Northern Kentucky, Quincy, Saint Joseph's (Ind.), Southern Illinois-Edwardsville, Southern Indiana, Wisconsin-Parkside.

GULF SOUTH CONFERENCE

Mailing Address: 4 Office Park Circle, Suite 218, Birmingham, AL 25223. **Telephone:** (205) 870-9750. **FAX:** (205) 870-4723. **E-Mail Address:** gcsid@mind-spring.com. **Website:** www.gulfsouthconference.org.

Baseball Members: Alabama-Huntsville, Arkansas-Monticello, Arkansas Tech, Central Arkansas, Christian Brothers, Delta State, Harding, Henderson State, Lincoln Memorial, Montevallo, North Alabama, Ouachita Baptist, Southern Arkansas, Valdosta State, West Alabama, West Florida, West Georgia.

LONE STAR CONFERENCE

Mailing Address: 1221 W. Campbell Rd., No. 245, Richardson, TX 75080. **Telephone:** (972) 234-0033. **FAX:** (972) 234-4110. **E-Mail Address:** tinderj@lonestar-conference.org. **Website:** www.lonestarconference.org.

Baseball Members: Abilene Christian, Cameron, Central Oklahoma, East Central, Eastern New Mexico, Northeastern State, Southeastern Oklahoma State, Southwestern Oklahoma State, Tarleton State, Texas A&M-Kingsville, West Texas A&M.

MID-AMERICA INTERCOLLEGIATE ATHLETICS ASSOCIATION

Mailing Address: 10551 Barkley, Suite 501, Overland Park, KS 66212. **Telephone:** (913) 341-3839/3080. **FAX:** (913) 341-5887/2995. **E-Mail Address:** rmc-fillen@themiaa.com. **Website:** www.themiaa.com.

Baseball Members: Central Missouri State, Emporia State, Missouri-Rolla, Missouri Southern State, Missouri Western State, Northwest Missouri State, Pittsburg State, Southwest Baptist, Truman State, Washburn.

NEW YORK COLLEGIATE ATHLETIC CONFERENCE

Mailing Address: 320 Sea Cliff Ave., Sea Cliff, NY 11579. **Telephone:** (516) 609-2714. **FAX:** (516) 609-0881. **E-Mail:** gonycac@hotmail.com. **Website:** www.nycac.net.

Baseball Members: Adelphi, Bridgeport, Concordia (N.Y.), C.W. Post, Dowling, Mercy, Molloy, New Haven, Philadelphia, Queens, St. Thomas Aquinas.

NORTH CENTRAL INTERCOLLEGIATE ATHLETIC CONFERENCE

Mailing Address: 3200 W. Maple St., Ramkota Inn, Sioux Falls, SD 57107. **Telephone:** (605) 338-0907. **FAX:** (605) 373-9018. **E-Mail Address:** info@northcentralcon-ference.org. **Website:** www.northcentralconference.org.

Baseball Members: Augustana (S.D.), Minnesota State-Mankato, Nebraska-Omaha, North Dakota, North Dakota State, St. Cloud State, South Dakota, South Dakota State.

NORTHEAST-10 CONFERENCE

Mailing Address: 16 Belmont St., South Easton, MA 02375. **Telephone:** (508) 230-9844. **FAX:** (508) 230-9845. **E-Mail:** kbelbin@northeast10.org. **Website:** www.northeast10.org.

Baseball Members: American International, Assumption, Bentley, Bryant, Franklin Pierce, Massachusetts-Lowell, Merrimack, Saint Anselm, Saint Rose, Southern Connecticut State, Southern New Hampshire, Stonehill.

NORTHERN SUN INTERCOLLEGIATE CONFERENCE

Mailing Address: 2800 University Ave., Suite 203, Minneapolis, MN 55414. **Telephone:** (612) 379-1498. **FAX:** (612) 379-3272. **E-Mail:** lockr100@hotmail.com. **Website:** www.northernsun.org.

Baseball Members: Bemidji State, Concordia-St. Paul, Minnesota-Crookston, Minnesota-Duluth, Minnesota-Morris, Northern State, Southwest Minnesota State, Wayne State (Neb.), Winona State.

PEACH BELT CONFERENCE

Mailing Address: P.O. Box 204290, Augusta, GA 30917. **Telephone:** (706) 860-8499. **FAX:** (706) 650-8113. **E-Mail Address:** sports@peachbelt.com. **Website:** www.peachbelt.com.

Baseball Members: Armstrong Atlantic State, Augusta State, Columbus State, Francis Marion, Georgia College & State, Kennesaw State, Lander, UNC Pembroke, North Florida, South Carolina-Aiken, South Carolina-Spartanburg.

PENNSYLVANIA STATE ATHLETIC CONFERENCE

Mailing Address: 204 Annex Building, Susquehanna Ave., Lock Haven, PA 17745. **Telephone:** (570) 893-2780. **FAX:** (570) 893-2206. **E-Mail Address:** wadair@lhup.edu. **Website:** www.psacsports.org.

Baseball Members: Bloomsburg, California (Pa.), Clarion, Indiana (Pa.), Kutztown, Lock Haven, Mansfield, Millersville, Shippensburg, Slippery Rock, West Chester.

ROCKY MOUNTAIN ATHLETIC CONFERENCE

Mailing Address: 219 West Colorado Ave., Suite 110, Colorado Springs, CO 80903. **Telephone:** (719) 471-0066. **FAX:** (719) 471-0088. **E-Mail Address:** tkrmac@qwest.net. **Website:** www.rmacsports.org.

Baseball Members: Colorado School of Mines, Fort Hays State, Mesa State, Metro State, Nebraska-Kearney, New Mexico Highlands, Regis, Southern Colorado.

SOUTH ATLANTIC CONFERENCE

Mailing Address: Gateway Plaza, Suite 130, 226 N. Park Dr., Rock Hill, SC 29730. **Telephone:** (803) 981-5240. **FAX:** (803) 981-9444. **E-Mail Address:** thesac@comporium.net. **Website:** www.thesac.com.

Baseball Members: Carson-Newman, Catawba, Lenoir-Rhyne, Mars Hill, Newberry, Presbyterian, Tusculum, Wingate.

SOUTHERN INTERCOLLEGIATE ATHLETIC CONFERENCE

Mailing Address: 3469 Lawrenceville Hwy., Suite 103, Tucker, GA 30084. **Telephone:** (770) 908-0482. **FAX:** (770) 408-2772. **Website:** www.thesiac.com.

Baseball Members: Albany State (Ga.), Clark Atlanta, Kentucky State, Lane, LeMoyne-Owen, Miles, Paine, Tuskegee.

SUNSHINE STATE CONFERENCE

Mailing Address: 7061 Grand National Dr., Suite 140, Orlando, FL 32819. **Telephone:** (407) 248-8460. **FAX:** (407) 248-8325. **E-Mail Address:** info@ssconference.org. **Website:** www.ssconference.org.

Baseball Members: Barry, Eckerd, Florida Southern, Florida Tech, Lynn, Rollins, Saint Leo, Tampa.

WEST VIRGINIA INTERCOLLEGIATE ATHLETIC CONFERENCE

Mailing Address: 1422 Main St., Princeton, WV 24740. **Telephone:** (304) 487-6298. **FAX:** (304) 487-6299. **E-Mail Address:** will@wviac.org. **Website:** www.wviac.org.

Baseball Members: Alderson-Broaddus, Bluefield State, Charleston, Concord, Davis & Elkins, Fairmont State, Ohio Valley, Salem International, Shepherd, West Liberty State, West Virginia State, West Virginia University Tech, West Virginia Wesleyan.

*Recruiting coordinator

AIR FORCE ACADEMY Falcons
Conference: Mountain West.
Mailing Address: 2169 Field House Dr., USAF Academy, CO 80840. **Website:** www.airforcesports.com.
Head Coach: Mike Hutcheon. **Assistant Coaches:** Chris Humphrey, *Ryan Thompson. **Telephone:** (719) 333-7898. ■ **Baseball SID:** Nick Arsenick. **Telephone:** (719) 333-2313. **FAX:** (719) 333-3798.

AKRON Zips
Conference: Mid-American.
Mailing Address: 325 Carroll St., Akron, OH 44325. **Website:** www.gozips.com.
Head Coach: Tim Berenyi. **Assistant Coaches:** *Scott Demetral, Trent McIlvain. **Telephone:** (330) 972-7290. ■ **Baseball SID:** Shawn Nestor. **Telephone:** (330) 972-6292. **FAX:** (330) 374-8844.

ALABAMA Crimson Tide
Conference: Southeastern (West).
Mailing Address: P.O. Box 870323, Tuscaloosa, AL 35487. **Website:** www.rolltide.com.
Head Coach: Jim Wells. **Assistant Coaches:** *Todd Butler, Jim Gatewood, B.J. Green. **Telephone:** (205) 348-4029. ■ **Baseball SID:** Barry Allen. **Telephone:** (205) 348-6084. **FAX:** (205) 348-8841.
Home Field: Sewell-Thomas Stadium. **Seating Capacity:** 6,118. **Outfield Dimensions:** LF—325, CF—400, RF—325. **Press Box Telephone:** (205) 348-4927.

ALABAMA-BIRMINGHAM Blazers
Conference: Conference USA.
Mailing Address: 1530 3rd Ave. S., Birmingham, AL 35294. **Website:** www.uabsports.com.
Head Coach: Larry Giangrosso. **Assistant Coach:** *Frank Walton. **Telephone:** (205) 934-5181. ■ **Baseball SID:** Mark Crawford. **Telephone:** (205) 934-0722. **FAX:** (205) 934-7505.

ALABAMA A&M Bulldogs
Conference: Southwestern Athletic.
Mailing Address: P.O. 1597, Normal, AL 35762. **Website:** www.aamu.edu/pr/sports/athletics.htm.
Head Coach: Thomas Wesley. **Telephone:** (256) 372-4004. ■ **Baseball SID:** Steve Underwood. **Telephone:** (256) 372-4005. **FAX:** (256) 372-5919.

ALABAMA STATE Hornets
Conference: Southwestern Athletic.
Mailing Address: 915 S. Jackson St., Montgomery, AL 36101. **Website:** www.alasu.edu/athletic/index.html
Head Coach: Larry Watkins. **Telephone:** (334) 229-4228. ■ **Baseball SID:** Albert Moore. **Telephone:** (334) 229-4511. **FAX:** (334) 229-2971.

ALBANY Great Danes
Conference: America East.
Mailing Address: P.E. 125, 1400 Washington Ave., Albany, NY 12222. **Website:** www.albany.edu/sports.
Head Coach: Jon Mueller. **Assistant Coaches:** Garrett Baron, Mark Lavenia, Matt Quatraro. **Telephone:** (518) 442-4391. ■ **Baseball SID:** Gene Brtalik. **Telephone:** (518) 442-3359. **FAX:** (518) 442-3139.

ALCORN STATE Braves
Conference: Southwestern Athletic.
Mailing Address: 1000 ASU Drive, P.O. Box 510, Alcorn State, MS 39096. **Website:** www.alcorn.edu/athletics.
Head Coach: Willie McGowan. **Assistant Coaches:**
*Marqus Johnson, Nathan Kennedy, Kevin Montgomery. **Telephone:** (601) 877-6279. ■ **Baseball SID:** Marqus Johnson. **Telephone:** (601) 877-6466. **FAX:** (601) 877-3821.

APPALACHIAN STATE Mountaineers
Conference: Southern.
Mailing Address: Owens Fieldhouse, Boone, NC 28608. **Website:** www.goasu.com.
Head Coach: Troy Huestess. **Assistant Coach:** Ski Chernisky. **Telephone:** (828) 262-6097. ■ **Baseball SID:** Kelby Siler. **Telephone:** (828) 262-2268. **FAX:** (828) 262-6106.

ARIZONA Wildcats
Conference: Pacific-10.
Mailing Address: Room 106, McKale Center, Tucson, AZ 85721. **Website:** www.arizonaathletics.com.
Head Coach: Andy Lopez. **Assistant Coach:** *Mark Wasikowski. **Telephone:** (520) 621-4102. ■ **Baseball SID:** Matt Rector. **Telephone:** (520) 621-0914. **FAX:** (520) 621-2681.
Home Field: Frank Sancet Field. **Seating Capacity:** 6,500. **Outfield Dimensions:** LF—360, CF—400, RF—360. **Press Box Telephone:** (520) 621-4440.

ARIZONA STATE Sun Devils
Conference: Pacific-10.
Mailing Address: Arizona State University, Tempe, AZ 85287. **Website:** www.thesundevils.com.
Head Coach: Pat Murphy. **Assistant Coaches:** Mike Rooney, Graham Rossini, *Jay Sferra, Chris Sinacori. **Telephone:** (480) 965-5717. ■ **Baseball SID:** Jeff Evans. **Telephone:** (480) 965-6594. **FAX:** (480) 965-5408.
Home Field: Packard Stadium/Bobby Winkles Field. **Seating Capacity:** 4,500. **Outfield Dimensions:** LF—340, CF—395, RF—340. **Press Box Telephone:** (480) 727-7253.

ARKANSAS Razorbacks
Conference: Southeastern (West).
Mailing Address: Broyles Athletic Center, Maple Street and Razorback Road, Fayetteville, AR 72701. **Website:** www.hogwired.com.
Head Coach: Dave Van Horn. **Assistant Coaches:** *Matt Deggs, Dave Jorn, Tom Pagnozzi. **Telephone:** (479) 575-3655. ■ **Baseball SID:** Bob Grant. **Telephone:** (479) 575-2751. **FAX:** (479) 575-7481.
Home Field: Baum Stadium. **Seating Capacity:** 9,477. **Outfield Dimensions:** LF—320, CF—400, RF—320. **Press Box Telephone:** (479) 575-4141.

ARKANSAS-LITTLE ROCK Trojans
Conference: Sun Belt.
Mailing Address: 2801 S. University Ave., Little Rock, AR 72204. **Website:** www.ualrtrojans.com.
Head Coach: Brian Rhees. **Assistant Coaches:** Clint Culbertson, Bobby Pierce. **Telephone:** (501) 663-8095. ■ **Baseball SID:** John Evans. **Telephone:** (501) 569-3077. **FAX:** (501) 683-7002.

ARKANSAS-PINE BLUFF Golden Lions
Conference: Southwestern Athletic.
Mailing Address: 1200 University Dr., Pine Bluff, AR 71601. **Website:** www.uapb.edu.
Head Coach: Elbert Bennett. **Assistant Coach:** *Michael Bumpers. **Telephone:** (870) 575-8938. ■ **Baseball SID:** Tamara Williams. **Telephone:** (870) 575-8675. **FAX:** (870) 543-8013.

ARKANSAS STATE Indians
Conference: Sun Belt.
Mailing Address: P.O. Box 1000, State University, AR 72467. **Website:** www.asuindians.com.
Head Coach: Keith Kessinger. **Assistant Coaches:** Brad Henderson, Brian Hicks, *Christian Ostrander. **Telephone:** (870) 972-2700. ■ **Baseball SID:** Gina Bowman. **Telephone:** (870) 972-3876. **FAX:** (870) 910-8119.

ARMY Cadets
Conference: Patriot.
Mailing Address: 639 Howard Rd., West Point, NY 10996. **Website:** www.goarmysports.com.
Head Coach: Joe Sottolano. **Assistant Coach:** Dave Borowicz, Brendan Dougherty, Fritz Hamburg. **Telephone:** (845) 938-3712. ■ **Baseball SID:** Bob Beretta. **Telephone:** (845) 938-6416. **FAX:** (845) 446-2556.

AUBURN Tigers
Conference: Southeastern (West).
Mailing Address: P.O. Box 351, Auburn, AL 36830. **Website:** www.auburntigers.com.
Head Coach: Steve Renfroe. **Assistant Coaches:** Chris Finwood, Mark Fuller. **Telephone:** (334) 844-4975. ■ **Baseball SID:** Kirk Sampson. **Telephone:** (334) 844-9803. **FAX:** (334) 844-9807.
Home Field: Hitchcock Field at Plainsman Park. **Seating Capacity:** 4,096. **Outfield Dimensions:** LF—315, CF—385, RF—331. **Press Box Telephone:** (334) 844-4138.

AUSTIN PEAY STATE Governors
Conference: Ohio Valley.
Mailing Address: P.O. Box 4515, Clarksville, TN 37044. **Website:** www.apsu.edu/letsgopeay.
Head Coach: Gary McClure. **Assistant Coaches:** Casey Callaway, *Brian Hetland, Greg Troy. **Telephone:** (931) 221-6266. ■ **Baseball SID:** Cody Bush. **Telephone:** (931) 221-7561. **FAX:** (931) 221-7562.

BALL STATE Cardinals
Conference: Mid-American.
Mailing Address: HP 128, Muncie, IN 47306. **Website:** www.ballstatesports.com.
Head Coach: Greg Beals. **Assistant Coaches:** *Clint Albert, Mike Stafford. **Telephone:** (765) 285-8226. ■ **Baseball SID:** Brad Caudill. **Telephone:** (765) 285-8242. **FAX:** (765) 285-8929.
Home Field: Ball Diamond. **Seating Capacity:** 1,700. **Outfield Dimensions:** LF—330, CF—400, RF—330. **Press Box Telephone:** (765) 285-8932.

BAYLOR Bears
Conference: Big 12.
Mailing Address: 150 Bear Run, Waco, TX 76711. **Website:** www.baylorbears.com.
Head Coach: Steve Smith. **Assistant Coaches:** Chris Berry, Steve Johnigan, *Mitch Thompson. **Telephone:** (254) 710-3029. ■ **Baseball SID:** Jeff Brown. **Telephone:** (254) 710-3065. **FAX:** (254) 710-1369.
Home Field: Ferrell Field at Baylor Ballpark. **Seating Capacity:** 5,000. **Outfield Dimensions:** LF—330, CF—400, RF—330. **Press Box Telephone:** (254) 754-5546.

BELMONT Bruins
Conference: Atlantic Sun.
Mailing Address: 1900 Belmont Blvd., Nashville, TN 37212. **Website:** www.belmont.edu/athletics.
Head Coach: Dave Jarvis. **Assistant Coaches:** Matt Barnett, Brian Schaeffer, *Jason Stein. **Telephone:** (615) 460-6166. ■ **Baseball SID:** Matt Wilson. **Telephone:** (615) 460-6698. **FAX:** (615) 460-5584.

BETHUNE-COOKMAN Wildcats
Conference: Mid-Eastern Athletic.
Mailing Address: 640 Dr. Mary McLeod Bethune Blvd., Daytona Beach, FL 32114. **Website:** www.cookman.edu/athletics/baseball.
Head Coach: Mervyl Melendez. **Assistant Coaches:** Willie Brown, *Joel Sanchez, Jose Vasquez. **Telephone:** (386) 481-2224. ■ **Baseball SID:** Opio Mashariki. **Telephone:** (386) 481-2206. **FAX:** (386) 481-2265.

BINGHAMTON Bearcats
Conference: America East.
Mailing Address: P.O. Box 6000, Binghamton, NY 13902. **Website:** athletics.binghamton.edu.
Head Coach: Tim Sinicki. **Assistant Coaches:** *Mike Collins, Tim Harkness. **Telephone:** (607) 777-2525. **Baseball SID:** John Hartrick. **Telephone:** (607) 777-6800. **FAX:** (607) 777-4597.

BIRMINGHAM-SOUTHERN Panthers
Conference: Big South.
Mailing Address: 900 Arkadelphia Rd., Birmingham, AL 35254. **Website:** www.bscsports.net.
Head Coach: Brian Shoop. **Assistant Coaches:** Brian Autry, *Bob Keller. **Telephone:** (205) 226-4797. **Baseball SID:** Will Chandler. **Telephone:** (205) 226-7736. **FAX:** (205) 226-3049.

BOSTON COLLEGE Eagles
Conference: Big East.
Mailing Address: 140 Commonwealth Ave., Chestnut Hill, MA 02467. **Website:** www.bceagles.com.
Head Coach: Pete Hughes. **Assistant Coaches:** *Mikio Aoki, Steve Englert, Mike Gambino. **Telephone:** (617) 552-1131. ■ **Baseball SID:** Kara McGillicudy. **Telephone:** (617) 552-2094. **FAX:** (617) 552-4903.
Home Field: Commander Shea Field. **Seating Capacity:** 1,500. **Outfield Dimensions:** LF—330, CF—400, RF—320. **Press Box Telephone:** None.

BOWLING GREEN STATE Falcons
Conference: Mid-American.
Mailing Address: Perry Stadium East, Bowling Green, OH 43403. **Website:** www.bgsufalcons.com.
Head Coach: Danny Schmitz. **Assistant Coaches:** *Tod Brown, Chris Hoiles, Dave Whitmire. **Telephone:** (419) 372-7065. ■ **Baseball SID:** Kris Kamann. **Telephone:** (419) 372-7077. **FAX:** (419) 372-6015.

BRADLEY Braves
Conference: Missouri Valley.
Mailing Address: 1501 W. Bradley Ave., Peoria, IL 61625. **Website:** www.bubraves.com.
Head Coach: Dewey Kalmer. **Assistant Coaches:** Mike Dunne, *Perry Roth. **Telephone:** (309) 677-2684. ■ **Baseball SID:** Bobby Parker. **Telephone:** (309) 677-2624. **FAX:** (309) 677-2626.

BRIGHAM YOUNG Cougars
Conference: Mountain West.
Mailing Address: 30 SFH, Provo, UT 84602. **Website:** www.byucougars.com.
Head Coach: Vance Law. **Assistant Coach:** *Ryan Roberts. **Telephone:** (801) 378-5049. ■ **Baseball SID:** Ralph Zobell. **Telephone:** (801) 422-9769. **FAX:** (801) 422-0633.
Home Field: Larry Miller Field. **Seating Capacity:** 2,204. **Outfield Dimensions:** LF—345, CF—400, RF—345. **Press Box Telephone:** (801) 378-4041.

BROWN Bears
Conference: Ivy League (Rolfe).
Mailing Address: 235 Hope St., Providence, RI

02912. **Website:** www.brownbears.com.
Head Coach: *Marek Drabinski. **Assistant Coach:** Raphael Cerrato, Jim Foster. **Telephone:** (401) 863-3090. ■ **Baseball SID:** Kristen DiCharo. **Telephone:** (401) 863-2219. **FAX:** (401) 863-1436.

BUCKNELL Bison
Conference: Patriot.
Mailing Address: Davis Gym, Lewisburg, PA 17837. **Website:** www.bucknellbison.com.
Head Coach: Gene Depew. **Assistant Coaches:** *R.J. Grant, Brian Hoyt. **Telephone:** (570) 577-3593. ■ **Baseball SID:** Andrew Borders. **Telephone:** (570) 577-3068. **FAX:** (570) 577-1660.

BUFFALO Bulls
Conference: Mid-American.
Mailing Address: 102 Alumni Arena, Buffalo, NY 14260. **Website:** www.buffalobulls.com.
Head Coach: Bill Breene. **Assistant Coaches:** Dave Borsuk, *Ron Torgalski. **Telephone:** (716) 645-6808. ■ **Baseball SID:** Jon Fuller. **Telephone:** (716) 645-6311. **FAX:** (716) 645-6840.

BUTLER Bulldogs
Conference: Horizon.
Mailing Address: 510 W. 49th St., Indianapolis, IN 46208. **Website:** www.butlersports.com.
Head Coach: Steve Farley. **Assistant Coach:** Bob Keeney, Luke Murphy. **Telephone:** (317) 940-9721. ■ **Baseball SID:** Jim McGrath. **Telephone:** (317) 940-9414. **FAX:** (317) 940-9808.

CALIFORNIA Golden Bears
Conference: Pacific-10.
Mailing Address: 210 Memorial Stadium, Berkeley, CA 94720. **Website:** www.calbears.com.
Head Coach: David Esquer. **Assistant Coaches:** *Dan Hubbs, Matt Priess, Ron Witmeyer. **Telephone:** (510) 643-6006. ■ **Baseball SID:** Scott Ball. **Telephone:** (510) 643-1741. **FAX:** (510) 643-7778.
Home Field: Evans Diamond. **Seating Capacity:** 2,500. **Outfield Dimensions:** LF—320, CF—395, RF—320. **Press Box Telephone:** (510) 642-3098.

UCLA Bruins
Conference: Pacific-10.
Mailing Address: P.O. Box 24044, Los Angeles, CA 90024. **Website:** www.uclabruins.com.
Head Coach: Gary Adams. **Assistant Coaches:** *Vince Beringhele, Tim Leary, John Violette **Telephone:** (310) 794-8210. ■ **Baseball SID:** Neila Matheny. **Telephone:** (310) 206-4008. **FAX:** (310) 825-8664.
Home Field: Jackie Robinson Stadium. **Seating Capacity:** 1,250. **Outfield Dimensions:** LF—330, CF—390, RF—330. **Press Box Telephone:** (310) 794-8213.

UC IRVINE Anteaters
Conference: Big West.
Mailing Address: 1394 Crawford Hall, Irvine, CA 92697. **Website:** www.athletics.uci.edu.
Head Coach: *John Savage. **Assistant Coaches:** Jason Gill, Matt Jones, Pat Shine. **Telephone:** (949) 824-4292. ■ **Baseball SID:** Fumi Kimura. **Telephone:** (949) 824-9474. **FAX:** (949) 824-5260.
Home Field: Anteater Stadium. **Seating Capacity:** 3,200. **Outfield Dimensions:** LF—335, CF—405, RF—335. **Press Box Telephone:** (949) 824-9905.

UC RIVERSIDE Highlanders
Conference: Big West.
Mailing Address: 900 University Ave., Riverside, CA 92521. **Website:** www.athletics.ucr.edu.

Head Coach: Jack Smitheran **Assistant Coach:** Andrew Checketts, *Doug Smith, Estavan Valencia. **Telephone:** (909) 787-5441. ■ **Baseball SID:** Brian Blank. **Telephone:** (909) 787-5438. **FAX:** (909) 787-5889.
Home Field: Riverside Sports Complex. **Seating Capacity:** 2,500. **Outfield Dimensions:** LF—330, CF—400, RF—330. **Press Box Telephone:** (909) 787-6415.

UC SANTA BARBARA Gauchos
Conference: Big West.
Mailing Address: Robertson Gym, Santa Barbara, CA 93106. **Website:** www.ucsbgauchos.com.
Head Coach: Bob Brontsema. **Assistant Coach:** *Dan Ricabal, Bob Townsend. **Telephone:** (805) 893-3690. ■ **Baseball SID:** Bryan DeSena. **Telephone:** (805) 893-3428. **FAX:** (805) 893-4537.
Home Field: Caesar Uyesaka Stadium. **Seating Capacity:** 1,000. **Outfield Dimensions:** LF—335, CF—400, RF—335. **Press Box Telephone:** (805) 893-4671.

CAL POLY Mustangs
Conference: Big West.
Mailing Address: One Grand Ave., San Luis Obispo, CA 93407. **Website:** www.gopoly.com.
Head Coach: Larry Lee. **Assistant Coaches:** Jarek Krukow, Jerry Weinstein, *Jesse Zepeda. **Telephone:** (805) 756-6367. ■ **Baseball SID:** Eric Burdick. **Telephone:** (805) 756-6550. **FAX:** (805) 756-2650.
Home Field: Robin Baggett Stadium. **Seating Capacity:** 1,534. **Outfield Dimensions:** LF—335, CF—405, RF—335. **Press Box Telephone:** (805) 756-7456.

CAL STATE FULLERTON Titans
Conference: Big West.
Mailing Address: 800 N. State College Blvd., Fullerton, CA 92834. **Website:** www.titansports.org.
Head Coach: George Horton. **Assistant Coaches:** Chad Baum, *Dave Serrano, Rick Vanderhook. **Telephone:** (714) 278-3780. ■ **Baseball SID:** Ryan Ermeling. **Telephone:** (714) 278-3081. **FAX:** (714) 278-3141.
Home Field: Goodwin Field. **Seating Capacity:** 3,500. **Outfield Dimensions:** LF—330, CF—400, RF—330. **Press Box Telephone:** (714) 278-5327.

CAL STATE NORTHRIDGE Matadors
Conference: Big West.
Mailing Address: 18111 Nordhoff St., Northridge, CA 91330. **Website:** www.gomatadors.com.
Head Coach: Steve Rousey. **Assistant Coaches:** *Grant Hohman, Mark Kertenian, Rob McKinley. **Telephone:** (818) 677-7055. ■ **Baseball SID:** Tony La Torra. **Telephone:** (818) 677-3243. **FAX:** (818) 677-4950.
Home Field: Matador Field. **Seating Capacity:** 1,200. **Outfield Dimensions:** LF—325, CF—400, RF—330. **Press Box Telephone:** (818) 677-4239.

CAMPBELL Fighting Camels
Conference: Atlantic Sun.
Mailing Address: P.O. Box 10, Buies Creek, NC 27506. **Website:** www.gocamels.com.
Head Coach: Chip Smith. **Assistant Coaches:** *Jeff Bock, Kent Cox. **Telephone:** (910) 893-1354. ■ **Baseball SID:** Chris Kilcoyne. **Telephone:** (910) 814-4367. **FAX:** (910) 893-1330.

CANISIUS Golden Griffins
Conference: Metro Atlantic.
Mailing Address: 2001 Main St., Buffalo, NY 14208. **Website:** www.gogriffs.com.
Head Coach: *Mark Notaro. **Assistant Coaches:** Don Bell, Tim Smith. **Telephone:** (716) 888-3251. ■ **Baseball SID:** Marc Gignac. **Telephone:** (716) 888-2978.

FAX: (716) 888-3178.

CENTENARY Gents

Conference: Mid-Continent.

Mailing Address: 2911 Centenary Blvd., Shreveport, LA 71134. **Website**: www.centenary.edu/athletics.

Head Coach: Ed McCann. **Assistant Coaches**: *Ben Adams, Jeremy Cantrell, Zach Cazzelle. **Telephone**: (318) 869-5298. ■ **Baseball SID**: David Pratt. **Telephone**: (318) 869-5092. **FAX**: (318) 869-5128.

CENTRAL CONNECTICUT STATE Blue Devils

Conference: Northeast.

Mailing Address: 1615 Stanley St., New Britain, CT 06050. **Website**: www.ccsubluedevils.com.

Head Coach: Charlie Hickey. **Assistant Coaches**: *Paul LaBella, Jim Ziogas. **Telephone**: (860) 832-3074. ■ **Baseball SID**: Tom Pincince. **Telephone**: (860) 832-3089. **FAX**: (860) 832-3084.

CENTRAL FLORIDA Golden Knights

Conference: Atlantic Sun.

Mailing Address: 4000 Central Florida Blvd., Orlando, FL 32816. **Website**: www.ucfathletics.com.

Head Coach: Jay Bergman. **Assistant Coaches**: *Craig Cozart, Derek Wolfe. **Telephone**: (407) 823-0140. ■ **Baseball SID**: Jason Baum. **Telephone**: (407) 823-0994. **FAX**: (407) 823-5266.

Home Field: Jay Bergman Field. **Seating Capacity**: 1,980. **Outfield Dimensions**: LF—375, CF—400, RF—375. **Press Box Telephone**: (407) 823-4487.

CENTRAL MICHIGAN Chippewas

Conference: Mid-American (West).

Mailing Address: 100 Rose Arena, Mount Pleasant, MI 48859. **Website**: www.cmuchippewas.com.

Head Coach: Steve Jaksa. **Assistant Coaches**: Brad Strohmdal, *Mike Villano. **Telephone**: (989) 774-4392. ■ **Baseball SID**: Fred Stabley. **Telephone**: (989) 774-3277. **FAX**: (989) 774-7324.

CHARLESTON Cougars

Conference: Southern.

Mailing Address: 30 George St., Charleston, SC 29424. **Website**: www.cougars.cofc.edu.

Head Coach: John Pawlowski. **Assistant Coaches**: *Scott Foxhall, Rob Reinstetle, Seth Von Behren. **Telephone**: (843) 953-5916. ■ **Baseball SID**: Tony Ciuffo. **Telephone**: (843) 953-953-5465. **FAX**: (843) 953-6534.

Home Field: Patriots Point Stadium. **Seating Capacity**: 2,000. **Outfield Dimensions**: LF—300, CF—405, RF—330. **Press Box Telephone**: (843) 953-9141.

CHARLESTON SOUTHERN Buccaneers

Conference: Big South.

Mailing Address: P.O. Box 118087, Charleston, SC 29423. **Website**: www.csusports.com.

Head Coach: Gary Murphy. **Telephone**: (843) 863-7591. ■ **Baseball SID**: David Shelton. **Telephone**: (843) 863-7688. **FAX**: (843) 863-7676.

CHARLOTTE 49ers

Conference: Conference USA.

Mailing Address: 9201 University City Blvd., Charlotte, NC 28223. **Website**: www.charlotte49ers.com.

Head Coach: *Loren Hibbs. **Assistant Coaches**: Bo Durkac, *Brandon Hall. **Telephone**: (704) 687-3935. ■ **Baseball SID**: Brent Stastny. **Telephone**: (704) 687-6313. **FAX**: (704) 687-4918.

Home Field: Tom and Lib Phillips Field. **Seating Capacity**: 2,000. **Outfield Dimensions**: LF—335, CF—390, RF—335. **Press Box Telephone**: (704) 687-3148.

CHICAGO STATE Cougars

Conference: Mid-Continent.

Mailing Address: 9501 S. King Dr., Chicago, IL 60628. **Website**: www.csu.edu/athletics.

Head Coach: Terrence Jackson. **Assistant Coaches**: *Dennis Bonebreak, Jose Ramirez, Dan Soria. **Telephone**: (773) 995-3659. ■ **Baseball SID**: Ben Greenberg. **Telephone**: (773) 995-2217. **FAX**: (773) 995-3656.

CINCINNATI Bearcats

Conference: Conference USA.

Mailing Address: One Edwards Center, Suite 1110, Cincinnati, OH 45221. **Website**: www.ucbearcats.com.

Head Coach: Brian Cleary. **Assistant Coaches**: *Brad Meador, Ty Neal, Bill Thistlethwaite. **Telephone**: (513) 556-0566. ■ **Baseball SID**: Shawn Sell. **Telephone**: (513) 556-0618. **FAX**: (513) 556-0619.

THE CITADEL Bulldogs

Conference: Southern.

Mailing Address: McAlister Field House, Charleston, SC 29407. **Website**: www.citadelsports.com.

Head Coach: Fred Jordan. **Assistant Coaches**: David Beckley, David Griffin, *Chris Lemonis. **Telephone**: (843) 953-5901. ■ **Baseball SID**: Kevin Rhodes. **Telephone**: (843) 953-5120. **FAX**: (843) 953-5058.

Home Field: Joseph P. Riley Park. **Seating Capacity**: 6,000. **Outfield Dimensions**: LF—305, CF—398, RF—337. **Press Box Telephone**: (843) 965-4151.

CLEMSON Tigers

Conference: Atlantic Coast.

Mailing Address: P.O. Box 31, 100 Perimeter Rd., Clemson, SC 29633. **Website**: www.clemsontigers.com.

Head Coach: Jack Leggett. **Assistant Coaches**: Bradley LeCroy, *Kevin O'Sullivan, Tom Riginos. **Telephone**: (864) 656-1940. ■ **Baseball SID**: Brian Hennessy. **Telephone**: (864) 656-1921. **FAX**: (864) 656-0299.

Home Field: Doug Kingsmore Stadium. **Seating Capacity**: 5,000. **Outfield Dimensions**: LF—320, CF—400, RF—330. **Press Box Telephone**: (864) 656-7731.

CLEVELAND STATE Vikings

Conference: Horizon.

Mailing Address: 2000 Prospect Ave., Cleveland, OH 44115. **Website**: www.csuvikings.com.

Head Coach: Jay Murphy. **Assistant Coaches**: Brian Donohew, Dave Sprochi. **Telephone**: (216) 687-4822. ■ **Baseball SID**: Kevin Zeise. **Telephone**: (216) 687-4818. **FAX**: (216) 523-7257.

COASTAL CAROLINA Chanticleers

Conference: Big South.

Mailing Address: 132 Chanticleer Drive Way, Room 103, Conway, SC 29528. **Website**: www.coastal.edu/athletics.

Head Coach: Gary Gilmore. **Assistant Coaches**: Clint Ayers, *Bill Jarman, Kevin Schnall. **Telephone**: (843) 349-2816. ■ **Baseball SID**: Kurt Reichert. **Telephone**: (843) 349-2840. **FAX**: (843) 349-2819.

Home Field: Watson Stadium. **Seating Capacity**: 2,000. **Outfield Dimensions**: LF—320, CF—390, RF—320. **Press Box Telephone**: (843) 234-3476.

COLUMBIA Lions

Conference: Ivy League (Gehrig).

Mailing Address: 3030 Broadway, M.C. 1910, New York, NY 10027. **Website**: www.gocolumbialions.com.

Head Coach: Paul Fernandes. **Assistant Coaches**: *Bryan Haley, Bob Koehler, Grisha Pavida. **Telephone**: (212) 854-2543. ■ **Baseball SID**: Darlene Camacho. **Telephone**: (212) 854-2535. **FAX**: (212) 854-8118.

CONNECTICUT Huskies

Conference: Big East.
Mailing Address: 2095 Hillside Road, Storrs, CT 06269. **Website:** www.uconnhuskies.com.
Head Coach: Jim Penders. **Assistant Coaches:** Chris Podeszwa, *Dave Turgeon. **Telephone:** (860) 486-4089. ■ **Baseball SID:** Patrick McKenna. **Telephone:** (860) 486-3531. **FAX:** (860) 486-5085.
Home Field: J.O. Christian Field. **Seating Capacity:** 2,000. **Outfield Dimensions:** LF—340, CF—405, RF—340. **Press Box Telephone:** (860) 486-2018.

COPPIN STATE Eagles

Conference: Mid-Eastern Athletic.
Mailing Address: 2500 W. North Ave., Baltimore, MD 21216. **Website:** www.coppin.edu/athletics.
Head Coach: *Guy Robertson. **Assistant Coaches:** Ruffin Bell, Peter Buck, Patrick Rosko. **Telephone:** (410) 951-3740. ■ **Baseball SID:** Kevin Paige. **Telephone:** (410) 951-3729. **FAX:** (410) 951-3717.

CORNELL Big Red

Conference: Ivy League (Rolfe).
Mailing Address: Teagle Hall, Campus Road, Ithaca, NY 14853. **Website:** www.cornellbigred.com.
Head Coach: Tom Ford. **Assistant Coaches:** Scott Marsh, Bill Walkenbach. **Telephone:** (607) 255-6604. ■ **Baseball SID:** Laura Stange. **Telephone:** (607) 255-5627. **FAX:** (607) 255-9791.

CREIGHTON Blue Jays

Conference: Missouri Valley.
Mailing Address: 2500 California Plaza, Omaha, NE 68178. **Website:** www.gocreighton.com.
Head Coach: Ed Servais. **Assistant Coaches:** Mike Bahun, Dan Heefner, *Travis Wyckoff. **Telephone:** (402) 280-2483. ■ **Baseball SID:** Matt Beltz. **Telephone:** (402) 280-5801. **FAX:** (402) 280-2495.
Home Field: Creighton Sports Complex. **Seating Capacity:** 1,000. **Outfield Dimensions:** LF—332, CF—402, RF—332. **Press Box Telephone:** (402) 280-2787.

DARTMOUTH Big Green

Conference: Ivy League (Rolfe).
Mailing Address: 6083 Alumni Gym, Hanover, NH 03755. **Website:** athletics.dartmouth.edu.
Head Coach: Bob Whalen. **Assistant Coach:** *Tony Baldwin, Brian Bishop. **Telephone:** (603) 646-2477. ■ **Baseball SID:** Matt Dougherty. **Telephone:** (603) 646-0424. **FAX:** (603) 646-3348.

DAVIDSON Wildcats

Conference: Southern.
Mailing Address: P.O. Box 7158, Davidson, NC 28035. **Website:** www.davidson.edu.
Head Coach: Dick Cooke. **Assistant Coaches:** Mike McAlpin, Chris Moore, *Andrew Riepe. **Telephone:** (704) 894-2368. ■ **Baseball SID:** Rick Bender. **Telephone:** (704) 894-2123. **FAX:** (704) 894-2636.

DAYTON Flyers

Conference: Atlantic-10 (West).
Mailing Address: 300 College Park, Dayton, OH 45469. **Website:** www.daytonflyers.com.
Head Coach: *Tony Vittorio. **Assistant Coaches:** Terry Bell, Jason Frazier, Todd Linklater. **Telephone:** (937) 229-4456. ■ **Baseball SID:** John Popelar. **Telephone:** (937) 229-4460. **FAX:** (937) 229-4461.

DELAWARE Fightin' Blue Hens

Conference: Colonial Athletic.
Mailing Address: Bob Carpenter Center, Newark, DE 19716. **Website:** www.udel.edu/sportsinfo

Head Coach: Jim Sherman. **Assistant Coaches:** Casey Fahy, Dan Hammer, *Greg Mamula. **Telephone:** (302) 831-8596. ■ **Baseball SID:** Pete DiVito. **Telephone:** (302) 831-2186. **FAX:** (302) 831-8653.

DELAWARE STATE Hornets

Conference: Mid-Eastern Athletic.
Mailing Address: 1200 N. DuPont Hwy., Dover, DE 19901. **Website:** www.dsc.edu/athletics.
Head Coach: J.P. Blandin. **Assistant Coaches:** Michael August, *Sean Moran, Mike O'Dea. **Telephone:** (302) 857-6035. ■ **Baseball SID:** Dennis Jones. **Telephone:** (302) 857-6065. **FAX:** (302) 857-6069.

DETROIT Titans

Conference: Horizon.
Mailing Address: P.O. Box 19900, Detroit, MI 48219. **Website:** www.detroittitans.com.
Head Coach: Chris Czarnik. **Assistant Coaches:** Juston Davenport, Stu Rose, *Mark Van Ameyde, Al Willett. **Telephone:** (313) 993-1725. ■ **Baseball SID:** Sean Palchick. **Telephone:** (313) 993-1745. **FAX:** (313) 993-1765.

DUKE Blue Devils

Conference: Atlantic Coast.
Mailing Address: P.O. Box 90555, Durham, NC 27708. **Website:** www.goduke.com.
Head Coach: Bill Hillier. **Assistant Coaches:** *Bill Hillier Jr., Jon Smith, *John Yurkow. **Telephone:** (919) 684-2358. ■ **Baseball SID:** Melanie McCullough. **Telephone:** (919) 684-2668. **FAX:** (919) 684-2489.
Home Field: Jack Coombs Stadium. **Seating Capacity:** 2,000. **Outfield Dimensions:** LF—330, CF—400, RF—330. **Press Box Telephone:** Unavailable.

DUQUESNE Dukes

Conference: Atlantic-10 (West).
Mailing Address: A.J. Palumbo Center, 600 Forbes Ave., Pittsburgh, PA 15282. **Website:** www.goduquesne.com.
Head Coach: Mike Wilson. **Assistant Coach:** Will Swisher. **Telephone:** (412) 396-5245. ■ **Baseball SID:** George Nieman. **Telephone:** (412) 396-5376. **FAX:** (412) 396-6210.

EAST CAROLINA Pirates

Conference: Conference USA.
Mailing Address: 117 Scales Field House, Greenville, NC 27858. **Website:** www.ecupirates.com.
Head Coach: Randy Mazey. **Assistant Coaches:** Tommy Eason, *Allen Osborne, Nick Schnabel. **Telephone:** (252) 328-1981. ■ **Baseball SID:** Jody Jones. **Telephone:** (252) 328-4523. **FAX:** (252) 328-4528.
Home Field: Harrington Field. **Seating Capacity:** 2,500. **Outfield Dimensions:** LF—325, CF—390, RF—325. **Press Box Telephone:** (252) 328-0068.

EAST TENNESSEE STATE Buccaneers

Conference: Southern.
Mailing Address: P.O. Box 70707, Johnson City, TN 37614. **Website:** www.etsubucs.com.
Head Coach: Tony Skole. **Assistant Coach:** *Nate Goulet. **Telephone:** (423) 439-4496. ■ **Baseball SID:** Matt Snellings. **Telephone:** (423) 439-5263. **FAX:** (423) 439-6138.

EASTERN ILLINOIS Panthers

Conference: Ohio Valley.
Mailing Address: 600 W. Lincoln, Charleston, IL 61920. **Website:** www.eiu.edu/panthers.
Head Coach: Jim Schmitz. **Assistant Coach:** Chris Martin, *Mitch Rosenthal. **Telephone:** (217) 581-2522.

■ **Baseball SID:** Patrick Osterman. **Telephone:** (217) 581-7020. **FAX:** (217) 581-6434.

EASTERN KENTUCKY Colonels
Conference: Ohio Valley.
Mailing Address: Alumni Coliseum, Room 115, Richmond, KY 40475. **Website:** www.ekusports.com.
Head Coach: Elvis Dominguez. **Assistant Coach:** *John Corbin, Brad Husz. **Telephone:** (859) 622-2128.
■ **Baseball SID:** Amy Ratliff. **Telephone:** (859) 622-2006. **FAX:** (859) 622-1230.

EASTERN MICHIGAN Eagles
Conference: Mid-American.
Mailing Address: 799 Hewitt Road, Convocation Center, Ypsilanti, MI 48197. **Website:** www.emich.edu/goeagles.
Head Coach: Roger Coryell. **Assistant Coach:** *Jake Boss. **Telephone:** (734) 487-0315. ■ **Baseball SID:** Bernadette Vielhaber. **Telephone:** (734) 487-0317. **FAX:** (734) 485-3840.
Home Field: Oestrike Stadium. **Seating Capacity:** 2,500. **Outfield Dimensions:** LF—330, CF—390, RF—330. **Press Box Telephone:** (734) 481-9328.

ELON Phoenix
Conference: Southern.
Mailing Address: Elon College, 2500 Campus Box, NC 27244. **Website:** www.elon.edu/athletics.
Head Coach: Mike Kennedy. **Assistant Coaches:** *Austin Alexander, Robbie Huffstettler, Greg Starbuck. **Telephone:** (336) 278-6741. ■ **Baseball SID:** Chris Rash. **Telephone:** (336) 278-6712. **FAX:** (336) 278-6768.
Home Field: Latham Park. **Seating Capacity:** 500. **Outfield Dimensions:** LF—317, CF—385, RF—327. **Press Box Telephone:** (336) 278-6788.

EVANSVILLE Purple Aces
Conference: Missouri Valley.
Mailing Address: 1800 Lincoln Ave., Evansville, IN 47722. **Website:** www.gopurpleaces.com.
Head Coach: Dave Schrage. **Assistant Coaches:** Tyler Herbst, Kevin Koch, *Scott Lawler. **Telephone:** (812) 479-2059. ■ **Baseball SID:** Tom Benson. **Telephone:** (812) 488-1152. **FAX:** (812) 479-2090.
Home Field: Braun Stadium. **Seating Capacity:** 1,200. **Outfield Dimensions:** LF—330, CF—400, RF—330. **Press Box Telephone:** (812) 479-2587.

FAIRFIELD Stags
Conference: Metro Atlantic.
Mailing Address: 1073 N. Benson Rd., Fairfield, CT 06430. **Website:** www.fairfieldstags.com.
Head Coach: John Slosar. **Assistant Coach:** Bill Consiglio, Dennis Whalen. **Telephone:** (203) 254-4000. ■ **Baseball SID:** Patrick Moran. **Telephone:** (203) 254-4000. **FAX:** (203) 254-4117.

FAIRLEIGH DICKINSON Knights
Conference: Northeast.
Mailing Address: 1000 River Rd., Teaneck, NJ 07666. **Website:** www.fduknights.com.
Head Coach: Dennis Sasso. **Assistant Coaches:** Don Hahn, John Kroeger. **Telephone:** (201) 692-2245. ■ **Baseball SID:** Drew Brown. **Telephone:** (201) 692-2204. **FAX:** (201) 692-9361.

FLORIDA Gators
Conference: Southeastern (East).
Mailing Address: P.O. Box 14485, Gainesville, FL 32604. **Website:** www.gatorzone.com.
Head Coach: Pat McMahon. **Assistant Coaches:** Tom Slater, Brian Fleetwood, *Ross Jones. **Telephone:** (352) 375-4683. ■ **Baseball SID:** Brian Dietz. **Telephone:**

(352) 375-4683. **FAX:** (352) 375-4809.
Home Field: McKethan Stadium. **Seating Capacity:** 5,000. **Outfield Dimensions:** LF—330, CF—400, RF—325. **Press Box Telephone:** (352) 375-4683.

FLORIDA A&M Rattlers
Conference: Mid-Eastern Athletic.
Mailing Address: 1500 Wahnish Way, Tallahassee, FL 32307. **Website:** www.famu.edu/athletics.
Head Coach: Joe Durant. **Assistant Coach:** K.C. Carter, *Brett Richardson. **Telephone:** (850) 599-3202.
■ **Baseball SID:** Brett Richardson. **Telephone:** (850) 599-3200. **FAX:** (850) 599-3206.

FLORIDA ATLANTIC Blue Wave
Conference: Atlantic Sun.
Mailing Address: 777 Glades Rd., Boca Raton, FL 33431. **Website:** www.fausports.com.
Head Coach: Kevin Cooney. **Assistant Coaches:** *John McCormack, George Roig. **Telephone:** (561) 297-3956. ■ **Baseball SID:** Dawn Elston. **Telephone:** (561) 297-3513. **FAX:** (561) 297-3499.
Home Field: FAU Field. **Seating Capacity:** 2,500. **Dimensions:** LF—330, CF—400, RF—330. **Press Box Telephone:** (561) 297-3455.

FLORIDA INTERNATIONAL Golden Panthers
Conference: Sun Belt.
Mailing Address: 11200 SW Eighth St., Miami, FL 33199. **Website:** www.fiusports.com.
Head Coach: Danny Price. **Assistant Coaches:** *Marc Calvi, Tony Casas, Chris Holick. **Telephone:** (305) 348-3166. ■ **Baseball SID:** Danny Kambel. **Telephone:** (305) 348-2084. **FAX:** (305) 348-2963.
Home Field: University Park. **Seating Capacity:** 2,000. **Outfield Dimensions:** LF—325, CF—400, RF—325. **Press Box Telephone:** (812) 243-6429.

FLORIDA STATE Seminoles
Conference: Atlantic Coast.
Mailing Address: P.O. Box 2195, Tallahassee, FL 32316. **Website:** www.seminoles.com.
Head Coach: Mike Martin. **Assistant Coaches:** Mike Martin Jr., *Jamey Shouppe. **Telephone:** (850) 644-1073. ■ **Baseball SID:** Jeff Purinton. **Telephone:** (850) 644-0615. **FAX:** (850) 644-3820.
Home Field: Dick Howser Stadium. **Seating Capacity:** 6,000. **Outfield Dimensions:** LF—340, CF—400, RF—320. **Press Box Telephone:** (850) 644-1553.

FORDHAM Rams
Conference: Atlantic-10 (East).
Mailing Address: 441 E. Fordham Rd., Bronx, NY 10458. **Website:** www.fordhamsports.com.
Head Coach: Dan Gallagher. **Assistant Coaches:** Bob Caputo, *Nick Restaino, Jim Shevlin. **Telephone:** (718) 817-2178. ■ **Baseball SID:** Scott Kwiatkowski. **Telephone:** (718) 817-2509. **FAX:** (718) 817-4244.

FRESNO STATE Bulldogs
Conference: Western Athletic.
Mailing Address: 5305 N. Campus Dr., Room 153, Fresno, CA 93740. **Website:** www.gobulldogs.com.
Head Coach: Mike Batesole. **Assistant Coaches:** Matt Curtis, *Tim Montez, Chad Thornhill. **Telephone:** (559) 278-2509. ■ **Baseball SID:** Darren Moradian. **Telephone:** (559) 278-6187. **FAX:** (559) 278-4689.
Home Field: Beiden Field. **Seating Capacity:** 6,575. **Outfield Dimensions:** LF—330, CF—400, RF—330. **Press Box Telephone:** (559) 278-7678.

FURMAN Paladins
Conference: Southern.
Mailing Address: 3300 Poinsett Hwy., Greenville, SC 29613. **Website:** www.furmanpaladins.com.
Head Coach: Ron Smith. **Assistant Coaches:** Jon Placko, Rockie Pittman. **Telephone:** (864) 294-2146. ■ **Baseball SID:** Robby Campbell. **Telephone:** (864) 294-3062. **FAX:** (864) 294-3061.

GARDNER-WEBB Runnin' Bulldogs
Conference: Atlantic Sun.
Mailing Address: P.O. Box 7237, Boiling Springs, NC 28017. **Website:** www.gwusports.com.
Head Coach: Rusty Stroupe. **Assistant Coaches:** Todd Interdonato, *Dan Roszel, Robbie Wilson. **Telephone:** (704) 406-4421. ■ **Baseball SID:** Marc Rabb. **Telephone:** (704) 406-4355. **FAX:** (704) 406-4739.

GEORGE MASON Patriots
Conference: Colonial Athletic.
Mailing Address: MSN 3A5, 4400 University Dr., Fairfax, VA 22030. **Website:** www.gmusports.com.
Head Coach: Bill Brown. **Assistant Coach:** *Shawn Stiffler. **Telephone:** (703) 993-3282. ■ **Baseball SID:** Ben Trittipoe. **Telephone:** (703) 993-3260. **FAX:** (703) 993-3259.

GEORGE WASHINGTON Colonials
Conference: Atlantic-10 (West).
Mailing Address: 600 22nd St. NW, Washington, DC 20037. **Website:** www.gwsports.com.
Head Coach: Tom Walter. **Assistant Coaches:** Chris Ebrahimoff, *Dennis Healy, Tag Montague. **Telephone:** (202) 994-7399. ■ **Baseball SID:** Lars Thorn. **Telephone:** (202) 994-0339. **FAX:** (202) 994-2713.
Home Field: Barcroft Field. **Seating Capacity:** 500. **Outfield Dimensions:** LF—325, CF—370, RF—325. **Press Box Telephone:** (703) 671-2151.

GEORGETOWN Hoyas
Conference: Big East.
Mailing Address: McDonough Arena, 37th & O Streets NW, Washington, DC 20057. **Website:** www.guhoyas.com.
Head Coach: Pete Wilk. **Assistant Coaches:** Steve Alhona, *Doc Beeman. **Telephone:** (202) 687-2462. ■ **Baseball SID:** Scott Homas. **Telephone:** (202) 687-5214. **FAX:** (202) 687-2491.
Home Field: Shirley Povich Field. **Seating Capacity:** 1,500. **Outfield Dimensions:** LF—330, CF—375, RF—330. **Press Box Telephone:** None.

GEORGIA Bulldogs
Conference: Southeastern (East).
Mailing Address: P.O. Box 1472, Athens, GA 30603. **Website:** www.georgiadogs.com.
Head Coach: David Perno. **Assistant Coaches:** Jason Eller, Don Norris, *Butch Thompson. **Telephone:** (706) 542-7971. ■ **Baseball SID:** Christopher Lakos. **Telephone:** (706) 542-1621. **FAX:** (706) 542-7993.
Home Field: Foley Field. **Seating Capacity:** 3,291. **Outfield Dimensions:** LF—350, CF—410, RF—320. **Press Box Telephone:** (706) 542-6161.

GEORGIA SOUTHERN Eagles
Conference: Southern.
Mailing Address: P.O. Box 8085, Statesboro, GA 30460. **Website:** www.georgiasoutherneagles.com.
Head Coach: Rodney Hennon. **Assistant Coaches:** Brett Lewis, *Mike Tidick. **Telephone:** (912) 486-7360. ■ **Baseball SID:** Shawn Reed. **Telephone:** (912) 681-5288. **FAX:** (912) 681-0046.
Home Field: J.I. Clements Stadium. **Seating**

Capacity: 2,000. **Outfield Dimensions:** LF—330, CF—380, RF—330. **Press Box Telephone:** (912) 681-2508.

GEORGIA STATE Panthers
Conference: Atlantic Sun.
Mailing Address: 125 Decatur St., Suite 201, Atlanta, GA 30303. **Website:** www.georgiasports.com.
Head Coach: Mike Hurst. **Assistant Coaches:** *David Hartley, Josh Hopper, Shane West. **Telephone:** (404) 244-5804. ■ **Baseball SID:** Brett Bahnsen. **Telephone:** (404) 651-4629. **FAX:** (404) 651-0842.

GEORGIA TECH Yellow Jackets
Conference: Atlantic Coast.
Mailing Address: 150 Bobby Dodd Way, Atlanta, GA 30332. **Website:** www.ramblinwreck.com.
Head Coach: Danny Hall. **Assistant Coaches:** Bobby Moranda, Jon Palmieri, *Scott Stricklin. **Telephone:** (404) 894-5471. ■ **Baseball SID:** Chris Capo. **Telephone:** (404) 894-5445. **FAX:** (404) 894-1248.
Home Field: Russ Chandler Stadium. **Seating Capacity:** 4,157. **Outfield Dimensions:** LF—328, CF—400, RF—334. **Press Box Telephone:** (404) 894-3167.

GONZAGA Bulldogs
Conference: West Coast.
Mailing Address: 502 E. Boone Ave., Spokane, WA 99258. **Website:** www.gozags.com.
Head Coach: *Mark Machtolf. **Assistant Coaches:** Scott Asan, Danny Evans, Chris Sheehan. **Telephone:** (509) 323-4226. ■ **Baseball SID:** Rich Moser. **Telephone:** (509) 323-5484. **FAX:** (509) 323-5730.
Home Field: Avista Stadium. **Seating Capacity:** 7,800. **Outfield Dimensions:** LF—330, CF—400, RF—330. **Press Box Telephone:** Unavailable.

GRAMBLING STATE Tigers
Conference: Southwestern Athletic.
Mailing Address: P.O. Box 868, Grambling, LA 71245. **Website:** www.gram.edu.
Head Coach (interim): James Randall. **Telephone:** (318) 274-6121. ■ **Baseball SID:** Roderick Mosley. **Telephone:** (318) 274-6265. **FAX:** (318) 274-2761.

HARTFORD Hawks
Conference: America East.
Mailing Address: 200 Bloomfield Ave., West Hartford, CT 06117. **Website:** www.hartfordhawks.com.
Head Coach: Harvey Shapiro. **Assistant Coaches:** Al Furrow, Mike Susi. **Telephone:** (860) 768-4656. ■ **Baseball SID:** Mike Vigneux. **Telephone:** (860) 768-4656. **FAX:** (860) 768-5047.

HARVARD Crimson
Conference: Ivy League (Rolfe).
Mailing Address: Murr Center, 65 N. Harvard St., Boston, MA 02163. **Website:** www.gocrimson.com.
Head Coach: Joe Walsh. **Assistant Coaches:** Gary Donovan, *Matt Hyde, Paul Sullivan. **Telephone:** (617) 495-2629. ■ **Baseball SID:** Kevin Anderson. **Telephone:** (617) 495-2206. **FAX:** (617) 495-2130.

HAWAII Rainbows
Conference: Western Athletic.
Mailing Address: 1337 Lower Campus Rd., Honolulu, HI 96822. **Website:** www.uhathletics.hawaii.edu.
Head Coach: Mike Trapasso. **Assistant Coaches:** Brian Green, *Chad Konishi, Keith Komeiji. **Telephone:** (808) 956-6247. ■ **Baseball SID:** Pakalani Bello. **Telephone:** (808) 956-7506. **FAX:** (808) 956-4470.
Home Field: Les Murakami Stadium. **Seating Capacity:** 4,500. **Outfield Dimensions:** LF—325, CF—385, RF—325. **Press Box Telephone:** (808) 956-6253.

HAWAII-HILO Vulcans

Conference: Independent.
Mailing Address: 200 W. Kawili St., Hilo, HI 96720. **Website:** vulcans.uhh.hawaii.edu.
Head Coach: Joey Estrella. **Assistant Coaches:** David Miller, Brendan Sagara. **Telephone:** (808) 974-7700. ■ **Baseball SID:** Kelly Leong. **Telephone:** (808) 974-7606. **FAX:** (808) 974-7711.

HIGH POINT Panthers

Conference: Big South.
Mailing Address: 833 Montlieu Ave., High Point, NC 27262. **Website:** www.highpointpanthers.com.
Head Coach: Sal Bando Jr. **Assistant Coach:** *Michael Lowman, Phil Maier. **Telephone:** (336) 841-9190. ■ **Baseball SID:** Lee Owen. **Telephone:** (336) 841-4605. **FAX:** (336) 841-9182.

HOFSTRA Flying Dutchmen

Conference: Colonial Athletic.
Mailing Address: 147 Hofstra University, Hempstead, NY 11549. **Website:** www.hofstra.edu/sports.
Head Coach: Chris Dotolo. **Assistant Coaches:** *Mike Fahid, Pete Graham. **Telephone:** (516) 463-5065. ■ **Baseball SID:** Jim Sheehan. **Telephone:** (516) 463-6764. **FAX:** (516) 463-5033.

HOLY CROSS Crusaders

Conference: Patriot.
Mailing Address: One College St., Worcester, MA 01610. **Website:** www.holycross.edu.
Head Coach: Fran O'Brien. **Assistant Coaches:** John Jeniski, Craig Najarian. **Telephone:** (508) 793-2221. ■ **Baseball SID:** Patrick Maloney. **Telephone:** (508) 793-2583. **FAX:** (508) 793-2309.

HOUSTON Cougars

Conference: Conference USA.
Mailing Address: 3100 Cullen Rd., Houston, TX 77204. **Website:** www.uhcougars.com.
Head Coach: Rayner Noble. **Assistant Coaches:** Sean Allen, *Kirk Blount, Nick Torina. **Telephone:** (713) 743-9396. ■ **Baseball SID:** Jeff Conrad. **Telephone:** (713) 743-9410. **FAX:** (713) 743-9411.
Home Field: Cougar Field. **Seating Capacity:** 3,500. **Outfield Dimensions:** LF—330, CF—390, RF—330. **Press Box Telephone:** (713) 743-0840.

ILLINOIS Fighting Illini

Conference: Big Ten.
Mailing Address: 1700 S. Fourth St., Champaign, IL 61820. **Website:** www.fightingillini.com.
Head Coach: Richard "Itch" Jones. **Assistant Coaches:** *Dan Hartleb, Eric Snider. **Telephone:** (217) 333-8605. ■ **Baseball SID:** Michelle Warner. **Telephone:** (217) 244-3707. **FAX:** (217) 333-5540.
Home Field: Illinois Field. **Seating Capacity:** 2,000. **Outfield Dimensions:** LF—330, CF—400, RF—330. **Press Box Telephone:** (217) 333-1227.

ILLINOIS-CHICAGO Flames

Conference: Horizon.
Mailing Address: 839 W. Roosevelt Rd., Chicago, IL 60608. **Website:** www.uicflames.com.
Head Coach: Mike Dee. **Assistant Coaches:** *Sean McDermott, Mike Nall, Scott Stahoviak. **Telephone:** (312) 996-8645. ■ **Baseball SID:** Matt Brendich. **Telephone:** (312) 996-5881. **FAX:** (312) 996-5882.

ILLINOIS STATE Redbirds

Conference: Missouri Valley.
Mailing Address: Campus Box 7130, Normal, IL 61790. **Website:** www.redbirds.org.

Head Coach: Jim Brownlee. **Assistant Coaches:** *Tim Brownlee, Kyle Ehrhardt, Seth Kenny. **Telephone:** (309) 438-5151. ■ **Baseball SID:** Aaron Johnston. **Telephone:** (309) 438-3598. **FAX:** (309) 438-5643.
Home Field: Redbird Field. **Seating Capacity:** 1,500. **Outfield Dimensions:** LF—330, CF—400, RF—330. **Press Box Telephone:** (309) 438-3504.

INDIANA Hoosiers

Conference: Big Ten.
Mailing Address: 1001 E. 17th St., Assembly Hall, Bloomington, IN 47408. **Website:** www.iuhoosiers.com.
Head Coach: Bob Morgan. **Assistant Coaches:** Jeff Calcaterra, *Tony Kestranek, Chris Moore **Telephone:** (812) 855-1680. ■ **Baseball SID:** Jeff Smith, Christy Tolin. **Telephone:** (812) 856-0146. **FAX:** (812) 855-9401.
Home Field: Sembower Field. **Seating Capacity:** 3,500. **Outfield Dimensions:** LF—333, CF—385, RF—333. **Press Box Telephone:** (812) 855-4787.

INDIANA-PURDUE UNIVERSITY Mastodons

Conference: Independent.
Mailing Address: 2101 Coliseum Blvd., Fort Wayne, IN 46805. **Website:** www.ipfw.edu/athletics.
Head Coach: Billy Gernon. **Assistant Coach:** Nick Otte, Tom Tornincasa. **Telephone:** (260) 481-6648. ■ **Baseball SID:** Rudy Yovich. **Telephone:** (260) 481-6646. **FAX:** (260) 481-6002.

INDIANA STATE Sycamores

Conference: Missouri Valley.
Mailing Address: Fourth and Chestnut St., Terre Haute, IN 47809. **Website:** www.indstate.edu/athletics.
Head Coach: Bob Warn. **Assistant Coaches:** Jim Fredwell, *C.J. Keating, Chad Zaucha. **Telephone:** (812) 237-4051. ■ **Baseball SID:** Adam Rouse. **Telephone:** (812) 237-4073. **FAX:** (812) 237-4157.
Home Field: Sycamore Field. **Seating Capacity:** 2,000. **Outfield Dimensions:** LF—340, CF—402, RF—340. **Press Box Telephone:** (812) 237-4187 or 4188.

IONA Gaels

Conference: Metro Atlantic.
Mailing Address: 715 North Ave., New Rochelle, NY 10801. **Website:** www.iona.edu.
Head Coach: Al Zoccolillo. **Assistant Coaches:** Forrest Irwin, *Chris Lombardo. **Telephone:** (914) 633-2319. ■ **Baseball SID:** Mike Laprey. **Telephone:** (914) 633-2334. **FAX:** (914) 633-2072.

IOWA Hawkeyes

Conference: Big Ten.
Mailing Address: 1 Elliot Drive, Iowa City, IA 52242. **Website:** www.hawkeyesports.com.
Head Coach: Jack Dahm. **Assistant Coaches:** Spencer Allen, *Ryan Brownlee, Nick Zumsande. **Telephone:** (319) 335-9390. ■ **Baseball SID:** James Allan. **Telephone:** (319) 335-9411. **FAX:** (319) 335-9417.
Home Field: Duane Banks Field. **Seating Capacity:** 3,000. **Outfield Dimensions:** LF—330, CF—400, RF—330. **Press Box Telephone:** (319) 335-9520.

JACKSON STATE Tigers

Conference: Southwestern Athletic.
Mailing Address: 1400 John R. Lynch St., Jackson, MS 39217. **Website:** www.jsums.edu.
Head Coach: *Mark Salter. **Assistant Coach:** Omar Johnson. **Telephone:** (601) 979-3928. ■ **Baseball SID:** Deidra Jones. **Telephone:** (601) 979-2291. **FAX:** (601) 979-2000.

JACKSONVILLE Dolphins

Conference: Atlantic Sun.
Mailing Address: 2800 University Blvd. N., Jacksonville, FL 32211. **Website:** www.judolphins.com.
Head Coach: Terry Alexander. **Assistant Coaches:** Chris Hayes, John Howard, Les Wright. **Telephone:** (904) 256-7476. ■ **Baseball SID:** Jamie Zeitz. **Telephone:** (904) 256-7409. **FAX:** (904) 256-7179.
Home Field: Alexander Brest Field. **Seating Capacity:** 2,300. **Outfield Dimensions:** LF—340, CF—405, RF—340. **Press Box Telephone:** (904) 256-7422.

JACKSONVILLE STATE Gamecocks

Conference: Ohio Valley.
Mailing Address: 700 Pelham Road N., Jacksonville, AL 36265. **Website:** www.jsugamecocksports.com.
Head Coach: Jim Case. **Assistant Coaches:** Steve Gillispie, Matt Ishee. **Telephone:** (256) 782-5367. ■ **Baseball SID:** Greg Seitz. **Telephone:** (256) 782-5279. **FAX:** (256) 782-5958.

JAMES MADISON Dukes

Conference: Colonial Athletic.
Mailing Address: MSC 2301 Godwin Hall, Harrisonburg, VA 22807. **Website:** www.jmusports.com.
Head Coach: Spanky McFarland. **Assistant Coaches:** *Chuck Bartlett, Dustin Bowman, Jay Sullenger. **Telephone:** (540) 568-3932. ■ **Baseball SID:** Curt Dudley. **Telephone:** (540) 568-6154. **FAX:** (540) 568-3703.
Home Field: Long Field/Mauck Stadium. **Seating Capacity:** 1,200. **Outfield Dimensions:** LF—340, CF—400, RF—320. **Press Box Telephone:** Unavailable.

KANSAS Jayhawks

Conference: Big 12.
Mailing Address: 1651 Naismith Dr., Lawrence, KS 66045. **Website:** www.kuathletics.com.
Head Coach: Ritch Price. **Assistant Coaches:** Steve Abney, Reggie Christiansen, *Ryan Graves. **Telephone:** (785) 864-7907. ■ **Baseball SID:** Scott Meyer. **Telephone:** (785) 864-7314. **FAX:** (785) 864-7944.
Home Field: Hoglund Ballpark. **Seating Capacity:** 2,500. **Outfield Dimensions:** LF—330, CF—392, RF—330. **Press Box Telephone:** (785) 864-4037.

KANSAS STATE Wildcats

Conference: Big 12.
Mailing Address: 1800 College Ave., Manhattan, KS 66502. **Website:** www.k-statesports.com.
Head Coach: Brad Hill. **Assistant Coaches:** *Sean McCann, Tommy Myers. **Telephone:** (785) 532-5723. ■ **Baseball SID:** Kenny Lannou. **Telephone:** (785) 532-6735. **FAX:** (785) 532-6093.
Home Field: Tointon Family Stadium. **Seating Capacity:** 2,331. **Outfield Dimensions:** LF—340, CF—400, RF—325. **Press Box Telephone:** (785) 532-5801.

KENT STATE Golden Flashes

Conference: Mid-American.
Mailing Address: 234 Mac Center, Kent, OH 44242. **Website:** www.kent.edu/athletics.
Head Coach: Rick Rembielak. **Assistant Coaches:** *Mike Birkbeck, Jeff Waggoner. **Telephone:** (330) 672-6396. ■ **Baseball SID:** Will Roleson. **Telephone:** (330) 672-2110. **FAX:** (330) 672-2112.
Home Field: Gene Michael Field. **Seating Capacity:** 2,000. **Outfield Dimensions:** LF—330, CF—400, RF—330. **Press Box:** (330) 672-2036.

KENTUCKY Wildcats

Conference: Southeastern (East).
Mailing Address: Memorial Coliseum, Room 23, Lexington, KY 40506. **Website:** www.ukathletics.com.
Head Coach: John Cohen. **Assistant Coaches:** Brad Bohannon, *Gary Henderson, Phillip Sledge, Jan Weisberg. **Telephone:** (859) 257-1419. ■ **Baseball SID:** Patrick Mitchell. **Telephone:** (859) 257-3838. **FAX:** (859) 323-4310.
Home Field: Cliff Hagan Stadium. **Seating Capacity:** 3,000. **Outfield Dimensions:** LF—340, CF—390, RF—310. **Press Box Telephone:** (859) 257-9013.

LAFAYETTE Leopards

Conference: Patriot.
Mailing Address: Kirby Sports Center, Pierce and Hamilton Streets, Easton, PA 18042. **Website:** www.goleopards.com.
Head Coach: *Joe Kinney. **Assistant Coaches:** Gregg Durrah, Paul Englehardt, Scott Stewart. **Telephone:** (610) 330-5476. ■ **Baseball SIDs:** Philip LaBella. **Telephone:** (610) 330-5123. **FAX:** (610) 330-5519.

LAMAR Cardinals

Conference: Southland.
Mailing Address: Box 10066, Beaumont, TX 77710. **Website:** www.athletics.lamar.edu.
Head Coach: Jim Gilligan. **Assistant Coaches:** Scott Hatten, *Jim Ricklefsen. **Telephone:** (409) 880-8315. ■ **Baseball SID:** Daucy Crizer. **Telephone:** (409) 880-8329. **FAX:** (409) 880-2338.
Home Field: Vincent-Beck Stadium. **Seating Capacity:** 3,500. **Outfield Dimensions:** LF—325, CF—380, RF—325. **Press Box Telephone:** (409) 880-8327.

LA SALLE Explorers

Conference: Atlantic-10 (West).
Mailing Address: 1900 W. Olney Ave., Philadelphia, PA 19141. **Website:** www.goexplorers.com.
Head Coach: Lee Saverio. **Assistant Coaches:** John Duffy, Mike Lake. **Telephone:** (215) 951-1995. ■ **Baseball SID:** Kale Beers. **Telephone:** (215) 951-1513. **FAX:** (215) 951-1694.

LEHIGH Mountain Hawks

Conference: Patriot.
Mailing Address: 641 Taylor St., Bethlehem, PA 18015. **Website:** www.lehigh.edu.
Head Coach: *Sean Leary. **Assistant Coaches:** Dave Cerminaro, Josh Perich. **Telephone:** (610) 758-4315. ■ **Baseball SID:** Jeff Tourial. **Telephone:** (610) 758-3158. **FAX:** (610) 758-4407.

LE MOYNE Dolphins

Conference: Metro Atlantic.
Mailing Address: 1419 Salt Springs Rd., Syracuse, NY 13214. **Website:** www.lemoyne.edu/athletics.
Head Coach: Steve Owens. **Assistant Coaches:** *Pete Hoy, Scott Landers, Bob Nandin. **Telephone:** (315) 445-4415. ■ **Baseball SID:** Mike Donlin. **Telephone:** (315) 445-4412. **FAX:** (315) 445-5678.

LIBERTY Flames

Conference: Big South.
Mailing Address: 1971 University Blvd., Lynchburg, VA 24502. **Website:** www.liberty.edu/athletics.
Head Coach: Matt Royer. **Assistant Coaches:** *Randy Tomlin, Terry Weaver. **Telephone:** (434) 582-2103. ■ **Baseball SID:** Joey Mullins. **Telephone:** (434) 582-2292. **FAX:** (434) 582-2076.

LIPSCOMB Bisons

Conference: Atlantic Sun.
Mailing Address: 3901 Granny White Pike, Nashville, TN 37204. **Website:** www.lipscombsports.com.
Head Coach: Wynn Fletcher. **Assistant Coaches:** Jay

Chittam, Jay Powell. **Telephone:** (615) 279-5716. ■
Baseball SID: Tim Beekman. **Telephone:** (615) 279-5862. **FAX:** (615) 269-1806.

LONG BEACH STATE 49ers
Conference: Big West.
Mailing Address: 1250 Bellflower Blvd., Long Beach, CA 90840. **Website:** www.longbeachstate.com.
Head Coach: Mike Weathers. **Assistant Coaches:** Don Barbara, *Troy Buckley, Tim McConnell. **Telephone:** (562) 985-7548. ■ **Baseball SID:** Niall Adler. **Telephone:** (562) 985-7565. **FAX:** (562) 985-1549.
Home Field: Blair Field. **Seating Capacity:** 3,000. **Outfield Dimensions:** LF—348, CF—400, RF—348. **Press Box Telephone:** (562) 433-8605.

LONG ISLAND Blackbirds
Conference: Northeast.
Mailing Address: One University Plaza, Brooklyn, NY 11201. **Website:** www.liu.edu.
Head Coach: Frank Giannone. **Assistant Coaches:** *Chris Bagley, Mike Ryan. **Telephone:** (718) 488-1538. ■ **Baseball SID:** Derek Crudele. **Telephone:** (718) 488-1307. **FAX:** (718) 488-3302.

LOUISIANA-LAFAYETTE Ragin' Cajuns
Conference: Sun Belt.
Mailing Address: 201 Reinhardt Dr., Lafayette, LA 70506. **Website:** www.ragincajuns.com.
Head Coach: Tony Robichaux. **Assistant Coaches:** Anthony Babineaux, *John Szefc. **Telephone:** (337) 482-6189. ■ **Baseball SID:** Chris Herbert. **Telephone:** (337) 851-2255. **FAX:** (337) 482-6649.
Home Field: Moore Field. **Seating Capacity:** 4,000. **Outfield Dimensions:** LF—330, CF—400, RF—330. **Press Box Telephone:** (337) 482-2255.

LOUISIANA-MONROE Indians
Conference: Southland.
Mailing Address: 308 Stadium Dr., Monroe, LA 71209. **Website:** www.ulmathletics.com.
Head Coach: Brad Holland. **Assistant Coaches:** Terry Burrows, Britten Oubre, Jeremy Talbot. **Telephone:** (318) 342-3591. ■ **Baseball SID:** Fred Sington. **Telephone:** (318) 342-5463. **FAX:** (318) 342-5464.

LOUISIANA STATE Tigers
Conference: Southeastern (West).
Mailing Address: P.O. Box 25095, Baton Rouge, LA 70894. **Website:** www.lsusports.net
Head Coach: Smoke Laval. **Assistant Coaches:** Jody Autery, *Turtle Thomas, Brady Wiederhold. **Telephone:** (225) 578-4148. ■ **Baseball SID:** Bill Franques. **Telephone:** (225) 578-2527. **FAX:** (225) 578-1861.
Home Field: Alex Box Stadium. **Seating Capacity:** 7,760. **Outfield Dimensions:** LF—330, CF—405, RF—330. **Press Box Telephone:** (225) 578-4149.

LOUISIANA TECH Bulldogs
Conference: Western Athletic.
Mailing Address: P.O. Box 3166, Ruston, LA 71272. **Website:** www.latechsports.com.
Head Coach: Wade Simoneaux. **Assistant Coaches:** Fran Andermann, *Brian Rountree, Toby White. **Telephone:** (318) 257-4111. ■ **Baseball SID:** Robby Lockwood. **Telephone:** (318) 257-3144. **FAX:** (318) 257-3757.
Home Field: J.C. Love Field. **Seating Capacity:** 3,500. **Outfield Dimensions:** LF—325, CF—385, RF—315. **Press Box Telephone:** (318) 257-3144.

LOUISVILLE Cardinals
Conference: Conference USA.
Mailing Address: 2100 S. Floyd St., Louisville, KY

40208. **Website:** www.uoflsports.com.
Head Coach: Lelo Prado. **Assistant Coaches:** *Brian Mundorf, Jim Zerilla. **Telephone:** (502) 852-0103. ■
Baseball SID: Sean Moth. **Telephone:** (502) 852-2159. **FAX:** (502) 852-7401.
Home Field: Cardinal Stadium. **Seating Capacity:** 33,000. **Outfield Dimensions:** LF—360, CF—405, RF—305. **Press Box Telephone:** (502) 852-3601.

LOYOLA MARYMOUNT Lions
Conference: West Coast.
Mailing Address: One LMU Drive, Los Angeles, CA 90045. **Website:** www.lmulions.com.
Head Coach: Frank Cruz. **Assistant Coaches:** Robbie Moen, *Jon Strauss. **Telephone:** (310) 338-2765. ■
Baseball SID: Alissa Zito. **Telephone:** (310) 338-7638. **FAX:** (310) 338-2703.
Home Field: Page Stadium. **Seating Capacity:** 600. **Outfield Dimensions:** LF—326, CF—413, RF—330. **Press Box Telephone:** (310) 338-3046.

MAINE Black Bears
Conference: America East.
Mailing Address: 5747 Memorial Gym, Orono, ME 04469. **Website:** www.goblackbears.com.
Head Coach: Paul Kostacopoulos. **Assistant Coaches:** *Scott Friedholm, Jason Largay. **Telephone:** (207) 581-1090. ■ **Baseball SID:** Laura Reed. **Telephone:** (207) 581-3646. **FAX:** (207) 581-3297.

MANHATTAN Jaspers
Conference: Metro Atlantic.
Mailing Address: 4513 Manhattan College Pkwy., Riverdale, NY 10471. **Website:** www.gojaspers.com.
Head Coach: Steve Trimper. **Assistant Coaches:** Kevin Leighton, *Tom Sowinski. **Telephone:** (718) 862-7486. ■ **Baseball SID:** Mike Antonaccio. **Telephone:** (718) 862-7228. **FAX:** (718) 862-8020.

MARIST Red Foxes
Conference: Metro Atlantic.
Mailing Address: 290 North Rd., Poughkeepsie, NY 12601. **Website:** www.GoRedFoxes.com.
Head Coach: Joe Raccuia. **Assistant Coaches:** Brian Anderson, Matt Griffiths, Ryan Mau. **Telephone:** (845) 575-3699. ■ **Baseball SID:** Chris O'Connor. **Telephone:** (845) 575-3321. **FAX:** (845) 471-0466.

MARSHALL Thundering Herd
Conference: Mid-American.
Mailing Address: P.O. Box 1360, Huntington, WV 25715. **Website:** www.herdzone.com.
Head Coach: Dave Piepenbrink. **Assistant Coaches:** *Tom Carty, Chad Miller, Zeke Mitchem. **Telephone:** (304) 696-5277. ■ **Baseball SID:** Bob Pristash. **Telephone:** (304) 696-4662. **FAX:** (304) 696-2325.

MARYLAND Terrapins
Conference: Atlantic Coast.
Mailing Address: Comcast Center, Terrapin Trail, College Park, MD 20742. **Website:** www.umterps.com.
Head Coach: Terry Rupp. **Assistant Coaches:** Ben Bachmann, *Gregg Kilby, Greg Olsen. **Telephone:** (301) 314-7122. ■ **Baseball SID:** Sean O'Connor. **Telephone:** (301) 314-7064. **FAX:** (301) 314-9094.
Home Field: Shipley Field. **Seating Capacity:** 2,500. **Outfield Dimensions:** LF—320, CF—380, RF—320. **Press Box Telephone:** (301) 314-0379.

MARYLAND-BALTIMORE COUNTY Retrievers
Conference: America East.
Mailing Address: 1000 Hilltop Circle, Baltimore, MD 21228. **Website:** www.umbcretrievers.com.

Head Coach: *John Jancuska. Assistant Coaches: Chuck Bragg, Bob Mumma. Telephone: (410) 455-2239. ■ Baseball SID: Steve Levy. Telephone: (410) 455-2639. FAX: (410) 455-3994.

MARYLAND-EASTERN SHORE Fighting Hawks
Conference: Mid-Eastern Athletic.
Mailing Address: William P. Hytche Athletic Center, Princess Anne, MD 21853. Website: www.umeshawks.com.
Head Coach: Bobby Rodriguez. Assistant Coaches: Ed Erisman, Bobby McCauley, Justin Watson. Telephone: (410) 651-8158. ■ Baseball SID: Stan Bradley. Telephone: (410) 651-6499. FAX: (410) 651-7514.

MASSACHUSETTS Minutemen
Conference: Atlantic-10 (East).
Mailing Address: Baseball Office, 248 Boyden Building, Amherst, MA 01003. Website: www.umassathletics.com.
Head Coach: Mike Stone. Assistant Coaches: Dave Bettencourt, Jason Gappa, Ernie May. Telephone: (413) 545-3120. ■ Baseball SID: Michael Coyne. Telephone: (413) 545-2439. FAX: (413) 545-1556.

McNEESE STATE Cowboys
Conference: Southland.
Mailing Address: 700 E. McNeese., Lake Charles, LA 70607. Website: www.mcneese.edu.
Head Coach: Chad Clement. Assistant Coaches: Darryl Byrd, *Mike Trahan. Telephone: (337) 475-5482. ■ Baseball SID: Louis Bonnette. Telephone: (337) 475-5207. FAX: (337) 475-5202.

MEMPHIS Tigers
Conference: Conference USA.
Mailing Address: 570 Normal, Memphis, TN 38152. Website: www.gotigersgo.com.
Head Coach: Dave Anderson. Assistant Coaches: George Holt, *Larry Owens, Nate Sams. Telephone: (901) 678-2452. ■ Baseball SID: Ryan Powell. Telephone: (901) 678-2337. FAX: (901) 678-4134.
Home Field: Nat Buring Stadium. Seating Capacity: 2,000. Outfield Dimensions: LF—315, CF—400, RF—315. Press Box Telephone: (901) 678-1300.

MERCER Bears
Conference: Atlantic Sun.
Mailing Address: 1400 Coleman Ave., Macon, GA 31207. Website: www.mercer.edu.
Head Coach: Craig Gibson. Assistant Coach: Jason Jackson, *Link Jarrett. Telephone: (478) 301-2396. ■ Baseball SID: Jeff Lamp. Telephone: (478) 301-2396. FAX: (478) 301-2061.

MIAMI Hurricanes
Conference: Independent.
Mailing Address: 6201 San Amaro Dr., Coral Gables, FL 33146. Website: www.hurricanesports.com.
Head Coach: Jim Morris. Assistant Coaches: J.D. Arteaga, *Gino DiMare, Greg Lovelady. Telephone: (305) 284-4171. ■ Baseball SID: Josh Maxson. Telephone: (305) 284-3241. FAX: (305) 284-2807.
Home Field: Mark Light Stadium. Seating Capacity: 5,000. Outfield Dimensions: LF—330, CF—400, RF—330. Press Box Telephone: (305) 284-5626.

MIAMI RedHawks
Conference: Mid-American.
Mailing Address: 230 Millett Hall, Oxford, OH 45056. Website: www.MURedHawks.com.
Head Coach: Tracy Smith. Assistant Coaches: Scott Googins, Fred Nori, *Dan Simonds. Telephone: (513) 529-6631. ■ Baseball SID: Ryan Erb. Telephone: (513)

529-1601. FAX: (513) 529-6729.
Home Field: Hayden Park at McKie Field. Seating Capacity: 1,000. Outfield Dimensions: LF—332, CF—400, RF—343. Press Box Telephone: (513) 529-4331.

MICHIGAN Wolverines
Conference: Big Ten.
Mailing Address: 1000 S. State St., Ann Arbor, MI 48109. Website: www.mgoblue.com.
Head Coach: Rich Maloney. Assistant Coaches: John Lowery, Scott Mallernee, *Jason Murray. Telephone: (734) 647-4550. ■ Baseball SID: Jim Schneider. Telephone: (734) 763-4423. FAX: (734) 647-1188.
Home Field: Ray Fisher Stadium. Seating Capacity: 4,000. Outfield Dimensions: LF—330, CF—400, RF—330. Press Box Telephone: (734) 647-1283.

MICHIGAN STATE Spartans
Conference: Big Ten.
Mailing Address: 304 Jenison Field House, East Lansing, MI 48824. Website: www.msuspartans.com.
Head Coach: Ted Mahan. Assistant Coaches: Dylan Putnam, John Young. Telephone: (517) 355-4486. ■ Baseball SID: Lindsay Carpenter. Telephone: (517) 355-5271. FAX: (517) 353-9636.
Home Fields Kobs Field. Seating Capacity: 3,000. Outfield Dimensions: LF—340, CF—410, RF—301. Press Box Telephone: Unavailable.

MIDDLE TENNESSEE STATE Blue Raiders
Conference: Sun Belt.
Mailing Address: 1301 E. Main St., Murfreesboro, TN 37132. Website: www.goblueraiders.com.
Head Coach: Steve Peterson. Assistant Coaches: Kevin Erminio, Andy Haines, *Jim McGuire. Telephone: (615) 898-2984. ■ Baseball SID: JoJo Freeman. Telephone: (615) 898-5270. FAX: (615) 898-5626.
Home Field: Reese Smith Field. Seating Capacity: 2,600. Outfield Dimensions: LF—325, CF—390, RF—325. Press Box Telephone: (615) 898-2117.

MINNESOTA Golden Gophers
Conference: Big Ten.
Mailing Address: 244 Bierman Field Athletic Building, 516 15th Ave. SE, Minneapolis, MN 55455. Website: www.gophersports.com.
Head Coach: John Anderson. Assistant Coaches: *Rob Fornasiere, Todd Oakes, Lee Swenson. Telephone: (612) 625-0869. ■ Baseball SID: Steve Geller. Telephone: (612) 624-9396. FAX: (612) 625-0359.
Home Fields (Seating Capacity): Siebert Field (1,100), Metrodome (48,678). Outfield Dimensions: Siebert Field/LF—330, CF—380, RF—330; Metrodome/LF—343, CF—408, RF—327. Press Box Telephones: Siebert Field/(612) 625-4031; Metrodome/(612) 627-4400.

MISSISSIPPI Rebels
Conference: Southeastern (West).
Mailing Address: P.O. Box 1848, University, MS 38677. Website: www.OleMissSports.com.
Head Coach: Mike Bianco. Assistant Coaches: Kyle Bunn, Stuart Lake, *Dan McDonnell. Telephone: (662) 915-6643. ■ Baseball SID: Rick Stupak. Telephone: (662) 915-7522. FAX: (662) 915-7006.
Home Field: Oxford-University Stadium/Swayze Field. Seating Capacity: 3,500. Outfield Dimensions: LF—330, CF—400, RF—330. Press Box Telephone: (662) 236-1931.

MISSISSIPPI STATE Bulldogs
Conference: Southeastern (West).
Mailing Address: P.O. Box 5327, Starkville, MS

39762. **Website:** www.mstateathletics.com.
Head Coach: Ron Polk. **Assistant Coaches:** Russ McNickle, Tommy Raffo, *Daron Schoenrock. **Telephone:** (662) 325-3597. ■ **Baseball SID:** Joe Dier. **Telephone:** (662) 325-8040. **FAX:** (662) 325-3654.
Home Field: Dudy Noble Field/Polk-DeMent Stadium. **Seating Capacity:** 15,000. **Outfield Dimensions:** LF—330, CF—390, RF—325. **Press Box Telephone:** (662) 325-3776.

MISSISSIPPI VALLEY STATE Delta Devils
Conference: Southwestern Athletic.
Mailing Address: 14000 Hwy. 82 W., No. 7246, Itta Bena, MS 38941. **Website:** www.mvsu.edu/athletics.
Head Coach: Doug Shanks. **Assistant Coaches:** Philip Dawson, *Jay Rayborn, Aaron Stevens, Chuck Welch. **Telephone:** (662) 254-3834. ■ **Baseball SID:** Marlon Reed. **Telephone:** (662) 254-3551. **FAX:** (662) 254-3639.

MISSOURI Tigers
Conference: Big 12.
Mailing Address: P.O. Box 677, Columbia, MO 65211. **Website:** www.mutigers.com.
Head Coach: Tim Jamieson. **Assistant Coaches:** Kevin Cullen, *Evan Pratte, Tony Vitello. **Telephone:** (573) 884-0731. ■ **Baseball SID:** Josh Murray. **Telephone:** (573) 884-0711. **FAX:** (573) 882-4720.
Home Field: Taylor Stadium at Simmons Field. **Seating Capacity:** 2,500. **Outfield Dimensions:** LF—340, CF—400, RF—340. **Press Box Telephone:** (573) 884-8912.

MONMOUTH Hawks
Conference: Northeast.
Mailing Address: 400 Cedar Ave., West Long Branch, NJ 07764. **Website:** www.monmouth.edu/athletics.
Head Coach: Dean Ehehalt. **Assistant Coaches:** *Jeff Barbalinardo, Dan Coia. **Telephone:** (732) 263-5186. ■ **Baseball SID:** Chris Tobin. **Telephone:** (732) 263-5180. **FAX:** (732) 571-3535.

MOREHEAD STATE Eagles
Conference: Ohio Valley.
Mailing Address: 150 University Blvd., UPO 1023, Morehead, KY 40351. **Website:** www.msueagles.com.
Head Coach: John Jarnagin. **Assistant Coaches:** Ryan Schmalz, *Rob Taylor. **Telephone:** (606) 783-2882. ■ **Baseball SID:** Randy Stacy. **Telephone:** (606) 783-2500. **FAX:** (606) 783-2550.

MOUNT ST. MARY'S Mountaineers
Conference: Northeast.
Mailing Address: 16300 Old Emmitsburg Rd., Emmitsburg, MD 21727. **Website:** www.mountathletics. com.
Head Coach: Scott Thomson. **Assistant Coaches:** Steve Mott, Steve Thomson. **Telephone:** (301) 447-3806. ■ **Baseball SID:** Mark Vandergrift. **Telephone:** (301) 447-5384. **FAX:** (301) 447-5300.

MURRAY STATE Thoroughbreds
Conference: Ohio Valley.
Mailing Address: 218 Stewart Stadium, Murray, KY 42071. **Website:** www.goracers.com.
Head Coach: Rob McDonald. **Assistant Coach:** Justus Scott, Charlie Ward, Paul Wyczawski. **Telephone:** (270) 762-4892. ■ **Baseball SID:** David Snow. **Telephone:** (270) 762-3351. **FAX:** (270) 762-6814.

NAVY Midshipmen
Conference: Patriot.
Mailing Address: 566 Brownson Rd., Annapolis, MD 21402. **Website:** www.navysports.com.
Head Coach: Steve Whitmyer. **Assistant Coaches:**

*Chris Murphy, Dan Nellum. **Telephone:** (410) 293-5571. ■ **Baseball SID:** Price Atkinson. **Telephone:** (410) 293-2700. **FAX:** (410) 293-8954.

NEBRASKA Cornhuskers
Conference: Big 12.
Mailing Address: 116 S. Stadium, Lincoln, NE 68588. **Website:** www.huskers.com.
Head Coach: Mike Anderson. **Assistant Coaches:** *Rob Childress, Andy Sawyers. **Telephone:** (402) 472-2269. ■ **Baseball SID:** Shamus McKnight. **Telephone:** (402) 472-7772. **FAX:** (402) 472-2005.
Home Field: Hawks Field at Haymarket Park. **Seating Capacity:** 8,486. **Outfield Dimensions:** LF—335, CF—395, RF—325. **Press Box Telephone:** (402) 434-6861.

NEVADA Wolf Pack
Conference: Western Athletic.
Mailing Address: 1664 N. Virginia St., Reno, NV 89557. **Website:** www.nevadawolfpack.com.
Head Coach: Gary Powers. **Assistant Coaches:** Chris Briones, Anthony Carano, *Stan Stolte, Jay Uhlman. **Telephone:** (775) 784-6900. ■ **Baseball SID:** Jack Kuestermeyer. **Telephone:** (775) 784-6900. **FAX:** (775) 784-4386.
Home Field: Peccole Park. **Seating Capacity:** 3,000. **Outfield Dimensions:** LF—340, CF—401, RF—340. **Press Box Telephone:** (775) 784-1585.

NEVADA-LAS VEGAS Rebels
Conference: Mountain West.
Mailing Address: 4505 Maryland Pkwy., Las Vegas, NV 89154. **Website:** www.unlvrebels.com.
Head Coach: Buddy Gouldsmith. **Assistant Coaches:** *Chuck Hazzard, Kevin Smoot. **Telephone:** (702) 895-3499. ■ **Baseball SID:** Brian Albertson. **Telephone:** (702) 895-3764. **FAX:** (702) 895-0989.
Home Field: Earl E. Wilson Stadium. **Seating Capacity:** 3,000. **Outfield Dimensions:** LF—335, CF—400, RF—335. **Press Box Telephone:** (702) 895-1595.

NEW MEXICO Lobos
Conference: Mountain West.
Mailing Address: Athletic Dept., MSC04 2680, 1 University of New Mexico, Albuquerque, NM 87131. **Website:** www.golobos.com.
Head Coach: Rich Alday. **Assistant Coaches:** *Ryan Brewer, Mark Martinez. **Telephone:** (505) 925-5720. ■ **Baseball SID:** Ben Phlegar. **Telephone:** (505) 925-5533. **FAX:** (505) 925-5529.
Home Field: Isotopes Park. **Seating Capacity:** 11,124. **Outfield Dimensions:** LF—340, CF—400, RF—340. **Press Box Telephone:** (505) 222-4093.

NEW MEXICO STATE Aggies
Conference: Sun Belt.
Mailing Address: P.O. Box 30001, Las Cruces, NM 88003. **Website:** www.nmstatesports.com.
Head Coach: Rocky Ward. **Assistant Coaches:** *Brad Dolejsi, Mike Pietrack, Chad Wolff. **Telephone:** (505) 646-5813. ■ **Baseball SID:** Sean Johnson. **Telephone:** (505) 646-1805. **FAX:** (505) 646-2425.
Home Field: Presley Askew Field. **Seating Capacity:** 1,000. **Outfield Dimensions:** LF—340, CF—400, RF—340. **Press Box Telephone:** (505) 646-5700.

NEW ORLEANS Privateers
Conference: Sun Belt.
Mailing Address: Lakefront Arena, New Orleans, LA 70122. **Website:** www.unoprivateers.com.
Head Coach: Randy Bush. **Assistant Coaches:** Kenny Bonura, Mikel Moreno. **Telephone:** (504) 280-7021. ■

Baseball SID: Jack Duggan. **Telephone:** (504) 280-7027. **FAX:** (504) 280-7240.

Home Field: Maestri Field. **Seating Capacity:** 4,200. **Outfield Dimensions:** LF—330, CF—405, RF—330. **Press Box Telephone:** (504) 280-7027.

NEW YORK TECH Bears

Conference: Independent.

Mailing Address: Northern Blvd., Old Westbury, NY 11568. **Website:** www.nyit.edu/athletics.

Head Coach: Bob Hirschfield. **Assistant Coaches:** James Arrante, Ray Giannelli. **Telephone:** (516) 686-7513. ■ **Baseball SID:** Ben Arcuri. **Telephone:** (516) 686-7504. **FAX:** (516) 686-1219.

NIAGARA Purple Eagles

Conference: Metro Atlantic.

Mailing Address: P.O. Box 2009, Niagara University, NY 14109. **Website:** www.purpleeagles.com.

Head Coach: *Mike McRae. **Assistant Coach:** Mike Kunigonis. **Telephone:** (716) 286-8624. ■ **Baseball SID:** Michele Dubert. **Telephone:** (716) 286-8588. **FAX:** (716) 286-8609.

NICHOLLS STATE Colonels

Conference: Southland.

Mailing Address: P.O. Box 2032, Thibodaux, LA 70310. **Website:** www.colonelsports.com.

Head Coach: B.D. Parker. **Assistant Coaches:** *Gerald Cassard, Jeff McCannon. **Telephone:** (985) 448-4808. ■ **Baseball SID:** Bobby Galinsky. **Telephone:** (985) 448-4281. **FAX:** (985) 448-4924.

NORFOLK STATE Spartans

Conference: Mid-Eastern Athletic.

Mailing Address: 700 Park Ave., Norfolk, VA 23504. **Website:** www.nsu.edu/athletics.

Head Coach: Marty Miller. **Assistant Coach:** Enrique Mendieta. **Telephone:** (757) 823-9539. ■ **Baseball SID:** Matt Michalec. **Telephone:** (757) 823-2628. **FAX:** (757) 823-8218.

NORTH CAROLINA Tar Heels

Conference: Atlantic Coast.

Mailing Address: P.O. Box 2126, Chapel Hill, NC 27515. **Website:** www.tarheelblue.com.

Head Coach: Mike Fox. **Assistant Coaches:** Ned French, *Chad Holbrook, Roger Williams. **Telephone:** (919) 962-2351. ■ **Baseball SID:** John Martin. **Telephone:** (919) 962-2123. **FAX:** (919) 962-0612.

Home Field: Boshamer Stadium. **Seating Capacity:** 2,500. **Outfield Dimensions:** LF—335, CF—400, RF—335. **Press Box Telephone:** (919) 962-3509.

UNC ASHEVILLE Bulldogs

Conference: Big South.

Mailing Address: One University Heights, Justice Center, Asheville, NC 28804. **Website:** www.unca.edu/athletics/baseball.

Head Coach: Matt Myers. **Assistant Coach:** Willie Stewart, Zack Whicker. **Telephone:** (828) 251-6920. ■ **Baseball SID:** Mike Gore. **Telephone:** (828) 251-6923. **FAX:** (828) 251-6386.

UNC GREENSBORO Spartans

Conference: Southern.

Mailing Address: P.O. Box 26168, Greensboro, NC 27402. **Website:** www.uncgspartans.com.

Head Coach: Mike Gaski. **Assistant Coaches:** *Mike Rodriguez, Andrew See, Mike Sollie. **Telephone:** (336) 334-3247. ■ **Baseball SID:** Chris Jones. **Telephone:** (336) 334-5615. **FAX:** (336) 334-3182.

Home Field: UNCG Baseball Stadium. **Seating**

Capacity: 3,000. **Outfield Dimensions:** LF—340, CF—405, RF—340. **Press Box Telephone:** (336) 334-3885.

UNC WILMINGTON Seahawks

Conference: Colonial Athletic.

Mailing Address: 601 S. College Rd., Wilmington, NC 28403. **Website:** www.uncwsports.com.

Head Coach: Mark Scalf. **Assistant Coaches:** Cliff Godwin, *Randy Hood, Scott Jackson. **Telephone:** (910) 962-3570. ■ **Baseball SID:** Tom Riordan. **Telephone:** (910) 962-4099. **FAX:** (910) 962-3686.

Home Field: Brooks Field. **Seating Capacity:** 3,500. **Outfield Dimensions:** LF—340, CF—380, RF—340. **Press Box Telephone:** (910) 395-5141.

NORTH CAROLINA A&T Aggies

Conference: Mid-Eastern Athletic.

Mailing Address: 1601 E. Market St., Moore Gym, Greensboro, NC 27411. **Website:** www.ncat.edu.

Head Coach: *Keith Shumate. **Assistant Coach:** Rod Gorham. **Telephone:** (336) 334-7371. ■ **Baseball SIDs:** Jim McNally. **Telephone:** (336) 334-7141. **FAX:** (336) 334-7181.

NORTH CAROLINA STATE Wolfpack

Conference: Atlantic Coast.

Mailing Address: P.O. Box 8501, Raleigh, NC 27695. **Website:** www.gopack.com.

Head Coach: Elliott Avent. **Assistant Coaches:** Josh Holliday, *Billy Jones, Chris Roberts. **Telephone:** (919) 515-3613. ■ **Baseball SID:** Bruce Winkworth. **Telephone:** (919) 515-2102. **FAX:** (919) 515-2898.

Home Field: Doak Field. **Seating Capacity:** 2,500. **Outfield Dimensions:** LF—330, CF—400, RF—330. **Press Box Telephone:** Unavailable.

NORTHEASTERN Huskies

Conference: America East.

Mailing Address: 360 Huntington Ave., Boston, MA 02115. **Website:** www.gonu.com/baseball.

Head Coach: Neil McPhee. **Assistant Coaches:** *Greg DiCenzo, Mike Grant, Steve Padovani, Tim Trovill. **Telephone:** (617) 373-3657. ■ **Baseball SID:** Adam Polgren. **Telephone:** (617) 373-4154. **FAX:** (617) 373-3152.

NORTHERN COLORADO Bears

Conference: Independent.

Mailing Address: 251 Butler-Hancock Hall, Greeley, CO 80639. **Website:** www.uncbears.com.

Head Coach: Kevin Smallcomb. **Assistant Coaches:** *Chris Forbes, Chris Humrich. **Telephone:** (970) 351-1714. ■ **Baseball SID:** Kyle Schwartz. **Telephone:** (970) 351-2522. **FAX:** (970) 351-1995.

NORTHERN ILLINOIS Huskies

Conference: Mid-American.

Mailing Address: 1525 W. Lincoln Hwy., DeKalb, IL 60115. **Website:** www.niuhuskies.com.

Head Coach: Ed Mathey. **Assistant Coaches:** Steve Joslyn, *Tim McDonough, Luke Sabers. **Telephone:** (815) 753-0147. ■ **Baseball SID:** Dave Retier. **Telephone:** (815) 753-3706. **FAX:** (815) 753-9540.

NORTHERN IOWA Panthers

Conference: Missouri Valley.

Mailing Address: UNI-Dome, NW Upper, Cedar Falls, IA 50614. **Website:** www.unipanthers.com.

Head Coach: Rick Heller. **Assistant Coaches:** *Dan Davis, Ryan Jacobs, Marty Sutherland. **Telephone:** (319) 273-6323. ■ **Baseball SID:** Jill Gansemer. **Telephone:** (319) 273-5455. **FAX:** (319) 273-3602.

Home Field: Waterloo Riverfront Stadium. **Seating**

Capacity: 4,277. **Outfield Dimensions:** LF—335, CF—380, RF—335. **Press Box Telephone:** (319) 232-5633.

NORTHWESTERN Wildcats
Conference: Big Ten.
Mailing Address: 1501 Central St., Evanston, IL 60208. **Website:** www.nusports.com.
Head Coach: Paul Stevens. **Assistant Coaches:** Joe Keenan, *Ron Klein, Tim Stoddard. **Telephone:** (847) 491-4652. ■ **Baseball SID:** Aaron Bongle. **Telephone:** (847) 491-7503. **FAX:** (847) 491-8818.
Home Field: Rocky Miller Park. **Seating Capacity:** 1,000. **Outfield Dimensions:** LF—330, CF—400, RF—330. **Press Box Telephone:** (847) 491-4200.

NORTHWESTERN STATE Demons
Conference: Southland.
Mailing Address: Athletic Fieldhouse, Natchitoches, LA 71497. **Website:** www.nsudemons.com.
Head Coach: Mitch Gaspard. **Assistant Coaches:** J.P. Davis, Travis Janssen. **Telephone:** (318) 357-4139. ■ **Baseball SID:** Matt Bonnette. **Telephone:** (318) 357-6468. **FAX:** (318) 357-4515.

NOTRE DAME Fighting Irish
Conference: Big East.
Mailing Address: 112 Joyce Center, Notre Dame, IN 46556. **Website:** www.und.com.
Head Coach: Paul Mainieri. **Assistant Coaches:** *David Grewe, Terry Rooney. **Telephone:** (574) 631-8466. ■ **Baseball SID:** Pete LaFleur. **Telephone:** (574) 631-7516. **FAX:** (574) 631-7941.
Home Field: Frank Eck Stadium. **Seating Capacity:** 2,500. **Outfield Dimensions:** LF—331, CF—401, RF—331. **Press Box Telephone:** (574) 631-9018.

OAKLAND Golden Grizzlies
Conference: Mid-Continent.
Mailing Address: Athletics Center, Rochester, MI 48309. **Website:** www.ougrizzlies.com.
Head Coach: Mark Avery. **Assistant Coaches:** Ben DiPonio, Chris Newell, Justin Robertson. **Telephone:** (248) 370-4059. ■ **Baseball SID:** Peter DiSanza. **Telephone:** (248) 370-3123. **FAX:** (248) 370-4056.

OHIO Bobcats
Conference: Mid-American.
Mailing Address: 215 Convocation Center, Richland Ave., Athens, OH 45701. **Website:** www.ohiobobcats.com.
Head Coach: *Joe Carbone. **Assistant Coaches:** Scott Malinowski, Bill Toadvine. **Baseball SID:** P.J. Gradowski. **Telephone:** (740) 593-0054. **FAX:** (740) 597-1838.
Home Field: Bob Wren Stadium. **Seating Capacity:** 6,000. **Outfield Dimensions:** LF—340, CF—380, RF—340. **Press Box Telephone:** (740) 593-0525.

OHIO STATE Buckeyes
Conference: Big Ten.
Mailing Address: Bill Davis Stadium, Room 114, Borror Drive, Columbus, OH 43210. **Website:** www.ohiostatebuckeyes.com.
Head Coach: Bob Todd. **Assistant Coaches:** Pat Bangston, *Greg Cypret, Erik Hagen. **Telephone:** (614) 292-1075. ■ **Baseball SID:** Todd Lamb. **Telephone:** (614) 688-0343. **FAX:** (614) 292-8547.
Home Field: Bill Davis Stadium. **Seating Capacity:** 4,450. **Outfield Dimensions:** LF—330, CF—400, RF—330. **Press Box Telephone:** (614) 292-0021.

OKLAHOMA Sooners
Conference: Big 12.
Mailing Address: 180 W. Brooks St., Room 2525,
Norman, OK 73019. **Website:** www.soonersports.com.
Head Coach: Larry Cochell. **Assistant Coaches:** Sunny Golloway, *Ray Hayward, Brian Hickman. **Telephone:** (405) 325-8354. ■ **Baseball SID:** Danielle Felter. **Telephone:** (405) 325-8372. **FAX:** (405) 325-7623.
Home Field: L. Dale Mitchell Park. **Seating Capacity:** 2,700. **Outfield Dimensions:** LF—335, CF—411, RF—335. **Press Box Telephone:** (405) 325-8363.

OKLAHOMA STATE Cowboys
Conference: Big 12.
Mailing Address: 220 OSU Athletics Center, Stillwater, OK 74075. **Website:** www.okstate.com.
Head Coach: Frank Anderson. **Assistant Coaches:** Jason Bell, *Greg Evans, Robbie Wine. **Telephone:** (405) 744-7141. ■ **Baseball SID:** Thomas Samuel. **Telephone:** (405) 744-7853. **FAX:** (405) 744-7754.
Home Field: Allie P. Reynolds Stadium. **Seating Capacity:** 4,000. **Outfield Dimensions:** LF—390, CF—400, RF—385. **Press Box Telephone:** (405) 744-5757.

OLD DOMINION Monarchs
Conference: Colonial Athletic.
Mailing Address: Hampton Boulevard, Norfolk, VA 23529. **Website:** www.odusports.com.
Head Coach: Tony Guzzo. **Assistant Coaches:** Eric Folmar, Scott Hearn, *Jimmy Tyrrell. **Telephone:** (757) 683-4230. ■ **Baseball SID:** Carol Hudson. **Telephone:** (757) 683-3372. **FAX:** (757) 683-3119.
Home Field: Bud Metheny Stadium. **Seating Capacity:** 2,500. **Outfield Dimensions:** LF—325, CF—395, RF—325. **Press Box Telephone:** (757) 683-5036.

ORAL ROBERTS Golden Eagles
Conference: Mid-Continent.
Mailing Address: 7777 S. Lewis Ave., Tulsa, OK 74171. **Website:** www.orugoldeneagles.com.
Head Coach: Rob Walton. **Assistant Coaches:** *Rob Cooper, Ryan Folmar, Ryan Neill. **Telephone:** (918) 495-7130. ■ **Baseball SID:** Cris Belvin. **Telephone:** (918) 495-7094. **FAX:** (918) 495-7142.
Home Field: J.L. Johnson Stadium. **Seating Capacity:** 2,418. **Outfield Dimensions:** LF—330, CF—400, RF—330. **Press Box Telephone:** (918) 495-7165.

OREGON STATE Beavers
Conference: Pacific-10.
Mailing Address: Gill Coliseum, Room 127, Corvallis, OR 97331. **Website:** www.osubeavers.com.
Head Coach: Pat Casey. **Assistant Coaches:** Donny Harrel, Marty Lees, *Dan Spencer. **Telephone:** (541) 737-2825. ■ **Baseball SID:** Kip Carlson. **Telephone:** (541) 737-7472. **FAX:** (541) 737-3072.
Home Field: Goss Stadium at Coleman Field. **Seating Capacity:** 2,000. **Outfield Dimensions:** LF—330, CF—400, RF—330. **Press Box Telephone:** (541) 737-7475.

PACE Setters
Conference: Independent.
Mailing Address: 861 Bedford Rd., Pleasantville, NY 10570. **Website:** www.pace.edu.
Head Coach: Hank Manning. **Assistant Coach:** *Trevor Brown, Jerry DeFabbia. **Telephone:** (914) 773-3413. ■ **Baseball SID:** Ken Sweeten. **Telephone:** (914) 773-3888. **FAX:** (914) 773-3491.

PACIFIC Tigers
Conference: Big West.
Mailing Address: 3601 Pacific Ave., Stockton, CA 95211. **Website Address:** www.pacifictigers.com.
Head Coach: Ed Sprague. **Assistant Coaches:** Tim Dixon, *Steve Pearse, Rob Selna. **Telephone:** (209) 946-

7309. ■ **Baseball SID:** Glen Sisk. **Telephone:** (209) 946-2730. **FAX:** (209) 946-2757.
Home Field: Billy Hebert Field. **Seating Capacity:** 6,000. **Outfield Dimensions:** LF—325, CF—390, RF—330. **Press Box Telephone:** (209) 644-1917.

PENNSYLVANIA Quakers
Conference: Ivy League (Gehrig).
Mailing Address: 235 S. 33rd St., James D. Donning Center, Philadelphia, PA 19104. **Website:** www.penn athletics.com.
Head Coach: *Bob Seddon. **Assistant Coaches:** Ralph Roesler, Bill Wagner. **Telephone:** (215) 898-6282. ■ **Baseball SID:** Carla Shultzberg. **Telephone:** (215) 898-6128. **FAX:** (215) 523-2095.

PENN STATE Nittany Lions
Conference: Big Ten.
Mailing Address: 101 Bryce Jordan Center, University Park, PA 16802. **Website:** www.gopsusports.com.
Head Coach: Joe Hindelang. **Assistant Coaches:** *Randy Ford, Jon Ramsey. **Telephone:** (814) 863-0230. ■ **Baseball SID:** Bob Volkert. **Telephone:** (814) 865-1757. **FAX:** (814) 863-3165.
Home Field: Beaver Field. **Seating Capacity:** 1,000. **Outfield Dimensions:** LF—350, CF—405, RF—350. **Press Box Telephone:** (814) 865-2552.

PEPPERDINE Waves
Conference: West Coast.
Mailing Address: 24255 Pacific Coast Hwy., Malibu, CA 90263. **Website:** www.pepperdinesports.com.
Head Coach: Steve Rodriguez. **Assistant Coaches:** *Rick Hirtensteiner, Ari Jacobs, Sean Kenny. **Telephone:** (310) 506-4371. ■ **Baseball SID:** Al Barba. **Telephone:** (310) 506-4455. **FAX:** (310) 506-4322.
Home Field: Eddy D. Field Stadium. **Seating Capacity:** 1,800. **Outfield Dimensions:** LF—330, CF—400, RF—330. **Press Box Telephone:** (310) 506-4598.

PITTSBURGH Panthers
Conference: Big East.
Mailing Address: P.O. Box 7436, Pittsburgh, PA 15213. **Website:** www.pittsburghpanthers.com.
Head Coach: Joe Jordano. **Assistant Coaches:** Joel Dombkowski, *Dan Ninemire, Todd Schiffhauer. **Telephone:** (412) 648-8208. ■ **Baseball SID:** Burt Lauten. **Telephone:** (412) 648-8240. **FAX:** (412) 648-8248.
Home Field: Trees Field. **Seating Capacity:** 200. **Outfield Dimensions:** LF—300, CF—400, RF—320. **Press Box Telephone:** None.

PORTLAND Pilots
Conference: West Coast.
Mailing Address: 5000 N. Willamette Blvd., Portland, OR 97203. **Website:** www.portlandpilots.com.
Head Coach: *Chris Sperry. **Assistant Coaches:** Matt Hollod, Gary Van Tol. **Telephone:** (503) 943-7707. ■ **Baseball SID:** Jason Brough. **Telephone:** (503) 943-7439. **FAX:** (503) 943-8082.
Home Field: Pilot Stadium. **Seating Capacity:** 1,500. **Outfield Dimensions:** LF—350, CF—390, RF—340. **Press Box Telephone:** (503) 943-7253.

PRAIRIE VIEW A&M Panthers
Conference: Southwestern Athletic.
Mailing Address: P.O. Box 97, Prairie View, TX 77446. **Website:** www.pvamu.edu/sports.
Head Coach: Michael Robertson. **Assistant Coach:** Waskyla Cullivan. **Telephone:** (936) 857-4290. ■ **Baseball SID:** Stefann Robinson. **Telephone:** (936) 857-2114. **FAX:** (936) 857-2395.

PRINCETON Tigers
Conference: Ivy League (Gehrig).
Mailing Address: P.O. Box 71, Jadwin Gym, Princeton, NJ 08544. **Website:** www.goprincetontigers.com.
Head Coach: Scott Bradley. **Assistant Coaches:** Lloyd Brewer, Pete Silletti. **Telephone:** (609) 258-5059. ■ **Baseball SID:** Yariv Amir. **Telephone:** (609) 258-5701. **FAX:** (609) 258-2399.

PURDUE Boilermakers
Conference: Big Ten.
Mailing Address: 302C Mollenkopf, West Lafayette, IN 47907. **Website:** www.purduesports.com.
Head Coach: Doug Schreiber. **Assistant Coaches:** *Todd Murphy, Rob Smith. **Telephone:** (765) 494-3998. ■ **Baseball SID:** Mark Leddy. **Telephone:** (765) 494-3281. **FAX:** (765) 494-5447.
Home Field: Lambert Field. **Seating Capacity:** 1,100. **Outfield Dimensions:** LF—340, CF—408, RF—340. **Press Box Telephone:** (765) 494-1522.

QUINNIPIAC Braves
Conference: Northeast.
Mailing Address: 275 Mount Carmel Ave., Hamden, CT 06518. **Website:** www.qunnipiacbobcats.com.
Head Coach: Dan Gooley. **Assistant Coaches:** Dan Scarpa, Marc Stonaha. **Telephone:** (203) 582-8966. ■ **Baseball SID:** Ben Dickie. **Telephone:** (203) 582-5387. **FAX:** (203) 582-5385.

RADFORD Highlanders
Conference: Big South.
Mailing Address: P.O. Box 6913, Radford, VA 24142. **Website:** www.radford.edu/athletics/index.html.
Head Coach: Lew Kent. **Assistant Coach:** Ryan Brittle, Robert Brown. **Telephone:** (540) 831-5881. ■ **Baseball SID:** Aaron Barter. **Telephone:** (540) 831-5211. **FAX:** (540) 831-5036.

RHODE ISLAND Rams
Conference: Atlantic-10.
Mailing Address: 3 Keaney Rd., Suite One, Kingston, RI 02881. **Website:** www.gorhody.com.
Head Coach: Frank Leoni. **Assistant Coaches:** Stephen Breitbach, *Jim Mason, Bob Wells. **Telephone:** (401) 874-4550. ■ **Baseball SID:** Mark Kwolek. **Telephone:** (401) 874-2409. **FAX:** (401) 874-5354.

RICE Owls
Conference: Western Athletic.
Mailing Address: 6100 Main St., Houston, TX 77005. **Website:** www.RiceOwls.com.
Head Coach: Wayne Graham. **Assistant Coaches:** Zane Curry, *David Pierce, Mike Taylor. **Telephone:** (713) 348-8864. ■ **Baseball SID:** John Sullivan. **Telephone:** (713) 348-5636. **FAX:** (713) 348-6019.
Home Field: Reckling Park. **Seating Capacity:** 3,500. **Outfield Dimensions:** LF—330, CF—400, RF—330. **Press Box Telephone:** (713) 348-4931.

RICHMOND Spiders
Conference: Atlantic-10 (West).
Mailing Address: Baseball Office, Robins Center, Richmond, VA 23173. **Website:** www.richmond spiders.com.
Head Coach: Ron Atkins. **Assistant Coaches:** Jason Johnson, Mike Loyd, *Adam Taylor. **Telephone:** (804) 289-1933. ■ **Baseball SID:** Stephanie Palewicz. **Telephone:** (804) 289-8391. **FAX:** (804) 289-8820.
Home Field: Pitt Field. **Seating Capacity:** 2,000. **Outfield Dimensions:** LF—320, CF—390, RF—320. **Press Box Telephone:** Unavailable.

RIDER Broncs

Conference: Metro Atlantic.
Mailing Address: 2083 Lawrenceville Rd., Lawrenceville, NJ 08648. **Website:** www.gobroncs.com.
Head Coach: Sonny Pittaro. **Assistant Coaches:** *Rick Freeman, Tom Petroff, Jeff Plunkett. **Telephone:** (609) 896-5055. ■ **Baseball SID:** Bud Focht. **Telephone:** (609) 896-5138. **FAX:** (609) 896-0341.

RUTGERS Scarlet Knights

Conference: Big East.
Mailing Address: 83 Rockefeller Rd., Piscataway, NJ 08854. **Website:** www.scarletknights.com.
Head Coach: Fred Hill. **Assistant Coaches:** Tom Baxter, Jay Blackwell, *Glen Gardner. **Telephone:** (732) 445-7833. ■ **Baseball SID:** Pat McBride. **Telephone:** (732) 445-7884. **FAX:** (732) 445-3063.
Home Field: Class of '53 Baseball Complex. **Seating Capacity:** 1,500. **Outfield Dimensions:** LF—330, CF—410, RF—320. **Press Box Telephone:** (732) 921-6743.

SACRAMENTO STATE Hornets

Conference: Independent.
Mailing Address: 6000 J St., Sacramento, CA 95819. **Website:** www.hornetsports.com.
Head Coach: John Smith. **Assistant Coaches:** Jim Barr, Rusty McLain. **Telephone:** (916) 278-7225. ■ **Baseball SID:** Brian Berger. **Telephone:** (916) 278-4313. **FAX:** (916) 278-5429.

SACRED HEART Pioneers

Conference: Northeast.
Mailing Address: 5151 Park Ave., Fairfield, CT 06825. **Website:** www.sacredheartpioneers.com.
Head Coach: Nick Giaquinto. **Assistant Coaches:** Bob Andrews, *Seth Kaplan. **Telephone:** (203) 365-7632. ■ **Baseball SID:** Gene Gumbs. **Telephone:** (203) 396-8127. **FAX:** (203) 371-7889.

ST. BONAVENTURE Bonnies

Conference: Atlantic-10 (East).
Mailing Address: Reilly Center, St. Bonaventure, NY 14778. **Website:** www.gobonnies.com.
Head Coach: Larry Sudbrook. **Assistant Coaches:** *Mark Evers, Kyle Stark. **Telephone:** (716) 375-2641. ■ **Baseball SID:** Steve Mest. **Telephone:** (716) 375-2319. **FAX:** (716) 375-2383.

ST. FRANCIS Terriers

Conference: Northeast.
Mailing Address: 180 Remsen St., Brooklyn Heights, NY 11201. **Website:** www.stfranciscollege.edu.
Head Coach: Frank Del George. **Assistant Coaches:** Robert Cruz, Walter Paller, Tommy Weber. **Telephone:** (718) 489-5490. ■ **Baseball SID:** Angela Merlino. **Telephone:** (718) 489-5369. **FAX:** (718) 797-2140.

ST. JOHN'S Red Storm

Conference: Big East.
Mailing Address: 8000 Utopia Pkwy., Jamaica, NY 11439. **Website:** www.redstormsports.com.
Head Coach: Ed Blankmeyer. **Assistant Coaches:** Scott Brown, *Mike Hampton. **Telephone:** (718) 990-6148. ■ **Baseball SID:** Mike Carey. **Telephone:** (718) 990-1521. **FAX:** (718) 969-8468.
Home Field: The Ballpark at St. John's. **Seating Capacity:** 3,500. **Outfield Dimensions:** LF—325, CF—390, RF—325. **Press Box Telephone:** (718) 990-2725.

ST. JOSEPH'S Hawks

Conference: Atlantic-10 (East).
Mailing Address: 5600 City Ave., Philadelphia, PA 19131. **Website:** www.sjuhawks.com.

Head Coach: Jim Ertel. **Assistant Coaches:** Mike DeLorenzo, *Kevin Sharp, Joe Tremoglie. **Telephone:** (610) 660-1718. ■ **Baseball SID:** Phil Denne. **Telephone:** (610) 660-1738. **FAX:** (610) 660-1724.

SAINT LOUIS Billikens

Conference: Conference USA.
Mailing Address: 3672 W. Pine Blvd., St. Louis, MO 63103. **Website:** www.slubillikens.com.
Head Coach: Bob Hughes. **Assistant Coach:** *Mike Reid. **Telephone:** (314) 977-3172. ■ **Baseball SID:** Diana Koval. **Telephone:** (314) 977-3463. **FAX:** (314) 977-7193.

ST. MARY'S Gaels

Conference: West Coast.
Mailing Address: 1928 St. Mary's Rd., Moraga, CA 94575. **Website:** www.smcgaels.com.
Head Coach: Jedd Soto. **Assistant Coaches:** Steve Roberts, Gabe Zappin. **Telephone:** (925) 631-4637. ■ **Baseball SID:** Ryan Reggiani. **Telephone:** (925) 631-4950. **FAX:** (925) 631-4405.
Home Field: Louis Guisto Field. **Seating Capacity:** 500. **Outfield Dimensions:** LF—340, CF—415, RF—340. **Press Box Telephone:** (925) 376-3906.

ST. PETER'S Peacocks

Conference: Metro Atlantic.
Mailing Address: 2641 John F. Kennedy Blvd., Jersey City, NJ 07306. **Website:** www.spc.edu/athletics/.
Head Coach: Jimmy Walsh. **Telephone:** (201) 915-9459. ■ **Baseball SID:** Tim Camp. **Telephone:** (201) 915-9101. **FAX:** (201) 915-9102.

SAM HOUSTON STATE Bearkats

Conference: Southland.
Mailing Address: P.O. Box 2268, Huntsville, TX 77341. **Website:** bearkats.shsu.edu.
Head Coach: Chris Rupp. **Assistant Coach:** Phillip Ghutzman. **Telephone:** (936) 294-1731. ■ **Baseball SID:** Paul Ridings. **Telephone:** (936) 294-1764. **FAX:** (936) 294-3538.

SAMFORD Bulldogs

Conference: Ohio Valley.
Mailing Address: 800 Lakeshore Dr., Birmingham, AL 35229. **Website:** www.samfordsports.com.
Head Coach: Tim Parenton. **Assistant Coaches:** *Jeramie Moore, *Jeff Newman, Gerald Tuck. **Telephone:** (205) 726-2134. ■ **Baseball SID:** Joey Mullins. **Telephone:** (205) 726-2799. **FAX:** (205) 726-2545.

SAN DIEGO Toreros

Conference: West Coast.
Mailing Address: 5998 Alcala Park, San Diego, CA 92110. **Website:** usdtoreros.com.
Head Coach: Rich Hill. **Assistant Coaches:** *Mike Kramer, Eric Valenzuela. **Telephone:** (619) 260-5953. ■ **Baseball SID:** Nick Mirkovich. **Telephone:** (619) 260-4745. **FAX:** (619) 260-2213.
Home Field: Cunningham Stadium. **Seating Capacity:** 1,500. **Outfield Dimensions:** LF—309, CF—395, RF—335. **Press Box Telephone:** None.

SAN DIEGO STATE Aztecs

Conference: Western Athletic.
Mailing Address: Department of Athletics, 5302 55th St., San Diego, CA 92182. **Website:** www.goaztecs.com.
Head Coach: Tony Gwynn. **Assistant Coaches:** *Rusty Filter, Anthony Johnson, Jay Martel. **Telephone:** (619) 594-6889. ■ **Baseball SID:** Dave Kuhn. **Telephone:** (619) 594-5242. **FAX:** (619) 582-6541.
Home Field: Tony Gwynn Stadium. **Seating Capacity:** 3,000. **Outfield Dimensions:** LF—340, CF—410, RF—

340. **Press Box Telephone:** (619) 594-4103.

SAN FRANCISCO Dons
Conference: West Coast.
Mailing Address: Memorial Gym, 2130 Fulton St., San Francisco, CA 94117. **Website:** www.usfdons.com.
Head Coach: Nino Giarratano. **Assistant Coaches:** *Greg Moore, Dutch Mendenhall, Troy Nakamura. **Telephone:** (415) 422-2934. ■ **Baseball SID:** Ryan McCrary. **Telephone:** (415) 422-6162. **FAX:** (415) 422-2510.
Home Field: Benedetti Diamond. **Seating Capacity:** 500. **Outfield Dimensions:** LF—313, CF—465, RF—321. **Press Box Telephone:** (415) 422-2919.

SAN JOSE STATE Spartans
Conference: Western Athletic.
Mailing Address: One Washington Square, San Jose, CA 95192. **Website:** www.sjsuspartans.com.
Head Coach: Sam Piraro. **Assistant Coaches:** Brian Kohndrow, *Dean Madsen, *Doug Thurman. **Telephone:** (408) 924-1255. ■ **Baseball SID:** Lawrence Fan. **Telephone:** (408) 924-1217. **FAX:** (408) 924-1291.
Home Field: Municipal Stadium. **Seating Capacity:** 5,000. **Outfield Dimensions:** LF—330, CF—400, RF—330. **Press Box Telephone:** (408) 924-7276.

SANTA CLARA Broncos
Conference: West Coast.
Mailing Address: 500 El Camino Real, Santa Clara, CA 95053. **Website:** www.santaclarabroncos.com.
Head Coach: Mark O'Brien. **Assistant Coaches:** Tom Myers, *Mike Oakland, Mike Zirelli. **Telephone:** (408) 554-4680. ■ **Baseball SID:** David Wahlstrom. **Telephone:** (408) 554-4670. **FAX:** (408) 554-6942.
Home Field: Buck Shaw Stadium. **Seating Capacity:** 6,800. **Outfield Dimensions:** LF—350, CF—400, RF—320. **Press Box Telephone:** (408) 554-4752.

SAVANNAH STATE Tigers
Conference: Independent.
Mailing Address: 3219 College St. Savannah, GA 31404. **Website:** www.savstate.edu.
Head Coach: Jamie Rigdon. **Assistant Coaches:** Robert Lampkin, Luis Marquez. **Telephone:** (912) 356-2801. ■ **Baseball SID:** Lee Pearson. **Telephone:** (912) 356-2446. **FAX:** (912) 353-3073.

SETON HALL Pirates
Conference: Big East.
Mailing Address: 400 S. Orange Ave., South Orange, NJ 07079. **Website:** www.shupirates.com.
Head Coach: Rob Sheppard. **Assistant Coaches:** Phil Cundari, Jim Duffy. **Telephone:** (973) 761-9557. ■ **Baseball SID:** Jeff Mead. **Telephone:** (973) 761-9493. **FAX:** (973) 761-9061.
Home Field: Owen T. Carroll Field. **Seating Capacity:** 1.000. **Outfield Dimensions:** LF—320, CF—400, RF—320. **Press Box Telephone:** (973) 818-1166.

SIENA Saints
Conference: Metro Atlantic.
Mailing Address: 515 New Loudon Rd., Loudonville, NY 12211. **Website:** www.sienasaints.com.
Head Coach: Tony Rossi. **Assistant Coaches:** *Bill Cilento, Matt Mueller, Paul Thompson. **Telephone:** (518) 786-5044. ■ **Baseball SID:** Jason Rich. **Telephone:** (518) 783-2411. **FAX:** (518) 783-2992.

SOUTH ALABAMA Jaguars
Conference: Sun Belt.
Mailing Address: 1209 Mitchell Center, Mobile, AL 36688. **Website:** www.usajaguars.com.

Head Coach: Steve Kittrell. **Assistant Coaches:** Tony David, Ronnie Powell, *Scot Sealy. **Telephone:** (251) 460-6876. ■ **Baseball SID:** Matt Smith. **Telephone:** (251) 460-7035. **FAX:** (251) 460-7297.
Home Field: Eddie Stanky Field. **Seating Capacity:** 3,500. **Outfield Dimensions:** LF—330, CF—400, RF—330. **Press Box Telephone:** (251) 460-7126.

SOUTH CAROLINA Gamecocks
Conference: Southeastern (East).
Mailing Address: 1300 Rosewood Dr., Columbia, SC 29208. **Website:** www.uscsports.com.
Head Coach: Ray Tanner. **Assistant Coaches:** Monty Lee, Jerry Meyers, *Jim Toman. **Telephone:** (803) 777-0116. ■ **Baseball SID:** Andrew Kitick. **Telephone:** (803) 777-5257. **FAX:** (803) 777-2967.
Home Field: Sarge Frye Field. **Seating Capacity:** 6,000. **Outfield Dimensions:** LF—330, CF—390, RF—320. **Press Box Telephone:** (803) 777-6648.

SOUTH FLORIDA Bulls
Conference: Conference USA.
Mailing Address: 4202 E. Fowler Ave., Tampa, FL 33620. **Website:** www.gousfbulls.com.
Head Coach: Eddie Cardieri. **Assistant Coaches:** Nelson North, *Bryan Peters. **Telephone:** (813) 974-2504. ■ **Baseball SID:** John Gerdes. **Telephone:** (813) 974-4086. **FAX:** (813) 974-5328.
Home Field: Red McEwen Field. **Seating Capacity:** 1,500. **Outfield Dimensions:** LF—340, CF—400, RF—340. **Press Box Telephone:** (813) 974-3604.

SOUTHEAST MISSOURI STATE Indians
Conference: Ohio Valley.
Mailing Address: One University Plaza, MS0200, Cape Girardeau, MO 63701. **Website:** www.gosoutheast.com.
Head Coach: Mark Hogan. **Assistant Coaches:** Jeff Dodson, Scott Southard. **Telephone:** (573) 651-2645. ■ **Baseball SID:** Ron Hines. **Telephone:** (573) 651-2294. **FAX:** (573) 651-2810.
Home Field: Capaha Field. **Seating Capacity:** 2,000. **Outfield Dimensions:** LF—335, CF—400, RF—335. **Press Box Telephone:** (573) 651-9139.

SOUTHEASTERN LOUISIANA Lions
Conference: Southland.
Mailing Address: SLU Station 10309, 800 Galloway Dr., Hammond, LA 70402. **Website:** www.lionsports.net.
Head Coach: Dan Canevari. **Assistant Coaches:** Fred Burnside, *Stephen Labbe, Graham Martin. **Telephone:** (985) 549-2896. ■ **Baseball SID:** David Steinle. **Telephone:** (985) 549-2142. **FAX:** (985) 549-3773.

SOUTHERN Jaguars
Conference: Southwestern Athletic.
Mailing Address: P.O. Box 9942, Baton Rouge, LA 70813. **Website:** www.subr.edu/baseball.
Head Coach: Roger Cador. **Assistant Coaches:** Jason Anderson, Arnold Brathwaite, *Barret Rey. **Telephone:** (225) 771-2513. ■ **Baseball SID:** Christopher Jones. **Telephone:** (225) 771-2601. **FAX:** (225) 771-2896.

SOUTHERN CALIFORNIA Trojans
Conference: Pacific-10.
Mailing Address: Dedeaux Field Building, Los Angeles, CA 90089. **Website:** www.usctrojans.com.
Head Coach: Mike Gillespie. **Assistant Coaches:** Rob Klein, *Dave Lawn, Andy Nieto. **Telephone:** (213) 740-5762. ■ **Baseball SID:** Jason Pommier. **Telephone:** (213) 740-8480. **FAX:** (213) 740-7584.
Home Field: Dedeaux Field. **Seating Capacity:** 2,500.

Outfield Dimensions: LF—335, CF—395, RF—335. Press Box Telephone: (213) 748-3449.

SOUTHERN ILLINOIS Salukis

Conference: Missouri Valley.
Mailing Address: 130 B Lingle Hall, Carbondale, IL 62901. Website: www.siusalukis.com.
Head Coach: Dan Callahan. Assistant Coaches: *Ken Henderson, Kevin Kimball, Bryan Wolff. Telephone: (618) 453-2802. ■ Baseball SID: Jeff Honza. Telephone: (618) 453-5470. FAX: (618) 453-2648.
Home Field: Abe Martin Field. Seating Capacity: 2,000. Outfield Dimensions: LF—340, CF—390, RF—340. Press Box Telephone: (618) 453-3794.

SOUTHERN MISSISSIPPI Golden Eagles

Conference: Conference USA.
Mailing Address: P.O. Box 5161, Hattiesburg, MS 39406. Website: www.southernmiss.com.
Head Coach: Corky Palmer. Assistant Coaches: Scott Berry, *Lane Burroughs, Allen Winningham. Telephone: (601) 266-5427. ■ Baseball SID: Mike Montoro. Telephone: (601) 266-5947. FAX: (601) 266-4507.
Home Field: Pete Taylor Park at Hill Denson Field. Seating Capacity: 3,678. Outfield Dimensions: LF—340, CF—400, RF—340. Press Box Telephone: (601) 266-5684.

SOUTHERN UTAH Thunderbirds

Conference: Mid-Continent.
Mailing Address: 351 W. Center St., Cedar City, UT 84720. Website: www.suu.edu/athletics.
Head Coach: *Kurt Palmer. Assistant Coach: Rick Wilding. Telephone: (435) 586-7932. ■ Baseball SID: Steve Johnson. Telephone: (435) 586-7752. FAX: (435) 865-8037.

SOUTHWEST MISSOURI STATE Bears

Conference: Missouri Valley.
Mailing Address: 901 S. National Ave., Springfield, MO 65804. Website: www.smsbears.net.
Head Coach: Keith Guttin. Assistant Coaches: Sam Carel, *Paul Evans, Brent Thomas. Telephone: (417) 836-5242. ■ Baseball SID: Jeff Williams. Telephone: (417) 836-5402. FAX: (417) 836-4868.
Home Fields (Seating Capacity): Hammons Field (8,000). Outfield Dimensions: LF—315, CF—400, RF—330. Press Box Telephone: (417) 343-8217.

STANFORD Cardinal

Conference: Pacific-10.
Mailing Address: Arrillaga Family Sports Center, Stanford, CA 94305. Website: www.gostanford.com.
Head Coach: Mark Marquess. Assistant Coaches: Tom Kunis, David Nakama, *Dean Stotz. Telephone: (650) 723-4528. ■ Baseball SID: Kyle McRae. Telephone: (650) 725-2959. FAX: (650) 725-2957.
Home Field: Sunken Diamond. Seating Capacity: 4,000. Outfield Dimensions: LF—335, CF—400, RF—335. Press Box Telephone: (650) 723-4629.

STETSON Hatters

Conference: Atlantic Sun.
Mailing Address: P.O. Box 8359, 421 N. Woodland Blvd., DeLand, FL 32723. Website: www.stetson.edu/athletics.
Head Coach: Pete Dunn. Assistant Coaches: Mitch Markham, Frank Martello, *Jeremy Tyson. Telephone: (386) 822-8106. ■ Baseball SID: Jamie Bataille. Telephone: (386) 822-8130. FAX: (386) 822-8133.
Home Field: Melching Field at Conrad Park. Seating Capacity: 2,500. Outfield Dimensions: LF—335, CF—

403, RF—335. Press Box Telephone: (386) 736-7360.

STONY BROOK Seawolves

Conference: America East.
Mailing Address: USB Sports Complex, Stony Brook, NY 11794. Website: www.goseawolves.org.
Head Coach: Matt Senk. Assistant Coaches: Tom Nielsen, Gerry Sputo. Telephone: (631) 632-9226. ■ Baseball SID: Robert Emmerich. Telephone: (631) 632-6312. FAX: (631) 632-8841.

TEMPLE Owls

Conference: Atlantic-10 (East).
Mailing Address: Vivacqua Hall, 4th Floor, 1700 N. Broad St., Philadelphia, PA 19122. Website: www.owl-sports.com.
Head Coach: Skip Wilson. Assistant Coaches: Shawn Dowds, Toby Fisher, *John McArdle. Telephone: (215) 643-1053. ■ Baseball SID: Chet Zukowski. Telephone: (215) 204-6912. FAX: (215) 204-7499.

TENNESSEE Volunteers

Conference: Southeastern (East).
Mailing Address: P.O. Box 15016, Knoxville, TN 37901. Website: www.utsports.com.
Head Coach: Rod Delmonico. Assistant Coaches: Fred Corral, Larry Simcox. Telephone: (865) 974-2057. ■ Baseball SID: Jeff Muir. Telephone: (865) 974-1212. FAX: (865) 974-1269.
Home Field: Lindsey Nelson Stadium. Seating Capacity: 4,000. Outfield Dimensions: LF—335, CF—404, RF—330. Press Box Telephone: (865) 974-3376.

TENNESSEE-MARTIN Skyhawks

Conference: Ohio Valley.
Mailing Address: 1037 Elam Center, Martin, TN 38238. Website: www.utm.edu.
Head Coach: *Bubba Cates. Assistant Coaches: Marshall Canosa, Jason Sullivan. Telephone: (731) 587-7337. ■ Baseball SID: Joe Lofaro. Telephone: (731) 587-7632. FAX: (731) 587-7624.

TENNESSEE TECH Golden Eagles

Conference: Ohio Valley.
Mailing Address: P.O. Box 5057, Cookeville, TN 38505. Website: www.tntech.edu.
Head Coach: Matt Bragga. Assistant Coaches: *Ryan Edwards, Craig Moore. Telephone: (931) 372-3925. ■ Baseball SID: Joanna Riley. Telephone: (931) 372-3088. FAX: (931) 372-6139.

TEXAS Longhorns

Conference: Big 12.
Mailing Address: P.O. Box 7399, Austin, TX 78713. Website: www.TexasSports.com.
Head Coach: Augie Garrido. Assistant Coaches: Dennis Cook, *Tommy Harmon, Tom Holliday. Telephone: (512) 471-5732. ■ Baseball SID: Mike Forcucci. Telephone: (512) 471-6039. FAX: (512) 471-6040.
Home Field: Disch-Falk Field. Seating Capacity: 6,649. Outfield Dimensions: LF—340, CF—400, RF—325. Press Box Telephone: (512) 471-1146.

TEXAS-ARLINGTON Mavericks

Conference: Southland.
Mailing Address: 1309 W. Mitchell St., Arlington, TX 76013. Website: utamavs.ocsn.com.
Head Coach: Jeff Curtis. Assistant Coaches: Scott Malone, *Darin Thomas. Telephone: (817) 272-2060. ■ Baseball SID: John Brush. Telephone: (817) 272-5706. FAX: (817) 272-2254.
Home Field: Clay Gould Ballpark. Seating Capacity: 1,600. Outfield Dimensions: LF—330, CF—400, RF—

330. **Press Box Telephone:** (817) 462-4225.

TEXAS-PAN AMERICAN Broncs
Conference: Independent.
Mailing Address: 1201 W. University Dr., Edinburg, TX 78541. **Website:** www.panam.edu/dept/athletics/.
Head Coach: Willie Gawlik. **Assistant Coaches:** *John Johnson, Kiki Trevino. **Telephone:** (956) 381-2235. ■
Baseball SID: Dave Geringer. **Telephone:** (956) 381-2240. **FAX:** (956) 381-2398.
Home Field: Edinburg Baseball Stadium. **Seating Capacity:** 4,000. **Outfield Dimensions:** LF—340, CF—410, RF—340. **Press Box Telephone:** Unavailable.

TEXAS-SAN ANTONIO Roadrunners
Conference: Southland.
Mailing Address: 6900 N. Loop 1604 W., San Antonio, TX 78249. **Website:** www.goutsa.com.
Head Coach: Sherman Corbett. **Assistant Coaches:** Jim Blair, *Jason Marshall. **Telephone:** (210) 458-4805. ■ **Baseball SID:** Erin Molina. **Telephone:** (210) 458-4930. **FAX:** (210) 458-4569.

TEXAS A&M Aggies
Conference: Big 12.
Mailing Address: P.O. Box 30017, College Station, TX 77843. **Website:** www.aggieathletics.com.
Head Coach: Mark Johnson. **Assistant Coaches:** David Coleman, Jason Hutchins, *Jim Lawler. **Telephone:** (979) 845-4810. ■ **Baseball SID:** Chuck Glenewinkel. **Telephone:** (979) 845-3239. **FAX:** (979) 845-0564.
Home Field: Olsen Field. **Seating Capacity:** 7,053. **Outfield Dimensions:** LF—330, CF—400, RF—330. **Press Box Telephone:** (979) 458-3604.

TEXAS A&M-CORPUS CHRISTI Islanders
Conference: Independent.
Mailing Address: 6300 Ocean Dr., Corpus Christi, TX 78412. **Website:** www.goislanders.com.
Head Coach: Hector Salinas. **Telephone:** (361) 825-3252. **Baseball SID:** John Gilger. **Telephone:** (361) 825-3410. **FAX:** (361) 825-3218.

TEXAS CHRISTIAN Horned Frogs
Conference: Conference USA.
Mailing Address: TCU Box 297600, Fort Worth, TX 76129. **Website:** www.gofrogs.com.
Head Coach: Jim Schlossnagle. **Assistant Coaches:** Heath Autrey, Mike Dilley, Matt Siegel, *Todd Whitting. **Telephone:** (817) 257-5354. ■ **Baseball SID:** Brandie Davidson. **Telephone:** (817) 257-7479. **FAX:** (817) 257-7964.
Home Field: Lupton Stadium. **Seating Capacity:** 2,500. **Outfield Dimensions:** LF—330, CF—400, RF—330. **Press Box Telephone:** (817) 257-7966.

TEXAS SOUTHERN Tigers
Conference: Southwestern Athletic.
Mailing Address: 3100 Cleburne St., Houston, TX 77004. **Website:** www.tsu.edu/athletics/.
Head Coach: Candy Robinson. **Assistant Coaches:** Rudy Courseault, Sonny Garcia, *Brian White. **Telephone:** (713) 313-7993. ■ **Baseball SID:** Lyshalle Thomas. **Telephone:** (713) 313-7271. **FAX:** (713) 313-1045.

TEXAS STATE Bobcats
Conference: Southland.
Mailing Address: 601 University Dr., San Marcos, TX 78666. **Website:** www.txstatebobcats.com.
Head Coach: Ty Harrington. **Assistant Coaches:** Howard Bushong, *Marcus Hendry, Greg Swindell. **Telephone:** (512) 245-7566. ■ **Baseball SID:** Max Kosub. **Telephone:** (512) 245-2988. **FAX:** (512) 245-2967.

Home Field: Bobcat Field. **Seating Capacity:** 1,800. **Outfield Dimensions:** LF—330, CF—404, RF—330. **Press Box Telephone:** (512) 245-3654.

TEXAS TECH Red Raiders
Conference: Big 12.
Mailing Address: P.O. Box 43021, Lubbock, TX 79409. **Website:** www.texastech.com.
Head Coach: Larry Hays. **Assistant Coaches:** Joe Dillon, *Daren Hays, Travis Walden. **Telephone:** (806) 742-3355. ■ **Baseball SID:** Blayne Beal. **Telephone:** (806) 742-2770. **FAX:** (806) 742-1970.
Home Field: Dan Law Field. **Seating Capacity:** 5,050. **Outfield Dimensions:** LF—330, CF—405, RF—330. **Press Box Telephone:** (806) 742-3688.

TOLEDO Rockets
Conference: Mid-American.
Mailing Address: 2801 W. Bancroft St., Toledo, OH 43606. **Website:** www.utrockets.com.
Head Coach: Cory Mee. **Assistant Coaches:** Mike Amrhein, Josh Bradford, *Matt Husted. **Telephone:** (419) 530-6263. ■ **Baseball SID:** Brian DeBenedictis. **Telephone:** (419) 530-4919. **FAX:** (419) 530-4930.

TOWSON Tigers
Conference: Colonial Athletic.
Mailing Address: 8000 York Rd., Towson, MD 21252. **Website:** www.towsontigers.com.
Head Coach: *Mike Gottlieb. **Assistant Coaches:** Mel Bacon, Liam Healy, Tony Quatraro. **Telephone:** (410) 704-3775. ■ **Baseball SID:** Dan O'Connell. **Telephone:** (410) 704-2232. **FAX:** (410) 704-3861.

TROY STATE Trojans
Conference: Atlantic Sun.
Mailing Address: Davis Field House, 100 George Wallace Dr., Troy, AL 36082. **Website:** www.troystate.com.
Head Coach: Bobby Pierce. **Assistant Coaches:** Todd Lamberth, *Mark Smartt. **Telephone:** (334) 670-3489. ■ **Baseball SID:** Josh Underwood. **Telephone:** (334) 670-5655. **FAX:** (334) 670-5665.

TULANE Green Wave
Conference: Conference USA.
Mailing Address: Wilson Center, Ben Weiner Drive, New Orleans, LA 70118. **Website:** www.tulanegreenwave.com.
Head Coach: Rick Jones. **Assistant Coaches:** Matthew Boggs, *Mark Kingston, Sean Teague. **Telephone:** (504) 862-8239. ■ **Baseball SID:** Richie Weaver. **Telephone:** (504) 314-7232. **FAX:** (504) 865-5512.
Home Field: Turchin Stadium. **Seating Capacity:** 3,600. **Outfield Dimensions:** LF—325, CF—400, RF—325. **Press Box Telephone:** (504) 862-8224.

UTAH Utes
Conference: Mountain West.
Mailing Address: 1825 E. South Campus Dr., Salt Lake City, UT 84112. **Website:** www.utahutes.com.
Head Coach: Tim Esmay. **Assistant Coaches:** Bryan Conger, *Matt Eeles, Chris Simonsen. **Telephone:** (801) 581-3526. ■ **Baseball SID:** Hope Wagner. **Telephone:** (801) 581-3771. **FAX:** (801) 581-4358.
Home Field: Franklin Covey Field. **Seating Capacity:** 15,500. **Outfield Dimensions:** LF—345, CF—420, RF—315. **Press Box Telephone:** (801) 464-6969.

UTAH VALLEY STATE Wolverines
Conference: Independent.
Mailing Address: 800 W. University Parkway, Orem, UT 84058. **Website:** www.wolverinesports.net.
Head Coach: Steve Gardner. **Assistant Coaches:** Eric Madsen, Nate Mathis. **Telephone:** (801) 863-8647. ■

Baseball SID: Todd Fairbourne. Telephone: (801) 863-8599. FAX: (801) 863-8813.

VALPARAISO Crusaders

Conference: Mid-Continent.

Mailing Address: Athletic Recreation Center, Valparaiso, IN 46383. Website: www.valpo.edu/athletics.

Head Coach: Paul Twenge. Assistant Coaches: Brian O'Connor, John Olson, Mark Waite Telephone: (219) 464-5239. ■ Baseball SID: Bill Rogers. Telephone: (219) 464-6953. FAX: (219) 464-6953.

VANDERBILT Commodores

Conference: Southeastern (East).

Mailing Address: 2601 Jess Neely Dr., Nashville, TN 37212. Website: www.vucommodores.com.

Head Coach: Tim Corbin. Assistant Coaches: *Erik Bakich, Michael Holder, Derek Johnson. Telephone: (615) 322-7725. ■ Baseball SID: Tammy Boclair. Telephone: (615) 343-4121. FAX: (615) 343-7064.

Home Field: Hawkins Field. Seating Capacity: 1,575. Outfield Dimensions: LF—310, CF—400, RF—330. Press Box Telephone: (615) 320-0436.

VERMONT Catamounts

Conference: America East.

Mailing Address: 226 Patrick Gym, Burlington, VT 05405. Website: www.uvmathletics.com.

Head Coach: Bill Currier. Assistant Coaches: Jim Carter, Mike Cole, *Anthony DeCicco. Telephone: (802) 656-7701. ■ Baseball SID: Bruce Bosley. Telephone: (802) 656-1109. FAX: (802) 656-8328.

VILLANOVA Wildcats

Conference: Big East.

Mailing Address: Jake Nevin Field House, 800 Lancaster Ave., Villanova, PA 19085. Website: www.villanova.com.

Head Coach: Joe Godri. Assistant Coaches: *Rick Clagett, Rod Johnson, Doc Kennedy. Telephone: (610) 519-4529. ■ Baseball SID: Jonathan Gust. Telephone: (610) 519-4122. FAX: (610) 519-7323.

Home Field: Villanova Ballpark at Plymouth Community Center. Seating Capacity: 750. Outfield Dimensions: LF—320, CF—405, RF—320. Press Box Telephone: (610) 937-2517.

VIRGINIA Cavaliers

Conference: Atlantic Coast.

Mailing Address: P.O. Box 400853, Charlottesville, VA 22904. Website: www.virginiasports.com.

Head Coach: Brian O'Connor. Assistant Coaches: Karl Kuhn, *Kevin McMullan, James Molinari. Telephone: (434) 982-4932. ■ Baseball SID: Adam Jones. Telephone: (434) 982-5131. FAX: (434) 982-5525.

Home Field: Virginia Baseball Field. Seating Capacity: 2,000. Outfield Dimensions: LF—352, CF—408, RF—352. Press Box Telephone: (434) 295-9262.

VIRGINIA COMMONWEALTH Rams

Conference: Colonial Athletic.

Mailing Address: 1300 W. Broad St., Richmond, VA 23284. Website: www.vcurams.vcu.edu.

Head Coach: *Paul Keyes. Assistant Coaches: Tim Haynes, Mark McQueen, Ryan Morris, Matt Reid. Telephone: (804) 828-4820. ■ Baseball SID: Niki DeSantis. Telephone: (804) 828-7000. FAX: (804) 828-7526.

Home Field: The Diamond. Seating Capacity: 12,134. Outfield Dimensions: LF—330, CF—402, RF—330. Press Box Telephone: (804) 359-1565.

VIRGINIA MILITARY INSTITUTE Keydets

Conference: Big South.

Mailing Address: Baseball Office, Cameron Hall, Lexington, VA 24450. Website: www.vmikeydets.com.

Head Coach: Marlin Ikenberry. Assistant Coaches: Chris Booth, Matt Kirby, *Andrew Slater. Telephone: (540) 464-7609. ■ Baseball SID: Ted Leshinski. Telephone: (540) 464-7015. FAX: (540) 464-7583.

VIRGINIA TECH Hokies

Conference: Big East.

Mailing Address: Room 460, Jameson Athletic Center, Blacksburg, VA 24061. Website: www.hokiesports.com.

Head Coach: Chuck Hartman. Assistant Coaches: Jon Hartness, *Jay Phillips. Telephone: (540) 231-3671. ■ Baseball SID: Dave Smith. Telephone: (540) 231-6726. FAX: (540) 231-6984.

Home Field: English Field. Seating Capacity: 1,500. Outfield Dimensions: LF—330, CF—400, RF—330. Press Box Telephone: (540) 231-4013.

WAGNER Seahawks

Conference: Northeast.

Mailing Address: One Campus Road, Staten Island, NY 10301. Website: www.wagner.edu/athletics.

Head Coach: *Joe Litterio. Assistant Coach: Jim Agnello, Jeff Toth. Telephone: (718) 390-3154. ■ Baseball SID: Todd Vatter. Telephone: (718) 390-3343. FAX: (718) 390-3347.

WAKE FOREST Demon Deacons

Conference: Atlantic Coast.

Mailing Address: P.O. Box 7426, Winston-Salem, NC 27109. Website: www.wakeforestsports.com.

Head Coach: George Greer. Assistant Coaches: Curtis Brown, Scott Daeley, *Jamie Mabe. Telephone: (336) 758-5570. ■ Baseball SID: Mike Vest. Telephone: (336) 758-1880. FAX: (336) 758-5140.

Home Field: Hooks Stadium. Seating Capacity: 2,500. Outfield Dimensions: LF—340, CF—400, RF—315. Press Box Telephone: (336) 759-9711.

WASHINGTON Huskies

Conference: Pacific-10.

Mailing Address: Graves Bldg., Box 354070, Seattle, WA 98195. Website: www.gohuskies.com.

Head Coach: Ken Knutson. Assistant Coaches: Travis Jewett, *Joe Ross, Gregg Swenson. Telephone: (206) 616-4335. ■ Baseball SID: Jeff Bechthold. Telephone: (206) 543-2230. FAX: (206) 543-5000.

Home Field: Husky Ballpark. Seating Capacity: 1,500. Outfield Dimensions: LF—327, CF—395, RF—317. Press Box Telephone: (206) 685-1994.

WASHINGTON STATE Cougars

Conference: Pacific-10.

Mailing Address: P.O Box 641602, Pullman, WA 99164. Website: www.wsucougars.com.

Head Coach: *Tim Mooney. Assistant Coaches: Mike Cummins, Gary Picone. Telephone: (509) 335-0211. ■ Baseball SID: Rachel Engrissei. Telephone: (509) 335-2684. FAX: (509) 335-0267.

Home Field: Bailey-Brayton Field. Seating Capacity: 3,500. Outfield Dimensions: LF—330, CF—400, RF—335.

WEST VIRGINIA Mountaineers

Conference: Big East.

Mailing Address: P.O. Box 0877, Morgantown, WV 26507. Website: www.msnsportsnet.com.

Head Coach: Greg Van Zant. Assistant Coaches: *Bruce Cameron, Jeff Ditch, Wayne Smith. Telephone:

(304) 293-2308. ■ **Baseball SID:** Tim Goodenow. **Telephone:** (304) 293-2821. **FAX:** (304) 293-4105.
Home Field: Hawley Field. **Seating Capacity:** 1,500. **Outfield Dimensions:** LF—325, CF—390, RF—325. **Press Box Telephone:** (304) 293-5988.

WESTERN CAROLINA Catamounts

Conference: Southern.
Mailing Address: Ramsey Center, Cullowhee, NC 28723. **Website:** www.catamountsports.com.
Head Coach: Todd Raleigh. **Assistant Coaches:** *Eric Filipek, Paul Menhart, Bergin Tatham. **Telephone:** (828) 227-2021. ■ **Baseball SID:** Mike Cawood. **Telephone:** (828) 227-2339. **FAX:** (828) 227-7688.
Home Field: Childress Field at Hennon Stadium. **Seating Capacity:** 1,500. **Outfield Dimensions:** LF—325, CF—390, RF—325. **Press Box Telephone:** (828) 227-7020.

WESTERN ILLINOIS Leathernecks

Conference: Mid-Continent.
Mailing Address: 204 Western Hall, 1 University Circle, Macomb, IL 61455. **Website:** www.wiuathletics.com.
Head Coach: Stan Hyman. **Assistant Coaches:** Mark Hilyard, Brigham John, Brian Lewis, *Greg Schaub. **Telephone:** (309) 298-1521. ■ **Baseball SID:** Shana Daniels. **Telephone:** (309) 298-1133. **FAX:** (309) 298-3366.

WESTERN KENTUCKY Hilltoppers

Conference: Sun Belt.
Mailing Address: One Big Red Way, Bowling Green, KY 42101. **Website:** www.wkusports.com.
Head Coach: Joel Murrie. **Assistant Coaches:** Luis Rodriguez, Mike McLaury, Dan Mosier. **Telephone:** (270) 745-6023. ■ **Baseball SID:** Chris Glowacki. **Telephone:** (270) 745-5388. **FAX:** (270) 745-3444.

WESTERN MICHIGAN Broncos

Conference: Mid-American.
Mailing Address: West Michigan Ave., Kalamazoo, MI 49008. **Website:** www.wmubroncos.com.
Head Coach: Fred Decker. **Assistant Coaches:** Mike Diaz, *Ken Jones. **Telephone:** (269) 387-8149. ■ **Baseball SID:** Paula Haughn. **Telephone:** (269) 387-4123. **FAX:** (269) 387-4139.

WICHITA STATE Shockers

Conference: Missouri Valley.
Mailing Address: 1845 Fairmount St., Campus Box 18, Wichita, KS 67260. **Website:** www.goshockers.com.
Head Coach: Gene Stephenson. **Assistant Coaches:** *Brent Kemnitz, Mike Stover, Jim Thomas. **Telephone:** (316) 978-3636. ■ **Baseball SID:** Tami Cutler. **Telephone:** (316) 978-5559. **FAX:** (316) 978-3336.
Home Field: Tyler Field-Eck Stadium. **Seating Capacity:** 7,851. **Outfield Dimensions:** LF—330, CF—390, RF—330. **Press Box Telephone:** (316) 978-3390.

WILLIAM & MARY Tribe

Conference: Colonial Athletic.
Mailing Address: P.O. Box 399, Williamsburg, VA 23187. **Website:** www.tribeathletics.com.
Head Coach: Jim Farr. **Assistant Coaches:** Rick Ciccionne, *Ryan Wheeler. **Telephone:** (757) 221-3399. ■ **Baseball SID:** Chris Poore. **Telephone:** (757) 221-3370. **FAX:** (757) 221-3412.
Home Field: Plumeri Park. **Seating Capacity:** 1,000. **Outfield Dimensions:** LF—315, CF—390, RF—315.

Press Box Telephone: (757) 221-3562.

WINTHROP Eagles

Conference: Big South.
Mailing Address: Winthrop Coliseum, Rock Hill, SC 29733. **Website:** www.winthropeagles.com.
Head Coach: Joe Hudak. **Assistant Coaches:** Kyle DiEduardo, Scott Forbes, *Jeremy Keller. **Telephone:** (803) 323-2129. ■ **Baseball SID:** John Verser. **Telephone:** (803) 366-0647. **FAX:** (803) 323-2433.
Home Field: Winthrop Ballpark. **Seating Capacity:** 2,000. **Outfield Dimensions:** LF—330, CF—390, RF—330. **Press Box Telephone:** (803) 323-2114/2155.

WISCONSIN-MILWAUKEE Panthers

Conference: Horizon.
Mailing Address: Athletic Dept., North Bldg., P.O. Box 413, Milwaukee, WI 53201. **Website:** www.uwmpanthers.com.
Head Coach: Jerry Augustine. **Assistant Coach:** Cory Bigler, *Scott Doffek. **Telephone:** (414) 229-5670. ■ **Baseball SID:** Kevin O'Connor. **Telephone:** (414) 229-5674. **FAX:** (414) 229-6759.

WOFFORD Terriers

Conference: Southern.
Mailing Address: 429 N. Church St., Spartanburg, SC 29303. **Website:** www.wofford.edu/athletics.
Head Coach: Steve Traylor. **Assistant Coaches:** Scott Brickman, Brandon McKillop. **Telephone:** (864) 597-4126. ■ **Baseball SID:** Mark Cohen. **Telephone:** (864) 597-4093. **FAX:** (864) 597-4129.

WRIGHT STATE Raiders

Conference: Horizon.
Mailing Address: 3640 Col. John Glenn Hwy., Dayton, OH 45435. **Website:** www.wsuraiders.com.
Head Coach: Ron Nischwitz. **Assistant Coaches:** Doug Long, *Jake Long. **Telephone:** (937) 775-2771. ■ **Baseball SID:** Greg Campbell. **Telephone:** (937) 775-4687. **FAX:** (937) 775-2818.

XAVIER Musketeers

Conference: Atlantic-10 (West).
Mailing Address: 3800 Victory Pkwy., Cincinnati, OH 45207. **Website:** www.xavier.edu/athletics.
Head Coach: John Morrey. **Assistant Coaches:** J.D. Heilmann, *Joe Regruth. **Telephone:** (513) 745-2890. ■ **Baseball SID:** Bill Thomas. **Telephone:** (513) 745-3416. **FAX:** (513) 745-2825.

YALE Bulldogs

Conference: Ivy League (Rolfe).
Mailing Address: 20 Tower Pkwy., New Haven, CT 06520. **Website:** www.yalebulldogs.com.
Head Coach: John Stuper. **Assistant Coaches:** Bill Asermely, Glenn Lungarini. **Telephone:** (203) 432-1466. ■ **Baseball SID:** Ernie Bertothy. **Telephone:** (203) 432-1448. **FAX:** (203) 432-1454.

YOUNGSTOWN STATE Penguins

Conference: Horizon.
Mailing Address: One University Plaza, Youngstown, OH 44555. **Website:** www.ysu.edu/sports.
Head Coach: *Mike Florak. **Assistant Coaches:** Craig Antush, Mark Thomas. **Telephone:** (330) 941-3485. ■ **Baseball SID:** Trevor Parks. **Telephone:** (330) 941-3192. **FAX:** (330) 941-3191.

SMALL COLLEGES

NCAA DIVISION II • NCAA DIVISION III • NAIA

School	Mailing Address	Head Coach	Telephone
Abilene Christian U.	ACU Station, Box 27916, Abilene, TX 79699	Britt Bonneau	(325) 674-2325
Adelphi U.	South Ave., Garden City, NY 11530	Ron Davies	(516) 877-4240
Adrian College	110 S. Madison St., Adrian, MI 49221	Craig Rainey	(517) 264-3977
Alabama-Huntsville, U. of	205 Spragins Hall, Huntsville, AL 35899	David Keel	(256) 824-2206
Albany State U.	504 College Dr., Albany, GA 31705	Edward Taylor	(229) 430-1829
Albertson College	2112 Cleveland Blvd., Caldwell, ID 83605	Shawn Humberger	(208) 459-5861
Albertus Magnus College	700 Prospect St., New Haven, CT 06511	Joe Tonelli Jr.	(203) 773-8578
Albion College	4830 Kellogg Center, Albion, MI 49224	Scott Carden	(517) 629-0517
Albright College	PO Box 15234, Reading, PA 19612	Jeff Feiler	(610) 921-7678
Alderson-Broaddus	500 College Hill Rd., Philippi, WV 26416	Kit Laird	(304) 457-6265
Alice Lloyd College	100 Purpose Rd., Pippa Passes, KY 41844	Scott Cornett	(606) 368-6120
Allegheny College	PO Box AC, Meadville, PA 16335	Mike Ferris	(814) 332-2830
Alma College	614 W. Superior St., Alma, MI 48801	John Leister	(989) 463-7265
Alvernia College	400 Saint Bernardine St., Reading, PA 19607	Yogi Lutz	(610) 796-8476
American Int'l Coll.	1000 State St., Springfield, MA 01109	Chuck Lelas	(413) 205-3574
Amherst College	PO Box 5000, Amherst, MA 01002	Bill Thurston	(413) 542-2284
Anderson College	316 Boulevard St., Anderson, SC 29621	Joe Miller	(864) 231-2013
Anderson U.	1100 E. 5th St., Anderson, IN 46012	Don Brandon	(765) 641-4488
Anna Maria College	50 Sunset Lane, Paxton, MA 01612	Rich Coleman	(508) 849-3446
Aquinas College	1607 Robinson Rd. SE, Grand Rapids, MI 49506	Doug Greenslate	(616) 632-2935
Arcadia University	450 S. Easton Rd., Glenside, PA 19038	Stan Exeter	(215) 572-2976
Arkansas Tech	1604 Coliseum Dr., Russellville, AR 72801	Billy Goss	(479) 968-0648
Arkansas-Monticello, U. of	UAM Box 3066, Monticello, AR 71656	Kevin Downing	(870) 460-1257
Armstrong Atlantic State U.	11935 Abercorn St., Savannah, GA 31419	Joe Roberts	(912) 921-5686
Asbury College	1 Macklem Dr., Wilmore, KY 40390	Joe Reed	(859) 858-3511
Ashland U.	916 King Rd., Ashland, OH 44805	John Schaly	(419) 289-5444
Assumption College	500 Salisbury St., Worcester, MA 01609	Jim Vail	(508) 767-7232
Atlanta Christian College	2605 Ben Hill Rd., East Point, GA 30344	Alan Wilson	(404) 761-8861
Auburn U.-Montgomery	7301 Senators Dr., Montgomery, AL 36124	Q.V. Lowe	(334) 244-3237
Augsburg College	2211 Riverside Ave., Minneapolis, MN 55454	Doug Schildgen	(612) 330-1395
Augusta State U.	2500 Walton Way #10, Augusta, GA 30904	Stanley Fite	(706) 731-7917
Augustana College	3500 5th Ave., Rock Island, IL 61201	Greg Wallace	(309) 794-7521
Augustana College	2001 S. Summit Ave, Sioux Falls, SD 57197	Jeff Holm	(605) 274-5541
Aurora U.	347 S. Gladstone Ave, Aurora, IL 60506	Shaun Neitzel	(630) 844-6515
Austin College	900 N. Grand Ave, Suite 6A, Sherman, TX 75090	Bruce Mauppin	(903) 813-2516
Averett University	420 W. Main St., Danville, VA 24541	Ed Fulton	(434) 791-5030
Avila U.	11901 Wornall Rd., Kansas City, MO 64145	Ryan Howard	(816) 501-3739
Azusa Pacific U.	901 E. Alosta Ave., Azusa, CA 91702	Paul Svagdis	(626) 815-6000
Babson College	Webster Center, Babson Park, MA 02457	Matt Noone	(781) 239-5823
Bacone College	2299 Old Bacone Rd., Muskogee, OK 74403	Matt Cloud	(918) 781-7237
Baker U.	PO Box 65, Baldwin City, KS 66006	Phil Hannon	(785) 594-8493
Baldwin-Wallace College	275 Eastland Rd., Berea, OH 44017	Bob Fisher	(440) 826-2182
Barber-Scotia College	145 Cabarrus Ave. West, Concord, NC 28025	Lane Mears	(704) 789-2959
Barry U.	11300 NE 2nd Ave., Miami Shores, FL 33161	Juan Ranero	(305) 899-3558
Barton College	401 Rountree St., Wilson, NC 27893	Todd Wilkinson	(252) 399-6552
Baruch College	One Bernard Baruch Way, New York, NY 10010	Miguel Iglesias	(616) 312-5040
Bates College	130 Central Ave., Lewiston, ME 04240	Craig Vandersea	(207) 786-6063
Becker College	964 Main St., Leicester, MA 01524	Walter Beede	(508) 791-9241
Belhaven College	1500 Peachtree St., Jackson, MS 39202	Hill Denson	(601) 968-8898
Bellarmine College	2001 Newburg Rd., Louisville, KY 40205	Scott Wiegandt	(502) 452-8496
Bellevue U.	1000 Galvin Rd. S., Bellevue, NE 68005	Mike Evans	(402) 293-3782
Belmont Abbey College	100 Belmont-Mount Holly Rd., Belmont, NC 28012	Kermit Smith	(704) 825-6804
Beloit College	700 College St., Beloit, WI 53511	Dave DeGeorge	(608) 363-2039
Bemidji State U.	1500 Birchmont Dr. NE, Bemidji, MN 56601	Chris Brown	(218) 755-4620
Benedict College	1600 Harden St., Columbia, SC 29204	Derrick Johnson	(803) 733-7421
Benedictine College	1020 N. 2nd St., Atchison, KS 66002	Dan Griggs	(913) 367-5340
Benedictine U.	5700 College Rd., Lisle, IL 60532	John Ostrowski	(630) 829-6147
Bentley College	175 Forest St., Waltham, MA 02452	Bob DeFelice	(781) 891-2332
Berea College	CPO 2187, Berea, KY 40404		(859) 985-3429
Berry College	PO Box 495015, Mount Berry, GA 30149	David Beasley	(706) 236-1743
Bethany College	Hummel Fieldhouse, Bethany, WV 26032	Rick Carver	(304) 829-7246
Bethany College	800 Bethany Dr., Scotts Valley, CA 95066	Giuseppe Chiaramonte	(831) 438-3800
Bethany College	421 N. First, Lindsborg, KS 67456	Matt Tramel	(785) 227-3380
Bethel College	1001 McKinley Ave, Mishawaka, IN 46545	Seth Zartman	(574) 257-3287
Bethel College	3900 Bethel Dr., St. Paul, MN 55112	Greg Indlecoffer	(651) 638-6143

College	Address	Contact	Phone
Bethel College	325 Cherry Ave., McKenzie, TN 38201	Glenn Hayes	(731) 352-4206
Biola U.	13800 Biola Ave, La Mirada, CA 90639	John Verhoeven	(562) 944-0351
Blackburn College	700 College Ave., Carlinville, IL 62626	Mike Neal	(217) 854-3231
Bloomfield College	467 Franklin St., Bloomfield, NJ 07003	Matt Belford	(973) 748-9000
Bloomsburg U.	400 E. 2nd St., Bloomsburg, PA 17815	Matt Haney	(570) 389-4375
Bluefield College	3000 College Dr., Bluefield, VA 24605	Billy Berry	(276) 326-4545
Bluefield State College	219 Rock St., Bluefield, WV 24701	Geoff Hunter	(304) 327-4084
Bluffton College	280 West College Ave, Bluffton, OH 45817	James Grandey	(419) 358-3227
Bowdoin College	9000 College Station, Brunswick, ME 04011	Michael Connolly	(207) 725-3734
Brandeis U.	Gosman Sports Center, MS 007, Waltham, MA 02454	Pete Varney	(781) 736-3639
Brescia U.	717 Frederica St., Owensboro, KY 42301	Jason Vittone	(270) 686-4207
Brevard College	400 N. Broad St., Brevard, NC 28712	Gil Payne	(828) 884-8273
Brewton Parker College	Hwy. 280, Mt. Vernon, GA 30445	Chad Parker	(912) 583-3177
Briar Cliff U.	PO Box 2100, Sioux City, IA 51104	Boyd Pitkin	(712) 279-5553
Bridgeport, U. of	120 Waldemere Ave., Bridgeport, CT 06601	John Anquillare	(203) 576-4229
Bridgewater College	402 E. College St., Bridgewater, VA 22812	Curt Kendall	(540) 828-5407
Bridgewater State College	Room 200, Bridgewater, MA 02325	Rick Smith	(508) 531-2898
British Columbia, U. of	6081 University Blvd., Vancouver, B.C. V6T 1Z1	Terry McKaig	(604) 822-4270
Bryan College	721 Bryan Dr., Dayton, TN 37321	Preston Douglas	(423) 775-7569
Bryant College	1150 Douglas Pike, Smithfield, RI 02917	Jon Sjogren	(401) 232-6397
Buena Vista U.	610 West 4th St., Storm Lake, IA 50588	Steve Eddie	(712) 749-2298
C.W. Post/Long Island U.	720 Northern Blvd., Brookville, NY 11548	Dick Vining	(516) 299-2938
Caldwell College	9 Ryerson Ave., Caldwell, NJ 07006	Chris Reardon	(973) 618-3462
UC Davis	One Shields Ave., Davis, CA 95616	Rex Peters	(530) 752-7513
UC San Diego	9500 Gilman Dr., La Jolla, CA 92093	Dan O'Brien	(858) 534-4211
Cal Poly Pomona	3801 West Temple Ave., Pomona, CA 91768	Mike Ashman	(909) 869-2829
Cal State Chico	1st & Orange Sts., Chico, CA 95929	Lindsay Meggs	(530) 898-4374
Cal State Dominguez Hills	1000 E. Victoria St., Carson, CA 90747	George Wing	(310) 243-3765
Cal State Hayward	25800 Carlos Bee Blvd., Hayward, CA 94542	Dirk Morrison	(510) 885-3046
Cal State Los Angeles	5151 State University Dr., Los Angeles, CA 90032	John Herbold	(323) 343-3093
Cal State San Bernardino	5500 University Pwy., San Bernardino, CA 92407	Don Parnell	(909) 880-5021
Cal State Stanislaus	801 W. Monte Vista Ave., Turlock, CA 95382	Kenny Leonesio	(209) 667-3272
Cal Tech	1200 E. California Blvd., Pasadena, CA 91125	John D'Auria	(626) 395-3263
California Baptist U.	8432 Magnolia Ave., Riverside, CA 92504	Gary Adcock	(909) 343-4382
California Lutheran U.	60 W. Olsen Rd., Thousand Oaks, CA 91360	Marty Slimak	(805) 493-3398
California U. (Pa.)	250 University Ave., California, PA 15419	Mike Conte	(724) 938-4388
Calumet College	2400 New York Ave., Whiting, IN 46394	Frank Eccles	(219) 473-4327
Calvin College	3201 Burton St. SE, Grand Rapids, MI 49546	Jeff Pettinga	(616) 957-6021
Cameron U.	2800 West Gore Blvd., Lawton, OK 73505	Todd Holland	(580) 581-2479
Campbellsville U.	1316 University Dr., Campbellsville, KY 42718	Beauford Sanders	(270) 789-5056
Capital U.	2199 E. Main St., Columbus, OH 43209	Greg Weyrich	(614) 236-6203
Cardinal Stritch U.	6801 N. Yates Rd., Milwaukee, WI 53217	Michael Zolecki	(414) 410-4519
Carleton College	1 N. College St., Northfield, MN 55057	Bill Nelson	(507) 646-4051
Carroll College	100 N. East Ave, Waukesha, WI 53186	Stephen Dannhoff	(262) 524-7105
Carson-Newman College	2130 Branner Ave., Jefferson City, TN 37760	Brent Achord	(865) 471-3465
Carthage College	2001 Alford Park Dr., Kenosha, WI 53140	Augie Schmidt	(262) 551-5935
Case Western Reserve U.	10900 Euclid Ave., Cleveland, OH 44106	Jerry Seimon	(216) 368-5379
Castleton State College	One Glennbrook Rd., Castleton, VT 05735	Ted Shipley	(802) 468-1485
Catawba College	2300 W. Innes St., Salisbury, NC 28144	Jim Gantt	(704) 637-4469
Catholic U.	3606 McCormack Rd. NE, Washington, DC 20064	Ross Natoli	(202) 319-6092
Cazenovia College	Liberty Street, Cazenovia, NY 13035	Peter Liddell	(315) 655-7141
Cedarville U.	251 N. Main St., Cedarville, OH 45314	Greg Hughes	(937) 766-3246
Centenary College	400 Jefferson St., Hackettstown, NJ 07840	Dave Sawicki	(908) 852-1400
Central Arkansas, U. of	314 Western Ave., Conway, AR 72032	Doug Clark	(501) 450-3407
Central Christian College	PO Box 1403, McPherson, KS 67460	Jared Hamilton	(620) 241-0723
Central College	812 University St., Pella, IA 50219	Adam Stevens	(641) 628-5348
Central Methodist College	411 CMC Square, Fayette, MO 65248	Jim Dapkus	(660) 248-6352
Central Missouri State U.	500 Washington St., Warrensburg, MO 64093	Darin Hendrickson	(660) 543-4800
Central Oklahoma, U. of	100 N. University Dr., Edmond, OK 73034	Wendell Simmons	(405) 974-2506
Central Washington U.	400 E. 8th Ave., Ellensburg, WA 98926	Desi Storey	(509) 963-3018
Centre College	600 W. Walnut St., Danville, KY 40422	Ed Rall	(859) 238-5489
Chapman U.	One University Dr., Orange, CA 92866	Tom Tereschuk	(714) 997-6662
Charleston, U. of	2300 MacCorkle Ave. SE, Charleston, WV 25304	Tom Nozica	(304) 357-4823
Chicago, U. of	5530 S. Ellis Ave., Chicago, IL 60637	Brian Baldea	(773) 702-4643
Chowan College	200 Jones Dr., Murfreesboro, NC 27855	Steve Flack	(252) 398-6228
Christian Brothers U.	650 E. Parkway South, Memphis, TN 38104	Phil Goodwin	(901) 321-3375
Christopher Newport U.	1 University Place, Newport News, VA 23606	John Harvell	(757) 594-7054
Circleville Bible Coll.	PO Box 458, Circleville, OH 43113	Larry Olson	(740) 477-7761
Claflin U.	400 Magnolia St., Orangeburg, SC 29115	Bill Newsome	(803) 535-5295
Claremont-Mudd-Scripps Coll	500 E. 9th St., Claremont, CA 91711	Randy Town	(909) 607-3796
Clarion U.	Wood St./Tippin Gym, Room 112 Clarion, PA 16214	Scott Feldman	(814) 393-1651
Clark Atlanta U.	223 Brawley Dr., Atlanta, GA 30314	Chris Atwell	(404) 880-6648

College	Address	Contact	Phone
Clark U.	950 Main St., Worcester, MA 01610	Jason Falcon	(508) 421-3832
Clarke College	1550 Clarke Dr., Dubuque, IA 52001	Eric Frese	(563) 588-6601
Clarkson U.	Box 5830, Alumni Gym, Potsdam, NY 13699	Jim Kane	(315) 268-3759
Clearwater Christian	3400 Gulf-to-Bay Blvd., Clearwater, FL 33759	Mark Bates	(727) 726-1153
Coe College	1220 First Ave. NE, Cedar Rapids, IA 52402	Steve Cook	(319) 399-8849
Coker College	300 E. College Ave., Hartsville, SC 29550	Dave Schmotzer	(843) 383-8105
Colby College	4900 Mayflower Hill, Waterville, ME 04901	Tom Dexter	(207) 872-3369
Colby-Sawyer College	541 Main St., New London, NH 03257	Jim Broughton	(603) 526-3607
Colorado School of Mines	1500 Illinois St., Golden, CO 80401	Mike Mulvaney	(303) 273-3367
Colorado State U.-Pueblo	2200 N. Bonforte Blvd., Pueblo, CO 81001	Stan Sanchez	(719) 549-2065
Columbia Union College	7600 Flower Ave., Takoma Park, MD 20912	Rhett Ross	(301) 891-4026
Columbus State U.	4225 University Ave., Columbus, GA 31907	Greg Appleton	(706) 568-2444
Concord College	Campus Box 77, Athens, WV 24712	Kevin Garrett	(304) 384-5340
Concordia College (Ala.)	1804 Green St., Selma, AL 36703	Frank Elliott	(334) 874-7143
Concordia College (Minn.)	901 8th Street S., Moorhead, MN 56562	Don Burgau	(218) 299-3209
Concordia College (N.Y.)	171 White Plains Rd., Bronxville, NY 10708	Bob Greiner	(914) 337-9300
Concordia U. (Calif.)	1530 Concordia West, Irvine, CA 92612	Tony Barbone	(949) 584-8002
Concordia U. (Ill.)	7400 Augusta St., River Forest, IL 60305	Spiro Lempesis	(708) 209-3125
Concordia U. (Mich.)	4090 Geddes Rd., Ann Arbor, MI 48105	Karl Kling	(734) 995-7343
Concordia U. (Minn.)	275 Syndicate St. N., St. Paul, MN 55104	Mark McKenzie	(651) 603-6208
Concordia U. (Neb.)	800 N. Columbia Ave, Seward, NE 68434	Jeremy Geidel	(402) 643-7347
Concordia U. (Ore.)	2811 NE Holman St., Portland, OR 97211	Rob Vance	(503) 280-8691
Concordia U. (Texas)	3400 I-35 North, Austin, TX 78705	Mike Gardner	(512) 486-1160
Concordia U. (Wis.)	12800 N. Lake Shore Dr., Mequon, WI 53097	Val Keiper	(262) 243-4266
Cornell College	600 1st Street W., Mount Vernon, IA 52314	Frank Fisher	(319) 895-4257
Cortland State	Pashley Dr., Cortland, NY 13045	Joe Brown	(607) 753-4950
Crown College	6425 County Road 30, St. Bonafacius, MN 55375	Kelly Spann	(952) 446-4146
Culver-Stockton College	One College Hill, Canton, MO 63435	Doug Bletcher	(217) 231-6374
Cumberland College	7526 College Station Dr., Williamsburg, KY 40769	Brad Shelton	(606) 539-4387
Cumberland U.	One Cumberland Sq., Lebanon, TN 37087	Woody Hunt	(615) 444-2562
Curry College	1071 Blue Hill Ave., Miller Gym, Milton, MA 02186	Dave Perdios	(617) 333-2055
D'Youville College	320 Porter Ave., Buffalo, NY 14201	Jeff Johnson	(716) 912-2717
Dakota State U.	820 N. Washington Ave, Madison, SD 57042	Pat Dolan	(605) 256-5232
Dakota Wesleyan U.	1200 W. University Ave, Mitchell, SD 57301	Adam Neisius	(605) 995-2853
Dallas Baptist U.	3000 Mountain Creek Pkwy., Dallas, TX 75211	Mike Bard	(214) 333-5326
Dallas, U. of	1845 E. Northgate Dr., Irving, TX 75062	Sam Blackmon	(972) 721-5117
Dana College	2848 College Dr., Blair, NE 68008	Chad Gorman	(402) 426-7374
Daniel Webster College	20 University Dr., Nashua, NH 03063	Brian Aloia	(603) 577-6491
Davis & Elkins College	100 Campus Dr., Elkins, WV 26241	Ryan Brisbin	(304) 637-1342
Defiance College	701 N. Clinton St., Defiance, OH 43512	Chad Donsbach	(419) 783-2341
Delaware Valley College	700 E. Butler Ave., Doylestown, PA 18901	Bob Altieri	(215) 489-2379
Delta State U.	PO Box 3161, Cleveland, MS 38733	Mike Kinnison	(662) 846-4291
Denison U.	PO Box 111, Granville, OH 43023	Barry Craddock	(740) 587-6714
De Pauw U.	Lilly Center, Greencastle, IN 46135	Matt Walker	(765) 658-4939
DeSales U.	2755 Station Ave., Center Valley, PA 18034	Tim Nieman	(610) 282-1100
Dickinson College	PO Box 1773, High Street, Carlisle, PA 17013	Russell Wrenn	(717) 245-1320
Dickinson State U.	291 Campus Dr., Dickinson, ND 58601	Duane Monlux	(701) 483-2716
Doane College	1014 Boswell Ave., Crete, NE 68333	Jack Hudkins	(402) 826-8646
Dominican College	470 Western Hwy., Orangeburg, NY 10962	Rick Giannetti	(845) 398-3008
Dominican U.	7900 W. Division St., River Forest, IL 60305	Tom Uraski	(708) 524-6542
Dordt College	498 4th Ave. NE, Sioux Center, IA 51250	Jeff Scholten	(712) 722-6232
Dowling College	150 Idle Hour Blvd., Oakdale, NY 11769	Carmen Carcone	(631) 244-3229
Drew U.	36 Madison Ave., Madison, NJ 07940	Vince Masco	(973) 408-3443
Dubuque, U. of	2000 University Ave., Dubuque, IA 52001	Shane Schmellschmidt	(563) 589-3124
Earlham College	801 National Rd. W., Richmond, IN 47374	Tom Parkevich	(765) 983-1237
East Central U.	1100 East 14th St., Ada, OK 74820	Ron Hill	(580) 436-4940
East Stroudsburg U.	Smith & Normal Streets, East Stroudsburg, PA 18301	Roger Barren	(570) 422-3263
East Texas Baptist U.	1209 N. Grove St., Marshall TX 75670	Robert Riggs	(903) 923-2228
Eastern U.	1300 Eagle Rd., St. Davids, PA 19087	Brian Burke	(610) 341-1736
Eastern Connecticut State U.	83 Windham St., Willimantic, CT 06226	Bill Holowaty	(860) 465-5185
Eastern Mennonite U.	1200 Park Rd., Harrisonburg, VA 22802	Rob Roeschley	(540) 432-4333
Eastern Nazarene College	23 East Elm Ave., Quincy, MA 02170	Todd Reid	(617) 745-3648
Eastern New Mexico U.	Greyhound Arena, Station 17, Portales, NM 88130	Phil Clabaugh	(505) 562-2889
Eastern Oregon U.	One University Blvd., La Grande, OR 97850	Wes McAllaster	(541) 962-3110
Eckerd College	4200 54th Ave. S., St. Petersburg, FL 33711	Bill Mathews	(727) 864-8253
Edgewood College	1000 Edgewood College Dr., Madison, WI 53711	Al Brisack	(608) 663-3289
Edward Waters College	1658 Kings Rd., Jacksonville, FL 32209	Carl Burden	(904) 366-2796
Elizabeth City State U.	Campus Box 900, Elizabeth City, NC 27909	Terrance Whittle	(252) 335-3392
Elizabethtown College	One Alpha Dr., Elizabethtown, PA 17022	Matt Jones	(717) 361-1463
Elmhurst College	190 Prospect Ave., Elmhurst, IL 60126	Clark Jones	(630) 617-3143
Embry-Riddle U.	600 S. Clyde Morris Blvd., Daytona Beach, FL 32114	Greg Guilliams	(386) 323-5010

Emerson College	120 Boylston St., Boston, MA 02116	Mitch Lebowitz	(617) 824-8904
Emmanuel College	PO Box 129, Franklin Springs, GA 30639	Ryan Gray	(706) 245-7226
Emory & Henry College	King Athletic Center, Emory, VA 24327	Dewey Lusk	(276) 944-6855
Emory U.	600 Asbury Circle, Atlanta, GA 30322	Mike Twardoski	(404) 727-0877
Emporia State U.	12th & Commercial Streets, Emporia, KS 66801	Bob Fornelli	(620) 341-5930
Endicott College	376 Hale St., Beverly, MA 01915	Larry Hiser	(978) 232-2304
Erskine College	2 Washington St., Due West, SC 29639	Kevin Nichols	(864) 379-8777
Eureka College	300 E. College Ave., Eureka, IL 61530	Airren Nylin	(309) 467-6376
Evangel U.	1111 North Glenstone Ave, Springfield, MO 65802	Al Poland	(417) 865-2815
Fairleigh Dickinson U.-Madison	285 Madison Ave., M130A, Madison, NJ 37940	Doug Radziewicz	(973) 443-8826
Fairmont State College	1201 Locust Ave., Fairmont, WV 26554	Ray Bonnett	(304) 367-4220
Faulkner U.	5345 Atlanta Hwy., Montgomery, AL 36109	Brent Barker	(334) 386-7318
Felician College	262 S. Main St., Lodi, NJ 07644	Steve Svenson	(201) 559-3509
Ferrum College	PO Box 1000, Route 40 W., Ferrum, VA 24088	Abe Naff	(540) 365-4488
Findlay, U. of	1000 N. Main St., Findlay, OH 45840	Troy Berry	(419) 434-6684
Finlandia U.	601 W. Quincy St., Hancock, MI 49930	Matt Farrell	(906) 487-7212
Fisher College	118 Beacon St., Boston, MA 02116	Scott Dulin	(617) 236-8877
Fisk U.	17 Avenue N., Nashville, TN 37208	Shannon Hill	(615) 329-8782
Fitchburg State College	160 Pearl St., Fitchburg, MA 01420	Pete Egbert	(978) 665-4681
Flagler College	74 King St., St. Augustine, FL 32084	Dave Barnett	(904) 829-6252
Florida Gulf Coast U.	10501 FGCU Blvd., South, Fort Myers, FL 33965	Dave Tollett	(941) 590-7051
Florida Memorial College	15800 NW 42nd Ave., Opa Locka, FL 33054	Robert Smith	(305) 626-3168
Florida Southern College	111 Lake Hollingsworth Dr., Lakeland, FL 33801	Pete Meyer	(863) 680-4264
Florida Tech	150 W. University Blvd., Melbourne, FL 32901	Paul Knight	(321) 674-8193
Fontbonne College	6800 Wydown St., St. Louis, MO 63105	Scott Cooper	(314) 719-8064
Fort Hays State U.	600 Park St., Hays, KS 67601	Matt Ranson	(785) 628-4357
Framingham State College	100 State St., Framingham, MA 01701	Mike Sarno	(508) 626-4566
Francis Marion U.	PO Box 100547, Florence, SC 29501	Art Inabinet	(843) 661-1242
Franciscan U.	400 North Bluff Blvd., Clinton, IA 52732	Desi Druschel	(563) 242-4023
Franklin & Marshall College	PO Box 3003, Lancaster, PA 17604	Brett Boretti	(717) 358-4530
Franklin College	501 E. Monroe St., Franklin, IN 46131	Lance Marshall	(317) 738-8136
Franklin Pierce College	20 College Rd., Rindge, NH 03461	Jayson King	(603) 899-4084
Fredonia State U.	Dods Hall, Fredonia, NY 14063	Matt Palisin	(716) 673-3743
Freed-Hardeman U.	158 E. Main St., Henderson, TN 38340	Chuck Box	(731) 989-6904
Friends U.	2100 W. University St., Wichita, KS 67213	Mark Carvalho	(316) 295-5769
Frostburg State U.	101 Braddock Rd, Frostburg, MD 21532	Chris McKnight	(301) 687-4273
Gallaudet U.	800 Florida Ave. NE, Washington, DC 20002	Kris Gould	(202) 651-5603
Gannon U.	109 University Square, Erie, PA 16541	Rick Iacobucci	(814) 871-5846
Geneva College	3200 College Ave., Beaver Falls, PA 15010	Alan Sumner	(724) 847-6647
George Fox U.	414 N. Meridian St., Newberg, OR 97132	Pat Bailey	(503) 554-2914
Georgetown College	400 E. College St., Georgetown, KY 40324	Jim Hinerman	(502) 863-8207
Georgia College & State U.	Campus Box 65, Milledgeville, GA 31061	Steve Mrowka	(478) 445-5319
Georgia Southwestern	800 Wheatley St., Americus, GA 31709	Barry Davis	(229) 931-2220
Gettysburg College	300 N. Washington St, Gettysburg, PA 17325	John Campo	(717) 337-6413
Gordon College	255 Grapevine Rd., Wenham, MA 01984	Bob Dickerman	(978) 867-4858
Goshen College	1700 S. Main St., Goshen, IN 46526	Brent Hoober	(574) 535-7495
Grace College	200 Seminary Dr., Winona Lake, IN 46590	Dennis Boyd	(574) 372-5100
Graceland U.	One University Pl., Lamoni, IA 50140	Brady McKillip	(641) 784-5351
Grand Canyon U.	PO Box 11097, Phoenix, AZ 85061	Dave Stapleton	(602) 589-2817
Grand Valley State U.	1 Campus Dr., Allendale, MI 49401	Steve Lyon	(616) 331-8800
Grand View College	1200 Grandview Ave., Des Moines, IA 50316	Lou Yacinich	(515) 263-2897
Greensboro College	815 W. Market St., Greensboro, NC 27401	Ken Carlyle	(336) 272-7102
Greenville College	PO Box 159, Greenville, IL 62246	Lynn Carlson	(618) 664-6623
Grinnell College	1118 10th Ave., Grinnell, IA 50112	Tim Hollibaugh	(641) 269-3822
Grove City College	100 Campus Dr., Grove City, PA 16127	Rob Skaricich	(724) 458-3836
Guilford College	5800 W. Friendly Ave., Greensboro, NC 27410	Gene Baker	(336) 316-2161
Gustavus Adolphus College	800 W. College Ave., St. Peter, MN 56082	Mike Carroll	(507) 933-6297
Gwynedd Mercy College	1325 Sumneytown Pike, Gwynedd Valley, PA 19437	Paul Murphy	(215) 646-7300
Hamilton College	198 College Hill Rd., Clinton, NY 13323	John Keady	(315) 859-4763
Hamline U.	1536 Hewitt Ave., St. Paul, MN 55104	Jason Verdugo	(651) 523-2035
Hampden-Sydney College	1 Kirby Field House Lane, Hampden-Sydney, VA 23943	Jeff Kinne	(434) 223-6981
Hannibal-LaGrange College	2800 Palmyra Rd., Hannibal, MO 63401	Clay Biggs	(573) 221-3675
Hanover College	PO Box 108, Hanover, IN 47243	Dick Naylor	(812) 866-7374
Hardin-Simmons U.	PO Box 16185, Abilene, TX 79698	Steve Coleman	(325) 670-1493
Harding U.	Box 12281, Searcy, AR 72149	Shane Fullerton	(501) 279-4344
Harris-Stowe State College	3026 Laclede Ave., St. Louis, MO 63103	Darren Munns	(314) 340-5971
Hartwick College	Binder PE Center, Oneonta, NY 13820	Doug Kimbler	(607) 431-4706
Hastings College	7th & Turner, Hastings, NE 68902	Jim Boeve	(402) 461-7468
Haverford College	370 Lancaster Ave., Haverford, PA 19041	Dave Beccaria	(610) 896-1172
Hawaii Pacific U.	1060 Bishop St., Honolulu, HI 96813	Allan Sato	(808) 543-8021

Heidelberg College	310 E. Market St., Tiffin, OH 44883	Matt Palm	(419) 448-2009
Henderson State U.	PO Box 7630, Arkadelphia, AR 71999	Pete Southall	(870) 230-5071
Hendrix College	1600 Washington Ave., Conway, AR 72032	Lane Stahl	(501) 450-3898
Hilbert College	5200 S. Park Ave, Hamburg, NY 14075	Sam Rutkowski	(716) 649-7900
Hillsdale College	201 Oak St., Hillsdale, MI 49242	Paul Noce	(517) 607-3146
Hillsdale Freewill Baptist	3701 S. I-35, Moore, OK 73160	Ryan Wade	(405) 912-9000
Hiram College	PO Box 1777, Hiram, OH 44234	Howard Jenter	(330) 569-5348
Hope College	137 E. 12th St., Holland, MI 49422	Stuart Fritz	(616) 395-7692
Houston Baptist U.	7502 Fondren Rd., Houston, TX 77074	Brian Huddleston	(281) 649-3332
Howard Payne U.	508 2nd St., Brownwood, TX 76801	Mike Kennemer	(325) 649-8117
Huntingdon College	1500 E. Fairview Ave, Montgomery, AL 36106	Scot Patterson	(334) 833-4501
Huntington College	2303 College Ave., Huntington, IN 46750	Mike Frame	(260) 359-4082
Huron U.	333 9th Street SW, Huron, SD 57350	Josue Prado	(305) 352-2010
Husson College	1 College Circle, Husson, ME 04401	John Winkin	(207) 941-7700
Huston-Tillotson College	900 Chicon St., Austin, TX 78702	Alvin Moore	(512) 505-3151
Illinois College	1101 W. College Ave., Jacksonville, IL 62650	Jay Eckhouse	(217) 245-3387
Illinois Tech	3300 S. Federal St., Chicago, IL 60616	John Fitzgerald	(312) 567-7128
Illinois Wesleyan U.	PO Box 2900, Bloomington, IL 61702	Dennis Martel	(309) 556-3335
Incarnate Word, U. of the	4301 Broadway St., San Antonio, TX 78209	Danny Heep	(210) 829-3830
Indiana Tech	1600 E. Washington Blvd., Fort Wayne, IN 46803	Steve Devine	(620) 422-5561
Indiana U. (Pa.)	660 South 11th St., Indiana, PA 15705	Tom Kennedy	(724) 357-7830
Indiana U.-Northwest	3400 Broadway, Gary, IN 46408	Tom Bainbridge.	(219) 980-6500
Indiana U.-Southeast	4201 Grant Line Rd., New Albany, IN 47150	Rick Parr	(812) 941-2450
Indiana Wesleyan U.	4201 S. Washington St., Marion, IN 46953	Mark DeMichael	(765) 677-2324
Indianapolis, U. of	1400 E. Hanna Ave., Indianapolis, IN 46227	Gary Vaught	(317) 788-3414
Iowa Wesleyan College	601 N. Main St., Mount Pleasant, IA 52641	Todd Huckabone	(319) 385-6349
Ithaca College	935 Danby Rd., Ithaca, NY 14850	George Valesente	(607) 274-3749
Jamestown College	PO Box 6088, Jamestown, ND 58405	Tom Hager	(701) 252-3467
Jarvis Christian College	PO Box 1470, Hawkins, TX 75765	Robert Thomas	(903) 769-5763
John Carroll U.	20700 N. Park Blvd., University Heights, OH 44118	Marc Thibeault	(216) 397-4660
John Jay College	899 10th Ave., New York, NY 10019	Dan Palumbo	(212) 237-8369
Johns Hopkins U.	Newton White Athletic Center, Baltimore, MD 21218	Bob Babb	(410) 516-7485
Johnson & Wales U.	7150 Montview Blvd., Denver, CO 80220	Mark Gentry	(303) 256-9307
Johnson Bible College	7900 Johnson Dr., Knoxville, TN 37998	Jack Barr	(865) 251-7765
Judson College	1151 N. State St., Elgin, IL 60123	Loren Torres	(847) 628-2523
Juniata College	1700 Moore St., Huntingdon, PA 16652	George Zanic	(814) 641-3515
Kalamazoo College	1200 Academy St., Kalamazoo, MI 49006	Steve Wideen	(616) 337-7287
Kansas Wesleyan U.	100 E. Claflin Ave, Salina, KS 67401	Tim Bellew	(785) 827-5541
Kean U.	1000 Morris Ave., Union, NJ 07083	Neil Loviero	(908) 737-5452
Keene State College	229 Main St., Keene, NH 03435	Ken Howe	(603) 358-2809
Kennesaw State U.	1000 Chastain Rd. NW, Kennesaw, GA 30144	Mike Sansing	(770) 423-6264
Kentucky State U.	400 E. Main St., Frankfort, KY 40601	Elwood Johnson	(502) 597-6018
Kentucky Wesleyan College	PO Box 1039, Owensboro, KY 42302	Todd Lillpop	(270) 852-3342
Kenyon College	Athletic Dept., Duff Street, Gambier, OH 43022	Matt Burdette	(740) 427-5810
Keuka College	Weed Physical Arts Center, Keuka Park, NY 14478	Jeff Cleanthes	(315) 279-5687
Keystone College	One College Green, La Plume, PA 18440	Jamie Shevchik	(570) 945-5141
King College	1350 King College Rd., Bristol, TN 37620	Craig Kleinmann	(423) 652-6017
King's College	133 N. River St., Wilkes-Barre, PA 18711	Jerry Greeley	(570) 208-5855
Knox College	2 E. South St., Galesburg, IL 61401	Jami Isaacson	(309) 341-7456
Kutztown U.	Keystone Hall, Kutztown, PA 19530	Chris Blum	(610) 683-4063
LaGrange College	601 Broad St., La Grange, GA 30240	Kevin Howard	(706) 880-8295
Lake Erie College	391 W. Washington St., Painesville, OH 44077	Ken Krsolovic	(440) 375-7470
Lakeland College	PO Box 359, Sheboygan, WI 53082	John Weber	(920) 565-1411
Lambuth U.	705 Lambuth Blvd., Jackson, TN 38301	Wayne Albury	(731) 425-3385
Lancaster Bible College	901 Eden Rd., Lancaster, PA 17608	Peter Beers	(717) 560-8267
Lander U.	CPO 6016, Greenwood, SC 29649	Mike McGuire	(864) 388-8961
Lane College	545 Lane Ave., Jackson, TN 38301	Anthony Sawyer	(731) 426-7571
La Roche College	9000 Babcock Blvd., Pittsburgh, PA 15237	Rich Pasquaze	(412) 536-1046
La Verne, U. of	1950 3rd St., La Verne, CA 91750	Scott Winterburn	(909) 593-3511
Lawrence U.	PO Box 599, Appleton, WI 54912	Korey Krueger	(920) 832-7346
Lebanon Valley College	101 N. College Ave., Annville, PA 17003	Keith Evans	(717) 867-6271
Lee U.	1120 N. Ocoee St., Cleveland, TN 37311	Dave Altopp	(423) 614-8445
Lehman College	250 Bedford Park Blvd. W., Bronx, NY 10468	Kiko Reyes	(718) 960-7746
LeMoyne-Owen College	807 Walker Ave., Memphis, TN 38126	Willie Patterson	(901) 942-7327
Lenoir-Rhyne College	PO Box 7356, Hickory, NC 28603	Frank Pait	(828) 328-7136
LeTourneau U.	PO Box 7001, Longview, TX 75602	Bernie Martinez	(903) 233-3372
Lewis & Clark College	0615 SW Palatine Hill Rd., Portland, OR 97219	Reed Rainey	(503) 768-7059
Lewis U.	One University Pkwy, Romeoville, IL 60446	Irish O'Reilly	(815) 836-5255
Lewis-Clark State College	500 8th Ave., Lewiston, ID 83501	Ed Cheff	(208) 792-2272

Limestone College	1115 College Dr., Gaffney, SC 29340	Chico Lombardo	(864) 488-4565
Lincoln Christian College	100 Campus View Dr., Lincoln, IL 62656	Donnie Bowman	(217) 732-3168
Lincoln Memorial U.	PO Box 2028, Harrogate, TN 37752	Jeff Sziksai	(423) 869-6345
Lincoln U.	820 Chestnut St., Jefferson City, MO 65102	Earl Wheeler	(573) 681-5334
Lincoln U.	PO Box 179, Lincoln University, PA 19352	Paul Johnson	(610) 932-8300
Lindenwood U.	209 S. Kings Highway, St. Charles, MO 63301	Brian Behrens	(636) 949-4185
Lindsey Wilson College	210 Lindsey Wilson St., Columbia, KY 42728	Mike Talley	(270) 384-8074
Linfield College	900 SE Baker St., McMinnville, OR 97128	Scott Carnahan	(503) 434-2229
Lock Haven U.	Thomas Fieldhouse, Lock Haven, PA 17745	Smokey Stover	(570) 893-2245
Longwood U.	201 High St., Farmville, VA 23909	Buddy Bolding	(434) 395-2352
Loras College	1450 Alta Vista St., Dubuque, IA 52004	Carl Tebon	(563) 588-7732
Louisiana College	1140 College Dr., Pineville, LA 71359	Mike Byrnes	(318) 487-7322
Loyola U.	6363 St. Charles Ave., New Orleans, LA 70118	Gregg Mucerino	(504) 864-7392
LSU-Shreveport	One University Place, Shreveport, LA 71115	Rocke Musgraves	(318) 798-4107
Lubbock Christian U.	5601 W. 19th St., Lubbock, TX 79407	Nathan Blackwood	(806) 720-7853
Luther College	700 College Dr., Decorah, IA 52101	Brian Gillogly	(563) 387-1590
Lynchburg College	1501 Lakeside Dr., Lynchburg, VA 24501	Percy Abell	(434) 544-8496
Lyndon State College	PO Box 919, Lyndonville, VT 05851	Skip Pound	(802) 626-6477
Lynn U.	3601 N. Military Trail, Boca Raton, FL 33431	Rudy Garbalosa	(561) 237-7242
Lyon College	PO Box 2317, Batesville, AR 72503	Kirk Kelley	(870) 698-4337
Macalester College	1600 Grand Ave., St. Paul, MN 55105	Matt Parrington	(651) 696-6770
Mac Murray College	447 E. College Ave, Jacksonville, IL 62650	Kevin Vest	(217) 479-7153
Madonna U.	36600 Schoolcraft Rd., Livonia, MI 48150	Greg Haeger	(734) 432-5609
Maine-Farmington, U. of	111 South St., Farmington, ME 04938	Dick Meader	(207) 778-7148
Maine-Presque Isle, U. of	181 Main St., Presque Isle, ME 04769	Leo Saucier	(207) 768-9421
Malone College	515 25th St. NW, Canton, OH 44709	Tom Crank	(330) 471-8286
Manchester College	604 E. College Ave., North Manchester, IN 46962	Rick Espeset	(260) 982-5390
Manhattanville College	2900 Purchase St., Purchase, NY 10577	Joe Ferraro	(914) 323-7284
Mansfield U.	Academy St., Mansfield, PA 16933	Harry Hillson	(570) 662-4457
Maranatha Baptist College	745 W. Main St., Watertown, WI 53094	Jerry Terrill	(920) 206-2380
Marian College	45 S. National Ave., Fond du Lac, WI 54935	Jason Bartelt	(920) 923-8090
Marian College	3200 Cold Spring Rd., Indianapolis, IN 46222	Kurt Guldner	(317) 955-6310
Marietta College	215 5th St., Marietta, OH 45750	Brian Brewer	(740) 376-4517
Mars Hill College	100 Athletic St., Mars Hill, NC 28754	Daniel Taylor	(828) 689-1173
Martin Luther College	1995 Luther Court, New Ulm, MN 56073	Drew Buck	(507) 354-8221
Martin Methodist College	433 W. Madison St., Pulaski, TN 38478	Jeff Dodson	(931) 363-9827
Mary, U. of	7500 University Dr., Bismarck, ND 58504	Van Vanetta	(701) 355-8270
Mary Hardin-Baylor U.	UMHB Box 8010, Belton, TX 76513	Micah Wells	(254) 295-4619
Mary Washington College	Goolrick Gymnasium, Fredericksburg, VA 22401	Tom Sheridan	(540) 654-1882
Maryville College	502 E. Lamar Alexander Pkwy., Maryville, TN 37804	Eric Etchison	(865) 981-8283
Maryville U.-St. Louis	13550 Conway Rd., St. Louis, MO 63141	Tracy Schmidt	(314) 529-9483
Marywood U.	2300 Adams Ave., Scranton, PA 18509	Joe Ross	(570) 961-4724
Mass College of Liberal Arts	375 Church St., North Adams, MA 01247	Jeff Puleri	(413) 662-5403
Mass. Institute of Technology	PO Box 397404, Cambridge, MA 02139	Andy Barlow	(617) 258-7310
Mass Maritime Academy	101 Academy Dr., Buzzards Bay, MA 02532	Bob Corradi	(508) 830-5055
Mass-Boston Harbor, U. of	100 Morrissey Blvd., Boston, MA 02125	Mark Bettencourt	(617) 287-7817
Mass-Dartmouth, U. of	285 Old Wesport Rd., North Dartmouth, MA 02747	Bruce Wheeler	(508) 999-8721
Mass-Lowell, U. of	1 University Ave, Costello Gym, Lowell, MA 01854	Ken Connerty	(978) 934-2344
Master's College, The	21726 Placerita Canyon Rd., Santa Clarita, CA 91321	Monte Brooks	(661) 259-3540
Mayville State U.	330 3rd St. NE, Mayville, ND 58257	Scott Berry	(701) 788-2301
McDaniel College	2 College Hill, Westminster, MD 21157	David Seibert	(410) 857-2583
McKendree College	701 College Rd., Lebanon, IL 62254	Jim Boehne	(618) 537-6906
McMurry U.	South 14th St. & Sayles Blvd., Abilene, TX 79697	Lee Driggers	(951) 793-4650
Medaille College	18 Agassiz Circle, Buffalo, NY 14214	Jim Koernehead	(716) 884-3281
Menlo College	1000 El Camino Real, Atherton, CA 94027	Ken Bowman	(650) 543-3932
Mercy College	555 Broadway, Dobbs Ferry, NY 10522	Billy Sullivan	(914) 674-7566
Mercyhurst College	501 E. 38th St., Erie, PA 16546	Joe Spano	(814) 824-2441
Merrimack College	315 Turnpike St., North Andover, MA 01845	Barry Rosen	(978) 837-5000
Mesa State College	1100 North Ave., Grand Junction, CO 81501	Chris Hanks	(970) 248-1891
Messiah College	One College Ave., Grantham, PA 17027	Frank Montgomery	(717) 766-2511
Methodist College	5400 Ramsey St., Fayetteville, NC 28311	Tom Austin	(910) 630-7176
Metropolitan State U.	PO Box 173362, Campus Box 9, Denver, CO 80217	Vince Porreco	(303) 556-3301
Mid-America Bible College	3500 SW 119th St., Oklahoma City, OK 73170	Gerre Griffin	(405) 692-3141
Mid-America Nazarene	2030 E. College Way, Olathe, KS 66062	Todd Garrett	(913) 791-3462
Mid-Continent College	99 Powell Rd. E., Mayfield, KY 42066	Seth Zartman	(270) 247-8521
Middlebury College	Memorial Fieldhouse, Middlebury, VT 05753	Robert Smith	(802) 443-5264
Midland Lutheran College	900 N. Clarkson St., Fremont, NE 68025	Jeff Field	(402) 941-6371
Miles College	5500 Myron Massey Blvd., Birmingham, AL 35208	Willie Patterson	(205) 929-1617
Millersville U.	PO Box 1002, Millersville, PA 17551	Glenn Gallagher	(717) 871-2411
Milligan College	PO Box 500, Milligan College, TN 37682	Danny Clark	(423) 461-8722
Millikin U.	1184 W. Main St., Decatur, IL 62522	Josh Manning	(217) 424-3608
Millsaps College	1701 N. State St., Jackson, MS 39210	Jim Page	(601) 974-1196

Institution	Address	Contact	Phone
Milwaukee Engineering	1025 N. Broadway, Milwaukee, WI 53202	Len VandenBoom	(414) 277-7154
Minnesota Bible College	920 Mayowood Road SW, Rochester, MN 55902	Mark Comeaux	(507) 288-4563
Minnesota-Crookston, U. of	Sports Center, Crookston, MN 56716	Steve Olson	(218) 281-8419
Minnesota-Duluth, U. of	1216 Ordean Court, Duluth, MN 55812	Scott Hanna	(218) 726-7563
Minnesota-Morris, U. of	E. 2nd St., Morris, MN 56267	Mark Fohl	(320) 589-6421
Minnesota State U.-Mankato	135 Myers Fieldhouse, Mankato, MN 56001	Dean Bowyer	(507) 389-2689
Minot State U.	500 University Ave. W., Minot, ND 58707	Dick Limmke	(701) 858-4328
Misericordia College	301 Lake St., Dallas, PA 18612	Chuck Edkins	(570) 674-6397
Mississippi College	PO Box 4049, Clinton, MS 39058	Lee Kuyrkendall	(601) 925-3346
Missouri Baptist U.	1 College Park Dr., St. Louis, MO 63141	Eddie Uschold	(314) 392-2384
Missouri Southern State Coll.	3950 E. Newman Rd, Joplin, MO 64801	Warren Turner	(417) 625-9312
Missouri-Rolla, U. of	Athletic Dept., Rolla, MO 65409	Travis Boulware	(573) 341-4191
Missouri-St. Louis, U. of	8001 Natural Bridge Rd., St. Louis, MO 63141	Jim Brady	(314) 516-5647
Missouri Valley College	500 E. College St., Marshall, MO 65340	Dan Bowers	(660) 831-4113
Missouri Western State	4525 Downs Dr., St. Joseph, MO 64507	Buzz Verduzco	(816) 271-4484
Mobile, U. of	5735 College Pkwy, Mobile, AL 36663	Mike Jacobs	(251) 442-2228
Molloy College	1000 Hempstead Ave., Rockville Centre, NY 11570	Bernie Havern	(251) 256-2228
Monmouth College	700 E. Broadway, Monmouth, IL 61462	Roger Sander	(309) 457-2176
Montclair State U.	One Normal Ave., Upper Montclair, NJ 07043	Norm Schoenig	(973) 655-5281
Montevallo, U. of	Station 6600, Montevallo, AL 35115	Bob Riesener	(205) 665-6760
Montreat College	310 Gaither Circle, Montreat, NC 28757	Darin Chaplain	(828) 669-8011
Moravian College	1200 Main St., Bethlehem, PA 18018	Ed Little	(610) 861-1536
Morehouse College	830 Westview Dr. SW, Atlanta, GA 30314	Bernard Pattillo	(404) 681-2800
Morningside College	1501 Morningside Ave, Sioux City, IA 51106	Jim Scholten	(712) 274-5248
Morris College	100 W. College St., Sumter, SC 29150	Clarence Houck	(803) 934-3235
Mount Marty College	1105 West 8th St., Yankton, SD 57078	Kelly Heller	(605) 668-1548
Mount Mercy College	1330 Elmhurst Drive NE, Cedar Rapids, IA 52402	Justin Schulte	(319) 363-1323
Mount Olive College	634 Henderson St., Mount Olive, NC 28365	Carl Lancaster	(919) 658-7669
Mount St. Joseph College	5701 Delhi Rd., Cincinnati, OH 45233	Chuck Murray	(513) 244-4402
Mount St. Mary College	330 Powell Ave., Newburgh, NY 12550	Matt Dembinsky	(845) 569-3287
Mount Union College	1972 Clark Ave., Alliance, OH 44601	Paul Hesse	(330) 823-4878
Mount Vernon Nazarene Coll.	800 Martinsburg Rd., Mt. Vernon, OH 43050	Keith Veale	(740) 392-6868
Muhlenberg College	2400 W. Chew St., Allentown, PA 18104	Bob Macaluso	(484) 664-3684
Muskingum College	163 Stormont St., New Concord, OH 43762	Gregg Thompson	(740) 826-8318
Nebraska-Kearney, U. of	Hwy 30 & 15th Ave., Kearney, NE 68849	Tony Murray	(308) 865-8022
Nebraska-Omaha, U. of	6001 Dodge St., Omaha, NE 68182	Bob Herold	(402) 554-3388
Nebraska Wesleyan U.	5000 St. Paul Ave., Lincoln, NE 68504	Mark Mancuso	(402) 465-2171
Neumann College	One Neumann Dr., Aston, PA 19014	Len Schuler	(610) 558-5625
New England College	Clement Arena, 24 Bridge St., Henniker, NH 03242	Dave Anderson	(603) 428-2407
New Haven, U. of	300 Orange Ave., West Haven, CT 06516	Frank Vieira	(203) 932-7018
New Jersey City U.	2039 Kennedy Blvd., Jersey City, NJ 07305	Ken Heaton	(201) 200-3079
New Jersey Tech	323 Martin Luther King Blvd., Newark, NJ 07102	Brian Callahan	(973) 596-5827
New Jersey, College of	PO Box 7718, Ewing, NJ 08628	Rick Dell	(609) 771-2374
New Mexico Highlands U.	Athletic Dept Fieldhouse, Las Vegas, NM 87701	Steve Jones	(505) 425-3587
Newberry College	2100 College St., Newberry, SC 29108	Tim Medlin	(803) 321-5162
Newman U.	3100 McCormick Ave., Wichita, KS 67213	Kevin Ulwelling	(316) 942-4291
Nichols College	PO Box 5000, Dudley, MA 01571	Steve Nadeau	(508) 213-2363
North Alabama, U. of	Box 5072, Florence, AL 35632	Mike Lane	(256) 765-4615
North Carolina Wesleyan	3400 Wesleyan Blvd., Rocky Mount, NC 27804	Charlie Long	(252) 985-5219
North Carolina-Pembroke, U. of	PO Box 1510, Pembroke, NC 28372	Paul O'Neil	(910) 521-6810
North Central College	30 N. Brainard St., Naperville, IL 60540	Brian Michalak	(630) 637-5512
North Dakota State U.	1600 N. University Dr., Fargo, ND 58105	Mitch McLeod	(701) 231-8853
North Dakota, U. of	PO Box 9013, Grand Forks, ND 58203	Kelvin Ziegler	(701) 777-4038
North Florida, U. of	4567 St. Johns Bluff Rd. S., Jacksonville, FL 32224	Dusty Rhodes	(904) 620-2556
North Georgia College	130 College Ave., Dahlonega, GA 30597	Tom Cantrell	(706) 867-2754
North Greenville College	PO Box 1892, Tigerville, SC 29688	Tim Nihart	(864) 977-7156
North Park U.	3225 W. Foster Ave, Chicago, IL 60625	Steve Vanden Branden	(773) 244-5675
Northeastern State U.	600 N. Grand Ave., Tahlequah, OK 74464	Sergio Espinal	(918) 456-5511
Northern Colorado, U. of	251 Butler-Hancock Hall, Greeley, CO 80639	Kevin Smallcomb	(970) 351-1714
Northern Kentucky U.	1 Nunn Drive, Highland Heights, KY 41099	Todd Asalon	(859) 572-6474
Northern State U.	1200 South Jay St., Aberdeen, SD 57401	Curt Fredrickson	(605) 626-7735
Northland College	1411 Ellis Ave., Ashland, WI 54806	Joel Barta	(715) 682-1387
Northwest Missouri State	800 University Dr., Maryville, MO 64468	Darin Loe	(660) 562-1304
Northwest Nazarene U.	623 Holly St., Nampa, ID 83686	Tim Onofrei	(208) 467-8351
Northwestern College	101 7th St. SW, Orange City, IA 51041	Dave Nonnemacher	(712) 707-7366
Northwestern College	3003 Snelling Ave. N., St. Paul, MN 55113	Dave Hieb	(651) 631-5345
Northwestern Okla. State	709 Oklahoma Blvd., Alva, OK 73717	Joe Phillips	(580) 327-8635
Northwood U.	2600 N. Military Tr., West Palm Beach, FL 33409	Rick Smoliak	(561) 478-5552
Northwood U.	4000 Whiting Drive, Midland, MI 48640	Joe DiBenedetto	(989) 837-4427
Northwood U.	1114 West FM 1382, Cedar Hill, TX 75104	Pat Malcheski	(972) 293-5439
Norwich U.	158 Harmon Dr., Northfield, VT 05663	Bill Barrale	(802) 485-2239
Nova Southeastern U.	3301 College Ave., Fort Lauderdale, FL 33314	Michael Mominey	(954) 262-8252

Nyack College	1 South Blvd., Nyack, NY 10960	Jason Beck	(845) 358-1710
Oakland City U.	143 Lucretia St., Oakland City, IN 47660	Ray Fletcher	(812) 749-1576
Oberlin College	200 Woodland Ave., Oberlin, OH 44074	Eric Lahetta	(440) 775-8502
Occidental College	1600 Campus Rd., Los Angeles, CA 90041	Jeff Henderson	(323) 259-2683
Oglethorpe U.	4484 Peachtree Rd. NE, Atlanta, GA 30319	Bill Popp	(404) 364-8417
Ohio Dominican College	1216 Sunbury Rd., Columbus, OH 43219	Paul Page	(614) 251-4535
Ohio Northern U.	525 S. Main, Ada, OH 45810	Milan Rasic	(419) 772-2442
Ohio Valley College	1 Campus View Dr., Vienna, WV 26105	Bob Crawford	(304) 865-6048
Ohio Wesleyan U.	61 S. Sandusky St., Delaware, OH 43015	Bengie Rodriguez	(740) 368-3738
Oklahoma, U. of Science/Arts	1727 W. Alabama, Chickisha, OK 73018	L.J. Powell	(405) 574-1228
Oklahoma Baptist U.	500 W. University St., Shawnee, OK 74801	Bobby Cox	(405) 878-2139
Oklahoma City U.	2501 N. Blackwelder, Oklahoma City, OK 73106	Denny Crabaugh	(405) 521-5156
Oklahoma Panhandle State U.	PO Box 430, Goodwell, OK 73939	Ron Clark	(580) 349-1340
Oklahoma Wesleyan Coll.	2201 Silver Lake Rd., Bartlesville, OK 74006	Jason Zielenski	(918) 335-6848
Olivet College	320 S. Main St., Olivet, MI 49076	Carlton Hardy	(269) 749-4184
Olivet Nazarene U.	One University Ave., Bourbonnais, IL 60914	Elliot Johnson	(815) 939-5119
Oneonta State U.	Ravine Pkwy., Oneonta, NY 13820	Rick Ferchen	(607) 436-2661
Oregon Tech	3201 Campus Dr., Klamath Falls, OR 97601	Pete Whisler	(541) 885-1722
Ottawa U.	1001 South Cedar St., Ottawa, KS 66067	Jarrod Titus	(785) 242-5200
Otterbein College	160 Center St., Westerville, OH 43081	George Powell	(614) 823-3521
Ouachita Baptist U.	410 Ouachita, Arkadelphia, AR 71998	B.J. Brown	(870) 245-5083
Ozarks, College of the	PO Box 17, Point Lookout, MO 65726	Patrick McGaha	(417) 334-6411
Ozarks, U. of the	415 N. College Ave., Clarksville, AR 72830	Jimmy Clark	(501) 979-1409
Pacific Lutheran U.	12180 Park Ave. S., Tacoma, WA 98447	Geoff Loomis	(253) 535-8789
Pacific U.	2043 College Way, Forest Grove, OR 97116	Greg Bradley	(503) 359-2142
Paine College	1235 15th St., Augusta, GA 30901	Stanley Stubbs	(706) 821-8228
Palm Beach Atlantic Coll.	901 S. Flagler Dr., West Palm Beach, FL 33416	Kyle Forbes	(561) 803-2523
Park U.	8700 NW River Park Dr., Parkville, MO 64152	Cary Lundy	(816) 584-6746
Paul Quinn College	3837 Simpson Stuart Rd., Dallas, TX 75241	Don Cofer	(214) 801-1168
Penn State Behrend College	5091 Station Rd., Erie, PA 16563	Paul Benim	(814) 898-6322
Penn State-Altoona	3000 Ivyside Park, Altoona, PA 16601	Joe Piotti	(814) 949-5226
Penn State-Berks/Lehigh Valley	PO Box 7009, Tupelhocken Rd., Reading, PA 19610	Joe Smull	(610) 396-6154
Penn State-Hazelton	76 University Dr., Hazelton, PA 18202	Cy Falatko	(570) 450-3164
Penn State-McKeesport	4000 University Dr., McKeesport, PA 15132	Mike Cherepko	(412) 675-9487
Peru State College	PO Box 10, Peru, NE 68421	Mark Bayliss	(402) 872-2443
Pfeiffer U.	PO Box 960, Misenheimer, NC 28109	Chris Pollard	(704) 463-1360
Philadelphia, U. of Sciences	600 S. 43rd St., Philadelphia, PA 19104	Jack Bilbee	(215) 895-1109
Philadelphia U.	School House Lane & Henry Ave., Philadelphia, PA 19144	Don Flynn	(215) 951-2630
Philadelphia Biblical U.	200 Manor Ave., Langhorne, PA 19047	Bill Marshall	(215) 702-4405
Piedmont College	PO Box 10, Demorest, GA 30535	Jim Peeples	(706) 778-3000
Pikeville College	147 Sycamore St., Pikeville, KY 41501	Johnnie LeMaster	(606) 218-5370
Pittsburg State U.	1701 S. Broadway, Pittsburg, KS 66762	Steve Bever	(620) 232-7951
Pittsburgh-Bradford, U. of	300 Campus Dr., Bradford, PA 16701	Bret Butler	(814) 362-5093
Pittsburgh-Greensburg, U. of	1150 Mt. Pleasant Rd., Greensburg, PA 15601	Joe Hill	(724) 836-7185
Pittsburgh-Johnstown, U. of	450 School House Rd., Johnstown, PA 15904	Todd Williams	(814) 269-7170
Plymouth State College	PE Center #32, Holderness Rd., Plymouth, NH 03264	Dennis McManus	(603) 535-2756
Point Loma Nazarene U.	3900 Lomaland Dr., San Diego, CA 92106	Scott Sarver	(619) 849-2765
Point Park College	201 Wood St., Pittsburgh, PA 15222	Al Liberi	(412) 392-3845
Polytechnic U.	6 Metro Tech Ctr., Brooklyn, NY 11201	Roger Perez	(718) 875-6083
Pomona-Pitzer College	220 E. 6th St., Claremont, CA 91711	Paul Svagdis	(909) 621-8422
Presbyterian College	105 Ashland, Clinton, SC 29325	Doug Kovash	(864) 833-8236
Presentation College	1500 N. Main, Aberdeen, SD 57401	Rick Kline	(605) 229-8406
Principia College	1 Maybeck Place, Elsah, IL 62028	Mike Barthelmen	(618) 374-5036
Puget Sound, U. of	1500 N. Warner St., Tacoma, WA 98416	Brian Billings	(253) 879-3414
Purdue U.-North Central	1401 U.S. Hwy. 421 S., Westville, IN 46391	Ryan Brown	(219) 785-5273
Queens College	65-30 Kissena Blvd., Flushing, NY 11367	Frank Battaglia	(718) 997-2781
Quincy U.	1800 College Ave., Quincy, IL 62301	Greg McVey	(217) 228-5268
Ramapo College	505 Ramapo Valley Rd., Mahwah, NJ 07430	Rich Martin	(201) 684-7098
Randolph-Macon College	PO Box 5005, Ashland, VA 23005	Gregg Waters	(804) 752-7303
Redlands, U. of	PO Box 3080, Redlands, CA 92373	Scott Laverty	(909) 335-4005
Regis U.	Athletic Dept., Denver, CO 80221	Dan McDermott	(303) 458-3519
Rensselaer Poly Institute	110 8th St., Troy, NY 12180	Karl Steffen	(518) 276-6185
Rhode Island College	600 Mt. Pleasant Ave., Providence, RI 02908	Jay Grenier	(401) 456-8641
Rhodes College	2000 N. Parkway, Memphis, TN 38112	Alan Reynolds	(901) 843-3456
Richard Stockton College	PO Box 195, Pomona, NJ 08240	Marty Kavanagh	(609) 652-4217
Rio Grande, U. of	218 N. College Ave, Rio Grande, OH 45674	Brad Warnimont	(740) 245-7486
Ripon College	300 Seward St., Ripon, WI 54971	Gordon Gillespie	(920) 748-8776
Rivier College	420 Main St., Nashua, NH 03060	Scott Thomas	(603) 888-1311
Roanoke College	221 College Lane, Salem, VA 24153	Richard Morris	(540) 378-5147

Robert Morris College	401 S. State St., Chicago, IL 60605	Woody Urchak	(312) 935-6801
Rochester, U. of	Goergen Athletic Center, Rochester, NY 14627	Joe Reina	(716) 275-6027
Rochester College	800 W. Avon Rd., Rochester Hills, MI 48307	Virgil Smith	(248) 218-2135
Rochester Tech	51 Lomb Memorial Dr., Rochester, NY 14623	Rob Grow	(716) 475-2210
Rockford College	5050 E. State St., Rockford, IL 61108	William Langston	(815) 226-4048
Rockhurst U.	1100 Rockhurst Rd., Kansas City, MO 64110	Gary Burns	(816) 501-4130
Roger Williams U.	1 Old Ferry Rd., Bristol, RI 02809	Derek Carlson	(401) 254-3163
Rollins College	1000 Holt Ave, Winter Park, FL 32789	Bob Rikeman	(407) 646-2328
Rose-Hulman Tech	5500 Wabash Ave., Terre Haute, IN 47803	Jeff Jenkins	(812) 877-8209
Rowan U.	201 Mullica Hill Rd., Glassboro, NJ 08028	John Cole	(856) 256-4687
Rust College	150 E. Rust Ave., Holly Springs, MS 38635	Avery Mason	(662) 252-4661
Rutgers U.-Camden	3rd & Linden Streets, Camden, NJ 08102	Keith Williams	(856) 225-6197
Rutgers U.-Newark	42 Warren St., Newark, NJ 07102	Mark Rizzi	(973) 353-5474
Saginaw Valley State	7400 Bay Rd., University Center, MI 48710	Walt Head	(989) 964-7334
St. Ambrose U.	518 W. Locust St., Davenport, IA 52803	Jim Callahan	(563) 333-6237
St. Andrews Presbyterian	1700 Dogwood Mile St., Laurinburg, NC 28352	Bobby Simmons	(910) 277-5426
St. Anselm College	100 St. Anselm Dr., Manchester, NH 03102	Ken Harring	(603) 656-6016
St. Augustine's College	1315 Oakwood Ave., Raleigh, NC 27610	Henry White	(919) 516-4174
St. Cloud State U.	720 4th Ave. S., St. Cloud, MN 56301	Denny Lorsung	(320) 255-3208
St. Edwards U.	3001 S. Congress Ave., Austin, TX 78704	Jerry Farber	(512) 448-8497
St. Francis, U. of	500 Wilcox St., Joliet, IL 60435	Tony Delgado	(815) 740-3406
St. Francis, U. of	2701 Spring St., Fort Wayne, IN 46808	Doug Coate	(260) 434-7414
St. Gregory's U.	1900 W. MacArthur Dr., Shawnee, OK 74804	Chris Pingry	(405) 878-5151
St. John Fisher College	3690 East Ave., Rochester, NY 14618	Dan Pepicelli	(716) 385-8419
St. John's U.	PO Box 7277, Collegeville, MN 56321	Jerry Haugen	(320) 363-2756
St. Joseph's College	PO Box 875, Rensselaer, IN 47978	Rick O'Dette	(219) 866-6399
St. Joseph's College	278 Whites Bridge Rd., Standish, ME 04084	Will Sanborn	(207) 893-6675
St. Joseph's College	155 Roe Blvd., Patchogue, NY 11772	Randy Caden	(631) 447-3349
St. Lawrence U.	Park Street, Canton, NY 13617	Tom Fay	(315) 229-5882
St. Leo U.	PO Box 6665, St. Leo, FL 33574	Ed Stabile	(352) 588-8227
St. Louis Christian College	1360 Grandview Dr., Florissant, MO 63033	Mike Pabarcus	(314) 837-6777
St. Martin's College	5300 Pacific Ave. SE, Lacey, WA 98503	Joe Dominiak	(360) 438-4351
St. Mary, U. of	4100 S. 4th St., Leavenworth, KS 66048	Rob Miller	(913) 758-6160
St. Mary's College	Somerset Hall, St. Mary's City, MD 20686	Lew Jenkins	(240) 895-4312
St. Mary's U.	700 Terrace Heights #47, Winona, MN 55987	Nicholas Whaley	(507) 457-1577
St. Mary's U.	1 Camino Santa Maria St., San Antonio, TX 78228	Charlie Migl	(210) 436-3034
St. Michael's College	One Winooski Park, Colchester, VT 05439	Perry Bove	(802) 654-2725
St. Norbert College	100 Grant St., De Pere, WI 54115	Tom Winske	(920) 403-3545
St. Olaf College	1520 St. Olaf Ave., Northfield, MN 55057	Matt McDonald	(507) 646-3638
St. Paul's College	115 College Dr., Lawrenceville, VA 23868	Oliver Harrison	(804) 848-3111
St. Rose, College of	432 Western Ave., Albany, NY 12203	Bob Bellizzi	(518) 458-2040
St. Scholastica, College of	1200 Kenwood Ave., Duluth, MN 55811	John Baggs	(218) 723-6298
St. Thomas, U. of	2115 Summit Ave., St. Paul, MN 55105	Dennis Denning	(651) 962-5924
St. Thomas Aquinas	125 Route 340, Sparkill, NY 10976	Scott Muscat	(845) 398-4027
St. Thomas U.	16400 NW 32nd Ave., Miami, FL 33054	Manny Mantrana	(305) 628-6730
St. Vincent College	300 Fraser Purchase Rd., Latrobe, PA 15650	Mick Janosko	(724) 539-9761
St. Xavier U.	3700 W. 103rd St., Chicago, IL 60655	Mike Dooley	(773) 298-3103
Salem-International U.	223 W. Main St., Salem, WV 26426	Rich Leitch	(304) 782-5632
Salem State College	352 Lafayette St., Salem, MA 01970	Ken Perrone	(978) 542-7260
Salisbury U.	1101 Camden Ave., Salisbury, MD 21801	Doug Fleetwood	(410) 543-6034
Salve Regina U.	100 Ochre Point Ave., Newport, RI 02840	Steve Cirella	(401) 341-2267
San Francisco State U.	1600 Holloway Ave., San Francisco, CA 94132	Matt Markovich	(415) 338-1226
Savannah Art & Design	PO Box 3146, Savannah, GA 31402	Doug Wollenburg	(912) 525-4782
Schreiner College	2100 Memorial Blvd., Kerrville, TX 78028	Joe Castillo	(830) 792-7292
Scranton, U. of	John J. Long Center, Scranton, Pa. 18510	Mike Bertoletti	(570) 941-7440
Seton Hall U.	PO Box 287, Greensburg, PA 15601	Marc Marizzaldi	(724) 830-1169
Shaw U.	118 E. South St., Raleigh, NC 27601	Bobby Sanders	(919) 546-8281
Shawnee State U.	940 2nd St., Portsmouth, OH 45662	Tom Bergan	(740) 351-3537
Shenandoah U.	1460 University Dr., Winchester, VA 22601	Kevin Anderson	(540) 665-4531
Shepherd College	James Butcher Center, Shepherdstown, WV 25443	Wayne Riser	(304) 876-5472
Shippensburg U.	1871 Old Main Dr., Shippensburg, PA 17257	Bruce Peddie	(717) 477-1508
Shorter College	315 Shorter Ave., Rome, GA 30165	Matt Larry	(706) 233-7510
Siena Heights U.	1247 E. Siena Heights Dr., Adrian, MI 49221	Gordie Theisen	(517) 264-7872
Simpson College	2211 College View Dr., Redding, CA 96003	Jon Mason	(530) 226-4157
Simpson College	701 North C St., Indianola, IA 50125	John Sirianni	(515) 961-1620
Sioux Falls, U. of	1101 W. 22nd St., Sioux Falls, SD 57105	Luke Langenfeld	(605) 331-6638
Skidmore College	North Broadway, Saratoga Springs, NY 12866	Ron Plourde	(518) 580-5380
Slippery Rock U.	102 Morrow Fieldhouse, Slippery Rock, PA 16057	Jeff Messer	(724) 738-2813
Sonoma State U.	1801 E. Cotati Ave., Rohnert Park, CA 94928	John Goelz	(707) 664-2524
South Carolina-Aiken, U. of	471 University Parkway, Aiken, SC 29801	Kenny Thomas	(803) 641-3410
South Carolina-Spartanburg, U. of	800 University Way, Spartanburg, SC 29303	Matt Fincher	(864) 503-5135
South Dakota, U. of	414 E. Clark St., Vermillion, SD 57069	Brian Atchison	(605) 677-6259

South Dakota State U.	16th Ave. & 11th St., Brookings, SD 57007	Mark Ekeland	(605) 688-5027
South, U. of the	735 University Ave., Sewanee, TN 37383	Scott Baker	(931) 598-1545
Southeastern College	1000 Longfellow Blvd, Lakeland, FL 33801	Frank Yurchak	(863) 667-5038
Southeastern Oklahoma State	1405 N. 4th, PMB 4049, Durant, OK 74701	Mike Metheny	(580) 745-2478
Southern Arkansas U.	100 E. University St., Magnolia, AR 71753	Steve Goodheart	(870) 235-4127
Southern Connecticut State	125 Wintergreen Ave., New Haven, CT 06515	Tim Shea	(203) 392-6021
Southern Illinois U.-Edwardsville	SIUE Box 1129, Edwardsville, IL 62026	GaryCollins	(618) 650-2872
Southern Indiana, U. of	8600 University Blvd, Evansville, IN 47712	Mike Goedde	(812) 464-1943
Southern Maine, U. of	37 College Ave., Gorham, ME 04038	Ed Flaherty	(207) 780-5474
Southern Nazarene U.	6729 NW 39th Expy., Bethany, OK 73008	Scott Selby	(405) 491-6630
Southern New Hampshire U.	2500 N. River Rd., Manchester, NH 03106	Bruce Joyce	(603) 645-9637
Southern Tech	1100 S. Marietta Pkwy., Marietta, GA 30060	Matt Griffin	(770) 528-5445
Southern Vermont College	982 Mansion Dr., Bennington, VT 05201	Ryan Marks	(802) 447-4658
Southern Virginia U.	1 College Hill Dr., Buena Vista, VA 24416	Jerry Schlegelmilch	(540) 261-4276
Southern Wesleyan U.	1 Wesleyan Dr., Central, SC 29630	Mike Gillespie	(864) 644-5035
Southwest, College of the	6610 N. Lovington Hwy., Hobbs, NM 88240	Jim Marshall	(505) 392-6561
Southwest Baptist U.	1600 University Ave., Bolivar, MO 65613	Sam Berg	(417) 328-1794
Southwest Minnesota State U.	1501 State St., Marshall, MN 56258	Paul Blanchard	(507) 537-7268
Southwestern Assemblies of God	1200 Sycamore, Waxahachie, TX 75165	Paul Borgard	(972) 937-4010
Southwestern Oklahoma State	100 Campus Dr., Weatherford, OK 73096	Charles Teasley	(580) 774-3263
Southwestern U.	1001 E. University, Georgetown, TX 78626	Jim Mallon	(512) 863-1383
Spalding U.	851 S. 4th St., Louisville, KY 40203	Kevin Kocks	(502) 452-2580
Spring Arbor College	106 E. Main St., Spring Arbor, MI 49283	Hank Burbridge	(517) 750-6503
Spring Hill College	4000 Dauphin St., Mobile, AL 36608	Frank Sims	(251) 380-3486
Springfield College	263 Alden St., Springfield, MA 01109	Mark Simeone	(413) 748-3274
Staten Island, College of	2800 Victory Blvd., Staten Island, NY 10314	Bill Cali	(718) 982-3171
Sterling College	125 W. Cooper, Sterling, KS 67579	Scott Norwood	(620) 278-4227
Stevens Tech	Castle Point on Hudson, Hoboken, NJ 07030	John Crane	(201) 216-8033
Stillman College	3600 Stillman Blvd., Tuscaloosa, AL 35401	Bobby Parker	(205) 366-8915
Stonehill College	320 Washington St., North Easton, MA 02357	Patrick Boen	(508) 565-1351
Suffolk U.	41 Temple St., Boston, MA 02114	Cary McConnell	(617) 573-8379
Sul Ross State U.	Box C-17, Hwy. 90 E., Alpine, TX 79832	Mike Pallanez	(915) 837-8231
SUNY Brockport	350 New Campus Dr., Brockport, NY 14420	Mark Rowland	(716) 395-5329
SUNY Farmingdale	Rte. 110 & Melville Rd., Farmingdale, NY 11735	Ken Rocco	(631) 420-2253
SUNY Maritime College	6 Pennyfield Ave., Bronx, NY 10465	Frank Menna	(718) 409-7331
SUNY New Paltz	75 S. Manheim Blvd., New Paltz, NY 12561	Mike Juhl	(845) 257-3915
SUNY Old Westbury	PO Box 210, Old Westbury, NY 11568	John Lonardo	(516) 876-3241
SUNY Oswego	Route 104, Oswego, NY 13126	Frank Paino	(315) 312-2405
SUNY Plattsburg	101 Broad St., Plattsburg, NY 12901	Kris Doorey	(518) 564-4136
SUNY Utica-Rome	PO Box 3050, Utica, NY 13504	Kevin Edick	(315) 792-7520
Susquehanna U.	514 University Ave., Selinsgrove, PA 17870	Tim Briggs	(570) 372-4417
Swarthmore College	500 College Ave., Swarthmore, PA 19081	Frank Agovino	(610) 328-8216
Tabor College	400 S. Jefferson St., Hillsboro, KS 67063	John Sparks	(620) 947-3121
Talladega College	627 Battle Street W., Talladega, AL 35160	Rodney Lipscomb	(256) 761-6238
Tampa, U. of	401 W. Kennedy Blvd., Tampa, FL 33606	Joe Urso	(813) 253-6240
Tarleton State U.	Box T-80, Stephenville, TX 76402	Trey Felan	(254) 968-9528
Taylor U.	236 W. Reade Ave, Upland, IN 46989	Mark Raikes	(765) 998-4635
Teikyo-Post U.	800 Country Club Rd., Waterbury, CT 06723	Wayne Mazzoni	(203) 596-4690
Tennessee Temple U.	1815 Union Ave., Chattanooga, TN 37404	Kevin Templeton	(423) 493-4220
Tennessee Wesleyan College	40 Green St., Athens, TN 37371	Ashley Lawson	(423) 746-5277
Texas A&M-Kingsville	MSC 202, Kingsville, TX 78363	Russell Stockton	(361) 593-3487
Texas College	PO Box 4500, Tyler, TX 75712	Malcolm Walker	(903) 593-8311
Texas-Dallas, U. of	Box 830688 AB 10, Richardson, TX 75083	Shane Shewmake	(972) 883-2392
Texas Lutheran U.	1000 W. Court St., Seguin, TX 78155	Bill Miller	(830) 372-8124
Texas Wesleyan U.	1201 Wesleyan St., Fort Worth, TX 76105	Mike Jeffcoat	(817) 531-7547
Thiel College	75 College Ave., Greenville, PA 16125	Joe Schaly	(724) 589-2139
Thomas College	West River Rd., Waterville, ME 04901	Greg King	(207) 859-1208
Thomas U.	1501 Millpond Rd., Thomasville, GA 31792	Mike Lee	(229) 226-1621
Thomas More College	333 Thomas More Pkwy., Crestview Hills, KY 41017	Jeff Hetzer	(859) 344-3532
Tiffin U.	155 Miami St., Tiffin, OH 44883	Lonny Allen	(419) 448-3359
Toccoa Falls College	PO Box 800818, Toccoa Falls, GA 30598	Joel Johnson	(706) 886-6831
Transylvania U.	300 N. Broadway, Lexington, KY 40508	Shayne Stock	(859) 233-8699
Trevecca Nazarene U.	333 Murfreesboro Rd., Nashville, TN 37210	Jeff Forehand	(615) 248-1276
Tri-State U.	1 University Ave., Angola, IN 46703	Greg Perschke	(260) 665-4135
Trinity Christian College	6601 W. College Dr., Palos Heights, IL 60463	Matt Schans	(708) 239-4780
Trinity College	Ferris Center, Summit St., Hartford, CT 06106	William Decker	(860) 297-2066
Trinity International U.	500 NE 1st Ave., Miami, FL 33132	Jud Damon	(305) 577-4600
Trinity International U.	2065 Half Day Rd., Deerfield, IL 60015	Mike Manes	(847) 317-7093
Trinity U.	715 Stadium Dr., San Antonio, TX 78212	Tim Scannell	(210) 999-8287
Truman State U.	100 E. Normal St., Kirksville, MO 63501	Larry Scully	(660) 785-6003
Tufts U.	161 College Ave., Medord, MA 02155	John Casey	(617) 627-5218
Tusculum College	PO Box 5090, Greeneville, TN 37743	Doug Jones	(423) 636-7322

Tuskegee U.	321 James Center, Tuskegee, AL 36088	Reggie Ruffin	(334) 724-4229
Union College	310 College St., Barbourville, KY 40906	Bart Osborne	(606) 546-1355
Union College	Alumni Gym, Union Ave., Schenectady, NY 12308	Gary Reynolds	(518) 388-6548
Union U.	1050 Union University Dr., Jackson, TN 38305	Andy Rushing	(731) 661-5333
U.S. Coast Guard Academy	15 Mohegan Ave., New London, CT 06320	Pete Barry	(860) 701-6132
U.S. Merchant Marine	300 Steamboat Rd., Kings Point, NY 11024	Dennis Gagnon	(516) 773-5620
Upper Iowa U.	Box 1857, Fayette, IA 52142	Mark Danker	(563) 425-5290
Urbana U.	579 College Way, Urbana, OH 43078	Scott Spriggs	(937) 454-1377
Ursinus College	601 Main St., Collegeville, PA 19426	Brian Thomas	(610) 409-3611
Utica College	1600 Burnstone Rd., Utica, NY 13502	Don Guido	(315) 752-3378
Valdosta State U.	1500 N. Patterson St, Valdosta, GA 31698	Tommy Thomas	(229) 259-5562
Valley City State U.	101 College St. SW, Valley City, ND 58072	Cory Anderson	(701) 845-7413
Valley Forge Christian	1401 Charlestown Rd., Phoenixville, PA 19460	Roger Burke	(610) 917-1467
Vanguard U.	55 Fair Dr., Costa Mesa, CA 92626	Kevin Kasper	(714) 556-3610
Vassar College	124 Raymond Ave., Poughkeepsie, NY 12604	Andy Barlow	(845) 437-5344
Vermont Tech	Randolph Center, VT 05061	Aaron Hill	(802) 728-1382
Villa Julie College	1525 Greenspring Valley Rd., Stevenson, MD 21153	Ray Kosmicky	(410) 602-7334
Virginia Intermont	1013 Moore St., Bristol, VA 24201	Chris Holt	(276) 466-7945
Virginia State U.	PO Box 9058, Petersburg, VA 23806	Herb Wheat	(804) 524-5816
Virginia Wesleyan College	1584 Wesleyan Dr., Norfolk, VA 23502	Nick Boothe	(757) 455-3348
Virginia-Wise, U. of	1 College Ave., Wise, VA 24293	Hank Banner	(276) 376-4504
Viterbo College	900 Viterbo Dr., La Crosse, WI 54601	Larry Lipker	(608) 796-3824
Voorhees College	PO Box 678, Voorhees Rd., Denmark, SC 29042	Adrian West	(803) 703-7142
Wabash College	301 West Wabash Ave., Crawfordsville, IN 47933	Bill Boone	(765) 361-6209
Waldorf College	106 S. 6th St., Forest City, IA 50436	Brian Grunzke	(641) 585-8263
Walsh U.	2020 Easton St. NW, North Canton, OH 44720	Tim Mead	(330) 490-7013
Warner Southern College	13895 Hwy. 27, Lake Wales, FL 33853	Jeff Sikes	(863) 638-7259
Wartburg College	100 Wartburg Blvd., Waverly, IA 50677	Joel Holst	(319) 352-8532
Washburn U.	1700 SW College Ave., Topeka, KS 66621	Steve Anson	(785) 231-1010
Washington & Jefferson College	60 S. Lincoln, Washington, PA 15301	Mark Mason	(724) 250-3306
Washington & Lee U.	P.O. Drawer 928, Lexington, VA 24450	Jeff Stickley	(540) 463-8680
Washington College	300 Washington Ave, Chestertown, MD 21620	Al Streelman	(410) 778-7239
Washington U.	Campus Box 1067, St. Louis, MO 63130	Ric Lessmann	(314) 935-5945
Wayland Baptist U.	1900 W.7th St., Plainview, TX 79072	Brad Bass	(806) 291-1132
Wayne State College	1111 Main St., Wayne, NE 68787	John Manganaro	(402) 375-7499
Wayne State U.	5101 Lodge Dr., Detroit, MI 48202	Jay Alexander	(313) 577-4280
Waynesburg College	51 W. College St., Waynesburg, PA 15370	Duane Lanzy	(724) 852-3229
Webber International U.	1201 N. Scenic Hwy. 27 South, Babson Park, FL 33827	Brad Niethammer	(863) 638-2951
Webster U.	470 E. Lockwood Ave, Webster Groves, MO 63119	Marty Hunsucker	(314) 961-2660
Wentworth Tech	550 Huntington Ave., Boston, MA 02115	Tom Randolph	(617) 989-4824
Wesley College	120 N. State St., Dover, DE 19901	Matt Addonizio	(302) 735-5939
Wesleyan U.	Freeman Athletic Center, Middletown, CT 06459	Mark Woodworth	(860) 685-2924
West Alabama, U. of	UWA Station 5, Livingston, AL 35470	Gary Rundles	(205) 652-3870
West Chester U.	Sturzebecker Center, West Chester, PA 19383	Chris Calciano	(610) 436-2152
West Florida, U. of	11000 University Pkwy., Pensacola, FL 32514	Jim Spooner	(850) 474-2488
West Georgia, State U. of	1600 Maple St., Carrollton, GA 30118	Doc Fowlkes	(770) 836-6533
West Liberty State College	Bartell Fieldhouse, West Liberty, WV 26074	Bo McConnaughy	(304) 336-8235
West Texas A&M U.	WTAMU Box 60049, Canyon, TX 79016	Mark Jones	(806) 651-2676
West Virginia State College	210 Fleming Hall, Institute, WV 25112	Cal Bailey	(304) 766-3165
West Virginia Tech	405 Fayette Pike, Route 61, Montgomery, WV 25136	Tim Epling	(304) 442-3121
West Virginia Wesleyan	College Ave., Buckhannon, WV 26201	Randy Tenney	(304) 473-8054
Western Baptist College	5000 Deer Park Drive SE, Salem, OR 97301	Paul Gale	(503) 589-8183
Western Connecticut State	181 White St., Danbury, CT 06810	John Susi	(203) 837-8608
Western New England College	1215 Wilbraham Rd., Springfield, MA 01119	Matt LaBranche	(413) 782-1792
Western Oregon U.	345 Monmouth Ave N., Monmouth, OR 97361	Terry Baumgartner	(503) 838-8448
Westfield State College	577 Western Ave., Westfield, MA 01086	Tom LoRicco	(413) 572-5633
Westminster College	501 Westminster Ave, Fulton, MO 65251	Scott Pritchard	(573) 592-5333
Westminster College	Market St., New Wilmington, PA 16172	Sean Kelly	(724) 946-7311
Westmont College	955 La Paz Rd., Santa Barbara, CA 93108	Robert Crawford	(805) 565-6012
Wheaton College	501 East College Ave, Wheaton, IL 60187	Bobby Elder	(630) 752-7164
Wheaton College	Haas Athletic Center, Norton, MA 02766	Eric Podbelski	(508) 286-3988
Whitman College	345 Boyer Ave., Walla Walla, WA 99362	Travis Feezell	(509) 527-4931
Whittier College	13406 E. Philadelphia St., Whittier, CA 90608	Mike Rizzo	(562) 907-4967
Whitworth College	300 W. Hawthorne Rd., Spokane, WA 99251	Keith Ward	(509) 777-4394
Widener U.	1 University Place, Chester, PA 19013	Sean Matkowski	(610) 499-4446
Wiley College	711 Wiley Ave., Marshall, TX 75670	Eddie Watson	(903) 927-3292
Wilkes U.	PO Box 111, Wilkes-Barre, PA 18703	Joe Folek	(570) 408-4020
Willamette U.	900 State St., Salem, OR 97301	David Wong	(503) 370-6011
William Carey Col	498 Tuscan Ave., Hattiesburg, MS 39401	Bobby Halford	(601) 318-6110
William Jewell Col	500 College Hill, Liberty, MO 64068	Mike Stockton	(816) 781-7700

William Paterson U.	300 Pompton Rd., Wayne, NJ 07470	Jeff Albies	(973) 720-2210
William Penn College	201 Trueblood Ave., Oskaloosa, IA 52577	Mike Laird	(641) 673-1023
William Woods U.	1 University Drive, Fulton, MO 65251	Ryan Bay	(573) 592-1187
Williams Baptist College	PO Box 3387, College City, AR 72476	John Katrosh	(870) 759-4192
Williams College	22 Spring St., Williamstown, MA 01267	Dave Barnard	(413) 597-3326
Wilmington College	320 N. DuPont Highway, New Castle, DE 19720	Matt Brainard	(302) 328-9435
Wilmington College	251 Ludovic St., Wilmington, OH 45177	Tony Haley	(937) 382-6661
Wingate U.	315 E. Wilson St., Wingate, NC 28174	Bill Nash	(704) 233-8242
Winona State U.	PO Box 5838, Winona, MN 55987	Kyle Poock	(507) 457-2332
Wisconsin Lutheran College	8800 W. Bluemound Rd., Milwaukee, WI 53226	Brook Smith	(414) 443-8990
Wisconsin-La Crosse, U. of	Mitchell Hall, La Crosse, WI 54601	George Williams	(608) 785-6540
Wisconsin-Oshkosh, U. of	800 Algoma Blvd., Oshkosh, WI 54901	Tom Lechnir	(920) 424-0374
Wisconsin-Parkside, U. of	900 Wood Rd., Kenosha, WI 53141	Tracy Archuleta	(262) 595-2317
Wisconsin-Platteville, U. of	1 University Plaza, Platteville, WI 53818	Jamie Sailors	(608) 342-1843
Wisconsin-Stevens Point, U. of	134 HEC, Stevens Point, WI 54481	Brian Nelson	(715) 346-4412
Wisconsin-Stout, U. of	Johnson Fiedhouse, Menomonie, WI 54751	Craig Walter	(715) 232-1459
Wisconsin-Superior, U. of	1800 Grand Ave., Superior, WI 54880	James Stukel	(715) 394-8272
Wisconsin-Whitewater, U. of	800 W. Main St., Whitewater, WI 53190	Jim Miller	(262) 472-5649
Wittenberg U.	PO Box 720, Springfield, OH 45501	Jay Lewis	(937) 327-6494
Wooster, College of	1189 Beall Ave., Wooster, OH 44691	Tim Pettorini	(330) 263-2180
Worcester State College	486 Chandler St., Worcester, MA 01602	Dirk Baker	(508) 929-8852
Worcester Tech	100 Institute Rd., Worcester, MA 01609	Chris Robertson	(508) 831-5624
York College	1125 E. 8th St., York, NE 68467	Jerry Laird	(402) 363-5736
York College	Country Club Road, York, PA 17405	Paul Saikia	(717) 815-1245

JUNIOR COLLEGES

School	Mailing Address	Head Coach	Telephone
Abraham Baldwin College	ABAC 41, 2802 Moore Hwy, Tifton, GA 31793	Steve Janousek	(229) 386-3931
Adirondack CC	640 Bay Road, Queensbury, NY 12804	John Hayes	(518) 743-2269
Alabama Southern CC	PO Box 2000, Monroeville, AL 36461	Mike Kandler	(251) 575-3156
Alfred State Col	Orvis Center, Alfred, NY 14802	Tom Kenney	(607) 587-4369
Allan Hancock Col	800 S. College Dr., Santa Maria, CA 93454	Chris Stevens	(805) 922-6966
Allegany College	12401 Willowbrook Rd., Cumberland, MD 21502	Steve Bazarnic	(301) 784-5265
Allegheny CCAC	808 Ridge Ave., Pittsburgh, PA 15212	Bob Janeda	(412) 237-2503
Allegheny County CC -Boyce	595 Beatty Rd., Monroeville, PA 15146	Bill Holmes	(724) 325-6621
Allegheny County CC -South	1750 Clairton Rd., West Mifflin, PA 15122	Jeff Minick	(412) 469-6388
Allen County CC	1801 N. Cottonwood St., Iola, KS 66749	Val McLean	(620) 365-5116
Alvin CC	3110 Mustang Rd., Alvin, TX 77511	Bryan Alexander	(281) 756-3696
American River CC	4700 College Oak Dr., Sacramento, CA 95841	Doug Jumelet	(916) 484-8294
Ancilla College	9601 S. Union Rd., Donaldson, IN 46513	Gene Reese	(574) 936-8898
Andrew College	413 College St., Cuthbert, GA 39840	Chip Reese	(229) 732-5953
Angelina College	PO Box 1768, Lufkin, TX 75902	Jeff Livin	(936) 633-5284
Anne Arundel CC	101 College Parkway, Arnold, MD 21012	Lou DiMenna	(410) 777-2322
Anoka-Ramsey CC	11200 Mississippi Blvd. NW, Coon Rapids, MN 55433	Tom Yelle	(763) 422-3521
Antelope Valley Col	3041 W. Avenue K, Lancaster, CA 93536	Jeffrey Leonard	(661) 722-6300
Arapahoe CC	5900 S. Santa Fe Dr., Littleton, CO 80160	Mark Laschanzky	(303) 797-5853
Arizona Western College	PO Box 929, Yuma, AZ 85366	John Stratton	(928) 344-7542
Arkansas-Fort Smith	5210 Grand Ave., PO Box 3649 Fort Smith, AR 72913	Dale Harpenau	(479) 788-7597
Bakersfield College	1801 Panorama Dr., Bakersfield, CA 93305	Tim Painton	(661) 395-4261
Baltimore CC-Liberty	2901 Liberty Heights Ave, Baltimore, MD 21215	Lance Mauck	(410) 462-7752
Barstow CC	2700 Barstow Rd., Barstow, CA 92311	Mike Gorman	(760) 252-2411
Barton County CC	245 NE 30th Rd., Great Bend, KS 67530	Mike Warren	(620) 792-9378
Bellevue CC	3000 Landerholm Circle SE, Bellevue, WA 98007	Mark Yoshino	(425) 564-2351
Bergen CC	400 Paramus Rd., Paramus, NJ 07652	John Decker	(201) 447-7183
Bethany Lutheran Col	700 Luther Dr., Mankato, MN 56001	Derek Woodley	(507) 344-7451
Bevill State CC- Fayette	2631 Temple Ave N., Fayette, AL 35555	Joey May	(205) 932-3221
Bevill State CC- Sumiton	PO Box 800, Sumiton, AL 35148	Ed Langham	(205) 648-3271
Big Bend CC	7662 Chanute St., Moses Lake, WA 98837	Don Lindgren	(509) 762-5351
Bishop State CC	351 N. Broad St., Mobile, AL 36603	Johnny Watkins	(251) 690-6436
Bismarck State CC	1500 Edwards Ave., Bismarck, ND 58506	Len Stanley	(701) 224-5736
Black Hawk College	6600 34th Ave., Moline, IL 61265	Tim McChesney	(309) 796-5607
Blinn College	902 College Ave., Brenham, TX 77833	Brian Roper	(979) 830-4171
Blue Mountain CC	2411 NW Carden Ave., Pendleton, OR 97801	Brett Bryan	(541) 278-5900
Blue Ridge CC	College Drive, Flat Rock, NC 28731	Damon Towe	(828) 694-1778
Bossier Parish CC	2719 Airline Dr., Bossier City, LA 71111	Jay Artigues	(318) 746-9851
Brevard CC	3865 N. Wickham Rd., Melbourne FL 32940	Ernie Rosseau	(321) 433-5601
Briarcliffe College	1055 Stewart Ave., Bethpage, NY 11714	Pete Alfero/Dave Rivera	(516) 918-3731
Brigham Young U.-Idaho	Hart Bldg., 264 Athletic Office, Rexburg, ID 83460	Don Schiess	(208) 356-2127
Bronx CC	W. 181st & Washington, Bronx, NY 10453	Adolfo DeJesus	(718) 289-5274
Brookdale CC	765 Newman Springs Rd., Lincroft, NJ 07738	Johnny Johnson	(732) 224-2379

Brookhaven College	3939 Valley View Lane, Farmers Branch, TX 75244	Denny Dixon	(972) 860-4121
Broome CC	901 Front St., Binghamton, NY 13902	Brett Carter	(607) 778-5568
Broward CC-Downtown	3501 SW Davie Rd., Davie, FL 33314	Mike Silvestri	(954) 475-6949
Broward CC-Central	3501 Davie Rd., Davie, FL 33314	Bob Detchsman	(954) 201-6949
Brown Mackie CC	2106 S. Ninth, Salina, KS 67401	Steve Bartow	(785) 825-5422
Bucks County CC	275Swamp Rd, Newton, PA 18940	Craig Scioscia	(215) 968-8450
Bunker Hill CC	250 New Rutherford Ave, Boston, MA 02129	Scott Blumsack	(617) 228-2088
Burlington County CC	County Route 530, Pemberton, NJ 08068	John Holt	(609) 894-9311
Butler County CC	901 S. Haverhill Rd., El Dorado, KS 67042	Steve Johnson	(316) 322-3201
Butler County CC	PO Box 1203, Butler, PA 16003	Tom Roper	(724) 287-8711
Butte College	3536 Butte Campus Dr., Oroville, CA 95965	Anthony Ferro	(530) 895-2521
Cabrillo College	6500 Soquel Dr., Aptos, CA 95003	Rich Weidinger	(831) 479-6100
Camden County College	PO Box 200, Blackwood, NJ 08012	Frank Angeloni	(856) 227-7200
Canada College	4200 Farm Hill Blvd., Redwood City, CA 94061	Tonny Lucca	(650) 306-3269
Canyons, College of the	26455 Rockwell Canyon Rd., Santa Clarita, CA 91355	Chris Cota	(661) 259-7800
Carl Albert State College	1507 S. McKenna St., Poteau, OK 74953	Mark Pollard	(918) 647-1280
Carl Sandburg College	2400 Tom L. Wilson Blvd., Galesburg, IL 61401	Mike Bailey	(309) 341-5227
CCBC-Catonsville	800 S. Rolling Rd., Baltimore, MD 21228	Dan Blue	(410) 455-6996
CCBC-Dundalk	7200 Sollers Point Rd., Baltimore, MD 21222	Scott Roane	(410) 285-9741
CCBC-Essex	7201 Rossville Blvd., Baltimore, MD 21237	George Henderson	(410) 780-6346
Cecil CC	One Seahawk Dr., North East, MD 21901	Charlie O'Brien	(410) 287-1080
Cedar Valley College	3030 N. Dallas Ave., Lancaster, TX 75134	Kyle Koehler	(972) 860-8184
Central Alabama CC	1675 Cherokee Rd., Alexander City, AL 35010	Don Ingram	(256) 215-4320
Central Arizona College	8470 N. Overfield Rd., Coolidge, AZ 85228	Clint Myers	(520) 426-4336
Central Florida CC	3001 SW College Rd., Ocala, FL 34474	Marty Smith	(352) 854-2322
Central Lakes College	501 W. College Dr., Brainerd, MN 56401	Warren Mertens	(218) 855-8210
Centralia College	600 W. Locust St., Centralia, WA 98531	Bruce Pocklington	(360) 736-9391
Cerritos College	11110 East Alondra Blvd., Norwalk, CA 90650	Geraldo Perez	(562) 860-3099
Cerro Coso CC	3000 College Heights Blvd., Ridgecrest, CA 93555	Dick Adams	(760) 384-6386
Chabot College	25555 Hesperian Blvd., Hayward, CA 94545	Steve Friend	(510) 723-6934
Chaffey College	5885 Haven Ave., Rancho Cucamonga, CA 91739	Jeff Harlow	(909) 941-2328
Chandler-Gilbert CC	2626 E. Pecos Rd., Chandler, AZ 85225	Doyle Wilson	(480) 732-7177
Chattahoochee Valley CC	2602 College Dr., Phenix City, AL 36869	Adam Thomas	(334) 291-4908
Chattanooga State Tech CC	4501 Amnicola Hwy., Chattanooga, TN 37406	Greg Dennis	(423) 697-3397
Chemeketa CC	4000 Lancaster Dr. NE, Salem, OR 97309	John Doran	(503) 399-7953
Chesapeake College	1000 College Dr., PO Box 8, Wye Mills, MD 21679	Frank Szymanski	(410) 827-5828
Chipola JC	3094 Indian Circle, Marianna, FL 32446	Jeff Johnson	(850) 718-2237
Citrus College	1000 W. Foothill Blvd., Glendora, CA 91741	Sean Severns	(626) 914-8674
Clackamas CC	19600 S. Molalla Ave., Oregon City, OR 97045	Robin Robinson	(503) 657-6958
Clarendon College	PO Box 968, Clarendon, TX 79226	Cory Hall	(806) 874-3571
Clark State CC	570 E. Leffel Ln., Springfield, OH 45501	Tim Rigel	(937) 328-6027
Cleveland State CC	PO Box 3570, Cleveland, TN 37320	Mike Policastro	(423) 478-6219
Clinton CC	136 Clinton Point Dr., Plattsburgh, NY 12901	Tom Neale	(518) 562-4220
Cloud County CC	Box 1002, Concordia, KS 66901	Greg Brummett	(785) 243-1435
Coahoma JC	3240 Friars Point Rd., Clarksdale, MS 38614	Billy Fields	(662) 621-4231
Cochise County CC	4190 W. Hwy. 80, Douglas, AZ 85607	Todd Inglehart	(520) 417-4095
Coffeyville CC	400 W. 11th St., Coffeyville, KS 67337	Ryan McCune	(620) 252-7095
Colby CC	1255 S. Range Ave, Colby, KS 67701	Ryan Carter	(785) 462-3984
Collin County CC	2800 E. Spring Creek Pkwy., Plano, TX 75074	Greg Dennis	(972) 881-5150
Colorado Northwestern CC	500 Kennedy Dr., Rangely, CO 81648	Dustin Colborn	(970) 675-3317
Columbia Basin CC	2600 N. 20th Ave., Pasco, WA 99301	Scott Rogers	(509) 547-0511
Columbia State CC	PO Box 1315, Columbia, TN 38402	Jim Painter	(931) 540-2632
Columbia-Greene CC	4400 Route 23, Hudson, NY 12534	Bob Godlewski	(518) 828-4181
Columbus State CC	550 E. Spring St., Columbus, OH 43215	Eric Welch	(614) 287-2616
Compton CC	111 East Artesia Blvd., Compton, CA 90221	Simon Peters	(310) 900-1600
Connecticut -Avery Point, U. of	1084 Shennescossett Rd., Groton, CT 06340	Roger Bidwell	(860) 405-9183
Connors State College	Rt. 1, Box 1000, Warner, OK 74469	Perry Keith	(918) 463-6231
Contra Costa College	2600 Mission Bell Dr., San Pablo, CA 94806	Marvin Webb	(510) 235-7800
Copiah-Lincoln JC	PO Box 649, Wesson, MS 39191	Keith Case	(601) 643-8381
Corning CC	1 Academic Dr., Corning, NY 14830	Brian Hill	(607) 962-9383
Cosumnes River CC	8401 Center Pkwy., Sacramento CA 95823	Tony Bloomfield	(916) 691-7397
Cowley County CC	125 S. 2nd St., Arkansas City, KS 67005	Dave Burroughs	(620) 441-5246
Crowder College	601 Laclede Ave., Neosho, MO 64850	Chip Durham	(417) 451-3223
Crowley's Ridge College	100 College Dr., Paragould, AR 72450	James Scott	(870) 236-6901
Cuesta College	PO Box 8106, San Luis Obispo, CA 93403	Bob Miller	(805) 546-3100
Cumberland County College	PO Box 1500, Vineland, NJ 08362	Cruz Comez	(856) 691-8600
Cuyahoga CC-West	11000 Pleasant Valley Rd., Parma, OH 44130	Brian Harrison	(216) 987-5459
Cypress College	9200 Valley View St., Cypress, CA 90630	Scott Pickler	(714) 484-7000
Dakota County Tech College	14200 Cedar Ave., Apple Valley, MN 55124	Kerry Lurken	(952) 997-9577
Danville Area CC	2000 E. Main St., Danville, IL 61832	Tim Bunton	(217) 443-8807
Darton College	2400 Gillionville Rd., Albany, GA 31707	Glenn Eames	(229) 430-6788

College	Address	Contact	Phone
Dawson CC	PO Box 421, Glendive, MT 59330	Brent Diegel	(406) 377-9450
Daytona Beach CC	1200 Int'l Speedway Rd., Daytona Beach, FL 32120	Tim Touma	(386) 506-4505
Dean College	99 Main St., Franklin, MA 02038	Kevin Burr	(508) 541-1814
De Anza College	21250 Stevens Creek Blvd., Cupertino, CA 95014	Scott Hertler	(408) 864-8741
Delaware County CC	901 S. Media Line Rd., Media, PA 19063	Paul Motta	(610) 359-5354
Delaware Tech & CC-Owens	PO Box 610, Route 18, Georgetown, DE 19947	Curtis Brock	(302) 855-1636
Delgado CC	615 City Park Ave., New Orleans, LA 70119	Joe Scheuermann	(504) 483-4381
Des Moines Area CC-Boone	1125 Hancock Dr., Boone, IA 50036	John Smith	(515) 433-5050
Desert, College of the	43500 Monterey Ave., Palm Desert, CA 92260	David Buttles	(760) 773-2585
Diablo Valley College	321 Golf Club Rd., Pleasant Hill, CA 94523	Larry Quirico	(925) 685-1230
Dixie State College	225 S. 700 E., St. George, UT 84770	Mike Littlewood	(435) 652-7526
Dodge City CC	2501 N. 14th Ave., Dodge City, KS 67801	Erick Wright	(620) 227-9347
DuPage, College of	425 Fawell Blvd., Glen Ellyn, IL 60137	Dan Kusinski	(630) 942-2426
Dutchess CC	53 Pendell Rd., Poughkeepsie, NY 12601	Joe DeRosa	(845) 431-8468
Dyersburg State CC	1510 Lake Rd., Dyersburg, TN 38024	Robert White	(731) 286-3252
East Central CC	PO Box 129, Decatur, MS 39327	Jake Yarborough	(601) 635-2111
East Central College	1964 Prairie Dell Rd., Union, MO 63084	Gale Wallis	(314) 583-5195
East Los Angeles College	1301 Avenida Cesar Chavez, Monterey Park, CA 91754	James Hines	(323) 265-8650
East Mississippi JC	PO Box 158, Scooba, MS 39358	Bill Baldner	(662) 476-5128
Eastern Arizona JC	615 N. Stadium Dr., Thatcher, AZ 85552	Jim Bagnall	(928) 428-8414
Eastern Oklahoma State	1301 W. Main St., Wilburton, OK 74578	Todd Shelton	(918) 465-2361
Eastern Utah, College of	451 E. 400 N., Price, UT 84501	Eric Madsen	(435) 613-5357
Eastfield College	3737 Motley Dr., Mesquite, TX 75150	Michael Martin	(972) 860-7643
Edison CC	8099 College Pkwy. SW, Fort Myers, FL 33919	John Cedarburg	(941) 489-9486
Edmonds CC	20000 68th Ave. W., Lynnwood, WA 98036	Don Marbut	(425) 640-1415
El Camino College	16007 Crenshaw Blvd., Torrance, CA 90506	Nick Van Lue	(310) 660-3679
El Paso CC	PO Box 20500, El Paso, TX 79998	Ken Jacome	(915) 831-2277
Elgin CC	1700 Spartan Dr., Elgin, IL 60123	Bill Angelo	(847) 214-7552
Ellsworth CC	1100 College Ave., Iowa Falls, IA 50126	Joel Lueken	(800) 322-9235
Enterprise -Ozark CC	PO Box 1300, Enterprise, AL 36331	Tim Hulsey	(334) 347-2623
Erie CC	6205 Main St., Williamsville, NY 14221	Joe Bauth	(716) 851-1290
Everett CC	2000 Tower St., Everett, WA 98201	Levi Lacey	(425) 388-9328
Faulkner State CC	1900 Hwy. 31 South, Bay Minette, AL 36507	Wayne Larker	(251) 580-2160
Finger Lakes CC	4355 Lakeshore Dr., Canandaigua, NY 14424	Jason Rich	(585) 394-3500
Florida CC	11901 Beach Blvd., Jacksonville, FL 32246	Chris Blaquiere	(904) 646-2205
Florida College	119 N. Glen Arven Ave., Temple Terrace, FL 33617	Kerry Keenan	(813) 899-6789
Fort Scott CC	2108 S. Horton St., Fort Scott, KS 66701	Chris Moddelmog	(620) 223-2700
Frank Phillips College	PO Box 5118, Borger, TX 79008	Guy Simmons	(806) 274-5961
Frederick CC	7932 Opossumtown Pike, Frederick, MD 21702	Rodney Bennett	(301) 846-2501
Fresno City College	1101 E. University Ave., Fresno, CA 93741	Ron Scott	(559) 442-4600
Fullerton College	321 E. Chapman Ave., Fullerton, CA 92832	Nick Fuscardo	(714) 992-7401
Fulton-Montgomery CC	2805 State Highway 67, Johnstown, NY 12095	Mike Mulligan	(518) 762-4651
Gadsden State CC	PO Box 227, Gadsden, AL 35902	Bill Lockridge	(256) 549-8311
Galveston College	4015 Avenue Q, Galveston, TX 77550	Ruben Felix	(409) 763-6551
Garden City CC	801 Campus Dr., Garden City, KS 67846	Rick Sabath	(620) 276-9599
Garrett College	687 Mosser Rd., McHenry, MD 21541	Lee Bradley	(301) 387-3052
Gateway CC	60 Sargent Dr., New Haven, CT 06511	Darryl Morhardt	(203) 285-2213
Gavilan College	5055 Santa Teresa Blvd., Gilroy, CA 95020	Neal Andrade	(408) 848-4916
Genesee CC	1 College Rd., Batavia, NY 14020	Barry Garigen	(585) 345-6898
George C. Wallace CC-Dothan	1141 Wallace Dr., Dothan, AL 36303	Mackey Sasser	(334) 983-3521
George C. Wallace CC-Selma	3000 Earl Goodwin Pkwy, PO Box 2530, Selma, AL 36702	EJ Brophy	(334) 876-9292
Georgia Perimeter College	3251 Panthersville Rd., Decatur, GA 30034	Ted Wallen	(404) 244-5765
Glen Oaks CC	62249 Shimmel Rd., Centreville, MI 49032	Chad Newhard	(269) 467-9945
Glendale CC	6000 W. Olive Ave., Glendale, AZ 85302	David Grant	(623) 845-3040
Glendale College	1500 N. Verdugo Rd., Glendale, CA 91208	Chris Cicuto	(818) 240-1000
Globe Tech	291 Broadway, New York, NY 10007	Justin Timmerman	(212) 349-4330
Gloucester County College	1400 Tanyard Rd., Sewell, NJ 08080	Rob Valli	(856) 415-2257
Golden West College	15744 Golden West St., Huntington Beach, CA 92647	Roberto Villarreal	(714) 895-8260
Gordon College	419 College Dr., Barnesville, GA 30204	Travis McClanahan	(770) 358-5061
Grand Rapids CC	143 Bostwick Ave. NE, Grand Rapids, MI 49503	Doug Wabeke	(616) 234-4270
Grays Harbor College	1620 Edward P. Smith Dr., Aberdeen, WA 98520	Shon Schreiber	(360) 538-4062
Grayson County College	6101 Grayson Dr., Denison, TX 75020	Tim Tadlock	(903) 463-8719
Green River CC	12401 SE 320th St., Auburn, WA 98092	Matt Acker	(253) 833-9111
Grossmont College	8800 Grossmont College Dr., El Cajon, CA 92020	Ed Olsen	(619) 644-7447
Gulf Coast CC	5230 W. Highway 98, Panama City, FL 32401	Darren Mazeroski	(850) 872-3897
Hagerstown CC	11400 Robinwood Dr., Hagerstown, MD 21742	Scott Jennings	(301) 790-2800
Harford CC	401 Thomas Run Rd., Bel Air, MD 21015	Bill Greenwell	(410) 836-4321
Harper College	1200 W. Algonquin Rd., Palatine, IL 60067	Vern Hasty	(847) 925-6957
Hartnell CC	156 Homestead Ave., Salinas, CA 93901	Dan Teresa	(831) 755-6840

Henry Ford CC	5101 Evergreen Rd., Dearborn, MI 48128	Darnell Walker	(313) 845-9647
Herkimer County CC	100 Reservoir Rd., Herkimer, NY 13350	Henry Testa	(315) 866-0300
Hesston College	325 S. College Dr., Box 3000, Hesston, KS 67062	Art Mullet	(620) 327-8278
Hibbing CC	1515 E. 25th St., Hibbing, MN 55746	Mike Turnbull	(218) 262-6748
Highland CC	2998 W. Pearl City Rd., Freeport, IL 61032	Mike Edmonds	(815) 599-3465
Highland CC	606 W. Main, Highland, KS 66035	Rick Eberly	(785) 442-6039
Hill College	PO Box 619, Hillsboro, TX 76645	Gary Benton	(254) 582-2555
Hillsborough CC	PO Box 30030, Tampa, FL 33630	Gary Calhoun	(813) 253-7311
Hinds CC	PO Box 1100, Raymond, MS 39154	Rick Clarke	(601) 857-3325
Hiwassee College	225 Hiwassee College Dr., Madisonville, TN 37354	Travis McClanahan	(423) 442-2001
Holmes CC	PO Box 369, Goodman, MS 39079	Kenny Dupont	(662) 472-9065
Holyoke CC	303 Homestead Ave., Holyoke, MA 01040	Dan O'Neill	(413) 552-2163
Hostos CC	500 Grand Concourse, Bronx, NY 10451	John Sanchez	(718) 518-6879
Howard College	1001 Birdwell Lane, Big Spring, TX 79720	Britt Smith	(432) 264-5041
Hudson Valley CC	80 Vandenburg Ave., Troy, NY 12180	Tom Reinisch	(518) 629-7415
Hutchinson CC	1300 N. Plum St., Hutchinson, KS 67501	Jon Wente	(620) 665-3586
Illinois Central College	One College Dr., East Peoria, IL 61635	Brett Kelley	(309) 694-5427
Illinois Valley CC	815 N. Orlando Smith St., Oglesby, IL 61348	Bob Koopmann	(815) 224-0471
Imperial Valley College	PO Box 158, Imperial, CA 92251	Dave Drury	(760) 355-6323
Independence CC	PO Box 708, Independence, KS 67301	Jon Olsen	(620) 331-4100
Indians Hills CC	721 N. 1st St., Centerville, IA 52544	Cam Walker	(800) 670-3641
Indian River CC	3209 Virginia Ave., Fort Pierce, FL 34981	Mike Easom	(772) 462-4772
Iowa Central CC	330 Avenue M, Fort Dodge, IA 50501	Rick Pederson	(515) 576-0099
Iowa Lakes CC	300 S. 18th St., Estherville, IA 51334	Jason Nell	(712) 362-7915
Iowa Western CC	2700 College Rd., Council Bluffs, IA 51503	Marc Radin	(712) 325-3331
Irvine Valley College	5500 Irvine Center Dr., Irvine, CA 92618	Kent Madole	(949) 451-5763
Itasca CC	1851 E. Hwy. 169, Grand Rapids, MN 55744	Justin Lamppa	(218) 327-4226
Itawamba CC	602 W. Hill St., Fulton, MS 38843	Rick Collier	(662) 862-8122
Jackson State CC	2046 N. Parkway, Jackson, TN 38301	Steve Cornelison	(731) 425-2649
Jamestown CC	525 Falconer St., Jamestown, NY 14701	Kerry Kellogg	(716) 665-5220
Jefferson CC	1220 Coffeen St., Watertown, NY 13601	Paul Alteri	(315) 786-2497
Jefferson College	1000 Viking Dr., Hillsboro, MO 63050	Dave Oster	(636) 797-3000
Jefferson Davis CC	PO Box 958, Brewton, AL 36427	Jim Morrill	(251) 809-1622
Jefferson State CC	2601 Carson Rd., Birmingham, AL 35215	Ben Short	(205) 856-7879
John A. Logan College	700 Logan College Rd., Carterville, IL 62918	Jerry Halstead	(618) 985-2828
Johnson County CC	12345 College Blvd., Overland Park, KS 66210	Kent Shelley	(913) 469-3820
John Wood CC	1301 S. 48th St., Quincy, IL 62301	Greg Wathen	(217) 641-4306
Joliet JC	1215 Houbolt Rd., Joliet, IL 60431	Wayne King	(815) 280-2210
Jones County JC	900 S. Court St., Ellisville, MS 39437	Bobby Glaze	(601) 477-4088
Kalamazoo Valley CC	PO Box 4070, Kalamazoo, MI 49003	Bernie Vallier	(269) 488-4781
Kankakee CC	PO Box 888, River Rd., Kankakee, IL 60901	Todd Post	(815) 802-8616
Kansas City CC	7250 State Ave., Kansas City, KS 66112	Steve Burleson	(913) 288-7150
Kaskaskia CC	27210 College Rd., Centralia, IL 62801	Larry Smith	(618) 545-3146
Kellogg CC	450 North Ave., Battle Creek, MI 49017	Russ Bortell	(269) 965-4151
Kingsborough CC	2001 Oriental Blvd., Brooklyn, NY 11235	Jim Ryan	(718) 368-5737
Kirkwood CC	PO Box 2068, Cedar Rapids, IA 52406	John Lewis	(319) 398-5589
Kishwaukee College	21193 Malta Rd., Malta, IL 60150	Mike Davenport	(815) 825-2086
Labette CC	200 S. 14th St., Parsons, KS 67357	Tom Hilton	(620) 820-1011
Lackawanna JC	501 Vine St., Scranton, PA 18509	Tony DiMattia	(570) 961-7869
Lake City CC	RR 19, Box 1030, Lake City, FL 32025	Tom Clark	(386) 754-4363
Lake County, College of	19351 W. Washington St., Grayslake, IL 60030	Gene Hanson	(847) 543-2046
Lake Land College	5001 Lake Land Blvd., Mattoon, IL 61938	Jim Jarrett	(217) 234-5296
Lake Michigan College	2755 E. Napier Ave., Benton Harbor, MI 49022	Keith Schreiber	(269) 927-8165
Lake-Sumter CC	9501 US Hwy. 441, Leesburg, FL 32788	Mike Matulia	(352) 323-3643
Lakeland CC	7700 Clocktower Dr., Kirtland, OH 44094	Howie Krause	(440) 953-7350
Lamar CC	2401 S. Main St., Lamar, CO 81052	Scott Crampton	(719) 336-1681
Lane CC	4000 E. 30th Ave., Eugene, OR 97405	Donny Harrel	(541) 463-5599
Laney College	900 Fallon St., Oakland, CA 94607	Francisco Zapata	(510) 464-3476
Lansing CC	PO Box 40010, Lansing, MI 48901	Frank Deak	(517) 483-1622
Laredo CC	West End, Washington St., Laredo, TX 78040	John Maley	(956) 721-5326
Lassen College	PO Box 3000, Susanville, CA 96130	Glen Yonan	(530) 251-8815
Lenoir CC	PO Box 188, Kinston, NC 28502	Lind Hartsell	(252) 527-6223
Lewis & Clark CC	5800 Godfrey Rd., Godfrey, IL 62035	Randy Martz	(618) 468-6230
Lincoln College	300 Keokuk St., Lincoln, IL 62656	Tony Thomas	(217) 732-3155
Lincoln Land CC	5250 Shepherd Rd., Springfield, IL 62794	Ron Riggle	(217) 786-2581
Lincoln Trail College	11220 State Hwy. 1, Robinson, IL 62454	Mitch Hannahs	(618) 544-5299
Linn-Benton CC	6500 Pacific Blvd. SW, Albany, OR 97321	Greg Hawk	(541) 917-4242
Lon Morris College	800 College Ave., Jacksonville, TX 75766	Josh Stewart	(903) 589-4076
Long Beach City College	4901 E. Carson St., Long Beach, CA 90808	Casey Crook	(562) 938-4242

Longview CC	500 SW Longview Rd., Lee's Summit, MO 64081	Mark Lyford	(816) 672-2440
Los Angeles City College	855 N. Vermont Ave., Los Angeles, CA 90029	Robert McKinley	(323) 953-4000
Los Angeles Harbor College	1111 Figueroa Pl., Wilmington, CA 90744	Jay Uhlman	(310) 522-8464
Los Angeles Pierce College	6201 Winnetka Ave., Woodland Hills, CA 91371	Bob Lofrano	(818) 710-2823
Los Angeles Valley College	5800 Fulton Ave., Valley Glen, CA 91401	Chris Johnson	(818) 947-2509
Los Medanos College	2700 E. Leland Rd., Pittsburg, CA 94565	Matt Jones	(925) 439-2185
Louisburg College	501 N. Main St., Louisburg, NC 27549	Billy Godwin	(919) 497-3266
Lower Columbia College	PO Box 3010, Longview, WA 98632	Kelly Smith	(360) 442-2870
LSU-Eunice	PO Box 1129, Eunice, LA 70535	Jeff Willis	(337) 550-1394
Lurleen B. Wallace State JC	PO Box 1418, Andalusia, AL 36420	Steve Helms	(334) 222-6591
Macomb CC	14500 E. 12 Mile Rd., Warren, MI 48088	Mike Kaczmarek	(586) 445-7119
Madison Area Tech	3550 Anderson St., Madison, WI 53704	Steve Hauser	(608) 246-6099
Manatee CC	5840 26th St. W, Bradenton, FL 34207	Tim Hill	(941) 752-5575
Manchester CC	Great Path MS No. 20 Manchester, CT 06045	Chris Strahowski	(860) 512-3353
Manhattan CC	199 Chambers St., New York, NY 10007	Juan Colon	(212) 220-8260
Maple Woods CC	2601 NE Barry Rd., Kansas City, MO 64156	Chris Mihlfeld	(816) 437-3175
Marin, College of	835 College Ave., Kentfield, CA 94904	Steve Berringer	(415) 485-9589
Marshalltown CC	3700 S. Center St., Marshalltown, IA 50158	Kevin Benzing	(641) 752-7106
Massachusetts Bay CC	50 Oakland St., Wellesley Hills, MA 02481	Bob Hanson	(508) 270-4065
Massasoit CC	1 Massasoit Blvd., Brockton, MA 02302	Thomas Frizzell	(508) 588-9100
McCook CC	1205 E. 3rd St., McCook, NE 69001	Ryan Jones	(308) 345-6303
McHenry County College	8900 U.S. Hwy. 14, Crystal Lake, IL 60012	Kim Johnson	(815) 455-8580
McLennan CC	1400 College Dr., Waco, TX 76708	David Wrzesinski	(254) 299-8811
Mendocino CC	1000 Hensley Creek Rd, Ukiah, CA 95482	Matthew Gordon	(707) 468-3142
Merced College	3600 M St., Merced, CA 95348	Chris Pedretti	(209) 384-6028
Mercer County CC	1200 Old Trenton Rd., Trenton, NJ 08690	Kip Harrison	(609) 586-4800
Mercyhurst-North East	16 W. Division St., North East, PA 16428	Ryan Smith	(814) 725-6104
Meridian CC	910 Hwy. 19 N., Meridian MS 39307	Mike Federico	(601) 484-8670
Mesa CC	1833 W. Southern Ave., Mesa, AZ 85202	Tony Cirelli	(480) 461-7562
Mesabi Range College	1001 Chestnut St W., Virginia, MN 55792	Brad Scott	(218) 748-2424
Miami-Dade CC	11011 SW 104 St., Miami, FL 33176	Steve Hertz	(305) 237-3086
Miami U.-Middletown	4200 E. University Blvd., Middletown, OH 45042	Kenneth Prichard	(513) 727-3273
Middle Georgia College	1100 2nd St. SE, Cochran, GA 31014	Craig Young	(478) 934-3044
Middlesex County College	2600 Woodbridge Ave., Edison, NJ 08818	Michael Lepore	(732) 906-2558
Midland College	3600 N. Garfield St., Midland, TX 79705	Steve Ramharter	(432) 685-5561
Miles CC	2715 Dickinson St., Miles City, MT 59301	Rob Bishop	(406) 874-6169
Milwaukee Area Tech	700 W. State St., Milwaukee, WI 53233	Scott Garland	(414) 297-7872
Mineral Area College	PO Box 1000., Park Hills, MO 63601	Jim Gerwitz	(573) 518-2146
Minn. State Comm & Tech - FF	1414 College Way, Fergus Falls, MN 56357	Kent Bothwell	(218) 739-7541
Minnesota West Comm. & Tech	1450 College Way, Worthington, MN 56187	Brian Iverson	(507) 372-3488
Minot State U.	105 Simrall Blvd., Bottineau, ND 58318	Jason Harris	(701) 228-5452
Mission College	3000 Mission College Blvd., Santa Clara, CA 95054	Todd Eagen	(408) 855-5366
Mississippi Delta CC	PO Box 668, Moorhead, MS 38761	Terry Thompson	(662) 246-6478
Mississippi Gulf Coast JC	Box 548, Perkinston, MS 39573	Cooper Farris	(601) 928-6348
Mitchell College	437 Pequot Ave., New London, CT 06320	Len Farquhar	(860) 701-5047
Modesto JC	435 College Ave., Modesto, CA 95350	Paul Aiello	(209) 575-6274
Mohawk Valley CC	1101 Sherman Dr., Utica, NY 13501	Dave Warren	(315) 792-5674
Monroe CC	1000 E. Henrietta Rd., Rochester, NY 14623	Skip Bailey	(585) 292-2088
Monterey Peninsula College	980 Fremont St., Monterey, CA 93940	Kenny Leonesio	(831) 646-4223
Montgomery College-Rockville	51 Mannakee St., Rockville, MD 20850	Tom Shaffer	(301) 251-7985
Montgomery-Germantown	20200 Observation Dr., Germantown, MD 20876	Tom Cassera	(301) 353-7727
Moorpark College	7075 Campus Rd., Moorpark, CA 93021	Mario Porto	(805) 378-1457
Moraine Valley CC	10900 S. 88th Ave., Palos Hills, IL 60465	Al Budding	(708) 974-5213
Morris, County College of	214 Center Grove Rd., Randolph, NJ 07869	Ed Moskal	(973) 328-5252
Morton College	3801 S. Central Ave., Cicero, IL 60804	Tony Hubbard	(708) 656-8000
Motlow State CC	PO Box 8500, Lynchburg, TN 37352	Don Rhoton	(931) 393-1615
Mott CC	1401 E. Court St., Flint, MI 48503	Dan LaNoue	(810) 762-0419
Mount Hood CC	26000 SE Stark St., Gresham, OR 97030	Gabe Sandy	(503) 491-7352
Mount San Antonio College	1100 N. Grand Ave., Walnut, CA 91789	Stacy Parker	(909) 594-5611
Mount San Jacinto CC	1499 N. State St., San Jacinto, CA 92583	Steve Alonzo	(909) 487-6752
Murray State College	1 Murray Campus, Tishomingo, OK 73460	Mike McBrayer	(580) 371-2371
Muscatine CC	152 Colorado St., Muscatine, IA 52761	Bob Allison	(563) 288-6001
Muskegon CC	221 S. Quarterline Rd., Muskegon, MI 49442	Cap Pohlman	(231) 777-0381
Napa Valley College	2277 Napa-Vallejo Hwy., Napa, CA 94558	Bob Freschi	(707) 253-3232
Nassau CC	One Education Dr., Garden City, NY 11530	Larry Minor	(516) 572-7522
Naugatuck Valley Tech	750 Chase Pkwy., Waterbury, CT 06708	Steve Baldwin	(203) 575-8073
Navarro College	3200 W. 7th Ave., Corsicana, TX 75110	Skip Johnson	(903) 875-7487
Neosho County CC	800 W. 14th St., Chanute, KS 66720	Steve Murry	(620) 431-2820
New Hampshire Tech	31 College Dr., Concord, NH 03301	Tom Neal	(603) 271-7127
New Mexico JC	5317 N. Lovington Hwy., Hobbs, NM 88240	Ray Birmingham	(505) 392-5503
New Mexico Military Inst.	101 W. College Blvd., Roswell, NM 88201	Marty Zeller	(505) 624-8271

Niagara County CC	3111 Saunders Settlement Rd., Sanborn, NY 14132	Dave Nemi	(716) 614-6271
North Arkansas Tech	1515 Pioneer Dr., Harrison, AR 72601	Phil Wilson	(870) 391-3287
North Central Missouri College	1301 Main St.., Trenton, MO 64683	Bob Shields	(660) 359-3948
North Central Texas College	1525 W. California St., Gainesville, TX 76240	Kevin Darwin	(940) 668-7731
North Florida CC	1000 Turner Davis Dr., Madison, FL 32340	Steve Givens	(850) 973-1628
North Hennepin CC	7411 85th Ave. N., Brooklyn Park, MN 55445	Greg Thorstad	(763) 424-0796
North Iowa Area CC	500 College Dr., Mason City, IA 50401	Todd Rima	(641) 422-4281
North Lake CC	5001 N. MacArthur Blvd., Irving, TX 75038	Steve Cummings	(972) 273-3518
North Shore CC	One Ferncroft Rd., Danvers, MA 01923	Charles Lyttle	(781) 477-2123
Northampton CC	3835 Green Pond Rd., Bethlehem, PA 18020	John Sweeney	(610) 861-5369
Northeast Mississippi CC	101 Cunningham Blvd., Booneville, MS 38829	Ray Scott	(662) 720-7352
Northeast Texas CC	PO Box 1307, Mount Pleasant, TX 75456	Chad Tidwell	(903) 572-1911
Northeastern JC	100 College Dr., Sterling, CO 80751	Bryan Shepherd	(970) 521-6641
Northeastern Oklahoma A&M	200 I Street NE, Miami, OK 74354	Roger Ward	(918) 540-6131
Northern Oklahoma-Enid	PO Box 2300, Enid, OK 73701	Raydon Leaton	(580) 548-2329
Northern Essex CC	100 Elliot Way, Haverhill, MA 01830	Kerry Quinlan	(978) 556-3820
Northland Tech	1101 Highway 1 E., Thief River Falls, MN 56701	Guy Finstrom	(218) 681-0739
Northern Oklahoma College	PO Box 310., Tonkawa, OK 74653	Terry Ballard	(580) 628-6218
Northwest Mississippi CC	4975 Hwy. 51 N., Senatobia, MS 38668	Donny Castle	(662) 562-3422
Northwest Shoals CC	800 George Wallace Blvd., Muscle Shoals, AL 35661	David Langston	(256) 331-5366
Norwalk CC	188 Richards Ave., Norwalk, CT 06854	Mark Lambert	(203) 857-7155
Oakton CC	1600 E. Golf Rd., Des Plaines, IL 60016	Mike Pinto	(847) 635-1753
Ocean County College	PO Box 2001, Toms River, NJ 08754	Ernie Leta	(732) 255-0345
Odessa College	201 W. University Blvd., Odessa, TX 79764	Rick Zimmerman	(432) 335-6850
Ohio State U. at Lima	4240 Campus Dr., Lima, OH 45804	Robert Livchak	(419) 221-1641
Ohlone College	43600 Mission Blvd., Fremont, CA 94539	Paul Moore	(510) 659-6056
Okaloosa-Walton CC	100 College Blvd., Niceville, FL 32578	Keith Griffin	(850) 729-5268
Olive-Harvey College	10001 S. Woodlawn Ave., Chicago, IL 60628	Mike Mayden	(773) 291-6272
Olney Central College	305 West St., Olney, IL 62450	Dennis Conley	(618) 395-7777
Olympic College	1600 Chester Ave., Bremerton, WA 98337	Michael Reese	(360) 475-7460
Onondaga CC	4941 Onondaga Rd., Syracuse, NY 13215	Chris Cafalone	(315) 498-2657
Orange Coast College	PO Box 5005, Costa Mesa, CA 92628	John Altobelli	(714) 432-5892
Orange County CC	115 South St., Middletown, NY 10940	Wayne Smith	(845) 341-4211
Otero JC	1802 Colorado Ave., La Junta, CO 81050	Mark Priegnitz	(719) 384-6833
Owens CC	PO Box 10000, Toledo, OH 43699	Robert Schultz	(419) 661-7974
Oxnard College	4000 S. Rose Ave., Oxnard, CA 93033	Jon Larson	(805) 986-5800
Palm Beach CC	4200 S. Congress Ave., Lake Worth, FL 33461	Craig Gero	(561) 868-3007
Palomar College	1140 W. Mission Rd., San Marcos, CA 92069	Bob Vetter	(760) 744-1150
Panola College	1109 W. Panola St., Carthage, TX 75633	Don Clinton	(903) 693-2062
Paris JC	2400 Clarksville St., Paris, TX 75460	Deron Clark	(903) 782-0218
Parkland College	2400 W. Bradley Ave., Champaign, IL 61820	Dave Seifert	(217) 351-2297
Pasadena City College	1570 E. Colorado Blvd., Pasadena, CA 91106	Mike Scolinos	(626) 585-7789
Pasco-Hernando CC	10230 Ridge Rd., New Port Richey, FL 34654	Steve Winterling	(727) 816-3340
Pearl River CC	101 Hwy. 11 N., Poplarville, MS 39470	Jay Artigues	(601) 403-1326
Penn State-Abington	1600 Woodland Rd., Abington, PA 19001	Bobby Spratt	(215) 881-7440
Penn State-Beaver	100 University Dr., Monaca, PA 15061	John Bellaver	(724) 773-3879
Penn State-Delaware	25 Yearsley Mill Rd., Media, PA 19063	Jeff Vickers	(610) 892-1470
Penn State-Fayette	PO Box 519, Uniontown, PA 15401	Joe Gessner	(724) 430-4271
Penn State-New Kensington	3550 7th Street Rd., New Kensington, PA 15068	Dave Montgomery	(724) 295-9544
Penn State-Wilkes-Barre	PO Box PSU, Lehman, PA 18627	Jack Monick	(717) 675-9262
Penn State-Worthington	120 Ridgeview Dr., Dunmore, PA 18512	Jeff Mallas	(570) 963-2611
Pennsyvania Tech	One College Ave., Williamsport, PA 17701	Michael Stanzione	(570) 327-4763
Pensacola JC	1000 College Blvd., Pensacola, FL 32504	Bill Hamilton	(850) 484-1304
Philadelphia, CC of	1700 Spring Garden St., Philadelphia, PA 19130	David Olmo	(215) 751-8964
Phoenix College	1202 W. Thomas Rd., Phoenix, AZ 85013	Mike Poplin	(602) 285-7122
Pierce College	9401 Farwest Dr. SW, Lakewood, WA 98498	Brett Muche	(253) 964-6613
Pima CC	2202 W. Anklam Rd., Tucson, AZ 85709	Edgar Soto	(520) 206-6045
Pitt CC	P.O. Drawer 7007, Greenville, NC 27835	Monte Little	(252) 321-4633
Polk CC	999 Avenue H NE, Winter Haven, FL 33881	Johnny Wiggs	(863) 297-1017
Porterville College	100 E. College Ave., Porterville, CA 93257	Bret Davis	(559) 791-2335
Potomac State College	101 Fort Ave., Keyser, WV 26726	Craig Rotruck	(304) 788-6879
Prairie State College	202 S. Halstead St., Chicago Heights, IL 60411	Michael Pohlman	(708) 709-3950
Pratt CC	348 NE Hwy. 61, Pratt, KS 67124	Jeff Brewer	(620) 672-5641
Prince George's CC	301 Largo Rd., Largo, MD 20774	William Vaughan	(301) 322-0513
Queensborough CC	22205 56th Ave., Bayside, NY 11364	Craig Everett	(718) 631-6322
Quinsigamond CC	670 W. Boylston St., Worcester, MA 01606	Barry Glinski	(508) 854-4266
Ranger College	1100 College Circle, Ranger, TX 76470	Don Flowers	(254) 647-3234
Raritan Valley CC	PO Box 3300, Route 28, Sommerville, NJ 08876	George Repetz	(908) 526-1200
Redlands CC	1300 S. Country Club Rd., El Reno, OK 73036	Matt Newgent	(405) 422-1280

School	Address	Contact	Phone
Redwoods, College of the	7351 Tompkins Hill Rd., Eureka, CA 95501	Bob Brown	(707) 476-4239
Reedley College	Reed & Manning Ave, Reedley, CA 93654	Jack Hacker	(559) 638-0303
Rend Lake JC	468 N. Ken Gray Pkwy., Ina, IL 62846	Bob Simpson	(618) 437-5321
Rhode Island, CC of	400 East Ave. Warwick, RI 02886	Jay Grenier	(401) 825-2114
Richland College	12800 Abrams Rd., Dallas, TX 75243	Bill Wharton	(972) 238-6261
Ridgewater College	2101 15th Ave. NW, Willmar, MN 56201	Dwight Katila	(320) 231-7696
Rio Hondo College	3600 Workman Mill Rd., Whittier, CA 90601	Mike Salazar	(562) 692-0921
Riverland CC	1900 8th Ave. SW, Austin, MN 55912	Lee Brand	(507) 433-0543
Riverside CC	4800 Magnolia Ave., Riverside, CA 92506	Dennis Rogers	(909) 222-8333
Roane State CC	276 Patton Lane, Harriman, TN 37748	Larry Works	(865) 882-4538
Rochester Tech CC	851 30th Ave. SE, Rochester, MN 55904	Brian LaPlante	(507) 285-7106
Rockingham CC	PO Box 38, Wentworth, NC 27375	John Barrow	(336) 342-4261
Rock Valley College	3301 N. Mulford Rd., Rockford, IL 61114	Jeremy Warren	(815) 921-3806
Rockland CC	145 College Rd., Suffern, NY 10901	Patrick Carey	(845) 574-4452
Rose State College	6420 SE 15th St., Midwest City, OK 73110	Lloyd Cummings	(405) 733-7421
Roxbury CC	1234 Columbus Ave., Roxbury Crossing, MA 02120	Ed Neal	(617) 541-2455
Sacramento City College	3835 Freeport Blvd., Sacramento, CA 95822	Andy McKay	(916) 558-2684
Saddleback CC	28000 Marguerite Pkwy., Mission Viejo, CA 92692	Jack Hodges	(949) 582-4642
St. Catharine College	2735 Bardstown Rd., St. Catharine, KY 40061	Brad Shelton	(859) 336-5082
St. Charles CC	4601 Mid Rivers Mall Dr., St. Peters, MO 63376	Chris Gober	(636) 922-8211
St. Clair County CC	323 Erie St., Port Huron, MI 48060	Rick Smith	(810) 989-5671
St. Johns River CC	5001 St. Johns Ave., Palatka, FL 32177	Sam Rick	(386) 312-4162
St. Louis CC-Florissant Valley	3400 Pershall Rd., St. Louis, MO 63135	Donnie Hillerman	(314) 595-4534
St. Louis CC-Forest Park	5600 Oakland Ave., St. Louis, MO 63110	Roy Tippett	(314) 644-9601
St. Louis CC-Meramec	11333 Big Bend Rd., St. Louis, MO 63122	Joe Swiderski	(314) 984-7786
St. Petersburg CC	PO Box 13489, St. Petersburg, FL 33733	Dave Pano	(727) 791-2662
Salem CC	460 Hollywood Ave., Carney's Point, NJ 08069	Ron Palmer	(856) 351-2695
Salt Lake CC	4600 S. Redwood Rd., Salt Lake City, UT 84130	D.G. Nelson	(801) 957-4861
San Bernardino Valley JC	701 S. Mt. Vernon Ave., San Bernardino, CA 92410	Bill Mierzwik	(909) 384-8643
San Diego City College	1313 12th Ave., San Diego, CA 92101	Chris Brown	(619) 388-3705
San Diego Mesa College	7250 Mesa College Dr., San Diego, CA 92111	Kevin Hazlett	(619) 388-5804
San Francisco, City College of	50 Phelan Ave., San Francisco, CA 94112	John Vanocini	(415) 239-3811
San Jacinto College-North	5800 Uvalde Rd., Houston, TX 77049	Tom Arrington	(281) 459-7613
San Joaquin Delta College	5151 Pacific Ave., Stockton, CA 95207	Jim Yanko	(209) 954-5189
San Jose City College	2100 Moorpark Ave., San Jose, CA 95128	Doug Robb	(408) 288-3730
San Mateo, College of	1700 W. Hillsdale Blvd., San Mateo, CA 94402	Doug Williams	(650) 358-6875
Santa Ana College	1530 W. 17th St., Santa Ana, CA 92706	Don Sneddon	(714) 564-6911
Santa Barbara City College	721 Cliff Dr., Santa Barbara, CA 93109	Teddy Warrecker	(805) 965-0581
Santa Fe CC	3000 NW 83rd St., Gainesville, FL 32606	Harry Tholen	(352) 395-5536
Santa Rosa JC	1501 Mendocino Ave., Santa Rosa, CA 95401	Ron Myers	(707) 527-4389
Sauk Valley CC	173 State Route 2, Dixon, IL 61021	Terry Cox	(815) 288-5511
Schenectady County CC	78 Washington Ave., Schenectady, NY 12305	Tim Andi	(518) 381-1356
Scottsdale CC	9000 E. Chaparral Rd., Scottsdale, AZ 85256	Ed Yeager	(480) 423-6616
Seminole CC	100 Weldon Blvd., Sanford, FL 32773	Mike Nicholson	(407) 328-2148
Seminole State College	2701 Boren Blvd., Seminole, OK 74868	Eric Myers	(405) 382-9201
Sequoias, College of the	915 S. Mooney Blvd., Visalia, CA 93277	Jody Allen	(559) 737-6196
Seward County CC	1801 N. Kansas, Liberal, KS 67905	Galen McSpadden	(620) 629-2730
Shasta College	PO Box 496006, Redding, CA 96049	Brad Rupert	(530) 225-4919
Shawnee CC	8364 Shawnee College Rd., Ullin, IL 62992	Greg Sheppard	(618) 634-3244
Shelby State CC	PO Box 780, Memphis, TN 38104	Doug Darnall	(901) 333-5143
Shoreline CC	16101 Greenwood Ave. N., Seattle, WA 98133	Matt Barker	(206) 546-4740
Sierra College	5000 Rocklin Rd., Rocklin, CA 95677	Rob Wilson	(916) 781-0583
Shelton State	9500 old Greensboro Rd., Tuscaloosa, AL 35405	Bobby Sprowl	(205) 391-2206
Sinclair CC	444 W. 3rd St., Dayton, OH 45402	Mike Goldschmidt	(937) 512-3039
Siskiyous, College of the	800 College Ave., Weed, CA 96094	Steve Neel	(530) 938-5231
Skagit Valley College	2405 E. College Way, Mount Vernon, WA 98273	Mark Linden	(360) 416-7690
Skyline College	3300 College Dr., San Bruno, CA 94066	Dino Nomicos	(650) 738-4197
Snead State CC	220 N. Walnut St., Boaz, AL 35957	Gerry Ledbetter	(256) 593-5120
Solano CC	4000 Suisun Valley Rd., Suisun City, CA 94534	Scott Stover	(707) 863-7822
South Carolina-Salkehatchie	PO Box 617, Allendale, SC 29810	Joe Baxter	(803) 584-3446
South Florida CC	600 W. College Dr., Avon Park, FL 33825	Rick Hitt	(863) 453-6661
South Georgia College	100 W. College Park Dr., Douglas, GA 31533	Scott Sims	(912) 389-4252
South Mountain CC	7050 S. 24th St., Phoenix, AZ 85040	Todd Eastin	(602) 243-8245
South Suburban College	15800 S. State St., South Holland, IL 60473	Steve Ruzich	(708) 596-2000
Southeastern CC	PO Box 151, Whiteville, NC 28472	Chuck Baldwin	(910) 642-7141
Southeastern CC	1500 W. Agency Rd., West Burlington, IA 52655	Lonnie Winston	(319) 752-2731
Southeastern Illinois College	3575 College Rd., Harrisburg, IL 62946	Adam Hines	(618) 252-5400
Southern Idaho, College of	315 Falls Ave., Twin Falls, ID 83303	Jim Walker	(208) 732-6491
Southern Maine Tech	Fort Rd., South Portland, ME 04106	Philip Desjardins	(207) 839-6563
Southern Maryland, Col of	PO Box 910, La Plata, MD 20646	Joe Blandford	(301) 934-2251
Southern Nevada, CC of	700 College Dr., Henderson, NV 89015	Tim Chambers	(702) 651-3013
Southern Union State CC	PO Box 1000, Wadley, AL 36726	Joe Jordan	(256) 395-2211

College	Address	Contact	Phone
Southwest Mississippi CC	2000 College Drive, Summit, MS 39666	Butch Holmes	(601) 276-2000
Southwest Tennessee CC	PO Box 780, Memphis, TN 38101	Johnny Ray	(901) 333-6060
Southwestern CC	1501 W. Townline Rd., Creston, IA 50801	Mike Cook	(641) 782-1459
Southwestern College	900 Otay Lakes Rd., Chula Vista, CA 91910	Jerry Bartow	(619) 482-6370
Southwestern Illinois College	2500 Carlyle Ave., Belleville, IL 62221	Neil Fiala	(618) 222-5371
Southwestern Oregon CC	1988 Newmark Ave., Coos Bay, OR 97420	Corky Franklin	(541) 888-7348
Spartanburg Methodist JC	1200 Textile Rd., Spartanburg, SC 29301	Tim Wallace	(864) 587-4267
Spokane Falls CC	3410 W. Fort George Wright Dr., Spokane, WA 99224	David Keller	(509) 533-3390
Spoon River College	23235 N. County Rd 22, Canton, IL 61520	Joe Moore	(309) 649-6303
Springfield College	1500 N. 5th St., Springfield, IL 62702	Steve Torricelli	(217) 525-1420
Springfield Tech CC	1 Armory Sq., Springfield, MA 01102	J.C. Fernandes	(413) 755-4070
Suffolk CC-West	Crooked Hill Road, Brentwood, NY 11717	Gary Puccio	(631) 851-6706
Suffolk County CC-Selden	533 College Rd., Selden, NY 11784	Eric Brown	(631) 732-2929
SUNY Cobleskill	Route 7, Cobleskill, NY 12043	Jason Trufant	(518) 255-5131
SUNY Morrisville	PO Box 901, Morrisville, NY 13408	Carl Lohman	(315) 684-6072
Surry CC	PO Box 304, Dobson, NC 27017	Mark Tucker	(336) 386-3217
Sussex County CC	1 College Hill Rd., Newton, NJ 07860	Todd Poltersdorf	(973) 300-2253
Taft College	29 Emmers Park Dr., Taft, CA 93268	Tony Thompson	(661) 763-7740
Tallahassee CC	444 Appleyard Dr., Tallahassee, FL 32304	Mike McLeod	(850) 201-8588
Temple College	2600 S. First St., Temple, TX 76504	Craig McMurtry	(254) 298-8524
Texarkana College	2500 N. Robison Rd., Texarkana, TX 75599	James Mansinger	(903) 832-5565
Texas-Brownsville, U. of	80 Fort Brown, Brownsville, TX 78520	Eliseo Herrera	(956) 544-8293
Three Rivers CC	2080 Three Rivers Blvd., Poplar Bluff, MO 63901	Stacey Burkey	(573) 840-9613
Treasure Valley CC	650 College Blvd., Ontario, OR 97914	Rick Baumann	(503) 889-6493
Trinidad State JC	600 Prospect St., Trinidad, CO 81082	Scott Douglas	(719) 846-5510
Triton College	2000 N. 5th Ave., River Grove, IL 60171	Bob Symonds	(708) 456-0300
Truett McConnell College	100 Alumni Dr., Cleveland, GA 30528	Jim Waits	(706) 865-2134
Tyler JC	PO Box 9020, Tyler, TX 75711	Jon Groth	(903) 510-2320
Ulster County CC	Stone Ridge, NY 12484	Ryan Snair	(845) 687-5278
Union County College	1033 Springfield Ave., Cranford, NJ 07016	Mark Domashinski	(908) 709-7093
Ventura College	4667 Telegraph Rd., Ventura, CA 93003	Don Adams	(805) 654-6348
Vermilion CC	1900 E. Camp St., Ely, MN 55731	Ray Podominick	(218) 365-7230
Vernon Regional JC	4400 College Dr., Vernon, TX 76384	Kevin Lallman	(940) 552-6291
Victor Valley CC	18422 Bear Valley Rd., Victorville, CA 92392	Nate Lambdin	(760) 245-4271
Vincennes University	1002 N. 1st St., Vincennes, IN 47591	Jerry Blemker	(812) 888-4478
Volunteer State CC	1480 Nashville Pike, Gallatin, TN 37066	Jeff Smith	(615) 230-3448
Wabash Valley College	2200 College Dr., Mount Carmel, IL 62863	Rob Fournier	(618) 263-4999
Waldorf College	206 John K. Hanson Dr., Forest City, IA 50436	Brian Grunzke	(641) 585-8263
Walla Walla CC	500 Tausick Way, Walla Walla, WA 99362	Chad Miltenberger	(509) 527-4494
Wallace CC Selma	3000 Earl Goodwin Pkwy., Selma, AL 36702	E.J. Brophy	(334) 876-9340
Wallace State CC Hanceville	PO Box 2000, Hanceville, AL 35077	Randy Putman	(256) 352-8121
Walters State CC	500 S. Davy Crockett Pkwy., Morristown, TN 37813	Ken Campbell	(423) 585-6759
Waubonsee College	Route 47 at Waubonsee Dr., Sugar Grove, IL 60554	Dave Randall	(630) 466-2527
Waukesha County Tech	800 Main St., Pewaukee, WI 53072	Roy Jeske	(262) 691-5545
Wenatchee Valley CC	1300 5th St., Wenatchee, WA 98801	Bob Duda	(509) 682-6886
Weatherford College	225 College Park Dr., Weatherford, TX 76086	Jeff Lightfoot	(817) 598-0412
West Hills College	300 W. Cherry Lane, Coalinga, CA 93210	Paul Hodson	(559) 934-2458
West Valley College	14000 Fruitvale Ave., Saratoga, CA 95070	Mike Perez	(408) 741-2176
Westchester CC	75 Grasslands Rd., Valhalla, NY 10595	Larry Massanori	(914) 785-6150
Western Nebraska CC	1601 E. 27th St., Scottsbluff, NE 69361	Mike Jones	(308) 635-6198
Western Oklahoma State	2801 N. Main St., Altus, OK 73521	Kurt Russell	(580) 477-7800
Western Texas College	6200 College Ave., Snyder, TX 79549	Billy Hefflinger	(325) 573-8511
Western Wisconsin Tech	304 North Sixth St., La Crosse, WI 54602	Mitch Baker	(608) 785-9442
Westmoreland County CC	400 Armburst Rd., Youngwood, PA 15697	Mike Draghi	(724) 327-4546
Wharton County JC	911 E. Boling Hwy., Wharton, TX 77488	Bob Nottebart	(979) 532-6480
Wilkes CC	PO Box 120, Wilkesboro, NC 28697	Tim Lackey	(336) 838-6189
Williamson Free School	106 S. New Middletown Rd., Media, PA 19063	Sal Intelisano	(610) 566-1176
Williston State College	PO Box 1326, Williston, ND 58802	Dave Richter	(701) 744-4242
Wisconsin, U. of-Barron	1800 College Dr., Rice Lake, WI 54868	Brad Randle	(715) 234-8176
Yakima Valley CC	PO Box 22520, Yakima, WA 98907	Bob Garretson	(509) 574-4724
Yavapai College	1100 E. Sheldon St., Prescott, AZ 86301	Sky Smeltzer	(928) 776-2292
Young Harris College	1 College St., Young Harris, GA 30582	Rick Robinson	(706) 379-4311
Yuba CC	2088 N. Beale Rd., Marysville, CA 95901	Tim Gloyd	(530) 634-7725

AMATEUR

INTERNATIONAL

INTERNATIONAL OLYMPIC COMMITTEE
Mailing Address: Chateau de Vidy, 1007 Lausanne, Switzerland.
Telephone: (41-21) 621-6111. **FAX:** (41-21) 621-6216. **Website:** www.olympic.org.
President: Jacques Rogge. **Director, Communications:** Giselle Davies.
Games of the XXVIII Olympiad: Aug. 13-29, 2004, at Athens, Greece. **Participating Countries, 2004 Olympics:** Australia, Canada, Cuba, Greece (host country), Italy, Japan, The Netherlands, Taiwan.

U.S. OLYMPIC COMMITTEE
Mailing Address: One Olympic Plaza, Colorado Springs, CO 80909. **Telephone:** (719) 866-4500. **FAX:** (719) 866-4654.
Chief Executive Officer: Jim Scherr. **Chief Communications Officer:** Darryl Seibel.
Games of the XXVIII Olympiad: Aug. 13-29, 2004, at Athens, Greece.

INTERNATIONAL BASEBALL FEDERATION
Mailing Address: Avenue de Mon-Repos 24, Case Postale 131, 1000 Lausanne 5, Switzerland. **Telephone:** (41-21) 318-8240. **FAX:** (41-21) 318-8241. **E-Mail Address:** ibaf@baseball.ch. **Website:** www.baseball.ch.
Year Founded: 1938.
President: Aldo Notari (Italy). **Secretary General:** Eduardo De Bello (Panama). **Treasurer:** Frans van Aalen (The Netherlands). **First Vice President:** Eiichiro Yamamoto (Japan). **Second Vice President:** Rodolfo Puente (Cuba). **Third Vice President:** Miguel Pozueta (Spain). **Members, At Large:** Mark Alexander (South Africa), Petr Ditrich (Czech Republic), Paul Seiler (United States).
Continental Vice Presidents: Africa—Ishola Williams (Nigeria). America—Hector Pereyra (Dominican Republic). Asia—Tom C.H. Peng (Taiwan). Europe—Alexander Ratner (Russia). Oceania—Mark Peters (Australia).
Executive Director: Miquel Ortin. **Communications Manager:** Enzo Di Gesu.

2004 Events
II World University Championship	Tainan, Taiwan, July 22-31
I Women's World Cup	Edmonton, Alberta, July 30-Aug. 8
XV World Children's Baseball Fair	Hyogo Prefecture, Japan, July 31-Aug. 5
Olympic Games Tournament	Athens, Greece, Aug. 15-25
XXII AAA World Junior Championship	Taipei, Taiwan, Sept. 3-12

CONFEDERATION PAN AMERICANA DE BEISBOL (COPABE)
Mailing Address: Calle 3, Francisco Filos, Vista Hermosa Edificio 74 Primer Alto, Local No. 2, Panama City, Panama.
Telephone: (507) 2361-5677. **FAX:** (507) 261-5215. **E-Mail Address:** copabe@sinfo.net.
President: Eduardo De Bello (Panama). **Executive Director:** Jose Calazan (Panama).

2004 Events
*AA Pan Am Championship	Site, date unavailable

*Qualifying tournament for 2005 World Youth Championship

BASEBALL CANADA
Mailing Address: 2212 Gladwin Cres., Suite A7, Ottawa, Ontario K1B 5N1. **Telephone:** (613) 748-5606. **FAX:** (613) 748-5767. **E-Mail Address:** info@baseball.ca. **Website:** www.baseball.ca.
Director General: Jim Baba. **Head Coach/Director, National Teams:** Greg Hamilton. **Manager, Baseball Operations:** Andre Lachance. **Program Coordinator:** Kelly Benoit.
Head Coach, Canadian Olympic Team: Ernie Whitt.

2004 Events
2004 Olympic Games	Athens, Greece, Aug. 15-25
Baseball Canada Cup (17 and under)	Thunder Bay, Ontario, Aug. 18-23

AFRICAN BASEBALL/SOFTBALL ASSOCIATION
Mailing Address: Paiko Road, Changaga, Minna, Niger State, PMB 150, Nigeria. **Telephone:** (234-66) 224-555, (234-66) 224-711. **FAX:** (234-66) 224-555. **E-Mail Address:** absasec@yahoo.com.
President: Ishola Williams (Nigeria). **Executive Director:** Friday Ichide (Nigeria).

BASEBALL FEDERATION OF ASIA
Mailing Address: Mainichi Palaceside Bldg., 1-1-1, Hitotsubahi, Chiyoda-ku, Tokyo 100, Japan. **Telephone:** (81-3) 320-11155, (81-3) 321-36776. **FAX:** (81-3) 320-10707.
President: Eiichiro Yamamoto (Japan).

EUROPEAN BASEBALL CONFEDERATION
Mailing Address: Avenue de Mon-Repos 24, Case postale 131, 1000 Lausanne 5, Switzerland. **Telephone:** (32-3) 219-0440. **FAX:** (32-3) 772 7727. **E-Mail Address:** info@baseballeurope.com. **Website:** baseballeurope.com.
President: Aldo Notari (Italy).

BASEBALL CONFERERATION OF OCEANIA
Mailing Address: 48 Partridge Way, Mooroolbark, Victoria 3138, Australia. **Telephone:** (61-3) 9727-1779. **FAX:** (61-3) 9727-5959. **E-Mail Address:** chetg@ozemail.com.au.
President: Mark Peters (Australia).

INTERNATIONAL SPORTS GROUP
Mailing Address: 142 Shadowood Dr., Pleasant Hill, CA 94523. **Telephone:** (925) 798-4591. **FAX:** (925) 680-1182.
E-Mail Address: ISGbaseball@aol.com.
President: Jim Jones. **Vice President:** Tom O'Connell. **Secretary/Treasurer:** Randy Town.

NATIONAL

USA BASEBALL
Mailing Address, Corporate Headquarters: P.O. Box 1131, Durham, NC 27702. **Telephone:** (919) 474-8721. **FAX:** (919) 474-8822. **E-Mail Address:** info@usabaseball.com. **Website:** www.usabaseball.com.
Chairman: Lindsay Burbage. **President:** Mike Gaski. **Executive Vice President:** Steve Shaad. **Secretary:** Jack Kelly. **Treasurer:** Abraham Key. **Executive Officer:** Stephen Keener.
Executive Director, Chief Executive Officer: Paul Seiler. **Director, National Teams:** Eric Campbell. **Director, Finance:** Miki Partridge. **Director, Marketing/Licensing:** David Perkins. **Director, Communications:** Dave Fanucchi. **Associate Directors, National Teams:** Ray Darwin, Jeff Singer. **Marketing Coordinator:** Jake Fehling. **Marketing Assistant:** David Shoemaker.
National Members: Amateur Athletic Union (AAU), American Amateur Baseball Congress (AABC), American Baseball Coaches Association (ABCA), American Legion Baseball, Babe Ruth Baseball, Dixie Baseball, Little League Baseball, National Amateur Baseball Federation (NABF), National Association of Intercollegiate Athletics (NAIA), National Baseball Congress (NBC), National Collegiate Athletic Association (NCAA), National Federation of State High School Athletic Associations, National High School Baseball Coaches Association, National Junior College Athletic Association (NJCAA), Police Athletic League (PAL), PONY Baseball, T-Ball USA, USSSA, YMCAs of the USA.

2004 Events
Team USA—Collegiate Level
National Team Trials	Durham, NC, June 20-22
II World University Championship	Tainan, Taiwan, July 22-31

Team USA—Junior Level (18 and under)
Tournament of Stars	Joplin, MO, June 21-28
National Team Trials	Joplin, MO, June 28-July 4
World Junior Championship	Tainan, Taiwan, Aug. 27-Sept. 13

Team USA—Youth Level (16 and under)
Junior Olympic Championship—West	Peoria/Surprise, AZ, June 18-26
Junior Olympic Championship—East	Palm Beach County, FL, June 18-26
National Team Trials	Site, dates unavailable
COPABE Pan Am Championship	Site, dates unavailable

AMERICAN BASEBALL FOUNDATION
Mailing Address: 1313 13th St. S., Birmingham, AL 35205. **Telephone:** (205) 558-4235. **FAX:** (205) 918-0800. **E-Mail Address:** abf@asmi.org. **Website:** www.americanbaseball.org.
Executive Director: David Osinski.

NATIONAL BASEBALL CONGRESS
Mailing Address: P.O. Box 1420, Wichita, KS 67201. **Telephone:** (316) 267-3372. **FAX:** (316) 267-3382.
Year Founded: 1931.
President: Robert Rich Jr.
General Manager: Eric Edelstein. **Assistant GM/Director of Baseball and Stadium Operations:** Josh Robertson. **Assistant GM/Director of Sales and Marketing:** Kyle Ebers. **Operations Manager:** Mike Quick. **Tournament Director:** Jerry Taylor. **Marketing Manager:** Matt Rogers.
2004 NBC World Series (Collegiate, ex-professional, unlimited age): July 31-Aug. 14 at Wichita, KS (Lawrence Dumont Stadium).

ATHLETES IN ACTION
Mailing Address: 651 Taylor Dr., Xenia, OH 45385. **Telephone:** (937) 352-1000. **FAX:** (937) 352-1245. **E-Mail Address:** baseball@ai.com. **Website:** www.aiabaseball.org.
Director, AIA Baseball: Jason Lester (AIA-Texas). **General Managers, AIA Teams:** Chris Beck (AIA-Alaska), J.D. Bickle (AIA-New York), Todd Johnson (AIA-Mexico), John McLaughlin (AIA-Latin America).

SUMMER COLLEGE LEAGUES

NATIONAL ALLIANCE OF COLLEGIATE SUMMER BASEBALL

Mailing Address: 1073 Mineral Spring Ave., North Providence, RI 02904. **Telephone:** (800) PLAY-BALL. **FAX:** (401) 722-5916.

Executive Director: Rick Gesualdi. **Secretary:** Roger Ingles.

NCAA Sanctioned Leagues: Atlantic Collegiate League, Cape Cod League, Central Illinois Collegiate League, Great Lakes League, New England Collegiate League, New York Collegiate League, Northwoods League, Southern Collegiate League, Valley League.

ALASKA BASEBALL LEAGUE

Mailing Address: 207 E. Northern Lights Blvd., Suite 106, Anchorage, AK 99503. **Telephone:** (907) 274-3627. **FAX:** (907) 274-3628.

Year Founded: 1969 (reunited, 1998).

President: Chuck Shelton. **First Vice President:** Pete Christopher. **Vice President, Marketing:** Dennis Mattingly. **VP, Rules:** Chris Beck. **VP, Schedule:** Don Dennis. **VP, Umpiring:** Mike Baxter.

Division Structure: None.

2004 Opening Date: June 8. **Closing Date:** Aug. 1.

Regular Season: 35 league games.

Playoff Format: Top two teams qualify for National Baseball Congress World Series.

Roster Limit: 22, plus exemption for Alaska residents.

Player Eligibility Rule: Players with college eligibility, except drafted seniors.

ALASKA GOLDPANNERS

Mailing Address: P.O. Box 71154, Fairbanks, AK 99707. **Telephone:** (907) 451-0095. **FAX:** (907) 456-6429. **E-Mail Address:** todd@goldpanners.com. **Website:** www.goldpanners.com.

President: Bill Stroecker. **General Manager:** Don Dennis. **Assistant GM:** Todd Dennis. **Head Coach:** Ed Cheff (Lewis-Clark State, Idaho).

ANCHORAGE BUCS

Mailing Address: P.O. Box 240061, Anchorage, AK 99524. **Telephone:** (907) 561-2827. **FAX:** (907) 561-2920. **E-Mail Address:** admin@anchoragebucs.com. **Website:** www.anchoragebucs.com.

President: Eugene Furman. **General Manager:** Dennis Mattingly. **Head Coach:** Matt Priess (U. of California).

ANCHORAGE GLACIER PILOTS

Mailing Address: 207 E. Northern Lights Blvd., Suite 106, Anchorage, AK 99503. **Telephone:** (907) 274-3627. **FAX:** (907) 274-3628. **E-Mail Address:** gpilots@alaska.net. **Website:** www.glacierpilots.com.

President: David Foreman. **General Manager:** Chuck Shelton. **Head Coach:** Kris Didion (Washington State U.).

ATHLETES IN ACTION-ALASKA

Mailing Address: 651 Taylor Dr., Xenia, OH 45385. **Telephone:** (937) 352-1000. **FAX:** (937) 352-1245. **E-Mail Address:** chris.beck@aia.com. **Website:** www.aiabaseball.org.

General Manager: Chris Beck. **Head Coach:** Dan Fitzgerald (North Iowa Area CC).

MAT-SU MINERS

Mailing Address: P.O. Box 2690, Palmer, AK 99645. **Telephone:** (907) 746-4914. **FAX:** (907) 746-5068. **E-Mail Address:** pdkkc@gci.net. **Website:** www.matsu miners.org.

General Manager: Pete Christopher. **Vice President:** Mark Alger. **Head Coach:** Kevin Edwards (Chemeketa, Ore., CC).

PENINSULA OILERS

Mailing Address: P.O. Box 318, Kenai, AK 99611. **Telephone:** (907) 283-7133. **FAX:** (907) 283-6186. **E-Mail Address:** admin@oilersbaseball.com. **Website:** www.oilersbaseball.com.

President: Karen Kester. **General Manager:** Mike Baxter. **Head Coach:** Aric Thomas (U. of Oklahoma).

ATLANTIC COLLEGIATE LEAGUE

Mailing Address: 401 Timber Dr., Berkeley Heights, NJ 07922. **Telephone/FAX:** (908) 464-8042. **E-Mail Address:** acbl@vs-inc.com. **Website:** www.acbl-online.com.

Year Founded: 1967.

Commissioner: Robert Pertsas. **President:** Tom Bonekemper. **Vice President/Treasurer:** Jerry Valonis. **Secretary/Public Relations:** Ben Smookler.

Division Structure: Wolff—Jersey Pilots, Lehigh Valley (Pa.) Cats, New Jersey Colts, Quakertown (Pa.) Blazers. **Kaiser**—Long Island (N.Y.) Collegians, Metro New York Cadets, New York Generals, Stamford (Conn.) Robins.

2004 Opening Date: June 1. **Closing Date:** August 15.

Regular Season: 40 games.

Playoff Format: Top two teams in each division meet in best-of-3 semifinals. Winners meet in one-game championship.

Roster Limit: 23 (college-eligible players only).

JERSEY PILOTS

Mailing Address: 401 Timber Dr., Berkeley Heights, NJ 07922. **Telephone:** (908) 464-8042.

President/General Manager: Ben Smookler. **Head Coach:** Chris Reardon.

LEHIGH VALLEY CATZ

Mailing Address: 103 Logan Dr., Easton, PA 18045. **Telephone:** (610) 533-9349. **E-Mail Address:** valley catz@hotmail.com. **Website:** www.lvcatz.com.

Owner/President: Tommy Lisinicchia. **General Manager:** Pat O'Connell. **Head Coach:** Adrian Yaguez.

LONG ISLAND COLLEGIANS

Mailing Address: 431 Centre Island Rd., Oyster Bay, NY 11771. **Telephone:** (516) 686-7513. **FAX:** (516) 626-0750.

Owner/General Manager: Bob Hirschfield. **Head Coach:** Nick Restaino.

METRO NEW YORK CADETS

Mailing Address: 158-50 90th St., Howard Beach, NY 11414. **Telephone:** (718) 224-8320. **FAX:** (718) 225-5695. **E-Mail Address:** metronycadets@aol.com.

Owner: Gus Antico. **General Manager:** Charles Papetti. **Head Coach:** Unavailable.

NEW YORK GENERALS
Mailing Address: 123 Euclid Ave., Ardsley, NY 10502. **Telephone/FAX:** (914) 693-4542. **E-Mail Address:** apol-loto@aol.com.
Owner/General Manager: Nick Disciullo. **Head Coach:** Rich Salerno.

NEW JERSEY COLTS
Mailing Address: 8 Millbrook Dr., Middletown, NJ 07748. **Telephone:** (732) 671-0616. **E-Mail Address:** njcolts@comcast.net.
General Manager: Bob Hoffman. **Head Coach:** Chris Erwin.

QUAKERTOWN BLAZERS
Mailing Address: Memorial Field, 4th and Mill Streets, Quakertown, PA. **Telephone:** (215) 258-1175.
General Manager: Todd Zartman. **Head Coach:** Carl Giuranna.

STAMFORD ROBINS
Mailing Address: P.O. Box 113254, Stamford, CT 06911. **Telephone:** (212) 522-5543. **E-Mail Address:** coachwolff@aol.com, michaelhalo3131@aol.com.
General Manager/Coach: Rick Wolff. **Scouting Liaison:** Mike D'Angelo.

CALIFORNIA COLLEGIATE LEAGUE

Mailing Address: 4299 Carpinteria Ave., Suite 201, Carpinteria, CA 93013. **Telephone:** (805) 684-0657. **FAX:** (805) 684-8596. **E-Mail Address:** pintard@sb foresters.org.
Year Founded: 1993.
President: Bill Pintard.
Member Clubs: Marin Seals, Salinas Packers, San Luis Obispo Blues, Santa Barbara Foresters, Solano Thunderbirds, Yuba-Sutter Gold Sox.
Division Structure: None.
Playoff Format: League champion advances to National Baseball Congress World Series.
2004 Opening Date: June 1. **Closing Date:** Aug. 5.
Regular Season: 40 games.
Roster Limit: 33.

CAPE COD LEAGUE

Mailing Address: P.O. Box 266, Harwich Port, MA 02646. **Telephone:** (508) 385-6260. **FAX:** (508) 385-6322. **E-Mail Address:** info@capecodbaseball.org. **Website:** www.capecodbaseball.org.
Year Founded: 1885.
Commissioner: Paul Galop. **President:** Judy Scarafile.
Vice Presidents: Phil Edwards, Peter Ford, Jim Higgins.
Deputy Commissioners: Dick Sullivan, Sol Yaz.
Treasurer: Steve Wilson. **Director, Public Relations/Broadcast Media:** John Garner. **League Communications:** Jim McGonigle. **Director, Publications:** Lou Barnicle. **Official Photographer:** Jan Volk.
Division Structure: East—Brewster, Chatham, Harwich, Orleans, Yarmouth-Dennis. **West**—Bourne, Cotuit, Falmouth, Hyannis, Wareham.
2004 Opening Date: June 17. **Closing Date:** Aug. 8.
Regular Season: 44 games.
Playoff Format: Top two teams in each division meet in best-of-3 semifinals. Winners meet in best-of-3 series for league championship.
All-Star Game: July 24 at Orleans.
Roster Limit: 23 (college-eligible players only).

BOURNE BRAVES
Mailing Address: P.O. Box 895, Monument Beach, MA 02553. **Telephone:** (508) 888-5080. **FAX:** (508) 833-9250. **E-Mail Address:** lynn.ladetto@verizon.net. **Website:** www.bournebraves.org.
President: Lynn Ladetto. **General Manager:** Michael Carrier.
Head Coach: Harvey Shapiro (U. of Hartford).

BREWSTER WHITE CAPS
Mailing Address: P.O. Box 2349, Brewster, MA 02631. **Telephone:** (617) 835-7130. **FAX:** (781) 934-0506. **E-Mail Address:** dpmfs@aol.com.
President: Hester Grue. **General Manager:** Dave Porter.
Head Coach: Bob Macaluso (Muhlenberg, Pa., College).

CHATHAM A's
Mailing Address: P.O. Box 428, Chatham, MA 02633. **Telephone:** (508) 945-3841. **FAX:** (508) 945-4787. **E-Mail Address:** cthoms@comcast.net. **Website:** www.chathamas.com.
President: Arthur Dunn. **General Manager:** Charles Thoms.
Head Coach: John Schiffner (Plainville, Conn., HS).

COTUIT KETTLEERS
Mailing Address: P.O. Box 411, Cotuit, MA 02635. **Telephone:** (508) 428-3358. **FAX:** (508) 420-5584. **E-Mail Address:** kettleers@hotmail.com. **Website:** www.kettleers.org.
President: Martha Johnson. **General Manager:** Bruce Murphy.
Head Coach: Mike Roberts.

FALMOUTH COMMODORES
Mailing Address: 33 Wintergreen Rd., Mashpee, MA 02649. **Telephone:** (508) 477-5724. **FAX:** (508) 862-6011. **E-Mail Address:** chuckhs@comcast.net. **Website:** www.falcommodores.org.
President: Darin Weeks. **General Manager:** Chuck Sturtevant.
Head Coach: Jeff Trundy (The Gunnery School, Conn.).

HARWICH MARINERS
Mailing Address: P.O. Box 201, Harwich Port, MA 02646. **Telephone:** (508) 432-2000. **FAX:** (508) 432-5357. **Website:** www.harwichmariners.org. **E-Mail Address:** mehendy@comcast.net.
President: Mary Henderson. **General Manager:** Mike DeAnzeris.
Head Coach: Steve Englert (Boston College).

HYANNIS METS
Mailing Address: P.O. Box 852, Hyannis, MA 02601. **Telephone:** (508) 420-0962. **FAX:** (508) 428-8199. **E-Mail Address:** jhowitt932@comcast.net. **Website:** www.hyannismets.org.
President: Jeff Converse. **General Manager:** John Howitt.
Head Coach: Greg King (Thomas, Maine, College).

ORLEANS CARDINALS
Mailing Address: P.O. Box 504, Orleans, MA 02653. **Telephone/FAX:** (508) 255-0793. **FAX:** (508) 255-2237. **Website:** www.orleanscardinals.com.
President: Mark Hossfeld. **General Manager:** Sue Horton.
Head Coach: Carmen Carcone (Dowling, N.Y., College).

WAREHAM GATEMEN
Mailing Address: 71 Towhee Rd., Wareham, MA

02571. **Telephone:** (508) 295-3956. **FAX:** (508) 295-8821. **Website:** www.gatemen.org.
President, General Manager: John Wylde.
Head Coach: Cooper Farris (Mississippi Gulf Coast CC).

YARMOUTH-DENNIS RED SOX
Mailing Address: P.O. Box 814, South Yarmouth, MA 02664. **Telephone:** (508) 394-9387. **FAX:** (508) 398-2239. **E-Mail Address:** jf.martin@verizon.net. **Website:** ydredsox.org.
President: Bob Mayo. **General Manager:** Jim Martin. **Head Coach:** Scott Pickler (Cypress, Calif., CC).

CENTRAL ILLINOIS COLLEGIATE LEAGUE
Mailing Address: 200 Glasgow, Springfield, IL 62702. **Telephone:** (217) 793-6538. **FAX:** (217) 786-2788. **E-Mail Address:** commissioner@ciclbaseball.com, info@ciclbaseball.com. **Website:** www.ciclbaseball.com.
Year Founded: 1963.
Commissioner: Ron Riggle. **President:** Duffy Bass. **Administrative Assistant:** Mike Woods.
Division Structure: None.
2004 Opening Date: June 10. **Closing Date:** Aug. 13.
Regular Season: 44 games.
Playoff Format: Top four teams meet in best-of-3 series. Winners meet in best-of-3 series for league championship.
All-Star Game: July 6 at Bluff City.
Roster Limit: 23 (college-eligible players only).

BLUFF CITY BOMBERS
Mailing Address: P.O. Box 141, Bethalto, IL 62010. **Telephone:** (618) 377-8040. **E-Mail Address:** actjac@hotmail.com. **Website:** www.leaguelineup.com/bluffcitybombers.
General Manager: Jack Tracz. **Head Coach:** Chris Erwin.

DANVILLE DANS
Mailing Address: 138 E. Raymond, Danville, IL 61832. **Telephone:** (217) 446-5521. **FAX:** (217) 442-2137. **E-Mail Address:** jc@soltec.net. **Website:** www.soltec.net/dansbaseball.
General Manager: Rick Kurth. **Assistant GM:** Jeanie Cooke. **Head Coach:** Greg Moore.

GALESBURG PIONEERS
Mailing Address: P.O. Box 1387, Galesburg, IL 61402. **Telephone:** (309) 345-3683. **FAX:** (309) 343-2311. **E-Mail Address:** rsensabaugh@ci.galesburg.il.us.
General Manager: Roger Sensabaugh. **Head Coach:** Jami Isaacson.

INDIANA CARDINALS
Mailing Address: Unavailable. **Telephone:** (812) 661-1324. **FAX:** (513) 792-3852. **E-Mail Address:** kkearns@rytelandassociates.com.
General Manager: Kevin Kearns. **Head Coach:** Chris Barney.

QUINCY GEMS
Mailing Address: 300 Civic Center Plaza, Quincy, IL 62301. **Telephone:** (217) 223-1000. **FAX:** (217) 223-1330. **E-Mail Address:** jjansen@quincygems.com. **Website:** www.quincygems.com.
Executive Director: Jeff Jansen. **Head Coach:** Luke Sabers.

SPRINGFIELD RIFLES
Mailing Address: 100 Cartwright, Springfield, IL 62704. **Telephone:** (217) 698-9591. **FAX:** (217) 698-9891. **E-Mail Address:** sqular@aol.com.

General Manager: Larry Squires. **Head Coach:** Eric Weaver.

TWIN CITY STARS
Mailing Address: 907 N. School St., Normal, IL 61761. **Telephone:** (309) 452-3317. **FAX:** (217) 452-0377. **E-Mail Address:** duffybass@aol.com.
General Manager: Duffy Bass. **Head Coach:** Jake Perganson.

CLARK GRIFFITH COLLEGIATE LEAGUE
Mailing Address: 6601 Cottonwood Dr., Franconia, VA 22310. **Telephone:** (703) 971-4716. **FAX:** (703) 860-0143. **E-Mail Address:** sellcarl@aol.com. **Website:** www.clarkgriffithbaseball.com.
Year Founded: 1945.
President: Carl Sell. **Vice President:** Frank Fannan. **Treasurer:** Tom Dellinger. **Media Director:** Ben Trittipoe. **VP/Rules Enforcement:** Byron Zeigler.
Division Structure: None.
2004 Opening Date: June 4. **Closing Date:** Aug. 1.
Regular Season: 40 games.
Playoff Format: Top two teams meet in best-of-5 series for league championship. Winner advances to All-America Amateur Baseball Association World Series.
All-Star Game: July 2 at Bethesda, MD (Shirley Povich Field)
Roster Limit: 25 (players 20 and under).

BALTIMORE PRIDE
Mailing Address: The Baseball Factory, 9176 Red Branch Rd., Suite M, Columbia, MD 21045. **Telephone:** (800) 641-4487. **FAX:** (410) 715-1975. **E-Mail Address:** jeff@baseballfactory.com. **Website:** www.baseballfactory.com.
President: Steve Sclafani. **General Manager:** Jeff Brazier. **Head Coach:** Bob Mumma (U. of Maryland-Baltimore County).

BETHESDA BIG TRAIN
Mailing Address: Bethesda Community Baseball Club, P.O. Box 30306, Bethesda, MD 20824. **Telephone:** (301) 652-4019. **FAX:** (301) 652-0691. **E-Mail Address:** bruce@greaterwash.org. **Website:** www.bigtrain.org.
President: Bruce Adams. **General Manager:** Elda Hacopian. **Assistant GM:** Alex Thompson. **Head Coach:** Derek Hacopian.

FAUQUIER GATORS
Mailing Address: 345 Winchester St., Warrenton, VA 20189. **Telephone:** (540) 347-0194. **FAX:** (540) 347-5199. **E-Mail Address:** hootbil@aol.com. **Website:** www.fauquiergators.com.
President: Steve Athey. **General Manager:** Sam Johnson. **Head Coach:** Paul Koch.

HERNDON BRAVES
Mailing Address: 1305 Kelly Court, Herndon, VA 20170. **Telephone:** (703) 481-3767. **FAX:** Unavailable. **E-Mail Address:** llombo@sigkit.com. **Website:** www.farisbaseball.com.
President: Lisa Lombardozzi. **General Manager:** John Lombardozzi. **Head Coach:** Chuck Faris.

RESTON HAWKS
Mailing Address: 12606 Magna Carta Rd., Herndon, VA 20171. **Telephone:** (703) 860-4780. **FAX:** (703) 860-0143. **E-Mail Address:** fannanfj@erols.com. **Website:** Unavailable.
President: Mike Torres. **General Manager:** Frank Fannan. **Head Coach:** Mike Torres.

SILVER SPRING-TAKOMA THUNDERBOLTS

Mailing Address: 326 Lincoln Ave., Takoma Park, MD 20912. **E-Mail Address:** tboltsoconn@aol.com. **Website:** www.tbolts.org.

President/General Manager: Richard O'Connor. **VP, Development/Recruiting:** Fred Rodriguez. **Head Coach:** Nate Harvey.

VIENNA SENATORS

Mailing Address: 3298 Wilson Blvd., Arlington, VA 22201. **Telephone:** (703) 247-3065. **FAX:** (703) 247-3070. **E-Mail Address:** cburr17@hotmail.com. **Website:** www.arlingtonsenator.org.

President: Bill McGillicuddy. **General Manager:** Chris Burr. **Head Coach:** Tag Montague (George Washington U.).

COASTAL PLAIN LEAGUE

Mailing Address: 4900 Waters Edge Dr., Suite 201, Raleigh, NC 27606.

Telephone: (919) 852-1960. **FAX:** (919) 852-1973. **Website:** www.coastalplain.com.

Year Founded: 1997.

Chairman/Chief Executive Officer: Jerry Petitt.

President: Pete Bock. **Director, Media Relations:** Justin Sellers.

Director, Administration: Erin Callahan.

Division Structure: North—Edenton, Outer Banks, Peninsula, Petersburg;

South—Fayetteville, Florence, Wilmington, Wilson; **West**—Asheboro, Gastonia, Spartanburg, Thomasville.

2004 Opening Date: June 3. **Closing Date:** Aug. 4.

Regular Season: 52 games (split schedule).

Playoff Format: Eight-team tournament (single-elimination first day, double-elimination from there on out), Aug. 6-8 in Hampton, VA.

All-Star Game: July 20 at Florence, SC.

Roster Limit: 22 (college-eligible players only).

ASHEBORO COPPERHEADS

Mailing Address: P.O. Box 4425, Asheboro, NC 27204. **Telephone:** (336) 636-5796. **FAX:** (336) 636-5400. **E-Mail Address:** baseball@asheboro.com.

Website: www.copperheadsbaseball.com.

President/General Manager: Pat Brown. **Head Coach:** Jon Smith (Duke).

EDENTON STEAMERS

Mailing Address: P.O. Box 86, Edenton, NC 27932. **Telephone:** (252) 482-4080. **FAX:** (252) 482-1717. **E-Mail Address:** edentonsteamers@hotmail.com. **Website:** www.edentonsteamers.com.

General Manager: Jeff Roemer. **Head Coach:** Joel Tremblay (Wayne State, Mich., College).

FAYETTEVILLE SWAMPDOGS

Mailing Address: P.O. Box 64691, Fayetteville, NC 28306. **Telephone:** (910) 426-5900. **FAX:** (910) 426-3544. **E-Mail:** info@fayettevilleswampdogs.com. **Website:** www.fayettevilleswampdogs.com.

General Manager: Steve Belcher. **Assistant GM:** Jard Schjei. **Director of Sales and Marketing:** Dallas Parks. **Head Coach:** Sandy Moore (Catawba, N.C., College).

FLORENCE REDWOLVES

Mailing Address: P.O. Box 809, Florence, SC 29503. **Telephone:** (843) 629-0700. **FAX:** (843) 629-0703. **E-Mail Address:** Jamie@florenceredwolves.com. **Website:** www.florenceredwolves.com.

President: Kevin Barth. **General Manager:** Jamie Young. **Head Coach:** Scott Brickman (Wofford U.).

GASTONIA GRIZZLIES

Mailing Address: P.O. Box 177, Gastonia, NC 28053. **Telephone:** (704) 866-8622. **FAX:** (704) 864-6122. **E-Mail Address:** jthompson@gastoniagrizzlies.com. **Website:** www.gastoniagrizzlies.com.

President: Ken Silver. **Vice Presidents:** Dr. Michael Silver, Kevin Silver.

General Manager: Jack Thompson. **Assistant GM:** Justin Rawlings. **Head Coach:** Travis Little (Montreat, N.C., College).

OUTER BANKS DAREDEVILS

Mailing Address: P.O. Box 1747, Nags Head, NC 27959. **Telephone:** (252) 202-1842. **FAX:** (252) 473-5070. **E-Mail Address:** obxdaredevils@yahoo.com. **Website:** www.outerbanksdaredevils.com

President: Warren Spivey. **General Manager:** Joe McGowan. **Head Coach:** Chris Francis (Virginia Wesleyan College).

PENINSULA PILOTS

Mailing Address: P.O. Box 7376, Hampton, VA 23666. **Telephone:** (757) 245-2222. **FAX:** (757) 245-8032. **E-Mail Address:** hank@peninsulapilots.com.

Website: www.peninsulapilots.com.

President: Henry Morgan. **General Manager:** Hank Morgan Jr. **Head Coach:** Ryan Morris (Virginia Commonwealth U.).

PETERSBURG GENERALS

Mailing Address: P.O. Box 1905, Petersburg, VA 23805. **Telephone:** (804) 722-0141. **FAX:** (804) 733-7370. **E-Mail Address:** pbgenerals@aol.com. **Website:** www.petersburgsports.com/generals.

President: Larry Toombs. **General Manager:** Jeremy Toombs. **Head Coach:** Tim Haynes (Virginia Commonwealth U.).

SPARTANBURG STINGERS

Mailing Address: P.O. Box 5493, Spartanburg, SC 29304. **Telephone:** (864) 591-2250. **FAX:** (864) 591-2131. **E-Mail Address:** gostingers@hotmail.com. **Website:** www.spartanburgstingers.com.

General Manager: Kevin Ferris. **Head Coach:** Kevin Flanagan (Virginia Wesleyan College).

THOMASVILLE HI-TOMS

Mailing Address: P.O. Box 3035, Thomasville, NC 27361. **Telephone:** (336) 472-8667. **FAX:** (336) 472-7198. **E-Mail Address:** greg@hitoms.com. **Website:** www.hitoms.com

President: Greg Suire. **General Manager:** Garrett Ball. **Head Coach:** Rob Huffstetler (Elon U.).

WILMINGTON SHARKS

Mailing Address: P.O. Box 15233, Wilmington, NC 28412. **Telephone:** (910) 343-5621. **FAX:** (910) 343-8932. **E-Mail Address:** info@wilmingtonsharks.com. **Website:** www.wilmingtonsharks.com.

President: Jim Morrison. **General Manager:** Curt Venderzee. **Head Coach:** Kyle DiEduardo (Winthrop).

WILSON TOBS

Mailing Address: P.O. Box 633, Wilson, NC 27894. **Telephone:** (252) 291-8627. **FAX:** (252) 291-1224. **E-Mail Address:** chris@wilsontobs.com. **Website:** www.wilsontobs.com.

President: Greg Turnage. **General Manager:** Chris Allen. **Head Coach:** Todd Wilkinson (Barton, N.C., College).

FLORIDA COLLEGIATE INSTRUCTIONAL LEAGUE

Mailing Address: IMG Academies/Bollettieri Campus,

5500 34th St. W., Bradenton, FL 34210. **Telephone:** (941) 727-0303. **FAX:** (941) 727-2962. **E-Mail Address:** tpluto@gte.net. **Website:** www.zonebaseball.com.

Year Founded: 2001.

President: Tom Pluto. **Secretary:** Flody Suarez.

2004 Opening Date: June 12. **Closing Date:** Aug. 1.

Regular Season: 36 games (split schedule).

Playoff Format: One-game playoff between first- and second-half winners.

All-Star Game: July 13 at Bradenton, FL (McKechnie Stadium).

Roster Limit: Open. **Player Eligibility Rule:** (college-eligible players only).

GREAT LAKES LEAGUE

Mailing Address: 690 Bunty Station Rd., Delaware, OH 43015. **Telephone:** (740) 368-3738. **FAX:** (740) 368-3799. **E-Mail Address:** RDIngles@owu.edu. **Website:** www.greatlakesleague.org.

Year Founded: 1986.

President, Commissioner: Roger Ingles. **Assistant Commissioner:** Kim Lance.

Division Structure: Red—Columbus, Delaware, Grand Lake, Indianapolis, Lima. Blue—Murraysville, Pitt, Southern Ohio, Stark County, Youngstown.

2004 Opening Date: June 12. **Closing Date:** Aug. 5.

Regular Season: 44 games.

Playoff Format: Top six teams meet in double-elimination tournament.

All-Star Game: July 17 at Delaware, OH.

Roster Limit: 27 (college-eligible players only).

COLUMBUS ALL-AMERICANS

Mailing Address: 3800 Municipal Way, Hilliard, OH 43026. **Telephone:** (614) 876-7361, ext. 500.

General Manager: Rodney Garnett. **Head Coach:** Brian Mannino.

DELAWARE COWS

Mailing Address: 3800 Criswell Dr., Columbus, OH 43220. **Telephone:** (614) 771-7070. **FAX:** (614) 771-7078.

General Manager, Head Coach: Bruce Heine.

GRAND LAKE MARINERS

Mailing Address: 717 W. Walnut St., Coldwater, OH 45828. **Telephone:** (419) 678-3607. **FAX:** (419) 586-4735.

General Manager: Wayne Miller. **Head Coach:** Mike Stafford.

Indianapolis One Crown

Mailing Address: 8888 Fitness Lane, Fishers, IN 46038. **Telephone:** (317) 842-2555. **FAX:** (317) 558-1162.

General Manager, Coach: Greg Lymberopoulos.

LIMA LOCOS

Mailing Address: 3700 S. Dixie Hwy., Lima, OH 45806. **Telephone:** (419) 991-4296. **FAX:** (419) 999-4586.

General Manager: Barry Ruben. **Head Coach:** Robert Livchak.

MURRYSVILLE MAULERS

Mailing Address: 709 Stonehaven Dr., Greensburg, PA 15601. **Telephone:** (724) 934-7238. **FAX:** (724) 934-7296.

General Manager, Head Coach: Bob Bozzuto.

PITTSBURGH PANDAS

Mailing Address: 118 Hetherton Dr., Pittsburgh, PA 15237. **Telephone:** (412) 759-4444. **FAX:** (412) 366-

2064.

General Manager: Frank Gilbert. **Head Coach:** Mark Schmidt.

SOUTHERN OHIO COPPERHEADS

Mailing Address: Grover E 146, Ohio University, Athens, OH 45701. **Telephone:** (740) 593-4666. **FAX:** (740) 0539.

General Manager: Andrew Kreutzer. **Head Coach:** Todd Linklater.

STARK COUNTY TERRIERS

Mailing Address: 1019 35th St. NW, Canton, OH 44709. **Telephone:** (330) 492-9220. **FAX:** (330) 492-9236.

General Manager: Greg Trbovich. **Head Coach:** Joe Gilhousen.

YOUNGSTOWN EXPRESS

Mailing Address: 945 Windham Ct., Suite 5, Boardman, OH 44512. **Telephone:** (330) 726-8028. **FAX:** (330) 726-6384.

General Manager: Chuck Whitman. **Head Coach:** Bill Sizemore.

JAYHAWK LEAGUE

Mailing Address: 5 Adams Pl., Halstead, KS 67056. **Telephone/FAX:** (316) 755-1285.

Year Founded: 1976.

Commissioner: Bob Considine. **President:** J.D. Schneider. **Vice President:** Curt Bieber. **Secretary:** Christi Billups.

2004 Opening Date: June 8. **Closing Date:** July 29.

Regular Season: 40 games.

Playoff Format: Top two teams qualify for National Baseball Congress World Series.

Roster Limit: 30 to begin season; 25 at midseason.

EL DORADO BRONCOS

Mailing Address: 865 Fabrique, Wichita, KS 67218. **Telephone:** (316) 687-2309. **FAX:** (316) 942-2009. **Website:** www.eldoradobroncos.org.

General Manager: J.D. Schneider.

ELKHART DUSTERS

Mailing Address: P.O. Box 793, Elkhart, KS 67950. **Telephone:** (620) 697-2095. **FAX:** (620) 697-2826. **Website:** my.elkhart.com/dusters.

General Manager: Brian Elsen.

HAYS LARKS

Mailing Address: 3409 Summer Lane, Hays, KS 67601. **Telephone:** (785) 625-3486. **FAX:** (785) 625-8542.

General Manager: Curt Bieber. **Manager:** Frank Leo.

LIBERAL BEEJAYS

Mailing Address: P.O. Box 352, Liberal, KS 67901. **Telephone:** (620) 624-1904. **FAX:** (620) 624-1906.

General Manager: Kim Snell.

NEVADA GRIFFONS

Mailing Address: Box 601, Nevada, MO 64772. **Telephone:** (417) 667-8308. **FAX:** (417) 667-8108.

General Manager: Dr. Jason Meisenheimer.

TOPEKA CAPITOLS

Mailing Address: 2005 SW Sims, Topeka, KS 66604. **Telephone:** (785) 234-5881. **FAX:** (785) 273-0220.

General Manager: Don Carlile.

MOUNTAIN COLLEGIATE BASEBALL LEAGUE

(Begins Play 2005)

Mailing Address: Unavailable. **Telephone:** (818) 887-

5447. **E-Mail Address:** info@mcbl.net **Website:** www.mcbl.net

Director: Kurt Colicchio.
Roster limit: 25 (college-eligible players only)
Member Clubs: Boulder (Colo.), Cheyenne (Wyo.), Fort Collins (Colo.), Grand Junction (Colo.), Greeley (Colo.), Laramie (Wyo.).

NEW ENGLAND COLLEGIATE LEAGUE
Mailing Address: 290 Harbor Place, Stamford, CT 06902. **Telephone:** (860) 646-4048. **FAX:** (860) 432-1665. **E-Mail Address:** commissioner@necbl.com. **Website:** www.necbl.com.
Year Founded: 1993.
President: Fay Vincent Jr. **Executive Vice President:** Joel Cooney. **Commissioner:** Kevin MacIlvane. **Deputy Commissioner:** Pete Dupuis. **Treasurer:** Ed Slegeski. **Secretary:** Rich Rossiter. **Director, Umpire Development:** Ed Vargo.
Division Structure: North—Berkshire, Concord, Keene, Mill City, North Adams, Sanford, Vermont. **South**—Danbury, Holyoke, Manchester, Newport, Riverpoint, Torrington.
2004 Opening Date: June 11. **Closing Date:** Aug. 10.
Regular Season: 42 games.
Playoff Format: Top four teams in each division meet in best-of-3 quarterfinals; winners meet in best-of-3 semifinals; winners meet in best-of-3 final for league championship.
All-Star Game: July 27 at Concord.
Roster Limit: 25 (college-eligible players only).

BERKSHIRE DUKES
Mailing Address: P.O. Box 2021, Hinsdale, MA 01235. **Telephone:** (413) 655-8077. **FAX:** (413) 655-8635. **Website:** www.berkshiredukes.com.
President/General Manager: Dan Duquette. **Director:** Kent Qualls. **Head Coach:** Steve Alonzo.

CONCORD QUARRY DOGS
Mailing Address: P.O. Box 404, Concord, NH 03302. **Telephone:** (603) 224-6508. **E-Mail Address:** info@quarrydogs.org. **Website:** www.quarrydogs.org
President: Curtis Barry. **General Manager:** Pete Dupuis. **Head Coach:** Ken Connerty (U. of Massachusetts-Lowell).

DANBURY WESTERNERS
Mailing Address: 37 Grammar School Dr., Danbury, CT 96811. **Telephone/FAX:** (203) 744-5874. **Website:** www.danburywesterners.com
General Manager: Mario Tiani. **Head Coach:** John Fitzgerald.

HOLYOKE GIANTS
Mailing Address: 56 Clearview Dr., Wallingford, CT 06492. **Telephone:** (203) 949-0025. **E-Mail Address:** cam@snet.net.
General Manager: Cal Moffie. **Head Coach:** Unavailable.

KEENE SWAMP BATS
Mailing Address: 31 W. Surry Rd., Keene, NH 03431. **Telephone:** (603) 357-2578. **FAX:** (603) 354-7842.
General Manager: Vicki Bacon. **Head Coach:** Mike Sweeney (Amherst, Mass., College).

MANCHESTER SILKWORMS
Mailing Address: 16 West St., Manchester, CT 06040. **Telephone:** (860) 559-3126. **FAX:** (860) 432-1665. **Website:** www.manchestersilkworms.org
General Manager: Ed Slegeski. **Head Coach:** Anthony

DeCicco (U. of Vermont).

MILL CITY ALL-AMERICANS
Mailing Address: P.O. Box 218, Chelmsford, MA 01863. **Telephone:** (978) 454-5058. **FAX:** (978) 251-1211. **E-Mail Address:** millcityallamericans@hotmail.com.
General Manager: Harry Ayotte. **Head Coach:** Chip Forrest.

NEWPORT GULLS
Mailing Address: P.O. Box 777, Newport, RI 02840. **Telephone:** (401) 845-6832. **Website:** www.newportgulls.com
President/General Manager: Chuck Paiva. **Head Coach:** Dennis Healy (George Washington U.)

NORTH ADAMS STEEPLECATS
Mailing Address: P.O. Box 812, North Adams, MA 01247. **Telephone:** (413) 652-1031. **Website:** www.steeplecats.com
General Manager: Sean McGrath. **Head Coach:** Unavailable.

RIVERPOINT ROYALS
Mailing Address: P.O. Box 206, West Warwick, RI 02893. **Telephone:** (401) 732-6667.
President/General Manager: Pete Fontaine. **Head Coach:** Jon Palmieri (Georgia Tech).

SANFORD MAINERS
Mailing Address: 924 Main St., Sanford, ME 04073. **Telephone:** (207) 324-0010. **FAX:** (207) 324-2227.
General Manager: Neil Olson. **Head Coach:** Scott Brown (SUNY-Cortland).

TORRINGTON TWISTERS
Mailing Address: 4 Blinkoff Ct., Torrington, CT 06790. **Telephone/FAX:** (860) 482-0450.
General Manager: Kirk Fredriksson. **Head Coach:** Gregg Hunt.

VERMONT MOUNTAINEERS
Mailing Address: P.O. Box 586, Montpelier, VT 05602. **Telephone:** (802) 223-5224.
President: Ed Walbridge. **General Manager:** Brian Gallagher. **Head Coach:** Chris Jones (St. John's U.)

NEW YORK COLLEGIATE LEAGUE
Summer Address: 28 Dunbridge Heights, Fairport, NY 14450. **Winter Address:** P.O. Box 2516, Tarpon Springs, FL 34688. **Telephone:** (585) 223-2328, (727) 942-9120.
Year Founded: 1986.
Commissioner: Dave Chamberlain. **President:** Al Visingard. **Vice Chairman:** Tom Kenney. **Treasurer:** Dan Russo. **Secretary:** Ted Ford.
Member Clubs: Alleghany County Nitros, Amsterdam Mohawks, Athletes In Action-Alfred, Geneva Redwings, Gennessee Valley River Bats, Glens Fall Golden Eagles, Hornell Dodgers, Ithaca Classics, Mohawk Valley Cobras, Plattsburgh Thunder, Penn Yan Raging Steamers, Saratoga Phillies, Watertown Wizards, Wayne County Raptors.
2004 Opening Date: June 3. **Closing Date:** July 31.
Regular Season: 42 games.
Playoff Format: Top four teams meet in best-of-3 series. Winners meet in best-of-3 series for league championship.
All-Star Game: June 28, site unavailable.
Roster Limit: 24 (college-eligible players only).

NORTHWOODS LEAGUE
Office Address: 403 E. Center St., Rochester, MN

55904. **Mailing Address:** P.O. Box 12, Rochester, MN 55903. **Telephone:** (507) 536-4579. **FAX:** (507) 289-1866. **E-Mail Address:** nwl@chartermi.net. **Website:** www.northwoodsleague.com.

Year Founded: 1994.

President: Dick Radatz Jr. **Director, Operations:** Jon Olson.

Division Structure: North—Alexandria, Duluth, Mankato, St. Cloud, Thunder Bay. **South**—La Crosse, Madison, Rochester, Waterloo, Wisconsin.

2004 Opening Date: June 2. **Closing Date:** Aug. 15.

Regular Season: 64 games (split schedule).

Playoff Format: First-half and second-half division winners meet in best-of-3 series. Winners meet in best-of-3 series for league championship.

All-Star Game: July 14 at Wausau.

Roster Limit: 25 (college-eligible players only).

ALEXANDRIA BEETLES

Mailing Address: 418 3rd Ave. E., Suite 111, Alexandria, MN 56308. **Telephone:** (320) 763-8151. **FAX:** (320) 763-8152. **E-Mail Address:** beetles@alexandria beetles.com. **Website:** www.alexandriabeetles.com.

General Manager: Ron Voz. **Head Coach:** Mark Magdaleno (Centaurus HS, Lafayette, CO).

DULUTH HUSKIES

Mailing Address: Suite 238, Holiday Center, 207 W. Superior St., Duluth, MN 55802. **Telephone:** (218) 786-9909. **FAX:** (218) 786-9001. **E-Mail Address:** huskies@duluthhuskies.com. **Website:** www.duluth huskies.com.

General Manager: Craig Smith. **Head Coach:** Jeff Casper (U. of Arizona).

LA CROSSE LOGGERS

Mailing Address: 1223 Caledonia St., La Crosse, WI 54601. **Telephone:** (608) 796-9553. **FAX:** (608) 796-9032. **E-Mail Address:** info@lacrosseloggers.com. **Website:** www.lacrosseloggers.com.

General Manager: Chris Goodell. **Head Coach:** Estevan Valencia (UC Riverside).

MADISON MALLARDS

Mailing Address: 2920 N. Sherman Ave., Madison, WI 53704. **Telephone:** (608) 246-4277. **FAX:** (608) 246-4163. **E-Mail Address:** vern@mallardsbaseball.com. **Website:** www.mallardsbaseball.com.

Director, Marketing/Baseball Operations: Vern Stenman. **Head Coach:** Darrell Handelsman.

MANKATO MOONDOGS

Mailing Address: 310 Belle Ave., Suite L-10, Mankato, MN 56001. **Telephone:** (507) 625-7047. **FAX:** (507) 625-7059. **E-Mail Address:** office@mankatomoon dogs.com. **Website:** www.mankatomoondogs.com.

General Manager: Kyle Mrozek. **Head Coach:** Brad Ruppert (Shasta, Calif., JC).

ROCHESTER HONKERS

Office Address: Mayo Field, 403 E. Center St., Rochester, MN 55904. **Mailing Address:** P.O. Box 482, Rochester, MN 55903. **Telephone:** (507) 289-1170. **FAX:** (507) 289-1866. **E-Mail Address:** honkers@rochester honkers.com. **Website:** www.rochesterhonkers.com.

General Manager: Dan Litzinger. **Head Coach:** Dave Parra (Neosho County, KS, CC).

ST. CLOUD RIVER BATS

Office Address: Athletic Park, 5001 8th St. N., St. Cloud, MN 56303. **Mailing Address:** P.O. Box 5059, St. Cloud, MN 56302. **Telephone:** (320) 240-9798. **FAX:** (320) 255-5228. **E-Mail Address:** riverbat@cloudnet.com.

Website: www.riverbats.com.

General Manager: Scott Schreiner. **Head Coach:** Tom Fleenor (U. of South Carolina-Spartanburg).

THUNDER BAY BORDER CATS

Office Address: 425 Winnipeg Ave., Thunder Bay, ON P7B 6P9. **Mailing Address:** P.O. Box 29105, Thunder Bay, ON P7B 6P9. **Telephone:** (807) 766-2287. **FAX:** (807) 345-8299. **E-Mail Address:** baseball@tbaytel.net.

General Manager: Dan Wolfert. **Head Coach:** Mitch Dunn (Chipola, Fla., JC).

WATERLOO BUCKS

Office Address: Riverfront Stadium, 850 Park Rd., Waterloo, IA 50703. **Mailing Address:** P.O. Box 4124, Waterloo, IA 50704. **Telephone:** (319) 232-0500. **FAX:** (319) 232-0700. **E-Mail Address:** garyrima23@hot-mail.com. **Website:** www.waterloobucks.com.

General Manager: Gary Rima. **Head Coach:** Andy Haines (Middle Tennessee State U.).

WISCONSIN WOODCHUCKS

Office Address: Washington Square, 300 Third St., L4, Wausau, WI 54402. **Telephone:** (715) 845-5055. **FAX:** (715) 845-5015. **E-Mail Address:** info@woodchucks.com.

General Manager: Clark Eckhoff. **Head Coach:** Darin Everson.

PACIFIC INTERNATIONAL LEAGUE

Mailing Address: 504 Yale Ave. N., Seattle, WA 98109 **Telephone:** (206) 623-8844. **FAX:** (206) 623-8361 **Email Address:** spotter@potterprinting.com **Website:** www.pacificinternationalleague.com **Year Founded:** 1992

President: Steve Konek Sr. **Commissioner:** Seth Dawson. **Vice President:** Dan Segel. **Secretary:** Steve Potter. **Treasurer:** Mark Dow. **Chairman of the Board:** Paul Ables.

Member Clubs: National Division—Aloha (Ore.) Knights, Bend (Ore.) Elks, Everett (Wash.) Merchants, Kirkland (Wash.) Kodiaks, Portland (Ore.) Kings, Seattle (Wash.) Studs. **International Division**—Bellingham (Wash.) Bells, Kelowna (B.C.) Falcons, Langley (B.C.) Blaze, Spokane (Wash.) RiverHawks, Wenatchee (Wash.) AppleSox.

2004 Opening Date: June 4. **Closing Date:** Aug. 15.

Regular Season: 36 games.

Playoff Format: National Division winner earns automatic berth in National Baseball Congress World Series. The next two finishers in National Division compete and top two finishers in International Division meet in best-of-3 semisimals; winners meet in best-of-3 series for league championship.

SOUTHERN COLLEGIATE BASEBALL LEAGUE

Mailing Address: 9300 Fairway Ridge Rd., Charlotte, NC 28277.

Telephone: (704) 847-5075. **FAX:** (704) 847-1455. **E-Mail Address:** SCBLCommissioner@aol.com. **Website:** www.scbl.org.

Year Founded: 1999.

Commissioner: Bill Capps. **President:** Jeff Carter. **Vice President:** Brian Swords. **Treasurer:** Steve Cunningham.

2004 Opening Date: June 1. **Closing Date:** Aug. 8.

Regular Season: 44 games.

All-Star Game: July 14 at Spartanburg.

Division Structure: North—Asheville, Carolina Copperheads, Kernersville, Lenoir, Rowan, Tennessee. **South**—Athens, Carolina Chaos, Carolina Warriors, Rock

Hill, Seneca, Spartanburg.

Playoff Format: Division winners meet in best-of-5 series for league championship.

Roster Limit: 30 (College-eligible players only).

ASHEVILLE REDBIRDS

Mailing Address: P.O. Box 1515, Johnson City, TN 37605. **Telephone:** (423) 854-9282, (423) 914-0621. **FAX:** (423) 854-9594. **E-Mail Address:** EntSport@aol.com. **Website:** www.scbl.org.

Owner/General Manager: Lyn Jeffers. **Head Coach:** Chris Mayes.

ATHENS PIRATE KINGS

Mailing Address: P.O. Box 462, Nicholson, GA 30565. **Telephone:** (706) 354-6789, (706) 296-4054. **E-Mail Address:** bpark@nbank.net. **Website:** www.eteamz.com/athenspirates

General Manager/Head Coach: Bill Park.

CAROLINA CHAOS

Mailing Address: 142 Orchard Dr., Liberty, SC 29657. **Telephone:** (864) 843-3232, (864) 901-4331. **E-Mail Address:** brian_swords@carolinachaos.com. **Website:** www.carolinachaos.com.

General Manager/Head Coach: Brian Swords.

CAROLINA COPPERHEADS

Mailing Address: 17606 Westward Reach, Cornelius, NC 28031. **Telephone:** (704) 892-1041, (704) 564-9211. **E-Mail Address:** Jcarter@standpointtech.com. **Website:** www.CarolinaCopperheadBaseball.org.

Owner: Carolina Copperhead Baseball, Inc. **General Manager:** Jeff Carter. **Head Coach:** Jamie Billings.

CAROLINA WARRIORS

Mailing Address: P.O. Box 286, Anderson, SC 29622. **Telephone:** (864) 222-9914, (864) 940-3392. **E-Mail Address:** rbmcclure58@aol.com. **Website:** www.scbl.org.

Owner/General Manager: Bruce McClure. **Head Coach:** Dave Delgado.

KERNERSVILLE BULLDOGS

Mailing Address: 7057 Avenbury Circle, Kernersville, NC 27284. **Telephone:** (336) 993-8195, (336) 462-9058. **FAX:** (888) 777-5412. **E-Mail Address:** dogpound@triad.rr.com. **Website:** www.scbl.org.

Owner/General Manager: Art Wedemeyer. **Head Coach:** Dale Ijames.

LENOIR OILERS

Mailing Address: 1848 Bellcroft Lane, Lenoir, NC 28645. **Telephone:** (828) 757-9375, (828) 217-2116. **E-Mail Address:** 3tadavis@charter.net. **Website:** www.scbl.org.

President: Buck Deal. **General Manager:** Freddie Davis. **Head Coach:** Unavailable.

ROCK HILL SOX

Mailing Address: 9300 Fairway Ridge Rd., Charlotte, NC 28277. **Telephone:** (704) 847-5075, (704) 621-0940. **FAX:** (704) 847-1455. **E-Mail Address:** CarolinaSox@aol.com. **Website:** www.CarolinaSoxBaseball.com.

Owner/General Manager: Bill Capps. **Head Coach:** Jeremy Keller.

ROWAN PIRATES

Mailing Address: 9300 Fairway Ridge Rd., Charlotte, NC 28277. **Telephone:** (704) 847-5075, (704) 621-0940. **FAX:** (704) 847-1455. **E-Mail Address:** RowanPirates@aol.com. **Website:** www.StanlyPirates.com.

Owner/General Manager: Bill Capps. **Head Coach:** Jeff Gregory. **Manager:** Kevin Frady.

SENECA INDIANS

Mailing Address: P.O. Box 286, Anderson, SC 29662.

Telephone: (864) 304-2866. **FAX:** (864) 226-9556. **E-Mail Address:** hitters@aol.com. **Website:** www.scbl.org. **Owner/General Manager:** Bob Hall. **Head Coach:** Kevin Nichoals.

SPARTANBURG CRICKETS

Mailing Address: P.O. Box 1429, Cowpens, SC 29330. **Telephone:** (864) 463-6667, (864) 266-3727. **E-Mail Address:** crickets@direcway.com. **Website:** www.scbl.org.

Owner/General Manager: Steve Cunningham. **Head Coach:** Mike Noble.

TENNESSEE THUNDER

Mailing Address: P.O. Box 1515, Johnson City, TN 37605. **Telephone:** (423) 854-9282, (423) 914-0621. **FAX:** (423) 854-9594. **E-Mail Address:** EntSport@aol.com. **Website:** www.scbl.org.

Owner/General Manager: Lyn Jeffers. **Head Coach:** Glen Davis.

TEXAS COLLEGIATE LEAGUE

Mailing Address: P.O. Box 200988, Arlington, TX 76006. **Telephone:** (214) 333-5340. **FAX:** (817) 838-3122. **E-Mail Addresses:** info@texascollegiateleague.com. **Website:** www.texascollegiateleague.com.

Year Founded: 2004.

Commissioner/President: Wayne Poage. **Director, Media Relations:** Rob Harman.

Member Clubs: Coppell Copperheads, Graham Roughnecks, Granbury Generals, Highland Park Blue Sox, McKinney Marshals, Mineral Wells Steam, Southlake Lone Stars, Weatherford Wranglers.

2004 Opening Date: June 8. **Closing Date:** Aug. 8.

Regular Season: 54 games.

Playoff Format: Top four teams meet in best-of-3 semifinals; winners meet in best-of-3 final for league championship.

All Star Game: July 12.

Roster Limit: Unavailable (college-eligible players only).

VALLEY LEAGUE

Mailing Address: 58 Bethel Green Rd., Staunton, VA 24401. **Telephone:** (540) 885-8901. **FAX:** (540) 885-2068. **E-Mail Addresses:** dudleycm@jmu.edu, davidb@fisherautoparts.com. **Website:** www.valleyleaguebaseball.com.

Year Founded: 1961.

President: David Biery. **Executive Vice President:** Warren Shand. **Director, Public Relations:** Curt Dudley. **League Statistician:** Mark Hoskins.

2004 Opening Date: June 4. **Closing Date:** July 29.

Regular Season: 44 games.

All-Star Game: July 11 at Waynesboro.

Division Structure: North—Front Royal, Loudoun, Luray, New Market, Winchester. **South**—Covington, Harrisonburg, Staunton, Waynesboro, Woodstock.

Playoff Format: Top four teams in each division meet in best-of-3 quarterfinals; winners meet in best-of-5 semifinals; winners meet in best-of-5 series for league championship.

Roster Limit: 28 (college eligible players only).

COVINGTON LUMBERJACKS

Mailing Address: P.O. Box 171, Covington, VA 24457. **Telephone/FAX:** (540) 863-5225. **E-Mail Address:** jacksbaseball28@aol.com. **Website:** www.jacksbaseball.com.

Owners: Clyde Helmintoller, Jason Helmintoller. **Recruiting Coordinator/Head Coach:** Brian Kraft

(Oklahoma City U.).

FRONT ROYAL CARDINALS
Mailing Address: P.O. Box 995, Front Royal, VA 22630. **Telephone:** (540) 636-1882. **FAX:** (540) 635-6498. **E-Mail Address:** sminkeen@shentel.net. **Website:** www.frcardinalbaseball.com.
President: Linda Keen. **Head Coach:** Unavailable.

HARRISONBURG TURKS
Mailing Address: 1489 S. Main St., Harrisonburg, VA 22801. **Telephone:** (540) 434-5919. **E-Mail Address:** hbgturks@vaix.net. **Website:** www.harrisonburgturks.com.
General Manager/Head Coach: Bob Wease. **Operations Manager:** Teresa Wease. **Public Relations:** Curt Dudley.

LOUDOUN RANGERS
Mailing Address: Unavailable. **Telephone:** Unavailable. **General Manager:** Unavailable. **Head Coach:** Unavailable.

LURAY WRANGLERS
Mailing Address: 1203 E. Main St., Luray, VA 22835. **Telephone:** (540) 743-3338. **E-Mail Addresses:** bturner@shentel.net, luraywranglers@hotmail.com, gmoyer@shentel.net.
President: Bill Turner. **General Manager:** Greg Moyer. **Head Coach:** Mike Bocock.

NEW MARKET REBELS
Mailing Address: P.O. Box 902, New Market, VA 22844. **Telephone:** (540) 740-4247, (540) 740-8569. **E-Mail Address:** nmrebels@shentel.net. **Website:** www.rebelsbaseballonline.com.
General Manager: Bruce Alger. **Public Relations:** Dick Golden. **Secretary/Treasurer:** Lynn Alger. **Head Coach:** Mac McClarrinon (Francis Marion, S.C., College).

STAUNTON BRAVES
Mailing Address: 14 Shannon Place, Staunton, VA 24401. **Telephone:** (540) 886-0987. **FAX:** (540) 886-0905. **E-Mail Address:** sbraves@hotmail.com. **Website:** www.stauntonbraves.com.
Director, Operations: Kay Snyder. **General Manager:** Steve Cox. **Head Coach:** Lawrence Nesselrodt (West Virginia State U.).

WAYNESBORO GENERALS
Mailing Address: P.O. Box 615, Waynesboro, VA 22980. **Telephone:** (540) 949-0370, (540) 942-2474. **FAX:** (540) 949-0653. **E-Mail Address:** jim_critzer@hotmail.com.
Owner: Jim Critzer. **President:** Rennie Dobbins. **General Manager:** Dale Coffey. **Assistant GM:** Jim Stohlmann. **Head Coach:** Derek McDaniel.

WINCHESTER ROYALS
Mailing Address: P.O. Box 2485, Winchester, VA 22604. **Telephone:** (540) 667-9227, (540) 662-4466. **FAX:** (540) 662-3299. **E-Mail Addresses:** tgt@shentel.net, jimphill@shentel.net. **Website:** www.winchesterroyals.com.
President: Todd Thompson. **Vice President:** Jim Phillips. **Public Relations:** Mark Sawyer. **Baseball Operations:** Brian Burke. **Head Coach:** Jason Johnson.

WOODSTOCK RIVER BANDITS
Mailing Address: 2115 Battlefield Run Ct., Richmond, VA 23231. **Telephone:** (804) 795-5128. **FAX:** (804) 226-8706. **E-Mail Addresses:** woodstockriverbandits@yahoo.com. **Website:** www.woodstockriverbandits.org.
President: Stu Richardson. **Vice President:** Glenn Berger. **General Manager:** Jerry Walters. **Assistant GM:** Harry Combs. **Head Coach:** Ricky Ware (St. Leo, Fla., College).

HIGH SCHOOL/ YOUTH

HIGH SCHOOL
BASEBALL

NATIONAL FEDERATION OF STATE HIGH SCHOOL ASSOCIATIONS
Mailing Address: P.O. Box 690, Indianapolis, IN 46206. **Telephone:** (317) 972-6900. **FAX:** (317) 822-5700. **E-Mail Address:** baseball@nfhs.org. **Website:** www.nfhs.org.

Executive Director: Robert Kanaby. **Chief Operating Officer:** Bob Gardner. **Assistant Director/Baseball Rules Editor:** Elliot Hopkins. **Director, Publications/Communications:** Bruce Howard.

NATIONAL HIGH SCHOOL BASEBALL COACHES ASSOCIATION
Mailing Address: P.O. Box 5128, Bella Vista, AR 72714. **Telephone:** (479) 876-2591. **FAX:** (479) 876-2596. **E-Mail Address:** homeplate@baseballcoaches.org. **Website:** www.baseballcoaches.org.

Executive Director: Jerry Miles. **Administrative Assistant:** Elaine Miles. **President:** Bob Colburn, St. Andrew's School, Middletown, DE. **First Vice President:** Stan McKeever, La Cueva HS, Albuquerque, NM. **Second Vice President:** Frank Carey, North Reading HS, Reading, MA.

2004 National Convention: Dec. 2-5, Grapevine, TX.

GATORADE CIRCLE OF CHAMPIONS
(National High School Player of the Year Award)

Mailing Address: The Gatorade Company, 321 N. Clark St., Suite 24-3, Chicago, IL 60610. **Telephone:** (312) 553-1240. **Website:** www.gatorade.com.

Mailing Address, Scholastic Coach and Athletic Director: 557 Broadway, New York, NY 10012. **Telephone:** (212) 343-6131. **FAX:** (212) 343-6376. **E-Mail Address:** mwallace@scholastic.com. **Website:** coachadguide.com. **Publisher:** Bruce Weber. **Marketing Manager:** Mike Wallace.

NATIONAL TOURNAMENTS

In-Season
BASEBALL AT THE BEACH
Mailing Address: P.O. Box 1717, Georgetown, SC 29442. **Telephone:** (843) 546-3800. **FAX:** (843) 527-1816. **Tournament Director:** Jim Owens.

2004 Tournament: Feb. 26-29 at Coastal Federal Stadium/Myrtle Beach High School (8 teams).

FIRST BANK CLASSIC
Mailing Address: 106 N. Vale Ave., Lubbock, TX 79416. **Telephone:** (806) 766-0706.

Tournament Director: Fred Oliver.

2004 Tournament: March 11-13 (16 teams).

HORIZON NATIONAL INVITATIONAL
Mailing Address: Horizon High School, 5601 E. Greenway Rd., Scottsdale, AZ 85254. **Telephone:** (602) 867-9003.

Tournament Director: Eric Kibler.

2004 Tournament: March 22-25 (16 teams).

INTERNATIONAL PAPER CLASSIC
Mailing Address: 4723 Johnson Rd., Georgetown, SC 29940. **Telephone:** (843) 527-9606. **FAX:** (843) 546-8521 **E-Mail Address:** ipclassic@yahoo.com.

Tournament Director: Alicia Johnson.

2004 Tournament: March 4-7 (8 teams).

LIONS INVITATIONAL
Mailing Address: 6626 Airoso Ave., San Diego CA 92120. **Telephone:** (619) 583-2633, (619) 444-3190. **FAX:** (619) 583-6605.

Tournament Director: Jim Gordon. **Assistant Director:** Bob Hinshaw.

2004 Tournament: April 5-8 (80 teams).

MARCH MADNESS
Mailing Address: Westminster Academy, 5601 N. Federal Hwy., Fort Lauderdale, FL 33308. **Telephone:** (954) 735-1841. **FAX:** (954) 334-6160.

Tournament Director: Rich Hofman.

2004 Tournament: March 15-18 (16 teams).

MIDLAND TOURNAMENT OF CHAMPIONS
Mailing Address: Midland High School, 906 W. Illinois Ave., Midland, TX 79701. **Telephone:** (432) 689-1337.

Tournament Director: Barry Russell.

2004 Tournament: March 4-6 (8 teams).

SARASOTA CLASSIC
Mailing Address: 2384 Seattle Slew Dr., Sarasota, FL 34240. **Telephone:** (941) 955-0181. **FAX:** (941) 378-5853.

Tournament Director: Clyde Metcalf.

2004 Tournament: March 29-April 2 at Sarasota, FL (16 teams).

TOYO TIRES NATIONAL CLASSIC
Mailing Address: P.O. Box 338, Placentia, CA 92870. **Telephone:** (714) 993-2838. **FAX:** (714) 993-5350. **E-Mail Address:** placentiamustang@aol.com. **Website:** national-classic.com.

Tournament Director: Todd Rogers.

2004 Tournament: April 12-15 at Cal State Fullerton (16 teams).

USA CLASSIC
Mailing Address: 5900 Walnut Grove Rd., Memphis, TN 38120. **Telephone:** (901) 872-8326. **FAX:** (901) 681-9443. **Website:** www.usabaseballstadium.org.

Tournament Organizers: John Daigle, Buster Kelso.

2004 Tournament: April 7-10 at USA Baseball Stadium, Millington, TN (16 teams).

WEST COAST CLASSIC
Mailing Address: 5000 Mitty Way, San Jose, CA 95129. **Telephone:** (408) 342-4273. **E-Mail Address:** hutton@mitty.com.

Tournament Director: Bill Hutton.

2004 Tournament: April 13-15 at Archbishop Mitty HS, San Jose, CA (16 teams).

WESTMINSTER NATIONAL CLASSIC
Mailing Address: Westminster Academy, 5601 N. Federal Hwy., Fort Lauderdale, FL 33308. **Telephone:**

(954) 735-1841. **FAX:** (954) 334-6160.
Tournament Director: Rich Hofman.
2004 Tournament: April 3-8 (16 teams).

Postseason
SUNBELT BASEBALL CLASSIC SERIES
Mailing Address: 505 North Blvd., Edmond, OK 73034. **Telephone:** (405) 348-3839. **FAX:** (405) 340-7538.
Chairman: Gordon Morgan. **Director:** John Schwartz.
2004 Senior Series: Norman, OK, June 22-26. (8 teams: Arizona, California, Florida, Georgia, Maryland, Ohio, Oklahoma, Texas).
2004 Junior Series: McAlester and Hartshorne, OK, June 11-15 (10 teams: Arizona, California, Canada, Georgia, Mississippi, Missouri, Oklahoma Blue, Oklahoma Gold, Tennessee, Texas).
2004 Sophomore Series: Edmond, OK, June 4-6 (4 teams: Oklahoma Red, Oklahoma White, Tennessee, Texas).

NATIONAL HIGH SCHOOL CHAMPIONSHIP
Mailing Address: c/o Champions Baseball Academy, 10701 Plantside Dr., Louisville, KY 40299. **Telephone:** (502) 261-9200. **FAX:** (502) 261-9278. **E-Mail Address:** champ8@aol.com. **Website:** championsbaseball.com.
Tournament Directors: John Marshall, Bill Miller, Justin Duncan.
2004 Tournament (high school/open): July 7-11 (64 teams).

ALL-STAR GAMES

AFLAC HIGH SCHOOL CLASSIC
Mailing Address: 10 S. Adams St., Rockville, MD 20850. **Telephone:** (301) 762-7188. **FAX:** (301) 762-1491.
Event Organizer: Sports America, Inc. **President, Chief Executive Officer:** Robert Geoghan.
2004 Game: High School Class of 2005, East vs. West, Aberdeen, MD, Aug. 6.

TALENT
SHOWCASES

PROFESSIONAL BASEBALL SCOUTING COMBINES

AREA CODE GAMES
Mailing Address: P.O. Box 213, Santa Rosa, CA 95402. **Telephone:** (707) 975-7894. **FAX:** (707) 525-0214. **E-Mail Address:** rwilliams@areacodebaseball.org. **Website:** www.areacodebaseball.org.
President, Goodwill Series, Inc.: Bob Williams.
2004 Area Code Games: Aug. 4-9 at Long Beach, CA (Blair Field).
Regional Scouting Combines: Milwaukee Brewers tryouts—June 12-13 at Sacramento, CA (Sacramento State U.); June 22-23 at Long Beach, CA (Blair Field). Montreal Expos tryout—June 19-20 at Charlottesville, VA (U. of Virginia). Texas Rangers tryout—June 28 at College Station, TX (Texas A&M U.); June 29 at Arlington, TX (U. of Texas-Arlington). Chicago White Sox tryouts—June 28 at Springfield, MO (Southwest Missouri State U.); June 30 at Indianapolis, IN (Butler U.); July 6 at Naperville, IL (North Central JC).
14th International Friendship Series: Aug. 9-18 at Beijing, China.
10th Annual Australia Goodwill Series: Dec. 16-31 at Adelaide, Canberra and Perth, Australia.

EAST COAST PROFESSIONAL BASEBALL SHOWCASE
Mailing Address: 601 S. College Rd., Wilmington, NC 28403. **Telephone:** (910) 962-3570.
Facility Directors: Mark Scalf, Randy Hood, Scott Jackson.
2004 Showcase: July 27-Aug. 1 at Wilmington, NC (UNC Wilmington).

HIGH SCHOOL SHOWCASE EVENTS

ALL-AMERICAN BASEBALL TALENT SHOWCASES
Mailing Address: 6 Bicentennial Ct., Erial, NJ 08081. **Telephone:** (856) 354-0201. **FAX:** (856) 354-0818. **E-Mail Address:** hitdoctor@thehitdoctor.com **Website:** thehitdoctor.com.
National Director: Joe Barth.

ARIZONA FALL CLASSIC
Mailing Address: 6102 W. Maui Lane, Glendale, AZ 85306. **Telephone:** (602) 978-2929. **FAX:** (602) 439-4494. **E-Mail Address:** azbaseballted@msn.com. **Website:** www.fallclassic.com.
Directors: Ted Heid, Tracy Heid.

2004 Events
Memorial Day Classic	Peoria Sports Complex, Peoria, AZ, May 28-31
Four Corner Classic	Peoria Sports Complex, Peoria, AZ, June 4-6
Senior Fall Classic (HS seniors)	Peoria Sports Complex, Peoria, AZ, Oct. 15-17
Junior Fall Classic (HS jr./soph)	Peoria Sports Complex, Peoria, AZ, Oct. 22-24
Halloween Classic	Peoria Sports Complex, Peoria, AZ, Oct. 29-31

BASEBALL FACTORY
Office Address: 9176 Red Branch Rd., Suite M, Columbia, MD 21045. **Telephone:** (800) 641-4487, (410) 715-5080. **FAX:** (410) 715-1975. **E-Mail Address:** info@baseballfactory.com. **Website:** www.baseballfactory.com.
Chief Executive Officer: Steve Sclafani. **President:** Rob Naddelman. **Vice President, Baseball Operations:** Steve Bernhardt.

BATS Program: Year-round, various locations.

BLUE-GREY CLASSIC

Mailing Address: Pro-Motion Sports, 83 E. Bluff Rd., Ashland, MA 01721. **Telephone:** (508) 881-2782. **E-Mail Address:** gus@impactprospects.com. **Website:** www.impactprospects.com.

Director: Gus Bell.

2004 Showcases: Pre-Draft Evaluation—May 2 at Tampa, FL (Progress Energy Park). Classic I—July 19-21 at Jacksonville, FL (Jacksonville U.). Classic II—Fort Worth, TX (Texas Christian U.), dates unavailable. National Battle of the States I—July 23-25 at Tampa, FL (Progress Energy Park). Classic III—Aug. 6-8 at Knoxville, TN (U. of Tennessee). Classic IV—Aug. 10-12 at Winston-Salem, NC (Wake Forest U.). Classic V—Aug. 16-18 at Williamsburg, VA (College of William & Mary). Classic VI—Aug. 20-22 at Conway, SC (Coastal Carolina U.). ShowTime I—Aug. 27-29 at Kissimmee, FL (Houston Astros Complex). National Battle of the States II—Oct. 29-31 at Kissimmee, FL (Houston Astros Complex). Underclassmen ShowTime—Dec. 4-5 at Clearwater, FL (Philadelphia Phillies complex).

DOYLE BASEBALL SELECT SHOWCASES

Mailing Address: P.O. Box 9156, Winter Haven, FL 33883. **Telephone:** (863) 439-1000. **FAX:** (863) 439-7086. **E-Mail Address:** doyleinfo@doylebaseball.com. **Website:** www.doylebaseball.com.

President: Denny Doyle. **Director, Satellite School:** Rick Siebert.

IMPACT BASEBALL

Mailing Address: P.O. Box 47, Sedalia, NC 27342. **Telephone:** Unavailable. **E-Mail Address:** andypartin@aol.com. **Website:** www.impactbaseball.com.

Operator: Andy Partin.

2004 Showcases: June 14 at Columbia, SC (U. of South Carolina); June 29 at Rock Hill, SC (Winthrop U.); July 21-23 at Chapel Hill, NC (U. of North Carolina).

MID-AMERICA FIVE STAR BASEBALL SHOWCASE

Mailing Address—Cincinnati: Champions Baseball Academy, 510 E. Business Way, Cincinnati, OH 45241. **Telephone:** (513) 247-9511. **FAX:** (513) 247-0040. **Mailing Address—Louisville:** Champions Baseball Academy, 10701 Plantside Dr., Louisville, KY 40299. Telephone: (502) 261-9200. FAX: (502) 261-9278. **E-Mail Address:** champ8@aol.com.

President: John Marshall.

2004 Showcases: July 11-14 at Louisville, KY (Louisville Slugger Field); July 27-30 at Cincinnati, OH.

MIDWEST PROSPECTS SHOWCASE

Mailing Address: 3212 NW 54th St., Oklahoma City, OK 73157. **Telephone:** (405) 942-5455. **FAX:** (405) 942-3012. **E-Mail Address:** midwestprospects@cox.net. **Website:** www.midwestprospects.com.

Director: Brian Rupe.

2004 Camps: June 28-30 at Stillwater, OK (Oklahoma State U.); July 30-Aug. 1 at Huntsville, TX (Sam Houston State U.); Aug. 6-8 at Arlington, TX (U. of Texas-Arlington).

PACIFIC NORTHWEST CHAMPIONSHIP

Mailing Address: 20170 SW Avery Court, Tualatin, OR 97062. **Telephone:** (503) 885-1126. **E-Mail Address:** mckay@baseballnorthwest.com. **Website:** www.baseballnorthwest.com.

Tournament Organizer: Jeff McKay.

2004 Events: Aug. 17-20 at Portland, OR (PGE Park). **Oregon Prospect Games:** June 22-23 at Corvallis, OR (Oregon State U.). **Washington Prospect Games:** East—Unavailable; West—June 28-29 at Tacoma (Cheney Stadium). **Idaho Selection Games:** Unavailable.

PERFECT GAME USA

Mailing Address: 1203 Rockford Road SW, Cedar Rapids, IA 52404. **Telephone:** (319) 298-2923, (800) 447-9362. **FAX:** (319) 298-2924. **E-Mail Address:** pgjerry@qwest.net. **Website:** www.perfectgame.org.

President, Director: Jerry Ford. **National Supervisors:** Andy Ford, Jason Gerst, Tyson Kimm. **International Supervisor:** Kentaro Yasutake. **National Coordinators:** Jim Arp, Tom Battista, Taylor McCollough.

Scouting Director, World Wood Bat Association: David Rawnsley.

National Identification Camp Director: Greg Legg. **Regional ID Camp Directors:** Doug Baker (California), Cecil Espy (South), John Freitas (Southwest), Garth Iorg (Southeast), Bobby McKinney (Northeast), Aaron Puffer (Midwest), Omar Washington (South). **Area Scouts:** Kirk Gardner (Midwest), Steve Merchant (Southeast), Mike Manning (Northeast), Bugs Moran (Northeast), Sandy Shofner (South).

Directors, Instruction: Bruce Kimm, Jim VanScoyac.

Director, Public Relations: Andrea Bachman. **Marketing Director:** Frank Fulton.

Business Manager: Don Walser. **Office Manager:** Betty Ford. **Website Manager:** Tim Barcz. **Merchandise Director:** Tom Jackson. **Merchandise Manager:** Dick Vaske. **Umpire Director:** Scott Behn. **National Softball Director:** Wendi Krejca.

Spring Top Prospect Showcase: May 1-2 at Cedar Rapids, IA. **National Pre-Draft Camp:** May 18 at Cedar Rapids, IA (Veterans Memorial Stadium). **Sunshine West Showcase:** June 12-13, site unavailable. **Sunshine East Showcase:** June 12-13 at Fort Myers, FL. **National Academic Showcase:** June 15-16 at Fort Myers, FL. **Top Unsigned Prospects Showcase:** June 15-16 at Fort Myers, FL. **Perfect Game National Showcase:** June 18-20 at St. Petersburg, FL (Tropicana Field). **South Top Prospect Showcase:** July 25-27 at Waco, TX (Baylor U.). **South Underclassmen Showcase:** July 29-31 at Waco, TX (Baylor U.). **Midwest Underclassmen Showcase:** Aug. 9-11 at Bourbonnais, IL. **Southeast Underclassmen Showcase:** Aug. 9-11, site unavailable. **Southeast Top Prospect Showcase:** Aug. 13-15 at Chapel Hill, NC (U. of North Carolina). **Northeast Underclassmen Showcase:** Aug. 16-18 at Wareham, MA (Clem Spillane Field). **Northeast Top Prospect Showcase:** Aug. 20-22 at Wareham, MA (Clem Spillane Field). **Western**

Underclassmen Showcase: Sept. 18-19, site unavailable. **Midwest Top Prospect Showcase:** Sept. 18-19 at Cedar Rapids, IA.
WWBA Underclassmen Championship (16 and under/fall): Oct. 1-4 at Fort Myers, FL (City of Palms Complex).
Perfect Game/Baseball America WWBA Championship (fall): Oct. 24-27, site unavailable.

PREMIER BASEBALL
Mailing Address: 2411 Teal Ave., Sarasota, FL 34237. **Telephone:** (941) 371-0989. **FAX:** (941) 371-0917.
Camp Directors: John Crumbley, Rich Hofman, Clyde Metcalf.

SELECTFEST BASEBALL
Mailing Address: 60 Franklin Place, Morris Plains, NJ 07950. **Telephone:** (973) 539-4781. **E-Mail Address:** selectfest@optonline.net.
Camp Directors: Brian Fleury, Bruce Shatel.
2004 Showcase: June 25-26 at Piscataway, NJ (Rutgers U.).

TEAM ONE SHOWCASES
Mailing Address: P.O. Box 8843, Cincinnati, OH 45208. **Telephone:** (859) 466-8326. **E-Mail Address:** TeamOneBB@aol.com. **Website:** www.teamonebaseball.com.
President, Team One Sports: Jeff Spelman. **Assistant Director:** Stan Brzezicki. Telephone: (814) 899-8407. E-Mail Address: Tricky023@aol.com. **Assistant:** Bob Pincus. Telephone: (352) 365-6130. E-Mail Address: BobT1BB@aol.com.
2004 Team One National Showcase: Dates unavailable, Las Vegas, NV (U. of Nevada-Las Vegas).
2004 Regional Showcases: West—June 26-28 at Tempe, AZ (Diablo Stadium); South—July 17-19 at Atlanta (Georgia Tech); North—July 23-25 at South Bend, IN (U. of Notre Dame).

TOP 96 INVITATIONAL SHOWCASE
Mailing Address: P.O. Box 5481, Wayland, MA 01778. **Telephone:** (508) 651-0165. **E-Mail Address:** kennethp50@comcast.net. **Website:** www.top96.com.
Showcase Organizers: Dave Callum, Doug Henson, Ken Hill.
2004 Showcase: Aug. 6-7 at Lowell, MA (Alumni Field).

COLLEGE PROSPECT DEVELOPMENT CAMPS

COLLEGE SELECT SHOWCASE
Mailing Address: P.O. Box 783, Manchester, CT 06040. **Telephone:** (800) 782-3672. **E-Mail Address:** TRhit@msn.com. **Website:** www.collegeselect.org.
Consulting Director: Tom Rizzi.
2003 Showcases: June 28-30 at Norwich, CT; July 8-11 at Warwick, RI; Aug. 9-11 at Binghamton, NY.

TOP GUNS SHOWCASE
Mailing Address: 7890 N. Franklin Rd., Suite 2, Coeur d'Alene, ID 83815. **Telephone/FAX:** (208) 762-1100. **E-Mail Address:** topgunsbss@hotmail.com. **Website:** www.topgunsbaseball.com.
President: Larry Rook. **National Director, Field Operations:** Gary Ward. **Assistant Director, National Scouting:** Nick Rook. **Scouting/Field Operations:** Cody Rook, Jason Rook.
2004 National Development Camp: June 29-July 1 at Henderson, NV (CC of Southern Nevada).
Regional Development Camps: July 7-9 at Greensboro, NC (UNC Greensboro); July 12-14 at Waco, TX (Baylor U.); July 19-21 at Auburn, AL (Auburn U.); Aug. 2-4 at Davis, CA (UC Davis); Aug. 9-11 at Indianapolis, IN (U. of Indianapolis).

SCOUTING SERVICES/HIGH SCHOOL, COLLEGE

BASEBALL FACTORY
Office Address: 9176 Red Branch Rd., Suite M, Columbia, MD 21045. **Telephone:** (800) 641-4487, (410) 715-5080. **FAX:** (410) 715-1975. **E-Mail Address:** info@baseballfactory.com. **Website:** www.baseballfactory.com.
Chief Executive Officer: Steve Sclafani. **President:** Rob Naddelman. **Vice President, Baseball Operations:** Steve Bernhardt.

PROSPECTS PLUS/THE SCOUTING REPORT
(A Joint Venture of Baseball America and Perfect Game USA)
Mailing Address: Baseball America, P.O. Box 2089, Durham, NC 27702. **Telephone:** (800) 845-2726. **FAX:** (919) 682-2880. **E-Mail Addresses:** allansimpson@baseballamerica.com; jerry@perfectgame.org. **Website:** www.baseballamerica.com; www.perfectgame.org.
Editor, Baseball America: Allan Simpson. **Director, Perfect Game USA:** Jerry Ford.

SKILLSHOW, INC.
Mailing Address: 290 King of Prussia Rd., Suite 102, Radnor, PA 19087. **Telephone:** (610) 687-9072. **FAX:** (610) 687-9629. **E-Mail Address:** info@skillshow.com. **Website:** www.skillshow.com.
Chief Executive Officer: Tom Koerick Jr. **President/Director, Sales:** Tom Koerick Sr. **Vice President, Marketing:** Louis Manon.

TEAM ONE SHOWCASES
Mailing Address: P.O. Box 8843, Cincinnati, OH 45208. **Telephone:** (859) 466-8326. **E-Mail Address:** TeamOneBB@aol.com. **Website:** www.teamonebaseball.com.
President, Team One Sports: Jeff Spelman.

YOUTH BASEBALL

ALL AMERICAN AMATEUR BASEBALL ASSOCIATION (AAABA)

Mailing Address: 331 Parkway Dr., Zanesville, OH 43701. **Telephone:** (740) 453-8531. **FAX:** (740) 453-3978. **E-Mail Address:** clw@aol.com. **Website:** www.aaaba.com.
Year Founded: 1944.
President: Robert Mingo. **Executive Director/Secretary:** Bob Wolfe.
2004 National Tournament (21 and under): Aug. 15-21 at Johnstown, PA (16 teams). **AAABA Regionals:** Aug. 2-6 at Altoona, PA, Schenectady, NY and Zanesville, OH.

AMATEUR ATHLETIC UNION OF THE UNITED STATES, INC. (AAU)

Mailing Address: P.O. Box 10000, Lake Buena Vista, FL 32803. **Telephone:** (407) 934-7200. **FAX:** (407) 934-7242. **E-Mail Address:** jeremy@aausports.org. **Website:** www.aaubaseball.org.
Year Founded: 1982.
Senior Sports Manager/Baseball: Jeremy Bullock.

DIVISION I
Age Classifications, National Championships

8 and under	Concord, NC, July 14-18
9 and under	*Orlando, July 9-17
10 and under (46/60 foot)	Des Moines, IA, July 16-24
10 and under (48/65 foot)	Charlotte, NC, July 18-24
11 and under (46/60 foot)	Des Moines, IA, July 16-24
11 and under (50/70 foot)	*Orlando, July 16-24
12 and under (46/60 foot)	Lakeland, FL, July 14-18
12 and under (50/70 foot)	Burnsville/Lakeville, MN, July 25-31
13 and under (54/80 foot)	Knoxville, TN, July 16-24
13 and under (60/90 foot)	Myrtle Beach, SC, July 23-31
14 and under (60/90 foot)	Sarasota, FL, July 23-31
15 and under	Virginia Beach, VA, July 23-31
Junior Olympics (16 and under)	Des Moines, IA, July 27-Aug. 7
17 and under	Kingsport, TN, July 16-23
18 and under	*Orlando, July 9-17

DIVISION II
Age Classifications, National Championships

10 and under (46/60 foot)	Des Moines, IA, July 16-24
10 and under (48/65 foot)	Charlotte, NC, July 18-24
11 and under	*Orlando, July 16-24
12 and under	Burnsville/Lakeville, MN, July 16-24
13 and under (54/80 foot)	Knoxville, TN, July 18-26
13 and under (60/90 foot)	Myrtle Beach, SC, July 23-31
14 and under (60/90 foot)	*Orlando, July 23-31
15 and under	*Orlando, July 16-24
16 and under	*Orlando, July 16-24

WEST COAST NATIONALS

10 and under (48/65 foot)	Portland, OR/Vancouver, WA, Sept. 2-5
10 and under (46/60 foot)	Portland, OR/Vancouver, WA, Sept. 2-5
11 and under (50/70 foot)	Portland, OR/Vancouver, WA, Sept. 2-5
12 and under (50/70 foot)	Portland, OR/Vancouver, WA, Sept. 2-5
13 and under (54/80 foot)	Arc Park, TX, July 27-Aug. 1
14 and under (54/80 foot)	Arc Park, TX, July 27-Aug. 1

International Championships

10 and under (46/60 foot)	*Orlando, June 11-17
12 and under (50/70 foot)	*Orlando, June 11-17

*Disney's Wide World of Sports Complex, Lake Buena Vista.

AMERICAN AMATEUR BASEBALL CONGRESS (AABC)

National Headquarters: 118-119 Redfield Plaza, P.O. Box 467, Marshall, MI 49068. **Telephone:** (269) 781-2002. **FAX:** (269) 781-2060. **E-Mail Address:** aabc@voyager.net. **Website:** www.aabc.us.
Year Founded: 1935.
President: Joe Cooper.

Age Classifications, World Series

Roberto Clemente (8 and under)	McDonough, GA, July 22-25

Willie Mays (9) .... Tulsa, OK, July 31-Aug. 4
Willie Mays (10 and under) .... Catano, PR, July 29-Aug. 1
Pee Wee Reese (11) .... Brooklyn, NY, Aug. 5-8
Pee Wee Reese (12 and under) .... Toa Baja, PR, Aug. 5-8
Sandy Koufax (13) .... Troy, MI, July 29-Aug. 1
Sandy Koufax (14 and under) .... Rockford, IL, July 29-Aug. 1
Mickey Mantle (15) .... Edmond, OK, July 30-Aug. 3
Mickey Mantle (16 and under) .... McKinney, TX, Aug. 4-8
Connie Mack (18 and under) .... Farmington, NM, Aug. 6-12
Stan Musial (unlimited) .... Battle Creek, MI, Aug. 12-15

AMERICAN AMATEUR YOUTH BASEBALL ALLIANCE

Mailing Address: 3851 Iris Lane, Bonne Terre, MO 63628. **Telephone:** (573) 518-0319. **FAX:** (314) 822-4974. **E-Mail Address:** clwjr28@aol.com. **Website:** www.aayba.com.
President, Baseball Operations: Carroll Wood.

Age Classifications, Open World Series

8 and under ....St. Louis, July 2-11
9 and under .... St. Louis, July 2-11
10 and under .... St. Louis, July 16-25
11 and under .... St. Louis, July 16-25
12 and under .... St. Louis, July 2-11
13 and under .... St. Louis, July 16-25
14 and under .... St. Louis, July 2-11

All-Star Nationals

9 and under .... St. Louis, July 30-Aug. 8
10 and under .... Chicago Heights, IL, Aug. 7-14
11 and under .... St. Louis, July 30-Aug. 8
12 and under .... St. Louis, July 30-Aug. 8
13 and under .... St. Louis, July 30-Aug. 8
14 and under .... Chicago Heights, IL, Aug. 7-14

AMERICAN LEGION BASEBALL

National Headquarters: National Americanism Commission, P.O. Box 1055, Indianapolis, IN 46206. **Telephone:** (317) 630-1213. **FAX:** (317) 630-1369. **E-Mail Address:** acy@legion.org. **Website:** www.baseball.legion.org.
Year Founded: 1925.
Program Coordinator: Jim Quinlan.
2004 World Series (19 and under): Aug. 20-24 at Hansen Stadium on Taylor Field, Corvallis, OR (8 teams).
2004 Regional Tournaments (Aug. 12-16, 8 teams): **Northeast**—Middletown, CT; **Mid-Atlantic**—Boyertown, PA; **Southeast**—Columbia, TN; **Mid-South**—Crowley, LA; **Great Lakes**—Harrison, OH; **Central Plains**—Omaha, NE; **Northwest**—Roseburg, OR; **Western**—Greeley, CO.

BABE RUTH BASEBALL

International Headquarters: 1770 Brunswick Pike, P.O. Box 5000, Trenton, NJ 08638. **Telephone:** (609) 695-1434. **FAX:** (609) 695-2505. **Website:** www.baberuthleague.org.
Year Founded: 1951.
President, Chief Executive Officer: Ron Tellefsen.
Executive Vice President/Chief Financial Officer: Rosemary Schoellkopf. **Vice President, Operations/Marketing:** Joe Smiegocki. **Vice President, Planning/Development:** Debra Horn. **Commissioners:** Robert Faherty, Steven Tellefsen (baseball), Jamie Horn (softball). **Executive Director, Special Events:** David Frolich.

Age Classifications, World Series

10 and under .... Vincennes, IN, Aug. 7-14
Cal Ripken (11-12) .... Aberdeen, MD, Aug. 14-22
13 .... Van Buren AR, Aug. 14-21
14 .... Wilson County, NC, Aug. 21-28
13-15 .... Longview WA, Aug. 20-28
16 .... Loudoun County, VA, Aug. 14-21
16-18 .... Newark, OH, Aug. 14-21

CONTINENTAL AMATEUR BASEBALL ASSOCIATION (CABA)

Mailing Address: 82 University St., Westerville, OH 43081. **Telephone:** (740) 382-4620. **E-Mail Address:** rtremaine@cababaseball.com. **Website:** www.cababaseball.com.
Year Founded: 1984.
Commissioner: John Mocny. **President:** Carl Williams. **Vice Presidents:** Larry Redwine, Fran Pell. **Secretary:** Janis Hogg. **Computer Advisor:** Guane Buck. **Legal Advisor:** Arturo Perez-Figaredo. **Executive Director:** Roger Tremaine.

Age Classifications, Ultimate World Series

9 and under .... Charles City, IA, July 30-Aug. 7
10 and under .... Marietta, GA, July 25-Aug. 1
11 and under .... Marion, OH, July 16-24
12 and under .... Cincinnati, July 23-31
13 and under .... Broken Arrow, OK, July 24-31

14 and under	Dublin, OH, July 16-24
14 and under/Southwest	Monterey Park, CA, July 23-31
15 and under	Crystal Lake, IL, July 23-Aug. 1
16 and under	Marietta, GA, July 18-25
High school age	Euclid, OH, July 17-23
18 and under	Homestead, FL, July 16-23
18 and under (Wood Bat)	Charleston, SC, July 25-Aug. 1

Age Classifications, Quality World Series

9 and under	Lynwood, IL, July 24-Aug. 1
10 and under	Lynwood, IL, July 24-Aug. 1
11 and under	Broken Arrow, OK, July 25-Aug. 1
12 and under	Marion, OH, July 24-31
13 and under	Cincinnati, July 23-Aug. 1
14 and under	Mentor, OH, July 23-31
15 and under	Lynwood, IL, July 24-Aug. 1

Age Classifications, House World Series

8-13 and under/Southeast	Miami, July 9-15
14-15 and under/Southeast	Miami, July 16-22
9-13 and under/Midwest	Lynwood, IL, July 24-Aug. 1
14-15 and under/Midwest	Lynwood, IL, July 24-Aug. 1
8-11 and under/Great Plains	Broken Arrow, OK, July 18-24
12-15 and under/Great Plains	Broken Arrow, OK, July 18-24
10, 12, 14 and under/Ohio Valley	Cincinnati, Aug. 5-9
11, 13, 15 and under/Ohio Valley	Cincinnati, Aug. 12-16
8, 10, 12, 14 and under/Southwest	Monterey Park, CA, July 23-31
9, 11, 13, 15 and under/Southwest	Monterey Park, CA, July 16-24
10 and under/Mid-Atlantic	Morgantown, WV, July 23-31
12-13 and under	Morgantown, WV, July 16-24
14 and under	Beckley, WV, July 23-31
15 and under	Beckley, WV, July 16-24

DIXIE BASEBALL, INC.

Mailing Address: P.O. Box 877, Marshall, TX 75671. **Telephone:** (903) 927-2255. **FAX:** (903) 927-1846. **Website:** www.dixie.org.

Year Founded: 1955.

Executive Director: Jim Quigley, 24 Pipes Loop, Covington, LA 70435. Telephone: (985) 893-1290. **Office Manager:** Rhonda Skelton.

Age Classifications, World Series

Dixie Youth (9-10)	Muscle Shoals, AL, Aug. 8-14
Dixie Youth (12 and under)	Muscle Shoals, AL, Aug. 8-14
Junior Dixie Boys (13)	Aiken, SC, July 31-Aug. 6
Dixie Boys (13-14)	LaGrange, GA, July 31-Aug. 6
Dixie Pre-Majors (15-16)	Guntersville, AL, July 31-Aug. 6
Dixie Majors (15-18)	Monroe, LA, July 31-Aug. 6

DIZZY DEAN BASEBALL, INC.

Mailing Address: P.O. Box 856, Hernando, MS 38632. **Telephone:** (662) 429-4365, (850) 455-8827.

Year Founded: 1962.

Commissioner: Danny Phillips. **Treasurer/Administrator:** D.B. Stewart.

Age Classifications, World Series

6 and under	Harrison, TN, July 16-21
7 and under	Rossville, GA, July 16-21
8 and under	Southaven, MS, July 23-28
9 and under	Southaven, MS, July 23-28
10 and under	Moody, AL, July 16-21
11 and under	Jasper, TN, July 16-21
12 and under	Moody, AL, July 16-21
13 and under	Southaven, MS, July 23-28
14 and under	Southaven, MS, July 23-28
Junior (15-16)	Southaven, MS, July 23-28
Senior (17-18)	Southaven, MS, July 23-28
High school	Starkville, MS, July 7-12

HAP DUMONT YOUTH BASEBALL

(A Division of the National Baseball Congress)

Mailing Address: 1325 N. Westlink, Wichita, KS 67212. **Telephone:** (316) 721-1779. **FAX:** (316) 721-8054. **Website:** hapdumontbaseball.com.

Year Founded: 1974.

National Chairman: Jerry Crowell. **Vice Chairman:** Jerald Vogt. **Executive Director:** Jim Barr.

Age Classifications, World Series

8 and under .... Midwest City, OK, July 23-28
9 and under .... Bartlett, TN, July 23-28
10 and under .... Harrison, AR, July 23-28
11 and under .... Oklahoma City, July 23-28
12 and under .... Greenfield, IN, July 23-28
13 and under .... Tunica, MS, July 23-28
14 and under .... Casper, WY, July 23-28
15 and under .... Kearny, MO, July 23-28
16 and under .... Horn Lake, MS, July 23-28
18 and under .... Wichita, July 23-38

LITTLE LEAGUE BASEBALL, INC.

International Headquarters: P.O. Box 3485, Williamsport, PA 17701. **Telephone:** (570) 326-1921. **FAX:** (570) 326-1074. **Website:** www.littleleague.org.
Year Founded: 1939.
Chairman: Dwight Raiford.
President/Chief Executive Officer: Steve Keener. **Director, Media Relations/Communications:** Lance Van Auken. **Director, Publications:** Scott Miller. **Director, Special Projects:** Scott Rosenberg.

Age Classifications, World Series

Little League (11-12) .... Williamsport, PA, Aug. 20-29
Junior League (13-14) .... Taylor, MI, Aug. 15-21
Senior League (14-16) .... Bangor, ME, Aug. 15-21
Big League (16-18) .... Easley, SC, July 30-Aug. 7

NATIONAL AMATEUR BASEBALL FEDERATION (NABF)

Mailing Address: P.O. Box 705, Bowie, MD 20718. **Telephone:** (301) 464-5460. **FAX:** (301) 352-0214. **E-Mail Address:** nabf1914@aol.com. **Website:** www.nabf.com.
Year Founded: 1914.
Executive Director: Charles Blackburn.

Age Classifications, World Series

Freshman (12 and under) .... Hopkinsville, KY, July 14-19
Sophomore (14 and under) .... Joplin, MO, July 23-27
Junior (16 and under) .... Northville, MI, July 22-26
High School (17 and under) .... Millington, TN, July 23-27
Senior (18 and under) .... Jackson, TN, July 29-Aug. 2
College (22 and under) .... Toledo, OH, Aug. 5-9
Major (unlimited) .... Louisville, KY, Aug. 12-15

NABF Classics (Invitational)

9 and under .... Southaven, MS, July 5-9
10 and under .... Hopkinsville, KY, July 5-9
11 and under .... Southaven, MS, July 5-9
13 and under .... Southaven, MS, July 5-9
15 and under .... Nashville, July 22-26
Major (unlimited) .... Orlando, Sept. 1-5

NATIONAL ASSOCIATION OF POLICE ATHLETIC LEAGUES

Mailing Address: 618 U.S. Highway 1, Suite 201, North Palm Beach, FL 33408. **Telephone:** (561) 844-1823. **FAX:** (561) 863-6120. **E-Mail Address:** copnkid@nationalpal.org. **Website:** www.nationalpal.org.
Year Founded: 1914.
Executive Director: Brad Hart. **National Program Manager:** Jeremy Phillips.

Age Classifications, World Series

14 and under .... Unavailable
16 and under .... Unavailable

PONY BASEBALL, INC.

International Headquarters: P.O. Box 225, Washington, PA 15301. **Telephone:** (724) 225-1060. **FAX:** (724) 225-9852. **E-Mail Address:** pony@pulsenet.com. **Website:** www.pony.org.
Year Founded: 1951.
President, Chief Executive Officer: Abraham Key. **Director, Baseball Operations:** Don Clawson.

Age Classifications, World Series

Shetland (5-6) .... No National Tournament
Pinto (7-8) .... No National Tournament
Mustang (9-10) .... Irving, TX, Aug. 4-7
Bronco (11-12) .... Monterey, CA, Aug. 5-10
Pony (13) .... Chino Hills, CA, July 29-Aug. 2
Pony (13-14) .... Washington, PA, Aug. 14-21
Colt (15-16) .... Lafayette, IN, Aug. 3-10
Palomino (17-18) .... Santa Clara, CA, Aug. 6-9

REVIVING BASEBALL IN INNER CITIES (RBI)

Mailing Address: 245 Park Ave., New York, NY 10167. **Telephone:** (212) 931-7897. **FAX:** (212) 949-5695.
Year Founded: 1989.
Founder: John Young. **Vice President, Community Affairs:** Thomas Brasuell. **Director, Marketing Communications:**
Kathleen Fineout.

Age Classifications, World Series

Junior Boys (13-15)	Detroit, Aug. 4-12
Senior Boys (16-18)	Detroit, Aug. 4-12

SUPER SERIES BASEBALL OF AMERICA

National Headquarters: 4036 East Grandview St., Mesa, AZ 85205. **Telephone:** (480) 664-2998. **FAX:** (480) 664-2997. **E-Mail Address:** info@superseriesbaseball.com. **Website:** www.superseriesbaseball.com.
President: Mark Mathew.

Age Classifications, World Series

8 and under (player pitch)	Colorado Springs, CO, July 10-17
8 and under (coach pitch)	Colorado Springs, CO, July 10-17
8 and under (machine pitch)	Colorado Springs, CO, July 10-17
9 and under (National)	Waco, TX, July 24-31
9 and under (American/Minors)	Gulfport, MS, July 17-24
10 and under (National/American/Minors)	Broken Arrow, OK, July 10-17
11 and under (National/Minors)	St. Louis, July 24-31
11 and under (American)	Sherwood, AR, July 23-30
12 and under (National/Minors)	Gulfport, MS, July 17-24
12 and under (American)	Collierville, TN, July 17-24
13 and under (National)	Waco, TX, July 10-17
13 and under (American)	Tulsa, OK, July 17-24
13 and under (Minors)	Waco, TX, July 24-31
14 and under (National, 54/80)	Dallas, July 10-17
14 and under (American 54/80)	Liberty, MO, July 10-17
14 and under (Minors 54/80)	Liberty, MO, July 24-31
14 and under (National/American 60/90)	Peoria, AZ, July 25-Aug. 1
15 and under (National/American)	Peoria, AZ, July 10-17
16 and under	Peoria, AZ, July 17-24
17-18	Peoria, AZ, July 17-24

T-BALL USA ASSOCIATION, INC.

Office Address: 2499 Main St., Stratford, CT 06615. **Telephone:** (203) 381-1449. **FAX:** (203) 381-1440. **E-Mail Address:** teeballusa@aol.com. **Website:** www.teeballusa.org.
Year Founded: 1993.
President: Bing Broido. **Executive Vice President:** Lois Richards.

TRIPLE CROWN SPORTS

Mailing Address: 3930 Automation Way, Fort Collins, CO 80525. **Telephone:** (970) 223-6644. **FAX:** (970) 223-3636. **Websites:** www.triplecrownsports.com.
Director, Baseball Operations: Sean Hardy.

Age Classifications, National Championships

9, 12, 13, 15, 16 World Series	Steamboat Springs, CO, July 20-25
10, 11, 14, 18 World Series	Steamboat Springs, CO, July 27-Aug. 1
10, 12, 13 World Series	Steamboat Springs, CO, Aug. 3-8
9, 11, 13, 15 Fall Nationals	Las Vegas, NV, Sept. 10-12
10, 12, 14, 16, 18 Fall Nationals	Las Vegas, NV, Sept. 17-19
10,12,14,15,18 Fall Nationals	St. Augustine, FL. Oct. 15-17
9,11,13, 16 Fall Nationals	St. Augustine, FL, Oct. 22-24

U.S. AMATEUR BASEBALL ASSOCIATION (USABA)

Mailing Address: 7101 Lake Ballinger Way, Edmonds, WA 98026. **Telephone/FAX:** (425) 776-7130. **E-Mail Address:** usaba@usaba.com. **Website:** www.usaba.com.
Year Founded: 1969.
Executive Director: Al Rutledge. **Secretary:** Roberta Engelhart.

Age Classifications, World Series

11 and under	Los Angeles, Aug. 7-14
12 and under	Compton, CA, Aug. 7-14
13 and under	Hoquiam, WA, July 30-Aug. 7
14 and under	Pasco, WA, Aug. 6-14
15 and under	Miarer, NV, July 23-31
16 and under	Richland, WA, Aug. 10-17
17 and under	Unavailable
18 and under	Compton, CA, Aug. 7-14

U.S. AMATEUR BASEBALL FEDERATION (USABF)

Mailing Address: 911 Stonegate Court, Chula Vista, CA 91913. **Telephone:** (619) 934-2551. **FAX:** (619) 271-6659. **E-Mail Address:** usabf@cox.net. **Website:** www.usabf.com.
  Year Founded: 1997.
  Senior CEO/President: Tim Halbig.

Age Classifications, World Series

10 and under	San Diego, Aug. 4-8
11 and under	San Diego, Aug. 4-8
12 and under	San Diego, Aug. 4-8
13 and under	San Diego, Aug. 4-8
14 and under	San Diego, Aug. 5-14
15 and under	San Diego, Aug. 5-14
16 and under	San Diego, Aug. 5-14
18 and under	San Diego, Aug. 5-14
Open	San Diego, July 29-Aug. 1

UNITED STATES SPECIALTY SPORTS ASSOCIATION (USSSA)

Executive Vice President, Baseball: Rick Fortuna, 6324 N. Chatham Ave., No. 136, Kansas City, MO 64151. **Telephone:** (816) 587-4545. **FAX:** (816) 587-4549. **E-Mail Address:** linda@kcsports.org. **Website:** kcsports.org.
  Year Founded: (1965)/Baseball (1996).

Age Classifications, World Series

7 and under (machine pitch)	Edmond, OK, July 13-18
7 and under (coach pitch)	Sulphur, LA, July 13-18
8 and under (machine pitch)	Edmond, OK, July 13-18
8 and under (machine pitch)	Thomas, GA, July 13-18
8 and under (coach pitch)	Sulphur, LA, July 13-18
8 and under/West	Chino Hills, CA, July 20-25
8 and under/East	Kansas City, MO, July 13-18
9 and under	St. Louis, July 18-25
10 and under (Major)	Henderson, NV, July 18-25
10 and under (AAA)	Southaven, MS, July 11-18
11 and under (Major Elite)	Orlando, Aug. 1-6
11 and under (Major)	Nevada, MO, July 11-18
11 and under (AAA)	Overland Park, KS, July 11-18
12 and under (Major Elite)	Orlando, Aug. 1-6
12 and under (Major)	Kansas City, MO, July 11-18
12 and under (AAA)	Hutchinson, KS, July 11-18
13 and under (Major)	Kansas City, MO, July 11-18
13 and under (AAA)	Canton, MI, July 18-25
13 and under (Major Elite)	Orlando, Aug. 1-6
14 and under (Major, 54/80)	Nevada, MO, July 11-18
14 and under (AAA, 54/80)	Tulsa, OK, July 11-18
14 and under (Major Elite, 60/90)	Orlando, Aug. 1-6
15 and under (Major/AAA)	Orlando, July 18-25
16 and under (Major/AAA)	Orlando, July 25-Aug. 1
17 and under (Major/AAA)	Lexington, KY, July 18-25
18 and under (Major/AAA)	Nashville, TN, July 25-Aug. 1

USA JUNIOR OLYMPIC BASEBALL CHAMPIONSHIP

Mailing Address: USA Baseball, 4825 Creekstone Dr., Suite 200, Durham, NC 27703. **Telephone:** (919) 474-8721. **FAX:** (919) 474-8822. **E-Mail Address:** jeffsinger@usabaseball.com. **Website:** www.usabaseball.com.
  Assistant Director, Baseball Operations: Jeff Singer.

Age Classifications, Championships

16 and under/West (72 teams)	Peoria/Surprise, AZ, June 18-26
16 and under/East (72 teams)	Palm Beach County, FL, June 18-26

WORLD WOOD BAT ASSOCIATION
(A Division of Perfect Game USA)

Mailing Address: 1203 Rockford Road SW, Cedar Rapids, IA 52404. **Telephone:** (319) 298-2923, (800) 447-9362. **FAX:** (319) 298-2924. **Website:** www.worldwoodbat.com.
  League Commisioner: Jerry Ford. **League President:** Andy Ford. **National Director:** Greg Legg. **Scouting Director:** David Rawnsley.

Age Classifications, World Series

2012 graduates/10 and under	Boubonnais, IL, July 29-Aug. 3
2011 graduates/11 and under	Boubonnais, IL, July 29-Aug. 3
2010 graduates/12 and under	Boubonnais, IL, July 29-Aug. 3
2009 graduates/13 and under	Boubonnais, IL, July 19-25
2008 graduates/14 and under	Boubonnais, IL, July 19-25
2007 graduates/15 and under	Marietta, GA, Aug. 4-8

2006 graduates/16 and under	Boubonnais, IL, July 19-25
2005 graduates/17 and under	Marietta, GA, July 6-11
2004 graduates/18 and under	Marietta, GA, July 12-18
World underclassmen	Fort Myers, FL, Oct. 1-4
Fall Championships/10-18	Site unavailable, Oct. 1-4
Fall Championship/high school	Site unavailable, Oct. 22-25

YOUTH BASEBALL TOURNAMENT CENTERS

BASEBALL USA

Mailing Address: 2626 W. Sam Houston Pkwy. N., Houston, TX 77043. **Telephone:** (713) 690-5055. **FAX:** (713) 690-9448. **E-Mail Address:** info@baseballusa.com. **Website:** www.baseballusa.com.

President: Charlie Maiorana. **Tournament Director:** Steve Olson. **Building Manager, Accounting:** Ken Ahrens. **Director, Marketing/Development:** Trip Couch. **League Baseball:** Kevin Nichols. **Pro Shop Manager:** Don Lewis.

Activities: Camps, baseball/softball spring and fall leagues, instruction, indoor cage and field rentals, youth tournaments, World Series events, corporate days, summer college league, pro shop.

CALIFORNIA COMPETITIVE YOUTH BASEBALL

Mailing Address: P.O. Box 338, Placentia, CA 92870. **Telephone:** (714) 993-2838. **FAX:** (714) 961-6078. **E-Mail Address:** ccybnet@aol.com.

Tournament Director: Todd Rogers.

2004 Tournament (ages 10-14): Aug. 1-7 at Fullerton, CA.

COCOA EXPO SPORTS CENTER

Mailing Address: 500 Friday Rd., Cocoa, FL 32926. **Telephone:** (321) 639- 3296. **Telephone:** (321) 639-3976. **FAX:** (321) 639-0598. **E-Mail Address:** athleticdirector@cocoaexpos.com. **Website:** www.cocoaexpo.com.

Executive Director: Jeff Biddle.

Activities: Spring training program, instructional camps, team training camps, youth tournaments.

2004 Events/Tournaments (ages 10-18): First Pitch Festival, May 21-23. Cocoa Expo Internationale, June 29-July 4. Cocoa Expo Summer Classic, Aug. 3-8. Labor Day Challenge, Sept. 3-6. Cocoa Expo Fall Classic, Oct. 15-17.

COOPERSTOWN BASEBALL WORLD

Mailing Address: P.O. Box 398, Bergenfield, NJ 07621. **Telephone:** (888) 229-8750. **FAX:** (888) 229-8720. **E-Mail Address:** cbw@cooperstownbaseballworld.com. **Website:** www.cooperstownbaseballworld.com.

Complex Address: Cooperstown Baseball World, SUNY-Oneonta, Ravine Parkway, Oneonta, NY 13820.

President/Chairman: Eddie Einhorn. **Vice President:** Debra Sirianni. **Senior Coordinator, Special Events:** Jennifer Einhorn.

Invitational Tournaments: 12 and under, 13 and under, 15 and under: June 26-July 2. 12 and under, 13 and under, 14 and under: July 3-9, July 10-16, July 31-Aug. 6. 12 and under, 14 and under: July 17-23. 12 and under, 13 and under, 15 and under: July 24-30. 12 and under, 13 and under: Aug. 7-Aug. 13.

COOPERSTOWN DREAMS PARK

Mailing Address: 101 E. Fisher St., 3rd Floor, Salisbury, NC 28144. **Telephone:** (704) 630-0050. **FAX:** (704) 630-0737. **E-Mail Address:** info@cooperstowndreamspark.com. **Website:** www.cooperstowndreamspark.com.

Complex Address: 4450 State Highway 28, Cooperstown, NY 13807.

Chief Executive Officer: Lou Presutti, **Program Director:** Phil Kehr.

Invitational Tournaments (64 teams per week): 10 and under—June 19-25; 12 and under—June 26-July 2, July 3-9, July 10-16, July 17-23, July 24-30, July 31-Aug. 6, Aug. 7-13, Aug. 14-20, Aug. 21-27.

National American Tournament of Champions: 12 and under—Aug. 28-Sept. 3.

DISNEY'S WIDE WORLD OF SPORTS

Mailing Address: P.O. Box 10000, Lake Buena Vista, FL 32830. **Telephone:** (407) 938-3802. **FAX:** (407) 938-3412. **E-Mail Address:** wdw.sports.baseball@disney.com. **Website:** www.disneyworldsports.com.

Manager, Sports Events: Kevin Reynolds. **Sports Manager:** Kevin Russell. **Tournament Director:** Al Schlazer. **Sales Manager, Baseball:** Rick Morris. **Sports Sales Coordinator, Baseball:** Kirk Stanley.

2004 Events/Tournaments: Disney's Sun & Surf Baseball Bash (8 and under coach pitch, 10 and under, 11, 12, 14, 16, 18), May 28-31. **Disney's Salute to Baseball Festival** (8 and under coach pitch, 10 and under, 11, 12, 14, 16, 18), July 3-9. **Disney's Turn Back the Clock Weekend** (8 and under coach pitch, 10 and under, 11, 12, 14, 16, 18), Sept. 2-6. **Disney's Sunshine Showdown** (8 and under coach pitch, 10 and under, 11, 12, 14, 16, 18), Oct. 22-24. **Disney's New Year's Baseball Classic** (10 and under, 11, 12, 14, 16, 18), Dec. 28-Jan. 1, 2005.

KC SPORTS TOURNAMENTS

Mailing Address: KC Sports, 6324 N. Chatham Ave., No. 136, Kansas City, MO 64151. **Telephone:** (816) 587-4545. **FAX:** (816) 587-4549. **E-Mail Addresses:** rick@kcsports.org, wally@kcsports.org, angelo@kcsports.org, linda@kcsports.org. **Website:** www.kcsports.org.

Activities: Youth tournaments (ages 6-18).

Tournament Organizers: Rick Fortuna, Wally Fortuna, Angela Giacalone, Linda Hottovy.

U.S. AMATEUR BASEBALL FEDERATION (USABF)

Mailing Address: 911 Stonegate Court, Chula Vista, CA 91913. **Telephone:** (619) 934-2551. **FAX:** (619) 271-6659. **E-Mail Address:** usabf@cox.net. **Website:** www.usabf.com.

Senior Chief Executive Officer/President: Tim Halbig.

ACADEMY OF PRO PLAYERS
Mailing Address: 317 Midland Ave., Garfield, NJ 07026. **Telephone:** (973) 772-3355. **FAX:** (973) 772-4839. **Website:** www.academypro.com.
Camp Director: Lar Gilligan.

ALDRETE BASEBALL ACADEMY
Office Address: P.O. Box 4048, Monterey, CA 93942. **Telephone:** (831) 884-0400. **FAX:** (831) 884-0800. **E-Mail Address:** aldretebaseball@aol.com. **Website:** www.aldretebaseball.com.
Camp Director: Rich Aldrete.
Manager: Dave Snow.

ALL-STAR BASEBALL ACADEMY
Mailing Addresses: 650 Parkway Blvd., Broomall, PA 19008; 52 Penn Oaks Dr., West Chester, PA 19382. **Telephone:** (610) 355-2411, (610) 399-8050. **FAX:** (610) 355-2414. **E-Mail Address:** info@allstarbaseballacademy.com. **Website:** www.allstarbaseballacademy.com.
Directors: Mike Manning, Chris Madonna.

THE BASEBALL ACADEMY
Mailing Address: IMG Academies, 5500 34th St. W., Bradenton, FL 34210. **Telephone:** (800) 872-6425, (941) 755-1000. **FAX:** (941) 752-2531. **E-Mail Address:** netsales@imgworld.com. **Website:** www.imgacademies.com.
Camp Director, Baseball: Ken Bolek.

BUCKY DENT BASEBALL SCHOOL
Mailing Address: 490 Dotterel Rd., Delray Beach, FL 33444. **Telephone:** (561) 265-0280. **FAX:** (561) 278-6679. **E-Mail Address:** staff@dentbaseball.com. **Website:** www.dentbaseball.com.
Vice President: Larry Hoskin.

DOYLE BASEBALL SCHOOL
Mailing Address: P.O. Box 9156, Winter Haven, FL 33883. **Telephone:** (863) 439-1000. **FAX:** (863) 439-7086. **E-Mail Address:** doyleinfo@doylebaseball.com. **Website:** www.doylebaseball.com.
President: Denny Doyle. **Chief Executive Officer:** Blake Doyle. **Director, Satellite School:** Rick Siebert.

FROZEN ROPES TRAINING CENTERS
Mailing Address: 12 Elkay Dr., Chester, NY 10918. **Telephone:** (877) 846-5699. **FAX:** (845) 469-6742. **E-Mail Address:** specialevents@frozenropes.com. **Website:** www.frozenropes.com.
Corporate Director: Tony Abbatine. **Camp Director:** Dan Hummel.

MARK CRESSE BASEBALL SCHOOL
Mailing Address: P.O. Box 4041, Seal Beach, CA 90740. **Telephone:** (714) 892-6145. **FAX:** (714) 892-1881. **E-Mail Address:** info@markcresse.com. **Website:** www.markcresse.com.
Owner/Founder: Mark Cresse. **Executive Director:** Jeff Courvoisier.

MICKEY OWEN BASEBALL SCHOOL
Mailing Address: P.O. Box 88, Miller, MO 65707. **Telephone:** (800) 999-8369, (417) 882-2799. **FAX:** (417) 889-6978. **E-Mail Address:** info@mickeyowen.com. **Website:** www.mickeyowen.com.
President: Ken Rizzo. **General Manager:** Mark Daniel. **Camp Director:** Bobby Doe. **Clinician:** Joe Fowler. **Advisor:** Howie Bedell.

NORTH CAROLINA BASEBALL ACADEMY
Mailing Address: 1137 Pleasant Ridge Rd., Greensboro, NC 27409. **Telephone:** (336) 931-1118. **E-Mail Address:** ncba@att.net. **Website:** www.ncbaseball.com.
Owner/Director: Scott Bankhead. **Assistant Director:** Matt Schirm. **Academy Director:** Tommy Jackson.

PENNSYLVANIA DIAMOND BUCKS BASEBALL CAMP
Mailing Address: 2320 Whitetail Court, Hellertown, PA 18055. **Telephone:** (610) 838-1219, (610) 442-6998. **E-Mail Address:** jciganick@moravian.edu.
Camp Director: Chuck Ciganick.

PERFECT GAME USA
Mailing Address: 1203 Rockford Rd. SW, Cedar Rapids, IA 52404. **Telephone:** (319) 298-2923. **FAX:** (319) 298-2924. **E-Mail Address:** services@perfectgame.org. **Website:** www.perfectgame.org.
President, Director: Jerry Ford. **National Supervisor:** Andy Ford. **Directors, Instruction:** Bruce Kimm, Jim VanScoyac.

PROFESSIONAL BASEBALL INSTRUCTION
Mailing Address: 107 Pleasant Ave., Upper Saddle River, NJ 07458. **Telephone:** (800) 282-4638 (NY/NJ), (877) 448-2220 (rest of U.S.). **FAX:** (201) 760-8820. **E-Mail Address:** info@baseballclinics.com. **Website:** www.baseballclinics.com.
President: Doug Cinnella.

RIPKEN BASEBALL CAMPS
Mailing Address: 1427 Clarkview Rd., Suite 100, Baltimore, MD 21209. **Telephone:** (800) 486-0850. **E-Mail Address:** information@ripkenbaseball.com. **Website:** www.ripkenbaseball.com.
Director, Operations: Bill Ripken.

ROOKIES BASEBALL INSTRUCTION, LLC
Mailing Address: 376 Hollywood Ave., Suite 209, Fairfield, NJ 07004. **Telephone:** (973) 808-7222. **FAX:** (973) 882-9311. **E-Mail Address:** info@rookiesbaseball.com. **Website:** www.rookiesbaseball.com.
Founders: Pat Byrnes, Joe Huffman.

SAN DIEGO SCHOOL OF BASEBALL
Mailing Address: P.O. Box 1492, La Mesa, CA 91944. **Telephone:** (619) 491-4000. **FAX:** (619) 469-5572. **E-Mail Address:** sdsbb@aol.com. **Website:** www.sandiegoschoolofbaseball.com.
Chief Executive Officer: Bob Cluck. **Vice Presidents:** Dave Smith, Alan Trammell, Reggie Waller. **Consultants:** Steve Finley, Luis Gonzalez.

SHO-ME BASEBALL CAMP
Mailing Address: P.O. Box 2270, Branson West, MO 65737. **Telephone:** (800) 993-2267, (417) 338-5838. **FAX:** (417) 338-2610. **E-Mail Address:** info@shome-baseball.com. **Website:** www.shomebaseball.com.
Camp Director: Christopher Schroeder. **Head of Instruction:** Dick Birmingham.

SOUTHWEST PROFESSIONAL BASEBALL SCHOOL
Mailing Address: 462 S. Gilbert Rd., Mesa, AZ 85204. **Telephone:** (888) 830-8031. **FAX:** (480) 830-7455. **E-Mail Address:** leonard@swpbs.com. **Website:** www.swpbs.com
Camp Directors: Leonard Garcia, Joe Maddon.

UTAH BASEBALL ACADEMY
Mailing Address: 8385 South Allen St., Suite 103, Sandy, UT 84070. **Telephone:** (801) 561-1700. **FAX:** (801) 571-5965. **E-Mail Address:** info@utahbaseballacademy.com. **Website:** www.utahbaseballacademy.com.

AGENT
DIRECTORY

SERVICE
DIRECTORY

INDEX

AGENT DIRECTORY

Aces Inc.
Seth Levinson, Esq., Sam Levinson
Keith Miller, Peter Pedalino, Esq.
Eric Amador, Michael Zimmerman
188 Montague St.
Brooklyn NY 11201
718-237-2900
fax 718-522-3906
acesinc2@aol.com

Anslow Sherrard Sports Management, LLC
Richard I. Anslow
195 Route 9 South
Manalapan NJ 07726
732-409-1212
fax 732-577-1188
ranslow@anslowlaw.com

Baseball Management International
Jesse Frescas Jr.
53-805 Avenida Martinez
La Quinta CA 92253
706-771-5109
fax 760-771-5143
jfrescas@dc.rr.com

Bouza, Klein & Goosenberg
Joseph Klein, David Goosenberg
950 S. Flower St. #100
Los Angeles CA 90015
213-488-0675
213-488-1316
jklein@bkglaw.com

David S. Abramson, Esq.
Verrill & Dana, LLP
One Portland Square
Portland, Maine 04112-0586
207-774-4000
fax 207-774-7499
dabramson@sportslaw.com
dabramson@verrilldana.com

DRM Brothers Sports Management Group
William S. Rose, Brian Doyle,
Todd Middlebrooks, Esq., Jim Munsey
31 Compass Lane
Ft. Lauderdale FL 33308
954-609-1505
fax 954-267-0336
ltdnyy@aol.com
drmsportsmgmt.com

Focus Management, Inc
Frank A. Blandino
P.O. Box 5777
Hillsborough NJ 08844
908-217-3226
fax 908-281-0596
focusmanagement@rcn.com

Golden Gate Sports Firm
Miles McAfee, PhD, Marcus Leazer,
Miles E. McAfee, Esq.
7677 Oakport Street Suite 1050
Oakland CA 94621
510-567-1390
fax 510-567-1395
goldengatesports1.com
milesmcafee@aol.com

Impact Management Company LLC
555 Ada Drive SE
P.O. Box 692
Ada MI 49301-0692
616-676-2086
fax 616-672-2278
imcsports.com
gregm@imcsports.com

Jennings, Taylor, Wheeler & Bouwkamp, P.C., Attorneys At Law
David L. Taylor, James E. Zoccola,
Quinn A. Moore
1171 N. Pennsylvania St. Suite 250
Carmel, IN 46032
317-575-7979
fax 317-575-7977
dave_taylor@jtwblaw.com

Jet Sports Management
B.B. Abbott
3514 West Obispo St.
Tampa FL 33629
813-902-9511
fax 813-902-0900
jetsports.us
bbabbott@jetsports.us

Law Office of James R. Kauffman
James R. Kauffman
877 Balboa Lane
Foster City CA 94404
650-377-0815
fax 650-377-0885
jrklaw@pacbell.net

Legends Management Group
Tom O'Connell
101 E. Kennedy Blvd. Suite 1790
Tampa FL 33602
813-223-5505
fax 813-275-9295
legendsmanagement.com
toclegends1@aol.com

King & King LLC
Stanley O. King, Esq
231 South Broad Street
Woodbury, NJ 08096
856-845-3001
fax 856-845-3079
stan@kingslaw.com

McDowell & Associates
Jim McDowell
Craig Wallenbrock
10061 Riverside Drive Number 870
Toluca Lake CA 91602
818-597-9948
fax 818-597-3212

Monaco Law Office
610 Newport Center Drive Suite 450
Newport Beach CA 92660
949-719-2669
fax 949-719-2607
randell@monacolawoffice.com

Northstar Sports Management
Barry Praver
105 Angelfish Lane
Jupiter FL 33477
561-775-6313
fax 561-775-7633
northstarsports@aol.com

Panco Sports Enterprises
Vince Panettiere
1841 N. Fuller Ave
Los Angeles CA 90046
323-876-5984
fax 323-876-5076
bbrep@yahoo.com

Peter E. Greenberg & Associates
Peter E. Greenberg, Esq., Edward L.
Greenberg, Chris Leible
200 Madison Avenue Suite 2225
New York NY 10016
212-334-6880
fax 212-334-6895

Pierce Sports Management
Steve Pierce, Lisa Pierce
6539 East Dreyfus
Scottsdale AZ 85254
480-991-1830/480-221-6884
fax 480-991-2762
optimumsportsla@aol.com
pierceandassoc@aol.com

Pro Agents Inc.
Billy Martin Jr., David P. Pepe
90 Woodbridge Center Dr. Suite 901
Woodbridge NJ 07095
800-795-3454
fax 732-855-6117
pepeda@wilentz.com

Professional Sports Management Group
Alan Meersand
865 Manhattan Beach Blvd. Suite 205
Manhattan Beach CA 90266
310-546-3400
fax 310-546-4046
meersand@aol.com

ProSport Management, Inc.
1831 N. Belcher Road G-3
Clearwater FL 33765
727-791-7556
fax 727-791-1489
vkrivacs@tampabay.44.om

Pro Star Management Inc.
Joe Bick
250 East Fifth Street Suite 1500
Cincinnati OH 45202
513-762-7676
fax 513-721-4628
prostar@fuse.net

Pro-Talent, Inc.
Christopher Fanta, Eduardo Diaz,
Jason Browning
3753 North Western Ave.
Chicago IL 60618
773-583-3411
fax 773-583-4277
protalentchicago@aol.com

**Reich, Katz & Landis
Baseball Group**
2370 One PPG Place
Pittsburgh PA 15222
412-391-2626
fax 412-391-2613

Reynolds Sports Management
3880 Lemon Street Suite 200
Riverside CA 92501
909-784-6333
fax 909-784-1451
reynddssports@aol.com

Riverfront Sports Management
Brian M. Goldberg
4300 Carew Tower
441 Vine Street
Cincinnati OH 45202
513-721-3111
fax 513-721-3077

RMG Sports Management
Robert Garber, Esq., Brett Laurvick,
Robert Lisanti
115 South Vine St. Suite 1E
Hinsdale IL 60521
630-986-2500
fax 630-986-0171

SKA Sports and Entertainment
Steve Greenberg
499 North Cannon Drive 3rd Floor
Beverly Hills CA 90210
310-551-0381
fax 310-551-0386
skasports@aol.com

Sosnick Cobbe Sports, Inc.
Matt Sosnick, Paul Cobbe
1601 N. California Blvd. Suite 150
Walnut Creek CA 94596
650-697-7070
fax 925-944-0361
mattsoz@aol.com

Stephen J. McLoughin, Esq
2555 Richmond Avenue
Staten Island NY 10304
718-983-1500
fax 718-983-5919
sjmcl14@aol.com

**Sports Management Group
Worldwide, Inc.**
10560 Main Street Suite 308
Fairfax VA 22030
703-273-4640
fax 703-273-1733
sportsmgt.net
dpilli@bwwonline.com

Tanzer Sports Consultants Inc.
Tommy Tanzer, Steve Alexander,
Jeff Kahn, Jamie Appel, Kenny
Felder, Bob Rischitelli, Brian James
P.O. Box 680340
Park City UT 84068
435-649-7603
fax 303-730-6304
tanzrball@aol.com
stevealexander@quest.net

Turner-Gary Sports Inc.
Jim Turner, Rex Gary, Chris Wimmer
101 S. Hanley Road Suite 1720
St. Louis MO 63105
314-863-6611
fax 314-863-9911

**West Coast Sports
Management LLC**
Len Strelitz, Bill Shupper, Jim Lentine
369 80 Fairoaks
Pasadena CA 91105
323-854-4001
fax 818-952-1527
proballfirm.com
bills@proballfirm.com

Add your company to the Baseball America
2005 Agent Directory or Service Directory.
Call (919) 682-9635 x104 for details.

SERVICE DIRECTORY

ACCESSORIES

JKP Sports, JUGS
19333 SW 118th Avenue
Tualatin OR 97062
800-547-6843
fax 503-691-1100
www.jugssports.com
stevec@jkpsports.com

APPAREL

All Pro Sports
16919 Ventura Blvd
Encino CA 91316
818-981-5264
fax 818-981-3020
allprosportsshoes.com
allprosports@socal.rr.com

Minor Leagues Major Dreams
P.O. Box 6098
Anaheim CA 92816
800-345-2421
fax 714-939-0655
minorleagues.com
mlmd@minorleagues.com

The Paul Pryor Company
12401 66th Street North
Largo FL 33773
727-531-8400
fax 727-530-1255
paulpryorbags.com
ppryorco@att.net

ARTWORK

Low and Inside
2022 N. Ferry Street Suite 3100
Minneapolis MN 55303
763-797-0777
fax 763-767-5510
lowandinside.com
creative@lowandinside.com

ATHLETIC INSURANCE

Francis L. Dean & Associates, Inc.
2800 S. Hulen Street #200
Fort Worth TX 76109
800-375-0552
fax 817-924-7884
athletic-insurance.com
jfaulder@fdean.com

K&K Insurance Group, Inc.
P.O. Box 2338
Fort Wayne, IN 46801
800-441-3994
fax 260-459-5120
Kandkinsurance.com
[See our ad after Page 224]

The Monument Sports Group
508 North Allison Street #1
Richmond VA 23220
804-354-9020
fax 804-354-9022
monumentsports.com
msg@monumentsports.com

BACKSTOPS

L.A. Steelcraft Products
PO Box 90365
Pasadena CA 91109
800-371-2438
fax 626-798-1482
lasteelcraft.com
info@lasteelcraft.com

BAGS

Diamond Sports
11130 Warland Drive
Cypress CA 90630
562-598-9717
fax 562-598-0906
diamond-sports.com
info@diamond-sports.com

The Paul Pryor Company
12401 66th Street North
Largo FL 33773
727-531-8400
fax 727-530-1255
paulpryorbags.com
ppryorco@att.net

BASEBALLS

Diamond Sports
11130 Warland Drive
Cypress CA 90630
562-598-9717
fax 562-598-0906
diamond-sports.com
info@diamond-sports.com

JKP Sports, JUGS
19333 SW 118th Avenue
Tualatin OR 97062
800-547-6843
fax 503-691-1100
jugssports.com
stevec@jkpsports.com

Markwort Sporting Goods Co.
4300 Forest Park Ave.
St Louis MO 63108
314-652-3757
fax 314-652-6241
markwort.com
sales@markwort.com

Phoenix Sports, Inc
301 Boren Avenue North
Seattle, WA 98109
800-776-9229
fax 800-776-4422
phoesports@aol.com

BASEBALL CARDS

Choice Marketing Sportscards
369 Turner Industrial Way
Aston PA 19014
800-999-2464
fax 610-494-8074
choicesportscards.com
info@choicesportscards.com

Grandstand Cards
22647 Ventura BL #192
Woodland Hills CA 91364
818-992-5642
fax 818-348-9122
gscards@pacbell.net

BALL/BAT/JERSEY DISPLAYS

BallQube Inc.
RR 2 Box 190
Cushing TX 75760
800-543-1470
fax 903-863-5571
ballqube.com
sales@ballqube.com

BASES

C&H Baseball
2215 60th Drive East
Bradenton FL 34203
941-727-1533
fax 941-727-0588
chbaseball.com
info@chbaseball.com

BATS

Akadema
317 Midland Avenue
Garfield NJ 07026
973-772-7669
fax 973-772-4839
akademapro.com
akadema@akademapro.com

Brett Bros. Sports International
East 9514 Montgomery #25
Spokane WA 99206
509-891-6435
fax 509-981-4156
brettbros.com
brettbats@aol.com

BWP
Rd. 1 Box 409A
Brookville PA 15825
814-849-0089
fax 814-849-8584
bwpbats.com
sales@bwpbats.com

D-Bat
1400 Preston Rd. Suite 110
Plano TX 75093
888-398-3393
fax 972-398-1001
batsales@dbatinc.com

Glomar Bats
116 W. Walnut Ave.
Fullerton CA 92832
714-871-5956
fax 714-871-5958
glomarbats.com
[See our ad on Page 5]

Hoosier Bat Company
4511 Evans Ave.
Valparaiso IN 46383
800-228-3787
fax 219-465-0877
hoosierbat.com
baseball@netnitco.com

Louisville Slugger
800 W. Main Street   See our ads
Louisville KY 40202   on Pages
888-444-2287   7 & 11

Old Hickory Bat Co., Inc.
1735 Hwy 31W
Goodlettsville, TN 37072
866-PROBATS toll-free
phone/fax (615) 285-0588
www.oldhickorybats.com
mail@oldhickorybats.com

Phoenix Bat Company
P.O. Box 921
Hilliard OH 43026
877-598-BATS
614-851-9448
phoenixbats.com

Zinger-X Professional Bats
939 W. Center A
Lindon UT 84042
801-372-1117
fax 801-226-5448
zingerx.com

BATTING CAGES

C&H Baseball
2215 60th Drive East
Bradenton FL 34203
941-727-1533
fax 941-727-0588
chbaseball.com
info@chbaseball.com

Cages Plus
518 Fair Lane
Napa ID 83686
866-475-9148
cagesplus.com

Horan Sports
P.O. Box 963
Conshohocken PA 19428
484-919-8547
fax 610-792-9737
horansports@aol.com
horansports.com

JKP Sports, JUGS
19333 SW 118th Avenue
Tualatin OR 97062
800-547-6843
fax 503-691-1100
jkpsports.com
stevec@jkpsports.com

Lanier Rollaway Cages
206 S. Three Notch
Andalusia AL 36420
800-716-9189
fax 334-222-3323
alaweb.com/~battingcages.com

Miller Net Company, Inc.
P.O. Box 18787
Memphis TN 38181
901-744-3804
fax 901-743-6580
millernets.com

National Batting Cages, Inc.
P.O. Box 250
Forest Grove OR 97116-0250
800-547-8800
fax 503-357-3727
nationalbattingcages.com
fred@nationalbattingcages.com

Russell Batting Cages
2045 Hickory Rd.
Birmingham AL 35216
888-722-2243
russellbattingcages.com

Vantage Products International
7895 Stage Hills Blvd. Suite 105
Memphis TN 38133
800-244-4457
fax 800-321-5882
vpisports.com
vpisports@aol.com

BATTING GLOVES

Akadema
317 Midland Avenue
Garfield NJ 07026
973-772-7669
fax 973-772-4839
akademapro.com
akadema@akademapro.com

All Pro Sports
16919 Ventura Blvd
Encino CA 91316
818-981-5264
fax 818-981-3020
allprosportsshoes.com
allprosports@socal.rr.com

Louisville Slugger
800 W. Main Street   See our ads
Louisville KY 40202   on Pages
888-444-2287   7 & 11

CAMPS/SCHOOLS

Mickey Owen Baseball School
P.O. Box 4504
Springfield MO 65808
417-882-2799
fax 417-889-6978
mickeyowen.com
ken@mickeyowen.com

Professional Baseball Instruction
107 Pleasant Avenue
Upper Saddle River NJ 07458
877-448-2220
fax 201-760-8820
baseballclinics.com
info@baseballclinics.com

San Diego School of Baseball
P.O. Box 1492
La Mesa CA 91944
619-491-4000
fax 619-469-5572
sandiegoschoolofbaseball.com
sdsbb@aol.com

Sho-Me Baseball Camp
P.O. Box 2270
Branson West MO 65737
800-993-2287
fax 417-338-2610
shomebaseball.com

The Baseball Academy
5500 34th Street West
Bradenton FL 34210
800-993-2267
fax 941-752-2531
imgacadimes.com
netsales@imgworld.com

CATCHERS & UMPIRES GEAR

Diamond Sports
11130 Warland Drive
Cypress CA 90630
562-598-9717
fax 562-598-0906
diamond-sports.com
info@diamond-sports.com

CAPS/HEADWEAR

Minor Leagues Major Dreams
P.O. Box 6098
Anaheim CA 92816
800-345-2421
fax 714-939-0655
minorleagues.com
mlmd@minorleagues.com

CHAMPIONSHIP RINGS

Balfour Sports
7211 Circle S Road   See our ad
Austin TX 78745   on Page 15
512-440-2017
fax 512-440-2661

CLEATS/FOOTWEAR

All Pro Sports
16919 Ventura Blvd
Encino CA 91316
818-981-5264
fax 818-981-3020
allprosportsshoes.com
allprosports@socal.rr.com

CONCESSIONS

Houston's Peanuts
P.O. Box 160
Dublin NC 28332
800-334-8383
fax 910-862-8076
houstonspeanuts.com
peanutprocessors@carolina.net

CUP HOLDERS

Caddy Products
72-064 Adelaid Street
Thousand Palms CA 92276
800-845-0591
fax 760-343-7598 | See our ad on Page 13
caddyproducts.com
sales@caddyproducts.com

EDUCATIONAL ASSOCIATIONS

Sports Turf Managers Association
1027 S. 3rd Street
Council Bluffs IA 51502-6875
800-323-3875
fax 712-366-9119
sportsturfmanager.com
stmahq@st.omhcoxmail.com

EMPLOYMENT

Henrys Baseball Club
Independent and Single A
719 Moody Street
Waltham MA 02453-5005
781-891-0621

MinorLeagueJobs.com
P.O. Box 1671
West Jordan UT 84084
801-542-0012
fax 801-542-0029 | See our ad on Page 23
minorleaguejobs.com

ENTERTAINMENT

BirdZerk!
P.O. Box 36061
Louisville KY 40233
800-219-0899
502-458-4020
fax 502-458-0867
birdzerk.com
johnny@birdzerk.com

Mark Out Productions, Inc.
P.O. Box 770440
Lakewood OH 44107
866-gameops
fax 978-418-0058
gameops.com
info@gameops.com

ZOOperstars!
P.O. Box 36061
Louisville KY 40233
800-219-0899
502-458-4020
fax 502-458-0867
zooperstars.com
johnny@zooperstars.com

FIELD COVERS/TARPS

C&H Baseball
2215 60th Drive East
Bradenton FL 34203
941-727-1533
fax 941-727-0588
chbaseball.com
info@chbaseball.com

Covermaster Inc.
100 Westmore Dr. 11-D
Rexdale ON M9V5C3
800-387-5808
fax 416-742-6837
covermaster.com
info@covermaster.com

Vantage Products International
7895 Stage Hills Blvd. Suite 105
Memphis TN 38133
800-244-4457
fax 800-321-5882
vpisports.com
vpisports@aol.com

FIELD EQUIPMENT

Diamond Sports
11130 Warland Drive
Cypress CA 90630
562-598-9717
fax 562-598-0906
diamond-sports.com
info@diamond-sports.com

FIELD WALL PADDING

C&H Baseball
2215 60th Drive East
Bradenton FL 34203
941-727-1533
fax 941-727-0588
chbaseball.com
info@chbaseball.com

Covermaster Inc.
100 Westmore Dr. 11-D
Rexdale ON M9V5C3
800-387-5808
fax 416-742-6837
covermaster.com
info@covermaster.com

Horan Sports
P.O. Box 963
Conshohocken PA 19428
484-919-8547
fax 610-792-9737
horansports@aol.com
horansports.com

FIREWORKS

Fireworks Productions Inc.
P.O. Box 294
Maryland Line MD 21105
800-765-2264
fax 410-357-0187
fireworksproductionsinc.com
larry@fireworksproductionsinc.com

S. Vitale Pyrotechnic Industries Inc. d/b/a Pyrotecnico
P.O. Box 149
302 Wilson Road
New Castle PA 16103
800-854-4705
fax 724-652-1288
pyrotecnico.com
svitale@pyrotecnico.com

Zambelli Fireworks
20 S Mercer St
New Castle PA 16103
724-658-6611
fax 724-658-8318
zambellifireworks.com
zambelli@zambellifireworks.com

FOOD SERVICE

Concession Solutions Inc.
16022-26th Ave. NE
Shoreline WA 98155
206-440-9203
fax 206-440-9213
concessionsolutions.com
theresa@concessionsolutions.com

Mini Melts
126 SE 5th Court
Deerfield Beach FL 33441
954-570-3555
fax 954-570-8240
minimelts.com
minimelts@aol.com

GLOVES

Akadema
317 Midland Avenue
Garfield NJ 07026
973-772-7669
fax 973-772-4839
akademapro.com
akadema@akademapro.com

All Pro Sports
16919 Ventura Blvd
Encino CA 91316
818-981-5264
fax 818-981-3020
allprosportsshoes.com
allprosports@socal.rr.com

Brett Bros. Sports International
East 9514 Montgomery #25
Spokane WA 99206
509-891-6435
fax 509-981-4156
brettbros.com
brettbats@aol.com

Louisville Slugger
800 W. Main Street
Louisville KY 40202
888-444-2287 | See our ads on Pages 7 & 11

GRAPHIC DESIGN

Low and Inside
2022 N. Ferry Street Suite 3100
Minneapolis MN 55303
763-797-0777
fax 763-767-5510
lowandinside.com
creative@lowandinside.com

INFLATABLES

Inflatable Images
2880 Interstate Parkway
Brunswick OH 44212
800-783-5717 ext 134
fax 330-273-3212
inflatableimages.com
m.yates@scherba.com

INSURANCE

Francis L. Dean & Associates, Inc.
2800 S. Hulen St. #200
Fort Worth TX 76109
800-375-0552
fax 817-924-7884
jfaulder@fdean.com
athletic-insurance.com

K&K Insurance Group, Inc.
P.O. Box 2338
Fort Wayne, IN 46801
800-441-3994
fax 260-459-5120
Kandkinsurance.com

See our ad after Page 224

MASCOTS

Olympus Flag & Banner
9000 West Heather Ave.
Milwaukee WI 53224
414-355-2010
fax 414-355-1931
olympus-flag.com
olympus@olympus-flag.com

MUSIC/SOUND EFFECTS

Game Ops Commander
1 Center Ct. Suite 200
Portland OR 97227
800-346-8037
fax 503-736-5066
gameopscommander.com
info@gameopscommander.com

Sound and Video Creations
2820 Azalea Place
Nashville TN 37204
615-460-7330
fax 615-460-7331
clickeffects.com
fran2nz@aol.com

See our ad on Page 17

NETTING/POSTS

C&H Baseball
2215 60th Drive East
Bradenton FL 34203
941-727-1533
fax 941-727-0588
chbaseball.com
info@chbaseball.com

Vantage Products International
7895 Stage Hills Blvd. Suite 105
Memphis TN 38133
800-244-4457
fax 800-321-5882
vpisports.com
vpisports@aol.com

PENNANTS/NOVELTIES

Rico Industries, Inc./Tag Express
1712 South Michigan Ave.
Chicago IL 60616
800-423-5856
fax 312-427-0190
ricoinc.com
jimz@ricoinc.com

PITCHING MACHINES

American Iron Sports
120 N. 3rd
Ponca City OK 74601
866-709-4189
fax 580-327-5456
americanironsports.com
info@americanironsports.com

C&H Baseball
2215 60th Drive East
Bradenton FL 34203
941-727-1533
fax 941-727-0588
chbaseball.com
info@chbaseball.com

Horan Sports
P.O. Box 963
Conshohocken PA 19428
484-919-8547
fax 610-792-9737
horansports@aol.com
horansports.com

JKP Sports, JUGS
19333 SW 118th Avenue
Tualatin OR 97062
800-547-6843
fax 503-691-1100
jugssports.com
stevec@jkpsports.com

Master Pitching Machines
4200 Northeast Birmingham Road
Kansas City MO 64117
800-878-8228
masterpitch.com

Vantage Products International
7895 Stage Hills Blvd. Suite 105
Memphis TN 38133
800-244-4457
fax 800-321-5882
vpisports.com
vpisports@aol.com

PLAYING FIELD PRODUCTS

C&H Baseball
2215 60th Drive East
Bradenton FL 34203
941-727-1533
fax 941-727-0588
chbaseball.com
info@chbaseball.com

Adscreen Group
8010 Leavenworth
Omaha NE 68114
877-393-5111
fax 402-393-4682
adscreengroup.com
steve@adscreengroup.com

Diamond Pro TXI
1341 West Mockingbird Lane
Dallas TX 75247
800-228-2987
fax 800-640-6735
diamondpro.com

L.A. Steelcraft Products
PO Box 90365
Pasadena CA 91109
800-371-2438
fax 626-798-1482
lasteelcraft.com
info@lasteelcraft.com

Midwest Athletic Surfaces
112 West State St.
Marshfield WI 54449
715-384-7027
fax 715-384-7027
webpages.charter.net/warningtrack
warningtrack@charter.net

Stabilizer Solutions, Inc.
205 S. 28th St.
Phoenix AZ 85034
800-336-2468
fax 602-225-5902
stabilizersolutions.com
lphubbs@stabilizersolutions.com

PLUSH & MASCOT DOLLS

Market Identity
2290 Agate Court
Simi Valley, CA 93065
800-927-8070
fax 805-579-6066
nbleier@iagtm.com

PORTABLE PITCHING MOUNDS

Horan Sports
P.O. Box 963
Conshohocken PA 19428
484-919-8547
fax 610-792-9737
horansports@aol.com
horansports.com

PRINTING

Low and Inside
2022 N. Ferry Street Suite 3100
Minneapolis MN 55303
763-797-0777
fax 763-767-5510
lowandinside.com
creative@lowandinside.com

PROMOTIONAL ITEMS

BallQube Inc.
RR 2 Box 190
Cushing TX 75760
800-543-1470
fax 903-863-5571
ballqube.com
sales@ballqube.com

Fungo Baseball Game Co.
642 Hilliard St.
Manchester CT 06040
860-432-1132
playfungo.com
tony@playfungo.com

Mark Out Productions, Inc.
P.O. Box 770440
Lakewood OH 44107
866-gameops
fax 978-418-0058
gameops.com
info@gameops.com

Rico Industries, Inc./Tag Express
1712 South Michigan Ave.
Chicago IL 60616
800-423-5856
fax 312-427-0190
ricoinc.com
jimz@ricoinc.com

Sport Beads
2828 Hedberg Drive
Minnetonka MN 55305
877-521-7631
fax 952-417-8146
sportbeads.com
adam@cardemporium.com

PROMOTIONAL PRIZE COVERAGE

SCA Promotions
8300 Douglas Ave 6th Floor
Dallas TX 75225
888-860-3700
fax 214-860-3723
scapromotions.com
info@scapromo.com

RADAR EQUIPMENT

**Applied Concepts/
Stalker Radar**
2609 Technology Drive
Plano TX 75074-7467
800-STALKER
stalkerradar.com

JKP Sports, JUGS
19333 SW 118th Avenue
Tualatin OR 97062
800-547-6843
fax 503-691-1100
jkpsports.com
stevec@jkpsports.com

RADIO SPONSOR SALES

Pioneer Radio & Sports
580 Naches Ave. SW #100
Renton WA 98055
425-738-3800
fax 425-738-3815
pioneerradioandsports.com
markm@pioneerradioandsports.com

SCOREBOARDS

Nevco Scoreboard Company
301 East Harris Avenue
Greenville IL 62246
618-664-0360
fax 618-664-0398
nevcoscoreboards.com
nevco@nevcoscoreboards.com

SEATING

Clarin
Steven J. Luttazi
927 North Shore Drive
Lake Bluff IL 60044
800-323-9062
fax 847-234-9001
clarinseating.com
sluttazi@clarinseating.com

Southern Bleacher Company
P.O. Box ONE
Graham TX 76450
800-433-0912
fax 940-549-1265
southernbleacher.com
info@southernbleacher.com

Starena International USA
30 Bentwater Court
Acworth GA 30101
877-827-3624
fax 678-574-7771
starenaintusa.com
info@starenaintusa.com

Sturdisteel
P.O. Box 2655
Waco TX 76702-2655
800-433-3116
fax 254-666-4472
info@sturdisteel.com
rgroppe@sturdisteel.com

SHOWCASE TRAINING

**Matt Merullo: The Pro
Advantage Baseball Center**
4 Nod Place
Clinton CT 06414
203-453-5661
www.proadvantagebaseball.com

SOFTWARE

E Solutions Corporation
400 North Tampa Street 16th Floor
Tampa FL 33602
888-840-4999
fax 813-342-2123
esnet.com
mmorizio@esnet.com

SOUVENIRS

Sport Beads
2828 Hedberg Drive
Minnetonka MN 55305
877-521-7631
fax 952-417-8146
sportbeads.com
adam@cardemporium.com

SPORTING GOODS

All Pro Sports
16919 Ventura Blvd
Encino CA 91316
818-981-5264
fax 818-981-3020
allprosportsshoes.com
allprosports@socal.rr.com

Frank's Sport Shop
430 East Tremont Ave.
New York NY 10457
718-299-9628
fax 718-583-1652
frankssportshop.com

JugheadSports
107 Pleasant Avenue
Upper Saddle River NJ 07458
877-448-2220
fax 201-760-8820
jugheadsports.com
info@baseballclinics.com

SPORTS MEDICINE

Cho-Pat Inc.
P.O. Box 293
Hainesport NJ 08036
609-261-1336
fax 609-261-7593
cho-pat.com
sales@cho-pat.com

STADIUM ARCHITECTS

Clarke Caton Hintz
400 Sullivan Way
Trenton NJ 08728
609-883-8383
fax 609-883-4044
ccharchitects.com
mainbox@cchnj.com

HOK Sport + Venue + Event
323 West 8th Street Suite 700
Kansas City MO 64105
816-221-1578
fax 816-221-1578
hok.com/sport
bruce.miller@hok.com

STADIUM DISPLAY SYSTEMS

BARCO
1651 N 1000 West
Logan UT 84321
435-753-2224
barcosports.com

TICKETS

Alliance Software Corporation
1505 N. Capitol St. NE
Washington DC 20002
www.alliance.biz
sales@alliance.biz
202-529-6730
fax 202-318-3026

Broach Baseball Tours
5821 Fairview Road Suite 118
Charlotte NC 28209
800-849-6345
fax 704-365-3800
BroachBaseballToursUSA.com
tbroach@broachsportstours.com

Etix.com
5171 Glenwood Ave.
Raleigh NC 27612
919-782-5010
fax 919-782-7727
etix.com

WorldWide Ticket & Label
1673 SW 1st Way #A-1
Deerfield Beach FL. 33441
www.wwticket.com
erikc@wwticket.com
877-426-5754 toll-free
fax 954-426-5761

TURNSTILE ADVERTISING

Entry Media Inc.
127 W. Fairbanks Ave. #417
Winter Park FL 32789
407-678-4446
fax 407-679-3590
entrymedia.com
entrymedia@att.net

TRAINING EQUIPMENT

Jump Stretch
1230 North Meridian Road
Youngstown OH 44509
800-344-3539
jumpstretch.com
slarosa@jumpstretch.com

TRASH CANS

United Receptacle
P.O. Box 870
Pottsville PA 17901
800-233-0314
fax 800-847-8551
unitedrecept.com
united@unitedrecept.com

TRAVEL

Broach Baseball Tours
5821 Fairview Road Suite 118
Charlotte NC 28209
800-849-6345
fax 704-365-3800
BroachBaseballToursUSA.com
tbroach@broachsportstours.com

Sports Travel and Tours
60 Main Street
Hatfield MA 01038
800-662-4424
sportstravelandtours.com
info@sportstravelandtours.com

TRAVEL, TEAM

**World Sports International
Sports Tours**
P.O. Box 661624
Los Angeles CA 90405
800-496-8687
fax 310-314-8872
worldsport-tours.com

TROPHIES/AWARDS

BallQube Inc.
RR 2 Box 190
Cushing TX 75760
800-543-1470
fax 903-863-5571
ballqube.com
sales@ballqube.com

UNIFORMS

Uniforms Express
2284 Old Middlefield Way #11
Mountain View CA 94043
650-691-4466
fax 888-661-7044
uesports.com
rob@uesports.com

WINDSCREENS

Adscreen Group
8010 Leavenworth
Omaha NE 68114
877-393-5111
fax 402-393-4682
adscreengroup.com
steve@adscreengroup.com

C&H Baseball
2215 60th Drive East
Bradenton FL 34203
941-727-1533
fax 941-727-0588
chbaseball.com
info@chbaseball.com

Covermaster Inc.
100 Westmore Dr. 11-D
Rexdale ON M9V5C3
800-387-5808
fax 416-742-6837
covermaster.com
info@covermaster.com

Promats, Inc.
P.O. Box 508
Fort Collins CO 80522
800-678-6287
fax 970-482-7740
promats.com
eileen@promats.com

Vantage Products International
7895 Stage Hills Blvd. Suite 105
Memphis TN 38133
800-244-4457
fax 800-321-5882
vpisports.com
vpisports@aol.com

2004 DIRECTORY
INDEX

MAJOR LEAGUE TEAMS
AMERICAN LEAGUE

Page	Club	Phone	FAX
36	Anaheim Angels	714-940-2000	714-940-2001
42	Baltimore Orioles	410-685-9800	410-547-6272
44	Boston Red Sox	617-267-9440	617-375-0944
48	Chicago White Sox	312-674-1000	312-674-5116
52	Cleveland Indians	216-420-4200	216-420-4396
56	Detroit Tigers	313-471-2000	313-471-2138
62	Kansas City Royals	816-921-8000	816-921-1366
68	Minnesota Twins	612-375-1366	612-375-7480
74	New York Yankees	718-293-4300	718-293-8431
76	Oakland Athletics	510-638-4900	510-562-1633
88	Seattle Mariners	206-346-4000	206-346-4400
90	Tampa Bay Devil Rays	727-825-3137	727-825-3111
92	Texas Rangers	817-273-5222	817-273-5110
94	Toronto Blue Jays	416-341-1000	416-341-1250

NATIONAL LEAGUE

Page	Club	Phone	FAX
38	Arizona Diamondbacks	602-462-6500	602-462-6599
40	Atlanta Braves	404-522-7630	404-614-1392
46	Chicago Cubs	773-404-2827	773-404-4129
50	Cincinnati Reds	513-765-7000	513-765-7342
54	Colorado Rockies	303-292-0200	303-312-2116
58	Florida Marlins	305-626-7400	305-626-7428
60	Houston Astros	713-259-8000	713-259-8981
64	Los Angeles Dodgers	323-224-1500	323-224-1269
66	Milwaukee Brewers	414-902-4400	414-902-4053
70	Montreal Expos	514-253-3434	514-253-8282
72	New York Mets	718-507-6387	718-507-6395
78	Philadelphia Phillies	215-463-6000	215-389-3050
80	Pittsburgh Pirates	412-323-5000	412-325-4412
82	St. Louis Cardinals	314-421-3060	314-425-0640
84	San Diego Padres	619-795-5000	619-795-5035
86	San Francisco Giants	415-972-2000	415-947-2800

MINOR LEAGUE TEAMS

Page	Club	League	Phone	FAX
203	Aberdeen	New York-Penn	410-297-9292	410-297-6653
153	Akron	Eastern	330-253-5151	330-253-3300
144	Albuquerque	Pacific Coast	505-924-2255	505-242-8899
153	Altoona	Eastern	814-943-5400	814-943-9132
166	Arkansas	Texas	501-664-1555	501-664-1834
195	Asheville	South Atlantic	828-258-0428	828-258-0320
203	Auburn	New York-Penn	315-255-2489	315-255-2675
195	Augusta	South Atlantic	706-736-7889	706-736-1122
171	Bakersfield	California	661-322-1363	661-322-6199
203	Batavia	New York-Penn	585-343-5454	585-343-5620
188	Battle Creek	Midwest	269-660-2287	269-660-2288
188	Beloit	Midwest	608-362-2272	608-362-0418
220	Billings	Pioneer	406-252-1241	406-252-2968
154	Binghamton	Eastern	607-723-6387	607-723-7779
160	Birmingham	Southern	205-988-3200	205-988-9698
215	Bluefield	Appalachian	276-326-1326	276-326-1318
210	Boise	Northwest	208-322-5000	208-322-6846
154	Bowie	Eastern	301-805-6000	301-464-4911
182	Brevard County	Florida State	321-633-9200	321-633-9210
215	Bristol	Appalachian	540-645-7275	540-669-7686
204	Brooklyn	New York-Penn	718-449-8497	718-449-6368
136	Buffalo	International	716-846-2000	716-852-6530
188	Burlington, IA	Midwest	319-754-5705	319-754-5882
215	Burlington, NC	Appalachian	336-222-0223	336-226-2498
195	Capital City	South Atlantic	803-256-4110	803-256-4338
160	Carolina	Southern	919-269-2287	919-269-4910
220	Casper	Pioneer	307-232-1111	307-265-7867

189	Cedar Rapids	Midwest	319-363-3887	319-363-5631
196	Charleston, SC	South Atlantic	843-723-7241	843-723-2641
196	Charleston, WV	South Atlantic	304-344-2287	304-344-0083
136	Charlotte	International	704-357-8071	704-329-2155
160	Chattanooga	Southern	423-267-2208	423-267-4258
182	Clearwater	Florida State	727-467-4457	727-712-4498
189	Clinton	Midwest	563-242-0727	563-242-1433
144	Colorado Springs	Pacific Coast	719-597-1449	719-597-2491
197	Columbus, GA	South Atlantic	706-571-8866	706-571-9984
137	Columbus, OH	International	614-462-5250	614-462-3271
216	Danville	Appalachian	434-797-3792	434-797-3799
190	Dayton	Midwest	937-228-2287	937-228-2284
182	Daytona	Florida State	386-257-3172	386-257-3382
197	Delmarva	South Atlantic	410-219-3112	410-219-9164
183	Dunedin	Florida State	727-733-9302	727-734-7661
137	Durham	International	919-687-6500	919-687-6560
145	Edmonton	Pacific Coast	780-414-4450	780-414-4475
216	Elizabethton	Appalachian	423-547-6440	423-547-6442
166	El Paso	Texas	915-755-2000	915-757-0671
155	Erie	Eastern	814-456-1300	814-456-7520
210	Eugene	Northwest	541-342-5367	541-342-6089
210	Everett	Northwest	425-258-3673	425-258-3675
183	Fort Myers	Florida State	239-768-4210	239-768-4211
190	Fort Wayne	Midwest	260-482-6400	260-471-4678
177	Frederick	Carolina	301-662-0013	301-662-0018
145	Fresno	Pacific Coast	559-442-1994	559-264-0795
166	Frisco	Texas	972-731-9200	972-731-7455
220	Great Falls	Pioneer	406-452-5311	406-454-0811
197	Greensboro	South Atlantic	336-333-2287	336-273-7350
217	Greeneville	Appalachian	423-638-0411	423-638-9450
161	Greenville	Southern	864-299-3456	864-277-7369
198	Hagerstown	South Atlantic	301-791-6266	301-791-6066
155	Harrisburg	Eastern	717-231-4444	717-231-4445
221	Helena	Pioneer	406-495-0500	406-495-0900
198	Hickory	South Atlantic	828-322-3000	828-322-6137
171	High Desert	California	760-246-6287	760-246-3197
204	Hudson Valley	New York-Penn	845-838-0094	845-838-0014
161	Huntsville	Southern	256-882-2562	256-880-0801
221	Idaho Falls	Pioneer	208-522-8363	208-522-9858
138	Indianapolis	International	317-269-3542	317-269-3541
171	Inland Empire	California	909-888-9922	909-888-5251
146	Iowa	Pacific Coast	515-243-6111	515-243-5152
162	Jacksonville	Southern	904-358-2846	904-358-2845
205	Jamestown	New York-Penn	716-664-0915	716-664-4175
217	Johnson City	Appalachian	423-461-4866	423-461-4864
184	Jupiter	Florida State	561-775-1818	561-691-6886
190	Kane County	Midwest	630-232-8811	630-232-8815
199	Kannapolis	South Atlantic	704-932-3267	704-938-7040
217	Kingsport	Appalachian	423-378-3744	423-392-8538
177	Kinston	Carolina	252-527-9111	252-527-0498
199	Lake County	South Atlantic	440-975-8085	440-975-8958
172	Lake Elsinore	California	909-245-4487	909-245-0305
184	Lakeland	Florida State	863-686-8075	863-688-9589
200	Lakewood	South Atlantic	732-901-7000	732-901-3967
172	Lancaster	California	661-726-5400	661-726-5406
191	Lansing	Midwest	517-485-4500	517-485-4518
146	Las Vegas	Pacific Coast	702-386-7200	702-386-7214
200	Lexington	South Atlantic	859-252-4487	859-252-0747
138	Louisville	International	502-212-2287	502-515-2255
205	Lowell	New York-Penn	978-459-2255	978-459-1674
177	Lynchburg	Carolina	434-528-1144	434-846-0768
206	Mahoning Valley	New York-Penn	330-505-0000	330-505-9696
147	Memphis	Pacific Coast	901-721-6000	901-892-1222
167	Midland	Texas	915-520-2255	915-520-8326
222	Missoula	Pioneer	406-543-3300	406-543-9463
162	Mobile	Southern	251-479-2327	251-476-1147
173	Modesto	California	209-572-4487	209-572-4490
163	Montgomery	Southern	334-323-2255	334-323-2225
178	Myrtle Beach	Carolina	843-918-6002	843-918-6001
147	Nashville	Pacific Coast	615-242-4371	615-256-5684
155	New Britain	Eastern	860-224-8383	860-225-6267
156	New Hampshire	Eastern	603-641-2005	603-641-2055
206	New Jersey	New York-Penn	973-579-7500	973-579-7502

148	New Orleans	Pacific Coast	504-734-5155	504-734-5118
139	Norfolk	International	757-622-2222	757-624-9090
156	Norwich	Eastern	860-887-7962	860-886-5996
222	Ogden	Pioneer	801-393-2400	801-393-2473
148	Oklahoma	Pacific Coast	405-218-1000	405-218-1001
149	Omaha	Pacific Coast	402-734-2550	402-734-7166
206	Oneonta	New York-Penn	607-432-6326	607-432-1965
139	Ottawa	International	613-747-5969	613-747-0003
185	Palm Beach	Florida State	561-775-1818	561-691-6886
140	Pawtucket	International	401-724-7300	401-724-2140
191	Peoria	Midwest	309-680-4000	309-680-4080
157	Portland, ME	Eastern	207-874-9300	207-780-0317
149	Portland, OR	Pacific Coast	503-553-5400	503-553-5405
178	Potomac	Carolina	703-590-2311	703-590-5716
218	Princeton	Appalachian	304-487-2000	304-487-8762
222	Provo	Pioneer	801-377-2255	801-377-2345
218	Pulaski	Appalachian	540-980-1070	540-980-1850
192	Quad Cities	Midwest	563-324-3000	563-324-3109
173	Rancho Cucamonga	California	909-481-5000	909-481-5005
157	Reading	Eastern	610-375-8469	610-373-5868
140	Richmond, VA	International	804-359-4444	804-359-0731
141	Rochester	International	585-454-1001	585-454-1056
201	Rome	South Atlantic	706-368-9388	706-368-6525
167	Round Rock	Texas	512-255-2255	512-255-1558
185	St. Lucie	Florida State	772-871-2100	772-878-9802
150	Sacramento	Pacific Coast	916-376-4700	916-376-4710
179	Salem	Carolina	540-389-3333	540-389-9710
211	Salem-Keizer	Northwest	503-390-2225	503-390-2227
150	Salt Lake	Pacific Coast	801-485-3800	801-485-6818
168	San Antonio	Texas	210-675-7275	210-670-0001
174	San Jose	California	408-297-1435	408-297-1453
185	Sarasota	Florida State	941-365-4460	941-365-4217
201	Savannah	South Atlantic	912-351-9150	912-352-9722
141	Scranton/Wilkes-Barre	International	570-969-2255	570-963-6564
192	South Bend	Midwest	574-235-9988	574-235-9950
211	Spokane	Northwest	509-535-2922	509-534-5368
207	Staten Island	New York-Penn	718-720-9265	718-273-5763
174	Stockton	California	209-644-1900	209-644-1931
142	Syracuse	International	315-474-7833	315-474-2658
151	Tacoma	Pacific Coast	253-752-7707	253-752-7135
186	Tampa	Florida State	813-875-7753	813-673-3174
163	Tennessee	Southern	865-286-2300	865-523-9913
142	Toledo	International	419-725-4367	419-725-4368
158	Trenton	Eastern	609-394-3300	609-394-9666
207	Tri-City, NY	New York-Penn	518-629-2287	518-629-2299
212	Tri-City, WA	Northwest	509-544-8789	509-547-9570
151	Tucson	Pacific Coast	520-434-1021	520-889-9477
168	Tulsa	Texas	918-744-5998	918-747-3267
212	Vancouver	Northwest	604-872-5232	604-872-1714
208	Vermont	New York-Penn	802-655-4200	802-655-5660
186	Vero Beach	Florida State	772-569-4900	772-567-0819
175	Visalia	California	559-625-0480	559-739-7732
193	West Michigan	Midwest	616-784-4131	616-784-4911
164	West Tenn	Southern	731-988-5299	731-988-5246
169	Wichita	Texas	316-267-3372	316-267-3382
208	Williamsport	New York-Penn	570-326-3389	570-326-3494
179	Wilmington	Carolina	302-888-2015	302-888-2032
180	Winston-Salem	Carolina	336-759-2233	336-759-2042
193	Wisconsin	Midwest	920-733-4152	920-733-8032
212	Yakima	Northwest	509-457-5151	509-457-9909

Phone and FAX numbers for minor league offices can be found on page 129.

INDEPENDENT LEAGUE TEAMS

Page	Club	League	Phone	FAX
270	Allentown	Northeast	610-437-6800	610-437-6804
262	Amarillo	Central	806-342-3455	806-467-9894
259	Atlantic City	Atlantic	609-344-8873	609-344-7010
270	Bangor	Northeast	207-947-1900	207-947-9900
259	Bridgeport	Atlantic	203-345-4800	203-345-4830
271	Brockton	Northeast	508-559-7000	508-587-2802
260	Camden	Atlantic	856-963-2600	856-963-8534
265	Chillicothe	Frontier	740-773-8326	740-773-8338

Page	Team	Division	Phone	FAX
262	Coastal Bend	Central	361-387-8585	361-387-3535
263	Edinburg	Central	956-289-8800	956-289-8833
271	Elmira	Northeast	607-734-1270	607-734-0891
266	Evansville	Frontier	812-435-8686	812-435-8688
273	Fargo-Moorhead	Northern	701-235-6161	701-297-9247
266	Florence	Frontier	859-594-4487	859-647-4639
263	Fort Worth	Central	817-226-2287	817-534-4620
273	Gary Southshore	Northern	219-882-2255	219-882-2259
266	Gateway	Frontier	618-337-3000	618-332-3625
263	Jackson	Central	601-362-2294	601-362-9577
274	Joliet	Northern	815-726-2255	815-726-9223
267	Kalamazoo	Frontier	269-388-8326	269-388-8333
274	Kansas City	Northern	913-328-2255	913-685-3642
275	Lincoln	Northern	402-474-2255	402-474-2254
260	Long Island	Atlantic	631-940-3825	631-940-3800
267	Mid-Missouri	Frontier	573-256-4004	573-256-4003
260	Nashua	Atlantic	603-883-2255	603-883-0880
271	New Haven County	Northeast	203-777-5636	203-777-4369
272	New Jersey	Northeast	973-746-7434	973-655-8021
261	Newark	Atlantic	973-848-1000	973-621-0095
272	North Shore	Northeast	781-592-0007	781-592-0004
261	Pennsylvania	Atlantic	—	—
264	Pensacola	Central	850-934-8444	850-934-8744
272	Quebec	Northeast	418-521-2255	418-521-2266
267	Richmond, IN	Frontier	765-935-7529	765-962-7047
268	River City	Frontier	636-240-2287	636-240-7313
268	Rockford	Frontier	815-964-2255	815-964-2462
275	St. Paul	Northern	651-644-3517	651-644-1627
264	San Angelo	Central	915-942-6587	915-947-9480
275	Schaumburg	Northern	877-891-2255	847-891-6441
264	Shreveport	Central	318-636-5555	318-636-5670
276	Sioux City	Northern	712-277-9467	712-277-9406
276	Sioux Falls	Northern	605-333-0179	605-333-0139
268	Springfield/Ozark, MO	Frontier	417-581-2868	417-581-8342
261	Somerset	Atlantic	908-252-0700	908-252-0776
269	Washington	Frontier	724-250-9555	724-250-2333
269	Windy City	Frontier	708-489-2255	708-489-2999
276	Winnipeg	Northern	204-982-2273	204-982-2274

INDEPENDENT LEAGUE OFFICES

Page	League	Phone	FAX
259	Atlantic League	856-541-9400	856-541-9410
262	Central League	919-956-8150	919-683-2693
265	Frontier League	740-452-7400	740-452-2999
270	Northeast League	919-956-8150	919-683-2693
273	Northern League	817-378-9898	817-378-9805
277	Southwestern League	505-523-4165	501-634-6181

OTHER ORGANIZATIONS

Page	Organization	Phone	FAX
360	AAABA	740-453-8531	740-453-3978
128	AAU Women's Baseball	330-923-3400	330-923-1967
119	ABC Sports Radio	212-456-5185	—
118	ABC-TV	212-456-4878	212-456-2877
367	Academy of Pro Players	973-772-3355	973-772-4839
357	AFLAC High School Classic	301-762-7188	301-762-1491
344	African Baseball/Softball Association	234-66-224-711	234-66-224-555
346	Alaska Baseball League	907-274-3627	907-274-3628
367	Aldrete Baseball Academy	831-884-0400	831-884-0800
360	All-American Amateur Baseball Association	740-453-8351	740-453-3978
357	All-American Baseball Talent Showcases	856-354-0201	856-354-0818
367	All-Star Baseball Academy	610-355-2411	610-355-2414
360	Amateur Athletic Union	407-934-7200	407-934-7242
360	American Amateur Baseball Congress	616-781-2002	616-781-2060
361	American Amateur Youth Baseball Alliance	573-518-0319	314-822-4974
297	American Baseball Coaches Association	989-775-3300	989-775-3600
345	American Baseball Foundation	205-558-4235	205-918-0800
361	American Legion Baseball	317-630-1213	317-630-1369
357	Area Code Games	707-975-7894	707-525-0214
357	Arizona Fall Classic	602-978-2929	602-439-4494
295	Arizona Fall League	480-496-6700	480-496-6384
119	Associated Press	212-621-1630	212-621-1639

127	Association of Professional Baseball Players	714-935-9993	714-935-0431
345	Athletes In Action	937-352-1000	937-352-1245
120	Athlon Sports Baseball	615-327-0747	615-327-1149
346	Atlantic Collegiate League	908-464-8042	908-464-8042
361	Babe Ruth Baseball	609-695-1434	609-695-2505
125	Babe Ruth Birthplace/Orioles Museum	410-727-1539	410-727-1652
367	The Baseball Academy	800-872-6425	941-752-2531
120	Baseball America	919-682-9635	919-682-2880
127	Baseball Assistance Team	212-931-7823	212-949-5691
356	Baseball At The Beach	843-546-3800	843-527-1816
344	Baseball Canada	613-748-5606	613-748-5767
127	Baseball Chapel	609-391-6444	—
344	Baseball Confederation of Oceania	61-3-9727-1779	61-3-9727-5959
120	Baseball Digest	847-491-6440	847-491-6203
357	Baseball Factory	410-715-5080	410-715-1975
344	Baseball Federation of Asia	81-3-320-11155	81-3-320-10707
121	Baseball Parent	865-523-1274	865-673-8926
127	Baseball Trade Show	727-822-6937	727-825-3785
366	Baseball USA	713-690-5055	713-690-9448
120	Baseball Writers Association of America	631-981-7938	631-585-4669
121	Beckett Publications	800-840-3137	972-991-8930
119	Bloomberg Sports News	609-750-4691	609-897-8397
358	Blue-Grey Classic	508-881-2782	—
367	Bucky Dent Baseball School	561-265-0280	561-278-6679
118	CBS Sports	212-975-5230	212-975-4063
344	COPABE	507-230-5399	507-230-4524
347	California Collegiate League	805-684-0657	805-684-8596
297	California Community College Commission on Athletics	916-444-1600	916-444-2616
125	Canadian Baseball Hall of Fame	519-284-1838	519-284-1234
119	Canadian Press	416-364-0321	416-364-0207
347	Cape Cod League	508-385-6260	508-385-6322
293	Caribbean Baseball Confederation	809-562-4737	809-565-4654
348	Central Illinois Collegiate League	217-793-6538	217-786-2788
288	China Baseball League	86-10-8582-6002	86-10-8582-5994
289	Chinese Pro Baseball League	886-2-2577-6992	886-2-2577-2606
348	Clark Griffith League	703-760-1684	703-821-8949
349	Coastal Plain League	919-852-1960	919-852-1973
366	Cocoa Expo Sports Center	321-639-3976	321-639-0598
359	College Select Baseball Showcase	800-782-3672	—
121	Collegiate Baseball	520-623-4530	520-624-5501
122	Coman Publishing	919-688-0218	919-682-1532
361	Continental Amateur Baseball Association	740-382-4620	—
366	Cooperstown Baseball World	888-229-8750	888-229-8720
366	Cooperstown Dreams Park	704-630-0050	704-630-0737
366	Disney's Wide World of Sports	407-938-3802	407-938-3412
362	Dixie Baseball, Inc.	903-927-2255	903-927-1846
362	Dizzy Dean Baseball	662-429-4365	—
293	Dominican League	809-567-6371	809-567-5720
287	Dominican Summer League	809-532-3619	809-532-3619
128	Donruss/Playoff Trading Cards	817-983-0300	817-983-0400
358	Doyle Baseball Select Showcases	863-439-1000	863-439-7086
290	Dutch Major League	31-30-607-6070	31-30-294-3043
117	ESPN/ESPN2-TV	860-766-2000	860-766-2213
120	ESPN The Magazine	212-515-1000	212-515-1290
119	ESPN Radio	860-766-2661	860-589-5523
357	East Coast Pro Baseball Showcase	910-962-3570	—
117	Elias Sports Bureau	212-869-1530	212-354-0980
344	European Baseball Confederation	32-3-219-0440	32-3-219-0440
126	Field of Dreams Movie Site	888-875-8404	319-875-7253
128	Fleer/Skybox Trading Cards	800-343-6816	856-231-0383
349	Florida Collegiate Instructional League	941-727-0303	941-727-2962
118	FOX Sports	212-556-2500	212-354-6902
367	Frozen Ropes Training Centers	508-563-1860	508-563-1875
356	Gatorade Circle of Champions	312-553-1240	—
128	Grandstand Cards	818-992-5642	818-348-9122
350	Great Lakes League	740-368-3738	740-368-3799
362	Hap Dumont Youth Baseball	316-721-1779	316-721-8054
125	Harry Wendelstedt Umpire School	386-672-4879	386-672-3212
356	Horizon National High School Invitational	602-867-9003	—
358	Impact Baseball Showcase	—	—
122	Indians Ink	440-953-2200	440-953-2202
124	Inside Edge Scouting	800-858-3343	508-526-6145
344	International Baseball Federation	41-21-318-8240	41-21-318-8241

344	International Olympic Committee	41-21-621-6111	41-21-621-6216
356	International Paper Classic	843-527-9606	843-546-8321
345	International Sports Group	925-798-4591	925-680-1182
290	Italian Serie A/1	39-06-36858297	39-06-36858201
288	Japan League	03-3502-0022	03-3502-0140
350	Jayhawk League	316-755-1285	316-755-1285
125	Jim Evans Academy of Professioinal Umpiring	512-335-5959	512-335-5411
121	Junior Baseball Magazine	818-710-1234	818-710-1877
366	KC Sports Tournaments	816-587-4545	816-587-4549
289	Korea Baseball Organization	02-3460-4643	02-3460-4649
122	Krause Publications	715-445-4612	715-445-4087
125	Lena Blackburn Rubbing Mud	856-764-7501	856-461-4089
363	Little League Baseball, Inc.	570-326-1921	570-326-1074
356	Lions High School Invitational	619-583-2633	619-583-6605
128	Los Angeles Dodgers Fantasy Camp	800-334-7529	772-229-6708
126	Louisville Slugger Museum	502-588-7228	502-585-1179
33	MLB Advanced Media (MLB.com)	212-485-3444	212-485-3456
33	MLB Commissioner's Office	212-931-7800	—
33	MLB International	212-931-7500	212-949-5795
127	MLB Players Alumni Association	719-477-1870	719-477-1875
124	MLB Players Association	212-826-0808	212-752-4378
33	MLB Productions	212-931-7777	212-931-7788
124	Major League Scouting Bureau	909-980-1881	909-980-7794
356	March Madness High School Tournament	954-735-1841	954-334-6160
367	Mark Cresse Baseball School	714-892-6145	714-892-1881
128	Men's Adult Baseball League	631-753-6725	631-753-4031
128	Men's Senior Baseball League	631-753-6725	631-753-4031
286	Mexican League	52-555-557-1007	52-555-395-2454
293	Mexican Pacific League	52-667-761-25-70	52-667-761-25-71
367	Mickey Owen Baseball School	800-999-8369	417-889-6978
356	Midland Tournament of Champions	432-689-1337	—
358	Mid-America Five Star Showcase	513-247-9511	513-247-0040
358	Midwest Prospects Showcase	405-942-5455	405-942-3012
129	Minor League Baseball	727-822-6937	727-821-5819
127	Minor League Baseball Alumni Association	727-477-6937	727-825-3785
350	Mountain Collegiate League	818-8875447	—
126	Museum of Minor League Baseball	901-722-0207	901-527-1642
297	NAIA	913-791-0044	913-791-9555
118	NBC-TV	212-664-2014	212-664-6365
297	NCAA	317-917-6222	317-917-6826
297	NJCAA	719-590-9788	719-590-7324
128	National Adult Baseball Association	800-621-6479	303-639-6605
346	National Alliance of College Summer Baseball	401-739-7875	401-739-9789
363	National Amateur Baseball Federation	301-464-5460	301-352-0214
345	National Baseball Congress	316-267-3372	316-267-3382
126	National Baseball Hall of Fame	607-547-7200	607-547-2044
120	National Collegiate Baseball Writers Association	312-553-0483	312-553-0495
356	National Federation of State High School Association	317-972-6900	317-822-5700
356	National High School Baseball Coaches Association	479-876-2591	479-876-2596
357	National High School Championship	502-261-9200	502-261-9278
126	Negro Leagues Baseball Museum	816-221-1920	816-221-8424
351	New England Collegiate League	603-483-0241	—
351	New York Collegiate League	585-223-2328	—
367	North Carolina Baseball Academy	336-931-1118	—
351	Northwoods League	507-536-4579	507-289-1866
122	Outside Pitch (Orioles)	410-234-8888	410-234-1029
352	Pacific International League	206-623-8844	602-623-8361
358	Pacific Northwest Championship	503-885-1126	—
367	Pennsylvania Diamond Bucks Camp	610-838-2119	—
358	Perfect Game USA	800-447-9362	319-298-2924
126	Peter McGovern Little League Museum	570-326-2267	570-326-2267
128	Phillies Adult Phantasy Camp	610-520-3400	—
363	Police Athletic Leagues	561-844-1823	561-863-6120
363	PONY Baseball, Inc.	724-225-1060	724-225-9852
359	Premier Baseball	941-371-0989	941-371-0917
125	Pro Baseball Athletic Trainers Society	404-875-4000	404-892-8560
127	Pro Baseball Employment Opportunities	866-397-7236	727-821-5819
367	Pro Baseball Instruction	877-448-2220	201-760-8820
125	Pro Baseball Umpire Corp.	727-822-6937	727-821-5819
124	Prospects Plus/The Scouting Report	800-845-2726	919-682-2880
294	Puerto Rican League	787-765-6285	787-767-3028
364	RBI	212-931-7897	212-949-5695
128	Randy Hundley's Fantasy Baseball Camps	847-991-9595	847-991-9595

122	Reds Report	614-486-2202	614-486-3650
367	Ripken Baseball Camps	800-486-0850	—
118	Rogers SportsNet	416-332-5000	416-332-5767
367	Rookies Baseball	973-872-6789	973-872-2533
128	Roy Hobbs Baseball	330-923-3400	330-923-1967
127	SABR	216-575-0500	216-575-0502
367	San Diego School of Baseball	619-491-4000	619-469-5572
356	Sarasota High School Baseball Classic	941-955-0181	941-378-5853
124	Scout of the Year Foundation	561-798-5897	561-798-4644
359	Selectfest Baseball	973-539-4781	—
367	Sho-Me Baseball Camp	800-993-2267	417-338-2610
125	Skillshow, Inc.	610-687-9072	610-687-9629
352	Southern Collegiate League	704-847-5037	704-847-1455
367	Southwest Professional Baseball School	888-830-8031	480-830-7455
120	The Sporting News	314-997-7111	314-997-0765
119	Sporting News Radio Network	847-509-1661	847-509-1677
119	Sports Byline USA	415-434-8300	415-391-2569
120	Sports Illustrated	212-522-1212	212-522-4543
121	Sports Illustrated for Kids	212-522-1212	212-522-0120
117	The Sports Network	215-441-8444	215-441-5767
118	The Sports Network (Canada)	416-332-5000	416-332-7658
119	SportsTicker	201-309-1200	201-860-9742
117	SportsTicker-Boston	617-951-0070	617-737-9960
121	Spring Training Yearbook	919-967-2420	919-967-6294
117	STATS, Inc.	847-583-2100	847-470-9160
121	Street and Smith's Baseball Yearbook	704-973-1575	704-973-1576
120	Street and Smith's Sports Business Journal	704-973-1400	704-973-1401
357	Sunbelt High School Baseball Classic Series	405-348-3839	405-340-7538
364	Super Series Baseball of America	480-664-2998	480-664-2997
364	T-Ball USA Association, Inc.	203-381-1449	203-381-1440
119	TBS	404-827-1700	404-827-1593
359	Team One Showcases	859-466-8326	—
126	Ted Williams Museum/Hitters Hall of Fame	352-527-6566	352-527-4163
353	Texas Collegiate League	214-333-5340	817-838-3122
359	Top 96 Showcase	508-651-0165	—
359	Top Guns Showcase	208-762-1100	208-762-1100
128	Topps	212-376-0300	212-376-0623
121	Total Baseball	416-466-0418	416-466-9530
356	Toyo Tires National Classic	714-993-2838	714-993-5350
364	Triple Crown Sports	970-223-6644	970-223-3636
128	Upper Deck	800-873-7332	760-929-6548
364	US Amateur Baseball Association	425-776-7130	425-776-7130
364	US Amateur Baseball Federation	619-435-2831	619-435-3148
345	USA Baseball	919-474-8721	919-474-8822
356	USA High School Classic	901-872-8326	901-681-9443
365	USSSA	816-587-4545	816-587-4549
344	US Olympic Committee	719-866-4500	719-866-4654
120	USA Today	703-854-5954	703-854-2072
120	USA Today Sports Weekly	703-854-6319	703-854-2034
367	Utah Baseball Academy	801-561-1700	801-561-1762
353	Valley League	540-885-8901	540-886-2068
294	Venezuelan League	58-212-761-4932	58-212-761-7661
287	Venezuelan Summer League	58-241-824-0321	58-241-824-0705
122	Vine Line (Cubs)	773-404-2827	773-404-4129
119	WGN	773-528-2311	773-528-6050
356	West Coast Classic	408-252-6670	—
356	Westminster National High School Classic	954-735-1841	954-735-1858
125	World Umpires Association	321-637-3471	321-633-7018
365	World Wood Bat Association	319-298-2923	319-298-2924
122	Yankees Magazine	800-469-2657	—